# Assembler Language Programming for the IBM 370

The Benjamin / Cummings Series in
Structured Programming

J. Brink and R. Spillman
**Computer Architecture and VAX Assembly Language Programming**

J. G. Brookshear
**Computer Science: An Overview, Second Edition**

F. M. Carrano
**Assembler Language Programming for the IBM 370**

F. M. Carrano
**Assembler Language Programming for the IBM 370, ASSIST Edition**

D. M. Etter
**Structured FORTRAN 77 for Engineers and Scientists, Second Edition**

C. Fischer and R. LeBlanc
**Crafting a Compiler**

P. Helman and R. Veroff
**Walls and Mirrors: Intermediate Problem Solving and Data Structures, Modula II Edition**

A. Kelley and I. Pohl
**A Book on C**

A. Kelley and I. Pohl
**C by Dissection**

T. King and B. Knight
**Programming the M68000, Second Edition**

N. Miller
**File Structures Using Pascal**

W. J. Savitch
**Pascal: An Introduction to the Art and Science of Programming, Second Edition**

W. J. Savitch
**Turbo Pascal, Second Edition**

R. Sebesta
**Structured Assembly Language Programming for the VAX-11**

R. Sebesta
**Structured Assembly Language Programming for the PDP-11**

M. Thorne
**Programming the 8086/8088 for the IBM and Compatibles**

# Assembler Language Programming for The IBM 370

**Frank M. Carrano**
University of Rhode Island

**The Benjamin/Cummings Publishing Company, Inc.**
Menlo Park, California • Reading, Massachusetts
Don Mills, Ontario • Wokingham, U.K. • Amsterdam • Sydney
Singapore • Tokyo • Madrid • Bogota • Santiago • San Juan

**Sponsoring Editor:** Alan R. Apt
**Production:** The Book Company: George Calmenson
**Production Supervisor:** Mary Picklum
**Copy Editor:** Lorraine Aochi
**Interior consulting, and cover designer:** The Book Company: Wendy Calmenson
**Illustrations:** Graphic Typesetting Service
**Composition:** Graphic Typesetting Service

The basic text of this book was designed using the Modular Design System, as developed by Wendy Earl and Design Office Bruce Kortebein.

**Cover Photo:** Michael Rochipp, The Image Bank



**Library of Congress Cataloging-in-Publication Data**

Carrano, Frank M.
Assembler language programming for the IBM 370.

Includes index.
1. IBM 370 (Computer)—Programming. 2. Assembler language (Computer program language) I. Title.
QA76.8.I123C35 1988 005.4′56 87–683
ISBN 0-8053-1811-9



ISBN 0-8053-1811-9

ABCDEFGHIJ-BA-8987

**THE BENJAMIN/CUMMINGS PUBLISHING COMPANY, INC.**
2727 Sand Hill Road
Menlo Park, California 94025

*This is dedicated to the ones I love*

# Preface

This introductory assembler language text is based upon my lecture notes that have evolved over the past 15 years. I offer an approach and an ordering of material that have worked for my students; yet I have built in flexibility to accommodate individual preferences and goals. Although the text is a comprehensive study of problem-state assembler language programming for the IBM System/370 or compatible computers, the presentation is based on instructional concerns that facilitate learning, rather than on an academic classification of topics, which, although common in other texts, is more suitable for students who already know assembler language. I assume that the reader has studied a high-level programming language such as Pascal or FORTRAN; typically, one such course is sufficient. This text is suitable for use in the standard course in assembler language programming (Course CS-3 of the ACM Curriculum Recommendations), and covers OS, CMS, and DOS.

## Approach

I stress concepts and a thorough understanding of the topic at hand. This emphasis is particularly important at the beginning of study since a strong foundation facilitates the writing and the debugging of future assembler language programs. With only a handful of instructions, the text carefully examines a simple machine language program, while it introduces concepts such as base-displacement addressing. Building toward assembler language from this beginning has proven to be an effective teaching strategy: when students know machine language, they understand assembler language at a deeper level. This understanding helps them to avoid programming errors.

It is important not to overwhelm students, particularly in the beginning of their study. Consequently, the information that the initial chapters present is not inclusive. The students encounter material only as needed, which makes it feasible to write programs as early as possible. Details that supplement the introductory concepts appear later when the students can assimilate them more easily.

## Numerous Examples

This text contains numerous examples that demonstrate the details, common usage, and pitfalls of each instruction that is discussed. Many program segments and complete programs demonstrate the broader view of instruction usage, the developmental aspects of assembler language programming, and the stylistic concerns that an assembler language programmer should have.

## Debugging

The text emphasizes error prevention and detection. A unique in-depth chapter (Chapter 6) teaches debugging techniques and strategies by analyzing several program listings and dumps. This chapter not only describes debugging tools, but also demonstrates the thought processes that are necessary to apply the tools in specific situations. Examples take the reader step-by-step through the debugging process of several programs that contain typical but nontrivial errors that novice programmers make. Thus, the chapter covers a topic that most texts leave for students to learn on their own by trial and error.

In addition to the debugging chapter, most chapters contain topic-specific **Debugging Hints,** which students can use either to locate or to avoid errors. Finally, an appendix describes the debugging tools that are available within the Conversational Monitor System (CMS).

## Learning Aids

Each chapter contains several aids to learning. First, each chapter begins with a **Chapter Overview** paragraph, and a list of **Objectives**, which are stated in terms of what the reader should be able to do after learning the new material. Second, **Self-Test Exercises,** whose solutions appear in an appendix, provide an opportunity for students to try out new concepts. Third, additional **Exercises and Programming Problems**, which are suitable for homework, appear at the end of each chapter. The solutions to these exercises appear in a separate *Instructor's Manual.* Finally, each chapter concludes with a **Summary** of important new ideas and a list of **New Instructions** with their definitions. This closing material is useful for both reference and review.

## Other Special Features

There are many other features that enhance learning and increase the usefulness of this text. **Structured pseudocode** is used to describe algorithms, and forms the basis of the comments within programs. Style and documentation are stressed within all sample programs. Most chapters also contain a section entitled **Stylistic Notes** that indicates the way to increase the readability of a program in specific situations. Many chapters contain **Case Studies** that demonstrate the new instructions within the broader context of a substantial program. Each case study contains both a flowchart and pseudocode to describe the logic of the algorithm, and an assembly listing of the program. When appropriate to particular instructions, the text includes information about the **extended architecture (370–XA).** Finally, supplementary **boxed material** enriches the presentation with historical and other related information.

## Flexibility

There are many possible paths through this text. After covering Chapters 1 through 7, which form a basic core, an instructor can either reorder or omit certain topics as desired. For example, external subprograms (Chapter 13), I/O under OS and DOS (Chapter 16), or macro definitions (Chapter 18) can be covered earlier than they appear in the text. The *Instructor's Manual* suggests several ways to use this text, and provides specific details about chapter dependencies.

## Chapter Outline

Chapter 1 introduces the concepts of machine language and assembler language, reviews the basic components of a computer in general, and provides a brief overview of the history and nature of IBM System/370.

Chapter 2 discusses the number systems that are immediately relevant in the next chapters for address computation and integer arithmetic. The chapter includes binary and hexadecimal integers, and both the sign-magnitude and the two's complement binary number systems. Related issues such as floating-point representation are left for later chapters.

Chapter 3 discusses System/370 machine language. It describes the organization of main storage, System/370 instruction formats, base-displacement addressing, and indexing. This chapter also defines a few basic instructions in their machine language form that load, store, add, and subtract binary integers; and then uses them in a simple, but complete, machine language program whose execution is traced through the CPU. A section that can be covered as an option describes a way to run the sample machine language program.

Chapter 4 introduces the rules for writing assembler language statements, illustrates the way to write a complete assembler language program, and describes the assembly process. The chapter differentiates between assembly-time errors and execution-time errors, and includes a description of the way to obtain storage and register dumps.

Chapter 5 defines new instructions that permit students to write more significant programs. The topics include controlling loops by using both the Compare instructions and the Branch on Condition instructions; processing arrays by using index registers; multiplying and dividing binary integers; and performing simple I/O under OS and DOS.

Chapter 6 is the debugging chapter that was described earlier in this preface.

Chapter 7 reviews the structure of loops and discusses new instructions (BCT, BXLE, and BXH) for loop control. The chapter also discusses internal subprograms.

Chapter 8 introduces logical and arithmetic shifting, and forms the basis for the eventual transition to byte manipulation.

Chapter 9 covers some miscellaneous instructions that involve binary integers: Load Multiple; the special Load Register instructions such as LTR; the instructions that involve halfword operands; and the logical Add and the logical Subtract instructions.

Chapters 10 and 11 discuss character strings and the instructions that manipulate bytes and bits.

Chapter 12 elaborates the way that the assembler chooses a base register and the way to use several base registers. This information is necessary for Chapter 13, which discusses external subprograms and data areas.

Chapter 14 introduces the two representations of decimal numbers and the various conversion instructions that involve them. Chapter 15 covers decimal arithmetic and discusses the way to perform computations with both integral and nonintegral data.

Chapter 16 discusses macro-level input and output under OS and DOS. The chapter covers the macro instructions to process sequential data sets under QSAM, BSAM, and SAM.

Chapter 17 introduces floating-point notation and instructions. The chapter includes program segments to convert between EBCDIC and floating-point representations, and between binary integer and floating-point representations.

Chapter 18 describes macro definitions and the conditional assembly language.

## *Acknowledgments*

I want to express my gratitude to the many people who helped me during this project. Alan Apt, Computer Science editor at Benjamin/Cummings, made this text possible. I thank him for his guidance and encouragement. Mary Ann Telatnik, Alan's assistant, dealt with many details that otherwise would have delayed my writing schedule. The production talents of George and Wendy Calmenson are evident in the final appearance of this text. Lorraine Aochi, my copy editor, was always there to show me the way out of grammatical tangles. I deeply appreciate the good humor and patience of all of these people.

I especially thank Bernard Lovell for his assistance with the BSAM and CMS material. In addition, I offer my sincere thanks to many others. Among them are David Tetreault, Nancy D'Antuono, Jenny DeGroot, Lorraine Berube, Marge White, Michael Hayden, Jan Pritchard, David Clayton, Nancy Rieser, Michael Sullivan, Loukas Mihalis, Dan Holloway, Charlene Yang, David Azzinaro, Irene Azzinaro, Lianne Armstrong, Ron Surprenant, Eric Miller, Tam Chapman, Frank Caraccia, Otto Carr, John Cardin, and Ted Emmott.

Finally, I thank my reviewers:

Stefan Burr
Ken Danhof
Bernard Lovell
Robert Sebesta
Gordon Springer

I invite you to share your comments, suggestions, and corrections with me.

F. M. C.

# Brief Contents

# Contents

## Chapter 1

### Preliminaries



## CHAPTER 2

### Number Systems



†Chapter End Material consists of Summary, Exercises, and where appropriate, New Instruction Summary and Programming Problems.



## CHAPTER 3

### Introduction to System/370 Machine Language

## CHAPTER 4

## Introduction to Assembler Language



## CHAPTER 5

## Loops, Arrays, and Binary Integer Arithmetic

## CHAPTER 6

### Debugging



## CHAPTER 7

### Loop Control and Internal Subprograms



## CHAPTER 8

### The Shift Instructions



## CHAPTER 9

### Miscellaneous Integer Instructions

## CHAPTER 10

## Character Manipulation



## CHAPTER 11

## Additional Bit and Byte Manipulations



## CHAPTER 12

## Multiple Base Registers

## CHAPTER 13

### Subprograms and Data Areas



## CHAPTER 14

### Decimal Representations and Conversions



## CHAPTER 15

### Decimal Arithmetic

## CHAPTER 16

## Input and Output under OS and DOS



## CHAPTER 17

## Floating-Point Operations

## CHAPTER 18

## Macro Definitions and the Conditional Assembly Language



## APPENDICES

# Assembler Language Programming for the IBM 370

# 1

# Preliminaries

CONTENTS



OVERVIEW

This chapter describes the nature of machine and assembler languages, and provides a rationale for studying them. It also outlines the structure of the IBM System/370 and its operating system.

OBJECTIVES

After studying this chapter, you should be able to:

1. Compare and contrast the nature of machine, assembler, and high-level languages.
2. Describe the importance of machine and assembler languages.
3. Describe the three major components of IBM System/370 computers.
4. Describe the general purpose of an operating system.

# Introduction

The **IBM Automatic Sequence Controlled Calculator**, also called the **Harvard Mark I**, was the first automatic digital computer. Completed in 1944, it was the result of a collaboration between Howard Aiken of Harvard University and IBM. The Mark I followed instructions that were punched onto a paper tape; a program was not stored internally within the machine. Calculations were carried out electromagnetically by using **relays**, which are mechanical switches that are activated by electromagnets.

At about the same time that Aiken was building his computer, John Atanasoff of Iowa State University designed and built the first electronic digital computer. Using Atanasoff's ideas, J. Presper Eckert and John Mauchly of the University of Pennsylvania completed the ENIAC in 1946. The ENIAC was the first large general-purpose electronic computer. Although these machines did not depend upon mechanical devices to perform their calculations, they were programmed by plugging wires into special boards and by setting thousands of switches.

**The stored program concept**

While work on the ENIAC progressed, Mauchly and Eckert, along with John von Neumann of Princeton University, proposed the stored program concept, whereby a computer's memory would contain both the program and the data to be manipulated. This concept was a significant advance in the development of computers and remains fundamental to all present computers.

## *Machine and Assembler Languages*

**Machine language instructions**

Programs stored in a computer's memory consist of **instructions** in a numeric form known as **machine language**. In general, each brand of computer has its own unique **instruction set** that is defined by the computer's designers. For example, the following is a sequence of three IBM 370 instructions that adds two numbers:

```
0101 1000 0010 0000 1100 0000 0000 1110
0101 1010 0010 0000 1100 0000 0001 0010
0101 0000 0010 0000 1100 0000 0001 0110
```

These instructions, like those of other computers, consist of strings of 1's and 0's. As such, they are binary integers whose digits are called **bits**.

In the late 1940s, programmers actually wrote machine language programs. Clearly, this was both tedious and error-prone, and produced programs that were difficult for humans to read and understand. Even so, you will occasionally have to work with machine language instructions. When this is necessary, the binary strings will be represented by a shorthand notation that replaces each group of 4 bits by a symbol in the range 0 through 9 or A through F, as shown here:

| | | | |
|---|---|---|---|
| 0000 = 0 | 0100 = 4 | 1000 = 8 | 1100 = C |
| 0001 = 1 | 0101 = 5 | 1001 = 9 | 1101 = D |
| 0010 = 2 | 0110 = 6 | 1010 = A | 1110 = E |
| 0011 = 3 | 0111 = 7 | 1011 = B | 1111 = F |

Thus, the machine language instructions shown earlier can be rewritten as

```
5820C00E
5A20C012
5020C016
```

As you will see in the next chapter, this notation is the hexadecimal number system. The notation is easier to write, but the instructions are still difficult to understand.

Assembler language

In the early 1950s, symbolic forms of machine languages called **assembler languages** were developed as an aid to programming. Typically, each machine language instruction is represented symbolically by one statement in an assembler language. For example, you can rewrite the three machine language instructions given earlier as

```
L     2,X     (Get X)
A     2,Y     (Add Y to it)
ST    2,Z     (Place the result in Z)
```

Here, L stands for **Load**, A for **Add**, and ST for **Store**; these define the operations to be performed. The data are represented by X and Y, and the result by Z. Clearly, these statements are more meaningful and easier to write than the corresponding machine language instructions. Moreover, anything that you can write in machine language can also be written in assembler language.

The assembler

An assembler language program must be translated into machine language before it can be executed. A program called the **assembler** performs this translation by reading the assembler language statements—known collectively as the **source program** or **source module**—and producing equivalent machine language instructions called the **object code** or **object module**. The assembler then produces an **assembly listing** that contains the source program and corresponding object code, an example of which is shown in Figure 1.1.

The linker

Usually, you must use a program called the **linker** to combine the object module with library subprograms before you can execute the program. The linker resolves the references to the subprograms to form a consolidated unit ready for execution, which is known as the **load module**. Another program called the **loader** then places the load module into memory. These ideas are illustrated in Figure 1.2. Note that IBM's linker is called the **Linkage Editor**. There is also an IBM **Loader**, which with certain restrictions combines the functions of linking and loading.

The mid-1950s saw the development of high-level languages that focused on problem solving and not on a particular machine language. A program that you write in one of these high-level languages must be translated into the machine language of a specific computer before it can be executed. This translation process is done by a program called the **compiler**. Machine language instructions are more primitive than the statements of a high-

**Figure 1.1**
An example of an assembly listing that contains the source program and object code.

| LOC | OBJECT CODE | ADDR1 | ADDR2 | STMT | SOURCE STATEMENT | | |
|---|---|---|---|---|---|---|---|
| 000000 | | | | 1 | EXAMPLE | CSECT | |
| | | | | 2 | * ADD TWO NUMBERS | | |
| 000000 | 05C0 | | | 3 | | BALR | 12,0 |
| 000002 | | | | 4 | | USING | BASE,12 |
| 000002 | 5820 C00E | | 00010 | 5 | BASE | L | 2,X |
| 000006 | 5A20 C012 | | 00014 | 6 | | A | 2,Y |
| 00000A | 5020 C016 | | 00018 | 7 | | ST | 2,Z |
| 00000E | 07FE | | | 8 | | BCR | 15,14 |
| 000010 | 0000000C | | | 9 | X | DC | F'12' |
| 000014 | 0000001E | | | 10 | Y | DC | F'30' |
| 000018 | | | | 11 | Z | DS | F |
| | | | | 12 | | END | EXAMPLE |

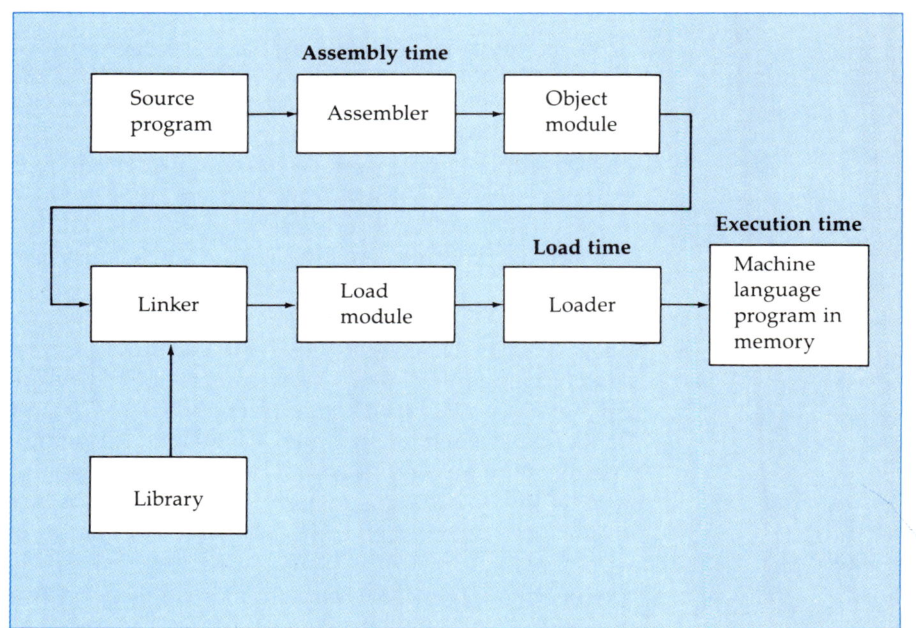


**Figure 1.2**
The steps required to execute an assembler language program.

level language; in fact, one statement in a high-level language generally can represent several machine language instructions. For example, the three machine language instructions given earlier perform the same task as the Pascal statement

```
Z := X + Y
```

Another example is shown in Figure 1.3, which lists the Pascal equivalent of the program in Figure 1.1.

In general, a machine or assembler language program written for one computer will not run on another computer by a different manufacturer. However, by writing different compilers for different computers, you can execute the same high-level language program on each of those computers. In addition, it is much easier to write a program in a high-level language than in an assembler language. The advantages of high-level languages may make you wonder about the need for assembler languages and the wisdom of studying them.

**Figure 1.3**
A Pascal program equivalent to the assembler language program of Figure 1.1.

```
program Example;
{Add two numbers}
   const X = 12;
         Y = 30;
   var Z: integer;
begin
   Z := X + Y
end.
```

## *Why Study Assembler and Machine Languages?*

Since high-level languages are designed for use with many computers, they may not be able to access all the features of a particular computer. With an assembler language, you have access to the full instruction set and, therefore, the full power of the computer. In addition, an assembler language allows total control over an instruction sequence. This is particularly important when efficient use of time and memory is a concern, as is the case when working with such computers as those on satellites. Even though some compilers can produce extremely efficient object code from high-level language programs, you may want to write your own assembler language instructions, rather than depend upon the skill of a compiler writer. You can choose the best of both approaches by writing assembler language subprograms for a program written in a high-level language.

Even if you do not plan to write assembler language programs, studying an assembler language will teach you many concepts about a computer, which in turn will help you to write better programs in high-level languages. You will learn about time and memory utilization, and of unusual occurrences such as arithmetic overflow. Knowing an assembler language removes the mystery from high-level languages and helps you to use them intelligently. Knowing an assembler language is also important if you plan to design new programming languages or computers.

*The Benefits of Learning about Machine Language.* You will rarely, if ever, have to write a machine language program. However, a knowledge of machine language is very important to the assembler language programmer. During

**AN HISTORICAL TIME LINE**

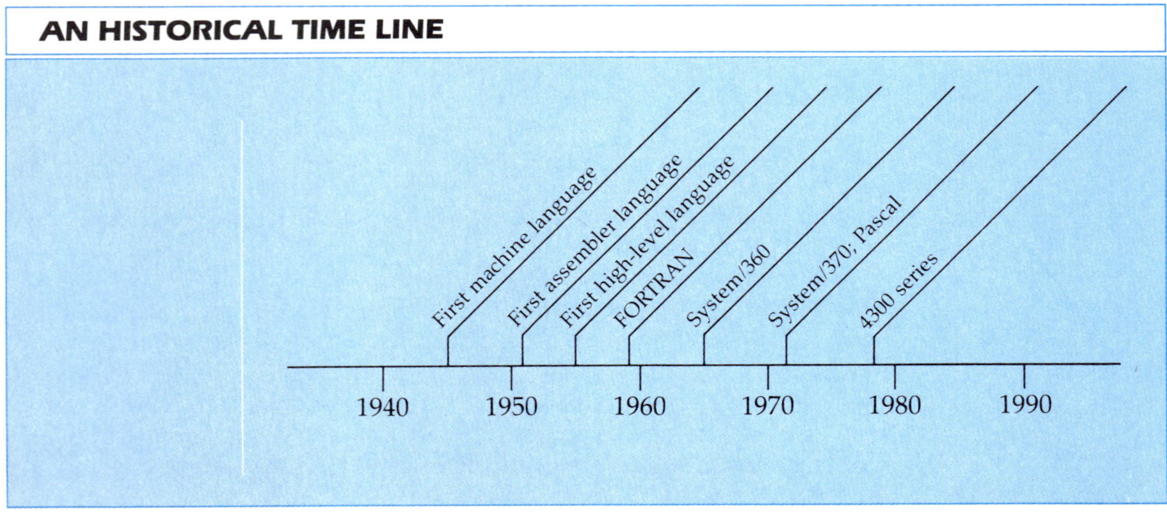

## THE IBM SYSTEM/360

On the morning of April 7, 1964, about 200 reporters boarded a chartered train in New York City bound for Poughkeepsie, New York. Why did they go to Poughkeepsie? They were headed to IBM's Poughkeepsie Laboratory for the unveiling of System/360—an event described that day by IBM's chairperson as the most important new product announcement in the company's 50-year history. That same day, similar press conferences in 62 U.S. cities and 14 foreign countries brought System/360 into the public eye with unprecedented fanfare. IBM's customers reacted enthusiastically, and the new system was an immediate commercial success.

What was so special about this product? The answers to this question are impressive—in fact, the fanfare was well deserved. System/360 made previous computers—even those of IBM—obsolete. It was the first computer to use microcircuitry, thereby initiating the Third generation of computer technology. The hybrid integrated circuits, as they were known, permitted a faster, more reliable computer.

Until 1964, computers were designed for either scientific applications or commercial applications, but not both. Scientific problems generally require many computations that use a relatively small amount of data. In contrast, business-oriented problems generally require limited manipulation of vast amounts of data. Computers had been designed for these special purposes, but the 360 was the first computer to integrate the characteristics of scientific and commercial computers, while serving the divergent needs of both science and business. It was consequently named for the 360 degrees of the compass—a tribute to its ability to handle a "full circle" of applications.

Another key innovation of System/360 was the concept of a family of program-compatible computers. A program written for one model would run correctly on other models that were at least as powerful. Thus, customers could begin with a small model and move up to a larger model, without paying for the cost of revising or replacing their programs. Since the introduction of the 360, compatibility between systems and models has been a major concern of computer designers.

The 360 was the first to have a standard interface for input, output, and storage devices. Previously, each computer had required its own personalized printers, terminals, and so on. Manufacturers of such **peripheral devices** had sold them to computer manufacturers, who then sold complete packages to their customers. Although IBM introduced about 40 such peripherals that could be used in numerous combinations with the various models within System/360, the standard interface enabled peripheral manufacturers to sell **plug-compatible** input, output, and storage devices directly to 360 owners, so that those manufacturers often competed with IBM itself.

System/360 was also significant to IBM's stockholders—first for its enormous development costs, and later for its tremendous sales record. *Fortune* magazine used a popular estimate when it referred to the project as "IBM's $5,000,000,000 Gamble,"[†] and one IBM executive joked, "We call this project, 'You bet your company.'" Looking back, no observer can doubt the wisdom of the gamble that produced one of the most successful—and original—computers ever built.

[†]Wise, T. A. "IBM's $5,000,000,000 Gamble." *Fortune* (September 1966): 228.

debugging, it is often necessary to examine the object code that appears in the assembly listing in order to verify the accuracy of an assembler language statement. In fact, you can avoid errors while writing assembler language statements if you try to be aware of the machine language instructions that they represent. Debugging also requires you to examine a **memory dump**, which prints the contents of memory after program execution. In doing so, you will have to be able to read machine language instructions.

### *Why Study the IBM System/370?*

In 1964, IBM introduced its System/360, the first family of program-compatible computers. With a few exceptions, an assembler language program written for one model in the family ran without change on a higher model. This concept continued with the introduction of System/370 in 1971 and the 4300 series, shown in Figure 1.4, in 1979.† IBM has made technological improvements to the computers and has added instructions to the instruction set, but programs written for System/360 computers in the 1960s will still run on the newest of models. Thus, it is reasonable to expect that the assembler language that you will learn now will still be used in the future.

System/370 assembler language is one of the most widely used assembler languages. In addition to the many System/370 installations, several computers outside of the IBM System/370 family also use the same assembler language. These include the IBM PC AT/370, shown in Figure 1.5, as well as those produced by several other manufacturers. If you must learn another assembler language for another computer, you will probably notice similarities between it and the one you will learn about in this text due to the influence that IBM has had on the computing industry. Even if this does not hold true in a particular case, all assembler languages share the same basic concepts, and the general programming techniques that you learn here will be applicable to other computers. Thus, once you have mastered the 370's assembler language, it will not be difficult to learn another.

†This text will use System/370 to describe all models in this family including the 4300 series, and will point out any differences with System/360 when necessary.

**Figure 1.4**
An IBM 4381 computing system. (*Courtesy of International Business Machines Corporation*)

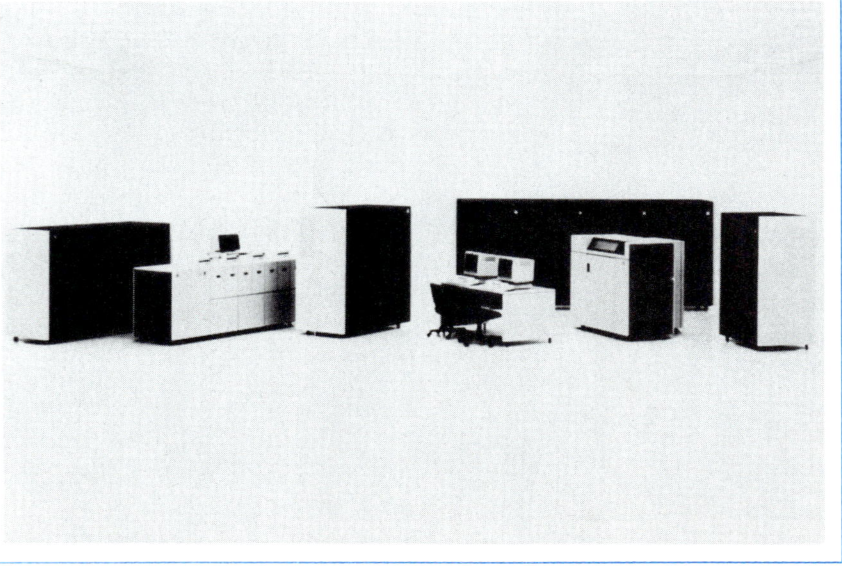

## The IBM SYSTEM/370

More than simply a follow-up to the 360, System/370 had its own influence on the computer industry. By 1970, IBM was by far the most observed company in the computer industry. Six years earlier, System/360 had launched the Third generation, and competitors and consumers were understandably eager to see IBM's forthcoming new system.

Two large models within System/370—the 155 and the 165—were introduced in June 1970. Many industry observers prematurely proclaimed the arrival of the Fourth generation, but some perceived the 370 as just a "beefed-up" 360. IBM was careful not to claim it had launched a new generation. (In fact, the distinctions between the Third and Fourth generations are still not unanimously agreed upon.) However, it soon became clear that the 370 was more than an enhanced 360.

System/370 was a commercial success, as customers looked forward to the faster execution times that it offered. The 370 expanded the concept of program compatibility, which the 360 introduced, to include not only models within System/370, but those within System/360 as well. Thus, programs written for the 360 could run without change on System/370 computers.

The 370's most important innovation first appeared on one of the smaller models, the Model 145 introduced in September 1970. This model was the first computer marketed with an all-semiconductor main memory. Semiconductors permitted faster—and much less expensive—memory than the magnetic cores that had been standard up to that time. The use of semiconductors affected the high technology industries that had moved to California's Santa Clara valley during the 1960s. For the first time, the valley's young semiconductor companies began to sell large quantities of their products to mainframe manufacturers. In this way, System/370 and its competitors helped make "Silicon Valley" a reality.

**Figure 1.5**
An IBM PC AT/370.
(*Courtesy of International Business Machines Corporation*)

## *Words of Encouragement*

Although learning your second assembler language may be easy, learning your first may not be. The nature of assembler language—particularly one as large as the 370's—can cause frustration. There are approximately 200 instructions in the System/370 instruction set and 40 **directives** to the assembler, which perform such tasks as defining symbols. Many elements in the language depend upon other language elements. At first, you may feel that you have to learn everything all at once. An assembler language requires that you think about many more details than are necessary when you use a high-level language. Many of these general characteristics are the same ones that you encountered when you learned your first programming language. Since you were successful then, you should now be well prepared to learn assembler language: all of the general concepts about problem solving, program design, style, documentation, testing, and debugging are still applicable.

### THE IBM 4300 SERIES

Imagine a manufacturer who improves its wares over an 8-year period to provide a product with increased performance to its customers. This is not unusual. Now, imagine that the manufacturer increases the efficiency of its production processes, allowing it to sell its new product at a lower price than the old product. This is noteworthy. However, if the product is a mainframe computer and its price is cut by 80 percent, the story is amazing.

In 1979, IBM announced its new line of computers, the 4300 series. This series provided a major increase in power over System/370, yet retained the program compatibility that was introduced with System/360. Prior to 1979, IBM used a memory chip that could store 2K bits of data. The 4300 series used a chip that could store 64K bits of data. This resulted in larger memories. (Chips that can store 256K bits of data are now common.)

Despite this increase in storage capacity, the introductory prices of the 4300 series were low, especially in comparison with the prices at which System/370 had been introduced 9 years earlier. The smallest model, the 4331, was priced at $65,000 in 1979. In 1970, the original price of the smallest 370 model had been $350,000—more than 5 times as much as the 4331. The top-of-the-line 4341 was introduced at $245,000—again, this was less than one-fifth of the original price of the largest 370 model. These price differences are even more impressive when you realize that the figures are not corrected for inflation.

Lower manufacturing costs were the chief reason for the low prices of the 4300 series, but there was another factor. Previously, IBM had priced hardware and the required software as a package—thus passing programming costs along to the hardware buyer. With the 4300 series, IBM moved away from this practice by pricing software and hardware separately. Although the basic software was provided without charge to the hardware buyer, enhancements and software maintenance were made available at additional cost. Consequently IBM could charge less for hardware, while software grew in importance as a separate product. The 4300 series was instrumental in changing hardware and software sales patterns.

# Introduction to the Structure of System/370

Before you can learn assembler language for the IBM 370, you must learn the terminology used to describe the general structure of this computing system. However, you will probably recognize many general concepts from your previous studies.

## *Component Overview*

The IBM 370, like typical digital computers, consists of three major components: **main storage** (also called **storage** or **memory**†), the **central processing unit** (the **CPU**), and the **input/output (I/O) system**. As each of these is described, refer to Figure 1.6, which pictures their interaction schematically.

†Like IBM documentation, this text will use *storage* instead of *memory*.

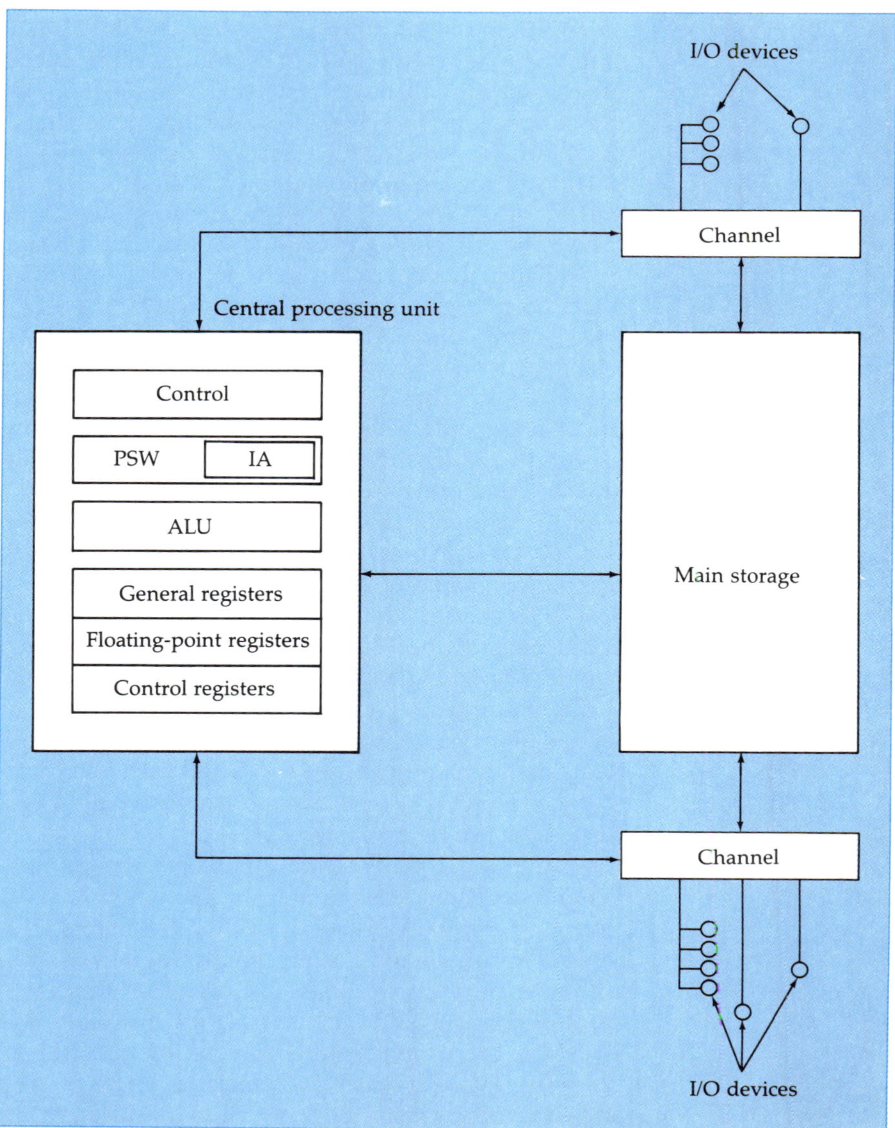


**Figure 1.6**
A block diagram of an IBM System/370.

Bytes

*Main Storage.* Main storage is a collection of cells or locations, each containing a piece of data. The storage locations of an IBM 370 are called **bytes**. Each byte contains an 8-bit binary quantity called its **contents**, and has a fixed numeric name known as its **address**. Addresses are simply binary integers that are assigned to the bytes consecutively, beginning with zero. You cannot change the address of a particular byte but you can change its contents. The common analogy between bytes and mailboxes in a post office is a good one: each box number (the address) is fixed, but the contents of the box can change. However, unlike a mailbox, a byte can contain only a single piece of data at a time; placing new data into a byte destroys the old data. Although the 8 bits in a byte permit a rather small range of numbers, you can group consecutive bytes to represent larger quantities. (Chapter 3 will elaborate on this concept.) Note that IBM first introduced the idea of organizing storage into bytes and groupings of bytes. The word *byte,* coined from "bite" and respelled, originally referred to a group of from 1 to 6 bits. However, System/360 pioneered the use of 8-bit bytes, which is a concept used by most computers today.

*The Central Processing Unit.* The instructions that compose a machine language program reside in consecutive bytes of main storage, and are executed by the central processing unit. Unless specifically instructed to do otherwise, the CPU executes instructions sequentially in the order in which they appear in storage. To control the sequence of instructions, the CPU places the address of the next instruction in the **instruction address (IA)** portion of the **program status word (PSW)**. The PSW is a special location within the CPU that indicates the status of the CPU in relation to a program. (The PSW will be described in detail in a later chapter.)

PSW

Initially, the operating system sets the IA to the address of the first instruction in the program, but thereafter the CPU maintains the IA. The CPU examines the IA to determine the address of the next instruction. After locating the instruction, the CPU updates the IA to the address of the next sequential instruction and executes the present instruction. This cycle continues repeatedly. There are instructions called **branch instructions**, whose execution changes the IA. Their use allows you either to write loops or to alter the sequential flow of your program.

The portion of the CPU that manipulates data specified by instructions is called the **arithmetic and logical unit (ALU)**. It performs arithmetic, comparisons, and other similar tasks. Associated with these operations are special locations called **registers**. Although they may look like storage locations, registers are contained in the CPU and have special addresses or names. Many instructions involve one or more registers. For example, to add two numbers, you would place one number into a register and add the second number to it; the sum would be developed within the register. Registers are used because the CPU can access data in them faster than in storage. However, registers are expensive so there are far fewer of them than there are bytes of storage.

Register types

The IBM 370 has several types of registers. Sixteen of these are called **general registers**: each represents 32 bits and is addressed by an integer from 0 to 15. You can use the general registers as accumulators for binary integer arithmetic or certain logical operations. You can also use them to compute the address of data in storage required by a particular instruction. Floating-point arithmetic uses 4 **floating-point registers** as accumulators. These registers are identified by the integers 0, 2, 4, and 6, and each is 64 bits long. There are also other registers that are used primarily by the operating system to keep track of status information, in addition to the infor-

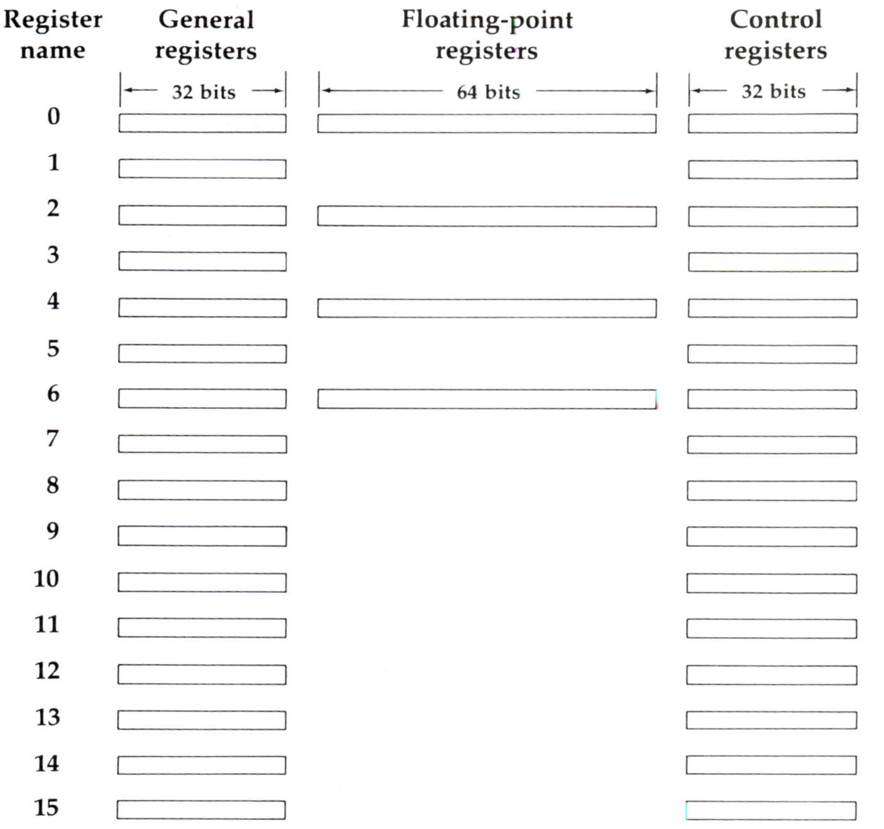

**Figure 1.7**
The general, floating-point, and control registers.

| Register name | General registers (32 bits) | Floating-point registers (64 bits) | Control registers (32 bits) |
|---|---|---|---|
| 0 | ☐ | ☐ | ☐ |
| 1 | ☐ | | ☐ |
| 2 | ☐ | ☐ | ☐ |
| 3 | ☐ | | ☐ |
| 4 | ☐ | ☐ | ☐ |
| 5 | ☐ | | ☐ |
| 6 | ☐ | ☐ | ☐ |
| 7 | ☐ | | ☐ |
| 8 | ☐ | | ☐ |
| 9 | ☐ | | ☐ |
| 10 | ☐ | | ☐ |
| 11 | ☐ | | ☐ |
| 12 | ☐ | | ☐ |
| 13 | ☐ | | ☐ |
| 14 | ☐ | | ☐ |
| 15 | ☐ | | ☐ |

mation stored in the PSW. Among these other registers are up to sixteen 32-bit **control registers**, which are also identified by the integers 0 to 15. The general, floating-point, and control registers are illustrated in Figure 1.7.

Notice that a register address does not distinguish its type; this is implied by the context in which an instruction uses a register. For now, this text will deal only with the general registers—often just calling them "registers"—until Chapter 17, which will introduce the use of floating-point registers. The study of control registers is beyond the scope of this book.

**The two states of the CPU**

The CPU can be in one of two states that are indicated by a bit in the PSW. The **problem state** allows you to run a program; such a program is called a **problem program** or a **user program**. However, there are certain instructions that are said to be **privileged**, which you cannot use when the CPU is in the problem state. These instructions are used by the operating system and can only be executed when the CPU is in **supervisor state**, which is discussed later. There are also **semiprivileged instructions**, which can be executed in the problem state under certain conditions, but are not normally part of a user program. The study of privileged and semiprivileged instructions is beyond the scope of this book.

**Interruptions**

Certain conditions, such as an execution-time error or the termination of an I/O operation, can cause an **interruption**. This hardware feature permits the CPU to transfer control rapidly from one program to another in response to an unusual situation. This means that the CPU can interrupt the execution of your program so that the operating system can issue an error message. When an interruption occurs, the CPU saves the contents of the PSW in a designated storage location according to the type of interruption. The CPU then replaces the contents of the PSW with a constant from another designated storage location. The IA portion of this new PSW contains the address of the program that will process the interruption. This processing program, for example, may issue an error message, keep track of the completion of an I/O operation, or terminate the interrupted program. If the processing program determines that the interrupted program can continue execution, it will ultimately restore the PSW to its original value.

*The Input/Output System.* The input/output system enables the computer to communicate with the outside world. You are already familiar with various **I/O devices**, such as terminals, card readers, printers, keyboards, video displays, tapes, and disks. Components called **channels** connect such devices to the rest of the computer, and are responsible for the flow of data between the devices and main storage. Data entered at an input device such as a keyboard is routed via a channel to the main storage. Data already in storage can be routed via a channel to an output device such as a printer. A typical computing system will contain several channels, each of which will be associated with perhaps many devices. After the CPU has initiated an I/O operation, a channel handles the details of the data transfer, thereby freeing the CPU for other processing. This concurrency of operation is a significant feature of large-scale computing systems.

## The Operating System

An **operating system** is a set of programs that provides services, which allow you to use a computer; for all practical purposes, it is an essential part of a computing system. When many users simultaneously share a large computing system such as System/370, the operating system schedules the available resources, protects each user from others, and allows for an efficient use of the computing system. The portion of the operating system chiefly responsible for these activities is called the **supervisor**.

One way that the operating system can provide protection is through the privileged instructions and the states of the CPU. The operating system executes while the CPU is in supervisor state, but a user program executes while the CPU is in problem state. Thus, only the operating system can execute privileged instructions. For example, since the I/O instructions are privileged, the user program must request the supervisor to perform I/O operations. Such requests cause the CPU to change from problem state to supervisor state. The supervisor then has complete control over the channels and can keep track of all I/O operations. The change from problem state to supervisor state makes interference with I/O operations by a user program impossible.

By making operations concurrent, the operating system also increases efficiency within the computing system. Since CPU processing and data transfer can occur simultaneously, the operating system can weave the execution of several user programs with itself to keep the CPU as busy as possible. With this technique, each user appears to have the total attention of the computing system, even though the CPU can only execute one instruction at a time.

Each user program is known as a **job**, which consists in general of several **job steps**. Some steps may require a processor, such as an assembler or a linkage editor, and access to collections of data called **files** or **data sets**.

For example, a file may contain the source program, the object module, the load module, or any other required data. The operating system schedules the required processors and provides access to the files. It also enables jobs to access a library of utility programs, such as text editors and file managers. You can specify the steps of a job and its file requirements with **job control language**, or **JCL**, statements.

Three classes of operating systems

Three classes of operating systems are available. They are **DOS** (Disk Operating System), **OS** (Operating System), and **VM** (Virtual Machine). Some examples of operating systems within these classes that you may encounter are DOS/VSE, MVS/370, MVS/XA, OS/VS1, and VM/370. DOS was first introduced for the smaller models of the 360 and is still available for the 370. OS is more complex and offers more services for users of larger computing systems. VM differs from OS and DOS because it allows each user to run any operating system on a simulated 370. For example, one user may choose DOS while another chooses OS. IBM also provides an interactive system called **CMS** (Conversational Monitor System), which runs under VM. For the most part, the choice of operating system has little effect on your assembler language programs. This text will point out any differences where appropriate; the most significant differences involve I/O and are discussed in Chapter 16.

## Summary

1. Each type of computer has its own set of numeric instructions known as its machine language.
2. An assembler language is a symbolic version of machine language. The assembler translates an assembler language program into a machine language program called the object module.
3. An assembler language provides access to a computer's full instruction set and may be better suited than a high-level language for certain applications.
4. Knowing machine language is important when debugging assembler language programs.
5. IBM's System/370 is a widely used family of program-compatible computers.
6. The smallest addressable unit of IBM 370 main storage is the byte.
7. The central processing unit (CPU) controls the execution and sequencing of instructions. Its registers are used by many instructions for such tasks as arithmetic calculations, comparisons, and address computation. The CPU also contains the program status word (PSW), which records the status of the CPU in relation to the user program and which contains the address of the next instruction.
8. The CPU has two states: supervisor state and problem state. The CPU is in supervisor state when the operating system executes and in problem state when the user program executes.
9. An interruption is a hardware feature that permits the CPU to transfer control rapidly from one program to another in response to an unusual situation.
10. The input/output system transmits data through a channel both from an I/O device to main storage and from main storage to an I/O device. After the CPU initiates an I/O operation, the channel takes over the details of the data transmission. I/O operations are privileged instructions, which the operating system executes at the request of a user program.

## Exercises

1. Find out how to run the assembler language program in Figure 1.1 and then try to run the program.
2. Find out the characteristics of the computing system that you will be using. For example, how many bytes are in its main storage? What are its I/O devices?

2

# Number Systems

CONTENTS



OVERVIEW

This chapter discusses number systems that are used by many computers, including those in the IBM/370 family. The binary and hexadecimal number systems are particularly important to assembler language programmers. The chapter describes the relationships of these number systems to each other and to decimal numbers, and covers the sign-magnitude and two's complement binary number systems within the context of finite number systems. Number representations, arithmetic, range, and overflow for each system are also considered.

**OBJECTIVES**

After studying this chapter, you should be able to:

1. Convert integers from one base to another.
2. Add and subtract unsigned binary and hexadecimal integers.
3. Represent integers, perform addition and subtraction, specify ranges, and detect overflow in a finite sign-magnitude binary number system.
4. Represent integers, perform addition and subtraction, specify ranges, and detect overflow in a two's complement binary number system.

## Introduction

Like most computers, computers in the IBM System/370 family represent instructions, addresses, numbers, and characters with a binary notation. As an assembler language programmer, you will frequently work at the machine language level during the writing and debugging stages of creating a program. For example, you may examine the object code to ensure that an assembler language statement is correct, check the contents of particular bytes in storage, or verify an address. Since working with long binary numbers can be tedious and prone to error, you frequently will substitute an equivalent, but shorter, **hexadecimal** (base 16) number. For example, the addresses and the object code that appear in assembly listings are given in hexadecimal, as are the contents of storage locations when they are printed in a dump. Translating from binary to hexadecimal is simple because there is a one-to-one relationship between the two number systems, as you learned in Chapter 1. The hexadecimal system is convenient to use since each hexadecimal digit represents 4 bits, a grouping that is fundamental to the design of IBM 370 instructions.

Computers cannot represent all numbers since the number of bits in a particular grouping of bytes is fixed. Number systems that result from this restriction are called **finite number systems**. The **range** of the number system specifies which numbers can be represented. There are two subdivisions of finite number systems that you will study. **Sign-magnitude numbers** are similar to the numbers that you are accustomed to except that they are always preceded by plus or minus signs. For example, this simple arithmetic expression uses sign-magnitude numbers: $+2 + (-5)$. The IBM 370 uses a sign-magnitude system to perform decimal and floating-point arithmetic. Another subdivision of finite number systems is the **two's complement binary number system**. This system permits a simpler design of a computer's arithmetic circuitry than is possible with sign-magnitude numbers. For this reason, most computers use the two's complement binary number system. In particular, System/370 computers use it to perform binary integer arithmetic.

## Unsigned Integers in a Positional Number System

While computers use binary numbers and although programmers represent them in hexadecimal for convenience, people continue to live in a decimal world. Therefore, you must be comfortable with all three systems and be able to convert from one to another with ease. This discussion is restricted to base 2, base 10, and base 16 numbers; however, you should note that the rules for all positional notation systems are the same.

This discussion begins with unsigned integers. Because binary unsigned integers are used as addresses by System/370 computers, you must be familiar with the concepts of number representation, counting, arithmetic, and conversion between bases.

### *Representations and Conversions*

**Positional number systems**

Ordinary decimal integers that you encounter everyday are characterized by a **positional notation**; an integer can contain a unit's digit, a ten's digit, and so on. Each digit represents a value based upon its position within the integer—thus, this system is called a **positional number system**. For example, the number 836 has a value equivalent to

$$\begin{aligned} & 8 \times 10^2 + 3 \times 10^1 + 6 \times 10^0 \\ = & 800 \quad + 30 \quad + 6 \end{aligned}$$

This representation is called an **expansion in powers of the base**. The leftmost digit of 836 is the **most-significant** or **high-order digit** because it is multiplied by the largest power of 10. Similarly, the rightmost digit is the **least-significant** or **low-order digit**.

**Symbols**

Conceptually, all positional number systems are the same. In general, a base $B$ number system uses $B$ symbols and the largest has a decimal value of $B - 1$. Decimal, or base 10, numbers use the 10 symbols 0 through 9. The value of the largest symbol, 9, is 1 less than the base, 10. Binary, or base 2, numbers use the 2 symbols 0 and 1. Again, the value of the largest symbol, 1, is 1 less than the base, 2. Hexadecimal, or base 16, numbers use the 16 symbols 0 through 9 and A through F. The letters represent the decimal values 10 through 15. Here again, the value of the largest symbol, F, is 1 less than the base.

Each digit position in the representation of a number represents a power of the base of the number system. Thus, you can compute the decimal equivalent of a base $B$ number by expanding it into powers of $B$, converting each of its digits to decimal, and using decimal arithmetic. This process is demonstrated for binary and hexadecimal integers in the next sections.

**A subscript notation designates the base of a number**

To emphasize the base of a number, the text uses a subscript notation. For example, $101101_2$ represents the binary integer 101101 and $101_{16}$ represents the hexadecimal integer 101. The term **hex** will sometimes be used to mean hexadecimal.

*Binary-to-Decimal Conversions.* When you use decimal arithmetic to expand the binary integer $b_1b_2 \ldots b_n$ into powers of its base, it is represented as

$$b_1 \times 2^{n-1} + b_2 \times 2^{n-2} + \ldots + b_{n-1} \times 2^1 + b_n \times 2^0$$

For example, the decimal equivalent of the binary integer 101101 is

**An expansion in powers of 2**

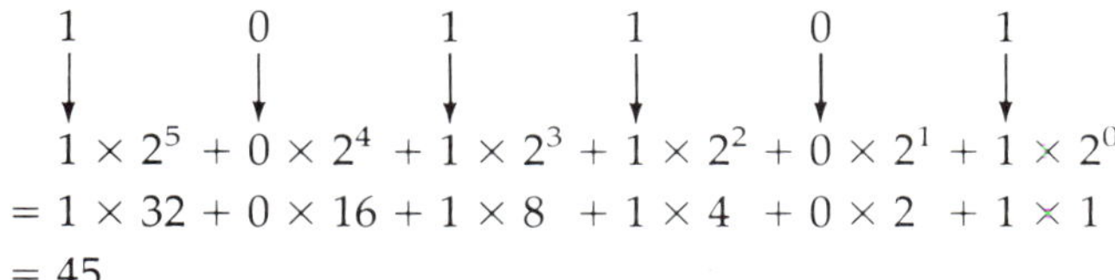

$$1 \times 2^5 + 0 \times 2^4 + 1 \times 2^3 + 1 \times 2^2 + 0 \times 2^1 + 1 \times 2^0$$
$$= 1 \times 32 + 0 \times 16 + 1 \times 8 + 1 \times 4 + 0 \times 2 + 1 \times 1$$
$$= 45$$

This example demonstrates a binary-to-decimal conversion that is easy to remember. The technique used is particularly useful when you have access to a table of powers of two.

However, you may prefer to nest the binary-to-decimal conversion of 101101, as shown here:

$$((((1 \times 2 + 0) \times 2 + 1) \times 2 + 1) \times 2 + 0) \times 2 + 1 = 45$$

Nesting the computation is equivalent to the **double-dabble method**, which is described as follows:

- Begin with the leftmost bit and double it.
- To this value, add the next bit to the right.
- Double the result and add in the next bit to the right.
- Continue doubling and adding (*dabbling*) until the last bit is added.

The computations may be arranged left to right:

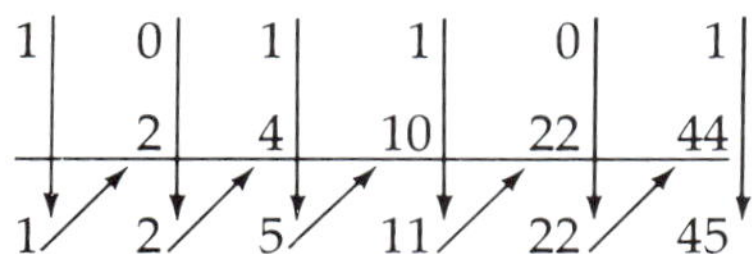

Here, the vertical arrows indicate addition and the diagonal arrows indicate multiplication by 2.

*Hexadecimal-to-Decimal Conversions.* When you use decimal arithmetic to expand the hexadecimal integer $h_1h_2 \ldots h_n$ into powers of its base, it is represented as

$$h_1 \times 16^{n-1} + h_2 \times 16^{n-2} + \ldots + h_{n-1} \times 16^1 + h_n \times 16^0$$

For example, the hexadecimal integer 29CF has a decimal value equivalent to the decimal computation

**An expansion in powers of 16**

$$\begin{array}{cccc} 2 & 9 & C & F \\ \downarrow & \downarrow & \downarrow & \downarrow \end{array}$$

$$2 \times 16^3 + 9 \times 16^2 + 12 \times 16^1 + 15 \times 16^0$$
$$= 2 \times 4096 + 9 \times 256 + 12 \times 16 + 15 \times 1$$
$$= 10703$$

This method is useful if you have a table of powers of 16. If you prefer, you can nest computation as

$$((2 \times 16 + 9) \times 16 + 12) \times 16 + 15$$

## A SHORT HISTORY OF NUMBER SYSTEMS

You probably would not sign up for a lecture course if you read that 11,000,000 students were already registered; and a discussion section with an enrollment of 1100 students might not look any more appealing. The reason for this is that you, like the rest of the culture, use the decimal number system. In fact, if binary numbers were in common use, you would automatically interpret 11,000,000 as 192, and 1100 as 12.

The decimal and binary number systems are examples of positional number systems, in which each digit's meaning is determined by its position. However, not all civilizations have used positional number systems. For example, in the Roman numeral system, the position of a symbol within a number does not affect the value of the symbol. Thus, in the number CCXX, each C represents 100 and each X represents 10. Roman numerals are just one instance of nonpositional representations. You would probably be confused if a class enrollment was listed as ↄ ∩ ∩ ∩ ∩ ∩ ∩ ∩ ∩ ∩ / /, but ancient Egyptians would have recognized it immediately as 192. A major disadvantage of number systems such as those used by the Romans and the Egyptians is that arithmetic is cumbersome.

### METHODS OF COUNTING

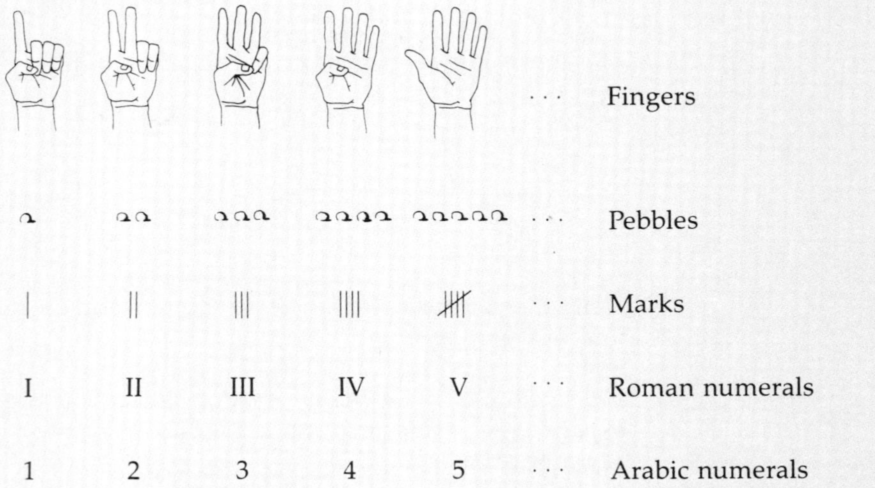

| | | | | | | |
|---|---|---|---|---|---|---|
| | | | | | … | Fingers |
| ○ | ○○ | ○○○ | ○○○○ | ○○○○○ | … | Pebbles |
| \| | \|\| | \|\|\| | \|\|\|\| | \|\|\|\|/ | … | Marks |
| I | II | III | IV | V | … | Roman numerals |
| 1 | 2 | 3 | 4 | 5 | … | Arabic numerals |

Among the cultures that did—and do—use positional number systems, there has been some variation in the selection of the systems' bases. Two noteworthy cases are the ancient Mesopotamians, who used a base 60 system around 1750 B.C., and the Mayans of Central America, who used a mixture of base 18 and base 20 some 17 centuries later. The present-day base 10 system is called the **Hindu-Arabic system**. It was developed by the Hindus around 600 A.D. It spread to Persia when some Hindu books were translated into Arabic, and reached Europe after an important Arabic text was translated into Latin. The standardization of the symbols 0 through 9 as a result of the invention of the printing press in the 1400s helped to bring the decimal number system into general use in all of Europe.

*(Continues)*

During the 1600s, two people—one from England and the other from Spain—separately had the idea of a binary notation for numbers. However, the mathematician Leibniz is usually credited with the discovery of binary arithmetic because he illustrated the four basic operations in base 2 in a publication in 1703. Leibniz was fascinated with binary notation: he saw it as a symbol of the creation of the world (1) from nothing (0).

Binary arithmetic was not used much during the next centuries. Even the earliest computers used decimal arithmetic. However, in 1946, Burks, Goldstine, and von Neumann proposed that a binary notation would be a more reliable and more economical way for computers to represent data. Today, binary arithmetic in computers is standard. So, even though you would be surprised to see an enrollment figure of 11,000,000, a computer would not. To a computer, 11,000,000 does not mean the population of Illinois; it is just enough to fill a lecture hall.

and arrange it left to right:

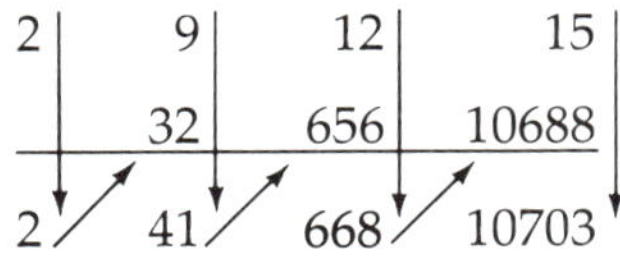


Here, the vertical arrows represent addition and the diagonal arrows represent multiplication by 16.

You may have noticed that the expansion in powers of a base is simply a polynomial that is evaluated at the base. For example, the expansion of 29CF just shown is the polynomial

$$2x^3 + 9x^2 + 12x + 15$$

evaluated at $x = 16$. You may perform this evaluation by using Horner's method† or synthetic division, which is identical to the nested computation just shown.

Each hex digit represents a 4-bit binary number

*Conversions Between Hexadecimal and Binary Integers.* As shown in Chapter 1, each of the 16 hexadecimal digits corresponds to one of the 16 possible 4-digit binary numbers. As noted earlier, this correspondence makes it convenient to use hexadecimal numbers as a shorthand for binary numbers. The ability to convert between binary and hexadecimal numbers with ease is an important skill for you to have. Figure 2.1 summarizes the relationships among decimal, binary, and hexadecimal numbers.

These conversions are simple mechanical processes. Given a binary integer, you first form groups of 4 bits beginning at the right. You then substitute the hexadecimal equivalent for each group. The process can be illustrated like this:

```
0111  1010  1100  0010
  |     |     |     |
  ↓     ↓     ↓     ↓
  7     A     C     2
```

†Knuth, D. E. *Seminumerical Algorithms.* Vol. 2 of *The Art of Computer Programming,* 467–468. 2d ed. Reading, Mass.: Addison-Wesley, 1981.

**Figure 2.1**
The relationships among decimal, binary, and hexadecimal numbers.

| Decimal | Binary | Hexadecimal |
|---|---|---|
| 0 | 0000 | 0 |
| 1 | 0001 | 1 |
| 2 | 0010 | 2 |
| 3 | 0011 | 3 |
| 4 | 0100 | 4 |
| 5 | 0101 | 5 |
| 6 | 0110 | 6 |
| 7 | 0111 | 7 |
| 8 | 1000 | 8 |
| 9 | 1001 | 9 |
| 10 | 1010 | A |
| 11 | 1011 | B |
| 12 | 1100 | C |
| 13 | 1101 | D |
| 14 | 1110 | E |
| 15 | 1111 | F |

Thus, $0111\ 1010\ 1100\ 0010_2 = 7AC2_{16}$. To check this result, convert both the binary integer and the hexadecimal integer to decimal. (The result is 31426.)

To convert from hexadecimal to binary, replace each hexadecimal digit by its 4-digit binary equivalent, as shown in this example:

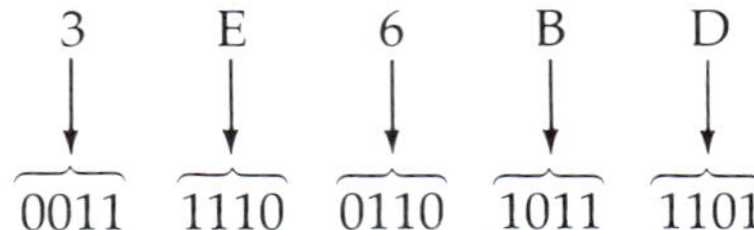


Thus, $3E6BD_{16} = 0011\ 1110\ 0110\ 1011\ 1101_2$.

*Decimal-to-Binary Conversions.* Suppose that you want to convert the decimal integer $I$ to binary. Assume that its binary equivalent has the form

$$b_1 b_2 \ldots b_n$$

If you expand this into powers of its base by using decimal arithmetic, you will get its decimal equivalent $I$. Therefore,

$$I = b_1 \times 2^{n-1} + b_2 \times 2^{n-2} + \ldots + b_{n-1} \times 2^1 + b_n$$

where the computations are decimal. Remember that $b_j$ is either 0 or 1. Divide $I$ by 2 and call the quotient $Q_1$. The remainder will be $b_n$; that is,

$$I \div 2 = Q_1 \text{ with a remainder of } b_n$$

So far, you have computed the rightmost bit, $b_n$, of the desired binary equivalent. Now, you are ready to work on $Q_1$:

$$Q_1 = b_1 \times 2^{n-2} + b_2 \times 2^{n-3} + \ldots + b_{n-2} \times 2^1 + b_{n-1}$$

You compute the next bit, $b_{n-1}$, by dividing $Q_1$ by 2:

$$Q_1 \div 2 = Q_2 \text{ with a remainder of } b_{n-1}$$

Continue the process until the quotient is 0 since, when $Q_n = 0$, the remainder is $b_1$, which is the first bit of the binary equivalent.

To illustrate this conversion process, consider $I = 13_{10}$:

**Perform divisions by 2**

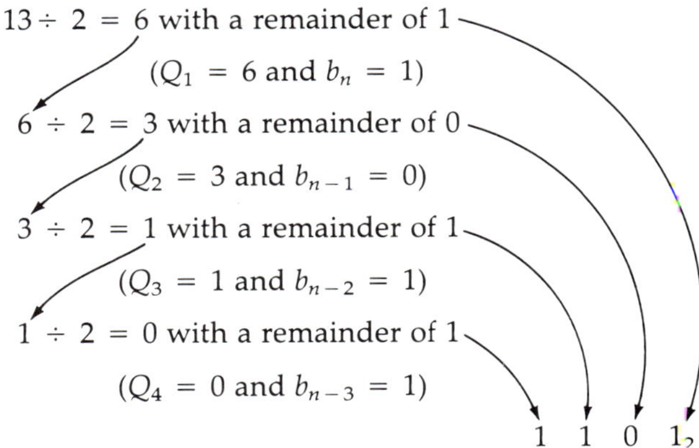


You form the binary equivalent by writing the remainders in an order opposite from which they were computed; thus, $13_{10} = 1101_2$. You could read the remainders from bottom to top, or write them from right to left on a line as you compute them. If you forget which way to read them, convert a number such as 13, whose binary equivalent is readily verified, but reads differently in each direction.

*Decimal-to-Hexadecimal Conversions.* The conversion from decimal to hexadecimal is analogous to the decimal-to-binary conversion just shown. As before, suppose $I$ is a decimal integer and that its hexadecimal equivalent is represented by

$$h_1 h_2 \ldots h_n$$

Then if $H_j$ is the decimal equivalent of the hexadecimal digit $h_j$, $I$ must appear as

$$I = H_1 \times 16^{n-1} + H_2 \times 16^{n-2} + \ldots + H_{n-1} \times 16^1 + H_n$$

Here, all computations are decimal. If you divide $I$ by 16, you will get a quotient $Q_1$ and a remainder $H_n$; that is,

$$I \div 16 = Q_1 \text{ with a remainder of } H_n$$

The desired hexadecimal digit $h_n$ is obtained by a simple conversion of $H_n$. You continue to divide each quotient by 16 until a zero quotient occurs. The remainders, when converted to hexadecimal, form the digits of the result. For example, consider $I = 1215_{10}$:

**Perform divisions by 16**

1215 ÷ 16 = 75 with a remainder of 15 = $F_{16}$

($Q_1 = 75$ and $H_n = 15$)

75 ÷ 16 = 4 with a remainder of 11 = $B_{16}$

($Q_2 = 4$ and $H_{n-1} = 11$)

4 ÷ 16 = 0 with a remainder of 4 = $4_{16}$

($Q_3 = 0$ and $H_{n-2} = 4$)

4 B $F_{16}$

You form the hexadecimal equivalent by writing the remainders in an order opposite from which they were computed; thus, $1215_{10} = 4BF_{16}$. You can verify this by converting $4BF_{16}$ to decimal.

Not only can you convert from decimal to any other base by using similar computations, you can convert from any base to any other base with arithmetic in the original base. This is considered in Exercise 15 at the end of this chapter.

## SELF-TEST EXERCISES

1. Convert the following unsigned binary integers to decimal:
   a. $11011_2$
   b. $111100_2$
   c. $1110101_2$
   d. $10100110_2$
   e. $1010011110_2$
2. Convert the binary integers in Self-Test Exercise 1 to hexadecimal.
3. Convert the following unsigned hexadecimal integers to decimal:
   a. $4D_{16}$
   b. $15A_{16}$
   c. $D67_{16}$
   d. $2EC8_{16}$
   e. $309BF_{16}$
4. Convert the hexadecimal integers in Self-Test Exercise 3 to binary.
5. Convert the following unsigned decimal integers to binary:
   a. 25
   b. 37
   c. 296
   d. 451
   e. 1628
6. Convert the decimal integers in Self-Test Exercise 5 to hexadecimal.

## *Unsigned Integer Arithmetic*

The same arithmetic rules apply to all positional number systems. However, you may find nondecimal arithmetic strange since you are unfamiliar with addition and multiplication tables in bases other than 10.

**Binary addition**

Since you will need to add and subtract hexadecimal and binary integers, first consider the addition of two 1-bit binary numbers. These are the possibilities:

$$\begin{array}{r} 0 \\ +\,0 \\ \hline 0 \end{array} \qquad \begin{array}{r} 0 \\ +\,1 \\ \hline 1 \end{array} \qquad \begin{array}{r} 1 \\ +\,0 \\ \hline 1 \end{array} \qquad \begin{array}{r} 1 \\ +\,1 \\ \hline 10 \end{array}$$

This information is often summarized in a binary addition table, as follows:

| + | 0 | 1 |
|---|---|---|
| 0 | 0 | 1 |
| 1 | 1 | 10 |

You add two $n$-bit binary integers by following the same rules that you use for decimal addition, but by using the binary addition table. Therefore, according to the addition rules, if a carry is generated in any position, you add the carry to the position at the immediate left. Thus, you may need to add three 1-digit binary numbers, which is equivalent to adding 0 or 1 to the results in the binary addition table just given. The only new result is

$$\begin{aligned} 1 + 1 + 1 &= (1 + 1) + 1 \\ &= 10 + 1 \\ &= 11 \end{aligned}$$

---

EXAMPLE 1

The following are some illustrations of adding unsigned binary integers:

a.
$$\begin{array}{r} 11 \quad \leftarrow \text{Carries} \\ 10111 \\ +\ 00010 \\ \hline 11001_2 \end{array}$$

b.
$$\begin{array}{r} 1\ 11 \quad \leftarrow \text{Carries} \\ 10111 \\ +\ 10010 \\ \hline 101001_2 \end{array}$$

c.
$$\begin{array}{r} 1\ \ 111 \quad \leftarrow \text{Carries} \\ 100111 \\ +\ 100111 \\ \hline 1001110_2 \end{array}$$

You can verify these results by converting the binary numbers to base 10 and performing the decimal addition, which is another—albeit tedious and error-prone—way to compute the sum of binary integers.

---

**Hexadecimal addition**

For hexadecimal addition, while you could refer to or memorize the hexadecimal addition table, this is probably more effort than is necessary because you will only do hexadecimal arithmetic occasionally. Thus, here is a procedure that you can follow. To add two hexadecimal digits, first convert each to decimal, perform the arithmetic in decimal, and then convert the result back to hexadecimal, adding any carry to the next position to the left. For example, consider the following hexadecimal addition:

$$\begin{array}{r} 11 \quad \leftarrow \text{Carries} \\ 4BF \\ +\ 7C3 \\ \hline C82 \end{array}$$

$(F + 3)_{16}$ is 15 plus 3, or 18, in decimal, which is $12_{16}$. You then write the 2 and carry the 1. Next, you compute $(1 + B + C)_{16}$: this is 1 plus 11 plus 12 in decimal, or $24_{10} = 18_{16}$. You write the 8 and carry the 1. Finally, you add $(1 + 4 + 7)_{16}$: this is 1 plus 4 plus 7 in decimal, or $12_{10} = C_{16}$. The conversion process involved in this addition is simple and more convenient than first converting 4BF and 7C3 to decimal, performing decimal arithmetic, and finally converting the result back to hexadecimal.

**Hexadecimal subtraction**

Subtracting binary or hexadecimal integers follows the same rules as those for decimal subtraction. Try doing this hexadecimal subtraction by using a technique similar to the one just demonstrated for addition:

$$\begin{array}{r} 7DF \\ -\ 320 \\ \hline 4BF \end{array}$$

First, $(F - 0)_{16}$ is $F_{16}$. Next, $(D - 2)_{16}$ is 13 minus 2 in decimal, or $11_{10} = B_{16}$. Finally, $7 - 3 = 4$ in either base.

As in decimal subtraction, it may be necessary to borrow. For example, in

```
 6 ¹5
 7̸ 6̸ ¹2
-1  A  3
---------
 5  B  F
```

Before you can subtract the 3 from the 2, you must borrow a 1 from the adjacent 6, reducing it to a 5. Now, $(12 - 3)_{16}$ is 18 minus 3 in decimal, or $15_{10} = F_{16}$. To subtract A from 5, you must borrow a 1 from the adjacent 7, reducing it to a 6. Then $(15 - A)_{16}$ becomes 21 minus 10 in decimal, or $11_{10} = B_{16}$. Finally, $6 - 1 = 5$. As a check, you can add the result to 1A3; you should get 762 back again.

**Binary subtraction**

The process of binary subtraction is similar to that of hexadecimal subtraction, but it is easy to become confused during the borrowing process. This is a simple example:

```
     0
 1 0 1̸ ¹0 0 1
-1 0 0  1 0 1
-------------
 0 0 0  1 0 0
```

Here, you borrow 1 from the digit on the left, making that digit a 0.

However, if there are intervening zeros between the present position and the next nonzero digit to the left, you borrow from that nonzero digit (changing it to 0) and convert the intervening zeros to ones, as shown:

```
   0 1 1
 1 1̸ 0̸ 0̸ ¹0 1
-1 0 0 1  1 1
-------------
 0 0 1 0  1 0
```

You can verify the result by adding it to 100111; you should get 110001 back again.

**Binary multiplication**

While you will seldom need to multiply or divide binary or hexadecimal integers, you should be familiar with the steps of the two processes. The rules are the same as for decimal multiplication and division. For example, the following binary multiplication is equivalent to the decimal computation $30 \times 21 = 630$:

```
          1 1 1 1 0
        × 1 0 1 0 1
        -----------
          1 1 1 1 0
        0 0 0 0 0
      1 1 1 1 0
    0 0 0 0 0
  1 1 1 1 0
  -------------------
1 0 0 1 1 1 0 1 1 0
```

## SELF-TEST EXERCISES

7. Perform the following binary arithmetic:

| | | | | | |
|---|---|---|---|---|---|
| **a.** | 11010 + 01110 | **d.** | 100111 + 101001 | **g.** | 101001 − 010010 |
| **b.** | 10111 + 10010 | **e.** | 11000 − 01111 | **h.** | 101001 − 010111 |
| **c.** | 100111 + 100011 | **f.** | 101000 − 010111 | | |

8. Perform the following hexadecimal arithmetic:

| | | | | | | | | | |
|---|---|---|---|---|---|---|---|---|---|
| **a.** | 4BF + 1A2 | **c.** | 2F1B + A0F3 | **e.** | 10111 + 10010 | **g.** | 661 − 1A2 | **i.** | 4F0B61 − 1E12AB |
| **b.** | ABC + DEF | **d.** | ABCDE + BCDEF | **f.** | 7DF − 320 | **h.** | D501 − 24BA | **j.** | 11000 − 01111 |

**Binary division**

The following binary division is equivalent to the decimal computation 437 ÷ 5 = 87 with a remainder of 2:

```
            1 0 1 0 1 1 1
1 0 1 ) 1 1 0 1 1 0 1 0 1
        1 0 1
            1 1 1
            1 0 1
              1 0 0 1
                1 0 1
                1 0 0 0
                  1 0 1
                  0 1 1 1
                    1 0 1
                      1 0 = remainder
```

## Finite Number Systems

**The largest integer**

Computers, by their nature, can only represent quantities having a finite number of digits. Thus, you can only represent a finite number of integers, of which one must be the largest integer. The largest integer that can be represented in $n$ digits in a base $B$ number system has a decimal equivalent of $B^n - 1$. For example, if $B = 10$ and $n = 3$, then

$$\begin{aligned} B^n - 1 &= 10^3 - 1 \\ &= 999 \end{aligned}$$

If $B = 2$ and $n = 3$, then

$$\begin{aligned} B^n - 1 &= 2^3 - 1 \\ &= 7 \\ &= 111_2 \end{aligned}$$

In general, the largest integer $L$ in a base $B$ number system is represented by $n$ repetitions of the largest digit, $B-1$. (Thus, $L$ is 999 in decimal and 111 in binary.) To demonstrate that $L$ has a decimal value of $B^n - 1$, you can use an expansion in powers of $B$. In decimal, the expansion is

$$\begin{aligned} L &= 999 \\ &= 9 \times 10^2 + 9 \times 10^1 + 9 \times 10^0 \end{aligned}$$

In binary, the expansion is

$$\begin{aligned} L &= 111_2 \\ &= 1 \times 2^2 + 1 \times 2^1 + 1 \times 2^0 \end{aligned}$$

The general format of the expansion in powers of $B$ is

$$\begin{aligned} L = {} & (B-1) \times B^{n-1} + (B-1) \times B^{n-2} + \ldots \\ & + (B-1) \times B^1 + (B-1) \times B^0 \end{aligned}$$

By performing the multiplication and regrouping terms, you obtain

$$\begin{aligned} L &= B^n + (-B^{n-1} + B^{n-1}) + \ldots + (-B + B) - 1 \\ &= B^n - 1 \end{aligned}$$

## Sign-Magnitude Number Systems

A **sign-magnitude number** consists of a sign attached to a magnitude, as shown by the decimal numbers $+56$, $-27$, and $+27$, and the binary numbers $-11_2$ and $+101_2$. As an illustration, this section will consider a finite sign-magnitude binary number system based upon the byte. Suppose that the leftmost bit is used to represent the sign; for example, let 0 represent plus and 1 represent minus. You then have 7 bits left to represent the magnitude of the number, as illustrated in Figure 2.2. For example, consider the following:

**An 8-bit sign-magnitude representation**

$+2_{10}$ is represented by 00000010
$-5_{10}$ is represented by 10000101

(sign: leftmost bit; magnitude: remaining 7 bits)

### *The Mechanics of Sign-Magnitude Addition*

The rules for adding two sign-magnitude numbers are the same rules that you use to compute the algebraic sum of two decimal numbers. For example, you know that

$$\begin{aligned} +5 + (-7) &= -2 \\ -5 + (-7) &= -12 \end{aligned}$$

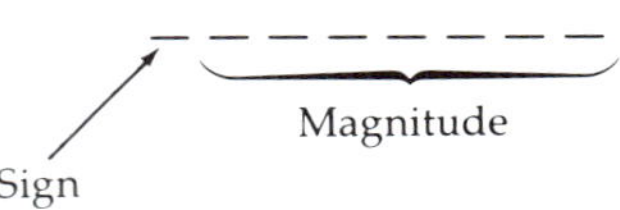


**Figure 2.2** An 8-bit sign-magnitude notation.

Although your response to these problems is fairly automatic, you have actually applied the following rules:

**The rules for sign-magnitude addition**

1. If the signs of the two numbers differ, then subtract the smaller magnitude from the larger to obtain the magnitude of the result. The sign of the result is the sign of the number having the larger magnitude.
2. If the signs of the two numbers are the same, then add the two magnitudes and attach the common sign.

You used the first rule to compute $+5 + (-7)$: you subtracted 5 from 7, and attached the minus sign to the difference to get the result $-2$. You used the second rule to compute $-5 + (-7)$: you computed $5 + 7$, and then attached a minus sign to the sum since both of the original numbers are negative. The result is then $-12$. The next examples repeat these computations and use an 8-bit sign-magnitude binary notation.

---

EXAMPLE 2

**Compute $+5 + (-7)$**

| | |
|---|---|
| 00000101 | 5 |
| 10000111 | −7 |
| 10000010 | −2 |

Since the numbers have opposite signs and $0000111_2$ is the larger magnitude, you compute $0000111_2 - 0000101_2 = 0000010_2$. You then attach a minus sign, represented by 1, since the number with the larger magnitude is negative. The result is $10000010_2$.

---

EXAMPLE 3

**Compute $-5 + (-7)$**

| | |
|---|---|
| 10000101 | − 5 |
| 10000111 | − 7 |
| 10001100 | −12 |

Since the numbers have the same sign, you compute $0000101_2 + 0000111_2 = 0001100_2$. You then attach a minus sign because that is the common sign of the original numbers. The final result is $10001100_2$.

---

## *The Range of Sign-Magnitude Integers*

If $L$ is the largest integer that can be represented in a given finite number system, a sign-magnitude notation allows you to represent integers from $-L$ to $+L$. In an 8-bit notation where 1 bit is reserved for the sign, there are 7 bits left for the magnitude. The largest magnitude is then $1111111_2$, so the range of the sign-magnitude integers is $-1111111_2$, which is represented as 11111111, to $+1111111_2$, which is represented as 01111111. This range in base 10 is $-(2^7 - 1)$ to $+(2^7 - 1)$. In general, a $d$-bit binary sign-magnitude representation in which the first bit denotes the sign has a range of

**The range of a *d*-bit binary sign-magnitude number system**

$$-(2^{d-1} - 1) \text{ to } +(2^{d-1} - 1)$$

### Overflow in a Sign-Magnitude Number System

When the result of a computation falls outside of the range of the number system, an **overflow** has occurred. In such cases, the magnitude of the result exceeds $d - 1$ bits. For example, in the following addition, the carry out of the left bit of the magnitude indicates that an overflow has occurred:

```
  0 1 1 1 1 1 1 1
+ 0 0 0 0 0 0 0 1
  0 ¹0 0 0 0 0 0 0     Overflow
```

The carry is lost: it does not affect the sign bit and the result is 00000000. Note that overflow is only feasible when the operands have like signs. (Can you explain why?)

### The Disadvantages of a Sign-Magnitude Number System

There are certain disadvantages of a sign-magnitude notation. First, the rules for addition require that the computer has circuitry for subtraction as well as addition. Although this sounds entirely reasonable, and while computers should be able to subtract as well as add, a separate subtract circuit is unnecessary if a complement notation is used as described next. A second disadvantage is that there are two zeros (+0 and −0), a less significant but bothersome characteristic.

Even with these disadvantages, sign-magnitude number systems are used. In fact, the IBM System/370 uses sign-magnitude number systems for floating-point and decimal arithmetic, which are discussed in later chapters.

## The Two's Complement Binary Number System

The **two's complement binary number system** allows you to represent integers and perform arithmetic in a way that permits a simpler design of a computer's arithmetic circuitry. For this reason, most computers today use this number system. The IBM System/370 uses this system for binary integer arithmetic.

This section starts by defining the procedure that the number system uses to transform a binary integer into another binary quantity called its **two's complement**. Since the number system is finite, all of the discussions are characterized by $d$-bit binary quantities. Typical values of $d$ used by many computers are 8, 16, 32, and 64.

### Taking the Two's Complement

**One definition of the two's complement**

The *two's complement* of a $d$-bit binary integer $N$ is equal to $2^d - N$, where the subtraction is performed in binary. For example, the two's complement of $00000101_2$ is computed as follows:

```
  100000000  ←  2^8
-  00000101  ←  N
   11111011  ←  Two's complement of N
```

A *complement* is defined as being either of two parts that together complete the whole. Thus, the two's complement of $N$ is that quantity that results in $2^d$ when added to $N$.

**Another definition of the two's complement**

The two's complement may also be computed by applying the following two rules to $N$:

1. Invert the bit values (the result is called the **one's complement**).
2. Add 1.

For example, the two's complement of 00000101 is computed by using these rules as follows:

```
00000101 --Invert the bit values--> 11111010
                                 +         1 <-- Add 1
                                    11111011 <-- Two's complement
```

You may use either method to compute the two's complement of a binary integer.

---

EXAMPLE 4

The following examples demonstrate both procedures for computing the two's complement of 8-bit binary integers.

**a.**

```
  100000000 = 2^8              00001000 = N
-  00001000 = N                11110111 <-- Invert bit values
   11111000 = 2^8 - N       +         1 <-- Add 1
                               11111000 <-- Two's complement
```

**b.**

```
  100000000 = 2^8              11111000 = N
-  11111000 = N                00000111 <-- Invert bit values
   00001000 = 2^8 - N       +         1 <-- Add 1
                               00001000 <-- Two's complement
```

The two's complement of 00001000 is 11111000; notice that if you take the two's complement of 11111000, you get 00001000 back again.

---

## *Representation of Integers*

**The two's complement binary number system**

You will now see a number system based upon the two's complement operation. Do not confuse the process of taking the two's complement with the two's complement binary number system. The examples here will use an 8-bit notation.

A positive number in this number system is the same as its sign-magnitude form. A negative number is represented by the two's complement of its magnitude. For example, to represent −5, you first represent +5 as 00000101. Then use its two's complement, 11111011, to represent −5.

EXAMPLE 5

The following are examples of 8-bit two's complement binary integers and their decimal equivalents:

| Decimal | Two's complement binary representation |
|---|---|
| +1 | 00000001 |
| −1 | 11111111 |
| +2 | 00000010 |
| −2 | 11111110 |
| +5 | 00000101 |
| −5 | 11111011 |
| +8 | 00001000 |
| −8 | 11111000 |
| +18 | 00010010 |
| −18 | 11101110 |
| +127 | 01111111 |
| −127 | 10000001 |

Although positive integers begin with a 0 and negative integers begin with a 1, the representations of negative integers are very different from those in a sign-magnitude system.

From what you have observed so far about the two's complement process, you know that if you now take the two's complement of 11101110 (−18), you will get 00010010 (+18) back again. This fact is the basis of the following rules to convert integers in the two's complement binary number system to decimal:

**Rules to convert to decimal**

1. If the number is positive (if it begins with a zero), convert it to base 10 just as if it were an unsigned binary integer.
2. If the number is negative (if it begins with a 1), compute its magnitude by taking the two's complement and converting that to base 10.

EXAMPLE 6

**Convert $11111001_2$ to Decimal**

Given that $11111001_2$ is an integer in the two's complement binary number system, you know that it is negative because it begins with a 1. Its two's complement is $00000111_2$, which is $+7_{10}$. Therefore, the original number represents $-7_{10}$.

**$10000000_2$ is an exceptional negative number**

One exception to the characteristics of negative numbers that have been discussed so far is that $10000000_2$ is *not* the two's complement of any 8-bit positive number in the number system. Indeed, taking the two's complement of 10000000 results in 10000000. This number is discussed later when the range of the number system is considered.

The next example demonstrates the effect of varying the number of bits, *d*, used in the number system.

EXAMPLE 7

The following are representations for $+5_{10}$ and $-5_{10}$ that use various values of $d$.

| $d$ | +5 | −5 |
|---|---|---|
| 9 | 000000101 | 111111011 |
| 8 | 00000101 | 11111011 |
| 7 | 0000101 | 1111011 |
| 6 | 000101 | 111011 |
| 5 | 00101 | 11011 |
| 4 | 0101 | 1011 |
| 3 | Insufficient number of bits | |

Notice that leading zeros are place holders for positive numbers, but ones are place holders for negative numbers.

The term *two's complement* can be confusing since it is used in more than one way. A two's complement number is a number in the two's complement binary number system. However, when you take the two's complement of a number, you are performing an arithmetic operation. This operation may be applied to both positive and negative numbers, so the result need not be negative.

### *Addition of Two's Complement Binary Integers*

You add two integers in the two's complement binary number system as if the integers were unsigned, without any concern about signs or the relative size of the magnitudes. In fact, you do not treat the leftmost bits separately; they participate in the addition just like any other bit, as shown in the following example.

EXAMPLE 8

**Addition in an 8-Bit Two's Complement Binary Number System**

| | Decimal | Binary | |
|---|---|---|---|
| **a.** | 7 | 00000111 | |
| | + 5 | + 00000101 | |
| | 12 | 00001100 | |
| **b.** | − 7 | 11111001 | |
| | + 5 | + 00000101 | |
| | −2 | 11111110 | |
| **c.** | − 7 | 11111001 | |
| | − 5 | + 11111011 | |
| | −12 | $^{1}$11110100 | Carry on left is discarded. |
| **d.** | 7 | 00000111 | |
| | − 5 | + 11111011 | |
| | 2 | $^{1}$00000010 | Carry on left is discarded. |

| | | | |
|---|---|---|---|
| **e.** | 7 | 00000111 | |
| | − 7 | + 11111001 | |
| | 0 | $^{1}$00000000 | Carry on left is discarded. |

The results of part **a** are not surprising because you are adding two positive numbers. In the other examples, however, the integers including the sign bits are simply *added*. Notice that any carry out of the leftmost bit is discarded and is not an indication of an error.

---

## *Overflow in a Two's Complement Binary Number System*

When a result cannot be represented in *d* bits, an overflow has occurred. As in sign-magnitude notation, overflow is impossible when you add numbers of opposite signs; therefore, this discussion will consider cases with the same signs. In parts **a** and **c** of Example 8, each result has the same sign as the integers added. These results were as expected and indicate that no overflow has occurred. There is another criterion that you can use, however. Note the carry behavior in and out of the leftmost bit: in part **a**, there are no carries involving this bit, but in part **c**, there is both a carry into and a carry out of the leftmost bit.

---

EXAMPLE 9

Consider the following cases of overflow that occur when adding in an 8-bit two's complement binary system.

| | | | | | |
|---|---|---|---|---|---|
| | | 1 | | | |
| **a.** | 126 | 01111110 | **b.** | −126 | 10000010 |
| | + 5 | + 00000101 | | − 5 | + 11111011 |
| | 131 ≠ | 10000011 | | −131 ≠ | $^{1}$01111101 |

Observe that the signs of both results are incorrect, so the results cannot possibly be correct. In part **a**, there is a carry into, but not out of the leftmost bit; in part **b**, there is a carry out of but not a carry into that bit position.

---

To summarize, an addition overflow can only occur when the numbers added are of like sign. You can choose from either of the following two criteria to detect such overflow:

**Use either criterion to detect overflow**

1. An overflow has occurred if the sign of the result differs from the common sign of the numbers added.
2. Or, an overflow has occurred if one of the following has occurred:
   - There is a carry into, but not out of the leftmost bit.
   - There is a carry out of, but not into the leftmost bit.

## *The Range of a Two's Complement Binary Number System*

Since positive numbers in the two's complement binary number system are the same as those in a sign-magnitude binary number system, the largest positive number is $2^{d-1} - 1$, as previously calculated. (If $d = 8$, this number is $01111111_2$.) Now $-(2^{d-1} - 1)$ is represented by the two's complement of $2^{d-1} - 1$. For $d = 8$, this is the two's complement of $01111111_2$, or $10000001_2$. To see if this is the smallest negative number, try to subtract 1 from it by adding $-1$:

| | |
|---|---|
| $-(2^{d-1} - 1)$ | 10000001 |
| $-\quad 1$ | + 11111111 |
| $-2^{d-1}$ | 10000000 |

This result is correct since there is no overflow. Therefore, $10000000_2$ must represent $-2^{d-1}$. Now, try to subtract 1 again:

| | | |
|---|---|---|
| $-2^{d-1}$ | 10000000 | |
| $-\quad 1$ | + 11111111 | |
| $-2^{d-1} - 1 \neq$ | 01111111 | Overflow |

**The range is $-2^{d-1}$ to $2^{d-1} - 1$**

When you try to form $-2^{d-1} - 1$, you obtain a positive result, which therefore must be incorrect. You can conclude that the range of the number system is $-2^{d-1}$ to $2^{d-1} - 1$. There is one more negative number than there are positive numbers.

The result of the last computation was actually the largest positive integer, $2^{d-1} - 1$: when you subtracted 1 from the smallest negative integer, you obtained the largest positive integer. Similarly, if you add 1 to the largest positive integer, you would obtain the smallest negative integer. Think of the integers in a two's complement binary number system as arranged around a circle, as shown in Figure 2.3.

Binary integer arithmetic on the IBM 370 uses 16-bit and 32-bit two's complement binary representations. In 16 bits, the range is $-2^{15}$ to $2^{15} - 1$ ($-32768$ to $32767$); in 32 bits, the range is $-2^{31}$ to $2^{31} - 1$ ($-2147483648$ to $2147483647$). These number systems are summarized in Figures 2.4 and 2.5.

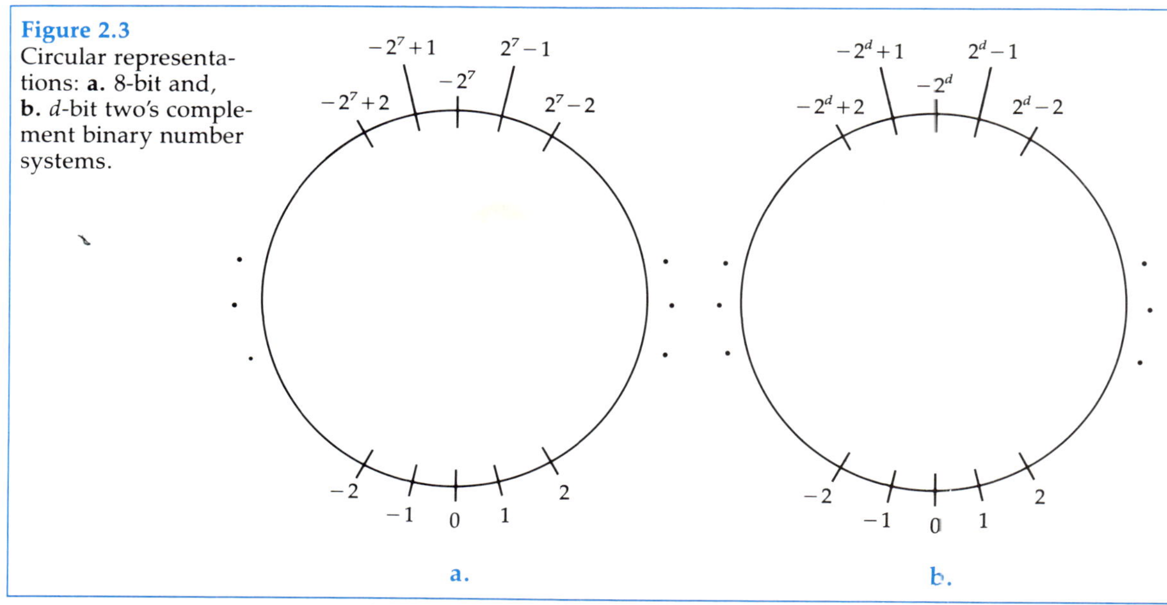


**Figure 2.3** Circular representations: **a.** 8-bit and, **b.** *d*-bit two's complement binary number systems.

**Figure 2.4**
The 16-bit two's complement binary number system.

| Decimal | Two's complement (Binary) | Two's complement (Hexadecimal) |
|---|---|---|
| $2^{15} - 1$ | 0111 1111 1111 1111 | 7FFF |
| $2^{15} - 2$ | 0111 1111 1111 1110 | 7FFE |
| . | . | . |
| . | . | . |
| . | . | . |
| 2 | 0000 0000 0000 0010 | 0002 |
| 1 | 0000 0000 0000 0001 | 0001 |
| 0 | 0000 0000 0000 0000 | 0000 |
| $-1$ | 1111 1111 1111 1111 | FFFF |
| $-2$ | 1111 1111 1111 1110 | FFFE |
| . | . | . |
| . | . | . |
| . | . | . |
| $-2^{15} + 2$ | 1000 0000 0000 0010 | 8002 |
| $-2^{15} + 1$ | 1000 0000 0000 0001 | 8001 |
| $-2^{15}$ | 1000 0000 0000 0000 | 8000 |

**Figure 2.5**
The 32-bit two's complement binary number system.

| Decimal | Two's complement (Binary) | Two's complement (Hexadecimal) |
|---|---|---|
| $2^{31} - 1$ | 0111 1111 1111 1111 1111 1111 1111 1111 | 7FFFFFFF |
| $2^{31} - 2$ | 0111 1111 1111 1111 1111 1111 1111 1110 | 7FFFFFFE |
| . | . | . |
| . | . | . |
| . | . | . |
| 2 | 0000 0000 0000 0000 0000 0000 0000 0010 | 00000002 |
| 1 | 0000 0000 0000 0000 0000 0000 0000 0001 | 00000001 |
| 0 | 0000 0000 0000 0000 0000 0000 0000 0000 | 00000000 |
| $-1$ | 1111 1111 1111 1111 1111 1111 1111 1111 | FFFFFFFF |
| $-2$ | 1111 1111 1111 1111 1111 1111 1111 1110 | FFFFFFFE |
| . | . | . |
| . | . | . |
| . | . | . |
| $-2^{31} + 2$ | 1000 0000 0000 0000 0000 0000 0000 0010 | 80000002 |
| $-2^{31} + 1$ | 1000 0000 0000 0000 0000 0000 0000 0001 | 80000001 |
| $-2^{31}$ | 1000 0000 0000 0000 0000 0000 0000 0000 | 80000000 |

### *Why Does the Two's Complement Binary Number System Work?*

The process of adding integers in the two's complement binary number system is somewhat remarkable because you do not have to worry about signs or the relative size of magnitudes. You can see why this is true by examining the following two computations, each expressed with signed-decimal, two's complement binary, and unsigned-decimal integers:

| | Signed decimal | Two's complement binary | Unsigned decimal |
|---|---|---|---|
| **1.** | $-7$ | 11111001 | $2^8 - 7$ |
| | $+5$ | + 00000101 | $+ \quad 5$ |
| | $-2$ | 11111110 | $2^8 - 2$ |
| **2.** | 7 | 00000111 | 7 |
| | $-5$ | + 11111011 | $+ \; 2^8 - 5$ |
| | 2 | $^1$00000010 | $2^8 + 2$ |

In the first computation, $2^8 - 7$ is the two's complement of $+7$ and, therefore, represents $-7$. Adding 5 gives you $2^8 - 2$, which is the two's complement of $+2$ and, therefore, represents the correct answer of $-2$.

In the second computation, $2^8 - 5$ is the two's complement of $+5$ and, therefore, represents $-5$. Adding 7 gives you $2^8 + 2$, which is too large by $2^8$. Notice, however, the carry out of the leftmost position of the binary addition: it represents $2^8$ and is discarded due to the finite nature of the arithmetic. This leaves only the 2, which is the correct answer. Discarding the carry is not a loss; it is necessary for a correct result.

The value of a result depends upon its interpretation. As an *unsigned* integer, 11111110 represents 254 ($2^8 - 2$). As a *signed* integer in a two's complement binary number system, 11111110 represents $-2$. Except for the detection of overflow, the addition of two's complement integers and the addition of unsigned integers are performed in the same manner.

## *The Advantages of Two's Complement Binary*

The difference of two numbers can be computed by taking the two's complement of one number and adding the result to the second number. Thus, the design of computers that use the two's complement binary number system can be simplified by using hardware elements for subtraction that are already required for addition. This simplification is the major reason that most present computers use this number system. Another less important advantage of using two's complement numbers is the existence of only one zero.

## *A Shortcut to Subtraction Using Hexadecimal*

When it becomes necessary to perform two's complement binary arithmetic, you most likely will have 16-bit or 32-bit integers represented in hexadecimal. The addition of such numbers can be performed directly in hexadecimal without difficulty; you only need to know the binary equivalent of the leftmost digits to recognize overflow. When you perform a subtraction such as

```
  9BC2
- C1DE
```

you could convert $C1DE_{16}$ to binary, take its two's complement, and then add the result to the binary equivalent of $9BC2_{16}$. However, you can save time by computing the two's complement of the binary integer represented by $C1DE_{16}$ directly in hexadecimal in one of two ways:

**Two ways to compute the two's complement by using hex representations**

1. Subtract each hex digit from F to get 3E21 and then add 1 to get 3E22. This process is equivalent to inverting the bit values of the binary integer and adding 1.
2. Or, compute $2^{16} - \text{C1DE}_{16}$, which is $10000_{16} - \text{C1DE}_{16} = \text{3E22}_{16}$.

Now, you can add 3E22 to 9BC2 to get the desired result. Notice that this addition is equivalent to

$$\text{9BC2} + 10000 - \text{C1DE} = \text{19BC2} - \text{C1DE}$$

Thus, you can perform the subtraction in its originally stated form by allowing a borrow, if necessary, for the leftmost position.

## SELF-TEST EXERCISES

9. Represent the following signed integers as 16-bit and 32-bit two's complement binary numbers, but indicate your answers in hexadecimal.
   - a. $\text{B40}_{16}$
   - b. $-\text{1C6}_{16}$
   - c. $10000010_2$
   - d. $-110101101_2$
   - e. $453_{10}$
   - f. $-300_{10}$

10. Perform the following decimal computations in an 8-bit sign-magnitude binary number system. Repeat the computations by utilizing an 8-bit two's complement binary number system. In each case, convert the result to decimal and indicate whether or not an overflow has occurred.
    - a. $4 + 3$
    - b. $-4 + 3$
    - c. $-30 + 3$
    - d. $64 + 64$
    - e. $-127 + 63$
    - f. $-64 - 64$

11. Perform the following decimal computations in a 7-bit sign-magnitude binary number system. Repeat the computations by utilizing a 7-bit two's complement binary number system. In each case, convert the result to decimal and indicate whether or not an overflow has occurred.
    - a. $35 + 16$
    - b. $-35 + 16$
    - c. $35 - 16$
    - d. $35 + 30$
    - e. $-35 - 30$

12. Assuming a 7-bit sign-magnitude binary number system, compute 1011011 + 0010100. Convert the result to decimal.

13. Repeat the computation in Self-Test Exercise 12, assuming a 7-bit two's complement binary number system. Convert the result to decimal.

14. The integers in the following computations are indicated in hexadecimal, but represent 16-bit two's complement binary numbers.

    a.
    ```
      560B
    + 0D97
    ```
    b.
    ```
      21F5
    + FE3C
    ```
    c.
    ```
      A08F
    - CF31
    ```
    d.
    ```
      E481
    - E78A
    ```
    e.
    ```
      D99B
    - AAAA
    ```

    Convert the hex integers to binary, perform the computations in binary, but report the results in hex. Repeat the computations directly in hexadecimal, without first converting to binary. You should get the same answers with both methods.

## Summary

1. Performing arithmetic on unsigned integers in a positional number system follows the same rules for arithmetic regardless of base.
2. To convert from any base to decimal, expand the number into powers of its base and use decimal arithmetic. The computation may be nested for evaluation.
3. To convert from decimal to another base, use repeated decimal division by that base until the quotient is zero. The remainders, when converted to the new base and written right to left, form the desired result.
4. Computers use finite number systems since storage locations can only represent a finite number of digits.
5. The largest $n$-digit integer in a base $B$ number system has a decimal equivalent of $B^n - 1$.
6. IBM System/370 computers use finite sign-magnitude number systems for floating-point and decimal integer arithmetic.
7. The range of a $d$-bit binary sign-magnitude number system is $-(2^{d-1} - 1)$ to $+(2^{d-1} - 1)$.
8. The $d$-bit two's complement of a binary integer $N$ is $2^d - N$.
9. The two's complement binary number system consists of positive and negative numbers that are the two's complement of each other. There is one exception, however: although $-2^{d-1}$ can be represented in $d$ bits, $+2^{d-1}$ cannot.
10. The range of a $d$-bit two's complement binary number system is $-2^{d-1}$ to $2^{d-1} - 1$.
11. The two's complement binary number system permits a simpler design of a computer's arithmetic circuits than a binary sign-magnitude system, and is therefore an attractive choice for computer designers. The IBM System/370 uses this number system for binary integer arithmetic.
12. With the exception of overflow, the addition of two's complement binary integers proceeds as if the integers were unsigned.
13. Addition overflow is possible only when the numbers to be added have the same signs. If the result in such cases has the opposite sign, an overflow has occurred. This is true for both sign-magnitude and two's complement binary number systems.
14. A binary integer cannot be correctly interpreted unless you are told whether it is an unsigned, a sign-magnitude, or a two's complement number.

## Exercises

1. Convert the following unsigned binary integers to decimal:

   a. 11100 e. 10101100
   b. 101001 f. 101011101
   c. 111111 g. 11101111011
   d. 1111110 h. 100001001101

2. Convert the binary integers in Exercise 1 to hexadecimal.
3. Convert the following unsigned hexadecimal integers to decimal:

   a. 201 e. 15A8
   b. 4BF f. 2BC4
   c. D36 g. 70E9D
   d. 1010 h. A10FF

4. Convert the hexadecimal integers in Exercise 3 to binary.
5. Convert the following unsigned decimal integers to binary:

   a. 14 e. 287
   b. 31 f. 370
   c. 97 g. 502
   d. 152 h. 1501

6. Convert the decimal integers in Exercise 5 to hexadecimal.
7. Perform the following binary arithmetic:

```
a.     1110        e.   10101010
     + 0111           + 11111111

b.   111010        f.   11101101
   + 110111           + 10110111

c.  1101110        g.      11011
  + 1011010                01101
                         + 00010

d.  1110101        h.     111011
  + 1011101               101101
                        + 111011
```

8. Perform the following binary arithmetic:

   a. 11010 − 10111
   b. 10100 − 00101
   c. 110001 − 011010
   d. 110001 − 010111
   e. 1001110 − 0110101
   f. 1000001 − 0101111
   g. 11110100 − 01101001
   h. 11101101 − 10110111

9. Perform the following binary arithmetic:

   a. 1001 × 11001
   b. 11010 × 1111
   c. 10011101 ÷ 1101
   d. 11000111 ÷ 1010

10. Perform the following hexadecimal arithmetic:

    a. 9C8 + 1A4
    b. 7DF + 92F
    c. 9876 + 9876
    d. DBE4 + EA1D
    e. ABC94 + 234A8
    f. DEFDE + F4AB7
    g. 4F0B61 + 1E12AB
    h. B39FDA + DB84DA

11. Perform the following hexadecimal arithmetic:

    a. 97A − 77C
    b. 2EC0 − 1FEF
    c. EA1D − CBE4
    d. 2C70D − 1DD8E
    e. 20D00 − 1AA41
    f. 2C70D − 1DD8E
    g. AD96A5 − E46342
    h. 9AD12E − 3BDE8A

12. Represent the following signed integers as 16-bit and 32-bit two's complement binary numbers, but indicate your answers in hexadecimal:

    a. $73E_{16}$
    b. $-B0C_{16}$
    c. $11101001_2$
    d. $-110110101_2$
    e. $301_{10}$
    f. $-452_{10}$

13. The integers in the following computations are indicated in hexadecimal, but represent 16-bit two's complement binary numbers.

    a. FE89 + 132D
    b. 867B + E8F9
    c. 867B − E8F9
    d. EA1D − CBE4

    Convert the hex integers to binary, perform the computations in binary, but report the results in hex; indicate any overflows that might occur. Repeat the computations directly in hexadecimal. You should get the same answers with both methods.

14. The integers in the following computations are indicated in hexadecimal, but represent 32-bit two's complement binary numbers. Perform the operations directly in hexadecimal and indicate any overflows that might occur.

    a. BF0A7DC0 + 70CFBA4D
    b. A463422E + ED96A58A
    c. FEDC8417 + 680ABCF7
    d. 70CFBA4D − BF0A7DC0
    e. E9DC9812 − E9DF502A
    f. A463422E − ED96A58A

15. Consider base $S$ and base $T$ number systems. Suppose that the integer $I$ has a known base $S$ representation of $s_1s_2 \ldots s_n$. Describe a process that uses base $S$ arithmetic to convert $I$ to base $T$. (The process will parallel the one used to convert integers from decimal to binary.) Use your procedure to convert the binary integer 111010 to base 3.

16. Repeat Exercise 15 by using base $T$ arithmetic to convert $I$ to base $T$. Use your procedure to convert $121_3$ to binary.

17. Consider the octal (base 8) number system, which uses the symbols 0, 1, . . . , 7.

    a. What is the largest three-digit unsigned octal integer? What is its decimal equivalent?
    b. Convert the octal numbers 765, 102, and 546 to base 10.
    c. Convert the octal numbers 765, 102, and 546 to binary.
    d. Convert the decimal numbers 57, 240, and 471 to octal.
    e. Perform the following octal arithmetic:

       777 + 357    123 + 675    6071 − 2275    1000 − 321

    f. Under what circumstances would it be convenient to represent binary integers as octal numbers? Name a computer for which this is true.

18. The two's complement of a binary integer may be computed by inverting all bit values to the left of the rightmost 1 and leaving the other bits as is. Can you prove that this is true?

19. A base 1 number system has 0 as its only symbol. Convert the unsigned base 1 integer 00000 to decimal by expanding it in powers of its base.

# 3

# Introduction to System/370 Machine Language

CONTENTS

**OVERVIEW**

This chapter begins with a brief description of the ways that bytes in storage are grouped. After a general summary of the characteristics of System/370 machine language instructions, the RR and RX instruction formats are presented in detail. As examples of these formats, a few instructions are defined, including Load, Store, Add, and Subtract. Using these instructions, the chapter presents a simple machine language program and traces its execution through the CPU.

**OBJECTIVES**

After studying this chapter, you should be able to:

1. Determine whether a given address is a halfword, fullword, or doubleword boundary.
2. Describe the general internal (machine language) form of RR and RX instructions.
3. Define base-displacement addressing.
4. Compute the effective address specified by the index register, base register, and displacement of a given RX instruction.
5. Initialize a base register.
6. Define the Load and Store instructions, and the binary integer Add and Subtract instructions, and determine their effect in a given situation.
7. Compute the displacement required to address a particular storage operand.
8. Write simple machine language programs using the instructions presented in this chapter.

## Introduction

The machine language instructions of the IBM System/370 have several formats, which vary in length. After providing a brief overview of these, this chapter will introduce a few machine language instructions that are representative of the two formats RR and RX. **RR instructions** operate only upon registers, and **RX instructions** involve both a register and a storage location. Using these simple instructions, the chapter will demonstrate how you can write a machine language program.

Remember that, although you will seldom, if ever, write an actual machine language program, you should understand machine language primarily for debugging purposes. The subsequent discussion of assembler language, however, will be more meaningful if you have a sound understanding of the machine language that the assembler language represents.

## Bytes and Groups of Bytes

**Addresses**

Each byte in main storage is addressed by an unsigned binary integer that begins with zero. Some models within System/370 have 24-bit addresses. Other models, notably those within the 4300 series, have an **extended architecture** (denoted as **370-XA**) that permits either 24-bit or 31-bit addresses. This text assumes 24-bit addresses; however, for the most part, the length of addresses will make no difference. Those instructions that are affected by the length of the address will be indicated. A 24-bit address allows a maximum of 16,777,216, or $2^{24}$, bytes. This maximum can also be stated as 16 megabytes (16M). A 31-bit address allows a maximum of 2,147,483,648, or $2^{31}$, bytes. This can be stated as 2 gigabytes (2G). A particular machine may have fewer bytes installed than is indicated by these limits. Although addresses are in binary, they are usually represented in hexadecimal for convenience. Imagine that the bytes are placed end to end in a long horizontal row, numbered from left to right, as shown in Figure 3.1 where 24-bit addresses are assumed.

**Special groups of bytes**

Recall that while each byte contains an 8-bit binary quantity, it is possible to group consecutive bytes to represent larger quantities. Groups of 2, 4, and 8 bytes are given special names when they begin on specific addresses. These addresses are called **integral boundaries**. An integral boundary for a particular group is an address that is a multiple of the group's length in bytes. Thus, a **halfword** is a group of 2 consecutive bytes beginning at an address that is a multiple of 2. In hexadecimal, such addresses end in 0, 2, 4, 6, 8, A, C, or E; in binary, they end in 0. This type of integral boundary is called a **halfword boundary** or a **2-byte boundary**. A **fullword** (**word**†)

†Although *fullword* appears in IBM documentation, *word* is used more often. In this text, however, *fullword* will be used to ensure clarity.

**Figure 3.1**
Storage pictured as a string of bytes.

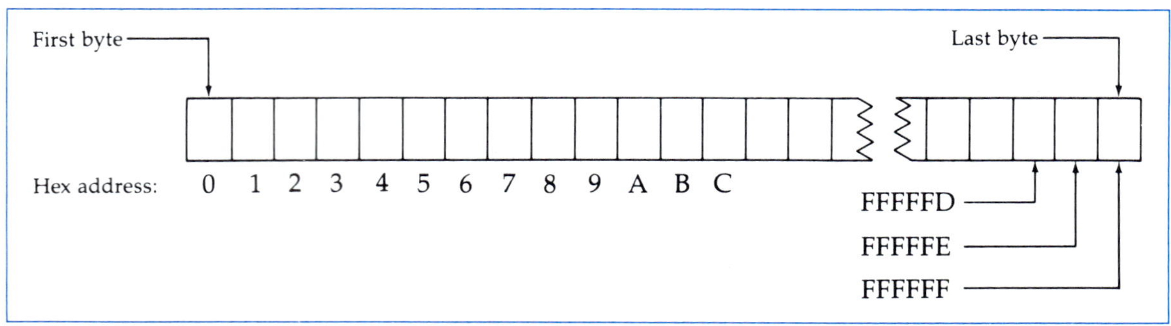

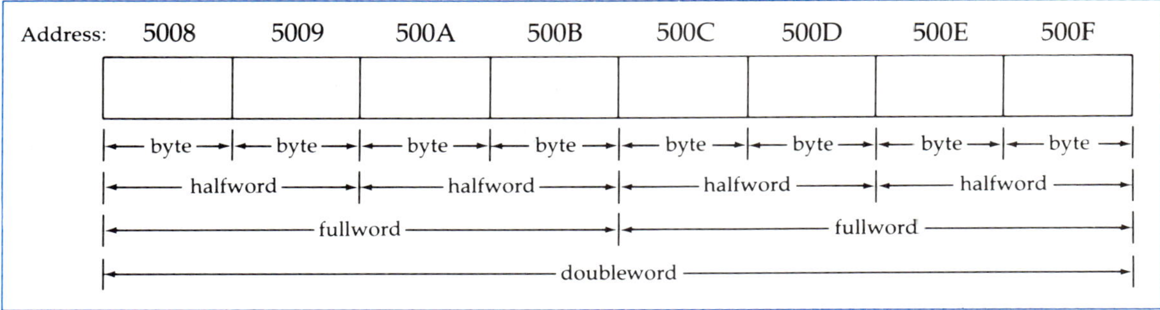


**Figure 3.2**
Bytes that are grouped as halfwords, fullwords, or a doubleword.

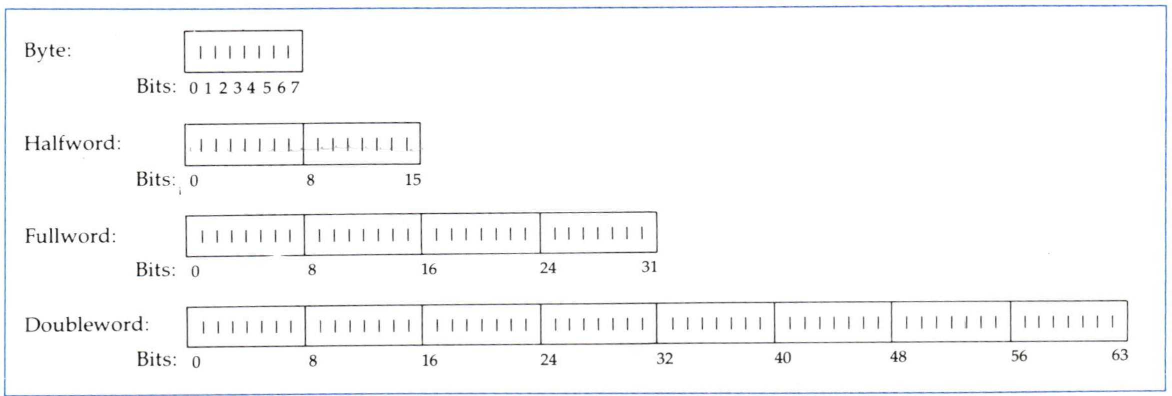


**Figure 3.3**
The bits in a byte or grouping are numbered for reference.

consists of 4 consecutive bytes beginning at an address that is a multiple of 4. In hexadecimal, such addresses end in 0, 4, 8, or C; in binary, they end in 00. This type of integral boundary is called a **fullword boundary** or a **4-byte boundary**. A **doubleword** consists of 8 consecutive bytes beginning at an address that is a multiple of 8. In hexadecimal, such addresses end in 0 or 8; in binary, they end in 000. This type of integral boundary is called a **doubleword boundary** or an **8-byte boundary**. Groupings of bytes are addressed by the address of the leftmost byte in the group. Thus, you might speak of the byte at address $5008_{16}$ or of the halfword, fullword, or doubleword at that same address. These concepts are illustrated in Figure 3.2.

**Bits are numbered for discussion purposes**

Sometimes, this discussion will refer to particular bits within a byte or a group of bytes. By convention, bits are numbered left to right beginning with zero. For example, the bits within a byte are numbered 0 to 7, while those within a fullword are numbered 0 to 31, as shown in Figure 3.3. This numbering is not a physical entity, and you should not confuse it with the concept of address. Individual bits cannot be directly addressed; remember that the byte is the smallest unit of storage that you can address. The numbering scheme is merely a convenience used when describing the effect of instructions. This same scheme will also be used to refer to the bits of a register or of the PSW.

## Instruction Fundamentals

Three instruction lengths

Instructions are unsigned binary integers that are 2, 4, or 6 bytes in length; they must begin on halfword boundaries. The first byte (and in a few cases, the first 2 bytes) of every instruction contains the **operation code**, or **op code**. This code not only specifies the purpose of the instruction, but also implies the length of the instruction itself. Following the operation code are operand designations. **Operands** are those quantities that are involved in the operation defined by the op code. For example, if you add 2 numbers, the numbers are operands. There are 3 types of operands. A **register operand** is an operand in a register; a **storage operand** is an operand in storage. An **immediate operand** consists of an 8-bit binary quantity that is contained within the instruction itself. Immediate operands are discussed in Chapter 10.

Three types of operands

Register operands can be in the general, the floating-point, or the control registers; the type of register is implied by the op code. A register operand is designated within the instruction by a 4-bit representation of the register name. The designation ranges from 0000 to 1111 in binary (0 to 15 in decimal), which allows any register to be specified.

The address of a storage operand is not written explicitly within the instruction. Instead, the address is computed by adding a portion of the instruction itself to quantities contained in one or two general registers that are designated in the instruction. This computation is called **base-displacement addressing** and will be described later in this chapter.

A storage operand may be a single byte or a grouping of bytes. For some instructions, the length of a storage operand is implied by the op code; for others, the length is stated explicitly within the instruction or within a general register. Instructions whose op codes imply storage operands of 2, 4, or 8 bytes in length will execute significantly faster if those operands are on integral boundaries; that is, if the operands are halfwords, fullwords, or doublewords. Therefore, it is desirable and almost always possible to adhere to this restriction. Most models of the IBM 360 actually require that the operands be on integral boundaries.

Eight instruction formats

Instructions are classified into eight formats labeled RR, RX, RS, SI, SS, S, RRE, and SSE, as pictured in Figure 3.4. In general, RR and RRE instructions specify two register operands; RX instructions specify one register operand and one storage operand; RS instructions specify two register operands and one storage operand; SI instructions specify one storage operand and an immediate operand; S instructions specify one storage operand; and SS and SSE instructions specify two storage operands. The text will describe the RR, RX, RS, SI, and SS formats in detail, as necessary, omitting the third variation of the SS format, which is used for certain semiprivileged instructions. Most of the instructions in the RRE, S, and SSE formats are privileged or semiprivileged, and will not be covered in this text. These three formats alone allow a 2-byte operation code, and they were unavailable on the IBM 360.

System/370 computers can perform binary integer and floating-point arithmetic by using fixed-length operands (halfwords, fullwords, or doublewords), decimal integer arithmetic by using variable-length operands, and character operations by using fixed- or variable-length operands. Eventually, this text will cover all of these topics and present most of the instructions that are available to you in the problem state. This chapter considers a few machine language instructions that assume binary integer operands.

# The RR Format

The operands of RR instructions are registers; RR stands for **register-and-register**. These instructions are the simplest to describe, the shortest in length, and the fastest to execute in general. Each RR instruction is 2 bytes long. The first byte contains the operation code; the second byte typically designates 2 register operands. Since a byte can contain two 4-bit quantities, a byte can address 2 registers. For example, if the second byte of an RR instruction contains the binary quantity

1001 1011

it would designate Registers 9 and 11.

Figure 3.4 shows you the general form of an RR instruction. *R1* and *R2* denote the registers that contain the operands. *R1* is sometimes called the **first operand location** and *R2* the **second operand location**. The **first register operand** is made up of the contents of the first operand location, which is denoted by C(*R1*). Similarly, the **second register operand** is the contents of the second operand location and is denoted by C(*R2*).

## *The Load Register Instruction*

An example of an RR instruction is the Load Register instruction. This replaces the contents of a general register by a copy of the contents of another general register. Suppose Registers 9 and 11 appear in binary as follows:

| | |
|---|---|
| Register 9 | 0000 0000 1010 1011 0010 0000 0101 0001 |
| Register 11 | 1111 1100 1001 1101 0111 1111 1000 1010 |

If you wanted to replace the current contents of Register 9 with a copy of the current contents of Register 11, you would write the following binary instruction:

**Load Register 9 with the contents of Register 11**

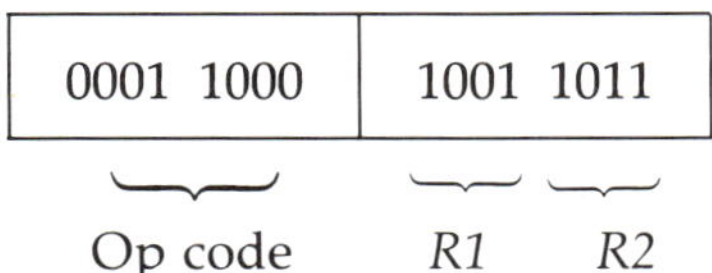


After execution of this instruction, Registers 9 and 11 would appear as follows:

| | |
|---|---|
| Register 9 | 1111 1100 1001 1101 0111 1111 1000 1010 |
| Register 11 | 1111 1100 1001 1101 0111 1111 1000 1010 |

Register 9 contains a copy of the contents of Register 11, while Register 11 is unchanged. It is said that Register 9 has been *loaded* with the contents of Register 11.

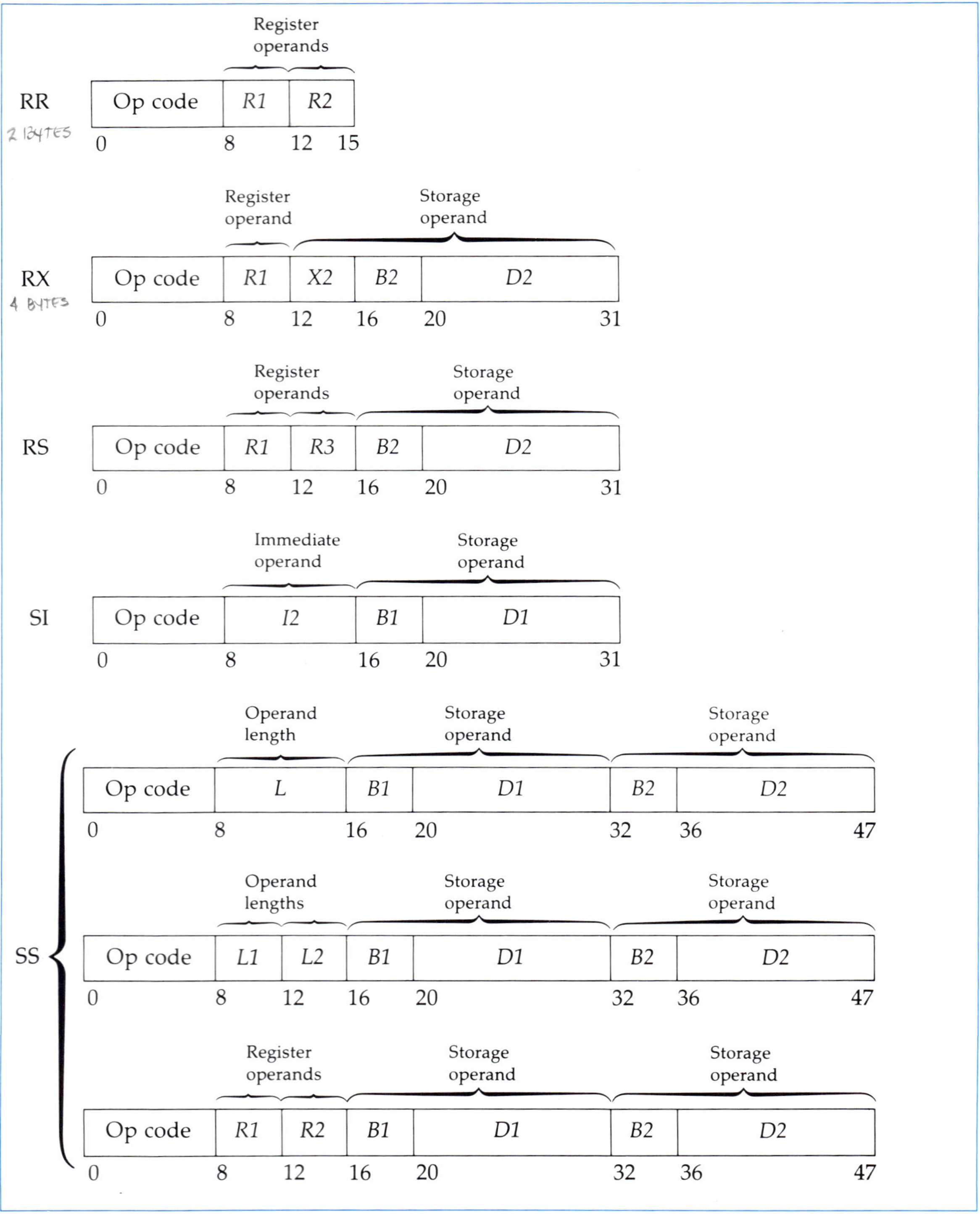


**Figure 3.4**
The machine language instruction formats.

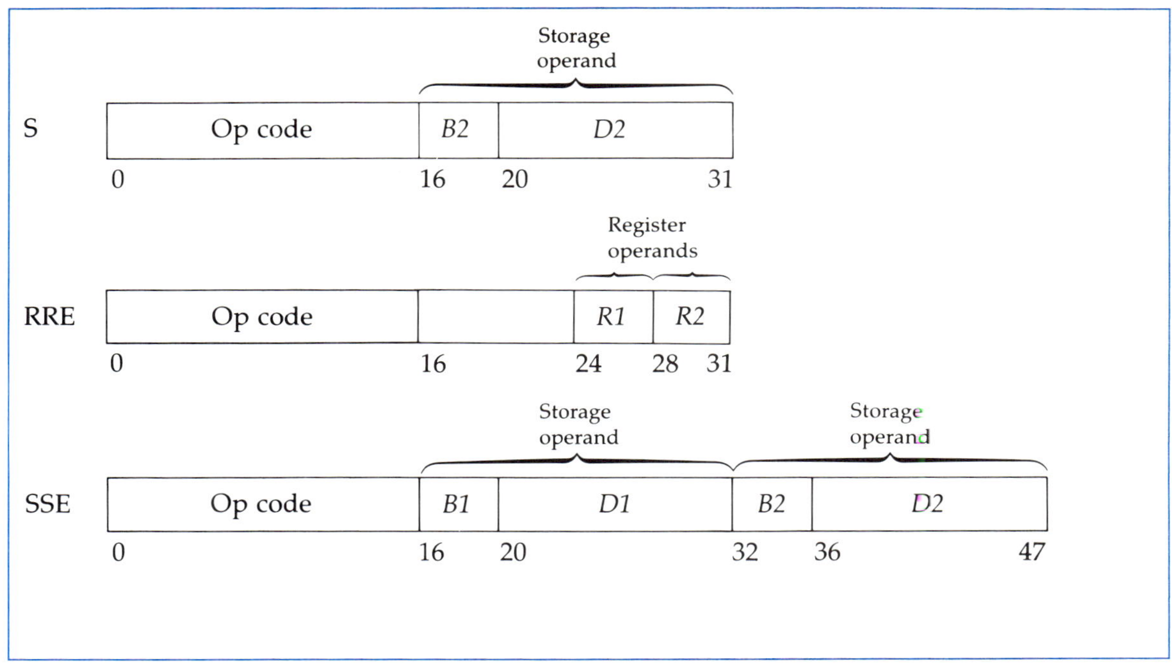


**Figure 3.4**
(*Continued*)

This text uses the following notation to describe this action in general:

C(*R1*) ← C(*R2*)

In other words, the contents (C) of the first operand location are loaded with the second register operand (which is made up of the contents of the second operand location). Since C(*R2*), the second register operand, is not explicitly replaced, you can assume that it is unchanged.

You could rewrite the binary instruction just given in hexadecimal as

189B

From now on, instructions, addresses, and the contents of registers and storage will usually be written in hexadecimal rather than binary since it will be easier to do so. However, register names within the text will be given in decimal.

### *The Add Register Instruction*

The Add Register instruction adds binary integers contained in general registers, assuming the two's complement binary number system. The general form and definition of this instruction are as follows:

| 1A | *R1* | *R2* |
|---|---|---|

Op code

C(*R1*) ← C(*R1*) + C(*R2*)

The instruction adds the integers in the designated registers, and the sum replaces the contents of the first operand location. The second register operand is left unchanged.

EXAMPLE 1

**1A4B**

The hexadecimal instruction 1A4B adds the contents of Register 11 to the contents of Register 4; the sum replaces the contents of Register 4. For example, consider the following register contents given in hexadecimal:

| | **Reg. 4** | **Reg. 11** |
|---|---|---|
| Before execution: | FFFFFFFF | 00000006 |
| After execution: | 00000005 | 00000006 |

Although the CPU performs the addition in binary, you can add the operands as if they were hexadecimal quantities.

### *The Subtract Register Instruction*

The Subtract Register instruction computes the difference between two binary integers that are assumed to be in the two's complement binary number system. The general form and definition of this instruction are as follows:

| 1B | *R1* | *R2* |
|---|---|---|

Op code

C(*R1*) ← C(*R1*) − C(*R2*)

The instruction subtracts the second register operand from the first register operand. The difference replaces the first register operand and the second register operand is unchanged. The CPU performs subtraction by adding the two's complement of the second operand to the first operand.

EXAMPLE 2

**1B0A**

The hexadecimal instruction 1B0A subtracts the integer in Register 10 from the integer in Register 0; the difference replaces the contents of Register 0. For example, consider the following register contents given in hexadecimal:

| | **Reg. 0** | **Reg. 10** |
|---|---|---|
| Before execution: | 12345678 | 0000002E |
| After execution: | 1234564A | 0000002E |

**Use Subtract Register to clear a register to zero.**

You can use the Subtract Register instruction to clear a register to zero. For example, the instruction 1B55 subtracts the contents of Register 5 from itself to generate a zero result. This technique to clear a register is used often because there is no instruction designed specifically for this purpose.

**SELF-TEST EXERCISE**

1. Assume the following register status:

   Reg. 0 = 12345678  Reg. 2 = 11111111
   Reg. 1 = 87654321  Reg. 3 = (Unknown)

   What are the contents of Registers 0, 1, 2, and 3 after the following sequence of instructions has been executed? Indicate any overflows that occur.

   ```
   1A00
   1B12
   1832
   1A30
   ```

# The RX Format

RX instructions involve one register operand and one storage operand. RX stands for **register and indexed storage**. This section begins with a description of how any System/370 instruction specifies the address of a storage operand. The method used is an indirect addressing scheme, whereby a 24- or 31-bit address is computed from quantities designated by a maximum of 20 bits of the instruction.

## *Base-Displacement Addressing*

To specify an address indirectly, you choose a point of reference called the **base address**, and count forward from this point until you reach the desired storage location. The actual address of this location is called the **effective address**, and the difference between it and the base address is called the **displacement**. This scheme is known as **base-displacement addressing,** or **relative addressing** since the effective address is specified in relation to a base address.

You place the base address into one of the general registers, which then becomes the **base register**. Any register except Register 0 may be used as a base register, although you will learn later of some conventions that may affect your choice. The name of the base register is specified by 4 bits of the instruction. Note that the base address remains fixed for the duration of program execution.

The displacement, designed to be a 12-bit unsigned binary integer, can range from 0 to $2^{12} - 1$, or 4095. The displacement and the base address are added together to form the effective address. The instruction then uses the result as the address of the operand. The text represents this computation with the notation†

**Base address plus displacement**

$$C(B)_{8-31} + D$$

The displacement, denoted by $D$, is added to the 24-bit base address found in bits 8 to 31 of the base register represented by $B$. The rightmost 24 bits

†The subscript notation, used here to indicate a portion of a register, will also be used with storage operands.

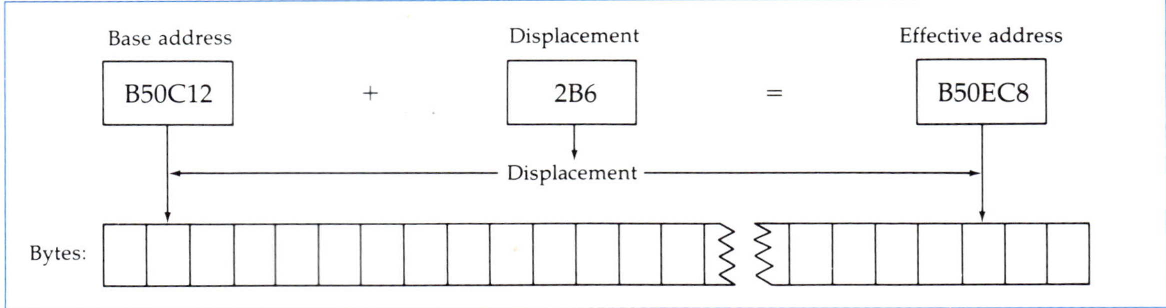


**Figure 3.5**
Computing an effective address from a base address and a displacement.

of the sum are taken as the effective address. Note that only 16 bits—12 bits for the displacement and 4 bits for the name of the base register—are required to designate a 24-bit address.

The computation of an effective address is illustrated in Figure 3.5. Since a displacement can range from 0 to 4095, an effective address that is computed from a base address and a displacement can range from the base address to a value that is 4095 larger.

## *The Effective Address Specified by an RX Instruction*

All instructions that address storage use the base-displacement addressing scheme. However, RX instructions optionally can include a modifier to affect the address computation just described. This modifier is analogous to an array subscript of a high-level language and is called the **index**. If present, the index is a 24-bit binary integer, which is added to the sum of the base address and the displacement when the CPU computes the effective address. You place the index into any general register other than 0; this register then becomes the **index register**. Like the name of the base register, the name of the index register is designated by 4 bits within the instruction. To summarize, the effective address specified by an RX instruction is defined to be the sum of the base address, the displacement, and the index. This computation is shown in Figure 3.6, and can be described as

**Effective address**

$$E = C(B)_{8-31} + D + C(X)_{8-31}$$

where $E$ is the effective address, $B$ is the name of the base register, $D$ is the 12-bit displacement, and $X$ is the name of the index register. The rightmost 24 bits of the result are retained as the effective address; overflow is ignored. (The extended architecture allows a 31-bit effective address. The rest of this text assumes 24-bit addresses.)

**Figure 3.6**
Computing an effective address from a base address, a displacement, and an index.

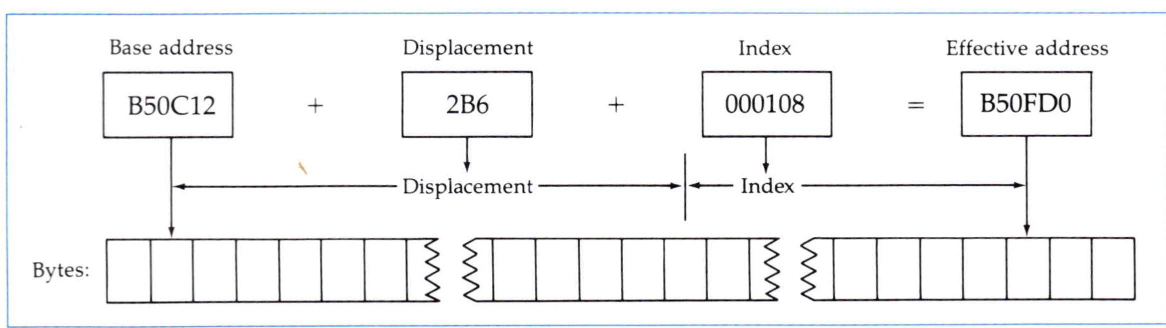

**Do not use Register 0 as a base register or as an index register**

Recall that you cannot use Register 0 as a base or index register. This characteristic allows a designation of zero for *B* or *X* to indicate the absence of a base or index register. In this way, either or both of these components can be omitted from the computation of an effective address.

It is possible to have a negative index. This is considered in Exercise 8 at the end of the chapter.

---

EXAMPLE 3

Assume these register contents:

| Reg. 0 | Reg. 1 | Reg. 2 |
|---|---|---|
| 00000008 | 0000000C | 000004AC |

| Reg. 10 | Reg. 11 | Reg. 12 |
|---|---|---|
| 9FFFFE68 | 000BF4C2 | 007F0FD6 |

The following 24-bit effective addresses are calculated from the given hexadecimal designations for index registers, base registers, and displacements:

| Index register | Base register | Displacement | Effective address |
|---|---|---|---|
| – | C | 056 | 7F102C |
| – | B | FFE | 0C04C0 |
| – | A | 000 | FFFE68 (Rightmost 24 bits) |
| 0 | A | ABC | 000924 (No index) |
| 1 | C | 912 | 7F18F4 |
| 2 | B | 216 | 0BFB84 |
| B | B | 008 | 17E98C |
| 2 | 0 | FA0 | 00144C (No base) |
| 0 | 0 | FA0 | 000FA0 (No index, no base) |

---

## COMPUTING THE EFFECTIVE ADDRESS WITHIN THE EXTENDED ARCHITECTURE

The extended architecture available with the newest models in the System/370 family permits several additional features, including a larger main storage with 31-bit addresses. For compatibility with earlier models, the extended architecture allows **bimodal addressing**, whereby the computer will assume either 24- or 31-bit addresses according to a bit in the PSW. The base address and the index, if applicable, are each 32 bits long and are contained in their respective registers; the displacement is still 12 bits. The computer adds the quantities and, ignoring overflow, uses the rightmost 24 or 31 bits of the result as the effective address.

The index and base registers may contain negative values. Bit 0 is always ignored and, in the 24-bit addressing mode, bits 1 to 7 are also ignored.

**SELF-TEST EXERCISE**

2. Assume the following register status:

| | | |
|---|---|---|
| Reg. 0 = 09A12F68 | Reg. 2 = 00000004 | Reg. 12 = 00BF5A02 |
| Reg. 1 = FFFFFFFE | Reg. 11 = 0007D9AE | |

a. Calculate the effective addresses designated by the following index registers, base registers, and displacements:

| Index register | Base register | Displacement |
|---|---|---|
| – | C | 2FE |
| – | B | 104 |
| – | 0 | D14 |
| 2 | 1 | FFE |
| 1 | B | 008 |
| 0 | B | 000 |

b. Which of the addresses just computed are doubleword boundaries? Which are fullword boundaries? Which are halfword boundaries?

## *The Format of an RX Instruction*

The format of an RX instruction was illustrated in Figure 3.4. There is an operation code in the first byte of the instruction. The first operand is in a register designated by *R1*. The second operand is a storage operand at the effective address *E2*, which is computed from an index register *X2*, a base register *B2*, and a displacement *D2*. (The *2* denotes the second operand.) The required portions of this instruction occupy 32 bits (2 halfwords).

The following instructions are examples of the RX format. For simplicity, the discussions omit the index register; why and how an index is used will be described in Chapter 5.

## *The Load Instruction*

The Load instruction replaces the contents of a register with a copy of the contents of the four bytes at the effective address *E2*. This action is denoted by

$$C(R1) \leftarrow C(E2)_{0-31}$$

The register is *loaded* with the storage operand. Notice that the storage operand is unaffected by the instruction. The operation code of the Load instruction is $58_{16}$.

EXAMPLE 4

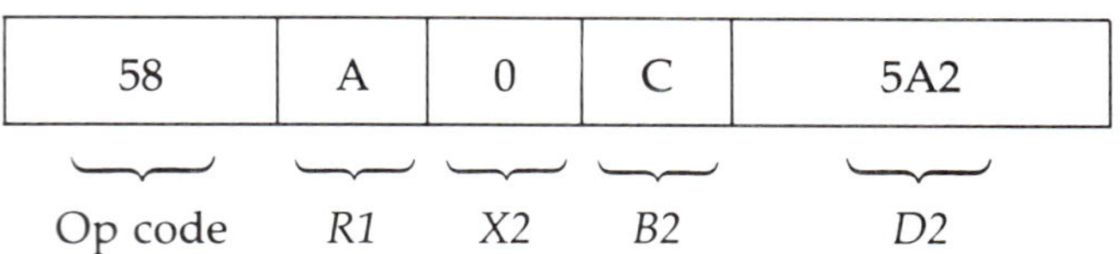

Assume the following status before execution:

| Reg. 10 | Reg. 12 | The bytes at address EFABA2 |
|---|---|---|
| FEDCBA98 | 00EFA602 | 12 34 **56 78 9A BC** DE F1 23 |

You compute the effective address of the second operand by adding the displacement, 5A2, to the base address contained in Register 12. The zero in the *X2* portion of the instruction indicates that there is no index register. Thus, the effective address is

$$\begin{aligned} E2 &= C(B2)_{8-31} + D2 \\ &= \text{EFA602} + \text{5A2} \\ &= \text{EFABA4} \end{aligned}$$

The result, EFABA4, is a fullword integral boundary. Register 10 is then loaded with the contents of the fullword at this effective address. Thus, after execution the register contents are as follows:

| Reg. 10 | Reg. 12 |
|---|---|
| 56789ABC | 00EFA602 |

Note that the base register (Register 12) is unchanged, as are the bytes in storage.

## *The Store Instruction*

The Store instruction performs the reverse operation of the Load instruction: the storage operand is replaced by a copy of the contents of a register, and the register remains unchanged. The register is *stored* and you can represent this by

$$C(E2)_{0-31} \leftarrow C(R1)$$

The operation code of the Store instruction is $50_{16}$.

EXAMPLE 5

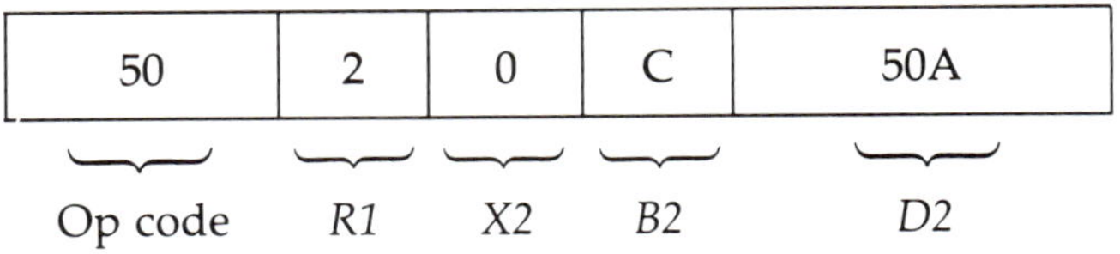


Assume the following status before execution:

| Reg. 2 | Reg. 12 | The fullword at BF560C |
|---|---|---|
| FEDCBA98 | 00BF5102 | 12345678 |

To compute the effective address specified by the instruction, add the displacement 50A to the base address BF5102. The result is BF560C. Register 2 is then stored at this effective address; thus, after execution:

| Reg. 2 | Reg. 12 | The fullword at BF560C |
|---|---|---|
| FEDCBA98 | 00BF5102 | FEDCBA98 |

---

**There is no RR Store instruction.**

There is no RR version of the Store instruction. Storing Register *a* into Register *b* would be equivalent to loading Register *b* with Register *a*; an RR Store would be superfluous.

### *The Add Instruction*

The RX Add instruction is analogous to the RR Add instruction: the sum of two 32-bit binary integers is computed by using the two's complement binary number system. The storage operand is added to the register operand; the sum replaces the contents of the register, and storage is unchanged. You can denote this operation by

$$C(R1) \leftarrow C(R1) + C(E2)_{0-31}$$

The operation code of the Add instruction is $5A_{16}$.

---

EXAMPLE 6

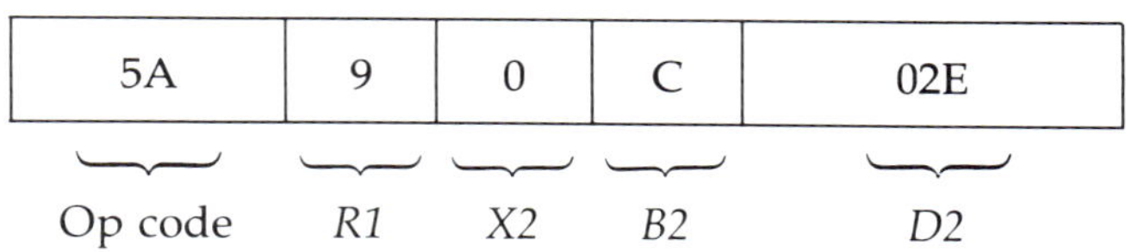


Assume the following status before and after execution:

| | Reg. 9 | Reg. 12 | The fullword at BF5130 |
|---|---|---|---|
| Before execution: | 12345678 | 00BF5102 | AB12C042 |
| After execution: | BD4716BA | 00BF5102 | AB12C042 |

The contents of the fullword at the effective address BF5130 (BF5102 + 02E) are added to the contents of Register 9, which are replaced by the sum.

---

### *The Subtract Instruction*

The RX Subtract instruction is analogous to the RR Subtract instruction: the difference between two 32-bit binary integers is computed by subtracting the storage operand from the register operand. The difference replaces the original contents of the register; storage is unchanged. You can denote this operation by

$$C(R1) \leftarrow C(R1) - C(E2)_{0-31}$$

The operation code of the Subtract instruction is $5B_{16}$.

## SELF-TEST EXERCISES

3. Assume the following status of bytes beginning at the address $5002_{16}$:

| 12 | 34 | 56 | 78 | 9A | BC | DE | F0 | 12 | 34 | 56 | 78 |
|---|---|---|---|---|---|---|---|---|---|---|---|

Also assume the following register status:

Reg. 0 = 00000001 Reg. 10 = 12004FE0
Reg. 3 = FFFFFFFF Reg. 12 = 00005002

**a.** What effective address is specified by the instruction 5830C002, and what are the contents of Register 3 after this instruction is executed?

**b.** Repeat part **a**, substituting the instruction 5830A028.

**c.** Are the effective addresses computed in parts **a** and **b** fullword boundaries? Which, if any, are doubleword boundaries?

4. Assume the following status of the bytes beginning at the address 1AB5A8:

| 00 | 00 | 00 | 08 | 9A | FF | FF | FF | 70 | 47 | 00 | 00 |
|---|---|---|---|---|---|---|---|---|---|---|---|

Also assume the following register status:

Reg. 0 = 00000004 Reg. 11 = 321AA5B2
Reg. 1 = 70000004 Reg. 12 = 001AB420

**a.** What effective address is specified by each of the following instructions:

```
5840C188
5A10BFFE
5B00C18C
```

**b.** What are the results of executing the instructions in part **a**? Indicate any overflows that occur.

---

EXAMPLE 7

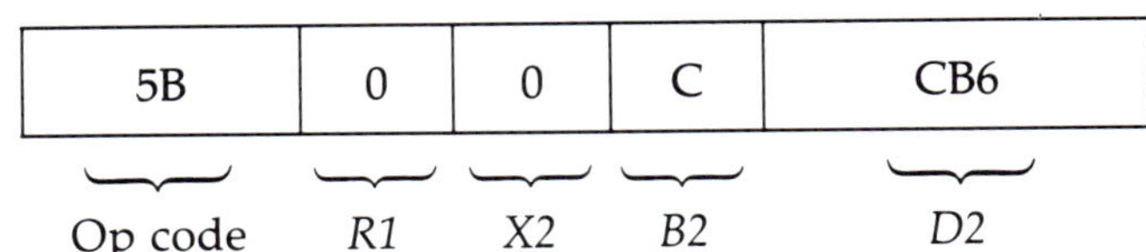


The following indicates the effect of this instruction:

| | **Reg. 0** | **Reg. 12** | **The fullword at BF5DB8** |
|---|---|---|---|
| Before execution: | 87654321 | 00BF5102 | DEF01234 |
| After execution: | A87530ED | 00BF5102 | DEF01234 |

The effective address is BF5DB8 (BF5102 + CB6). To perform the subtraction, add the two's complement of DEF01234 to 87654321 to get the result A87530ED.

Notice that $R1 = 0$ indicates that the first register operand is Register 0, but that $X2 = 0$ indicates the absence of an index register.

---

## Sample Machine Language Program

Now consider a simple machine language program that uses some of the instructions that you have studied.

### *Problem Statement*

Suppose that three 32-bit binary integers—called $x$, $y$, and $z$ here—are stored in fullwords. Also suppose that you want to compute $x - y + z$ and place the result into a fullword called $w$. The steps necessary to accomplish this are as follows.

**Step 1: Load $x$ into a register $R$.**
You first must get the value of $x$ and place it into a register since the arithmetic instructions that you have require at least one register operand.

**Step 2: Subtract $y$ from $R$.**
Next, you subtract $y$ from $x$; the difference will be in the register.

**Step 3: Add $z$ to $R$.**
You then add $z$ to the difference in the register, completing the computation.

**Step 4: Store the contents of $R$ into $w$.**
Finally, you copy the result from the register and place it into storage.

These steps are depicted as a flowchart in Figure 3.7. Since this is the first program that you have encountered in this text, the algorithm has been described in much more detail than is normally done; each step will correspond to exactly one instruction in the program.

Now that you have a clear picture of the program logic, you can begin to think about the instructions. First, you should choose a register to use for the arithmetic; let Register 2 serve this purpose. Since you must refer to data in storage, you will use some RX instructions and, therefore, will require a base register. Any general register other than 0 can be a base register, but typically Register 12 is chosen.

The base register must contain the base address. How does it get there? You must load the base address into the base register. What is the base address? You do not know. In fact, you do not even know the address at which the program begins since the operating system—particularly the loader—selects the **starting address**. Thus, you need a new instruction to help you.

### *A Simplified Definition of the Branch and Link Instruction*

The Branch and Link instruction is available in both RR and RX formats, but a special case of its RR form is used to establish base registers. The complete definition of the instruction will be given in Chapter 7. The simplified form appears as

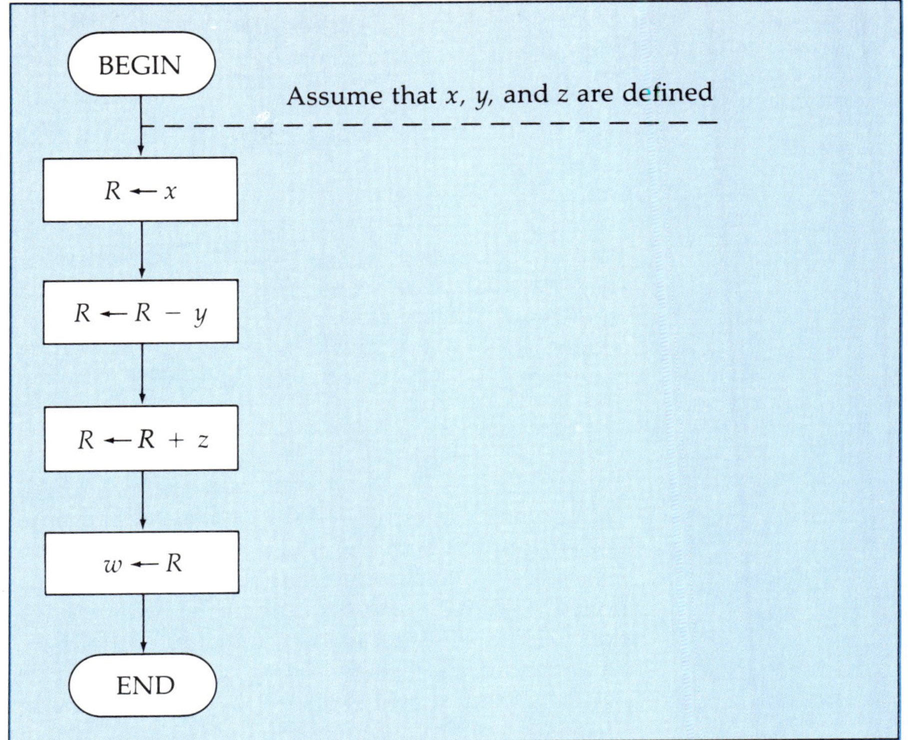


**Figure 3.7**
The flowchart for a program to compute $w = x - y + z$.

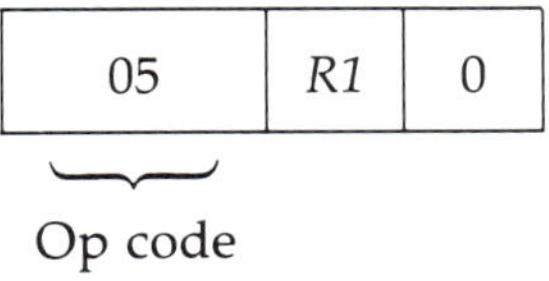


The address of the byte that follows the instruction is loaded into the register designated by *R1*. For this particular instruction, the zero in the *R2* portion implies the absence of an operand and does not denote Register 0. This is an exception to the typical interpretation of an RR instruction.

## *Writing the Program*

**Load the base register**

You can now use the Branch and Link instruction in the program. Suppose you write 05C0 as the first instruction. Assume that the program has a starting address called *S*. The address of the byte that follows the instruction 05C0 is then $S + 2$ since 05C0 occupies two bytes. The address $S + 2$ is loaded into Register 12 and will serve as the base address for the program. You do not know exactly what the base address is since *S* is unknown, but knowing that the base address is $S + 2$ will be sufficient.

The instructions of the program will be loaded into sequential bytes of storage. As you write the instructions, record their addresses in terms of *S*; that is, in relation to the starting address. You could also record these addresses in relation to the base address identified here as *B*. Place $x$, $y$, $z$, and $w$ after the instructions. As you write RX instructions, you will need to compute displacements to reference these storage operands, but you will

**Figure 3.8**
A partially completed machine language program to compute $w = x - y + z$.

| Instruction | Address of leftmost byte | Remark |
|---|---|---|
| 05C0 | $S$ | Load base register |
| 5820C___ | $S$ + 002 = $B$ | Load register with $x$ |
| 5B20C___ | $S$ + 006 = $B$ + 004 | Subtract $y$ |
| 5A20C___ | $S$ + 00A = $B$ + 008 | Add $z$ |
| 5020C___ | $S$ + 00E = $B$ + 00C | Store the result in $w$ |
| 07FE | $S$ + 012 = $B$ + 010 | Return |
| FFFFFFEA | $S$ + 014 = $B$ + 012 | $x = -22$ |
| 00000002 | $S$ + 018 = $B$ + 016 | $y = 2$ |
| 00000014 | $S$ + 01C = $B$ + 01A | $z = 20$ |
| 00000000 | $S$ + 020 = $B$ + 01E | $w$ |

not be able to determine the exact placement of $x$, $y$, $z$ and $w$ since you have not written the entire program. To avoid this problem, omit the displacements at first, and compute them later after $x$, $y$, $z$, and $w$ have been positioned. Figure 3.8 presents the partially completed program. The instruction 07FE labeled Return is the logical end of the program, and is simply an unconditional transfer that—under OS—returns control to the operating system. The text will explain more about it shortly; Chapter 5 presents it formally. Under DOS, use the instruction 0A0E instead of the instruction 07FE to return control to the operating system.

**Compute the displacements**

Next, you compute the displacement necessary in the Load instruction, which is the second instruction. This instruction will load a register with the contents of the fullword, $x$, that begins at address $S$ + 014. Thus, the effective address of the second operand of the instruction must be $S$ + 014. Recall that in the absence of an index register, you have

$$\text{Effective address} = \text{Base address} + \text{Displacement}$$

which can be restated as

$$\text{Displacement} = \text{Effective address} - \text{Base address}$$

Therefore, you can compute the displacement as follows:

$$\begin{aligned}\text{Displacement} &= S + 014 - B \\ &= S + 014 - (S + 002) \\ &= 012\end{aligned}$$

As was shown in Figure 3.8, the address of $x$ is given as $S$ + 014 and as $B$ + 012. The displacement 012 can be read directly from this latter entry. So you can compute the displacement in one of two ways: either by taking the difference between the desired effective address and the base address, or by reading it directly from the rightmost portion of the address column. When you wrote this column, you actually computed all possible displacements. Notice that you compute displacements without knowing the actual starting or base addresses; this is a very important observation as it makes it possible to write machine language programs and, more importantly, enables the assembler to translate an assembler language program into machine language. Figure 3.9 contains the completed program.

**Ensure boundary alignment**

Recall that $x$, $y$, $z$, and $w$ were described as fullwords. As such, they must begin on fullword integral boundaries in the program. How can you be sure that this is the case? You have seen that $x$ begins at the address $S$ + 014. This address will be a fullword boundary if $S$ is a doubleword

**Figure 3.9**
A complete machine language program to compute $w = x - y + z$.

| Instruction | Address of leftmost byte | Relative address | Remark |
|---|---|---|---|
| 05C0 | $S$ | 000 | Load base register |
| 5820C012 | $S + 002 = B$ | 002 | Load register with $x$ |
| 5B20C016 | $S + 006 = B + 004$ | 006 | Subtract $y$ |
| 5A20C01A | $S + 00A = B + 008$ | 00A | Add $z$ |
| 5020C01E | $S + 00E = B + 00C$ | 00E | Store the result in $w$ |
| 07FE | $S + 012 = B + 010$ | 012 | Return |
| FFFFFFEA | $S + 014 = B + 012$ | 014 | $x = -22$ |
| 00000002 | $S + 018 = B + 016$ | 018 | $y = 2$ |
| 00000014 | $S + 01C = B + 01A$ | 01C | $z = 20$ |
| 00000000 | $S + 020 = B + 01E$ | 020 | $w$ |

boundary; in fact, the operating system will always choose the starting address of the program to be a doubleword boundary. If you define the **relative address** to be the number of bytes beyond the beginning of the program, it is sufficient to apply the criterion for an integral boundary to the relative address, instead of to the actual address. In this case, the relative address of $x$ is 014; since the address ends in a 4, it must be a fullword boundary. If the relative address of $x$ was 016, then $x$ would not begin on a fullword boundary. To force it to do so, you could skip two bytes just prior to the definition of $x$ by inserting two bytes of zeros. This process is called **forcing boundary alignment**.

## *Tracing Program Execution Through the CPU*

**The starting and return addresses**

Imagine what happens when you run the program under OS. First, the operating system must load the program into storage. The loader selects a starting address at a doubleword boundary and places it into Register 15 for possible use by the program. Next, the loader places into Register 14 the **return address**, which is an address within the operating system to which the program should return upon completion. (These conventions will be described in more detail in later chapters. Note that DOS does not load Registers 14 and 15. Other than this difference, the discussion here is applicable to both OS and DOS.) The loader then places the starting address into the instruction address (IA) portion of the PSW. Recall that the CPU determines the address of the next instruction from this location. Therefore, at this point, the next instruction to be executed is the first one of the program.

**Suppose the starting address is $6500_{16}$**

Suppose that the starting address is $6500_{16}$ and the program appears in storage as shown in part **a** of Figure 3.10. When the CPU looks at the contents of the byte at the starting address, it will find the operation code of the first instruction of the program. From this code, the CPU can determine the instruction length and, hence, the instruction itself. However, before the CPU executes the instruction, it updates the IA by this instruction length to get the address of the next instruction. The length of this first instruction is two bytes, so the IA is updated to 006502. The first instruction is 05C0: it loads Register 12 with the address of the byte that follows it. Notice that this address is conveniently in the IA. Register 12 will now contain the base address 6502.

Next, the CPU determines from the IA that the next instruction is at the address 6502. The operation code at that address is 58: it implies an instruc-

Figure 3.10
The program of Figure 3.9 as it would appear in storage at **a.** the starting address $6500_{16}$ and **b.** the starting address $7500_{16}$.

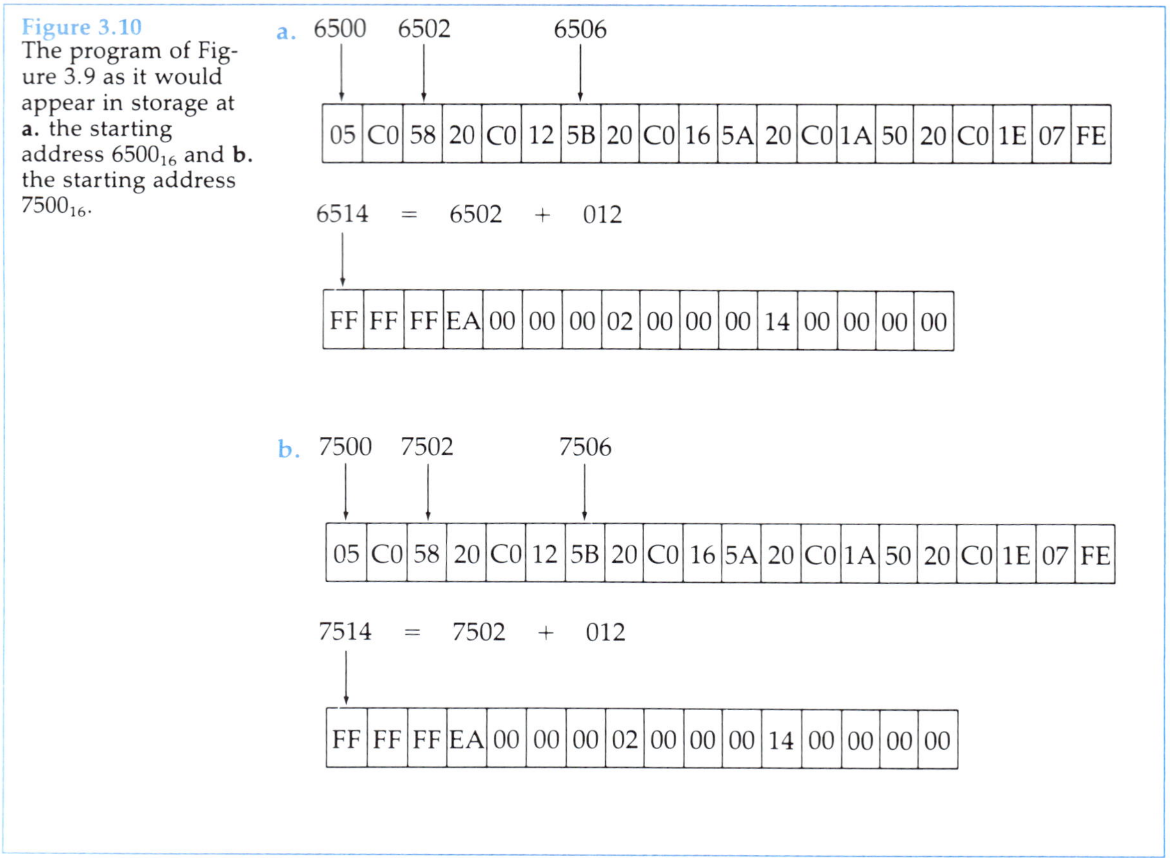


tion length of 4 bytes. The CPU adds 4 to the IA to get 6506, the address of the third instruction. Then the second instruction, 5820C012, is executed. Because it is an RX instruction, the effective address of its second operand must be computed. The CPU adds the base address, 6502, to the displacement, 012, to get an effective address of 6514. This is the address of the fullword called *x*; it is at 014 bytes beyond the starting address.

Now suppose the starting address is $7500_{16}$

Now consider how this process would be different if the program had started at $7500_{16}$ instead and appeared in storage as shown in part **b** of Figure 3.10. If you trace through the execution, you will find that the base address is 7502, the address of *x* is 7514, and the effective address of the second operand of the Load instruction is 7502 + 012, or 7514.

Base-displacement addressing enables you to write a program without knowing the starting address. More importantly the program will run correctly, regardless of the starting address—assuming, however, that it is a doubleword boundary. Such a program is said to be **relocatable** since it not only can start anywhere, but also can be moved by the operating system as necessary during its execution and can still produce correct results if the operating system simply changes the contents of the base register. This is an important advantage of base-displacement addressing.

## *A Closer Look at the Instruction 07FE*

The instruction 07FE, used to transfer control back to OS, is an example of the RR form of the Branch on Condition instruction, shown here:

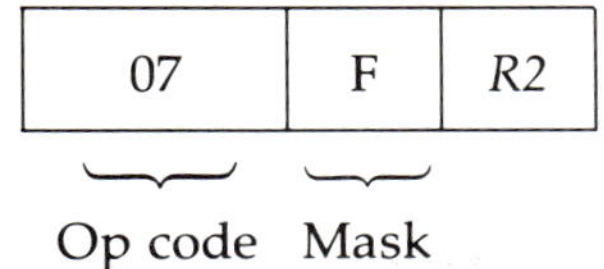


The first operand is not a register, but rather a code called a **mask**, which indicates whether or not the transfer is unconditional. In this case, the $F_{16}$ denotes an unconditional transfer or **branch**. The second register operand is the address of the instruction that is executed after the branch takes place. In the instruction 07FE, the second register operand is in Register 14. Remember that OS loads Register 14 with the return address. Thus, 07FE branches to the address in Register 14 and thereby returns control to the operating system. (For now, this is all that you need know about this instruction.)

**SELF-TEST EXERCISE**

5. In each of the following, compute the displacement required to load Register 0 with the contents of the first fullword that follows the instruction 07FE. (You may have to force boundary alignment.)

**a.**
```
05A0
5800A___
07FE
```

**b.**
```
05C0
5800C___
1A22
07FE
```

## Running a Machine Language Program

Although you usually will not write and run a machine language program, it can be instructive to do so. You can use the assembler even though the program is in machine language. Figure 3.11 shows the format of the statements necessary to run such a program. The program itself begins with CSECT and ends with END. Think of CSECT as a signal to the assembler that indicates the beginning of the program, and END as another signal that indicates the end.

Each machine language instruction is written as a hexadecimal constant. In the program, each DC tells the assembler to define a constant and the X indicates that the constant is hexadecimal. (These elements of assembler language will be detailed in the next chapter.) The address columns and remarks are ignored by the assembler, but are written for your use. The descriptive information prior to the instructions consists of comment statements: ignored by the assembler, they begin with an asterisk and will appear in the listing.

If you were to run this program as written in Figure 3.11, you would not get a storage dump: there would be no way of observing the result of the computation since it is only stored, but not printed. One way to get a dump is to cause an execution-time error. You can do this by replacing the last instruction, 07FE, by an illegal instruction, such as 0000. When the

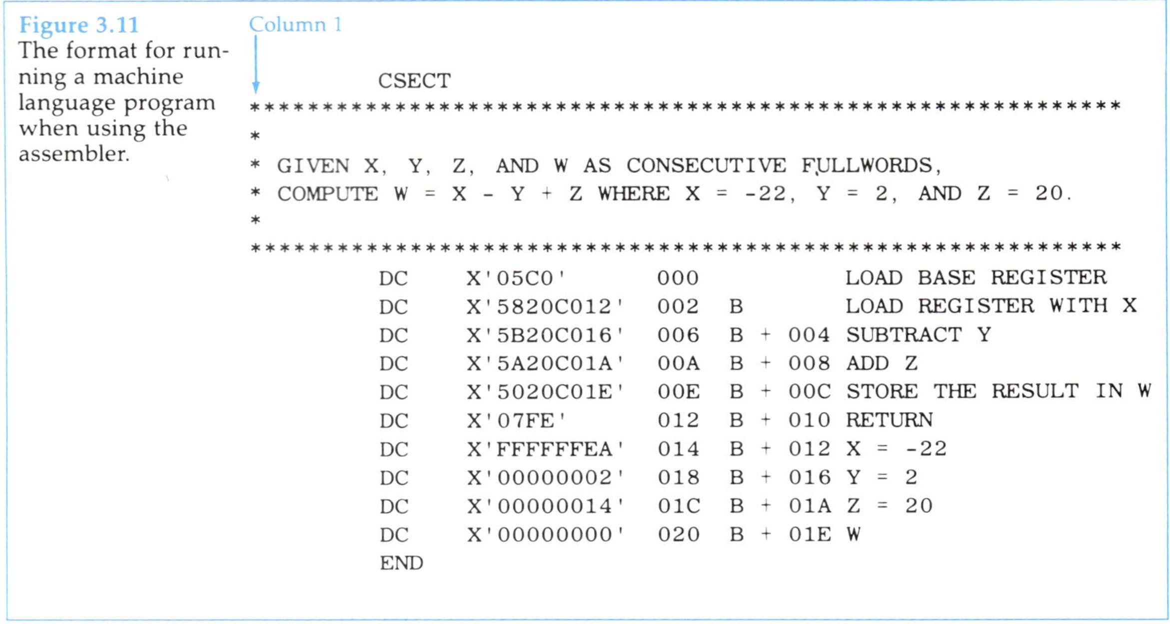

```
Column 1
         CSECT
****************************************************************
*
* GIVEN X, Y, Z, AND W AS CONSECUTIVE FULLWORDS,
* COMPUTE W = X - Y + Z WHERE X = -22, Y = 2, AND Z = 20.
*
****************************************************************
         DC    X'05C0'       000           LOAD BASE REGISTER
         DC    X'5820C012'   002  B        LOAD REGISTER WITH X
         DC    X'5B20C016'   006  B + 004  SUBTRACT Y
         DC    X'5A20C01A'   00A  B + 008  ADD Z
         DC    X'5020C01E'   00E  B + 00C  STORE THE RESULT IN W
         DC    X'07FE'       012  B + 010  RETURN
         DC    X'FFFFFFEA'   014  B + 012  X = -22
         DC    X'00000002'   018  B + 016  Y = 2
         DC    X'00000014'   01C  B + 01A  Z = 20
         DC    X'00000000'   020  B + 01E  W
         END
```

**Figure 3.11** The format for running a machine language program when using the assembler.

```
  LOC  OBJECT CODE    ADDR1 ADDR2  STMT   SOURCE STATEMENT
000000                                1          CSECT
                                      2 ****************************************************************
                                      3 *
                                      4 *    GIVEN X, Y, Z, AND W AS CONSECUTIVE FULLWORDS,
                                      5 *    COMPUTE W = X - Y + Z WHERE X = -22, Y = 2, AND Z = 20.
                                      6 *
                                      7 ****************************************************************
                                      8 *
000000 05C0                           9          DC    X'05C0'      000          LOAD BASE REGISTER
000002 5820C012                      10          DC    X'5820C012'  002  B       LOAD REGISTER WITH X
000006 5B20C016                      11          DC    X'5B20C016'  006  B + 004 SUBTRACT Y
00000A 5A20C01A                      12          DC    X'5A20C01A'  00A  B + 008 ADD Z
00000E 5020C01E                      13          DC    X'5020C01E'  00E  B + 00C SAVE THE RESULT IN W
000012 0000                          14          DC    X'0000'      012  B + 010 CRASH
000014 FFFFFFEA                      15          DC    X'FFFFFFEA'  014  B + 012 X = -22
000018 00000002                      16          DC    X'00000002'  018  B + 016 Y = 2
00001C 00000014                      17          DC    X'00000014'  01C  B + 01A Z = 20
000020 00000000                      18          DC    X'00000000'  020  B + 01E W
                                     19          END

                                          ASSEMBLER DIAGNOSTICS AND STATISTICS

NO STATEMENTS FLAGGED IN THIS ASSEMBLY
HIGHEST SEVERITY WAS     0

                                                VS LOADER

OPTIONS USED - PRINT,MAP,LET,NOCALL,NORES,NOTERM,SIZE=98304,NAME=**GO

     NAME   TYPE   ADDR          NAME   TYPE   ADDR          NAME   TYPE   ADDR          NAME   TYPE   ADDR          NAME   TYPE   ADDR

  $PRIVATE    PC    EC010
IEW1161
```

(Continues)

**Figure 3.12** The results of executing the program in Figure 3.11.

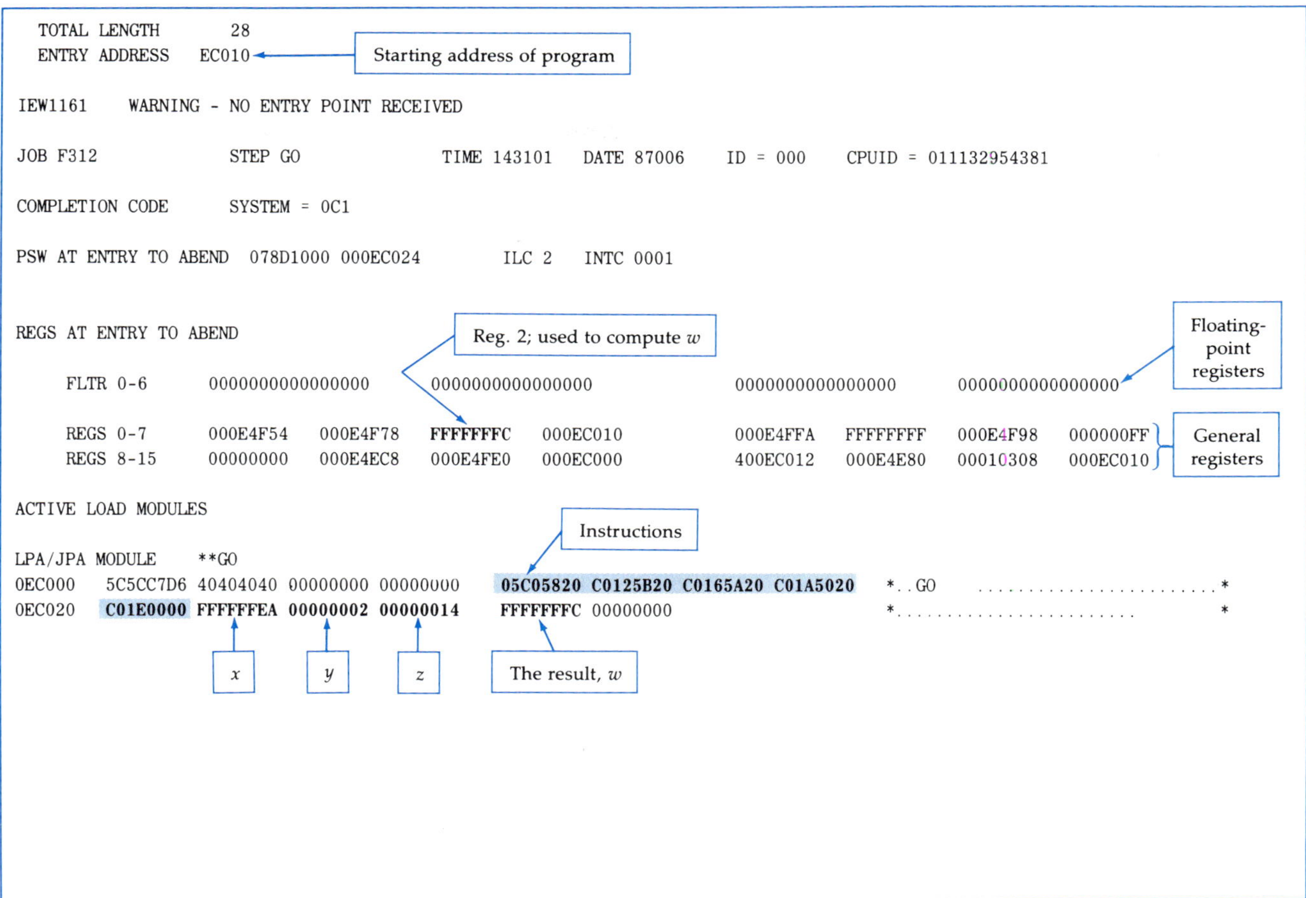


**Figure 3.12**
(*Continued*)

CPU attempts to execute this zero constant, it will detect that it is not a valid instruction. The operating system will print an error message and, more importantly, will print a storage dump. Figure 3.12 shows a portion of such a dump with the instructions and the result, *w*, indicated. You will learn more about dumps in later chapters.

## Summary

1. Each byte of storage contains 8 bits and has an address that is an unsigned 24-bit or 31-bit binary integer.
2. Consecutive bytes can be grouped to represent larger quantities than can be represented by a single byte. Special groupings of 2, 4, and 8 bytes are called, respectively, halfwords, fullwords, and doublewords. Each grouping must start at an address that is a multiple of the group length in bytes. Such an address is called an integral boundary.
3. RR instructions involve one or two register operands. RX instructions involve a register operand and a storage operand.
4. Base-displacement addressing is used to address storage operands. An effective address is computed by adding the base address and the displacement together. For RX instructions, an index value can also be added. RX instructions are the only instructions that permit an index register.
5. The primary advantage of base-displacement addressing is that it allows the instructions of a program to be written independently of its starting address. A secondary advantage is that it takes fewer bits to designate a base register, an index register, and a displacement than it would to write an address explicitly.

6. When you load a register, its contents are replaced by a copy of either a register operand or a storage operand, according to whether the instruction is in RR or RX format.
7. When you store a register, a copy of its contents is placed into storage. The Store instruction is in the RX format; there is no RR version.
8. Both the Add instruction and the Subtract instruction are available in RR and RX formats. Their results always replace their first register operands.
9. The Branch and Link instruction is used to load the base register.
10. When writing a machine language program, you must remember operation codes, compute relative addresses, take into account integral boundaries, and compute displacements.

## New Instruction Summary

| Instruction Name | Op Code | Format | Action |
|---|---|---|---|
| LOAD REGISTER | 18 | RR | $C(R1) \leftarrow C(R2)$ |
| LOAD | 58 | RX | $C(R1) \leftarrow C(E2)_{0-31}$ |
| STORE | 50 | RX | $C(E2)_{0-31} \leftarrow C(R1)$ |
| ADD REGISTER | 1A | RR | $C(R1) \leftarrow C(R1) + C(R2)$ |
| ADD | 5A | RX | $C(R1) \leftarrow C(R1) + C(E2)_{0-31}$ |
| SUBTRACT REGISTER | 1B | RR | $C(R1) \leftarrow C(R1) - C(R2)$ |
| SUBTRACT | 5B | RX | $C(R1) \leftarrow C(R1) - C(E2)_{0-31}$ |
| BRANCH AND LINK | 05 | RR | $C(R1) \leftarrow$ Address of the byte following this instruction. |
| BRANCH ON CONDITION | 07 | RR | 07FE returns control to OS by branching to the address in Register 14. |

## Exercises

1. Consider the following machine language program:

```
05C0
5820C012
1A22
1812
5B10C012
1801
1B00
07FE
F02AB73C
D980E4FA
```

   **a.** What are the contents of Registers 0, 1, and 2 after this program is executed?

   **b.** Assume that the program is loaded at the address BF02A8. What are the contents of Register 12?

   **c.** With the assumption given in part **b**, what is the address of the fullword that follows the instruction 07FE? What integral boundary is it?

2. Assume the following register status:

   Reg. 0 = 00000120 Reg. 12 = AE0CD988

   **a.** What effective address is specified by the instruction 5000C82C?

   **b.** What type of integral boundary does *not* describe the effective address computed in part **a**?

   **c.** What are the contents of Registers 0 and 12 after execution of the instruction 1B0C?

3. Assume the following register status:

Reg. 0 = 00000144  Reg. 11 = 00EFFC86
Reg. 4 = 000FFF74  Reg. 12 = 000AB25A

a. Calculate the effective addresses designated by the following index registers, base registers, and displacements:

| Index register | Base register | Displacement |
|---|---|---|
| - | C | 252 |
| - | B | 426 |
| 0 | C | 252 |
| 4 | B | 426 |
| B | C | 20E |
| B | 4 | 000 |
| C | 0 | 252 |

b. Which of the addresses computed in part **a** are doubleword boundaries? Which are fullword boundaries? Which are halfword boundaries?

4. Assume the following register status:

Reg. 0 = 00000004  Reg. 11 = 00FFFE9A
Reg. 1 = 0000002C  Reg. 12 = 00ABCDEA

Each effective address in the following table is computed from the given designations for index and base registers and an unknown displacement. Compute the required displacements.

| Effective address | Index register | Base register | Displacement |
|---|---|---|---|
| ABDDC8 | – | C | |
| ABCDF4 | 0 | C | |
| 000100 | 1 | B | |
| ABCC84 | B | C | |

5. Assume the following register status:

Reg. 11 = 01BF02FE  Reg. 12 = 00BEFDB2

Also assume that the contents of the consecutive bytes beginning at address BF0858 are

FF FF FF FD 12 34 56 78 9A BC DE F0

What are the contents of Register 0 after each of the following instructions is executed? Indicate any overflows that occur.

```
5800CAAE
5B00CAAA
5A00B55A
```

6. The following program should load a register with the contents of the fullword labeled X, double it, and store the result in the fullword labeled Y.

```
05A0
5890A___
1A99
5090A___
07FE
0000
00000004   X
00000000   Y
```

a. Compute the required displacements assuming Register 10 is the base register.
b. Is X at a doubleword boundary? Explain.

7. In each of the following, compute the displacement required to load Register 2 with the contents of the first fullword that follows the instruction 07FE. Force boundary alignment if necessary.

| a. | b. | c. |
|---|---|---|
| 05C0 | 05C0 | 1B22 |
| 1B11 | 5820C___ | 05C0 |
| 5820C___ | 1830 | 5820C___ |
| 07FE | 1B22 | 1831 |
| | 07FE | 07FE |

8. Suppose that Register 1 contains FFFFFFFC and Register 12 contains 000C4FB6.
a. Compute the effective address specified by the instruction 5831C002.
b. Note that the index value specified here behaves as $-4_{10}$. Explain why this is so.

## Programming Problems

1. Assume that $x$, $y$, and $z$ are consecutive fullwords in storage. Prior to execution, $x$ and $y$ contain the decimal constants $-24$ and 12, respectively. Write a machine language program that computes $y + y - x$ and stores the result in $z$. The given constants must remain unchanged.

2. Run the program of Programming Problem 1 by using the technique that is described at the end of this chapter. Circle $x$, $y$, and $z$ in the storage dump.

# 4

# Introduction to Assembler Language

CONTENTS

## OVERVIEW

This chapter presents the format of IBM System/370 assembler language statements by using as examples the instructions that were introduced in Chapter 3. Although the chapter introduces no new machine instructions, it defines several new instructions to the assembler. These include DC to define a constant, DS to reserve storage, USING to declare a base register, and EQU to define symbols that make the program more readable. The chapter also defines the listing control instructions that affect the appearance of the assembly listing, and presents the steps necessary to run a complete assembler language program. Finally, the logic of the assembly process is described.

## OBJECTIVES

After studying this chapter, you should be able to:

1. Define and give examples of terms, self-defining terms, symbols, and expressions.
2. Define, give examples of, and identify absolute and relocatable expressions.
3. Write operand entries of machine instructions by using explicit or implicit designations as appropriate for given situations.
4. Write syntactically correct assembler language statements.
5. Use in a program the directives DC to define constants, DS to reserve storage, USING to declare a base register, and EQU to define new symbols.
6. Use the listing control directives within a program.
7. Write and run a simple assembler language program.
8. Describe the assembly process.
9. Distinguish between assembly-time and execution-time errors, and give examples of each.

## Introduction

By now, you are aware of the extra effort involved when machine language is used instead of a high-level language. Most of this effort is attributable to the inherent differences between the languages. Machine language instructions are basic: you must take more steps to accomplish the same task as one statement in a high-level language. Even so, some of the tedium involved in machine language—such as looking up operation codes, computing displacements, and converting from one number base to another—can be alleviated through the use of assembler language. Since each machine instruction can be specified symbolically by one assembler language statement, you retain complete control over the instruction set; anything that you can write in machine language can be written with equivalent assembler language statements.

You may feel that much of this chapter is an endless list of related rules. However, you will become more comfortable with these rules as you practice writing programs, especially after new machine instructions have been introduced in subsequent chapters. Try to understand the major ideas now and return to the details later as necessary.

A few aspects of the language, particularly those involving limits, differ according to the assembler in question. This text will consider the OS and DOS assemblers and point out their differences where appropriate.

## The Format of Assembler Language Statements

**Three types of instructions**

Assembler language statements specify either instructions or comments. Instructions are either machine instructions, assembler instructions, or macro instructions. A **machine instruction** is an assembler language statement that represents a single executable machine language instruction. An **assembler instruction** (also called a **directive**) either provides information to the assembler, or requests it to perform such functions as reserving storage or defining constants. Except for directives that define constants, these instructions do not produce object code. Two examples of directives mentioned in Chapter 3 are CSECT and END, which are used to mark the beginning and the end of a program. **Macro instructions** can simplify the programmer's task as each instruction represents a sequence of machine instructions, assembler instructions, or both that are generated according to a predefined pattern. You use macro instructions to perform tasks that can occur frequently, such as I/O requests or subprogram calls. The pattern or macro definition either can reside in a system library, in which case it is called a **library-macro definition** or a **system macro,** or can be included within the source program. Those in the source program are described in detail in Chapter 18.

### *The Format of Instructions*

The character set used for machine and assembler instructions consists of letters, digits, and several special characters. In this set, letters include $, #, and @, as well as A through Z. The valid special characters are as follows:

& + − , = . * ( ) ' / blank

Note that blanks are meaningful characters; they are not ignored, as they are in some high-level languages.

Symbols

A **symbol** is a sequence of one to eight letters and digits that begin with a letter. Although a symbol may look like a variable in Pascal or FORTRAN, it is not the same. Some symbols are used to represent addresses. For example, a symbol that represents the address of a fullword in storage is similar to a variable in Pascal or FORTRAN, but a symbol that represents the address of an instruction is similar to a Pascal label or a FORTRAN statement number. However, symbols can represent other language components, such as the name of a register.

---

EXAMPLE 1

The following are some examples of valid and invalid symbols.

| Valid symbols | Invalid symbols | |
|---|---|---|
| X | 2ND | First character is not a letter |
| R5 | 15 | First character is not a letter |
| CONSTANT | SECTION10 | More than eight characters |
| $DATA1 | $DATA.1 | "." is illegal in a symbol |
| #1234567 | CAR_TAX | Illegal character (_) |
| @##$$@@ | | |

---

Operation codes

Operation codes are specified symbolically, rather than numerically. A short string of alphabetic characters that suggests the name of the operation is used to represent the operation code. For example, L means Load and ST means Store. Such operation codes are said to be **mnemonic** because they help you remember their meanings. A list of the mnemonic operation codes for the instructions introduced in Chapter 3 is provided in Figure 4.1. Directives and macro instructions are also said to have mnemonic op codes.

Each instruction in assembler language contains up to four entries† separated by one or more blanks. The entries, in the order that they appear in an instruction, are defined as follows:

†Although some programmers use the term *field,* IBM's *Assembler Language* manual uses *entry.* This text will use *entry* also.

**Figure 4.1**
The mnemonic operation codes for the instructions that were introduced in Chapter 3.

| Mnemonic | Instruction name |
|---|---|
| L | Load |
| LR | Load Register |
| ST | Store |
| A | Add |
| AR | Add Register |
| S | Subtract |
| SR | Subtract Register |
| BALR | Branch and Link |
| BCR | Branch on Condition |

Four entries of an assembler language statement

- The **name entry** is a symbol that begins in column 1 and that is used to identify the statement. This entry is optional and, if omitted, column 1 must be blank.
- The **operation entry** is required and consists of the mnemonic operation code of the instruction.
- The **operand entry** designates the operands of the instruction. For a machine instruction, this entry designates the operands of the corresponding machine language instruction. For directives and macros, the operand entry provides information required by the operation. In general, the operand designations are separated by commas without intervening blanks. Several definitions and rules are necessary for constructing this entry, and will be detailed shortly. Some directives omit or optionally use this entry. If you omit the operand entry but still desire to use a remarks entry, you must write a single comma as the operand entry.
- The **remarks entry** explains the statement to you and to other programmers. As such, the assembler ignores it. The entry can consist of any characters including blanks.

These four entries are written in a free format. With the exception of the name entry, which must begin in column 1, the entries do not need to begin in specific columns. You only have to remember to separate each entry from the preceding entry by at least one blank. Leave column 1 blank when you omit the name entry so that the assembler can distinguish between a name entry and an operation code. Although you can use free format, you can greatly enhance program readability by beginning the entries in particular columns. Generally, programmers begin the operation entry in column 10, the operand entry in column 16, and the remarks in a convenient but fixed column between 30 and 40.

## *The Comments Statement*

Comments statements, which begin with an asterisk (*), are ignored by the assembler but appear in the assembly listing. While the remarks entry of an instruction describes the particular details of that instruction, you use comments statements at the beginning of the program to describe its purpose, and throughout the program to explain the intent of groups of instructions. You will see this technique used in later examples.

## *Statement Length*

Columns 1 to 71 of a line or card specify assembler language statements. It is possible, though not usual, for a statement to exceed this space. If so, you can continue the statement onto the next line by first entering a nonblank character (called the **continuation indicator**) into column 72, and then continuing the statement at column 16 of the next line. (You must leave columns 1 to 15 blank.) If necessary, you may repeat this procedure once more for a maximum total of 3 lines per statement. (This restriction applies to machine instructions and directives, but not to macro instructions.)

EXAMPLE 2

Figure 4.2 provides some examples of assembler language statements. Statement 1 is an example of an instruction that does not require an operand entry. Since a remarks entry is desired, the operand entry consists of a single comma. The long remark is continued onto successive lines by using a continuation indicator in column 72. Although you can continue unusually long operand entries in this manner, it is easier to write the remainder of a long remark on successive comments statements, as demonstrated by Statements 8, 9, and 10. Note the way that the continued portion is indented to distinguish the continuation from the statements that follow.

Although it is correct to continue a comments statement with a continuation indicator, it is easier to use several separate comments statements, each with an asterisk in column 1. However, be careful not to type the comment beyond column 71 since a character in column 72 will be interpreted to be a continuation indicator; the assembler will then assume that the subsequent instruction is part of the comments statement and ignore it.

```
STMT    SOURCE STATEMENT
   1 EXAMPLE  CSECT ,              THE OPERAND WAS OMITTED SO A COMMA IS    X
               NECESSARY IN THE OPERAND ENTRY.  THIS STATEMENT NOW IS   X
               TOO LONG FOR ONE LINE.  NOTE HOW IT IS CONTINUED.
   2 *
   3 * THE ABOVE STATEMENT MAY NOT BE CONTINUED ONTO A FOURTH LINE.
   4 *
   5 * A REMARKS ENTRY IS BEST CONTINUED BY INSERTING COMMENTS STATEMENTS
   6 * AS NEEDED, AND NOT AS IN STMT 1.  FOR EXAMPLE:
   7 *
   8 LOOP     AR    3,2            THE NAME ENTRY REPRESENTS THE ADDRESS
   9 *                                OF THIS INSTRUCTION.  NOTE HOW
  10 *                                THIS REMARK IS CONTINUED.
  11 *
  12          AR    3,2            HERE, THE NAME ENTRY IS OMITTED.
  13 *
  14 * IT IS BEST NOT TO CONTINUE COMMENTS STATEMENTS AS IN STATEMENT 1.
  15 * INSTEAD, USE ADDITIONAL COMMENTS STATEMENTS AS IS DONE HERE.
  16 * BE CAREFUL NOT TO TYPE INTO COLUMN 72, HOWEVER, AS YOU WILL
  17 * INADVERTENTLY INDICATE A CONTINUATION.
```

**Figure 4.2**
Examples of assembler language statements.

## SELF-TEST EXERCISE

1. Which of the following are not valid symbols? Explain.

| | | |
|---|---|---|
| **a.** AB$ | **e.** A12345678 | **i.** X(4) |
| **b.** DATA.SET | **f.** $AB | **j.** $12 |
| **c.** 3D | **g.** #DEF | **k.** $$$$ |
| **d.** AB4DEFGH | **h.** *ABC | **l.** @**** |

## Defining Constants and Storage

Two directives are available to allocate storage and, if desired, to assign symbolic addresses. Both have similar forms. The DC directive establishes values in storage that are used either as constants or as initial values. The DS directive reserves storage, but does not assign initial values.

### *The Define Constant (DC) Directive*

**Initializing storage**

You can establish constants (or initial values) in storage, and let the assembler take care of base conversions and boundary alignment with the Define Constant directive. Several types of constants are possible; this section will introduce a few now and save the others for later.

The DC directive is summarized as follows:

| Name | Operation | Operand | Instruction Name | Action |
|---|---|---|---|---|
| *symbol* or *blank* | **DC** | *dt'c'* | DEFINE CONSTANT | Defines *d* copies of the constant *c* of type *t*. |

The optional *symbol* in the name entry represents the address of the constant defined. The operand entry describes the number of duplicate constants (*d*), if any, that are desired, the type of constant (*t*), and the constant itself (*c*). You write the constant according to its type. Some possible values of *t* are as follows:

**Some constant types for DC**

- F Specifies a fullword constant. The constant *c* is a signed, decimal integer that is converted by the assembler into a 32-bit two's complement binary integer, and is placed into the next available fullword of storage. The constant must be in the range −2147483648 to 2147483647 ($-2^{31}$ to $2^{31} - 1$). Any bytes skipped as a result of boundary alignment are set to zero.
- H Specifies a halfword constant analogously to F. The assembled constant is 16 bits long and is placed into the next halfword of storage. Its value must be in the range −32768 to 32767 ($-2^{15}$ to $2^{15} - 1$).
- X Specifies a hexadecimal constant. The constant *c* is an unsigned hexadecimal integer that is assembled into the minimum number of bytes required to accommodate it. Since each byte can represent 2 hexadecimal digits, if there is an odd number of digits, the assembler pads the left side of the constant with a zero digit. Hexadecimal constants cannot exceed 256 bytes in length. No boundary alignment occurs; instead the next available bytes are used. (Recall that machine language instructions in Chapter 3 were specified as hexadecimal constants.)
- B Specifies a binary constant in a fashion analogous to X. The constant is padded on the left with zeros, if necessary, so that its length is a multiple of 8 bits.

The **duplication factor** *d* indicates that the constant will be generated *d* times. The factor may be specified as an unsigned decimal integer and is an optional entry; if it is omitted, the assembler assumes it to be 1.

EXAMPLE 3

The following are examples of the DC directive.

| | | | |
|---|---|---|---|
| CON1 | DC | F'21' | This directive defines a fullword that contains $00000015_{16}$, which is equivalent to the decimal constant 21, at the next fullword boundary. Note that any bytes skipped as a result of achieving boundary alignment are not considered to be part of the assembled constant. Thus, the symbol CON1 represents the address of the fullword constant, but not the address of the skipped bytes. |
| CON2 | DC | 2F'-1' | This directive defines 2 consecutive fullwords, each containing $FFFFFFFF_{16}$, which is equivalent to the decimal constant −1. The first fullword begins at the next fullword boundary; the symbol CON2 represents its address. |
| CON3 | DC | H'14' | This directive defines a halfword containing $000E_{16}$, which is equivalent to the decimal constant 14, at the next halfword boundary. The symbol CON3 represents the address of the halfword. |
| CON4 | DC | X'ABCDE' | This defines the hexadecimal constant 0ABCDE in the next 3 bytes. Since there is an odd number of digits in the constant, it is padded on the left with a zero. No boundary alignment occurs. CON4 represents the address of the constant. |
| CON5 | DC | B'11010' | This directive defines the binary constant 00011010 in the next available byte. No boundary alignment occurs. CON5 represents the address of the constant. |

## *The Define Storage (DS) Directive*

Reserving storage

You must reserve storage if, for example, you plan to store the results of a computation. You can use the DC directive to do this if you want the reserved storage to contain an initial value, but the DS directive reserves storage without initializing the contents of the reserved bytes. Its general form is very similar to the DC instruction, as follows:

| Name | Operation | Operand | Instruction Name | Action |
|---|---|---|---|---|
| *symbol* or *blank* | **DS** | *dt'c'* | DEFINE STORAGE | Reserves *d* units of storage. Uses *t* (D = doubleword, F = fullword, H = halfword, X = byte, B = byte) to give the type of unit. |

The name and operand entries have the same meanings as for the DC directive†; however, DS does not define a constant even if you include one. In fact, the '*c*' portion is usually omitted. For example,

```
SUM      DS    F
```

reserves a fullword whose address is represented by the symbol SUM. Any bytes skipped in achieving the proper boundary alignment are not initialized, as they are with the DC directive.

---

EXAMPLE 4

The following are examples of the DS directive.

| | | | |
|---|---|---|---|
| A | DS | 2F | This directive reserves 2 consecutive fullwords at the next fullword boundary. The symbol A represents the address of the first fullword. |
| B | DS | 100H | This reserves an array of 100 consecutive halfwords at the next halfword boundary. The symbol B represents the first halfword. |
| SAVE | DS | 9D | This reserves an array of 9 consecutive doublewords at the next doubleword boundary. The symbol SAVE represents the first doubleword. |
| | DS | 3X | This reserves the next 3 bytes and no boundary alignment occurs. |
| | DS | 3B | This has exactly the same meaning to the assembler as the directive just given. You would choose B over X if you thought of the contents of the bytes as binary instead of hexadecimal. |

---

If a constant is specified within the operand of a DS, the assembler reserves sufficient space to accommodate it. For example, you could reserve the 3 bytes necessary to accommodate a 5-digit hexadecimal number by writing

```
DS    3X
```

or

```
DS    3B
```

Or you could reserve them by specifying any 5-digit hexadecimal constant in the operand; thus,

```
DS    X'12345'
```

also reserves 3 bytes. It is important to realize that the constant is *not*

†The D-type constant in the DC directive is a floating-point constant that you will encounter in Chapter 17.

assembled and the reserved bytes are not initialized. For this reason, you should use this technique with extreme caution, if at all.

**Forcing boundary alignment**

It is possible to specify a duplication factor of zero. If you do this with a constant type of either D, F, or H, alignment to the indicated integral boundary occurs without reservation of additional storage. Usually when programmers use a zero duplication factor, they follow it with a DC directive. For example, suppose that you wanted to define a fullword hexadecimal constant. The instruction

```
DC     X'ABCDEF12'
```

defines the constant, but there is no boundary alignment. The solution is to write

```
DS     0F
DC     X'ABCDEF12'
```

Note that you may also use a zero duplication factor with the DC directive. The specified constant is not assembled and any bytes skipped as a result of boundary alignment are set to zero. If setting the skipped bytes to zero is important in a given situation, use DC instead of DS in the solution just given.

### SELF-TEST EXERCISES

2. Write one or more DC and DS directives to create each of the following:
   a. An array of 3 halfwords that contains the integers 11, 12, and 13.
   b. An array of 3 bytes that contains the integers 11, 12, and 13.
   c. An array of 832 bytes that begins at a halfword boundary.
   d. A fullword named T that contains the hexadecimal integer ABCDEF.
3. Assume that W is at a doubleword boundary. What are the contents in hexadecimal of the consecutive bytes beginning at W, as defined by each of the following?

a.
```
W      DC     X'A'
       DC     2H'-1'
       DC     F'49'
```

b.
```
W      DC     2X'4'
       DC     0F'0'
       DC     4X'12'
```

c.
```
W      DC     H'-5'
       DS     0F
       DC     2X'12ABC'
```

## Operand Designations

This section will define the terminology and state the rules necessary to designate operands. These designations are said to be explicit or implicit. For example, to write an RX instruction with an explicit designation of its storage operand, you would specify the index and base registers, as well as the displacement. If you designated an RX storage operand implicitly, as is usually the case, the assembler would specify the base register and calculate the displacement. However, you always designate the operands of RR instructions explicitly because they are always in registers.

| | DOS | | | OS | | |
|---|---|---|---|---|---|---|
| | *Maximum number of digits* | *Minimum value* | *Maximum value* | *Maximum number of digits* | *Minimum value* | *Maximum value* |
| Decimal | 8 | 0 | $2^{24} - 1$ | 10 | 0 | $2^{31} - 1$ |
| Binary | 24 | 0 | $2^{24} - 1$ | 32 | $-2^{31}$ | $2^{31} - 1$ |
| Hex | 6 | 0 | $2^{24} - 1$ | 8 | $-2^{31}$ | $2^{31} - 1$ |
| Character | 3 | 0 | $2^{24} - 1$ | 4 | 0 | $2^{31} - 1$ |

**Figure 4.3**
The limits on self-defining terms.

## *Self-Defining Terms*

**Self-defining terms** are constants written in decimal, binary, hexadecimal, or character form that designate such instruction components as registers, masks, and displacements within the operand entry. They are called *self-defining* because their values are inherent in their definitions. For example, 3 is a decimal self-defining term. Regardless of their form, self-defining terms have a 24-bit value in DOS and a 32-bit value in OS. The following are descriptions of the types of self-defining terms:

**Four types of self-defining terms**

- A **decimal self-defining term** is an unsigned decimal integer.
- A **binary self-defining term** is a binary integer within apostrophes and preceded by a B, as in B'1101'.
- A **hexadecimal self-defining term** is a hexadecimal integer within apostrophes and preceded by an X, as in X'5A4'.
- A **character self-defining term** is a character string, which is typically a single character, within apostrophes and preceded by a C, as in C'Z'. This form of self-defining term will not be used until character manipulation is discussed in Chapter 10.

The limits on self-defining terms are summarized in Figure 4.3.

## *Explicit Operand Designations*

Explicit operand designations allow you to define each portion of the corresponding machine language instruction explicitly. You can use self-defining terms for this purpose, although there are other ways, which will be noted later. Most RR instructions have two register operands that are denoted by *R1* and *R2*, and that are designated explicitly in assembler language by

*R1,R2*

For example,

```
LR    3,10
```

loads Register 3 with the contents of Register 10. Recall that, in RX format, *R1* denotes the register operand, and the effective address of the storage operand is computed from the index register, base register, and displacement, which are denoted by *X2*, *B2*, and *D2*, respectively. These are specified explicitly in assembler language as

*R1,D2(X2,B2)*

**Figure 4.4**
The format of explicit operand designations for RR and RX instructions.

| Instruction format | Operand format | Example |
|---|---|---|
| RR | *R1,R2* | `LR 3,10` |
| RX | *R1,D2(X2,B2)* | `L 8,206(2,12)` |
| RX; No index register | *R1,D2(0,B2)* | `L 8,206(0,12)` |
| | *R1,D2(,B2)* | `L 8,206(,12)` |
| RX; No base register | *R1,D2(X2,0)* | `L 8,206(2,0)` |
| | *R1,D2(X2)* | `L 8,206(2)` |
| RX; No index or base register | *R1,D2(0,0)* | `L 8,206(0,0)` |
| | *R1,D2* | `L 8,206` |

There are some contractions of this form that you can use when you omit the index register or the base register, as indicated in Figure 4.4.

The examples provided in Figure 4.4 use decimal self-defining terms. However, you would generally use whatever base was most convenient. For example, the following three instructions are equivalent:

```
L     8,206(2,12)
L     8,X'CE'(2,12)
L     B'1000',206(2,X'C')
```

RX instructions in explicit form require you to compute displacements and thus do not provide much advantage over machine language. Although you will use explicit operand designations with certain RX instructions that will be given later, you will typically designate RX operands in implicit form.

---

EXAMPLE 5

Figure 4.5 lists an assembler language version of the machine language program of Figure 3.9. This version uses explicit operand designations throughout. It is somewhat easier to write and read, but it still requires you to count bytes and compute displacements.

**Figure 4.5**
The assembler language version of the machine language program of Figure 3.9, which uses explicit operand designations.

```
EXAMPLE  CSECT
*************************************************************
*
*     GIVEN X, Y, Z, AND W AS CONSECUTIVE FULLWORDS,
*     COMPUTE W = X - Y + Z WHERE X = -22, Y = 2, AND Z = 20.
*
*************************************************************
*
         BALR   12,0                000  LOAD BASE REGISTER
         L      2,X'012'(0,12)      002  LOAD REGISTER WITH X
         S      2,X'016'(0,12)      006  SUBTRACT Y
         A      2,X'01A'(0,12)      00A  ADD Z
         ST     2,X'01E'(0,12)      00E  STORE THE RESULT IN W
         BCR    X'F',14             012  RETURN
         DC     F'-22'              014  X = -22
         DC     F'2'                018  Y = 2
         DC     F'20'               01C  Z = 20
         DS     F                   020  W
         END    EXAMPLE
```

## *Implicit Operand Designations*

Consider the constant defined by

```
K       DC      F'25'
```

Suppose that you want to load this constant into Register 4. As you have seen, with a knowledge of the base address, you could compute the necessary displacement and write a Load instruction explicitly as, for example,

```
L       4,X'026'(0,12)
```

However, it would be far simpler to write

```
L       4,K
```

and let the assembler compute the displacement. This in fact is a Load instruction with an implicit operand designation. K, along with other aspects of the program that you will consider later, implies the base register and the displacement.

Let *S2* represent a symbolic address. You can write the operand entry of an RX instruction implicitly as either

*R1,S2*    as in    `L       4,K`

or

*R1,S2(X2)*    as in    `L       4,K(6)`

where *X2* is the index register (Register 6 in this case). The assembler will compute the displacements by using information about the base register that you must provide with the USING directive described in the next section.

## *The USING Directive*

When you computed displacements in Chapter 3, you had to know something about the base address. Since the assembler will essentially perform the same computation that you did, you must give it the name of the base register and the symbolic value of the base address. You might wonder why the assembler cannot figure this out on its own. Suppose you load the base register by using the instruction

```
BALR        12,0
```

Although you have not yet seen other uses for the BALR instruction, you should be aware that it has other uses than loading a base register. Also, a base register can be loaded with instructions other than the BALR instruction. Therefore, the assembler cannot look for the instruction that loaded the base register. Thus, you must tell the assembler the name of the base register that you have selected. Having done this, you now wonder if the assembler simply can look in the base register for the base address. To answer this, a careful distinction between assembly (translation) time and execution time must be made. During the translation of your program, the base register does not contain the base address that it will eventually contain after the program begins execution. In fact, the assembler might use this register since, after all, it is itself a program. Therefore, not only do you have to tell the assembler the name of the base register, but also you have to tell it to assume a certain value for the base address. You accomplish this with the USING directive.

**Declaring a base register**

The USING directive is summarized as follows:

| Name | Operation | Operand | Instruction Name | Action |
|---|---|---|---|---|
| *blank* | **USING** | *S,R* | DECLARE BASE REGISTER | Causes the assembler to assume that Register *R* is a base register and that it contains the address *S*. |

The *blank* indicates that you must omit the name entry. *S* represents the base address in a symbolic form and *R* is the name of the base register. The instruction tells the assembler to use Register *R* as the base register and to assume that that register will contain the address *S*. Again, at the time of assembly, Register *R* does not contain this address and the USING directive does *not* load the base register; you must do that with a separate instruction, such as a BALR. The USING instruction does not generate machine language instructions; it only provides information to the assembler.

---

EXAMPLE 6

In the following instructions, the USING directive informs the assembler that, from this point on and until further notice, it can use Register 12 as a base register and that it can *assume* that Register 12 will contain the address represented by the symbol BASE.

```
PROGRAM  CSECT
         BALR    12,0
         USING   BASE,12
BASE     SR      2,2
```

It remains your responsibility to ensure that the base register will contain this base address before it is first required. Here, this is accomplished with the BALR instruction. Since USING does not generate machine language instructions, the BALR and SR instructions will be adjacent to each other in storage. BALR loads Register 12 with the address of the SR instruction; the symbol BASE represents this address.

---

EXAMPLE 7

The program in Figure 4.6 is another version of the program of Figure 4.5. It uses implicit operand designations for the RX instructions. This is the way that your programs will typically appear.

**Figure 4.6**
The program of Figure 4.5 rewritten with implicit operand designations for the RX instructions.

```
EXAMPLE  CSECT
****************************************************************
*
*    GIVEN X, Y, Z, AND W AS CONSECUTIVE FULLWORDS,
*    COMPUTE W = X - Y + Z WHERE X = -22, Y = 2, AND Z = 20.
*
****************************************************************
*
         BALR  12,0                LOAD BASE REGISTER
         USING BASE,12             DECLARE BASE ADDRESS AND REGISTER
BASE     L     2,X                 LOAD A REGISTER WITH X
         S     2,Y                 SUBTRACT Y
         A     2,Z                 ADD Z
         ST    2,W                 STORE THE RESULT IN W
         BCR   X'F',14             RETURN
X        DC    F'-22'
Y        DC    F'2'
Z        DC    F'20'
W        DS    F
         END   EXAMPLE
```

## *Additional Definitions Required for Operand Designations*

Terms and expressions

Both implicit and explicit operand designations can be written more generally than the previous examples indicate. You can specify them by using **expressions,** which are defined to be either a **term** or an arithmetic combination of terms. So far, you have encountered only two kinds of terms: symbols and self-defining terms. There are others, which will be presented later. Expressions essentially adhere to the rules of FORTRAN or Pascal, but there are some restrictions, which are detailed in Figure 4.7. Note that expressions, like other operand designations, cannot contain embedded blanks. Expressions are evaluated at assembly time, not at execution time. They represent addresses or values that are used to define machine language instructions; they do not refer to the contents of registers or of storage.

Absolute expressions

Relocatable expressions

Expressions are said to be either *absolute* or *relocatable.* **Absolute expressions** are those whose values are independent of the actual starting address of the program. For example, a self-defining term is absolute; the self-defining term 3 is 3, regardless of where the program starts. As the opposite of absolute expressions, **relocatable expressions** do depend upon the starting address of the program. A symbol in the name entry of a DC instruction is an example of a relocatable expression since it represents the address of a constant in storage. The actual address clearly depends upon the program's starting address.

Suppose that X and Y are defined by

```
X       DC     F'17'
Y       DS     F
```

The expression Y−X is absolute; regardless of the program's starting address, the addresses represented by X and Y will differ by 4. In general, the expression formed by the difference of two relocatable expressions is absolute.

**Figure 4.7**
The rules for constructing operand expressions.

An *expression* is either a term or a combination of terms, arithmetic operators (+, −, ∗, / ), and pairs of parentheses that adhere to the following rules:

1. A term may not be adjacent to another term, and an operator may not be adjacent to another operator.
2. An expression may not contain embedded blanks unless they are part of a character string within apostrophes.
3. There are limits on the number of operators and levels of parentheses (excluding the parentheses that are used to specify the operand). With DOS, the limit is 15 operators and 5 levels of parentheses; in OS, the limit is 19 operators and 6 levels of parentheses.
4. Parenthesized subexpressions are evaluated first. Within this constraint, operations are performed left to right, with multiplication and division carried out before addition and subtraction.
5. The value of an expression lies within 0 to $2^{24} - 1$ in DOS and $-2^{31}$ to $2^{31} - 1$ in OS.
6. The result of a division is always truncated to an integer. Division by zero produces a zero result.
7. Relocatable terms cannot be used wth multiplication or division.

Arithmetic combinations of absolute expressions are also absolute. Thus, if you let *rel* represent a relocatable expression and *abs* represent an absolute expression, then the following expressions

*rel* − *rel*
*abs* • *abs*

are absolute where • represents +, −, *, or /.

In contrast, the expression X+4 is relocatable since it represents the address that is 4 bytes beyond the address represented by X. Thus, X+4 represents the same address as Y. Note that X+4 does not mean 21. In general, the following are relocatable expressions:

*rel* + *abs*
*rel* − *abs*

The following general rules are also applicable:

1. Relocatable expressions must contain an odd number of relocatable terms. All but one of the relocatable terms must occur in pairs, where a *pair* is two terms of opposite signs. The unpaired term must be added, but not subtracted.
2. Absolute expressions must contain an even number of relocatable terms. All relocatable terms must be paired as defined in the previous rule.

In the earlier definitions of explicit and implicit operand designations, *R1*, *R2*, *X2*, *B2*, and *D2* can each be an absolute expression, and *S2* can be a relocatable expression. In the definition of USING, *R* can be an absolute expression and *S* can be a relocatable expression. The duplication factor *d* used with the DC and DS directives can also be a positive absolute expression within parentheses, as well as a self-defining term.

---

EXAMPLE 8

Assume that X, Y, and Z are relocatable symbols and that A is an absolute symbol.

The following are examples of relocatable expressions:

```
X+Y-Z+4
X+A-8
X+4
```

The following are examples of absolute expressions:

```
4*A-8
X-Y
2*(X-Y)/A+1
A+4
X+Y-Z-Z-A
```

---

## SELF-TEST EXERCISES

4. Which of the following expressions are absolute? Which are relocatable? Which are invalid? Assume that A and B are absolute symbols, and X and Y are relocatable symbols.

| | | | |
|---|---|---|---|
| a. X'ABC' | e. X − Y | i. X − A * B | m. 98 + A/(B + 4) |
| b. X + X'9C' | f. B'ABC + 1' | j. X * Y | n. (X + 4) − Y |
| c. X + A | g. Y + 4 + X | k. B − B'1011' | |
| d. X + Y | h. Y + B + 4 | l. (X − Y) + X | |

5. Which of the following assembler statements are invalid? Explain. Assume that R2, R4, and R12 are absolute symbols, and X and Y are relocatable symbols.

| | | | | | |
|---|---|---|---|---|---|
| a. | L | R2,X(R4) | h. | L | R4,X(R2)+4 |
| b. | L | X'A',Y+R4 | i. | L | R2,500 |
| c. | L | R2,X(0,R4) | j. | L | R2,Y-4(R4) |
| d. | L | 7,Y(R2,R12) | k. | L | R2,Y+4(R4,12) |
| e. | L | R4,4(R2) | l. | LR | R2,R3 |
| f. | L | X'10',X'10'(3,R12) | m. | LR | R4,Y |
| g. | L | 0,0(R4,R12) | n. | LR | R4,X'F' |

6. Assume that DATA represents an address that is $156_{10}$ bytes beyond the base address, and that Register 12 is the base register. For each of the following instructions, write an equivalent instruction by using explicit operand designations. Also write the machine language instruction that is represented by each.

| | | | | | |
|---|---|---|---|---|---|
| a. | L | 8,DATA | d. | ST | 8,DATA+4(3) |
| b. | A | 8,DATA+4 | e. | L | 8,DATA-4(2) |
| c. | S | 8,DATA(3) | | | |

7. Assume that Y represents an address that is $252_{10}$ bytes beyond the base address, and that Register 10 is the base register. Rewrite each of the following explicit operand designations in an implicit form in terms of Y.

| | | |
|---|---|---|
| a. 252(,10) | c. 256(0,10) | e. 250(,10) |
| b. 252(3,10) | d. 256(2,10) | f. 250(3,10) |

## The EQU Directive

You have seen that symbols are defined and, hence, given meaning when they appear as the name entry of an instruction. In fact, each symbol must appear as one and only one name entry; otherwise, the symbol either would be undefined or would have multiple definitions.

**Defining new symbols**

EQU is an assembler instruction whose sole purpose is to define a symbol. It is summarized as follows:

| Name | Operation | Operand | Instruction Name | Action |
|---|---|---|---|---|
| *symbol* | **EQU** | *expression* | EQUATE SYMBOL | Defines the *symbol*; its value is that of the *expression* in the operand. |

The assembler assigns to the *symbol* the value of the *expression*, which is either relocatable or absolute. Although all of the symbols that have been defined so far have represented addresses and, therefore, were relocatable, it is possible to define absolute symbols. For example,

```
R8      EQU    8
```

equates the symbol R8 with the self-defining term 8. Therefore, R8 is absolute. You can use these two quantities interchangeably in the assembler language to specify, for example, a register. Thus,

```
SR    R8,R8
```

is the same as

```
SR    8,8
```

However, notice that the EQU does not equate R8 with Register 8; it equates R8 simply with 8. R8 means Register 8 only if it is used as *R1, R2, X2,* or *B2,* but not if it is used as a displacement or within an expression.

You can also use EQU to provide alternate names for symbols or expressions—whether they are absolute or relocatable. When symbols appear within the operand entry of an EQU, their definitions must precede the EQU; that is, the symbols must be previously defined in the program. Beyond this restriction, the EQU may appear anywhere in the program and need not precede the use of the symbol that it defines.

---

EXAMPLE 9

The following sequence of instructions demonstrates the EQU directive:

```
R4      EQU   4          R4 is an absolute symbol.
        L     R4,W       Equivalent to  L    4,W
        AR    R4,R4      Equivalent to  AR   4,4
        ST    R4,W4      Equivalent to  ST   4,W+4
        ST    R4,WORD    Equivalent to  ST   4,W+8
        .
        .
        .
W       DC    F'21'
        DS    F
W4      EQU   W+4        W must be previously defined.
WORD    EQU   W4+R4      W4 and R4 must be previously defined.
```

Notice that the definitions of W4 and WORD do not precede their use in the Store instructions; they could precede it, but they do not have to. However, the definition of W must precede the definition of W4 since W appears in the operand entry of the EQU defining W4. Similarly, the definitions of both W4 and R4 must precede the definition of WORD.

Notice also that R4 in the definition of WORD does not represent Register 4. This use of R4 can be confusing and, therefore, is stylistically poor, but was used here to illustrate the meaning of R4 to the assembler.

---

It is important to realize that EQU does not generate machine language instructions; it merely informs the assembler about new symbols that you want to use in your program. You define symbols in this way to make the program more meaningful and, therefore, you should choose them with this in mind. For example, it is a good idea to name all of the registers symbolically, as Registers 4 and 8 had been in the previous examples. Most programmers include in their programs the statements listed in Figure 4.8,

**Symbolic register names**

**Figure 4.8**
The definition of symbols to be used as register names.

```
R0       EQU   0
R1       EQU   1
R2       EQU   2
R3       EQU   3
R4       EQU   4
R5       EQU   5
R6       EQU   6
R7       EQU   7
R8       EQU   8
R9       EQU   9
R10      EQU   10
R11      EQU   11
R12      EQU   12
R13      EQU   13
R14      EQU   14
R15      EQU   15
```

and all future examples will assume that this has been done. You can use the remarks entries of these EQU statements to indicate how the registers are used in the program. In addition, the symbols R0, R1, and so on to R15 will appear in a **cross-reference table** in the assembly listing. This table contains all symbols defined in the program and indications as to where each symbol was defined and used. This information can be very helpful during debugging.

Do not confuse the notation *R1* and *R2* for the first and second register operands with the symbols R1 and R2 that are generally used to represent Registers 1 and 2. The notation was chosen to be consistent with IBM's *System/370 Reference Summary.*

Figure 4.9 contains a listing of the program of Figure 4.6 that has been rewritten with EQU directives. The TITLE directive that appears there is described in the next section.

## SELF-TEST EXERCISES

8. Write statements to perform the following:
   a. Equate the symbol X to the hex value AB.
   b. Equate the symbol Y to the symbol X.
   c. Equate the symbol Z to the address that is 2 bytes before that represented by WORD.
9. Explain the difference between

```
R     EQU   4
```

and

```
R     DC    F'4'
```

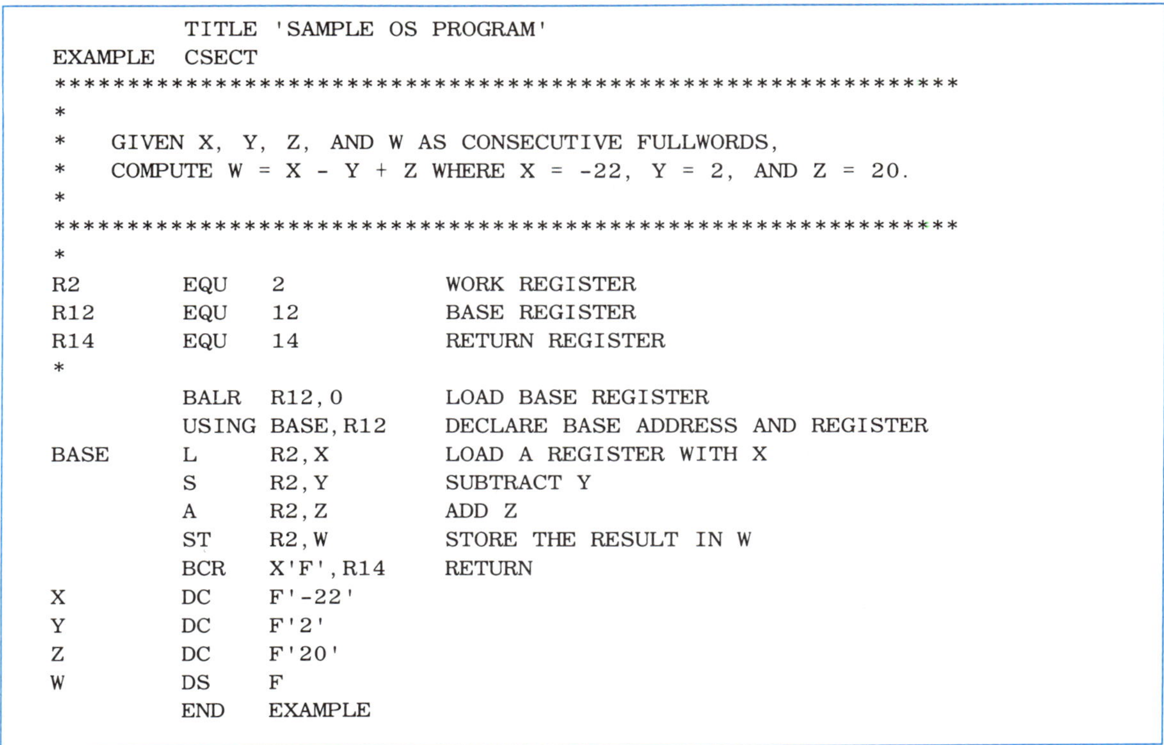

```
         TITLE 'SAMPLE OS PROGRAM'
EXAMPLE  CSECT
**************************************************************
*
*    GIVEN X, Y, Z, AND W AS CONSECUTIVE FULLWORDS,
*    COMPUTE W = X - Y + Z WHERE X = -22, Y = 2, AND Z = 20.
*
**************************************************************
*
R2       EQU   2           WORK REGISTER
R12      EQU   12          BASE REGISTER
R14      EQU   14          RETURN REGISTER
*
         BALR  R12,0       LOAD BASE REGISTER
         USING BASE,R12    DECLARE BASE ADDRESS AND REGISTER
BASE     L     R2,X        LOAD A REGISTER WITH X
         S     R2,Y        SUBTRACT Y
         A     R2,Z        ADD Z
         ST    R2,W        STORE THE RESULT IN W
         BCR   X'F',R14    RETURN
X        DC    F'-22'
Y        DC    F'2'
Z        DC    F'20'
W        DS    F
         END   EXAMPLE
```

**Figure 4.9** The program of Figure 4.6 rewritten with EQU directives.

## Completing an Assembler Language Program

This section formally defines the CSECT and END directives, outlines certain conventions about register usage that you must follow, and defines some directives that are used to affect the appearance of the assembly listing. To run an assembler language program, you must use control statements appropriate to the computing and operating systems available to you. These control statements are described in Appendix I.

### *The Program Delimiters CSECT and END*

**Indicating a program's beginning and end**

You indicate the beginning of your program with the CSECT directive. CSECT means **control section.** As you will see in Chapter 13, programs can be divided into modules known as control sections. For now, your programs will consist of only one control section. The directive is summarized as follows:

| Name | Operation | Operand | Instruction Name | Action |
|---|---|---|---|---|
| *symbol* or *blank* | **CSECT** | None | DEFINE CONTROL SECTION | Signals either the beginning of a control section or, for present purposes, the beginning of the program. |

The *symbol* represents the starting address of the control section. This address will always be a doubleword boundary. You can precede CSECT with comments statements if desired.

The last statement of a program is the END directive, which is summarized as follows:

| Name | Operation | Operand | Instruction Name | Action |
|---|---|---|---|---|
| *blank* | **END** | *relocatable expression* | END SOURCE MODULE | Signals the end of a control section or program. |

The operand entry indicates the address of the first instruction to be executed. This is usually the symbol in the name entry of the CSECT. Thus, CSECT and END are signals to the assembler that delimit the program.

## *Register Conventions*

The simple programs that you have studied so far do not follow most of the conventions that this section describes. Although their simplicity allows these programs to execute correctly, generally you must follow the conventions that are described here.

**Registers 0, 1, 13, 14, and 15 are special**

By convention, Registers 0, 1, 13, 14, and 15 are reserved for special purposes. Only a few convention details are important right now; Chapter 13 will describe all of the particulars. Both the operating system and the source program use these registers to link the various subprograms necessary to support program execution. Registers 0 and 1 are usually associated with the arguments of subprograms, although they do have other uses. Register 13 contains the address of an area in storage—called the **save area**—where subprograms and OS main programs save the contents of all other general registers.

A save area consists of either 18 fullwords in OS or 9 doublewords in DOS. Assuming that SAVE represents the address of the save area that you define in your program, you should begin your programs with the **standard entry**, as shown here:

**In OS**

```
PROG     CSECT
  (EQUs to define registers)
         STM    R14,R12,12(R13)
         BALR   R12,0
         USING  BASE,R12
BASE     ST     R13,SAVE+4
         LA     R13,SAVE
```

**In DOS**

```
PROG     CSECT
  (EQUs to define registers)
         BALR   R12,0
         USING  BASE,R12
BASE     LA     R13,SAVE
```

The STM instruction stores all general registers except Register 13 into the save area that OS provides. The LA instruction loads Register 13 with the address of the save area that you define in your program. You will learn more about the LA instruction in Chapter 7 and the STM instruction in Chapter 9.

To terminate program execution and to return to the operating system, write the **standard exit**, as shown here:

| In OS | | In DOS |
|---|---|---|
| L | R13,SAVE+4 | EOJ |
| LM | R14,R12,12(R13) | |
| BCR | X'F',R14 | |

The L and LM instructions restore the contents of the registers to the status that they had before you executed your program. (You will learn about the LM instruction in Chapter 9.) Recall that OS loads Register 14 with the return address: you use this register when you return control to OS with the BCR instruction. EOJ is a system macro instruction that returns control to DOS.

Finally, Register 15 initially contains the starting address of an OS program. You can sometimes take advantage of this fact by using Register 15 as a base register, but generally this is not a good idea.

**Register 2 through 12 are for user programs**

To summarize, you can use Registers 2 through 12 within your programs as needed. You can use Registers 0 and 1 as long as you understand that their contents may be destroyed when you invoke a subprogram or system macro. Remember that once you have selected a base register, you should not use it for anything else.

### *The Listing Controls TITLE, EJECT, SPACE, and PRINT*

Simple directives are available that affect the appearance of the assembly listing. The TITLE directive provides a heading for each page of the listing. It is summarized as follows:

| Name | Operation | Operand | Instruction Name | Action |
|---|---|---|---|---|
| *blank* | **TITLE** | *'string'* | CREATE HEADER | Provides a heading for each page of the assembly listing; *string* consists of up to 100 characters. |

The *string* is a string of up to 100 characters. A new TITLE directive may appear anywhere in the program to change the heading for subsequent pages. TITLE causes the listing to advance immediately to a new page. The TITLE instruction itself is not printed in the assembly listing.

The EJECT directive causes the next line of the source program to be printed at the top of a new page. EJECT is summarized as follows:

| Name | Operation | Operand | Instruction Name | Action |
|---|---|---|---|---|
| *blank* | **EJECT** | *blank* | SKIP TO A NEW PAGE | Prints the next line of the source program at the top of a new page. |

The EJECT instruction itself is not printed in the assembly listing.

The SPACE directive inserts one or more blank lines, as indicated by its operand entry, into the listing of the source program. It is summarized as follows:

| Name | Operation | Operand | Instruction Name | Action |
|---|---|---|---|---|
| *blank* | **SPACE** | *n* | INSERT BLANK LINES | Inserts *n* blank lines into the listing of the source program. The assembler assumes *n* is 1 if it is omitted. |

Here, *n* is a decimal self-defining term that indicates the number of blank lines to be inserted. If *n* is omitted, it is assumed to be 1. If *n* is larger than the number of lines left on the page, the instruction has the same effect as EJECT. The SPACE instruction itself is not printed in the assembly listing.

You can use the PRINT directive to affect certain details in the assembly listing. For example, although the assembly listing usually displays the instructions that macro instructions represent, you can suppress their appearance by using the PRINT directive in the following form:

| Name | Operation | Operand | Instruction Name | Action |
|---|---|---|---|---|
| *blank* | **PRINT** | NOGEN | PRINT DETAILS | Suppresses the printing of the instructions that a macro instruction represents. |

The instruction `PRINT NOGEN` is particularly useful when you write the system macro instructions that you will learn in this chapter and in Chapter 5. You also can use the PRINT directive with other operands either to affect how constants appear in the assembly listing, or to suppress the assembly listing entirely. The complete definition of the PRINT directive appears in Appendix F.

## The Assembly Process

When you write or debug assembler language programs, it is helpful to have a basic understanding of the assembly process. The logic used by an assembler to translate an assembler language source program into a machine language object program is fairly intuitive. As the steps involved are described, keep in mind the steps that you took when writing a machine language program.

**Location counter**

There are two features of the assembler that are fundamental to the assembly process. The first is the **location counter.** It points to the next byte available for assignment to the program. Initially zero, it is incremented by the number of bytes that are required by an instruction as soon as that number is determined. At any particular time, the location counter represents the number of bytes assigned to the program so far. You can think of the location counter as containing the relative address of a particular instruction. When you wrote machine language programs, you noted this information next to each instruction. Do not confuse the location counter, which is part of the assembler, with the instruction address portion of the PSW, which is part of the computer.

**Symbol table**

The second feature is the **symbol table,** which is an array that contains all of the symbols that appear as name entries in the program, their values, and information about whether the symbol is absolute or relocatable. If the symbol is absolute, its value is the absolute quantity to which it has been equated. If the symbol is relocatable, its value is the relative address that it represents. This relative address is the value of the location counter at the time that the symbol was encountered as a name entry.

**Assembly in two passes**

Typically, the assembler processes the source program in two *passes.* During the first pass, the assembler translates the mnemonic operation codes, maintains the location counter, and constructs the symbol table. The assembler usually does not translate the operand entries at this time since they may contain symbols that it has not encountered before. However, it does consider operands of DC and DS instructions during the first pass since they affect the location counter. By using the newly created symbol table, the assembler translates the remaining operands during a second pass of the source program.

Figure 4.10 provides an example of the assembly process. (For simplicity, the example omits the standard entry and the standard exit.) The symbol table is constructed during the first pass as just described. Note that the operand of the DS only affects the location counter; DS does not initialize reserved bytes.

In Figure 4.10, also observe how the operand of the Load instruction is translated during the second pass. When the assembler encounters the USING statement, it notes that the base register is 12 and that BASE represents the base address. The symbol table confirms that BASE is relocatable and has a value of 002. The assembler then locates the symbols R2 and Y of the Load instruction in the symbol table. Since R2 represents the first register operand, it must be absolute. The assembler confirms this by checking the symbol table. R2 has a value of 2, so the first operand location is 2. The symbol table indicates that Y is relocatable and has a value of 020. Y

**Figure 4.10**
An example of **a.** the assembly process and **b.** the symbol table as constructed during the first pass.

| Source program | | | Location counter | Object Code Pass 1 | Object Code Pass 2 |
|---|---|---|---|---|---|
| PROGRAM | CSECT | | 000 | | |
| R2 | EQU | 2 | | | |
| | BALR | 12,0 | 000 | 05 | C0 |
| | USING | BASE,12 | | | |
| BASE | L | R2,Y | 002 | 58 | 20C01E |
| | A | R2,Z | 006 | 5A | 20C022 |
| | ST | R2,X | 00A | 50 | 20C012 |
| | ST | R2,X2 | 00E | 50 | 20C016 |
| | BCR | X'F',14 | 012 | 07 | FE |
| X | DS | 3F | 014 | | |
| X2 | EQU | X+4 | | | |
| Y | DC | F'2' | 020 | 00000002 | |
| Z | DC | F'3' | 024 | 00000003 | |
| | END | PROGRAM | | | |

a.

| Symbol | Value | R/A |
|---|---|---|
| PROGRAM | 000 | R |
| R2 | 002 | A |
| BASE | 002 | R |
| X | 014 | R |
| X2 | 018 | R |
| Y | 020 | R |
| Z | 024 | R |

(R = relocatable; A = absolute)

b.

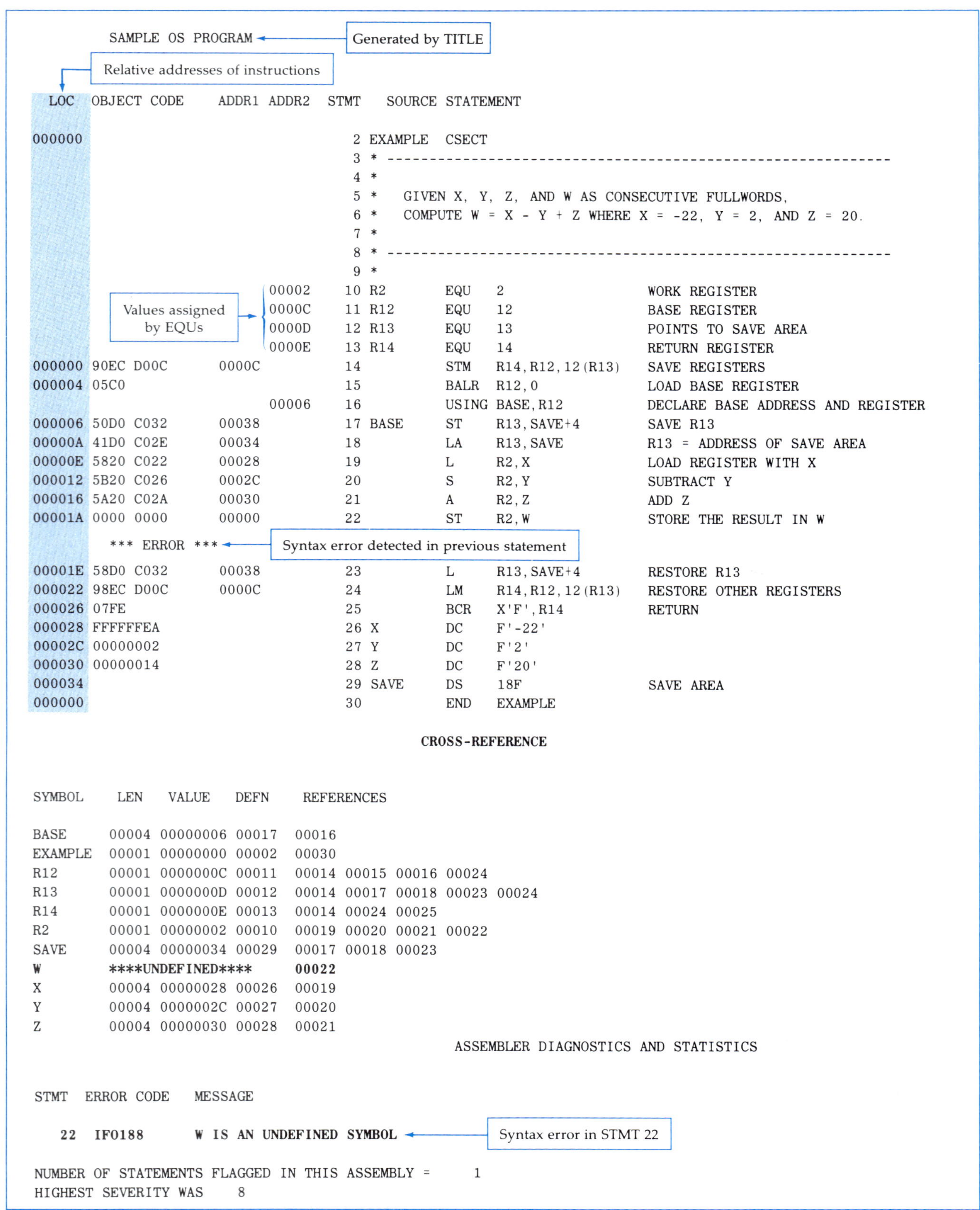

```
         SAMPLE OS PROGRAM

  LOC  OBJECT CODE    ADDR1 ADDR2  STMT   SOURCE STATEMENT

000000                                2 EXAMPLE  CSECT
                                      3 * ------------------------------------------------------
                                      4 *
                                      5 *   GIVEN X, Y, Z, AND W AS CONSECUTIVE FULLWORDS,
                                      6 *   COMPUTE W = X - Y + Z WHERE X = -22, Y = 2, AND Z = 20.
                                      7 *
                                      8 * ------------------------------------------------------
                                      9 *
                            00002    10 R2       EQU   2                   WORK REGISTER
                            0000C    11 R12      EQU   12                  BASE REGISTER
                            0000D    12 R13      EQU   13                  POINTS TO SAVE AREA
                            0000E    13 R14      EQU   14                  RETURN REGISTER
000000 90EC D00C      0000C          14          STM   R14,R12,12(R13)     SAVE REGISTERS
000004 05C0                          15          BALR  R12,0               LOAD BASE REGISTER
                            00006    16          USING BASE,R12            DECLARE BASE ADDRESS AND REGISTER
000006 50D0 C032      00038          17 BASE     ST    R13,SAVE+4          SAVE R13
00000A 41D0 C02E      00034          18          LA    R13,SAVE            R13 = ADDRESS OF SAVE AREA
00000E 5820 C022      00028          19          L     R2,X                LOAD REGISTER WITH X
000012 5B20 C026      0002C          20          S     R2,Y                SUBTRACT Y
000016 5A20 C02A      00030          21          A     R2,Z                ADD Z
00001A 0000 0000      00000          22          ST    R2,W                STORE THE RESULT IN W
         *** ERROR ***
00001E 58D0 C032      00038          23          L     R13,SAVE+4          RESTORE R13
000022 98EC D00C      0000C          24          LM    R14,R12,12(R13)     RESTORE OTHER REGISTERS
000026 07FE                          25          BCR   X'F',R14            RETURN
000028 FFFFFFEA                      26 X        DC    F'-22'
00002C 00000002                      27 Y        DC    F'2'
000030 00000014                      28 Z        DC    F'20'
000034                               29 SAVE     DS    18F                 SAVE AREA
000000                               30          END   EXAMPLE
```

**CROSS-REFERENCE**

```
SYMBOL    LEN    VALUE    DEFN    REFERENCES

BASE     00004 00000006 00017  00016
EXAMPLE  00001 00000000 00002  00030
R12      00001 0000000C 00011  00014 00015 00016 00024
R13      00001 0000000D 00012  00014 00017 00018 00023 00024
R14      00001 0000000E 00013  00014 00024 00025
R2       00001 00000002 00010  00019 00020 00021 00022
SAVE     00004 00000034 00029  00017 00018 00023
W        ****UNDEFINED****     00022
X        00004 00000028 00026  00019
Y        00004 0000002C 00027  00020
Z        00004 00000030 00028  00021
```

ASSEMBLER DIAGNOSTICS AND STATISTICS

```
STMT  ERROR CODE   MESSAGE

  22   IF0188       W IS AN UNDEFINED SYMBOL

NUMBER OF STATEMENTS FLAGGED IN THIS ASSEMBLY =      1
HIGHEST SEVERITY WAS    8
```



**Figure 4.11**
A sample OS assembly listing with an assembly-time error message.

then represents an address that requires a base address and a displacement. The displacement, 01E, is the difference between the values of the symbols Y and BASE.

Syntax errors

The assembler generates an error message whenever it detects a syntax error. For example, R2 is used as a first register operand. If the symbol table lists R2 as a relocatable symbol, then something is wrong; the assembler will report this error. Similarly, if you forget to define R2, the assembler would report this as an error. It is important to distinguish between *assembly-time errors* and *execution-time errors*. This chapter discusses several execution-time errors later.

Assembly listing

The sample assembly listing in Figure 4.11 includes a syntax error message since the definition of W has been omitted. (The program is derived from the one in Figure 4.9.) The leftmost column (labeled LOC) contains the relative addresses of machine instructions, DCs, and DSs. These entries, along with the statement (STMT) numbers, are used in the cross-reference table, which appears after the program. In this table, each symbol appears followed by a length (which you should ignore for now), its symbol-table value, the number of the statement that defines the symbol, and the numbers of the statements that reference the symbol.

Cross-reference table

**SELF-TEST EXERCISE**

10. Consider the following assembler language program:

```
PROG     CSECT
R5       EQU   5
R12      EQU   12
         BALR  R12,0
         USING BASE,12
BASE     L     R5,X
         AR    R5,R5
         ST    R5,X+4
         BCR   X'F',14
X        DC    2F'-1'
         END   PROG
```

a. What object code is produced by the assembler?
b. What are the contents of the symbol table, which is constructed by the assembler?
c. What are the contents of the fullwords at X after the program is executed?

## Storage and Register Dumps

You can print the contents—in hexadecimal—of the registers and of storage at any time during program execution.

### *Obtaining a Dump under OS*

In OS, you can obtain a dump by using the system macro instruction SNAP. However, SNAP requires that you write other macro instructions elsewhere in the program and an additional control statement within the job. SNAP has the following form:

| Name | Operation | Operand | Action |
|---|---|---|---|
| *symbol* or *blank* | **SNAP** | STORAGE=(*S1*,*S2*), PDATA=(REGS, PSW), DCB=*snapdcb*, ID=*n* | Produces a dump of either storage, registers, the PSW, or any combination of these, according to the operands. |

The notation in this instruction is defined as follows:

| | |
|---|---|
| *S1* and *S2* | Relocatable expressions that specify the starting address and the ending address, respectively, of the storage that you want to dump. |
| REGS | A request for a dump of both the general registers and the floating-point registers. |
| PSW | A request for the contents of the PSW. |
| *snapdcb* | The symbol in the name entry of the associated DCB macro instruction, which will be described shortly. |
| *n* | An integer between 0 and 127 that labels the dump. |

You can request less information by omitting either the STORAGE operand or the PDATA operand. You also can omit either REGS or PSW.

Figure 4.12
Using the SNAP instruction within a program.

```
         TITLE 'HOW TO USE SNAP'
EXAMPLE  CSECT
         PRINT NOGEN
         (Standard entry)
         OPEN   (SNAPDCB,OUTPUT)
         .
         .
         .
         SNAP   STORAGE=(ARRAY,Z),DCB=SNAPDCB,ID=1
         SNAP   STORAGE=(SAVE,SAVE+72),PDATA=(REGS),DCB=SNAPDCB,ID=2
         .
         .
         .
         CLOSE  (SNAPDCB)
         (Standard exit)
ARRAY    DC     50F'0'
X        DC     F'4'
Y        DC     F'5'
Z        DC     F'6'
SAVE     DS     18F
SNAPDCB  DCB    DSORG=PS,MACRF=W,RECFM=VBA,BLKSIZE=1632,LRECL=125,         X
                DDNAME=SNAP
         END    EXAMPLE
/*
//GO.SNAP DD SYSOUT=A
//GO.SYSIN DD *
/*
```

Before you execute a SNAP for the first time, you must execute the following instruction:

```
OPEN        (snapdcb, OUTPUT)
```

After you execute the last SNAP in your program, you must execute the following instruction:

```
CLOSE       (snapdcb)
```

In the OPEN instruction and the CLOSE instruction, *snapdcb* is the symbol that appears both in the operand entry of the SNAP instruction and in the name entry of the following DCB instruction:

```
snapdcb  DCB  DSORG=PS,MACRF=W,RECFM=VBA,BLKSIZE=1632,LRECL=125,        X
              DDNAME=snapdd
```

You must include the DCB instruction in an area of your program—such as after the DC and DS instructions—where it will not be executed. The instruction specifies a symbol *snapdd*, which is the same symbol that appears in the following DD statement:

```
//GO.snapdd  DD  SYSOUT=A
```

You place this DD statement before the //GO.SYSIN DD statement.

The OPEN instruction and the CLOSE instruction can affect the contents of Registers 0, 1, 14, and 15. Therefore, it is a good idea to write the OPEN instruction immediately after the standard entry, and the CLOSE instruction immediately before the standard exit.

---

EXAMPLE 10

## How to Use the SNAP Instruction

Figure 4.12 provides an example of how to use the SNAP instruction within your program.

---

EXAMPLE 11

## A Sample Dump

Figure 4.13 shows both a portion of the assembly listing and the dumps that result when you execute the program given in Figure 4.12. Each line of a storage dump lists the hexadecimal contents of up to 8 fullwords and begins with an addresss. In Figure 4.13, the first line of the storage dump, which is labeled with ID = 001, begins with the address 0EC180. However, in this first line, the contents of the fullword at 0EC180 are not printed. In comparison, the second line of this storage dump begins with the address 0EC1A0 and lists the contents of 8 fullwords, beginning with the fullword at 0EC1A0. By using the second line as a guide, you can determine the address of the first fullword that is printed in the first line of the storage dump: this address is 0EC190.

Since the first SNAP instruction (Statement 19) requests a storage dump that begins at ARRAY, the symbol ARRAY must represent the address 0EC190.

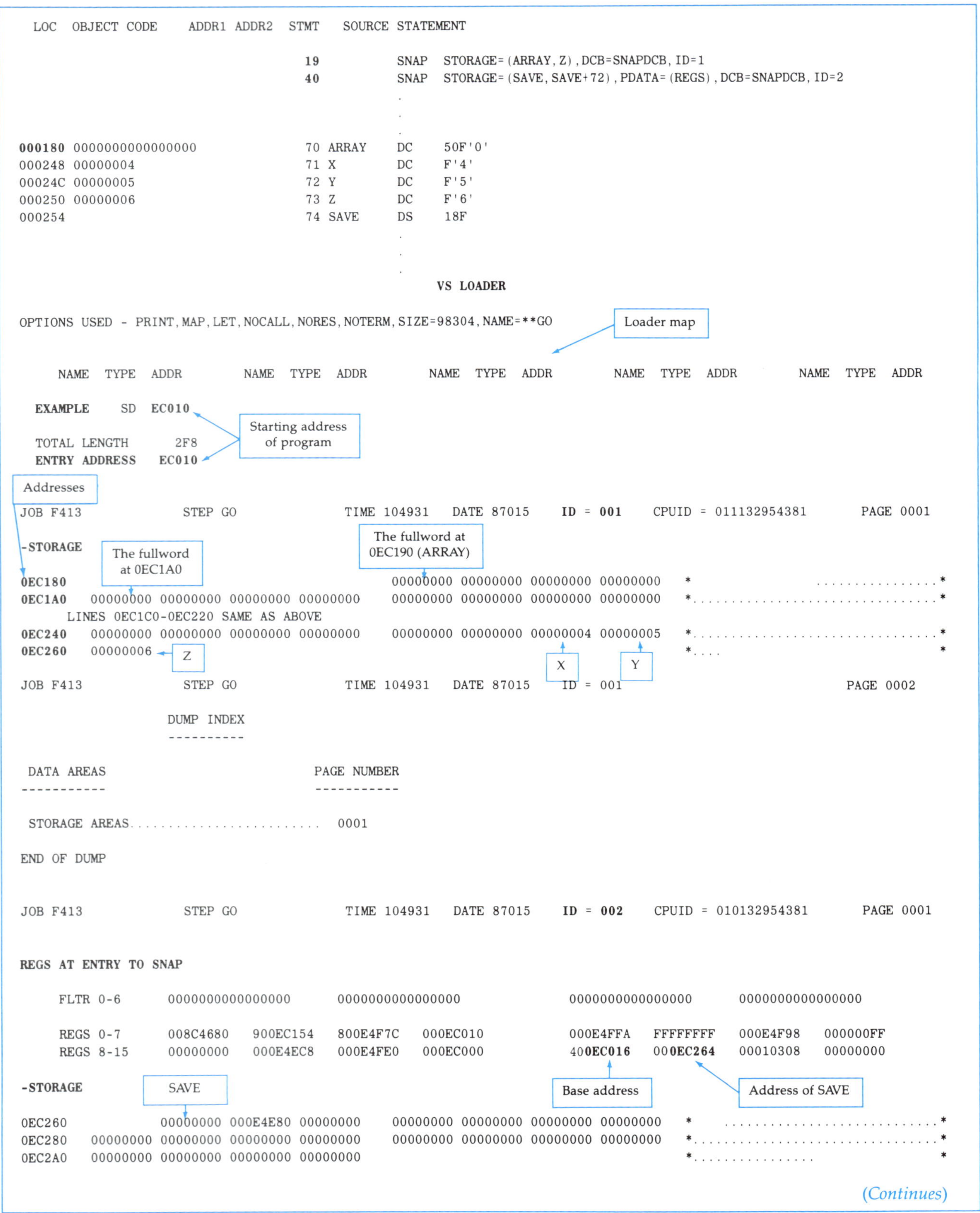

```
  LOC  OBJECT CODE     ADDR1 ADDR2  STMT    SOURCE STATEMENT

                                     19          SNAP   STORAGE=(ARRAY,Z),DCB=SNAPDCB,ID=1
                                     40          SNAP   STORAGE=(SAVE,SAVE+72),PDATA=(REGS),DCB=SNAPDCB,ID=2
                                                  .
                                                  .
                                                  .
000180 0000000000000000              70 ARRAY    DC     50F'0'
000248 00000004                      71 X        DC     F'4'
00024C 00000005                      72 Y        DC     F'5'
000250 00000006                      73 Z        DC     F'6'
000254                               74 SAVE     DS     18F
                                                  .
                                                  .
                                                  .
                                                         VS LOADER

OPTIONS USED - PRINT,MAP,LET,NOCALL,NORES,NOTERM,SIZE=98304,NAME=**GO

    NAME  TYPE  ADDR      NAME  TYPE  ADDR      NAME  TYPE  ADDR      NAME  TYPE  ADDR      NAME  TYPE  ADDR

  EXAMPLE    SD  EC010

  TOTAL LENGTH     2F8
  ENTRY ADDRESS   EC010

JOB F413           STEP GO           TIME 104931   DATE 87015    ID = 001    CPUID = 011132954381      PAGE 0001

-STORAGE

0EC180                                            00000000 00000000 00000000 00000000   *                ................*
0EC1A0   00000000 00000000 00000000 00000000      00000000 00000000 00000000 00000000   *................................*
     LINES 0EC1C0-0EC220 SAME AS ABOVE
0EC240   00000000 00000000 00000000 00000000      00000000 00000000 00000004 00000005   *................................*
0EC260   00000006                                                                       *....                            *

JOB F413           STEP GO           TIME 104931   DATE 87015    ID = 001                              PAGE 0002

                  DUMP INDEX
                  ----------

 DATA AREAS                        PAGE NUMBER
 -----------                       -----------

 STORAGE AREAS.........................   0001

END OF DUMP

JOB F413           STEP GO           TIME 104931   DATE 87015    ID = 002    CPUID = 010132954381      PAGE 0001

REGS AT ENTRY TO SNAP

    FLTR 0-6      0000000000000000   0000000000000000       0000000000000000   0000000000000000

    REGS 0-7      008C4680   900EC154   800E4F7C   000EC010      000E4FFA   FFFFFFFF   000E4F98   000000FF
    REGS 8-15     00000000   000E4EC8   000E4FE0   000EC000      400EC016   000EC264   00010308   00000000

-STORAGE

0EC260            00000000 000E4E80 00000000      00000000 00000000 00000000 00000000   *    ............................*
0EC280   00000000 00000000 00000000 00000000      00000000 00000000 00000000 00000000   *................................*
0EC2A0   00000000 00000000 00000000 00000000                                            *................                *
```



(Continues)

Figure 4.13
A sample dump, as described in Example 11.

```
JOB F413            STEP GO             TIME 104931   DATE 87015    ID = 002                        PAGE 0002

                   DUMP INDEX
                   ----------

 DATA AREAS                          PAGE NUMBER
-----------                          -----------

 REGISTERS..............................  0001
 STORAGE AREAS..........................  0001

END OF DUMP
```

**Figure 4.13**
(*Continued*)

You can confirm this fact by performing a simple computation. First, by examining the assembly listing, you can determine that ARRAY was assembled at the relative address 000180. Next, by looking at the **map** that the loader produces, you can determine that the program begins at the address 0EC010: the map contains both the symbol EXAMPLE, which is defined by CSECT, and the address that EXAMPLE represents. The map also labels this same address as the entry address. To calculate the address at which ARRAY appears in the dump, you add the starting address 0EC010 to the relative address 000180 and obtain 0EC190. Conversely, to go from an address in the storage dump back to the assembly listing, you subtract the starting address of the program from the address in the dump; you then will obtain the corresponding relative address in the assembly listing. Note that the contents of ARRAY, X, Y, and Z are indicated in the dump.

The second SNAP instruction (Statement 40) prints the contents of the save area and the contents of the registers. The resulting dump is labeled with ID = 002. Note the base address in Register 12 and the address of SAVE in Register 13.

---

### *Obtaining a Dump under DOS*

The procedure to obtain a dump under DOS is much simpler than under OS. The following instruction causes a dump of both the general registers and the storage in the range from *S1* to *S2*, where *S1* and *S2* are relocatable expressions:

```
PDUMP      S1,S2
```

You need no other instructions or control statements.

## Execution-Time Errors

Execution-time errors are not detected by the assembler, but are errors in the program logic. They either can cause abnormal termination of the program or can be so subtle that you may not detect them for quite some time.

As you begin to write and execute simple assembler language programs, you will probably encounter this type of error. This section will help you understand some of the errors that you will most likely make at this time.

Certain errors can cause the CPU to suspend execution of your program and give control to the operating system, which will analyze the situation and usually provide a message. Often the message is of the form

```
COMPLETION CODE        SYSTEM=0Cn
```

where *n* is a hex digit. The **completion code** 0C*n* indicates the nature of the error. The following is a list of some common completion codes and their meanings.

- 0C1. A 0C1 error occurs when the CPU encounters an illegal operation code. Often, this happens because you have omitted the instruction that returns control to the operating system (BCR or EOJ). Thus, the CPU tries to execute the constants of your program as if they were instructions. Look at Figure 3.12 again: you caused a 0C1 error when you replaced the instruction 07FE with 0000 to obtain a storage dump.
- 0C4. There can be several user programs and portions of the operating system in storage simultaneously. A combination of hardware and software features offers degrees of protection for each program from access by another. Therefore, you may not be able to reference (for example, load from or store into) certain storage locations beyond those that have been assigned to your program. If you attempt to do so, the operating system will terminate execution of your program and will assign a completion code of 0C4. Probable sources of this error include a failure to reserve sufficient storage for an array, incorrectly designated index or base registers, incorrect index values or base addresses, or incorrect displacements.
- 0C5. If an instruction attempts to address storage that is beyond the amount physically available to the particular computer, a 0C5 error occurs. The sources of this error are similar to those that cause a 0C4 error, including problems with the index registers, base registers, and displacements.
- 0C6. If you run your program on an IBM System/360, each storage operand of 2, 4, or 8 bytes whose length is implied by the instruction's op code must be aligned to an integral boundary. Failure to adhere to this restriction will result in a 0C6 error. Although this is not true when your program is run on System/370, such an error can occur for other reasons with instructions that you will study later.

## Debugging Hints

Future chapters will have a section called *Debugging Hints*. The information provided in those sections will often be stated as preventative or antibugging measures. Although you can use an antibugging hint to avoid an error while writing a program, you can also restate the hint for use during debugging. Thus, these sections will not distinguish between antibugging and debugging. However, keep these hints in mind while writing a program and during the debugging process later.

## Stylistic Notes

You have considered stylistic issues in your previous studies, and you will recognize the same general themes in the discussions of programming style in this text. Although people generally agree on the broad issues of style within an assembler language program, there are no universal standards for their implementation. While variety in style abounds, your style cannot be so individual that other people have difficulty understanding your intent. The guidelines offered in this section in future chapters will help you develop a sense of style that will make your programs readable, not only by yourself, but by others. Also realize that you must be aware of other stylistic viewpoints because programmers do not just write programs. They maintain and, therefore, must read many programs written by a variety of people, with each person having an individual interpretation of style. In addition, you may find that you will have to adapt your style to someone else's if you are part of a programming group, since organizations typically have their own documentation standards that you must follow.

## Summary

1. A symbol is a sequence of one to eight letters and digits that begins with a letter. (Letters are A through Z, $, #, @.)
2. An assembler language statement contains four entries: name, operation, operand, and remarks. The name entry must begin in the first column. Other entries are in a free format and are separated from each other by at least one blank.
3. Self-defining terms are decimal, binary, hexadecimal, or character constants that are used to specify registers, masks, and displacements.
4. Self-defining terms and symbols are examples of terms.
5. Expressions are arithmetic combinations of terms that you use to designate operands. The assembler evaluates expressions at assembly time.
6. An expression is absolute if its value is independent of the starting address of the program. An expression is relocatable if its value depends upon the starting address of the program.
7. Explicit operand designations are written with absolute expressions. All RR instructions designate operands as *R1,R2*. You can write RX instructions with explicit operand designations of the form *R1,D2(X2,B2)*.
8. Implicit operand designations are written with relocatable expressions and, for RX instructions, appear as *R1,S2* or *R1,S2(X2)*, where *S2* is relocatable, and *R1* and *X2* are absolute.
9. The DC directive can be used to define constants.
10. The DS directive can be used to reserve storage.
11. The USING directive is used to declare a base address and base register.
12. The EQU directive is used to define new symbols.
13. The CSECT and END directives delimit an assembler language program.
14. In general, Registers 2 through 12 are available for use within a user program.
15. The directives TITLE, EJECT, SPACE, and PRINT affect the appearance of the source program listing.
16. An assembler uses two passes to translate an assembler language program into machine language. During the first pass, the assembler maintains a location counter, constructs a symbol table, and translates the operation codes. During the second pass, the assembler translates the operands.
17. SNAP (under OS) and PDUMP (under DOS) are macro instructions that request a dump of registers and storage.
18. Assembly-time errors are syntax errors that are detected by the assembler. Execution-time errors are errors in program logic. Certain unusual situations that occur during execution can cause the termination of execution.

## New Instruction Summary

| Name | Operation | Operand | Instruction Name | Action |
|---|---|---|---|---|
| *symbol* or *blank* | **DC** | *dt'c'* | DEFINE CONSTANT | Defines *d* copies of the constant *c* of type *t*. Aligns fullword ($t$ = F) and halfword ($t$ = H) constants to integral boundaries; however, does not so align hexadecimal ($t$ = X) and binary ($t$ = B) constants. |
| *symbol* or *blank* | **DS** | *dt'c'* | DEFINE STORAGE | Reserves *d* units of storage. Uses *t* (D = doubleword, F = fullword, H = halfword, X = byte, B = byte) to give the type of unit. |
| *blank* | **USING** | *S,R* | DECLARE BASE REGISTER | Causes the assembler to assume that Register *R* is a base register and that it contains the address *S*. |
| *symbol* | **EQU** | *expression* | EQUATE SYMBOL | Defines the *symbol;* its value is that of the *expression* in the operand. |
| *symbol* or *blank* | **CSECT** | *blank* | DEFINE CONTROL SECTION | Signals either the beginning of a control section or, for present purposes, the beginning of the program. |
| *blank* | **END** | *relocatable expression* | END SOURCE MODULE | Signals the end of a source module. |
| *blank* | **TITLE** | *'string'* | CREATE HEADER | Provides a heading for each page of the assembly listing; *string* consists of up to 100 characters. |
| *blank* | **SPACE** | *n* | INSERT BLANK LINES | Inserts *n* blank lines into the listing of the source program. The assembler assumes *n* is 1 if it is omitted. |
| *blank* | **EJECT** | *blank* | SKIP TO A NEW PAGE | Prints the next line of the source program at the top of a new page. |
| *blank* | **PRINT** | NOGEN | PRINT DETAILS | Suppresses the printing of the instructions that a macro instruction represents. |

| Name | Operation | Operand | Action |
|---|---|---|---|
| *symbol* or *blank* | **PDUMP** | *S1,S2* | Under DOS, produces a dump of both the general registers and the storage in the range from *S1* to *S2*. |
| *symbol* or *blank* | **SNAP** | STORAGE= (*S1*,*S2*), PDATA= (REGS, PSW), DCB=*snapdcb*, ID=*n* | Under OS, produces a dump of either storage, registers, the PSW, or any combination of these, according to the operands. |

## Exercises

1. Which of the following are not valid symbols? Explain.
   a. A1234567
   b. #456
   c. @XYZ
   d. $88#23456
   e. $88#
   f. ####
   g. $12.34
   h. @@@@@
   i. AB(5)
2. Write DC and DS directives to create each of the following:
   a. An array of 3 halfwords with the names X, Y, and Z.
   b. An array of 567 bytes starting at a fullword boundary.
   c. An array of 3 halfwords containing the hex integers AB12, C30, and F.
   d. An array of 3 bytes containing the binary integers 11, 101111, and 0111000.
3. Assume that Y is at the hex address 6000. What are the contents in hexadecimal of the consecutive bytes beginning at Y, as defined by each of the following?

```
a. Y    DC    F'-18'
        DC    X'A'
        DC    H'12'
b. Y    DS    0F
        DC    3B'1010'
        DC    F'-18'
c. Y    DC    2X'DEF'
        DC    0H'2'
        DC    2H'-31'
        DS    0F
        DC    X'2A'
```

4. Which of the following expressions are absolute? Which are relocatable? Which are invalid? Assume that A and B are absolute symbols, and that X and Y are relocatable symbols.
   a. X'1011'+1
   b. X−X'5B2'
   c. Y+(B+2)
   d. 2*Y+A
   e. (X−4)+Y
   f. (X−Y)/4+Y
   g. X+Y−A
   h. (X'5A4'−X)+Y
5. Which of the following assembler statements are invalid? Explain. Assume that R8, R9, and R10 are absolute symbols, and that X and Y are relocatable symbols.

```
a. A    R8,X(,R10)
b. A    R8,R9(R10)
c. A    R8,X(R10)
d. A    R9,X+2*R9
e. A    R9,Y(R8,0)
f. A    R8,Y(R8)+8
g. A    R9,Y+4(R8)
h. A    B'1111',0(X,R8)
i. A    B'1111',R9(R8,R10)
```

6. Assume that WORD represents an address that is $302_{10}$ bytes beyond the base address, and that Register 12 is the base register. Also assume that R2 and R4 have been equated to 2 and 4, respectively. For each of the following instructions, write an equivalent instruction by using explicit operand designations. Also write the machine language instruction represented by each.

```
a. L    R4,WORD
b. ST   R4,WORD+4
c. A    R4,WORD(R2)
d. S    R4,WORD-4(R2)
e. ST   R4,WORD+8(R2)
```

7. Assume that G represents an address that is $946_{10}$ bytes beyond the base address, and that Register 12 is the base register. Rewrite each of the following explicit operand designations in an implicit form in terms of G.
   a. 946(,12)
   b. 946(2,12)
   c. 950(0,12)
   d. 950(2,12)
   e. 944(,12)
   f. 944(2,12)
8. Write assembler language statements to accomplish each of the following:
   a. Compute the sum of the integers in the fullwords at A, B, and C.
   b. Interchange the contents of the fullwords at Y and Z.

9. Translate the following assembler language program into machine language, and indicate the contents of the symbol table that is generated by the assembler. The program is not logically meaningful.

```
PROG     CSECT
R3       EQU   3
R4       EQU   4
R10      EQU   10
         BALR  R10,0
         USING BASE,R10
BASE     SR    R4,R4
         L     R3,Z
         A     R3,Z+4(R4)
         S     R3,0(R4,R10)
         L     R3+R4,W(R4)
         ST    R3,Z+2*R4(R3)
         BCR   B'1111',X'E'
Z        DC    F'-2'
         DS    10F
W        EQU   Z
         END   PROG
```

## Programming Problems

1. Experiment with assembly-time errors by altering the program in Figure 4.9 in each of the following ways:
   a. Omit one or more of the EQU statements.
   b. Omit the symbol BASE from the Load instruction.
   c. Omit the USING statement.
   d. Omit a DC statement.
   e. Define a new symbol with an EQU or DC directive.
   f. Precede an EQU statement with a comments statement that extends into column 72.
   g. Insert a blank between the comma and the X in the Load instruction.
   h. Omit the END statement.
   i. Insert the instruction

      ```
      DS   5000X
      ```

      between the definitions of Z and W.
   j. Insert

      ```
      BCR   X'F',EXAMPLE
      ```

      after the ST instruction.
   k. Try to create other assembly-time errors.

2. Experiment with execution-time errors by altering the program in Figure 4.9 in each of the following ways:
   a. Omit the BALR instruction.
   b. Omit the BCR instruction.
   c. Replace the Store instruction with

      ```
      ST      R2,W+4000
      ```

3. Assume A = −251, B = 5281, C = 98765, and D = −42146. Write an assembler language program to compute T = A + B − C + D.

4. Define an array of fullwords that contain the integers 1 through 10. Write an assemblef language program to perform the following computations:
   a. Compute the sum of the even integers in the array.
   b. Compute the sum of the odd integers in the array.
   c. Compute the difference of these two sums.

# 5

# Loops, Arrays, and Binary Integer Arithmetic

CONTENTS

## OVERVIEW

This chapter introduces several instructions that will enable you to write more complex programs that perform binary integer computations. Loop control, which is essential to this goal, is described by using the Compare and Branch on Condition instructions. Instructions to multiply and divide two's complement binary integers are defined and used in several examples with the previously defined instructions to add and subtract.

The chapter discusses and illustrates the fundamentals of good programming style. In addition, it also introduces literals, which provide another way to define constants. The chapter concludes with a description of the ways that you can perform input and output operations.

## OBJECTIVES

After studying this chapter, you should be able to:

1. State the effect that any instruction in a given situation has upon the condition code.
2. Change the logical sequence of instruction execution, which is based upon the value of the condition code, either by specifying the mask in a Branch on Condition instruction or by using an extended mnemonic instruction.
3. Write simple loops.
4. Use an index register to process an array.
5. Describe the results of the M, MR, D, and DR instructions when given particular operand values.
6. Determine if a 64-bit product can be correctly represented in only 32 bits.
7. Create a 64-bit dividend from a fullword operand.
8. Use literals to define constants.
9. Describe the EBCDIC representation of characters.

10. Define character constants.
11. Perform simple I/O operations.
12. Write programs to perform binary integer arithmetic that incorporate techniques of good programming style.

## Introduction

This chapter begins with a description of the instructions that are necessary to write loops or to alter the sequential flow of a program. These concepts are essential if you are to go beyond writing the simple programs of the previous chapter. Using the index register offers another level of power because it enables you to utilize arrays. While you will encounter both looping and indexing in many situations throughout this text, this chapter will apply them to binary integer arithmetic.

Chapter 3 introduced instructions to add and subtract integers in the two's complement binary number system. This chapter now continues the discussion of binary integer arithmetic by presenting the fullword multiply and divide instructions. These four arithmetic operations—addition, subtraction, multiplication, and division—are the only ones that can be performed when using the binary integer instructions of the System/370. You must program operations such as raising a number to a power (exponentiation) or taking the square root of a number by using the four basic operations.

Binary integer arithmetic has its limitations when applied to extensive mathematical computations. However, the System/370 instruction set includes two other types of arithmetic operations that may be more suitable in a given situation. First, the decimal instructions, which are discussed in Chapter 15, operate upon sign-magnitude base 10 numbers. Second, floating-point instructions, which are discussed in Chapter 17, provide a flexible way of treating numbers that have both integral and fractional portions.

The last portion of this chapter includes topics relevant to programs in general. It will cover the elements of style as applied to assembler language programs, and introduce literals as a preferable way to define most constants—both for convenience and stylistic reasons. Finally, the chapter will consider the internal representation of characters and some instructions to perform input and output operations.

## The Condition Code

Certain instructions affect the value of a 2-bit binary quantity within the PSW. Known as the **condition code (CC)**, this quantity has a binary value of 00, 01, 10, or 11, or a decimal value of 0, 1, 2 or 3. For example, the Add and Subtract instructions A, AR, S, and SR set the condition code, as indicated in Figure 5.1. You can interrogate the condition code and, depending upon its value, change the sequence of instruction execution, as you will soon see.

**Figure 5.1**
The values of the condition code after execution of A, AR, S, or SR.

| Result of addition or subtraction | Condition code |
|---|---|
| Zero, no overflow | 0 |
| Negative, no overflow | 1 |
| Positive, no overflow | 2 |
| Overflow | 3 |

---

EXAMPLE 1

```
SR      5,5
```

This instruction subtracts Register 5 from itself. The result is 0 and the condition code is set to 0.

---

EXAMPLE 2

```
AR      3,3
```

| | **Reg. 3** | |
|---|---|---|
| Before execution: | 4FFFFFFF | |
| After execution: | 9FFFFFFE | *Condition code* = 3 |

Since the sign of the result is opposite that of the original operands, you can tell that an overflow has occurred. The condition code is set to 3. Notice that even though the result appears to be negative, the condition code is *not* set to 1. (A fixed-point overflow exception also occurs.)

---

As new instructions are introduced, the text will indicate their effect, if any, upon the condition code. The following instructions do nothing except alter the condition code.

### *The Compare (CR and C) Instructions*

The Compare instructions are available in RR and RX formats. Both versions algebraically compare two 32-bit binary integers and set the condition code to reflect the result of this comparison. Only the condition code is affected; the operands remain unchanged. The instructions are summarized as follows:

| Operation | Operand | Format | Instruction Name | Action |
|---|---|---|---|---|
| **CR** | *R1,R2* | RR | COMPARE REGISTERS | Compares C(*R1*) with C(*R2*)<br>Condition code = $\begin{cases} 0 \text{ if } C(R1) = C(R2) \\ 1 \text{ if } C(R1) < C(R2) \\ 2 \text{ if } C(R1) > C(R2) \end{cases}$ |
| **C** | *R1,S2*<br>or *R1,S2(X2)*<br>or *R1,D2(X2,B2)* | RX | COMPARE | Compares C(*R1*) with $C(E2)_{0\text{-}31}$<br>Condition code = $\begin{cases} 0 \text{ if } C(R1) = C(E2)_{0\text{-}31} \\ 1 \text{ if } C(R1) < C(E2)_{0\text{-}31} \\ 2 \text{ if } C(R1) > C(E2)_{0\text{-}31} \end{cases}$ |

In the RR format, the binary integers to be compared are in registers; in the RX format, one binary integer is in a register and the other is in a fullword of storage. The storage operand is at the effective address *E2*, which is computed from the second operand designations in the instruction. The various contractions of the explicit form of the RX operand entry have been omitted to conserve space.

---

EXAMPLE 3

```
CR      10,0
```

The following table indicates the relationship between the hexadecimal contents of Registers 10 and 0, and the corresponding effect of the Compare instruction upon the condition code.

| Reg. 10 | Relationship | Reg. 0 | Condition code |
|---|---|---|---|
| 77777777 | = | 77777777 | 0 |
| 00000008 | > | 00000000 | 2 |
| 98765432 | < | 12345678 | 1 |
| 98765432 | > | 98765431 | 2 |

In the last two examples, 98765432 represents a negative number; as such, it is less than the positive number 12345678, but greater than the negative number 98765431. Convert these numbers to binary to show that this is true in the two's complement binary number system.

---

**SELF-TEST EXERCISE**

1. What is the condition code after each of the following instructions is executed? Assume that Registers 0, 2, and 4, and the fullwords at X and Y are as indicated before the execution of each instruction.

   Reg. 0 = ABCDEF12 Reg. 4 = 12345678 Y = 00000000
   Reg. 2 = 8F000000 X = 7654ABCD

| | | | | | | | | |
|---|---|---|---|---|---|---|---|---|
| **a.** | AR | 0,2 | **g.** | CR | 0,2 | **l.** | C | 0,Y |
| **b.** | SR | 0,2 | **h.** | CR | 2,0 | **m.** | C | 2,X |
| **c.** | AR | 4,4 | **i.** | CR | 2,4 | **n.** | C | 4,X |
| **d.** | SR | 4,4 | **j.** | CR | 4,2 | **o.** | LR | 3,4 |
| **e.** | AR | 2,0 | **k.** | CR | 4,4 | **p.** | L | 3,Y |
| **f.** | SR | 2,0 | | | | | | |

## *The Branch on Condition (BCR and BC) Instructions*

Test condition code

A Branch on Condition instruction tests the condition code and determines which instruction will be executed next. If the condition code is as specified by the instruction, a **branch** takes place: the instruction sequencing is altered. Otherwise, the next sequential instruction is executed. In either case, the

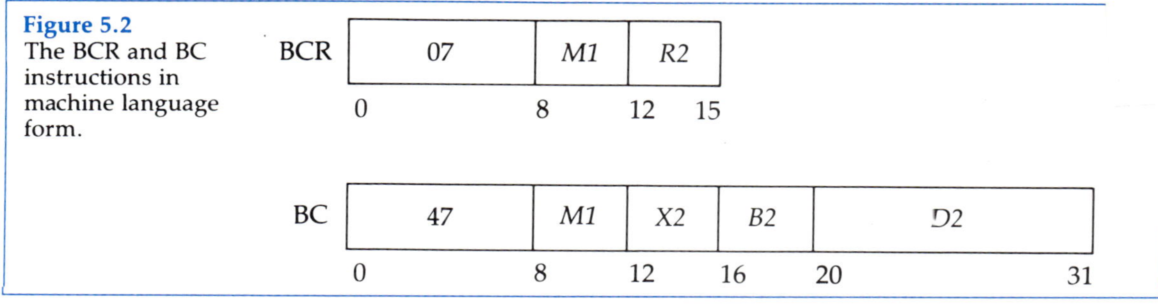


**Figure 5.2** The BCR and BC instructions in machine language form.

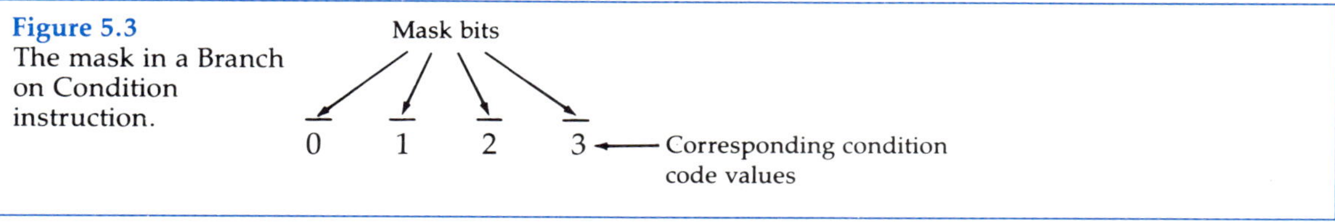


**Figure 5.3** The mask in a Branch on Condition instruction.

condition code is unaffected. These instructions are in the RR and RX formats, respectively. However, the first operand designation, which is in bits 8 through 11 of the instruction, does not name a register, as was the case for previous instructions. These bits are called a **mask** and are used to specify the particular values of the condition code in which you are interested. In the machine language formats illustrated in Figure 5.2, the mask is denoted by *M1*. To construct the mask, first label bits 8 through 11 as 0, 1, 2 and 3, as shown in Figure 5.3. These labels represent the possible condition code values. Then place ones in those positions that correspond to the desired condition code settings, and place zeros elsewhere. For example, a mask of 1010 will specify a branch if the condition code is 0 or 2. Other mask values are summarized in Figure 5.4.

Mask

The second operand specifies the address of the next instruction to be executed when the condition code is as specified by the mask. This address is called the **branch address**. In the RX case, the branch address is the effective address *E2*; in the RR case, the branch address is contained in the register that is designated by *R2*. Note that you cannot use Register 0 for this purpose; if *R2* = 0, no branch will take place. This restriction applied to the BALR instruction and is a characteristic of all RR instructions that branch.

Branch address

The Branch on Condition instructions are summarized as follows. Note that *M1* is an absolute quantity.

| Operation | Operand | Format | Instruction Name | Action |
|---|---|---|---|---|
| **BCR** | *M1,R2* | RR | BRANCH ON CONDITION | If the condition code is as specified by *M1*, branches to the address in *R2*; if it is not, sequences. Does not branch if *R2* = 0. |
| **BC** | *M1,S2*<br>or *M1,S2(X2)*<br>or *M1,D2(X2,B2)* | RX | BRANCH ON CONDITION | If the condition code is as specified by *M1*, branches to the effective address *E2*; if it is not, sequences. |

**Figure 5.4**
A summary of typical masks for the Branch on Condition instructions.

| Mask (Binary) | Branch if condition code is: | Branch if result of addition or subtraction is: | Branch if result of comparison is: |
|---|---|---|---|
| 1000 | 0 | = 0 | = |
| 0100 | 1 | < 0 | < |
| 0010 | 2 | > 0 | > |
| 0001 | 3 | Overflow | (No branch) |
| 1100 | 0 or 1 | ⩽ 0 | ⩽ |
| 1010 | 0 or 2 | ⩾ 0 | ⩾ |
| 0110 | 1 or 2 | < 0 or > 0 | ≠ |
| 1001 | 0 or 3 | = 0 or Overflow | = |
| 0111 | 1, 2, or 3 | ≠ 0 or Overflow | ≠ |
| 0101 | 1 or 3 | < 0 or Overflow | < |
| 0011 | 2 or 3 | > 0 or Overflow | > |
| 1101 | 0, 1, or 3 | ⩽ 0 or Overflow | ⩽ |
| 1011 | 0, 2, or 3 | ⩾ 0 or Overflow | ⩾ |
| 1110 | 0, 1, or 2 | No overflow | (Unconditional branch) |
| 1111 | 0, 1, 2, or 3 | (Unconditional branch) | (Unconditional branch) |
| 0000 | (No branch) | (No branch) | (No branch) |

An illustration of an RX Branch on Condition instruction appears in Figure 5.5.

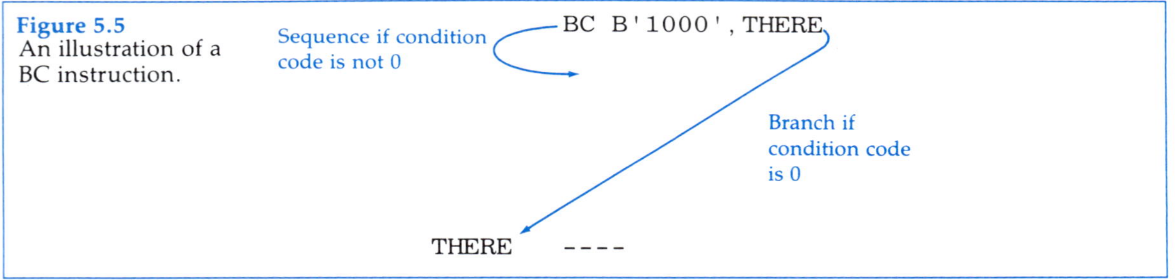


**Figure 5.5**
An illustration of a BC instruction.

---

EXAMPLE 4

```
BC      X'A',LOOP
```

The mask $A_{16} = 1010_2$ indicates that a branch will occur if the present value of the condition code is 0 or 2. If so, the branch will be to the instruction labeled LOOP. If the condition code is 1 or 3, a branch will not occur and the next sequential instruction will be executed.

This is an example of a conditional branch. If it follows a Compare instruction, then the Branch on Condition instruction will branch if the first operand of the comparison is greater than or equal to the second operand. If it follows an Add or Subtract instruction, then a branch will occur if the result of the arithmetic operation is positive or zero.

You may also specify the mask by using a binary or a decimal self-defining term, or a symbol that is equated to a self-defining term. Thus, the following BC instructions are equivalent to the previous one:

```
         BC    B'1010',LOOP
         BC    10,LOOP
         BC    GE,LOOP
GE       EQU   X'A' or B'1010' or 10
```

---

EXAMPLE 5

**BCR X'F',14**

The mask $F_{16} = 1111_2$ indicates that a branch will occur if the present value of the condition code is 0, 1, 2, or 3. The condition code must be one of these, so this is an unconditional branch to the address in Register 14. Since—under OS—the operating system places the return address into Register 14, this instruction returns control to the operating system.

---

It is interesting to note how the CPU actually executes a Branch on Condition instruction. In Figure 5.6, consider the RX instruction 4780CA60 at the address BF41D8. If Register 12, the base register, contains BF4002, then the effective address that is specified by the instruction is BF4A62. The instruction will either branch to this effective address if the condition code is equal to zero, or sequence if it is not equal to zero since the mask is $1000_2$. To accomplish this, the CPU takes the following steps to execute the Branch instruction:

**BC and BCR affect the IA**

1. Update the instruction address (IA) portion of the PSW to BF41DC. It now points to the instruction after the Branch on Condition instruction.
2. Test the condition code. If it is nonzero, execution of this instruction is complete; if it is zero, the IA is replaced by the effective address, BF4A62.

The Branch on Condition instruction then simply changes the IA. Following execution of the Branch, the CPU looks at the IA to get the address of the next instruction. This address is either the branch address or the address of the instruction that follows the Branch instruction.

*Extended Mnemonics.* Computing branch masks is both tedious and prone to error. The assembler will make these computations if you specify the Branch on Condition instructions with the **extended mnemonic operation codes** (also called **extended mnemonics**).

For example, after a Compare instruction, you can write

```
BL    LOOP
```

instead of

```
BC    4,LOOP
```

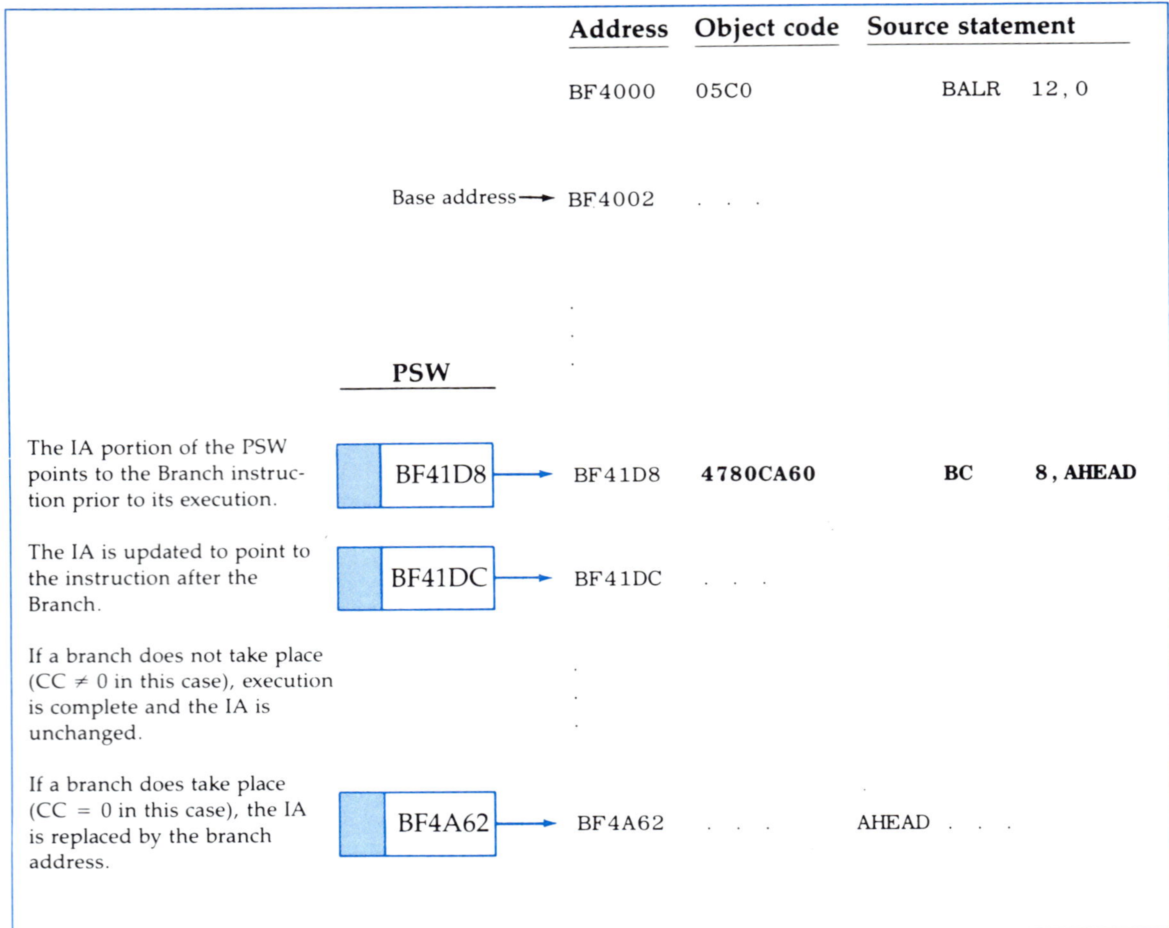


**Figure 5.6**
The effect of a Branch on Condition instruction on the instruction address (IA) portion of the PSW.

to branch to LOOP if the comparison is "less than." Both forms result in the same machine language instruction that branches when the condition code is 1. Read the extended mnemonic BL as "Branch on Low." BL represents the op code ($47_{16}$, in this case) and the *M1* portion of the instruction. Only the branch address is designated in the operand entry of an extended mnemonic instruction.

You can test for a negative result after an addition or subtraction by using the extended mnemonic BM, which is read as "Branch on Minus." Both BL and BM test for a condition code of 1, and they both produce the same machine language instruction. You would choose one over the other, according to your situation. Figure 5.7 summarizes the extended mnemonics that are relevant right now. (A complete list is in Appendix C.) Although the RX operand entries have been designated as *S2* to save space, all explicit and implicit variations are valid.

Notice that the extended mnemonics are quite literal. BNM means "Branch on Not Minus" and is used following an arithmetic instruction. The assembler interprets BNM as a branch if the condition code is anything other than 1—that is 0, 2, or 3. Therefore, a branch will occur if the result is zero, positive, or incorrect due to an overflow. This is quite different from the

**Figure 5.7**
A partial list of extended mnemonics.

| Name of extended mnemonic | | Extended form | | Equivalent BC instruction | |
|---|---|---|---|---|---|
| Branch unconditionally | | B | *S2* | BC | 15,*S2* |
| | | BR | *R2* | BCR | 15,*R2* |
| No Operation | | NOP | *S2* | BC | 0,*S2* |
| | | NOPR | *R2* | BCR | 0,*R2* |
| *After comparing the first operand A with the second operand B:* | | | | | |
| Branch on Equal | (A = B) | BE | *S2* | BC | 8,*S2* |
| | | BER | *R2* | BCR | 8,*R2* |
| Branch on High | (A > B) | BH | *S2* | BC | 2,*S2* |
| | | BHR | *R2* | BCR | 2,*R2* |
| Branch on Low | (A < B) | BL | *S2* | BC | 4,*S2* |
| | | BLR | *R2* | BCR | 4,*R2* |
| Branch on Not Equal | (A ≠ B) | BNE | *S2* | BC | 7,*S2* |
| | | BNER | *R2* | BCR | 7,*R2* |
| Branch on Not High | (A ≤ B) | BNH | *S2* | BC | 13,*S2* |
| | | BNHR | *R2* | BCR | 13,*R2* |
| Branch on Not Low | (A ≥ B) | BNL | *S2* | BC | 11,*S2* |
| | | BNLR | *R2* | BCR | 11,*R2* |
| *After arithmetic instructions:* | | | | | |
| Branch on Zero | | BZ | *S2* | BC | 8,*S2* |
| | | BZR | *R2* | BCR | 8,*R2* |
| Branch on Plus | | BP | *S2* | BC | 2,*S2* |
| | | BPR | *R2* | BCR | 2,*R2* |
| Branch on Minus | | BM | *S2* | BC | 4,*S2* |
| | | BMR | *R2* | BCR | 4,*R2* |
| Branch on Overflow | | BO | *S2* | BC | 1,*S2* |
| | | BOR | *R2* | BCR | 1,*R2* |
| Branch on Not Zero | | BNZ | *S2* | BC | 7,*S2* |
| | | BNZR | *R2* | BCR | 7,*R2* |
| Branch on Not Plus | | BNP | *S2* | BC | 13,*S2* |
| | | BNPR | *R2* | BCR | 13,*R2* |
| Branch on Not Minus | | BNM | *S2* | BC | 11,*S2* |
| | | BNMR | *R2* | BCR | 11,*R2* |
| Branch on No Overflow | | BNO | *S2* | BC | 14,*S2* |
| | | BNOR | *R2* | BCR | 14,*R2* |

common "branch on greater than or equal to," and in fact a mnemonic does not exist for this condition alone. You must be careful not to invent mnemonics that sound reasonable, but do not exist. While extended mnemonics can be helpful, they do not entirely relieve you of the burden of computing branch masks in certain situations.

## SELF-TEST EXERCISES

2. Write the decimal masks that will cause a Branch on Condition instruction to branch when the condition code equals the following:
   a. 2 or 3
   b. any value except 0
3. Write the decimal masks that will cause a Branch on Condition instruction to sequence to the next instruction when the condition code equals the following:
   a. 3
   b. 0 or 3
4. Assume that each of the following Branch on Condition instructions is executed immediately after

```
C     3,X
```

   What relationship must exist between the contents of Register 3 and the fullword X to cause each instruction to branch to OUT?
   a. `BC 6,OUT`
   b. `BC 10,OUT`
   c. `BC 9,OUT`
   d. `BNL OUT`
   e. `BNP OUT`
5. Assume that each of the following Branch on Condition instructions is executed immediately after

```
S     3,X
```

   In each case, describe the circumstances that will cause a branch to SPOT.
   a. `BC 9,SPOT`
   b. `BC 14,SPOT`
   c. `BC 1,SPOT`
   d. `BC 3,SPOT`
   e. `BNZ SPOT`
   f. `BNM SPOT`
   g. `BNP SPOT`

# Sample Program

### *Problem Statement*

Given the binary integers $n$ and $z$, compute the product $n * z$ by using repeated addition. Assume that $n$ and $z$ are fullwords in storage, and that $n > 0$.

### *Program Logic*

This problem requires you to add $z$ to a register $n$ times. The desired algorithm is described in pseudocode as follows:

```
r := 0
REPEAT n times
    r := r + z
END REPEAT
Save the result r
```

Figure 5.8 describes this algorithm in flowchart form.

A counter controls the required loop. The counter is simply a register whose value counts in increments of 1. Since it is convenient to place zero into a register with the SR instruction, let the counter count from 0 to $n - 1$. Rather than compute $n - 1$, you will compare the counter with $n$ and branch as long as the comparison is "less than." The detailed flowchart in Figure 5.9 illustrates this process. The OS version and the DOS version of the program that implements the algorithm appear in Figure 5.10.

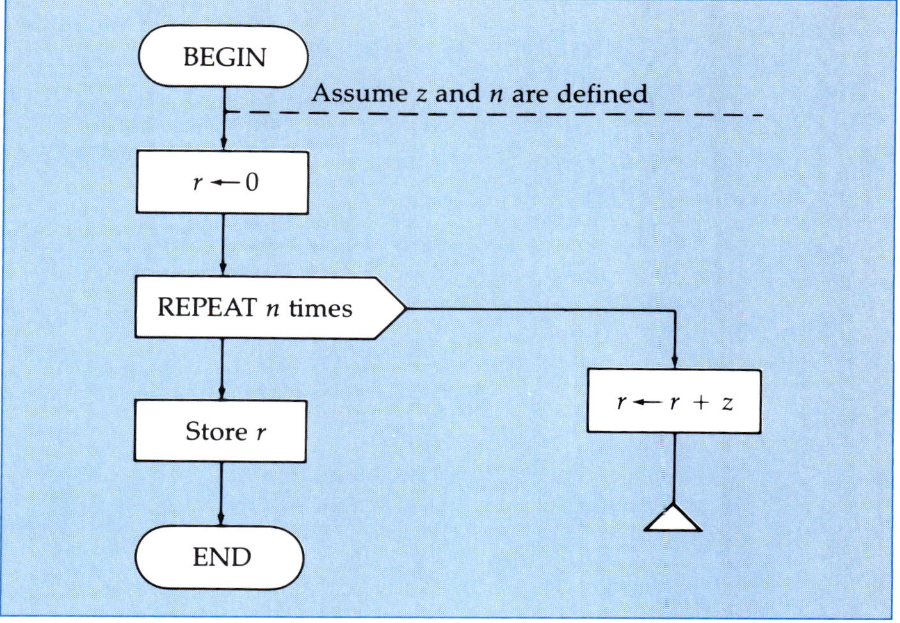


**Figure 5.8**
The flowchart for a program to compute $n * z$ by using addition.

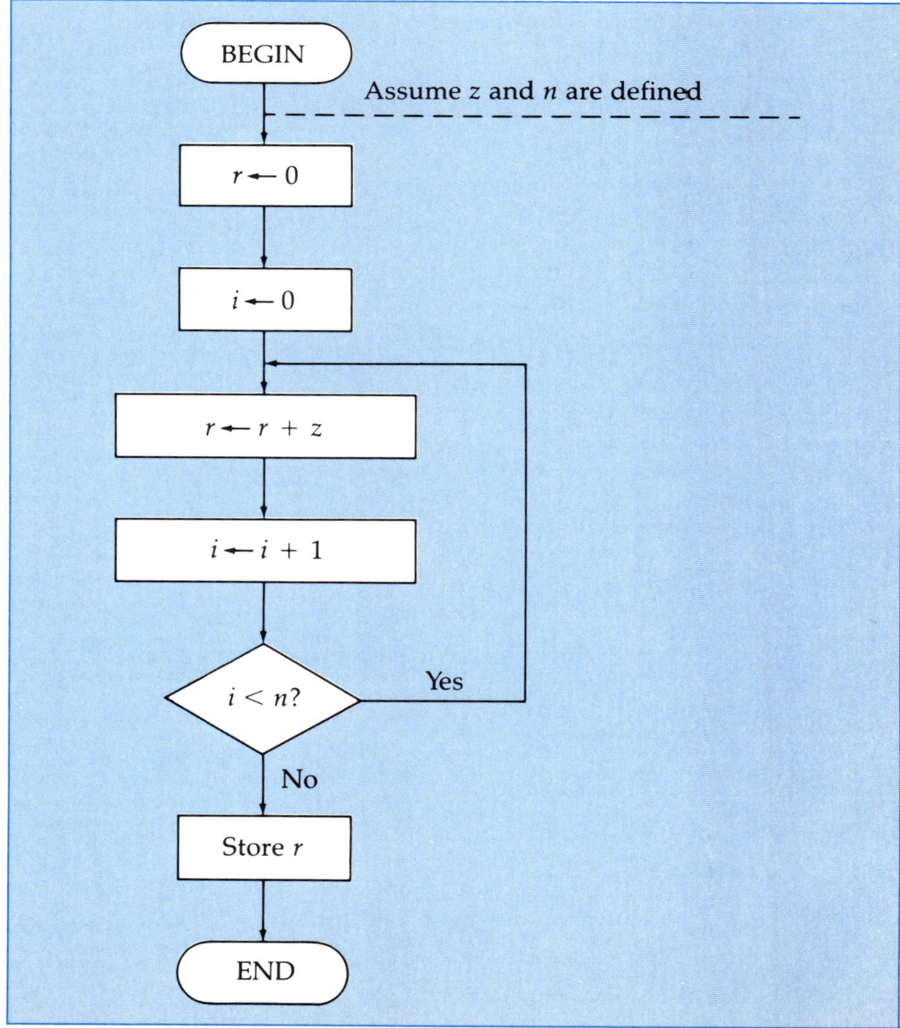


**Figure 5.9**
A more-detailed flowchart for a program to compute $n * z$ by using addition.

**a.**

```
         TITLE 'MULTIPLE OF Z: OS VERSION'
MULTIPLE CSECT
************************************************************
*
* GIVEN THE FULLWORD BINARY INTEGERS N AND Z, COMPUTE N * Z
* BY USING ADDITION.
*
************************************************************
         PRINT NOGEN           SUPPRESS MACRO EXPANSIONS
R0       EQU   0               WORK REGISTER TO COMPUTE PRODUCT
R2       EQU   2               COUNTER
R12      EQU   12              BASE REGISTER
R13      EQU   13              SAVE AREA POINTER
R14      EQU   14              RETURN REGISTER
* STANDARD ENTRY AND INITIALIZATION:
         STM   R14,R12,12(R13) SAVE REGISTERS
         BALR  R12,0           LOAD BASE REGISTER
         USING BASE,R12        DECLARE BASE ADDRESS AND REGISTER
BASE     ST    R13,SAVE+4      SAVE R13
         LA    R13,SAVE        R13 = ADDRESS OF SAVE AREA
         OPEN  (SNAPDCB,OUTPUT) PREPARE FOR DUMP
         SR    R0,R0           CLEAR WORK REGISTER
         SR    R2,R2           CLEAR COUNTER
* REPEAT N TIMES:
LOOP     A     R0,Z            ADD Z TO WORK REGISTER
         A     R2,ONE          ADD 1 TO COUNTER
         C     R2,N            COMPARE COUNTER WITH N
         BL    LOOP            REPEAT IF COUNTER IS < N
* END REPEAT
         ST    R0,RESULT       SAVE THE RESULT
         SNAP  STORAGE=(RESULT,RESULT),DCB=SNAPDCB,ID=1
         CLOSE (SNAPDCB)
* STANDARD EXIT:
         L     R13,SAVE+4      RESTORE R13
         LM    R14,R12,12(R13) RESTORE REMAINING REGISTERS
         BR    R14             RETURN TO OS
*
Z        DC    F'33'           GIVEN VALUE OF Z
N        DC    F'15'           GIVEN VALUE OF N
ONE      DC    F'1'            COUNTER INCREMENT
RESULT   DS    F               COMPUTED VALUE OF N * Z
SAVE     DS    18F             SAVE AREA
SNAPDCB  DCB   DSORG=PS,MACRF=W,RECFM=VBA,BLKSIZE=1632,LRECL=125,     X
               DDNAME=SNAP
         END   MULTIPLE
```

*(Continues)*

**Figure 5.10**
A program to compute $n * z$ by using addition: **a**. the OS version and, **b**. the DOS version.

**b.**

```
         TITLE 'MULTIPLE OF Z: DOS VERSION'
MULTIPLE CSECT
************************************************************
*
* GIVEN THE FULLWORD BINARY INTEGERS N AND Z, COMPUTE N * Z
* BY USING ADDITION.
*
************************************************************
         PRINT NOGEN             SUPPRESS MACRO EXPANSIONS
R0       EQU   0                 WORK REGISTER TO COMPUTE PRODUCT
R2       EQU   2                 COUNTER
R12      EQU   12                BASE REGISTER
R13      EQU   13                SAVE AREA POINTER
* STANDARD ENTRY AND INITIALIZATION:
         BALR  R12,0             LOAD BASE REGISTER
         USING BASE,R12          DECLARE BASE ADDRESS AND REGISTER
BASE     LA    R13,SAVE          R13 = ADDRESS OF SAVE AREA
         SR    R0,R0             CLEAR WORK REGISTER
         SR    R2,R2             CLEAR COUNTER
* REPEAT N TIMES:
LOOP     A     R0,Z              ADD Z TO WORK REGISTER
         A     R2,ONE            ADD 1 TO COUNTER
         C     R2,N              COMPARE COUNTER WITH N
         BL    LOOP              REPEAT IF COUNTER IS < N
* END REPEAT
         ST    R0,RESULT         SAVE THE RESULT
         PDUMP RESULT,RESULT     DUMP THE RESULT
         EOJ                     RETURN TO DOS
*
Z        DC    F'33'             GIVEN VALUE OF Z
N        DC    F'15'             GIVEN VALUE OF N
ONE      DC    F'1'              COUNTER INCREMENT
RESULT   DS    F                 COMPUTED VALUE OF N * Z
SAVE     DS    9D                SAVE AREA
         END   MULTIPLE
```

**Figure 5.10** *(Continued)*

## Indexing

Reconsider the program just given, and assume that you want to save all intermediate multiples of $z$ ($z$, $2z$, . . . , $nz$) in an array of consecutive fullwords. In Pascal or FORTRAN, you would refer to the elements of the array with a subscript; in assembler language, you use an index register.

First, consider the pseudocode solution, which is given in Figure 5.11, to this new problem and the corresponding flowchart, which is given in Figure 5.12. Here, the array is $m$ and its elements are $m_0$, $m_1$, $m_2$, and so on. During each pass through the loop, $r$ is stored into the next fullword of the array $m$. You must accomplish this with one Store instruction that cannot be changed after it is written. Even so, it must store into a different fullword each time that it is executed. The base address should remain fixed throughout the program and, once the displacement has been computed, it will not change. Recall the complete definition of the effective address for an RX instruction:

**Figure 5.11**
The pseudocode solution for a program that computes and stores the multiples of $z$.

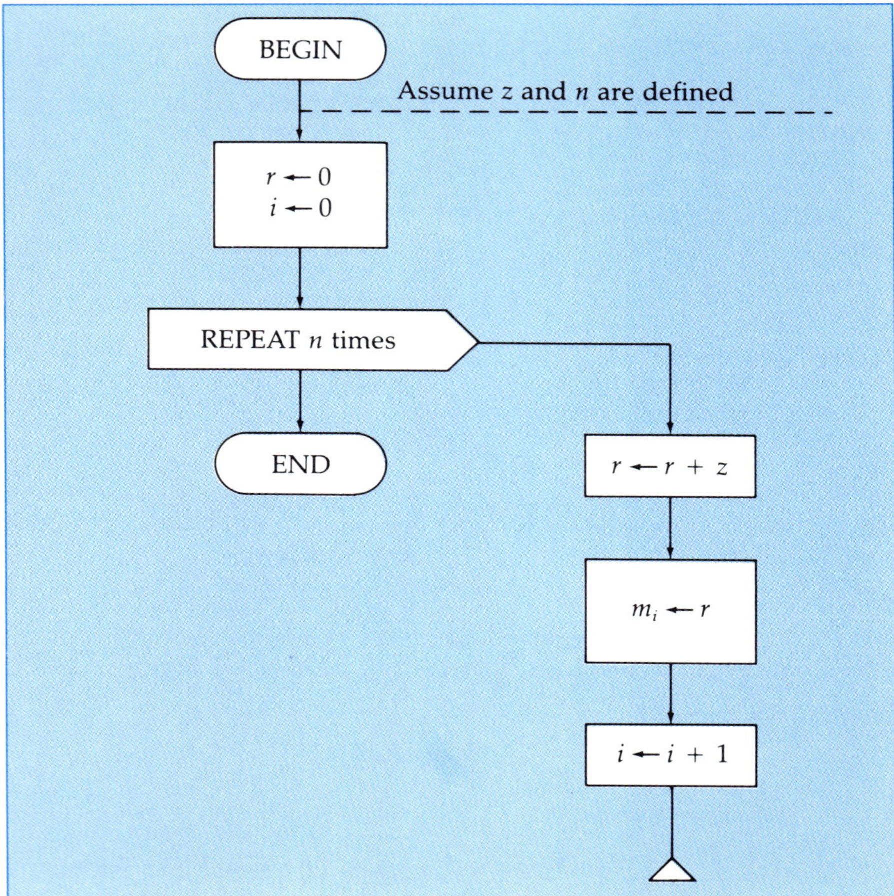


**Figure 5.12**
The flowchart for a program that computes and stores the multiples of $z$.

$$E2 = C(X2)_{8\text{-}31} + C(B2)_{8\text{-}31} + D2$$

If the base address and the displacement are to remain fixed, then you must vary the contents of the index register to alter the effective address. If the index register is incremented by 4, the effective address will change by 4. For example, as Register 2 changes in Figure 5.13, the instruction 5002C07A will store Register 0 into consecutive fullwords of the array $m$. In assembler language, this instruction could appear as

```
ST      R0,M(R2)
```

**Figure 5.13**
The effective address specified by an RX instruction changes as the index changes.

| Machine language | Assembler language | |
|---|---|---|
| 5002C07A | ST | R0,M(R2) |

| Base Register 12 | Index Register 2 | Effective address | Array element |
|---|---|---|---|
| EC016 | 00000000 | EC090 | $m_0$ |
| | 00000004 | EC094 | $m_1$ |
| | 00000008 | EC098 | $m_2$ |
| | 0000000C | EC09C | $m_3$ |
| | 00000010 | EC0A0 | $m_4$ |
| | 00000014 | EC0A4 | $m_5$ |

The assembler language program and the equivalent object code for this problem appear in Figure 5.14. (The program begins at address $EC010_{16}$.) Since the index register, Register 2, contains zero, the first time that the Store instruction (Statement 38) is executed, the store will be into the first element ($m_0$) of the array. Then as the index register counts by increments of 4, the effective address will also count by increments of 4—thus, pointing to the fullwords of the array.

The index register need not begin at zero, but it is convenient to do so. The index register serves as a counter for the loop, so a separate counter is unnecessary. Since the index counts by increments of 4, you must compare it with $4 * n$, instead of $n$. (The program assumes a value of $n = 15$.) Such adjustments are made when you write the program, and are not indicated in the pseudocode or the flowchart. Compare this program with the one given in Figure 5.10.

## Binary Integer Multiplication and Division

Like the Add and Subtract instructions, the Multiply and Divide instructions each operate upon two integers, and are available in the RR and RX formats. When you multiply two 32-bit integers, the product is 64 bits long. The Multiply instruction is designed to retain this entire product. As a companion to multiplication, the Divide instruction divides a 64-bit integer by a 32-bit integer. Just as with the pencil-and-paper division that you learned in elementary school, the Divide instruction produces an integer quotient and an integer remainder. Each of these quantities is 32 bits long. What to do with a 64-bit product or how to utilize a remainder are questions that you as the programmer must face.

### *Even-Odd Register Pairs*

The product generated by a Multiply instruction and the dividend used by a Divide instruction each is a 64-bit two's complement binary integer. In

```
        COMPUTE AND STORE MULTIPLES OF Z

  LOC  OBJECT CODE    ADDR1 ADDR2  STMT   SOURCE STATEMENT
000000                               2 MULTIPLE CSECT
                                     3          PRINT NOGEN         SUPPRESS MACRO EXPANSIONS
                                     4 ********************************************************
                                     5 **  GIVEN THE FULLWORD BINARY INTEGER, Z, COMPUTE
                                     6 **  Z, 2 * Z, ... , 15 * Z AND STORE THEM INTO AN ARRAY
                                     7 **  OF CONSECUTIVE FULLWORDS.
                                     8 ********************************************************
                            00000    9 R0       EQU   0                WORK REGISTER
                            00002   10 R2       EQU   2                INDEX REGISTER
                            0000C   11 R12      EQU   12               BASE REGISTER
                            0000D   12 R13      EQU   13               SAVE AREA POINTER
                            0000E   13 R14      EQU   14               RETURN REGISTER (OS)
                                    14 *
                                    15 * STANDARD ENTRY AND INITIALIZATION:
                                    16 ** OS:
000000 90EC D00C      0000C         17          STM   R14,R12,12(R13)  SAVE REGISTERS
000004 05C0                         18          BALR  R12,0            LOAD BASE REGISTER
                            00006   19          USING BASE,R12         DECLARE BASE ADDRESS AND REGISTER
000006 50D0 C0BA      000C0         20 BASE     ST    R13,SAVE+4       SAVE R13
00000A 41D0 C0B6      000BC         21          LA    R13,SAVE         R13 = ADDRESS OF SAVE AREA
                                    22          OPEN  (SNAPDCB,OUTPUT) PREPARE FOR DUMP
                                    28 ** DOS*******
                                    29 *        BALR  R12,0            LOAD BASE REGISTER
                                    30 *        USING BASE,R12         DECLARE BASE ADDRESS AND REGISTER
                                    31 *BASE    LA    R13,SAVE         R13 = ADDRESS OF SAVE AREA
                                    32 ******
                                    33 * INITIALIZE:
00001A 1B22                         34          SR    R2,R2            CLEAR INDEX REGISTER
00001C 1B00                         35          SR    R0,R0            CLEAR WORK REGISTER
                                    36 * REPEAT N TIMES:
00001E 5A00 C06E      00074         37 LOOP     A     R0,Z             ADD Z TO WORK REGISTER
000022 5002 C07A      00080         38          ST    R0,M(R2)         SAVE MULTIPLE IN THE ARRAY
000026 5A20 C072      00078         39          A     R2,FOUR          INCREMENT INDEX REGISTER
00002A 5920 C076      0007C         40          C     R2,LIMIT         FINISHED?
00002E 4740 C018      0001E         41          BL    LOOP             IF NOT, REPEAT
                                    42 * END REPEAT
                                    43 * DUMP AND EXIT:
                                    44 ** OS:
                                    45          SNAP  STORAGE=(M,M+56),DCB=SNAPDCB,ID=1
                                    66          CLOSE (SNAPDCB)
00006A 58D0 C0BA      000C0         72          L     R13,SAVE+4       RESTORE R13
00006E 98EC D00C      0000C         73          LM    R14,R12,12(R13)  RESTORE REMAINING REGISTERS
000072 07FE                         74          BR    R14              RETURN TO OS
                                    75 ** DOS*******
                                    76 *        PDUMP M,M+56           DUMP ARRAY
                                    77 *        EOJ                    RETURN TO DOS
                                    78 ******
000074 00000021                     79 Z        DC    F'33'            THE GIVEN INTEGER Z
000078 00000004                     80 FOUR     DC    F'4'             INCREMENT
00007C 0000003C                     81 LIMIT    DC    F'60'            15 * 4 = 60 (LOOP CONTROL)
000080                              82 M        DS    15F              THE ARRAY OF MULTIPLES
0000BC                              83 SAVE     DS    18F              SAVE AREA (9D IN DOS)
                                    84 SNAPDCB  DCB   DSORG=PS,MACRF=W,RECFM=VBA,BLKSIZE=1632,LRECL=125,      X
                                                      DDNAME=SNAP
000000                             135          END   MULTIPLE
-STORAGE                                   M
0EC080                                         00000021 00000042 00000063 00000084   *                ................*
0EC0A0   000000A5 000000C6 000000E7 00000108   00000129 0000014A 0000016B 0000018C   *.......F...X....................*
0EC0C0   000001AD 000001CE 000001EF                                                   *............                   *
```

**Figure 5.14**
A program to compute and store the multiples of $z$.

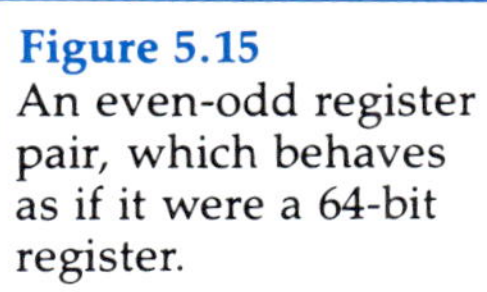

**Figure 5.15**
An even-odd register pair, which behaves as if it were a 64-bit register.

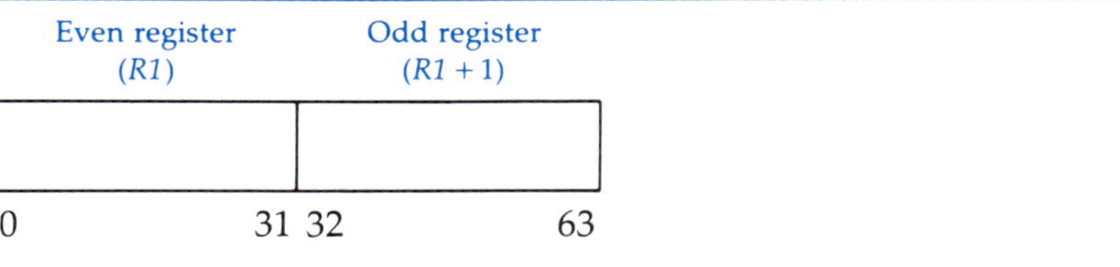


**Even/odd register pairs**

both cases, this quantity is contained in two adjacent registers that can behave as if they are a single 64-bit register. The consecutive registers must consist of an even-numbered register and the next odd-numbered register. These registers are called an **even-odd register pair**, and are shown in Figure 5.15. There are 8 such pairs: Registers 0 and 1, 2 and 3, 4 and 5, and so on to Registers 14 and 15; no other combinations are possible. You will encounter other instructions in later chapters that also use even-odd register pairs.

**Specification exception**

You write the even-numbered register to designate an even-odd register pair. The instruction's operation code implies that such a designation denotes a register pair and not just a single register. In the case of multiplication and division, *R1* designates the pair *R1,R1* + 1; the notation C(*R1,R1* + 1) represents their contents. Note that failure to specify *R1* as an even number usually will cause an assembly-time error message; if not, a *specification exception* will occur, which causes a program interruption.

## *The Multiply (MR and M) Instructions*

**64-bit product**

The Multiply instructions each compute a 64-bit product from two 32-bit integers called the *multiplicand* and the *multiplier.* The MR instruction involves register operands, while the M instruction multiplies a fullword in storage by the contents of a register. The product is formed in an even-odd register pair. The instructions are summarized as follows:

| Operation | Operand | Format | Instruction Name | Action |
|---|---|---|---|---|
| **MR** | *R1,R2* | RR | MULTIPLY REGISTERS | $C(R1,R1+1) \leftarrow C(R1+1) * \begin{cases} C(R2) \text{ for MR} \\ C(E2)_{0\text{-}31} \text{ for M} \end{cases}$ |
| **M** | *R1,S2*<br>or *R1,S2(X2)*<br>or *R1,D2(X2,B2)* | RX | MULTIPLY | |

The multiplicand is in the odd-numbered register of the even-odd pair *R1,R1* + 1. The multiplier is either in register *R2* if the instruction is MR, or in a fullword of storage that is specified as the second operand if the instruction is M. The 64-bit product is formed in the even-odd register pair and destroys their prior contents. Figure 5.16 illustrates this action. Notice that the prior contents of *R1* do not participate in the multiplication and are destroyed. Since it is impossible to generate a product that is longer than 64 bits from two 32-bit operands, overflow cannot occur. The condition code is unchanged.

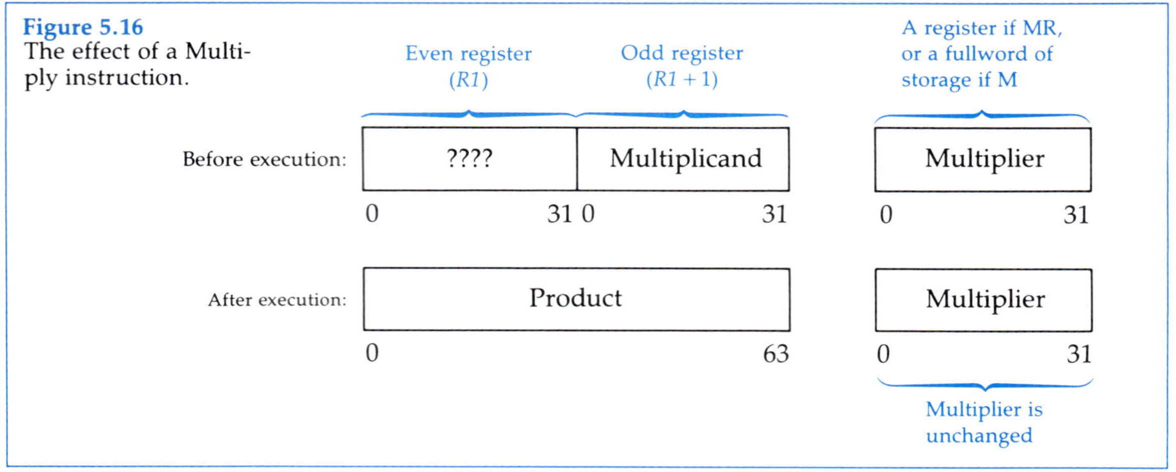


**Figure 5.16**
The effect of a Multiply instruction.

---

EXAMPLE 6

```
MR      2,5 ← This register contains the multiplier.
```

↑ This specifies an even-odd register pair. (The odd register (Register 3) contains the multiplicand.

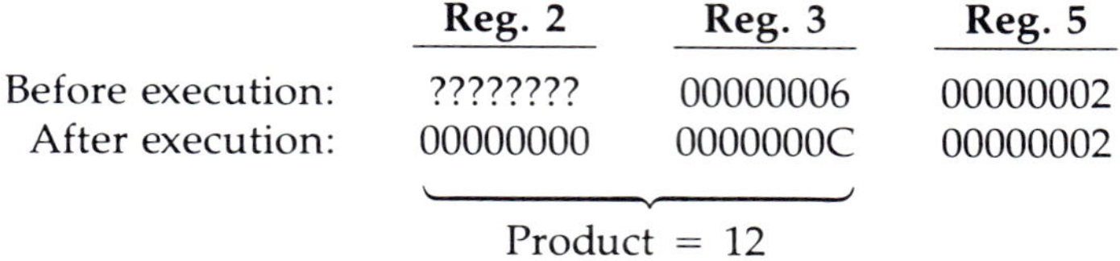

| | Reg. 2 | Reg. 3 | Reg. 5 |
|---|---|---|---|
| Before execution: | ???????? | 00000006 | 00000002 |
| After execution: | 00000000 | 0000000C | 00000002 |

Product = 12

---

EXAMPLE 7

```
M       10,Y    where    Y    DC    F'-2'
```

↑ This specifies an even-odd register pair. Register 11 contains the multiplicand.

The multiplier is in a fullword of storage.

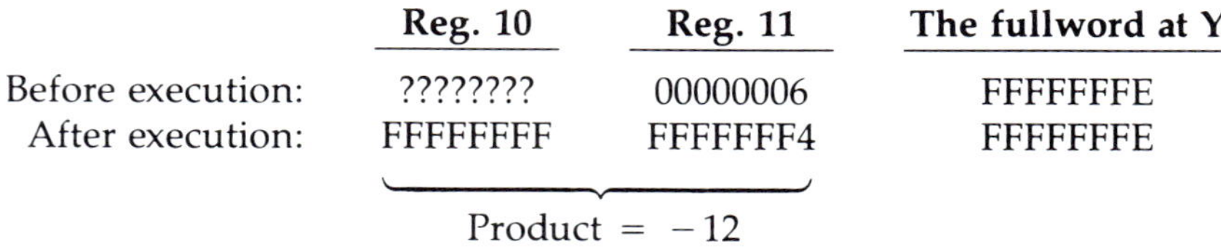

| | Reg. 10 | Reg. 11 | The fullword at Y |
|---|---|---|---|
| Before execution: | ???????? | 00000006 | FFFFFFFE |
| After execution: | FFFFFFFF | FFFFFFF4 | FFFFFFFE |

Product = −12

---

EXAMPLE 8

```
MR      4,5  SQUARE THE CONTENTS OF REG. 5
```

↑ This implies that Register 5 contains the multiplicand.

The multiplier is in Register 5.

| | Reg. 4 | Reg. 5 |
|---|---|---|
| Before execution: | ???????? | 01000000 |
| After execution: | 00010000 | 00000000 |

The *R1* entry (4) implies both that the multiplicand is in Register 5, and that the product will be placed into Registers 4 and 5. The *R2* entry (5) indicates that the multiplier is also in Register 5. In this case, both the multiplicand and the multiplier are the same, so the effect is to square the contents of Register 5.

Here, Register 5 originally contains the equivalent of $16^6$; its square is $16^{12}$. This product is developed in Registers 4 and 5, and replaces their prior contents.

---

EXAMPLE 9

Assume that I, J, and K are fullwords in storage. The following sequence computes the product of the integers in I and J, and stores it into K. (In Pascal, you would write K := I * J.) Assume that the product can be represented by 32 bits.

```
L     3,I       PLACE I INTO AN ODD REGISTER
M     2,J       MULTIPLY IT BY J
ST    3,K       STORE THE RESULT INTO K
```

---

**Multiply does not indicate when a product exceeds 32 bits**

The Multiply instructions do not indicate when a product exceeds 32 bits. You must write separate instructions to determine if the 64-bit product can be represented correctly by its low-order 32 bits. The binary products that are illustrated in Figure 5.17 begin to demonstrate when this is possible. Product **a** is positive. Since the odd register contains a positive integer and the even register contains zero, you can ignore the even register. Thus, the odd register contains a correct 32-bit version of the product. However, this is not the case for Product **b** since it is positive, but the contents of the odd register, when taken alone, are negative in a 32-bit two's complement binary number system. In Product **c**, there are significant bits in the even register that cannot be ignored.

**Figure 5.17**
A study of 64-bit products.

| | | Product: Even register | Product: Odd register | Value of 64-bit product correctly represented by odd register? |
|---|---|---|---|---|
| *Positive products* | **a.** | 0 . . . 0 | 0? . . . ? | Yes |
| | **b.** | 0 . . . 0 | 1? . . . ? | No |
| | **c.** | ≠ 0 | ? . . . ? | No |
| *Negative products* | **d.** | 1 . . . 1 | 1? . . . ? | Yes |
| | **e.** | 1 . . . 1 | 0? . . . ? | No |
| | **f.** | ≠ all 1's | ? . . . ? | No |

## SELF-TEST EXERCISES

6. Assume that, before each of the subsequent instructions is executed, Registers 0 through 3 and the fullwords X and Y contain the following decimal quantities:

| | | |
|---|---|---|
| Reg. 0 = 0 | Reg. 2 = 2 | X = 7 |
| Reg. 1 = −16 | Reg. 3 = 8 | Y = −3 |

What are the contents, in decimal and in hex, of the designated even-odd register pairs after execution of the following Multiply instructions?

a. `MR 0,2`
b. `M 2,X`
c. `M 2,Y`
d. `MR 0,1`
e. `MR 2,2`

7. Given the fullwords X, Y, and Z, compute

   Z = 3 * X + 4 * Y

8. Square the contents in Register 6 and place the result into Register 6. Assume that the result can be contained in 32 bits.
9. Assume an integer $n$ is in Register 3. Compute $n^3 - n$ in Register 5.
10. Which of the following 64-bit two's complement binary products that are contained in an even-odd register pair can be correctly represented by the 32 bits of the odd register?

| | Even Register | Odd Register |
|---|---|---|
| a. | 0 . . . 00 | 00 . . . 01 |
| b. | 0 . . . 01 | 10 . . . 00 |
| c. | 0 . . . 00 | 010 . . . 00 |
| d. | 0 . . . 00 | 10 . . . 00 |
| e. | 1 . . . 11 | 11 . . . 11 |
| f. | 1 . . . 11 | 10 . . . 00 |
| g. | 1 . . . 11 | 00 . . . 00 |
| h. | 1 . . . 10 | 10 . . . 00 |

You can make similar comments when the product is negative. In Product **d**, the contents of the odd register are negative in a 32-bit number system and, since the even register contains all ones, which are just placeholders in the 64-bit product, you can ignore them. This is not the case in Product **e** since the odd register by itself appears to contain a positive integer. Finally, in Product **f**, the even register contains significant bits that cannot be ignored.

To summarize, a 64-bit product can be represented correctly by its low-order 32 bits when either of the following conditions occur:

**Determination of when a product exceeds 32 bits**

1. The even register is zero and the odd register begins with a 0 (is non-negative).
2. Or, the even register contains all 1's and the odd register begins with a 1 (is negative).

The flowchart in Figure 5.18 and the instructions in Figure 5.19 demonstrate these criteria. In Chapter 8, you will see that a single arithmetic shift instruction can replace the instructions written here.

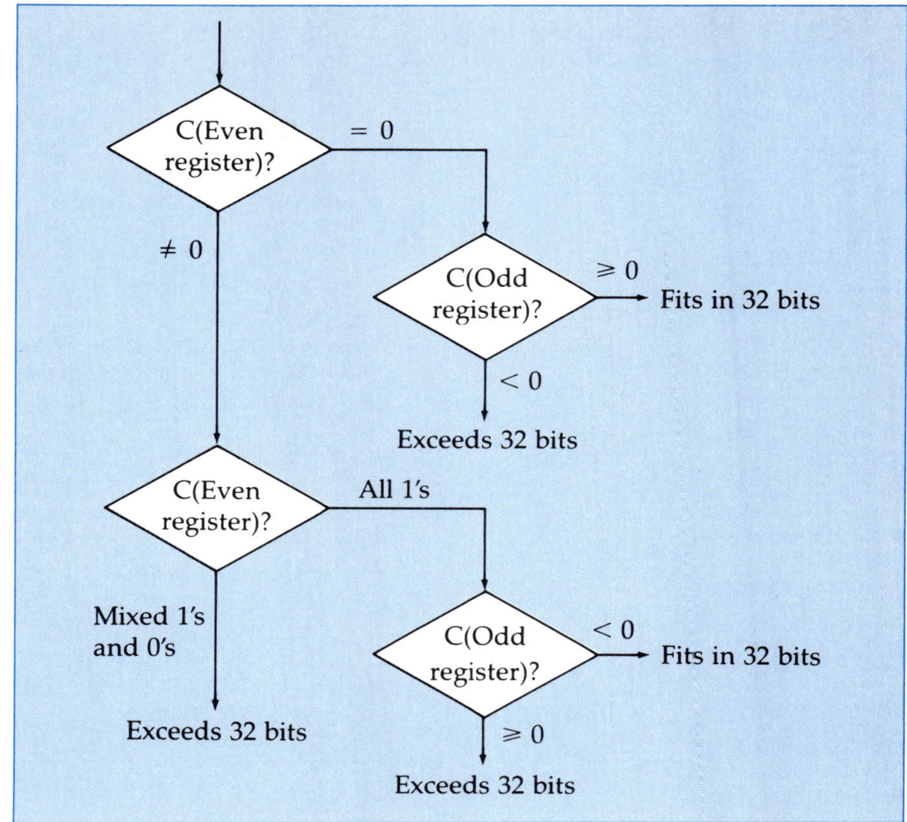


**Figure 5.18**
A flowchart of the algorithm to determine if a product can be represented by 32 bits.

When you expect a product to exceed 32 bits, it may be preferable to use floating-point arithmetic, which is discussed in Chapter 17. However, you can make use of 64-bit integer quantities. Chapter 9 shows how you can compute the sum of 64-bit integers.

## *The Divide (DR and D) Instructions*

**Quotient and remainder**

The Divide instructions each divide a 64-bit integer called the *dividend* by a 32-bit integer called the *divisor* to produce a *quotient* and a *remainder*. An even-odd register pair initially contains the dividend. The divisor is in a register or a fullword in storage, according to whether the instruction is DR or D. The quotient and the remainder replace the dividend. The Divide instructions are summarized as follows:

| Operation | Operand | Format | Instruction Name | Action |
|---|---|---|---|---|
| **DR** | *R1*,*R2* | RR | DIVIDE REGISTERS | C(*R1*+1) ← Quotient of C(*R1*,*R1*+1) ÷ Divisor<br>C(*R1*) ← Remainder of C(*R1*,*R1*+1) ÷ Divisor |
| **D** | *R1*,*S2*<br>or *R1*,*S2*(*X2*)<br>or *R1*,*D2*(*X2*,*B2*) | RX | DIVIDE | where Divisor = { C(*R2*) for DR; $C(E2)_{0\text{-}31}$ for D } |

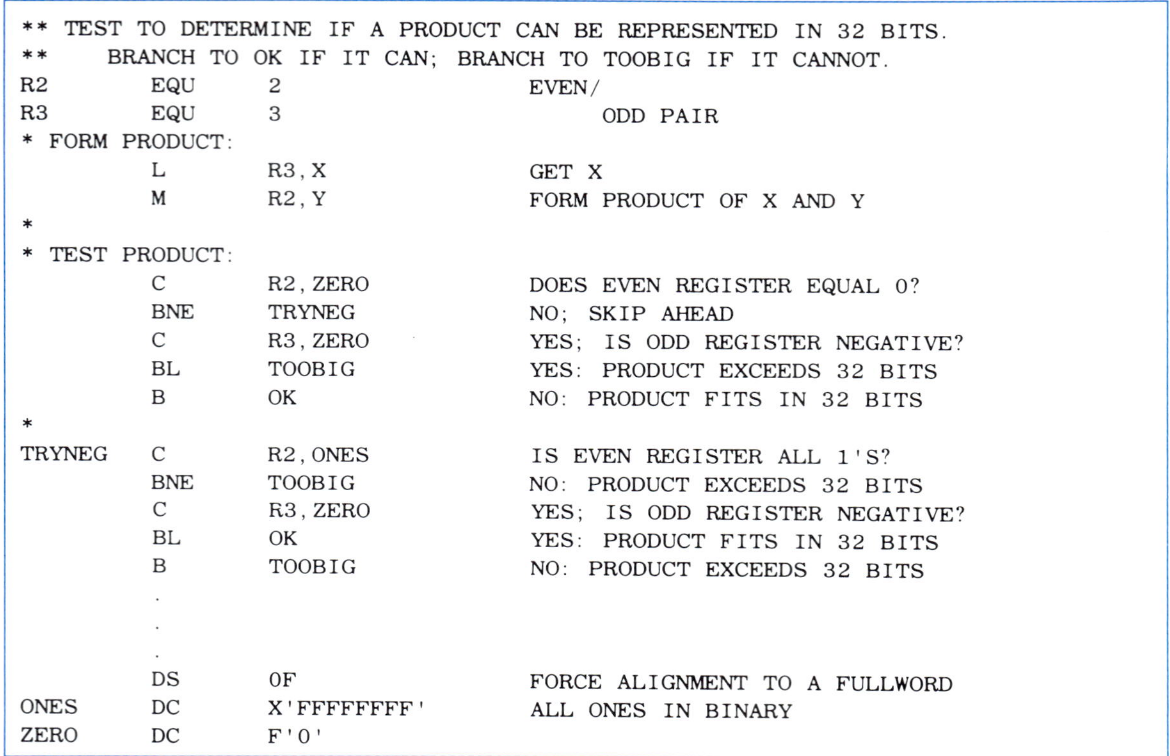

```
** TEST TO DETERMINE IF A PRODUCT CAN BE REPRESENTED IN 32 BITS.
**     BRANCH TO OK IF IT CAN; BRANCH TO TOOBIG IF IT CANNOT.
R2       EQU    2                   EVEN/
R3       EQU    3                        ODD PAIR
* FORM PRODUCT:
         L      R3,X                GET X
         M      R2,Y                FORM PRODUCT OF X AND Y
*
* TEST PRODUCT:
         C      R2,ZERO             DOES EVEN REGISTER EQUAL 0?
         BNE    TRYNEG              NO; SKIP AHEAD
         C      R3,ZERO             YES; IS ODD REGISTER NEGATIVE?
         BL     TOOBIG              YES: PRODUCT EXCEEDS 32 BITS
         B      OK                  NO: PRODUCT FITS IN 32 BITS
*
TRYNEG   C      R2,ONES             IS EVEN REGISTER ALL 1'S?
         BNE    TOOBIG              NO: PRODUCT EXCEEDS 32 BITS
         C      R3,ZERO             YES; IS ODD REGISTER NEGATIVE?
         BL     OK                  YES: PRODUCT FITS IN 32 BITS
         B      TOOBIG              NO: PRODUCT EXCEEDS 32 BITS
         .
         .
         .
         DS     0F                  FORCE ALIGNMENT TO A FULLWORD
ONES     DC     X'FFFFFFFF'         ALL ONES IN BINARY
ZERO     DC     F'0'
```

**Figure 5.19**
The instructions to determine if a product can be represented in 32 bits.

**64-bit dividend**

The 64-bit dividend is in the even-odd register pair *R1*,*R1*+1. The divisor is in register *R2* if the instruction is DR, or in a fullword of storage that is specified as the second operand if the instruction is D. The division results in an integer quotient in the odd register *R1*+1 and an integer remainder in the even register *R1*. The dividend is destroyed. Figure 5.20 illustrates this effect of the Divide instruction.

The quotient is positive if the signs of the operands are the same or if the quotient is zero; it is negative if not. If the remainder is nonzero, it has the sign of the dividend. The condition code is unchanged.

An attempted division by zero or a division that will cause a quotient to exceed 32 bits will cause a **fixed-point divide exception**, which in turn will cause a program interruption. The dividend will remain unchanged.

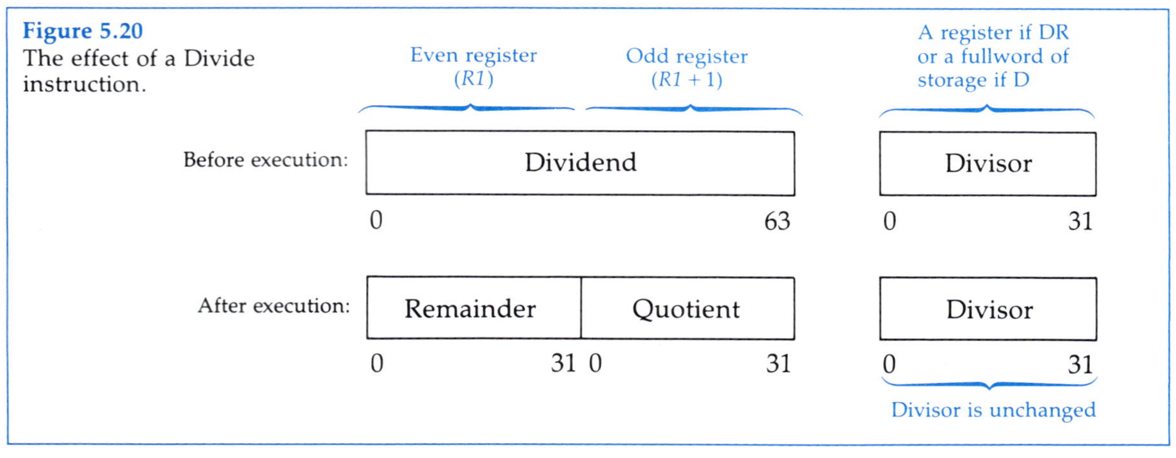


**Figure 5.20**
The effect of a Divide instruction.

EXAMPLE 10

```
DR    2,7 ←— This register contains the divisor.
        ↑
```

This specifies the even-odd register pair—Registers 2 and 3—that contains the dividend.

**a.** If you divide +9 by +4, you will get a quotient of +2 and a remainder of +1, as shown here:

| | Reg. 2 | Reg. 3 | Reg. 7 |
|---|---|---|---|
| Before execution: | 00000000 | 00000009 | 00000004 |
| After execution: | 00000001 | 00000002 | 00000004 |
| | Remainder | Quotient | Divisor |

**b.** If you divide +9 by −4, you will get a quotient of −2 (negative since the signs of the dividend and the divisor differ) and a remainder of +1 (positive since the dividend is positive). The following shows this result:

| | Reg. 2 | Reg. 3 | Reg. 7 |
|---|---|---|---|
| Before execution: | 00000000 | 00000009 | FFFFFFFC |
| After execution: | 00000001 | FFFFFFFE | FFFFFFFC |
| | Remainder | Quotient | Divisor |

**c.** If you divide −9 by +4, you will get a quotient of −2 (negative since the dividend and divisor have opposite signs) and a remainder of −1 (negative since the dividend is negative). The following shows this result:

| | Reg. 2 | Reg. 3 | Reg. 7 |
|---|---|---|---|
| Before execution: | FFFFFFFF | FFFFFFF7 | 00000004 |
| After execution: | FFFFFFFF | FFFFFFFE | 00000004 |
| | Remainder | Quotient | Divisor |

EXAMPLE 11

```
D     10,TWO    where    TWO     DC   F'2'
```

The dividend is in Registers 10 and 11. — The divisor is a fullword in storage.

**a.** If you divide −8 by +2, you will get a quotient of −4 and a remainder of 0, as shown here:

| | Reg. 10 | Reg. 11 | The fullword at TWO |
|---|---|---|---|
| | Dividend = −8 | | |
| Before execution: | FFFFFFFF | FFFFFFF8 | 00000002 |
| After execution: | 00000000 | FFFFFFFC | 00000002 |
| | Remainder | Quotient | Divisor |

Since the remainder is zero, it does not have the sign of the dividend.

**b.** If you divide $2^{32}$ by 2, a fixed-point divide exception occurs since the quotient ($2^{31}$) cannot be represented in 32 bits. The division is suppressed and the dividend is unchanged, as shown here:

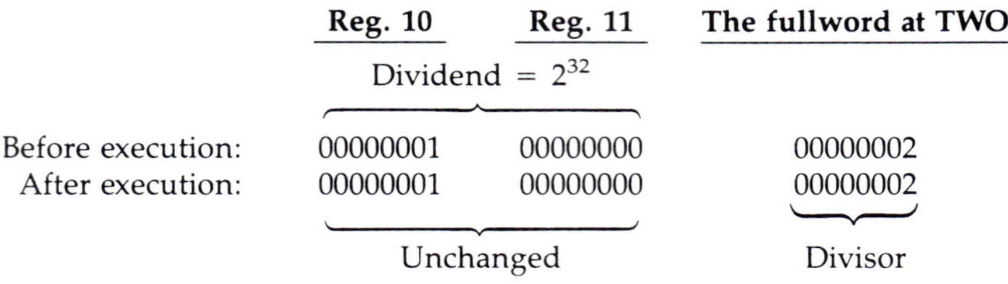

| | Reg. 10 | Reg. 11 | The fullword at TWO |
|---|---|---|---|
| | Dividend = $2^{32}$ | | |
| Before execution: | 00000001 | 00000000 | 00000002 |
| After execution: | 00000001 | 00000000 | 00000002 |
| | Unchanged | | Divisor |

EXAMPLE 12

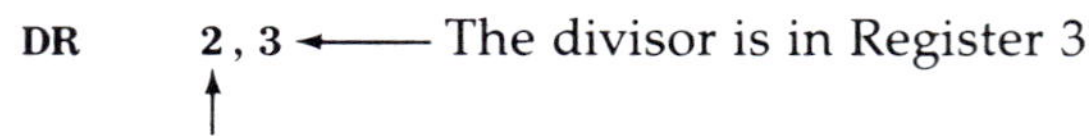

```
DR      2,3 <—— The divisor is in Register 3
```

↑ The dividend is in Registers 2 and 3

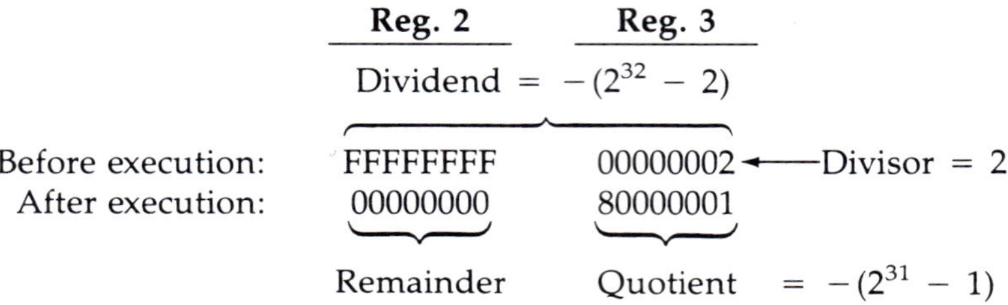

| | Reg. 2 | Reg. 3 | |
|---|---|---|---|
| | Dividend = $-(2^{32} - 2)$ | | |
| Before execution: | FFFFFFFF | 00000002 | ← Divisor = 2 |
| After execution: | 00000000 | 80000001 | |
| | Remainder | Quotient | = $-(2^{31} - 1)$ |

Here, Registers 2 and 3 contain the dividend, and Register 3 contains the divisor. After the division, Register 2 contains the remainder and Register 3 contains the quotient.

*Preparing the Dividend.* Often, integers that you may want to divide are not available as doublewords. Therefore, you must take steps prior to the division to construct a 64-bit dividend. Here are some possibilities when the dividend originally is a fullword.

CASE 1 *Positive Dividend*

- Load the dividend into the odd register.
- Zero the even register.

In this example

| | | | Reg. 6 | Reg. 7 |
|---|---|---|---|---|
| | L | 7,DVDND | ???????? | 00000FFF |
| | SR | 6,6 | 00000000 | 00000FFF |
| | . | | | |
| | . | | | |
| | . | | | |
| DVDND | DC | F'4095' | | |

Register 7 contains a 32-bit representation of 4095 but, when it is combined with the zeros in Register 6, a 64-bit representation exists.

CASE 2 *Sign of the Dividend Is Unknown*

- Load the dividend into the odd register.
- Multiply the odd register by 1 to generate a 64-bit representation of the dividend.

In this example

```
                                Reg. 6      Reg. 7
         L     7,DVDND         ????????    FFFFF001
         M     6,ONE           FFFFFFFF    FFFFF001
         .
         .
         .
ONE      DC    F'1'
DVDND    DC    F'-4095'
```

multiplication by +1 effectively changes a 32-bit representation of an integer into a 64-bit representation. If DVDND contains a negative number as it does here, Register 6 will contain FFFFFFFF after the multiplication. However, if DVDND contains a positive number, the multiplication will set Register 6 to zero.

In essence, this procedure will propagate the leftmost bit of the 32-bit dividend throughout the even register. Another approach to this task is to use an arithmetic shift; this will be discussed in Chapter 8.

## SELF-TEST EXERCISES

11. Assume that, before each of the subsequent instructions is executed, Registers 0 through 5 and the fullword X contain the following decimal quantities:

    Reg. 0 = −1  Reg. 2 = 0  Reg. 4 = 0  X = −3
    Reg. 1 = −4  Reg. 3 = 7  Reg. 5 = −1

    What are the contents, in decimal and in hex, of the designated even-odd register pairs after the following Divide instructions are executed?

    **a.** DR 2,1  **c.** D 0,X
    **b.** DR 0,3  **d.** DR 4,1

12. Given the fullword integers in X and Y, write instructions to compute

    X/3 + Y/4

    Ignore any remainders.

13. Assume that Register 6 contains a positive integer. Compute the quotient when this integer is divided by −3.
14. Assume that Register 11 contains a negative integer. Compute the remainder after this integer is divided by the contents of Register 0.

### *Multiplications and Divisions in the Same Arithmetic Expression*

Often, divisions follow multiplications and the inverse also occurs. Here, this section examines a product that is divided and a quotient that is multiplied. The examples will use Pascal-like expressions to describe the desired arithmetic. Assume that each variable mentioned represents a fullword in storage, and that R4 and R5 represent an even-odd register pair.

---

EXAMPLE 13

**Compute (L*M)/N**

Ignore the remainder after the division and store the result into J.

```
L      R5,L        PREPARE FOR MULTIPLY
M      R4,M        L*M IS IN EVEN-ODD PAIR
D      R4,N        COMPUTE QUOTIENT
ST     R5,J        SAVE QUOTIENT; IGNORE REMAINDER
```

Notice that, when a division immediately follows a multiplication, a separate step to prepare the dividend is unnecessary since the product is already a 64-bit quantity.

---

EXAMPLE 14

**Compute (M/N)*L**

Assume that M is positive and ignore the remainder after the division. Also assume that the product can be correctly represented in 32 bits.

```
L      R5,M        GET DIVIDEND
SR     R4,R4       EXTEND DIVIDEND TO 64 BITS
D      R4,N        COMPUTE QUOTIENT
M      R4,L        MULTIPLY QUOTIENT BY L
ST     R5,J        SAVE 32-BIT PRODUCT
```

Here, the remainder of the division is in R4 and is ignored by the Multiply instruction.

---

**SELF-TEST EXERCISE**

15. Write instructions to compute each of the following expressions. Ignore any remainders that follow the divisions.
    **a.** ((L + 2) / K − 3) * N
    **b.** (X + 1) * (Y − 15) / (Z − 3)

## Sample Computations

The following program segments demonstrate the concepts introduced so far in this chapter. Since each segment is part of a larger program, assume that base registers and necessary arrays have already been defined.

---

EXAMPLE 15

### Compute the Average of the First *n* Elements of an Array

The following is a pseudocode solution to this problem:

*Sum* := 0
REPEAT *n* TIMES
    Add next array element to *Sum*
END REPEAT
*Average* := *Sum* ÷ *n*

Assume that the array consists of fullword integers at the address ARRAY, and N is a fullword that contains a positive integer $n$. The desired program segment appears in Figure 5.21. As in past examples, you require an index register to address the fullwords of ARRAY. The index register can conveniently start at zero, and count by increments of 4 until it attains its last value of $4 * (n-1)$. Notice how the loop is controlled: A limit of $4 * n$ is computed and stored at LIMIT since it is easier to compute than $4 * (n-1)$ and works just as well. The Branch on Condition instruction that controls the loop branches if the index is less than the limit. This means that the last value of the index is $4 * (n-1)$ as required.

**Figure 5.21**
A program segment to compute the average of the first $n$ elements of an array.

```
** PROGRAM SEGMENT TO AVERAGE THE FIRST N ELEMENTS OF ARRAY.
** ASSUME ARRAY AND N ARE DEFINED AND N > 0.
*
** REGISTER DEFINITIONS:
*
R2       EQU   2                                            EVEN/
R3       EQU   3      LIMIT   (LOOP CONTROL)                   ODD PAIR
R4       EQU   4                                            EVEN/
R5       EQU   5      SUM                                      ODD PAIR
R6       EQU   6      INDEX
*
** INITIALIZATION:
*     SUM (R5) = 0
*     INDEX (R6) = 0
*     LIMIT (R3) = 4*N
         SR    R5,R5             CLEAR SUM AREA
         SR    R6,R6             CLEAR INDEX REGISTER
         L     R3,N              GET N
         M     R2,FOUR           LIMIT = 4*N FOR LOOP CONTROL
*
```

(Continues)

**Figure 5.21**
*(Continued)*

```
** COMPUTE SUM OF INTEGERS IN ARRAY:
* REPEAT N TIMES:
LOOP     A     R5,ARRAY(R6)       ADD NEXT ELEMENT TO SUM
         A     R6,FOUR            INDEX = INDEX + 4
         CR    R6,R3              DONE?
         BL    LOOP               IF NOT, REPEAT
* END REPEAT
*
** COMPUTE AVERAGE:
         M     R4,ONE             PREPARE FOR DIVIDE
         D     R4,N               COMPUTE AVERAGE
         ST    R5,AVERAGE         SAVE IT, IGNORING REMAINDER
         .
         .
         .
ARRAY    DS    50F                ARRAY OF FULLWORD INTEGERS
N        DS    F                  NO. OF INTEGERS TO CONSIDER
FOUR     DC    F'4'               INDEX INCREMENT
ONE      DC    F'1'               CONSTANT
AVERAGE  DS    F                  RESULT
```

---

EXAMPLE 16

### Determine If a Given Year Is a Leap Year

Leap years are those years that are exactly divisible by 4. Possible exceptions are centenary years: they must be divisible by 400. For example, 1900 was not a leap year (it is not divisible by 400), but 2000 will be. Thus, to determine if a year is a leap year, you first check to see if it ends in 00—that is, if it is divisible by 100. If it is, it must also be divisible by 400 to be called a leap year. If the year does not end in 00, then it simply must be divisible by 4 to be a leap year. This algorithm can be described more clearly with the pseudocode in Figure 5.22 or the flowchart in Figure 5.23. Figure 5.24 lists the program segment to accomplish leap-year calculations.

**Figure 5.22**
The pseudocode to determine if a year is a leap year.

```
IF year is divisible by 100
    THEN
       IF year is divisible by 400
           THEN year is a leap year
           ELSE year is not a leap year
       END IF
    ELSE
       IF year is divisible by 4
           THEN year is a leap year
           ELSE year is not a leap year
       END IF
END IF
```

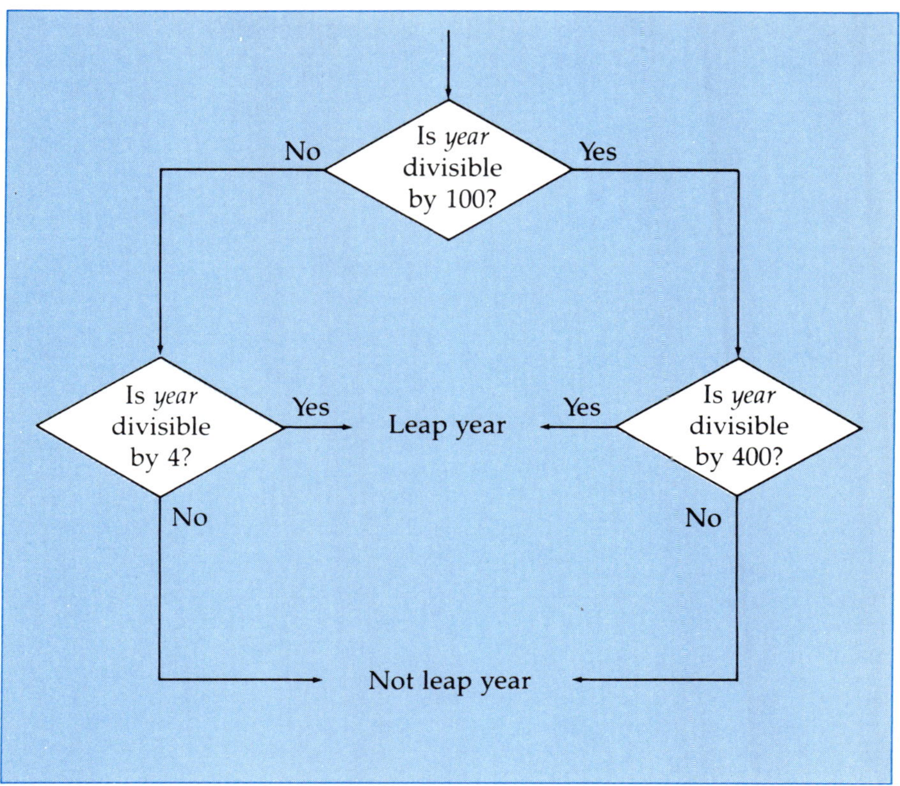


**Figure 5.23**
A flowchart to determine if a year is a leap year.

**Figure 5.24**
A program segment to determine if a year is a leap year.

```
** PROGRAM SEGMENT TO DETERMINE IF A YEAR IS A LEAP YEAR
**     ASSUME YEAR IS DEFINED;
**     BRANCH TO LEAP IF YEAR IS A LEAP YEAR;
**     BRANCH TO NOTLEAP IF IT IS NOT.
*
** REGISTER DEFINITIONS:
*
R2       EQU    2                  EVEN/
R3       EQU    3                       ODD PAIR
*
* IF YEAR IS DIVISIBLE BY 100:
         L      R3,YEAR            GET YEAR
         SR     R2,R2              PREPARE FOR DIVIDE
         D      R2,HUNDRED         DIVIDE BY 100
         C      R2,ZERO            CHECK REMAINDER
         BNE    NOT100
* - THEN:
* - - IF YEAR IS DIVISIBLE BY 400:
         D      R2,FOUR            R3=YEAR/100 SO DIVIDE BY 4;
*                                  R2=0 SO ALL SET TO DIVIDE
         C      R2,ZERO            CHECK REMAINDER
* - - - THEN IT IS A LEAP YEAR
         BE     LEAP
* - - - ELSE IT IS NOT
         B      NOTLEAP
* - - END IF
* - ELSE:
```

(Continues)

**Figure 5.24**
*(Continued)*

```
* - - IF YEAR IS DIVISIBLE BY 4:
NOT100   L      R3,YEAR          GET YEAR AGAIN
         SR     R2,R2            PREPARE FOR DIVIDE
         D      R2,FOUR          DIVIDE BY 4
         C      R2,ZERO          CHECK REMAINDER
* - - - THEN IT IS A LEAP YEAR
         BE     LEAP
* - - - ELSE IT IS NOT
         B      NOTLEAP
* - - END IF
* END IF
         .
         .
         .
YEAR     DS     F
HUNDRED  DC     F'100'
FOUR     DC     F'4'
ZERO     DC     F'0'
```

## Programming Style

Good style is an important aspect of any program, but is especially so in assembler language programs. The program segments in Figures 5.21 and 5.24, and the program in Figure 5.32, which is given later, illustrate the following stylistic points:

1. *Begin with a TITLE and a Prologue.* A *prologue* consists of several comments statements that provide an overall description of the program. It should include a clear statement of the program's purpose, any assumptions made, its input and output, and the algorithm used. You can use lines of asterisks to set off the prologue from the rest of the program.
2. *Define Symbolic Register Names.* Chapter 4 pointed out the importance of using the EQU directive to define symbolic names for the registers. You should group these definitions at the beginning or the end of the program, and use their remarks entries to describe the purpose of each register.
3. *Choose Mnemonic Symbols.* You should try to make your program as self-documenting as possible. All symbols should suggest meaning to the reader. Try to avoid lengthy symbols or symbols that have similar names because they cause confusion and invite typographical errors.
4. *Divide the Program into Sections.* It is easier to see and comprehend program sections that are relatively short and clearly delineated. Use comments statements to create such divisions and to describe the overall effect of each section. Anyone should be able to read through these comments in order to get an overall understanding of the program. Detailed descriptions of each step in the algorithm are left for the remarks entries of individual instructions.

   The comments statements that precede the sections in Figures 5.21 and 5.24 are identified with two asterisks, but you can delineate major sections in a lengthy program with entire lines of blanks, asterisks, or dashes. However, be aware that too many comments statements can hide the instructions of a program and make it as difficult to read as a program without comments.

5. *Indicate the Program's Structure.* Assembler language by its very nature is not a structured language. There are no control structures as found in a language such as Pascal. However, you can use the structured pseudocode that you write to describe your algorithms as the basis for comments that give a sense of structure to the program. In Figure 5.24, notice how the indentations of the pseudocode are preserved and highlighted. There is one blank between the asterisk and the pseudocode of first-level control structures. Each indentation consists of two additional spaces beyond the blank, and contains a dash and a blank. This practice makes the depth of indentation and, hence, the level of nesting of the control structure visually apparent.
6. *Use Meaningful Remarks.* Since instructions can be self-documenting, you should try to avoid redundancy in the remarks entry. For example, in Figure 5.24, the statement

```
C       R2,ZERO              CHECK REMAINDER
```

is more descriptive than if you had written

```
C       R2,ZERO              COMPARE R2 WITH ZERO
```

COMPARE R2 WITH ZERO provides no more information than can be inferred from the instruction itself. You should choose symbols to provide as much information as possible to the reader, and your remarks should augment, not duplicate, this information.

## Literals

Many of the programs and program segments considered so far used values that remained constant. These values were defined with the DC directive. For example, the following instruction subtracts 4 from Register 7:

```
          S       R7,FOUR
```

where

```
FOUR      DC      F'4'
```

As an alternative, you could write the Subtract instruction as

```
          S       R7,=F'4'
```

**Literals and literal constants**

The designation =F'4' is called a **literal**. It essentially looks like the operand entry of a DC, except that an equal sign (=) precedes it. When the assembler encounters a literal for the first time, it defines a constant —in this case, a fullword containing 00000004—within an area of the program reserved for this purpose. The constant is called a **literal constant**. Essentially =F'4' has the same effect as the DC statement that defines FOUR. If you use the literal, you would not use the DC. If you use the same literal again in another instruction in the program, the assembler will recognize this and not generate a duplicate constant; rather, it will refer to the constant defined earlier. Two literals are the same if their specifications are identical, and not if the assembled constants happen to be the same.

The assembler translates a literal into a base register and a displacement so that the corresponding literal constant will be addressed at execution time.

**Restrictions**

There are some restrictions that limit what you can do with literals:

1. Do not store into a literal.
2. Do not combine a literal with terms to form an expression.
3. Do not specify an index register.
4. Do not use a zero duplication factor.

With the possible exception of the first restriction, it is not likely that you will want to take any of these actions. If you ever consider storing into a literal, remember that a literal defines a constant: all occurrences of a particular literal refer to the same constant in storage, so you should not change it.

The assembler places all constants that are defined by literals into an area called the **literal pool**. The literal pool begins on a doubleword boundary and is divided into four segments. The constants are assigned to a segment according to their assembled length in bytes. The first segment contains those constants whose lengths are multiples of eight. These are followed by remaining constants whose lengths are multiples of four, and then by those remaining with lengths that are multiples of two. All other constants will have odd lengths and will appear last. Here is an example of the significance of the literal pool structure: if you write

```
S      R2,=X'00000004'
```

the constant $00000004_{16}$ will appear on a fullword boundary. Unless you specify otherwise, the assembler places the literal pool at the end of the program. A later chapter will describe how to alter the location of the literal pool and why you would want to.

**Constants versus initial values**

You cannot change the values of literals at execution time; they are truly constants. In contrast, you can change the values established with a DC directive during program execution. You can think of these values as initial values analogous to those assigned to variables in a high-level language. Thus, "Define Constant" is in essence a misnomer. However, you sometimes do define constants with DC directives, rather than with literals. In cases where you want control over the location of the constant, use a DC. If you find it necessary to define some constants or data structures in several steps, the DC is essential. Finally, tables of constants are defined with several DCs. Later, this chapter will discuss the use of literals and the DC directive further.

## Character Representation

You can represent a character such as a letter or a digit in one byte by using a binary code. IBM uses an 8-bit encoding scheme called **EBCDIC (Extended Binary Coded Decimal Interchange Code)**. Although it would be possible to represent 256 different characters by using 8-bit codes, only uppercase

### SPECIAL GRAPHIC CHARACTERS

| Hex | Symbol | Name |
|---|---|---|
| 40 | | blank |
| 4A | ¢ | cent sign |
| 4B | . | period |
| 4C | < | less than |
| 4D | ( | left parenthesis |
| 4E | + | plus |
| 4F | \| | logical OR |
| 50 | & | ampersand |
| 5A | ! | exclamation |
| 5B | $ | dollar sign |
| 5C | * | asterisk |
| 5D | ) | right parenthesis |
| 5E | ; | semicolon |
| 5F | ¬ | logical NOT |
| 60 | - | minus, hyphen |
| 61 | / | slash |
| 6A | ¦ | vertical line |
| 6B | , | comma |
| 6C | % | percent |
| 6D | _ | underscore |
| 6E | > | greater than |
| 6F | ? | question mark |
| 79 | ` | grave accent |
| 7A | : | colon |
| 7B | # | number sign |
| 7C | @ | at sign |
| 7D | ' | apostrophe |
| 7E | = | equal sign |
| 7F | " | quotation mark |
| A1 | ~ | tilde |
| C0 | { | left brace |
| CC | ⑀ | hook |
| CE | ⑂ | fork |
| D0 | } | right brace |
| E0 | \ | reverse slash |
| EC | ⑁ | chair |
| FA | \| | long vertical mark |

### LOWERCASE LETTERS

| Hex | Letter | Hex | Letter | Hex | Letter |
|---|---|---|---|---|---|
| 81 | a | 91 | j | | |
| 82 | b | 92 | k | A2 | s |
| 83 | c | 93 | l | A3 | t |
| 84 | d | 94 | m | A4 | u |
| 85 | e | 95 | n | A5 | v |
| 86 | f | 96 | o | A6 | w |
| 87 | g | 97 | p | A7 | x |
| 88 | h | 98 | q | A8 | y |
| 89 | i | 99 | r | A9 | z |

### UPPERCASE LETTERS

| Hex | Letter | Hex | Letter | Hex | Letter |
|---|---|---|---|---|---|
| C1 | A | D1 | J | | |
| C2 | B | D2 | K | E2 | S |
| C3 | C | D3 | L | E3 | T |
| C4 | D | D4 | M | E4 | U |
| C5 | E | D5 | N | E5 | V |
| C6 | F | D6 | O | E6 | W |
| C7 | G | D7 | P | E7 | X |
| C8 | H | D8 | Q | E8 | Y |
| C9 | I | D9 | R | E9 | Z |

### DIGITS

| Hex | Digit |
|---|---|
| F0 | 0 |
| F1 | 1 |
| F2 | 2 |
| F3 | 3 |
| F4 | 4 |
| F5 | 5 |
| F6 | 6 |
| F7 | 7 |
| F8 | 8 |
| F9 | 9 |

**Figure 5.25**
Printable EBCDIC characters.

and lowercase letters, the 10 digits, and a number of special characters and punctuation marks constitute the printable character set represented in EBCDIC, as shown in Figure 5.25.

Character representation is important at this point because all input and output that involve devices, such as terminals, card readers, or printers, are performed with character data. For example, imagine that you read the

## THE EVOLUTION OF BCDIC, EBCDIC, AND ASCII

Three distinct, but related, codes are commonly used to represent data on today's computers: EBCDIC, ASCII, and ASCII-8. The codes are descended from an unlikely ancestor—a weaving technique developed in 19th-century France. From this surprising common root, however, they have evolved into separate codes.

In 1801, Joseph Jacquard devised a new weaving system that used cards with holes punched in them. The placement of the holes allowed certain threads into the loom, while others were blocked by the card. Herman Hollerith, a statistician, used this idea in a machine that he invented for tabulating the results of the 1890 U.S. Census. Hollerith translated the 10 digits and 2 special symbols into 12 patterns of holes to be punched in cards. In his machine, the holes allowed certain electrical circuits to be completed and, therefore, the patterns could be detected.

By the 1950s, computers routinely used expanded versions of Hollerith's original code. Each position on a card could either be punched or not, thereby representing one of two possible states. These codes were said to be *binary coded* and IBM's first code was called the **Binary Coded Decimal Interchange Code** or **BCDIC**. BCDIC was a 6-bit code that permitted $2^6$, or 64, possible combinations of 0's and 1's. Other manufacturers developed other codes, but 6-bit codes were the most popular type. The situation was soon changed, however, by two major American institutions: the U.S. Government and IBM.

The first major change came from IBM. In the late 1950s, the byte went from 6 bits to 8 bits. With this change came the first 8-bit code: **EBCDIC**, or **Extended BCDIC**. This code satisfied a goal of IBM's designers to represent more than the 64 characters permitted by BCDIC. Subsequently, codes proliferated in the U.S., with over 2 dozen in use, frustrating communication between computers. In an attempt to solve this problem, the American Standards Association created the *Subcommittee X3.2 on Coded Character Sets and Data Formats* and assigned it the task of establishing a single U.S. standard code.

The subcommittee's first order of business was to decide how many bits were necessary for such a code. It was agreed that a 7-bit code, allowing 128 characters, was the minimum necessary to provide all of the characters needed for scientific, commercial, and government purposes. There were arguments in favor of the economy of an 8-bit code, but these were matched by other factors that favored 7 bits. In a subcommittee vote, the 7-bit code won and, in June 1963, it was approved as an American standard: the **American Standard Code for Information Interchange**, or **ASCII**.

Less than a year later, IBM unveiled its System/360, complete with 8-bit EBCDIC. To avoid complete incompatibility with the new U.S. standard, IBM also provided **ASCII-8**, an 8-bit code based upon ASCII. Today, EBCDIC, ASCII, and ASCII-8 are all in frequent use, and data is routinely translated from one code to another. Coding differences among American data sets remain, despite the efforts of Subcommittee X3.2.

**ASCII DEVICES**

Although IBM I/O devices use EBCDIC, some devices attached to your computing system—notably, terminals designed by other manufacturers—use another character code known as ASCII (American Standard Code for Information Interchange). The operating system converts ASCII input to EBCDIC and EBCDIC output to ASCII as necessary. A complete list of EBCDIC and ASCII codes appears in Appendix D.

number −183 from an input device and place it into storage. Each character will be represented by its 1-byte EBCDIC code, as follows

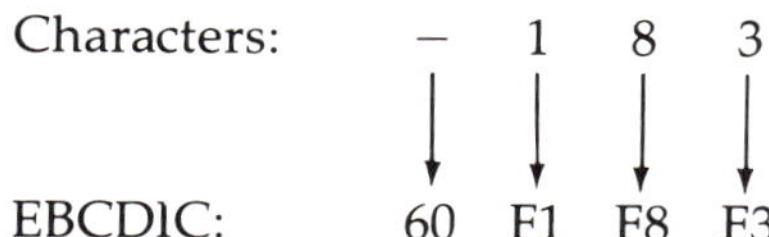


The EBCDIC codes are given in hexadecimal. The EBCDIC form is inappropriate for binary integer arithmetic and must first be converted to the two's complement binary representation, which is shown here:

FFFFFF49

Similarly, before you can print an arithmetic result, you must convert it from its numeric form to EBCDIC characters. The next section will introduce instructions to perform character input and output, and to convert between EBCDIC and binary integer representations. However, first consider how to define character constants. You can use such character strings to label a program's printed output.

## *Defining Character Constants*

One way to define a character string is to look up the EBCDIC codes for each character and to write a hexadecimal constant with the DC directive. For example

```
LABEL     DC     X'E3C8C9E240C9E240E3C8C540C1D5E2E6C5D9'
```

defines the following character string:

THIS IS THE ANSWER

**C-type constants**

An easier approach is to have the assembler look up the codes for you by writing a character constant:

```
LABEL     DC     C'THIS IS THE ANSWER'
```

This is exactly equivalent to the previous hexadecimal constant, and each byte represents one character. (Note that when you want an apostrophe or an ampersand to appear in the assembled constant, you must write two apostrophes or two ampersands in the character string.)

In general, you may use a constant type of C within a DC directive or a literal to define a character string, or within the DS directive to reserve storage. Like constant types B and X, a constant type C does not cause boundary alignment. Within a DS, C has the same effect as B or X: each reserves bytes.

## Simplified Input and Output Operations

You will want to perform I/O operations in most of the programs that you will write. The IBM System/370 requires that you write system macro instructions whenever you want an I/O operation to take place. A complete discussion of these macro instructions will occur in Chapter 16. However, this section demonstrates how you can perform simple character input and output operations.

In addition, you will learn how to convert decimal integers that you read from character form to binary integer form. You also will learn how to convert binary integers into decimal integers that are in character form so that you can print them. A complete discussion of the instructions that perform these conversions appears in later chapters. In the meantime, you do not need to know how these new instructions work; you only need to be able to write them.

### *Character Input and Output*

**Execute an OPEN instruction prior to I/O.**

Before you can perform I/O operations, you must execute one of the following OPEN macro instructions:

| In OS | In DOS |
|---|---|
| OPEN (READER, INPUT, PRINTER, OUTPUT) | OPEN READER, PRINTER |

**Include DCB or DTF instructions in a nonexecutable portion of your program.**

Usually, you will execute this instruction once in your program. Associated with the OPEN instruction are statements that you must include in your program in an area where they will not be executed, such as after the DC and DS instructions. They are as follows:

**In OS**

```
READER   DCB   DSORG=PS,MACRF=GM,DDNAME=SYSIN,RECFM=F,LRECL=rlen,            X
               BLKSIZE=rlen,EODAD=endaddr
PRINTER  DCB   DSORG=PS,MACRF=PM,DDNAME=SYSPRINT,RECFM=FA,LRECL=plen,        X
               BLKSIZE=plen
```

**In DOS**

```
READER   DTFCD DEVADDR=SYSIPT,DEVICE=2540,IOAREA1=INBUF,RECFORM=FIXUNB,X
               BLKSIZE=rlen,TYPEFLE=INPUT,WORKA=YES,EOFADDR=endaddr
PRINTER  DTFPR DEVADDR=SYSLST,DEVICE=3203,IOAREA1=OUTBUF,WORKA=YES,     X
               RECFORM=FIXUNB,BLKSIZE=plen,CTLCHAR=ASA
INBUF    DS    80C       INPUT BUFFER (MAX RECORD LENGTH IS 80)
OUTBUF   DS    133C      OUTPUT BUFFER (MAX LINE LENGTH IS 132)
```

version indicates the control statements that follow the program and that delineate the input data set.

Each time that GET is executed, a new data record is read. The program continues to read data until there are no more records left—at which time, program execution terminates. Each time that PUT is executed, a new line is printed. Notice that the character count that either the DCB instruction or the DTFPR instruction at PRINTER specifies includes the carriage-control character, which is at LINE.

---

## *Conversions Between Binary Integers and EBCDIC*

You have learned that GET reads EBCDIC characters and that PUT prints EBCDIC characters. However, the arithmetic instructions that you know operate upon two's complement binary integers. Now, you will learn how to convert decimal integers that you read from character form to two's

```
         TITLE 'READ AND PRINT RECORDS'
EX17     CSECT
         PRINT NOGEN                   SUPPRESS MACRO EXPANSIONS
R12      EQU   12                      BASE REGISTER
R13      EQU   13                      SAVE AREA POINTER
* STANDARD ENTRY:
         BALR  R12,0                   LOAD BASE REGISTER
         USING BASE,R12                DECLARE BASE ADDRESS AND REGISTER
BASE     LA    R13,SAVE                R13 = ADDRESS OF SAVE AREA
* READ AND PRINT RECORDS:
         OPEN  READER,PRINTER          PREPARE FOR I/O
LOOP     GET   READER,DATA             READ NEXT INPUT RECORD
         PUT   PRINTER,LINE            PRINT THE RECORD ON NEXT LINE
         B     LOOP                    REPEAT UNTIL END-OF-FILE
ENDDATA  CLOSE READER,PRINTER          END-OF-FILE: I/O COMPLETE
         EOJ                           RETURN TO DOS
*
LINE     DC    C' '                    CARRIAGE CONTROL
DATA     DS    80C                     DATA AREA
SAVE     DS    9D                      SAVE AREA
INBUF    DS    80C                     INPUT BUFFER
OUTBUF   DS    81C                     OUTPUT BUFFER
READER   DTFCD DEVADDR=SYSIPT,DEVICE=2540,IOAREA1=INBUF,RECFORM=FIXUNB,X
               BLKSIZE=80,TYPEFLE=INPUT,WORKA=YES,EOFADDR=ENDDATA
PRINTER  DTFPR DEVADDR=SYSLST,DEVICE=3203,IOAREA1=OUTBUF,WORKA=YES,     X
               RECFORM=FIXUNB,BLKSIZE=81,CTLCHAR=ASA
         END   EX17
/*
// EXEC LNKEDT
// EXEC
THIS RECORD WILL BE READ THE FIRST TIME THAT GET IS EXECUTED.
THIS RECORD WILL BE READ THE SECOND TIME THAT GET IS EXECUTED.
(Other data records)
/*
/&
```

**Figure 5.28**
A DOS program that reads records and prints them, as described in Example 17.

complement binary representation so that you can perform arithmetic. You also will see how to convert binary integers into decimal integers that are in character form; you perform this conversion so that you can print the results of your arithmetic. To simplify the conversions, several requirements are necessary:

- Each decimal integer that you write in an input record must consist of 10 characters, and each character string in storage that represents a decimal integer must occupy 10 bytes. There can be leading blanks or leading zeros; however, for now, there can be no sign.
- NUM represents the 10-byte character string in storage that was just described.
- TEMP represents a doubleword.

To convert the 10 characters at NUM into a binary representation that is placed into Register 2, you can write the following instructions:

Instructions to convert unsigned decimal integers in EBCDIC to binary.

```
PACK   TEMP(8),NUM(10)      IF NUM = 10 CHARACTERS,
CVB    R2,TEMP              THEN R2 = BINARY EQUIVALENT
```

To convert the binary integer that is in Register 2 into an EBCDIC representation at NUM, you can write the following instructions:

Instructions to convert nonnegative binary integers to decimal integers in EBCDIC.

```
CVD    R2,TEMP              IF R2 = BINARY INTEGER,
OI     TEMP+7,X'0F'
UNPK   NUM(10),TEMP(8)      THEN NUM = EBCDIC EQUIVALENT
```

---

EXAMPLE 18

**Read Two Unsigned Integers and Print Their Sum**

Suppose that you have a data record that contains two 10-character unsigned decimal integers. One integer begins in column 1 of the record and the second integer begins in column 21. The program segment in Figure 5.29 reads this data record and prints the sum of the two integers. To save space, this segment assumes that the necessary OPEN, CLOSE, DCB, and DTF instructions are the same as those that appear in Figures 5.27 and 5.28. Therefore, the segment in Figure 5.29 reserves 80 bytes for the data record and 81 bytes for each line of print. You can shorten these areas by changing *rlen* or *plen* in either the DCB instructions or the DTF instructions.

Suppose that the input data record appears as follows:

The printed line will appear as

```
THE SUM OF THE INTEGERS IS 0000003467
```

(Note the leading zeros: you will learn how to remove these characters in Chapter 14.)

If an end-of-data condition occurs, a branch to ENDDATA, where an error message is printed, will occur.

---

By adding a few instructions to the conversion instructions just presented, you can accommodate negative integers. However, you must place the minus sign in the leftmost position of the 10-character string that has been assumed; thus, −000000012 represents −12. Positive integers must be unsigned. To convert the 10 characters at NUM—regardless of their sign—into a binary representation that is placed into Register 2, you can write these instructions:

**Instructions to convert decimal integers in EBCDIC to binary.**

```
         PACK     TEMP(8),NUM(10)       IF NUM = 10 CHARACTERS,
         CVB      R2,TEMP               R2 = MAGNITUDE IN BINARY
         CLI      NUM,C'-'              IS THERE A MINUS SIGN?
         BNE      NN                    IF NOT, ASSUME NONNEGATIVE
         LNR      R2,R2                 IF SO, MAKE R2 NEGATIVE
NN       ----                           R2 = BINARY EQUIVALENT
```

```
** COMPUTE THE SUM OF 2 UNSIGNED DECIMAL INTEGERS.  ONE DATA RECORD
** CONTAINS BOTH INTEGERS.  ONE INTEGER BEGINS IN COL. 1; THE OTHER
** BEGINS IN COL. 21.  EACH INTEGER CONSISTS OF 10 CHARACTERS.
         GET      READER,DATA           READ DATA RECORD
         PACK     TEMP(8),NUM1(10)      CONVERT FIRST INTEGER FROM
         CVB      R3,TEMP                 EBCDIC TO BINARY.
         PACK     TEMP(8),NUM2(10)      CONVERT SECOND INTEGER FROM
         CVB      R4,TEMP                 EBCDIC TO BINARY.
         AR       R3,R4                 ADD THE INTEGERS
         CVD      R3,TEMP               CONVERT THE SUM FROM
         OI       TEMP+7,X'0F'            BINARY TO
         UNPK     NUM3(10),TEMP(8)          EBCDIC.
         PUT      PRINTER,LINE          PRINT THE RESULT
         B        EXIT                  ALL DONE
ENDDATA  PUT      PRINTER,ERROR         PRINT ERROR MESSAGE IF NO DATA
EXIT     ----                           STANDARD EXIT
         .
         .
         .
DATA     DS       0C                    DATA RECORD (80 CHARACTERS):
NUM1     DS       10C                     FIRST INTEGER (COLS. 1 - 10)
         DS       10C                     SPACER (COLS. 11 - 20)
NUM2     DS       10C                     SECOND INTEGER (COLS. 21 - 30)
         DS       50C                     REST OF RECORD (COLS. 31 - 80)
* LINE OF PRINT (81 CHARACTERS):
LINE     DC       C' THE SUM OF THE INTEGERS IS '
NUM3     DS       10C                   RESULT
         DC       43C' '                PAD TO 81 CHARACTERS
*
TEMP     DS       D                     WORK AREA FOR CONVERSIONS
ERROR    DC       C' MISSING DATA RECORD'  ERROR MESSAGE
         DC       61C' '                PAD TO 81 CHARACTERS
```

**Figure 5.29**
A program segment that reads 2 unsigned integers and prints their sum, as described in Example 18.

To convert the binary integer—regardless of sign—that is in Register 2 into an EBCDIC representation at NUM, you can write the following instructions:

**Instructions to convert binary integers to decimal integers in EBCDIC.**

```
         CVD    R2,TEMP              IF R2 = BINARY INTEGER,
         OI     TEMP+7,X'0F'
         UNPK   NUM(10),TEMP(8)      NUM = MAGNITUDE IN EBCDIC
         MVI    NUM,C' '             MAKE SIGN BLANK
         C      R2,=F'0'             IS BINARY INTEGER NEGATIVE?
         BNM    NN                   IF NOT, LEAVE BLANK FOR SIGN
         MVI    NUM,C'-'             IF SO, MAKE SIGN MINUS
NN       ----                        NUM = EBCDIC EQUIVALENT
```

There is room for only nine decimal digits at NUM. Thus, these instructions restrict the magnitude of the binary integer that Register 2 contains to one whose decimal equivalent contains nine or fewer digits.

## Case Study

### *Problem Statement*

**Determine the day of the week for a given date.**

If you have used an IBM PC, you know that the operating system asks you to enter the current date. Later, when the operating system reports the date, it includes the day of the week, even though you never entered that information.

This case study demonstrates one way that you can make such a determination. The algorithm used provides an exercise in binary integer arithmetic, and the program illustrates the use of literals and the I/O macro instructions.

### *Discussion*

The algorithm used by this program is called Zeller's congruence.[†] According to the definition of the algorithm, a date such as December 31, 1993 is first divided into four components:

$M$ is the month number, but one that is different than what you are used to. As illustrated in Figure 5.30, March is 1, April is 2, and so on to December, which is 10. The algorithm considers January and February as months 11 and 12 of the preceding year; thus, for these months, you must subtract 1 from the year before proceeding.

[†]Archibald, R. G. *An Introduction to the Theory of Numbers*, 264–266. Columbus, Ohio: Charles E. Merrill Publishing Company, 1970.

Gruenberger, F., and G. Jaffray. *Problems for Computer Solution.* New York: John Wiley & Sons, 1965.

Uspensky, J. V., and M. A. Heaslet. *Elementary Number Theory*, 206–211. New York: McGraw-Hill Book Company, 1939.

| Previous year | | Present year | | | | | | | | | |
|---|---|---|---|---|---|---|---|---|---|---|---|
| Jan | Feb | Mar | Apr | May | Jun | Jul | Aug | Sep | Oct | Nov | Dec |
| 11 | 12 | 1 | 2 | 3 | 4 | 5 | 6 | 7 | 8 | 9 | 10 |

**Figure 5.30**
The month numbers for Zeller's congruence.

$D$ is the day of the month, as you are used to.
$C$ is equal to the first two digits of the year.
$Y$ is equal to the last two digits of the year.

For example, December 31, 1993 is represented by

$M = 10$
$D = 31$
$C = 19$
$Y = 93$

January 2, 1800 is represented by

$M = 11$
$D = 2$
$C = 17$
$Y = 99$

(Since the month is January, you consider the previous year 1799.) To continue Zeller's congruence, you would compute

$$F = [(26 * M - 2)/10] + D + Y + [Y/4] + [C/4] - 2 * C$$

where the square brackets indicate that any remainders after division are discarded. You would then compute

$$W = F \pmod 7$$

as follows: First, divide $F$ by 7 and save the remainder. Since it is possible for $F$ to be negative, the remainder will not always be positive. If the remainder is greater than or equal to zero, then it is the value of $W$. If the remainder is less than zero, add 7 to the remainder to obtain $W$.

$W$ represents the day of the week of the given date: $W = 0$ indicates a Sunday, $W = 1$ indicates a Monday, and so on.

---

EXAMPLE 19

The computation for December 31, 1993 is given in Figure 5.31 and proceeds as follows: Since $M = 10$, $26 * M - 2$ is 258. Divide by 10 and ignore the remainder; the result is 25. Add 31 for $D$ and 93 for $Y$. Then $[Y/4]$ is 23 and, since $C$ is 19, $[C/4]$ is 4 and $-2 * C$ is $-38$. Add these results to get $F$, which is 138. Divide $F$ by 7 and retain the remainder 5. This number is $W$ and represents Friday.

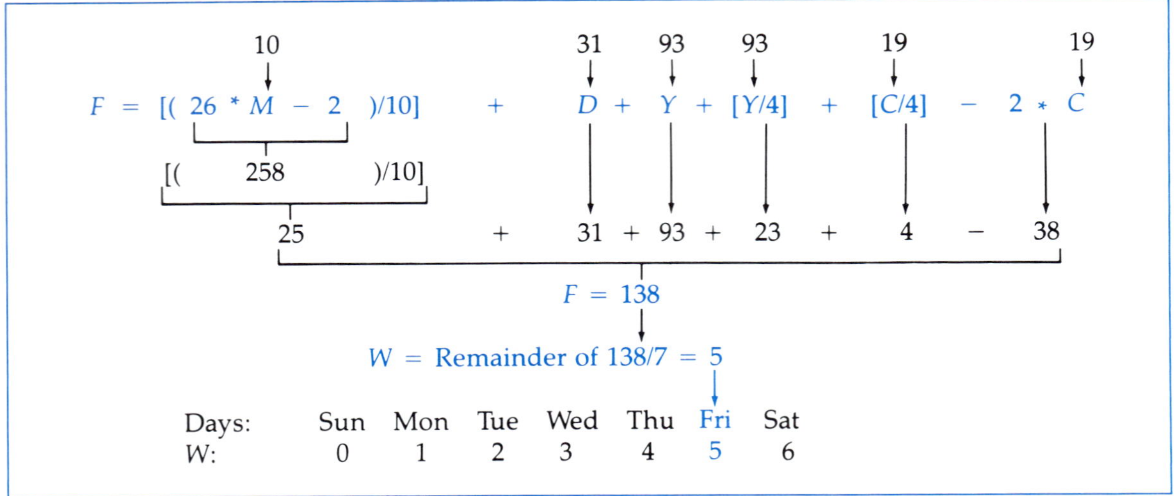


**Figure 5.31**
The computation for December 31, 1993.

*Implementation of the Algorithm.* Assume that *MONTH, DAY,* and *YEAR* do not represent the date as in the algorithm, but in the conventional way. For December 31, 1993 (12/31/1993), $MONTH = 12$, $DAY = 31$, and $YEAR = 1993$. Note that the required value of *M* is 10, which is equal to $MONTH - 2$. For most months, this equation will work; but for January and February, $MONTH - 2$ is less than or equal to zero. In such cases, adding 12 will give the required value of *M*, as illustrated in Figure 5.32.

The pseudocode in Figure 5.33 and the flowchart in Figure 5.34 describe the required algorithm. Figure 5.35 lists the assembler language program.

**Figure 5.32**
The calculation of *M* from *MONTH.*

| *MONTH* | | *MONTH − 2* | | *M* |
|---|---|---|---|---|
| Jan: | 1 | −1 | Add 12 | 11 |
| Feb: | 2 | 0 | | 12 |
| Mar: | 3 | 1 | Leave as is | 1 |
| Apr: | 4 | 2 | | 2 |
| May: | 5 | 3 | | 3 |
| Jun: | 6 | 4 | | 4 |
| Jul: | 7 | 5 | | 5 |
| Aug: | 8 | 6 | | 6 |
| Sep: | 9 | 7 | | 7 |
| Oct: | 10 | 8 | | 8 |
| Nov: | 11 | 9 | | 9 |
| Dec: | 12 | 10 | | 10 |

**Figure 5.33**
The pseudocode solution for Zeller's congruence.

```
D := DAY
M := MONTH - 2
IF M ≤ 0 THEN
    M := M + 12
    YEAR := YEAR - 1
END IF
C := quotient of YEAR / 100
Y := remainder of YEAR / 100
F := [(26 * M - 2) / 10] + D + Y + [Y / 4] + [C / 4] - 2 * C
W := remainder of F / 7
IF W < 0 THEN
    W := W + 7
END IF
```

## Debugging Hints

1. Remember that you cannot use Register 0 as an index register. An attempt to do so by specifying 0 for *X2* is interpreted as the absence of an index register. The assembler will not issue an error message.
2. Remember that the Multiply instruction destroys the contents of the even register. Be particularly careful of this when you are multiplying small numbers: since you would anticipate a product that easily fits into one register, you may forget that the even register is also affected by the instruction.
3. Failure to initialize the even register prior to a Divide instruction can lead to a fixed-point divide exception or, worse, incorrect results without any error message. Since the Divide instruction assumes that the even register contains the high-order portion of the dividend, failure to load the even register will almost certainly make the presumed dividend incorrect. The magnitude of the presumed dividend might be large enough to produce a quotient that exceeds 32-bits, which results in a fixed-point divide exception. If the quotient does not exceed 32 bits, it will almost certainly be incorrect without warning.
4. The macro instructions that you use for I/O generally alter the contents of Registers 0, 1, 14, and 15. Therefore, you must plan carefully the use of these registers.

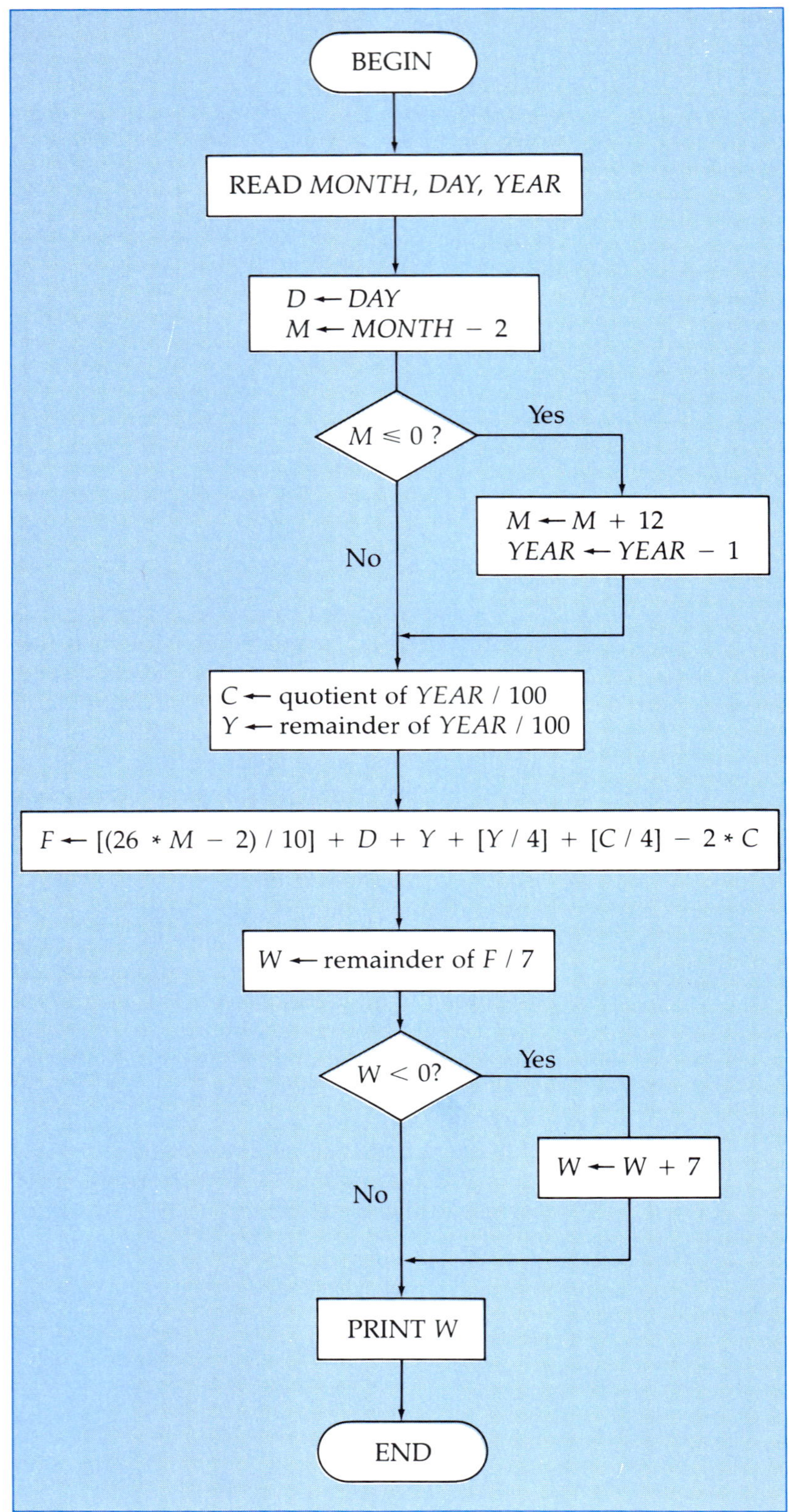


**Figure 5.34** A flowchart for Zeller's congruence.

```
         ZELLER'S CONGRUENCE

  LOC  OBJECT CODE    ADDR1 ADDR2  STMT   SOURCE STATEMENT
000000                                2 ZELLER    CSECT
                                      3           PRINT NOGEN             SUPPRESS MACRO EXPANSIONS
                                      4 **************************************************************
                                      5 **
                                      6 **                    ZELLER'S CONGRUENCE
                                      7 **
                                      8 ** THIS PROGRAM COMPUTES THE DAY OF THE WEEK FOR ANY GIVEN DATE
                                      9 ** BY USING ZELLER'S CONGRUENCE:
                                     10 **    M = MONTH: MARCH = 1, APRIL = 2, ..., DECEMBER = 10
                                     11 **        JANUARY & FEBRUARY ARE 11 AND 12 OF THE PRECEDING
                                     12 **        YEAR.
                                     13 **    D = DAY OF THE MONTH
                                     14 **    C = FIRST 2 DIGITS OF YEAR (ADJUSTED IF JAN. & FEB.)
                                     15 **    Y = LAST 2 DIGITS OF YEAR
                                     16 **    F = (26*M-2)/10 + D + Y + Y/4 + C/4 - 2*C
                                     17 **        ALL DIVISIONS ARE TRUNCATED TO AN INTEGER. IT IS
                                     18 **        POSSIBLE FOR F TO BE NEGATIVE.
                                     19 **    W = F(MOD 7) WILL DENOTE THE RESULTANT DAY OF THE
                                     20 **        WEEK (0 = SUN, 1 = MON, ... , 6 = SAT)
                                     21 **
                                     22 ** INPUT:  MONTH, DAY, AND YEAR.  EACH IS A NUMBER THAT IS
                                     23 **         RIGHT-JUSTIFIED IN A FIELD OF 10 CHARACTERS.  THESE
                                     24 **         3 FIELDS ARE ADJACENT TO EACH OTHER ON ONE RECORD.
                                     25 ** OUTPUT: THE VALUE OF W.
                                     26 **
                                     27 **************************************************************
                                     28 *
                                     29 ** REGISTER DEFINITIONS:
                         00002       30 R2        EQU   2                             EVEN/
                         00003       31 R3        EQU   3     M                            ODD PAIR
                         00004       32 R4        EQU   4     Y = LAST 2 DIGITS OF YEAR.  EVEN/
                         00005       33 R5        EQU   5     C = FIRST 2 DIGITS OF YEAR.  ODD PAIR
                         00006       34 R6        EQU   6                             EVEN/
                         00007       35 R7        EQU   7                                  ODD PAIR
                         00008       36 R8        EQU   8     W                       EVEN/
                         00009       37 R9        EQU   9     F                            ODD PAIR
                         0000C       38 R12       EQU   12               BASE REGISTER
                         0000D       39 R13       EQU   13               SAVE AREA POINTER
                         0000E       40 R14       EQU   14               RETURN REGISTER (OS)
                                     41 ** STANDARD ENTRY AND INITIALIZATION:
                                     42 ** OS:
000000 90EC D00C    0000C            43           STM   R14,R12,12(R13)  SAVE REGISTERS
000004 05C0                          44           BALR  R12,0            LOAD BASE REGISTER
                         00006       45           USING BASE,R12         DECLARE BASE ADDRESS AND REGISTER
000006 50D0 C14E    00154            46 BASE      ST    R13,SAVE+4       SAVE R13
00000A 41D0 C14A    00150            47           LA    R13,SAVE         R13 = ADDRESS OF SAVE AREA
                                     48           OPEN  (READER,INPUT,PRINTER,OUTPUT)  PREPARE FOR I/O
                                     56 ** DOS*******
                                     57 *         BALR  R12,0            LOAD BASE REGISTER
                                     58 *         USING BASE,R12         DECLARE BASE ADDRESS AND REGISTER
                                     59 *BASE     LA    R13,SAVE         R13 = ADDRESS OF SAVE AREA
                                     60 *         OPEN  READER,PRINTER   PREPARE FOR I/O
                                     61 ******
                                     62 ** READ DATA:
                                     63           GET   READER,DATE      READ DATE
00002C F279 C142 C0D2 00148 000D8    68           PACK  TEMP(8),NUM1(10) CONVERT MONTH
000032 4F30 C142    00148            69           CVB   R3,TEMP            TO BINARY
000036 F279 C142 C0DC 00148 000E2    70           PACK  TEMP(8),NUM2(10) CONVERT DAY
00003C 4F50 C142    00148            71           CVB   R5,TEMP            TO BINARY
000040 5050 C122    00128            72           ST    R5,DAY           SAVE DAY FOR LATER
000044 F279 C142 C0E6 00148 000EC    73           PACK  TEMP(8),NUM3(10) CONVERT YEAR
00004A 4F50 C142    00148            74           CVB   R5,TEMP            TO BINARY
```

*(Continues)*

**Figure 5.35** The program to determine the day of the week by using Zeller's congruence.

```
                                 ** DEFINE M FROM MONTH INFORMATION, AND ADJUST YEAR IF JAN. OR FEB.:
                                 *
                                 * M = MONTH - 2
                                 *
00004E 5B30 C252       00258              S      R3,=F'2'          RESULT IS -1 IF JAN., 0 IF FEB.,
                                 *                                   1 IF MAR.,...,10 IF DEC.
                                 * IF M <= 0 THEN
                                 * - M = M + 12
                                 * - YEAR = YEAR - 1
                                 *
000052 4720 C058       0005E              BH     SKIP              IF > 0, M IS OK;
000056 5A30 C256       0025C              A      R3,=F'12'         OTHERWISE ADJUST SO JAN=11, FEB=12
00005A 5B50 C25A       00260              S      R5,=F'1'          AND CONSIDER PREVIOUS YEAR
                                 * END IF
                                 *
                                 ** DIVIDE YEAR INTO C AND Y:
                                 *   C = QUOTIENT OF YEAR/100
                                 *   Y = REMAINDER OF YEAR/100
                                 *
00005E 1B44                      SKIP     SR     R4,R4             CLEAR EVEN REG. FOR DIVIDE
000060 5D40 C25E       00264              D      R4,=F'100'        SPLIT YEAR INTO Y AND C
                                 *
                                 ** F = (26*M-2)/10 + D + Y + Y/4 + C/4 - 2*C COMPUTED IN R9:
                                 *
                                 * COMPUTE FIRST TERM (26*M-2)/10. DISCARD REMAINDER, RESULT IS IN R3.
                                 *
000064 5C20 C262       00268              M      R2,=F'26'         26*M WILL BE IN R3
000068 5B30 C252       00258              S      R3,=F'2'          26*M - 2
00006C 5D20 C266       0026C              D      R2,=F'10'         (26*M - 2)/10
                                 *                                   (EVEN REG. WAS ZEROED BY MULTIPLY)
000070 1893                               LR     R9,R3             PLACE FIRST TERM IN R9
                                 *
                                 * ADD D + Y - 2*C:
000072 5A90 C122       00128              A      R9,DAY            ADD D (D AND DAY ARE EQUIVALENT)
000076 1A94                               AR     R9,R4             ADD Y
000078 1B95                               SR     R9,R5             SUBTRACT C TWICE
00007A 1B95                               SR     R9,R5
                                 *
                                 * ADD Y/4 + C/4
                                 *
00007C 1874                               LR     R7,R4             GET Y
00007E 1B66                               SR     R6,R6             PREPARE FOR DIVIDE
000080 5D60 C26A       00270              D      R6,=F'4'          Y/4 IS IN R7
000084 1A97                               AR     R9,R7             ADD Y/4 TO ACCUMULATOR
000086 1B44                               SR     R4,R4             PREPARE FOR DIVIDE
000088 5D40 C26A       00270              D      R4,=F'4'          C/4 IS IN R5
00008C 1A95                               AR     R9,R5             ADD C/4 TO ACCUMULATOR
                                 *
                                 ** COMPUTE W = F(MOD 7):
                                 *
                                 * FIRST COMPUTE W = REMAINDER OF F/7
                                 *
00008E 5C80 C25A       00260              M      R8,=F'1'          PREPARE FOR DIVIDE, NOTE: F CAN
                                 *                                   BE NEGATIVE.
000092 5D80 C26E       00274              D      R8,=F'7'          REMAINDER WILL BE IN R8
                                 *
                                 * IF W < 0
                                 *
000096 5980 C272       00278              C      R8,=F'0'          CHECK SIGN OF REMAINDER
00009A 47B0 C09C       000A2              BNL    STORE             IF POSITIVE, WE'RE DONE
                                 *
                                 * - THEN W = W + 7
                                 *
00009E 5A80 C26E       00274              A      R8,=F'7'          IF NEG., ADD 7 TO FINISH MODULO
                                 *
                                 * END IF
```

*(Continues)*

**Figure 5.35** *(Continued)*

```
                                       141 *
0000A2 4E80 C142      00148            142 STORE    CVD   R8,TEMP            CONVERT AND
0000A6 960F C149      0014F            143          OI    TEMP+7,X'0F'         STORE DAY OF
0000AA F397 C133 C142 00139 00148      144          UNPK  W(10),TEMP(8)          WEEK (W)
                                       145          PUT   PRINTER,RESULT     PRINT W
                                       150 *
                                       151 ** STANDARD EXIT
                                       152 ** OS:
                                       153 ENDDATA  CLOSE (READER,,PRINTER) I/O IS COMPLETE
0000CE 58D0 C14E      00154            161          L     R13,SAVE+4         RESTORE R13
0000D2 98EC D00C      0000C            162          LM    R14,R12,12(R13)    RESTORE REMAINING REGISTERS
0000D6 07FE                            163          BR    R14                RETURN TO OS
                                       164 ** DOS*******
                                       165 *ENDDATA CLOSE READER,PRINTER     I/O IS COMPLETE
                                       166 *        EOJ                      RETURN TO DOS
                                       167 ******
                                       168 ** INPUT AND INPUT AREAS:
0000D8                                 169 DATE     DS    80C                INPUT RECORD:
                                000D8  170 NUM1     EQU   DATE                 MONTH
                                000E2  171 NUM2     EQU   DATE+10              DAY
                                000EC  172 NUM3     EQU   DATE+20              YEAR
000128                                 173 DAY      DS    F                  WORK AREA FOR DAY
00012C 40E3C8C540C4C1E8                174 RESULT   DC    C' THE DAY IS: '   OUTPUT LABEL
000139                                 175 W        DS    10C                CODE FOR DAY OF WEEK
000148                                 176 TEMP     DS    D                  WORK AREA FOR CONVERSIONS
000150                                 177 SAVE     DS    18F                SAVE AREA (9D IN DOS)
                                       178 *
                                       179 ** DCB'S FOR I/O:
                                       180 READER   DCB   DSORG=PS,MACRF=GM,DDNAME=SYSIN,RECFM=F,LRECL=80,         X
                                                          BLKSIZE=80,EODAD=ENDDATA
                                       234 PRINTER  DCB   DSORG=PS,MACRF=PM,DDNAME=SYSPRINT,RECFM=FA,LRECL=23,     X
                                                          BLKSIZE=23
                                       288 ** DOS*******
                                       289 ** DTF'S FOR I/O:
                                       290 *READER  DTFCD DEVADDR=SYSIPT,DEVICE=2540,IOAREA1=INBUF,RECFORM=FIXUNB,X
                                                          BLKSIZE=80,TYPEFLE=INPUT,WORKA=YES,EOFADDR=ENDDATA
                                       291 *PRINTER DTFPR DEVADDR=SYSLST,DEVICE=3203,IOAREA1=OUTBUF,WORKA=YES,     X
                                                          RECFORM=FIXUNB,BLKSIZE=23,CTLCHAR=ASA
                                       292 *INBUF   DS    80C
                                       293 *OUTBUF  DS    23C
000000                                 294          END   ZELLER
000258 00000002                        295                =F'2'
00025C 0000000C                        296                =F'12'
000260 00000001                        297                =F'1'
000264 00000064                        298                =F'100'
000268 0000001A                        299                =F'26'
00026C 0000000A                        300                =F'10'
000270 00000004                        301                =F'4'
000274 00000007                        302                =F'7'
000278 00000000                        303                =F'0'

                                  CROSS-REFERENCE

SYMBOL    LEN   VALUE    DEFN    REFERENCES

BASE     00004 00000006 00046  00045
DATE     00001 000000D8 00169  00065 00170 00171 00172
DAY      00004 00000128 00173  00072 00108
NUM1     00001 000000D8 00170  00068
NUM2     00001 000000E2 00171  00070
NUM3     00001 000000EC 00172  00073
PRINTER  00004 000001F8 00238  00054 00146 00159
READER   00004 00000198 00184  00052 00064 00157
RESULT   00013 0000012C 00174  00147
```

(*Continues*)

**Figure 5.35** (*Continued*)

```
R12       00001 0000000C 00038  00043 00044 00045 00162
R13       00001 0000000D 00039  00043 00046 00047 00161 00162
R14       00001 0000000E 00040  00043 00162 00163
R2        00001 00000002 00030  00101 00103
R3        00001 00000003 00031  00069 00079 00086 00102 00105
R4        00001 00000004 00032  00094 00094 00095 00109 00115 00119 00119 00120
R5        00001 00000005 00033  00071 00072 00074 00087 00110 00111 00121
R6        00001 00000006 00034  00116 00116 00117
R7        00001 00000007 00035  00115 00118
R8        00001 00000008 00036  00127 00129 00133 00138 00142
R9        00001 00000009 00037  00105 00108 00109 00110 00111 00118 00121
SAVE      00004 00000150 00177  00046 00047 00161
SKIP      00002 0000005E 00094  00085
STORE     00004 000000A2 00142  00134
TEMP      00008 00000148 00176  00068 00069 00070 00071 00073 00074 00142 00143 00144
W         00001 00000139 00175  00144
ZELLER    00001 00000000 00002  00294
                                                       LITERAL CROSS-REFERENCE


SYMBOL    LEN   VALUE    DEFN    REFERENCES

=F'2'     00004 00000258 00295  00079 00102
=F'12'    00004 0000025C 00296  00086
=F'1'     00004 00000260 00297  00087 00127
=F'100'   00004 00000264 00298  00095
=F'26'    00004 00000268 00299  00101
=F'10'    00004 0000026C 00300  00103
=F'4'     00004 00000270 00301  00117 00120
=F'7'     00004 00000274 00302  00129 00138
=F'0'     00004 00000278 00303  00133
                                                       ASSEMBLER DIAGNOSTICS AND STATISTICS


NO STATEMENTS FLAGGED IN THIS ASSEMBLY
HIGHEST SEVERITY WAS    0
OPTIONS FOR THIS ASSEMBLY
  ALIGN, ALOGIC, BUFSIZE(STD), NODECK, ESD, FLAG(0), LINECOUNT(55), LIST, NOMCALL, YFLAG, WORKSIZE(2097152)
  NOMLOGIC, NONUMBER, OBJECT, NORENT, RLD, NOSTMT, NOLIBMAC, NOTERMINAL, NOTEST, XREF(SHORT)
  SYSPARM()
WORK FILE BUFFER SIZE/NUMBER =10750/ 1
TOTAL RECORDS READ FROM SYSTEM INPUT        170
TOTAL RECORDS READ FROM SYSTEM LIBRARY     3408
TOTAL RECORDS PUNCHED                        13
TOTAL RECORDS PRINTED                       248

                                                          VS LOADER

OPTIONS USED - PRINT,MAP,LET,NOCALL,NORES,NOTERM,SIZE=98304,NAME=**GO


     NAME   TYPE   ADDR         NAME   TYPE   ADDR         NAME   TYPE   ADDR         NAME   TYPE   ADDR         NAME   TYPE   ADDR

  ZELLER      SD   EC010

  TOTAL LENGTH       280
  ENTRY ADDRESS    EC010


THE DAY IS: 0000000005 <---- Output from program
```

**Figure 5.35** *(continued)*

## Stylistic Notes

1. Do not complicate a program's logic by writing sequences such as the following:

```
                BE      LABEL1
                B       LABEL2
LABEL1          ----
```

   Instead, write the following:

```
                BNE     LABEL2
LABEL1          ----
```

2. Do not initialize the even register prior to a Multiply instruction. Such a step is superfluous since the prior contents of the even register will not participate in the operation.
3. Generally, use literals instead of a DC to define constants. Literals are easy to use and have obvious meanings. However, be sure that you intend for such quantities to remain constant throughout program execution.
4. Sometimes it is better to use a DC rather than a literal to define a constant. Before choosing a technique, determine the likelihood that you will change your mind about the value of the constant during the programming process. If there are parameters with tentative values that are referenced many times within the program, then you should define them with the DC directive. If you change your mind about a particular value, it will be easier for you to change a single DC, rather than change all of the references to that value, which would be necessary had you used a literal. It is also better to define lengthy constants, especially if they are referenced often, with a DC than a literal. Typing a lengthy literal again and again is not only tedious, but, more importantly, is prone to error.
5. Use comments to indicate clearly whether a DC directive defines a constant or an initial value. Where you use several of each type, consider grouping them if possible. This can help you to avoid making an accidental reference to an initial value at a point after that value has been changed.
6. Distinguish between initialization at assembly time and initialization during execution. It is often a good idea to initialize storage at execution time, rather than at assembly time. However, some people reserve and initialize all storage by using DCs instead of DSs as a debugging aid. The next chapter will elaborate on this practice.

## Summary

1. The condition code is a 2-bit binary quantity within the PSW. Certain instructions, including Add, Subtract, and Compare, set the value of the condition code. Unless an instruction explicitly changes the condition code, its value remains unchanged.
2. The Branch on Condition instructions or the equivalent extended mnemonic operations can test the condition code without changing it. You use these instructions both to alter the sequential flow of execution and to program loops.
3. Index registers can be used to process arrays.

4. Each Multiply instruction multiplies two 32-bit integers and forms a 64-bit product, which is placed into an even-odd register pair.
5. Overflow cannot occur during multiplication.
6. The Multiply instructions do not indicate when a product exceeds 32 bits. You must write separate instructions to determine if the 64-bit product can be represented correctly by its low-order 32 bits.
7. The Divide instructions use an even-odd register pair to represent the 64-bit dividend prior to the division. The divisor, the quotient, and the remainder are each 32-bit integers.
8. A fixed-point divide exception will occur if either of the following occurs:
   a. You attempt a division by zero.
   b. Or, you attempt a division whose quotient would exceed 32 bits.

   In either case, the division does not occur.
9. The Multiply and Divide instructions do not change the condition code.
10. An assembly-time error message or a specification exception will occur if the first operand of a Multiply or Divide instruction is not an even-numbered register.
11. Literals provide a convenient way to define constants.
12. Adhere to the following stylistic points:
    a. Begin the program with a TITLE and a prologue.
    b. Define symbolic register names.
    c. Choose mnemonic symbols.
    d. Divide the program into sections.
    e. Indicate the program's structure.
    f. Use meaningful remarks.
13. One-byte codes represent characters. IBM uses EBCDIC, but non-IBM I/O devices use ASCII. You can define character strings with a DC or with a literal, by using C-type constants.
14. You can use system macro instructions to perform I/O in assembler language programs. However, programs that use system macro instructions require that you use the standard entry and the standard exit conventions. Character I/O requires that you convert between EBCDIC and two's complement binary representations whenever you perform binary integer arithmetic.

## New Instruction Summary

| Operation | Operand | Format | Instruction Name | Action |
|---|---|---|---|---|
| **CR** | *R1,R2* | RR | COMPARE REGISTERS | Compares C(*R1*) with C(*R2*)<br>Condition code = $\begin{cases} 0 \text{ if } C(R1) = C(R2) \\ 1 \text{ if } C(R1) < C(R2) \\ 2 \text{ if } C(R1) > C(R2) \end{cases}$ |
| **C** | *R1,S2*<br>or *R1,S2(X2)*<br>or *R1,D2(X2,B2)* | RX | COMPARE | Compares C(*R1*) with $C(E2)_{0\text{-}31}$<br>Condition code = $\begin{cases} 0 \text{ if } C(R1) = C(E2)_{0\text{-}31} \\ 1 \text{ if } C(R1) < C(E2)_{0\text{-}31} \\ 2 \text{ if } C(R1) > C(E2)_{0\text{-}31} \end{cases}$ |
| **BCR** | *M1,R2* | RR | BRANCH ON CONDITION | If the condition code is as specified by *M1*, branches to the address in *R2*; if not, sequences. Does not branch if *R2* = 0. |
| **BC** | *M1,S2*<br>or *M1,S2(X2)*<br>or *M1,D2(X2,B2)* | RX | BRANCH ON CONDITION | If the condition code is as specified by *M1*, branches to the effective address *E2*; if not, sequences. |
| **MR** | *R1,R2* | RR | MULTIPLY REGISTERS | $C(R1,R1+1) \leftarrow C(R1+1) * C(R2)$ |
| **M** | *R1,S2*<br>or *R1,S2(X2)*<br>or *R1,D2(X2,B2)* | RX | MULTIPLY | $C(R1,R1+1) \leftarrow C(R1+1) * C(E2)_{0\text{-}31}$ |

| Operation | Operand | Format | Instruction Name | Action |
|---|---|---|---|---|
| **DR** | *R1,R2* | RR | DIVIDE REGISTERS | C(*R1*+1) ← Quotient of C(*R1*,*R1*+1) ÷ C(*R2*)<br>C(*R1*) ← Remainder of C(*R1*,*R1*+1) ÷ C(*R2*) |
| **D** | *R1,S2*<br>or *R1,S2(X2)*<br>or *R1,D2(X2,B2)* | RX | DIVIDE | C(*R1*+1) ← Quotient of C(*R1*,*R1*+1) ÷ $C(E2)_{0\text{-}31}$<br>C(*R1*) ← Remainder of C(*R1*,*R1*+1) ÷ $C(E2)_{0\text{-}31}$ |

## New Constant Type with DC and DS Directives

| Operation | Operand | Action |
|---|---|---|
| **DC** | *d*C'*c*' | Defines an array of 1-byte EBCDIC codes, 1 code per character, as specified by the constant *c*. No boundary alignment occurs. (You can use this constant type in a literal of the form =*d*C'*c*'.) |
| **DS** | *d*C | Reserves *d* bytes without boundary alignment. |

## Exercises

1. What is the condition code after each of the following instructions is executed? Assume that Registers 6 and 7 are as indicated before the execution of each instruction.

   Reg. 6 = 000000AB  Reg. 7 = 88000000

   | | | | | | |
   |---|---|---|---|---|---|
   | **a.** | AR | 6,7 | **f.** | CR | 7,6 |
   | **b.** | AR | 7,6 | **g.** | CR | 6,7 |
   | **c.** | AR | 7,7 | **h.** | BR | 14 |
   | **d.** | SR | 7,6 | **i.** | MR | 6,7 |
   | **e.** | LR | 2,6 | **j.** | DR | 6,7 |

2. Consider the following instruction sequence:

   ```
   C      2,X
   BC     MASK,LOOP
   ```

   **a.** What two hex values can each be equated to MASK so that a branch to LOOP will occur when the comparison is one of the following?
   i) not equal
   ii) less than or equal to
   iii) greater than

   **b.** What extended mnemonic instruction can replace BC in each case of Exercise 2a?

3. Consider the following instruction sequence:

   ```
   A      2,Y
   BC     MASK,AHEAD
   ```

   **a.** What hex value must be equated to MASK so that a branch to AHEAD will occur when the results of the addition are one of the following?
   i) Negative or incorrect due to overflow.
   ii) Negative or positive.
   iii) Zero or positive.
   iv) Zero, negative, or incorrect due to overflow.
   v) Correct.

   **b.** For each case of Exercise 3a, replace the BC instruction by one or two extended mnemonic instructions.

4. Assume that R2 and R3 are registers, and that X and Y are fullwords in storage. In the following pseudocode segments, these symbols represent the contents of the relevant registers or fullwords. Write an equivalent sequence of assembler language instructions for each of the following pseudocode segments:

   **a.** IF X < Y
   THEN X := X − Y
   END IF

   **b.** IF R2 ≥ X
   THEN R2 := 0
   END IF

   **c.** IF R2 < 0
   THEN R3 := 1
   ELSE R3 := −1
   END IF

5. Assume that R2 is a register, and that X, Y, and Z are fullword integers. Write a sequence of assembler language instructions to perform each of the following tasks:
   a. Load R2 with the larger of X and Y.
   b. Load R2 with the largest of X, Y, and Z.
   c. Load R2 with the absolute value of X.
   d. Branch to ZERO if the contents of R2 are zero, branch to NEG if they are negative, and sequence if they are positive.

6. Replace each of the following by a single instruction:

a.
```
         BNZ   SKIP
         B     OUT
SKIP     -----
```

b.
```
         BL    SKIP
         BH    OUT
SKIP     -----
```

c.
```
         BNH   TEST
         B     SKIP
TEST     BE    OUT
SKIP     -----
```

7. The segment

```
         L     R2,X
         S     R2,Y
         BP    ACTION2
         BM    ACTION3
ACTION1  -----
```

was intended to implement the following pseudocode:

IF X = Y THEN action 1
IF X > Y THEN action 2
IF X < Y THEN action 3

However, the segment does not always work correctly. Explain.

8. What are the results after each of the following instructions is executed? Assume that Registers 6 through 9, and the fullwords at X and Y are as indicated before the execution of each instruction.

| | | | |
|---|---|---|---|
| Reg. 6 | = 00000001 | Reg. 9 | = 88000000 |
| Reg. 7 | = 000000AB | X | = FFFFFFFE |
| Reg. 8 | = F0000000 | Y | = 00000002 |

a. `M 6,X` c. `M 8,X`
b. `M 6,Y` d. `M 8,Y`

9. What are the results after each of the following instructions is executed? Assume that Registers 4 through 9, and the fullwords at X and Y are as indicated before the execution of each instruction.

| | | | |
|---|---|---|---|
| Reg. 4 | = 00000000 | Reg. 8 | = 00000001 |
| Reg. 5 | = 0000000E | Reg. 9 | = 00000000 |
| Reg. 6 | = FFFFFFFF | X | = 00000004 |
| Reg. 7 | = FFFFFFEE | Y | = FFFFFFFC |

a. `D 4,X` d. `D 6,Y`
b. `D 4,Y` e. `D 8,X`
c. `D 6,X`

10. Assume that $n$ is an integer in Register 2. Write instructions to compute each of the following, and leave the results in a register.
    a. $n^3$
    b. $n^4$
    c. $n^5$
    d. $n^3 - n^2$

11. Assume that X, Y, and Z represent fullword integers. Write instructions to compute each of the following. Assume that products can be represented by 32 bits; ignore all remainders. In each case, store the result in the fullword RESULT.
    a. X + Y * Z
    b. (X + Y)/Z
    c. The sum of the remainders of X/2 and X/3
    d. X * (X − 1)/2
    e. $(X^2 + Y^2)/2$
    f. $(X^2 + 5 * X)/(Y + 3)$
    g. (X/2) * (Y/3)
    h. (X − Y) * (Y + 4)/(X * Y − 1)

12. Consider the Divide instruction. Suppose that the dividend can be represented in 32 bits and the divisor is nonzero. Is it possible for a fixed-point divide exception to occur? Explain your answer and illustrate it with examples.

## Programming Problems

*For the following programs, you can either define the given quantities with DCs and use SNAP or PDUMP to verify the results of the computations, or use macro instructions to perform I/O.*

1. Write an assembler language program to compute the number of negative integers in the array of N fullwords that is stored at Z.

2. Write an assembler language program to sort an array of N fullword integers that is stored at Z.

3. Given an array of N fullword integers stored at X, write an assembler language program to compute the array R such that its elements consist of the fullword integers in X, stored in the

reverse order: for example, if X = 8, −4, 0, 2, then R = 2, 0, −4, 8.

4. The Fibonacci sequence appears as follows:

0 1 1 2 3 5 8 13 21 34 55 . . .

Each term after the second term is the sum of the preceding 2 terms. Write a program to compute 15 terms of this sequence and store them in an array of fullwords.

5. An integer is called a **perfect square** when its square root is also an integer. Thus, 1, 4, 9, 16, 25, and 36 are the first 6 perfect squares. Note that these are simply the squares of the integers 1 through 6.

Write a program to compute the first 20 perfect squares and store them into an array of fullwords. Do this in two different ways, as follows:

**a.** Do not use the Multiply and Divide instructions and keep in mind the following observations. First, note that the differences between adjacent perfect squares

Perfect squares: 1 4 9 16 25 . . .

Differences: 3 5 7 9 . . .

are the odd integers. Thus, you can generate the perfect squares greater than 1 by adding consecutive odd integers:

1 + 3 = 4
1 + 3 + 5 = 9
1 + 3 + 5 + 7 = 16
1 + 3 + 5 + 7 + 9 = 25

**b.** Use the Multiply instruction. You can compute the desired perfect squares by squaring the integers 1 through 20.

6. Write an assembler language program to compute $n!$ for $n$ = 1, 2, and so on until $n!$ exceeds $2^{31} - 1$. Store the factorials into an array of fullwords.

7. Assume that Z is an array of N fullword integers. Write an assembler language program that implements the following pseudocode:

```
i := 0
REPEAT N times
    Qi := Quotient of Zi ÷ N
    Ri := Remainder of Zi ÷ N
    i := i + 1
END REPEAT
```

8. Write an assembler language program to compute $16^n$ for $n$ = 1, 2, and so on until $16^n$ exceeds $2^{31} - 1$. Store these values into an array of fullwords.

9. Repeat Programming Problem 8 by using 2 fullwords for each computed value. Compute until $16^n$ exceeds $2^{63} - 1$.

10. Given two arrays X and Y, each containing N fullword integers, write an assembler language program to compute $X_1 * Y_1 + X_2 * Y_2 + \ldots + X_N * Y_N$.

11. Two-dimensional arrays in FORTRAN are stored columnwise. For example, the elements of the M by N array X are defined as consecutive fullwords in the following order:

X(1,1); X(2,1); . . . X(M,1); X(1,2); X(2,2); . . . X(M,2); . . . X(1,N); X(2,N); . . . X(M,N)

Write an assembler language program to compute I and J such that X(I,J) is the first zero element that is encountered in storage beginning at X(1,1).

12. Write a program segment that uses *W* as computed by Zeller's congruence to print a message such as the following:

THE DAY IS FRI

# 6

# Debugging

CONTENTS



OVERVIEW

By using examples, this chapter demonstrates how you can find and correct assembly-time and execution-time errors. It describes the contents of the PSW and the information contained in a dump.

OBJECTIVES

After studying this chapter, you should be able to:

1. Determine the source of an assembly-time error, when given the error message produced by the assembler.
2. Determine by examining the corresponding object code if a particular syntactically correct assembler language statement performs the desired task.
3. In the event of a program interruption, determine by examining the dump the type of exception that caused the interruption; the address and length of the instruction that caused the interruption; and the value of the condition code and the contents of the program mask at the time of the interruption.
4. Debug your programs.

## Introduction

Although future chapters will contain debugging and antibugging hints, this chapter examines several examples that will help you develop a mindset for debugging assembler language programs. The chapter begins with syntax errors that generate misleading error messages or whose source is not obvious. Next, it considers execution-time errors and shows how a dump can provide clues that help you detect the error or errors. Dumps contain more information than simply the contents of the registers and storage. As an example, the contents of the PSW will be printed. This chapter will examine the general format of the PSW and show you how this knowledge is helpful.

By now, you should realize that debugging is an important skill for a programmer to have and, like other problem-solving skills, is one that is developed through practice. The examples provided here cannot possibly illustrate all of the errors that you will make in your present programs, but they include some common errors that were made by other novice assembler language programmers. However, you cannot acquire successful debugging skills by simply memorizing the examples in this chapter. Do not expect that comparing your problem with samples of error situations will enable you to recognize the source of your error quickly and easily. Only experience and a familiarity with many errors will give you the intuition that tells you where to begin your search.

Learn to ask the right questions. The examples in this chapter will demonstrate the thought process involved in each case. You will learn little about debugging by simply asking someone else to find your error. After doing so, even if you understand the source of your error, and even if this understanding helps make you less likely to make that error again, you will not have learned anything about debugging unless you understand the steps that the person used to locate the error. It is much easier for anyone, including your instructor, to locate and explain an error than it is to demonstrate exactly how the error was located. When your debugging efforts fail, by all means, seek help—but play an active role in understanding how the error is found. Asking the other person to explain each step in the debugging process can be helpful.

Note that the program listings in this chapter were produced under OS. However, the debugging concepts that this chapter describes and demonstrates apply also to DOS.

### A BUG IN THE MARK II

Bugs have plagued people for decades. Even Thomas Edison complained of a bug in his phonograph. Just like Mr. Edison, most students of programming quickly discover the necessity of debugging. However, one early debugging exercise did not involve a syntax error, but rather a real bug—the six-legged kind.

In the summer of 1945, Grace Murray Hopper and other researchers were working with the Mark II computer as part of the U.S. war effort. It was a hot summer, and often the windows of the aging Navy building were left open to improve the ventilation. One afternoon in early September, the Mark II stopped running. Hopper and her colleagues searched for the problem and found a relay that had failed. When they investigated further, they discovered a moth; it had flown in through an open window and made its way into the computer where it had been beaten to death by the relay.

In addition to its small revenge of temporarily stopping the Mark II, the insect gained a permanent place in computer history. The amused researchers extracted it with tweezers and taped it in their log book, carefully labeling it with the hour and minute of its discovery. Today, visitors to the Naval Museum in Dahlgren, Virginia can view "the first bug"—still taped to the log-book page of September 9, 1945.

## Examples of Assembly-Time Errors

Error messages that are produced by various assemblers range from helpful descriptions of the error to the all-inclusive *"Syntax Error."* Regardless of their level of usefulness, assembler error messages do not always point to the actual error. Remember that an assembler produces an error message when it first detects that something is amiss. The point at which this occurs in your program is not always at the source of the error, as the following examples demonstrate. A basic understanding of the assembly process will help to interpret these messages.

---

EXAMPLE 1

### An Example of an Addressability Error

The program in Figure 6.1 contains an **addressability error,** which the assembler discovered while translating the Store instruction. Notice that the assembler prints `*** ERROR ***` immediately after the Store instruction, but prints the error message after the source program. An addressability error means that the assembler cannot represent an implicitly designated address—SAVE+4, in this case—in a base-displacement form. In particular, a base address is not available that permits a displacement between 0 and 4095, which is the range imposed by this 12-bit quantity. In fact, the assembler has no base address at all because there is no USING statement. A BALR instruction alone is insufficient to establish a base register; USING

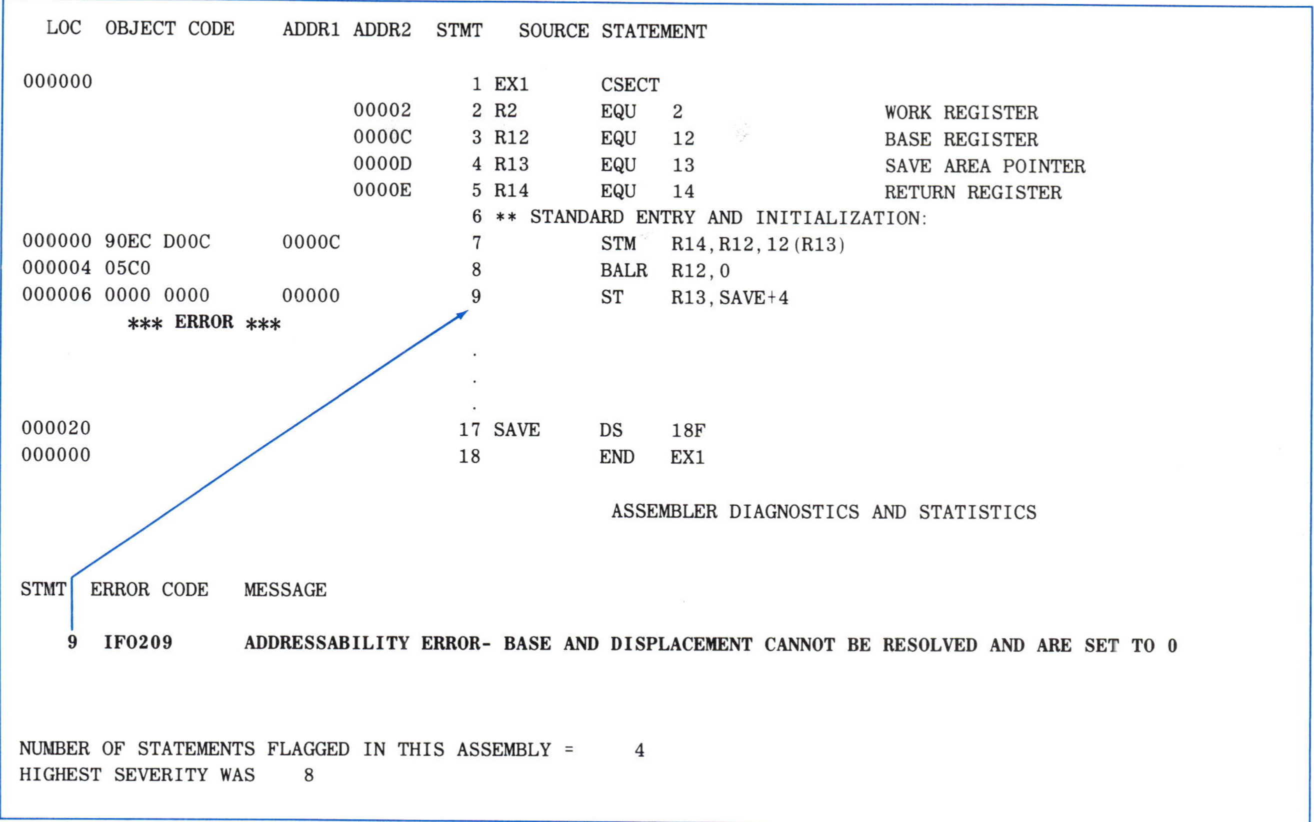

```
  LOC  OBJECT CODE    ADDR1 ADDR2  STMT   SOURCE STATEMENT

000000                                1 EX1      CSECT
                            00002     2 R2       EQU   2                 WORK REGISTER
                            0000C     3 R12      EQU   12                BASE REGISTER
                            0000D     4 R13      EQU   13                SAVE AREA POINTER
                            0000E     5 R14      EQU   14                RETURN REGISTER
                                      6 ** STANDARD ENTRY AND INITIALIZATION:
000000 90EC D00C      0000C           7          STM   R14,R12,12(R13)
000004 05C0                           8          BALR  R12,0
000006 0000 0000      00000           9          ST    R13,SAVE+4
        *** ERROR ***
                                      .
                                      .
                                      .
000020                               17 SAVE     DS    18F
000000                               18          END   EX1

                                          ASSEMBLER DIAGNOSTICS AND STATISTICS

STMT  ERROR CODE   MESSAGE

   9  IF0209       ADDRESSABILITY ERROR- BASE AND DISPLACEMENT CANNOT BE RESOLVED AND ARE SET TO 0


NUMBER OF STATEMENTS FLAGGED IN THIS ASSEMBLY =     4
HIGHEST SEVERITY WAS    8
```

**Figure 6.1**
A program that contains an addressability error, as described in Example 1.

must also be present. Note that, although the error message points to the Store instruction, it is not in error.

There are other sources of an addressability error. For example, if a correct USING statement existed in Figure 6.1, but if SAVE+4 was more than 4095 bytes beyond the base address, then the necessary displacement would be too large. This is the case for a program that contains large arrays or numerous instructions. However, this is unlikely to happen now, and further discussion of these sources of error will not occur until Chapter 12.

---

EXAMPLE 2

### Examples of Syntax Errors

Consider the errors in the program listed in Figure 6.2. The first error message implies that the second operand designation X in Statement 14 should not be a relocatable expression, but rather should be an absolute expression. Since X is defined with a DC, it is a relocatable symbol and, as such, is inappropriate to the RR form of the Multiply instruction. However, the problem is not X, but an incorrect mnemonic op code. The instruction should have been written with M instead of MR.

```
  LOC   OBJECT CODE     ADDR1 ADDR2  STMT    SOURCE STATEMENT

000000                                  1 EX2        CSECT
                              00002     2 R2         EQU   2
                              00003     3 R3         EQU   3
                              0000C     4 R12        EQU   12
                              0000D     5 R13        EQU   13
                              0000E     6 R14        EQU   14
                                        7 ** STANDARD ENTRY AND INITIALIZATION:
000000 90EC D00C        0000C           8            STM   R14,R12,12(R13)
000004 05C0                             9            BALR  R12,0
                              00006    10            USING BASE,R12
000006 50D0 C02E        00034          11 BASE       ST    R13,SAVE+4
00000A 41D0 C02A        00030          12            LA    R13,SAVE
00000E 5830 C072        00078          13            L     R3,=F'486'
000012 0000                            14            MR    R2,X
               *** ERROR ***
000014 0000 0000        00000          15            A     R3,W
               *** ERROR ***
000018 0000 0000        00000          16            ST    R3,Y
               *** ERROR ***
                                       17 ** STANDARD EXIT
00001C 58D0 C02E        00034          18            L     R13,SAVE+4
000020 98EC D00C        0000C          19            LM    R14,R12,12(R13)
000024 07FE                            20            BR    R14
                                       21 ***********************************************************************
                                          W          DC    F'18'

               *** ERROR ***
000026 0000
000028 FFFFFFF4                        22 X          DC    F'-12'
                                       23 Y          DX    F

               *** ERROR ***
00002C                                 24 BASE       DS    F
               *** ERROR ***
000030                                 25 SAVE       DS    18F
000000                                 26            END   EX2
000078 000001E6                        27                  =F'486'

                                       ASSEMBLER DIAGNOSTICS AND STATISTICS


STMT  ERROR CODE    MESSAGE

 14   IF0217        RELOCATABILITY ERROR NEAR OPERAND COLUMN 5
 15   IF0188        W IS AN UNDEFINED SYMBOL
 16   IF0188        Y IS AN UNDEFINED SYMBOL
 21   IF0026        CHARACTERS APPEAR BETWEEN THE BEGIN AND CONTINUE COLUMNS ON CONTINUATION CARD
 23   IF0078        UNDEFINED OP CODE
 24   IF0196        BASE HAS BEEN PREVIOUSLY DEFINED

NUMBER OF STATEMENTS FLAGGED IN THIS ASSEMBLY =      6
HIGHEST SEVERITY WAS   12
```

**Figure 6.2**
A program that contains several errors, as described in Example 2.

The second error message indicates that W in Statement 15 is an undefined symbol. However, W does appear in the name entry of the DC instruction that immediately follows Statement 21, which is a comments statement. Notice that no statement number labels the DC instruction. A closer look at the comments statement reveals that it contains 72 asterisks. A character such as an asterisk in column 72 indicates that the statement continues onto the next line. Thus, the assembler treats the definition of W as part of the comment, so W remains undefined. However, columns 1 to 15 of a continuation line must be blank: the error message that follows the DC instruction alerts you that these columns are not blank, and suggests that an error has been made.

The Store instruction in Statement 16 also contains an undefined symbol. The program did define Y, but used DX instead of DS when doing so. The last error message indicates that BASE has been defined more than once; it appears as the name entry of more than one statement.

## Program Interruptions

You know that certain execution-time errors can cause the CPU to suspend execution of your program and then give control to the operating system. As mentioned in Chapter 1, this suspension of execution is called an **interruption**. Interruptions that are caused by the execution of a user program are called **program interruptions**; the unusual conditions responsible for these interruptions are called **exceptions**. Each interruption corresponds to an **interruption code**, which is a 4-digit hex integer.

Although this chapter will show you where to find the interruption code, it is usually sufficient to determine the **completion code**, which Chapter 4 introduced. Figure 6.3 contains a complete list of completion codes and their causes. In all but one case, each completion code corresponds to one exception. However, any of several exceptions—each of which corresponds to a separate interruption code—can cause a completion code of 0C4. These exceptions involve an effective address that the CPU is unable to access for one of several reasons. One reason is that the effective address references a protected area of storage, which your program may not access.

**Figure 6.3** The completion codes and their causes.

| Completion code | Cause |
|---|---|
| 0C1 | Operation exception |
| 0C2 | Privileged operation exception |
| 0C3 | Execute exception |
| 0C4 | Invalid address |
| 0C5 | Addressing exception |
| 0C6 | Specification exception |
| 0C7 | Data exception |
| 0C8 | Fixed-point overflow exception |
| 0C9 | Fixed-point divide exception |
| 0CA | Decimal overflow exception |
| 0CB | Decimal divide exception |
| 0CC | Exponent overflow exception |
| 0CD | Exponent underflow exception |
| 0CE | Significance exception |
| 0CF | Floating-point divide exception |

Although the other reasons are beyond the scope of this text, the sources of a 0C4 error are the same: as Chapter 4 noted, these sources include insufficient storage for an array, incorrectly designated index registers or base registers, and incorrect index values or base addresses.

You can determine the address of the instruction that causes an interruption by examining the PSW and by knowing the instruction's length, which the CPU records as the **instruction length code (ILC)**. Usually, the instruction address (IA) portion of the PSW contains the address of the instruction that follows the one that caused the interruption. In this case, you can subtract the ILC from the IA to determine the address of the instruction that caused the interruption. However, the IA sometimes points directly to the instruction that caused the interruption. You can distinguish between these two possibilities of the IA by examining the interruption code. When the interruption code is either 0010 or 0011, the IA contains the address of the instruction that caused the interruption; in such cases, the ILC might be incorrect but, since you do not have to subtract the ILC from the IA, this error is usually of little consequence. When the interruption code is neither 0010 nor 0011, the IA contains the address of the instruction that follows the one that causes an interruption. Even though a full discussion of these facts is beyond the scope of this text, you can still debug many programs without knowing more about them. Note that, later, this chapter will show you the way to locate the PSW, the ILC, and the interruption code in a dump.

There are four exceptions that, at your option, need not cause a program interruption. They are the **fixed-point overflow**, **decimal overflow**, **exponent overflow**, and **significance exceptions**. A fixed-point overflow exception takes place if an overflow occurs during a binary integer addition or subtraction. If you want either to ignore the overflow or to test the condition code so that you can deal with the overflow yourself, then you would not want a program interruption to occur. You can ignore any of the four exceptions just given by using the **program mask**, which is 4 bits in the PSW. Each bit within this mask corresponds to one of the four exceptions. For example, the first bit in the program mask corresponds to fixed-point overflow exceptions. If this bit is 1, then a fixed-point overflow exception will cause a program interruption; if this bit is 0, the exception will not cause an interruption, and execution of your program will continue. In this latter case, the exception has been **masked off**. Similarly, you use the remaining bits in the program mask to affect the other exceptions, which will be explained later in this text. (Chapter 15 covers decimal overflow exceptions, and Chapter 17 describes both the exponent overflow and significance exceptions.)

By examining the PSW in a dump, you can determine the initial value of the program mask. You can change this value at any time by using the Set Program Mask (SPM) instruction, which will be defined in Chapter 8.

## The Anatomy of a Dump

You can find execution-time errors in an assembler language program by using the register and storage dumps that can occur. As a prelude to the next section, which will demonstrate the use of dumps in debugging, this section will examine the general form of dumps.

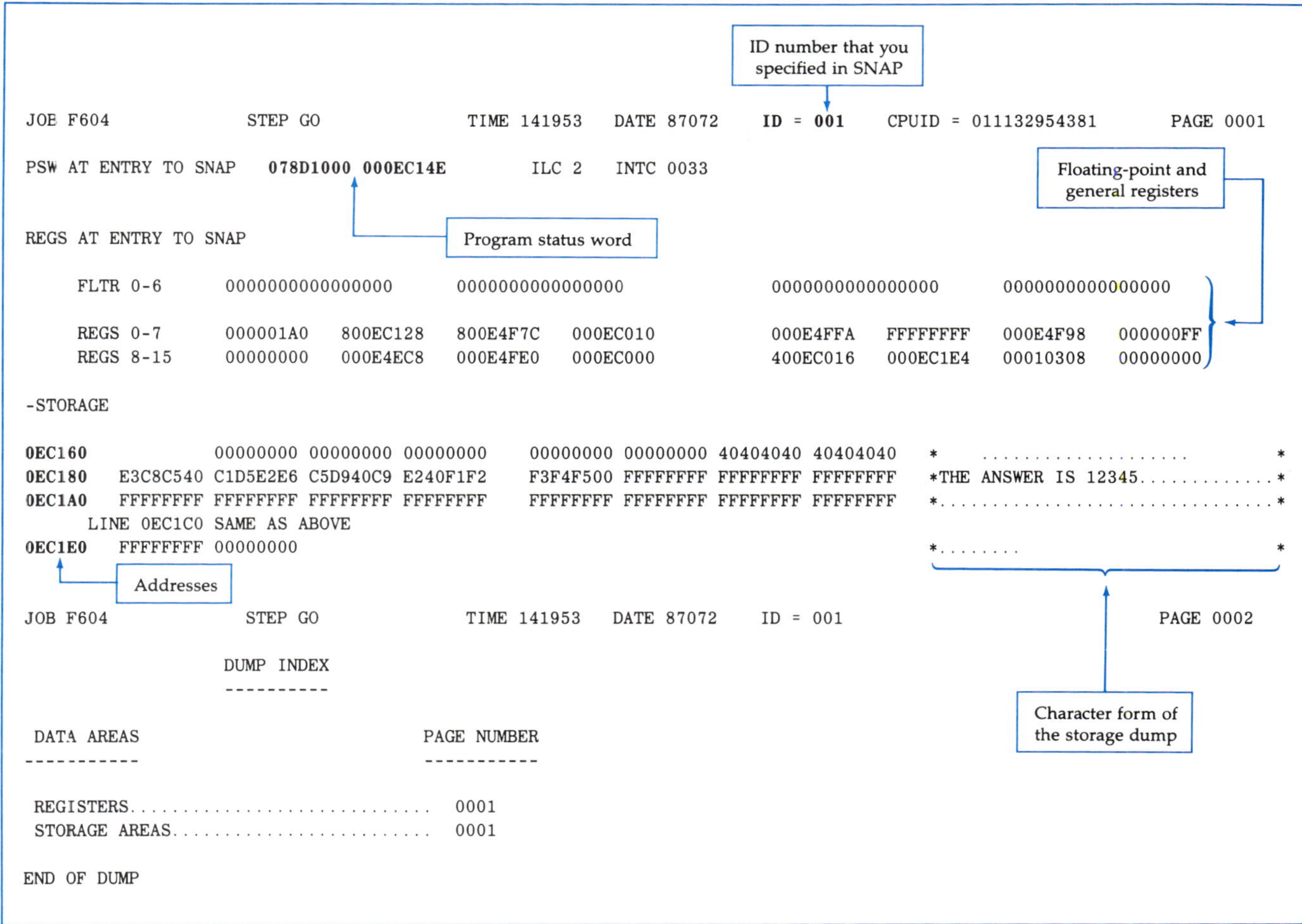

```
JOE F604            STEP GO             TIME 141953   DATE 87072    ID = 001    CPUID = 011132954381        PAGE 0001

PSW AT ENTRY TO SNAP    078D1000 000EC14E        ILC 2    INTC 0033

REGS AT ENTRY TO SNAP

     FLTR 0-6      0000000000000000     0000000000000000          0000000000000000     0000000000000000

     REGS 0-7      000001A0   800EC128   800E4F7C   000EC010        000E4FFA   FFFFFFFF   000E4F98   000000FF
     REGS 8-15     00000000   000E4EC8   000E4FE0   000EC000        400EC016   000EC1E4   00010308   00000000

-STORAGE

0EC160              00000000 00000000 00000000    00000000 00000000 40404040 40404040   *     ....................       *
0EC180     E3C8C540 C1D5E2E6 C5D940C9 E240F1F2    F3F4F500 FFFFFFFF FFFFFFFF FFFFFFFF   *THE ANSWER IS 12345.............*
0EC1A0     FFFFFFFF FFFFFFFF FFFFFFFF FFFFFFFF    FFFFFFFF FFFFFFFF FFFFFFFF FFFFFFFF   *................................*
      LINE 0EC1C0 SAME AS ABOVE
0EC1E0     FFFFFFFF 00000000                                                            *........                        *

JOB F604            STEP GO             TIME 141953   DATE 87072    ID = 001                                PAGE 0002

                     DUMP INDEX
                     ----------

 DATA AREAS                          PAGE NUMBER
-----------                          -----------

 REGISTERS.............................   0001
 STORAGE AREAS.........................   0001

END OF DUMP
```



**Figure 6.4**
A sample snapshot dump that SNAP produces.

## *Types of Dumps*

A dump provides the status of the registers and storage at a particular time during program execution. There are two basic types of dumps: snapshot and abend. **Snapshot dumps** are those that you request with the SNAP instruction in OS or the PDUMP instruction in DOS. **Abend dumps** occur when a program ends abnormally because of an error.

Figure 6.4 contains the snapshot dump that is caused by the instruction

```
SNAP   STORAGE=(ARRAY,SAVE),PDATA=(REGS,PSW),DCB=SNAPDCB,ID=1
```

**Snapshot dumps**

The dump begins with the identification number *n* that you specify by writing ID = *n* in the operand entry of the SNAP instruction. Next in the dump are the contents of the PSW at the time that the dump occurred; later, this chapter will describe the PSW in detail. The hexadecimal contents of the floating-point registers and the general registers appear next. Finally, the dump lists the contents of the storage that is within the range of addresses that SNAP requests. Recall that each line of a storage dump begins with an

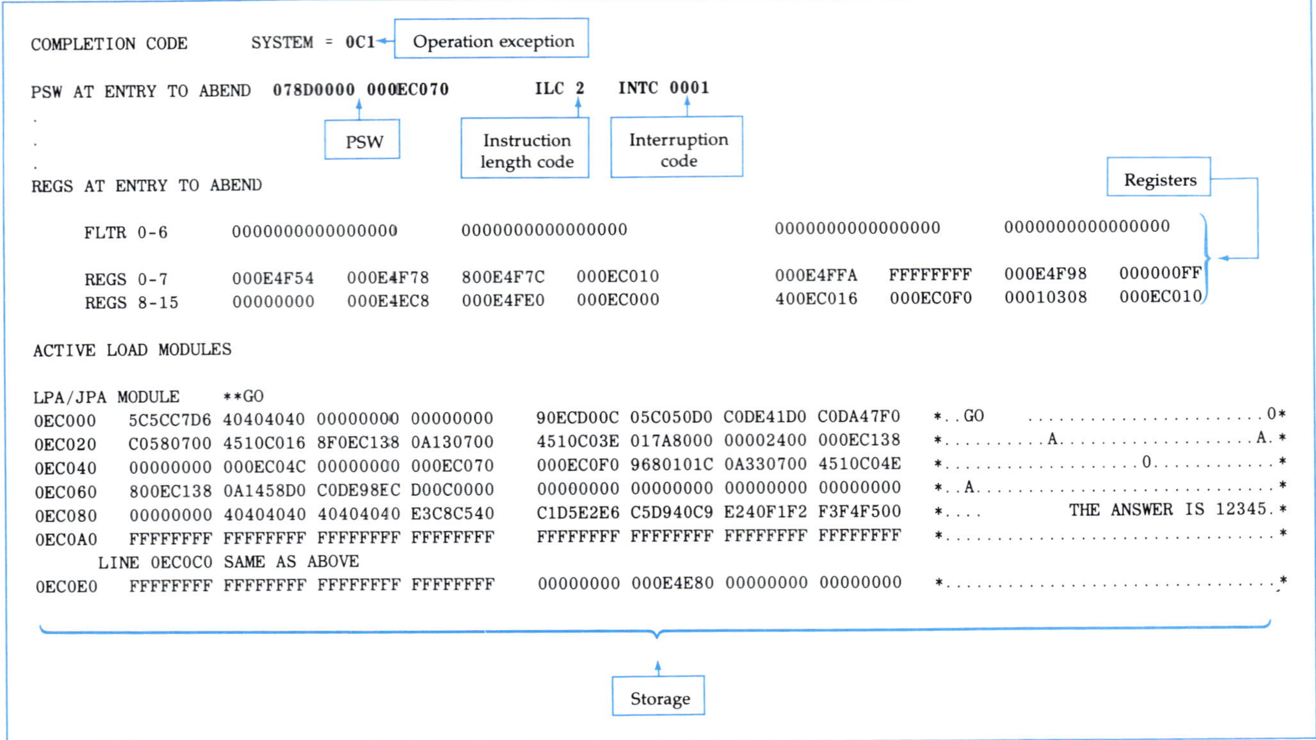

```
COMPLETION CODE        SYSTEM = 0C1

PSW AT ENTRY TO ABEND  078D0000 000EC070          ILC 2    INTC 0001
.
.
.
REGS AT ENTRY TO ABEND

     FLTR 0-6      0000000000000000   0000000000000000        0000000000000000   0000000000000000

     REGS 0-7      000E4F54  000E4F78  800E4F7C  000EC010     000E4FFA  FFFFFFFF  000E4F98  000000FF
     REGS 8-15     00000000  000E4EC8  000E4FE0  000EC000     400EC016  000EC0F0  00010308  000EC010

ACTIVE LOAD MODULES

LPA/JPA MODULE    **GO
0EC000    5C5CC7D6 40404040 00000000 00000000    90ECD00C 05C050D0 C0DE41D0 C0DA47F0    *..GO    .......................0*
0EC020    C0580700 4510C016 8F0EC138 0A130700    4510C03E 017A8000 00002400 000EC138    *..........A..................A.*
0EC040    00000000 000EC04C 00000000 000EC070    000EC0F0 9680101C 0A330700 4510C04E    *..................0............*
0EC060    800EC138 0A1458D0 C0DE98EC D00C0000    00000000 00000000 00000000 00000000    *..A............................*
0EC080    00000000 40404040 40404040 E3C8C540    C1D5E2E6 C5D940C9 E240F1F2 F3F4F500    *....           THE ANSWER IS 12345.*
0EC0A0    FFFFFFFF FFFFFFFF FFFFFFFF FFFFFFFF    FFFFFFFF FFFFFFFF FFFFFFFF FFFFFFFF    *...............................*
      LINE 0EC0C0 SAME AS ABOVE
0EC0E0    FFFFFFFF FFFFFFFF FFFFFFFF FFFFFFFF    00000000 000E4E80 00000000 00000000    *...............................*
```



**Figure 6.5**
A sample abend dump.

address, and contains the hexadecimal contents of a maximum of 32 bytes that are arranged as fullwords. Also recall that in Example 11 of Chapter 4 you learned how to locate quantities within a storage dump. To the right of the hex dump is the character representation of all bytes that contain an EBCDIC code for a letter, digit, or blank. Periods represent all other codes. You can use this portion to locate the general area of interest within the dump; doing so is particularly helpful when the dump is long.

**Abend dumps**

Unlike a snapshot dump, an abend dump produces an overwhelming amount of information, most of which is irrelevant to your immediate needs. Figure 6.5 contains a portion of an abend dump that was caused by a program interruption. The dump begins with the completion code, which indicates the nature of the error. Here, 0C1 indicates that an operation exception caused the interruption. Next, the dump lists the PSW, the instruction length code (ILC), and the interruption code (INTC), as they were at the time of the error.

An abend dump also contains the contents of the floating-point and general registers, and the contents of the storage that is assigned to the program. This information appears as it does in a snapshot dump.

Note that when an abend dump occurs, the operating system does not print it unless you have written the proper job control statement. In OS, you must write

```
//GO.SYSUDUMP   DD   SYSOUT=A
```

before the //GO.SYSIN DD statement; in DOS, you must specify DUMP in the OPTION statement. Appendix I contains more information about job control statements.

| Channel masks | E | Key | 0MWP | Interruption code | ILC | CC | Program mask | Instruction address |
|---|---|---|---|---|---|---|---|---|
| 0 7 | 8 | | 12 | 16 | 32 | 34 | 36 | 40 63 |

| Bits | Contents |
|---|---|
| 0–6 | Channel masks |
| 7 | (E) External mask |
| 8–11 | Protection key |
| 12 | 0 for BC mode |
| 13 | (M) Machine-check mask |
| 14 | (W) Wait state (1) or not (0) |
| 15 | (P) Problem state (1) or supervisor state (0) |
| 16–31 | Interruption code |
| 32–33 | Instruction length code (ILC) |
| 34–35 | Condition code (CC) |
| 36–39 | Program mask: |
| | 36: Fixed-point overflow mask |
| | 37: Decimal overflow mask |
| | 38: Exponent underflow mask |
| | 39: Significance mask |
| 40–63 | Instruction address |

**Figure 6.6**
The PSW in BC mode.

## *PSW Formats*

**There are three formats for the PSW**

Recall that the 64-bit program status word contains information about the status of the CPU in relation to the program in execution and that the CPU uses the PSW to control the sequence of instruction execution. As you will see, there are three format variations of the PSW within the System/370 family. However, the PSW always contains the address of the next instruction to be executed in the instruction address (IA) portion, and the condition code.

Computers without the extended architecture can operate in either the **basic-control (BC) mode** or the **extended-control (EC) mode,** and each mode has a different PSW format. A third format occurs with extended architecture machines: collectively, BC mode and EC mode are referred to as **System/370 mode,** in contrast to the **370-XA** (extended architecture) **mode.**

**BC mode**

The format of the PSW in the BC mode, as shown in Figure 6.6, is compatible with the System/360 PSW. The rightmost 3 bytes (bits 40 through 63) contain the 24-bit instruction address (IA). The length of the current instruction, recorded in halfwords, is contained in bits 32 and 33. This is the instruction length code (ILC); it has a binary value of 01, 10, or 11, which indicate an instruction length of 1, 2, or 3 halfwords, respectively. Bits 34 and 35 contain the binary condition code (CC). When an interruption occurs, the interruption code is recorded in bits 16 through 31. The 4-bit program mask is in bits 36 through 39.

The remainder of the PSW is not relevant to the topics in this book so the description about it will be brief. Bits 8 through 11 contain a bit pattern known as the **protection key,** which offers levels of storage protection. Under certain conditions, the CPU can access storage only if this key matches

| 0R00 0TIE | Key | 1MWPS | 0 | CC | Program mask | 0000 0000 0000 0000 | Instruction address |
|---|---|---|---|---|---|---|---|
| 0 | 8 | 12 | 17 | 18 | 20 | 24 | 40 – 63 |

| Bits | Contents |
|---|---|
| 1 | (R) Program-event-recording mask |
| 5 | (T) Dynamic-address-translation (DAT) mode |
| 6 | (I) Input/output mask |
| 7 | (E) External mask |
| 8–11 | Protection key |
| 12 | 1 for EC mode |
| 13 | (M) Machine-check mask |
| 14 | (W) Wait state (1) or not (0) |
| 15 | (P) Problem state (1) or supervisor state (0) |
| 16 | (S) Address-space control mode |
| 18–19 | Condition code (CC) |
| 20–23 | Program mask:<br>20: Fixed-point overflow mask<br>21: Decimal overflow mask<br>22: Exponent underflow mask<br>23: Significance mask |
| 40–63 | Instruction address |

**Figure 6.7**
The PSW in EC mode.

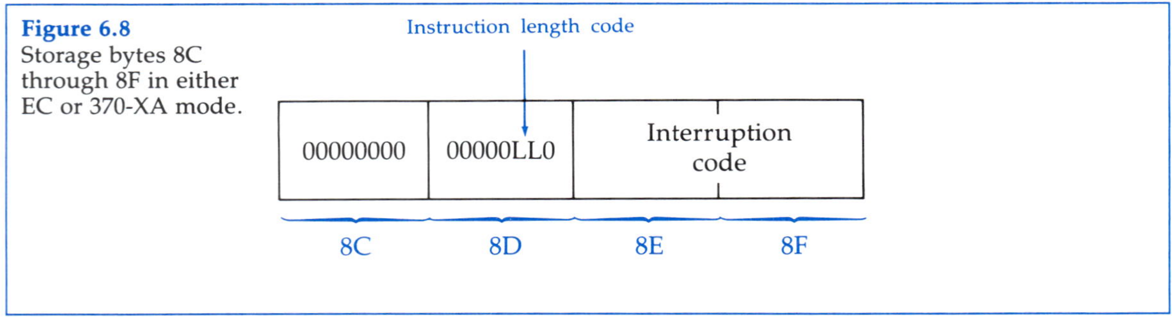


**Figure 6.8**
Storage bytes 8C through 8F in either EC or 370-XA mode.

another pattern that is associated with the desired storage. If a match is not made, a protection exception occurs. Bit 12 is 0 in BC mode. The System/360 PSW used this bit to determine whether certain instructions used EBCDIC or ASCII, and is the only difference between a BC mode PSW and a System/360 PSW. Bit 15 indicates the state of the CPU; it is 1 if the CPU is in problem state, or 0 if it is in supervisor state. The remaining bits of the PSW affect classes of interruptions other than program interruptions in a similar manner to the program mask.

**EC mode**

Figure 6.7 illustrates an EC mode PSW. The instruction address (IA) portion is still in bits 40 through 63, but the condition code (bits 18 and 19) and the program mask (bits 20 through 23) are in positions that differ from

| 0R00 0TIE | Key | 1MWPS | 0 | CC | Program mask | 0000 0000 | A | Instruction address |
|---|---|---|---|---|---|---|---|---|
| 0 | 8 | 12 | 17 | 18 | 20 | 24 | 32 | 33 … 63 |

| Bits | Contents |
|---|---|
| 1 | (R) Program-event-recording mask |
| 5 | (T) Dynamic-address-translation (DAT) mode |
| 6 | (I) Input/output mask |
| 7 | (E) External mask |
| 8–11 | Protection key |
| 12 | 1 |
| 13 | (M) Machine-check mask |
| 14 | (W) Wait state (1) or not (0) |
| 15 | (P) Problem state (1) or supervisor state (0) |
| 16 | (S) Address-space control mode |
| 18–19 | Condition code (CC) |
| 20–23 | Program mask:<br>20: Fixed-point overflow mask<br>21: Decimal overflow mask<br>22: Exponent underflow mask<br>23: Significance mask |
| 32 | (A) Addressing mode (1 = 31 bits, 0 = 24 bits) |
| 33–63 | Instruction address |

**Figure 6.9**
The PSW in 370-XA mode.

the BC mode. Instead of appearing in the PSW, the instruction length code (ILC) and the interruption code are placed into storage, as illustrated in Figure 6.8. The ILC is stored in bits 5 and 6 of the byte at hex address 8D, and the interruption code is stored into bytes 8E and 8F. The remaining bits of byte 8D and all of byte 8C must be zero.

Bits 1, 5, 6, and 16 of the EC mode PSW have meanings that differ from BC mode, but you do not have to be concerned about them now. Notice that bits 0, 2, 3, 4, 17, and 24 through 39 are unused and must be zero. Bit 12 is 1 in EC mode.

**370-XA mode**

Figure 6.9 illustrates a 370-XA mode PSW. Here, the instruction address (IA) portion occupies 31 bits (bits 33 through 63). Bit 32 (A) indicates the addressing mode used. If bit 32 is 0, then the CPU assumes 24-bit addresses and the first 7 bits of the IA must be zero. If bit 32 is 1, then the CPU assumes 31-bit addresses. The instruction length code and interruption code are stored in bytes 8C through 8F, just as in EC mode.

Note that the PSW in 370-XA mode with 24-bit addressing has the same format as an EC mode PSW.

---

EXAMPLE 3

### Examples of PSWs

The contents of the PSW appear within a dump in hexadecimal. A BC mode PSW is shown here; portions have been rewritten in binary where appropriate.

**BC mode**

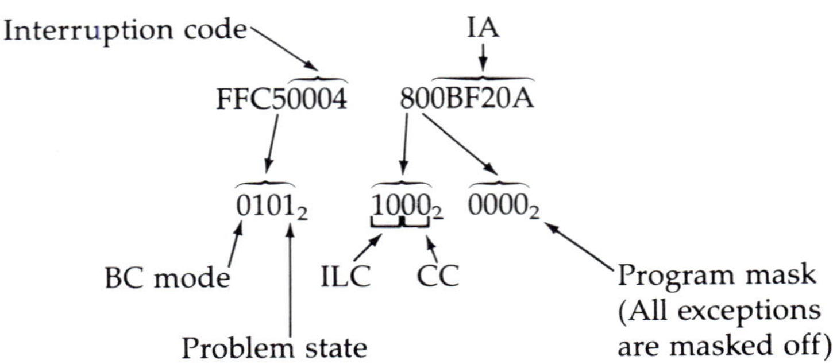


An EC mode PSW is shown next. It is in hexadecimal and, once again, portions have been rewritten in binary.

**EC mode**

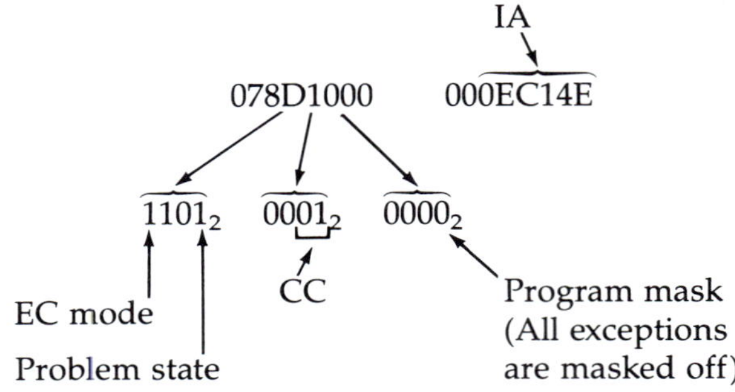


Finally, a 370-XA mode PSW is shown next.

**370-XA mode**

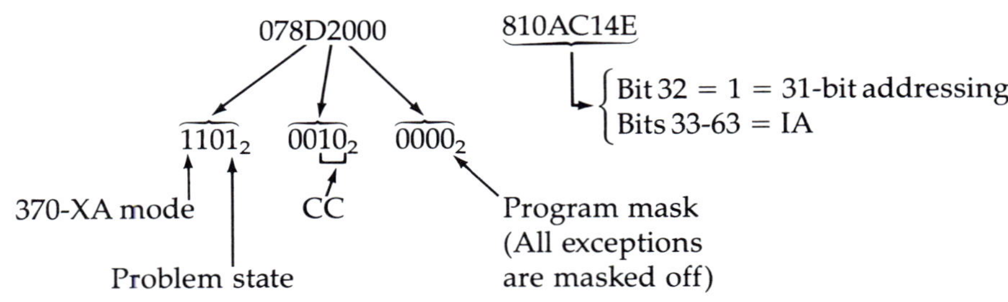


---

## SELF-TEST EXERCISE

1. For each of the following PSWs, determine the condition code, the instruction address (IA), and the program mask. If BC mode is indicated, also determine the instruction length code and the interruption code. (*Hint:* first determine whether BC, EC, or 370-XA mode is indicated.)
   **a.** FFC50008 9FE2B184 **c.** 47CDBF00 80F94DA2
   **b.** 47CD9800 0001A9BE **d.** 47C50005 6CF28A06

## Examples of Execution-Time Errors

This section will consider errors that cannot be detected by the assembler. These include errors in logic and certain typing mistakes. Not all execution-time errors cause error messages; those that do not are sometimes called **silent errors.** Failure to notice incorrect results in such cases can be disastrous.

---

EXAMPLE 4

### A Silent Error

The program in Figure 6.10 executes without an error message. However, the results of execution are incorrect. The program attempts to compute the product of X and Y, and should get $21_{10}$. Instead Registers 2 and 3 contain

$00000000\ 0002C028_{16}$

which is clearly incorrect.

In Figure 6.10, the programmer intended to multiply Register 3 by Register 4. Although you might not notice an error in the Multiply instruction in Statement 24, examining the corresponding object code should make the error evident. Notice that the machine language instruction is in RX format, and that it multiplies the contents of Register 3 by the contents of the fullword at the effective address 4. The problem then is with the mnemonic op code: it is M instead of MR. Since the statement is syntactically correct, the assembler cannot detect the error, and takes R4 as a displacement, not as a register. Compare this example with Example 2, in which an incorrect op code led to an assembler error message.

```
  LOC   OBJECT CODE     ADDR1 ADDR2  STMT    SOURCE STATEMENT

000000                                 1 EX4      CSECT
                                       2 ** COMPUTE X*Y
                                       3          PRINT NOGEN            SUPPRESS MACRO EXPANSIONS
                              00002    4 R2       EQU   2                                     EVEN/
                              00003    5 R3       EQU   3                WORK REGISTER        ODD PAIR
                              00004    6 R4       EQU   4                WORK REGISTER
                              0000C    7 R12      EQU   12               BASE REGISTER
                              0000D    8 R13      EQU   13               SAVE AREA POINTER
                              0000E    9 R14      EQU   14               RETURN REGISTER
                                      10 ** STANDARD ENTRY AND INITIALIZATION:
000000 90EC D00C        0000C         11          STM   R14,R12,12(R13)  SAVE REGISTERS
000004 05C0                           12          BALR  R12,0            LOAD BASE REGISTER
                              00006   13          USING BASE,R12         DECLARE BASE ADDRESS AND REGISTER
000006 50D0 C062        00068         14 BASE     ST    R13,SAVE+4       SAVE R13
00000A 41D0 C05E        00064         15          LA    R13,SAVE         R13 = ADDRESS OF SAVE AREA
                                      16          OPEN  (SNAPDCB,OUTPUT) PREPARE FOR DUMP
00001A 5830 C056        0005C         22          L     R3,X             GET X
00001E 5840 C05A        00060         23          L     R4,Y             GET Y
000022 5C20 0004        00004         24          M     R2,R4            COMPUTE X * Y
                                      25          SNAP  PDATA=(REGS),DCB=SNAPDCB,ID=1   DUMP REGISTERS
                                      43          CLOSE (SNAPDCB)        DUMP IS COMPLETE
```

*(Continues)*

**Figure 6.10**
An incorrect program that does not produce error messages, as described in Example 4.

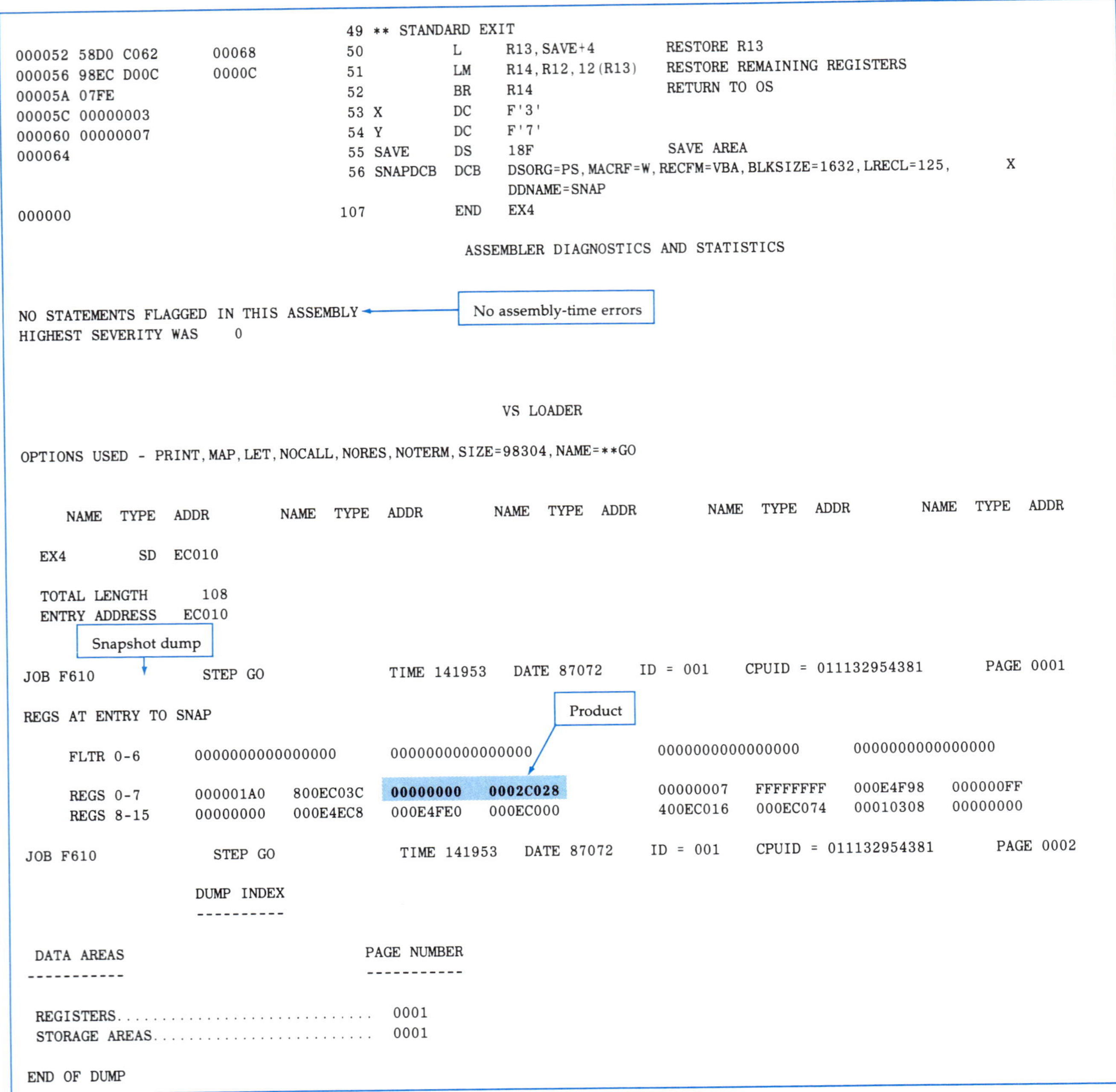

```
                                    49 ** STANDARD EXIT
000052 58D0 C062        00068       50          L     R13,SAVE+4          RESTORE R13
000056 98EC D00C        0000C       51          LM    R14,R12,12(R13)     RESTORE REMAINING REGISTERS
00005A 07FE                         52          BR    R14                 RETURN TO OS
00005C 00000003                     53 X        DC    F'3'
000060 00000007                     54 Y        DC    F'7'
000064                              55 SAVE     DS    18F                  SAVE AREA
                                    56 SNAPDCB  DCB   DSORG=PS,MACRF=W,RECFM=VBA,BLKSIZE=1632,LRECL=125,        X
                                                      DDNAME=SNAP
000000                             107          END   EX4

                                          ASSEMBLER DIAGNOSTICS AND STATISTICS

NO STATEMENTS FLAGGED IN THIS ASSEMBLY
HIGHEST SEVERITY WAS     0

                                          VS LOADER

OPTIONS USED - PRINT,MAP,LET,NOCALL,NORES,NOTERM,SIZE=98304,NAME=**GO

    NAME  TYPE  ADDR        NAME  TYPE  ADDR        NAME  TYPE  ADDR        NAME  TYPE  ADDR        NAME  TYPE  ADDR

  EX4         SD  EC010

  TOTAL LENGTH       108
  ENTRY ADDRESS    EC010

JOB F610             STEP GO              TIME 141953   DATE 87072    ID = 001    CPUID = 011132954381       PAGE 0001

REGS AT ENTRY TO SNAP

    FLTR 0-6      0000000000000000    0000000000000000    0000000000000000    0000000000000000

    REGS 0-7      000001A0  800EC03C  00000000  0002C028  00000007  FFFFFFFF  000E4F98  000000FF
    REGS 8-15     00000000  000E4EC8  000E4FE0  000EC000  400EC016  000EC074  00010308  00000000

JOB F610             STEP GO              TIME 141953   DATE 87072    ID = 001    CPUID = 011132954381       PAGE 0002

                  DUMP INDEX
                  ----------

  DATA AREAS                        PAGE NUMBER
  -----------                       -----------

  REGISTERS.............................  0001
  STORAGE AREAS.........................  0001

END OF DUMP
```



**Figure 6.10** *(Continued)*

---

EXAMPLE 5

## A Program Interruption

The program in Figure 6.11 tries to compute multiples of $z$ and store them in an array of consecutive fullwords. (The program is based upon the one in Figure 5.14.) The completion code 0C4 indicates that the CPU has encountered an invalid address during execution; a program interruption occurs. From the abend dump, you can see that the PSW at the time of the interruption is as follows:

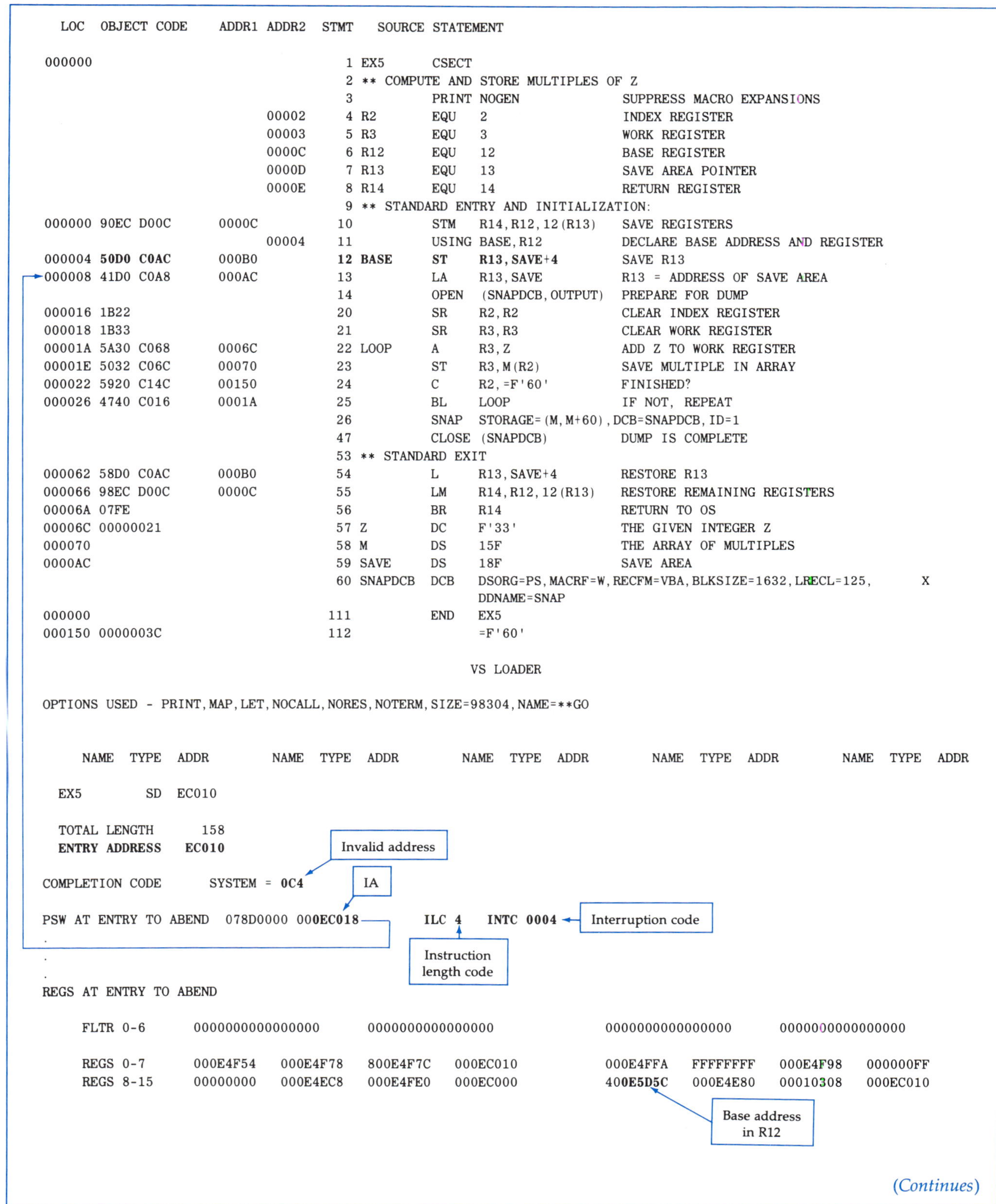

```
  LOC   OBJECT CODE     ADDR1 ADDR2  STMT    SOURCE STATEMENT

000000                                  1 EX5      CSECT
                                        2 ** COMPUTE AND STORE MULTIPLES OF Z
                                        3          PRINT NOGEN               SUPPRESS MACRO EXPANSIONS
                             00002      4 R2       EQU    2                  INDEX REGISTER
                             00003      5 R3       EQU    3                  WORK REGISTER
                             0000C      6 R12      EQU    12                 BASE REGISTER
                             0000D      7 R13      EQU    13                 SAVE AREA POINTER
                             0000E      8 R14      EQU    14                 RETURN REGISTER
                                        9 ** STANDARD ENTRY AND INITIALIZATION:
000000 90EC D00C        0000C          10          STM    R14,R12,12(R13)    SAVE REGISTERS
                             00004     11          USING BASE,R12            DECLARE BASE ADDRESS AND REGISTER
000004 50D0 C0AC        000B0          12 BASE     ST     R13,SAVE+4         SAVE R13
000008 41D0 C0A8        000AC          13          LA     R13,SAVE           R13 = ADDRESS OF SAVE AREA
                                       14          OPEN   (SNAPDCB,OUTPUT)   PREPARE FOR DUMP
000016 1B22                            20          SR     R2,R2              CLEAR INDEX REGISTER
000018 1B33                            21          SR     R3,R3              CLEAR WORK REGISTER
00001A 5A30 C068        0006C          22 LOOP     A      R3,Z               ADD Z TO WORK REGISTER
00001E 5032 C06C        00070          23          ST     R3,M(R2)           SAVE MULTIPLE IN ARRAY
000022 5920 C14C        00150          24          C      R2,=F'60'          FINISHED?
000026 4740 C016        0001A          25          BL     LOOP               IF NOT, REPEAT
                                       26          SNAP   STORAGE=(M,M+60),DCB=SNAPDCB,ID=1
                                       47          CLOSE  (SNAPDCB)          DUMP IS COMPLETE
                                       53 ** STANDARD EXIT
000062 58D0 C0AC        000B0          54          L      R13,SAVE+4         RESTORE R13
000066 98EC D00C        0000C          55          LM     R14,R12,12(R13)    RESTORE REMAINING REGISTERS
00006A 07FE                            56          BR     R14                RETURN TO OS
00006C 00000021                        57 Z        DC     F'33'              THE GIVEN INTEGER Z
000070                                 58 M        DS     15F                THE ARRAY OF MULTIPLES
0000AC                                 59 SAVE     DS     18F                SAVE AREA
                                       60 SNAPDCB  DCB    DSORG=PS,MACRF=W,RECFM=VBA,BLKSIZE=1632,LRECL=125,        X
                                                          DDNAME=SNAP
000000                                111          END    EX5
000150 0000003C                       112                 =F'60'

                                   VS LOADER

OPTIONS USED - PRINT,MAP,LET,NOCALL,NORES,NOTERM,SIZE=98304,NAME=**GO

    NAME   TYPE   ADDR       NAME   TYPE   ADDR       NAME   TYPE   ADDR       NAME   TYPE   ADDR       NAME   TYPE   ADDR

  EX5        SD   EC010

  TOTAL LENGTH       158
  ENTRY ADDRESS    EC010

COMPLETION CODE       SYSTEM = 0C4

PSW AT ENTRY TO ABEND   078D0000 000EC018      ILC 4    INTC 0004
.
.
.
REGS AT ENTRY TO ABEND

    FLTR 0-6      0000000000000000      0000000000000000           0000000000000000      0000000000000000

    REGS 0-7      000E4F54   000E4F78   800E4F7C   000EC010        000E4FFA   FFFFFFFF   000E4F98   000000FF
    REGS 8-15     00000000   000E4EC8   000E4FE0   000EC000        400E5D5C   000E4E80   00010308   000EC010
```



(Continues)

**Figure 6.11**
A program in which a program interruption occurs, as described in Example 5.

```
ACTIVE LOAD MODULES                                         The ST instruction
                                                                (STMT 12)
LPA/JPA MODULE      **GO
0EC000    5C5CC7D6 40404040 00000000 00000000    90ECD00C 50D0C0AC 41D0C0A8 4510C010    *..GO      ........................*
0EC020    8F0EC104 0A131B22 1B335A30 C0685032    C06C5920 C14C4740 C0160700 4510C04C    *..A...............A..  ........*
0EC040    017A8000 00000000 000EC104 00000000    000EC058 00000000 000EC080 000EC0BC    *..........A....................*
0EC060    9680101C 0A330700 4510C05C 800EC104    0A1458D0 C0AC98EC D00C07FE 00000021    *..............A................*
0EC080    00000000 00000000 00000000 00000000    00000000 00000000 00000000 00000000    *...............................*
      LINES 0EC0A0-0EC0E0 SAME AS ABOVE
0EC100    00000000 00000000 00000000 00000000    00000000 00000000 00000001 00004000    *...............................*
0EC120    00000001 00000001 54000000 E2D5C1D7    40404040 02000020 00000001 00000001    *............SNAP     ..........*
0EC140    00000660 00000000 00000001 00000001    00000001 0000007D 00000001 00000000    *...............................*
0EC160    0000003C 00000000                                                             *........                       *
```

**Figure 6.11**
*(Continued)*

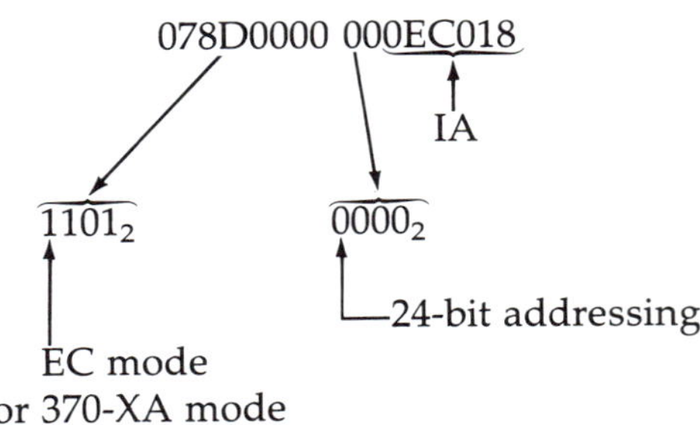


You can see that 24-bit addressing is in effect. (The machine is either in EC mode, which implies 24-bit addressing, or in 370-XA mode with 24-bit addressing.) The IA portion of the PSW contains 0EC018, which is the address of the instruction that follows the one that caused the interruption—since the interruption code (INTC) is not 0010 or 0011. Appearing in the dump immediately to the right of the PSW is the instruction length code (ILC) at the time of the interruption. The ILC is 4, which indicates that the last executed instruction was 4 bytes in length. By subtracting the ILC from the IA, you get the address of the instruction that caused the interruption; in this case, the address is 0EC014, which is the address of the instruction in Statement 12. Usually, you do not need to make this computation and can simply look in the program listing for the instruction that precedes the one that the IA indicates. (Recall that, to compute the relative address of the instruction at 0EC014, you subtract the entry address, which is 0EC010, from 0EC014. The result is 000004, which is the relative address of the Store instruction in Statement 12.)

Now, examine the suspected instruction:

```
BASE      ST      R13,SAVE+4
```

You are looking for an error that produced an effective address beyond the bounds of the program. This often occurs because an index register has an incorrect value, but the Store instruction here does not specify an index. The instruction is written correctly and, as you can tell, SAVE+4 is within the program. The object code that is produced by the assembler is correct, and a check of the storage dump verifies that the instruction was not altered or destroyed prior to its execution. Another possible source of error is an incorrect base address. Register 12 is the base register. The contents of Register 12, at the time of the interruption, are shown in the abend dump as 400E5D5C, which is incorrect because the base address 0E5D5C precedes the starting address 0EC010 of the program. Therefore, the program did

## SELF-TEST EXERCISE

2. Use the dump in Figure 6.11 to answer the following questions:
   a. At the time of the interruption, what are the following?
      - The contents of Register 2.
      - The contents of bits 2 and 3 of the byte at address 0EC033.
      - The address of the fullword literal constant that is defined by =F'60'.
      - The contents of the byte that follows the literal constant.
      - The value of the condition code.
   b. Will a fixed-point overflow exception during the execution of this program cause a program interruption? Explain.

not establish a base register correctly. A closer look at the source program reveals that the BALR instruction was omitted. The assembler did not detect this error since the assembler depends solely on the USING statement for information about the base register. Thus, at execution time, the CPU uses the incorrect contents of Register 12 to compute the effective address that was specified by the Store instruction. This address happens to be within a protected area of storage and so an interruption occurs.

---

EXAMPLE 6

### Another Silent Error

The program in Figure 6.12 is supposed to compute the sum of the N fullwords at ARRAY. The program executes and terminates normally, but the results are incorrect. The dump shows the computed value, −5, in the fullword at SUM (Location 0EC0AC). Since there are only 5 values in the array—all of them known—it is clear that this result is incorrect. In practice, this fact may not be as obvious, but often you know something about the expected answer, such as its sign or its approximate value.

Tracing the execution of portions of the program can help isolate the error. The program first computes 4 * N, and stores the result as LIMIT (Location 0EC0A8) for use in loop control. Looking in the storage dump verifies that this value is correct. A trace of the logic of the loop is illustrated in Figure 6.13. The loop appears to be controlled correctly, and the dump indicates that Register 3 contains a correct final value of $14_{16}$, which is 20 in decimal. Yet, the computed sum is wrong. Apparently, Register 3 counts correctly, so you might suspect something stranger than a logic error. A check of the base address in bits 8 through 31 of Register 12 indicates that it is correct.

Detecting this error will probably require very careful scrutiny of the assembler language statements and the object code that they produce. Although the instruction in Statement 29 that adds an array element to Register 2 may appear to be correct, examining the object code reveals the problem. The corresponding machine language instruction, 5A20C07A, does not specify an index register as it should. The assembler language statement incorrectly contains an embedded blank in its operand entry, as shown here:

```
LOOP      A        R2,ARRAY (R3)
                           ↑
                         Blank
```

The assembler treats *(R3)* as part of the remarks entry and, therefore, ignores it. Thus, the program adds the first element in the array, −1, to Register 2 five times, and computes a sum of −5. As this example has shown, it is important not only to find the error, but also to demonstrate that it caused the incorrect result. In this way, you are certain that you have not overlooked an error.

```
  LOC   OBJECT CODE    ADDR1 ADDR2  STMT    SOURCE STATEMENT

000000                                 1 EX6      CSECT
                                       2 ** COMPUTE THE SUM OF THE N FULLWORD-INTEGERS AT ARRAY
                                       3          PRINT NOGEN           SUPPRESS MACRO EXPANSIONS
                              00002    4 R2       EQU   2               WORK REGISTER    EVEN/
                              00003    5 R3       EQU   3               INDEX REGISTER         ODD PAIR
                                       6 * R2 AND R3 SERVE TWO ROLES: AS AN EVEN/ODD PAIR FOR MULTIPLICATION,
                                       7 * AND AS SEPARATE WORK AND INDEX REGISTERS.
                              0000C    8 R12      EQU   12              BASE REGISTER
                              0000D    9 R13      EQU   13              SAVE AREA POINTER
                              0000E   10 R14      EQU   14              RETURN REGISTER
                                      11 ** STANDARD ENTRY AND INITIALIZATION:
000000 90EC D00C        0000C         12          STM   R14,R12,12(R13)    SAVE REGISTERS
000004 05C0                           13          BALR  R12,0           LOAD BASE REGISTER
                              00006   14          USING BASE,R12        DECLARE BASE ADDRESS AND REGISTER
000006 50D0 C09E        000A4         15 BASE     ST    R13,SAVE+4      SAVE R13
00000A 41D0 C09A        000A0         16          LA    R13,SAVE        R13 = ADDRESS OF SAVE AREA
                                      17          OPEN  (SNAPDCB,OUTPUT)   PREPARE FOR DUMP
00001A 5830 C08E        00094         23          L     R3,N            GET NUMBER OF ELEMENTS
00001E 5C20 C13A        00140         24          M     R2,=F'4'        COMPUTE LIMIT FOR LOOP CONTROL
000022 5030 C092        00098         25          ST    R3,LIMIT        SAVE IT
000026 1B22                           26          SR    R2,R2           CLEAR WORK REGISTER
000028 1B33                           27          SR    R3,R3           CLEAR INDEX REGISTER
                                      28 * REPEAT N TIMES:
00002A 5A20 C07A        00080         29 LOOP     A     R2,ARRAY (R3)   ADD NEXT ARRAY ELEMENT
00002E 5A30 C13A        00140         30          A     R3,=F'4'        INCREMENT INDEX
000032 5930 C092        00098         31          C     R3,LIMIT        FINISHED?
000036 4740 C024        0002A         32          BL    LOOP            REPEAT IF THERE ARE MORE ELEMENTS TO ADD
                                      33 * END REPEAT
00003A 5020 C096        0009C         34          ST    R2,SUM          STORE SUM
                                      35          SNAP  PDATA=(REGS),STORAGE=(ARRAY,ARRAY+200),DCB=SNAPDCB,ID=1
                                      56          CLOSE (SNAPDCB)       DUMP IS COMPLETE
                                      62 ** STANDARD EXIT
000076 58D0 C09E        000A4         63          L     R13,SAVE+4      RESTORE R13
00007A 98EC D00C        0000C         64          LM    R14,R12,12(R13)   RESTORE REMAINING REGISTERS
00007E 07FE                           65          BR    R14             RETURN TO OS
000080 FFFFFFFF                       66 ARRAY    DC    F'-1'           ARRAY OF N FULLWORDS
000084 00000062                       67          DC    F'98'
000088 00000011                       68          DC    F'17'
00008C FFFFFFFD                       69          DC    F'-3'
000090 0000003D                       70          DC    F'61'
000094 00000005                       71 N        DC    F'5'            NUMBER OF INTEGERS IN ARRAY
000098                                72 LIMIT    DS    F               INDEX LIMIT FOR LOOP CONTROL
00009C                                73 SUM      DS    F               SUM OF INTEGERS IN ARRAY
0000A0                                74 SAVE     DS    18F             SAVE AREA
                                      75 SNAPDCB  DCB   DSORG=PS,MACRF=W,RECFM=VBA,BLKSIZE=1632,LRECL=125,        X
                                                        DDNAME=SNAP
000000                               126          END   EX6
000140 00000004                      127                =F'4'
```

*(Continues)*

**Figure 6.12**
A program that is supposed to compute the sum of N fullwords, as discussed in Example 6.

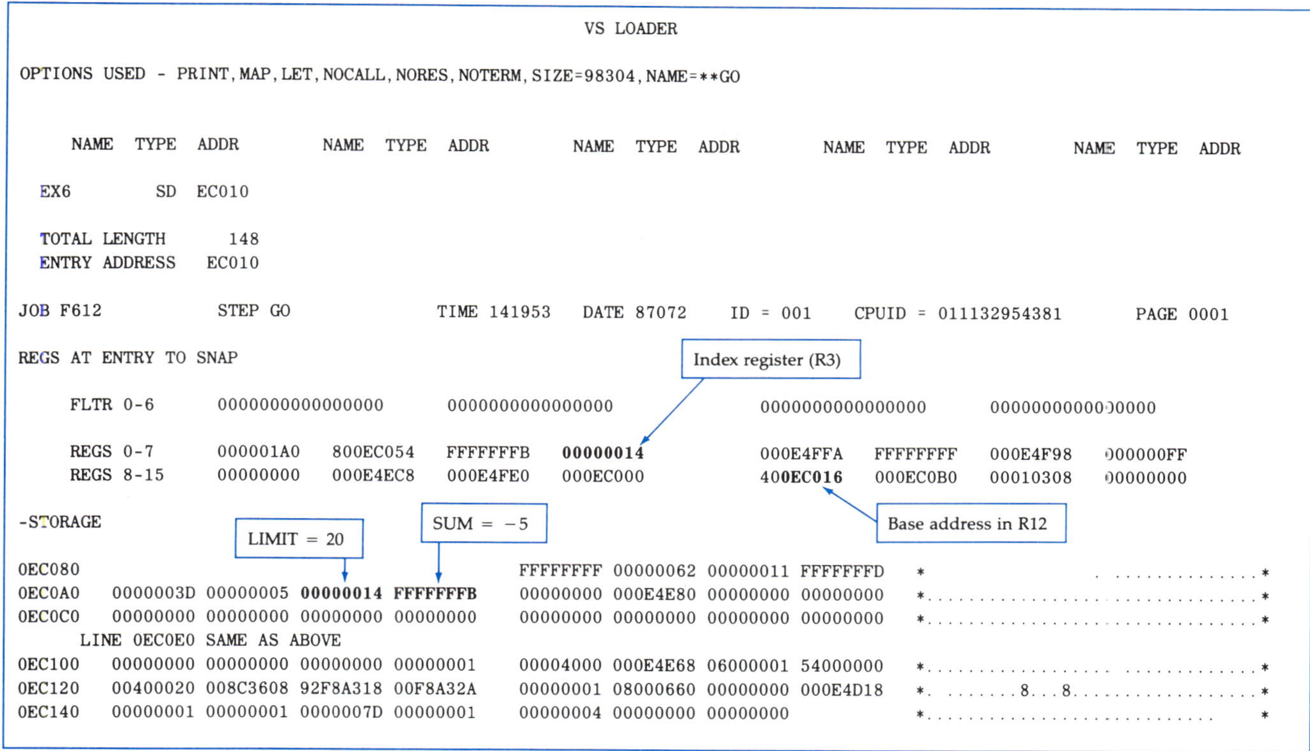

```
                                        VS LOADER

OPTIONS USED - PRINT,MAP,LET,NOCALL,NORES,NOTERM,SIZE=98304,NAME=**GO

     NAME   TYPE   ADDR          NAME   TYPE   ADDR          NAME   TYPE   ADDR          NAME   TYPE   ADDR          NAME   TYPE   ADDR

  EX6         SD   EC010

  TOTAL LENGTH       148
  ENTRY ADDRESS    EC010

JOB F612          STEP GO           TIME 141953   DATE 87072    ID = 001    CPUID = 011132954381      PAGE 0001

REGS AT ENTRY TO SNAP

     FLTR 0-6      0000000000000000      0000000000000000         0000000000000000      0000000000000000

     REGS 0-7      000001A0   800EC054   FFFFFFFB   00000014      000E4FFA   FFFFFFFF   000E4F98   000000FF
     REGS 8-15     00000000   000E4EC8   000E4FE0   000EC000      400EC016   000EC0B0   00010308   00000000

-STORAGE

0EC080                                             FFFFFFFF 00000062 00000011 FFFFFFFD   *               ...............*
0EC0A0   0000003D 00000005 00000014 FFFFFFFB   00000000 000E4E80 00000000 00000000   *................................*
0EC0C0   00000000 00000000 00000000 00000000   00000000 00000000 00000000 00000000   *................................*
     LINE 0EC0E0  SAME AS ABOVE
0EC100   00000000 00000000 00000000 00000001   00004000 000E4E68 06000001 54000000   *................ ..............*
0EC120   00400020 008C3608 92F8A318 00F8A32A   00000001 08000660 00000000 000E4D18   *. .......8...8..................*
0EC140   00000001 00000001 0000007D 00000001   00000004 00000000 00000000            *..........................     *
```



**Figure 6.12** *(Continued)*

| Statement | | | C(R3) | Effective address of ARRAY element | C(R2) | Comparison | Branch? |
|---|---|---|---|---|---|---|---|
| | | | 0 | | 0 ← Initial values | | |
| 29 LOOP | A | R2,ARRAY(R3) | 0 | ARRAY | −1 | | |
| 30 | A | R3,=F'4' | 4 | | −1 | | |
| 31 | C | R3,LIMIT | | | | < | |
| 32 | BL | LOOP | | | | | Yes |
| 29 LOOP | A | R2,ARRAY(R3) | 4 | ARRAY + 4 | 97 | | |
| 30 | A | R3,=F'4' | 8 | | 97 | | |
| 31 | C | R3,LIMIT | | | | < | |
| 32 | BL | LOOP | | | | | Yes |
| 29 LOOP | A | R2,ARRAY(R3) | 8 | ARRAY + 8 | 114 | | |
| 30 | A | R3,=F'4' | 12 | | 114 | | |
| 31 | C | R3,LIMIT | | | | < | |
| 32 | BL | LOOP | | | | | Yes |
| 29 LOOP | A | R2,ARRAY(R3) | 12 | ARRAY + 12 | 111 | | |
| 30 | A | R3,=F'4' | 16 | | 111 | | |
| 31 | C | R3,LIMIT | | | | < | |
| 32 | BL | LOOP | | | | | Yes |
| 29 LOOP | A | R2,ARRAY(R3) | 16 | ARRAY + 16 | 172 | | |
| 30 | A | R3,=F'4' | 20 | | 172 | | |
| 31 | C | R3,LIMIT | | | | = | |
| 32 | BL | LOOP | | | | | No |

**Figure 6.13**
A trace of the logic Statements 29 through 32 of the program in Figure 6.12.

```
  LOC  OBJECT CODE    ADDR1 ADDR2  STMT   SOURCE STATEMENT

000000                                1 EX7      CSECT
                                      2 ** COMPUTE THE SUM OF THE N FULLWORD-INTEGERS AT ARRAY
                                      3          PRINT NOGEN               SUPPRESS MACRO EXPANSIONS
                            00002     4 R2       EQU   2                   INDEX REGISTER
                            00003     5 R3       EQU   3                   LOOP COUNTER
                            00004     6 R4       EQU   4                   WORK REGISTER
                            0000C     7 R12      EQU   12                  BASE REGISTER
                            0000D     8 R13      EQU   13                  SAVE AREA POINTER
                            0000E     9 R14      EQU   14                  RETURN REGISTER
                                     10 ** STANDARD ENTRY AND INITIALIZATION:
000000 90EC D00C      0000C          11          STM   R14,R12,12(R13)     SAVE REGISTERS
000004 05C0                          12          BALR  R12,0               LOAD BASE REGISTER
                            00006    13          USING BASE,R12            DECLARE BASE ADDRESS AND REGISTER
000006 50D0 C0C2      000C8          14 BASE     ST    R13,SAVE+4          SAVE R13
00000A 41D0 C0BE      000C4          15          LA    R13,SAVE            R13 = ADDRESS OF SAVE AREA
                                     16          OPEN  (SNAPDCB,OUTPUT)    PREPARE FOR DUMP
00001A 1B22                          22          SR    R2,R2               CLEAR INDEX REGISTER
00001C 1B33                          23          SR    R3,R3               CLEAR LOOP COUNTER
00001E 1B44                          24          SR    R4,R4               CLEAR WORK REGISTER
                                     25 * REPEAT N TIMES:
000020 5A42 C106      0010C          26 LOOP     A     R4,ARRAY(R2)        ADD NEXT ARRAY ELEMENT
000024 5AC0 C122      00128          27          A     12,=F'4'            INCREMENT INDEX
000028 5A30 C126      0012C          28          A     R3,=F'1'            INCREMENT LOOP COUNTER
00002C 5930 C11A      00120          29          C     R3,N                FINISHED?
000030 4740 C01A      00020          30          BL    LOOP                REPEAT IF LOOP COUNTER IS < N
                                     31 * END REPEAT
000034 5040 C11E      00124          32          ST    R4,SUM              STORE SUM
                                     33          SNAP  PDATA=(REGS),STORAGE=(ARRAY,ARRAY+40),DCB=SNAPDCB,ID=1
                                     54 ** STANDARD EXIT
000062 58D0 C0BE      000C4          55          L     R13,SAVE + 4        RESTORE R13
000066 98EC D00C      0000C          56          LM    R14,R12,12(R13)     RESTORE REMAINING REGISTERS
00006A 07FE                          57          BR    R14                 RETURN TO OS
                                     58 *
                                     59 SNAPDCB  DCB   DSORG=PS,MACRF=W,RECFM=VBA,BLKSIZE=1632,LRECL=125,      X
                                                       DDNAME=SNAP
0000C4                              110 SAVE     DS    18F                 SAVE AREA
00010C FFFFFFFF                     111 ARRAY    DC    F'-1'               ARRAY OF N FULLWORDS:
000110 00000062                     112          DC    F'98'
000114 00000011                     113          DC    F'17'
000118 FFFFFFFD                     114          DC    F'-3'
00011C 0000003D                     115          DC    F'61'
000120 00000005                     116 N        DC    F'5'                NUMBER OF INTEGERS IN ARRAY
000124 00000000                     117 SUM      DC    F'0'                SUM OF INTEGERS IN ARRAY
000000                              118          END   EX7
000128 00000004 } <-- Literal       119                =F'4'
00012C 00000001 }     constants     120                =F'1'
```

*(Continues)*

**Figure 6.14**
Another program that is supposed to compute the sum of N fullwords, as discussed in Example 7.

---

EXAMPLE 7

## Another Silent Error

The purpose of the program in Figure 6.14 is the same as the one given in Figure 6.12. However, the loop control differs in that Register 3 counts the number of times that the loop is repeated. Like the previous program, this program executes and terminates normally, but the computed sum is incorrect. The snapshot dump reveals that SUM (Location 0EC134) contains zero, which is also its initial value. The following observations lead to the detection of the error:

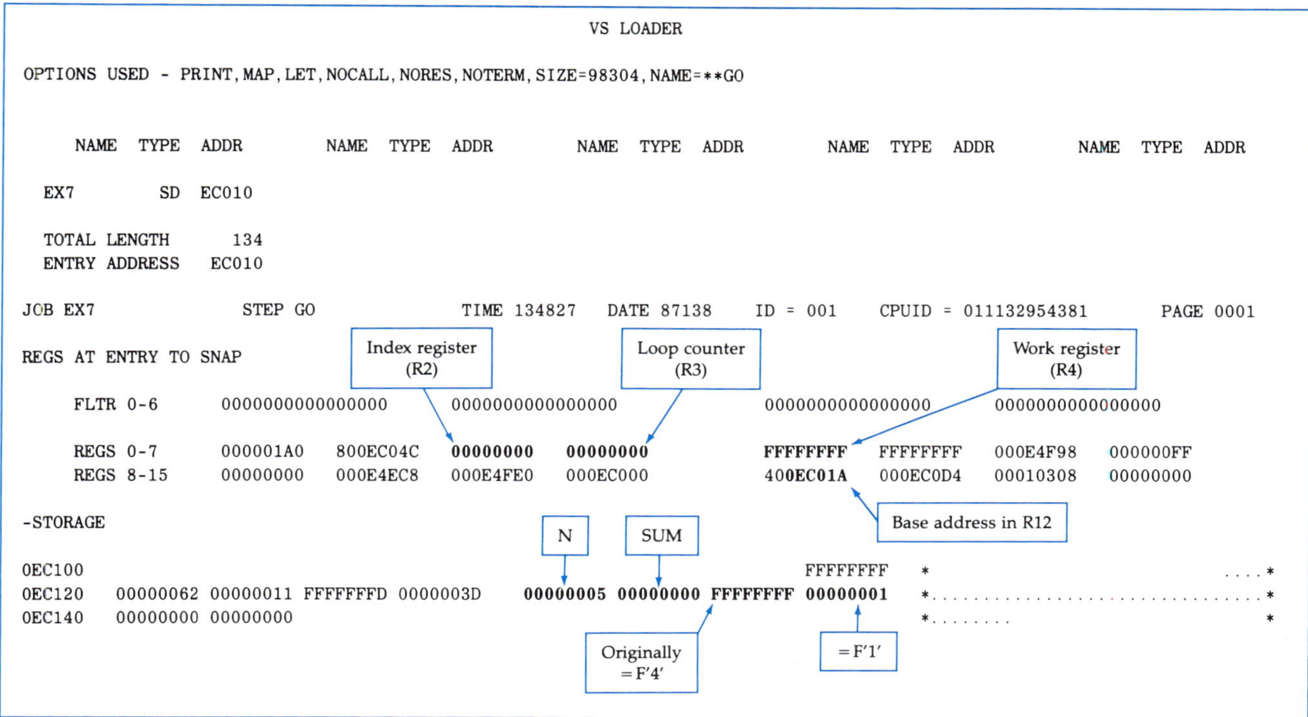

```
                                        VS LOADER

OPTIONS USED - PRINT,MAP,LET,NOCALL,NORES,NOTERM,SIZE=98304,NAME=**GO

     NAME  TYPE  ADDR          NAME  TYPE  ADDR          NAME  TYPE  ADDR          NAME  TYPE  ADDR          NAME  TYPE  ADDR

  EX7          SD  EC010

  TOTAL LENGTH       134
  ENTRY ADDRESS    EC010

JOB EX7             STEP GO              TIME 134827   DATE 87138    ID = 001    CPUID = 011132954381       PAGE 0001

REGS AT ENTRY TO SNAP

     FLTR 0-6        0000000000000000      0000000000000000      0000000000000000      0000000000000000

     REGS 0-7        000001A0  800EC04C  00000000  00000000  FFFFFFFF  FFFFFFFF  000E4F98  000000FF
     REGS 8-15       00000000  000E4EC8  000E4FE0  000EC000  400EC01A  000EC0D4  00010308  00000000

-STORAGE

0EC100                                                        FFFFFFFF   *                                 ....*
0EC120    00000062 00000011 FFFFFFFD 0000003D   00000005 00000000 FFFFFFFF 00000001   *................................*
0EC140    00000000 00000000                                                           *........                         *
```



**Figure 6.14** *(Continued)*

1. Register 4 (R4), which should contain the sum, contains −1. This is the same value as that of the first array element, but possibly this is coincidence. Notice that, although R4 was stored in SUM at Statement 32, SUM does not contain −1.
2. Register 2 (R2), the index register, contains zero. The program never got beyond the point of adding the first element of the array (−1) to R4. You can see now that the value of R4 is not coincidence.
3. Register 3 (R3), the loop counter, contains zero. Although Statement 23 initializes Register 3 to zero, the Add instruction in Statement 28 should add 1 to Register 3. However, this addition does not appear to occur. The Add instruction and its equivalent object code appear to be correct. Checking the storage dump should verify that the Add instruction has not been destroyed but, since the dump does not include this portion of the program, you should arrange to check this on the next run if you cannot locate the error now.
4. It is possible that the literal constant that is defined by =F'1' in Statement 28 was destroyed. However, location 0EC13C in the storage dump indicates that such is not the case.
5. While examining the literal constant that =F'1' defines, notice that the literal constant that =F'4' defines (Location 0EC138) contains −1, and not 4. Could it be that the Store instruction stored into this constant instead of SUM? If you assume that the Store instruction is correct and has not been destroyed, its erroneous behavior would suggest an incorrect base address. (Again, since you do not have a dump of the program, you cannot verify at this time that the Store instruction has not been destroyed. Thus, you should note this and proceed.)
6. The base address in Register 12 is 0EC01A. It is 4 larger than it should be. Since this value is not random, it is plausible that something was

inadvertently added to Register 12. A careful examination of the program reveals that Statement 27 is in error. The instruction adds 4 to Register 12 instead of to Register 2; thus, 12 was typed instead of R2. In a long program, this error could be difficult to find.

**Verification that the error explains all of the symptoms**

To verify that this error explains all of the symptoms, you can trace its effect on the program. Prior to the first time that Statement 27 is executed, R4 contains −1, which is the first element of the array. Statement 27 then adds 4 to the base register: subsequent RX instructions will not execute correctly since all effective addresses will be 4 larger than they should be. For example, consider the effective address that is specified by the displacement and base register of the Add instruction in Statement 28. It points to the fullword after the literal constant defined by =F'1', instead of to the literal constant itself. Since this fullword contains zero and since R3 was zero, R3 will remain zero as a result of the Add instruction. The Compare instruction in Statement 29 compares Register 3 with the contents of the fullword that is 4 bytes beyond the address represented by N—again, due to the incorrect base address. This fullword is the same one at SUM, and at this time, contains zero. Therefore, the comparison is "equal" and the loop falls through. Register 4, which contains −1, is then stored into the fullword after SUM—once again due to the incorrect base register. Thus, the program destroys the literal constant that =F'4' defines. In conclusion, all of the unusual observations are attributable to this one typing error.

This program contains two more errors, which Exercise 6 at the end of this chapter considers.

---

**Initializing storage as a debugging aid**

Example 7 demonstrates—in the definition of SUM—the use of the DC directive to provide an initial value, which can be useful for debugging, but which is irrelevant to the logic of the program. Finding this initial value in the dump can suggest that the program did not store into a particular location. However, there is no guarantee that the program did not compute and store—by coincidence—a value that is identical to your initial value. Furthermore, no guarantee is generally possible, regardless of the initial value. However, an initial value that is more distinctive than zero can be a better choice, if it allows more definitive conclusions.

---

EXAMPLE 8

### Reading Beyond the Last Data Record

The program in Figure 6.15 tries to read integers and store their binary equivalents into an array of fullwords. It assumes that each integer is on a separate data record. The following execution-time error message occurs:

```
COMPLETION CODE        SYSTEM = 337
```

This means that the program read beyond the last data record. (You can determine the meaning of any completion code by consulting an IBM manual, such as *System Codes*.) Using the following analysis will lead you to the error:

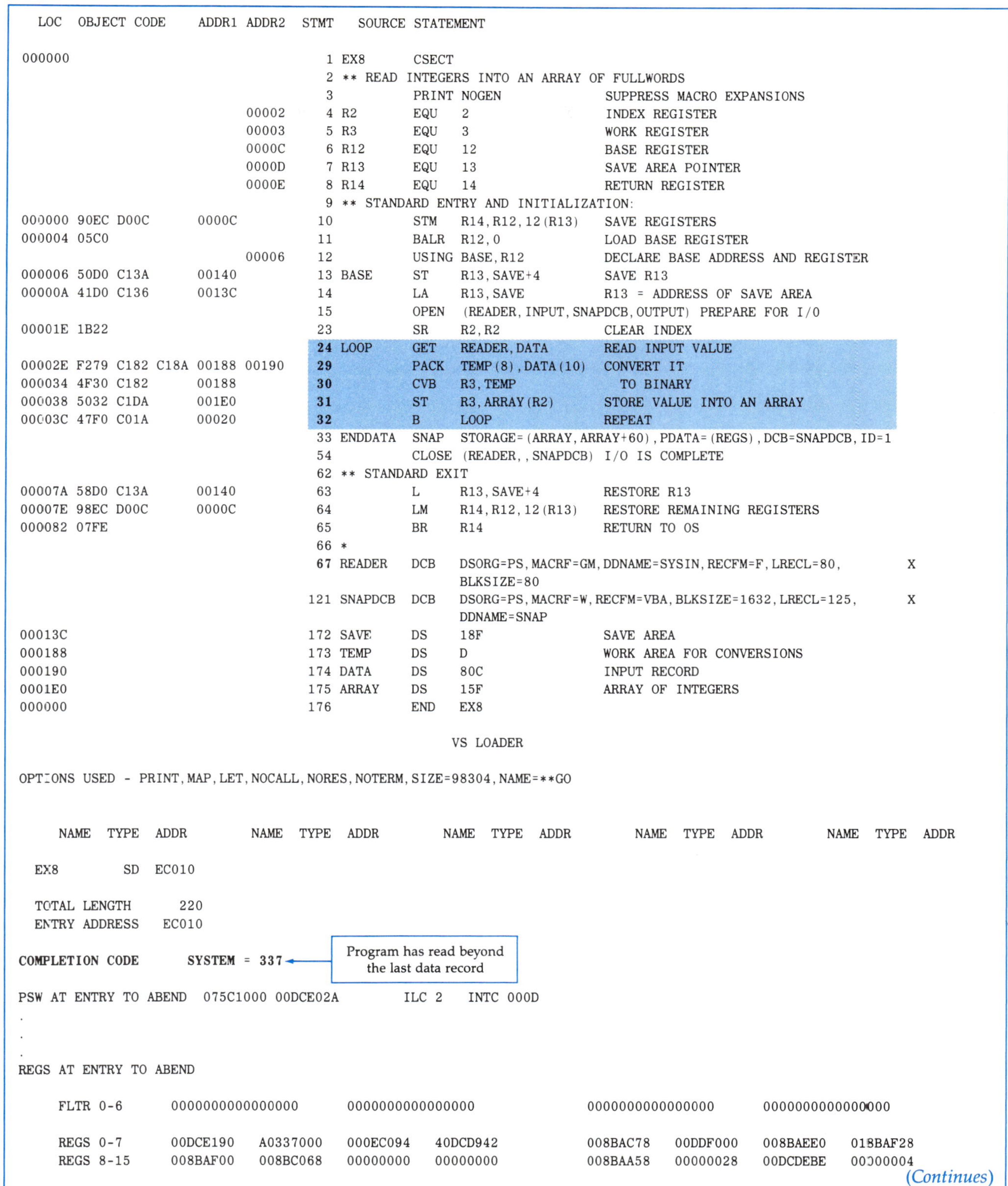

```
  LOC  OBJECT CODE    ADDR1 ADDR2  STMT   SOURCE STATEMENT

000000                                1 EX8      CSECT
                                      2 ** READ INTEGERS INTO AN ARRAY OF FULLWORDS
                                      3          PRINT NOGEN              SUPPRESS MACRO EXPANSIONS
                             00002    4 R2       EQU    2                 INDEX REGISTER
                             00003    5 R3       EQU    3                 WORK REGISTER
                             0000C    6 R12      EQU    12                BASE REGISTER
                             0000D    7 R13      EQU    13                SAVE AREA POINTER
                             0000E    8 R14      EQU    14                RETURN REGISTER
                                      9 ** STANDARD ENTRY AND INITIALIZATION:
000000 90EC D00C       0000C         10          STM    R14,R12,12(R13)   SAVE REGISTERS
000004 05C0                          11          BALR   R12,0             LOAD BASE REGISTER
                             00006   12          USING  BASE,R12          DECLARE BASE ADDRESS AND REGISTER
000006 50D0 C13A       00140         13 BASE     ST     R13,SAVE+4        SAVE R13
00000A 41D0 C136       0013C         14          LA     R13,SAVE          R13 = ADDRESS OF SAVE AREA
                                     15          OPEN   (READER,INPUT,SNAPDCB,OUTPUT) PREPARE FOR I/O
00001E 1B22                          23          SR     R2,R2             CLEAR INDEX
                                     24 LOOP     GET    READER,DATA       READ INPUT VALUE
00002E F279 C182 C18A 00188 00190    29          PACK   TEMP(8),DATA(10)  CONVERT IT
000034 4F30 C182       00188         30          CVB    R3,TEMP             TO BINARY
000038 5032 C1DA       001E0         31          ST     R3,ARRAY(R2)      STORE VALUE INTO AN ARRAY
00003C 47F0 C01A       00020         32          B      LOOP              REPEAT
                                     33 ENDDATA  SNAP   STORAGE=(ARRAY,ARRAY+60),PDATA=(REGS),DCB=SNAPDCB,ID=1
                                     54          CLOSE  (READER,,SNAPDCB) I/O IS COMPLETE
                                     62 ** STANDARD EXIT
00007A 58D0 C13A       00140         63          L      R13,SAVE+4        RESTORE R13
00007E 98EC D00C       0000C         64          LM     R14,R12,12(R13)   RESTORE REMAINING REGISTERS
000082 07FE                          65          BR     R14               RETURN TO OS
                                     66 *
                                     67 READER   DCB    DSORG=PS,MACRF=GM,DDNAME=SYSIN,RECFM=F,LRECL=80,          X
                                                        BLKSIZE=80
                                    121 SNAPDCB  DCB    DSORG=PS,MACRF=W,RECFM=VBA,BLKSIZE=1632,LRECL=125,        X
                                                        DDNAME=SNAP
00013C                              172 SAVE     DS     18F               SAVE AREA
000188                              173 TEMP     DS     D                 WORK AREA FOR CONVERSIONS
000190                              174 DATA     DS     80C               INPUT RECORD
0001E0                              175 ARRAY    DS     15F               ARRAY OF INTEGERS
000000                              176          END    EX8

                                                VS LOADER

OPTIONS USED - PRINT,MAP,LET,NOCALL,NORES,NOTERM,SIZE=98304,NAME=**GO


    NAME  TYPE  ADDR        NAME  TYPE  ADDR        NAME  TYPE  ADDR        NAME  TYPE  ADDR        NAME  TYPE  ADDR

  EX8         SD  EC010

  TOTAL LENGTH      220
  ENTRY ADDRESS    EC010

COMPLETION CODE      SYSTEM = 337   <-- Program has read beyond the last data record

PSW AT ENTRY TO ABEND  075C1000 00DCE02A        ILC 2   INTC 000D
 .
 .
 .
REGS AT ENTRY TO ABEND

    FLTR 0-6      0000000000000000    0000000000000000        0000000000000000    0000000000000000

    REGS 0-7      00DCE190  A0337000  000EC094  40DCD942      008BAC78  00DDF000  008BAEE0  018BAF28
    REGS 8-15     008BAF00  008BC068  00000000  00000000      008BAA58  00000028  00DCDEBE  00000004
```

*(Continues)*

**Figure 6.15**
A program that tries to read beyond the last data record, as described in Example 8.

```
ACTIVE LOAD MODULES

LPA/JPA MODULE     **GO
0EC000   5C5CC7D6 40404040 00000000 00000000   90ECD00C 05C050D0 C13A41D0 C1360700   *..GO   .................A...A...*
0EC020   4510C016 000EC094 8F0EC0F4 0A131B22   4110C07E 4100C18A 58F01030 05EFF279   *...........4..........A..0....2.*
0EC040   C182C18A 4F30C182 5032C1DA 47F0C01A   4510C05E 017A8000 00002000 000EC0F4   *A.A...A...A..0.................4*
0EC060   00000000 000EC06C 00000000 000EC1F0   000EC22C 9680101C 0A330700 4510C072   *..............A0..B.............*
0EC080   000EC094 800EC0F4 0A1458D0 C13A98EC   D00C07FE 00000000 00000000 00000000   *.......4....A...................*
0EC0A0   00000000 00000000 000E4A18 00004000   00000001 04000001 80000000 E2E8E2C9   *.............. .............SYSI*
0EC0C0   D5404040 02005000 00000001 00000001   08090050 00000000 00000001 000E4A70   *N   ............................*
0EC0E0   000E4A20 00000050 00000001 00000000   00000001 00000000 00000000 00000000   *................................*
0EC100   00000000 00000000 00000001 00004000   000E4D00 06000001 54000000 00540020   *.............. .................*
0EC120   008B8F08 92F8A318 00F8A32A 00000001   08000660 00000000 000E4BB0 00000001   *.....8...8......................*
0EC140   00000001 0000007D 00000001 00000000   000E4E80 00000000 400EC03E 12B489A6   *........................ .......*
0EC160   400EC03E 00B0D408 00000000 000EC094   000EC094 00000006 000E4FFA FFFFFFFF   * .....M..........................*
0EC180   000E4F98 000000FF 00B0D408 400EC03E   00B0D408 00000000 00000000 0000006F   *..........M.   .....M............*
0EC1A0 ┌→40404040 40404040 40F64040 40404040   40404040 40404040 40404040 40404040   *        6                       *
0EC1C0 │ 40404040 40404040 40404040 40404040   40404040 40404040 40404040 40404040   *                                *
0EC1E0 │ 40404040 40404040 40404040 40404040   00000006 00000000 00000000 00000000   *                ................*
0EC200 │ 00000000 00000000 00000000 00000000   00000000 00000000 00000000 00000000   *................................*
0EC220 │ 00000000 00000000 00000000 00000000                                         *................               *
       DATA
```

**Figure 6.15**
*(Continued)*

1. The immediate problem obviously occurred during the execution of the GET instruction.
2. The data records and the associated control statements are correct. They appear as follows:

```
//GO.SYSIN DD *
         2
         5
         6
/*
```

3. The storage dump shows that the first 10 bytes at DATA (Location 0EC1A0) contain 404040404040404040F6, which is the EBCDIC representation of 9 blanks and the digit 6. This observation confirms that the program read the last data record. The error occurred because GET was executed yet another time. An examination of the loop that Statements 24 through 32 define reveals no obvious exit from the loop. The only possible exit from this loop would be achieved if you wrote EODAD=*endaddr* in the operand entry of the DCB instruction at READER (Statement 67). Since this was not done here, program execution terminated abnormally.

Note that the IA portion of the PSW is not helpful in this case: it points to an instruction within the operating system that is executed as a result of the GET macro instruction.

The next example shows an attempt to fix this program. The DCB has been corrected, but the program does not run correctly: it still produces incorrect results.

EXAMPLE 9

The program listed in Figure 6.16 is the same as the one in Figure 6.15, but with the DCB at READER corrected: EODAD = ENDDATA has been added to this DCB instruction.

This program executes and terminates normally, but an examination of the storage dump reveals that the program has changed only the first fullword of ARRAY (Location 0EC1F0). The following analysis leads to the error:

1. You can verify that the input data set is correct. (It is the same as the one in the last example.)
2. Notice that the last value in the input data set is in Register 3 (R3) and in the array, which indicates that it must have been read. However, you might not know this in general or, if you did know the last data value, you might not know if there were other data values equal to the last value and, therefore, could not be sure that the entire data set was read.
3. To check the number of times that the read loop was executed, you can examine the contents of the index register (R2). It contains zero. This could indicate that the loop was executed only once but, in fact, this is not the case since neither R3 nor the array contains the first data value.
4. Why does R2 contain zero? By looking for instructions that affect R2, you will find that there is no instruction to increment R2. Since R2 is the index register, the program stores each of the input values into the same location—namely, the first fullword at ARRAY.

```
  LOC  OBJECT CODE     ADDR1 ADDR2  STMT   SOURCE STATEMENT

000000                                 1 EX9       CSECT
                                       2 ** READ INTEGERS INTO AN ARRAY OF FULLWORDS
                                       3           PRINT NOGEN                SUPPRESS MACRO EXPANSIONS
                             00002     4 R2        EQU   2                    INDEX REGISTER
                             00003     5 R3        EQU   3                    WORK REGISTER
                             0000C     6 R12       EQU   12                   BASE REGISTER
                             0000D     7 R13       EQU   13                   SAVE AREA POINTER
                             0000E     8 R14       EQU   14                   RETURN REGISTER
                                       9 ** STANDARD ENTRY AND INITIALIZATION:
000000 90EC D00C       0000C          10           STM   R14,R12,12(R13)      SAVE REGISTERS
000004 05C0                           11           BALR  R12,0                LOAD BASE REGISTER
                             00006    12           USING BASE,R12             DECLARE BASE ADDRESS AND REGISTER
000006 50D0 C13A       00140          13 BASE      ST    R13,SAVE+4           SAVE R13
00000A 41D0 C136       0013C          14           LA    R13,SAVE             R13 = ADDRESS OF SAVE AREA
                                      15           OPEN  (READER,INPUT,SNAPDCB,OUTPUT)  PREPARE FOR I/O
00001E 1B22                           23           SR    R2,R2                CLEAR INDEX
                                      24 LOOP      GET   READER,DATA          READ INPUT VALUE
00002E F279 C182 C18A 00188 00190     29           PACK  TEMP(8),DATA(10)     CONVERT
000034 4F30 C182       00188          30           CVB   R3,TEMP                TO BINARY
000038 5032 C1DA       001E0          31           ST    R3,ARRAY(R2)         STORE VALUE INTO AN ARRAY
00003C 47F0 C01A       00020          32           B     LOOP                 REPEAT
                                      33 ENDDATA   SNAP  STORAGE=(ARRAY,ARRAY+60),PDATA=(REGS),DCB=SNAPDCB,ID=1
                                      54           CLOSE (READER,,SNAPDCB)  I/O IS COMPLETE
```

(Continues)

Figure 6.16
A failed attempt to correct the program in Figure 6.15, as described in Example 9.

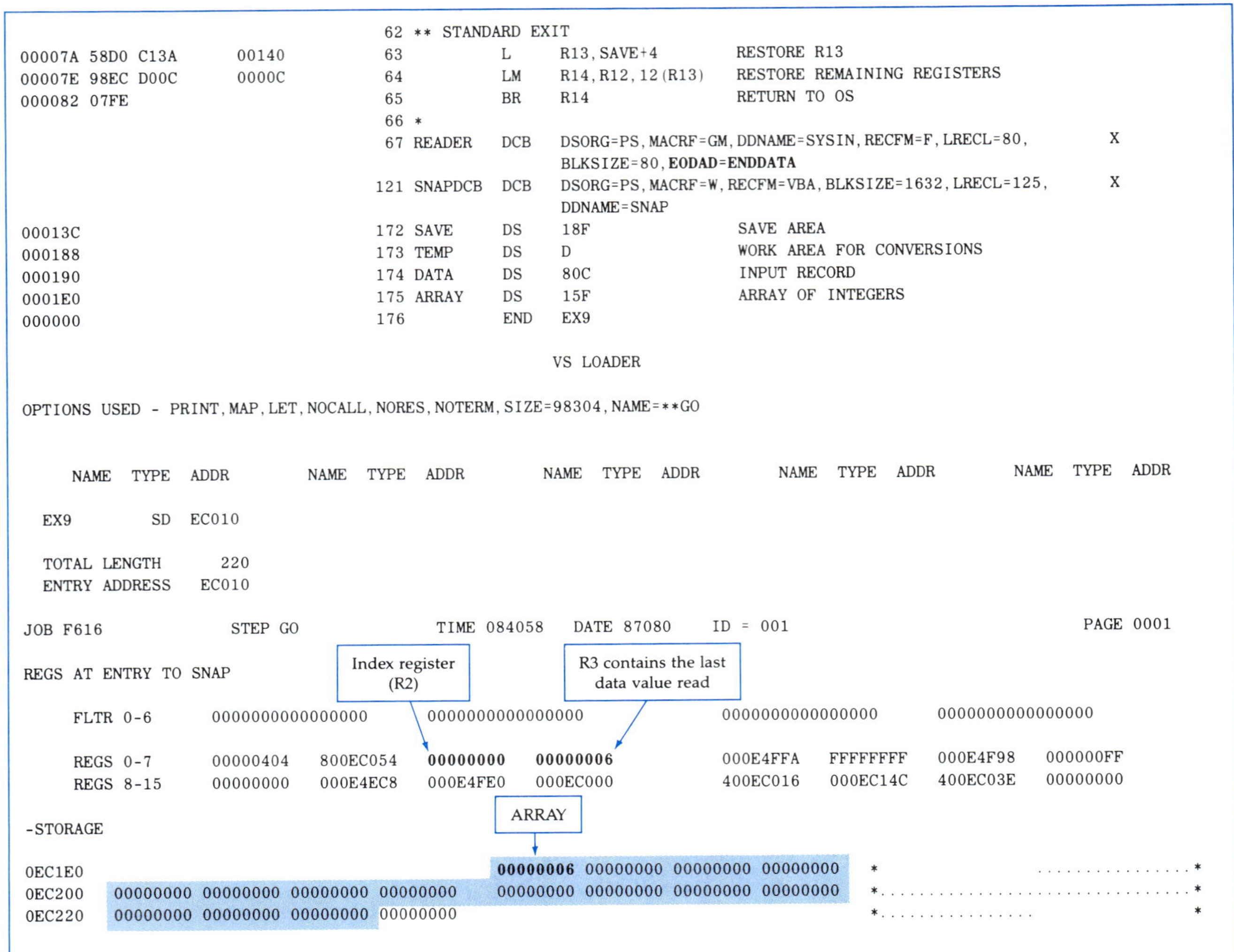

```
                                             62 ** STANDARD EXIT
00007A 58D0 C13A        00140                63            L     R13,SAVE+4           RESTORE R13
00007E 98EC D00C        0000C                64            LM    R14,R12,12(R13)      RESTORE REMAINING REGISTERS
000082 07FE                                  65            BR    R14                  RETURN TO OS
                                             66 *
                                             67 READER     DCB   DSORG=PS,MACRF=GM,DDNAME=SYSIN,RECFM=F,LRECL=80,            X
                                                                 BLKSIZE=80,EODAD=ENDDATA
                                            121 SNAPDCB    DCB   DSORG=PS,MACRF=W,RECFM=VBA,BLKSIZE=1632,LRECL=125,          X
                                                                 DDNAME=SNAP
00013C                                      172 SAVE       DS    18F                  SAVE AREA
000188                                      173 TEMP       DS    D                    WORK AREA FOR CONVERSIONS
000190                                      174 DATA       DS    80C                  INPUT RECORD
0001E0                                      175 ARRAY      DS    15F                  ARRAY OF INTEGERS
000000                                      176            END   EX9

                                                     VS LOADER

OPTIONS USED - PRINT,MAP,LET,NOCALL,NORES,NOTERM,SIZE=98304,NAME=**GO

      NAME   TYPE   ADDR         NAME   TYPE   ADDR         NAME   TYPE   ADDR         NAME   TYPE   ADDR         NAME   TYPE   ADDR

   EX9          SD   EC010

   TOTAL LENGTH       220
   ENTRY ADDRESS    EC010

JOB F616             STEP GO              TIME 084058    DATE 87080     ID = 001                                   PAGE 0001

REGS AT ENTRY TO SNAP

     FLTR 0-6       0000000000000000     0000000000000000           0000000000000000     0000000000000000

     REGS 0-7       00000404   800EC054   00000000   00000006         000E4FFA   FFFFFFFF   000E4F98   000000FF
     REGS 8-15      00000000   000E4EC8   000E4FE0   000EC000         400EC016   000EC14C   400EC03E   00000000

-STORAGE

0EC1E0                                          00000006 00000000 00000000 00000000    *                ................*
0EC200   00000000 00000000 00000000 00000000    00000000 00000000 00000000 00000000    *................................*
0EC220   00000000 00000000 00000000 00000000                                           *................                *
```



**Figure 6.16** *(Continued)*

---

EXAMPLE 10

## An Error Dependent on the Data Set

You can correct the previous program by adding 4 to Register 2 after storing the data value into ARRAY. To do this, insert an Add instruction between Statements 31 and 32 of Figure 6.16. The resulting program runs correctly when you use the same data set as in Examples 8 and 9. However, when you use a larger data set, a program interruption occurs, as indicated in Figure 6.17. The data set contains 21 records that have the values 1 up to 15 in increments of 1, and 4000 up to 9000 in increments of 1000. The following observations lead to the error:

1. The completion code is 0C4, which indicates that an instruction designates an invalid effective address. You can determine the address of this instruction from the instruction address (IA) portion of the PSW. Since the interruption code (INTC) is 0011, you can tell that the

```
  LOC  OBJECT CODE    ADDR1 ADDR2  STMT   SOURCE STATEMENT

000000                                1 EX10     CSECT
                                      2 ** READ INTEGERS INTO AN ARRAY OF FULLWORDS
                                      3          PRINT NOGEN                SUPPRESS MACRO EXPANSIONS
                            00002     4 R2       EQU   2                    INDEX REGISTER
                            00003     5 R3       EQU   3                    WORK REGISTER
                            0000C     6 R12      EQU   12                   BASE REGISTER
                            0000D     7 R13      EQU   13                   SAVE AREA POINTER
                            0000E     8 R14      EQU   14                   RETURN REGISTER
                                      9 ** STANDARD ENTRY LINKAGE AND INITIALIZATION:
000000 90EC D00C      0000C          10          STM   R14,R12,12(R13)      SAVE REGISTERS
000004 05C0                          11          BALR  R12,0                LOAD BASE REGISTER
                            00006    12          USING BASE,R12             DECLARE BASE ADDRESS AND REGISTER
000006 50D0 C13E      00144          13 BASE     ST    R13,SAVE+4           SAVE R13
00000A 41D0 C13A      00140          14          LA    R13,SAVE             R13 = ADDRESS OF SAVE AREA
                                     15          OPEN  (READER,INPUT,SNAPDCB,OUTPUT) PREPARE FOR I/O
00001E 1B22                          23          SR    R2,R2                CLEAR INDEX
                                     24 LOOP     GET   READER,DATA          READ INPUT VALUE
00002E F279 C182 C18A 00188 00190    29          PACK  TEMP(8),DATA(10)     CONVERT
000034 4F30 C182      00188          30          CVB   R3,TEMP                TO BINARY
000038 5032 C1DA      001E0          31          ST    R3,ARRAY(R2)         STORE VALUE INTO AN ARRAY
00003C 5A20 C21A      00220          32          A     R2,=F'4'             INCREMENT INDEX
000040 47F0 C01A      00020          33          B     LOOP                 REPEAT
                                     34 ENDDATA  SNAP  STORAGE=(ARRAY,ARRAY+60),PDATA=(REGS),DCB=SNAPDCB,ID=1
                                     55          CLOSE (READER,,SNAPDCB) I/O IS COMPLETE
                                     63 ** STANDARD EXIT
00007E 58D0 C13E      00144          64          L     R13,SAVE+4           RESTORE R13
000082 98EC D00C      0000C          65          LM    R14,R12,12(R13)      RESTORE REMAINING REGISTERS
000086 07FE                          66          BR    R14                  RETURN TO OS
                                     67 *
                                     68 READER   DCB   DSORG=PS,MACRF=GM,DDNAME=SYSIN,RECFM=F,LRECL=80,         X
                                                       BLKSIZE=80,EODAD=ENDDATA
                                    122 SNAPDCB  DCB   DSORG=PS,MACRF=W,RECFM=VBA,BLKSIZE=1632,LRECL=125,       X
                                                       DDNAME=SNAP
000140                              173 SAVE     DS    18F                  SAVE AREA
000188                              174 TEMP     DS    D                    WORK AREA FOR CONVERSIONS
000190                              175 DATA     DS    80C                  INPUT RECORD
0001E0                              176 ARRAY    DS    15F                  ARRAY OF INTEGERS
000000                              177          END   EX10
000220 00000004                     178                =F'4'

                                             VS LOADER

OPTIONS USED - PRINT,MAP,LET,NOCALL,NORES,NOTERM,SIZE=98304,NAME=**GO


     NAME  TYPE  ADDR         NAME  TYPE  ADDR         NAME  TYPE  ADDR         NAME  TYPE  ADDR         NAME  TYPE  ADDR

  EX10       SD  EC010

  TOTAL LENGTH      228
  ENTRY ADDRESS   EC010

COMPLETION CODE      SYSTEM = 0C4

PSW AT ENTRY TO ABEND  078D0000 000EC048        ILC 4    INTC 0011
  .
  .
  .
```

(Continues)

**Figure 6.17**
A failed attempt to correct the program in Figure 6.16—one that produces a program interruption, as described in Example 10.

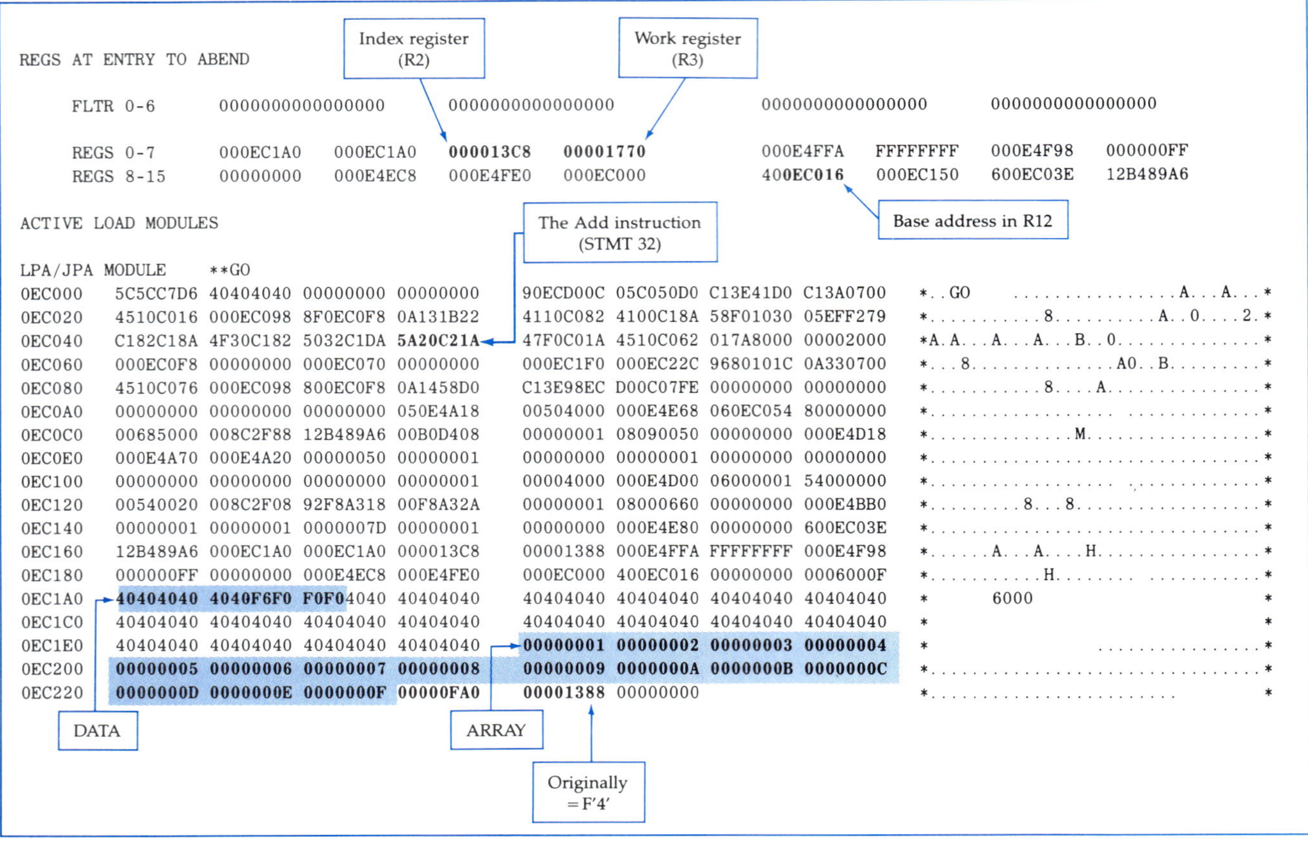


```
REGS AT ENTRY TO ABEND

    FLTR 0-6    0000000000000000    0000000000000000         0000000000000000    0000000000000000

    REGS 0-7    000EC1A0  000EC1A0  000013C8  00001770       000E4FFA  FFFFFFFF  000E4F98  000000FF
    REGS 8-15   00000000  000E4EC8  000E4FE0  000EC000       400EC016  000EC150  600EC03E  12B489A6

ACTIVE LOAD MODULES

LPA/JPA MODULE      **GO
0EC000    5C5CC7D6 40404040 00000000 00000000   90ECD00C 05C050D0 C13E41D0 C13A0700   *..GO   ................A...A...*
0EC020    4510C016 000EC098 8F0ECOF8 0A131B22   4110C082 4100C18A 58F01030 05EFF279   *...........8..........A..0....2.*
0EC040    C182C18A 4F30C182 5032C1DA 5A20C21A   47F0C01A 4510C062 017A8000 00002000   *A.A...A...A...B..0..............*
0EC060    000EC0F8 00000000 000EC070 00000000   000EC1F0 000EC22C 9680101C 0A330700   *...8..............A0..B.........*
0EC080    4510C076 000EC098 800EC0F8 0A1458D0   C13E98EC D00C07FE 00000000 00000000   *...........8....A...............*
0EC0A0    00000000 00000000 00000000 050E4A18   00504000 000E4E68 060EC054 80000000   *................................*
0EC0C0    00685000 008C2F88 12B489A6 00B0D408   00000001 08090050 00000000 000E4D18   *..............M.................*
0EC0E0    000E4A70 000E4A20 00000050 00000001   00000000 00000001 00000000 00000000   *................................*
0EC100    00000000 00000000 00000000 00000001   00004000 000E4D00 06000001 54000000   *................................*
0EC120    00540020 008C2F08 92F8A318 00F8A32A   00000001 08000660 00000000 000E4BB0   *.........8...8..................*
0EC140    00000001 00000001 0000007D 00000001   00000000 000E4E80 00000000 600EC03E   *................................*
0EC160    12B489A6 000EC1A0 000EC1A0 000013C8   00001388 000E4FFA FFFFFFFF 000E4F98   *......A...A....H................*
0EC180    000000FF 00000000 000E4EC8 000E4FE0   000EC000 400EC016 00000000 0006000F   *...........H....................*
0EC1A0    40404040 4040F6F0 F0F04040 40404040   40404040 40404040 40404040 40404040   *        6000                    *
0EC1C0    40404040 40404040 40404040 40404040   40404040 40404040 40404040 40404040   *                                *
0EC1E0    40404040 40404040 40404040 40404040   00000001 00000002 00000003 00000004   *                ................*
0EC200    00000005 00000006 00000007 00000008   00000009 0000000A 0000000B 0000000C   *................................*
0EC220    0000000D 0000000E 0000000F 00000FA0   00001388 00000000                     *........................       *
```

**Figure 6.17**
*(Continued)*

IA contains the address of the instruction that caused the interruption. Thus, the interruption occurred during the execution of the Store instruction at the address 0EC048 (Statement 31).

2. Register 2 (R2) contains $13C8_{16}$. When used as an index with ARRAY, this large value causes the interruption.
3. Register 3 (R3) contains $1770_{16}$, which is 6000 in decimal. This is the last value that was read and converted. You can confirm this fact by examining the dump and by observing that the first 10 bytes at DATA contain

   ```
   404040404040F6F0F0F0
   ```

4. From the storage dump, you can see that the consecutive fullwords that begin at ARRAY contain the values 1 through 15, 4000 ($FA0_{16}$), and 5000 ($1388_{16}$). Thus, after the program read and converted the value 6000, a program interruption occurred when the program attempted to store it.
5. The previous observation implies that the GET instruction was executed 18 times. However, the value of R2 is much larger than it should be. This might happen if the program failed to clear R2 prior to the loop, but this cannot be the case because the program read and stored 17 values correctly. In fact, R2 is initialized correctly. It is subsequently altered only by Statement 32, which seems to execute correctly at first, but which may not continue to do so.

6. To determine if there is a problem with the Add instruction in Statement 32, you can observe the following:
   - **a.** The instruction is correctly assembled, which is confirmed both by the object code and by the fact that it does execute correctly at first.
   - **b.** The instruction is correct in storage and it has not been destroyed.
   - **c.** The base address is correct.
   - **d.** The literal constant (Location 0EC230) that is defined by =F'4' has been destroyed. The last data value stored—namely, $1388_{16}$, which is 5000 in decimal—was stored on top of this constant.
7. The problem occurs when the program reads more than 15 data values, since only 15 fullwords were reserved for the array. You can correct the error by reserving more storage.

To confirm that this error causes all of the previous symptoms, you can trace execution from the time that the literal constant is destroyed by the Store instruction in Statement 31. Observation **6d** implies that, at this time, R3 must contain $1388_{16}$, which is 5000 in decimal, and R2 must contain $40_{16}$. (The address of the destroyed literal constant, 0EC230, is equal to ARRAY + $40_{16}$.) Following the Store, the Add instruction adds what is now in the place of the literal constant—namely, $1388_{16}$—to R2, which produces $13C8_{16}$. This value then causes the program interruption during the next time that it is used as an index value in the Store instruction.

---

# Debugging Hints

1. Take the time to desk-check your programs for both syntax and logical errors before you run them for the first time. Letting the computer find errors that you can easily locate is not economical since this practice often increases your overall debugging time.
2. Make liberal use of the remarks entries when writing the first draft of a program. Many novices add these after the program has been debugged; however, including carefully written remarks and comments can be very helpful during the debugging process.
3. Always attempt to find and correct as many errors as you can from a single run. Avoid the temptation to run the program again immediately after you fix the first error that you find. This will be particularly helpful when you are dealing with execution-time errors. Often, you can uncover errors by using the information in a dump, even though an explicit error message does not exist. By taking the time to find the errors early, you will decrease your total debugging time.
4. Even though a program under development executes and terminates normally, it is often necessary to check the contents of the registers and storage. However, the operating system does not automatically provide a dump in these situations. By always including a Dump instruction before the return to the operating system, you can avoid an extra run just to get a dump. Be sure to dump the program's instructions, as well as the data areas and registers. To avoid an addressability error, do not specify in the Dump instruction a symbol whose value is less than the base address.
5. When an assembler language statement does not work but looks as

if it should, do not blame the computer. Believing that you did not make an error can make it more difficult to find one. Often, a careful examination of the object code will reveal instances in which the assembler language statement is incorrect, even though the assembler did not detect the error.

6. If your program produces unusual results that defy explanation, perhaps you have accidentally destroyed the contents of the base register. Check a dump to see if this is the case.
7. Tracing the execution of portions of a program is a useful, and often necessary, debugging strategy. You can facilitate lengthy traces by including instructions to dump or print the contents of key storage locations or registers. You can then use this information to verify the accuracy of the trace as it progresses. Choose the location of these instructions carefully and be selective about what is dumped. Long dumps that contain too much information can frustrate your search for the error.
8. When your program terminates normally, carefully verify its results. Test the program with appropriate data that thoroughly checks the logic of the program, including all of its paths. Review what you have learned in your previous studies about creating test data sets, since that information is also applicable to assembler language programs.
9. Initializing storage prior to program execution can be helpful during debugging. You can do this by using DCs, instead of DSs, to reserve storage. Thus, you can examine a dump and readily determine storage locations that the program probably does not affect.

## Summary

1. When the assembler is unable to convert a relocatable expression into a base-displacement representation, it issues an addressability error message. Sources of this error include a missing USING statement or a base address that does not permit a valid displacement between 0 and 4095.
2. Assembler error messages do not always point to the actual source of the error.
3. You can request a snapshot dump at any time during execution. It is used to determine the status of either the registers or storage, so that you can verify the logic of a program.
4. An abend dump is produced when program execution is terminated due to an execution-time error, such as a program interruption. A completion code that indicates the nature of the termination is printed.
5. The format of the PSW depends upon whether the computer is in BC mode, EC mode, or 370-XA mode. Regardless of its format, the PSW will contain the instruction address (IA), the condition code (CC), the program mask, and the protection key.
6. The program mask is a portion of the PSW that controls whether or not four specific exceptions will cause a program interruption. Each mask bit corresponds to one exception. If the bit value is 0, the exception will be ignored; if the bit value is 1, the exception will cause a program interruption.
7. The instruction length code (ILC) is a 2-bit binary quantity that indicates the length in halfwords of the currently executing instruction. In BC mode, it appears in the PSW; in other modes, it is stored in a fixed location in storage.
8. When a program interruption occurs, the instruction address (IA) portion of the PSW typically points to the instruction that follows the one that caused the interruption. However, when the interruption code is 0010 or 0011, the IA portion of the PSW points directly to the instruction that caused the interruption. The completion code indicates the type of interruption.

## Exercises

1. The program in Figure 6.18 is supposed to compute 10 additional terms of the Fibonacci sequence after it is given the first 2 terms. (See Programming Problem 4 of Chapter 5.) The results of execution are incorrect. Correct the program. (*Hint:* The dump shows one error. You can locate a second error by carefully tracing the program's logic.)
2. The program in Figure 6.19 is supposed to read a value N. The program should then read N unsigned values, convert the values to binary, and store the results into consecutive fullwords of an array. The results of execution are incorrect. Determine the error. Note that the following data values were specified, as 10-character strings, one per input record:

   7, 2, 4, 6, 8, 10, 12, 14
3. The program in Figure 6.20 is supposed to determine the largest integer in an array, but a program interruption takes place. Correct the program.
4. The program in Figure 6.21 is supposed to compute the sum of the integers in an array, but a program interruption occurs. Correct the program.
5. The program in Figure 6.22 is supposed to determine the smallest integer in an array, but the results are incorrect. Correct the program.
6. Suppose you notice that the CLOSE instruction is missing from the program in Figure 6.14 (Example 7). The program in Figure 6.23 contains both the correction that Example 7 describes and the required CLOSE instruction. However, a program interruption occurs. Correct the program.

```
  LOC   OBJECT CODE     ADDR1 ADDR2  STMT    SOURCE STATEMENT

000000                                  1 FIBONACC CSECT
                                        2          PRINT NOGEN              SUPPRESS MACRO EXPANSIONS
                              00002     3 R2       EQU   2                  WORK REGISTER
                              00003     4 R3       EQU   3                  INDEX REGISTER
                              0000C     5 R12      EQU   12                 BASE REGISTER
                              0000D     6 R13      EQU   13                 SAVE AREA POINTER
                              0000E     7 R14      EQU   14                 RETURN REGISTER
                                        8 ** STANDARD ENTRY AND INITIALIZATION:
000000 90EC D00C        0000C           9          STM   R14,R12,12(R13)    SAVE REGISTERS
000004 05C0                            10          BALR  R12,0              LOAD BASE REGISTER
                              00006    11          USING BASE,R12           DECLARE BASE ADDRESS AND REGISTER
000006 50D0 C0A2        000A8          12 BASE     ST    R13,SAVE+4         SAVE R13
00000A 41D0 C09E        000A4          13          LA    R13,SAVE           R13 = ADDRESS OF SAVE AREA
                                       14          OPEN  (SNAPDCB,OUTPUT)   PREPARE FOR I/O
00001A 1B33                            20          SR    R3,R3              CLEAR INDEX
00001C 5820 C072        00078          21          L     R2,FIB1            GET SECOND TERM OF SEQUENCE
000020 5A23 C06E        00074          22 LOOP     A     R2,FIB(R3)         ADD PREVIOUS TERM
000024 5020 C06E        00074          23          ST    R2,FIB + 8(R3)     STORE IN NEXT LOCATION OF ARRAY
000028 5A30 C142        00148          24          A     R3,=F'4'           INCREMENT INDEX
00002C 5930 C146        0014C          25          C     R3,=F'36'          FINISHED?
000030 4740 C01A        00020          26          BL    LOOP               IF NOT, REPEAT
                                       27          SNAP  PDATA=(REGS),STORAGE=(BASE,BASE+360),DCB=SNAPDCB,ID=1
                                       48          CLOSE (SNAPDCB)          I/O IS COMPLETE
                                       54 ** STANDARD EXIT
00006A 58D0 C0A2        000A8          55          L     R13,SAVE+4         RESTORE R13
00006E 98EC D00C        0000C          56          LM    R14,R12,12(R13)    RESTORE REMAINING REGISTERS
000072 07FE                            57          BR    R14                RETURN TO OS
000074 00000000                        58 FIB      DC    F'0'               1ST FIBONACCI NUMBER
000078 00000001                        59 FIB1     DC    F'1'               2ND FIBONACCI NUMBER
00007C                                 60          DS    10F                NEXT 10 FIBONACCI NUMBERS
0000A4                                 61 SAVE     DS    18F                SAVE AREA
                                       62 SNAPDCB  DCB   DSORG=PS,MACRF=W,RECFM=VBA,BLKSIZE=1632,LRECL=125,      X
                                                         DDNAME=SNAP
000000                                113          END   FIBONACC
000148 00000004                       114                =F'4'
00014C 00000024                       115                =F'36'
.
.
.
  ENTRY ADDRESS   EC010
.
.
.
REGS AT ENTRY TO SNAP

     FLTR 0-6      0000000000000000     0000000000000000          0000000000000000     0000000000000000

     REGS 0-7      000001A0   800EC048   00000002   00000024          000E4FFA   FFFFFFFF   000E4F98   000000FF
     REGS 8-15     00000000   000E4EC8   000E4FE0   000EC000          400EC016   000EC0B4   00010308   00000000

-STORAGE

0EC000                                             05C050D0 C0A241D0 C09E0700   *                 .............*
0EC020   4510C012 8F0EC0FC 0A131B33 5820C072   5A23C06E 5020C06E 5A30C142 5930C146   *..........................A...A.*
0EC040   4740C01A 4510C052 017A8000 00002000   000EC0FC 00000000 000EC060 00000000   *. ..............................*
0EC060   000EC016 800EC17E 9680101C 0A330700   4510C062 800EC0FC 0A1458D0 C0A298EC   *......A.........................*
0EC080   D00C07FE 00000002 00000001 00000000   00000000 00000000 00000000 00000000   *................................*
0EC0A0   00000000 00000000 00000000 00000000   00000000 00000000 000E4E80 00000000   *................................*
0EC0C0   00000000 00000000 00000000 00000000   00000000 00000000 00000000 00000000   *................................*
     LINE 0EC0E0 SAME AS ABOVE
0EC100   00000000 00000000 00000000 00000000   00000001 00004000 000E4E68 06000001   *.....................  .........*
0EC120   54000000 00400020 008BA608 92F8A318   00F8A32A 00000001 08000660 00000000   *.....  ........8...8.............*
0EC140   000E4D18 00000001 00000001 0000007D   00000001 00000000 00000004 00000024   *................................*
0EC160   00000000 00000000 00000000 00000000   00000000 00000000 00000000 00000000   *................................*
```

**Figure 6.18**
A program that is supposed to produce 10 additional terms of a Fibonacci sequence, as given in Exercise 1.

```
  LOC   OBJECT CODE      ADDR1 ADDR2  STMT    SOURCE STATEMENT

000000                                   1 READ      CSECT
                                         2           PRINT NOGEN              SUPPRESS MACRO EXPANSIONS
                               00002     3 R2        EQU   2                  LOOP COUNTER
                               00003     4 R3        EQU   3                  WORK REGISTER
                               00004     5 R4        EQU   4                  INDEX REGISTER
                               0000C     6 R12       EQU   12                 BASE REGISTER
                               0000D     7 R13       EQU   13                 SAVE AREA POINTER
                               0000E     8 R14       EQU   14                 RETURN REGISTER
                                         9 ** STANDARD ENTRY AND INITIALIZATION:
000000 90EC D00C          0000C         10           STM   R14,R12,12(R13)    SAVE REGISTERS
000004 05C0                             11           BALR  R12,0              LOAD BASE REGISTER
                               00006    12           USING BASE,R12           DECLARE BASE ADDRESS AND REGISTER
000006 50D0 C10E          00114         13 BASE      ST    R13,SAVE+4         SAVE R13
00000A 41D0 C10A          00110         14           LA    R13,SAVE           R13 = ADDRESS OF SAVE AREA
                                        15           OPEN  (READER,INPUT,SNAPDCB,OUTPUT)  PREPARE FOR I/O
                                        23           GET   READER,N           READ N
00002C F279 C102 C09E 00108 000A4       28           PACK  TEMP(8),N(10)      CONVERT N
000032 4F20 C102          00108         29           CVB   R2,TEMP              TO BINARY
000036 1B44                             30           SR    R4,R4              CLEAR INDEX
                                        31 LOOP      GET   READER,DATA        READ NEXT ARRAY ELEMENT
000046 F279 C102 C0A8 00108 000AE       36           PACK  TEMP(8),DATA(10)   CONVERT IT
00004C 4F30 C102          00108         37           CVB   R3,TEMP              TO BINARY
000050 5034 C0B2          000B8         38           ST    R3,ARRAY(R4)       STORE IT IN ARRAY
000054 5A40 C20A          00210         39           A     R4,=F'4'           INCREMENT INDEX
000058 5B20 C20E          00214         40           S     R2,=F'1'           DECREMENT LOOP COUNTER
00005C 4720 C032          00038         41           BH    LOOP               REPEAT IF LOOP COUNTER > 0
                                        42 ENDDATA   SNAP  PDATA=(REGS),STORAGE=(BASE,BASE+530),DCB=SNAPDCB,ID=1
                                        63           CLOSE (READER,,SNAPDCB) I/O IS COMPLETE
                                        71 ** STANDARD EXIT
00009A 58D0 C10E          00114         72           L     R13,SAVE+4         RESTORE R13
00009E 98EC D00C          0000C         73           LM    R14,R12,12(R13)    RESTORE REMAINING REGISTERS
0000A2 07FE                             74           BR    R14                RETURN TO OS
0000A4                                  75 N         DS    10C                AREA FOR FIRST DATA RECORD
0000AE                                  76 DATA      DS    10C                AREA FOR SUBSEQUENT DATA RECORDS
0000B8                                  77 ARRAY     DS    20F                ARRAY OF INTEGERS READ
000108                                  78 TEMP      DS    D                  WORK AREA FOR CONVERSIONS
000110                                  79 SAVE      DS    18F                SAVE AREA
                                        80 READER    DCB   DSORG=PS,MACRF=GM,DDNAME=SYSIN,RECFM=F,LRECL=80,          X
                                                           BLKSIZE=80,EODAD=ENDDATA
                                       134 SNAPDCB   DCB   DSORG=PS,MACRF=W,RECFM=VBA,BLKSIZE=1632,LRECL=125,        X
                                                           DDNAME=SNAP
000000                                 185           END   READ
000210 00000004                        186                 =F'4'
000214 00000001                        187                 =F'1'
.
.
.
  ENTRY ADDRESS    EC010
.
.
.
REGS AT ENTRY TO SNAP

     FLTR 0-6     0000000000000000     0000000000000000          0000000000000000     0000000000000000

     REGS 0-7     000EC0BE  800EC074  00000000  0000000E         0000001C  FFFFFFFF  000E4F98  000000FF
     REGS 8-15    00000000  000E4EC8  000E4FE0  000EC000         400EC016  000EC120  600EC056  12B489A6
```

*(Continues)*

**Figure 6.19**
A program that is supposed to read integers into an array, as given in Exercise 2.

```
-STORAGE

0EC000                                         05C050D0 C10E41D0 C10A0700   *                ....A...A...*
0EC020   4510C016 000EC168 8F0EC1C8 0A134110   C1524100 C09E58F0 103005EF F279C102   *......A...AH....A......0....2.A.*
0EC040   C09E4F20 C1021B44 4110C152 4100C0A8   58F01030 05EFF279 C102C0A8 4F30C102   *....A.....A......0....2.A.....A.*
0EC060   5034C0B2 5A40C20A 5B20C20E 4720C032   4510C07E 017A8000 00002000 000EC1C8   *..... B...B..................AH*
0EC080   00000000 000EC08C 00000000 000EC016   800EC228 9680101C 0A330700 4510C092   *..................B.............*
0EC0A0   000EC168 800EC1C8 0A1458D0 C10E98EC   D00C07FE 40404040 40404040 40F74040   *..A...AH....A.......         7  *
0EC0C0   40404040 4040F1F4 40404040 40404040   40404040 40404040 40404040 40404040   *      14                        *
0EC0E0   0000000E 40404040 40404040 40404040   40404040 40404040 40404040 40404040   *....                            *
0EC100   40404040 40404040 40404040 40400000   00000000 00000000 00000000 0000014F   *              ..................*
0EC120   00000000 000E4E80 00000000 600EC056   12B489A6 000EC0BE 000EC0BE 00000001   *................................*
0EC140   0000000C 00000018 FFFFFFFF 000E4F98   000000FF 00000000 000E4EC8 000E4FE0   *...........................H....*
0EC160   000EC000 400EC016 00000000 00000000   00000000 00000000 00000000 050E4A18   *.... ...........................*
0EC180   00504000 000E4E68 060EC070 80000000   00685000 008B8F88 12B489A6 00B0D408   *.. ..........................M.*
0EC1A0   00000001 08090050 00000000 000E4D18   000E4A70 000E4A20 00000050 00000001   *................................*
0EC1C0   00000000 00000001 00000000 00000000   00000000 00000000 00000000 00000001   *................................*
0EC1E0   00004000 000E4D00 06000001 54000000   00400020 008B8F08 92F8A318 00F8A32A   *.. ............. .......8...8..*
0EC200   00000001 08000660 00000000 000E4BB0   00000001 00000001 0000007D 00000001   *................................*
0EC220   00000004 00000001 00000000                                                  *...........                     *
```

**Figure 6.19** *(Continued)*

```
  LOC  OBJECT CODE    ADDR1 ADDR2  STMT   SOURCE STATEMENT

000000                                1 MAX      CSECT
                                      2          PRINT NOGEN           SUPPRESS MACRO EXPANSIONS
                            00003     3 R3       EQU   3               LARGEST VALUE FOUND SO FAR
                            00004     4 R4       EQU   4               INDEX REGISTER
                            0000C     5 R12      EQU   12              BASE REGISTER
                            0000D     6 R13      EQU   13              SAVE AREA POINTER
                            0000E     7 R14      EQU   14              RETURN REGISTER
                                      8 ** STANDARD ENTRY AND INITIALIZATION:
000000 90EC D00C      0000C           9          STM   R14,R12,12(R13) SAVE REGISTERS
000004 05C0                          10          BALR  R12,0           LOAD BASE REGISTER
                            00006    11          USING BASE,R12        DECLARE BASE ADDRESS AND REGISTER
000006 50D0 C096      0009C          12 BASE     ST    R13,SAVE+4      SAVE R13
00000A 41D0 C092      00098          13          LA    R13,SAVE        R13 = ADDRESS OF SAVE AREA
                                     14          OPEN  (SNAPDCB,OUTPUT) PREPARE FOR DUMP
00001A 5830 C132      00138          20          L     R3,=X'80000000' GET SMALLEST POSSIBLE VALUE
00001E 5B40 0004      00004          21          S     R4,R4           CLEAR INDEX
000022 5934 C07A      00080          22 LOOP     C     R3,ARRAY(R4)    COMPARE LARGEST SO FAR WITH NEXT ELEMENT
000026 4720 C028      0002E          23          BH    CONTINUE        SKIP AHEAD IF R3 IS STILL LARGEST
00002A 5834 C07A      00080          24          L     R3,ARRAY(R4)    ELSE REPLACE R3 WITH LARGER VALUE
00002E 5A40 C136      0013C          25 CONTINUE A     R4,=F'4'        INCREMENT INDEX
000032 5940 C13A      00140          26          C     R4,=F'20'       FINISHED?
000036 4740 C01C      00022          27          BL    LOOP            IF NOT, REPEAT
00003A 5030 C08E      00094          28          ST    R3,LARGE        SAVE RESULT
                                     29          SNAP  PDATA=(REGS),STORAGE=(BASE,BASE+350),DCB=SNAPDCB,ID=1
                                     50          CLOSE (SNAPDCB)       DUMP IS COMPLETE
```

*(Continues)*

**Figure 6.20**
A program that is supposed to determine the largest integer in an array, as given in Exercise 3.

```
                                       56 ** STANDARD EXIT
000076 58D0 C096      0009C            57          L     R13,SAVE+4        RESTORE R13
00007A 98EC D00C      0000C            58          LM    R14,R12,12(R13)   RESTORE REMAINING REGISTERS
00007E 07FE                            59          BR    R14               RETURN TO OS
000080 FFFFFFF8                        60 ARRAY    DC    F'-8'             ARRAY OF FULLWORDS
000084 00002351                        61          DC    F'9041'
000088 00003039                        62          DC    F'12345'
00008C FFFFCFC7                        63          DC    F'-12345'
000090 00000000                        64          DC    F'0'
000094                                 65 LARGE    DS    F                 LARGEST INTEGER
000098                                 66 SAVE     DS    18F               SAVE AREA
                                       67 SNAPDCB  DCB   DSORG=PS,MACRF=W,RECFM=VBA,BLKSIZE=1632,LRECL=125,     X
                                                         DDNAME=SNAP
000000                                118          END   MAX
000138 80000000                       119                =X'80000000'
00013C 00000004                       120                =F'4'
000140 00000014                       121                =F'20'
.
.
.
  ENTRY ADDRESS   EC010

COMPLETION CODE     SYSTEM = 0C4

PSW AT ENTRY TO ABEND  078D2000 000EC032        ILC 4    INTC 0010
.
.
.
REGS AT ENTRY TO ABEND

     FLTR 0-6      0000000000000000     0000000000000000          0000000000000000     0000000000000000

     REGS 0-7      000001A0   008BAE60   800E4F7C   80000000      000D6542   FFFFFFFF   000E4F98   000000FF
     REGS 8-15     00000000   000E4EC8   000E4FE0   000EC000      400EC016   000EC0A8   00010308   00000000

ACTIVE LOAD MODULES

LPA/JPA MODULE    **GO
0EC000    5C5CC7D6 40404040 00000000 00000000    90ECD00C 05C050D0 C09641D0 C0920700    *..GO    ........................*
0EC020    4510C012 8F0EC0F0 0A135830 C1325B40    00045934 C07A4720 C0285834 C07A5A40    *.......0....A.. ............... *
0EC040    C1365940 C13A4740 C01C5030 C08E0700    4510C05E 017A8000 00002000 000EC0F0    *A.. A.. .......................0*
0EC060    00000000 000EC06C 00000000 000EC016    000EC174 9680101C 0A330700 4510C06E    *..................A.............*
0EC080    800EC0F0 0A1458D0 C09698EC D00C07FE    FFFFFFF8 00002351 00003039 FFFFCFC7    *...0...............8...........G*
0EC0A0    00000000 00000000 00000000 000E4E80    00000000 00000000 00000000 00000000    *................................*
0EC0C0    00000000 00000000 00000000 00000000    00000000 00000000 00000000 00000000    *................................*
      LINE 0EC0E0 SAME AS ABOVE
0EC100    00000000 00000001 00004000 000E4E68    06000001 54000000 00400020 008BA608    *.......... ............. ......*
0EC120    92F8A318 00F8A32A 00000001 08000660    00000000 000E4D18 00000001 00000001    *.8...8..........................*
0EC140    0000007D 00000001 80000000 00000004    00000014 00000000                      *.......................        *
```

**Figure 6.20** *(Continued)*

```
  LOC  OBJECT CODE    ADDR1 ADDR2  STMT   SOURCE STATEMENT

000000                                1 ADD      CSECT
                                      2          PRINT NOGEN            SUPPRESS MACRO EXPANSIONS
                            00002     3 R2       EQU   2                LOOP COUNTER
                            00003     4 R3       EQU   3                INDEX REGISTER
                            00004     5 R4       EQU   4                SUM
                            0000C     6 R12      EQU   12               BASE REGISTER
                            0000D     7 R13      EQU   13               SAVE AREA POINTER
                            0000E     8 R14      EQU   14               RETURN REGISTER
                                      9 ** STANDARD ENTRY AND INITIALIZATION:
000000 90EC D00C      0000C          10          STM   R14,R12,12(R13)  SAVE REGISTERS
000004 05C0                          11 BASE     BALR  R12,0            LOAD BASE REGISTER
                            00004    12          USING BASE,R12         DECLARE BASE ADDRESS AND REGISTER
000006 50D0 C094      00098          13          ST    R13,SAVE+4       SAVE R13
00000A 41D0 C090      00094          14          LA    R13,SAVE         R13 = ADDRESS OF SAVE AREA
                                     15          OPEN  (SNAPDCB,OUTPUT) PREPARE FOR DUMP
00001A 1B44                          21          SR    R4,R4            CLEAR SUM REGISTER
00001C 1B22                          22          SR    R2,R2            CLEAR LOOP COUNTER
00001E 1B33                          23          SR    R3,R3            CLEAR INDEX
                                     24 * REPEAT N TIMES:
000020 5A43 C074      00078          25 LOOP     A     R4,ARRAY(R3)     ADD NEXT ARRAY ELEMENT
000024 5AC0 C134      00138          26          A     R12,=F'1'        INCREMENT LOOP COUNTER
000028 5A30 C138      0013C          27          A     R3,=F'4'         INCREMENT INDEX REGISTER
00002C 5920 C088      0008C          28          C     R2,N             FINISHED?
000030 4740 C01C      00020          29          BL    LOOP             REPEAT IF LOOP COUNTER < N
                                     30 * END REPEAT
000034 5040 C08C      00090          31          ST    R4,SUM           STORE SUM
                                     32          SNAP  PDATA=(REGS),STORAGE=(ARRAY,ARRAY+28),DCB=SNAPDCB,ID=1
                                     53          CLOSE (SNAPDCB)        DUMP IS COMPLETE
                                     59 ** STANDARD EXIT
00006E 58D0 C094      00098          60          L     R13,SAVE+4       RESTORE R13
000072 98EC D00C      0000C          61          LM    R14,R12,12(R13)  RESTORE REMAINING REGISTERS
000076 07FE                          62          BR    R14              RETURN TO OS
000078 FFFFFFFF                      63 ARRAY    DC    F'-1'            ARRAY OF FULLWORDS
00007C 00000062                      64          DC    F'98'
000080 00000011                      65          DC    F'17'
000084 FFFFFFFD                      66          DC    F'-3'
000088 0000003D                      67          DC    F'61'
00008C 00000005                      68 N        DC    F'5'             NUMBER OF INTEGERS IN ARRAY
000090                               69 SUM      DS    F                SUM OF INTEGERS IN ARRAY
000094                               70 SAVE     DS    18F              SAVE AREA
                                     71 SNAPDCB  DCB   DSORG=PS,MACRF=W,RECFM=VBA,BLKSIZE=1632,LRECL=125,       X
                                                       DDNAME=SNAP
000000                              122          END   ADD
000138 00000001                     123                =F'1'
00013C 00000004                     124                =F'4'
.
.
.
  ENTRY ADDRESS   EC010

COMPLETION CODE      SYSTEM = 0C4

PSW AT ENTRY TO ABEND  078D2000 000EC038        ILC 4   INTC 0010
.
.
.
REGS AT ENTRY TO ABEND

     FLTR 0-6      0000000000000000   0000000000000000        0000000000000000   0000000000000000

     REGS 0-7      000E4F54  800EC024  00000000  00000000        FFFF0000  FFFFFFFF  000E4F98  000000FF
     REGS 8-15     00000000  000E4EC8  000E4FE0  000EC000        400FC016  000EC0A6  00010308  000EC010
```

(Continues)

**Figure 6.21**
A program that is supposed to compute the sum of integers in an array, as given in Exercise 4.

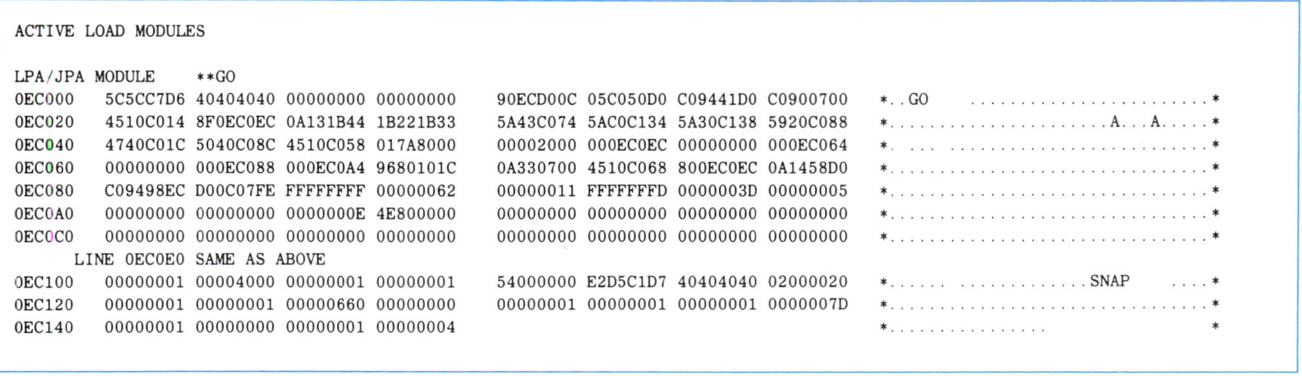

```
ACTIVE LOAD MODULES

LPA/JPA MODULE       **GO
0EC000    5C5CC7D6 40404040 00000000 00000000    90ECD00C 05C050D0 C09441D0 C0900700   *..GO     ........................*
0EC020    4510C014 8F0EC0EC 0A131B44 1B221B33    5A43C074 5AC0C134 5A30C138 5920C088   *.....................A...A.....*
0EC040    4740C01C 5040C08C 4510C058 017A8000    00002000 000EC0EC 00000000 000EC064   *. ... ..........................*
0EC060    00000000 000EC088 000EC0A4 9680101C    0A330700 4510C068 800EC0EC 0A1458D0   *................................*
0EC080    C09498EC D00C07FE FFFFFFFF 00000062    00000011 FFFFFFFD 0000003D 00000005   *................................*
0EC0A0    00000000 00000000 0000000E 4E800000    00000000 00000000 00000000 00000000   *................................*
0EC0C0    00000000 00000000 00000000 00000000    00000000 00000000 00000000 00000000   *................................*
      LINE 0EC0E0 SAME AS ABOVE
0EC100    00000001 00004000 00000001 00000001    54000000 E2D5C1D7 40404040 02000020   *...... .............SNAP    ....*
0EC120    00000001 00000001 00000660 00000000    00000001 00000001 00000001 0000007D   *................................*
0EC140    00000001 00000000 00000001 00000004                                          *................               *
```

**Figure 6.21** (*Continued*)

```
  LOC  OBJECT CODE    ADDR1 ADDR2  STMT   SOURCE STATEMENT

000000                                1 MIN      CSECT
                                      2          PRINT NOGEN             SUPPRESS MACRO EXPANSIONS
                            00003     3 R3       EQU   3                 SMALLEST VALUE FOUND SO FAR
                            00004     4 R4       EQU   4                 INDEX REGISTER
                            0000C     5 R12      EQU   12                BASE REGISTER
                            0000D     6 R13      EQU   13                SAVE AREA POINTER
                            0000E     7 R14      EQU   14                RETURN REGISTER
                                      8 ** STANDARD ENTRY AND INITIALIZATION:
000000 90EC D00C      0000C           9          STM   R14,R12,12(R13)   SAVE REGISTERS
000004 05C0                          10          BALR  R12,0             LOAD BASE REGISTER
                            00006    11          USING BASE,R12          DECLARE BASE ADDRESS AND REGISTER
000006 50D0 C092      00098          12 BASE     ST    R13,SAVE+4        SAVE R13
00000A 41D0 C08E      00094          13          LA    R13,SAVE          R13 = ADDRESS OF SAVE AREA
                                     14          OPEN  (SNAPDCB,OUTPUT)  PREPARE FOR DUMP
00001A 5830 C132      00138          20          L     R3,=X'7FFFFFFF'   GET LARGEST POSSIBLE VALUE
00001E 1B44                          21          SR    R4,R4             CLEAR INDEX
000020 5934 C076      0007C          22 LOOP     C     R3,ARRAY(R4)      COMPARE SMALLEST SO FAR W. NEXT ELEMENT
000024 47B0 C026      0002C          23          BNL   CONTINUE          SKIP AHEAD IF R3 IS STILL SMALLEST
000028 5834 C076      0007C          24          L     R3,ARRAY(R4)      ELSE REPLACE R3 WITH SMALLER VALUE
00002C 5A40 C136      0013C          25 CONTINUE A     R4,=F'4'          INCREMENT INDEX
000030 5940 C13A      00140          26          C     R4,=F'20'         FINISHED?
000034 4740 C01A      00020          27          BL    LOOP              IF NOT, REPEAT
000038 5030 C08A      00090          28          ST    R3,SMALL          SAVE RESULT
                                     29          SNAP  PDATA=(REGS),STORAGE=(BASE,BASE+316),DCB=SNAPDCB,ID=1
                                     50          CLOSE (SNAPDCB)         DUMP IS COMPLETE
                                     56 ** STANDARD EXIT
000072 58D0 C092      00098          57          L     R13,SAVE+4        RESTORE R13
000076 98EC D00C      0000C          58          LM    R14,R12,12(R13)   RESTORE REMAINING REGISTERS
00007A 07FE                          59          BR    R14               RETURN TO OS
00007C FFFFFFF8                      60 ARRAY    DC    F'-8'             ARRAY OF FULLWORDS
000080 00002351                      61          DC    F'9041'
000084 00003039                      62          DC    F'12345'
000088 FFFFCFC7                      63          DC    F'-12345'
00008C 00000000                      64          DC    F'0'
000090                               65 SMALL    DS    F                 SMALLEST INTEGER
000094                               66 SAVE     DS    18F               SAVE AREA
                                     67 SNAPDCB  DCB   DSORG=PS,MACRF=W,RECFM=VBA,BLKSIZE=1632,LRECL=125,       X
                                                       DDNAME=SNAP
000000                              118          END   MIN
000138 7FFFFFFF                     119                =X'7FFFFFFF'
00013C 00000004                     120                =F'4'
000140 00000014                     121                =F'20'
```

(*Continues*)

**Figure 6.22**
A program that is supposed to determine the smallest integer in an array, as given in Exercise 5.

```
.
.
.
 ENTRY ADDRESS   EC010
.
.
.
REGS AT ENTRY TO SNAP

     FLTR 0-6        0000000000000000     0000000000000000          0000000000000000     0000000000000000

     REGS 0-7        000001A0   800EC050   800E4F7C   7FFFFFFF          00000014   FFFFFFFF   000E4F98   000000FF
     REGS 8-15       00000000   000E4EC8   000E4FE0   000EC000          400EC016   000EC0A4   00010308   00000000

-STORAGE

0EC000                                                05C050D0 C09241D0 C08E0700   *                  ............*
0EC020    4510C012 8F0EC0EC 0A135830 C1321B44    5934C076 47B0C026 5834C076 5A40C136   *............A...............A.*
0EC040    5940C13A 4740C01A 5030C08A 4510C05A    017A8000 00002000 000EC0EC 00000000   *. A.. .........................*
0EC060    000EC068 00000000 000EC016 800EC152    9680101C 0A330700 4510C06A 800EC0EC   *..............A................*
0EC080    0A1458D0 C09298EC D00C07FE FFFFFFF8    00002351 00003039 FFFFCFC7 00000000   *..............8..........G....*
0EC0A0    7FFFFFFF 00000000 000E4E80 00000000    00000000 00000000 00000000 00000000   *..............................*
0EC0C0    00000000 00000000 00000000 00000000    00000000 00000000 00000000 00000000   *..............................*
     LINE 0EC0E0 SAME AS ABOVE
0EC100    00000001 00004000 000E4E68 06000001    54000000 00540020 008BA608 92F8A318   *...... ...................8..*
0EC120    00F8A32A 00000001 08000660 00000000    000E4D18 00000001 00000001 0000007D   *.8............................*
0EC140    00000001 00000000 7FFFFFFF 00000004    00000014                              *....................          *
```

**Figure 6.22** *(Continued)*

```
  LOC   OBJECT CODE    ADDR1 ADDR2  STMT   SOURCE STATEMENT

000000                                 1 ADD      CSECT
                                       2 ** COMPUTE THE SUM OF THE N FULLWORD-INTEGERS AT ARRAY
                                       3          PRINT NOGEN               SUPPRESS MACRO EXPANSIONS
                             00002     4 R2       EQU   2                   INDEX REGISTER
                             00003     5 R3       EQU   3                   LOOP COUNTER
                             00004     6 R4       EQU   4                   WORK REGISTER
                             0000C     7 R12      EQU   12                  BASE REGISTER
                             0000D     8 R13      EQU   13                  SAVE AREA POINTER
                             0000E     9 R14      EQU   14                  RETURN REGISTER
                                      10 ** STANDARD ENTRY AND INITIALIZATION:
000000 90EC D00C       0000C          11          STM   R14,R12,12(R13)     SAVE REGISTERS
000004 05C0                           12          BALR  R12,0               LOAD BASE REGISTER
                             00006    13          USING BASE,R12            DECLARE BASE ADDRESS AND REGISTER
000006 50D0 C076       0007C          14 BASE     ST    R13,SAVE+4          SAVE R13
00000A 41D0 C072       00078          15          LA    R13,SAVE            R13 = ADDRESS OF SAVE AREA
                                      16          OPEN  (SNAPDCB,OUTPUT)    PREPARE FOR DUMP
00001A 1B22                           22          SR    R2,R2               CLEAR INDEX REGISTER
00001C 1B33                           23          SR    R3,R3               CLEAR LOOP COUNTER
00001E 1B44                           24          SR    R4,R4               CLEAR WORK REGISTER
                                      25 * REPEAT N TIMES:
000020 5A42 C112       00118          26 LOOP     A     R4,ARRAY(R2)        ADD NEXT ARRAY ELEMENT
000024 5A20 C132       00138          27          A     R2,=F'4'            INCREMENT INDEX
000028 5A30 C136       0013C          28          A     R3,=F'1'            INCREMENT LOOP COUNTER
00002C 5930 C126       0012C          29          C     R3,N                FINISHED?
000030 4740 C01A       00020          30          BL    LOOP                REPEAT IF LOOP COUNTER IS < N
                                      31 * END REPEAT
000034 5040 C12A       00130          32          ST    R4,SUM              STORE SUM
                                      33          SNAP  PDATA=(REGS),STORAGE=(ARRAY,ARRAY+40),DCB=SNAPDCB,ID=1
                                      54          CLOSE (SNAPDCB)
```

*(Continues)*

**Figure 6.23**
A program that is supposed to compute the sum of N fullwords, as given in Exercise 6.

```
                                    60 ** STANDARD EXIT
00006E 58D0 C072      00078         61          L     R13,SAVE + 4       RESTORE R13
000072 98EC D00C      0000C         62          LM    R14,R12,12(R13)    RESTORE REMAINING REGISTERS
000076 07FE                         63          BR    R14                RETURN TO OS
                                    64 *
000078                              65 SAVE     DS    18F                SAVE AREA
                                    66 SNAPDCB  DCB   DSORG=PS,MACRF=W,RECFM=VBA,BLKSIZE=1632,LRECL=125,      X
                                                      DDNAME=SNAP
000118 FFFFFFFF                    117 ARRAY    DC    F'-1'              ARRAY OF N FULLWORDS:
00011C 00000062                    118          DC    F'98'
000120 00000011                    119          DC    F'17'
000124 FFFFFFFD                    120          DC    F'-3'
000128 0000003D                    121          DC    F'61'
00012C 00000005                    122 N        DC    F'5'               NUMBER OF INTEGERS IN ARRAY
000130 00000000                    123 SUM      DC    F'0'               SUM OF INTEGERS IN ARRAY
000000                             124          END   ADD
000138 00000004                    125                =F'4'
00013C 00000001                    126                =F'1'
.
.
.
  ENTRY ADDRESS   EC010

COMPLETION CODE       SYSTEM = 0C1

PSW AT ENTRY TO ABEND  078D0000 00000004        ILC 2   INTC 0001
.
.
.
REGS AT ENTRY TO ABEND

     FLTR 0-6      0000000000000000     0000000000000000          0000000000000000     0000000000000000

     REGS 0-7      00000000   078D2200   000E989A   075C3000          00DDF72C   070C3000   00D65F78   00000000
     REGS 8-15     00000000   078D2200   000F078C   007D6310          0C000000   00000000   00000000   000102B8

ACTIVE LOAD MODULES

LPA/JPA MODULE     **GO
0EC000    5C5CC7D6 40404040 00000000 00000000    90ECD00C 05C050D0 C07641D0 C0720700    *..GO     ........................*
0EC020    4510C012 8F0EC0D0 0A131B22 1B331B44    5A42C112 5A20C132 5A30C136 5930C126    *.................A...A...A...A.*
0EC040    4740C01A 5040C12A 4510C056 017A8000    00002000 000EC0D0 00000000 000EC064    *. ... A.........................*
0EC060    00000000 000EC128 800EC150 9680101C    0A330700 4510C066 800EC0D0 0A1458D0    *......A...A.....................*
0EC080    C07298EC D00C07FE 00000000 000E4E80    00000000 00000000 00000000 00000000    *................................*
0EC0A0    00000000 00000000 00000000 00000000    00000000 00000000 00000000 00000000    *................................*
      LINE 0EC0C0 SAME AS ABOVE
0EC0E0    00000000 00000001 00004000 00000001    04000001 54000000 E2D5C1D7 40404040    *.......... .............SNAP    *
0EC100    02000020 00000001 00000001 00000660    00000000 00000001 00000001 00000001    *................................*
0EC120    0000007D 00000001 FFFFFFFF 00000062    00000011 FFFFFFFD 0000003D 00000005    *................................*
0EC140    000000AC 00000000 00000004 00000001                                            *................               *
```

**Figure 6.23** *(Continued)*

# 7

# Loop Control and Internal Subprograms

CONTENTS



OVERVIEW

This chapter presents several new instructions that enhance your ability to control a loop. These instructions are LA, BCT, BCTR, BXLE, and BXH. The chapter includes examples of counted and conditional loops, which demonstrate how you can implement control structures such as FOR, REPEAT-UNTIL, and WHILE in assembler language. In addition, the application of the BAL and BALR instructions to subprograms is described.

OBJECTIVES

After studying this chapter, you should be able to:

1. Use the Load Address (LA) instruction to initialize and increment registers.
2. Describe the RS instruction format and compute the effective address that is designated by such an instruction.

3. Use the Branch on Count (BCT, BCTR), Branch on Index Low or Equal (BXLE), and Branch on Index High (BXH) instructions to control loops.
4. Implement FOR, REPEAT-UNTIL, and WHILE loops in assembler language.
5. Use the Branch and Link (BAL, BALR) instructions to invoke subprograms.

## Introduction

The two major topics of this chapter—loop control and internal subprograms—involve instructions that branch. This chapter will begin with an examination of loops and demonstrate how you use the new instructions LA, BCT, BCTR, BXLE, and BXH to control them. The first loops to be considered are controlled by the extended mnemonics of the BC instruction, and incorporate the Load Address (LA) instruction to initialize and increment registers efficiently. However, the LA instruction has other important uses apart from loop control; these will be shown here and in later chapters.

The chapter will also cover other more powerful instructions that combine the counting and testing functions of loop control. These are the Branch on Count (BCT and BCTR), Branch on Index Low or Equal (BXLE), and Branch on Index High (BXH) instructions. Of these, BCT and BCTR are the most important and the easiest to use. Many of the loop examples will demonstrate how to implement familiar control structures such as FOR, REPEAT-UNTIL, and WHILE in assembler language.

Lastly, the chapter will reconsider the Branch and Link (BAL and BALR) instructions, and complete the simplified definition given earlier. These instructions enable you to branch to subsections of a program called internal subprograms and thereby improve the program's design.

## Loop Control

**Parts of a loop**

All of the loops that you encountered when you wrote programs in a high-level language and the ones that you have studied so far in assembler language consist of three basic parts. There is an *initialization* section at the beginning of the loop. This section defines steps that are executed once. It is here that the program sets counters, index registers, and work registers to initial values. The *body* of the loop defines the processing that will be repeated. The *control* portion of the loop determines the number of times that the body is executed. You can control loops by using a counter, by using some condition that occurs within the loop, or by using a combination of both. You can do this in two steps: a *change step* and a *test step*. In the change step, you make changes to such things as counters, index registers, and the data to be processed in preparation for the next execution of the body of the loop. You then test the results of some or all of these changes to determine if execution of the loop is complete. You already should be familiar with these concepts, and you should be able to design loops and to describe them with a pseudocode notation. However, the following brief review will present the notation used in this chapter.

**Counted loops**

You have already used the following pseudocode structure for *counted loops:*

REPEAT *n* TIMES
  *body*
END REPEAT

This structure clearly indicates that the body of the loop is executed exactly *n* times. It is sometimes desirable to describe a counted loop with a FOR structure, as follows:

FOR *i* = 1 TO *n*
  *body*
END FOR

This structure allows you to use the counter *i* within the body of the loop for such things as array subscripts.

**Conditional loops**

More general structures permit control of the loop not only by counting, but also by conditions that are determined by computation or by the data itself. Two such structures are REPEAT-UNTIL and WHILE. The REPEAT-UNTIL appears in pseudocode as follows:

REPEAT
  *body*
UNTIL *condition*
END REPEAT

The body of the loop is repeated until a certain condition is true. In this type of loop, the condition is tested after the body is executed; thus, the body is always executed at least once.

The WHILE structure appears in pseudocode like this:

WHILE *condition* DO
  *body*
END WHILE

Here, the body of the loop is executed as long as the condition is true. The condition is tested before the body of the loop so it is possible that the body will not be executed at all if the condition is initially false. This relationship between the test and the body of the loop is the major distinction between REPEAT-UNTIL and WHILE loops.

One goal of this section is to show you how to implement these control structures in assembler language. Using the loops of Chapter 5 as a basis, this section begins with an instruction that is often used to initialize or change the contents of registers within a loop.

## The Load Address (LA) Instruction

**LA loads the effective address**

Although the Load Address instruction has a rather simple definition, it can challenge your understanding of effective address, the differences between relocatable and absolute expressions, and the differences between explicit and implicit operands. The Load Address instruction is summarized as follows:

| Operation | Operand | Format | Instruction Name | Action |
|---|---|---|---|---|
| LA | *R1,D2(X2,B2)*<br>or *R1,S2*<br>or *R1,S2(X2)* | RX | LOAD ADDRESS | With 24-bit addressing,<br>$C(R1)_{0-7} \leftarrow 0$<br>$C(R1)_{8-31} \leftarrow E2$<br>With 31-bit addressing,<br>$C(R1)_0 \leftarrow 0$<br>$C(R1)_{1-31} \leftarrow E2$ |

The instruction computes the effective address *E2* in the same way as any RX instruction, and places it into the register that is designated by *R1*. Compare this with the Load instruction: both compute an effective address *E2* in exactly the same manner. Load places the contents of the fullword at *E2* into *R1*, while Load Address places *E2* itself into *R1*. The following examples demonstrate some typical uses for the Load Address instruction. These examples are valid regardless of the addressing mode.

---

EXAMPLE 1

**Initialize a Register:** `LA 2,4`

| | Reg. 2 |
|---|---|
| Before execution: | ???????? |
| After execution: | 00000004 |

**LA is often used with explicit operand designations**

The effective address that is specified by this instruction is simply the displacement 4, which replaces the previous contents of Register 2. The LA instruction provides a good way to load a register with a constant. Since the displacement must lie between 0 and 4095, the constant must also lie within this range.

---

EXAMPLE 2

**Increment a Register:** `LA 7,4(7)`

| | Reg. 7 |
|---|---|
| Before execution: | 000000A8 |
| After execution: | 000000AC |

The general form of the operand entry of this particular instruction is *R1,D2(X2)*. The effective address is equal to the sum of the displacement and the index value, and is placed into *R1*. Often, when you use the instruction in this form, *R1* and *X2* designate the same register as they do in this example. The effect of the instruction is to add the displacement to the specified register.

This form of the instruction provides you with a simple way to increment a register by a positive constant that does not exceed 4095; this feature is particularly useful for loop counters and index registers. Since Load Address places zero into the first bit of *R1* regardless of addressing mode, the result is always positive.

Notice that

```
LA      0,4(0)
```

does not increment Register 0 by 4, but instead loads Register 0 with 4. Since you cannot use Register 0 as an index register, the effective address is simply the displacement; the prior contents of Register 0 are irrelevant.

---

EXAMPLE 3

**LA 4,ARRAY**

**An implicit operand designation**

Assume that ARRAY is a relocatable symbol that represents the hexadecimal address 9AF0. (For example, you might define ARRAY by using a DC.) As shown here, this instruction loads Register 4 with the actual effective address that is represented by ARRAY:

| | **Reg. 4** |
|---|---|
| Before execution: | ???????? |
| After execution: | 00009AF0 |

---

EXAMPLE 4

**Load Address versus Load**

This example compares the Load Address instruction with the Load instruction when the operands of both instructions are the same. Consider the following definitions:

```
FOUR     EQU   4
EIGHT    DC    F'8'
```
(Assume that this is at the address $AB09C4_{16}$.)

Note how each of the following instructions affects Register 2:

**FOUR is a displacement (it is absolute).**

**a.** **LA 2,FOUR**

| | **Reg. 2** |
|---|---|
| Before execution: | ???????? |
| After execution: | 00000004 |

The operand entry of this instruction is equivalent to 2,4 since FOUR is absolute. The effective address is equal to the displacement 4, so the instruction loads Register 2 with 4.

**b.** **L 2,FOUR**

| | Reg. 2 |
|---|---|
| Before execution: | ???????? |
| After execution: | ???????? |

As in part **a**, the operand entry is equivalent to 2,4 and the effective address is 4. The Load instruction attempts to load the contents of the fullword at the address 4, which you generally will not know. This is not the way to load a register with the constant 4. This error can be elusive: there will be no error message at assembly time since the instruction is syntactically correct. If you examine the corresponding object code, 58200004, you should be able to see that the instruction is in error since the effective address is 4.

**EIGHT is relocatable.**

**c.**
```
L         2,EIGHT
```

| | Reg. 2 |
|---|---|
| Before execution: | ???????? |
| After execution: | 00000008 |

The effective address that is represented by the symbol EIGHT is AB09C4. The Load instruction places the contents of the fullword at this effective address into Register 2.

**d.**
```
LA        2,EIGHT
```

| | Reg. 2 |
|---|---|
| Before execution: | ???????? |
| After execution: | 00AB09C4 |

The effective address is AB09C4, as in part **c**, and is placed into Register 2.

---

## SELF-TEST EXERCISES

1. Assume the definitions

```
X         DC        F'5'
Y         DC        F'6'
SEVEN     EQU       7
```

where X represents the address $54A8_{16}$. What are the contents of the indicated registers after execution of each instruction in the following *sequence?* When necessary, assume that the prior contents of a register are as set by the instructions that are given earlier in the list.

| | | | | | |
|---|---|---|---|---|---|
| **a.** | LA | 1,X | **g.** | LA | 7,0(2) |
| **b.** | LA | 2,4 | **h.** | LA | 8,0(2,2) |
| **c.** | L | 3,X(2) | **i.** | LA | 9,SEVEN |
| **d.** | LA | 4,X(2) | **j.** | LA | 10,SEVEN(2,3) |
| **e.** | L | 5,0(4) | **k.** | LA | 11,X(SEVEN) |
| **f.** | LA | 6,0(4) | | | |

2. Assume that base register 12 contains $5002_{16}$. What object code is produced by each of the instructions in Self-Test Exercise 1?

## *Structured Loops in Assembler Language*

This section demonstrates how you can implement structured loops in assembler language by using the LA instruction and other instructions that you know. The examples include loops that are controlled by counting, by a condition other than counting, and by more than one condition.

*Counted Loops.* Although you have written counted loops in assembler language before, consider another simple example that compares and illustrates the use of the LA instruction in a loop. Suppose that you have an array X of 50 elements—$X_0$, $X_1$, through $X_{49}$—that you want to initialize to zero at execution time. Figure 7.1 contains the pseudocode and the flowchart that describe the required loop, and Figure 7.2 contains the corresponding assembler language instructions. Notice the close relationship between the instructions and the steps pictured in the flow chart.

*Conditional Loops.* A condition other than counting determines the number of times that the body of a conditional loop is executed. For example, sup-

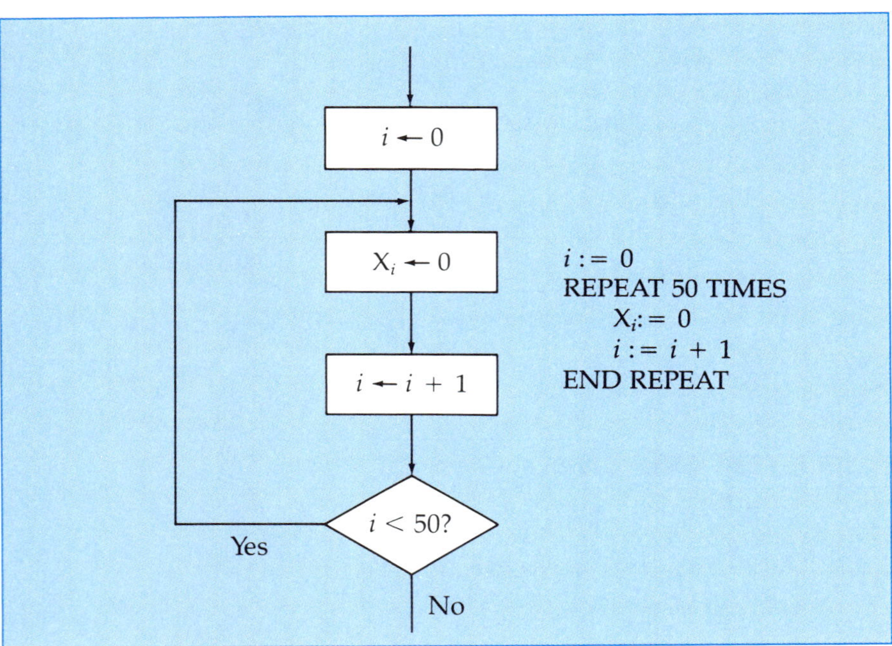


**Figure 7.1**
The flowchart and the pseudocode to initialize an array X to zero.

**Figure 7.2**
The program segment for the logic of Figure 7.1, which initializes an array X to zero.

```
** INITIALIZE AN ARRAY TO ZERO
              LA     R2,0            R2 = INDEX REGISTER = 0
              LA     R3,0            R3 = CONSTANT = 0
* REPEAT 50 TIMES:
LOOP          ST     R3,X(R2)        CLEAR ARRAY ELEMENT
              LA     R2,4(R2)        INCREMENT INDEX
              C      R2,=F'200'      FINISHED? (LIMIT = 4*50 = 200)
              BL     LOOP            IF NOT, REPEAT
* END REPEAT
```

pose that you have an array Y, which contains several nonzero elements that are followed by an element that is zero. The array may look like this:

| 34 | −1 | 2 | 98 | −41 | 0 |
|---|---|---|---|---|---|
| $Y_0$ | $Y_1$ | $Y_2$ | $Y_3$ | $Y_4$ | $Y_5$ |

Figure 7.3 describes a REPEAT-UNTIL loop to accumulate the sum of the integers until the zero element is encountered. Since the body of the loop is executed at least once, you must assume that $Y_0$ is not the zero element that you seek since it is added to SUM without testing.

Figure 7.4 uses a WHILE structure to write the loop. Each element, including $Y_0$, is compared with zero *before* it is added to SUM. Therefore, no restriction on $Y_0$ is necessary; it can be zero without causing adverse effects on the logic of the loop.

Figure 7.5 contains the assembler language statements that implement these loops. Notice that the WHILE loop contains an additional branch instruction, which generally makes it somewhat slower than the REPEAT-UNTIL loop.

*Multiconditional Loops.* You can also control loops by using a test of more than one condition. Consider the case in which both a counter and a test for zero control the loop. The example used here is similar to the one just given. Suppose that you have an array Z of $n$ elements:

$$Z_0, Z_1, \ldots, Z_{n-1}$$

However, this time, it is possible that none of the elements are zero. To accumulate the sum of the elements until you either reach the end of the array or encounter a zero element, you must compute

$$Z_0 + Z_1 + \ldots + Z_m$$

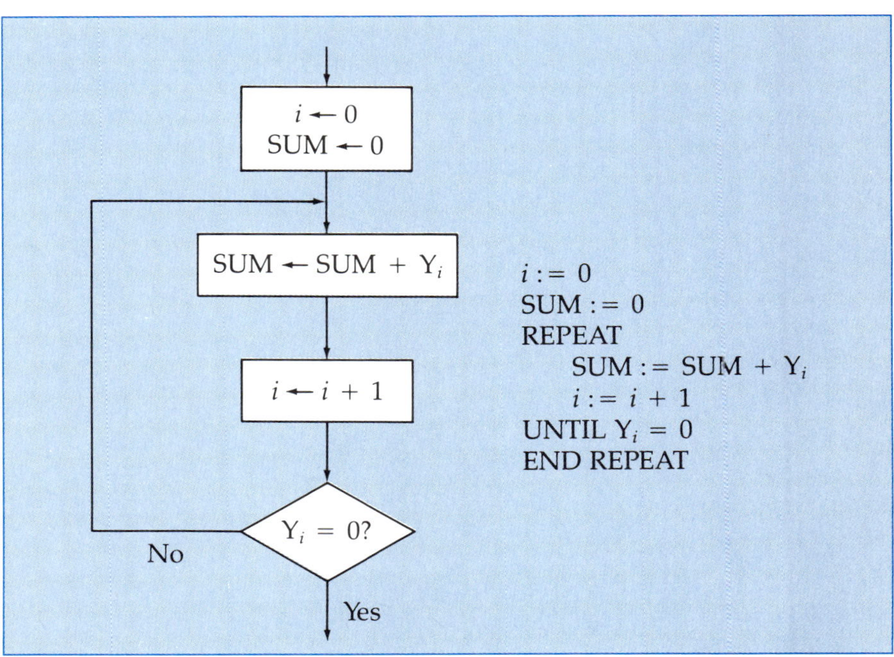


**Figure 7.3**
A REPEAT-UNTIL loop to add the integers in an array Y until the zero element is encountered ($Y_0 \neq 0$).

**Figure 7.4**
A WHILE loop to add the integers in an array Y until the zero element is encountered (no restriction on $Y_0$).

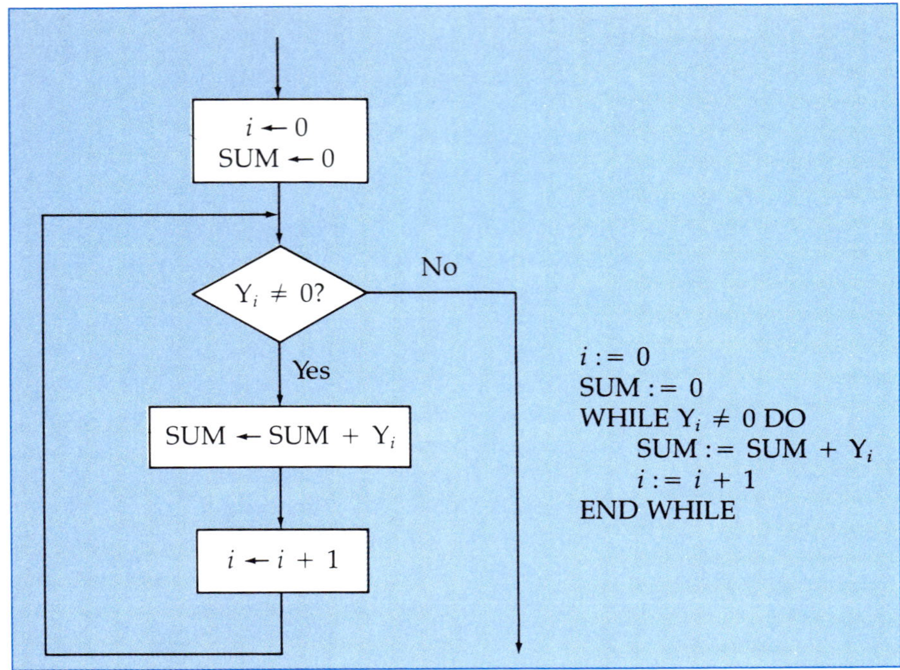


**Figure 7.5**
The program segments to add the integers in an array until the zero element is encountered by using, **a**. REPEAT-UNTIL and, **b**. WHILE.

**a.**

```
** ADD ARRAY ELEMENTS UNTIL A ZERO IS FOUND.
* INITIALIZE REGISTERS:
          LA     R2,0          R2 = INDEX REGISTER = 0
          LA     R3,0          R3 = WORK REGISTER = 0
          LA     R4,0          R4 = CONSTANT = 0
* REPEAT:
LOOP      A      R3,Y(R2)      ADD NEXT ELEMENT TO WORK REGISTER
          LA     R2,4(R2)      INCREMENT INDEX
* UNTIL ARRAY ELEMENT = 0
          C      R4,Y(R2)      ZERO FOUND?
          BNE    LOOP          IF NOT, REPEAT
* END REPEAT
** SUM IS IN R3
```

**b.**

```
** ADD ARRAY ELEMENTS WHILE THEY ARE NONZERO.
* INITIALIZE REGISTERS:
          LA     R2,0          R2 = INDEX REGISTER = 0
          LA     R3,0          R3 = WORK REGISTER = 0
          LA     R4,0          R4 = CONSTANT = 0
* WHILE ARRAY ELEMENT IS NOT 0 DO:
LOOP      C      R4,Y(R2)      ZERO FOUND?
          BE     OUT           IF YES, EXIT
          A      R3,Y(R2)      ELSE, ADD NEXT ELEMENT TO WORK REGISTER
          LA     R2,4(R2)      INCREMENT INDEX
          B      LOOP          REPEAT
* END WHILE
** SUM IS IN R3
OUT       ----
```

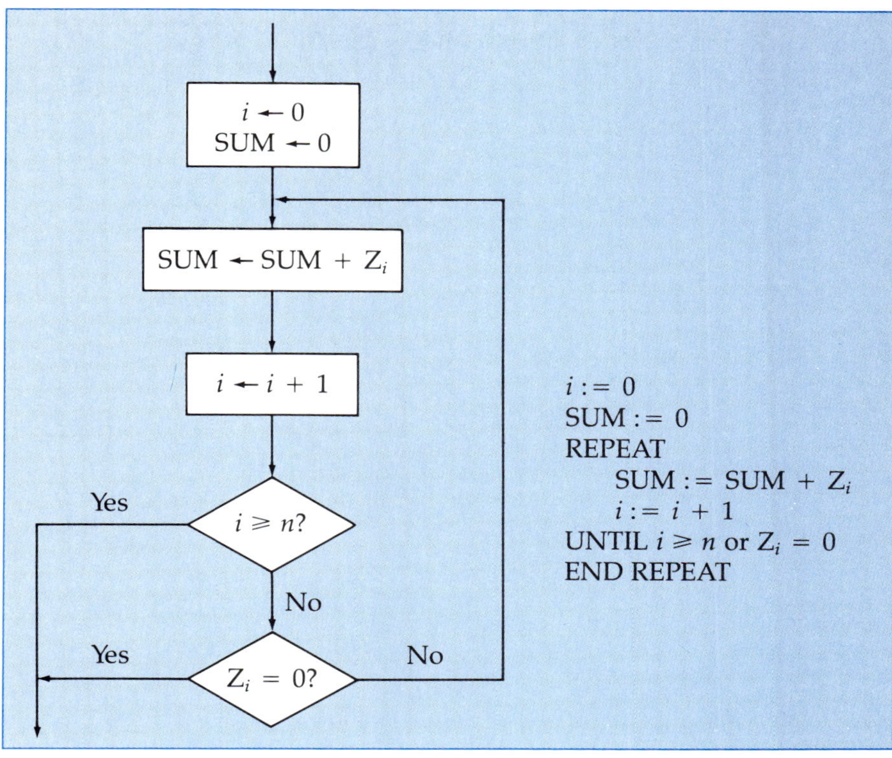


**Figure 7.6** The flowchart and pseudocode to compute $Z_0 + Z_1 + \ldots + Z_m$, where $m = n-1$ or $Z_{m+1} = 0$ (assuming $Z_0 \neq 0$ and $n \geq 1$).

**Figure 7.7** The program segment for the logic of Figure 7.6, which computes $Z_0 + Z_1 + \ldots + Z_m$, where $m = n-1$ or $Z_{m+1} = 0$.

```
** ADD ELEMENTS OF ARRAY Z UNTIL A ZERO IS ENCOUNTERED OR
**     THE END OF ARRAY IS REACHED.  ASSUME LIMIT = 4*N.
* INITIALIZE REGISTERS:
     LA    R2,0        R2 = INDEX REGISTER = 0
     LA    R3,0        R3 = WORK REGISTER = 0
     LA    R4,0        R4 = CONSTANT = 0
* REPEAT:
LOOP A     R3,Z(R2)    ADD NEXT ELEMENT TO WORK REGISTER
     LA    R2,4(R2)    INCREMENT INDEX
* UNTIL INDEX >= LIMIT OR ARRAY ELEMENT = 0
     C     R2,LIMIT    FINISHED?
     BNL   OUT         IF SO, EXIT
     C     R4,Z(R2)    ZERO FOUND?
     BNE   LOOP        IF NOT, REPEAT
* END REPEAT
** SUM IS IN R3
OUT  ----
```

where $m = n - 1$ or $Z_{m+1} = 0$. Figure 7.6 provides a solution to this problem by using a REPEAT-UNTIL structure. As in the example given previously, since the body of the loop is executed at least once, $Z_0$ is not compared with zero. You must assume, then, that the first element $Z_0$ does not contain the zero that you seek. This assumption implies that there is at least one nonzero element in the array; that is, $n \geq 1$. To avoid referencing the undefined element $Z_n$ after $i$ is incremented, you must compare $i$ with $n$ before you look at $Z_i$. Figure 7.7 gives the program segment for this loop.

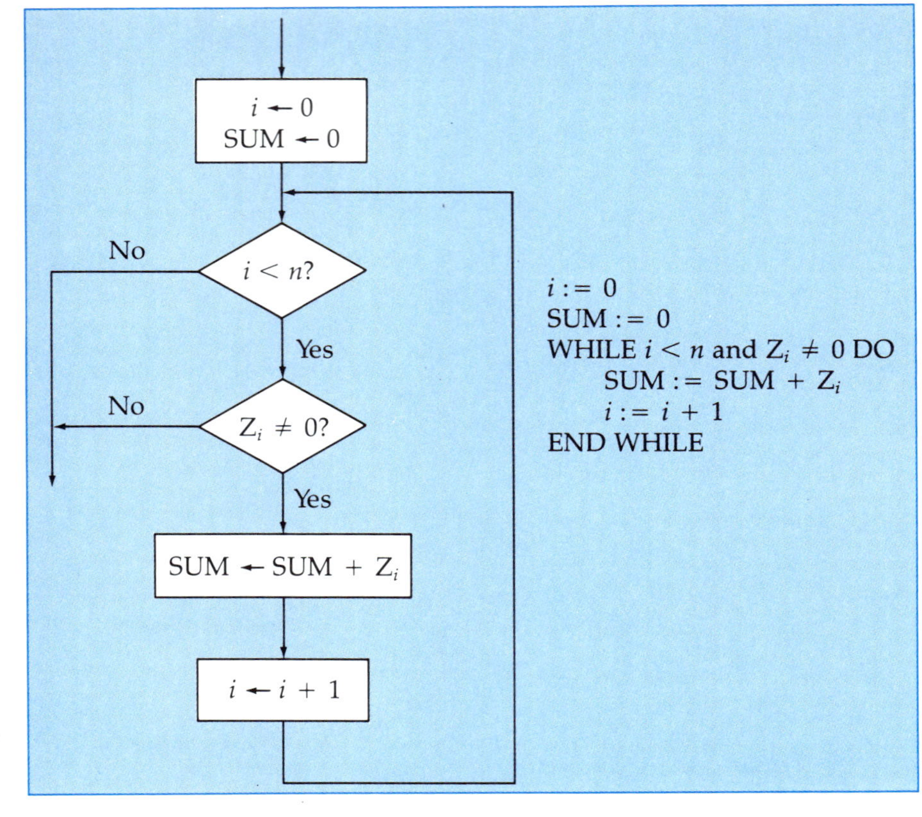


**Figure 7.8**
The flowchart and pseudocode to compute $Z_0 + Z_1 + \ldots + Z_m$, where $m = n-1$ or $Z_{m+1} = 0$.

**Figure 7.9**
The program segment for the logic of Figure 7.8, which computes $Z_0 + Z_1 + \ldots + Z_m$, where $m = n-1$ or $Z_{m+1} = 0$.

```
** ADD ELEMENTS OF ARRAY Z UNTIL A ZERO IS ENCOUNTERED OR
**    THE END OF ARRAY IS REACHED.  ASSUME LIMIT = 4*N.
* INITIALIZE REGISTERS:
     LA    R2,0        R2 = INDEX REGISTER = 0
     LA    R3,0        R3 = WORK REGISTER = 0
     LA    R4,0        R4 = CONSTANT = 0
* WHILE INDEX < LIMIT AND ARRAY ELEMENT .NE. 0 DO:
LOOP C     R2,LIMIT    FINISHED?
     BNL   OUT         IF SO, EXIT
     C     R4,Z(R2)    ZERO FOUND?
     BE    OUT         IF YES, EXIT
     A     R3,Z(R2)    ELSE, ADD NEXT ELEMENT TO WORK REGISTER
     LA    R2,4(R2)    INCREMENT INDEX
     B     LOOP        REPEAT
* END WHILE
** SUM IS IN R3
OUT  ----
```

In Figure 7.8, a WHILE structure solves this problem. There is no restriction on $Z_0$ since it is compared with zero before it is added to SUM. Notice that there is also no restriction on $n$; for example, if $n = 0$, the body of the loop is bypassed. Figure 7.9 lists the instructions for this loop.

### *The Branch on Count (BCT and BCTR) Instructions*

**Loop control by counting backward by increments of one**

The Branch on Count instructions combine both the counting and the testing portions of loop control. The associated counter always counts backward by one until it reaches zero. The instruction is summarized as follows:

| Operation | Operand | Format | Instruction Name | Action |
|---|---|---|---|---|
| **BCT** | *R1,S2*<br>or *R1,S2(X2)*<br>or *R1,D2(X2,B2)* | RX | BRANCH ON COUNT | C(*R1*) ← C(*R1*) − 1<br>Branches to *E2*<br>if C(*R1*) ≠ 0 |
| **BCTR** | *R1,R2* | RR | BRANCH ON COUNT | C(*R1*) ← C(*R1*) − 1<br>Branches to address in *R2* if C(*R1*) ≠ 0<br>and *R2* ≠ 0 |

The register that is designated by *R1* is a counter that counts backward by one each time that the Branch on Count is executed. If the new value of the counter is not zero, the instruction branches; but if the new value is zero, the next sequential instruction is executed. The branch address either is the effective address that is specified by the operand entry of the BCT instruction, or is contained in the register that is designated by the BCTR instruction as *R2*. Notice that if *R2* = 0, the BCTR instruction never branches.

The BCT and BCTR instructions do not change the condition code, even though they perform a subtraction when decrementing *R1*. If an overflow occurs during this subtraction, it is ignored.

---

EXAMPLE 5

```
BCT     8,LOOP
```

**A typical use of BCT**

This is an example of the most commonly used form of BCT, which appears as follows:

BCT *R1,S2*

Here, LOOP represents the address of another instruction in the program. The following indicates the effect of executing this instruction for various initial values of Register 8.

| Reg. 8 before execution | Reg. 8 after execution | Effect of execution |
|---|---|---|
| 3 | 2 | Branch to LOOP |
| 2 | 1 | Branch to LOOP |
| 1 | 0 | Sequence |
| 0 | −1 | Branch to LOOP |
| −1 | −2 | Branch to LOOP |

---

EXAMPLE 6

**A counted loop**

The following is an outline of a counted loop controlled by a BCT instruction:

```
         L       R3,N
LOOP     ----
         .
         .                       }  ←Body
         .
         BCT     R3,LOOP
```

Suppose that N is a fullword containing 50. Since Register 3 is decremented each time that BCT is executed, it takes on the values 50, 49, 48, and so on to 0. As a result, the body of the loop is executed 50 times.

Now, suppose that N contains zero. Since the BCT instruction sequences only when the counter becomes zero as a result of the subtraction, Register 3 will take on the following values:

$$-1, -2, \ldots, -2^{31}, 2^{31} - 1, 2^{31} - 2, \ldots, 1, 0$$

Notice that after Register 3 reaches $-2^{31}$ (the smallest negative number), its next value is $2^{31} - 1$ (the largest positive number). Similar results will occur if N is negative.

EXAMPLE 7

**BCTR 2,7**

| | Reg. 2 | Reg. 7 |
|---|---|---|
| Before execution: | 000000FF | 00AD401C |
| After execution: | 000000FE | 00AD401C |

This instruction subtracts one from Register 2. Since the result is not zero, a branch to the address in Register 7 (AD401C) takes place.

EXAMPLE 8

**BCTR 5,0**

| | Reg. 5 |
|---|---|
| Before execution: | 00000A58 |
| After execution: | 00000A57 |

This instruction subtracts one from Register 5, but does not branch since the *R2* entry is 0. (Remember that *R2* = 0 does not designate Register 0.) You can use this to subtract one from a register whenever it is unnecessary to test the sign of the result or to detect overflow. Although the purpose of the instruction may not be as obvious as a Subtract instruction, many programmers use this technique.

EXAMPLE 9

### Square the Integers in an Array

**Address computation that uses LA**

The program segment in Figure 7.10 replaces the first 3 integers in an array by their squares. (Assume that each square can be represented by 32 bits.) This simple BCT loop also demonstrates address computation using the LA instruction. Notice that Register 9 contains the address of each array element as it is considered. Statement 4 loads Register 9 with the address of the first integer in the array, and Statement 9 increments this value by 4 so that it points to the next integer. The Load and Store instructions (Statements 6 and 8) use Register 9 to compute the address of the desired array element.

Figure 7.11 provides a trace of this loop, which assumes that ARRAY is at the hex address A48. The effect of each instruction is highlighted.

**Figure 7.10**
A program segment to square the integers in an array, as described in Example 9.

```
 1 ** REPLACE ARRAY ELEMENTS BY THEIR SQUARES
 2 * INITIALIZE REGISTERS:
 3          LA    R4,3       R4 = LOOP COUNTER = NO. OF ARRAY ELEMENTS
 4          LA    R9,ARRAY   R9 = POINTER TO ARRAY ELEMENTS
 5 * REPEAT 3 TIMES:
 6 LOOP     L     R7,0(R9)   R7 = MULTIPLICAND
 7          MR    R6,R7      SQUARED INTEGER IN R6,R7
 8          ST    R7,0(R9)   REPLACE ARRAY ELEMENT WITH ITS SQUARE
 9          LA    R9,4(R9)   GET ADDRESS OF NEXT ELEMENT
10          BCT   R4,LOOP    DECREMENT COUNTER; REPEAT IF NONZERO
11 * END REPEAT
```

| STMT | R4 | R6 | R7 | R9 | ARRAY | | |
|---|---|---|---|---|---|---|---|
| 3 | 00000003 | | | | 00000008 | FFFFFFFF | 00000006 |
| 4 | 00000003 | | | 00000A48 | 00000008 | FFFFFFFF | 00000006 |
| 6 | 00000003 | | 00000008 | 00000A48 | 00000008 | FFFFFFFF | 00000006 |
| 7 | 00000003 | 00000000 | 00000040 | 00000A48 | 00000008 | FFFFFFFF | 00000006 |
| 8 | 00000003 | 00000000 | 00000040 | 00000A48 | 00000040 | FFFFFFFF | 00000006 |
| 9 | 00000003 | 00000000 | 00000040 | 00000A4C | 00000040 | FFFFFFFF | 00000006 |
| 10 | 00000002 | 00000000 | 00000040 | 00000A4C | 00000040 | FFFFFFFF | 00000006 |
| 6 | 00000002 | 00000000 | FFFFFFFF | 00000A4C | 00000040 | FFFFFFFF | 00000006 |
| 7 | 00000002 | 00000000 | 00000001 | 00000A4C | 00000040 | FFFFFFFF | 00000006 |
| 8 | 00000002 | 00000000 | 00000001 | 00000A4C | 00000040 | 00000001 | 00000006 |
| 9 | 00000002 | 00000000 | 00000001 | 00000A50 | 00000040 | 00000001 | 00000006 |
| 10 | 00000001 | 00000000 | 00000001 | 00000A50 | 00000040 | 00000001 | 00000006 |
| 6 | 00000001 | 00000000 | 00000006 | 00000A50 | 00000040 | 00000001 | 00000006 |
| 7 | 00000001 | 00000000 | 00000024 | 00000A50 | 00000040 | 00000001 | 00000006 |
| 8 | 00000001 | 00000000 | 00000024 | 00000A50 | 00000040 | 00000001 | 00000024 |
| 9 | 00000001 | 00000000 | 00000024 | 00000A54 | 00000040 | 00000001 | 00000024 |
| 10 | 00000000 | 00000000 | 00000024 | 00000A54 | 00000040 | 00000001 | 00000024 |

**Figure 7.11**
A trace of the BCT loop of Figure 7.10, which squared the integers in an array.

EXAMPLE 10

## Count the Negative Integers in an Array

**A comparison of looping techniques**

Each of the two program segments that are listed in Figure 7.12 counts the number of negative values in the array of 10 elements, which is represented by ARRAY. The first segment contains a loop that is controlled by the value of the index register (R3) using the C and BL instructions. The second segment uses an additional register (R2) and the BCT instruction to control the loop. The outlined portions of the two segments are identical. However, the BCT segment involves one more initialization instruction, one less instruction to perform the test, and one more register. The choice of one segment over the other depends upon the existing circumstances or the results that you desire. A comparison of the gross number of instructions that are used in two program segments generally does not indicate their relative execution times. Execution time depends upon the type of instructions, the nature of the operands, and the model of computer that is used. In this example, the significant difference between the segments is in the testing portion since it is executed repeatedly, whereas the initialization instructions are only executed once. Both tests involve a branch instruction, but the first test contains an additional instruction. Thus, you can expect the first test to take longer to execute. However, except in extreme cases or unless the loop is executed many, many times, such differences are usually negligible.

To summarize, if the array is very large and you are concerned with execution time, then this BCT loop would be preferable because it executes faster. However, if registers are at a premium, then using the BCT loop is disadvantageous. In either case, you must also consider your programming time since it is frequently at a greater premium than execution time. The BCT loop is more convenient to write since you only need to initialize the counter to the number of times that the loop is to execute. In contrast, loop control that is based upon the index register, as in the first segment, is more prone to error, since you must determine the last desired index value.

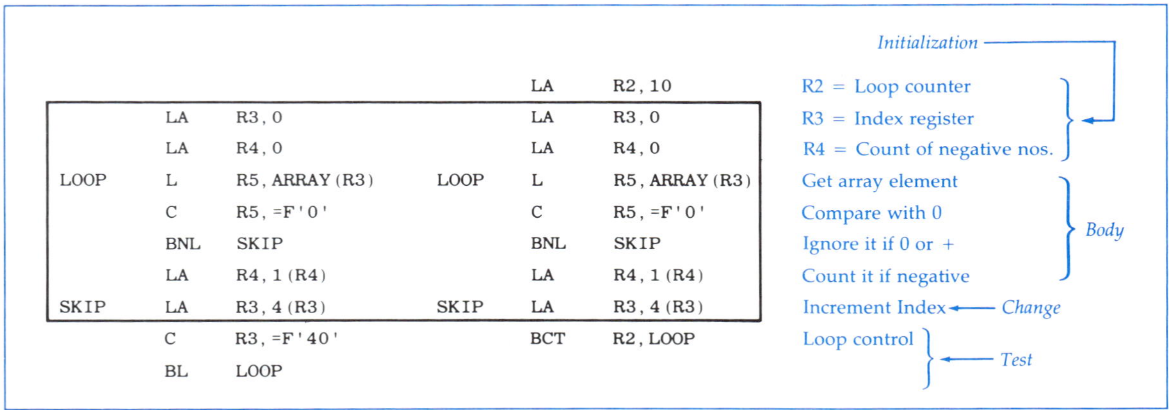


**Figure 7.12**
Two program segments to count the negative integers in an array, as described in Example 10.

## SELF-TEST EXERCISES

3. Assume the following register status:

| | |
|---|---|
| Reg. 0 = 000A54F2 | Reg. 6 = 00000000 |
| Reg. 2 = 00008C06 | Reg. 8 = 00000001 |
| Reg. 4 = FFFFFFFF | Reg. 9 = 00000004 |

How does each of the following instructions affect the status of the registers just given? Does each instruction branch and, if so, to where?

| | |
|---|---|
| **a.** BCT 0, LOOP | **g.** BCTR 8, 2 |
| **b.** BCT 2, LOOP (9) | **h.** BCTR 9, 2 |
| **c.** BCT 4, LOOP | **i.** BCTR 9, 0 |
| **d.** BCT 6, LOOP | **j.** BCTR 6, 2 |
| **e.** BCT 8, LOOP (9) | **k.** BCTR 6, 0 |
| **f.** BCTR 0, 2 | |

4. Assume a loop of the form

```
LOOP     ----
          .
          .
          .
         BCT     R7, LOOP
```

How many times will the instruction at LOOP be executed if Register 7 initially contains the following?

**a.** 1
**b.** 3
**c.** 0
**d.** $-2^{31}$

### *The BXLE and BXH Instructions*

Each of the instructions Branch on Index Low or Equal (BXLE) and Branch on Index High (BXH) incorporates counting and testing into a single instruction. As such, they are similar to BCT; however, they are much more flexible since you can increment or decrement the counter (or index) by any value, and compare it with any value. BXLE will branch if this comparison is "less than or equal to," and BXH will branch if the comparison is "greater than."

Both instructions are in an RS (register and storage) format, which is the third instruction format that you have encountered so far and which appears as follows:

**The RS instruction format**

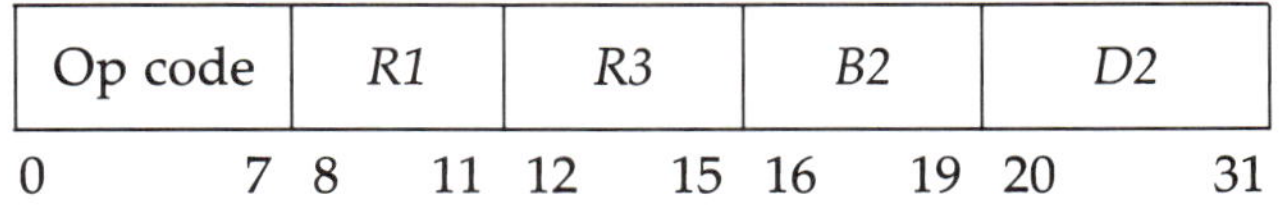


There are three operands: the first and third are register operands that are designated by *R1* and *R3*, and the second operand has an effective address *E2*, which is computed from the displacement *D2* and the base address in register *B2*. For example, with 24-bit addressing, the effective address is computed as follows:

$$E2 = C(B2)_{8-31} + D2$$

*Branch on Index Low or Equal (BXLE).* The BXLE instruction can be summarized as follows:

| Operation | Operand | Format | Instruction Name | Action |
|---|---|---|---|---|
| **BXLE** | *R1,R3,S2* or *R1,R3,D2(B2)* | RS | BRANCH ON INDEX LOW OR EQUAL | $C(R1) \leftarrow C(R1) + C(R3)$<br>Branches to *E2* if $C(R1) \leq \begin{cases} C(R3) \text{ if } R3 \text{ is odd} \\ C(R3+1) \text{ if } R3 \text{ is even} \end{cases}$ |

The register that is denoted by *R1* is the counter or index. The register that is denoted by *R3* is the increment and contains a value that is added to the contents of *R1* when the instruction is executed. Although *R3* is called an increment, it may contain either a positive or a negative value. After this addition is performed, the instruction compares the new value in *R1* with a limit. This limit is contained in an odd register, which is either *R3* or the register that follows *R3* (denoted by *R3*+1). If the counter is less than or equal to the limit, the instruction branches to the effective address *E2;* if the counter is greater than the limit, the instruction sequences.

The addition and comparison are 32-bit two's complement binary operations. The condition code is unchanged and any overflow that occurs is ignored.

---

EXAMPLE 11

```
BXLE    4,8,LOOP
```

| | Reg. 4 | Reg. 8 | Reg. 9 | |
|---|---|---|---|---|
| Before execution: | 00000000 | 00000001 | 00000002 | |
| After execution: | 00000001 | 00000001 | 00000002 | *Branch* |

The instruction increments the contents of Register 4 by the contents of Register 8. It then compares the result, 1, with the contents of Register 9. Since the comparison is "less than," a branch to LOOP takes place.

---

EXAMPLE 12

```
BXLE    6,8,LOOP
```

| | Reg. 6 | Reg. 8 | Reg. 9 | |
|---|---|---|---|---|
| Before execution: | 00000001 | 00000001 | 00000002 | |
| After execution: | 00000002 | 00000001 | 00000002 | *Branch* |

The instruction increments the contents of Register 6 by the contents of Register 8. Since the result, 2, is equal to the contents of Register 9, a branch to LOOP takes place.

---

EXAMPLE 13

**BXLE 6,9,LOOP**

The increment and limit are the same

| | Reg. 6 | Reg. 9 | |
|---|---|---|---|
| Before execution: | 00000001 | 00000002 | |
| After execution: | 00000003 | 00000002 | *Sequence* |

The instruction increments the contents of Register 6 by the contents of Register 9. Since the result, 3, is greater than the contents of Register 9, the instruction sequences.

EXAMPLE 14

**BXLE 9,8,LOOP**

| | Reg. 8 | Reg. 9 | |
|---|---|---|---|
| Before execution: | 00000001 | 00000002 | |
| After execution: | 00000001 | 00000003 | *Sequence* |

Register 9 is used for two purposes

Here, Register 9 is both the counter (*R1*) and the limit (*R3*+1). When you use a register for more than one purpose, it is helpful to consider the counter, the increment, and the limit as separate values that are initialized at the start of the instruction. Thus, initially, the counter is 2, the increment is 1, and the limit is 2. After execution of the instruction, the counter is 3, and since the counter is greater than the limit, the instruction sequences. In other words, the instruction increments the contents of Register 9 by the contents of Register 8. The result, 3, is greater than 2, which is the original contents of Register 9.

EXAMPLE 15

**Count the Negative Integers in an Array**

You can rewrite either of the two program segments listed in Figure 7.12 to use a BXLE loop, as indicated in Figure 7.13. To construct the loop, you first define three registers to serve as the index, the increment, and the limit. Think of the increment and the limit as an even-odd register pair; this example uses the pair R6, R7. The program segment initializes the three registers to appropriate values as follows: the index register (R3) begins at zero and will count by an increment (R6) of four. Since BXLE branches when the index is less than or equal to the limit (R7), R7 must contain the last desired value of the index register—which is 4 * (10 − 1), or 36. This value is different than the one used in the first segment of Figure 7.12.

Comparing a BXLE loop with previous techniques

If you compare this BXLE loop with the BCT loop in Figure 7.12 and ignore initialization, you find that the BXLE loop involves one less instruction, but one more register. You can usually write more efficient loops by using the BXLE instruction, but BXLE is more difficult to use and can be expensive in terms of register use. Remember, though, that the increment and the limit can sometimes occupy the same register. If this is possible, it can be advantageous to use BXLE. Although you cannot do this here, later you will see an example that uses one register for the increment and the limit of a BXH instruction.

```
** COUNT THE NEGATIVE INTEGERS IN AN ARRAY.
* INITIALIZE REGISTERS:
         LA    R3,0           R3 = INDEX REGISTER
         LA    R4,0           R4 = COUNT OF NEGATIVE INTEGERS
         LA    R6,4           R6 = INCREMENT FOR BXLE LOOP
         LA    R7,36          R7 = LIMIT FOR BXLE LOOP = 4 * (10 - 1)
* REPEAT 10 TIMES:
LOOP     L     R5,ARRAY(R3)   GET NEXT ARRAY ELEMENT
         C     R5,=F'0'       COMPARE IT WITH ZERO
         BNL   SKIP           IGNORE IT IF ZERO OR POSITIVE
         LA    R4,1(R4)       COUNT IT IF NEGATIVE
SKIP     BXLE  R3,R6,LOOP     INCREMENT INDEX, TEST, AND REPEAT
* END REPEAT
```

**Figure 7.13**
A program segment to count the negative integers in an array by using a BXLE loop, as described in Example 15.

---

*Branch on Index High (BXH).* The only difference between BXH and BXLE is in the comparison. BXH branches when the index is greater than the limit. The instruction can be summarized as follows:

| Operation | Operand | Format | Instruction Name | Action |
|---|---|---|---|---|
| **BXH** | *R1,R3,S2* or *R1,R3,D2(B2)* | RS | BRANCH ON INDEX HIGH | $C(R1) \leftarrow C(R1) + C(R3)$<br>Branches to *E2* if<br>$C(R1) > \begin{cases} C(R3) \text{ if } R3 \text{ is odd} \\ C(R3+1) \text{ if } R3 \text{ is even} \end{cases}$ |

---

EXAMPLE 16 **BXH 4,8,LOOP**

| | Reg. 4 | Reg. 8 | Reg. 9 | |
|---|---|---|---|---|
| Before execution: | 00000010 | FFFFFFFC | FFFFFFFF | |
| After execution: | 0000000C | FFFFFFFC | FFFFFFFF | *Branch* |

The instruction increments the contents of Register 4 ($16_{10}$) by the contents of Register 8 ($-4_{10}$). Since the result, $12_{10}$, is greater than the contents of Register 9 ($-1_{10}$), a branch to LOOP takes place.

---

EXAMPLE 17 **BXH 6,8,LOOP**

| | Reg. 6 | Reg. 8 | Reg. 9 | |
|---|---|---|---|---|
| Before execution: | 00000001 | FFFFFFFC | FFFFFFFF | |
| After execution: | FFFFFFFD | FFFFFFFC | FFFFFFFF | *Sequence* |

The instruction increments the contents of Register 6 by the contents of Register 8 (−4). Since the result, −3, is less than the contents of Register 9 (−1), the instruction sequences.

---

EXAMPLE 18

**BXH 6,9,LOOP**

**Increment and limit are the same**

| | Reg. 6 | Reg. 9 | |
|---|---|---|---|
| Before execution: | 00000001 | FFFFFFFF | |
| After execution: | 00000000 | FFFFFFFF | *Branch* |

The instruction increments the contents of Register 6 by the contents of Register 9 (−1). Since the result, 0, is greater than the contents of Register 9, a branch to LOOP takes place.

---

EXAMPLE 19

## Simple Table Look-up

**A BXH loop that counts backward**

Consider an array at TABLE of 10 fullwords, which contain unique values. Suppose that you have a value in Register 0 and wish to determine if that value occurs in the array. The program segment in Figure 7.14 accomplishes this by using a loop that is controlled by a BXH instruction. BXH lends itself to loop control that counts backward. Therefore, this search begins with the last fullword of the table and works towards the first fullword. Since the table entries are unique, you may search the table correctly in either order.

The index register (R3) starts at 4 * (10 − 1), which is 36, and counts backward by increments of 4 to zero. The increment (R4) must contain −4 and, since BXH branches when the index is greater than the limit (R5), R5 must contain a negative value such as −1. The index register R3 then counts 36, 32, and so on to 0.

Having written this loop, you can observe that the limit could just as well have been −4, although a smaller value would not work. (Can you explain why it would not?) If this is true, the increment and the limit are

**Figure 7.14**
A program segment to search a table backward by using a BXH loop, as described in Example 19.

```
** SEARCH TABLE BACKWARD FOR VALUE IN REGISTER 0
* INITIALIZE REGISTERS:
         LA    R3,36            R3 = INDEX REG. = 4 * 9 (POINTS TO END)
         L     R4,=F'-4'        R4 = INCREMENT FOR BXH LOOP
         L     R5,=F'-1'        R5 = LIMIT FOR BXH LOOP (ODD REGISTER)
* REPEAT UNTIL VALUE IS FOUND OR 10 ITEMS ARE SEARCHED:
LOOP     C     R0,TABLE(R3)     COMPARE GIVEN VALUE WITH TABLE ENTRY
         BE    FOUND            MATCH; EXIT LOOP
         BXH   R3,R4,LOOP       DECREMENT, TEST, AND REPEAT
* END REPEAT
* VALUE IS NOT FOUND
         .
         .
         .
FOUND    ----                   VALUE IS FOUND
```

**The increment and limit can be the same**

the same, and could in fact be in the same register. Thus, you could write the loop with one less register, as shown in Figure 7.15.

It is possible to search the table in a forward direction, while still using the BXH instruction. To accomplish this, the BXH instruction precedes the body of the loop, as demonstrated in Figure 7.16. The index register (R3) counts by increments of 4 from −4 to 40; however, only the values 0 to 36 are actually available within the loop. Since the testing step precedes the body of the loop, this construction is equivalent to a WHILE structure. The loop requires one more branch instruction than the loop in Figure 7.14.

```
** SEARCH TABLE BACKWARD FOR VALUE IN REGISTER 0
* INITIALIZE REGISTERS:
          LA    R3,36            R3 = INDEX REG.  = 4 * 9  (POINTS TO END)
          L     R5,=F'-4'        R5 = INCREMENT & LIMIT FOR BXH LOOP (ODD)
* REPEAT UNTIL VALUE IS FOUND OR 10 ITEMS ARE SEARCHED:
LOOP      C     R0,TABLE(R3)     COMPARE GIVEN VALUE WITH TABLE ENTRY
          BE    FOUND            MATCH; EXIT LOOP
          BXH   R3,R5,LOOP       DECREMENT, TEST, AND REPEAT
* END REPEAT
* VALUE IS NOT FOUND
          .
          .
          .
FOUND     ----                   VALUE IS FOUND
```

**Figure 7.15**
An improved version of the loop in Figure 7.14, which searches a table backward.

```
** SEARCH TABLE FORWARD FOR VALUE IN REGISTER 0
* INITIALIZE REGISTERS:
          L     R3,=F'-4'        R3 = INDEX REG.; -4 POINTS BEFORE TABLE
          LA    R4,4             R4 = INCREMENT FOR BXH LOOP
          LA    R5,36            R5 = LIMIT FOR BXH LOOP = 4 * 9
* REPEAT UNTIL VALUE IS FOUND OR 10 ITEMS ARE SEARCHED:
LOOP      BXH   R3,R4,EXITLOOP   INCREMENT, TEST, AND BRANCH WHEN DONE
          C     R0,TABLE(R3)     COMPARE GIVEN VALUE WITH TABLE ENTRY
          BE    FOUND            MATCH; EXIT LOOP
          B     LOOP             REPEAT
* END REPEAT
* VALUE IS NOT FOUND
EXITLOOP ----
          .
          .
          .
FOUND     ----                   VALUE IS FOUND
```

**Figure 7.16**
A program segment to search a table forward by using a BXH loop, as described in Example 19.

## SELF-TEST EXERCISES

5. Assume the following register status before the execution of each BXLE and BXH instruction:

| | |
|---|---|
| Reg. 2 = 00000004 | Reg. 3 = 00000010 |
| Reg. 6 = 0000000C | Reg. 7 = 00000000 |
| Reg. 8 = 00000018 | Reg. 9 = FFFFFFF8 |

Give the value of the first register operand after each of the following is executed and indicate whether the instruction branches to LOOP.

```
a. BXLE  6,2,LOOP        h. BXH  7,8,LOOP
b. BXLE  8,2,LOOP        i. BXH  9,2,LOOP
c. BXLE  7,2,LOOP        j. BXH  2,8,LOOP
d. BXLE  2,6,LOOP        k. BXH  9,6,LOOP
e. BXLE  2,9,LOOP        l. BXH  9,3,LOOP
f. BXLE  2,3,LOOP        m. BXH  8,9,LOOP
g. BXLE  9,7,LOOP        n. BXH  7,9,LOOP
```

6. Assume the following register status:

Reg. 2 = 0
Reg. 6 = 4
Reg. 7 = 8

Indicate the number of times that the instruction at LOOP is executed for each of the following loops.

```
a. LOOP  ----                     c. LOOP  ----
         .                                 BXH   2,6,OUT
         .                                 .
         .                                 .
         BXH   2,7,LOOP                    .
                                           B     LOOP
                                     OUT   ----
b. LOOP  ----
         .
         .
         .
         BXLE  2,6,LOOP
```

# Internal Subprograms

Modular design is as important for assembler language programs as it is for high-level language programs. The advantages of breaking a program into smaller units called **subprograms** do not depend on the programming language. Assembler language subprograms are classified as internal or external. **Internal subprograms** are subsections of the program to which you branch as desired. **External subprograms** are written so that you can assemble them separately from the rest of the program. As a result, external subprograms must follow several conventions that internal subprograms do not have to follow (although there are reasons why all subprograms should follow the conventions). Chapter 13 discusses subprogram conventions in detail. For now, this section will discuss how you can create internal subprograms, branch to them, and eventually return to the instruction after the branch. The Branch and Link instructions allow you to do this.

### *The Branch and Link (BAL and BALR) Instructions*

The Branch and Link instructions can be summarized as follows:

| Operation | Operand | Format | Instruction Name | Action |
|---|---|---|---|---|
| **BAL** | *R1,S2*<br>or *R1,S2(X2)*<br>or *R1,D2(X2,B2)* | RX | BRANCH AND LINK | C(*R1*) ← { ILC, CC, program mask, IA (24-bit addressing); 1, IA (31-bit addressing) }<br>Branches to the effective address *E2* |
| **BALR** | *R1,R2* | RR | BRANCH AND LINK REGISTER | Loads *R1* with the same value as BAL. Branches to the address in *R2* if *R2* ≠ 0. |

The Branch and Link instructions load the register that is designated by *R1*, as follows:

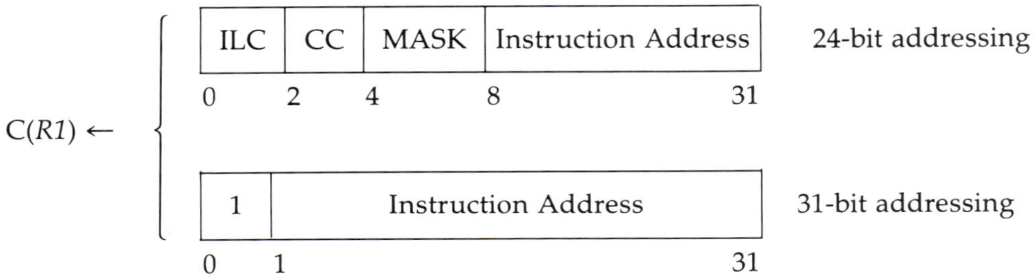

C(*R1*) ←

| ILC | CC | MASK | Instruction Address |
|---|---|---|---|
| 0 | 2 | 4 | 8 … 31 |

24-bit addressing

| 1 | Instruction Address |
|---|---|
| 0 | 1 … 31 |

31-bit addressing

The instruction address portion is simply the address of the next instruction. When 24-bit addressing is in effect, the register will also contain the instruction length code (ILC), the condition code (CC), and the program mask (MASK). Together, these elements appear in the same format as the right half of a BC mode PSW, regardless of the CPU's actual mode. In addition, BAL branches to the effective address that is specified by its operand entry; BALR branches to the address that is contained in the register designated by *R2*, unless *R2* is 0—in which case, no branch takes place.

**Use a BAL or BALR instruction to invoke a subprogram**

Consider a section of a program at the address SUB that you want to treat as a subprogram. As illustrated in Figure 7.17, you can branch to SUB from various places within the program and each time, the subprogram must eventually branch back to the point from which it was invoked. A Branch and Link instruction permits this, for not only does it branch to the subprogram, but also it places the address of the instruction immediately after it in a register called the **link register.** This address is called the **return address,** and serves as a link between the subprogram and the portion of the program that invoked it. Using the link register, you can write a BR

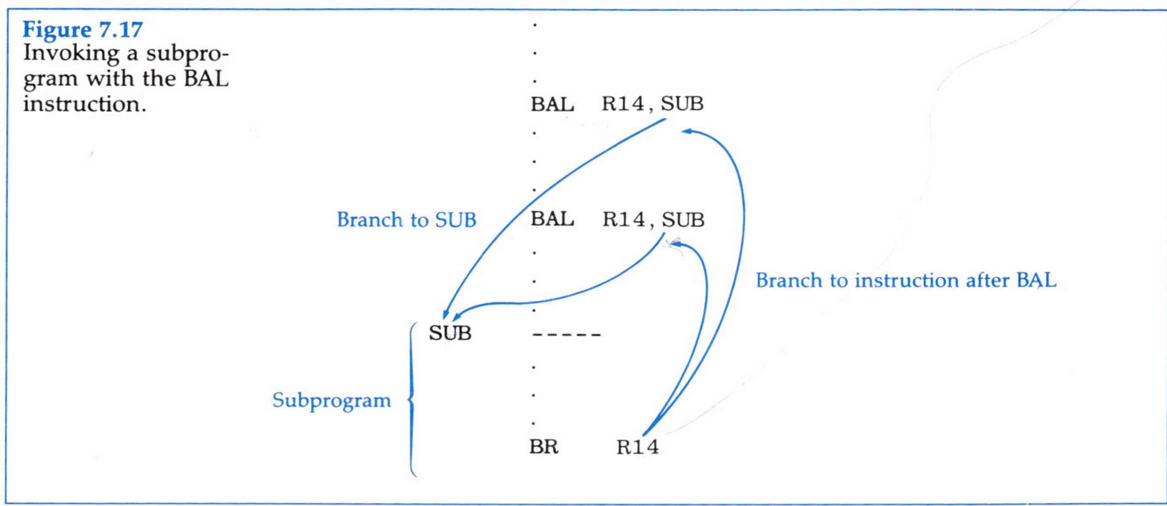


**Figure 7.17**
Invoking a subprogram with the BAL instruction.

instruction that branches to the return address without prior knowledge of that address.

Although it is possible to use any register other than Register 0 as the link register for internal subprograms, Register 14 is used by convention as the link register for external subprograms. Therefore, you should consider using Register 14 as the link register for internal subprograms as well. However, if you invoke another subprogram from within an internal subprogram, you first must save the contents of Register 14 before you use it again as a link register. In this way, you later can restore Register 14 to the correct return address. The macro instructions that you use to perform I/O or to request a dump invoke subprograms. Therefore, if your subprogram uses these macro instructions, you must first save and later restore the contents of Register 14.

The following example demonstrates the use of an internal subprogram that uses Register 14 as the link register. The case study that appears later in this chapter demonstrates the use of internal subprograms that perform I/O.

---

EXAMPLE 20

**Divide the Sum of the Integers in One Array by the Sum of the Integers in Another**

The program segment in Figure 7.18 divides the sum of the integers in one array by the sum of the integers in another array using an internal subprogram that computes the sum of the integers in an array. The program segment demonstrates some of the ways that you can communicate with an internal subprogram. First, you must give the subprogram an array and tell it how many integers the array contains. Here, Register 2 contains the address of the array and Register 3 contains the number of integers in the array. Next, the BAL instruction loads the link register (R14) with the address of the next instruction and branches to the subprogram. Finally, the subprogram returns the required sum in Register 5.

```
         LA     R2,ARRAY1      R2 = ADDRESS OF FIRST ARRAY
         LA     R3,10          R3 = NUMBER OF INTEGERS IN FIRST ARRAY
         BAL    R14,ADD        COMPUTE SUM OF INTEGERS IN FIRST ARRAY
         ST     R5,SUM         SAVE SUM FOR LATER
         LA     R2,ARRAY2      R2 = ADDRESS OF SECOND ARRAY
         LA     R3,16          R3 = NUMBER OF INTEGERS IN SECOND ARRAY
         BAL    R14,ADD        COMPUTE SUM OF INTEGERS IN SECOND ARRAY
         M      R4,=F'1'       CONVERT SUM TO 64-BIT FORM
         D      R4,SUM         DIVIDE SECOND SUM BY FIRST SUM
         .
         .
         .
SUM      DS     F               TEMPORARY STORAGE FOR SUM
ARRAY1   DS     10F             FIRST ARRAY
ARRAY2   DS     16F             SECOND ARRAY
***************************************************************
** SUBPROGRAM TO COMPUTE THE SUM OF THE INTEGERS IN AN ARRAY.
** INPUT:  R2  = ADDRESS OF THE ARRAY
**         R3  = NUMBER OF INTEGERS IN THE ARRAY
**         R14 = RETURN ADDRESS
** OUTPUT: R5  = SUM OF INTEGERS IN THE ARRAY
**         DESTROYS R2 AND R3
***************************************************************
ADD      SR     R5,R5           CLEAR SUM REGISTER
* REPEAT C(R3) TIMES:
ADDLOOP  A      R5,0(R2)        ADD NEXT ARRAY ELEMENT TO SUM
         LA     R2,4(R2)        POINT TO NEXT ELEMENT
         BCT    R3,ADDLOOP      DECREMENT COUNTER; REPEAT IF NOT 0
* END REPEAT
         BR     R14             RETURN
```

**Figure 7.18**
A program segment that uses an internal subprogram to divide the sum of the integers in one array by the sum of the integers in another, as described in Example 20.

You need not use registers to communicate with an internal subprogram. Instead, you can place data in particular storage locations and have the subprogram address those locations directly. You can also have the subprogram store its results in fixed-storage locations and access the results outside of the subprogram. This type of communication is demonstrated in the following case study.

# Case Study

## *Problem Statement*

**Compute the transpose of an N × N matrix.**

## *Discussion*

A matrix is a two-dimensional array of elements arranged in rows and columns. ARRAY(I,J), or $a_{I\,J}$, will represent the element in row I and column J. The **transpose** of a matrix is another matrix whose columns and rows are the rows and columns, respectively, of the original matrix, as pictured in Figure 7.19. You can replace a matrix by its transpose, as will be done here, by interchanging the elements $a_{I\,J}$ and $a_{J\,I}$. Note that the elements $a_{J\,J}$ on the diagonal remain unchanged.

The program described here uses three subprograms: the first to read N and the elements of a matrix, the second to print a matrix, and the third to replace a matrix by its transpose. The flowcharts of Figure 7.20 give an overview of this logic.

You can represent a matrix of integers with a two-dimensional array of fullwords, arranged by columns in storage. Thus, you can store the N integers of the first column into consecutive fullwords, then immediately store the N integers of the second column, and so on. Figure 7.21 depicts this order. It is possible to compute the address of the fullword that contains the element ARRAY(I,J) directly from the subscripts I and J (Programming Problem 6 will show you how), but this case study will not do this here. Instead, you will compute the required addresses without explicit use of the subscripts.

*The Read Subprogram.* You can simplify the logic necessary to read the matrix by requiring its elements to appear in the input data set in order of its columns, just as they must appear in storage. Thus, the address of the next element to be read is only 4 bytes greater than the address of the present element. The pseudocode in Figure 7.22 reflects this requirement.

*The Print Subprogram.* The matrix is printed by rows so that it has a standard two-dimensional appearance. The required logic of this subprogram is not as straightforward as that of the previous subprogram, since the elements in any particular row are not stored consecutively in storage. Two observations are used in formulating the required logic:

**Figure 7.19**
An N × N matrix and its transpose.

| **Original matrix** | **Transpose matrix** |
|---|---|
| $a_{11}\ a_{12}\ a_{13}\ \ldots\ a_{1N}$ | $a_{11}\ a_{21}\ a_{31}\ \ldots\ a_{N1}$ |
| $a_{21}\ a_{22}\ a_{23}\ \ldots\ a_{2N}$ | $a_{12}\ a_{22}\ a_{32}\ \ldots\ a_{N2}$ |
| $a_{31}\ a_{32}\ a_{33}\ \ldots\ a_{3N}$ | $a_{13}\ a_{23}\ a_{33}\ \ldots\ a_{N3}$ |
| $\cdot\ \ \cdot\ \ \cdot\ \ \ \ \cdot\ \ \cdot$ | $\cdot\ \ \cdot\ \ \cdot\ \ \ \ \cdot\ \ \cdot$ |
| $\cdot\ \ \cdot\ \ \cdot\ \ \ \ \cdot\ \ \cdot$ | $\cdot\ \ \cdot\ \ \cdot\ \ \ \ \cdot\ \ \cdot$ |
| $\cdot\ \ \cdot\ \ \cdot\ \ \ \ \cdot\ \ \cdot$ | $\cdot\ \ \cdot\ \ \cdot\ \ \ \ \cdot\ \ \cdot$ |
| $a_{N1}\ a_{N2}\ a_{N3}\ \ldots\ a_{NN}$ | $a_{1N}\ a_{2N}\ a_{3N}\ \ldots\ a_{NN}$ |

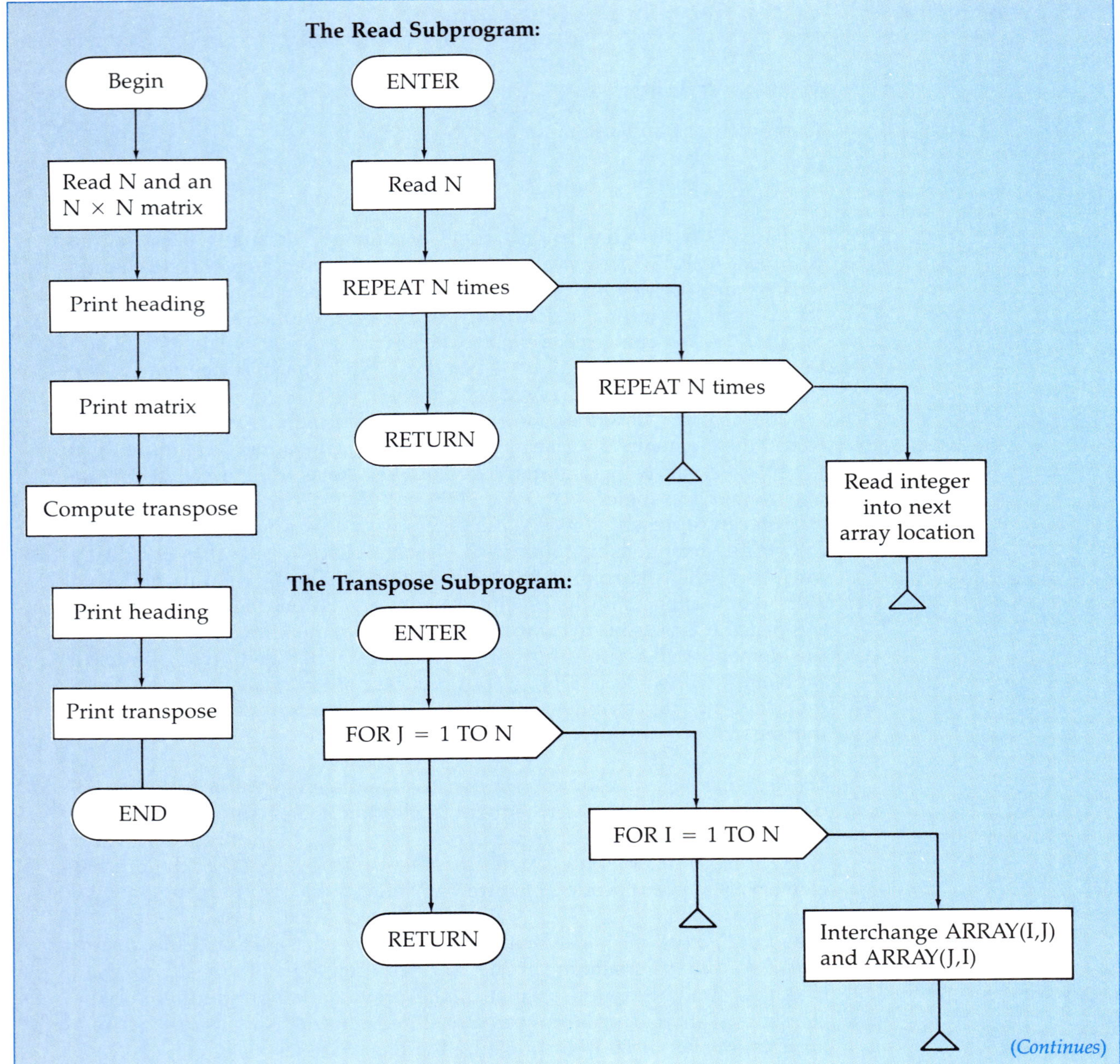


**Figure 7.20**
The flowcharts for a program to transpose a matrix.

- As shown in the portion labeled 1 in Figure 7.23, the first row begins with the address of the first element of the array. Each successive row begins at an address that is 4 bytes larger than the starting address of the previous row.
- As shown in the portion labeled 2 in Figure 7.23, successive elements within a row have addresses that differ by 4N bytes.

The subprogram uses a one-dimensional array LINE to form a line of print. As each row element is located in storage, the subprogram places it into this array. As soon as a row is completed, the contents of LINE are

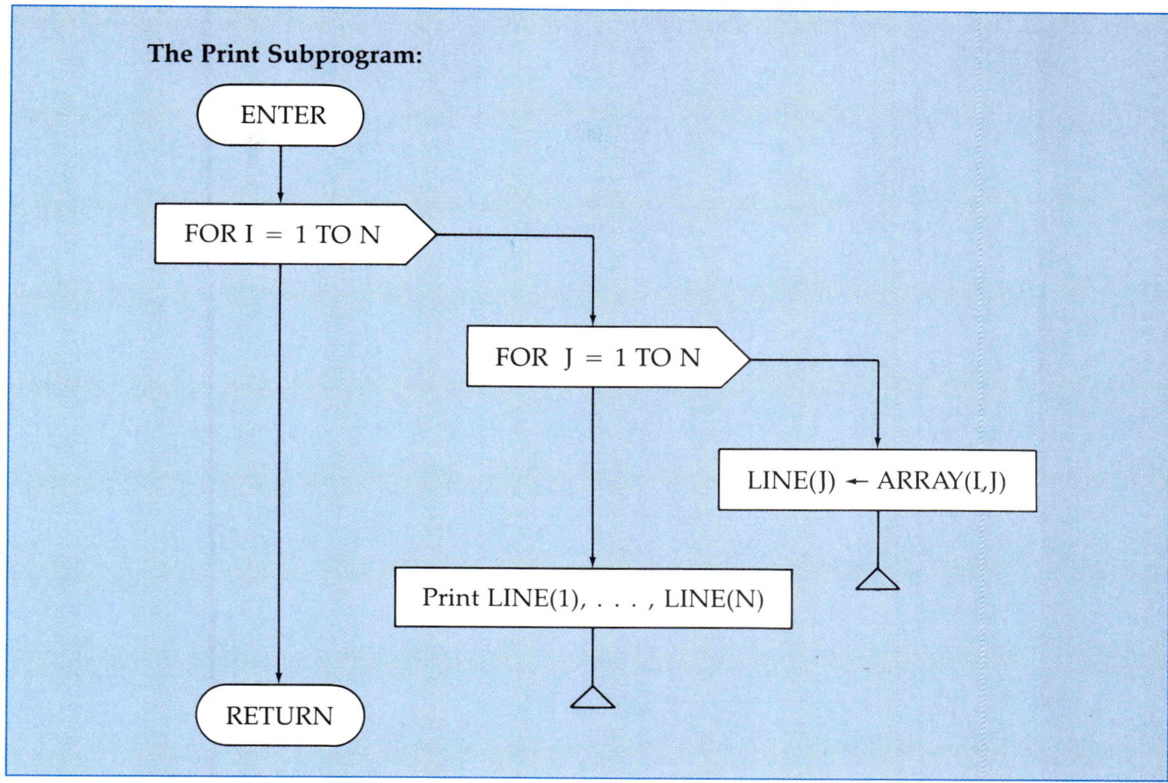


**Figure 7.20**
*(Continued)*

printed. The pseudocode of Figure 7.24 summarizes the logic of this subprogram. ROW represents the starting address of each row; A represents the address of each individual element in a row.

*The Transpose Subprogram.* Although the flowchart in Figure 7.20 does not exclude interchanging ARRAY(J,J) with itself, you clearly want to avoid this unnecessary step. You can interchange elements of the matrix, as illustrated in Figure 7.25, by performing the following steps:

1. Interchange the elements of the first column with those of the first row. Leave the element ARRAY(1,1) fixed.
2. Interchange elements of the second column that lie below the diagonal element ARRAY(2,2) with the elements of the second row that lie to the right of ARRAY(2,2).
3. In general, interchange elements of a particular column that lie below the diagonal with the elements of the corresponding row that lie to the right of the diagonal.

You can use the following observations to compute the addresses that are required in the steps just given:

- As shown in the portion labeled 1 in Figure 7.26, you can compute the address of the column element immediately below the diagonal from the address of the first element in the column. For the first column, these addresses differ by 4; for the second column, they differ by 8; and for the J-th column, they differ by 4 J.

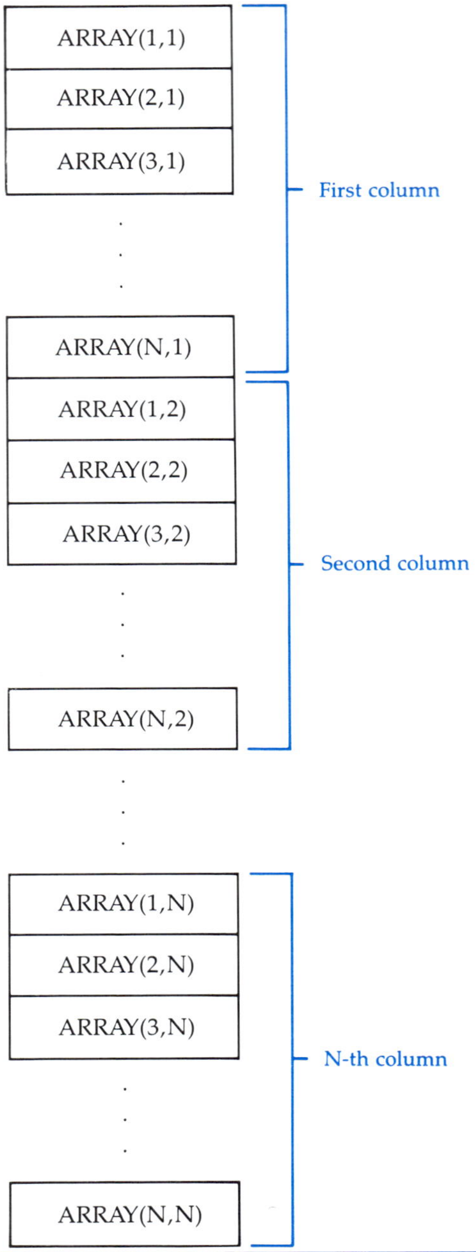

**Figure 7.21**
The storage order of a two-dimensional array.

ARRAY(1,1)
ARRAY(2,1)
ARRAY(3,1)
.
.
.
ARRAY(N,1)
— First column

ARRAY(1,2)
ARRAY(2,2)
ARRAY(3,2)
.
.
.
ARRAY(N,2)
— Second column

.
.
.

ARRAY(1,N)
ARRAY(2,N)
ARRAY(3,N)
.
.
.
ARRAY(N,N)
— N-th column

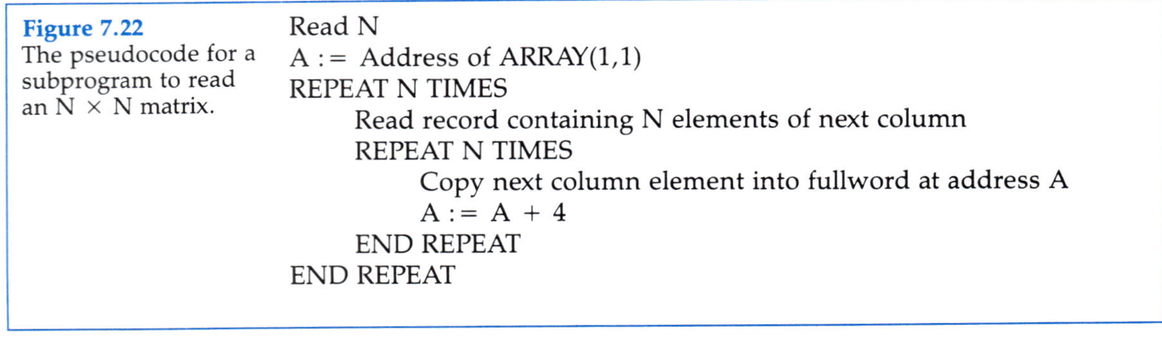

**Figure 7.22**
The pseudocode for a subprogram to read an N × N matrix.

```
Read N
A := Address of ARRAY(1,1)
REPEAT N TIMES
    Read record containing N elements of next column
    REPEAT N TIMES
        Copy next column element into fullword at address A
        A := A + 4
    END REPEAT
END REPEAT
```

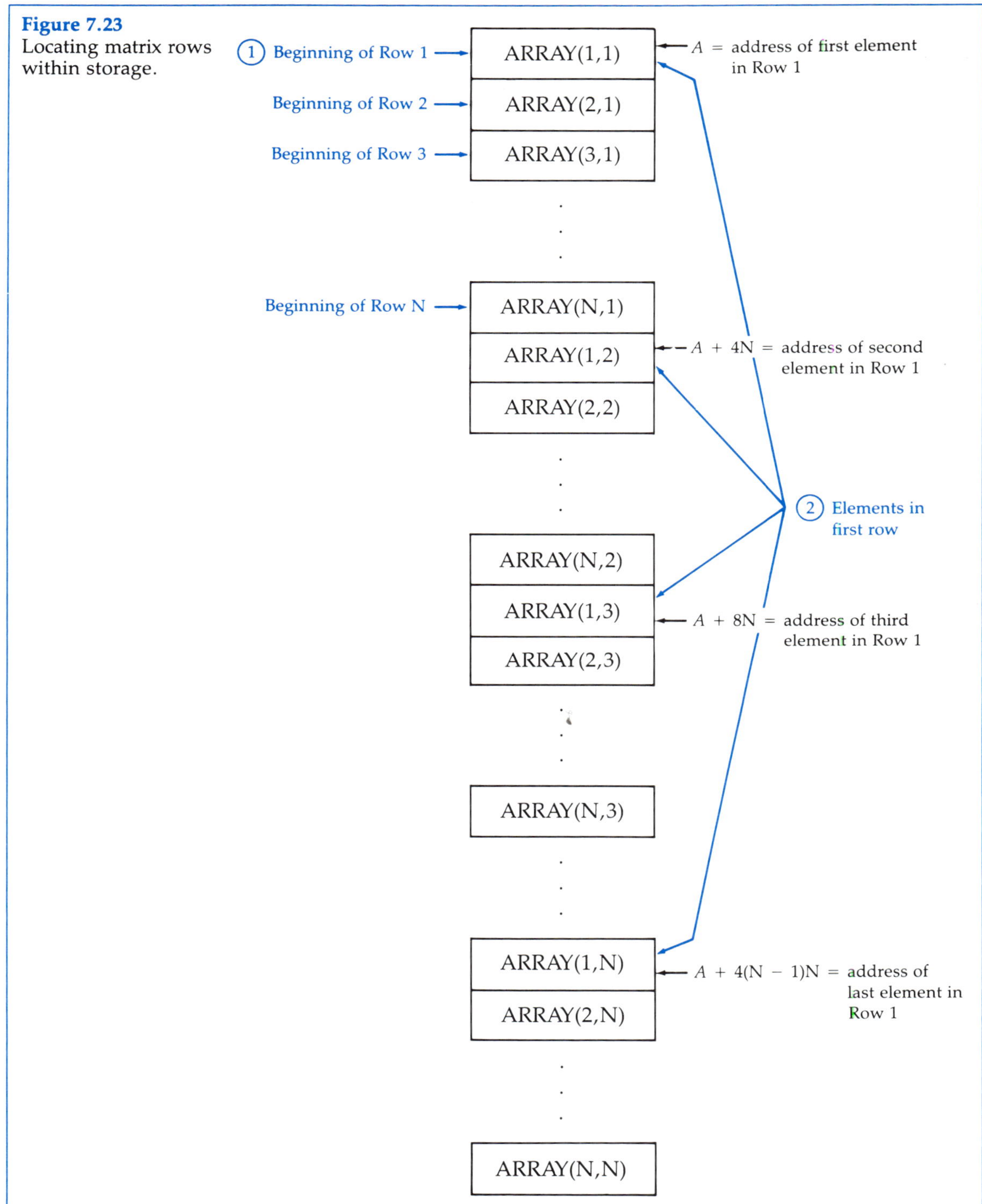


**Figure 7.23**
Locating matrix rows within storage.

- As shown in the portion labeled 2 in Figure 7.26, the addresses of consecutive elements within a column differ by 4.
- As shown in the portion labeled 3 in Figure 7.26, you can calculate the address of the beginning of a column by adding 4 to the address of the last element in the previous column. (This observation simply reflects the fact that the columns are stored consecutively.)

**Figure 7.24**
The pseudocode for a subprogram to print an N × N matrix.

```
ROW := Address of ARRAY(1,1)
REPEAT N TIMES
      A := ROW
      FOR J = 1 TO N
            LINE(J) := Element at address A
            A := A + 4N
      END FOR
      Print LINE(1), . . . , LINE(N)
      ROW := ROW + 4
END REPEAT
```

**Figure 7.25**
The elements to be interchanged while transposing a matrix.

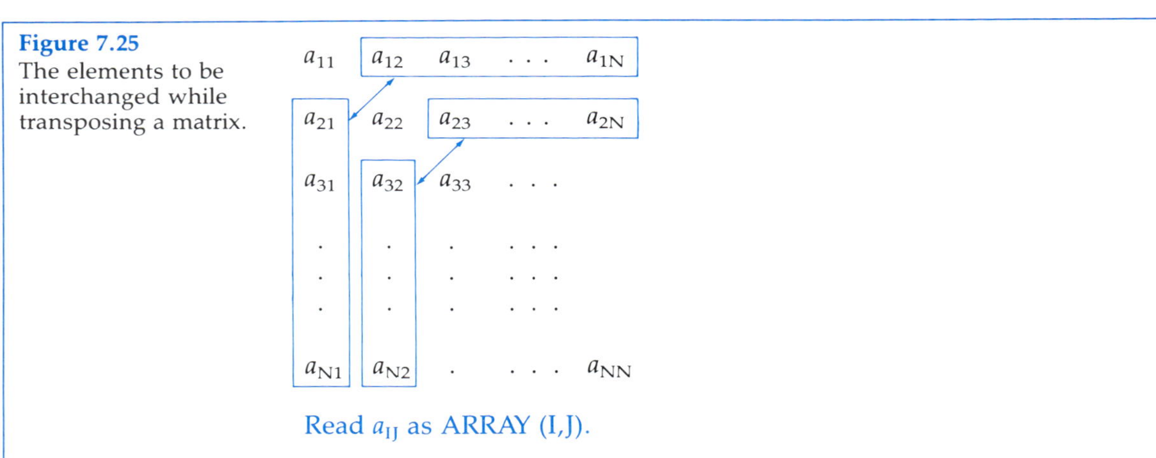


Read $a_{IJ}$ as ARRAY (I,J).

- As shown in Figure 7.27, you can compute the address of the element in Row J immediately to the right of the diagonal by adding 4(N − 1) to the address of the element in Column J immediately below the diagonal. (This is a convenient method because the address of the element in Column J immediately below the diagonal is already available.)
- As was shown in Figure 7.23, the addresses of adjacent row elements differ by 4N.

The pseudocode in Figure 7.28 uses these observations. Note that COL represents the address of a column entry and ROW represents the address of the corresponding row entry. You interchange these two entries. COL begins at the address of the first element in the array, which is also the first element in the first column. You then increment COL by ADJ so that COL points to the first element below the diagonal. (ADJ is initially 4 and is incremented by 4 during each time through the outer loop.) You use COL to compute ROW, the address of the first element to the right of the diagonal. The inner loop performs the interchange of the column with the corresponding row. Note that, when this loop falls through, COL points to the beginning of the next column. Each successive column contains one less element that must be interchanged. Thus, you must decrement the inner loop counter L by one each time that the inner loop falls through.

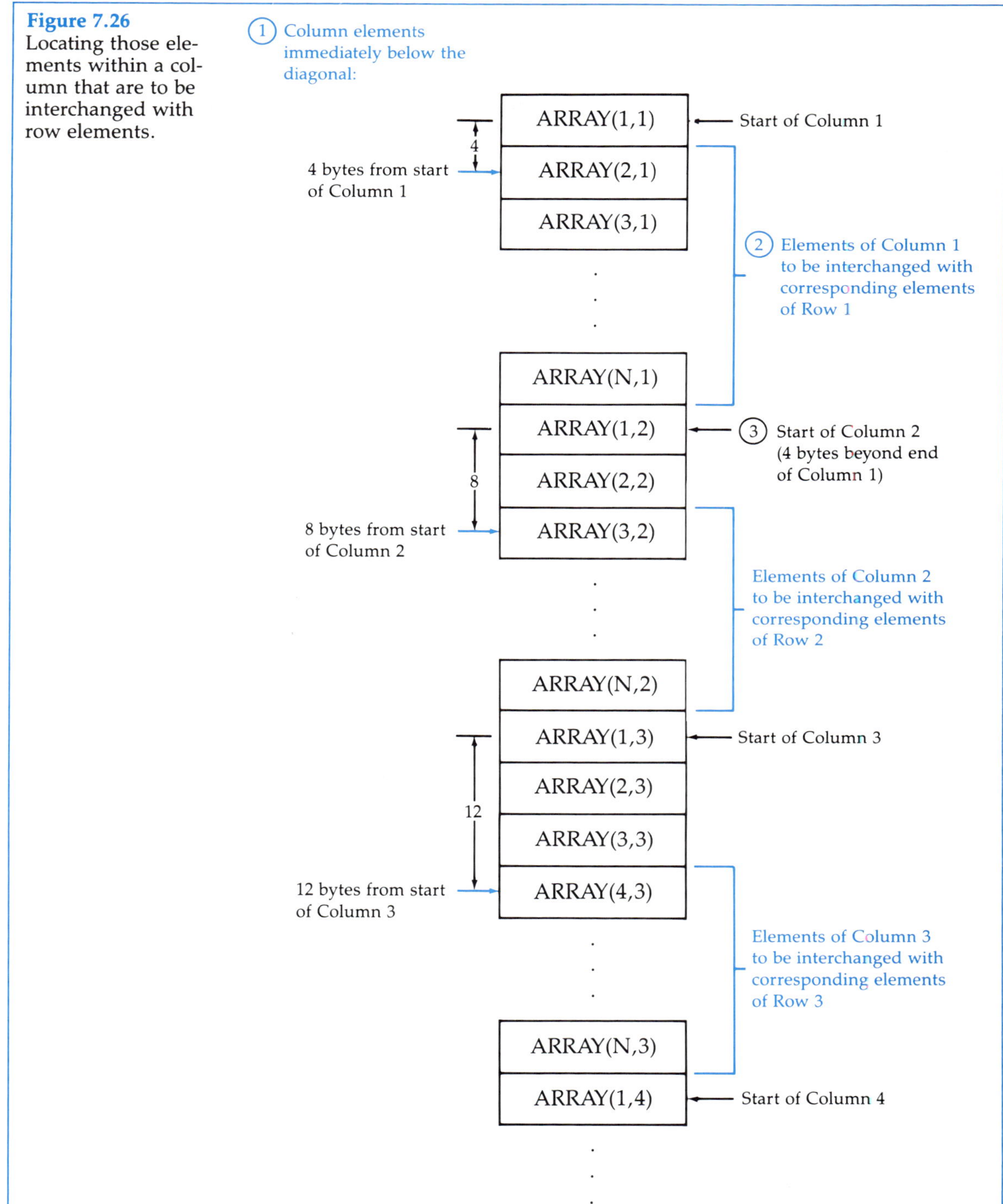


**Figure 7.26** Locating those elements within a column that are to be interchanged with row elements.

## *The Program*

Figure 7.29 lists the program, which is written with internal subprograms. For simplicity, the program restricts the input data as follows. Each element in the matrix is assumed to be a 9-digit integer. If either one blank or a minus sign precedes each element in the input record, then an 80-column

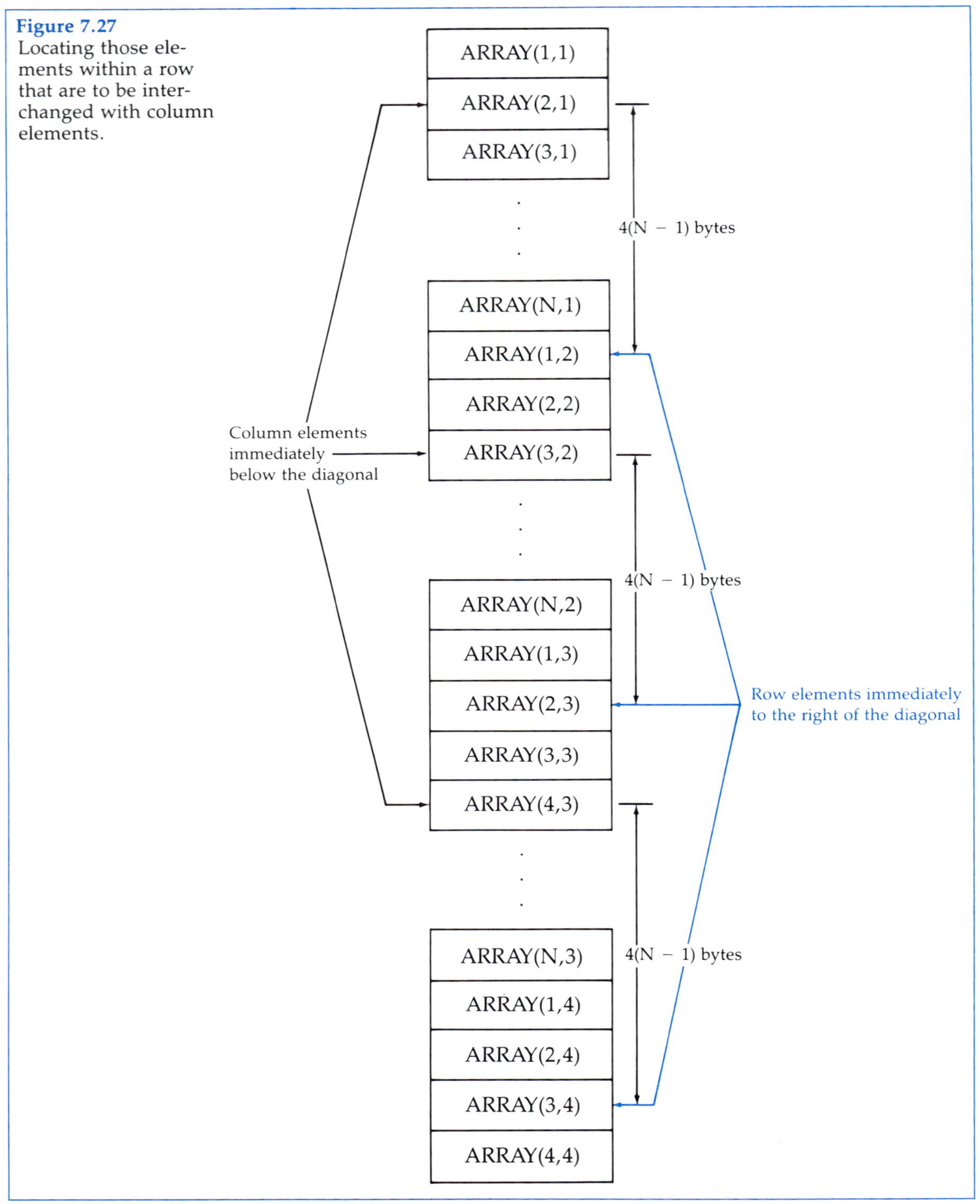


**Figure 7.27** Locating those elements within a row that are to be interchanged with column elements.

record can accommodate up to 8 elements. If you restrict N to be less than or equal to 8, each column can occupy a single record. This restriction also allows each row to be printed on a single line.

Since each input record contains more than one element, the PACK instruction that you use when you convert an element from character form

**Figure 7.28**
The pseudocode for a subprogram to transpose an N×N matrix.

```
L := N - 1
ADJ := 4
COL := Address of ARRAY(1,1)
REPEAT N - 1 TIMES
     COL := COL + ADJ
     ROW := COL + 4(N - 1)
     REPEAT L TIMES
          Interchange elements at addresses COL and ROW
          COL := COL + 4
          ROW := ROW + 4N
     END REPEAT
     ADJ := ADJ + 4
     L := L - 1
END REPEAT
```

to two's complement binary representation must use an operand entry that differs from the one that you learned in Chapter 5. Instead of writing

```
PACK    TEMP(8),NUM(10)
```

where NUM represents the address of a 10-character string, you can write

```
PACK    TEMP(8),0(10,R2)
```

where Register 2 contains the address of the character string. This instructions appears in Statement 102 of Figure 7.29. The LA instruction in Statement 99 initializes Register 2 to the address of the first element in the input record. Statement 109 adds 10 to Register 2 so that the register will point to the next element in the input record.

You can use a similar technique to print more than one element on a line. Instead of writing

```
UNPK    NUM(10),TEMP(8)
MVI     NUM,C' '
```

when you convert a binary integer to an EBCDIC representation, as you learned in Chapter 5, you can write

```
UNPK    0(10,R5),TEMP(8)
MVI     0(R5),C' '
```

Here, Register 5 must contain the address of the resulting character string. These instructions occur in Statements 140 and 141, and a similar MVI instruction appears in Statement 144. The LA instruction in Statement 132 initializes Register 5 to the address of the area that will contain the first element in the printed line. Statement 147 adds 11 to Register 5 so that the register will point to the area for the next element. By first initializing an array of 88 bytes to blanks in Statement 161, and by then adding 11 to Register 5 as was just described, you can separate the elements in the printed line with blanks.

Each of the internal subprograms READ, PRINT, and TRANS immediately saves the contents of Register 14 (Statements 82, 123, and 167) and later restores this register to its original contents (Statements 114, 157, and 196). This procedure is necessary for the READ and PRINT subprograms to operate properly because they perform I/O and, therefore, invoke subprograms that destroy Register 14 when they use Register 14 as a link register. Although this situation is not true for the subprogram TRANS, you may find it useful stylistically to make a practice of always saving and restoring Register 14 within an internal subprogram as was just described. In this way, you are free either to invoke another subprogram or to perform I/O.

In OS, the standard entry saves the contents of Register 14, and the standard exit restores Register 14 to its original value. These two steps allow you to use Register 14 as a link register for an internal subprogram without destroying the address within the operating system that you must branch to upon completion of program execution.

To reduce the chance of duplicate symbols, the instructions within a particular subprogram have been labeled with symbols that begin with the same letter or sequence of letters.

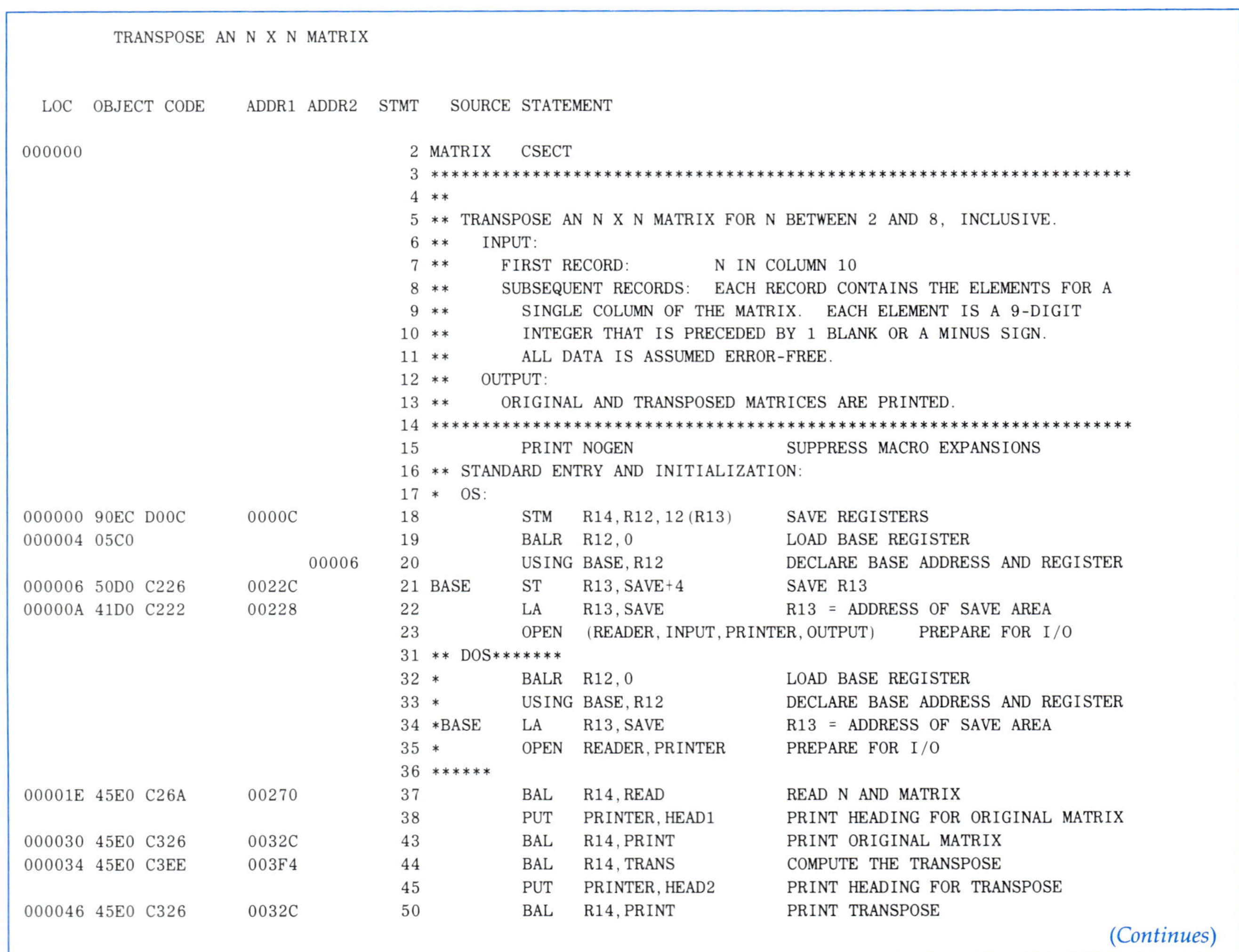

```
        TRANSPOSE AN N X N MATRIX

  LOC  OBJECT CODE    ADDR1 ADDR2  STMT   SOURCE STATEMENT

000000                                2 MATRIX   CSECT
                                      3 ***********************************************************************
                                      4 **
                                      5 ** TRANSPOSE AN N X N MATRIX FOR N BETWEEN 2 AND 8, INCLUSIVE.
                                      6 **    INPUT:
                                      7 **      FIRST RECORD:          N IN COLUMN 10
                                      8 **      SUBSEQUENT RECORDS:  EACH RECORD CONTAINS THE ELEMENTS FOR A
                                      9 **        SINGLE COLUMN OF THE MATRIX.  EACH ELEMENT IS A 9-DIGIT
                                     10 **        INTEGER THAT IS PRECEDED BY 1 BLANK OR A MINUS SIGN.
                                     11 **        ALL DATA IS ASSUMED ERROR-FREE.
                                     12 **    OUTPUT:
                                     13 **      ORIGINAL AND TRANSPOSED MATRICES ARE PRINTED.
                                     14 ***********************************************************************
                                     15          PRINT NOGEN                 SUPPRESS MACRO EXPANSIONS
                                     16 ** STANDARD ENTRY AND INITIALIZATION:
                                     17 *  OS:
000000 90EC D00C      0000C          18          STM   R14,R12,12(R13)       SAVE REGISTERS
000004 05C0                          19          BALR  R12,0                 LOAD BASE REGISTER
                            00006    20          USING BASE,R12              DECLARE BASE ADDRESS AND REGISTER
000006 50D0 C226      0022C          21 BASE     ST    R13,SAVE+4            SAVE R13
00000A 41D0 C222      00228          22          LA    R13,SAVE              R13 = ADDRESS OF SAVE AREA
                                     23          OPEN  (READER,INPUT,PRINTER,OUTPUT)    PREPARE FOR I/O
                                     31 ** DOS*******
                                     32 *        BALR  R12,0                 LOAD BASE REGISTER
                                     33 *        USING BASE,R12              DECLARE BASE ADDRESS AND REGISTER
                                     34 *BASE    LA    R13,SAVE              R13 = ADDRESS OF SAVE AREA
                                     35 *        OPEN  READER,PRINTER        PREPARE FOR I/O
                                     36 ******
00001E 45E0 C26A      00270          37          BAL   R14,READ              READ N AND MATRIX
                                     38          PUT   PRINTER,HEAD1         PRINT HEADING FOR ORIGINAL MATRIX
000030 45E0 C326      0032C          43          BAL   R14,PRINT             PRINT ORIGINAL MATRIX
000034 45E0 C3EE      003F4          44          BAL   R14,TRANS             COMPUTE THE TRANSPOSE
                                     45          PUT   PRINTER,HEAD2         PRINT HEADING FOR TRANSPOSE
000046 45E0 C326      0032C          50          BAL   R14,PRINT             PRINT TRANSPOSE
```

(*Continues*)

**Figure 7.29**
The program to transpose a matrix.

```
                                         51 ** STANDARD EXIT:
                                         52 ** OS:
                                         53            CLOSE  (READER,,PRINTER)    CLOSE I/O
00005A 58D0 C226         0022C           61            L      R13,SAVE+4           RESTORE R13
00005E 98EC D00C         0000C           62            LM     R14,R12,12(R13)      RESTORE REMAINING REGISTERS
000062 07FE                              63            BR     R14                  RETURN TO OS
                                         64 ** DOS*******
                                         65 *          CLOSE READER,PRINTER        CLOSE I/O
                                         66 *          EOJ                         RETURN TO DOS
                                         67 ******
000064                                   68 N          DS     F                    SIZE OF MATRIX (MAX = 8)
000068                                   69 ARRAY      DS     64F                  MATRIX (MAX SIZE = 8 X 8)
000168 F0D6D9C9C7C9D5C1                  70 HEAD1      DC     C'0ORIGINAL MATRIX   '
00017A 4040404040404040                  71            DC     71C' '               PAD TO LENGTH OF LINE
0001C1 F0E3D9C1D5E2D7D6                  72 HEAD2      DC     C'0TRANSPOSED MATRIX'
0001D3 4040404040404040                  73            DC     71C' '               PAD TO LENGTH OF LINE
000220                                   74 TEMP       DS     D                    WORK AREA FOR CONVERSIONS
000228                                   75 SAVE       DS     18F                  SAVE AREA (9D IN DOS)
                                         76 *****************************************************************
                                         77 ** SUBPROGRAM TO READ N AND AN N X N MATRIX.
                                         78 **    INPUT AS DESCRIBED IN MAIN PROLOGUE.
                                         79 **    ASSUME STORAGE FOR N AND ARRAY ARE DEFINED.
                                         80 *****************************************************************
                                         81 * READ, CONVERT, AND STORE N:
000270 50E0 C322         00328           82 READ       ST     R14,RSAVE14          SAVE SUBPROGRAM RETURN ADDRESS
                                         83            GET    READER,RECORD        READ N
000282 F279 C21A C2D2 00220 002D8        88            PACK   TEMP(8),RECORD(10)   CONVERT N TO BINARY;
000288 4FA0 C21A         00220           89            CVB    R10,TEMP               R10 = OUTER LOOP COUNTER
00028C 50A0 C05E         00064           90            ST     R10,N                SAVE N
000290 4180 0000         00000           91            LA     R8,0                 R8 = ARRAY INDEX = 0
                                         92 * REPEAT N TIMES:
000294 5890 C05E         00064           93 RDOUTLP    L      R9,N                 R9 = INNER LOOP COUNTER = N
                                         94            GET    READER,RECORD        READ NEXT COLUMN
0002A6 4120 C2D2         002D8           99            LA     R2,RECORD            R2 = POINTER TO EACH AREA IN
                                        100 *                                           INPUT RECORD
                                        101 * - REPEAT N TIMES:
0002AA F279 C21A 2000 00220 00000       102 RDINLP     PACK   TEMP(8),0(10,R2)     CONVERT
0002B0 4F40 C21A         00220          103            CVB    R4,TEMP                ELEMENT
0002B4 9560 2000         00000          104            CLI    0(R2),C'-'               TO
0002B8 4770 C2B8         002BE          105            BNE    RDNN                       SIGNED
0002BC 1144                             106            LNR    R4,R4                        BINARY
0002BE 5048 C062         00068          107 RDNN       ST     R4,ARRAY(R8)         STORE ELEMENT IN ARRAY
0002C2 4188 0004         00004          108            LA     R8,4(R8)             INCREMENT ARRAY INDEX
0002C6 4122 000A         0000A          109            LA     R2,10(R2)            POINT TO NEXT AREA IN INPUT RECORD
0002CA 4690 C2A4         002AA          110            BCT    R9,RDINLP            DECREMENT COUNTER; REPEAT IF NONZERO
                                        111 * - END REPEAT
0002CE 46A0 C28E         00294          112            BCT    R10,RDOUTLP          DECREMENT COUNTER; REPEAT IF NONZERO
                                        113 * END REPEAT
0002D2 58E0 C322         00328          114            L      R14,RSAVE14          RESTORE SUBPROGRAM RETURN ADDRESS
0002D6 07FE                             115            BR     R14                  RETURN
                                        116 *
0002D8                                  117 RECORD     DS     80C                  INPUT RECORD
000328                                  118 RSAVE14    DS     F                    SAVE AREA FOR RETURN ADDRESS
                                        119 *****************************************************************
                                        120 ** SUBPROGRAM TO PRINT AN N X N MATRIX.
                                        121 **    ASSUME N AND ARRAY ARE DEFINED.
                                        122 *****************************************************************
00032C 50E0 C3EA         003F0          123 PRINT      ST     R14,PSAVE14          SAVE SUBPROGRAM RETURN ADDRESS
000330 5830 C05E         00064          124            L      R3,N                 GET N
000334 0630                             125            BCTR   R3,0                 N - 1
000336 5C20 C502         00508          126            M      R2,=F'4'             R3 = BXLE LIMIT = 4*(N - 1)
00033A 4120 0004         00004          127            LA     R2,4                 R2 = BXLE INCREMENT = 4
00033E 4163 0004         00004          128            LA     R6,4(R3)             R6 = CONSTANT = 4*(N - 1) + 4 = 4*N
000342 41A0 0000         00000          129            LA     R10,0                R10 = OUTER LOOP COUNTER
```

*(Continues)*

**Figure 7.29**
*(Continued)*

```
                                            130 * REPEAT N TIMES:
000346 188A                                 131 PRTOUTLP LR     R8,R10              R8 = POINTER TO EACH ELEMENT IN ROW
000348 4150 C391        00397               132          LA     R5,LINE             R5 = POINTER TO EACH AREA IN OUTPUT
                                            133 *                                        LINE
00034C 5890 C05E        00064               134          L      R9,N                R9 = INNER LOOP COUNTER = N
                                            135 * - REPEAT N TIMES:
000350 5848 C062        00068               136 PRTINLP  L      R4,ARRAY(R8)        R4 = WORK REGISTER
                                            137 *                                      = NEXT ELEMENT IN ROW
000354 4E40 C21A        00220               138          CVD    R4,TEMP             CONVERT
000358 960F C221        00227               139          OI     TEMP+7,X'0F'          SIGNED
00035C F397 5000 C21A 00000 00220           140          UNPK   0(10,R5),TEMP(8)        ELEMENT
000362 9240 5000        00000               141          MVI    0(R5),C' '
000366 5940 C506        0050C               142          C      R4,=F'0'                  TO
00036A 47B0 C36C        00372               143          BNM    PRTNN
00036E 9260 5000        00000               144          MVI    0(R5),C'-'                  EBCDIC
000372 4188 6000        00000               145 PRTNN    LA     R8,0(R8,R6)         POINT TO NEXT ELEMENT IN ROW
                                            146 *                                     (R8 IS INCREMENTED BY 4*N)
000376 4155 000B        0000B               147          LA     R5,11(R5)           POINT TO NEXT AREA IN OUTPUT LINE
00037A 4690 C34A        00350               148          BCT    R9,PRTINLP          DECREMENT COUNTER; REPEAT IF NONZERO
                                            149 * - END REPEAT
                                            150          PUT    PRINTER,CC          PRINT ROW OF MATRIX
00038C 87A2 C340        00346               155          BXLE   R10,R2,PRTOUTLP     POINT TO NEXT ROW; REPEAT
                                            156 * END REPEAT
000390 58E0 C3EA        003F0               157          L      R14,PSAVE14         RESTORE SUBPROGRAM RETURN ADDRESS
000394 07FE                                 158          BR     R14                 RETURN
                                            159 *
000396 40                                   160 CC       DC     C' '                CARRIAGE CONTROL
000397 4040404040404040                     161 LINE     DC     88C' '              AREA FOR LINE OF PRINT
0003F0                                      162 PSAVE14  DS     F                   SAVE AREA FOR RETURN ADDRESS
                                            163 **********************************************************************
                                            164 ** SUBPROGRAM TO TRANSPOSE AN N X N MATRIX IN PLACE.
                                            165 **    ASSUME N AND ARRAY ARE DEFINED.
                                            166 **********************************************************************
0003F4 50E0 C43E        00444               167 TRANS    ST     R14,TSAVE14         SAVE SUBPROGRAM RETURN ADDRESS
0003F8 5830 C05E        00064               168          L      R3,N                GET N
0003FC 0630                                 169          BCTR   R3,0                N - 1
0003FE 18A3                                 170          LR     R10,R3              R10 = OUTER LOOP CONTROL = N - 1
000400 5C20 C502        00508               171          M      R2,=F'4'            R3 = CONSTANT = 4*(N - 1)
000404 4123 0004        00004               172          LA     R2,4(R3)            R2 = CONSTANT = 4*(N - 1) + 4 = 4*N
000408 4180 0000        00000               173          LA     R8,0                R8 = INDEX TO COLUMN ELEMENT = 0
00040C 4160 0004        00004               174          LA     R6,4                R6 = ADJ
                                            175 *                                      = NO. OF BYTES BETWEEN FIRST
                                            176 *                                        ELEMENT IN COLUMN AND ELEMENT
                                            177 *                                        IMMEDIATELY BELOW DIAGONAL
                                            178 * REPEAT N  -1 TIMES:
000410 189A                                 179 TROUTLP  LR     R9,R10              R9 = INNER LOOP COUNTER L=N-1,...,1
000412 4188 6000        00000               180          LA     R8,0(R8,R6)         R8 = INDEX TO COLUMN ELEMENT
                                            181 *                                        IMMEDIATELY BELOW DIAGONAL
000416 4178 3000        00000               182          LA     R7,0(R8,R3)         R7 = INDEX TO ROW ELEMENT
                                            183 *                                        IMMEDIATELY RIGHT OF DIAGONAL
                                            184 * - REPEAT L = C(R9) TIMES:
00041A 5848 C062        00068               185 TRINLP   L      R4,ARRAY(R8)        GET COLUMN ELEMENT
00041E 5857 C062        00068               186          L      R5,ARRAY(R7)        GET ROW ELEMENT
000422 5058 C062        00068               187          ST     R5,ARRAY(R8)        INTERCHANGE
000426 5047 C062        00068               188          ST     R4,ARRAY(R7)          THEM
00042A 4188 0004        00004               189          LA     R8,4(R8)            POINT TO NEXT COLUMN ELEMENT
00042E 4177 2000        00000               190          LA     R7,0(R7,R2)         POINT TO NEXT ROW ELEMENT
000432 4690 C414        0041A               191          BCT    R9,TRINLP           DECREMENT COUNTER; REPEAT IF NONZERO
                                            192 * - END REPEAT (R8 NOW POINTS TO TOP OF NEXT COLUMN)
000436 4166 0004        00004               193          LA     R6,4(R6)            ADJ = ADJ + 4
00043A 46A0 C40A        00410               194          BCT    R10,TROUTLP         DECREMENT COUNTER; REPEAT IF NONZERO
                                            195 * END REPEAT
00043E 58E0 C43E        00444               196          L      R14,TSAVE14         RESTORE SUBPROGRAM RETURN ADDRESS
000442 07FE                                 197          BR     R14                 RETURN
```

*(Continues)*

**Figure 7.29**
*(Continued)*

```
                                          198 *
000444                                    199 TSAVE14  DS    F                   SAVE AREA FOR RETURN ADDRESS
                                          200 * DCB'S FOR I/O:
                                          201 READER   DCB   DSORG=PS,MACRF=GM,DDNAME=SYSIN,RECFM=F,LRECL=80,            X
                                                             BLKSIZE=80
                                          255 PRINTER  DCB   DSORG=PS,MACRF=PM,DDNAME=SYSPRINT,RECFM=FA,LRECL=89,        X
                                                             BLKSIZE=89
                                          309 ** DOS*******
                                          310 *READER  DTFCD DEVADDR=SYSIPT,DEVICE=2540,IOAREA1=INBUF,                   X
                                                             RECFORM=FIXUNB,BLKSIZE=80,TYPEFLE=INPUT,WORKA=YES
                                          311 *PRINTER DTFPR DEVADDR=SYSLST,DEVICE=3203,IOAREA1=OUTBUF,WORKA=YES,        X
                                                             RECFORM=FIXUNB,BLKSIZE=89,CTLCHAR=ASA
                                          312 *INBUF   DS    80C                 INPUT BUFFER
                                          313 *OUTBUF  DS    89C                 OUTPUT BUFFER
                                          314 ******
                                          315 * REGISTER DEFINITIONS:
                                   00002  316 R2       EQU   2
                                   00003  317 R3       EQU   3                   USED TO COMPUTE N-1 AND 4*(N-1)
                                   00004  318 R4       EQU   4                   WORK REGISTER
                                   00005  319 R5       EQU   5
                                   00006  320 R6       EQU   6
                                   00007  321 R7       EQU   7
                                   00008  322 R8       EQU   8                   ARRAY INDEX
                                   00009  323 R9       EQU   9                   INNER LOOP COUNTER
                                   0000A  324 R10      EQU   10                  OUTER LOOP COUNTER
                                   0000C  325 R12      EQU   12                  BASE REGISTER
                                   0000D  326 R13      EQU   13                  SAVE AREA POINTER
                                   0000E  327 R14      EQU   14                  LINK TO SUBPROGRAMS AND OS
000000                                    328          END   MATRIX
000508 00000004                           329                =F'4'
0005CC 00000000                           330                =F'0'


ORIGINAL MATRIX
 000000001 -000000005  000000009 -000000013
 000000002 -000000006  000000010 -000000014
 000000003 -000000007  000000011 -000000015
 000000004 -000000008  000000012 -000000016

TRANSPOSED MATRIX
 000000001  000000002  000000003  000000004
-000000005 -000000006 -000000007 -000000008
 000000009  000000010  000000011  000000012
-000000013 -000000014 -000000015 -000000016
```

Output from program

**Figure 7.29**
*(continued)*

## Debugging Hints

1. Errors in writing the LA instruction that are undetected by the assembler are easy to make, particularly if you confuse absolute and relocatable expressions. If the results of execution indicate that an LA instruction does not behave as expected, examine its corresponding object code to confirm its accuracy. For example, if the instruction is to load Register 2 with the constant 4, then its machine language form should be 41200004. However, if it appears as 4120C5A4, then you probably wrote an instruction such as

   ```
   LA    R2,=F'4'
   ```

   or

   ```
   LA    R2,FOUR
   ```

   where FOUR labels a DC. You should have written

   ```
   LA    R2,4
   ```

2. Make certain to establish the correct starting and ending values that are involved in controlling a loop. Consideration of a specific example that involves only one or two repetitions of the loop can help with the general design. If your loop does not work correctly, verify that the starting and ending values of the counter are correct and consistent with the test that you used.
3. When you use a BCT instruction for loop control, be careful that the counter does not become zero or negative before the instruction is executed. If this happens, the loop may be executed many more times than you want. This could happen if you change the counter within the body of the loop, prior to the BCT itself. You might be tempted to do this, for example, in order to count by increments of 2 instead of 1. Avoid doing this; instead consider an alternate loop control instruction, such as BXLE or BXH.
4. If you use Register 14 as a link register for an internal subprogram that either invokes another subprogram, performs I/O, or requests a dump, be sure that you first save and later restore the original contents of Register 14. If you do not do this, you will not be able to branch back to the correct return address.

## Stylistic Notes

1. You can use both LA and SR to initialize a register to zero. The LA instruction executes faster than the SR instruction, but it is 2 bytes longer.
2. You may write REPEAT, FOR, and WHILE structures by using BCT, BXLE, or BXH instructions. Of the three structures, WHILE requires an additional branch instruction and will, therefore, be slower in general.
3. Both BXLE and BXH permit either positive or negative increments. Typically, your choices for loop control will conform to the following chart:

| Type of Loop | Sign of Increment: Positive | Negative |
|---|---|---|
| REPEAT-UNTIL | BXLE | BXH |
| WHILE | BXH | BXLE |

Generally, it is easier to use BXLE with positive increments, and BXH with negative increments.

4. When you first design a BXLE or a BXH loop, it is a good idea to define three different registers to serve as the counter, the increment, and the limit. After you write a draft of the loop, see if the increment and the limit have the same value, or if it is possible to change the limit so that it is the same as the increment. If so, use only one register to serve both these functions.
5. Execution time, memory utilization, register utilization, and programming time are frequently in direct conflict. You will often have to make decisions that are based upon these factors—particularly when writing loops; you should be aware of how your choice of a loop-control instruction affects each of these. Using the branch instructions defined in this chapter generally results in loops that use more registers than those controlled by the BC instruction; however, these loops can be easier to read and take less time to execute.
6. Each subprogram should have its own prologue, which describes its purpose, its assumptions, its required inputs, and the results of its execution.

## Summary

1. The Load Address (LA) instruction places the effective address that is designated by its operand entry into a register. It provides a simple way to initialize or increment a register by a constant between 0 and 4095.
2. The BCT and BCTR instructions cause a loop counter to count backward by increments of one until it becomes zero.
3. The BXLE and BXH instructions increment a counter by any desired value, and compare the result with any desired value. They permit execution-efficient loops, but generally require more registers than other methods of loop control.
4. Initially, design BXLE and BXH loops with separate registers for the index, the increment, and the limit. Revise the register allocation if it becomes apparent that a register will serve more than one function.
5. It is possible to implement REPEAT, FOR, and WHILE structures by using BC, BCT, BXLE, or BXH instructions.
6. The BAL and BALR instructions first load the address of the next instruction into a register and then branch. They can be used to invoke a subprogram.

## New Instruction Summary

| Operation | Operand | Format | Instruction Name | Action |
|---|---|---|---|---|
| **LA** | *R1,D2(X2,B2)* or *R1,S2* or *R1,S2(X2)* | RX | LOAD ADDRESS | With 24-bit addressing, $C(R1)_{0-7} \leftarrow 0$, $C(R1)_{8-31} \leftarrow E2$. With 31-bit addressing, $C(R1)_{0} \leftarrow 0$, $C(R1)_{1-31} \leftarrow E2$ |
| **BCT** | *R1,S2* or *R1,S2(X2)* or *R1,D2(X2,B2)* | RX | BRANCH ON COUNT | $C(R1) \leftarrow C(R1) - 1$ Branches to $E2$ if $C(R1) \neq 0$ |
| **BCTR** | *R1,R2* | RR | BRANCH ON COUNT | $C(R1) \leftarrow C(R1) - 1$ Branches to address in $R2$ if $C(R1) \neq 0$ and $R2 \neq 0$ |
| **BXLE** | *R1,R3,S2* or *R1,R3,D2(B2)* | RS | BRANCH ON INDEX LOW OR EQUAL | $C(R1) \leftarrow C(R1) + C(R3)$ Branches to $E2$ if $C(R1) \leq \begin{cases} C(R3) \text{ if } R3 \text{ is odd} \\ C(R3+1) \text{ if } R3 \text{ is even} \end{cases}$ |
| **BXH** | *R1,R3,S2* or *R1,R3,D2(B2)* | RS | BRANCH ON INDEX HIGH | $C(R1) \leftarrow C(R1) + C(R3)$ Branches to $E2$ if $C(R1) > \begin{cases} C(R3) \text{ if } R3 \text{ is odd} \\ C(R3+1) \text{ if } R3 \text{ is even} \end{cases}$ |
| **BAL** | *R1,S2* or *R1,S2(X2)* or *R1,D2(X2,B2)* | RX | BRANCH AND LINK | $C(R1) \leftarrow \begin{cases} \text{ILC,CC, program mask, IA (24-bit addressing)} \\ \text{1, IA (31-bit addressing)} \end{cases}$ Branches to the effective address $E2$. |
| **BALR** | *R1,R2* | RR | BRANCH AND LINK REGISTER | Loads $R1$ with the same value as BAL. Branches to the address in $R2$ if $R2 \neq 0$. |

## Exercises

1. Assume the following definitions:

```
FOUR     DC    F'4'
DATA     DC    F'5'
         DC    F'6'
SEVEN    EQU   7
```

FOUR represents the address $48C_{16}$. What are the contents of the indicated registers after execution of each instruction in the following sequence? When necessary, assume that the prior contents of a register are as set by the instructions that are given earlier in the list.

**a.** `LA 1,DATA`
**b.** `LA 2,4(1)`
**c.** `L 3,4(1)`
**d.** `LA 4,DATA(3)`
**e.** `LA 5,0(4)`
**f.** `LA 6,4`
**g.** `LA 7,FOUR`
**h.** `LA 8,FOUR(6)`
**i.** `LA 9,0(2)`
**j.** `LA 10,SEVEN(2,3)`
**k.** `LA 11,0(1,6)`

2. Assume that base register 12 contains $102_{16}$. What object code is produced by each of the instructions in Exercise 1?

3. Assume the following register status:

| | |
|---|---|
| Reg. 0 = 0000D002 | Reg. 4 = 00000008 |
| Reg. 2 = 00BF5046 | Reg. 5 = 00000000 |
| Reg. 3 = FFFFFFFE | Reg. 6 = 00000001 |

How does each of the following instructions affect this register status? Does each instruction branch and, if so, to where?

| | | | | | |
|---|---|---|---|---|---|
| a. | BCT 5, LOOP | g. | BCTR 3, 0 |
| b. | BCT 3, LOOP (4) | h. | BCTR 4, 2 |
| c. | BCT 0, LOOP | i. | BCTR 4, 0 |
| d. | BCT 6, LOOP (4) | j. | BCTR 5, 2 |
| e. | BCT 4, LOOP | k. | BCTR 6, 2 |
| f. | BCTR 0, 0 | l. | BCTR 6, 0 |

4. Assume the following register status before the execution of each BXLE and BXH instruction:

| | |
|---|---|
| Reg. 4 = FFFFFFFC | Reg. 5 = 00000008 |
| Reg. 6 = 00000004 | Reg. 7 = 00000020 |
| Reg. 8 = 00000004 | Reg. 9 = 00000000 |

Give the value of the first register operand after each of the following instructions is executed, and indicate whether the instruction branches to LOOP.

| | | | |
|---|---|---|---|
| a. | BXLE 4, 5, LOOP | k. | BXH 4, 6, LOOP |
| b. | BXLE 4, 8, LOOP | l. | BXH 4, 9, LOOP |
| c. | BXLE 5, 8, LOOP | m. | BXH 5, 6, LOOP |
| d. | BXLE 6, 4, LOOP | n. | BXH 6, 5, LOOP |
| e. | BXLE 7, 9, LOOP | o. | BXH 6, 8, LOOP |
| f. | BXLE 8, 4, LOOP | p. | BXH 7, 4, LOOP |
| g. | BXLE 8, 7, LOOP | q. | BXH 8, 5, LOOP |
| h. | BXLE 9, 6, LOOP | r. | BXH 8, 6, LOOP |
| i. | BXLE 9, 7, LOOP | s. | BXH 9, 4, LOOP |
| j. | BXLE 9, 8, LOOP | t. | BXH 9, 5, LOOP |

5. Assume the following register status:

Reg. 2 = 12
Reg. 6 = −4
Reg. 7 = 4

Indicate the number of times that the instruction at LOOP is executed for each of the following loops:

a.
```
LOOP    ----
        .
        .
        .
        BXH   2,6,LOOP
```

b.
```
LOOP    ----
        .
        .
        .
        BXLE  6,7,LOOP
```

c.
```
LOOP    ----
        BXH   6,7,OUT
        .
        .
        .
        B     LOOP
OUT     ----
```

d.
```
LOOP    ----
        BXLE  2,6,OUT
        .
        .
        .
        B     LOOP
OUT     ----
```

6. Consider a program that is terminated by the operating system because it exceeded its time limit. The dump indicates that the last instruction executed was in a loop that ended with

```
BXLE    R5,R6,LOOP
```

and that Registers 5, 6, and 7 are as follows:

Reg. 5 = C0000000
Reg. 6 = FFFFFFFC
Reg. 7 = 000000A4

What is a possible explanation for the termination?

## Programming Problems

*Write programs to solve the following problems by making liberal use of internal subprograms. It is possible to write the required loops in several ways by using the various instructions of this chapter. Practice these instructions by considering alternate solutions to each problem.*

1. Consider a one-dimensional array of fullword integers.
   a. Replace the negative values in the array by zeros.
   b. Delete the zero values in the array.
   c. Find the address of the smallest integer in the array.
   d. Compute another array whose entries are in the opposite order of the given array.

e. Reverse the order of the entries in the array without using a second array.
f. Print the array in reverse order without changing the array in storage and without using a second array.

2. Consider 2 one-dimensional arrays X and Y. Each array consists of N fullword integers that are arranged in ascending order.
   a. Compute the sum of the arrays. (The sum is a third array whose J-th entry is X(J) + Y(J).)
   b. Compute the scalar product defined by

      X(1) * Y(1) + X(2) * Y(2) + . . .
      + X(N) * Y(N)

   c. Compute the array that contains only those integers that occur in both X and Y. Assume that neither X nor Y contains duplicate entries.
   d. Repeat Programming Problem 2c to permit duplicate entries in X and Y. However, do not allow duplicates in the new array.
   e. Compute an array that consists of all integers in X and Y in ascending order.

3. Compute an array that consists of integers that are read from an input data set in such a way that duplicates are ignored.

4. Write a subprogram to sort a one-dimensional array of fullword integers into ascending order.

5. Suppose that ARRAY is an N × N array of fullwords, similar to the one described in the Case Study. The **trace** of such an array is defined as the sum of the diagonal elements. Write a subprogram to compute the trace by using the fact that the addresses of successive diagonal elements differ by 4(N + 1).

6. Suppose that ARRAY is a two-dimensional array of fullwords with N rows and M columns, whose elements are stored by columns. The address of the element ARRAY(I,J) is equal to

   [Address of ARRAY(1,1)] + 4 * N * (J − 1)
   + 4 * (I − 1)

   a. Write a subprogram to compute this address when given I and J.
   b. Using the subprogram that you wrote in Programming Problem 6a, compute the trace of an N × N array.
   c. Using the subprogram from Programming Problem 6a, compute the transpose of an N × N array. How does your solution compare with that given in Figure 7.29?

7. The product of the N × M array X and the M × N array Y is an N × N array whose I,J element is

   X(I,1) * Y (1,J) + X(I,2) * Y(2,J) + . . . + X(I,M)
   * Y(M,J)

   Write a subprogram to compute the product of X and Y.

8. Let X be an N × N array and let $X^T$ denote its transpose. Compute the trace of the product of X and $X^T$. Use the subprograms in the Case Study and those of Programming Problems 5 and 7.

# 8

# The Shift Instructions

CONTENTS



OVERVIEW

This chapter defines instructions to shift the bits in a register or in an even-odd register pair either to the left or to the right. The instructions allow you to work with data at the bit level. There are two types of shift instructions: logical and arithmetic. Logical shifts treat register contents as unsigned binary integers, and are often used to manipulate character or other non-numeric data. Arithmetic shifts assume that the registers contain two's complement binary integers, and can be used to multiply or divide the integers by a power of two.

The arithmetic Shift instructions can cause a fixed-point overflow exception. For certain applications, it is desirable to mask off this exception. Therefore, this chapter includes a description of the SPM instruction, which is used to set the program mask.

**OBJECTIVES**

After studying this chapter, you should be able to:

1. Describe the result of the Shift instructions when given particular operand values.
2. Describe how the number of bits shifted is designated in assembler language, and how it is computed at execution time.
3. Use the Shift instructions to isolate particular portions of a given quantity.
4. Use the Shift instructions to combine given bit patterns into a longer sequence of bits.
5. Use the arithmetic Shift instructions to multiply or divide the contents of a register or a register pair by a power of two.
6. Use the arithmetic Shift instructions to prepare an even-odd register pair for a Divide instruction, or to determine if you can represent the result of a Multiply instruction in 32 bits.
7. Set the program mask to any given value, including the value it had at the start of program execution.

## Introduction

Although previous chapters have introduced the internal representation of character data, most of the focus has been on numeric operations. This chapter will begin to change that focus by introducing the Shift instructions and by considering both nonnumeric and numeric data. You will manipulate both forms of data at the bit level. While it has been advantageous to think in hexadecimal up to now, it is better to think in binary when you consider shifting.

Nonnumeric data includes strings of 1's and 0's that represent a sequence of discrete logical quantities, with each quantity having one of two possible values. You can interpret these as true or false, yes or no, and so on. Known as **logical switches,** such binary quantities can keep track of events within a program that affect the logic of execution. Nonnumeric data can also represent characters; bits can be manipulated in groups such as those used to represent characters in EBCDIC or ASCII.

The Shift instructions operate only upon the general registers, either individually or as even-odd pairs. When you shift data within these registers, you move it either to the left or to the right as desired. The logical shift instructions treat the data as nonnumeric. In this case, shifting is used to isolate bits either as individuals or in groups, or to concatenate bits or bit patterns. The arithmetic Shift instructions assume that the registers contain integers in the two's complement binary number system. Shifting arithmetically is equivalent to multiplication or division by powers of two, and is a more efficient and convenient alternative to the Multiply and Divide instructions when powers of two are involved.

## The Logical Shift Instructions

The logical Shift instructions treat data as a string of discrete bits without any other assumed meaning, even though groups of bits may actually represent characters. When you shift the contents of a register, the bits are moved to the left or to the right within the register. Bits that are shifted beyond the edge of the register are lost; zeros fill in vacancies that are introduced at the other edge.

### *The Shift Left Logical (SLL) Instruction*

For example, suppose that you want to shift Register 2 to the left by 7 bits. If, prior to the shift, Register 2 appears in binary as

| 0000 1111 0000 1111 0000 1111 1111 1111 |
|---|

then, after the shift, it will look like this:

As the original contents of the register move to the left, the 7 bits on the left, 0000111, are discarded; 7 zeros replace the vacancies that are created on the right. The instruction to accomplish this is called Shift Left Logical and is written as

```
SLL     2,7
```

The register (2) to be shifted is designated first in the operand entry; the **shift amount**—in this case, 7—is written next. Figure 8.1 illustrates the effect of this instruction.

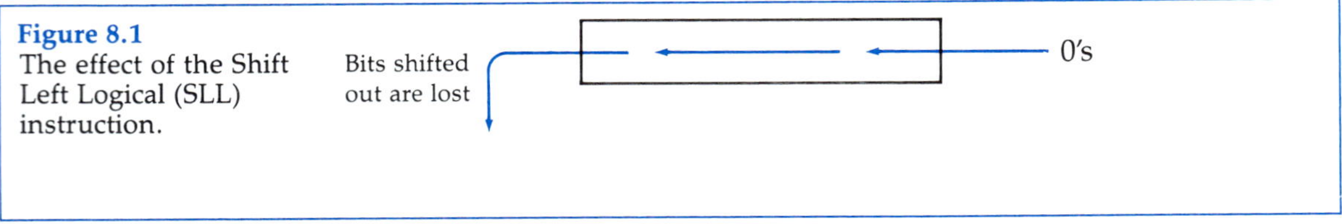


**Figure 8.1**
The effect of the Shift Left Logical (SLL) instruction.

## *The Shift Right Logical (SRL) Instruction*

Suppose that you now want to shift Register 2 back to the right by 7 bits. The required instruction is called Shift Right Logical and is written

```
SRL  2,7
```

Register 2 will now appear as follows:

| 0's shifted in → | Register 2 | Bits shifted out and lost → |
|---|---|---|
| | 0000 0001 0000 1111 0000 1111 1111 1111 | 0000 000 |

Bits shifted out of the right of the register are lost; zeros fill in vacancies that are introduced on the left. Notice that the original 7 leftmost bits of Register 2 were permanently lost during the left shift; they did not reappear during the subsequent right shift. Figure 8.2 illustrates the effect of this instruction.

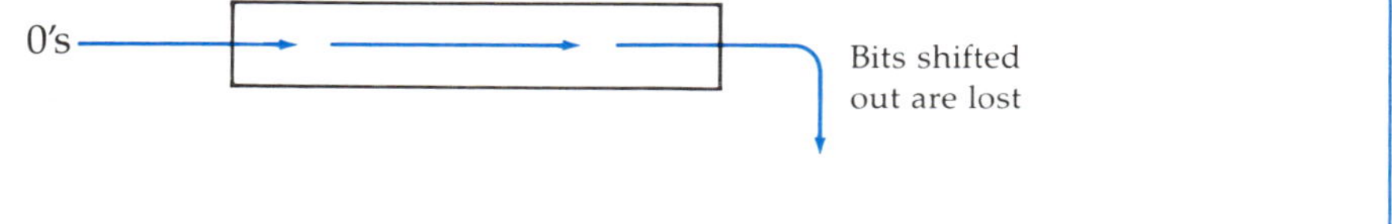


**Figure 8.2**
The effect of the Shift Right Logical (SRL) instruction.

## *The Shift Left Double Logical (SLDL) Instruction*

You can also shift the 64-bit quantity that is contained in an even-odd register pair to the left or right. Think of the pair of registers as if they were attached together, end-to-end, to form one 64-bit register. Shifting the contents of this imaginary register then is analogous to the operations described in the previous sections. You use the instruction Shift Left Double Logical (SLDL) to accomplish a left shift. For example, consider the instruction

```
SLDL   8,5
```

The first operand entry (8) designates the even register of the pair. If this register is not even, an assembler error message or a specification exception will occur, just as it did for the Multiply and Divide instructions. The second operand entry (5) is the shift amount. Suppose that Registers 8 and 9 appear as follows:

**Before execution of SLDL 8,5**

| Reg. 8 | Reg. 9 |
|---|---|
| 0000 1111 0000 1111 0000 1111 1111 1111 | 0101 0101 0101 0101 0101 0101 0101 0101 |

After the instruction is executed, the registers appear as

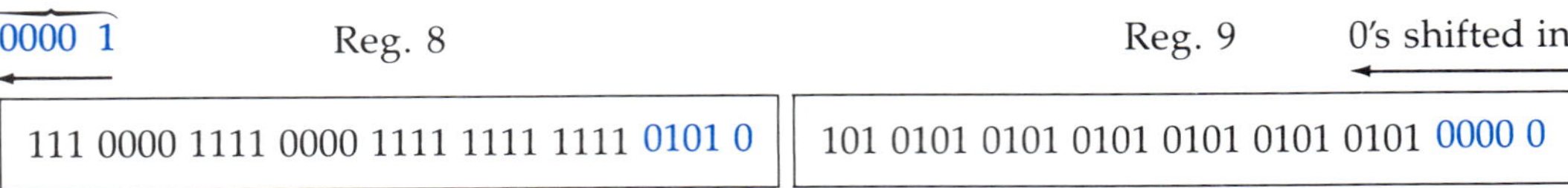


**After execution of SLDL 8,5**

The contents of Registers 8 and 9 are shifted left by 5 bits. The bits shifted out of the left of Register 8 are lost; zeros fill in vacancies that are introduced on the right of Register 9. The bits shifted out of the left of Register 9 replace the vacancies that are introduced on the right of Register 8. Figure 8.3 illustrates the effect of this instruction.

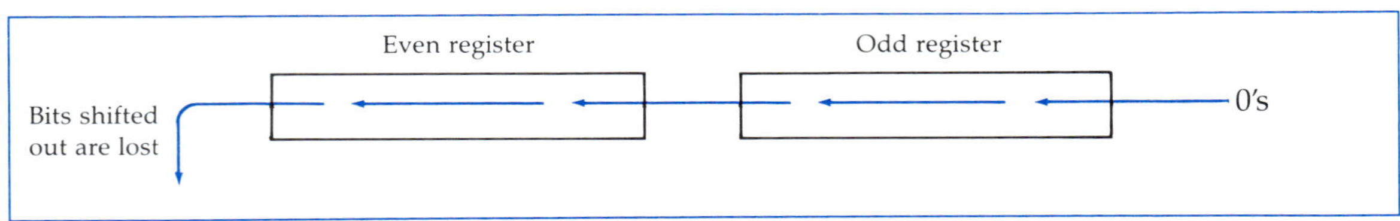


**Figure 8.3**
The effect of the Shift Left Double Logical (SLDL) instruction.

## *The Shift Right Double Logical (SRDL) Instruction*

The instruction Shift Right Double Logical is analogous to Shift Left Double Logical. For example, consider the following instruction:

```
SRDL    4,3
```

**Before execution of SRDL 4,3**

Before this instruction is executed, if Registers 4 and 5 appear as

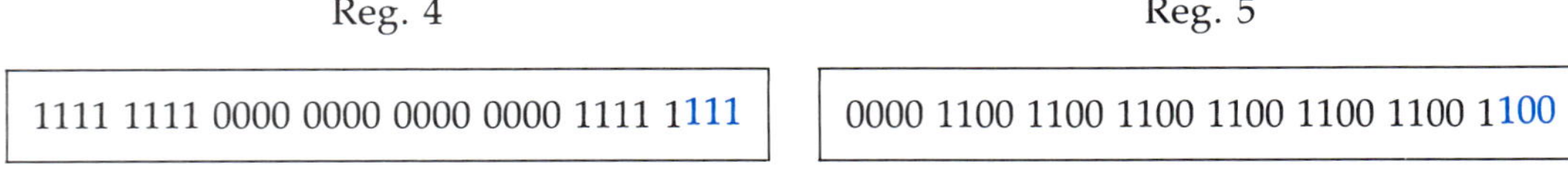


then after the shift takes place, the registers appear as follows:

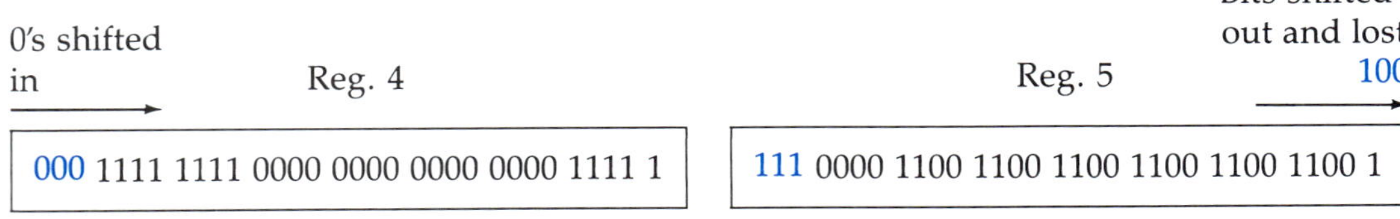


**After execution of SRDL 4,3**

The contents of Registers 4 and 5 are shifted to the right by 3 bits. The bits shifted out of the right of Register 5 are lost; zeros fill in vacancies that are introduced on the left of Register 4. The bits shifted out of the right of Register 4 replace the vacancies that are introduced on the left of Register 5. Figure 8.4 illustrates the effect of this instruction.

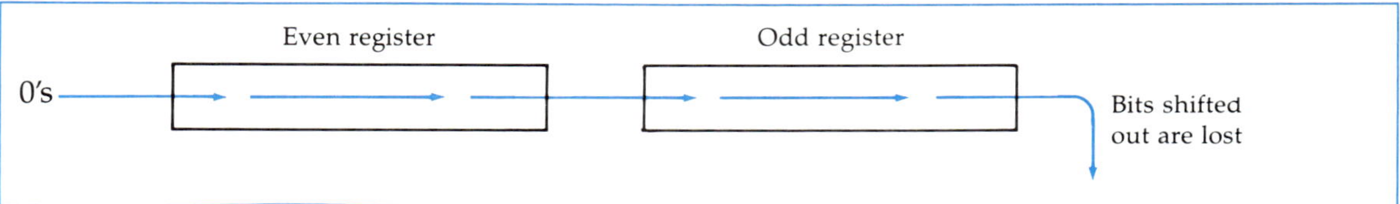


**Figure 8.4**
The effect of the Shift Right Double Logical (SRDL) instruction.

---

EXAMPLE 1

### Counting the 1-Bits in a Register

Suppose that you want to count the number of 1's that appear in the 32 bits of a register. Figure 8.5 contains program segments for four approaches to this problem. Method A assumes the given register is odd. It uses a double logical shift to isolate each bit in an even register so it can be compared with 1. The 1's are counted while the 0's are ignored. This logic is straightforward.

Method B takes the same approach to isolate each bit, but adds each bit to another register, R4—regardless of whether it is 1 or 0. This method is based upon the observation that the number of 1's in a register is equal to the sum of all of its bits. When you compare Methods A and B, you can see that it is easier to add all of the bits than it is to decide which to count and which to ignore.

**Figure 8.5**
Four program segments to count the 1's in a register, as described in Example 1.

```
** REGISTER DEFINITIONS:
R2       EQU   2                  AN EVEN/
                                     ODD REGISTER PAIR
R3       EQU   3
R4       EQU   4                  COUNTS NUMBER OF 1'S IN A REGISTER
R5       EQU   5                  A COUNTER FOR LOOP CONTROL
R6       EQU   6                  ANY REGISTER
*
* ----------------------------------------------------------------
*
** METHOD A: COUNT THE 1'S IN AN ODD REGISTER (R3)
         SR    R4,R4              CLEAR 1'S COUNTER
         LA    R5,32              INITIALIZE LOOP COUNTER
* REPEAT 32 TIMES:
LOOPA    SR    R2,R2              CLEAR REGISTER TO RECEIVE BIT
         SLDL  R2,1               SHIFT A BIT FROM R3 INTO R2
* - IF BIT = 1
         C     R2,=F'1'           IS THE BIT 1?
         BNE   SKIPA              IF NOT, DO NOT COUNT IT
* - - THEN COUNT = COUNT + 1
         LA    R4,1(R4)           INCREMENT 1'S COUNTER
* - END IF
SKIPA    BCT   R5,LOOPA           DECREMENT COUNTER; REPEAT IF NONZERO
* END REPEAT

** METHOD B: COUNT THE 1'S IN AN ODD REGISTER (R3)
         SR    R4,R4              CLEAR 1'S COUNTER
         LA    R5,32              INITIALIZE LOOP COUNTER
* REPEAT 32 TIMES:
LOOPB    SR    R2,R2              CLEAR REGISTER TO RECEIVE BIT
         SLDL  R2,1               SHIFT A BIT FROM R3 INTO R2
         AR    R4,R2              ADD THE BIT TO THE 1'S COUNTER
         BCT   R5,LOOPB           DECREMENT COUNTER; REPEAT IF NONZERO
* END REPEAT
```

(Continues)

**Figure 8.5**
*(Continued)*

```
** METHOD C: COUNT THE 1'S IN AN EVEN REGISTER (R2)
*          SR     R4,R4               CLEAR 1'S COUNTER
           LA     R5,32               INITIALIZE LOOP COUNTER
* REPEAT 32 TIMES:
LOOPC      SRDL   R2,1                SHIFT A BIT FROM R2 INTO R3
* - IF BIT = 1
           C      R3,=F'0'            THE BIT IS IN THE SIGN POSITION
           BNL    SKIPC               IF BIT IS 0, DO NOT COUNT IT
* - - THEN COUNT = COUNT + 1
           LA     R4,1(R4)            INCREMENT 1'S COUNTER
* - END IF
SKIPC      BCT    R5,LOOPC            DECREMENT COUNTER; REPEAT IF NONZERO
* END REPEAT
```

---

```
** METHOD D: COUNT THE 1'S IN ANY REGISTER (R6)
*          SR     R4,R4               CLEAR 1'S COUNTER
           LA     R5,32               INITIALIZE LOOP COUNTER
* REPEAT 32 TIMES:
* - IF THE LEFTMOST BIT IS 1
LOOPD      C      R6,=F'0'            THE BIT IS IN THE SIGN POSITION
           BNL    SKIPD               IF BIT IS 0, DO NOT COUNT IT
* - - THEN COUNT = COUNT + 1
           LA     R4,1(R4)            INCREMENT 1'S COUNTER
* - END IF
SKIPD      SLL    R6,1                MOVE NEXT BIT INTO LEFTMOST POSITION
           BCT    R5,LOOPD            DECREMENT COUNTER; REPEAT IF NONZERO
* END REPEAT
```

Method C returns to the idea of comparing and counting, but does so in an unusual way. It assumes that the given register is even. Here, each bit of R2 is shifted into the leftmost position of R3, where it behaves as if it were the sign of R3. You compare R3 with zero to determine if its first bit is 0 or 1. Since it does not matter what else is in R3, this method does not zero R3 prior to the shift. Thus, after all bits have been examined, the original contents of R2 will be in R3.

Method D is similar to Method C, but relaxes the requirement that the register be even because it does not use a double shift. It compares the register (R6) with zero to determine the value of its first bit. A logical left shift moves each bit in turn through the leftmost position, where it can then be examined.

Methods A, C, and D are similar because they examine each bit and count only the 1's. As such, they are longer than Method B. Of the four methods, Method A has the most obvious logic; Method B has the shortest loop, and probably executes the fastest since it uses the fewest Branch instructions; Method C does not destroy the original contents of the register; and Method D uses the fewest registers.

## Specifying the Shift Amount

In the examples just given, the shift amount was written explicitly as the second operand. Doing this is fine as long as you know the shift amount in advance, but there are occasions when you must compute the shift amount during program execution. To understand how to specify a variable shift amount, you must look at the machine language format of the shift instructions.

## *Format of the Shift Instructions*

Shift instructions are in the RS format, but they do not use the *R3* portion. Their machine language form appears as follows:

**The Shift instructions use a variation of the RS format**

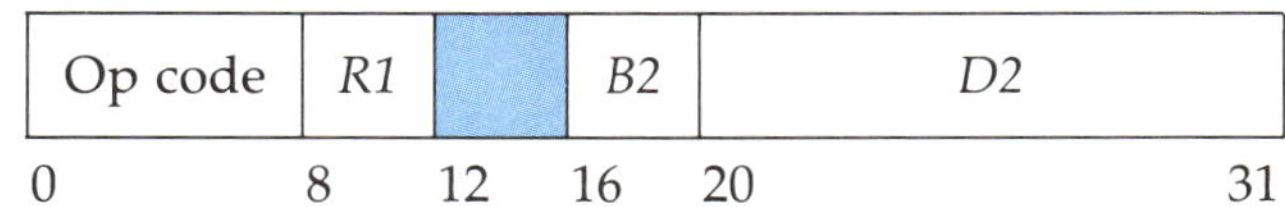


The operands are designated explicitly in assembler language as

*R1,D2(B2)*

In the RS format, the displacement *D2* and base register *B2* define an effective address *E2*, but for the Shift instructions, the effective address does not refer to storage. Rather, the rightmost 6 bits define the shift amount, *n*. Mathematically, you would write the following:

**The shift amount**

$$n = E2 \pmod{2^6}$$
$$= E2 \pmod{64}$$

The register designated by *B2* is not the base register of your program. Rather, it is a register that specifies the shift amount indirectly.

Note that the largest possible shift amount is 63 (111111, in binary). Although you can shift everything out of a single register (which results in zero), you cannot zero an even-odd register pair by using a Shift instruction.

---

EXAMPLE 2

```
SLL     4,6(2)
```

**A computed shift amount**

The following demonstrates the binary computation of the shift amount that is designated by this instruction, when given different values of Register 2 and when 24-bit addressing is assumed. The instruction adds the rightmost 24 bits of Register 2 to the displacement; the rightmost 6 bits of the sum constitute the shift amount. The decimal equivalents are noted.

| | | Binary | | Decimal |
|---|---|---|---|---|
| C(Reg. 2)$_{8-31}$ | = | 0000 0000 0000 0000 0000 1110 | = | 14 |
| Displacement | = | 0000 0000 0110 | = | 6 |
| Shift amount | = | 01 0100 | = | 20 |
| C(Reg. 2)$_{8-31}$ | = | 0000 0000 0000 0000 1101 1010 | = | 218 |
| Displacement | = | 0000 0000 0110 | = | 6 |
| Shift amount | = | 10 0000 | = | 32 |
| | | | = | (218 + 6) mod 64 |
| C(Reg. 2)$_{8-31}$ | = | 1111 1111 1111 1111 1111 1111 | = | −1 |
| Displacement | = | 0000 0000 0110 | = | 6 |
| Shift amount | = | 00 0101 | = | 5 |

| | | | | |
|---|---|---|---|---|
| $C(\text{Reg. }2)_{8-31}$ | = | 1111 1111 1111 1111 1111 1000 | = | −8 |
| Displacement | = | 0000 0000 0110 | = | 6 |
| Shift amount | = | 11 1110 | = | 62 |
| | | | = | (−8 + 6) mod 64 |

---

EXAMPLE 3

Assume the following register status:

| Reg. 2 | Reg. 3 |
|---|---|
| 5 | −34 |

The following table gives examples of shift amounts that are specified by various operand designations:

| *D2(B2)* | Shift Amount | |
|---|---|---|
| 9 | 9 | |
| 65 | 1 | 65 (mod 64) = 1 |
| 0 | 0 | |
| 0(2) | 5 | 0 + C(Reg. 2) = 5 |
| 3(2) | 8 | 3 + C(Reg. 2) = 8 |
| 70(2) | 11 | 70 + C(Reg. 2) (mod 64) = 75 (mod 64) = 11 |
| 44(3) | 10 | 44 + C(Reg. 3) (mod 64) = 10 |
| 0(3) | 30 | 0 + C(Reg. 3) (mod 64) = −34 (mod 64) = 30 |

---

EXAMPLE 4

Consider the shift amounts designated in the following sequence of instructions:

```
R2       EQU    2
R8       EQU    8
         L      R2,SHIFT       Reg. 2 is loaded with 5
         SLL    R8,0(R2)       Reg. 8 is shifted 5 bits to the left
         SLL    R8,4(R2)       Reg. 8 is shifted 9 bits to the left
         SLL    R8,R2          Reg. 8 is shifted 2 bits to the left
         SLL    R8,SHIFT       This is inappropriate
         .
         .
         .
SHIFT    DC     F'5'
```

The first two Shift instructions are correct ways to specify a computed shift amount. The third Shift instruction is syntactically correct, but R2 is a displacement and not a register; so 2 bits—not 5—are shifted. The last Shift instruction is incorrect: it is important to realize that this is not the way that you specify a shift amount of 5. The second operand is implicit: SHIFT is a relocatable symbol that represents an address within the program. Although the instruction can compute this effective address modulo 64, you cannot predict the result during the programming process. Therefore, this address is an inappropriate shift amount. For example, suppose that at execution time SHIFT represents an effective address of $BF1014_{16}$. The shift amount would then be equal to the rightmost 6 bits of this address:

$010100_2 = 20_{10}$

Although SHIFT as a second operand is inappropriate, the assembler will not find an error in the instruction. It will determine the required base register and displacement—thus, translating the instruction into machine language. Similarly, the use of a literal is an incorrect way to specify a shift amount.

---

**SELF-TEST EXERCISES**

1. What are the contents of Registers 4 and 5 after each of the following instructions is executed? Assume the following prior to each instruction:

   Reg. 4 = 73737373 Reg. 5 = 9B9B9B9B

   **a.** SLL 4,2
   **b.** SLDL 4,2
   **c.** SRL 4,4
   **d.** SRDL 4,4
   **e.** SLL 4,31
   **f.** SLL 4,32
   **g.** SLDL 4,63
   **h.** SLDL 4,64
   **i.** SRDL 4,32
   **j.** SRL 5,31
   **k.** SRL 4,0(5)
   **l.** SLL 4,2(5)

2. Write a sequence of instructions to store bits 9 through 30 of Register 2 into the rightmost portion of the fullword at DATA. (The remaining bits of DATA should contain zeros.)
3. Write a sequence of instructions to replace the contents of the fullword at WORD by a value whose leftmost 10 bits are the rightmost 10 bits of Register 4, and whose rightmost 22 bits are the rightmost 22 bits of Register 5.
4. Write a sequence of instructions to place the leftmost 13 bits of the fullword at X into Register 8 and the rightmost 19 bits of X into Register 9. These values should be right-justified in the registers.
5. Write a single instruction to shift Register 5 to the left logically by $n$ bits, where $n$ is in Register 3.

## The Arithmetic Shift Instructions

The arithmetic Shift instructions assume that the registers contain integers in the two's complement binary number system. Unlike a logical shift, an arithmetic shift does not change the first bit of the register or register pair, so that the sign of the result is the same as the sign of the original quantity.

### *The Shift Left Arithmetic (SLA) Instruction*

The SLA instruction can be summarized as follows:

| Operation | Operand | Format | Instruction Name | Action |
|---|---|---|---|---|
| **SLA** | *R1,D2(B2)* | RS | SHIFT LEFT ARITHMETIC | Shifts $C(R1)_{1-31}$ to the left by $n = E2$ (mod 64) bits. Bits that are shifted out of the left are lost; zeros fill in vacancies that are introduced on the right. The leftmost bit (bit 0) of *R1* remains unchanged. |

$$\text{Condition code} = \begin{cases} 0 \text{ if the result is zero} \\ 1 \text{ if the result is negative} \\ 2 \text{ if the result is positive} \\ 3 \text{ if an overflow occurs} \end{cases}$$

**Arithmetic left shifts are equivalent to multiplication by $2^n$**

**Overflow is possible**

Notice that an arithmetic shift to the left is the same as a binary integer multiplication by $2^n$. Thus, it is possible for the correct product to be too large to be represented in 32 bits. This will happen if a bit that differs from bit 0 is shifted out of the register. If the correct product is too large, a fixed-point overflow exception occurs and the condition code is set to 3. (A program interruption will also occur if the first bit of the program mask is 1, which is the same situation as an overflow during a binary integer addition or subtraction.) Figure 8.6 illustrates the effect of the SLA instruction.

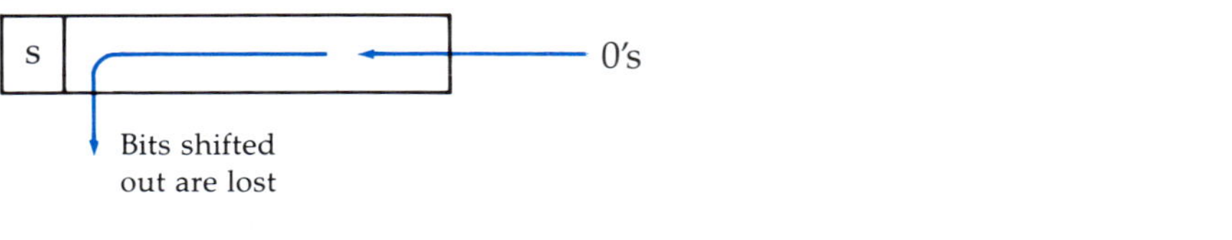


**Figure 8.6**
The effect of the Shift Left Arithmetic (SLA) instruction.

---

EXAMPLE 5

Assume that Register 9 contains

1 1110 1100 0001 1111 1111 1111 0000 011

Each of the following instructions affects this value and the value of the condition code, as indicated:

| Instruction | Effect of Instruction | |
|---|---|---|
| | *Reg. 9* | *CC* |
| `SLA 9,2` | 1 10 1100 0001 1111 1111 1111 0000 011 **00** | 1 |
| `SLA 9,3` | 1 0 1100 0001 1111 1111 1111 0000 011 **000** | 1 |
| `SLA 9,4` | 1 1100 0001 1111 1111 1111 0000 011 **0000** | 3 |
| `SLA 9,30` | 1 **1000 0000 0000 0000 0000 0000 0000 000** | 3 |
| `SLA 9,31` | 1 **0000 0000 0000 0000 0000 0000 0000 000** | 3 |
| `SLA 9,0` | 1 1110 1100 0001 1111 1111 1111 0000 011 | 1 |

Note that when the shift amount is zero, the instruction only affects the condition code.

---

## *The Shift Right Arithmetic (SRA) Instruction*

The SRA instruction can be summarized as follows:

| Operation | Operand | Format | Instruction Name | Action |
|---|---|---|---|---|
| SRA | *R1,D2(B2)* | RS | SHIFT RIGHT ARITHMETIC | Shifts $C(R1)_{1-31}$ to the right by $n = E2$ (mod 64) bits. Bits that are shifted out of the right are lost; copies of bit 0, which remains unchanged, fill in vacancies that are introduced on the left. |

$$\text{Condition code} = \begin{cases} 0 \text{ if the result is zero} \\ 1 \text{ if the result is negative} \\ 2 \text{ if the result is positive} \end{cases}$$

Note that overflow is impossible with this instruction. Figure 8.7 illustrates the effect of the SRA instruction.

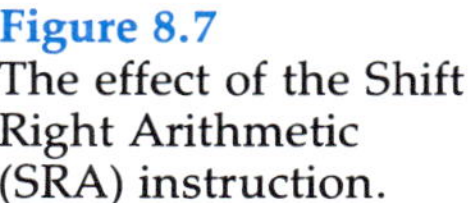

**Figure 8.7**
The effect of the Shift Right Arithmetic (SRA) instruction.

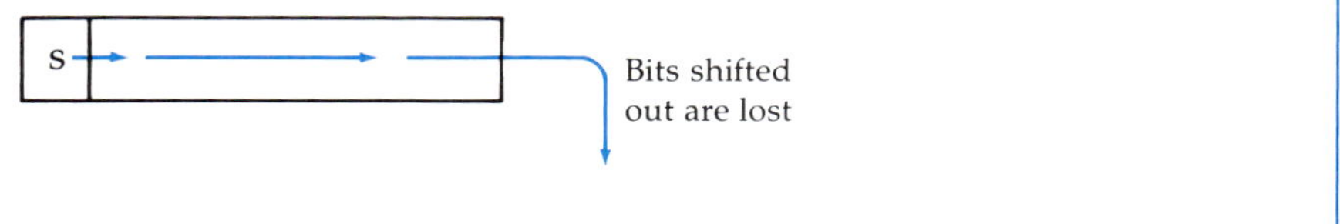


---

EXAMPLE 6

Assume that Register 9 contains

1 0000 1111 1111 0000 0000 0000 1111 111

Each of the following instructions affects this value and the value of the condition code, as indicated:

| Instruction | Effect of Instruction *Reg. 9* | *CC* |
|---|---|---|
| SRA 9,1 | 1 **1** 0000 1111 1111 0000 0000 0000 1111 11 | 1 |
| SRA 9,3 | 1 **111** 0000 1111 1111 0000 0000 0000 1111 | 1 |
| SRA 9,31 | 1 **111 1111 1111 1111 1111 1111 1111 1111** | 1 |
| SRA 9,0 | 1 0000 1111 1111 0000 0000 0000 1111 111 | 1 |

---

**Arithmetic right shifts are equivalent to division by $2^n$ with rounding down**

An arithmetic shift to the right is the same as division by $2^n$ with *rounding down*—that is, toward the next algebraically lower integer. For positive integers, a right shift will give the same quotient as division. For example, shifting the binary equivalent of 5 to the right by one bit will result in 2, as follows.

Before shift: 0000 0000 0000 0000 0000 0000 0000 0101 $= 5_{10}$
After shift: 0000 0000 0000 0000 0000 0000 0000 0010 $= 2_{10}$

Dividing 5 by 2 results in a quotient of 2 and a remainder of 1. Rounding this quotient down produces the result of 2. For negative numbers, the situation is a little different. The result of shifting the binary equivalent of −5 to the right by one bit is −3.

Before shift: 1111 1111 1111 1111 1111 1111 1111 1011 = $-5_{10}$
After shift: 1111 1111 1111 1111 1111 1111 1111 1101 = $-3_{10}$

Dividing −5 by 2 results in a quotient of −2 and a remainder of −1. If you round this quotient down, you will get −3, which is the same as the result of shifting.

## *The Shift Left Double Arithmetic (SLDA) Instruction*

The SLDA instruction can be summarized as follows:

| Operation | Operand | Format | Instruction Name | Action |
|---|---|---|---|---|
| **SLDA** | *R1*,*D2*(*B2*) | RS | SHIFT LEFT DOUBLE ARITHMETIC | Shifts $C(R1,R1+1)_{1-63}$ to the left by $n = E2$ (mod 64) bits. Bits shifted out of the left of the even register *R1* are lost; zeros fill in vacancies that are introduced on the right of the odd register. Bits that are shifted out of the left of the odd register replace the vacancies that are introduced on the right of the even register. The leftmost bit (bit 0) of *R1* remains unchanged. |

$$\text{Condition code} = \begin{cases} 0 \text{ if the result is zero} \\ 1 \text{ if the result is negative} \\ 2 \text{ if the result is positive} \\ 3 \text{ if an overflow occurs} \end{cases}$$

Registers *R1* and $R1+1$ compose an even-odd register pair that contains a 64-bit quantity. As with logical double shifts, *R1* must be even. The effect of this instruction is analogous to the SLA instruction, and is illustrated in Figure 8.8.

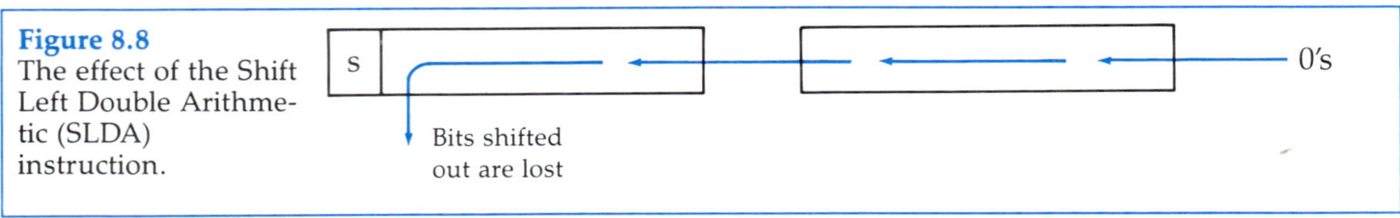


**Figure 8.8** The effect of the Shift Left Double Arithmetic (SLDA) instruction.

---

EXAMPLE 7

Assume the following register status prior to execution of each Shift instruction:

| Reg. 6 | Reg. 7 |
|---|---|
| 1 111 0000 1111 1111 1111 1111 1111 1111 | 0000 0000 0000 0000 0000 0000 1111 1111 |

Each of the following instructions affects these registers and the condition code, as indicated:

| Instruction | Effect of Instruction | | |
|---|---|---|---|
| | *Reg. 6* | *Reg. 7* | *CC* |
| SLDA 6,2 | 1 1 0000 1111 1111 1111 1111 1111 1111 **00** | 00 0000 0000 0000 0000 0000 1111 1111 **00** | 1 |
| SLDA 6,4 | 1 000 1111 1111 1111 1111 1111 1111 **0000** | 0000 0000 0000 0000 0000 1111 1111 **0000** | 3 |
| SLDA 6,63 | 1 **000 0000 0000 0000 0000 0000 0000 0000** | **0000 0000 0000 0000 0000 0000 0000 0000** | 3 |

## *The Shift Right Double Arithmetic (SRDA) Instruction*

The SRDA instruction can be summarized as follows:

| Operation | Operand | Format | Instruction Name | Action |
|---|---|---|---|---|
| **SRDA** | *R1*,*D2*(*B2*) | RS | SHIFT RIGHT DOUBLE ARITHMETIC | Shifts $C(R1,R1+1)_{1-63}$ to the right by $n = E2$ (mod 64) bits. Bits that are shifted out of the right of the odd register ($R1+1$) are discarded; copies of bit 0, which remains unchanged, fill in vacancies that are introduced on the left of the even register *R1*. Bits that are shifted out of the right of the even register replace the vacancies that are introduced on the left of the odd register. |

$$\text{Condition code} = \begin{cases} 0 \text{ if the result is zero} \\ 1 \text{ if the result is negative} \\ 2 \text{ if the result is positive} \end{cases}$$

Illustrated in Figure 8.9, the effect of this instruction is analogous to SLDA and SRA; like SLDA, *R1* must be even, and, like SRA, an overflow is impossible.

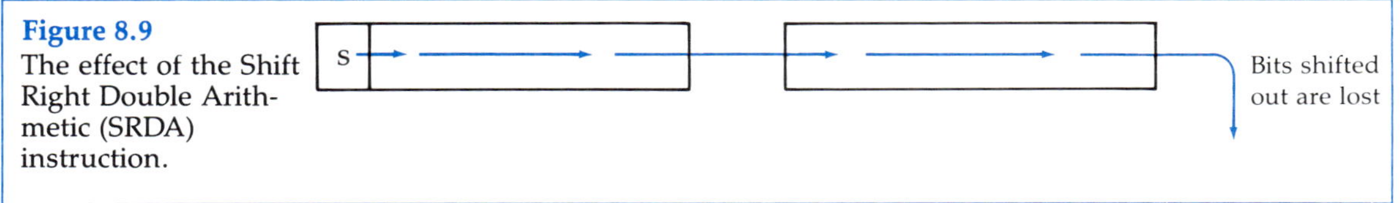


**Figure 8.9**
The effect of the Shift Right Double Arithmetic (SRDA) instruction.

EXAMPLE 8

Assume the following register status prior to execution of each Shift instruction:

| Reg. 6 | Reg. 7 |
|---|---|
| 1 111 0000 1111 1111 1111 1111 1111 1111 | 0000 0000 0000 0000 0000 0000 1111 1111 |

Each of the following instructions affects these registers and the condition code, as indicated:

| Instruction | Effect of Instruction | | |
|---|---|---|---|
| | *Reg. 6* | *Reg. 7* | CC |
| SRDA 6, 2 | 1 **11**111 0000 1111 1111 1111 1111 1111 11 | **11** 0000 0000 0000 0000 0000 0000 1111 11 | 1 |
| SRDA 6, 63 | 1 **111 1111 1111 1111 1111 1111 1111 1111** | **1111 1111 1111 1111 1111 1111 1111 1111** | 1 |

EXAMPLE 9 **SLDA 6, 0** or **SRDA 6, 0**

You can use either of these instructions to determine if both Registers 6 and 7 contain zero. If they do, the condition code is set to 0.

## SELF-TEST EXERCISES

6. Assume the following register status prior to each instruction:

   Reg. 4 = D2D2D2D2 Reg. 5 = 1F1F1F1F

   What are the contents of Registers 4 and 5, and the value of the condition code after each of the following instructions is executed?

| | | | | | |
|---|---|---|---|---|---|
| a. | SLA | 4, 1 | i. | SRA | 4, 32 |
| b. | SLA | 4, 3 | j. | SRA | 5, 3 |
| c. | SLA | 4, 32 | k. | SRA | 5, 32 |
| d. | SLA | 5, 2 | l. | SRDA | 4, 8 |
| e. | SLA | 5, 8 | m. | SLDA | 4, 8 |
| f. | SLA | 5, 31 | n. | SRDA | 4, 63 |
| g. | SRA | 4, 2 | o. | SLDA | 4, 63 |
| h. | SRA | 4, 31 | p. | SLA | 4, 0(5) |

7. Write a Shift instruction to multiply the 64-bit integer in Registers 10 and 11 by 64. What happens if the product exceeds 64 bits?
8. Write instructions that do not involve a Divide instruction to multiply Register 7 by 5/8. Represent the result in 64 bits, discarding any remainder.

### *Applications of Double Arithmetic Shifts*

Two common applications of the double arithmetic Shift instructions involve the Divide instructions and the Multiply instructions. This section demonstrates one new way to prepare a dividend for division and one new way to determine if you can correctly represent a product in only 32 bits.

*Dividend Preparation.* Prior to a division, the dividend must occupy the 64 bits of an even-odd register pair. Chapter 5 discussed two techniques to prepare these registers. You can use the following technique when the sign of the dividend is unknown:

```
L       R4, DVDND
SRDA    R4, 32
```

This technique loads the dividend, which is assumed here to be in a fullword at the address that is represented by DVDND, into an even register R4. The double arithmetic shift places the dividend into R5 and propagates the sign bit throughout R4, so that the register pair will contain a correct 64-bit representation of the dividend, as shown in these examples:

| | Reg. 4 | Reg. 5 |
|---|---|---|
| Before execution: | 1100 0011 1110 0000 0000 0000 0000 0000 | ???? ???? ???? ???? ???? ???? ???? ???? |
| After execution: | 1111 1111 1111 1111 1111 1111 1111 1111 | 1100 0011 1110 0000 0000 0000 0000 0000 |
| Before execution: | 0111 1111 1111 1111 1111 1111 1111 1111 | ???? ???? ???? ???? ???? ???? ???? ???? |
| After execution: | 0000 0000 0000 0000 0000 0000 0000 0000 | 0111 1111 1111 1111 1111 1111 1111 1111 |

You might wonder how this technique compares with the technique of multiplication by one, which was discussed in Chapter 5. If the dividend is in storage or is already in an even register, then the technique shown here is faster than multiplication. However, if the dividend is in an odd register, then multiplying the dividend by one is more convenient than moving it to an even register so that you can shift it to the right arithmetically.

*Testing a Product.* Chapter 5 discussed how to determine if a 64-bit product can be correctly represented by only 32 bits. Recall that several instructions were necessary to make this determination; however, a double arithmetic shift greatly simplifies this test. Figure 8.10 illustrates the form of a 64-bit product that has a value that can be represented by the 32 bits of the odd register. All bits in the even register and the first bit of the odd register must be either all 1's or all 0's. Thus, the first 33 bits of such a product are the same. If you shift this product—which is assumed to be in the register pair R4,R5—to the left arithmetically by 32 bits by using the instruction

```
SLDA   R4,32
```

then the leftmost bit will be retained. The remaining 32 copies will be shifted out, leaving the 32-bit product in the even register, as shown in this example:

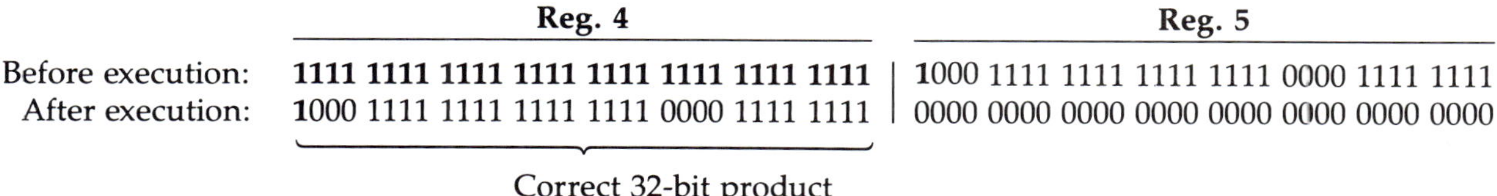

| | Reg. 4 | Reg. 5 |
|---|---|---|
| Before execution: | **1111 1111 1111 1111 1111 1111 1111 1111** | 1000 1111 1111 1111 1111 0000 1111 1111 |
| After execution: | 1000 1111 1111 1111 1111 0000 1111 1111 | 0000 0000 0000 0000 0000 0000 0000 0000 |
| | Correct 32-bit product | |

Following this shift, the condition code is 1.

However, if any of the first 33 bits of the original product differ from

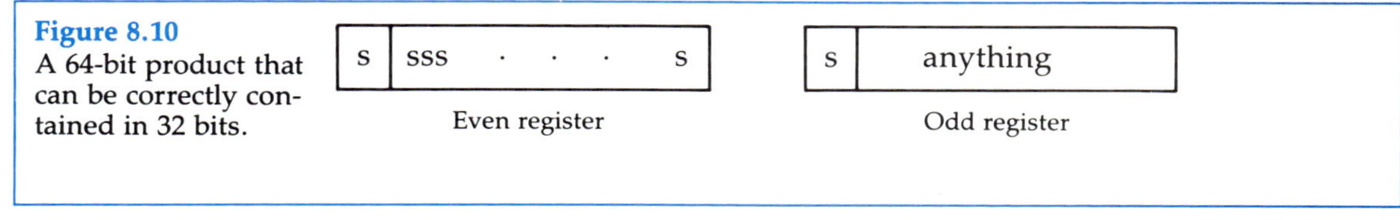


**Figure 8.10**
A 64-bit product that can be correctly contained in 32 bits.

the first bit, a fixed-point overflow exception will occur during the shift. Such is the case in the following example:

| | Reg. 4 | Reg. 5 |
|---|---|---|
| Before execution: | **0000 0000 0000 0000 0000 0000 0000 0011** | 0000 0000 0000 0000 0000 0000 0001 1111 |
| After execution: | 0000 0000 0000 0000 0000 0000 0001 1111 | 0000 0000 0000 0000 0000 0000 0000 0000 |

Product is destroyed

If you assume that the exception is masked off, the condition code will be set to 3. Notice that the product is destroyed.

Thus, the following sequence will test the product as just described:

```
SLDA   R4,32
BO     OVERFLOW
```

To ensure that a fixed-point overflow exception will not cause a program interruption, you must know that the first bit of the program mask is 0. If this is not the case, you can make it so by using the Set Program Mask (SPM) instruction, which is described next.

## *The Set Program Mask (SPM) and the Insert Program Mask (IPM) Instructions*

The SPM instruction can be summarized as follows:

| Operation | Operand | Format | Instruction Name | Action |
|---|---|---|---|---|
| **SPM** | *R1* | RR | SET PROGRAM MASK | Condition code ← $C(R1)_{2-3}$<br>Program mask ← $C(R1)_{4-7}$ |

The SPM instruction sets the condition code and the program mask of the PSW from bits 2 through 7 of the register operand that is designated by *R1*. The instruction ignores the remaining bits of the register. Notice that the instruction does not specify a second operand; in fact, bits 12 through 15 of the instruction are ignored. The following sequence sets all bits of the program mask to 0:

**Set program mask to 0's**

```
SR     R9,R9
SPM    R9
```

Sometimes, you must restore the program mask to its original value. To do so, observe that the Branch and Link instructions (BALR and BAL) in the 24-bit addressing mode load bits 2 through 7 of the register that is designated by *R1* with the condition code and the program mask. Thus, you could proceed as follows:

**Save, alter, and restore program mask**

```
BALR   R0,0        SAVE CC AND PROGRAM MASK
.
.
.
SPM    R9          CHANGE CC AND PROGRAM MASK.
```

```
      .
      .
      .
      SPM   R0          RESTORE CC AND PROGRAM MASK
```

If this sequence appears in a subprogram, you can use the link register (usually R14) instead of R0, which makes the previous BALR superfluous.

In the 370-XA mode, you would use the instruction Insert Program Mask (IPM), instead of BALR, to load bits 2 through 7 of a register with the condition code and the program mask. Thus, in the previous sequence, replace the BALR instruction with

```
      IPM   R0
```

The IPM instruction can be summarized as follows:

| Operation | Operand | Format | Instruction Name | Action |
|---|---|---|---|---|
| IPM | *R1* | RRE | INSERT PROGRAM MASK | $C(R1)_{0-1} \leftarrow 0$<br>$C(R1)_{2-3} \leftarrow$ Condition code<br>$C(R1)_{4-7} \leftarrow$ Program mask |

The IPM instruction is in the RRE format, which simply means that the instruction is 4 bytes long and has a 2-byte op code. Although you must use IPM when 31-bit addressing is in effect, you can use either IPM or BALR when 24-bit addressing is in effect.

## An Example with Shifts

As an example of how you can use the Shift instructions in a program, consider the conversion of a hexadecimal integer from an EBCDIC representation to its internal numeric form. Suppose that the 4 bytes at the address DATA contain the EBCDIC representation of an unsigned 4-digit hexadecimal integer. For example, if you read the characters 18A3 into the bytes at DATA, they would appear in hex as

F1F8C1F3

The integer's numeric representation that is suitable for fullword binary integer arithmetic is

000018A3

To make this conversion, you could proceed as follows.

Recall that the digits 0 through 9 are represented in EBCDIC by the hexadecimal values F0 through F9; the letters A through F are represented by C1 through C6. You must translate each byte of DATA according to this correspondence, as illustrated in Figure 8.11. Suppose that you define a table of the possible EBCDIC codes for the hexadecimal digits. The table is ordered so that the code for 0 is first, the code for 1 is second, and so on. If you take a byte of DATA and locate its value in the table, then you can determine the value's hexadecimal equivalent from its position in the table.

Since the Compare instruction compares the contents of a register with the contents of a fullword in storage, you would write the table as an array of fullwords, as pictured in Figure 8.12.

Figure 8.13 lists the program segment to perform the conversion. The SRDL instruction isolates each byte of DATA in a register; the program then compares the register with each fullword of the table until a match occurs. At the time of the match, the value of the index register (R4) is four times the corresponding numeric equivalent of the character. The SRA instruction divides this value by four. A double logical shift is used to concatenate the digits as they are formed to produce the final result.

A shorter, but less obvious, approach produces the numeric digit directly from its EBCDIC representation and, thereby, avoids the table look-up. This approach is considered in Programming Problem 1 at the end of this chapter.

Although this example and the case study that follows provide simple demonstrations of how you can use the Shift instructions, there are easier ways to perform these conversions by using the instructions CVB, CVD, PACK, and UNPK. Although you already have used these instructions, you will learn more about them in Chapter 14.

**Figure 8.11**
The correspondence between the hexadecimal digits and their EBCDIC representations.

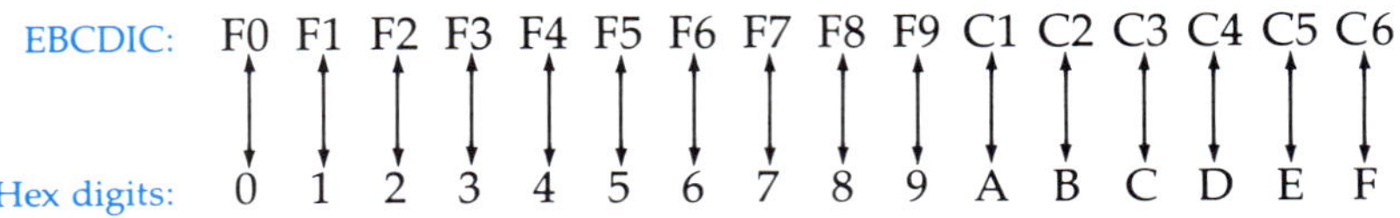


**Figure 8.12**
The table used to translate EBCDIC characters into hex digits.

| Table | Index | Corresponding Hex Digit |
|---|---|---|
| F0000000 | 0 | 0 |
| F1000000 | 4 | 1 |
| F2000000 | 8 | 2 |
| ⋮ | ⋮ | ⋮ |
| F9000000 | 24 | 9 |
| C1000000 | 28 | A |
| ⋮ | ⋮ | ⋮ |
| C6000000 | 3C | F |

```
** CONVERT A FOUR-DIGIT HEX INTEGER FROM EBCDIC TO NUMERIC FORM.
**     ASSUME THE EBCDIC FORM IS IN THE FULLWORD AT DATA;
**     THE NUMERIC RESULT WILL BE IN REGISTER R5.
** REGISTER DEFINITIONS:
R2       EQU    2              EVEN/
R3       EQU    3                   ODD PAIR TO ISOLATE CHARACTERS
R4       EQU    4              TABLE INDEX         (EVEN/
R5       EQU    5              THE NUMERIC RESULT         ODD PAIR)
R6       EQU    6              LOOP COUNTER
* INITIALIZE
         L      R2,DATA        GET EBCDIC FORM
         LA     R6,4           INITIALIZE LOOP COUNTER
*
* REPEAT 4 TIMES:
*    ISOLATE NEXT CHARACTER
OUTLOOP  SR     R3,R3          CLEAR R3 PRIOR TO ISOLATING CHARACTER
         SRDL   R2,8           R3=NEXT EBCDIC CHAR. FROM RIGHT OF R2
*    FIND CHARACTER IN TABLE
*    (R4 WILL POINT TO IT AND BE 4 TIMES ITS NUMERIC VALUE.)
         SR     R4,R4          INITIALIZE TABLE INDEX
INLOOP   C      R3,TABLE(R4)   IS CHARACTER IN TABLE?
         BE     FOUND          YES
         LA     R4,4(R4)       NO; INCREMENT INDEX
         B      INLOOP         CONTINUE SEARCH
*
*    CONVERT TO NUMERIC VALUE AND INSERT IN REGISTER R5
FOUND    SRA    R4,2           DIVIDE INDEX BY 4 TO GET NUMERIC
*                                EQUIVALENT OF CHARACTER.
         SRDL   R4,4           MOVE HEX DIGIT INTO R5
         BCT    R6,OUTLOOP     DECREMENT COUNTER; REPEAT IF NOT 0
* END REPEAT
         SRL    R5,16          RIGHT-JUSTIFY NUMERIC RESULT
         .
         .
         .
TABLE    DC     X'F0000000'
         DC     X'F1000000'
         DC     X'F2000000'
         DC     X'F3000000'
         DC     X'F4000000'
         DC     X'F5000000'
         DC     X'F6000000'
         DC     X'F7000000'
         DC     X'F8000000'
         DC     X'F9000000'
         DC     X'C1000000'
         DC     X'C2000000'
         DC     X'C3000000'
         DC     X'C4000000'
         DC     X'C5000000'
         DC     X'C6000000'
```

**Figure 8.13**
The program segment to convert a 4-digit hex integer from EBCDIC form to numeric form.

## Case Study

### Problem Statement

**Consider several data records, each of which contains 2 unsigned decimal integers in columns 1 through 4 and 9 through 12. For each record, compute the quotient and the remainder as a result of dividing the first integer by the second integer. Print the results. Assume that the data is error-free, the integers are right-justified in their fields of 4 columns, and the divisor is nonzero.**

### Discussion

There are two major computations to consider. First, you must convert each decimal integer, which is represented in EBCDIC by four bytes, to a 32-bit two's complement binary representation. Second, after you do this and perform the division, you must convert two 32-bit binary integers—the quotient and the remainder—to base 10 and then represent them in EBCDIC so that they can be printed.

*Conversion from Decimal Characters to Binary.* The decimal digits 0 through 9 are represented in EBCDIC by F0 through F9, and can be isolated readily by removing the F's with the Shift instructions. Since the EBCDIC for a blank character is 40, the same Shift instructions will remove the 4. Thus, leading blanks in a 4-byte field will be converted to 0's.

Recall that you can write a decimal integer as an expansion in powers of 10. For example, 1342 is equal to

$$1 \times 10^3 + 3 \times 10^2 + 4 \times 10^1 + 2 \times 10^0$$

If you isolate each of the digits—1, 3, 4, and 2—from their EBCDIC representations as just described, each digit will be in binary. If you multiply each of these by the appropriate power of ten, represented in binary, and if you accumulate the sum of these products, you will obtain the binary equivalent of the original decimal integer, as shown here:

| Decimal | | Binary |
|---|---|---|
| $1 \times 10^3$ | = | 0001 × 0011 1110 1000 = 0011 1110 1000 |
| $3 \times 10^2$ | = | 0011 × 0000 0110 0100 = 0001 0010 1100 |
| $4 \times 10^1$ | = | 0100 × 0000 0000 1010 = 0000 0010 1000 |
| $2 \times 10^0$ | = | 0010 × 0000 0000 0001 = 0000 0000 0010 |
| 1342 | = | 0101 0011 1110 |

The pseudocode for this conversion is in part **a** of Figure 8.14.

*Conversion from Binary to Decimal Characters.* The computed quotient and remainder will be binary integers that must be converted first to decimal and then to EBCDIC, so that you can print them. If you divide the decimal number 1234 by 10, the remainder would be 4 (the rightmost digit). You can then divide the quotient 123 by 10 to obtain a remainder of 3, which is the next digit. Thus, you can generate the decimal digits by taking the given binary quantity and dividing it successively by the binary equivalent of ten. If you start with 0100 1101 0010 (the binary equivalent of 1234), and note that the binary equivalent of ten is 1010, you will have the following binary divisions:

**Figure 8.14** The pseudocode to convert, **a.** from decimal characters to binary and, **b.** from binary to decimal characters.

```
BINARY := 0
i := 0
REPEAT 4 TIMES
    d := digit represented by the next character from
         the left
    BINARY := BINARY + d * 10^(3 - i)
    i := i + 1
END REPEAT
```

**a.**

```
q := binary number
CHARS := null
REPEAT 4 TIMES
    r := remainder of q ÷ 10
    q := quotient of q ÷ 10
    r := F16 | r
    CHARS := r | CHARS
END REPEAT
```

**b.**

Note: | denotes concatenation

```
          1111011               1100              1             0
1010 )010011010010     1010 )1111011     1010 )1100     1010 )1
       1010                   1010              1010            0
       10010                   1010              10 = 2₁₀       1 = 1₁₀
        1010                   1010
        10001                    11 = 3₁₀
         1010
          1110
          1010
          10001
           1010
            1110
            1010
             100 = 4₁₀
```

To convert the remainders to character form, each remainder is expressed as a 4-bit quantity and preceded by $1111_2$. The pseudocode for this conversion is in part **b** of Figure 8.14.

## *The Program*

From the flowchart in Figure 8.15, it is clear that you must convert two quantities from character form to numeric form, and two quantities from numeric form to character form. Rather than repeat the instructions for each conversion, it is preferable to treat the conversion processes as subprograms.

Figure 8.16 lists the program. Note the following two points: First, in the main portion of the program, the storage reserved for the input data

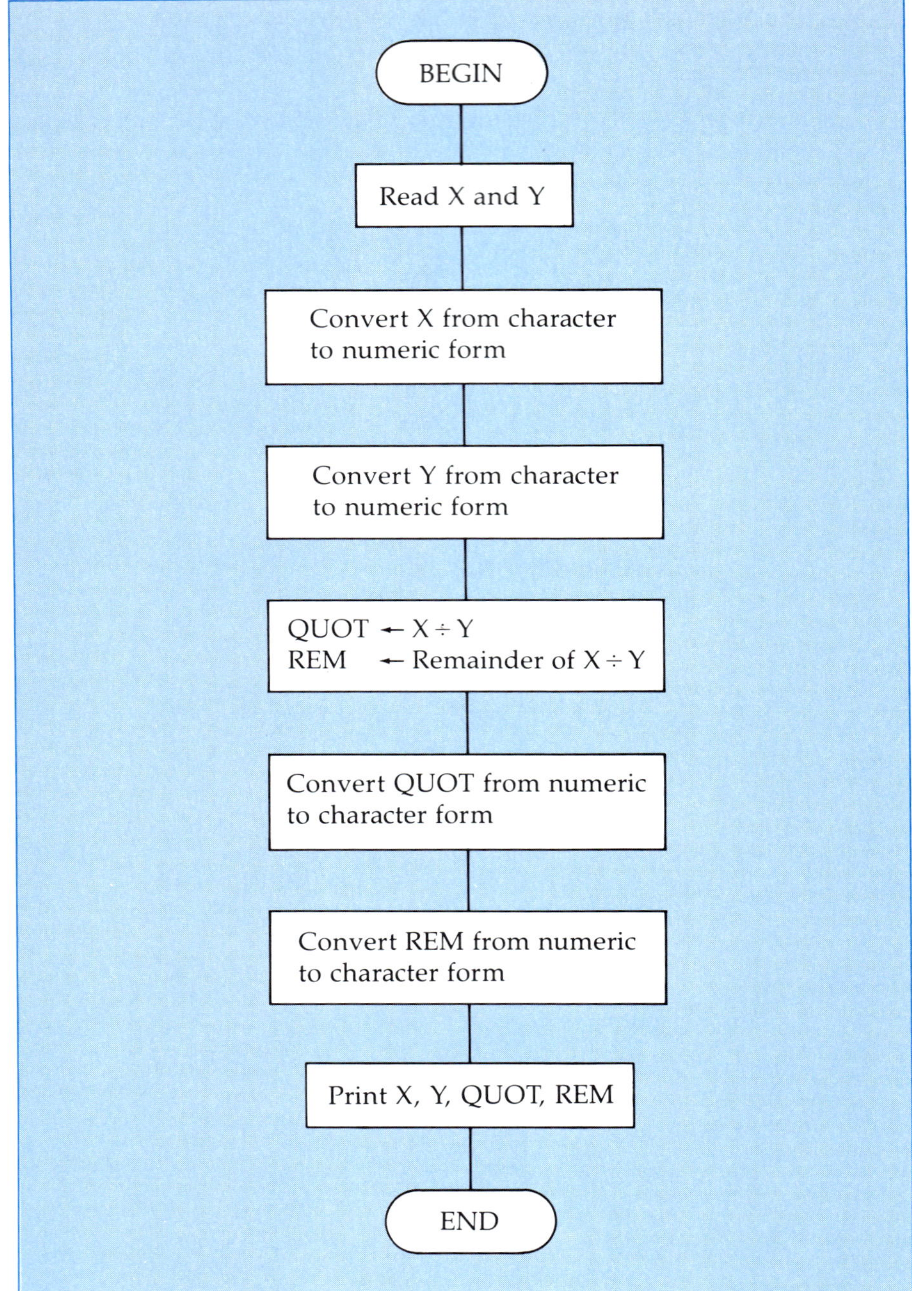


**Figure 8.15**
The flowchart for the case study.

record is defined by Statements 107 through 111 in several steps. In this way, the two integers expected in the data record can be given names, and these names can differ from the name of the data record itself. Notice that the program uses the same technique in Statements 113 through 120 to define storage for the line of output. Secondly, in the EBCDIC-to-binary subprogram (E2B), the powers of ten are defined in a short table (Statements 153 through 156), and are referenced in Statement 146 by a Multiply instruction that uses an index register. At the end of this chapter, Programming Problem 2 considers an alternate technique that does not require a table.

```
        DECIMAL TO BINARY CONVERSION


  LOC  OBJECT CODE     ADDR1 ADDR2  STMT   SOURCE STATEMENT

000000                                 2 DECBIN   CSECT
                                       3 ********************************************************************
                                       4 **
                                       5 **  DEMONSTRATION OF CONVERSION BETWEEN DECIMAL AND BINARY
                                       6 **
                                       7 **        INPUT:   EACH RECORD CONTAINS TWO UNSIGNED INTEGERS
                                       8 **                 RIGHT-JUSTIFIED IN COLS 1-4 AND 9-12.
                                       9 **                 ASSUME ERROR-FREE DATA AND A NONZERO SECOND INTEGER.
                                      10 **                 PROGRAM READS RECORDS UNTIL A BLANK RECORD IS FOUND.
                                      11 **
                                      12 **        OUTPUT:  FOR EACH RECORD READ, THE RESULT OF DIVIDING THE
                                      13 **                 FIRST INTEGER BY THE SECOND IS PRINTED WITH
                                      14 **                 APPROPRIATE LABELS.
                                      15 **
                                      16 ********************************************************************
                                      17 ** REGISTER DEFINITIONS:
                              00002   18 R2       EQU   2                  EVEN/
                              00003   19 R3       EQU   3                       ODD PAIR
                              00004   20 R4       EQU   4                  EVEN/
                              00005   21 R5       EQU   5                       ODD PAIR
                              00006   22 R6       EQU   6                  EVEN/
                              00007   23 R7       EQU   7                       ODD PAIR
                              00008   24 R8       EQU   8                  INDEX TO POWERS TABLE
                              00009   25 R9       EQU   9                  COUNTER FOR LOOP CONTROL
                              0000C   26 R12      EQU   12                 BASE REGISTER
                              0000D   27 R13      EQU   13                 SAVE AREA POINTER
                              0000E   28 R14      EQU   14                 LINK TO SUBPROGRAMS AND OS
                                      29 *  R3 = VALUE PASSED TO INTERNAL SUBPROGRAMS E2B AND B2E
                                      30 *  R4 = VALUE RETURNED FROM E2B
                                      31 *  R4,R5 = DIVIDEND; R4 = REMAINDER, R5 = QUOTIENT
                                      32 *  R7 = VALUE RETURNED FROM B2E
                                      33 *
                                      34          PRINT NOGEN              SUPPRESS MACRO EXPANSIONS
                                      35 ** STANDARD ENTRY AND INITIALIZATION:
                                      36 *  OS:
000000 90EC D00C        0000C         37          STM   R14,R12,12(R13)  SAVE REGISTERS
000004 05C0                           38          BALR  R12,0            LOAD BASE REGISTER
                              00006   39          USING BASE,R12         DECLARE BASE ADDRESS AND REGISTER
000006 50D0 C12A        00130         40 BASE     ST    R13,SAVE+4       SAVE R13
00000A 41D0 C126        0012C         41          LA    R13,SAVE         R13 = ADDRESS OF SAVE AREA
                                      42          OPEN  (READER,INPUT,PRINTER,OUTPUT)  PREPARE FOR I/O
                                      50 ** DOS*******
                                      51 *        BALR  R12,0            LOAD BASE REGISTER
                                      52 *        USING BASE,R12         DECLARE BASE ADDRESS AND REGISTER
                                      53 *BASE    LA    R13,SAVE         R13 = ADDRESS OF SAVE AREA
                                      54 *        OPEN  READER,PRINTER   PREPARE FOR I/O
                                      55 ******
                                      56 ** READ INPUT AND CHECK FOR TRAILER:
                                      57 READ     GET   READER,INPUT     READ A RECORD
00002C 5830 C09A        000A0         62          L     R3,Y             GET DIVISOR FROM INPUT RECORD
000030 5930 C282        00288         63          C     R3,=C'           CHECK FOR TRAILER CONDITION
000034 4780 C07A        00080         64          BE    EXIT             IF TRAILER, RETURN TO SYSTEM
                                      65 ** MOVE INPUT TO OUTPUT AREA AND CONVERT INPUT TO BINARY:
000038 5030 C0F6        000FC         66          ST    R3,DIVISOR       MOVE DIVISOR TO OUTPUT AREA
00003C 45E0 C16E        00174         67          BAL   R14,E2B          CONVERT IT TO BINARY (RESULT IN R4)
000040 5040 C122        00128         68          ST    R4,DENOM         SAVE IN TEMPORARY LOCATION
                                      69 *
000044 5830 C092        00098         70          L     R3,X             GET DIVIDEND FROM INPUT RECORD
000048 5030 C0E6        000EC         71          ST    R3,DIVDND        MOVE IT TO OUTPUT AREA
00004C 45E0 C16E        00174         72          BAL   R14,E2B          CONVERT IT TO BINARY (RESULT IN R4)
```

*(Continues)*

**Figure 8.16**
The program for the case study

```
                                     ** PERFORM THE DIVISION:
000050 8E40 0020        00020                 SRDA  R4,32              SET UP DIVIDEND
000054 5D40 C122        00128                 D     R4,DENOM           DIVIDE X BY Y
                                     ** CONVERT RESULTS TO EBCDIC AND PRINT:
000058 1835                                   LR    R3,R5              GET QUOTIENT
00005A 45E0 C1A2        001A8                 BAL   R14,B2E            CONVERT IT TO EBCDIC (RESULT IN R7)
00005E 5070 C102        00108                 ST    R7,QUOT            PLACE IN OUTPUT AREA
                                     *
000062 1834                                   LR    R3,R4              GET REMAINDER
000064 45E0 C1A2        001A8                 BAL   R14,B2E            CONVERT IT TO EBCDIC (RESULT IN R7)
000068 5070 C11E        00124                 ST    R7,REM             PLACE IN OUTPUT AREA
                                              PUT   PRINTER,OUTPUT     PRINT RESULTS
00007A 47F0 C018        0001E                 B     READ               GO BACK FOR MORE INPUT
                                     ** STANDARD EXIT:
                                     ** OS:
                                     EXIT     CLOSE (READER,,PRINTER)  I/O IS COMPLETE
00008E 58D0 C12A        00130                 L     R13,SAVE+4         RESTORE R13
000092 98EC D00C        0000C                 LM    R14,R12,12(R13)    RESTORE REMAINING REGISTERS
000096 07FE                                   BR    R14                RETURN TO OS
                                     ** DOS*******
                                     *EXIT    CLOSE READER,PRINTER     I/O IS COMPLETE
                                     *        EOJ                      RETURN TO DOS
                                     ******
000098                               INPUT    DS    0F                 INPUT RECORD:
000098                               X        DS    F                    DIVIDEND (COLS. 1-4)
00009C                                        DS    F                    SPACER (COLS. 5-8)
0000A0                               Y        DS    F                    DIVISOR  (COLS. 9-12)
0000A4                                        DS    17F                  PAD TO 80 BYTES
                                     *                                 LINE OF OUTPUT:
0000E8 F0404040                      OUTPUT   DC    C'0   '              CARRIAGE CONTROL
0000EC                               DIVDND   DS    F                    DIVIDEND
0000F0 40C4C9E5C9C4C5C4                       DC    C' DIVIDED BY '
0000FC                               DIVISOR  DS    F                    DIVISOR
000100 40C5D8E4C1D3E240                       DC    C' EQUALS '
000108                               QUOT     DS    F                    QUOTIENT
00010C 40E6C9E3C840C140                       DC    C' WITH A REMAINDER OF    '
000124                               REM      DS    F                    REMAINDER
                                     *
000128                               DENOM    DS    F                  TEMPORARY LOCATION FOR BINARY DIVISOR
00012C                               SAVE     DS    18F                SAVE AREA (9D IN DOS)
                                     ***********************************************************************
                                     **
                                     **  E2B:  EBCDIC TO BINARY CONVERSION
                                     **
                                     **      INPUT:  R3 = FOUR-CHARACTER DECIMAL INTEGER
                                     **      OUTPUT: R4 = EQUIVALENT BINARY INTEGER
                                     **
                                     **      PROCEDURE: FOR THE 4-DIGIT DECIMAL INTEGER WXYZ, COMPUTE:
                                     **                 W*10**3 + X*10**2 + Y*10**1 + Z*10**0
                                     **                 THIS IS THE BINARY EQUIVALENT.
                                     **
                                     ***********************************************************************
000174 1B88                          E2B      SR    R8,R8              R8 = INDEX FOR POWERS TABLE = 0
000176 1B44                                   SR    R4,R4              R4 = ACCUMULATOR = 0
000178 4190 0004        00004                 LA    R9,4               R9 = LOOP COUNTER = 0
                                     * REPEAT 4 TIMES:
                                     *   ISOLATE DIGIT ON LEFT:
00017C 8930 0004        00004        E2BLOOP  SLL   R3,4               GET RID OF FIRST 4 BITS OF EBCDIC
000180 1B22                                   SR    R2,R2              PREPARE FOR DOUBLE SHIFT
000182 8D20 0004        00004                 SLDL  R2,4               GET DIGIT FROM LEFT OF R3
                                     *   MULTIPLY BY APPROPRIATE POWER OF 10 AND ADD RESULT TO ACCUMULATOR:
000186 1872                                   LR    R7,R2              PREPARE FOR MULTIPLY
000188 5C68 C192        00198                 M     R6,POWERS(R8)      MULTIPLY BY APPROPRIATE POWER OF 10
00018C 1A47                                   AR    R4,R7              ADD PRODUCT TO ACCUMULATOR
00018E 4188 0004        00004                 LA    R8,4(R8)           INCREMENT INDEX
000192 4690 C176        0017C                 BCT   R9,E2BLOOP         DECREMENT COUNTER; REPEAT IF NONZERO
```

*(Continues)*

**Figure 8.16**
*(Continued)*

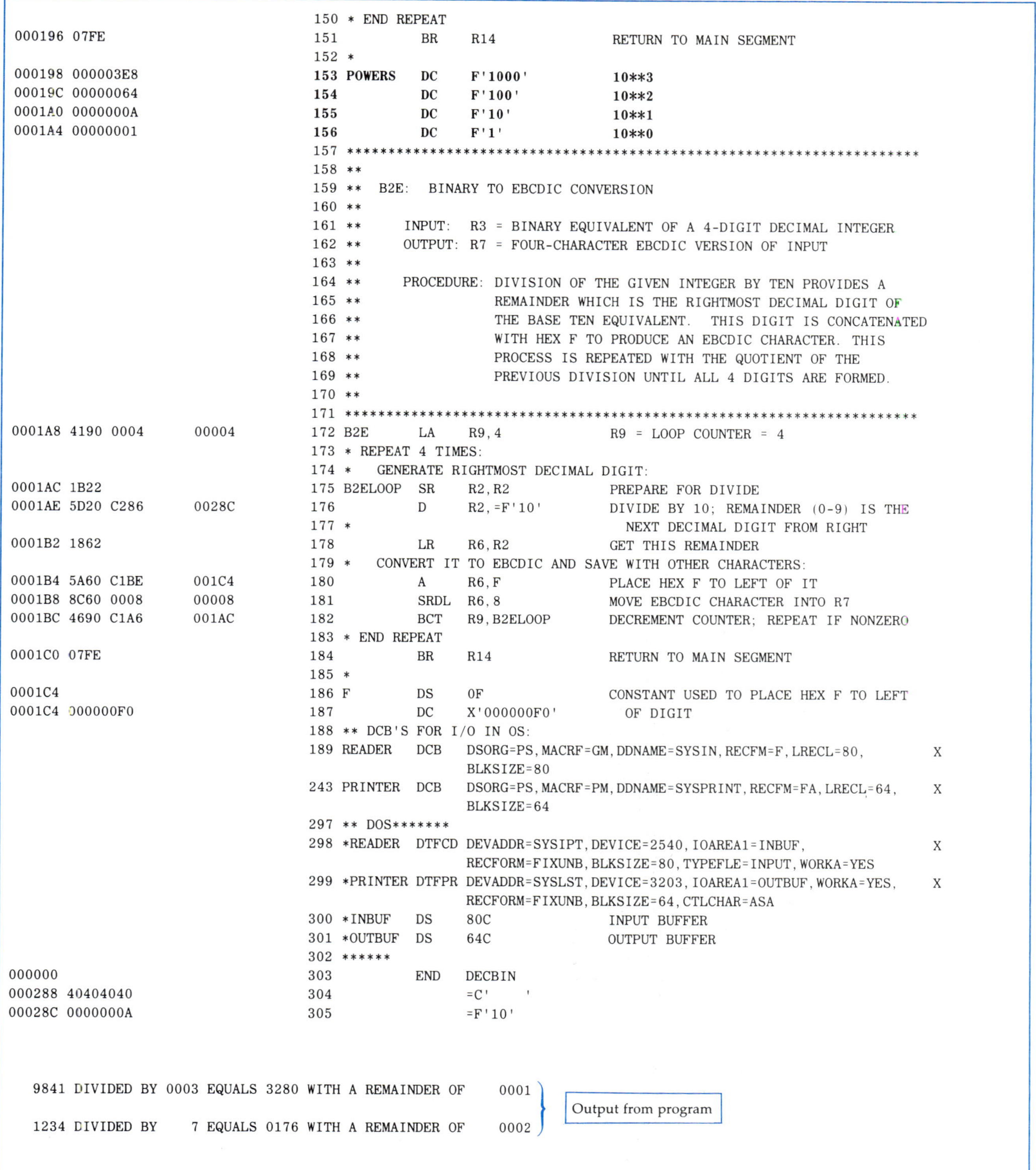

```
                                * END REPEAT
000196 07FE                             BR    R14              RETURN TO MAIN SEGMENT
                                *
000198 000003E8                 POWERS  DC    F'1000'          10**3
00019C 00000064                         DC    F'100'           10**2
0001A0 0000000A                         DC    F'10'            10**1
0001A4 00000001                         DC    F'1'             10**0
                                ***********************************************************************
                                **
                                **  B2E:  BINARY TO EBCDIC CONVERSION
                                **
                                **     INPUT:  R3 = BINARY EQUIVALENT OF A 4-DIGIT DECIMAL INTEGER
                                **     OUTPUT: R7 = FOUR-CHARACTER EBCDIC VERSION OF INPUT
                                **
                                **     PROCEDURE: DIVISION OF THE GIVEN INTEGER BY TEN PROVIDES A
                                **                REMAINDER WHICH IS THE RIGHTMOST DECIMAL DIGIT OF
                                **                THE BASE TEN EQUIVALENT.  THIS DIGIT IS CONCATENATED
                                **                WITH HEX F TO PRODUCE AN EBCDIC CHARACTER. THIS
                                **                PROCESS IS REPEATED WITH THE QUOTIENT OF THE
                                **                PREVIOUS DIVISION UNTIL ALL 4 DIGITS ARE FORMED.
                                **
                                ***********************************************************************
0001A8 4190 0004       00004    B2E     LA    R9,4             R9 = LOOP COUNTER = 4
                                * REPEAT 4 TIMES:
                                *   GENERATE RIGHTMOST DECIMAL DIGIT:
0001AC 1B22                     B2ELOOP SR    R2,R2            PREPARE FOR DIVIDE
0001AE 5D20 C286       0028C            D     R2,=F'10'        DIVIDE BY 10; REMAINDER (0-9) IS THE
                                *                                NEXT DECIMAL DIGIT FROM RIGHT
0001B2 1862                             LR    R6,R2            GET THIS REMAINDER
                                *   CONVERT IT TO EBCDIC AND SAVE WITH OTHER CHARACTERS:
0001B4 5A60 C1BE       001C4            A     R6,F             PLACE HEX F TO LEFT OF IT
0001B8 8C60 0008       00008            SRDL  R6,8             MOVE EBCDIC CHARACTER INTO R7
0001BC 4690 C1A6       001AC            BCT   R9,B2ELOOP       DECREMENT COUNTER; REPEAT IF NONZERO
                                * END REPEAT
0001C0 07FE                             BR    R14              RETURN TO MAIN SEGMENT
                                *
0001C4                          F       DS    0F               CONSTANT USED TO PLACE HEX F TO LEFT
0001C4 000000F0                         DC    X'000000F0'        OF DIGIT
                                ** DCB'S FOR I/O IN OS:
                                READER  DCB   DSORG=PS,MACRF=GM,DDNAME=SYSIN,RECFM=F,LRECL=80,         X
                                              BLKSIZE=80
                                PRINTER DCB   DSORG=PS,MACRF=PM,DDNAME=SYSPRINT,RECFM=FA,LRECL=64,     X
                                              BLKSIZE=64
                                ** DOS*******
                                *READER  DTFCD DEVADDR=SYSIPT,DEVICE=2540,IOAREA1=INBUF,               X
                                              RECFORM=FIXUNB,BLKSIZE=80,TYPEFLE=INPUT,WORKA=YES
                                *PRINTER DTFPR DEVADDR=SYSLST,DEVICE=3203,IOAREA1=OUTBUF,WORKA=YES,    X
                                              RECFORM=FIXUNB,BLKSIZE=64,CTLCHAR=ASA
                                *INBUF   DS    80C              INPUT BUFFER
                                *OUTBUF  DS    64C              OUTPUT BUFFER
                                ******
000000                                  END   DECBIN
000288 40404040                               =C'    '
00028C 0000000A                               =F'10'


   9841 DIVIDED BY 0003 EQUALS 3280 WITH A REMAINDER OF    0001 \
                                                                 } Output from program
   1234 DIVIDED BY    7 EQUALS 0176 WITH A REMAINDER OF    0002 /
```

(*Continues*)

**Figure 8.16**
(*Continued*)

## Debugging Hints

1. Be careful when specifying the shift amount. The second operand designation for a Shift instruction should be in an explicit form and use absolute quantities. If you use a relocatable expression, the shift amount will be computed from the address that is represented by the expression, and not from the contents of the address as you might have hoped. Remember that the assembler will compute a base and a displacement, which reference this address. Therefore, even though you should not have used a relocatable expression to specify the shift amount, you will not get an error message from the assembler. However, the resulting machine language instruction will contain the name of the program's base register; this should indicate to you that the instruction is in error.
2. Do not use Register 0 to specify the shift amount. Register 0 never participates in the computation of an effective address. Therefore, its contents will be ignored if you try to use it in this manner.

## Stylistic Notes

1. Generally, specifying a fixed shift amount symbolically is not a good idea. To do so will tend to hide those instances in which you accidentally used a relocatable symbol to state the shift amount.
2. It is important to practice register conservation now so that you will not run out of registers later when the demand for them increases. Look for registers that are used in one part of a program, but are available for use in another part. Rather than using two registers, you can use one for two different purposes. Practice register conservation up to the point when you must store and restore them. This is a last resort that you can always take.

## Summary

1. Shift instructions operate upon either individual general registers or even-odd register pairs.
2. Logical Shift instructions treat data as unsigned binary quantities. The 32- or 64-bit quantities are shifted to the left or right as desired. Bits shifted out of one end of a quantity are lost; zeros fill in vacancies that are introduced at the other end. The condition code is unchanged.
3. Arithmetic Shift instructions treat data as two's complement binary integers. The 32- or 64-bit integers are shifted to the left or right as desired. The leftmost bit remains fixed and does not participate in the shift. Bits shifted out of one end of the integer are lost; vacancies introduced at the other end are filled in with zeros if the shift is to the left, or with copies of the leftmost bit if the shift is to the right.
4. An overflow can occur during an arithmetic left shift. The CPU recognizes an overflow if a bit unlike the first bit is shifted out of the register. A fixed-point overflow exception occurs, which will cause a program interruption if the first bit of the program mask is 1. Overflow cannot occur during the execution of the other Shift instructions.
5. Arithmetic Shift instructions set the condition code to 0 if the result is zero, 1 if it is negative, 2 if it is positive, or 3 if an overflow occurs during a left shift.
6. You can use arithmetic Shift instructions to multiply or divide a quantity by a power of 2.

## New Instruction Summary

| Operation | Operand | Format | Instruction Name | Action |
|---|---|---|---|---|
| **SLL** | *R1*,*D2*(*B2*) | RS | SHIFT LEFT LOGICAL | Shifts C(*R1*) to the left (right) by $n = E2$ (mod 64) bits. Bits shifted out of the left (right) side are lost; zeros fill in vacancies that are introduced on the right (left). The condition code is unchanged. |
| **SRL** | *R1*,*D2*(*B2*) | RS | SHIFT RIGHT LOGICAL | |
| **SLDL** | *R1*,*D2*(*B2*) | RS | SHIFT LEFT DOUBLE LOGICAL | Shifts C(*R1*,*R1*+1) to the left (right) by $n = E2$ (mod 64) bits. Bits shifted out of the left (right) side are lost; zeros fill in vacancies that are introduced on the right (left). The condition code is unchanged. *R1* must be even. |
| **SRDL** | *R1*,*D2*(*B2*) | RS | SHIFT RIGHT DOUBLE LOGICAL | |
| **SLA** | *R1*,*D2*(*B2*) | RS | SHIFT LEFT ARITHMETIC | Shifts $C(R1)_{1-31}$ to the left by $n = E2$ (mod 64) bits. Bits shifted out of the left are lost; zeros fill in vacancies that are introduced on the right. The leftmost bit (bit 0) of *R1* remains unchanged.<br><br>Condition code = { 0 if the result is zero; 1 if the result is negative; 2 if the result is positive; 3 if an overflow occurs |
| **SRA** | *R1*,*D2*(*B2*) | RS | SHIFT RIGHT ARITHMETIC | Shifts $C(R1)_{1-31}$ right by $n = E2$ (mod 64) bits. Bits shifted out of the right are lost; copies of bit 0, which remains unchanged, fill in vacancies that are introduced on the left.<br><br>Condition code = { 0 if the result is zero; 1 if the result is negative; 2 if the result is positive |
| **SLDA** | *R1*,*D2*(*B2*) | RS | SHIFT LEFT DOUBLE ARITHMETIC | Shifts $C(R1,R1+1)_{1-63}$ to the left by $n = E2$ (mod 64) bits. Bits shifted out of the left of the even register *R1* are lost; zeros fill in vacancies that are introduced on the right of the odd register. Bits that are shifted out of the left of the odd register replace the vacancies that are introduced on the right of the even register. The leftmost bit (bit 0) of *R1* remains unchanged. The condition code is set in the same way as for the SLA instruction. |

| Operation | Operand | Format | Instruction Name | Action |
|---|---|---|---|---|
| SRDA | *R1*,*D2*(*B2*) | RS | SHIFT RIGHT DOUBLE ARITHMETIC | Shifts $C(R1,R1+1)_{1-63}$ to the right by $n = E2 \pmod{64}$ bits. Bits shifted out of the right of the odd register ($R1+1$) are discarded; copies of bit 0, which remains unchanged, fill in vacancies introduced on the left of the even register *R1*. Bits that are shifted out of the right of the even register replace the vacancies that are introduced on the left of the odd register. The condition code is set in the same way as for the SRA instruction. |
| SPM | *R1* | RR | SET PROGRAM MASK | Condition code $\leftarrow C(R1)_{2-3}$<br>Program mask $\leftarrow C(R1)_{4-7}$ |
| IPM | *R1* | RRE | INSERT PROGRAM MASK | $C(R1)_{0-1} \leftarrow 0$<br>$C(R1)_{2-3} \leftarrow$ Condition code<br>$C(R1)_{4-7} \leftarrow$ Program mask |

## Exercises

1. Assume the following register status prior to each instruction:

   Reg. 2 = C760000E
   Reg. 3 = 000000C3
   Reg. 4 = FFFFFFFC

   What are the contents of these registers after each of the following instructions is executed? If the value of the condition code is affected by an instruction, indicate its value.

   a. `SLL 2,3`
   b. `SLA 2,4`
   c. `SLL 2,8`
   d. `SLA 2,8`
   e. `SRL 3,2`
   f. `SRA 3,5`
   g. `SRL 4,4`
   h. `SRA 4,4`
   i. `SLDL 2,1`
   j. `SLDA 2,1`
   k. `SRDL 2,3`
   l. `SRDA 2,3`
   m. `SRA 3,X'C4'(4)`
   n. `SLL 4,0(3)`
   o. `SRDL 2,0(4)`
   p. `SLA 2,2(2)`

2. Write the Shift instructions to accomplish each of the following:
   a. Set the first 11 bits of Register 9 to zero.
   b. Set the first *n* bits of Register 7 to copies of its first bit. Assume that *n* is in the fullword at N.
   c. Divide Register 6 by $2^n$, where *n* is in Register 3 and $0 \leq n \leq 31$.
   d. Multiply Register 5 by $2^n$, where $n \geq 0$ is in Register 3. Treat the product as a 64-bit integer. If the product is correct, store it in the doubleword at PROD. If it is not correct, branch to ERROR.

3. Assume that Register 5 contains an integer *n* that is in the range 0 to 31. Write instructions to accomplish each of the following:
   a. Set bit *n* of Register 3 to 1 and the remaining bits of Register 3 to 0.
   b. Set bit *n* of Register 3 to 0 and the remaining bits of Register 3 to 1.

4. Write instructions to square the integer in Register 7. Treat the result as a 32-bit integer. If the result is correct, store it in the fullword at SQUARE. If it is not correct, cause a program interruption due to fixed-point overflow.

5. Write a sequence of instructions to replace the contents of the following registers with the values that are contained in the indicated portions of the fullword at W. (Values should be right-justified in the registers.)

   C(Register 2) $\leftarrow C(W)_{0-9}$
   C(Register 4) $\leftarrow C(W)_{10-11}$
   C(Register 5) $\leftarrow C(W)_{12-31}$

6. Write a sequence of instructions to replace the contents of the following registers with the values that are contained in the indicated portions of the fullword at Z. (Values should be right-justified in the registers.)

   C(Register 3) $\leftarrow C(Z)_{0-18}$
   C(Register 4) $\leftarrow C(Z)_{19-21}$
   C(Register 5) $\leftarrow C(Z)_{22-28}$
   C(Register 6) $\leftarrow C(Z)_{29-31}$

7. Write a sequence of instructions to replace the contents of the fullword at Y by a value that is composed of the rightmost portions of registers, as follows:

   $C(Y)_{0-11} \leftarrow$ rightmost 12 bits of Register 2
   $C(Y)_{12-13} \leftarrow$ rightmost 2 bits of Register 3
   $C(Y)_{14-31} \leftarrow$ rightmost 18 bits of Register 4

8. Write a sequence of instructions to replace the contents of the fullword at KEY by a value that is composed of the rightmost portions of registers, as follows:

   $C(KEY)_{0} \leftarrow$ rightmost bit of Register 5
   $C(KEY)_{1-20} \leftarrow$ rightmost 20 bits of Register 6
   $C(KEY)_{21-23} \leftarrow$ rightmost 3 bits of Register 7
   $C(KEY)_{24-31} \leftarrow$ rightmost 8 bits of Register 8

9. Write a sequence of instructions to reverse the bit order in a register.

10. Some computers have instructions that perform left or right logical circular shifts of a register. Bits shifted out of one end of the register are inserted into the other end.
    a. Write a sequence of IBM 370 instructions that performs a right logical circular shift of Register 3 by 5 bits.
    b. Repeat Exercise 10a, but shift Register 2 instead.

## Programming Problems

1. Revise the program segment in Figure 8.13 to eliminate the table look-up. You can compute each hex digit directly from its EBCDIC representation. For example, by subtracting F0 from F6, you get 6, which is the hex digit that is represented by F6.

2. Revise the subprogram E2B in Figure 8.16 so that the computation is nested as follows:

   $$1234 = ((1 * 10 + 2) * 10 + 3) * 10 + 4$$

   Nesting eliminates the need for the table at POWERS. Compare the two approaches.

3. Write a subprogram to compute $n!$ when given $n$. If $n!$ exceeds 32 bits, set the condition code to 3; if $n!$ does not exceed 32 bits, set it to 2.

4. Write a subprogram that prints the rightmost 4 bits of a register as a binary integer. Write another subprogram that prints the entire contents of Register 2 as a binary integer.

5. Write a subprogram that prints the rightmost 16 bits of a register as a hexadecimal integer. Write another subprogram that prints the entire contents of Register 2 as a hexadecimal integer.

6. Write a subprogram that prints the rightmost 12 bits of a register as an octal integer. Write another subprogram that prints the entire contents of Register 2 as an octal integer. (*Hint:* pad the octal result to 12 digits.)

7. Using the subprograms of Programming Problems 4 through 6, write a program that reads an unsigned decimal integer and prints it with its binary, hexadecimal, and octal equivalents.

8. Write a subprogram that converts a four-character string of ones and zeros as represented in EBCDIC into its binary integer equivalent. Use this subprogram in a program that reads a string of 32 ones and zeros, and computes the 32-bit binary integer that they represent.

9. Consider a data set of 80-character records that are followed by a trailer record, which contains a $ in the first column. Each data record consists of up to 20 four-character fields, with each field containing a 3-bit unsigned binary integer. Write a program that prints each data record and the sum (in binary) of the binary integers that are contained on that record. Use or modify the subprograms of Programming Problems 4 and 8.

10. You can compute the square root of a decimal number by using an algorithm described by the following pseudocode. Note that the symbol "|" is used to indicate concatenation.

    Beginning at the decimal point and proceeding in both directions, group the digits of the number into pairs. (The leftmost and rightmost "pairs" may in fact consist of a single digit.)

```
N := the number of pairs
REMAINDER := 0
ROOT := 0
REPEAT N TIMES
    REMAINDER := REMAINDER | next pair of digits from the left
    DIVISOR := 20 * ROOT
    D := Largest digit such that:
            (DIVISOR + digit) * digit ≤ REMAINDER
    ROOT := ROOT | D
    REMAINDER := REMAINDER − (DIVISOR + D) * D
END REPEAT
```

For example, the computation of the square root of 236196 appears as

```
   4  8  6
 ) 23 61 96
   16
    7 61
    7 04
       57 96
       57 96
           0
```

A trace of the pseudocode for this computation gives the following results:

| REMAINDER | DIVISOR | D | (DIVISOR + D) * D | ROOT |
|---|---|---|---|---|
| 0 | | | | 0 |
| 023 | 0 | 4 | 16 | 4 |
| 7 | | | | |
| 761 | 80 | 8 | 704 | 48 |
| 57 | | | | |
| 5796 | 960 | 6 | 5796 | 486 |
| 0 | | | | |

To compute the square root of a binary number, replace 20 by $100_2$ in the previous pseudocode. For example, the square root of the binary integer 1010001, which is $81_{10}$, is 1001. The computation is summarized as

```
   1  0  0  1
 ) 1 01 00 01
   1
   0 01
   0 00
      1 00
      0 00
      1 00 01
      1 00 01
            0
```

Write a program that implements the square root algorithm for 32-bit binary integers.

# 9

# Miscellaneous Integer Instructions

CONTENTS

**OVERVIEW**

This chapter presents several instructions that involve binary integers. These enable you to perform the following tasks: load or store several general registers with a single instruction, test or alter the sign of an integer, compute with halfword binary integers, and add or subtract unsigned binary integers. In addition, the chapter describes the location counter reference. Although it is a nonessential part of this assembler language, many people use it.

**OBJECTIVES**

After studying this chapter, you should be able to:

1. Load or store several registers by using LM or STM.
2. Use the LTR instruction to compare the contents of a register with zero.
3. Alter the sign of a binary integer by using LPR, LNR, or LCR.
4. Perform operations on halfword binary integers by using the instructions LH, STH, AH, SH, CH, and MH.
5. Add or subtract unsigned binary integers by using AL, ALR, SL, and SLR.
6. Use the location counter reference when defining base registers, symbols, or constants.

## Introduction

This chapter completes the discussion of instructions that manipulate binary integer quantities. These instructions vary in their degree of importance. Load Multiple and Store Multiple are significant in situations in which you are saving the contents of several registers in storage for later use. The Load Multiple and Store Multiple instructions are important when you use external subprograms, as will be discussed in Chapter 13. Four special Load Register instructions involve the sign of the binary integer. They are used either to compare an integer with zero or to alter the sign of an integer, such as when you compute the absolute value. The halfword instructions enable you to use halfword integers, which saves storage. Of particular interest is the Multiply Halfword instruction because you can use it to multiply the contents of *any* general register without being concerned about even/odd pairs. Finally, the Logical Add and Logical Subtract instructions treat the register contents as unsigned binary integers. Although they are used to program multiple precision arithmetic, they are of little other importance.

The chapter introduces the location counter reference, which is represented by an asterisk, because it is frequently used by programmers, especially when defining a base register. Since it is easy to make an error when you use the location counter reference while defining a base register, you may find that it is safer to avoid its use in this situation. Although its use is far from essential, the location counter reference has other applications that simplify the programming task and, ironically, help to avoid error.

## The Load Multiple (LM) and Store Multiple (STM) Instructions

**Load or store consecutive registers**

The Load Multiple instruction is used to load several consecutively numbered registers from consecutive fullwords of storage. The Store Multiple instruction stores several consecutively numbered registers into consecutive fullwords of storage. As RS format instructions, they designate a storage operand and two register names that specify the range of the consecutive registers affected. The instructions can be summarized as follows:

| Operation | Operand | Format | Instruction Name | Action |
|---|---|---|---|---|
| **LM** | *R1,R3,S2* or *R1,R3,D2(B2)* | RS | LOAD MULTIPLE | Loads the contents of the consecutive registers from *R1* to *R3*, inclusive, with the contents of the consecutive fullwords of storage that begin at the effective address *E2*. When *R1* is larger than *R3*, Register 0 is assumed to follow Register 15 when the instruction determines consecutive registers. |
| **STM** | *R1,R3,S2* or *R1,R3,D2(B2)* | RS | STORE MULTIPLE | Stores the contents of the consecutive registers from *R1* to *R3*, inclusive, into the consecutive fullwords of storage that begin at the effective address *E2*. As with LM, Register 0 follows Register 15 when the instruction determines consecutive registers. |

---

EXAMPLE 1 **Load Registers 2, 3, and 4**

```
         LM    2,4,DATA
         .
         .
         .
DATA     DC    F'10'
         DC    F'-1'
         DC    F'194'
```

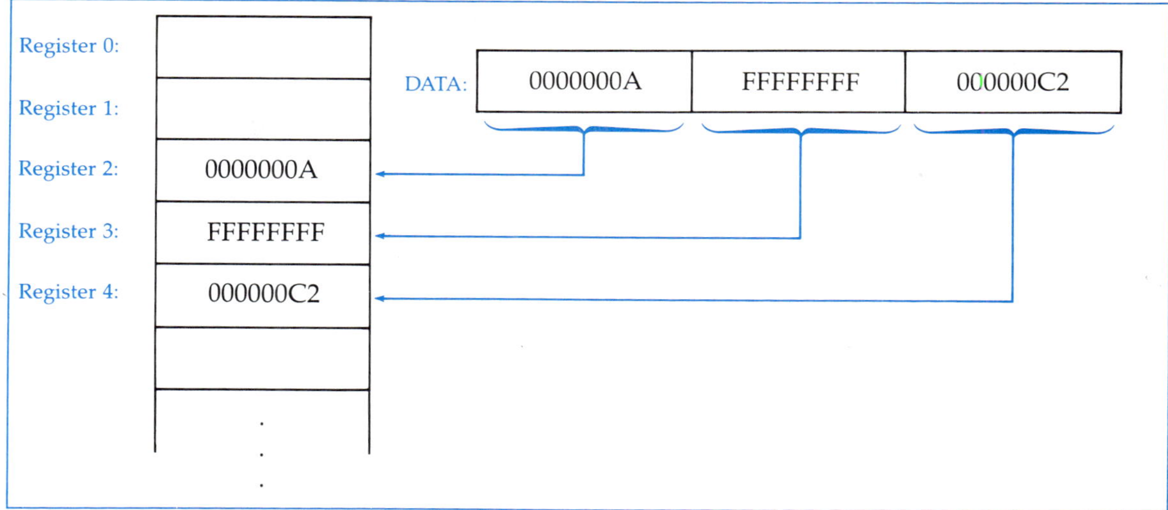


**Figure 9.1**
The effect of
LM 2,4,DATA
as described in
Example 1.

Registers 2, 3, and 4 are loaded with the contents of the fullwords at the addresses DATA, DATA + 4, and DATA + 8, respectively. Thus, after the execution of LM, the registers will appear as

| **Reg. 2** | **Reg. 3** | **Reg. 4** |
|---|---|---|
| 0000000A | FFFFFFFF | 000000C2 |

This example is represented schematically in Figure 9.1.

---

EXAMPLE 2

**Check the Length of a Product**

Without destroying the product, the following sequence determines if X*Y can be represented in 32 bits:

```
         L     R3,X              PLACE X INTO ODD REGISTER
         M     R2,Y              COMPUTE X*Y
         STM   R2,R3,PRODUCT     SAVE 64-BIT PRODUCT
         SLDA  R2,32             WILL PRODUCT FIT INTO 32 BITS?
         BNO   YES               YES, PRODUCT IS IN REG. 2
         LM    R2,R3,PRODUCT     NO, RETRIEVE 64-BIT PRODUCT
         .
         .
         .
PRODUCT  DS    2F
```

X and Y are assumed to be fullwords in storage. After computing their product, the instruction sequence saves it in the two consecutive fullwords at the address PRODUCT. If the product can be represented by 32 bits, then it will be in Register 2 and the program will branch to YES. If the product cannot be represented by 32 bits, the product is recovered and placed into Registers 2 and 3. At this point, the logic of the program may be complicated by this 64-bit integer. As an example of how you might deal with this situation, the chapter will consider the addition of 64-bit integers later.

---

EXAMPLE 3

**Compute (X*Y)/4 + (X*Y)/7**

In the following program segment, the product X*Y is computed once and saved for the second division. Remainders are ignored. Assume that R8 and R9 define an even/odd register pair, and that X and Y represent fullwords in storage.

```
          L     R9,X            PLACE X INTO ODD REGISTER
          M     R8,Y            COMPUTE X*Y
          STM   R8,R9,SAVE      SAVE IT FOR LATER
          D     R8,=F'4'        (X*Y)/4
          ST    R9,QUOTIENT     SAVE THE FIRST QUOTIENT
          LM    R8,R9,SAVE      GET X*Y AGAIN
          D     R8,=F'7'        (X*Y)/7
          A     R9,QUOTIENT     ADD BOTH QUOTIENTS
*   THE RESULT IS IN R9.
          .
          .
          .
SAVE      DS    2F
QUOTIENT  DS    F
```

EXAMPLE 4

**STM 14,1,SAVE**

Since *R1* is larger than *R3*, this instruction stores Registers 14, 15, 0, and 1 into the consecutive fullwords at the address SAVE. The effect of this instruction is illustrated in Figure 9.2.

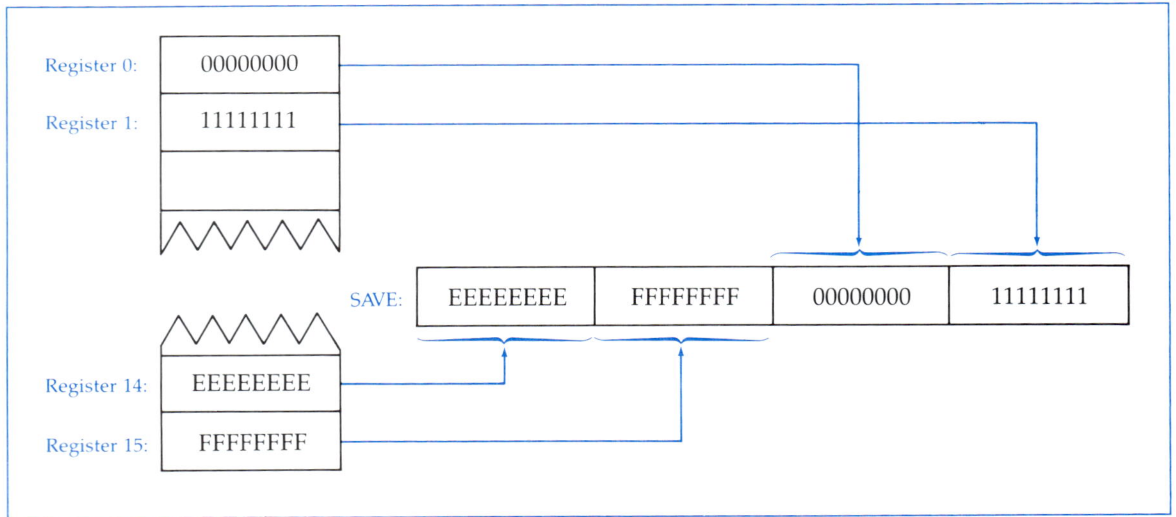


**Figure 9.2**
The effect of
STM 14,1,SAVE
as described in
Example 4.

**SELF-TEST EXERCISE**

1. Assume the following status of the registers and the bytes at AREA:

| | |
|---|---|
| Reg. 0 = 00000000 | Reg. 4 = 44444444 |
| Reg. 1 = 11111111 | Reg. 14 = EEEEEEEE |
| Reg. 2 = 22222222 | Reg. 15 = FFFFFFFF |
| Reg. 3 = 33333333 | |

AREA: ABCDEF01 23456789 FEDCBA98 76543210

What is the effect of each of the following instructions on these quantities?

| | | | | | |
|---|---|---|---|---|---|
| **a.** | STM | 0,2,AREA | **d.** | LM | 14,1,AREA |
| **b.** | STM | 15,2,AREA | **e.** | LM | 1,4,AREA |
| **c.** | STM | 14,15,AREA | **f.** | LM | 15,0,AREA |

## Variations of the Load Register Instruction

Each of the following four RR instructions loads a register and sets the condition code to reflect its new contents. These instructions are important because of the ease with which they allow you to test or change the sign of a binary integer.

### *The Load and Test Register (LTR) Instruction*

**Load a register and then compare it with zero**

In addition to loading a register as if it were the Load Register instruction, the Load and Test Register instruction compares the new value of the first register operand with zero and sets the condition code accordingly. The instruction can be summarized as follows:

| Operation | Operand | Format | Instruction Name | Action |
|---|---|---|---|---|
| **LTR** | *R1,R2* | RR | LOAD AND TEST REGISTER | $C(R1) \leftarrow C(R2)$<br>Condition code $= \begin{cases} 0 \text{ if } C(R1) = 0 \\ 1 \text{ if } C(R1) < 0 \\ 2 \text{ if } C(R1) > 0 \end{cases}$ |

EXAMPLE 5

```
LTR     2,4
```

| | Reg. 2 | Reg. 4 | |
|---|---|---|---|
| Before execution: | 12345678 | 90ABCDEF | |
| After execution: | 90ABCDEF | 90ABCDEF | *Condition code* = 1 |

This instruction has exactly the same effect as the sequence

```
LR      2,4
C       2,=F'0'
```

EXAMPLE 6

```
LTR     5,5
```

This instruction does not change the contents of Register 5, but does set the condition code. It is equivalent to the instruction

```
C       5,=F'0'
```

This form of the LTR instruction is the preferred way to compare the contents of a register with zero. As an RR instruction, LTR is shorter and faster than the Compare instruction, and does not require a zero constant.

---

### *The Load Positive Register (LPR) Instruction*

**Compute the absolute value (make the sign a plus)**

The Load Positive Register instruction is used to take the absolute value of a binary integer; the condition code is set to reflect the status of the result. The instruction can be summarized as follows:

| Operation | Operand | Format | Instruction Name | Action |
|---|---|---|---|---|
| **LPR** | *R1*,*R2* | RR | LOAD POSITIVE REGISTER | $C(R1) \leftarrow \lvert C(R2) \rvert$<br>Condition code $= \begin{cases} 0 \text{ if } C(R1) = 0 \\ 2 \text{ if } C(R1) > 0 \\ 3 \text{ if an overflow occurs} \end{cases}$ |

---

EXAMPLE 7

```
LPR     8,4
```

| | **Reg. 8** | **Reg. 4** | |
|---|---|---|---|
| Before execution: | 12345678 | FFFFFFFF | |
| After execution: | 00000001 | FFFFFFFF | *Condition code* = 2 |

Since the contents of Register 4 represent a negative number, the two's complement is taken and placed into Register 8. Since the new contents of Register 8 are positive, the condition code is set to 2.

---

EXAMPLE 8

```
LPR     5,5
```

| | **Reg. 5** | |
|---|---|---|
| Before execution: | FFFFFFFF | |
| After execution: | 00000001 | *Condition code* = 2 |

Since Register 5 contains a negative number, the two's complement is taken and the result replaces the original contents of Register 5. Because the result is positive, the condition code is set to 2.

EXAMPLE 9

**LPR 0,3**

| | Reg. 0 | Reg. 3 | |
|---|---|---|---|
| Before execution: | FFFFFFFF | 12345678 | |
| After execution: | 12345678 | 12345678 | *Condition code* = 2 |

Positive numbers (and zero) are unchanged by the LPR instruction.

EXAMPLE 10

**LPR 7,9**

| | Reg. 7 | Reg. 9 | |
|---|---|---|---|
| Before execution: | FFFFFFFF | 80000000 | |
| After execution: | 80000000 | 80000000 | *Condition code* = 3 |

Register 9 contains $-2^{31}$, but $+2^{31}$ cannot be represented in 32 bits. The contents of Register 9 remain unchanged, but they do replace the contents of Register 7. A fixed-point overflow exception occurs and the condition code is set to 3. If the first bit of the program mask is 1, a program interruption will take place.

## *The Load Negative Register (LNR) Instruction*

**Make the sign a minus**

The Load Negative Register instruction performs an operation opposite to that of LPR. If a number if positive, it is made negative; but if the number is negative or zero, it is unchanged. Since the largest positive number is $2^{31} - 1$ and the number $-(2^{31} - 1)$ can be represented, overflow cannot occur. The instruction can be summarized as follows:

| Operation | Operand | Format | Instruction Name | Action |
|---|---|---|---|---|
| **LNR** | *R1,R2* | RR | LOAD NEGATIVE REGISTER | $C(R1) \leftarrow -\lvert C(R2)\rvert$<br>Condition code = $\begin{cases} 0 \text{ if } C(R1) = 0 \\ 1 \text{ if } C(R1) < 0 \end{cases}$ |

EXAMPLE 11

**LNR 3,0**

| | Reg. 3 | Reg. 0 | |
|---|---|---|---|
| Before execution: | 12345678 | 00000001 | |
| After execution: | FFFFFFFF | 00000001 | *Condition code* = 1 |

Since Register 0 contains a positive number, the two's complement is taken and the result is placed into Register 3. The result is negative so the condition code is set to 1.

EXAMPLE 12 **LNR 8,8**

| | Reg. 8 | |
|---|---|---|
| Before execution: | 7FFFFFFF | |
| After execution: | 80000001 | *Condition code* = 1 |

Register 8 originally contains $2^{31} - 1$; the number $-(2^{31} - 1)$ can be represented and replaces the contents of Register 8. Remember that overflow cannot occur with this instruction.

EXAMPLE 13 **LNR 6,8**

| | Reg. 6 | Reg. 8 | |
|---|---|---|---|
| Before execution: | FFFFFFFF | 80000000 | |
| After execution: | 80000000 | 80000000 | *Condition code* = 1 |

This instruction does not change negative numbers.

EXAMPLE 14 **LNR 7,2**

| | Reg. 7 | Reg. 2 | |
|---|---|---|---|
| Before execution: | FFFFFFFF | 00000000 | |
| After execution: | 00000000 | 00000000 | *Condition code* = 0 |

This instruction does not change zero.

## *The Load Complement Register (LCR) Instruction*

**Change signs**

The Load Complement Register instruction takes the two's complement of a binary quantity and sets the condition code according to the result. The instruction can be summarized as follows:

| Operation | Operand | Format | Instruction Name | Action |
|---|---|---|---|---|
| **LCR** | *R1,R2* | RR | LOAD COMPLEMENT REGISTER | C(*R1*) ← The two's complement of C(*R2*)<br>Condition code = 0 if C(*R1*) = 0; 1 if C(*R1*) < 0; 2 if C(*R1*) > 0; 3 if an overflow occurs |

**SELF-TEST EXERCISES**

2. Assume the following register status:

| | |
|---|---|
| Reg. 0 = FFFFFFFC | Reg. 4 = 80000000 |
| Reg. 2 = 0000FFFF | Reg. 5 = 00000000 |
| Reg. 3 = 80000001 | Reg. 6 = 7FFFFFFF |

What is the effect of each of the following instructions on these quantities and the condition code?

| | | | | | | | | | | | |
|---|---|---|---|---|---|---|---|---|---|---|---|
| **a.** | LTR | 0,5 | **g.** | LPR | 0,0 | **m.** | LNR | 3,0 | **s.** | LCR | 3,0 |
| **b.** | LTR | 2,4 | **h.** | LPR | 6,4 | **n.** | LNR | 0,2 | **t.** | LCR | 0,2 |
| **c.** | LTR | 3,2 | **i.** | LPR | 3,3 | **o.** | LNR | 4,4 | **u.** | LCR | 4,4 |
| **d.** | LTR | 6,6 | **j.** | LPR | 5,6 | **p.** | LNR | 4,5 | **v.** | LCR | 4,5 |
| **e.** | LTR | 0,0 | **k.** | LPR | 6,5 | **q.** | LNR | 0,6 | **w.** | LCR | 0,6 |
| **f.** | LTR | 5,3 | **l.** | LPR | 2,2 | **r.** | LNR | 3,3 | **x.** | LCR | 3,3 |

3. Write a sequence of instructions that tests the integer in Register 9 and branches to ZERO if it is zero, branches to NEG if it is negative, and sequences if it is positive.

---

EXAMPLE 15 **LCR 1,1**

| | Reg. 1 | |
|---|---|---|
| Before execution: | FFFFFFFF | |
| After execution: | 00000001 | *Condition code* = 2 |

---

EXAMPLE 16 **LCR 5,2**

| | Reg. 5 | Reg. 2 | |
|---|---|---|---|
| Before execution: | 12345678 | 00000001 | |
| After execution: | FFFFFFFF | 00000001 | *Condition code* = 1 |

---

EXAMPLE 17 **LCR 3,9**

| | Reg. 3 | Reg. 9 | |
|---|---|---|---|
| Before execution: | FFFFFFFF | 80000000 | |
| After execution: | 80000000 | 80000000 | *Condition code* = 3 |

Register 9 contains $-2^{31}$, but $+2^{31}$ cannot be represented in 32 bits. The contents of Register 9 remain unchanged, but they do replace the contents of Register 3. A fixed-point overflow exception occurs and the condition code is set to 3. If the first bit of the program mask is 1, a program interruption will take place.

EXAMPLE 18

```
LCR    4,2
```

| | Reg. 4 | Reg. 2 | |
|---|---|---|---|
| Before execution: | FFFFFFFF | 00000000 | |
| After execution: | 00000000 | 00000000 | *Condition code* = 0 |

This instruction does not change zero.

## The Halfword Instructions

You can perform several binary integer operations with halfword operands instead of fullword operands. There are only six instructions, all of which are in the RX format, that use halfword operands. You can load or store halfwords, add a halfword to or subtract a halfword from a register, multiply a register by a halfword, or compare a register with a halfword. There is no halfword divide instruction.

You may use the halfword instructions whenever you happen to have halfword operands that are already defined. More likely, you will find that you want to perform some arithmetic with constants that are small enough to be represented by the 16 bits of a halfword. If this is the case, you can save storage by defining the constants as halfwords instead of as fullwords. You can do this with a DC or literal that uses the H-type constant. The range of such constants is $-2^{15}$ to $+2^{15} - 1$ or, $-32{,}768$ to $+32{,}767$.

**Range of 16-bit integers**

Except for the store operation, the halfword instructions involve all 32 bits of a general register. During the execution of most of these instructions, the halfword operand is temporarily expanded to a 32-bit quantity without actually affecting the halfword in storage. The result of this process is called the **fullword expansion** of a halfword. You can compute the expansion by preceding the halfword value with 16 copies of its leftmost bit. The text denotes the fullword expansion by

**Fullword expansion**

$$F[C(E2)_{0-15}]$$

where *E2* is the effective address of the halfword.

EXAMPLE 19

**Examples of Fullword Expansions**

The following fullword expansions are obtained by preceding positive halfword quantities by 16 zeros, and negative halfword quantities by 16 ones. The values are given in hex.

| Halfword | Fullword Expansion |
|---|---|
| 0001 | 00000001 |
| 8000 | FFFF8000 |
| 0000 | 00000000 |

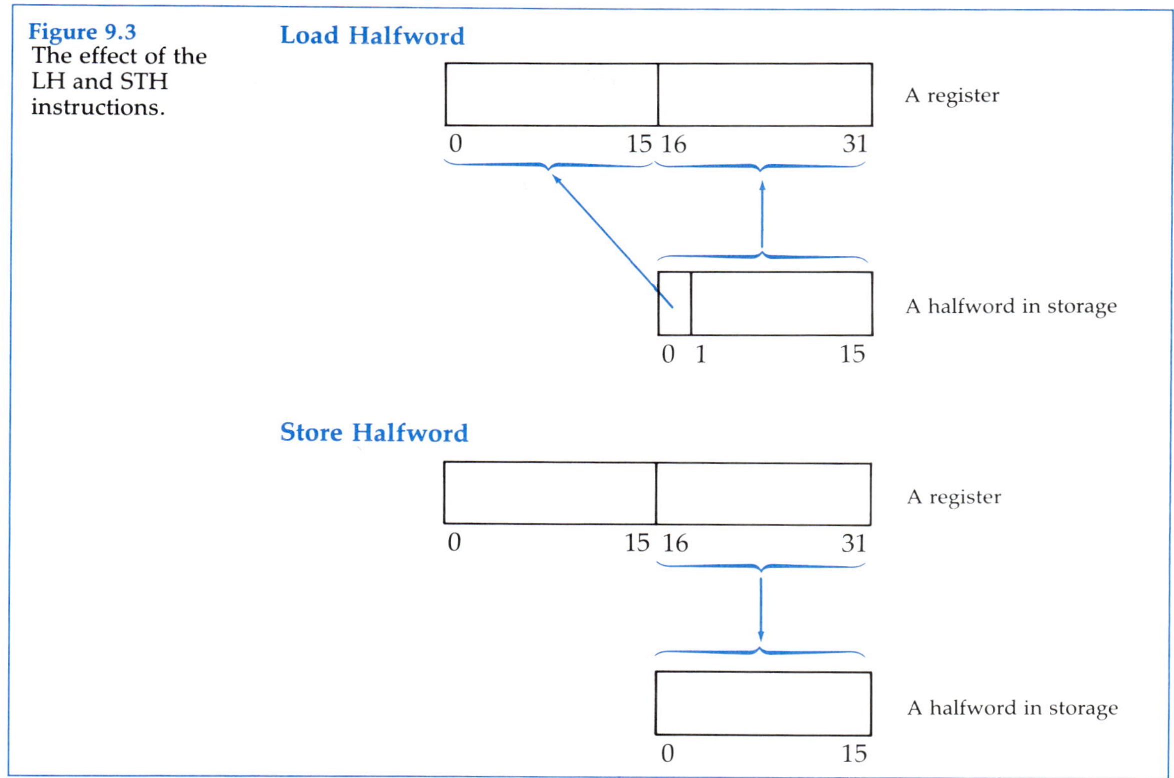


**Figure 9.3** The effect of the LH and STH instructions.

### *The Load Halfword (LH) and Store Halfword (STH) Instructions*

The Load Halfword instruction replaces the entire register operand with the fullword expansion of the halfword storage operand, without changing the halfword in storage. The Store Halfword instruction replaces the halfword in storage by the low-order 2 bytes of the register operand. STH ignores the high-order 2 bytes of the register, regardless of their contents. The contents of the register remain unchanged. These instructions are illustrated in Figure 9.3. The instructions can be summarized as follows:

| Operation | Operand | Format | Instruction Name | Action |
|---|---|---|---|---|
| **LH** | *R1*,*S2*<br>or *R1*,*S2*(*X2*)<br>or *R1*,*D2*(*X2*,*B2*) | RX | LOAD HALFWORD | $C(R1)_{0-31} \leftarrow F[C(E2)_{0-15}]$ |
| **STH** | *R1*,*S2*<br>or *R1*,*S2*(*X2*)<br>or *R1*,*D2*(*X2*,*B2*) | RX | STORE HALFWORD | $C(E2)_{0-15} \leftarrow C(R1)_{16-31}$ |

These instructions do not change the condition code.

EXAMPLE 20

```
LH      2,W
```

| | Reg. 2 | Halfword at W |
|---|---|---|
| Before execution: | ABEFEFFF | 1234 |
| After execution: | 00001234 | 1234 |

All of Register 2 is replaced by the fullword expansion of the contents of the halfword at the address that is represented by W. Since the contents of the halfword are positive, each of the first 16 bits of the register is set to zero.

EXAMPLE 21

```
LH      2,=X'90AB'
```

| | Reg. 2 | =X'90AB' |
|---|---|---|
| Before execution: | 12345678 | 90AB |
| After execution: | FFFF90AB | 90AB |

As in the previous example, all of Register 2 is replaced. Here, the contents of the halfword are negative, so each of the first 16 bits of the register is set to one.

EXAMPLE 22

```
STH     4,Y
```

| | Reg. 4 | Halfword at Y |
|---|---|---|
| Before execution: | 1234**5678** | 90AB |
| After execution: | 12345678 | 5678 |

Only the rightmost 16 bits of Register 4 are stored into the halfword of storage. The instruction ignores the rest of Register 4.

EXAMPLE 23

**Halfword Instructions with Fullword Operands**

Do not become confused when halfword instructions reference fullword storage operands. Remember that only the 2 bytes at the effective address participate in the instructions, even though register results are 32 bits. For example, consider the following:

```
LH      6,W     where     W       DC      F'4095'
```

| | Reg. 6 | The bytes at W |
|---|---|---|
| Before execution: | 12345678 | **0000**0FFF |
| After execution: | 00000000 | 00000FFF |

The *halfword* at W contains 0000; its fullword expansion replaces the contents of Register 6. Although there may be legitimate reasons for doing this, more likely the definition of W is in error and should be H'4095'.

Now, consider the instruction:

```
STH    6,Z    where    Z    DS    F
```

| | **Reg. 6** | **The bytes at Z** | |
|---|---|---|---|
| Before execution: | 0000**0001** | ???????? | ← Contents of Z are unknown |
| After execution: | 00000001 | 0001???? | |

The contents of the rightmost 2 bytes of Register 6 replace the contents of the 2 bytes at Z.

---

## *The Add Halfword (AH) and Subtract Halfword (SH) Instructions*

The Add Halfword and Subtract Halfword instructions are very similar to their fullword counterparts Add and Subtract. The only difference is that the second operand is a halfword in storage: the contents of this halfword are expanded to a fullword, and are either added to or subtracted from the *entire* (32-bit) register operand to produce a 32-bit result. The instructions can be summarized as follows:

| Operation | Operand | Format | Instruction Name | Action |
|---|---|---|---|---|
| **AH** | *R1,S2*<br>or *R1,S2(X2)*<br>or *R1,D2(X2,B2)* | RX | ADD HALFWORD | $C(R1)_{0-31} \leftarrow C(R1)_{0-31} + F[C(E2)_{0-15}]$ |
| **SH** | *R1,S2*<br>or *R1,S2(X2)*<br>or *R1,D2(X2,B2)* | RX | SUBTRACT HALFWORD | $C(R1)_{0-31} \leftarrow C(R1)_{0-31} - F[C(E2)_{0-15}]$ |

For both instructions, the condition code =
- 0 if the result is zero
- 1 if the result is negative
- 2 if the result is positive
- 3 if an overflow occurs

---

EXAMPLE 24

```
AH    2,X
```

| | **Reg. 2** | **Halfword at X** | |
|---|---|---|---|
| Before execution: | 12345678 | 4321 | |
| After execution: | 12349999 | 4321 | *Condition code* = 2 |

The contents of X are temporarily expanded into 00004321 without affecting X in storage. This quantity is added to Register 2; the result is positive.

---

EXAMPLE 25

```
AH      4,=H'-2'
```

| | Reg. 4 | =H′−2′ | |
|---|---|---|---|
| Before execution: | 00000073 | FFFE | |
| After execution: | 00000071 | FFFE | *Condition code* = 2 |

FFFE is temporarily expanded into the fullword FFFFFFFE without affecting the literal constant defined by =H′−2′. The fullword is added to Register 4; the result is positive.

EXAMPLE 26

```
SH      7,=H'3'
```

| | Reg. 7 | =H′3′ | |
|---|---|---|---|
| Before execution: | FFFFFFFF | 0003 | |
| After execution: | FFFFFFFC | 0003 | *Condition code* = 1 |

The fullword expansion of 0003 is 00000003. The subtraction is performed by adding the two's complement of 00000003 to Register 7; the result is negative.

## *The Compare Halfword (CH) Instruction*

The Compare Halfword instruction compares the 32-bit integer in a register with the fullword expansion of a halfword in storage, and sets the condition code. The instruction has the following form:

| Operation | Operand | Format | Instruction Name | Action |
|---|---|---|---|---|
| CH | *R1,S2*<br>or *R1,S2(X2)*<br>or *R1,D2(X2,B2)* | RX | COMPARE HALFWORD | Compares C(*R1*) with $F[C(E2)_{0-15}]$<br>Condition code = $\begin{cases} 0 \text{ if } C(R1) = F[C(E2)_{0-15}] \\ 1 \text{ if } C(R1) < F[C(E2)_{0-15}] \\ 2 \text{ if } C(R1) > F[C(E2)_{0-15}] \end{cases}$ |

EXAMPLE 27

```
CH      7,=H'-2'
```

| | Reg. 7 | =H′−2′ | |
|---|---|---|---|
| Before execution: | FFFFFFFF | FFFE | |
| After execution: | FFFFFFFF | FFFE | *Condition code* = 2 |

The contents of Register 7, which represent −1, are compared with FFFFFFFE, which is the fullword expansion of =H′−2′. Since −1 is greater than −2, the condition code is set to 2.

### *The Multiply Halfword (MH) Instruction*

The Multiply Halfword instruction is particularly useful. With MH, you can multiply the contents of *any* register by a halfword constant without worrying about even/odd register pairs. The instruction has the following form:

| Operation | Operand | Format | Instruction Name | Action |
|---|---|---|---|---|
| MH | *R1,S2*<br>or *R1,S2(X2)*<br>or *R1,D2(X2,B2)* | RX | MULTIPLY HALFWORD | $C(R1)_{0-31} \leftarrow C(R1)_{0-31} * C(E2)_{0-15}$ |

The 32-bit multiplicand is in the general register that is designated by *R1*. The multiplier is the 16-bit integer storage operand. Both of these quantities are assumed to use a two's complement binary notation. The product is at most 48 bits long; however, only the rightmost 32 bits are retained and replace the contents of *R1*. If the product is in the range of $-2^{31}$ to $2^{31}-1$, then the discarded high-order bits of the product will not be significant bits, and the product will be correctly contained in *R1*. If the product is not in that range, not only will the value of the result be incorrect, but it is possible that its sign will be incorrect also. No indication of this is given, and the condition code remains unchanged.

---

EXAMPLE 28

```
MH    1,=H'-2
```

| | Reg. 1 | =H'−2' |
|---|---|---|
| Before execution: | 00000003 | FFFE |
| After execution: | FFFFFFFA | FFFE |

The product of 3 and −2 is correctly represented in Register 1.

---

EXAMPLE 29

```
MH    9,=H'4'
```

| | Reg. 9 | =H'4' |
|---|---|---|
| Before execution: | 80000000 | 0004 |
| After execution: | 00000000 | 0004 |

Register 9 contains $-2^{31}$. The product of $-2^{31}$ and 4 is $-2^{33}$, which cannot be correctly represented in 32 bits. After execution, Register 9 contains only the rightmost 32 bits of the product. Clearly, this is an incorrect result; however, the condition code remains unchanged and an overflow exception does not occur.

---

**SELF-TEST EXERCISES**

4. Assume the following definitions and register status:

```
W         DS     H
X         DC     X'88881111'
          DC     X'22227777'
Y         DC     H'-4'
Z         DC     F'-8'
```

Reg. 1 = 87654321     Reg. 2 = ABCD0000

What is the effect of each of the following instructions on these quantities and the condition code?

| | | | | | | | | |
|---|---|---|---|---|---|---|---|---|
| **a.** | STH | 1,W | **g.** | LH | 2,X | **m.** | SH | 1,Y |
| **b.** | STH | 2,X | **h.** | LH | 2,X+6 | **n.** | SH | 2,Z |
| **c.** | STH | 2,X+2 | **i.** | CH | 1,X+6 | **o.** | MH | 2,Y |
| **d.** | STH | 1,Z | **j.** | CH | 2,X | **p.** | MH | 2,Z |
| **e.** | LH | 1,Y | **k.** | AH | 1,X | | | |
| **f.** | LH | 1,Z | **l.** | AH | 2,X+4 | | | |

5. Write a sequence of instructions to store the smaller of two halfword integers at H1 and H2 into a halfword at H3.
6. What is the one negative 16-bit (two's complement binary) integer whose absolute value cannot be represented as a halfword?

## An Example with Halfwords

**A subprogram that uses the new instructions introduced so far**

This example demonstrates several of the instructions introduced so far in this chapter, by considering an internal subprogram to compute

$$Z = \left| \frac{X_1 + 2X_2 + \ . \ . \ . + NX_N}{N} \right|$$

where X is an array of at most 50 halfword binary integers. Assume that N is stored as a halfword and Z is a fullword.

The subprogram that is listed in Figure 9.4 saves (with the STM instruction) and later restores (with the LM instruction) the contents of the registers it uses. Thus, when you use this subprogram, you can assume that it will not destroy the contents of the registers. This feature is typical of external subprograms and there are conventions, which are discussed in Chapter 13, that govern how this is accomplished. Although internal subprograms can, and perhaps should, follow these same conventions, for now you can invent your own.

The computation is performed with straightforward logic, so you will be able to concentrate on the use of the new instructions. Since a BCT instruction controls the required loop, you must convert the halfword at N to a 32-bit quantity and place it into a register (R2); you can accomplish this with the LH instruction. Use the LTR instruction to compare the result with zero to ensure that N contains a positive number. If this is not the case, the subprogram stores a negative value in Z as a signal that N is incorrect.

The terms of the sum are of the form $jX_j$, so you need both a counter

```
*****************************************************************
** SUBPROGRAM TO COMPUTE:
**                          | X(1) + 2*X(2) + . . . + N*X(N) |
**                      Z = | ------------------------------ |
**                          |                N               |
** ASSUME: X IS AN ARRAY OF AT MOST 50 HALFWORDS, N IS A HALFWORD,
**         AND Z IS A FULLWORD.  ALSO ASSUME THE FOLLOWING REGISTER
**         DEFINITIONS:
**     R2  = LOOP COUNTER; DIVISOR
**     R3  = INDEX REGISTER FOR ARRAY X
**     R4  = ACCUMULATOR FOR THE NUMERATOR; EVEN
**     R5  = THE QUOTIENT;                   /ODD PAIR
**     R6  = EACH TERM IN THE NUMERATOR
**     R14 = THE LINK REGISTER
** NOTE: IF N <= 0, Z IS SET TO -1.
*****************************************************************
EXAMPLE  STM   R14,R6,EXSAVE SAVE REGISTERS USED
** INITIALIZATION:
         LH    R2,N          INITIALIZE COUNTER
         LTR   R3,R2         COPY N AND COMPARE WITH ZERO
         BH    EXOK          CONTINUE IF N > 0
         LH    R5,=H'-1'     OTHERWISE, SET ERROR VALUE
         B     EXSTORE       STORE ERROR VALUE AND RETURN
EXOK     SH    R3,=H'1'      N - 1
         SLA   R3,1          R3 = 2*(N - 1) = INDEX TO X(N)
         SR    R4,R4         INITIALIZE ACCUMULATOR
** COMPUTE NUMERATOR IN REVERSE ORDER:
* REPEAT:
EXLOOP   LR    R6,R2         PREPARE FOR MULTIPLY
         MH    R6,X(R3)      COMPUTE TERM J*X(J)
         AR    R4,R6         ADD IT TO ACCUMULATOR
         SH    R3,=H'2'      DECREMENT INDEX
* UNTIL R2 (LOOP COUNTER) = 0
         BCT   R2,EXLOOP     DECREMENT COUNTER; REPEAT IF NONZERO
* END REPEAT
** DIVIDE BY N AND TAKE ABSOLUTE VALUE:
         SRDA  R4,32         PREPARE FOR DIVIDE
         LH    R2,N          GET DIVISOR AS FULLWORD
         DR    R4,R2         FORM QUOTIENT
         LPR   R5,R5         TAKE ABSOLUTE VALUE
EXSTORE  ST    R5,Z          SAVE RESULT
         LM    R14,R6,EXSAVE RESTORE REGISTERS
         BR    R14           RETURN
EXSAVE   DS    9F            REGISTER SAVE AREA
```

**Figure 9.4**
A subprogram to demonstrate new instructions.

to use as a multiplier and an index register to address the elements of the array. R2 can serve as the multiplier, but since the subprogram uses a BCT for loop control, R2 counts backward. Therefore, the subprogram will add the terms of the numerator in reverse order; the corresponding index register R3 must count backward from 2(N − 1) by increments of 2.

Although the array elements are halfwords, the subprogram treats the products and the sum as fullwords. Notice how the subprogram performs the division since there is no halfword divide instruction. Finally, LPR is used to compute the absolute value of the quotient.

# The Logical Addition and Subtraction Instructions

**Logical arithmetic uses unsigned binary integers**

IBM uses the term *logical* to describe certain instructions when unsigned integer data is involved. Such instructions, encountered here and in later chapters, have nothing to do with logic or Boolean algebra. For example, the Add Logical and Subtract Logical instructions use operands that are unsigned binary integers. However, given the nature of finite arithmetic, the numeric results of the Logical Add and Subtract instructions are the same as those of the instructions A and S. Yet, the condition code settings differ, and Add Logical and Subtract Logical do not cause an exception due to overflow. You can use the instructions to program multiple precision integer arithmetic, but other than this use, these instructions have little application. The rest of this text refers to both **signed integers,** a term that means integers in a two's complement binary number system, and to unsigned integers.

## *The Add Logical (AL and ALR) Instructions*

The Add Logical instructions can be summarized as follows:

| Operation | Operand | Format | Instruction Name | Action |
|---|---|---|---|---|
| **AL** | *R1,S2*<br>or *R1,S2(X2)*<br>or *R1,D2(X2,B2)* | RX | ADD LOGICAL | $C(R1) \leftarrow C(R1) + C(E2)_{0-31}$ |
| **ALR** | *R1,R2* | RR | ADD LOGICAL REGISTERS | $C(R1) \leftarrow C(R1) + C(R2)$ |

**The condition code settings differ from those of A and AR**

Both instructions set the condition code according to whether or not a carry out of the leftmost bit occurs.

- If no carry occurs, the condition code is set to:

  0 if the result is zero,
  1 if the result is nonzero.

- If a carry does occur, the condition code is set to:

  2 if the result is zero,
  3 if the result is nonzero.

---

EXAMPLE 30 **ALR 9,5**

| | Reg. 9 | Reg. 5 | |
|---|---|---|---|
| Before execution: | 7FFFFFFF | 7FFFFFFF | |
| After execution: | FFFFFFFE | 7FFFFFFF | *Condition code* = 1 |

Registers 9 and 5 each contain $2^{31} - 1$; their sum is $2^{32} - 2$. The addition appears in binary as

```
  011 ...  1
+ 011 ...  1
  111 ... 10
```

There is no carry out of the leftmost bit and, since the sum is nonzero, the condition code is set to 1.

If the instruction had been

```
AR      9,5
```

then the result in Register 9 would have been the same, but a fixed-point overflow exception would have occurred, which results in a condition code of 3.

---

EXAMPLE 31

```
ALR     1,1
```

| | Reg. 1 | |
|---|---|---|
| Before execution: | 80000000 | |
| After execution: | 00000000 | *Condition code* = 2 |

Register 1 originally contains the *unsigned* integer $2^{31}$. Adding this integer to itself results in $2^{32}$, which requires 33 bits for its binary representation (1 followed by 32 zeros). Register 1 contains the zeros, and the condition code, which is set to 2, reflects the carry out of the leftmost bit. If the instruction had been

```
AR      1,1
```

then Register 1 would have contained the same result. However, a fixed-point overflow exception would have occurred and the condition code would have been set to 3.

---

### *The Subtract Logical (SL and SLR) Instructions*

The Subtract Logical instructions can be summarized as follows:

| Operation | Operand | Format | Instruction Name | Action |
|---|---|---|---|---|
| **SL** | *R1,S2*<br>or *R1,S2(X2)*<br>or *R1,D2,(X2,B2)* | RX | SUBTRACT LOGICAL | $C(R1) \leftarrow C(R1) - C(E2)_{0-31}$ |
| **SLR** | *R1,R2* | RR | SUBTRACT LOGICAL REGISTERS | $C(R1) \leftarrow C(R1) - C(R2)$ |

**The condition code can be 1, 2, or 3**

Both instructions set the condition code: it can never be zero, as shown in Example 32, but remaining condition code settings are the same as for Add Logical.

Each instruction performs a subtraction by adding both 1 and the one's complement of the second operand to the first operand. When the second operand is zero, a carry is always generated, as shown in Example 33. The carries would be different if the instruction used the two's complement of the second operand.

---

EXAMPLE 32

```
SLR    9,9
```

| | Reg. 9 | |
|---|---|---|
| Before execution: | 00000004 | |
| After execution: | 00000000 | *Condition code* = 2 |

The computation is performed as follows:

```
  00000004   ← The original contents of Register 9
+ FFFFFFFB   ← The one's complement of 00000004
+        1   ← Plus one
 1 00000000
Carry   Result
```

When the result is zero, there is always a carry. Therefore, the condition code is set to 2; it can never be 0.

---

EXAMPLE 33

```
SL     1,=F'0'
```

| | Reg. 1 | =F'0' | |
|---|---|---|---|
| Before execution: | 00000012 | 00000000 | |
| After execution: | 00000012 | 00000000 | *Condition code* = 3 |

The computation is performed as follows:

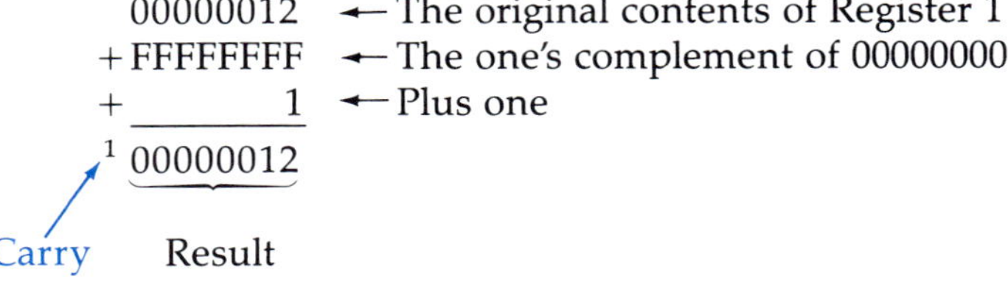


The condition code is set to 3.

---

**SELF-TEST EXERCISE**

7. What is the effect of each of the following instructions on Register 2 and the condition code if Register 2 contains 7FFFFFFF?

| | | | | | |
|---|---|---|---|---|---|
| **a.** AL | `2,=F'15'` | | **e.** SL | `2,=F'0'` |
| **b.** A | `2,=F'15'` | | **f.** S | `2,=F'0'` |
| **c.** AL | `2,=F'-1'` | | **g.** SLR | `2,2` |
| **d.** A | `2,=F'-1'` | | **h.** SR | `2,2` |

## *Multiple Precision Addition*

Remember that under certain conditions, you can represent a 64-bit product by using just 32 bits, and that you can then readily use the product in further computations. However, suppose that this is not the case: for example, you might have two 64-bit quantities whose sum you want to compute. You cannot perform this addition by using only one instruction, but rather you must use several instructions that consider a 64-bit integer in 32-bit portions.

Suppose that X and Y are each 64-bit binary integers. Figure 9.5 shows an example of two such integers and the computation of their sum. Each integer is partitioned into two 32-bit portions and is represented in hexadecimal. Consider the addition of the low-order portions of X and Y: if there is a carry out of the leftmost digit (and there is in this example), it is added into the sum of the high-order portions. This process is really nothing more than ordinary addition viewed in a slightly different way. Notice that the carry, if it occurs, must always be 1.

This procedure can be described in pseudocode. Let $X_H$ and $Y_H$ represent the high-order portions of X and Y, and $X_L$ and $Y_L$ represent their low-order portions. Then to compute X + Y, proceed as follows:

$SUM_L := X_L + Y_L$
IF there is a carry out of the leftmost bit
    THEN add 1 to $X_H$
END IF
$SUM_H := X_H + Y_H$

You can implement this pseudocode as follows. Use the Add Logical instruction to add the low-order portions $X_L$ and $Y_L$ so that, if a carry out of their sum occurs, you can detect it by examining the condition code. (It will be set to 2 or 3.) If X and Y represent signed quantities, then you should compute the sum of the high-order portions $X_H$ and $Y_H$ with an Add instruction so that you can use the condition code to detect overflow or to determine the sign of the result. If X and Y represent unsigned integers,

**Figure 9.5**
An example of a 64-bit addition (in hex).

```
                1
X:     12345678 \ FFFF0000
Y: +   00000013 \ 00012345
                  1
Z:     1234568C | 00002345
                  Carry
```

use the Add Logical instruction instead. This procedure can readily be extended to higher-order precisions.

To demonstrate the concepts just presented, consider computing the average of the squares of N signed binary integers stored in an array of fullwords. The squares will be positive 64-bit integers, but assume that their average will not exceed 32 bits. The program segment listed in Figure 9.6 performs this computation. Notice that, in the event of a carry, the program uses an Add instruction instead of an LA instruction to add one to the high-order portion of the sum. Although you might be tempted to use LA for this purpose, remember that LA places zero at least into the first bit of the register and could, therefore, destroy part of the sum.

```
** COMPUTE:  THE AVERAGE OF THE SUM OF THE SQUARES OF THE SIGNED
**           INTEGERS IN AN ARRAY OF FULLWORDS AND STORE IT IN THE
**           FULLWORD AT AVERAGE.
** ASSUME:   THE ARRAY IS DEFINED AT ARRAY AND THE NUMBER OF INTEGERS
**           IN THE ARRAY IS STORED IN THE HALFWORD AT N.
**           ALSO ASSUME THE FOLLOWING REGISTER DEFINITIONS:
**      R2 = INDEX REGISTER
**      R4 = HIGH-ORDER PART OF PRODUCT; EVEN/
**      R5 = LOW-ORDER PART OF PRODUCT;       ODD PAIR
**      R6 = HIGH-ORDER PART OF SUM;                 EVEN/
**      R7 = LOW-ORDER PART OF SUM; ALSO THE AVERAGE.   ODD PAIR
**      R9 = INCREMENT/LIMIT FOR LOOP CONTROL (ODD)
** BRANCH MASK:
NOCAR      EQU   B'1100'          NO CARRY AFTER LOGICAL ADD
** INITIALIZATION:
           LH    R9,=H'-4'        INCREMENT/LIMIT FOR LOOP CONTROL
           LH    R2,N             NUMBER OF ARRAY ELEMENTS
           SH    R2,=H'1'         N - 1
           SLA   R2,2             4*(N-1) = INDEX TO ARRAY(N)
           SR    R6,R6            CLEAR ACCUMULATOR (HIGH-ORDER)
           SR    R7,R7            CLEAR ACCUMULATOR (LOW-ORDER)
** ACCUMULATE THE 64-BIT SUM OF SQUARES:
**    (PROCESS THE ARRAY BACKWARD)
LOOP       L     R5,ARRAY(R2)     GET NEXT ARRAY ELEMENT
           MR    R4,R5            SQUARE IT
           ALR   R7,R5            ADD LOW-ORDER PORTION TO SUM
           BC    NOCAR,SKIP       CARRY?
           A     R6,=F'1'         IF SO, ADD IT TO HIGH-ORDER PART
SKIP       AR    R6,R4            ADD HIGH-ORDER PART OF PRODUCT
           BO    ERROR            ERROR IF OVERFLOW
           BXH   R2,R9,LOOP       INCREMENT AND TEST INDEX
** COMPUTE AVERAGE:
           LH    R2,N             CONVERT N TO FULLWORD FORM
           DR    R6,R2            DIVIDE SUM OF SQUARES BY N
           ST    R7,AVERAGE       SAVE RESULT
           .
           .
           .
ERROR      ----                   PRINT ERROR MESSAGE
```

**Figure 9.6**
A program segment that illustrates double precision addition.

## The Location Counter Reference

This text previously mentioned the location counter when it discussed the assembly process. As you recall, the assembler uses the location counter to count bytes as they are assigned to the object program. The location counter represents the relative address at any particular point in the program.

You can refer to the address at any point in the source program by using the **location counter reference.** This is denoted by an asterisk (*). Since the location counter reference represents an address, it is a relocatable term that may be combined with other terms to form expressions. When used in the operand of an EQU or USING directive, the location counter reference represents the address of the next available byte. When used in the operand of a machine instruction, it represents the address of the first byte of the instruction.

---

EXAMPLE 34

### In an EQU

Consider the following definitions:

```
TABLE     DS    5F
NEXT      EQU   *
LAST      EQU   *-4
LENGTH    EQU   *-TABLE
```

TABLE is the address of an array of five fullwords. NEXT is a relocatable symbol that represents the address of the byte *after* the array. An equivalent way to define NEXT is

```
NEXT      EQU   TABLE+20
```

However, this is not as convenient as using the location counter reference since you must count the number of bytes in the array; if you later change your mind about the definition of TABLE, you would have to change this byte count as well.

LAST is a relocatable symbol that represents the address of the fifth and last fullword in the array. LENGTH is an absolute symbol that represents the number of bytes in the array: 20, in this case. The operand * − TABLE is equivalent to NEXT − TABLE.

---

EXAMPLE 35

### Defining Base Registers

A common use of the location counter reference is in the definition of a base register, as follows:

```
          BALR  12,0
          USING *,12
BASE      ----
```

Here, BASE is the address of the next instruction. The asterisk denotes the address that is represented by the location counter at the point that the USING occurs; this is the same address that is represented by BASE. The sequence is equivalent to

```
          BALR   12,0
          USING  BASE,12
BASE      ----
```

You must be very careful when using an asterisk in this manner: the order of the USING directive and the BALR instruction is crucial to the proper definition of the base register. For example, the following sequence is *incorrect:*

**An incorrect way to define a base register**

```
          USING *,12
          BALR  12,0
```

Here, USING tells the assembler that Register 12 contains the address of the BALR instruction; but Register 12 actually contains the address of the byte *after* the BALR. While it is safer not to use the location counter reference in the USING directive, many people do, so you are bound to encounter it when reading other programs.

---

EXAMPLE 36

**Defining Base Registers**

Another way to define a base register is

```
PROGRAM   CSECT
          USING *,15
```

This has the same meaning as

```
PROGRAM   CSECT
          USING PROGRAM,15
```

Both cases tell the assembler to assume that Register 15 contains the starting address of the program. (The operating system has ensured that it does.)

---

EXAMPLE 37

```
      B      *
```

An asterisk in the operand entry of a machine instruction represents the address of that instruction. An easy way to remember this is to note that this Branch instruction branches to itself.

---

EXAMPLE 38

```
BRANCH    B      *+6
```

This instruction is equivalent to

```
BRANCH      B       BRANCH+6
```

Since the asterisk represents the address of the Branch instruction, this instruction will skip over a 2-byte instruction that follows. Some programmers use this technique to avoid defining additional symbols. In general, however, this practice is very dangerous and should be avoided since you must count the bytes in instructions. Even if you used this technique correctly, it is likely that the number of instructions between the Branch instruction and the branch address will change during the programming process. If so, you would also have to change any Branch operand entries that contained the location counter reference. This is a tedious step and one that you are likely to forget to do.

---

## SELF-TEST EXERCISES

8. Assume that the following sequence begins at hex address BF00:

```
                 LA      2,NEXT
                 LA      3,NEXT-ARRAY
                 LA      4,*
                 BR      14
ARRAY            DC      5H'0'
NEXT             EQU     *
```

   a. What are the contents of Registers 2, 3, and 4 after these instructions are executed?
   b. Rewrite this sequence without the asterisks.

9. a. If Register 5 contains 00000008, what address will the following branch to?

```
         B       *(5)
         B       POINTA
         B       POINTB
         B       POINTC
         B       POINTD
```

   b. Rewrite the first Branch instruction without the asterisk.

10. Use the following incorrect sequence in a program to determine what happens:

```
USING *,12
BALR  12,0
```

# Debugging Hints

1. Remember that it is possible to generate an incorrect product with the MH instruction. Use it only when one operand is a halfword and you can be sure that the product will be correctly contained in a fullword.

2. If you use the location counter reference to define a base register, be careful of the placement of the USING directive. If you make an error, you might receive an addressability error message, but it is probable that the assembler will not issue any error messages. In that case, the displacements will be incorrect, and so will the results of execution. An execution-time error message is probable, but it is possible that none will occur.

## Stylistic Notes

1. Consider using MH when it is necessary to compute a product. If it is feasible to use this instruction, do so since it functions without even/odd register pairs.
2. Develop the habit of writing the USING directive immediately after the instruction that loads the base register, rather than writing it before. This order is usually necessary if you use the location counter reference. Even if you do not use the location counter reference, the suggested order will help you to avoid base register errors that are undetected by the assembler. Chapter 12 will discuss this fully.
3. Generally, it is poor practice to use the location counter reference in the operand of a Branch instruction. It is safer not to use the location counter reference in the operand of the USING directive.

## Summary

1. Use STM and LM to save and restore the contents of several consecutively numbered registers. These instructions are useful when you use even/odd register pairs or subprograms.
2. Use LTR to compare the contents of a register with zero.
3. Use LPR, LNR, or LCR when you must alter the sign of a register. In particular, use LPR to compute the absolute value of a binary integer.
4. You can save storage by using halfwords to define constants that are in the range −32,768 to +32,767. The halfword instructions LH, STH, AH, SH, CH, and MH are used with such operands. These instructions are in the RX format only.
5. Use the MH instruction to multiply any register by a 16-bit integer.
6. There is no halfword divide instruction.
7. The Add Logical and Subtract Logical instructions assume the operands are unsigned binary integers. Except for the condition code settings and the absence of an overflow exception, these instructions give the same results as the fullword binary integer Add and Subtract instructions. Add Logical and Subtract Logical are used to program multiple precision integer arithmetic.
8. The location counter reference, which is designated by an asterisk, is a relocatable term used to represent the address at the point at which the asterisk appears.

## New Instruction Summary

| Operation | Operand | Format | Instruction Name | Action |
|---|---|---|---|---|
| **LM** | *R1*,*R3*,*S2* or *R1*,*R3*,*D2*(*B2*) | RS | LOAD MULTIPLE | C(*R1*), C(*R1*+1), . . . , C(*R3*) ← C(*E2*), C(*E2*+4), . . . |

| Operation | Operand | Format | Instruction Name | Action |
|---|---|---|---|---|
| **STM** | *R1,R3,S2*<br>or *R1,R3,D2(B2)* | RS | STORE MULTIPLE | $C(E2), C(E2+4), \ldots \leftarrow C(R1), C(R1+1), \ldots, C(R3)$ |
| **LTR** | *R1,R2* | RR | LOAD AND TEST REGISTER | $C(R1) \leftarrow C(R2)$<br>Condition code $= \begin{cases} 0 \text{ if } C(R1) = 0 \\ 1 \text{ if } C(R1) < 0 \\ 2 \text{ if } C(R1) > 0 \end{cases}$ |
| **LPR** | *R1,R2* | RR | LOAD POSITIVE REGISTER | $C(R1) \leftarrow \lvert C(R2) \rvert$<br>Cond. code $= \begin{cases} 0 \text{ if } C(R1) = 0 \\ 2 \text{ if } C(R1) > 0 \\ 3 \text{ if an overflow occurs} \end{cases}$ |
| **LNR** | *R1,R2* | RR | LOAD NEGATIVE REGISTER | $C(R1) \leftarrow -\lvert C(R2) \rvert$<br>Condition code $= \begin{cases} 0 \text{ if } C(R1) = 0 \\ 1 \text{ if } C(R1) < 0 \end{cases}$ |
| **LCR** | *R1,R2* | RR | LOAD COMPLEMENT REGISTER | $C(R1) \leftarrow$ The two's complement of $C(R2)$<br>Cond. code $= \begin{cases} 0 \text{ if } C(R1) = 0 \\ 1 \text{ if } C(R1) < 0 \\ 2 \text{ if } C(R1) > 0 \\ 3 \text{ if an overflow occurs} \end{cases}$ |
| **LH** | *R1,S2*<br>or *R1,S2(X2)*<br>or *R1,D2(X2,B2)* | RX | LOAD HALFWORD | $C(R1)_{0-31} \leftarrow F[C(E2)_{0-15}]$ |
| **STH** | *R1,S2*<br>or *R1,S2(X2)*<br>or *R1,D2(X2,B2)* | RX | STORE HALFWORD | $C(E2)_{0-15} \leftarrow C(R1)_{16-31}$ |
| **AH** | *R1,S2*<br>or *R1,S2(X2)*<br>or *R1,D2(X2,B2)* | RX | ADD HALFWORD | $C(R1)_{0-31} \leftarrow C(R1)_{0-31} + F[C(E2)_{0-15}]$<br>Condition code $= \begin{cases} 0 \text{ if } C(R1) = 0 \\ 1 \text{ if } C(R1) < 0 \\ 2 \text{ if } C(R1) > 0 \\ 3 \text{ if an overflow occurs} \end{cases}$ |
| **SH** | *R1,S2*<br>or *R1,S2(X2)*<br>or *R1,D2(X2,B2)* | RX | SUBTRACT HALFWORD | $C(R1)_{0-31} \leftarrow C(R1)_{0-31} - F[C(E2)_{0-15}]$<br>The condition code settings are the same as for AH. |
| **CH** | *R1,S2*<br>or *R1,S2(X2)*<br>or *R1,D2(X2,B2)* | RX | COMPARE HALFWORD | Compares $C(R1)$ with $F[C(E2)_{0-15}]$<br>Condition code $= \begin{cases} 0 \text{ if } C(R1) = F[C(E2)_{0-15}] \\ 1 \text{ if } C(R1) < F[C(E2)_{0-15}] \\ 2 \text{ if } C(R1) > F[C(E2)_{0-15}] \end{cases}$ |
| **MH** | *R1,S2*<br>or *R1,S2(X2)*<br>or *R1,D2(X2,B2)* | RX | MULTIPLY HALFWORD | $C(R1)_{0-31} \leftarrow C(R1)_{0-31} * C(E2)_{0-15}$<br>The condition code is unchanged. |

| Operation | Operand | Format | Instruction Name | Action |
|---|---|---|---|---|
| **AL** | *R1,S2*<br>or *R1,S2(X2)*<br>or *R1,D2(X2,B2)* | RX | ADD LOGICAL | $C(R1) \leftarrow C(R1) + C(E2)_{0-31}$<br>Condition code = 0 if no carry, zero result; 1 if no carry, nonzero result; 2 if carry, zero result; 3 if carry, nonzero result |
| **ALR** | *R1,R2* | RR | ADD LOGICAL REGISTERS | $C(R1) \leftarrow C(R1) + C(R2)$<br>The condition code settings are the same as for AL. |
| **SL** | *R1,S2*<br>or *R1,S2(X2)*<br>or *R1,D2(X2,B2)* | RX | SUBTRACT LOGICAL | $C(R1) \leftarrow C(R1) - C(E2)_{0-31}$<br>Condition code = 1 if no carry, nonzero result; 2 if carry, zero result; 3 if carry, nonzero result |
| **SLR** | *R1,R2* | RR | SUBTRACT LOGICAL REGISTERS | $C(R1) \leftarrow C(R1) - C(R2)$<br>The condition code settings are the same as for SL. |

## Exercises

1. Describe the effect of the following sequence of instructions:

```
         LA     13,SAVE
         STM    14,12,12(13)
         .
         .
         .
SAVE     DS     18F
```

2. Write a sequence of instructions to compute the one's complement of a 32-bit integer.
3. What are the contents of Register 2 after execution of each instruction in the following *sequence* of instructions?

```
L      2,=F'-4'
LNR    2,2
LCR    2,2
LCR    2,2
LNR    2,2
LNR    2,2
LCR    2,2
LPR    2,2
LCR    2,2
```

4. Consider the following sequence of instructions:

```
LNR    2,2
AH     2,=H'7'
LPR    2,2
LCR    2,2
LNR    2,2
MH     2,=H'2'
LCR    2,2
LCR    2,2
```

What are the final contents of Register 2 if it initially contains 4?

5. Assume the following definitions and that Register 5 contains $80000000_{16}$:

```
U        DC     F'65536'
V        DC     X'12345678'
W        DS     F
```

What is the effect of each of the following instructions on these quantities, the designated registers, and the condition code?

```
a. LH    2,=H'-4'          f. STH   5,W
b. LH    3,=F'-4'          g. AH    5,V
c. LH    4,U               h. SH    5,=H'-1'
d. CH    5,=H'-1'          i. MH    5,=H'-1'
e. STH   5,V
```

6. What are the contents of Registers 2 and 3 and the value of the condition code after each of the following instructions is executed? Assume that Register 3 contains $12345678_{16}$ prior to each instruction.

| | | | | | |
|---|---|---|---|---|---|
| **a.** | SLR | `2,2` | **e.** | ALR | `3,3` |
| **b.** | SR | `2,2` | **f.** | AR | `3,3` |
| **c.** | AL | `3,=F'-4'` | **g.** | SL | `3,=X'12345678'` |
| **d.** | A | `3,=F'-4'` | **h.** | S | `3,=X'12345678'` |

*For each of the following exercises, write a sequence of instructions to perform the indicated computation.*

7. Replace the integers in an array of fullwords with their absolute values. Branch to ERROR if an overflow occurs.

8. Replace the integers in an array of halfwords with their absolute values. Branch to ERROR if a result exceeds 32 bits.

9. Examine an array of halfwords and make any positive integers negative.

10. Compute the fullword sum of the positive halfword integers in an array.

11. Create an array of fullwords from an array of halfwords.

12. Determine if the contents of Register 2 can be correctly represented as a halfword.

13. Compute X − Y, X * Y, and X ÷ Y. Assume that X and Y are halfwords. Will these results always be correct?

14. Compute

$$W = (5X + 2)/Y - Z$$

where X, Y, and Z are halfwords in storage.

15. Compute X − Y, assuming that X and Y are 64-bit signed integers.

## Programming Problems

1. Write subprograms to compute the sum and difference of 96-bit signed integers.

2. Repeat Programming Problem 1 for unsigned integers.

3. Write a subprogram to compute the 128-bit product of two 64-bit signed integers. (*Hint:* If X is one of the operands, write it as $2^{32} * X_H + X_L$.)

# 10

# Character Manipulation

CONTENTS

**OVERVIEW**

This chapter introduces the basic instructions that manipulate bytes or groups of bytes. These instructions enable you to move bytes either between registers and storage, or from one portion of storage to another. Other instructions permit you to compare data as unsigned integers. Such comparisons are called logical comparisons and are possible between registers, registers and storage, or storage and storage. The chapter introduces two new instruction formats, SI and SS, that permit storage-to-storage operations. Finally, the chapter concludes with a description of some additional features of assembler language that are useful when you write programs that involve the new instructions introduced here.

**OBJECTIVES**

After studying this chapter, you should be able to:

1. Describe the SI and SS instruction formats.
2. Copy bytes either from a register to storage or from storage to a register by using the instructions IC, ICM, STC, and STCM.
3. Copy bytes from one portion of storage to another by using the instructions MVI, MVC, and MVCIN.
4. Perform logical comparisons of data either in registers or in registers and storage by using the instructions CLR, CL, and CLM.
5. Perform logical comparisons of data in storage by using the instructions CLI and CLC.
6. Define and use the length modifier for DC and DS directives.
7. Specify the duplication factor of DC and DS directives symbolically.
8. Define and use A-type address constants.
9. Determine the length attribute for any given symbol, and define and use the symbol length attribute reference.

## Introduction

Processing textual material or other character data is an important application for which the IBM 370 is well suited. Chapter 5 discussed how each character is represented in one byte by a code known as EBCDIC. This chapter will introduce instructions that manipulate data in storage at the byte level. With these new instructions, you can address individual bytes or groups of up to 256 consecutive bytes. Try to free yourself of the notion that data is solely numerical and is stored as fullwords or halfwords. The term **field** will be used to describe data stored in consecutive bytes. A field that contains only characters can also be called a **character string.**

Several instructions introduced in this chapter involve an operation called **move.** Moving field A to field B means that a copy of field A replaces field B. The first instructions presented move individual bytes between a register and storage. As such, they are a transition between the instructions that you already know and new ones that involve fields in storage, instead of fields in registers. The new instructions that involve fields in storage are in one of two formats, SI and SS, which will be discussed here. These instructions permit you to move fields from one place in storage to another, and to make logical comparisons of two fields in storage.

The chapter describes additional features of assembler language that are useful with the new instructions. They are the explicit length modifier and the symbolic duplication factor that are used in DC and DS directives; the A-type address constant; and the symbol length attribute reference.

## Moving Bytes Between Registers and Storage

This section describes the operations that you can use to move bytes between registers and storage.

### *The Insert Character (IC) and Store Character (STC) Instructions*

**RX byte-oriented instructions**

Insert Character and Store Character are RX instructions that involve only the rightmost byte of a register and one byte of storage. The rest of the register does not participate in the operation and remains unchanged. The effective address that is specified by the instruction's second operand entry is unrestricted by boundary alignment considerations. The instructions can be summarized as follows:

| Operation | Operand | Format | Instruction Name | Action |
|---|---|---|---|---|
| **IC** | *R1,S2*<br>or *R1,S2(X2)*<br>or *R1,D2(X2,B2)* | RX | INSERT CHARACTER | $C(R1)_{24-31} \leftarrow C(E2)_{0-7}$ |
| **STC** | *R1,S2*<br>or *R1,S2(X2)*<br>or *R1,D2(X2,B2)* | RX | STORE CHARACTER | $C(E2)_{0-7} \leftarrow C(R1)_{24-31}$ |

The condition code remains unchanged by these instructions.

The IC instruction is a type of load instruction. It loads the rightmost byte of the register operand with the contents of the one-byte storage operand. The STC instruction performs an analogous store operation. When you think of the name Insert Character alone, it is not particularly distinctive: do not confuse the instruction's meaning with Store Character. If you always think of these instructions together, it will be clear that IC is not a store operation. Also, of the nonprivileged instructions, only CVD (presented later in Chapter 14) and those whose mnemonics begin with ST perform register-to-storage operations. The IC and STC instructions are valuable because they are the only byte-oriented instructions in the RX format.

In the following examples, X represents the address of a byte in storage.

---

EXAMPLE 1

**IC 2,X**

| | **Reg. 2** | **The byte at X** |
|---|---|---|
| Before execution: | 12345678 | CD |
| After execution: | 123456**CD** | CD |

The instruction loads the rightmost byte of Register 2 with the contents of the byte at X.

---

EXAMPLE 2

**STC 2,X**

| | **Reg. 2** | **The byte at X** |
|---|---|---|
| Before execution: | 12345678 | CD |
| After execution: | 12345678 | 78 |

This instruction stores the rightmost byte of Register 2 into the byte at X.

---

## *The Insert Characters Under Mask (ICM) and Store Characters Under Mask (STCM) Instructions*

Insert Characters Under Mask and Store Characters Under Mask are RS instructions that are similar in effect to IC and STC, but involve up to 4 bytes instead of only 1. The bytes selected from the first register operand *need not be contiguous;* you designate their positions by using a 4-bit binary mask *M3* that is specified as the third operand of the RS format. A corresponding number of *consecutive* bytes in storage compose the second operand.

**Register bytes are selected according to a mask**

Each bit in the mask corresponds to a byte in the register, as pictured in Figure 10.1. The leftmost bit in the mask corresponds to the leftmost byte of the register, and so on. If a 1 appears in the mask, the corresponding register byte is selected; if not, it is ignored. Several examples of this selection are illustrated in Figure 10.2.

The ICM instruction loads the selected register bytes from the *consecutive* bytes in storage that are specified by the effective address. The remaining

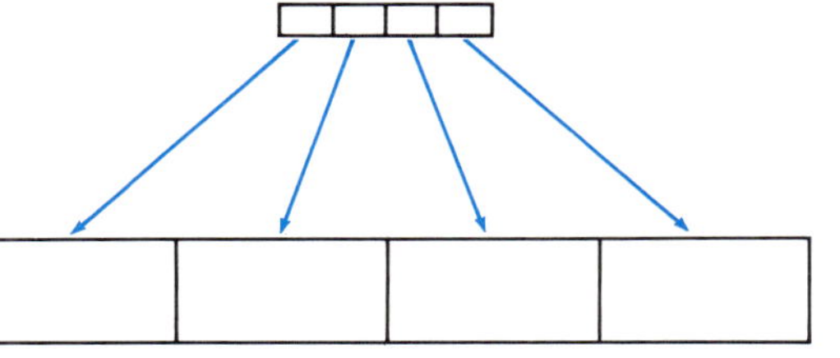


**Figure 10.1**
The bits in the mask for ICM and STCM correspond to the bytes of a register.

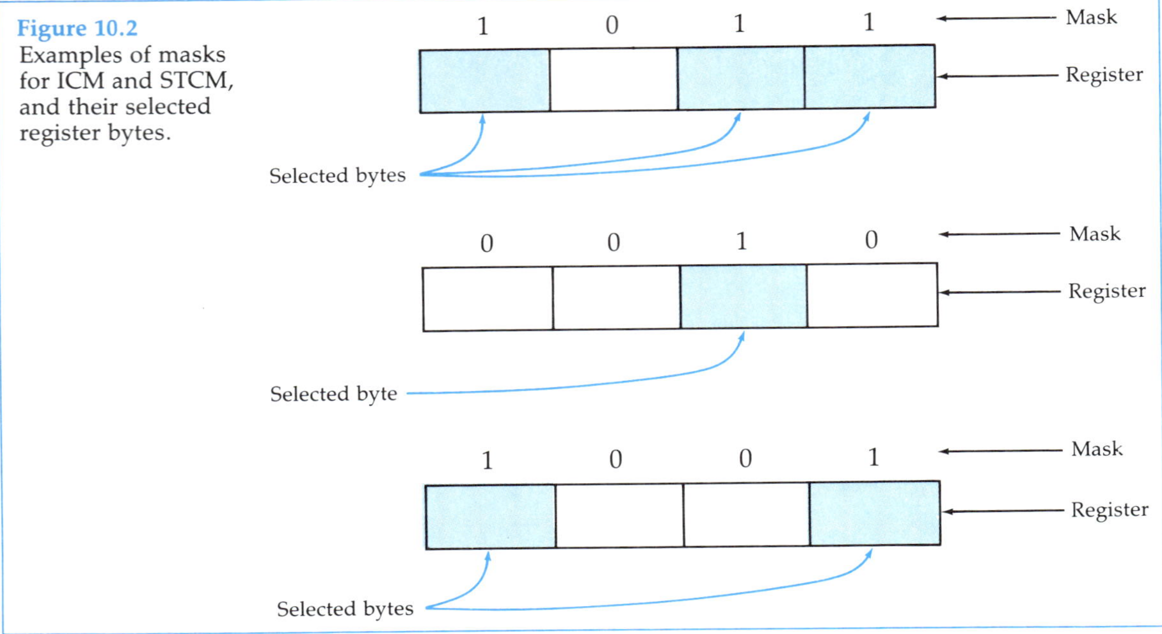


**Figure 10.2** Examples of masks for ICM and STCM, and their selected register bytes.

register bytes are unchanged. Conversely, STCM stores the selected register bytes into *consecutive* bytes of storage at the effective address. ICM sets the condition code, but STCM does not. The instructions can be summarized as follows:

| Operation | Operand | Format | Instruction Name | Action |
|---|---|---|---|---|
| **ICM** | *R1,M3,S2* or *R1,M3,D2(B2)* | RS | INSERT CHARACTERS UNDER MASK | Loads bytes in *R1*, which are selected according to the mask *M3*, from consecutive bytes at *E2* |
| | | | Cond. Code = | 0 if the inserted bytes are zero, or M3 = 0<br>1 if the leftmost bit of the inserted bytes is 1<br>2 if the inserted bytes are not zero, but the leftmost bit is 0 |
| **STCM** | *R1,M3,S2* or *R1,M3,D2(B2)* | RS | STORE CHARACTERS UNDER MASK | Stores bytes of *R1*, which are selected according to the mask *M3*, into the consecutive bytes at *E2*. The condition code is unchanged. |

Usually the clearest way to specify the mask *M3* is with a binary self-defining term.

In the following examples, X, Y, and Z represent addresses in storage. Be sure to notice that the mask selects only register bytes and not bytes in storage. The bytes in storage are always consecutive.

EXAMPLE 3

```
ICM     2,B'0101',X
```

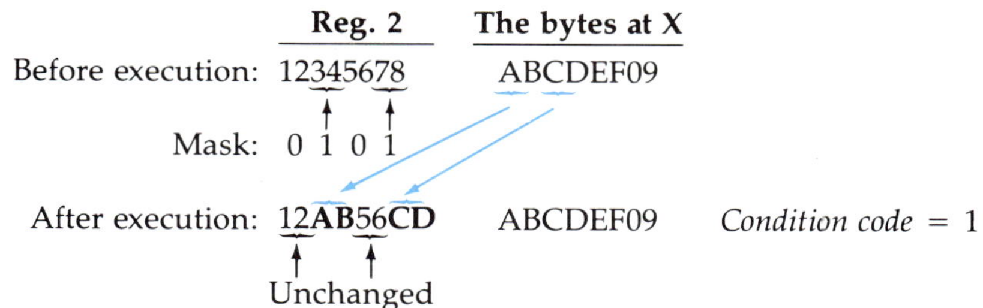


Since the second and fourth bits of the mask are 1, the second and fourth bytes of Register 2 are loaded from the consecutive bytes at X. Since the leftmost bit of the hexadecimal quantity ABCD is 1, the condition code is set to 1.

EXAMPLE 4

```
ICM     5,B'1111',Y
```

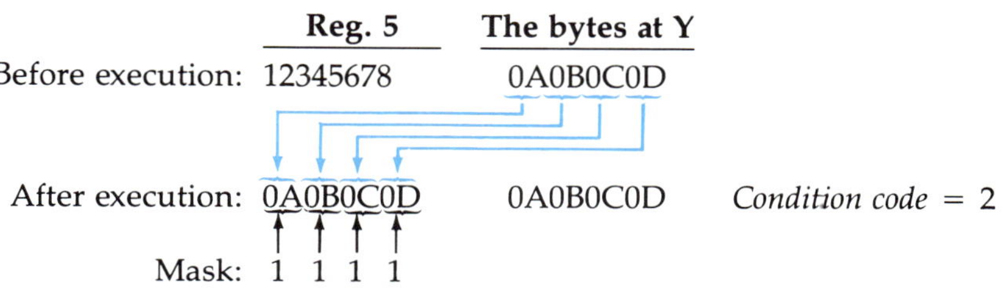


The mask selects all 4 bytes of Register 5 so that they are loaded from the 4 consecutive bytes at Y. Since the hexadecimal quantity 0A0B0C0D is nonzero and its leftmost bit is 0, the condition code is set to 2. In this form, the instruction has the same effect as the sequence

```
L       5,Y
LTR     5,5
```

EXAMPLE 5

```
STCM    7,B'1011',Z
```

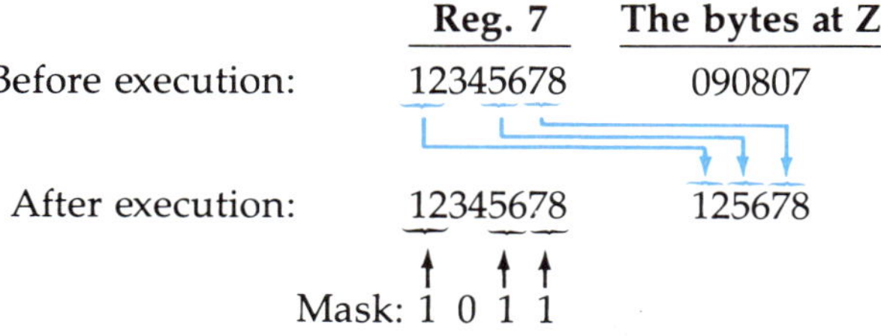


The first, third, and fourth bytes of Register 7 are stored into the three consecutive bytes at Z. The condition code is unchanged.

## SELF-TEST EXERCISES

1. Assume that the bytes at DATA contain F5F6F7F8. Also assume the following:

   Reg. 4 = 40F1F2F3  Reg. 7 = 00000002

   Indicate how each of the following instructions affects these quantities and the condition code.

   a. `IC 4,DATA`
   b. `IC 4,DATA+1`
   c. `STC 4,DATA`
   d. `STC 4,DATA(7)`
   e. `STC 4,DATA+3`
   f. `ICM 4,B'1001',DATA`
   g. `ICM 4,7,DATA`
   h. `ICM 4,B'0010',X'0'`
   i. `ICM 4,0,DATA+2`
   j. `ICM 4,B'0110',=C'$*'`
   k. `STCM 4,B'1101',DATA`
   l. `STCM 4,2,DATA+1`
   m. `STCM 4,X'1',DATA`
   n. `STCM 4,B'0110',DATA`
   o. `STCM 4,9,DATA`

2. Write the machine language instructions that are represented by the statements in Self-Test Exercise 1d and 1k. Assume that Register 12 is the base register and that DATA is 4A8 bytes beyond the base address.
3. For each of the following, write a STCM instruction that produces an equivalent effect:

   a. `ST 2,W`  b. `STH 2,H`  c. `STC 2,C`

4. a. Write an ICM instruction that has the same effect on Register 6 as

   ```
   IC      6,BYTE
   ```

   b. What is an advantage and a disadvantage of using the ICM instruction as a substitute for the IC instruction?

## Copying Bytes in Storage: The Move Instructions

The Move instructions copy data directly from one portion of storage to another. Of these, one instruction affects individual bytes, while another involves groups of up to 256 consecutive bytes. This section introduces two new instruction formats, SI and SS, to accomplish this.

### *The Storage and Immediate Data (SI) Instruction Format*

Instructions in the SI format require 4 bytes and specify 2 operands. The machine language form appears as follows:

**The SI format**

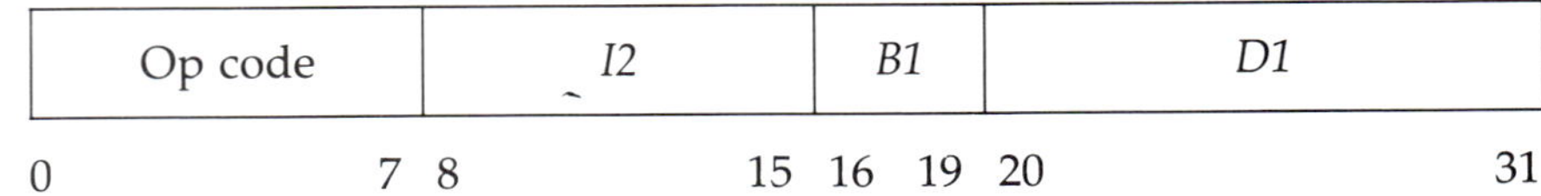


The first operand is a single byte in storage whose effective address *E1* is specified by a base register *B1* and a displacement *D1*. The second operand is an 8-bit quantity that is contained in the second byte of the instruction itself, rather than in a register or elsewhere in storage. This operand is denoted here as *I2* and is called **immediate data.** You specify *I2* in assembler language by writing either a self-defining term, an absolute symbol, or some other absolute expression. The use of immediate data is an unusual aspect that distinguishes the SI format from the other formats.

The mnemonic operation codes for most, but not all, SI instructions end in I.

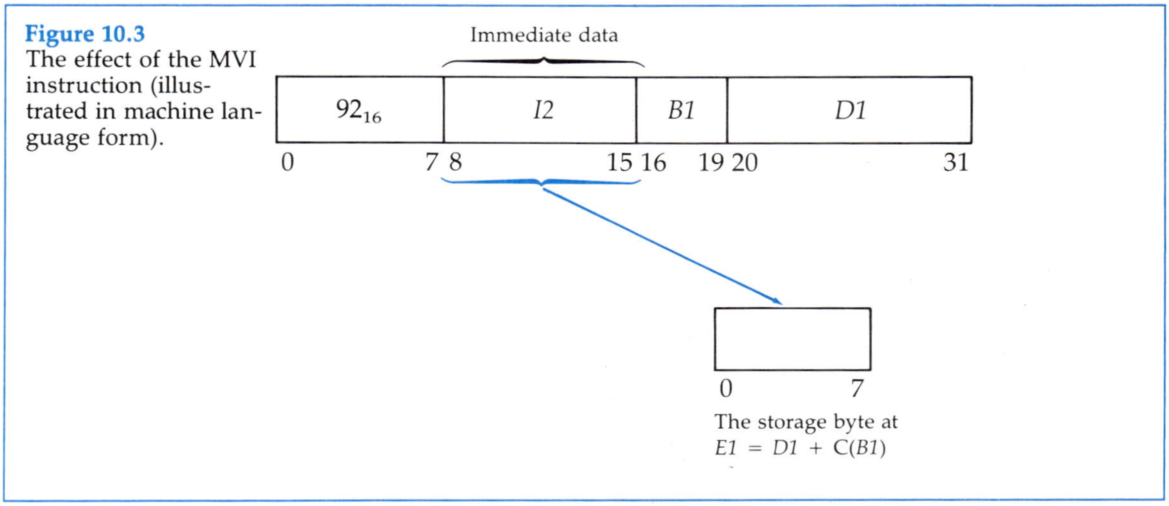


**Figure 10.3** The effect of the MVI instruction (illustrated in machine language form).

## *The Move Immediate (MVI) Instruction*

**Change the contents of a single byte**

The Move Immediate instruction, illustrated in Figure 10.3, replaces the contents of a single byte in storage with the immediate data that is contained in the second byte of the instruction. For notational convenience, let C(*E1*) denote $C(E1)_{0-7}$, the contents of the byte at the effective address *E1*. The instruction can be summarized as follows:

| Operation | Operand | Format | Instruction Name | Action |
|---|---|---|---|---|
| **MVI** | *S1,I2* or *D1(B1),I2* | SI | MOVE IMMEDIATE | C(*E1*) ← *I2* |

In the following examples, D represents the address of a byte in storage.

---

EXAMPLE 6

```
MVI     D,X'5B'
```

| | **The byte at D** |
|---|---|
| Before execution: | A1 |
| After execution: | 5B |

The contents of D are replaced by the second operand $5B_{16}$, which is contained in the second byte of the MVI instruction. The machine language form of this MVI instruction is

925BCE48

assuming that the base register is 12 and the effective address represented by D is $E48_{16}$ bytes beyond the base address.

*Do not confuse the self-defining term X'5B' with the literal =X'5B', which denotes a byte elsewhere in storage.*

---

Character self-defining terms are often used with SI instructions

*Character Self-Defining Terms.* Move instructions frequently involve character data. For example, you can use the MVI instruction to place a character in its EBCDIC form into a byte of storage. In fact, the self-defining term X'5B' that was used in Example 6 represents the EBCDIC form of the character $. Rather than using a hexadecimal self-defining term, you can have the assembler supply the correct EBCDIC value by writing a character self-defining term

C'*x*'

where *x* represents any character. Recall that you can use character self-defining terms interchangeably with decimal, binary, and hexadecimal self-defining terms as desired to specify absolute quantities in the operand entries of any instruction.

---

EXAMPLE 7

```
MVI     D,C'$'
```

| | The byte at D |
|---|---|
| Before execution: | A1 |
| After execution: | 5B |

Since C'$' and X'5B' have the same meaning, this instruction is exactly the same as the one in Example 6.

---

EXAMPLE 8

The following instructions are equivalent:

```
MVI  D,C'$'
MVI  D,X'5B'
MVI  D,B'01011011'
MVI  D,91
MVI  D,DOLLAR
```

Here, DOLLAR is defined by

DOLLAR EQU C'$' *or* X'5B' *or* B'01011011' *or* 91

In all cases, the second operand is specified by an absolute quantity and designates the same 8-bit pattern, which is the EBCDIC for the character $.

---

## *The Storage and Storage (SS) Instruction Format*

The SS instructions are distinctive in that they have two storage operands. There are three slightly different forms of the SS format; this section discusses one form now, and Chapter 14 will introduce a second form later. The third form, which is used for certain semiprivileged instructions, is beyond the scope of this text. In the form discussed here, each operand is a group of from 1 to 256 consecutive bytes; the operands are of the same length. They are designated in assembler language as

*S1(L),S2*
or *S1(L),D2(B2)*
or *D1(L,B1),S2*
or *D1(L,B1),D2(B2)*

The length *L*, when stated explicitly as it is here, must be an absolute quantity. However, you can omit *L* and have the assembler supply the length, as you shall see later.

In machine language, SS instructions require 6 bytes and, as such, they are the longest in the instruction set. The machine language form appears as follows:

**The SS format**

| Op code | *L* − 1 | *B1* | *D1* | *B2* | *D2* |
|---|---|---|---|---|---|
| 0 7 | 8 15 | 16 19 | 20 31 | 32 35 | 36 47 |

Notice that, although you designate the actual length *L* when writing the assembler language instruction, it is represented internally as *L* − 1. This is done so that the values 0 to 255 as represented by one byte can denote lengths from 1 to 256.

## *The Move Characters (MVC) Instruction*

**Copy a character string**

The Move Characters instruction copies (moves) *L* consecutive bytes, or characters, from one place in storage to another. In particular, the **source bytes** of the second operand are copied and replace the **destination bytes** of the first operand. The notation $C(E)_{L\ \text{bytes}}$ will be used to denote the contents of the *L* consecutive bytes at the effective address *E*. The instruction has the following form:

| Operation | Operand | Format | Instruction Name | Action |
|---|---|---|---|---|
| **MVC** | *S1(L),S2*<br>or *S1(L),D2(B2)*<br>or *D1(L,B1),S2*<br>or *D1(L,B1),D2(B2)* | SS | MOVE CHARACTERS | $C(E1)_{L\ \text{bytes}} \leftarrow C(E2)_{L\ \text{bytes}}$ |

EXAMPLE 9

```
MVC     B(5),A
```

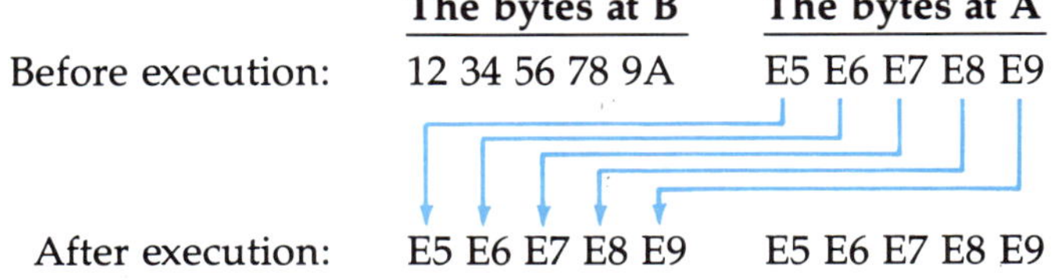


Copies of the 5 bytes at A replace the contents of the 5 bytes at B.

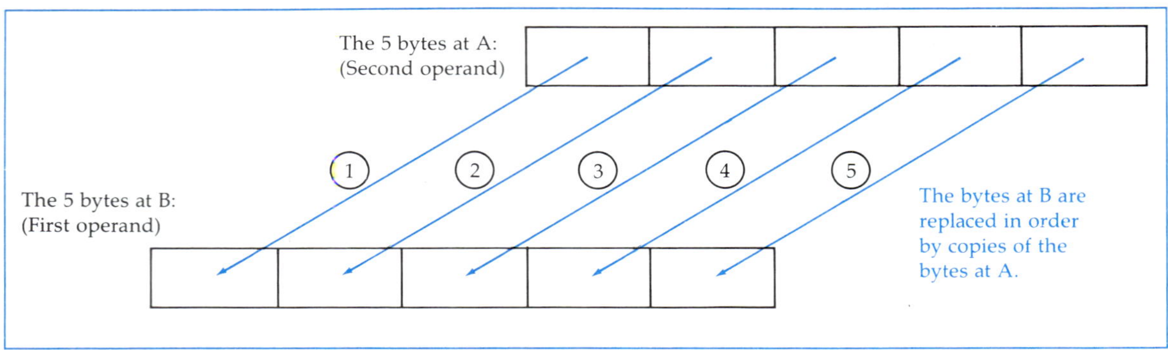


**Figure 10.4**
The effect of
`MVC B(5),A`
on the field at B.

MVC moves bytes one at a time from left to right. In Example 9, the leftmost byte at A was copied and replaced the leftmost byte at B. Next the byte at A + 1 was copied and replaced the byte at B + 1, and so on, as illustrated in Figure 10.4. Knowing this is important only when the two operands overlap, either partially or entirely, as in the next examples.

---

EXAMPLE 10

```
MVC     CH+1(5),CH
```

| | The bytes at CH as characters |
|---|---|
| Before execution: | R S T U V W |
| After execution: | R R R R R R |

The operands describe two fields: the 5 bytes at CH contain the characters RSTUV and the 5 bytes at CH+1 contain the characters STUVW. The leftmost character at CH (the R) is copied and replaces the leftmost character at CH+1 (the S). The second character at CH is now an R; it is copied and replaces the second character at CH+1 (the T). This continues until 5 characters are copied. At that time, each of the 6 bytes at CH contains the character R. The process is pictured in Figure 10.5.

You can use this technique to initialize each byte in a field to a single value, as shown in the next example.

---

EXAMPLE 11

**Initialize a Field to Blanks**

The following initializes each of the 200 bytes at AREA to the character blank:

```
MVI  AREA,C' '            SET THE BYTE AT AREA TO BLANK
MVC  AREA+1(199),AREA     PROPAGATE IT THROUGH THE FIELD
```

After the byte at AREA is initialized to a blank, it is propagated throughout the remaining consecutive bytes at AREA in the same manner that was used in Example 10. The prior contents of the bytes at AREA are irrelevant.

---

The 5 bytes at CH (Second operand)
Before execution:
R S T U V W
The 5 bytes at CH+1 (First operand)
R R T U V W
R R R U V W
R R R R V W
R R R R R W
After execution:
R R R R R R

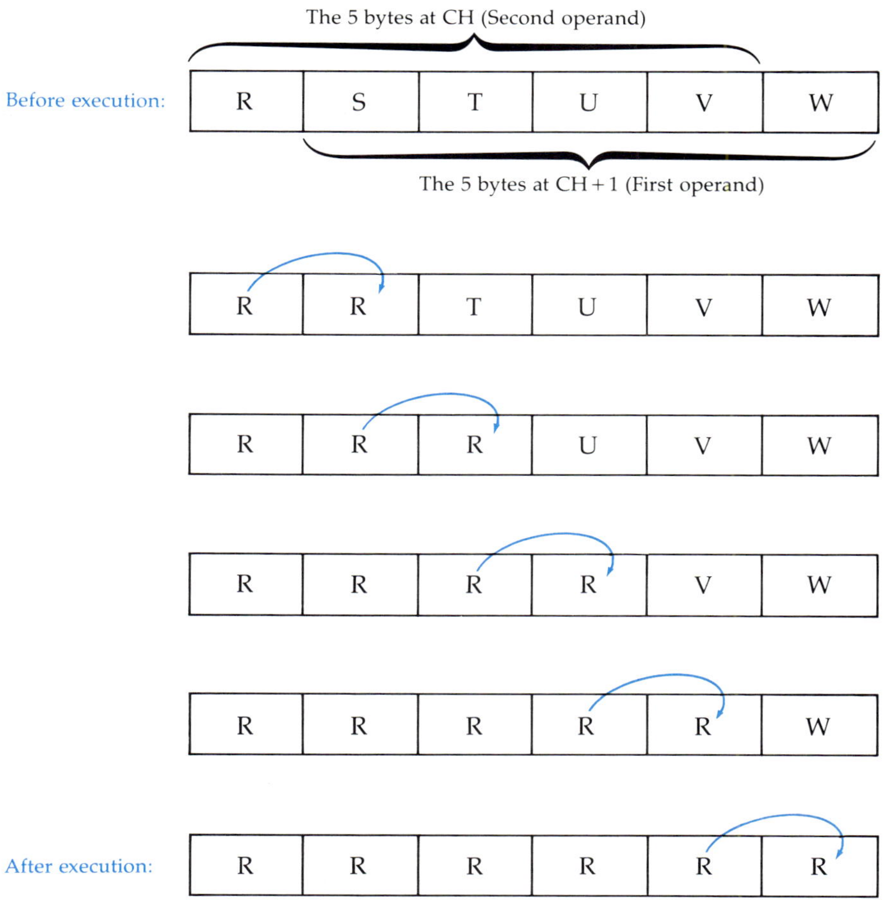

**Figure 10.5**
The effect of `MVC CH+1(5), CH` on the field at CH, as described in Example 10.

Source field
Overlap
Destination field

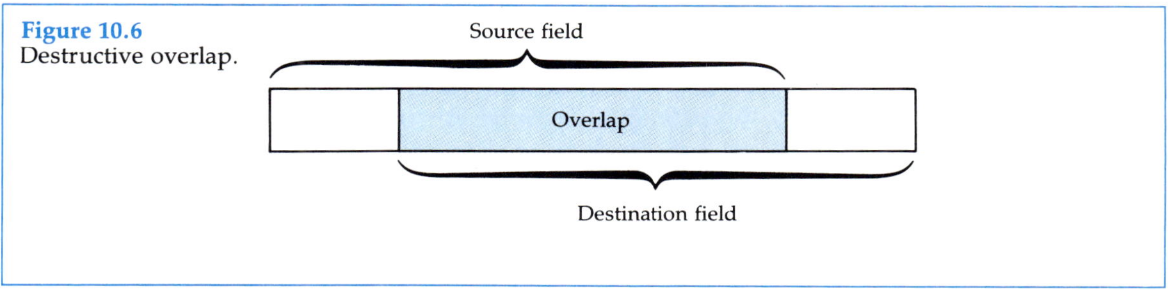

**Figure 10.6**
Destructive overlap.

Examples 10 and 11 demonstrated a situation known as **destructive overlap.** As illustrated in Figure 10.6, this situation occurs when, first, the source field (the second operand) overlaps with the destination field (the first operand) and, second, the destination field begins at an address higher than the beginning of the source field (or, equivalently, the first byte of the destination field is within the source field).

EXAMPLE 12

**Move a Character String Up in Storage (Operands Overlap)**

Sometimes, you must move a character string up (to a higher address) or down (to a lower address) in storage. No special considerations are necessary when the character string and the field to which it will be moved occupy distinct bytes. In Example 10, however, the intention may have been to move the characters RSTUV up in storage by one byte, but the operand overlap caused destruction of the characters and produced RRRRR. Instead, the following sequence is necessary. Assume that A and TEMP represent distinct areas of storage:

```
MVC   TEMP(5),A       MAKE A COPY OF THE CHARACTERS
MVC   A+1(5),TEMP     MOVE THEM INTO THEIR NEW PLACE
```

| | The bytes at TEMP as characters | The bytes at A as characters |
|---|---|---|
| Before execution: | X X X X X | R S T U V W |
| After execution of first MVC: | R S T U V | R S T U V W |
| After execution of second MVC: | R S T U V | R R S T U V |

The characters at A have been moved up in storage by one byte.

EXAMPLE 13

**Move a Character String Down in Storage (Operands Overlap)**

You can copy a character string to a lower address by using one MVC instruction, even though the operands overlap, as the following demonstrates:

```
MVC      X(6),X+4
```

| | The bytes at X as characters |
|---|---|
| Before execution: | A B C D E F G H I J (Second operand: E F G H I J) |
| After execution: | E F G H I J G H I J (First operand: E F G H I J; Unchanged: G H I J) |

Each of the two operands consists of 6 characters. The 6 bytes at X contain the characters ABCDEF, while the 6 bytes at X+4 contain the characters EFGHIJ. The last 2 bytes of the first operand are the same as the first 2 bytes of the second operand. Despite this overlap, copies of the 6 characters at X+4 replace the 6 bytes at X. However, a portion of the original contents of the second operand is changed due to the overlap.

**Figure 10.7**
Nondestructive overlap.

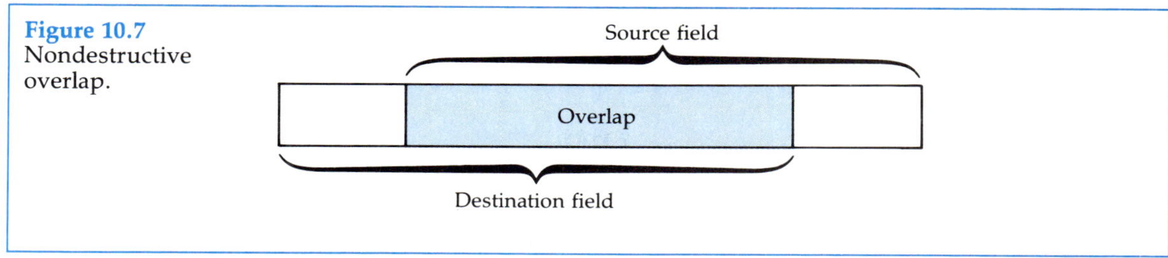


Example 13 demonstrated a situation known as **nondestructive overlap.** As is illustrated in Figure 10.7, this occurs when, first, the source field overlaps with the destination field and, second, the destination field begins at an address lower than the beginning of the source field (or equivalently, the first byte of the destination field is not within the source field).

---

EXAMPLE 14

```
MVC   B(1),A
MVC   B(0),A
```

These instructions are equivalent since the assembler generates the same machine language instruction in each case. You use the latter form in special cases when the actual length is modified during execution. The next chapter will cover this situation.

---

## *The Move Inverse (MVCIN) Instruction*

**Reverse the order of a string**

The Move Inverse instruction is available as an optional feature on the IBM 370 and 4300 series computers. It is similar to the MVC instruction, but the order of the bytes is reversed as they are copied. Thus, the instruction causes the *L* consecutive bytes of the first operand to be replaced left to right by the *L* consecutive bytes, taken right to left, of the second operand. There is an important distinction between the MVCIN instruction and all other SS-format instructions: the second operand entry designates the address of the *rightmost* byte of the second operand. The instruction can be summarized as follows:

| Operation | Operand | Format | Instruction Name | Action |
|---|---|---|---|---|
| **MVCIN** | *S1(L),S2*<br>or *S1(L),D2(B2)*<br>or *D1(L,B1),S2*<br>or *D1(L,B1),D2(B2)* | SS | MOVE INVERSE | $C(E1)_{L\ \text{bytes}} \leftarrow C(E2-L+1)_{L\ \text{bytes}}$ in reverse order |

The results of this instruction are unpredictable if the operands overlap by more than one byte.

EXAMPLE 15 **MVCIN B(5),A+4**

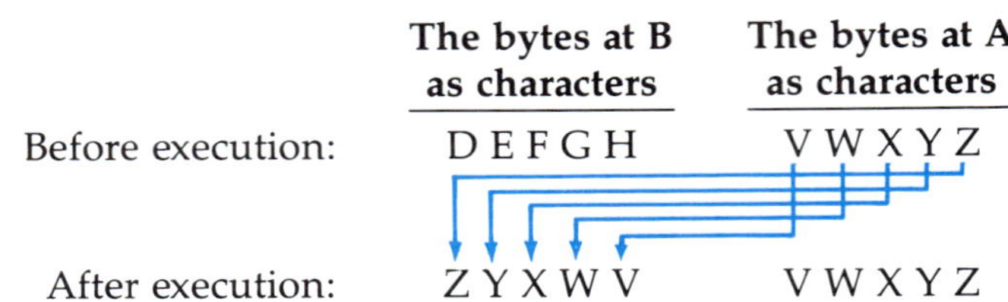


This instruction causes the contents of the 5 bytes at B to be replaced by copies of the 5 bytes at A taken in reverse order. The instruction proceeds as follows: the byte at A+4 (the Z) is moved to the byte at B; the byte at A+3 (the Y) is moved to the byte at B+1, and so forth. Note that the second operand is designated by A+4, the address of the second operand's rightmost byte.

## SELF-TEST EXERCISES

5. Assume the following sequence:

```
X        DC    C'AB'
Y        DC    C'CDEF'
```

Indicate the effect that each of the following instructions has on the bytes defined by X and Y.

**a.** `MVI Y,C'Z'`
**b.** `MVI Y+1,64`
**c.** `MVC X(4),Y`
**d.** `MVC Y(4),X`
**e.** `MVC X(3),=C'RST'`
**f.** `MVC Y(4),=4C'$'`
**g.** `MVCIN X(2),Y+2`
**h.** `MVCIN Y+1(3),Y`

6. Discuss the similarities and differences of the instructions

```
MVI   BYTE,C'$'
```

and

```
MVC   BYTE(1),=C'$'
```

7. Write instructions to move the 5 bytes at DATA up in storage by 3 bytes. For example, if DATA contains the characters ABCDEFGH, then after execution of the instructions, the bytes at DATA should contain ABCABCDE.

8. The instruction

```
MVC   HEADING(120),=12C'0123456789'
```

initializes a 120-byte array at HEADING to

01234567890123456789 . . . 0123456789

but uses a 120-byte literal constant. Write a sequence of two MVC instructions that accomplishes the same thing, but only uses a 10-byte literal constant.

# Logical Comparisons

**Quantities are compared as unsigned binary integers**

As was noted in Chapter 9, logical instructions treat their operands as unsigned binary integers. This section considers instructions that compare two such operands and then set the condition code according to whether the comparison is equal, less than, or greater than. As unsigned integers, $00000000_{16}$ is less than $FFFFFFFF_{16}$. (As signed integers, the opposite is true.) Frequently, unsigned binary quantities represent characters in EBCDIC. By design, the numeric codes for characters provide an order consistent with alphabetic order. The blank ($40_{16}$) appears first in this order. Next come punctuation marks and most other special symbols, followed by the lowercase letters, the uppercase letters, and finally the digits 0 through 9. (Refer to Figure 5.25 or Appendix D.)

Depending upon the format of the instruction, the quantities to be compared can be either in registers or in storage as fullwords or groups of 1 to 256 consecutive bytes. The comparison of two operands proceeds a byte at a time from left to right, until a comparison is unequal or until the end of the operands is encountered. Logical Compare instructions are available in RR, RX, SI, and SS formats.

## *Comparisons With a Register Operand: CLR, CL, and CLM*

**Fullword comparisons**

The instructions Compare Logical Register (CLR) and Compare Logical (CL) are analogous to CR and C, but the comparisons are logical instead of arithmetic. (The Compare Logical Under Mask instruction will be discussed later.) The CLR and CL instructions can be summarized as follows:

| Operation | Operand | Format | Instruction Name | Action |
|---|---|---|---|---|
| **CLR** | *R1,R2* | RR | COMPARE LOGICAL REGISTERS | Compares C(*R1*) with C(*R2*)<br>Condition code = { 0 if the comparison is equal; 1 if the first operand is less than the second; 2 if the first operand is greater than the second } |
| **CL** | *R1,S2*<br>or *R1,S2(X2)*<br>or *R1,D2(X2,B2)* | RX | COMPARE LOGICAL | Compares C(*R1*) with $C(E2)_{0-31}$<br>The condition code is set as for CLR. |

As you shall see in the next examples, logical and arithmetic comparisons have equivalent results if the operands, when treated as signed quantities, have the same sign.

EXAMPLE 16

**CLR 4,6**

| Reg. 4 | Reg. 6 | |
|---|---|---|
| F1ABC3E2 | 01ABC3E2 | *Condition code* = 2 |

As unsigned integers, the contents of Register 4 are greater than the contents of Register 6; thus, the condition code is set to 2. Had the instruction been CR, the condition code would have been 1 since, as signed integers, F1ABC3E2 is negative and 01ABC3E2 is positive.

EXAMPLE 17

**CL 7,X**

| Reg. 7 | The fullword at X | |
|---|---|---|
| FFFFFFFE | FFFFFFFF | *Condition code* = 1 |

As unsigned integers, the contents of Register 7 are less than the contents of the fullword at X. The condition code is set to 1. As signed quantities, FFFFFFFE represents −2 and FFFFFFFF represents −1; had the instruction been C instead of CL, the condition code would still be set to 1.

**Comparisons of 1-byte to 4-byte operands**

The Compare Logical Under Mask (CLM) instruction is an RS instruction that uses a mask *M3* as defined for ICM and STCM. Bytes of the first register operand, which is designated by *R1*, that correspond to 1's in the mask are treated as contiguous data. These bytes are compared with the same number of *consecutive* bytes that begin at the second operand address. The instruction can be summarized as follows:

| Operation | Operand | Format | Instruction Name | Action |
|---|---|---|---|---|
| **CLM** | *R1,M3,S2* or *R1,M3,D2(B2)* | RS | COMPARE LOGICAL UNDER MASK | Compares bytes of *R1*, selected according to *M3*, with the consecutive bytes at *E2* |

Condition code =
- 0 if the operands are equal, or *M3* = 0
- 1 if the first operand is less than the second
- 2 if the first operand is greater than the second

EXAMPLE 18

```
CLM    4,B'1010',X
```

| | Reg. 4 | The bytes at X | |
|---|---|---|---|
| | **12**34**56**78 | **1256**ABCD | *Condition code* = 0 |
| Mask: | 1 0 1 0 | | |

The instruction causes the first and third bytes of Register 4 to be selected since the first and third bits of the mask are 1. The bytes contain $1256_{16}$, which is equal to the contents of the first 2 bytes at X. Therefore, the condition code is set to 0.

## *Comparisons Without a Register Operand: CLI and CLC*

**Comparisons of single bytes or groups of bytes**

The instructions Compare Logical Immediate (CLI) and Compare Logical Characters (CLC) compare operands in storage as if they were unsigned integers. The instructions can be summarized as follows:

| Operation | Operand | Format | Instruction Name | Action |
|---|---|---|---|---|
| **CLI** | *S1,I2*<br>or *D1(B1),I2* | SI | COMPARE LOGICAL IMMEDIATE | Compares C(*E1*) with *I2* |
| **CLC** | *S1(L),S2*<br>or *S1(L),D2(B2)*<br>or *D1(L,B1),S2*<br>or *D1(L,B1),D2(B2)* | SS | COMPARE LOGICAL CHARACTERS | Compares $C(E1)_{L\ \text{bytes}}$ with $C(E2)_{L\ \text{bytes}}$ |

For both instructions, the condition code settings are the same as for CLR or CL.

EXAMPLE 19

```
CLI    X,C'$'
```

| The byte at X | |
|---|---|
| 5B | *Condition code* = 0 |

The byte at X contains a value equal to the value that is defined by the self-defining term C'$'. Therefore, the condition code is set to 0.

EXAMPLE 20

```
CLC     X(5),Y
```

| The bytes at X as characters | The bytes at Y as characters | |
|---|---|---|
| D E F G H | D E F G J | *Condition code* = 1 |

The string DEFGH is less than DEFGJ since H is less than J. The condition code is set to 1.

**SELF-TEST EXERCISE**

9. Assume that

Reg. 8 = 405BF9F0
Reg. 9 = C1C2C3C4

and that the bytes at W contain C1C2F1F2. Indicate how each of the following instructions affects the condition code.

**a.** `CLR    8,9`
**b.** `CR     8,9`
**c.** `CL     9,W`
**d.** `C      9,W`
**e.** `CLM    9,B'1100',W`
**f.** `CLM    8,B'0010',W+3`
**g.** `CLM    9,B'0101',=C'BD'`
**h.** `CLI    W,C'1'`
**i.** `CLI    W+3,X'40'`
**j.** `CLC    W(2),W+2`
**k.** `CLC    W+1(3),=C'BCD'`
**l.** `CLC    W(2),=C'$$'`
**m.** `CLC    W+2(2),=C'12'`

## Processing Character Arrays

Arrays of character data occur frequently in many applications. Such arrays might be character strings in which each array element is simply one byte. Other arrays might have elements that are themselves character strings, such as in a list of names. It is natural to reference array elements with a subscript, but an implementation with an index register is possible only if you use RX instructions. As mentioned earlier, the instructions IC and STC are the only byte-oriented RX instructions available and, although this fact makes them important, their application to these problems is limited. The SI and SS instructions are more useful, but they do not permit an index register. Even so, you can use SI and SS instructions to address array elements, as the next examples will demonstrate. The same technique is applicable to RS instructions, such as ICM, STCM, and CLM.

EXAMPLE 21

**Replace Every Tenth Character in a String**

**Two approaches to processing character arrays**

Suppose that you have a string of 120 characters at STRING and that you wish to replace the first and every tenth character thereafter with an asterisk. The instructions that are listed in Figure 10.8 accomplish this. The

**Figure 10.8**
The first solution of Example 21.

```
** REPLACE EVERY TENTH CHARACTER IN STRING BY AN ASTERISK
         LA    R2,12          R2 = LOOP COUNTER = 12
         LA    R4,STRING      R4 = STRING POINTER = BEGINNING ADDRESS
LOOP     MVI   0(R4),C'*'     REPLACE BYTE BY *
         LA    R4,10(R4)      INCREMENT POINTER BY 10
         BCT   R2,LOOP        DECREMENT COUNTER; REPEAT IF NOT ZERO
```

**Figure 10.9**
The second solution of Example 21.

```
** REPLACE EVERY TENTH CHARACTER IN STRING BY AN ASTERISK
         LA    R2,12          R2 = LOOP COUNTER = 12
         SR    R3,R3          R3 = STRING INDEX = 0
LOOP     LA    R4,STRING(R3)  R4 = STRING POINTER
         MVI   0(R4),C'*'     REPLACE BYTE BY *
         LA    R3,10(R3)      INCREMENT INDEX BY 10
         BCT   R2,LOOP        DECREMENT COUNTER; REPEAT IF NOT ZERO
```

affected bytes are at the addresses that are represented by STRING, STRING + 10, STRING + 20, and so on to STRING + 110. Notice how Register 4 points to these bytes and how the MVI instruction uses it to change their contents.

A variation of this solution is given in Figure 10.9: Register 3 counts 0, 10, 20, and so on to 110. An LA instruction uses this register as an index to compute the address of every tenth byte. As in the previous solution, Register 4 takes on the values STRING, STRING + 10, and so on, and is used in the same way by the MVI instruction.

If you compare the two solutions, you find that the second solution requires an additional register and has one more instruction in its loop. Using an index register is not always a more expensive approach but, even if it is, it can be convenient. Both techniques will be used again in later examples.

---

EXAMPLE 22

## Count the Number of Characters in a Nonblank String

A common problem is to determine the length of a particular character string. To do so, you must know where the string begins and have enough information to determine where the string ends. You can take several approaches to this problem. To see this, consider two solutions to the problem of counting the number of consecutive nonblank characters, if any, that exist at the beginning of an 80-byte area at the address DATA.

**Count each character**

*Solution 1.* The logic of the first solution is straightforward. Starting at the address DATA, you examine each byte and increment a counter each time that you encounter a nonblank character. Stop as soon as you find a blank, so that the counter will contain the number of consecutive nonblank characters beginning at DATA. The instructions to accomplish this are listed in Figure 10.10.

This solution counts only consecutive nonblank characters beginning at DATA and ignores other characters that may exist after a blank in the 80-byte area. If the first byte at DATA is blank, the counter will contain a value

**Figure 10.10**
The first solution of Example 22.

```
** DETERMINE THE LENGTH OF A CHARACTER STRING AT DATA
         SR    R2,R2           R2 = COUNTER
         LA    R3,DATA         R3 = STRING POINTER = BEGINNING ADDRESS
* WHILE CHARACTER IN STRING IS NOT BLANK DO:
LOOP     CLI   0(R3),C' '      IS CHARACTER BLANK?
         BE    OUT             IF SO, EXIT LOOP
         LA    R2,1(R2)        ELSE COUNT NONBLANK CHARACTER
         LA    R3,1(R3)        POINT TO NEXT CHARACTER
         B     LOOP            REPEAT
* END WHILE
OUT      ----
** AT THIS POINT, C(R2) = LENGTH OF CHARACTER STRING
         .
         .
         .
DATA     DS    80C
         DC    C' '            FORCED BLANK TO PREVENT AN INFINITE LOOP
```

**Figure 10.11**
An alternative to the first solution of Example 22.

```
** DETERMINE THE LENGTH OF A CHARACTER STRING AT DATA
         SR    R2,R2           R2 = INDEX AND COUNTER
* WHILE CHARACTER IN STRING IS NOT BLANK DO:
LOOP     LA    R3,DATA(R2)     R3 = POINTER TO NEXT CHARACTER IN STRING
         CLI   0(R3),C' '      IS CHARACTER BLANK?
         BE    OUT             IF SO, EXIT LOOP
         LA    R2,1(R2)        ELSE COUNT NONBLANK CHARACTER
         B     LOOP            REPEAT
* END WHILE
OUT      ----
** AT THIS POINT, C(R2) = LENGTH OF CHARACTER STRING
         .
         .
         .
DATA     DS    80C
         DC    C' '            FORCED BLANK TO PREVENT AN INFINITE LOOP
```

of zero. However, suppose that none of the 80 bytes at DATA is blank. Notice that the only exit from the loop occurs when a blank character is found. You could provide alternative loop control to guard against looping more than 80 times, but it is much easier to define a blank character (a *sentinel*) immediately after the eightieth byte of the area, as is done here.

An alternate implementation of this approach, listed in Figure 10.11, uses an index register. Both implementations use the same number of registers and have loops that contain the same instructions (although they use different operands and are in a different order). Here, the choice is one of personal preference.

**Locate the beginning and end of the string, and then compute its length**

*Solution 2.* A different approach is to determine the beginning of the string (here, you know that it begins at DATA) and the end of the string. The length of the string is the difference between the address of the byte after the end of the string and the address of the beginning of the string. Figure 10.12 illustrates calculating the length of the string ABCD. Here, DATA+4 represents the address of the byte after the string; the difference between DATA+4 and DATA is 4, which is the length of the string. The instructions for this approach are listed in Figure 10.13.

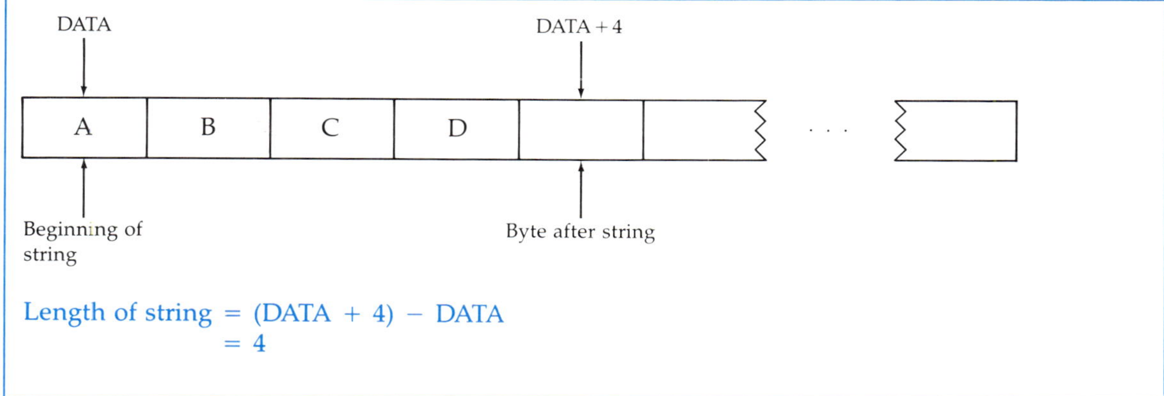


Length of string = (DATA + 4) − DATA
= 4

**Figure 10.12**
Determining the length of the character string ABCD.

**Figure 10.13**
The second solution of Example 22.

```
*** DETERMINE THE LENGTH OF A CHARACTER STRING AT DATA
         LA    R3,DATA          R3 = STRING POINTER = BEGINNING ADDRESS
** FIND BLANK AFTER STRING:
* WHILE CHARACTER IN STRING IS NOT BLANK DO:
LOOP     CLI   0(R3),C' '       IS CHARACTER BLANK?
         BE    OUT              IF SO, EXIT LOOP
         LA    R3,1(R3)         ELSE POINT TO NEXT CHARACTER
         B     LOOP             REPEAT
* END WHILE
*
** COMPUTE LENGTH OF STRING:
OUT      LA    R4,DATA          GET STARTING ADDRESS
         SR    R3,R4            COMPUTE LENGTH OF STRING
** AT THIS POINT, C(R3) = LENGTH OF CHARACTER STRING
         .
         .
         .
DATA     DS    80C
         DC    C' '             FORCED BLANK TO PREVENT AN INFINITE LOOP
```

---

EXAMPLE 23

**Locate and Move a Nonblank Character String**

This example uses some of the same ideas as given in the previous example. DATA is the address of an 80-byte area—perhaps the result of reading an input record. Somewhere within this area is a nonblank character string that need not start at DATA. Imagine that you want to locate the string and move it to FIELD. Figure 10.14 shows this process.

To determine the address of the beginning of the string, examine the bytes starting at DATA until you encounter the first nonblank character. You must save this beginning address. To determine the end of the string, proceed as in the second solution of Example 22 and skip over the nonblank characters, finally stopping when a blank is found. To ensure that this blank will always exist, you again define a blank character after the eightieth byte at DATA. There are two common approaches to this problem. Both will be discussed, but the second solution cannot be completed until the EX instruction is introduced in the next chapter.

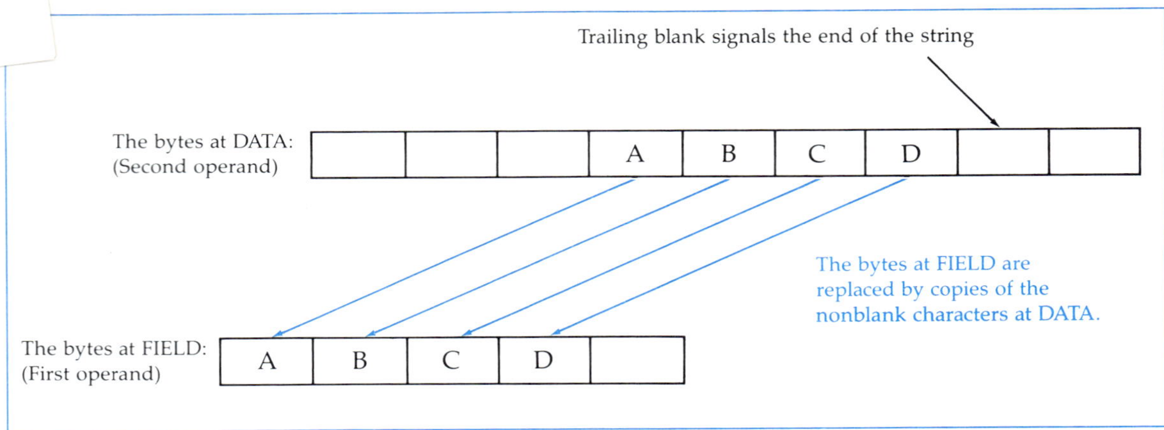


**Figure 10.14**
The process to locate and move a nonblank character string.

Both solutions begin by determining the starting address of the nonblank string.

**Move bytes one at a time**

*Solution 1.* After you have determined the starting address of the string, examine each successive byte one at a time until you find a blank. During your examination, move each of these nonblank characters to the consecutive bytes at FIELD. Figure 10.15 lists the instructions for this solution.

**Locate the beginning and end of a string, and then move it**

*Solution 2.* As before, determine the starting address of the string. Then skip over the nonblank characters and determine the address of the blank that follows the string. Do not move any characters to FIELD as you do this. Instead, compute the length of the string by subtracting its beginning

**Figure 10.15**
The first solution of Example 23.

```
*** LOCATE AND MOVE A NONBLANK CHARACTER STRING ONE BYTE AT A TIME
         LA    R3,DATA          R3 = DATA POINTER = BEGINNING ADDRESS
         LA    R4,FIELD         R4 = FIELD POINTER = BEGINNING ADDRESS
** FIND FIRST NONBLANK CHARACTER:
* WHILE CHARACTER IS BLANK DO:
LOOP     CLI   0(R3),C' '       BLANK?
         BNE   NONBLANK         IF NOT, EXIT LOOP
         LA    R3,1(R3)         POINT TO NEXT CHARACTER
         B     LOOP             REPEAT
* END WHILE
*
** MOVE NONBLANK CHARACTERS UNTIL BLANK IS FOUND:
* REPEAT:
NONBLANK MVC   0(1,R4),0(R3)    MOVE NONBLANK CHARACTER
         LA    R3,1(R3)         INCREMENT DATA POINTER
         LA    R4,1(R4)         INCREMENT FIELD POINTER
* UNTIL CHARACTER IS BLANK
         CLI   0(R3),C' '       BLANK?
         BNE   NONBLANK         IF NOT, REPEAT
* END REPEAT
         .
         .
         .
DATA     DS    80C
         DC    C' '             FORCED BLANK
FIELD    DS    80C
```

**Figure 10.16**
A part of the second solution of Example 23.

```
*** LOCATE AND MOVE A NONBLANK CHARACTER STRING
         LA    R3,DATA        R3 = DATA POINTER = BEGINNING ADDRESS
** FIND FIRST NONBLANK CHARACTER:
* WHILE CHARACTER IS BLANK DO:
LOOP     CLI   0(R3),C' '     BLANK?
         BNE   NONBLANK       IF NOT, EXIT LOOP
         LA    R3,1(R3)       POINT TO NEXT CHARACTER
         B     LOOP           REPEAT
* END WHILE
*
** MARK BEGINNING AND FIND END OF STRING:
NONBLANK LR    R5,R3          R5 = ADDRESS OF START OF STRING
* REPEAT:
LOOP2    LA    R3,1(R3)       POINT TO NEXT CHARACTER
* UNTIL CHARACTER IS BLANK
         CLI   0(R3),C' '     IS IT BLANK?
         BNE   LOOP2          IF NOT, REPEAT
* END REPEAT
** COMPUTE LENGTH OF STRING:
         SR    R3,R5          ADDRESS OF BLANK MINUS ADDRESS
*                               OF BEGINNING OF STRING
** AT THIS POINT, R3 CONTAINS THE LENGTH OF THE STRING.
** THE EX INSTRUCTION IS USED TO COMPLETE THIS PROGRAM SEGMENT.
         .
         .
         .
DATA     DS    80C
         DC    C' '           FORCED BLANK
FIELD    DS    80C
```

address from the address of the trailing blank. Figure 10.16 lists the instructions to accomplish this.

At this point, you know the beginning address of the string, you have computed its length, and you want to move it to FIELD. You should use the MVC instruction, but you cannot specify the length indirectly. This is important to note: the length specified in an SS instruction must be explicitly stated as an absolute quantity. You cannot specify it indirectly within a register in the same way that you can specify, for instance, a shift amount. For example, if you were to write

```
MVC   FIELD(R3),0(R4)
```

it would have exactly the same meaning as

```
MVC   FIELD(3),0(R4)
```

since R3 is an absolute symbol that was equated to 3. Three bytes would be moved to FIELD. In this context, R3 does not designate Register 3.

The SS instructions were not designed to accommodate this problem. The resolution to this difficulty is found in the Execute (EX) instruction, which will be discussed in the next chapter. This example will be completed at that time.

**SELF-TEST EXERCISES**

10. Write a sequence of instructions to count the number of commas in the 100-byte character string at STRING.
11. Write a sequence of instructions to count the number of times that the string ABC appears in the 240 characters at DATA.

## More Features of Assembler Language

This section introduces a few additional language constructs that are particularly useful in programs that involve character processing. These constructs also have other applications, which will be discussed in later chapters.

### *The Length Modifier for DC and DS*

The operand entry of both the DC and DS directives may optionally include a **length modifier** to state explicitly the length of the constant in bytes. The general form of the operand is then

*dt*L*n*'*c*'

where L*n* is the length modifier and where *n*, the constant length, is either a decimal self-defining term or a positive absolute expression that is enclosed in parentheses. The duplication factor *d* is the number of duplicate constants defined, *t* specifies the constant type, and *c* is the constant. The maximum value of *n* depends upon the constant type; the limits on *n* and the other characteristics of the length modifier are listed in Figure 10.17. When a length modifier is specified, no boundary alignment occurs.

**Figure 10.17** The characteristics of the length modifier for the DC and DS directives, according to the type of constant.

| Constant Type | Range of Length Modifier (bytes) | Truncation/ Padding Side | Padding With: |
|---|---|---|---|
| F | 1 to 8 | Left | 0's |
| H | 1 to 8 | Left | 0's |
| X | 1 to 256 | Left | 0's |
| B | 1 to 256 | Left | 0's |
| C | 1 to 256 | Right | Blanks |
| A | 1 to 4 | Left | 0's |

---

EXAMPLE 24

```
DC      CL5'ABC'
```

This instruction defines a 5-byte constant. The first 3 bytes contain the character codes for A, B, and C, respectively. The last 2 bytes contain blanks. Character constants are padded on the right with blanks if the explicit length is larger than necessary, as it is here.

EXAMPLE 25

```
DC      CL2'ABC'
```

This instruction defines a 2-byte constant that contains the characters A and B. For character constants, if the explicit length is smaller than required, truncation occurs on the right. This is a dangerous feature that you should not use ordinarily. Be alert for unintentional uses of this in your programs.

EXAMPLE 26

```
DC      XL3'123'
```

This instruction defines the hexadecimal constant 000123 in the next 3 bytes. The specified constant is padded on the left with zeros since the explicit length is larger than necessary.

EXAMPLE 27

```
DC      XL2'123456'
```

This instruction defines the 2-byte hexadecimal constant 3456. When the explicit length is less than that required by a specified numeric constant, truncation occurs on the left. This feature is as dangerous to use for numeric constants as it is for character constants.

EXAMPLE 28

```
DC      FL3'21'
```

This instruction defines a 3-byte constant that contains the two's complement binary equivalent of the decimal constant 21. In hexadecimal, the constant appears as 000015. No boundary alignment occurs even though the constant type is F. Certainly defining an F-type constant of length 3 seems to be a contradiction. Here, F is used to indicate that the specified constant is decimal and is to be converted to binary integer notation. Similar observations can be made for an H-type constant. Occasionally, this feature is convenient, but you should use it with care.

EXAMPLE 29

```
DS      FL3
```

The next 3 bytes are reserved; no boundary alignment occurs. This technique may be confusing and can be avoided with little, if any, loss.

Note that a length modifier affects a B-type constant in the same way as it affects an X-type; it affects an H-type constant in the same way as it affects an F-type. For types X, B, F, and H, padding with zeros or truncation occurs on the left of the specified constant. For character (type-C) constants, padding with blanks or truncation occurs on the right. Of these types, you would seldom write F and H with a length modifier.

It is possible to state lengths in terms of bits rather than bytes, but this will not be discussed in this text.

## *Reexamining the Duplication Factor*

**Symbolic duplication factors**

Usually the duplication factor *d* that is specified in a DC or DS directive is just a decimal self-defining term. However, it can be an absolute expression that is enclosed in parentheses. The value of such an expression must be greater than or equal to zero, and you must define the symbols in the expression previously. This feature permits symbolic duplication factors and is occasionally useful.

---

EXAMPLE 30

Suppose that you want to print column headings on one line and then print a line of dashes to separate them from the columns themselves. The following defines the same number of dashes as there are characters in the headings (not including the carriage-control character):

```
HEADING  DC    C' '                 CARRIAGE CONTROL
         DC    C'PURCHASE PRICE'
         DC    3C' '
         DC    C'SALES TAX'
HDLEN    EQU   *-HEADING
DASHES   DC    C' '                 CARRIAGE CONTROL
         DC    (HDLEN-1)C'-'
```

Printing the HDLEN characters at HEADING on one line followed by the same number of characters at DASHES on the next line produces the desired effect:

```
PURCHASE PRICE   SALES TAX
--------------------------
```

---

## *Address Constants*

You can define actual storage addresses as constants by using the DC directive and a new constant type. These constants are called **address constants.** You can use address constants when you load base registers, as you will see in Chapter 12, and to specify subprogram arguments, as you will see in Chapter 13. They are also useful when defining arrays or computing the length of character strings. There are several types of address constants, but only the A-type will be discussed here.

The operand entry that is used to define an address constant has a somewhat different form from other DC operands: the constant *c* is enclosed in parentheses rather than apostrophes. The entry appears as

**A-type address constants**

*d*AL*n*(*c*)

The constant type is A. As before, *d* is an optional duplication factor. The length modifier L*n* is also optional and is often omitted. In the absence of the length modifier, the assembler defines the constant as a fullword at the next fullword integral boundary. The constant *c* is an absolute or relocatable expression that is evaluated to 32 bits and truncated, if necessary, on the left. You can also define an address constant with a literal of the form

=*d*AL*n*(*c*)

If *c* is a relocatable expression, as it is in the next examples, the defined constant is the actual address that is assigned to the location represented by the expression. In this case, a length modifier, if used, can only specify a length of 3 or 4.

---

EXAMPLE 31

```
X       DC       A(Y+4)
```

Assume that Y is a relocatable symbol, which perhaps is defined by a DS directive, that represents the actual hexadecimal address AE1234. Then the address constant is 00AE1238 and is defined at a fullword integral boundary that is represented by X.

---

EXAMPLE 32

```
X       DC       AL3(Y+4)
```

The address constant is defined without boundary alignment and occupies the next 3 bytes. If Y is defined as in the previous example, the value of the address constant is AE1238.

---

EXAMPLE 33

```
X       DC       A(*)
```

The address constant is equal to the address that is indicated by the location counter reference. This constant has the same value as a constant defined by A(X).

---

The constant *c* can also be an absolute expression. The address constant is then equal to the value of the expression. However, this value usually is not an address and the terminology *address constant* can be misleading. Actually, the A-type constant defines the value of the specified expression, regardless of whether it is relocatable or absolute. If the expression is relocatable as in the previous examples, the value is an address; if the expression is absolute, the value need not be an address.

For address constants that are defined by absolute expressions, an explicit length can be from 1 to 4 bytes.

---

EXAMPLE 34

```
X       DC       A(21)
```

This has the same meaning as a constant that is defined by F'21'.

EXAMPLE 35

```
X        DC       A(J)
J        EQU      4
```

This has the same meaning as a constant that is defined by F'4'. Symbolic definitions like this can be stylistically useful, as you shall see later.

EXAMPLE 36

```
X        DC       AL2(3*J-1)
J        EQU      4
```

This has the same meaning as a constant that is defined by FL2'11'. There is no boundary alignment. The advantage of the A-type definition is that it provides the ability to define the constant as an expression.

EXAMPLE 37

```
Z        DC       5AL1(*-Z)
```

When you use a duplication factor and the location counter reference to define address constants, the value of the location counter reference varies with each constant. This is true because the assembler increments the location counter each time it assembles a constant. Thus, this DC instruction defines the hexadecimal constant 0001020304.

## *The Symbol Length Attribute*

The assembler assigns **attributes** to each symbol used in a program. One of these is the length in bytes of the item that is represented by the symbol. For example, the **length attribute** of the symbol W that is defined by

```
W        DS       F
```

is 4 since W is the address of a fullword. In the absence of an explicit length modifier, the length attribute of a symbol that is defined by a DC or DS is determined from its constant type. If FL3 defined W, however, the length attribute of W would be 3, which is the value of the explicit length modifier.

You must be careful not to confuse the length attribute with the duplication factor. For example, if 5H defined W, the length attribute of W would be 2, *not* 10. Figure 10.18 lists the rules that determine the length attribute for various symbol definitions, and Figure 10.19 provides some examples.

It is important to know about the length attribute in case you omit the length when writing an SS instruction. If the operand entry appears as

*S1,S2*

**Using an implicit length**

or

*S1,D2(B2)*

**Figure 10.18**
The rules that determine the symbol length attribute.

| Definition of Symbol | Length Attribute |
|---|---|
| DC or DS | Stated explicitly by length modifier or implied by constant type |
| Machine instruction | Instruction length (2, 4, or 6) |
| EQU | Length attribute of the first term of the operand expression |
| * in operand entry of a machine instruction | Instruction length (2, 4, or 6) |
| * appearing elsewhere | 1 |
| Self-defining term | 1 |

**Figure 10.19**
Some examples of the symbol length attribute.

| Definition of Symbol | | | Length Attribute of Symbol | |
|---|---|---|---|---|
| A | DC | XL3'123' | 3 | |
| B | DC | X'123' | 2 | |
| C | DC | X'000123' | 3 | |
| D | DS | 5H | 2 | |
| E | DS | 80C | 1 | |
| F | DS | CL80 | 80 | |
| G | AR | 8,10 | 2 | |
| H | EQU | A+4 | 3 | (Equal to that of A) |
| I | EQU | *+4 | 1 | (Equal to that of *) |
| J | EQU | 4 | 1 | |
| K | EQU | F-D | 80 | (Equal to that of F) |

then the assembler supplies a length called the **implicit length,** which is based upon the length attribute of *S1*. For example, if the length attribute of the symbol X is 6, then the instruction

```
MVC     X,Y
```

is equivalent to

```
MVC     X(6),Y
```

Many programmers take advantage of this equivalency so that once they have defined the lengths of certain fields, they do not need to write them explicitly again. This practice is fine if you are careful. However, if you unintentionally omit the length in an SS instruction, the assembler will not provide an error message since the instruction is syntactically correct. If the implicit length is not the length that you want, an error in execution will likely occur. You can check the length that the assembler supplied by looking at the second byte of the machine language instruction. Remember that the value in this byte is one less than the length of the field.

Other attributes will be discussed in Chapter 18.

*The Symbol Length Attribute Reference.* You can reference the length attribute of a symbol explicitly in assembler language statements by using the **symbol length attribute reference**. This is written as

L'*symbol*

which is simply the symbol preceded by L'. L'*symbol* is an absolute term that you may use within an expression.

---

EXAMPLE 38

```
MVC     X(L'Y),Y
```

If the length attribute of Y is 3, then this instruction is equivalent to

```
MVC     X(3),Y
```

---

EXAMPLE 39

```
MOVE     MVC     INSTR(L'*),MOVE
```

L'* denotes the length attribute of the instruction in which it appears—six, in this case. L'* has the same meaning as L'MOVE. This instruction moves a copy of its object form to the bytes at INSTR.

---

EXAMPLE 40

**Examples of Additional Assembler Features**

Figure 10.20 defines a table and, using the ideas of this section, some constants and symbols that can be useful in processing the table. TABLE represents the beginning address of an array of 10 elements, with each being 5 bytes long. NEXT represents the address of the byte after the array. BEGIN is the address of a fullword constant containing the beginning address of the array. Notice that the instruction

```
L       2,BEGIN
```

has the same effect as

```
LA      2,TABLE
```

The length of the array in bytes is contained in the fullword at TL. The statement that defines TL is equivalent to

```
TL        DC    F'50'
```

Notice that the instruction

```
L       2,TL
```

has the same effect as

```
LA      2,NEXT-TABLE
```

```
TABLE    DS     10CL5               AN ARRAY
NEXT     EQU    *                   ADDRESS OF BYTE AFTER THE ARRAY
BEGIN    DC     A(TABLE)            ADDRESS OF FIRST BYTE OF THE ARRAY
TL       DC     A(NEXT-TABLE)       LENGTH OF ARRAY IN BYTES
SIZE     EQU    L'TABLE             LENGTH OF ARRAY ELEMENT
S        DC     A(SIZE)             LENGTH OF ARRAY ELEMENT
NS       DC     A(0-SIZE)           MINUS THE LENGTH OF ARRAY ELEMENT
LAST     DC     A(NEXT-SIZE)        ADDRESS OF LAST ENTRY IN ARRAY
COPY     DS     (NEXT-TABLE)C       SPACE FOR A COPY OF TABLE
```

**Figure 10.20**
Some examples of additional assembler features, as described in Example 40.

NEXT – TABLE is an absolute expression that specifies the displacement in the LA instruction.

The absolute symbol SIZE represents the length of each entry in the array. The instruction

```
LA     2,SIZE
```

is exactly equivalent to

```
LA     2,L'TABLE
```

The length of each entry is also contained in the fullword at S. Each of the previous two instructions has the same effect as

```
L      2,S
```

The fullword at NS contains −5, and the fullword at LAST contains the address of the last entry in the array. Notice that L'TABLE can replace SIZE in the definitions of S, NS, and LAST. COPY is an array that contains the same number of bytes as TABLE. Note, however, that L'COPY is 1.

Although such definitions may seem indirect and even unnecessary, it can be advantageous to write programs in this manner because the symbols provide a measure of self-documentation and the assembler does the arithmetic for you. The latter reason is particularly useful if you change the definition of TABLE: the assembler recomputes everything else.

---

EXAMPLE 41

**Convert a Month Abbreviation to an Integer From 1 to 12 and to the Month's Full Name**

You will now use some of the ideas of this section to write a subprogram that involves a simple linear search of a table. Suppose that you have read an input record that contains a date, such as

```
OCT 12, 1492
```

Assume that the month is a three-letter abbreviation that begins anywhere in the record. Since you will focus only on this portion of the date, the rest of it can be in any format. The subprogram should examine the record, and convert the month abbreviation to the actual name of the month and to an appropriate integer from 1 to 12. Figure 10.21 lists the subprogram.

```
*********************************************************************
**
** SUBPROGRAM TO CONVERT A MONTH ABBREVIATION TO AN INTEGER FROM
** 1 TO 12 AND TO THE MONTH'S FULL NAME.
**
** INPUT:  R6 = ADDRESS OF A CHARACTER STRING THAT CONTAINS A 3-LETTER
**              MONTH ABBREVIATION, WHICH MAY BE PRECEDED BY BLANKS
**              AND IS FOLLOWED BY A NUMERIC DAY AND YEAR;
**              E.G.      OCT 12, 1492
**
** OUTPUT: R2 = ADDRESS OF MONTH NAME
**         R3 = NUMERIC EQUIVALENT OF MONTH (1 - 12), OR
**            = 0 IF ERROR IN ABBREVIATION
**         R6 = ADDRESS OF MONTH ABBREVIATION IN CHARACTER STRING
**         PRESERVES ALL OTHER REGISTERS
**
*********************************************************************
** INITIALIZE:
CONVERT  STM   R4,R5,SAVE           SAVE WORK REGISTERS
** SEARCH FOR BEGINNING OF DATE:
LOOP     CLI   0(R6),C' '           BLANK?
         BNE   NONBLANK             IF NOT, FOUND DATE; EXIT LOOP
         LA    R6,1(R6)             ELSE CONTINUE SEARCH
         B     LOOP                 REPEAT
** R6 = ADDRESS OF FIRST NONBLANK; ASSUMED BEGINNING OF ABBREVIATION.
** FIND ABBREVIATION IN TABLE:
NONBLANK LA    R2,ABBREV            R2 = ABBREVIATION TABLE POINTER
         LA    R4,L'ABBREV          R4 = INCREMENT = ABBREVIATION LENGTH
         L     R5,LAST              R5 = LOOP LIMIT = ADDR. LAST ABBREV.
* WHILE MONTH ABBREVIATION IS NOT CURRENT TABLE ENTRY:
LOOP2    CLC   0(L'ABBREV,R6),0(R2) ABBREVIATION VS. TABLE ENTRY
         BE    FOUND                IF EQUAL, EXIT LOOP
         BXLE  R2,R4,LOOP2          ELSE INCREMENT R2, TEST AND REPEAT
* END WHILE
ERROR    SR    R3,R3                ERROR; SET R3 TO 0 (ABBREV. NOT
         B     DONE                   FOUND); RETURN
** COMPUTE MONTH NUMBER AND ADDRESS OF MONTH NAME:
FOUND    S     R2,=A(ABBREV)        GET INDEX TO TABLE ENTRY
         SRDA  R2,32                PREPARE FOR DIVISION
         DR    R2,R4                R3 = INDEX/(ABBREV. LENGTH) (0 - 11)
         LR    R2,R3                SAVE THIS VALUE
         LA    R3,1(R3)             R3 = MONTH NUMBER (1 - 12)
         MH    R2,=AL2(L'NAMES)     R2 = INDEX TO NAMES TABLE
         LA    R2,NAMES(R2)         R2 = ADDRESS OF MONTH NAME
DONE     LM    R4,R5,SAVE           RESTORE WORK REGISTERS
         BR    R14                  FINISHED; RETURN
** TABLE OF ABBREVIATIONS:
ABBREV   DC    C'JAN'               REPRESENTATIVE ABBREVIATION
         DC    C'FEBMARAPRMAYJUNJULAUGSEPOCTNOVDEC'
NEXT     EQU   *                    ADDRESS OF BYTE AFTER THIS TABLE
LAST     DC    A(NEXT-L'ABBREV)     ADDRESS OF LAST ABBREVIATION
```

(Continues)

**Figure 10.21**
A subprogram to convert a month abbreviation to an integer from 1 to 12, and to the month's full name, as described in Example 41.

```
52 ** TABLE OF MONTH NAMES:
53 NAMES     DC    CL9'JANUARY'
54           DC    CL9'FEBRUARY'
55           DC    CL9'MARCH'
56           DC    CL9'APRIL'
57           DC    CL9'MAY'
58           DC    CL9'JUNE'
59           DC    CL9'JULY'
60           DC    CL9'AUGUST'
61           DC    CL9'SEPTEMBER'
62           DC    CL9'OCTOBER'
63           DC    CL9'NOVEMBER'
64           DC    CL9'DECEMBER'
65 SAVE      DS    2F                 SAVE AREA
```

**Figure 10.21**
*(Continued)*

The subprogram begins by locating the month abbreviation in the input record. This step requires a simple loop, which consists of Statements 21 to 24, to skip over the leading blanks. When this loop terminates, Register 6 contains the address of the first character in the abbreviation. To identify the abbreviation, the instructions in Statements 31 to 33 compare it with the successive entries in a table of possible values until a match occurs. If there is no match, then the input record contains an erroneous abbreviation and Register 3 is set to 0 to indicate an error condition (Statements 35 and 36).

If you assume that there is only 1 possible abbreviation for each month, then there are only 12 possible correct values. By arranging the table of abbreviations in the order that the months occur in the calendar, you can readily determine the proper month number. For example, if you have APR, the abbreviation for April, a match in the table will occur at the fourth entry. Thus, the month number is 4. To compute this, note that Register 2 contains the address of the table entry when a match occurs (Statement 31). As Figure 10.22 shows, subtracting the starting address of the table (represented by ABBREV) from Register 2 results in one of the values 0, 3, 6, and so on to 33. If you divide this value by 3 and add 1, you will get the desired result.

**Figure 10.22**
The month number and the index to NAMES is computed from the contents of Register 2 (R2).

| **C(R2)** | $i$ **= C(R2) − ABBREV** | $i$**/3** | $i$**/3 + 1** (Month number) | **9(**$i$**/3)** (Index to NAMES) | **NAMES** |
|---|---|---|---|---|---|
| ABBREV | 0 | 0 | 1 | 0 | JANUARY |
| ABBREV + 3 | 3 | 1 | 2 | 9 | FEBRUARY |
| ABBREV + 6 | 6 | 2 | 3 | 18 | MARCH |
| . | . | . | . | . | . |
| . | . | . | . | . | . |
| . | . | . | . | . | . |
| ABBREV + 33 | 33 | 11 | 12 | 99 | DECEMBER |

## SELF-TEST EXERCISES

12. What hex constants are defined by the following *sequence* of instructions? Assume that A represents the address 0BF1C4 and that L is equated to 7 with an EQU.

```
A        DC      2XL3'12'
B        DC      FL3'12'
C        DC      2CL3'*'
D        DC      CL1'ABC'
E        DC      XL1'123'
F        DC      A(3)
G        DC      A(2*L+4)
H        DC      A(B)
I        DC      A(D-4)
J        DC      AL3(A)
K        DC      (L)C'0'
```

13. What are the length attributes of the symbols in the name entries of the following *sequence* of instructions?

```
A        BR      14
B        DC      4H'1'
C        DC      10C'ABC'
D        DC      X'01234'
E        DC      2X'1'
F        DC      A(C)
G        DC      10CL5'ABC'
H        DC      100C' '
I        DC      50XL20'0'
J        EQU     F+4
K        EQU     *-2
L        EQU     G-E
M        EQU     9
```

14. Rewrite the instructions in Figure 10.13 to incorporate the literal =A(DATA).
15. Assume the following definitions:

```
A        DS      10CL80
B        DS      80C
C        DS      200F
```

Indicate the number of bytes that are moved by each of the following instructions:

**a.** MVC 0(L'A,2),B
**b.** MVC A,B
**c.** MVC A(L'A),B
**d.** MVC A(L'B),B
**e.** MVC A(L'C),B
**f.** MVC B,A
**g.** MVC C,B
**h.** MVC C,A
**i.** MVC 0(,2),C

16. Indicate whether or not each of the following instructions performs the action that is described by its remarks. If it does not, make the appropriate corrections.

**a.** MVC Y(8),=C' ' SET 8 BYTES AT Y TO BLANKS
**b.** CLC Z(5),=CL5'0' COMPARE 5 BYTES AT Z WITH C'00000'

Statements 38 to 42 of the subprogram perform this computation and place the month number into Register 3.

A second array, NAMES, contains the complete names of the months in their proper order (Statements 53 to 64). The longest month name, September, contains 9 characters, so each entry in this array is padded to a length of 9. The corresponding index values to use with NAMES are 0, 9, 18, and so on to 99, as was shown in Figure 10.22. Since Register 2 contains a value from 0 to 11 (Statement 41), you can obtain the correct index by multiplying Register 2 by 9 (Statement 43), which is the length of a month name. The subprogram uses this new index to compute the address of the desired name; this address replaces the contents of Register 2 (Statement 44).

Consider Statements 48 to 51:

```
48 ABBREV   DC    C'JAN'
49          DC    C'FEBMARAPRMAYJUNJULAUGSEPOCTNOVDEC'
50 NEXT     EQU   *
51 LAST     DC    A(NEXT-L'ABBREV)
```

The first DC defines a representative abbreviation so that L'ABBREV will be correct (3, in this case). Notice that the definition of LAST is *not* equivalent to

```
LAST        DC    A(*-L'ABBREV)
```

The asterisk here represents the same address as LAST, but this address need not be the same as NEXT; a gap may occur between the two addresses due to the boundary alignment of the A-type constant.

Notice that you can use a literal instead of the address constant LAST; a literal was not used so that the terminology LAST could be introduced into the program. Also, you can replace the instruction (Statement 29)

```
L       R5,LAST
```

with

```
LA      R5,NEXT-L'ABBREV
```

as long as the value of NEXT − L'ABBREV does not exceed 4095. Clearly, it does not exceed 4095 here, but the Load instruction provides a more general solution.

## Case Study

### *Problem Statement*

**As part of a course pre-registration system, tabulate the number of student requests for each course.** Course requests for a student appear on a single data record, such as

```
DOE,JANE/123456789/CSC311,ART120,MTH244,ENG300,SOC202
```

Beginning in the first column, the record contains the student's last name, followed by a comma, followed by the first name, followed by a slash, followed by the student's 9-digit identification number, followed by a slash, followed by up to five 6-character course codes, which are separated by commas. There are no blanks embedded within this data.

Produce a report that looks like this:

```
COURSE SELECTION AUDIT
LAST NAME                FIRST NAME STUDENT ID  COURSE SELECTIONS
-----------------------------------------------------------------------
DOE                      JANE       123456789   CSC311 ART120 MTH244 ENG300 SOC202
BROWN                    JACK       987654321   ART120 CSC311 ECN125
                                        .
                                        .
                                        .

TOTAL NUMBER OF REQUESTS BY COURSE:
CSC311 = 36
ART120 = 52
    .
    .
    .
```

### *Discussion*

The courses that are selected by a student are contained in a single input record and are printed on one line of the report. However, the format of the input record differs from the desired line of print, so each line must be composed in an array of storage before printing. Such an array is called a **buffer.**

The length of the student's name determines the positions of the remaining data in the input record. You use the delimiting commas and slashes to isolate the various fields, and then move them to their new positions within the output buffer. Move the letters of the last name one at a time until you encounter the comma. Then, move the letters of the first name one at a time until you encounter the slash. The student identification number is always nine digits so you can move it in one instruction. You can do the same for each course code because each is always six characters long. Move these until you encounter a blank.

As each course code is processed, you must determine if it has been previously encountered so that you can tabulate its occurrence properly. To do so, you construct an array called TABLE to contain only distinct course codes and a corresponding array of counters called TALLY. The *j*-th counter in TALLY contains the number of times that the *j*-th code in TABLE has occurred. Initially, the counters are zero and TABLE is empty; thus, you insert the first course code into TABLE and set its counter to one. For each subsequent code, you determine if it already exists in TABLE. If it does, you increment its counter. If it does not, you add the code to the end of the array and set its counter to one.

The pseudocode, flowchart, and program for this problem are contained in Figures 10.23, 10.24 and 10.25, respectively. The shaded portion of the pseudocode corresponds to the subprogram COUNT.

Notice the use of the ICM instruction in the program. Statement 83 loads the next character in the student name field into Register 4. The condition code is set according to whether its EBCDIC code begins with a 0 or a 1—thus, distinguishing between a letter, which begins with a 1, or a comma or slash, which begin with a 0. In the subprogram COUNT, Statement 177 loads Register 5 with N, which is the number of codes in TABLE, and tests it for 0. Notice that N is a single byte; since the number of course codes is

**Figure 10.23**
The pseudocode solution to the case study.

```
Assumptions:
    TABLE  is an array to contain distinct course codes.
    TALLY  is an array of counters corresponding to the codes in
           TABLE; all counters are initially zero.
    N      is the number of codes in TABLE; initially 0.

Print heading
WHILE there is data DO
    Read input record of student data
    Clear output buffer
    Set input pointer to start of input record
    Set output pointer to start of last name field
    REPEAT
        WHILE input character is a letter (not "/" or ",") DO
            Store character according to output pointer
        END WHILE
        Set output pointer to start of first name field
    UNTIL "/" is encountered
    END REPEAT
    Move student ID to output buffer
    Skip "/"
    REPEAT
        Copy next course code to output buffer
        IF course code is not in TABLE                       }
            THEN increment N and add code to TABLE           }
        END IF                                               } Subprogram
        Increment appropriate counter in TALLY               }
        Increment input and output pointers
    UNTIL blank is encountered
    END REPEAT
    Print line of output for this student
END WHILE
Print tally heading
REPEAT
    Print tally for next course code
UNTIL all course codes are processed
END REPEAT
```

limited to 100, this is sufficient. Single-byte counters can be useful when they are numerous; the program includes this one (N) for the sake of demonstration.

Observe the use of the absolute symbols OPLEN (Statement 217), LLEN (Statement 225), and HDLEN (Statement 243) to specify lengths that are best computed by the assembler, rather than by you. In particular, note the use of these symbols in the duplication factors of the DC directives in Statements 218, 226, 244, 247, and 248. You can replace 133, which appears in these duplication factors, with L'OUT since the length attribute of OUT is 133. Also note the use of OPLEN in the MVC instruction in Statement 77.

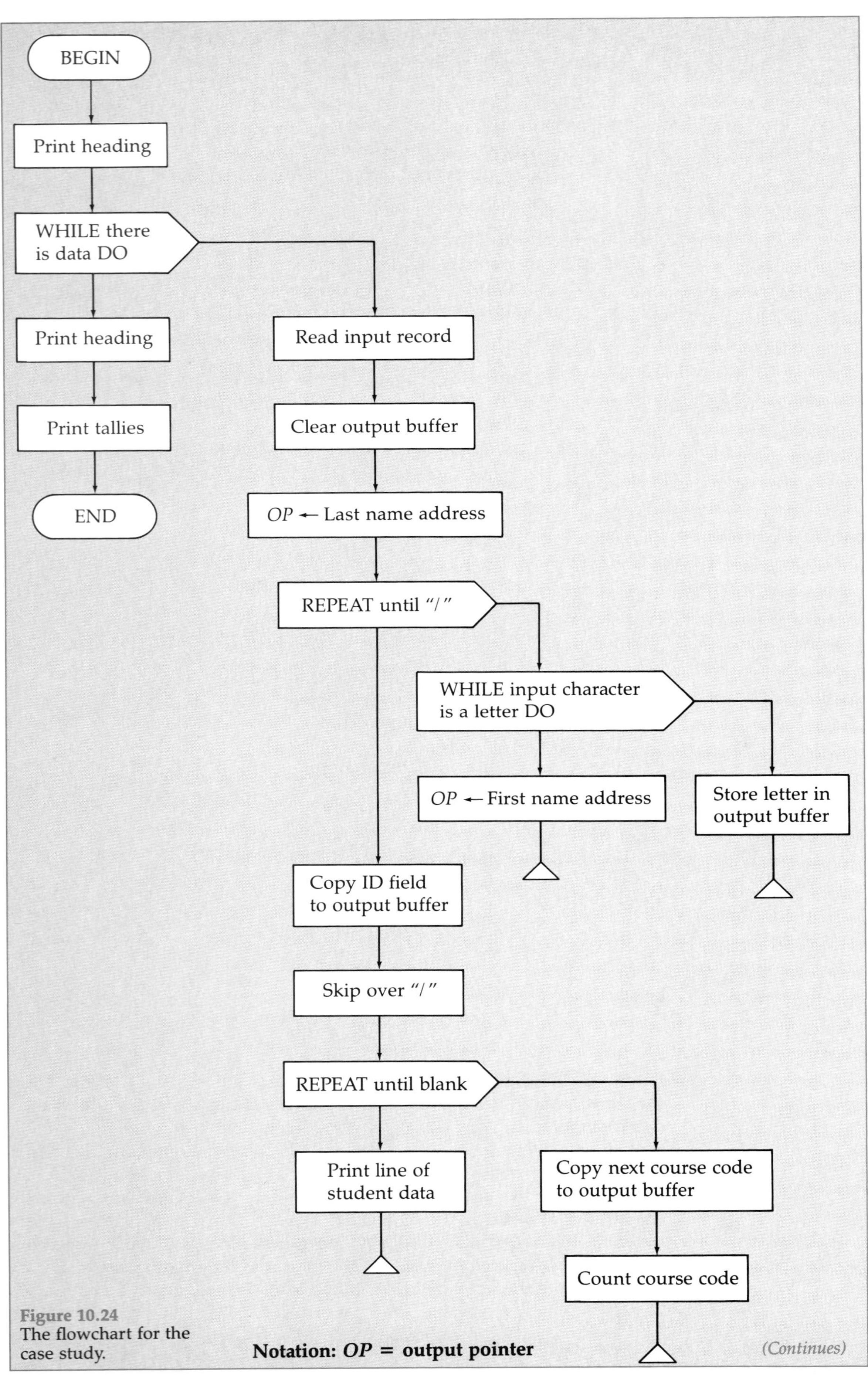


**Figure 10.24**
The flowchart for the case study.

**Notation: *OP* = output pointer**

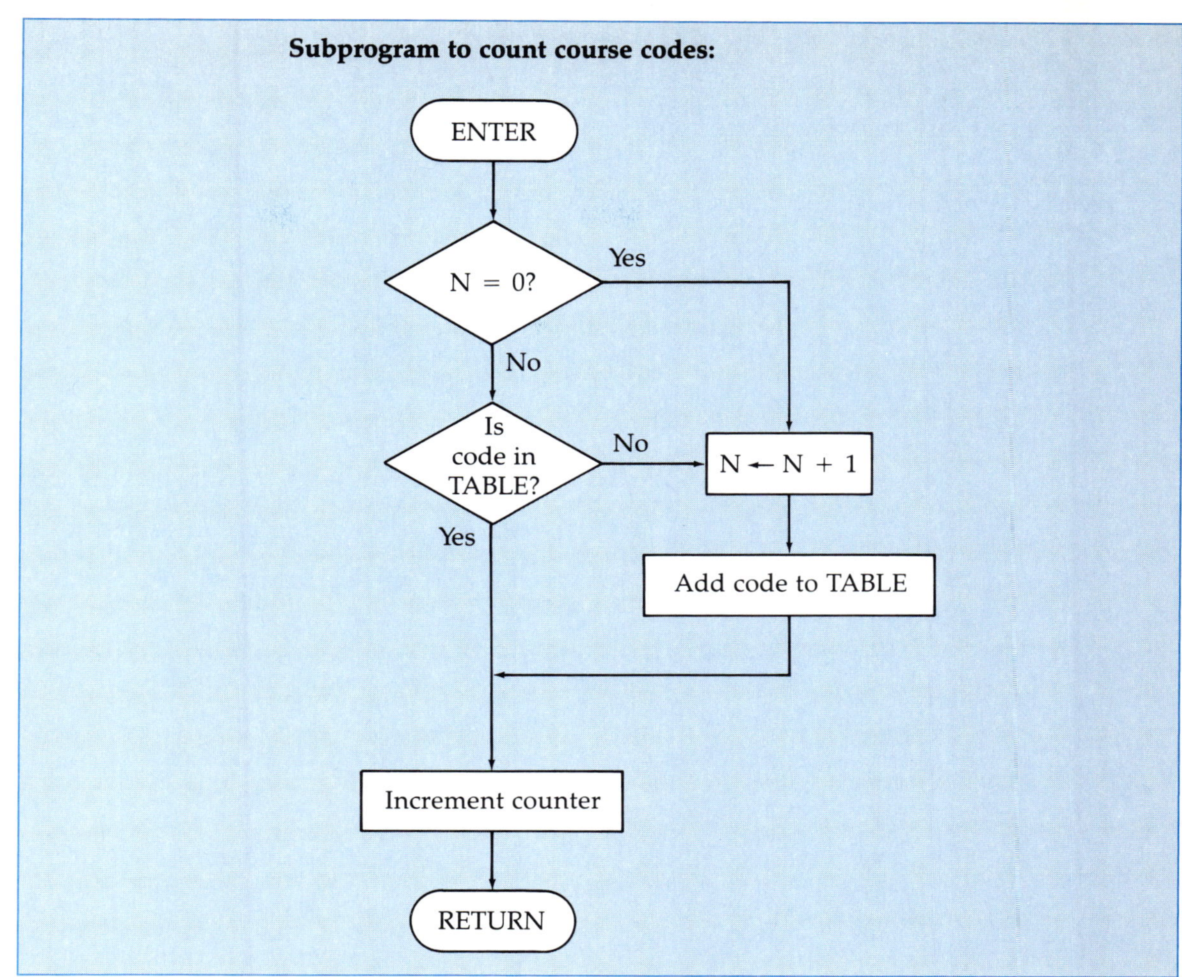


**Figure 10.24**
*(Continued)*

```
------------------------------------------------------
        PROGRAM TO LIST AND TALLY COURSE SELECTIONS


  LOC  OBJECT CODE    ADDR1 ADDR2  STMT   SOURCE STATEMENT

000000                                 2 LIST     CSECT
                                       3 ***********************************************************************
                                       4 **
                                       5 ** INPUT:  ONE 80-BYTE RECORD PER STUDENT:
                                       6 **           BEGINNING IN COLUMN 1, NO SPACES:
                                       7 **             LAST NAME, FIRST NAME
                                       8 **             SLASH
                                       9 **             STUDENT ID NUMBER
                                      10 **             SLASH
                                      11 **             UP TO FIVE 6-CHARACTER COURSE CODES SEPARATED BY COMMAS
                                      12 **         E.G. DOE,JANE/123456789/CSC311,ART120,MTH244,ENG300,SOC202
                                      13 **         DATA IS ASSUMED ERROR-FREE.  UP TO 100 DIFFERENT COURSES CAN
                                      14 **         BE ACCOMMODATED.
                                      15 ** OUTPUT: LISTING OF COURSE REQUESTS BY STUDENT NAME AND TOTAL NUMBER
                                      16 **         OF REQUESTS PER COURSE.
                                      17 **
                                      18 ***********************************************************************
                                      19          PRINT NOGEN              SUPPRESS MACRO EXPANSIONS
                                      20 ** REGISTER DEFINITIONS:
                           00002      21 R2       EQU   2                  INPUT RECORD POINTER; TALLY INDEX
                           00003      22 R3       EQU   3                  OUTPUT RECORD POINTER
                           00004      23 R4       EQU   4                  WORK REGISTER; COURSE TABLE POINTER
                           00005      24 R5       EQU   5                  LOOP COUNTER
                           0000C      25 R12      EQU   12                 BASE REGISTER
                           0000D      26 R13      EQU   13                 SAVE AREA POINTER
                           0000E      27 R14      EQU   14                 LINK TO SUBPROGRAMS AND OS
                                      28 ** MASKS:
                           00002      29 PUNC     EQU   B'0010'            CC=2 IF SELECTED BYTE BEGINS WITH 0
                                      30 *                                    DISTINGUISHES LETTERS FROM / OR ,
                                      31 ** STANDARD ENTRY AND INITIALIZATION:
                                      32 *  OS:
000000 90EC D00C     0000C            33          STM   R14,R12,12(R13)    SAVE REGISTERS
000004 05C0                           34          BALR  R12,0              LOAD BASE REGISTER
                           00006      35          USING BASE,R12           DECLARE BASE ADDRESS AND REGISTER
000006 50D0 C8E6     008EC            36 BASE     ST    R13,SAVE+4         SAVE R13
00000A 41D0 C8E2     008E8            37          LA    R13,SAVE           R13 = ADDRESS OF SAVE AREA
                                      38          OPEN  (READER,INPUT,PRINTER,OUTPUT)  PREPARE FOR I/O
                                      46 ** DOS*******
                                      47 *        BALR  R12,0              LOAD BASE REGISTER
                                      48 *        USING BASE,R12           DECLARE BASE ADDRESS AND REGISTER
                                      49 *BASE    LA    R13,SAVE           R13 = ADDRESS OF SAVE AREA
                                      50 *        OPEN  READER,PRINTER     PREPARE FOR I/O
                                      51 ******
                                      52 ** PRINT HEADINGS:
                                      53          PUT   PRINTER,HEAD1      REPORT HEADING
                                      58          PUT   PRINTER,HEAD2      COLUMN HEADINGS
                                      63          PUT   PRINTER,ULINE      UNDERLINE HEADINGS
                                      68 *
                                      69 * WHILE THERE IS DATA:
                                      70 ** READ INPUT RECORD, CLEAR OUTPUT BUFFER, INITIALIZE POINTERS:
                                      71 READ     GET   READER,IN          READ STUDENT RECORD
000056 9240 C1D0     001D6            76          MVI   OUT,C' '           SET OUTPUT BUFFER
00005A D24E C1D1 C1D0 001D7 001D6     77          MVC   OUT+1(OPLEN-1),OUT   TO BLANKS
000060 4120 C17E     00184            78          LA    R2,IN              R2 = INPUT RECORD POINTER
000064 4130 C1D1     001D7            79          LA    R3,LASTNAME        R3 = OUTPUT POINTER = LAST NAME ADDR.
                                      80 ** MOVE LAST NAME THEN FIRST NAME TO OUTPUT BUFFER:
```

*(Continues)*

**Figure 10.25**
The program listing for the case study.

```
                                    * - REPEAT:
                                    * - - WHILE INPUT CHARACTER IS A LETTER (NOT "/" OR ","):
000068 BF41 2000        00000       LOOP     ICM    R4,B'0001',0(R2)     GET NEXT INPUT CHARACTER; SET CC
00006C 4720 C07A        00080                BC     PUNC,COMSLASH        EXIT LOOP IF COMMA OR SLASH:
                                    *                                      (CC=2; EBCDIC CODE BEGINS WITH 0)
000070 4243 0000        00000                STC    R4,0(R3)             STORE LETTER IN OUTPUT BUFFER
000074 4122 0001        00001                LA     R2,1(R2)             INCREMENT INPUT POINTER
000078 4133 0001        00001                LA     R3,1(R3)             INCREMENT OUTPUT POINTER
00007C 47F0 C062        00068                B      LOOP                 CONTINUE PROCESSING CHARACTERS
                                    * - - END WHILE
                                    *
                                    * COMMA OR SLASH DETECTED:
000080 956B 2000        00000       COMSLASH CLI    0(R2),C','           COMMA IN INPUT RECORD?
000084 4770 C08E        00094                BNE    SLASH                IF NOT, MUST BE SLASH
                                    * PREPARE TO PROCESS FIRST NAME
000088 4130 C1E6        001EC                LA     R3,FIRST             R3 = FIRST NAME ADDRESS IN OUTPUT
00008C 4122 0001        00001                LA     R2,1(R2)             INCREMENT INPUT POINTER
000090 47F0 C062        00068                B      LOOP                 REPEAT
                                    * - UNTIL SLASH ENCOUNTERED
                                    * - END REPEAT
                                    ** MOVE STUDENT ID TO OUTPUT BUFFER (R2 POINTS TO PRECEDING "/"):
000094 D208 C1F1 2001 001F7 00001   SLASH    MVC    ID(9),1(R2)          ID NUMBER FOLLOWS "/"; COPY TO OUTPUT
00009A 4122 000B        0000B                LA     R2,11(R2)            ADVANCE TO FIRST COURSE CODE
00009E 4130 C1FD        00203                LA     R3,COURSES           R3 = COURSE CODE ADDRESS IN OUTPUT
                                    ** PROCESS COURSE CODES:
                                    * - REPEAT (FOR ALL COURSE CODES):
0000A2 D205 3000 2000 00000 00000   MORE     MVC    0(6,R3),0(R2)        COPY NEXT COURSE CODE TO OUTPUT
0000A8 45E0 C12E        00134                BAL    R14,COUNT            COUNT COURSE CODE
0000AC 4122 0007        00007                LA     R2,7(R2)             POINT TO NEXT COURSE CODE IN INPUT
0000B0 4133 0007        00007                LA     R3,7(R3)             POINT TO NEXT COURSE CODE IN OUTPUT
                                    * - UNTIL BLANK ENCOUNTERED
0000B4 9540 2000        00000                CLI    0(R2),C' '           ENDING BLANK?
0000B8 4770 C09C        000A2                BNE    MORE                 IF NOT, REPEAT
                                    * - END REPEAT
                                             PUT    PRINTER,OUT          ELSE PRINT LINE FOR THIS STUDENT
0000CA 47F0 C042        00048                B      READ                 CONSIDER NEXT INPUT RECORD
                                    * END WHILE
                                    *
                                    ** END-OF-DATA; PRINT TALLIES FOR ALL COURSES SELECTED:
                                    ENDDATA  PUT    PRINTER,HEAD3        PRINT TALLY HEADING
0000DC 1B55                                  SR     R5,R5                CLEAR R5 PRIOR TO INSERTING BYTE AT N
0000DE 4350 C6C2        006C8                IC     R5,N                 R5 = N = NUMBER OF DISTINCT COURSES
0000E2 4140 C2DA        002E0                LA     R4,TABLE             R4 = TABLE POINTER
0000E6 1B22                                  SR     R2,R2                R2 = TALLY INDEX
                                    * REPEAT:
0000E8 D205 C256 4000 0025C 00000   TLOOP    MVC    CODE(6),0(R4)        MOVE NEXT COURSE CODE FROM TABLE TO
                                    *                                      OUTPUT BUFFER CALLED LINE
0000EE 5832 C532        00538                L      R3,TALLY(R2)         GET NO. OF REQUESTS FOR THIS COURSE
0000F2 4E30 C8DA        008E0                CVD    R3,TEMP              CONVERT TO
0000F6 960F C8E1        008E7                OI     TEMP+7,X'0F'           EBCDIC AND
0000FA F397 C25F C8DA 00265 008E0            UNPK   TOTAL(10),TEMP(8)        STORE IN BUFFER
                                             PUT    PRINTER,LINE         PRINT COURSE CODE AND NO. OF REQUESTS
00010E 4122 0004        00004                LA     R2,4(R2)             INCREMENT TALLY INDEX
000112 4144 0006        00006                LA     R4,6(R4)             INCREMENT TABLE POINTER
                                    * UNTIL ALL COURSE CODES ARE PROCESSED
000116 4650 C0E2        000E8                BCT    R5,TLOOP             DECREMENT COUNTER; REPEAT IF NONZERO
                                    * END REPEAT
                                    ** STANDARD EXIT
                                    ** OS:
                                             CLOSE  (READER,,PRINTER)    I/O IS COMPLETE
00012A 58D0 C8E6        008EC                L      R13,SAVE+4           RESTORE R13
00012E 98EC D00C        0000C                LM     R14,R12,12(R13)      RESTORE REMAINING REGISTERS
000132 07FE                                  BR     R14                  RETURN TO OS
```

*(Continues)*

**Figure 10.25**
*(Continued)*

```
                                        ** DOS*******
                                        *          CLOSE READER,PRINTER      I/O IS COMPLETE
                                        *          EOJ                       RETURN TO DOS
                                        ***********************************************************************
                                        ** INTERNAL SUBPROGRAM TO COUNT REQUESTS FOR EACH COURSE
                                        ** INPUT:   R2 = ADDRESS OF COURSE CODE
                                        ** OUTPUT:  TABLE CONTAINS DISTINCT COURSE CODES ENCOUNTERED SO FAR;
                                        **          TALLY CONTAINS FREQUENCY COUNTS FOR EACH COURSE
                                        ** LIMITS:  MAXIMUM OF 100 DIFFERENT COURSE CODES;
                                        **          DESTROYS REGISTERS R4 AND R5
                                        ***********************************************************************
000134 4140 C2DA       002E0            COUNT    LA    R4,TABLE               R4 = TABLE POINTER
                                        * IF COURSE CODE IS NOT IN TABLE:
000138 1B55                                      SR    R5,R5                  CLEAR R5 PRIOR TO INSERTING BYTE AT N
00013A BF51 C6C2       006C8                     ICM   R5,B'0001',N           R5 = NUMBER OF COURSE CODES IN TABLE
00013E 4780 C152       00158                     BZ    CNULL                  TABLE IS EMPTY FIRST TIME
                                        * - REPEAT N TIMES OR UNTIL CODE FOUND IN TABLE:
000142 D505 2000 4000 00000 00000       CSEARCH  CLC   0(6,R2),0(R4)          GIVEN COURSE CODE VS. TABLE ENTRY
000148 4780 C160       00166                     BE    CMATCH                 EXIT LOOP IF CODE FOUND IN TABLE
00014C 4144 0006       00006                     LA    R4,6(R4)               ELSE INCREMENT POINTER
000150 4650 C13C       00142                     BCT   R5,CSEARCH             DECREMENT COUNTER; REPEAT IF NONZERO
                                        * - END REPEAT
                                        * THEN INCREMENT N AND ADD CODE TO TABLE:
000154 4350 C6C2       006C8                     IC    R5,N                   GET N (NUMBER OF TABLE ENTRIES)
000158 4155 0001       00001            CNULL    LA    R5,1(R5)               R5 = N + 1
00015C 4250 C6C2       006C8                     STC   R5,N                   N = N + 1
000160 D205 4000 2000 00000 00000                MVC   0(6,R4),0(R2)          ADD COURSE CODE TO TABLE
                                        * END IF
                                        *
                                        ** INCREMENT TALLY (MUST SUBTRACT A(TABLE) FROM R4, DIVIDE RESULT BY
                                        **    6, AND MULTIPLY BY 4 TO GET CORRESPONDING INDEX TO TALLY ARRAY):
000166 5B40 C9EA       009F0            CMATCH   S     R4,=A(TABLE)           R4 = INDEX TO COURSE CODE TABLE
                                        *                                        = 0, 6, 12, ...
00016A 8E40 0020       00020                     SRDA  R4,32                  PREPARE FOR DIVISION
00016E 5D40 C9EE       009F4                     D     R4,=F'6'               R5 = 0, 1, 2, ...
000172 8B50 0002       00002                     SLA   R5,2                   R5 = 0, 4, 8, ...
000176 5845 C532       00538                     L     R4,TALLY(R5)           R4 = # OF REQUESTS FOR COURSE SO FAR
00017A 5A40 C9F2       009F8                     A     R4,=F'1'               INCREMENT TALLY (# OF REQUESTS)
00017E 5045 C532       00538                     ST    R4,TALLY(R5)           STORE UPDATED TALLY
000182 07FE                                      BR    R14                    RETURN TO MAIN PROCESSING
                                        ***********************************************************************
000184                                  IN       DS    CL80                   INPUT RECORD
0001D4 4040                                      DC    2C' '                  FORCED BLANKS TO END LOOP IN CASE
                                        *                                       COURSE CODE ENDS IN 80-TH BYTE
                                        *                                       OF INPUT.
0001D6                                  OUT      DS    0CL133                 OUTPUT BUFFER FOR STUDENT DATA:
0001D6 40                                        DC    C' '                     CARRIAGE CONTROL
0001D7                                  LASTNAME DS    CL20                     LAST NAME
0001EB                                           DS    X                        SPACE
0001EC                                  FIRST    DS    CL10                     FIRST NAME
0001F6                                           DS    X                        SPACE
0001F7                                  ID       DS    CL9                      STUDENT ID NUMBER
000200                                           DS    3X                       SPACES
000203                                  COURSES  DS    5CL7                     5 COURSE CODES SEPARATED BY BLANKS
                                00050   OPLEN    EQU   *-OUT                    TOTAL LENGTH OF ABOVE FIELDS
000226 4040404040404040                          DC    (133-OPLEN)C' '          PAD WITH BLANKS TO 133 BYTES
                                        *
00025B                                  LINE     DS    0CL133                 OUTPUT BUFFER FOR TALLY LINE:
00025B 40                                        DC    C' '                     CARRIAGE CONTROL
00025C                                  CODE     DS    CL6                      COURSE CODE
000262 407E40                                    DC    C' = '
000265                                  TOTAL    DS    CL10                     NUMBER OF REQUESTS
                                00014   LLEN     EQU   *-LINE                   TOTAL LENGTH OF ABOVE FIELDS
00026F 4040404040404040                          DC    (133-LLEN)C' '           PAD WITH BLANKS TO 133 BYTES
```

*(Continues)*

**Figure 10.25**
*(Continued)*

```
                                        *
0002E0                                  TABLE    DS     100CL6            TABLE OF UNIQUE COURSE CODES
000538 0000000000000000                 TALLY    DC     100F'0'           CORRESPONDING COUNTS OF COURSE
                                        *                                   CODES; INITIALLY ZERO
0006C8 00                               N        DC     X'0'              NUMBER OF DISTINCT COURSE CODES;
                                        *                                   INITIALLY 0
                                        *
0006C9 F0C3D6E4D9E2C540                 HEAD1    DC     CL133'0COURSE SELECTION AUDIT'  REPORT HEADING
00074E                                  HEAD2    DS     0CL133            COLUMN HEADINGS AS FOLLOWS:
00074E 40D3C1E2E340D5C1                          DC     C' LAST NAME'
000758 4040404040404040                          DC     CL12' '
000764 C6C9D9E2E340D5C1                          DC     C'FIRST NAME'
00076E 40                                        DC     C' '
00076F E2E3E4C4C5D5E340                          DC     C'STUDENT ID'
000779 4040                                      DC     CL2' '
00077B C3D6E4D9E2C540E2                          DC     C'COURSE SELECTIONS'
                             0003E      HDLEN    EQU    *-HEAD2           LENGTH OF COLUMN HEADINGS
00078C 4040404040404040                          DC     (133-HDLEN)C' '   PAD WITH BLANKS TO 133 BYTES
                                        *
0007D3 40                               ULINE    DC     C' '              CARRIAGE CONTROL
0007D4 6060606060606060                          DC     (OPLEN-1)C'-'     DASHES TO UNDERLINE HEADING
000823 4040404040404040                          DC     (133-OPLEN)C' '   PAD WITH BLANKS TO 133 BYTES
000858 F0E3D6E3C1D340D5                 HEAD3    DC     CL133'0TOTAL NUMBER OF REQUESTS BY COURSE:'
0008E0                                  TEMP     DS     D                 WORK AREA FOR EBCDIC CONVERSION
0008E8                                  SAVE     DS     18F               SAVE AREA (9D IN DOS)
                                        ** DCB'S FOR I/O IN OS:
                                        READER   DCB    DSORG=PS,MACRF=GM,DDNAME=SYSIN,RECFM=F,LRECL=80,          X
                                                        BLKSIZE=80,EODAD=ENDDATA
                                        PRINTER  DCB    DSORG=PS,MACRF=PM,DDNAME=SYSPRINT,RECFM=FA,               X
                                                        LRECL=133,BLKSIZE=133
                                        ** DOS*******
                                        *READER  DTFCD  DEVADDR=SYSIPT,DEVICE=2540,IOAREA1=INBUF,BLKSIZE=80,      X
                                                        RECFORM=FIXUNB,TYPEFLE=INPUT,WORKA=YES,EOFADDR=ENDDATA
                                        *PRINTER DTFPR  DEVADDR=SYSLST,DEVICE=3203,IOAREA1=OUTBUF,WORKA=YES,      X
                                                        RECFORM=FIXUNB,BLKSIZE=133,CTLCHAR=ASA
                                        *INBUF   DS     80C               DOS INPUT BUFFER
                                        *OUTBUF  DS     133C              DOS OUTPUT BUFFER
                                        ******
000000                                           END    LIST
0009F0 000002E0                                         =A(TABLE)
0009F4 00000006                                         =F'6'
0009F8 00000001                                         =F'1'
```

```
COURSE SELECTION AUDIT
LAST NAME            FIRST NAME STUDENT ID  COURSE SELECTIONS
---------------------------------------------------------------------------
DOE                  JANE       123456789   CSC311 ART120 MTH244 ENG300 SOC202
BROWN                JACK       987654321   ART120 CSC311 ECN125
GREEN                MARK       555555555   ECN125 ART208 MTH244 CSC311

TOTAL NUMBER OF REQUESTS BY COURSE:
CSC311 = 0000000003
ART120 = 0000000002
MTH244 = 0000000002
ENG300 = 0000000001
SOC202 = 0000000001
ECN125 = 0000000002
ART208 = 0000000001
```

Output from program

**Figure 10.25**
*(Continued)*

## Debugging Hints

1. Do not confuse the instructions IC and STC. Remember that IC is a load operation and STC is a store operation.
2. Be sure that the *I2* entry for an SI instruction is an absolute quantity. Do not confuse self-defining terms with literals.
3. It is easy to make an error when writing the operands of an SI or SS instruction. The SI instructions do not specify a length for either operand. In this chapter, the SS instructions do not designate a length for the second operand; both operands are assumed to be of equal length. At execution time, if the length specified in an SS instruction appears to be in error, check the second byte of the machine language instruction. This byte should contain a value that is one less than the desired length. Remember that the length that you write in the assembler language instruction is the actual length. Also remember that, if you omit the length specification, the assembler will assume a length that is equal to the length attribute of the first operand. This may or may not be what you intended.

   SI and SS instructions cannot use an index register. If the operand designation is implicit, then use a relocatable expression; no registers should appear. If you use explicit operand designations, such as when processing an array, be sure that the specified items are absolute.
4. Remember that the mask in the instructions ICM, STCM, and CLM selects bytes of the first register operand only. The relevant storage bytes are consecutive, beginning at the specified effective address.
5. Be careful when you use the MVCIN instruction. The address of the second operand is that of its rightmost byte. In this respect, it differs from all other SS instructions.
6. Be aware of padding and truncation when you define constants with an explicit length modifier. Also be aware of the contrasting effect that the length modifier and the duplication factor have upon the length attribute of a symbol. For example, consider the following definitions (the hex constants are noted as remarks):

```
A     DC    CL3'0'    F04040
B     DC    3C'0'     F0F0F0
C     DC    XL3'0'    000000
D     DC    3X'0'     000000
E     DC    XL3'9'    000009
F     DC    3X'9'     090909
```

   A and B specify different constants and have different length attributes, as do E and F. Although C and D represent the same constant, they have different length attributes.

## Stylistic Notes

1. Avoid explicit length modifiers if they specify a length shorter than the implicit length of the defined constant. For example, do not write =XL2'123456789'.

2. Until you gain more experience with SS instructions, state operand lengths explicitly. However, you should define fields with correct length attributes. For example, define space for an input record as

```
DATA     DS     CL80
```

instead of

```
DATA     DS     80C
```

3. Consider an output buffer defined by

```
OUTPUT   DC     CL120' '
```

Fields moved into the buffer can be separated by the blanks remaining from the assembly-time initialization. Later, if you replace these fields by shorter fields, characters from the first fields will remain. Thus, you must also consider execution-time initialization: you could write

```
MVC      OUTPUT(120),=CL120' '
```

This requires a 120-byte literal constant, but allows an initialization with one instruction. To save storage at the expense of execution time, you can write

```
MVI      OUTPUT,C' '
MVC      OUTPUT+1(119),OUTPUT
```

The last technique is probably the best for most applications. Even though it is slower, such an operation is usually not used often enough in a program to be a problem.

## Summary

1. Each of the IC and STC instructions moves 1 byte, and each of the ICM and STCM instructions moves up to 4 bytes between a register and storage. IC and STC are the only available RX byte-oriented instructions.
2. SI instructions reference 1 byte in storage and use 1 byte of immediate data, which is stored within the instruction itself.
3. SS instructions permit storage-to-storage operations on groups of up to 256 consecutive bytes.
4. The MVI instruction changes the contents of a single byte in storage.
5. The MVC instruction copies up to 256 consecutive bytes from one area in storage to another.
6. MVCIN is the only SS instruction to reference an operand by the address of its rightmost byte. Use it to reverse the order of a character string.
7. Logical comparisons treat data as unsigned integers.
8. Each of the CLR, CL, and CLM instructions compares data in a register with data in storage.
9. The CLI instruction compares a byte in storage with any 8-bit value stored as immediate data.
10. The CLC instruction compares two fields in storage.
11. Array processing with SI and SS instructions cannot directly involve an index register. However, you can compute the effective address of the desired area of storage with a separate instruction, and then use it in the SI or SS instruction.
12. The length in bytes of a constant or area that is defined by a DC or DS may be designated explicitly with a length modifer L*n*.
13. The duplication factor *d* in a DC or DS directive can be either an absolute expression that is enclosed in parentheses or a decimal self-defining term.

14. Use A-type address constants to define constants whose values are equal to that of the designated absolute or relocatable expression.

15. Each symbol has a length attribute that is assigned by the assembler. You can reference it within an assembler language statement by using the symbol length attribute reference L'*symbol*.

## New Instruction Summary

| Operation | Operand | Format | Instruction Name | Action |
|---|---|---|---|---|
| **IC** | *R1,S2*<br>or *R1,S2(X2)*<br>or *R1,D2(X2,B2)* | RX | INSERT CHARACTER | $C(R1)_{24-31} \leftarrow C(E2)_{0-7}$ |
| **STC** | *R1,S2*<br>or *R1,S2(X2)*<br>or *R1,D2(X2,B2)* | RX | STORE CHARACTER | $C(E2)_{0-7} \leftarrow C(R1)_{24-31}$ |
| **ICM** | *R1,M3,S2*<br>or *R1,M3,D2(B2)* | RS | INSERT CHARACTERS UNDER MASK | Loads bytes in *R1*, selected according to the mask *M3*, from consecutive bytes at *E2*<br>Cond. code = 0 if the inserted bytes are zero, or *M3* = 0; 1 if the leftmost bit of the inserted bytes is 1; 2 if the inserted bytes are not zero, but the leftmost bit is 0 |
| **STCM** | *R1,M3,S2*<br>or *R1,M3,D2(B2)* | RS | STORE CHARACTERS UNDER MASK | Stores bytes of *R1*, selected according to the mask *M3*, into the consecutive bytes at *E2* |
| **MVI** | *S1,I2*<br>or *D1(B1),I2* | SI | MOVE IMMEDIATE | $C(E1) \leftarrow I2$ |
| **MVC** | *S1(L),S2*<br>or *S1,S2*<br>or *S1(L),D2(B2)*<br>or *S1,D2(B2)*<br>or *D1(L,B1),S2*<br>or *D1(L,B1),D2(B2)* | SS | MOVE CHARACTERS | $C(E1)_{L\text{ bytes}} \leftarrow C(E2)_{L\text{ bytes}}$ |
| **MVCIN** | *S1(L),S2*<br>or *S1,S2*<br>or *S1(L),D2(B2)*<br>or *S1,D2(B2)*<br>or *D1(L,B1),S2*<br>or *D1(L,B1),D2(B2)* | SS | MOVE INVERSE | $C(E1)_{L\text{ bytes}} \leftarrow C(E2-L+1)_{L\text{ bytes}}$ in reverse order |

| Operation | Operand | Format | Instruction Name | Action |
|---|---|---|---|---|
| **CLR** | *R1,R2* | RR | COMPARE LOGICAL REGISTERS | Compares C(*R1*) with C(*R2*)<br>Cond. code = { 0 if the comparison is equal; 1 if the first operand is less than the second; 2 if the first operand is greater than the second } |
| **CL** | *R1,S2*<br>or *R1,S2(X2)*<br>or *R1,D2(X2,B2)* | RX | COMPARE LOGICAL | Compares C(*R1*) with $C(E2)_{0-31}$. The condition code is set as for CLR. |
| **CLM** | *R1,M3,S2*<br>or *R1,M3,D2(B2)* | RS | COMPARE LOGICAL UNDER MASK | Compares bytes of *R1*, selected according to *M3*, with the consecutive bytes at *E2*<br>Cond. code = { 0 if the operands are equal, or *M3* = 0; 1 if the first operand is less than the second; 2 if the first operand is greater than the second } |
| **CLI** | *S1,I2*<br>or *D1(B1),I2* | SI | COMPARE LOGICAL IMMEDIATE | Compares C(*E1*) with *I2*. The condition code is set as for CLR. |
| **CLC** | *S1(L),S2*<br>or *S1,S2*<br>or *S1(L),D2(B2)*<br>or *S1,D2(B2)*<br>or *D1(L,B1),S2*<br>or *D1(L,B1),D2(B2)* | SS | COMPARE LOGICAL CHARACTERS | Compares $C(E1)_{L\ \text{bytes}}$ with $C(E2)_{L\ \text{bytes}}$. The condition code is set as for CLR. |

## New Directives

| Operation | Operand | Instruction Name | Action |
|---|---|---|---|
| **DC** | *d*AL*n*(*c*) | DEFINE ADDRESS CONSTANT | Defines *d* copies of a constant equal to the value of the expression *c*. In the absence of L*n*, each constant is a fullword at a fullword integral boundary. If L*n* is present, no boundary alignment occurs and each constant is of length *n*. |

## Exercises

1. Assume the following:

```
A        DS     CL4
B        DS     4C
R5       EQU    5
```

Which of the following are correct ways to copy 4 bytes from A to B? Justify each of your answers.

**a.** MVC A,B

**b.** MVC 0(4,B),0(A)

**c.** LA R5,B
MVC 0(4,R5),A

**d.** MVC B,A

**e.** LA R5,A
MVC 4(4,R5),0(R5)

2. Assume the following:

```
X        DS     C
DOLLAR   DC     C'$'
D        EQU    C'$'
R2       EQU    2
```

Which of the following will *not* move a $ into the byte at X? Justify each selection.

**a.** MVI X,DOLLAR

**b.** MVC X(1),DOLLAR

**c.** MVI X,D

**d.** MVC DOLLAR(1),X

**e.** IC R2,DOLLAR
STC R2,X

**f.** LA R2,DOLLAR
MVI X,0(R2)

**g.** MVCIN X(1),DOLLAR

**h.** LA R2,D
MVI X,R2

**i.** LA R2,DOLLAR
MVC X(1),0(R2)

**j.** LA R2,DOLLAR
MVC 0(1,R2),X

**k.** LA R2,X
MVI 0(R2),C'$'

**l.** ICM R2,B'0100',DOLLAR
STCM R2,B'0100',X

3. Assume the following:

```
X        DC     C'ABCDE'
Y        DC     C'FGHIJ'
Z        DC     C'KLMNO'
```

What are the contents of the 5 bytes at X and the 5 bytes at Y after the execution of these instructions?

```
MVC    X+1(4),X
MVC    Y(4),Y+1
```

4. Assume the following:

```
X        DC     C'ABCDE'
Y        DC     C'ABXYZ'
```

For each of the following instructions, indicate the operands compared and the resultant value of the condition code:

**a.** CLC X(3),Y

**b.** CLC Y(2),X

**c.** CLI X,C'2'

**d.** CLC Y,X

5. Assume that Register 4 contains an integer $n$. Which of the following are correct ways to determine if the byte at DATA+$n$ contains a blank? Correct any that are incorrect.

**a.** CLC DATA(1,R4),=C' '

**b.** LA R5,0
IC R5,DATA(R4)
CL R5,=CL4' '

**c.** LA R5,DATA
CLI 0(R4,R5),C' '

**d.** CLI DATA(R4),C' '

**e.** LA R5,DATA(R4)
CLC 0(1,R5),=C' '

**f.** IC R5,DATA(R4)
CLM R5,B'0001',=C' '

**g.** LA R5,DATA(R4)
CLI 0(R5),=C' '

6. Discuss the merits, if any, of not testing the condition code immediately after it is set in the following sequence. Assume that DATA represents a character string.

```
         LA     6,DATA-1
LOOP     CLI    1(6),C' '
         LA     6,1(6)
         BE     LOOP
```

*For each of the following exercises, write a sequence of instructions to perform the indicated computation.*

7. If the character at C is a $, change it to a #; if it is not a $, leave it alone.

8. If the 100-character array at Z contains 100 dollar signs, replace them with asterisks.

9. Replace any dollar signs in the 50-character array at W with asterisks. Do not change the other bytes.

10. Insert an asterisk into the beginning of the character string at STRING. (The byte at STRING should contain an asterisk and it should be followed by the original character string.)

11. Reverse the order of a character string without using the MVCIN instruction. Try this in two ways: first, by using a second array to contain the reversed string, and, second, without a second array.

12. Initialize the 1000 bytes at BLOCK to blanks by using several different approaches. Comment upon their relative advantages or disadvantages. Would your answer differ if 100,000 bytes were initialized?

13. Consider two strings at S1 and S2. Produce a third string that consists of characters taken alternately from the two strings. (That is, take the first character of S1, then the first character of S2, then the second character of S1, and so on.)

14. Consider the string of characters at S1. Produce a second string that consists of the same characters separated by single blanks.

15. The 80-byte area at DATA contains several nonblank alphabetic character strings that are separated by one or more blanks. Create a condensed version of this data at NEW by replacing any sequence of blanks with a single *.

16. The 80 bytes at DIGITS contain decimal digits in EBCDIC form. Count the number of occurrences of each digit by using 1-byte counters.

17. For each 15-character data record read, concatenate the first 5 characters with the last 5 characters to produce a 10-character string. Create an array of these strings.

18. Convert any lowercase letters that may occur in an input string to uppercase letters. Do not change any other characters.

## Programming Problems

1. Revise the program, which is listed in Figure 10.21, for Example 41 to eliminate the array of abbreviations. Note that each abbreviation consists of the first three letters of the month's name and these are available in the array NAMES.

2. Write a program that reads integers $a$ and $b$, and computes $a/b$ to 40 decimal places if $a < b$. Print a line such as 2/7 = 0.28571· · ·. If $a \geq b$, print an error message. An algorithm may be derived from the following computations for 2/7:

2/7

(2 * 10)/7 = **2** with a remainder of 6

(6 * 10)/7 = **8** with a remainder of 4

(4 * 10)/7 = **5** with a remainder of 5

(5 * 10)/7 = **7** with a remainder of 1

(1 * 10)/7 = **1** with a remainder of 3

3. Consider an input data set that contains sentences written entirely with lowercase letters. Write a program that replaces the first letter of each sentence by an uppercase letter. Assume that the sentences can end only with a period, a question mark, or an exclamation point, and that they can contain no other punctuation. Also assume that a single blank separates the sentences. Print both the original and the modified sentences.

4. Repeat Programming Problem 3 to allow the sentences to be separated by an arbitrary number of blanks. Produce sentences that are separated by exactly two blanks.

5. Using Zeller's congruence (see the case study in Chapter 5) and Example 41, write a program that reads a date such as 12/31/93 and that produces a line of output such as

FRIDAY DECEMBER 31, 1993

with no extra spaces. Assume that input dates contain no blanks, and that single-digit months or days do not contain leading zeros. Therefore, a date such as April 1, 2005 would be written as 4/1/05. Your program should be valid for 99 years from the present date. (You will need an array that contains the names of the days of the week. See if you can use an array in which the letters DAY are omitted from each name.)

6. Consider an array of up to 100 entries that are each 15 bytes long. Each entry is a 15-character string that consists of up to 14 letters followed by blanks. Initialize the array by reading data records that contain 5 strings, which begin in columns 1, 16, 31, 46, and 61. (The last record may contain fewer than 5 strings.) Print the data with an appropriate heading, and 5 strings per line. Alphabetize the strings in the array and print the results, 3 strings per line. (Arrange the output so that it is alphabetical by row; for example,

```
A··· B··· C···
D··· E··· F···
```

As an added challenge, arrange the output so that it is alphabetical by column; for example,

```
A··· D··· G···
B··· E··· H···
C··· F··· I···
```

7. Consider two arrays, each of which is as described in Programming Problem 6. Assume that the data set for each array consists of distinct strings given in alphabetical order. Although each array contains distinct entries, a string in one array may occur in the other array. Merge the two arrays into a third array, which is also in alphabetical order and which contains distinct entries. Print the three arrays so that each array forms one of three adjacent columns.

8. Revise Programming Problems 6 and 7 so that a single comma, instead of a blank, separates adjacent character strings in a data record. A comma must follow the last string in any record; a blank must follow the last string in the data set.

9. Consider an array of up to 100 character strings that are each 20 bytes long in collating sequence order. Given an arbitrary 20-character string, determine whether or not it occurs in the array and, if it does, determine its position in the array. Use a binary search.

10. The operation, operand, and remarks entries of an assembler language statement need not begin in fixed columns. You can write them in a free format, whereby the entries are separated by at least one blank. Write a program to read free-format assembler language statements, print a listing of them, and then print a revised listing so that name entries begin in Column 1, operation entries in Column 10, operand entries in Column 16, and remarks in Column 35. Assume the following:

    - Original and revised statements are at most 71 characters long and appear on a single line.
    - Comments statements are possible and should remain unchanged.
    - Only the operation entry is required. (Recall that if there is no operand entry, a comma replaces it if a remarks entry follows.)
    - Operand entries will not contain embedded blanks, such as in C' '.
    - Name, operation, and operand entries will fit in the allowed space on the revised line. If the remarks entry does not fit into Columns 35 to 71 of the revised line, truncate it.
    - There are at most 50 statements in the data set.

11. Write a program to generate several random four-line verses of the following form:

    Adjective, Plural noun, Adverb, Plural verb, Adjective, Plural noun
    Adjective, Plural noun, Plural verb, Adverb, Adjective, Plural noun
    Plural noun, Plural verb, Preposition, Article, Adjective, Singular noun
    Article, Singular noun, Singular verb, Preposition, Article, Singular noun

    First, establish a vocabulary of words that is classified according to the types just given. Use about 10 words of each type; you may assume a maximum of 8 letters per word. Read and print the vocabulary before you generate verses.

    To construct a verse, generate a random integer *R* (described later) and select the *R*-th adjective from your vocabulary. Continue by generating another random integer *R* and select the *R*-th plural noun, and so on until the four lines of the verse have been completed. Print the verse; at first, you may allow several spaces between words, but later try to print the words with only one space between them.

    To generate a random integer *R* between 1 and *N*, proceed as follows:

    - Initialize a fullword X to 65539. (Since you should do this only once in the program, do it at assembly time.)
    - $X := |X * 759375|$ (Retain only the rightmost 32 bits of the product; then take the absolute value.)

      $R := [(X * N)/2^{31}] + 1$ (The division is truncated. Note that you cannot represent $2^{31}$ as a fullword.)

12. Write a program that reads alphabetic text and produces a histogram of the frequency of each letter's occurrence in the text. For example, the beginning of the histogram could appear as

```
A ********************
B ***********
```

The number of asterisks that is used for a particular letter should be proportional to the frequency that the letter occurs.

13. Repeat Programming Problem 12, but print the asterisks vertically, as shown here:

```
*
*
* *
* *
A B ...
```

14. Consider a linked list in which each node contains a 16-byte data field that is followed by a 4-byte address that points to the next node in the list. The last node contains a zero address portion. The address of the first node is in the fullword at HEAD. (HEAD is zero if the list is empty.) Assume an available space list defined by statements such as

```
ASL      DC    A(SPACE)     HEAD OF AVAILABLE SPACE LIST
SPACE    DS    CL16         DATA
         DC    AL4(*+4)     LINK
         DS    CL16
         DC    AL4(*+4)
         .
         .
         .
         DS    CL16
         DC    AL4(0)
```

Assume that $n$ is an integer greater than zero in the fullword at N. Write subprograms to perform the following operations on the linked list:

**a.** Determine the character string that is stored in node $n$.

**b.** Delete node $n$ and return the space to the available space list.

**c.** Insert a node that contains a given 16-byte character string at the beginning of the list. (The list could be empty.)

**d.** Insert a node that contains a given 16-byte character string after node $n$.

**e.** Insert a given character string into its proper position in an ordered list.

**f.** Delete the node that contains a given 16-byte character string from an ordered list. Return the space to the available space list.

# 11

# Additional Bit and Byte Manipulations

CONTENTS



OVERVIEW

This chapter discusses several additional instructions that are used to operate on data at the bit or byte level. Included are instructions that perform the Boolean operations AND, OR, and EXCLUSIVE OR, which are used primarily to manipulate bits. In addition, the chapter introduces powerful instructions that facilitate character manipulation. With them, you can, for example, process fields whose length is specified at execution time, translate from one character code to another, rearrange fields in storage rapidly, scan a byte string for particular values, and copy or compare byte strings of arbitrary length.

**OBJECTIVES**

After studying this chapter, you should be able to:

1. Define the Boolean operations AND, OR, EXCLUSIVE OR, and NOT.
2. Use the instructions that implement AND, OR, and EXCLUSIVE OR to alter or test particular bits within a register or storage.
3. Use the same instructions to interchange the contents of two registers or areas of storage, to initialize an area of storage to zero, or to compare an area of storage with zero.
4. Use the Test Under Mask instruction to test selected bits of a byte.
5. Use the Execute instruction to alter the effect of other instructions. In particular, use it to specify at execution time, instead of at assembly time, the length of a field that is associated with an SS instruction.
6. Use the Translate instruction to translate from one character code to another, or to rearrange the order of fields in storage.
7. Use the Translate and Test instruction to locate or identify any desired values within a byte string.
8. Use the Move Characters Long instruction to initialize or copy fields that are arbitrarily long in storage.
9. Use the Compare Characters Long instruction to compare two arbitrarily long fields in storage.

## Introduction

This chapter begins with a discussion of Boolean operations and the instructions available to perform them. Boolean concepts are used in symbolic logic and circuit design; while you may encounter applications related to these areas, your main concern will be with their use in bit manipulation. Remember that the byte is the smallest addressable unit of storage, so you cannot address bits directly. However, the Boolean instructions allow you to alter or test individual bits in registers or in storage. In addition, the instruction Test Under Mask tests selected bits of a byte. Together, these instructions augment the Shift instructions and allow you to perform a wide range of bit-level operations.

This chapter also discusses additional, more powerful instructions to manipulate bytes. The Execute instruction enables the temporary modification of the second byte of other instructions. For example, this allows you to specify at execution time the length of the fields that are involved in an SS instruction. The Translate instruction alters the value of several bytes according to a programmer-designed translation table. For example, this permits you to translate characters that are written with one character code into another code. The Translate and Test instruction allows a character string to be scanned quickly for particular characters. Finally, the instructions Move Characters Long and Compare Characters Long permit operations with byte strings of arbitrary length.

## Bit Manipulation

The Boolean operations involve operands that can have only two values, and produce results that also have two values. In symbolic logic, these values are TRUE and FALSE; in Boolean algebra, they are 0 and 1. For simplicity, this text will use the values 0 and 1 and, when appropriate, interpret them as FALSE and TRUE, respectively.

Four common Boolean operations are of interest here. They are AND, OR, EXCLUSIVE OR, and NOT; each will be defined in turn. Suppose that *x* and *y* represent the operands of a Boolean operation. Then the operation AND is defined as follows:

AND

| *x* | *y* | *x* AND *y* |
|---|---|---|
| 0 | 0 | 0 |
| 0 | 1 | 0 |
| 1 | 0 | 0 |
| 1 | 1 | 1 |

Notice that *x* AND *y* is 1 if *both x* and *y* are 1; *x* AND *y* is 0, if they are not. You can interpret this to mean the following:

*x* AND *y* is TRUE if and only if both *x* and *y* are TRUE.

The operation OR is defined as follows:

OR

| *x* | *y* | *x* OR *y* |
|---|---|---|
| 0 | 0 | 0 |
| 0 | 1 | 1 |
| 1 | 0 | 1 |
| 1 | 1 | 1 |

Here, *x* OR *y* is 1 if *either or both* operands is 1; the only time that *x* OR *y* is 0 is if both operands are 0. Thus, you can interpret this to mean the following:

*x* OR *y* is TRUE if either *x* or *y* is TRUE

The operation EXCLUSIVE OR is defined as follows:

EXCLUSIVE OR

| $x$ | $y$ | $x$ EXCLUSIVE OR $y$ |
|---|---|---|
| 0 | 0 | 0 |
| 0 | 1 | 1 |
| 1 | 0 | 1 |
| 1 | 1 | 0 |

Note that $x$ EXCLUSIVE OR $y$ is 1 if exactly one of the operands is 1; it is 0 if not. You can interpret this to mean the following:

> $x$ EXCLUSIVE OR $y$ is TRUE if exactly one of x *or* y is TRUE, but not both.

The operation NOT is defined as follows:

NOT

| $x$ | NOT $x$ |
|---|---|
| 0 | 1 |
| 1 | 0 |

NOT operates upon a single operand to invert its value.

## A BIOGRAPHY OF GEORGE BOOLE

George Boole, the inventor of Boolean algebra, never took an algebra course. Born in 1815 in Lincoln, England, Boole's early education was shaped by his father, who was a poor cobbler with a strong interest in mathematics. Poverty forced Boole to leave school after only a few years, but his father and a family friend helped him to study mathematics and languages. When he was only 15, Boole was hired as a mathematics teacher; by the time that he was 20, he had established a school of his own and published his first scientific paper.

During Boole's time, logic was a branch of philosophy, not of mathematics. A Scottish philosopher once ridiculed one of Boole's friends, the mathematician Augustus De Morgan, about the inadequacy of mathematics in the development of logic. Boole came to De Morgan's defense and, in 1847, published the essay "The Mathematical Analysis of Logic," which proved that mathematics can be applied to logic. In doing so, he introduced the system that is now known as Boolean algebra.

While his essay was not as highly regarded as it is today, it did establish a reputation for Boole. In 1849, he was hired as a mathematics professor at Queen's College in Cork, Ireland. While there, he published the second of his landmark works, entitled "An Investigation of the Laws of Thought" in 1854. Today, this work is recognized as the foundation of symbolic logic.

During his career, he published 2 textbooks and about 50 papers, received 2 honorary degrees, and was named a Fellow of the Royal Society, England's leading scholarly association. He died in 1864 of pneumonia; always the dedicated teacher, he had walked 2 miles through the rain to class and, soaking wet, delivered his lecture.

## *Instructions to Perform Boolean Operations*

Of the four Boolean operations—AND, OR, EXCLUSIVE OR, and NOT—only the first three are implemented directly in the IBM 370 instruction set. However, you can implement the NOT operation in terms of an EXCLUSIVE OR instruction since the following is true:

NOT *x*

NOT *x* is equivalent to 1 EXCLUSIVE OR *x*

The Boolean instructions have operands that are bit strings. The operands either can be 32 bits long and can be contained in registers, or can be fields of from 1 to 256 consecutive bytes in storage. When 2 *n*-bit strings are involved in a Boolean operation, each bit of one string is combined with the corresponding bit of the second string to form the result. These *n* operations occur independently of one another. For example, consider the following AND operation on two 8-bit strings:

**Boolean instructions perform bitwise operations**

```
     1 1 1 1 0 0 0 0
AND  1 0 1 0 1 0 1 0
     1 0 1 0 0 0 0 0
```

Four instructions, each in a different format—RR, RX, SI, or SS—are available for each Boolean operation. In the following, the instructions are grouped by format and the symbol *op* is used to represent a Boolean operation.

| Operation | Operand | Format | Instruction Name | Action |
|---|---|---|---|---|
| **NR** | *R1,R2* | RR | AND REGISTER | C(*R1*) ← C(*R1*) *op* C(*R2*) |
| **OR** | | | OR REGISTER | |
| **XR** | | | EXCLUSIVE OR REGISTER | |
| **N** | *R1,S2*<br>or *R1,S2(X2)*<br>or *R1,D2(X2,B2)* | RX | AND | C(*R1*) ← C(*R1*) *op* $C(E2)_{0-31}$ |
| **O** | | | OR | |
| **X** | | | EXCLUSIVE OR | |
| **NI** | *S1,I2*<br>or *D1(B1),I2* | SI | AND IMMEDIATE | C(*E1*) ← C(*E1*) *op I2* |
| **OI** | | | OR IMMEDIATE | |
| **XI** | | | EXCLUSIVE OR IMMEDIATE | |
| **NC**† | *S1(L),S2*<br>or *D1(L,B1),D2(B2)* | SS | AND CHARACTERS | $C(E1)_{L\ \text{bytes}} \leftarrow C(E1)_{L\ \text{bytes}}\ op\ C(E2)_{L\ \text{bytes}}$ |
| **OC** | | | OR CHARACTERS | |
| **XC** | | | EXCLUSIVE OR CHARACTERS | |

For all of these instructions,

$$\text{Condition code} = \begin{cases} 0 & \text{if the result is zero} \\ 1 & \text{if the result is nonzero} \end{cases}$$

†The SS instructions in this chapter, like the ones in the previous chapter, have operand entries of the following forms:

*S1(L),S2*
or *S1,S2*
or *S1(L),D2(B2)*
or *S1,D2(B2)*
or *D1(L,B1),S2*
or *D1(L,B1),D2(B2)*

To save space, this chapter will list only the first and last forms.

As with the Shift instructions, it is usually more convenient to think in binary when you use the Boolean operations. Thus, the following examples use binary quantities.

---

EXAMPLE 1

```
NR      4,8
```

Before execution:

Reg. 4 = 1111 1111 1010 1010 1111 1111 1010 1010
Reg. 8 = 0000 0000 1111 1111 0000 0000 1111 1111

After execution:

Reg. 4 = 0000 0000 1010 1010 0000 0000 1010 1010
Reg. 8 = unchanged
*Condition code* = 1

Each bit in Register 4 is ANDed with a corresponding bit in Register 8. The result of these 32 AND operations replaces the contents of Register 4. Notice that only the 1-bits in Register 4 that correspond to 1-bits in Register 8 remain as 1; the other bits become 0. Also notice that bits in Register 4 that correspond to 0's in Register 8 become 0; the rest are unchanged.

Since the result is nonzero, the condition code is set to 1.

---

EXAMPLE 2

```
OI      X,B'11110000'
```

Before execution:

The byte at X = 01010101
Immediate data = 11110000

After execution:

The byte at X = 11110101
*Condition code* = 1

Each bit in the byte at X is ORed with a corresponding bit in the immediate data. The result of these 8 operations replaces the byte at X. The bits of X that correspond to 1's in the immediate data become 1; the rest are unchanged.

---

EXAMPLE 3

```
XC      A(2),B
```

Before execution:

The field at A = 11110000 11110000
The field at B = 11111111 00000000

After execution:

The field at A = 00001111 11110000
The field at B = unchanged
*Condition code* = 1

Each bit in the field at A is EXCLUSIVE ORed with a corresponding bit in the field at B. The result of these operations replaces the field at A. The bits of A that correspond to 1's in B are inverted in value; the remaining bits are unchanged.

---

EXAMPLE 4

```
NC      Y(256),Y
```

By examining the definition of the AND operation, you will see that

0 AND 0 is 0
1 AND 1 is 1

and, in general,

*x* AND *x* is *x*

Thus, anything ANDed with itself remains unchanged, so the instruction here does not affect the 256 bytes at Y. However, the condition code is set. This instruction provides a fast way to determine if the field at Y contains zero.

The same comments apply to the OR operation.

---

EXAMPLE 5

```
XC      B(256),B
```

By examining the definition of the EXCLUSIVE OR operation, you will see that

0 EXCLUSIVE OR 0 is 0
1 EXCLUSIVE OR 1 is 0

and, in general,

*x* EXCLUSIVE OR *x* is 0

Thus, anything EXCLUSIVE ORed with itself is changed to zero. Here, the instruction sets the 256 bytes at B to zero. This is a convenient and fast way to initialize a maximum of 256 bytes of storage to zero.

---

EXAMPLE 6

**Interchanging the Contents of Two Areas**

The following sequence of instructions interchanges the contents of the 256 bytes at A with the contents of the 256 bytes at B, without using intermediate storage:

```
XC      A(256),B
XC      B(256),A
XC      A(256),B
```

Although this sequence may be in the category of a programming trick, it is a widely used technique to exchange the contents of two areas of storage; it is particularly useful in a sort. (You can verify that this technique does indeed interchange A and B in Exercise 1 at the end of this chapter.) You can use an analogous sequence of RR instructions to interchange the contents of two registers without using a third register.

---

## *Changing Bits*

You may use the Boolean instructions to set bits selectively to 0 or to 1 as desired, or to invert the value of a particular bit.

*To Set Bits to 0 Selectively.* By examining the definition of the AND operation, you will observe the following rules:

**Use AND to set bits to 0**

0 AND $x$ = 0
1 AND $x$ = $x$

If you AND 0 with any bit, the result is 0; if you AND 1 with any bit, that bit is unchanged. You need to know both of these facts if you are to change particular bits to 0 without altering the other bits in the operand. You proceed by creating a mask with 0's in the positions that correspond to the bits that are to be set to 0, and with 1's elsewhere.

---

EXAMPLE 7

**Set the Third and Sixth Bits of a Byte to 0**

```
NI     BITS,B'11011011'
```

Before execution:

The byte at BITS = 01110010
Mask (immediate data) = 11011011

After execution:

The byte at BITS = 01010010
(third and sixth bits marked: Set to 0)

The mask, written here as immediate data, has a 0 for its third and sixth bits; the remaining bits are 1. The instruction sets the third and sixth bits of the byte at BITS to 0; it then leaves the remaining bits unchanged.

---

*To Set Bits to 1 Selectively.* By examining the definition of the OR operation, you will observe the following rules:

**Use OR to set bits to 1**

1 OR $x$ is 1
0 OR $x$ is $x$

If you OR 1 with any bit, the result is 1; if you OR 0 with any bit, that bit is unchanged. You proceed as before by creating a mask, but this time there are 1's in the positions that correspond to the bits that are to be set to 1, and there are 0's elsewhere.

---

EXAMPLE 8

**Set the Third and Sixth Bits of a Byte to 1**

```
OI      BITS,B'00100100'
```

Before execution:

The byte at BITS = 01110010
Mask = 00100100

After execution:

The byte at BITS = 01110110
(third and sixth bits: Set to 1)

The third and sixth bits of the mask are 1; the remaining bits are 0. The instruction sets the third and sixth bits of BITS to 1, regardless of their prior value; the rest are unchanged.

---

*To Invert Bit Values Selectively.* By examining the definition of the EXCLUSIVE OR operation, you will observe the following rules:

**Use EXCLUSIVE OR to invert bit values**

1 EXCLUSIVE OR $x$ is NOT $x$
0 EXCLUSIVE OR $x$ is $x$

If you EXCLUSIVE OR 1 with any bit, the bit value is inverted. If you EXCLUSIVE OR 0 with any bit, that bit is unchanged. The required mask is created in the same manner as before: there are 1's in the positions that correspond to the bits to be inverted, and there are 0's elsewhere.

---

EXAMPLE 9

**Invert the Values of the Third and Sixth Bits of a Byte**

```
XI      BITS,B'00100100'
```

Before execution:

The byte at BITS = 01110010
Mask = 00100100

After execution:

The byte at BITS = 01010110
(third and sixth bits: Values inverted)

The third and sixth bits of the byte at BITS, which correspond to the mask bits that are 1, are inverted. The remaining bits are unchanged.

---

## Testing Bits: The Test Under Mask (TM) Instruction

You may also use the Boolean instructions to test the value of selected bits without altering them. (Example 11 of the next section will demonstrate how this is done.) However, when the operand consists of only one byte, the Test Under Mask instruction facilitates this test. TM is an SI instruction whose immediate data *I2* is used as a mask. If a bit in the mask is 1, the instruction selects the corresponding bit in the first operand. If the mask bit is 0, the instruction ignores the corresponding bit in the first operand. All of the selected bits are examined and the condition code is set accordingly. The instruction is summarized as follows:

| Operation | Operand | Format | Instruction Name | Action |
|---|---|---|---|---|
| **TM** | *S1,I2* or *D1(B1),I2* | SI | TEST UNDER MASK | Tests bits of C(*E1*) selected according to *I2*<br>Condition code = { 0 if all selected bits are 0's or if *I2* = 0; 1 if some selected bits are 0's and if others are 1's; 3 if all selected bits are 1's |

Notice that the condition code is never 2.

---

EXAMPLE 10

```
TM      BYTE,B'00110000'
```

Selected bits

The byte at BYTE = 01010110 *Condition code* = 1

Mask = 00110000

The instruction causes the third and fourth bits of BYTE to be selected. Since they are neither all 1's nor all 0's, the condition code is set to 1. The contents of BYTE remain unchanged.

---

You can use the extended mnemonic branch instructions after a Test Under Mask. You have seen these before, although they had different meanings then. Even so, the generated branch masks are correct regardless of how you interpret them. Here are the relevant extended mnemonic branch instructions.

**Extended mnemonics to follow a TM instruction**

| | | |
|---|---|---|
| BZ | Branch if Zeros | (branches if the condition code = 0) |
| BM | Branch if Mixed | (branches if the condition code = 1) |
| BO | Branch if Ones | (branches if the condition code = 3) |
| BNZ | Branch if Not Zeros | (branches if the condition code ≠ 0) |
| BNM | Branch if Not Mixed | (branches if the condition code ≠ 1) |
| BNO | Branch if Not Ones | (branches if the condition code ≠ 3) |

RR versions of these instructions are also available.

## *Sample Applications of Bit Manipulation*

The instructions introduced so far in this chapter enable you to deal with individual bits, regardless of whether they are in a register or in storage. You can set a particular bit to 0, set it to 1, invert its value, test it without modification, or isolate it. These capabilities allow you to create a set of logical switches or flags that you can use to affect the execution of your program. For example, certain sort algorithms use a flag to indicate whether or not interchanges have been made during a pass through the data. Sometimes, several flags are necessary. For example, within the operating system, the status of many events such as input and output operations must be recorded. Since there are so many of them, you can save space by using an individual bit, rather than a byte or a group of bytes, to represent each flag.

---

EXAMPLE 11

### 32 Switches in a Fullword

Suppose there is a fullword at SWITCHES whose bits represent 32 logical on/off switches that are numbered left to right from 0 to 31. Assume that $n$ is an integer in the range 0 to 31 and that it is contained in Register 9. Given this information, set bit $n$ to 1 or to 0, or invert its value, or test it.

*Set Bit* n *to 1.* Remember that you can set a particular bit to 1, regardless of its present value, by ORing it with 1. Any of the OR instructions will affect more than a single bit and, since you do not want to alter the other bits in SWITCHES, you must OR them with 0's. For example, if you want to set bit 2 to 1—that is, turn Switch 2 on—you would perform the following OR operation:

```
SWITCHES:        xxxx . . . xx
              OR 0010 . . . 00
                 ------------
                 xx1x . . . xx
```

where $x$ denotes any bit value. The operation affects only the bit in position 2, and leaves the rest unchanged.

In general, you must create a 32-bit mask that has a 1 in position $n$ and 0's elsewhere. You can do this by loading

1000 . . . 00

into a register and shifting it to the right logically by $n$ bits. As you can see from the instructions in Figure 11.1, the right shift is performed by

```
SRL   R2,0(R9)
```

where again Register 9 contains $n$. The fullword SWITCHES is then ORed with Register 2, and the result stored back into SWITCHES.

*Set Bit* n *to 0.* This time, you must AND bit $n$ with 0 to set it to 0, regardless of its present value. You must AND other bits with 1's so that their values

**Figure 11.1**
The instructions to set bit $n$ to 1, as described in Example 11.

```
** SET BIT N OF SWITCHES TO 1.
** SWITCHES IS A FULLWORD IN STORAGE;
** REGISTER 9 CONTAINS AN INTEGER N BETWEEN 0 AND 31;
**
         L     R2,=X'80000000' LEFTMOST BIT IS 1
         SRL   R2,0(R9)        1 IN POSITION N,  0'S ELSEWHERE
         O     R2,SWITCHES     SET BIT N TO 1; REST ARE UNCHANGED
         ST    R2,SWITCHES     STORE BACK INTO SWITCHES
```

**Figure 11.2**
The instructions to set bit $n$ to 0, as described in Example 11.

```
** SET BIT N OF SWITCHES TO 0.
** SWITCHES IS A FULLWORD IN STORAGE;
** REGISTER 9 CONTAINS AN INTEGER N BETWEEN 0 AND 31;
**
         L     R2,=X'80000000' LEFTMOST BIT IS 1
         SRL   R2,0(R9)        1 IN POSITION N,  0'S ELSEWHERE
         X     R2,=X'FFFFFFFF' 0 IN POSITION N,  1'S ELSEWHERE
         N     R2.SWITCHES     SET BIT N TO 0; REST ARE UNCHANGED
         ST    R2,SWITCHES     STORE BACK INTO SWITCHES
```

are unchanged. For example, if you wanted to set bit 2 to 0—that is, turn Switch 2 off—you would perform the following AND operation:

| SWITCHES: | | *xxxx . . . xx* |
|---|---|---|
| | AND | 1101 . . . 11 |
| | | *xx*0*x . . . xx* |

The problem then is to create a mask with 0 in position $n$ and with 1's elsewhere. One way is to create the same mask as before by forming

0010 . . . 00

in a register and then by inverting each bit value by EXCLUSIVE ORing each bit value with 1. The instructions in Figure 11.2 show how this is done. (Another way to do this is described in Exercise 3 at the end of this chapter.)

*Test Bit* n. One way to test a bit is to first isolate it. Recall the following fact:

1 AND $x$ is $x$

By ANDing a 1 into bit position $n$, you will get the value of that bit as a result. ANDing 0's into the other bits will produce 0's; thus, you can isolate bit $n$. Once again, construct a mask with a 1 in position $n$ and with 0's elsewhere. The result of ANDing SWITCHES with this mask is the value of bit $n$, surrounded by 31 zeros. Now recall that the AND instruction sets the condition code according to whether the result is zero or not. Using this feature is all you need to complete the test. The necessary instructions are listed in Figure 11.3.

**Figure 11.3** The instructions to test bit $n$, as described in Example 11.

```
** TEST BIT N OF SWITCHES.
** SWITCHES IS A FULLWORD IN STORAGE;
** REGISTER 9 CONTAINS AN INTEGER N BETWEEN 0 AND 31;
**
         L      R2,=X'80000000'  LEFTMOST BIT IS 1
         SRL    R2,0(R9)         1 IN POSITION N, 0'S ELSEWHERE
         N      R2,SWITCHES      ISOLATE BIT N IN R2
         BZ     OFF              BIT N = 0  (SWITCH IS OFF)
         BNZ    ON               BIT N = 1  (SWITCH IS ON)
```

---

EXAMPLE 12

**Eight Flags in a Byte**

In this example, you will alter bits with the Boolean instructions, but you will test them with the TM instruction. There are two major distinctions between this example and Example 11. First, bit positions here are indicated directly as immediate data, rather than with a register. Second, the operand is one byte, rather than a fullword—although, as you will see, this does not preclude defining several arbitrary bytes of flags.

Assume that you have 2 bytes that are not necessarily consecutive, each of which represents 8 flags. For example, each byte might represent a different group having 8 possible characteristics that correspond to the 8 bits in the byte. If a bit is 1, then assume that the group has that characteristic.

To write instructions that alter or test one or more bit values requires several masks, as defined in Figure 11.4. The advantage to these definitions is to provide mnemonic terminology. Thus, you avoid the tedium and the possible errors involved in rewriting a mask each time that you need it in an instruction. Some sample operations are listed in Figure 11.5. In part **a** of Figure 11.5, CHAR4 is used instead of the mask B'00010000' to set the bit that represents the fourth characteristic to 1. In part **b** of Figure 11.5, notice how a characteristic is deleted. To set the seventh bit of GROUP2 to 0, the binary mask 11111101 must be ANDed with the byte at GROUP2. This mask is written as

```
DELETE-CHAR7
```

which is equivalent to

```
B'11111111'-B'00000010'
```

In part **c** of Figure 11.5, the TM instruction tests the sixth bit of GROUP1 for 0. CHAR6 represents the required mask and, if the bit is 0, the condition code is set to 0.

You can test for the simultaneous existence of more than one characteristic by combining masks. In part **d** of Figure 11.5, the instruction

```
TM      GROUP2,CHAR2+CHAR4
```

**Figure 11.4**
Mask definitions for Example 12.

```
CHAR1    EQU   B'10000000'   FIRST BIT
CHAR2    EQU   B'01000000'   SECOND BIT
CHAR3    EQU   B'00100000'   THIRD BIT
CHAR4    EQU   B'00010000'   FOURTH BIT
CHAR5    EQU   B'00001000'   FIFTH BIT
CHAR6    EQU   B'00000100'   SIXTH BIT
CHAR7    EQU   B'00000010'   SEVENTH BIT
CHAR8    EQU   B'00000001'   EIGHTH BIT
DELETE   EQU   B'11111111'   MASK TO INVERT BIT VALUES
```

**Figure 11.5**
Sample operations on flags in a byte, as described in Example 12.

**a.** Assign characteristic 4 to GROUP1:

```
OI    GROUP1,CHAR4          SET 4-TH BIT TO 1
```

**b.** Delete characteristic 7 from GROUP2:

```
NI    GROUP2,DELETE-CHAR7   SET 7-TH BIT TO 0
```

**c.** Branch to NO if GROUP1 is missing characteristic 6:

```
TM    GROUP1,CHAR6          TEST 6-TH BIT
BZ    NO                    BRANCH IF BIT IS 0
```

**d.** Branch to BOTH if GROUP2 has both characteristics 2 and 4:

```
TM    GROUP2,CHAR2+CHAR4    TEST 2-ND AND 4-TH BITS
BO    BOTH                  BRANCH IF BOTH BITS ARE 1
```

tests the second and fourth bits of GROUP2. This is equivalent to

```
TM    GROUP2,B'01010000'
```

since

```
CHAR2+CHAR4
```

is equivalent to

```
B'01000000'+B'00010000'
```

which is equivalent to

```
B'01010000'
```

## SELF-TEST EXERCISES

1. Assume the following register status:

   Reg. 4 = FFFFFFFF
   Reg. 5 = 00000000
   Reg. 6 = 0000000C

   Indicate the effect that each of the following instructions has upon this status and the condition code.

   a. NR 4,6
   b. NR 5,6
   c. NR 6,6
   d. OR 6,4
   e. OR 6,5
   f. OR 6,6
   g. XR 4,6
   h. XR 5,6
   i. XR 6,6
   j. O 6,=X'AB000001'
   k. N 6,=X'AB000001'
   l. N 6,=X'AB000004'
   m. X 6,=X'AB000004'

2. What is the effect of each of the following instructions on the condition code and the field that is defined by

   ```
   BITS     DC     X'ABCDEF'
   ```

   a. OI BITS,B'01010101'
   b. NI BITS+1,X'6B'
   c. XI BITS,0
   d. NC BITS(2),=H'0'
   e. XC BITS(3),BITS
   f. OC BITS,BITS
   g. XC BITS(3),=X'FFFFFF'

3. Write instructions to perform each of the following:
   a. Set the odd-numbered bits in Register 4 to 0, and leave the others alone.
   b. Set the odd-numbered bits in the doubleword at D to 1, and leave the others alone.
   c. Set bits 2 through 7 of Register 2 to 001111, invert the values of bits 10 through 16, and leave the rest alone.

4. Write instructions to compute the one's complement of the binary integer in Register 5.

5. With the definitions described in Example 12 and Figure 11.4, write instructions to perform each of the following:
   a. If GROUP1 does not have characteristic 7, assign it; if GROUP1 does have characteristic 7, delete it.
   b. Assign characteristics 5 and 8 to GROUP2.
   c. Delete characteristic 2 from both GROUP1 and GROUP2.
   d. Repeat the operation of Self-Test Exercise 5c in one instruction. Assume that GROUP2 follows GROUP1 immediately in storage.
   e. Branch to NEITHER if GROUP1 has neither characteristic 3 nor 5.
   f. Branch to ONE if GROUP2 has either characteristic 1 or 4, but not both.
   g. Branch to MISSING if GROUP1 is missing either or both of characteristics 5 and 6.

## The Execute (EX) Instruction

The Execute instruction allows you to execute another instruction whose second byte is temporarily altered. Recall that the second byte of an SS instruction contains the length of the fields that are involved. In an SI instruction, the second byte is the immediate data. For other instructions, the second byte designates registers or masks. For now, focus on the SS instructions. As the last chapter noted, you cannot specify the length of the fields that are involved in an SS instruction indirectly when you write the instruction. The EX instruction will now enable you to circumvent this problem.

The EX instruction is an RX instruction whose second operand entry specifies the address of another instruction called the **target instruction.** The target instruction is executed, either as is or modified, during the execution of the EX instruction. Essentially, the program behaves as if the target instruction replaces EX.

**Register 0 cannot be used with the EX instruction**

When *R1* is not 0, it designates a register operand whose rightmost byte (bits 24 through 31) is ORed with the second byte of the target instruction. This modification is made to a copy of the target instruction within the CPU; the actual target instructon in storage is unchanged. When *R1* is 0, it does not designate Register 0; instead, the target instruction is executed as is without modification. The instruction can be summarized as follows:

| Operation | Operand | Format | Instruction Name | Action |
|---|---|---|---|---|
| **EX** | *R1,S2*<br>or *R1,S2(X2)*<br>or *R1,D2(X2,B2)* | RX | EXECUTE | If $R1 \neq 0$, executes the target instruction at *E2* as if its second byte had been ORed with $C(R1)_{24-31}$; the target instruction is unchanged in storage. If $R1 = 0$, executes the target instruction as is without modification. |

The target instruction may be any instruction except another Execute (otherwise, an **Execute exception** occurs), and it must be located at a half-word boundary (otherwise, a specification exception occurs). The target instruction is executed as if it replaced EX in the program; thus, unless the target instruction is a Branch instruction, the instruction after EX is executed next. If the target instruction is a Branch instruction that branches, the next instruction is taken from the branch address; but if the target instruction is a Branch instruction that sequences, the next instruction is the one that immediately follows the EX.

**Position the target instruction near EX**

The target instruction can set the condition code and cause exceptions. Although the target instruction may be located anywhere in the program, it is typically positioned so that it will not be executed in its unmodified form. For example, you could place it with the DC and DS directives if they are nearby, but often the best practice is to write it near the EX instruction and branch around it. It is highly unlikely that you would ever want to place the target instruction immediately after the EX.

---

EXAMPLE 13

**Specifying the Operand Length of an MVC Instruction at Execution Time**

```
      LA    R2,5       L-1
      EX    R2,MOVE    MOVE 6 BYTES
      .
      .
      .
MOVE  MVC   B(0),A
```

The length as written in the MVC instruction is 0; therefore, the second byte of this instruction contains zero. The second byte is ORed with the rightmost byte of Register 2 when EX is executed as follows. (The quantities are given in binary.)

| | |
|---|---|
| C(Reg. $2)_{24-31}$: | 00000101 |
| Second byte of MVC: | 00000000 |
| Result: | 00000101 |

Remember that the internal operand length of an SS instruction is one less than the actual length.

The MVC instruction is then executed as if its second byte contained the result of this ORing. *Six* bytes are moved from A to B since the length in machine language—which is 5 in this case—is always one less than the desired length.

The MVC instruction is written with a length of 0 so that the assembled length is 0. Typically, you write the target instruction in this way. The value that is required for the second byte of the target instruction—which is one less than the actual length of the field to be moved—is then placed into the first register operand of the EX instruction since ORing with 0 leaves a value unchanged.

---

EXAMPLE 14

**Locate and Move a Nonblank Character String**

Consider Example 23 (Figure 10.16) of the previous chapter in which a string of nonblank characters was located somewhere within an 80-byte area: The address of the beginning of the string was in Register 5; the length of the string was in Register 3. The goal was to move the string to the bytes at FIELD. At that time, it was noted that you cannot specify the operand length in an SS instruction indirectly. You can now resolve this problem with the EX instruction, as follows:

```
* ASSUME REGISTER 3 CONTAINS THE STRING LENGTH
         BCTR   R3,0             COMPUTE INTERNAL LENGTH
         EX     R3,MOVE          MOVE STRING TO FIELD
         B      AROUND           SKIP OVER TARGET
* ASSUME REGISTER 5 CONTAINS THE ADDRESS OF THE STRING
MOVE     MVC    FIELD(0),0(R5)  TARGET INSTRUCTION
AROUND   ----
```

Since Register 3 contains the actual length of the string, you must subtract 1 from it before you can use it in the EX instruction.

Notice the position of the target instruction within this program segment.

---

EXAMPLE 15

**No Modification Occurs if *R1* Is 0**

```
         LA   0,5
         EX   0,MOVE
         .
         .
         .
MOVE     MVC  B(0),A
```

The contents of Register 0 are irrelevant to the EX instruction. The target instruction is executed without modification and, since the internal length in the MVC instruction is 0, 1 byte is copied from A to B. Although it is unlikely that you would use EX in this manner, it is important to remember how EX behaves when *R1* = 0 so that you will not use it inadvertently.

---

EXAMPLE 16

**The Target Instruction Should Not Immediately Follow EX**

```
         LA    R3,4             R3 = LENGTH - 1
         EX    R3,COMPARE       COMPARE STRINGS
COMPARE  CLC   S(0),C'AAAAAAA'  TARGET INSTRUCTION
         BE    EQUAL
         .
         .
         .
S        DC    C'ABCDEFG'
```

The EX instruction compares the strings ABCDE and AAAAA; each is 5 bytes long since the internal length is 4. The condition code is set to 2 since ABCDE is greater than AAAAA. The instruction immediately after EX is the CLC instruction, which is executed as written. It compares the strings A and A, each string being 1 byte long (again since the internal length is 0). The condition code is set to 0 and a branch to EQUAL occurs. However, this is not the desired result: the target instruction should not appear immediately after the EX instruction.

---

Although you will frequently use the EX instruction to designate the field lengths with SS instructions, it has other uses. The next example demonstrates an application with an RS instruction.

---

EXAMPLE 17

**Specify the Shift Register at Execution Time**

Suppose you want to shift Register *r* to the left where *r* is contained in Register 2. The leftmost 4 bits of the second byte of a Shift instruction designate the instruction's register operand. The EX instruction can affect this. For example, suppose that the target instruction is

This assembles as the hex instruction

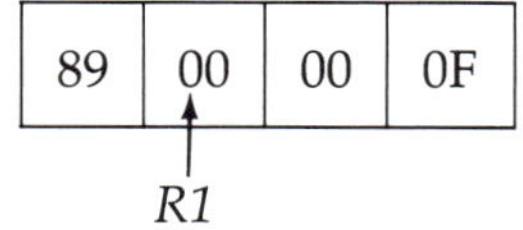


You can change the *R1* portion of the instruction to *r* by ORing the second byte with *r*0. The following sequence accomplishes this:

```
SLL    R2,4        (form r0 in rightmost byte)
EX     R2,SHIFT
```

---

**SELF-TEST EXERCISES**

6. Assume the following definitions:

```
STRING   DC    2CL5' '
MOVE1    MVC   STRING(0),=C'ABCDEFGH'
MOVE2    MVC   STRING,=C'ABCDEFGH'
```

Also assume the following register status:

Reg. 0 = 00000003
Reg. 7 = 00000004
Reg. 8 = 00000001

What is the effect of each of the following instructions on the bytes at STRING?

**a.** `EX 0,MOVE1` **c.** `EX 0,MOVE2`
**b.** `EX 7,MOVE1` **d.** `EX 8,MOVE2`

7. Write instructions before the following segment so that the effect is to add Register 10 to Register 7:

```
         EX    2,ADD
         B     AROUND
ADD      AR    0,0
AROUND   ----
```

# The Translate (TR) Instruction

The Translate instruction is a powerful SS instruction that replaces 8-bit quantities with other 8-bit quantities that are determined according to a **translation table** of your design. For example, you can use TR to translate between the ASCII and EBCDIC codes, or to rearrange fields in storage rapidly.

The first operand of the TR instruction consists of up to 256 consecutive bytes, which are to be translated into something else. These bytes are called the **arguments.** The translation table is a list of bytes at the second operand address. The instruction considers each argument byte in turn, from left to right, and replaces it by a byte called the **function byte,** which has been selected from the translation table.

**Argument bytes point to and are replaced by function bytes**

The correspondence between the arguments and the function bytes in the translation table is a bit peculiar. The 8-bit quantity in an argument byte is added to the effective address *E2* that is specified by the second operand entry. This addition is typical of address arithmetic: the 8-bit quantity is padded on the left with zeros. The effect is much like indexing, and the result of this addition is the address of the function byte.

The instruction can be summarized as follows:

| Operation | Operand | Format | Instruction Name | Action |
|---|---|---|---|---|
| **TR** | *S1(L),S2* or *D1(L,B1),D2(B2)* | SS | TRANSLATE | Translates *L* bytes as follows:<br>C(*E1*) ← C(*E2* + C(*E1*))<br>C(*E1*+1) ← C(*E2* + C(*E1*+1))<br>.<br>.<br>. |

The condition code is unchanged.

EXAMPLE 18

**Translate Numbers into Letters**

```
            TR    ARG(5),TABLE
            .
            .
            .
ARG         DC    X'0200010301'
TABLE       DC    C'ABCD'              OR X'C1C2C3C4'
```

This sequence replaces the bytes at ARG with bytes that are selected from those at TABLE. Each occurrence of $00_{16}$ is replaced by the character code for the letter A, each occurrence of $01_{16}$ by the letter B, and so on. The translation proceeds as follows. The first byte at ARG contains $02_{16}$; this is added to the address that is represented by TABLE. The byte at TABLE + 2 contains the character code for the letter C, which then replaces the first byte at ARG. The second byte at ARG contains 00. When this byte is added to TABLE, the result is TABLE. The byte at TABLE contains the character code for the letter A, which then replaces the second byte at ARG. This continues until all 5 bytes of the first operand are translated. At that time, the bytes at ARG contain the hex quantities

C3 C1 C2 C4 C2

which represent the character string

CABDB

EXAMPLE 19

**Translate Letters into Numbers**

Suppose that ARG contains a string of letters selected only from A to D. The following TR instruction replaces each letter in the string with a hexadecimal number: 01 for A, 02 for B, 03 for C, and 04 for D.

```
            TR    ARG(6),TABLE
            .
            .
            .
ARG         DC    C'ACCBDA'
TABLE       DC    193X'00'           (C'A' = X'C1' = 193)
            DC    X'01020304'
```

Designing this translation table requires a knowledge of EBCDIC. The character codes for A, B, C, and D are consecutive hexadecimal values that begin at C1. Since $C1_{16} = 193$, the first possible function byte is at TABLE + 193. Therefore, TABLE begins with 193 bytes that will be skipped in the translation process. You could define these bytes with a DS, but initializing them with a DC will help in the debugging process, in case you designed the table incorrectly or the bytes at ARG are in error.

After TR is executed, the bytes at ARG contain

01 03 03 02 04 01

Note that you can replace

```
TABLE       DC    193X'00'
```

by

```
TABLE      DC    (C'A')X'00'
```

which is both easier to write and less prone to error because you do not have to look up the decimal equivalent of C'A'.

Since you know that each character in ARG is restricted to A, B, C, or D, and that the first 193 bytes at TABLE are skipped, you can save storage by redefining the translation table to be only 4 bytes long, as follows:

```
TABLE      EQU   *-C'A'
           DC    X'01020304'
```

TABLE now represents an address that is 193 bytes before the constant that is defined by the DC directive; the previous TR instruction will have the same effect with this table as it did with the previous translation table. Since the characters at ARG are restricted, the TR instruction will never access the undefined bytes in the table. To avoid an addressability error due to a negative displacement when using this technique, you must ensure that the DC is at least 193 or C'A' bytes beyond the base address.

---

EXAMPLE 20

### Rearrange Bytes in Storage

Suppose that an array of consecutive bytes is defined at BLOCK. You can use the Translate instruction to copy some or all of these bytes so that they appear in any rearranged order that you choose. For example, you can copy the following bytes into the consecutive bytes at SELECT:

BLOCK+5, BLOCK+26, BLOCK+26, BLOCK+37, BLOCK+2, and BLOCK+31

**Figure 11.6** Illustration of the TR instruction in Example 20 that rearranges bytes in storage.

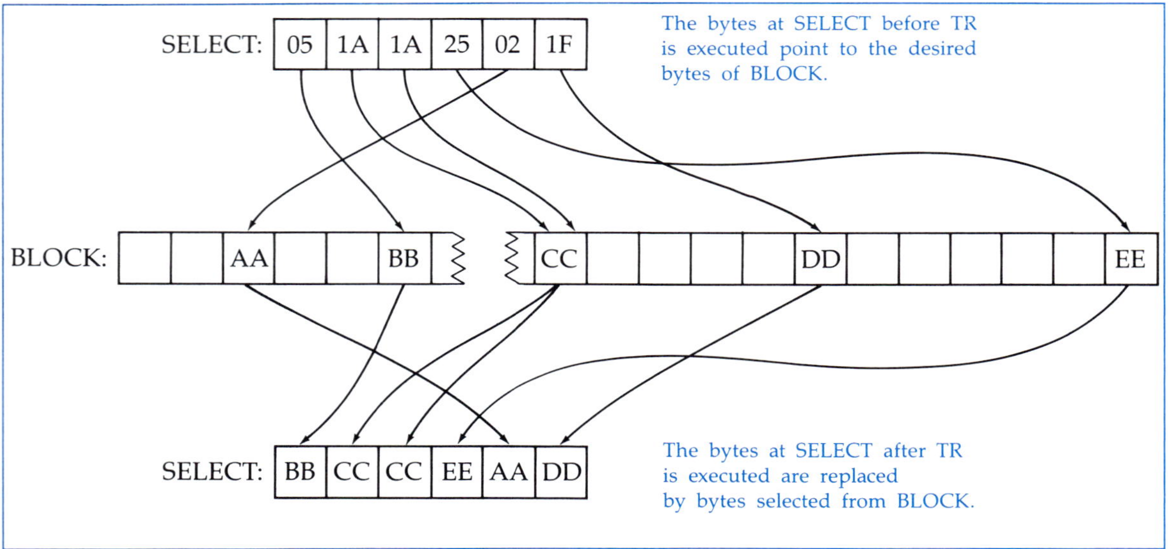

The required instructions are

```
         TR      SELECT(6),BLOCK
         .
         .
         .
SELECT   DC      X'051A1A25021F'
```

Figure 11.6 illustrates the operation: notice that the TR instruction destroys the bytes at SELECT. You should make a copy of them before the TR instruction is executed if you will need them later.

---

EXAMPLE 21

**Rearrange Fields in Storage**

You can also use the TR instruction to rearrange fields within storage. This is particularly useful when you need to fill an output buffer. For example, suppose that you have a record at INPUT that contains a person's name and Social Security number in three adjacent fixed-length fields, as follows:

| | | |
|---|---|---|
| Field 1: | First name | (10 characters) |
| Field 2: | Last name | (15 characters) |
| Field 3: | S. S. number | (9 characters) |

Now, suppose that you want to print this data on a single line that begins with the Social Security number and is followed by the last name and the first name. Unlike the fields at INPUT, the printed fields should be separated by blanks. To accomplish this, you must create an output buffer as illustrated in Figure 11.7. Suppose that this buffer is called OUTPUT.

The instructions in Figure 11.8 allow you to accomplish this task. The bytes at PATTERN specify the desired bytes from INPUT in the proper

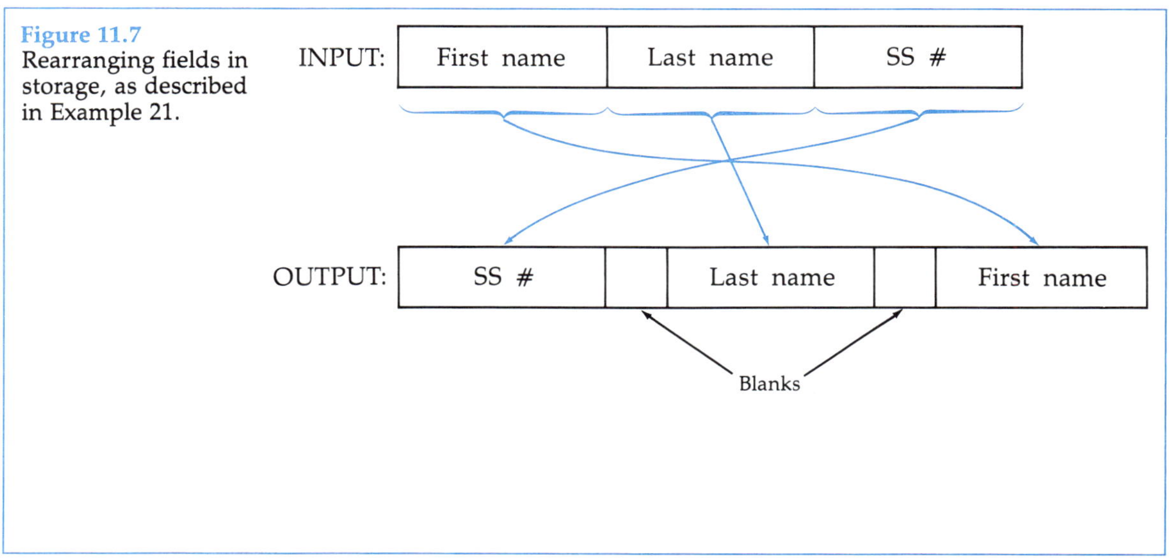


Figure 11.7
Rearranging fields in storage, as described in Example 21.

```
** ASSUME INPUT RECORD HAS BEEN READ
         MVC   OUTPUT(LP),PATTERN        COPY PATTERN TO OUTPUT BUFFER
         TR    OUTPUT(LP),INPUT-1        REARRANGE FIELDS
         .
         .
         .
         DC    C' '                              SPACER
INPUT    DS    CL34                              INPUT RECORD
*
PATTERN  DC    X'1A1B1C1D1E1F202122'             BYTES 26-34
         DC    3X'00'                            SPACE
         DC    X'0B0C0D0E0F101112131415161718191' BYTES 11-25
         DC    3X'00'                            SPACE
         DC    X'0102030405060708090A'           BYTES 1-10
LP       EQU   *-PATTERN                         LENGTH OF PATTERN
*
OUTPUT   DS    (LP)C                             OUTPUT BUFFER
```

**Figure 11.8**
The instructions to rearrange fields in storage, as described in Example 21.

order. You can copy this pattern into the output buffer with the MVC instruction so that you can reuse the pattern with the next input record if you desire. These pattern bytes serve as the arguments of the TR instruction. Constructing the pattern is not as difficult as it may first seem. Here, the bytes in the input record were numbered in hexadecimal from 1 to 22 (1 to $34_{10}$). You can use these numbers in the pattern if you designate the TR instruction's second operand address as INPUT − 1 instead of INPUT. For example, when a pattern byte that contains $01_{16}$ is added to INPUT − 1, the resultant effective address is INPUT, which is the address of the first byte at INPUT. Similarly, a pattern byte of 02 will point to the second byte at INPUT, and so on. Blanks can be conveniently specified as 00 if a blank is defined in the byte at INPUT − 1. Thus, after you establish the pattern, a single TR instruction will perform the desired rearrangement.

---

EXAMPLE 22

### Detect Erroneous Characters

Suppose that you want to print a string of 100 characters and then print a $ under each character that is not an uppercase letter. You can proceed first by making a copy of the string, and then by translating each uppercase letter into a blank and any other character into a $. Thus, if you print the original string on one line and print the translated copy on the next line, you will have the desired results. Figure 11.9 lists the required instructions.

**Translation tables usually are 256 bytes long, but can be shorter if you are careful**

Observe two aspects of the translation table at TABLE. First, since the table is 256 bytes long, it can accommodate any value that is stored in an argument byte, even if that value does not represent a printable character. This is the general case: translation tables can be shorter if you know that argument values are restricted, as they were in the previous examples. Second, the definition of TABLE is prone to error. You must be aware of the gap between the character codes for I and J, and between the character codes for R and S, and count carefully. Fortunately, you can define translation tables in another way by using the ORG directive, as described next. It will facilitate table definition and add a measure of self-documentation.

```
** ASSUME A CHARACTER STRING AT LINE.  CREATE ANOTHER STRING AT TYPOS
** WHOSE CHARACTERS ARE:
**     BLANK IF THEY CORRESPOND TO UPPERCASE LETTERS IN LINE;
**     $'S IF THEY CORRESPOND TO ANY OTHER CHARACTERS IN LINE.
*
         MVC   TYPOS(100),LINE   MAKE A COPY OF THE ORIGINAL STRING
         TR    TYPOS(100),TABLE  CONVERT LEGAL CHARACTERS TO BLANKS,
*                                  ILLEGAL CHARACTERS TO $'S.
         .
         .
         .
* TRANSLATION TABLE:
TABLE    DC    (C'A')C'$'
         DC    9C' '             A - I
         DC    7C'$'
         DC    9C' '             J - R
         DC    8C'$'
         DC    8C' '             S - Z
         DC    22C'$'
*
LINE     DS    CL100
TYPOS    DS    CL100
```

**Figure 11.9**
The instructions to detect erroneous characters, as described in Example 22.

---

## *The Origin (ORG) Directive*

**ORG sets the location counter**

The Origin directive instructs the assembler to change the value of the location counter. Typically, you use it to redefine areas of storage, and it is particularly useful when you define translation tables. The directive can be summarized as follows:

| Name | Operation | Operand | Instruction Name | Action |
|---|---|---|---|---|
| *symbol* or *blank* | ORG | *relocatable expression* or *blank* | ORIGIN | Sets the location counter to the value of the relocatable expression; in case the operand entry is omitted, resets the location counter to the highest value attained so far. |

(DOS: no symbol permitted in the name entry)

When there is an operand entry, ORG sets the location counter to the value that is represented by the relocatable expression in the operand entry. You must define any symbols that appear in the expression in an earlier statement. If the operand entry is blank, ORG resets the location counter to the highest value that it had attained so far; this value points to the next available byte.

Usually, the name entry is omitted; but if it is not, the symbol represents the location counter value *before* it is changed by the ORG. The next example illustrates this situation.

EXAMPLE 23

```
X        DC     3F'5'
Y        ORG    X+4
         DC     F'8'
         ORG
Z        DC     F'3'
```

The assembler initially defines three fullword constants at X, each of which contains 5. The first ORG sets the location counter back to X+4 so that the constant 8 replaces the second fullword at X. The second ORG resets the location counter so that it points to the byte after the three fullwords at X. At this point, the fullword at Z is defined.

The symbol Y represents the address of the byte *after* the three fullwords at X, since the assembler determines its value before the ORG alters the location counter. Thus, these statements are equivalent to

```
X        DC     F'5'
         DC     F'8'
         DC     F'5'
Y        EQU    *
Z        DC     F'3'
```

EXAMPLE 24

**Redefine the Translation Table of Example 22**

You can redefine the translation table in Figure 11.9 as

```
TABLE    DC    256C'$'            DEFINE 256 $'S
         ORG   TABLE+C'A'         BACK UP TO TABLE+193
         DC    (C'I'-C'A'+1)C' '  BLANKS FOR A - I
         ORG   TABLE+C'J'         ADVANCE TO TABLE+209
         DC    (C'R'-C'J'+1)C' '  BLANKS FOR J - R
         ORG   TABLE+C'S'         ADVANCE TO TABLE+226
         DC    (C'Z'-C'S'+1)C' '  BLANKS FOR S - Z
         ORG   ,                  RESET TO TABLE+256
```

Note the comma in the operand entry of the last ORG: it is necessary when a remark is present but an operand is not.

EXAMPLE 25

**Assign Names to the Fields Within a Data Area**

```
OUTPUT   DS    CL32     RESERVE OUTPUT BUFFER
         ORG   OUTPUT   BACK UP TO ASSIGN NAMES TO FIELDS
         DC    C' '       CARRIAGE CONTROL
FIRST    DS    CL10       FIRST NAME
         DC    C' '       SPACE
LAST     DS    CL20       LAST NAME
         ORG   ,        RETURN TO BYTE AFTER OUTPUT BUFFER
```

You can use the ORG directive to define fields within a data area and to assign them names. Here, OUTPUT is the name of a 32-byte output buffer whose length can be designated by L'OUTPUT. FIRST and LAST represent two fields within the buffer that contain a person's first and last names. The length attributes of FIRST and LAST are equal to the respective lengths of the fields the symbols represent. Thus, the ORG directive provides you with another way to define a data area. You will see this technique used in the case study given later in this chapter.

---

**SELF-TEST EXERCISES**

8. Describe the effect of

```
         TR    DATA(200),TABLE
```

where

```
TABLE    DC    256C'#'
         ORG   TABLE+C'0'
         DC    X'00010203040506070809'
         ORG
```

9. Assume that the 8 bytes at HEX contain values that are selected from the hex integers 0 to F. Write a TR instruction and its associated table to replace these values with the corresponding EBCDIC codes for the characters 0 through 9 and A through F.

10. Consider a 50-byte field at ALPHA that consists of characters selected from the letters A through Z and blanks. Write a TR instruction to convert each letter into a numeric that indicates its position in the alphabet. (That is, A = 1, B = 2, and so on.) Leave blanks alone.

11. Using TR, write instructions to reverse the order of the 10 bytes at STRING and store them into the 10 bytes at REVERSE.

12. What is wrong with the way that the following translation table is defined?

```
TABLE    DC    256C' '
         ORG   TABLE+C'A'
         DC    X'0A0B0C0D0E0F'
         ORG   TABLE+L'TABLE
```

## The Translate and Test (TRT) Instruction

The Translate and Test instruction is used to scan up to 256 consecutive bytes for a particular value. You can use the instruction to search character strings for certain significant characters. TRT is an SS instruction that has the same operands as the Translate instruction. Like Translate, the first operand consists of up to 256 argument bytes that reference a translation table of function bytes at the second operand address. However, unlike

**TRT does not alter its storage operands**

Translate, TRT does not alter the contents of either operand. Here, *translate* describes the process by which an argument byte references a function byte.

Each argument byte is considered in turn from left to right, and references a function byte in exactly the same manner as the Translate instruction. If the function byte is zero, the instruction ignores the argument byte and considers the next argument byte. If all of the argument bytes reference function bytes with values of zero, the condition code is set to zero and execution of the instruction is complete.

**In general, TRT affects Registers 1 and 2, and the condition code**

However, if the function byte is nonzero, the instruction loads the *address* of the corresponding argument byte into Register 1 and loads bits 24 through 31 of Register 2 with the *contents* of the function byte; the rest of Register 2 is unchanged. The condition code is also set and execution of the instruction terminates. If this argument byte is not the last, or rightmost, byte of the first operand, the condition code will be set to 1; if the argument byte is the last byte, the condition code is set to 2. The instruction can be summarized as follows:

| Operation | Operand | Format | Instruction Name |
|---|---|---|---|
| **TRT** | *S1(L),S2*<br>or *D1(L,B1),D2(B2)* | SS | TRANSLATE AND TEST |

**Action**

Each of a maximum of *L* consecutive argument bytes at *E1*, considered left to right, references a function byte in the table at *E2* in exactly the same manner as the TR instruction, except that the arguments are unchanged. This continues until one of the following occurs:

1. A nonzero function byte is referenced:
   $C(\text{Register } 1)_{8-31} \leftarrow$ Address of the argument byte that references the nonzero function byte
   (Note: With 31-bit addressing, the address is placed into bits 1 through 31 of Register 1 and bit 0 is 0.)
   $C(\text{Register } 2)_{24-31} \leftarrow$ Contents of the function byte
   Condition code = { 1 if the argument byte is not the last (rightmost) one in the first operand; 2 if the argument is the last one in the first operand }
2. All arguments are considered and all function bytes are zero:
   Condition code = 0
   Registers 1 and 2 remain unchanged.

Notice that the condition code is set to 1 if and only if all argument bytes are not examined (that is, if there are still more arguments to consider). You can use the extended mnemonic BM, which is interpreted as "Branch on More," to test for this situation. Also, notice that with 24-bit addressing, bits 0 through 7 of Register 1 are unchanged but, with 31-bit addressing, bit 0 is set to 0. This is important to remember when you use Register 1 in arithmetic, as often is the case.

Only Registers 1 and 2 are affected by this instruction. *Note that TRT is the only instruction that implicitly affects Register 2.*

The next examples demonstrate different aspects of the TRT instruction, as follows:

- Example 26 uses only the contents of Register 1 as set by TRT.
- Example 27 uses the contents of both Registers 1 and 2.
- Example 28 uses the contents of both Registers 1 and 2 as well as the condition code.

---

EXAMPLE 26

**Locate and Move a Nonblank Character String**

This example shows how to differentiate between blank and nonblank characters, and uses only the contents of Register 1 as set by TRT.

Consider the same problem that was discussed in Example 14. A nonblank character string exists somewhere in the area defined at DATA, and is followed by a blank character. The problem is to locate the string and move it to FIELD. This example uses the TRT instruction to locate the beginning and the end of the string.

In Figure 11.10, the first TRT instruction searches for a nonblank char-

**Figure 11.10**
The instructions to locate and move a nonblank character string, as described in Example 26.

```
** LOCATE THE NONBLANK STRING WITHIN THE AREA AT DATA; MOVE IT TO
**    FIELD.   (RESERVE REGISTERS 1 AND 2 FOR TRT)
*
         TRT   DATA(80),T1       SCAN TO FIRST NONBLANK CHARACTER
         LR    R5,R1             R5 = STARTING ADDRESS OF STRING
         TRT   1(80,R1),T2       BEGINNING WITH NEXT CHAR., LOCATE
*                                  FIRST BLANK AFTER THE STRING.
         SR    R1,R5             R1 = LENGTH, L, OF STRING
         BCTR  R1,0              L - 1; INTERNAL LENGTH FOR EX
         EX    R1,MOVE           MOVE STRING TO FIELD
         B     AROUND            SKIP TARGET INSTRUCTION
MOVE     MVC   FIELD(0),0(R5)    TARGET OF EX TO MOVE STRING TO FIELD
AROUND   ----
         .
         .
         .
DATA     DS    CL80              THE GIVEN AREA CONTAINING A STRING
         DC    C' '              FORCED BLANK TO ENSURE SECOND TRT STOPS
FIELD    DS    CL80              STRING IS MOVED HERE
*
** TRT TABLE TO IGNORE ONLY BLANKS:
T1       DC    256X'FF'          ANY NONZERO VALUES
         ORG   T1+C' '
         DC    X'00'             IGNORE BLANKS
         ORG
*
** TRT TABLE TO IGNORE EVERYTHING EXCEPT BLANKS:
T2       DC    256X'00'
         ORG   T2+C' '
         DC    X'FF'             DETECT BLANKS
         ORG
```

acter by beginning with the byte at DATA. The table at T1, which is illustrated in part **a** of Figure 11.11, is defined so that blanks are ignored, but any nonblank character will cause TRT to terminate and place the address of the character into Register 1. This address then is the starting address of the string and is saved in Register 5.

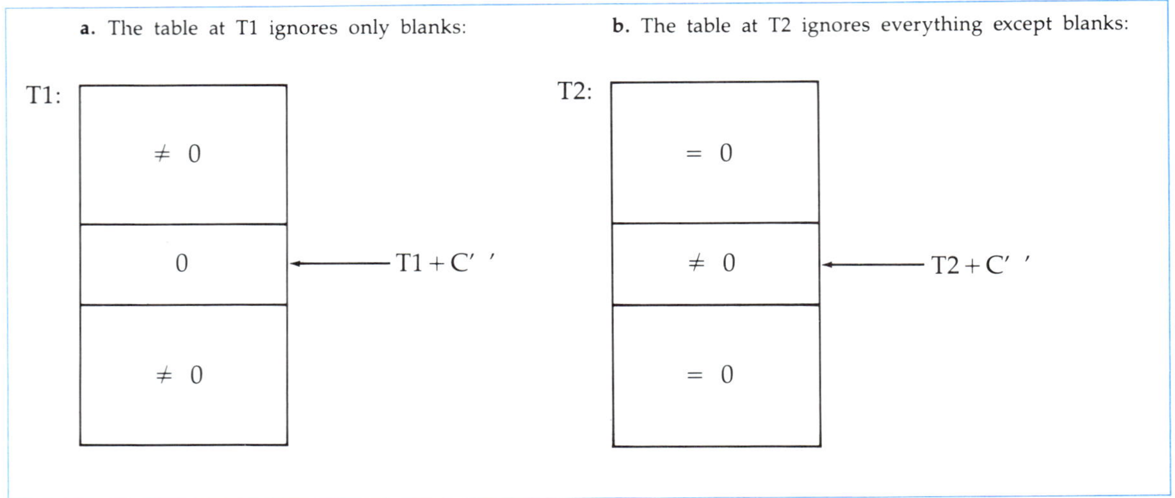


Figure 11.11
Translation tables of Example 26 that, **a.** ignore blanks and, **b.** ignore everything except blanks.

Scanning continues with the next byte by using a second TRT instruction. This time, you must ignore nonblank characters and search for the blank that follows the string. The table at T2, shown in part **b** of Figure 11.11, is defined with this process in mind. After the address of this trailing blank is determined, moving the string proceeds just as in Example 14.

Notice that the length entry that is written in the second TRT instruction is 80, even though you know that there are fewer argument bytes left to be scanned. You can do this here because you know that there is a blank after the string that will terminate execution of the TRT.

With 24-bit addressing, the first byte of Register 1 is unaffected by TRT

With 24-bit addressing, the TRT instruction does not affect the leftmost byte of Register 1. The unknown contents of this byte are copied into Register 5 and then subtracted out when the length of the string is computed. Thus, the unaffected byte of Register 1 does not cause a problem. However, there are computations where this byte would cause an error and, in such cases, you must initialize Register 1 to zero before the first TRT instruction is executed. You will see an example of this in the case study that is presented later in this chapter. As a precaution against error, you can routinely clear Register 1 prior to the first TRT instruction in your program.

---

EXAMPLE 27

### Distinguish Between Characters

This example shows how to differentiate between several characters, and acts according to the character; it uses the contents of both Registers 1 and 2.

Picture an input record that contains several fields separated by commas. A blank always follows the last field, but there are no other blanks within or between fields. Each field contains characters that specify a length in feet and inches. The apostrophe (′) and the quotation mark (″) are used to designate these units in the typical fashion. Assume that the record has been read into the bytes at DATA; Figure 11.12 pictures some possibilities.

In this example, the problem is to compute the average, in inches, of these lengths. Since this example will focus on how to use TRT to scan for these characters: ′ ″, and *blank*, the explanation here omits the details of the computation of the average, as well as the conversions from EBCDIC to binary and from feet to inches.

Figure 11.13 lists the solution. The translation table is defined so as to ignore all characters except the four just given. However, notice that the four function bytes that correspond to these characters do not contain just any nonzero values, but contain particular nonzero values. The program segment uses these values to distinguish between the four special characters.

**Only the rightmost byte of Register 2 is affected by TRT; remaining bytes are unchanged**

The first instruction initializes Register 2 to zero. This is necessary here because TRT only changes the rightmost byte of Register 2. Next, you must determine the beginning and end of each field, as well as the units that are represented by the value within the field. Register 4 contains the beginning address of each field. Initially, this is the address DATA. The loop is written so that it works not only for the first field, but also for subsequent fields. To see that this is true, look at Figure 11.14, which pictures the contents of Register 1 just after each of the three successive executions of TRT. After the first execution of TRT, Register 1 points to the apostrophe. The second execution of TRT begins at the character after the apostrophe and stops immediately because it is a comma; Register 1 contains its address. During the third execution, TRT again begins at the next character, the 1, and stops with Register 1 pointing to the quotation mark.

Each time that TRT terminates, you must determine the next action according to the special character encountered. If the character is an apostrophe, you must branch to instructions that first will convert the field from EBCDIC to binary and from feet to inches, and then will add the result to an accumulator. If the character is a quotation mark, you only need to convert from EBCDIC and add the binary value to the accumulator. If the character is a comma, you must count the field that was just processed for later use when the average is computed. Finally, if the character is a blank, you have reached the end of the data: you must count the last field, and then compute the average.

**Figure 11.12**
The possibilities for DATA in Example 27: **a.** the last field ends before byte 80 and, **b.** the last field ends at byte 80.

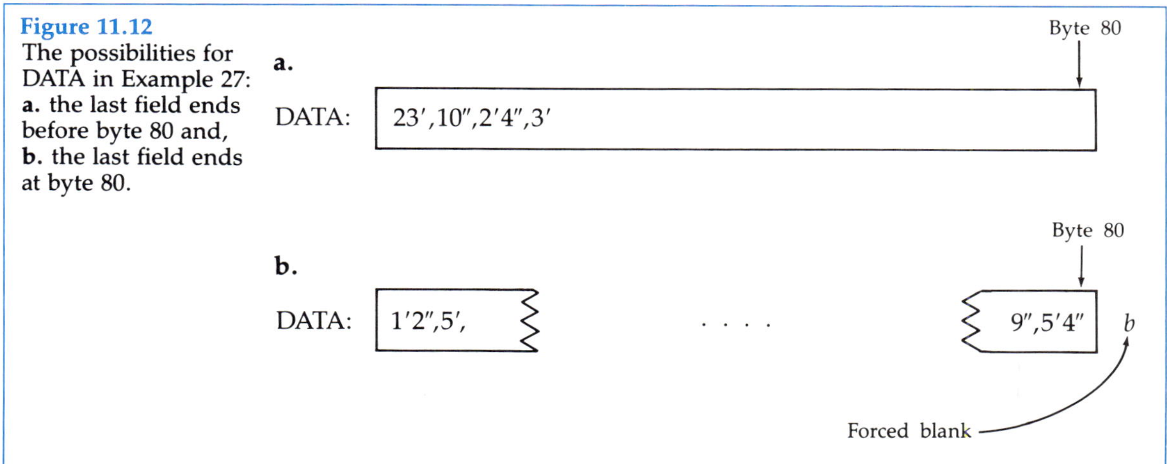

```
** DISTINGUISH BETWEEN APOSTROPHES, QUOTES, COMMAS, AND BLANKS
**    (RESERVE REGISTERS 1 AND 2 FOR TRT)
*
         SR    R2,R2               CLEAR FUNCTION BYTE REGISTER
         SR    R3,R3               R3 = FIELD COUNTER = 0
         LA    R1,DATA-1           PREPARE FOR FIRST TRT
LOOP     LA    R4,1(R1)            R4 = BEGINNING ADDRESS OF NEXT FIELD
         TRT   0(80,R4),TABLE      FIND  ' " , OR BLANK
** BRANCH TO FEET, INCHES, COMMA OR BLANK ACCORDING TO CHARACTER FOUND:
         SLA   R2,2                MULTIPLY FUNCTION BYTE BY 4
BRANCHES B     BRANCHES(R2)        BRANCH TO PROPER BRANCH INSTRUCTION.
** BRANCH TABLE.  ORDER OF INSTRUCTIONS IS IMPORTANT:
         B     FEET                PROCESS FEET
         B     INCHES              PROCESS INCHES
         B     COMMA               PROCESS COMMA
*                                  PROCESS BLANK
BLANK    LA    R3,1(R3)            COUNT PREVIOUS FIELD.
         B     AVERAGE             LAST FIELD; COMPUTE AVERAGE
*-----------------------------------------------------------------
COMMA    LA    R3,1(R3)            COUNT PREVIOUS FIELD.
         B     LOOP                GO BACK FOR NEXT FIELD
*
** CONVERT TO BINARY, THEN TO INCHES; ADD TO SUM:
FEET     ----
         .
         .
         .
         B     LOOP                GO BACK FOR NEXT FIELD
*
** CONVERT TO BINARY; ADD TO SUM:
INCHES   ----
         .
         .
         .
         B     LOOP                GO BACK FOR NEXT FIELD
*
** TRT TABLE:
TABLE    DC    256X'00'            IGNORE MOST CHARACTERS
         ORG   TABLE+C''''
         DC    X'01'               APOSTROPHE
         ORG   TABLE+C'"'
         DC    X'02'               QUOTE
         ORG   TABLE+C','
         DC    X'03'               COMMA
         ORG   TABLE+C' '
         DC    X'04'               BLANK
         ORG
*
DATA     DS    CL80                INPUT RECORD
         DC    C' '                FORCED BLANK (SENTINEL)
```

**Figure 11.13**
The instructions to distinguish between characters, as described in Example 27.

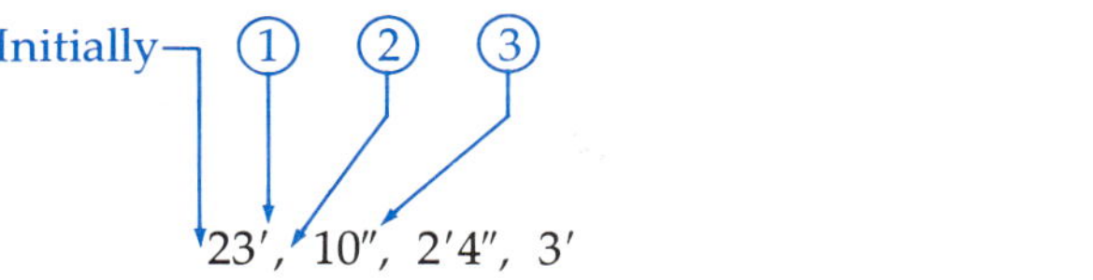


**Figure 11.14** Register 1 as TRT is executed three times in Example 27.

**Function bytes can be used to distinguish between characters**

Notice how the function byte in Register 2 is used to distinguish between the special characters: each character is associated with a value from 1 to 4; TRT then loads this value into Register 2. The SLA multiplies this value by four, before it is used as an index to a list of Branch instructions that specify the next action. As an alternative, you could define the function bytes in the translation table with the hex values 4, 8, C, and 10. This eliminates the need for the SLA instruction, but requires more care to ensure that the values are actually correct.

Fields that are converted by the segments at FEET and INCHES begin at the address in Register 4 and end one byte before the address in Register 1. It is important that these instructions do not destroy Register 1 because it is used to locate the next field.

Again, you can specify a length of 80 in the TRT instruction, even though this length is only correct during the first time that TRT is executed, since there is always a blank after the last field to terminate the TRT.

A further note: when an apostrophe is the character in a self-defining term, you must duplicate it. Thus, in the definition of TABLE, C'''' is equivalent to X'7D'.

---

EXAMPLE 28

## Distinguish Between Characters, But Ignore Blanks

In addition to utilizing the contents of Registers 1 and 2, this example tests the condition code after TRT is executed and demonstrates how to use EX with TRT.

You can extend the previous example to ignore blanks. This permits blanks to appear between or even within fields, but it creates a problem in determining the last field if the sentinel character after DATA is a blank. Clearly, one solution is to use a different character for the sentinel; however, for the sake of this demonstration, assume that either this is not possible or there is no sentinel. Then you can detect the last field by testing the condition code. You must specify the length of the first operand of the TRT at execution time by using the EX instruction.

In Figure 11.15, the translation table is similar to that of the previous example, except that a blank points to a zero function byte so that it will be ignored. The length of the remaining bytes of DATA to be scanned must be computed prior to each execution of TRT. This is done in such a way as to produce a result one less than the actual length so that the result may be used with EX. As with all SS instructions, the internal operand length of TRT is one less than the actual operand length.

The remaining steps are the same as in Example 27, except that if you permit blanks within the fields, the conversion routines must take this into account.

**Figure 11.15**
The instructions to distinguish between characters, but ignore blanks, as described in Example 28.

```
** DISTINGUISH BETWEEN APOSTROPHES, QUOTES, AND COMMAS; IGNORE BLANKS.
**    (RESERVE REGISTERS 1 AND 2 FOR TRT)
*
         SR    R2,R2              CLEAR FUNCTION BYTE REGISTER
         SR    R3,R3              R3 = FIELD COUNTER = 0
         LA    R1,DATA-1          PREPARE FOR FIRST TRT
LOOP     LA    R5,DATA+78         R5 = ADDRESS OF BYTE BEFORE LAST ONE
         SR    R5,R1              NO. OF REMAINING BYTES LESS 1
         BM    DONE               FINISHED; NO BYTES LEFT
         LA    R4,1(R1)           R4 = BEGINNING ADDRESS OF NEXT FIELD
         EX    R5,TEST            SCAN TO NEXT SPECIAL CHARACTER
         BZ    DONE               NONE FOUND; FINISHED
         B     AROUND             SKIP TARGET INSTRUCTION
TEST     TRT   0(0,R4),TABLE      TARGET FOR EX
** BRANCH TO FEET, INCHES, OR COMMA ACCORDING TO CHARACTER FOUND:
AROUND   SLA   R2,2               MULTIPLY FUNCTION BYTE BY 4
BRANCHES B     BRANCHES(R2)       BRANCH TO PROPER BRANCH INSTRUCTION.
** BRANCH TABLE.  ORDER OF INSTRUCTIONS IS IMPORTANT:
         B     FEET               PROCESS FEET
         B     INCHES             PROCESS INCHES
*                                 PROCESS COMMA
COMMA    LA    R3,1(R3)           COUNT PREVIOUS FIELD
         B     LOOP               GO BACK FOR NEXT FIELD
*
DONE     LA    R3,1(R3)           COUNT PREVIOUS FIELD
         B     AVERAGE            LAST FIELD. COMPUTE AVERAGE
*--------------------------------------------------------------------
** TRT TABLE:
TABLE    DC    256X'00'           IGNORE MOST CHARACTERS
         ORG   TABLE+C''''
         DC    X'01'              APOSTROPHE
         ORG   TABLE+C'"'
         DC    X'02'              QUOTE
         ORG   TABLE+C','
         DC    X'03'              COMMA
         ORG
*
DATA     DS    CL80               INPUT RECORD
```

## SELF-TEST EXERCISES

13. Assume the following register status:

    Reg. 1 = 00000000
    Reg. 2 = ABCDEFAB

    Describe the effect of the instruction

    ```
    TRT   ST(5),=X'000200000900'
    ```

    for each of the following values of ST. Assume that ST represents the address BF20.

    **a.** 0100040102 **c.** 0503030004
    **b.** 0205000302 **d.** 0200030401

14. Using TRT, write instructions to branch to YES if the 100-byte field at DIGITS contains only the EBCDIC codes for blanks and the digits 0 to 9.

15. Using TRT, write instructions to count the number of commas in the 80-byte character string at INPUT.

## Strings of Arbitary Length

This section describes the instructions that allow you to work with strings of arbitrary length.

### *The Move Characters Long (MVCL) Instruction*

**MVCL moves arbitrarily long character strings**

The Move Characters Long instruction permits you to copy bytes from one area of storage to another without worrying about the length restriction of 256, which is inherent in the MVC instruction. As such, the use of MVCL is powerful when you must copy or initialize very long fields. It also provides a way to move a field whose length is computed at execution time without using EX. The instruction requires more information than you can specify in an SS-format instruction, so it uses register pairs instead. For this reason, it does not replace the need for the MVC instruction. The instruction can be summarized as follows:

| Operation | Operand | Format | Instruction Name | Action |
|---|---|---|---|---|
| **MVCL** | *R1*,*R2* | RR | MOVE CHARACTERS LONG | *R1* and *R2* are even and define two even-odd register pairs. Each pair contains the starting address and length of a field in storage. The first field is replaced by copies of bytes taken from the second field, which is extended on the right if necessary by copies of $C(R2+1)_{0-7}$. If $L_1$ and $L_2$ denote the field lengths: Condition code = 0 if $L_1 = L_2$; 1 if $L_1 < L_2$; 2 if $L_1 > L_2$; 3 if no bytes are moved due to destructive overlap |

The destination bytes of the field that is described by the first even-odd register pair are replaced by copies of the source bytes of the field that is described by the second register pair. If the first field is longer than the second, it is filled in on the right with a value of your choosing that is contained in the **pad byte.** Figure 11.16 shows the addresses, lengths, and pad byte within the register pairs when 24-bit addressing is used. (With 31-bit addressing, the even-numbered registers contain addresses in bits 1 through 31 and bit 0 of each register is ignored.) The lengths $L_1$ and $L_2$ that are contained in the odd-numbered registers are the *actual* lengths of the two fields. This differs from SS instructions, in which the internal lengths are one less than the actual lengths. $L_1$ bytes are moved by proceeding left to right through the fields.

The even-odd register pairs are modified during execution of the instruction. After execution, they appear as illustrated in Figure 11.17, which assumes 24-bit addressing. The registers in the pair that is designated by *R1* are each changed by $L_1$: *R1* is incremented by $L_1$ so that it now points to the address of the byte after the last one in the first field; $R1+1$ is decremented by $L_1$ and it becomes zero. Each of the registers in the pair that is designated by *R2* are changed by the number of bytes that are copied from the second

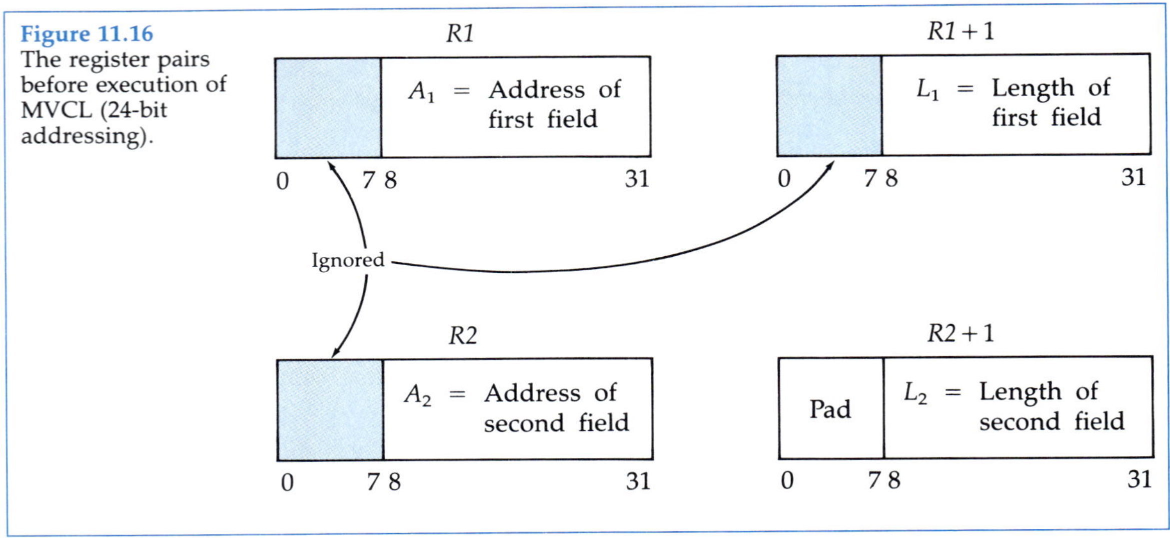


**Figure 11.16** The register pairs before execution of MVCL (24-bit addressing).

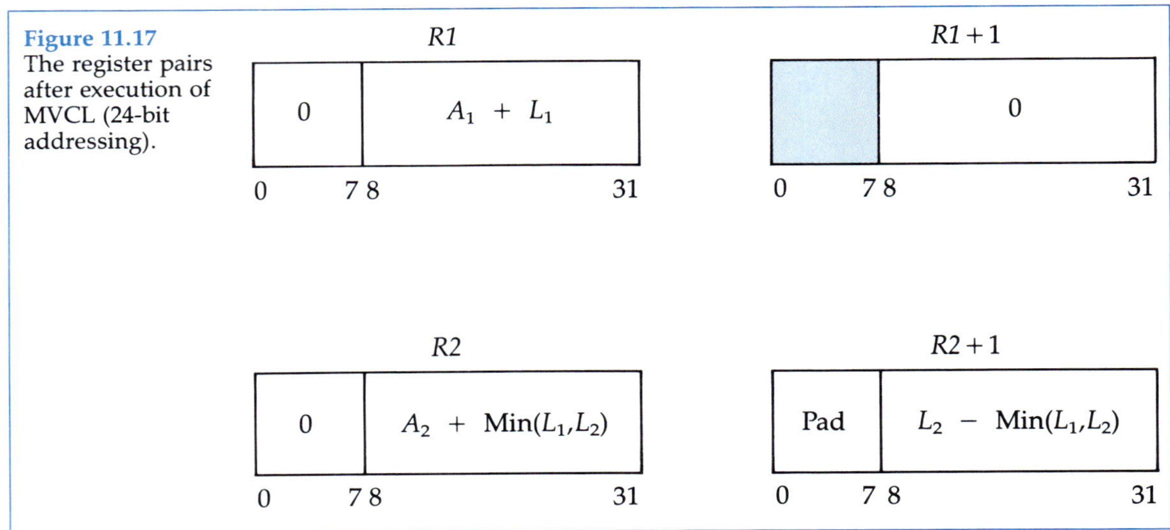


**Figure 11.17** The register pairs after execution of MVCL (24-bit addressing).

field. This number is the length of the shorter field and is denoted by Min($L_1$,$L_2$); the number is added to the even register and is subtracted from the odd register. The first byte of each of the even registers *R1* and *R2* is set to zero; the first byte of each of the odd registers remains unchanged. (With 31-bit addressing, only the first bit of each of the even registers is set to 0.)

**Destructive overlap is not permitted**

As described in the previous chapter, destructive overlap exists when the fields overlap and $A_1 > A_2$. If permitted, a byte moved into the first field would later be considered a source byte and would be copied again. However, destructive overlap of the fields is not permitted. (In this regard, MVCL differs from MVC.) If this situation arises, no bytes are copied, the condition code is set to 3, and bits to the left of the addresses in the even registers are set to zero. You can test for a condition code of 3 by using the extended mnemonic BO, which you can interpret as "Branch on Overlap." If $L_2$ is 0 or 1, there can be no destructive overlap.

If $L_2 = 0$, a copy of the pad byte replaces each byte in the first field. You can use this feature to initialize an area to a particular value. If $L_1 = 0$, no bytes are moved, the condition code is set (only 0 or 1 is possible), and bits to the left of the addresses in the even registers are set to zero. When an operand has a zero length, addressing and protection exceptions do not occur for that operand.

The following examples assume 24-bit addressing.

---

EXAMPLE 29

**Replace the $L_1$ Bytes at X with Copies from the $L_2$ Bytes at Y: $L_1 < L_2$**

```
MVCL    4,8
```

Let A(X) and A(Y) denote the addresses of X and Y.

Before execution:

*Reg. 4*

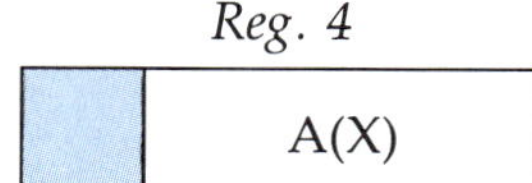


*Reg. 5*

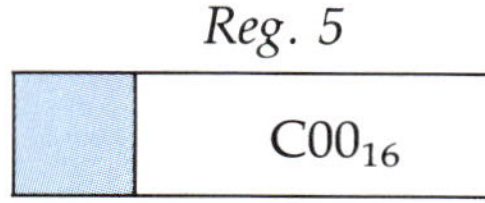


*Reg. 8*

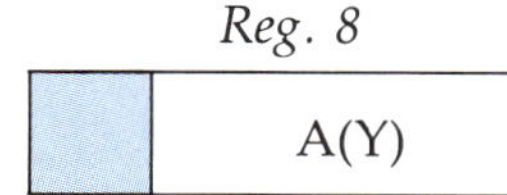


*Reg. 9*

After execution:

*Reg. 4*

| 00 | A(X) + $C00_{16}$ |
|---|---|

*Reg. 5*

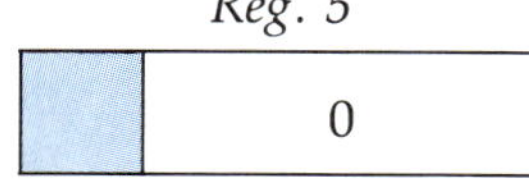


*Reg. 8*

| 00 | A(Y) + $C00_{16}$ |
|---|---|

*Reg. 9*

| 00 | $DE_{16}$ |
|---|---|

Since $L_1 < L_2$, $L_1 = 3072$ ($C00_{16}$) bytes are copied from Y and replace the bytes at X. The instruction sets the condition code to 1, and does not use the pad byte.

---

EXAMPLE 30

**Replace the $L_1$ Bytes at X with Copies from the $L_2$ Bytes at Y; $L_1 > L_2$**

```
MVCL    0,2
```

Before execution:

*Reg. 0*

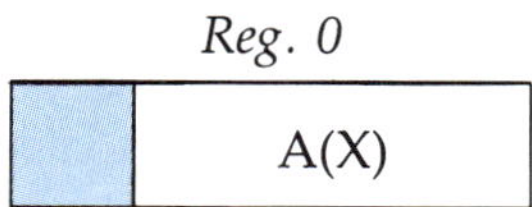


*Reg. 1*

| | $C00_{16}$ |
|---|---|

*Reg. 2*

| | A(Y) |
|---|---|

*Reg. 3*

| 40 | $200_{16}$ |
|---|---|

After execution:

*Reg. 0*

| 00 | A(X) + $C00_{16}$ |
|---|---|

*Reg. 1*

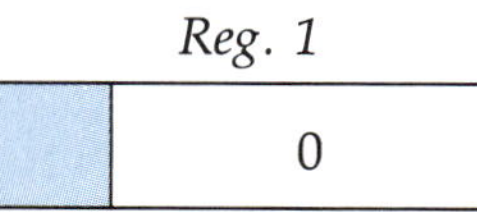


*Reg. 2*

| 00 | A(Y) + $200_{16}$ |
|---|---|

*Reg. 3*

| 40 | 0 |
|---|---|

Since $L_1 > L_2$, $L_2 = 512$ ($200_{16}$) bytes are copied from Y and replace the first 512 bytes at X. A copy of the pad byte, which contains the character blank in this case, replaces each of the remaining bytes at X. The condition code is set to 2.

Notice that this instruction uses Register 0 to address storage, even though this register cannot be used in the computation of the effective address that is specified by other instructions.

---

EXAMPLE 31

**Initialize the Field at X to Blanks**

```
         LM    4,5,INIT   DESCRIBE FIELD AT X
         IC    9,=C' '    GET PAD (BLANK)
         SLL   9,24       LEFT-JUSTIFY PAD; SET LENGTH
*                           OF SECOND FIELD TO ZERO.
         MVCL  4,8        SET FIELD AT X TO BLANKS
         .
         .
         .
INIT     DC    A(X)       ADDRESS OF FIELD
         DC    F'3000'    LENGTH OF FIELD
```

Since the length of the second field is zero, MVCL does not use the second field's beginning address; thus, it is unnecessary to initialize Register 8. Copies of the pad byte in Register 9 replace the 3000 bytes at X. The condition code is set to 2.

---

### *The Compare Characters Long (CLCL) Instruction*

**CLCL compares arbitrarily long character strings**

The Compare Characters Long instruction specifies two fields in storage and a pad byte by using the even-odd register pairs that are denoted by *R1* and *R2*. It does so in exactly the same manner as for MVCL. The CLCL instruction can be summarized as follows:

| Operation | Operand | Format | Instruction Name | Action |
|---|---|---|---|---|
| **CLCL** | *R1,R2* | RR | COMPARE CHARACTERS LONG | Logically compares the fields whose starting addresses and lengths are contained in the even-odd register pairs designated by *R1* and *R2* |

Condition code = 
- 0 if the fields are equal, or are both of zero length
- 1 if the first field is less than the second
- 2 if the first field is greater than the second

Before the comparison begins, the instruction extends a copy of the shorter field on the right with copies of the pad byte until both fields are of the same length. This step is done within the CPU and does not affect the fields in storage. The instruction then performs a logical comparison

**Figure 11.18** Comparing strings where the shorter one is padded on the right with blanks.

| String 1 | Comparison | String 2 |
|---|---|---|
| XY | < | XYZ |
| 1234 | > | 123 |
| ABCDE | < | BCD |

one byte at a time, proceeding left to right through the fields. Execution terminates as soon as an unequal comparison is made or there are no more bytes left to compare.

The condition code is set to reflect the results of the comparison, and the registers are altered as follows:

- If the comparison is not equal, the even-numbered registers point to the first bytes in their respective fields that are unequal. Each of the lengths in the odd-numbered registers is decremented by the number of equal byte comparisons made, except that neither can become negative.
- If the comparison is equal, the even-numbered registers point to the first byte after each field. The leftmost bits that are not part of the addresses in these registers are set to 0. The lengths in the odd-numbered registers are set to zero and bits 0 through 7 remain unchanged.

Figure 11.18 gives some examples of the comparison of strings with unequal lengths.

Unlike the MVCL instruction, CLCL permits fields that overlap.

---

EXAMPLE 32

**Compare the Field at X with the Field at Y**

```
LA    4,X       STARTING ADDRESS OF FIRST FIELD
LA    5,2000    LENGTH OF FIRST FIELD
LA    8,Y       STARTING ADDRESS OF SECOND FIELD
LA    9,1000    LENGTH OF SECOND FIELD (PAD = 0)
CLCL  4,8       COMPARE THE FIELDS
```

The pad byte contains 00 and is used to extend the field at Y temporarily for the purposes of the comparison.

---

EXAMPLE 33

**Compare the Field at X with the Field at Y**

```
LM    4,7,=A(X,2000,Y,1000) DESCRIBE THE FIELDS
ICM   7,B'1000',=C' '        SET PAD TO BLANK
CLCL  4,6                    COMPARE FIELDS
```

This example demonstrates another way to initialize the even-odd register pairs. It is possible to specify more than one constant either in the definition of a literal or in the operand of a DC. This can be convenient when you use an LM instruction, but address constants as defined in Example 31 are certainly adequate. Note that the pad byte differs from the previous example.

---

MVCL and CLCL are two of a few instructions that are said to be **interruptible.** As has been mentioned, there are classes of interruptions other than program interruptions. For example, an *input/output (I/O) interruption* occurs when an I/O operation, which is initiated by the operating system, terminates. Ordinarily, such an interruption is held until execution of the current instruction is complete. However, the MVCL and CLCL instructions are relatively slow in comparison to the other instructions, and it would be impractical to wait for their completion. Therefore, the CPU can interrupt their execution. When this occurs, data in the relevant even-odd register pairs are adjusted so that resumption of the instruction is possible after the operating system processes the interruption. If these instructions are the target of an EX instruction, you should not use registers in the even-odd pairs that are designated by the instructions in the *R1*, *X2*, or *B2* portions of the EX instruction.

## SELF-TEST EXERCISES

16. Assume four distinct, but adjacent, fields at the ascending addresses that are represented by FIELD1, FIELD2, FIELD3, and FIELD4. The fields have lengths (in hex) of 200, 1FE, 500, and 200, respectively. Furthermore, assume the following register status:

    Reg. 0 = A(FIELD1)　　Reg. 4 = A(FIELD3)
    Reg. 1 = 00000200　　Reg. 5 = 40000500
    Reg. 2 = A(FIELD2)　　Reg. 6 = A(FIELD4)
    Reg. 3 = 400001FE　　Reg. 7 = 40000200

    Describe the effect that each of the following instructions has upon the fields, the registers, and the condition code:

    **a.** `MVCL 0,2`
    **b.** `MVCL 0,4`
    **c.** `MVCL 2,4`
    **d.** `MVCL 0,6`
    **e.** `MVCL 4,0`

17. Assume the following definitions and register status:

```
FIELD1   DC   C'ABCDEFGHIJKLM'
FIELD2   DC   C'ABCDEX'
FIELD3   DC   C'ABCDEY'
```

    Reg. 0 = A(FIELD1)　　Reg. 3 = 40000005
    Reg. 1 = 4000000C　　Reg. 4 = A(FIELD3)
    Reg. 2 = A(FIELD2)　　Reg. 5 = 40000005

    What is the effect of each of the following instructions on the condition code and these registers?

    **a.** `CLCL 0,2`
    **b.** `CLCL 2,4`

# Case Study

## *Problem Statement*

**Create a data base that can be used with a computerized checkout system in a grocery store.**

In the data base, each product will have an entry that consists of these fields.

Field 1: The Universal Product Code (UPC); 11 EBCDIC characters.
Field 2: Flag byte; a bit is 1 if the corresponding description is true; it is 0 if it is not true.
- Bit 0: Taxable item
- Bit 1: Special sale item
- Bit 2: Bakery item
- Bit 3: Dairy item
- Bit 4: Grocery item
- Bit 5: Meat item
- Bit 6: Produce item
- Bit 7: Nonfood item.

Field 3: A short, 10-character description of the item. (Suitable for use on cash-register tapes.)
Field 4: A longer, 25-character description of the item. (Suitable for inventory lists.)
Field 5: Current price; 5 EBCDIC characters including a decimal point.
Field 6: Current inventory; 4 bytes.

Each item is specified in an input record that consists of six fields separated by slashes. The fields are as follows:

Field 1: An 11-digit UPC number.
Field 2: 1 to 3 single-letter codes written without spaces. The codes are the first letter of the names of the flags described earlier. For example, TGS indicates a taxable grocery item that is offered on special sale.
Fields 3 and 4: The short and long descriptions in fields of at most 10 and 25 characters, respectively. Thus, these descriptions are not of a fixed length.
Fields 5 and 6: The price and inventory in fixed-length fields of 5 and 4 characters, respectively.

For example, an input record might appear as

```
00001111222/SD/MILK/MILK, HALF-GALLON/01.25/0123
```

A record that contains an asterisk in column 1 signals the end of the input data set.

## *Discussion*

The overall logic of the program is straightforward and is described by the flowchart of Figure 11.19 and the pseudocode of Figure 11.20. These assume

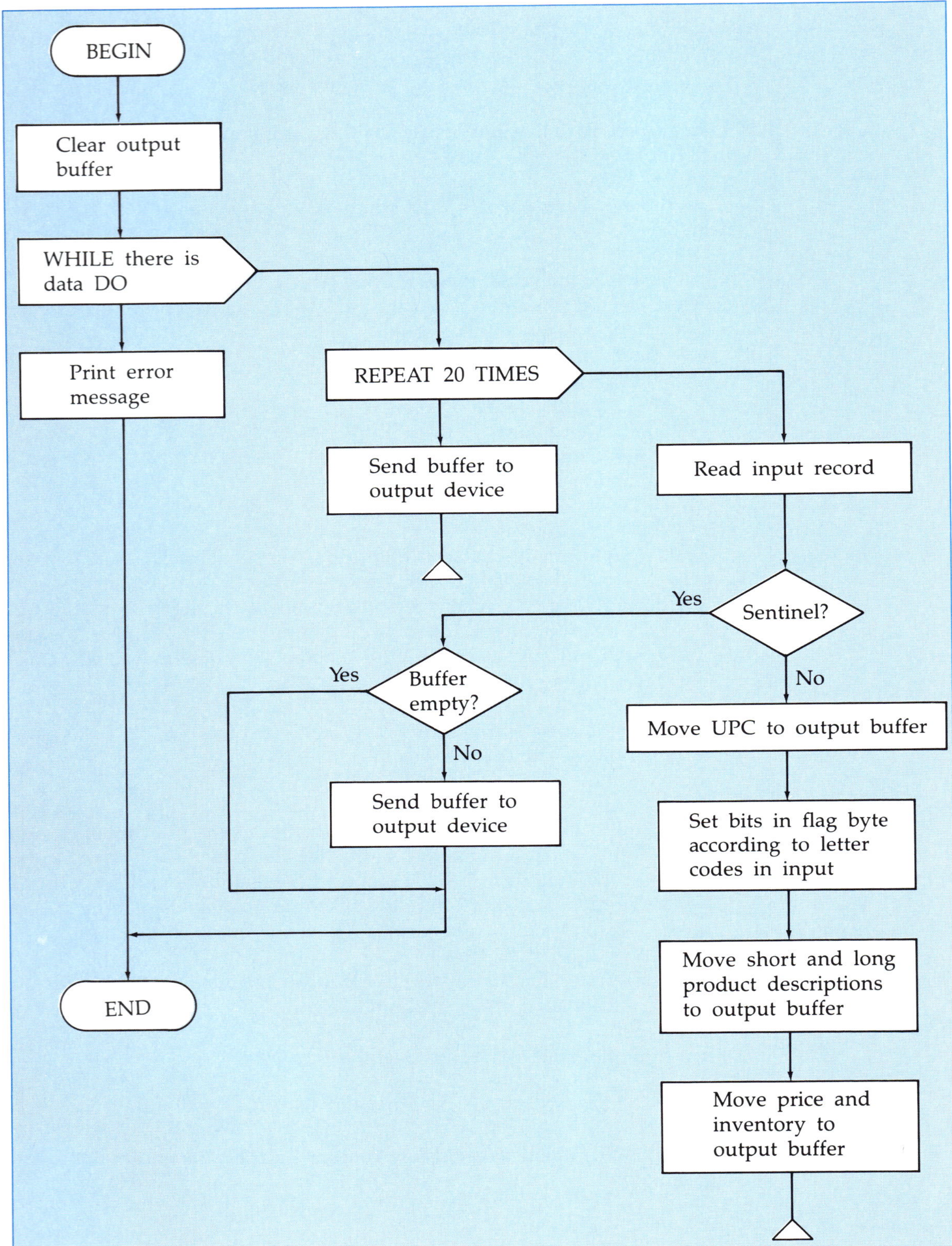


**Figure 11.19**
The flowchart for a program to create a UPC data base, as described in the case study.

```
Clear output buffer
WHILE there is data DO
    REPEAT 20 TIMES
        Read input record
        IF sentinel
            THEN
                IF buffer is not empty THEN send it to output device
                END IF
                Exit
            ELSE
                Move UPC to output buffer
                Determine number of letter flags in input
                Encode each letter flag into a single bit in a byte
                OR these bytes together to create flag byte
                Move flag byte to output buffer
                Determine length of short description
                Move short description to output buffer
                Determine length of long description
                Move long description to output buffer
                Move price to output buffer
                Move inventory to output buffer
        END IF
    END REPEAT
    Send buffer to output device
END WHILE
Print error message
```

**Figure 11.20**
The pseudocode solution for the case study.

that the data base will be written on a device such as a disk, and that a subprogram called IO is available to do this. To enhance the demonstration, an output buffer is filled with the data of 20 products before the subprogram is invoked.

Figure 11.21 lists the program. First, notice how the output buffer is defined at the end of the program: Statements 211 through 219 allocate space for 20 products and give names to the fields that are associated with a single product. L'OUTPUT represents the length of all data that is associated with one product, and LENOUT, defined in Statement 220, represents the length of the entire buffer.

The fact that TRT uses Registers 1 and 2 is clearly noted at the beginning of the program in Statements 27 and 28. Since the program does not utilize the contents of Register 2 as set by TRT, it is easy to forget that the TRT instruction changes the register. To avoid this problem, the program does not use the register at all (there are enough registers here to allow this), and does not define the symbol R2.

Since the short and long product descriptions have a fixed length in the data base, but may be shorter in the input record, it is desirable to initialize the output buffer to blanks. Statements 67 to 70 do this early in the program with an MVCL instruction. (*Text continues on page 11.46*)

```
        CREATE UPC DATA BASE

  LOC  OBJECT CODE    ADDR1 ADDR2  STMT   SOURCE STATEMENT

000000                               2 GROCERY  CSECT
                                     3 ***********************************************************************
                                     4 ** CREATE A DATA BASE FOR A COMPUTERIZED GROCERY STORE
                                     5 **
                                     6 ** INPUT:   EACH RECORD CONSISTS OF 6 FIELDS SEPARATED BY SLASHES IN
                                     7 **          THE FOLLOWING ORDER.  (FIELD LENGTHS ARE IN PARENTHESES):
                                     8 **          UPC (11)/LETTER-FLAGS (<=3)/SHORT DESCRIPTION (<=10)/
                                     9 **          LONG DESCRIPTION (<=25)/PRICE (5)/INVENTORY (4)
                                    10 **
                                    11 **          NB:  FLAG FIELD CONSISTS OF 1-3 LETTERS, WRITTEN WITHOUT
                                    12 **               SPACES AND SELECTED FROM T (TAXABLE ITEM),
                                    13 **               S (SPECIAL SALE), B (BAKERY), D (DAIRY), G (GROCERY),
                                    14 **               M (MEAT), P (PRODUCE), AND N (NONFOOD).
                                    15 **
                                    16 **          LAST RECORD IS A SENTINEL: IT CONTAINS * IN COL. 1
                                    17 **
                                    18 ** OUTPUT: EACH PRODUCT IS REPRESENTED IN THE DATA BASE BY 6 FIXED-
                                    19 **          LENGTH FIELDS IN THE SAME ORDER AS IN THE INPUT RECORD.
                                    20 **          FLAGS ARE REPRESENTED BY ONE BYTE SUCH THAT BIT 0 IS 1 IF
                                    21 **          THE FLAG IS T, BIT 1 IS 1 IF THE FLAG IS S, AND SO ON.
                                    22 **
                                    23 ** SUBPROGRAM:  IO; WRITES ON AN OUTPUT DEVICE SUCH AS A DISK.  (HERE
                                    24 **              IO IS A DUMMY THAT SIMPLY DUMPS THE OUTPUT BUFFER.)
                                    25 ***********************************************************************
                                    26 ** REGISTER DEFINITIONS:
                             00001  27 R1       EQU   1               TRT POINTER TO SLASH
                                    28 *              2               REG. 2 DESTROYED BY TRT; NOT USED
                             00003  29 R3       EQU   3               LENGTH FOR EX
                             00004  30 R4       EQU   4               OUTPUT FIELD POINTER
                             00005  31 R5       EQU   5               INDEX FOR OUTPUT FIELDS
                             00006  32 R6       EQU   6               INPUT FIELD POINTER
                             00007  33 R7       EQU   7               LOOP COUNTER
                             0000C  34 R12      EQU   12              BASE REGISTER
                             0000D  35 R13      EQU   13              SAVE AREA POINTER
                             0000E  36 R14      EQU   14              LINK TO SUBPROGRAMS AND OS
                                    37 * R4, R5, R6, R7 ALSO USED INITIALLY BY MVCL TO CLEAR BUFFER
                                    38          PRINT NOGEN           SUPPRESS MACRO EXPANSIONS
                                    39 ** STANDARD ENTRY AND INITIALIZATION:
                                    40 *  OS:
000000 90EC D00C       0000C        41          STM   R14,R12,12(R13) SAVE REGISTERS
000004 05C0                         42          BALR  R12,0           LOAD BASE REGISTER
                             00006  43          USING BASE,R12        DECLARE BASE ADDRESS AND REGISTER
000006 50D0 C82E       00834        44 BASE     ST    R13,SAVE+4      SAVE R13
00000A 41D0 C82A       00830        45          LA    R13,SAVE        R13 = ADDRESS OF SAVE AREA
                                    46          OPEN  (READER,INPUT,PRINTER,OUTPUT)   PREPARE FOR I/O
                                    54          OPEN  (SNAPDCB,OUTPUT) PREPARE FOR DUMP
                                    60 ** DOS*******
                                    61 *        BALR  R12,0           LOAD BASE REGISTER
                                    62 *        USING BASE,R12        DECLARE BASE ADDRESS AND REGISTER
                                    63 *BASE    LA    R13,SAVE        R13 = ADDRESS OF SAVE AREA
                                    64 *        OPEN  READER,PRINTER  PREPARE FOR I/O
```

*(Continues)*

**Figure 11.21**
The program to create a UPC data base, as described in the case study.

```
                                    65 ******
                                    66 *  CLEAR OUTPUT BUFFER:
00002A 9845 C98A       00990        67 LOOP     LM    R4,R5,=A(OUTPUT,LENOUT)  DESCRIBE OUTPUT BUFFER FOR MVCL
00002E 4170 0040       00040        68          LA    R7,C' '           GET BLANK PAD CHARACTER
000032 8970 0018       00018        69          SLL   R7,24             LEFT-JUSTIFY PAD AND SET LENGTH TO 0
000036 0E46                         70          MVCL  R4,R6             CLEAR OUTPUT BUFFER WITH BLANKS
                                    71 *
000038 1B55                         72          SR    R5,R5             CLEAR INDEX
00003A 4170 0014       00014        73          LA    R7,LENOUT/L'OUTPUT   R7 = # OF PRODUCTS BUFFER CAN HOLD
                                    74 **
                                    75 * WHILE THERE IS DATA:
                                    76 * - REPEAT C(R7) TIMES:
                                    77 READ     GET   READER,INPUT      READ DATA FOR NEXT PRODUCT
                                    82 * - - IF SENTINEL IS READ:
00004C 955C C176       0017C        83          CLI   INPUT,C'*'        SENTINEL?
000050 4770 C05E       00064        84          BNE   CONTINUE          NO, CONTINUE PROCESSING
                                    85 * - - - THEN:                    YES:
000054 5970 C992       00998        86          C     R7,=A(LENOUT/L'OUTPUT)  BUFFER EMPTY?
000058 4780 C11A       00120        87          BE    EXIT              IF YES, DONE
00005C 45E0 C136       0013C        88          BAL   R14,IO            ELSE OUTPUT REMAINING PORTION OF BUFFER
000060 47F0 C11A       00120        89          B     EXIT              DONE
                                    90 * - - - ELSE:
                                    91 ** PROCESS UPC:
000064 4145 C1C6       001CC        92 CONTINUE LA    R4,UPC(R5)        R4 = ADDR. OF UPC FIELD IN OUTPUT
000068 D20A 4000 C176 00000 0017C   93          MVC   0(11,R4),INPUT    MOVE UPC TO OUTPUT
                                    94 ** PROCESS LETTER-FLAGS TO CREATE FLAG BYTE:
00006E 4160 C182       00188        95          LA    R6,INFLAGS        R6 = ADDR. OF FIRST FLAG
000072 1B11                         96          SR    R1,R1             CLEAR FIRST BYTE OF R1
000074 DD03 C182 C626 00188 0062C   97          TRT   INFLAGS(4),SLASHTAB  LOOK FOR NEXT SLASH (3 FLAGS MAX)
00007A 1831                         98          LR    R3,R1             R3 = R1 = ADDR. OF SLASH AFTER FLAGS.
                                    99 *                                  DO NOT DESTROY R1; IT IS USED LATER.
00007C 1B36                        100          SR    R3,R6             R3 = NUMBER OF FLAGS
00007E 4430 C080       00086       101          EX    R3,TRANS          CONVERT LETTER FLAGS TO BIT VALUES. NB:
                                   102 *                                  CONVERTS / TOO, BUT WE WILL IGNORE IT
000082 47F0 C086       0008C       103          B     AROUND            SKIP TARGET INSTRUCTION
000086 DC00 C182 C726 00188 0072C  104 TRANS    TR    INFLAGS(0),FLAGTAB  TARGET FOR PREVIOUS EX
                                   105 *  OR FLAG BITS TOGETHER TO FORM SINGLE BYTE OF FLAGS:
                                   106 *  (RECALL THAT R3 = NUMBER OF FLAGS)
00008C D700 C826 C826 0082C 0082C  107 AROUND   XC    BYTE(1),BYTE      ZERO WORK BYTE
000092 D600 C826 6000 0082C 00000  108 ORLOOP   OC    BYTE(1),0(R6)     OR NEXT FLAG BIT TO BYTE
000098 4166 0001       00001       109          LA    R6,1(R6)          POINT TO NEXT FLAG
00009C 4630 C08C       00092       110          BCT   R3,ORLOOP         REPEAT FOR ALL FLAGS
0000A0 4145 C1D1       001D7       111          LA    R4,FLAGS(R5)      R4 = ADDR. OF FLAG BYTE IN OUTPUT
0000A4 D200 4000 C826 00000 0082C  112          MVC   0(1,R4),BYTE      MOVE FLAG BYTE TO OUTPUT BUFFER
                                   113 **
                                   114 ** MOVE SHORT DESCRIPTION:
0000AA 4161 0001       00001       115          LA    R6,1(R1)          POINT TO START OF SHORT DESCRIPTION
                                   116 *                      (SINCE R1 = ADDR. OF /, R6 = ADDR. NEXT FIELD)
0000AE DD0A 6000 C626 00000 0062C  117          TRT   0(L'SHORT+1,R6),SLASHTAB  LOOK FOR NEXT SLASH;
                                   118 *                                          R1 = ITS ADDRESS
0000B4 1831                        119          LR    R3,R1             R3 = R1 = ADDR. OF SLASH
0000B6 1B36                        120          SR    R3,R6             R3 = LENGTH OF SHORT DESCRIPTION
0000B8 4B30 C996       0099C       121          SH    R3,=H'1'          LENGTH MINUS 1 FOR EX
0000BC 4145 C1D2       001D8       122          LA    R4,SHORT(R5)      R4 = ADDR. OF SHORT DESCR. OUTPUT FIELD
0000C0 4430 C0C2       000C8       123          EX    R3,MOVE           MOVE SHORT DESCRIPTION TO OUTPUT BUFFER
0000C4 47F0 C0C8       000CE       124          B     AROUND2           SKIP TARGET INSTRUCTION
0000C8 D200 4000 6000 00000 00000  125 MOVE     MVC   0(0,R4),0(R6)     TARGET FOR PREVIOUS AND NEXT EX
```

*(Continues)*

**Figure 11.21**
*(Continued)*

```
                                        126 ** MOVE LONG DESCRIPTION:
0000CE 4161 0001       00001            127 AROUND2  LA    R6,1(R1)          POINT TO LONG DESCRIPTION (SKIP OVER /)
0000D2 DD19 6000 C626 00000 0062C       128          TRT   0(L'LONG+1,R6),SLASHTAB SEARCH FOR NEXT /; R1 = ITS ADDR
0000D8 1831                             129          LR    R3,R1             R3 = R1 = ADDR. OF SLASH
0000DA 1B36                             130          SR    R3,R6             R3 = LENGTH OF LONG DESCRIPTION
0000DC 4B30 C996       0099C            131          SH    R3,=H'1'          LENGTH MINUS 1 FOR EX
0000E0 4145 C1DC       001E2            132          LA    R4,LONG(R5)       R4 = ADDR. OF LONG DESCR. OUTPUT FIELD
0000E4 4430 C0C2       000C8            133          EX    R3,MOVE           MOVE LONG DESCRIPTION TO OUTPUT BUFFER
                                        134 ** MOVE PRICE AND INVENTORY:
0000E8 4161 0001       00001            135          LA    R6,1(R1)          POINT TO PRICE (SKIP OVER /)
0000EC 4145 C1F5       001FB            136          LA    R4,PRICE(R5)      R4 = ADDR. OF PRICE FIELD IN OUTPUT
0000F0 D204 4000 6000 00000 00000       137          MVC   0(L'PRICE,R4),0(R6)  MOVE PRICE TO OUTPUT BUFFER
0000F6 4145 C1FA       00200            138          LA    R4,INVEN(R5)      R4 = ADDR. OF INVENTORY FIELD IN OUTPUT
0000FA D203 4000 6006 00000 00006       139          MVC   0(L'INVEN,R4),L'PRICE+1(R6)  MOVE INVENTORY TO OUTPUT
                                        140 *
000100 4155 0038       00038            141          LA    R5,L'OUTPUT(R5)   INCREMENT OUTPUT INDEX
000104 4670 C038       0003E            142          BCT   R7,READ           DECREMENT LOOP COUNTER; REPEAT IF NOT 0
                                        143 * - - END IF
                                        144 * - END REPEAT
                                        145 ** OUTPUT BUFFER FULL; SEND TO OUTPUT DEVICE:
000108 45E0 C136       0013C            146          BAL   R14,IO            CALL OUTPUT ROUTINE
00010C 47F0 C024       0002A            147          B     LOOP              FILL BUFFER AGAIN
                                        148 * END WHILE
                                        149 ERROR    PUT   PRINTER,ERR       PRINT MISSING DATA MESSAGE
                                        154 ** STANDARD EXIT
                                        155 ** OS:
                                        156 EXIT     CLOSE (READER,,PRINTER,,SNAPDCB)  I/O IS COMPLETE
000132 58D0 C82E       00834            166          L     R13,SAVE+4        RESTORE R13
000136 98EC D00C       0000C            167          LM    R14,R12,12(R13)   RESTORE REMAINING REGISTERS
00013A 07FE                             168          BR    R14               RETURN TO OS
                                        169 ** DOS*******
                                        170 *EXIT    CLOSE READER,PRINTER    I/O IS COMPLETE
                                        171 *        EOJ                     RETURN TO DOS
                                        172 ******
                                        173 ** DUMMY I/O SUBPROGRAM:
                            0013C       174 IO       EQU   *
                                        175 * DUMP OUTPUT BUFFER
                                        176          SNAP  STORAGE=(OUTPUT,OUTPUT+LENOUT),DCB=SNAPDCB,ID=1
                                        197 ** DOS*******
                                        198 *        PDUMP OUTPUT,OUTPUT+LENOUT
                                        199 ******
000166 07FE                             200          BR    R14               RETURN
                                        201 **
                                        202 ** DATA AREA:
000168 40C5D9D9D6D97A40                 203 ERR      DC    C' ERROR: MISSING DATA'
                                        204 *
00017C                                  205 INPUT    DS    CL80              INPUT RECORD
0001CC                      0017C       206          ORG   INPUT             BACK UP TO ASSIGN NAME FOR FLAGS
00017C                                  207          DS    CL11                UPC IN INPUT
000187                                  208          DS    X                   / THAT FOLLOWS
000188                                  209 INFLAGS  DS    3C                  UP TO 3 FLAGS
00018B                      001CC       210          ORG   ,                 RETURN TO BYTE AFTER INPUT RECORD
0001CC                                  211 OUTPUT   DS    20CL56            OUTPUT BUFFER WITH FIELDS AS FOLLOWS:
00062C                      001CC       212          ORG   OUTPUT            BACK UP TO ASSIGN FIELD NAMES
0001CC                                  213 UPC      DS    CL11                UPC NUMBER
0001D7                                  214 FLAGS    DS    X                   FLAG BYTE
0001D8                                  215 SHORT    DS    CL10                SHORT PRODUCT DESCRIPTION
0001E2                                  216 LONG     DS    CL25                LONGER PRODUCT DESCRIPTION
0001FB                                  217 PRICE    DS    CL5                 PRICE WITH DECIMAL POINT (EBCDIC)
000200                                  218 INVEN    DS    CL4                 INVENTORY
000204                      0062C       219          ORG   ,                 RETURN TO BYTE AFTER OUTPUT BUFFER
                            00460       220 LENOUT   EQU   *-OUTPUT          LENGTH OF OUTPUT BUFFER
```

(*Continues*)

**Figure 11.21**
(*Continued*)

```
                                        221 *
                                        222 ** TRT TABLE TO DETECT SLASH:
00062C 0000000000000000                 223 SLASHTAB DC    256X'00'           IGNORE MOST CHARACTERS
00072C                        0068D     224          ORG   SLASHTAB+C'/'      SLASH
00068D 01                               225          DC    X'1'               ANY NONZERO
00068E                        0072C     226          ORG
                                        227 *
                                        228 ** TR TABLE TO CONVERT LETTER FLAG TO BIT PATTERN:
00072C 0000000000000000                 229 FLAGTAB  DC    256X'00'           CONVERT ILLEGALS TO ZEROS
00082C                        0080F     230          ORG   FLAGTAB+C'T'       T = TAXABLE ITEM
00080F 80                               231          DC    B'10000000'            BIT 0 IS 1
000810                        0080E     232          ORG   FLAGTAB+C'S'       S = SPECIAL SALE
00080E 40                               233          DC    B'01000000'            BIT 1 IS 1
00080F                        007EE     234          ORG   FLAGTAB+C'B'       B = BAKERY ITEM
0007EE 20                               235          DC    B'00100000'            BIT 2 IS 1
0007EF                        007F0     236          ORG   FLAGTAB+C'D'       D = DAIRY ITEM
0007F0 10                               237          DC    B'00010000'            BIT 3 IS 1
0007F1                        007F3     238          ORG   FLAGTAB+C'G'       G = GROCERY ITEM
0007F3 08                               239          DC    B'00001000'            BIT 4 IS 1
0007F4                        00800     240          ORG   FLAGTAB+C'M'       M = MEAT ITEM
000800 04                               241          DC    B'00000100'            BIT 5 IS 1
000801                        00803     242          ORG   FLAGTAB+C'P'       P = PRODUCE ITEM
000803 02                               243          DC    B'00000010'            BIT 6 IS 1
000804                        00801     244          ORG   FLAGTAB+C'N'       N = NONFOOD ITEM
000801 01                               245          DC    B'00000001'            BIT 7 IS 1
000802                        0082C     246          ORG
                                        247 *
00082C                                  248 BYTE     DS    X                  WORK BYTE
000830                                  249 SAVE     DS    18F                SAVE AREA (9D IN DOS)
                                        250 ** DCB'S FOR I/O IN OS:
                                        251 READER   DCB   DSORG=PS,MACRF=GM,DDNAME=SYSIN,RECFM=F,LRECL=80,          X
                                                           BLKSIZE=80,EODAD=ERROR
                                        305 PRINTER  DCB   DSORG=PS,MACRF=PM,DDNAME=SYSPRINT,RECFM=FA,LRECL=L'ERR,   X
                                                           BLKSIZE=L'ERR
                                        359 SNAPDCB  DCB   DSORG=PS,MACRF=W,RECFM=VBA,BLKSIZE=1632,LRECL=125,        X
                                                           DDNAME=SNAP
                                        410 ** DOS*******
                                        411 *READER  DTFCD DEVADDR=SYSIPT,DEVICE=2540,IOAREA1=INBUF,EOFADDR=ERROR,   X
                                                           RECFORM=FIXUNB,BLKSIZE=80,TYPEFLE=INPUT,WORKA=YES
                                        412 *PRINTER DTFPR DEVADDR=SYSLST,DEVICE=3203,IOAREA1=OUTBUF,WORKA=YES,      X
                                                           RECFORM=FIXUNB,BLKSIZE=L'ERR,CTLCHAR=ASA
                                        413 *INBUF   DS    80C                INPUT BUFFER
                                        414 *OUTBUF  DS    (L'ERR)C           OUTPUT BUFFER
                                        415 ******
000000                                  416          END   GROCERY
000990 000001CC00000460                 417                =A(OUTPUT,LENOUT)
000998 00000014                         418                =A(LENOUT/L'OUTPUT)
00099C 0001                             419                =H'1'
```

**Figure 11.21**
*(Continued)*

Since the position and length of the UPC number in the input record are known, the UPC number is readily moved to the output buffer, using Statements 92 and 93. The TRT instruction in Statement 97 locates the slash after the flags so that the number of flags can be determined. Notice that Statement 98 saves the address that is in Register 1 because it is needed later. To ensure that the subtraction in Statement 100 is correct when 24-bit addressing is used, you must clear Register 1 prior to the first TRT instruction. Here, Register 1 is cleared in Statement 96. Using the EX and TR instructions (Statements 101 and 104), the program translates each letter code into an 8-bit quantity: seven 0's and a single 1 in the proper bit position. For example, since T signals a taxable item, bit 0 of the flag byte must be set to 1. Therefore, the program converts T to the binary integer 10000000, S to the binary integer 01000000, and so on. The flag byte in the data base for a taxable (T) sale item (S) would be 11000000, which is obtained by ORing 10000000 and 01000000 together. This is done in Statements 107 through 112. Note that, although the program does not warn you if it encounters illegal flags, it translates such flags into 0's so they will not affect the flag byte. Also, notice that to save an instructon, the length that is specified by the EX instruction is one larger than it should be. Therefore, the program also translates the slash after the flags but, since it is skipped anyway, this causes no problem.

Statements 115 through 133 locate each variable-length description field within the input record with a TRT instruction and move it to a fixed-length field in the output buffer by using the EX and MVC instructions. Since the lengths of the remaining fields are known, they are readily moved (Statements 135 through 139).

The subprogram IO is invoked whenever the output buffer is full because 20 products have been processed, or whenever the sentinel record is read and the buffer is not empty. Clearly, the focus of this case study is on the instructions that fill the buffer and not on the IO subprogram. In fact, the subprogram used here is a dummy routine that simply dumps the buffer. Chapter 16 discusses the concept of a buffer in relation to I/O operations.

## Debugging Hints

1. If an Execute instruction executes the target instruction in its unmodified form contrary to your expectations, you may have erroneously used Register 0 as the first register operand of the EX instruction.
2. When you use EX to specify a field length for an SS instruction, be sure that the length that you compute is one less than the actual number of bytes in the field.
3. Initially define the translation table of a TR or TRT instruction to be 256 bytes long. You should consider reducing its length when feasible only after the program executes correctly. However, be careful when you design tables that are shorter than 256 bytes: unpredictable results will occur if argument bytes reference bytes outside of the table.
4. When you use the TRT instruction, do not use Registers 1 and 2 for purposes not related to TRT. This warning is particularly important to heed if you are planning to ignore the contents of one or both of these registers as set by TRT. In such cases, it is easy to forget that the instruction has probably modified their contents. This is particularly true of Register 2 and using it needlessly invites difficult-to-find errors.

5. When you use Register 1 in arithmetic after TRT, it may be necessary to zero the first byte of Register 1 previously if 24-bit addressing is in effect since the first byte is unchanged by TRT. As a precaution against error, you can routinely clear Register 1 before you execute the first TRT instruction in your program. This step is unnecessary if 31-bit addressing is used.

## Stylistic Notes

1. Place the target instruction of an EX near the EX itself. This not only simplifies your search for the target during debugging, but it can also improve performance in a virtual storage environment.
2. Use the ORG directive and character self-defining terms when you define translation tables to reduce arithmetic errors and to make them as self-documenting as possible. Clarify the definition with several comments.
3. It is easy to misinterpret the meaning of a symbol in the name entry of an ORG directive; avoid using a symbol there.

## Summary

1. Selectively set a bit to 1 by ORing it with 1.
2. Selectively set a bit to 0 by ANDing it with 0.
3. Selectively invert a bit value by EXCLUSIVE ORing it with 1.
4. You can use three consecutive EXCLUSIVE OR instructions to interchange the contents of two registers or two areas of storage.
5. You can use the TM instruction to test one or more bits of a byte selectively.
6. The EX instruction is used to modify temporarily and execute another instruction. An important application of the EX instruction is to specify at execution time the field length that is used by an SS instruction.
7. The TR instruction changes the contents of the bytes that are specified as the first operand. The instruction is used either to translate characters from one encoding scheme into another or to rearrange fields in storage.
8. The TRT instruction does not affect the contents of the bytes that are specified by its operands, but it does set the condition code and usually affects Registers 1 and 2. The instruction is used to detect the occurrence of any given values in a string of bytes.
9. The ORG directive, which is used to alter the contents of the location counter during the assembly process, facilitates the definition of translation tables for the TR and TRT instructions.
10. The MVCL and CLCL instructions are used with character strings of arbitrary length. You can also use them when you compute field lengths at execution time without having to use the EX instruction. These characteristics give them an advantage over the MVC and CLC instructions. However, they generally require four registers to specify the fields involved.

## New Instruction Summary

| Operation | Operand | Format | Instruction Name | Action |
|---|---|---|---|---|
| NR<br>OR<br>XR | *R1*,*R2* | RR | AND REGISTER<br>OR REGISTER<br>EXCLUSIVE OR REGISTER | C(*R1*) ← C(*R1*) *op* C(*R2*) |

Condition code = { 0 if the result is zero; 1 if the result is nonzero }

| Operation | Operand | Format | Instruction Name | Action |
|---|---|---|---|---|
| N<br>O<br>X | *R1,S2*<br>or *R1,S2(X2)*<br>or *R1,D2(X2,B2)* | RX | AND<br>OR<br>EXCLUSIVE OR | $C(R1) \leftarrow C(R1)\ op\ C(E2)_{0-31}$<br>Condition code: same as for RR Boolean instructions |
| NI<br>OI<br>XI | *S1,I2*<br>or *D1(B1),I2* | SI | AND IMMEDIATE<br>OR IMMEDIATE<br>EXCLUSIVE OR IMMEDIATE | $C(E1) \leftarrow C(E1)\ op\ I2$<br>Condition code: same as for RR Boolean instructions |
| NC<br>OC<br>XC | *S1(L),S2*<br>or *S1,S2*<br>or *S1(L),D2(B2)*<br>or *S1,D2(B2)*<br>or *D1(L,B1),S2*<br>or *D1(L,B1),D2(B2)* | SS | AND CHARACTERS<br>OR CHARACTERS<br>EXCLUSIVE OR CHARACTERS | $C(E1)_{L\ \text{bytes}} \leftarrow C(E1)_{L\ \text{bytes}}\ op\ C(E2)_{L\ \text{bytes}}$<br>Condition code: same as for RR Boolean instructions |
| TM | *S1,I2*<br>or *D1(B1),I2* | SI | TEST UNDER MASK | Tests bits of C(*E1*) that are selected according to *I2*<br>Condition code = { 0 if all selected bits are 0's, or *I2* = 0; 1 if some selected bits are 0's, and others are 1's; 3 if all selected bits are 1's } |
| EX | *R1,S2*<br>or *R1,S2(X2)*<br>or *R1,D2(X2,B2)* | RX | EXECUTE | If $R1 \neq 0$, executes the target instruction at *E2* as if its second byte had been ORed with $C(R1)_{24-31}$; the target instruction is unchanged in storage. If $R1 = 0$, executes the target instruction without modification. |
| MVCL | *R1,R2* | RR | MOVE CHARACTERS LONG | The even registers *R1* and *R2* define two even-odd register pairs. Each pair contains the starting address and length of a field in storage. The first field is replaced by copies of bytes taken from the second field, which is extended on the right if necessary by copies of $C(R2+1)_{0-7}$. If $L_1$ and $L_2$ denote the field lengths: |

| Operation | Operand | Format | Instruction Name | Action |
|---|---|---|---|---|
| | | | Condition code = | 0 if $L_1 = L_2$<br>1 if $L_1 < L_2$<br>2 if $L_1 > L_2$<br>3 if no bytes are moved due to destructive overlap |
| **CLCL** | *R1,R2* | RR | COMPARE CHARACTERS LONG | Logically compares the fields whose starting addresses and lengths are contained in the even-odd register pairs that are designated by *R1* and *R2* |
| | | | Condition code = | 0 if the fields are equal, or are both of zero length<br>1 if the first field is less than the second<br>2 if the first field is greater than the second |
| **TR** | *S1(L),S2*<br>or *S1,S2*<br>or *S1(L),D2(B2)*<br>or *S1,D2(B2)*<br>or *D1(L,B1),S2*<br>or *D1(L,B1),D2(B2)* | SS | TRANSLATE | Translates *L* bytes as follows:<br>C(*E1*) ← C(*E2* + C(*E1*))<br>C(*E1* + 1) ← C(*E2* + C(*E1* + 1))<br>.<br>.<br>. |
| **TRT** | *S1(L),S2*<br>or *S1,S2*<br>or *S1(L),D2(B2)*<br>or *S1,D2(B2)*<br>or *D1(L,B1),S2*<br>or *D1(L,B1),D2(B2)* | SS | TRANSLATE AND TEST | (*See below*) |

**Action**

Each of a maximum of *L* consecutive argument bytes at *E1*, which are considered left to right, references a function byte in the table at *E2* in exactly the same manner as the TR instruction, except that the arguments are unchanged. This continues until one of the following occurs.

1. A nonzero function byte is referenced:
   $C(\text{Reg. }1)_{8-31}$ ← Address of the argument byte that references the nonzero function byte
   (Note: With 31-bit addressing, the address is placed in bits 1 through 31 of Register 1 and bit 0 is 0.)
   $C(\text{Reg. }2)_{24-31}$ ← Contents of the function byte
   Condition code = { 1 if the argument byte is not the last (rightmost) one in the first operand; 2 if the argument is the last one in the first operand }
2. All arguments are considered and all functon bytes are zero:
   Condition code = 0
   Registers 1 and 2 remain unchanged

## New Directives

| Name | Operation | Operand | Instruction Name | Action |
|---|---|---|---|---|
| *symbol* or *blank* | ORG | *relocatable expression* or *blank* | ORIGIN | Sets the location counter to the value of the relocatable expression. In case the operand entry is omitted, resets the location counter to the highest value attained so far. |

(DOS: no symbol permitted in the name entry.)

## Exercises

1. Verify that you can use three EXCLUSIVE OR instructions to interchange the contents of two registers or two fields in storage, as described in Example 6.
2. Write one instruction to compute the one's complement of the 32-bit integer in Register 5.
3. Rewrite the instructions in Figure 11.2 so that only one Boolean instruction is necessary instead of two. (Hint: Think of another way to form the required mask.) You can do this with one less instruction, but one more register than used in Figure 11.2.
4. Assume that SWITCHES is a fullword that represents 32 switches numbered from 0 to 31, as in Example 11. If $n$ is in Register 9, write instructions that will invert the value of switch $n$.
5. With SWITCHES defined as in Exercise 4, write instructions to isolate the first three switches and place them left-justified in Register 5.
6. Assume that Register 2 contains an integer $n$ and that BITS is a halfword in storage. Write instructions to manipulate bit $n$ of BITS as follows: set it to 1, set it to 0, invert its value, and test it. Repeat this process but assume that BITS is a doubleword. Write the instructions once more, but assume that BITS is a byte.
7. Write instructions to change bits within the 250-byte field at AREA as follows:
   Set to 0 the first bit of each of bytes 1, 3, 5, and so on to 249.
   Set to 1 the first bit of each of bytes 2, 4, 6, and so on to 250.
   Invert the value of the last bit of every byte.
   Leave all other bits alone.
8. Assuming the definitions of Example 12 and Figure 11.4, write instructions to perform each of the following:
   a. Delete all characteristics from GROUP1.
   b. Delete characteristics 3 and 6 from GROUP2 by using one instruction.
   c. Assign characteristics 2, 4, and 8 to GROUP1.
   d. Branch to EITHER if GROUP2 has either or both of characteristics 1 or 4.
   e. Branch to BOTH if GROUP2 has either both characteristics 2 and 8 or neither of them.
   f. Branch to ONE if GROUP2 is missing exactly one of characteristics 5 and 6.
   g. Branch to SOME if GROUP1 has one or more of characteristics 1, 3, and 7.
   h. Branch to NOTALL if GROUP2 has one or two, but not all, of characteristics 1, 3, and 7.
   i. Branch to NONE if GROUP1 has none of the characteristics 1, 3, or 7.
   j. Branch to TWO if GROUP1 has exactly two of characteristics 4, 6, and 8.
   k. Branch to ONLYONE if GROUP2 has exactly one of characteristics 4, 6, and 8.
9. You can use a Boolean operation to implement the circular shift that is described in Exercise 10 of Chapter 8. Is such a solution better than one that uses only shifts?
10. Consider the following:

```
                 EX      2,SUB
                 B       AROUND
        SUB      S       0,N
        AROUND   ----
```

Write instructions before this segment so that the EX instruction has the same effect as

```
        S       9,N
```

Repeat so that it has the same effect as

```
        S       9,N(4)
```

11. Revise the instructions in Figure 11.8 (Example 21) so that the Social Security number will be printed with dashes, as in 000-00-0000.

12. Suppose that there were no TR instruction. Write a loop that would do the same thing but, of course, in a less efficient manner.

13. Given a character string of uppercase and lowercase letters, periods, commas, and blanks, write instructions that will print the string with dollar signs beneath only the lowercase letters.

14. Write instructions to translate a string of lowercase letters to uppercase.

15. Write instructions to translate any lowercase letter in a string of letters to uppercase, leaving uppercase letters unchanged.

16. Write instructions to translate the string of ASCII uppercase letters at STRING into EBCDIC.

17. Write some instructions to translate an ASCII character string into EBCDIC, and other instructions to translate an EBCDIC character string into ASCII. If a character in one code does not exist in the other, translate it into 00.

18. Write the translate table that is necessary to reverse the order of bits in a byte. With this table, write instructions to reverse the order of the bits in a field of 4 bytes. Repeat with a field of $n$ bytes, where $1 \leq n \leq 256$ and $n$ is in Register 3.

19. Write the translate table necessary to count the number of bits in a byte. Using this table, write instructions to count the number of bits in a field of 4 bytes. (You may destroy the contents of the field.) Repeat with a field of $n$ bytes, where $1 \leq n \leq 256$ and $n$ is in Register 3.

20. Using TRT, write instructions to determine if the 100 characters at STRING consist of anything other than the letters A to Z or blanks.

21. Using TRT, write instructions to determine the number of periods and the number of commas that occur in the 50-byte character string at DATA.

22. Write instructions to print only those input records that contain no other characters than uppercase letters or blanks.

23. Write instructions to count the number of bytes in a 100-byte field that have zeros in their first 4 bits. Solve this both with and without a TRT instruction.

24. What is wrong with each of the following definitions?

a.
```
AREA     DS    0CL50
FIELD1   DS    CL22
FIELD2   DS    CL38
         ORG   AREA+L'AREA
```

b.
```
T        DC    128X'0'
         ORG   T + C'$'
         DC    X'01'
         ORG
```

c.
```
TABLE    DC    100C' '
         ORG   TABLE+C'A'
         DC    X'2'
         ORG
```

## Programming Problems

1. Given the UPC data base that is described in the case study and given an input data set of the UPC numbers for products purchased, write a program to print a cash-register tape. For each purchase, print a label that categorizes the product (taxable, grocery, and so on), the product's short description, and its price. Note that the tape is only 25 characters wide. Do not compute the tax or total sale; it is best to do such computations with the decimal instructions that are covered in Chapter 15. (For simplicity, you can define the UPC data base with DCs.)

2. Consider a data structure that consists of a collection of sequentially allocated items called records. Each record contains a character string that is preceded by its length, in hex, in a single byte. A zero-valued byte follows the last record. For example, the following three records contain the character strings AB, CDE, and F:

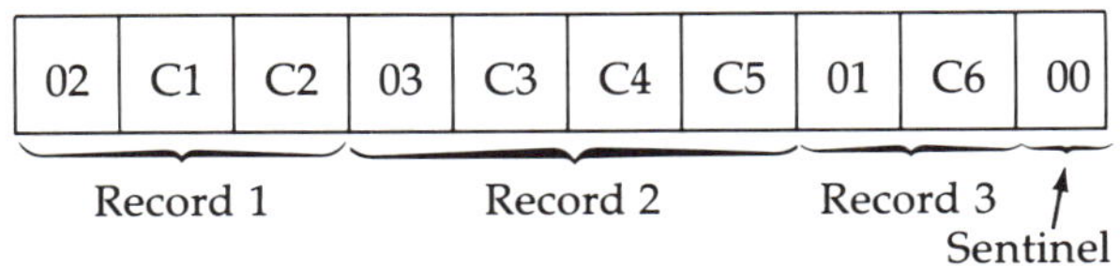


Write a program to perform the following:

**a.** Read character strings, one per input record, and create the described data structure.

**b.** Search the data structure for the character string that is lowest in the collating sequence.

**c.** Given any character string, determine if it exists in the data structure.

**d.** Print the character strings, without lengths, in the order that they appear in the data structure.

**e.** Print the character strings in collating order.

As you develop the program, you can write and test the instructions that you write for parts **b** through **e** independently of the instructions that you write for part **a** by defining a data structure with DCs, as shown here:

```
DATA    DC    AL1(L'ST1)
ST1     DC    C'AB'
        DC    AL1(L'ST2)
ST2     DC    C'CDE'
        DC    AL1(L'ST3)
ST3     DC    C'F'
        DC    X'0'
```

3. Assume input records that each contains a person's name anywhere within a field of 40 characters. Names appear with the first name first and with or without a middle initial. If there is a middle initial, it can appear with or without a period. Thus, the following are possible:

   JOHN DOE
   JANE S. DOE
   JILL A DOE

   Write a program to create a 500-byte array that contains names, each of which is followed by a slash and is written with the last name first followed by a comma, the first name, and the middle initial, if any, without a period. The only permitted blanks are between the first name and the middle initial. For example, the names just given would appear as

   DOE,JOHN/DOE,JANE S/DOE,JILL A/

   When no more names will completely fit into the array, print its contents by using lines of no more than 100 characters each. Each printed line should contain as many complete names as can fit, in the order they appear in the array, and each must end with a complete name and its slash.

4. Consider 80-character input records that contain names, each of which is followed by a slash and is written with the last name first, followed by a comma, the first name, and the middle initial, if any, without a period. The only blanks appear between the first name and the middle initial, as follows:

   DOE,JOHN/DOE,JANE S/DOE,JILL A/DOE,MICHAEL/

   Each record ends with a complete name and its slash, followed possibly by blanks. Produce a printed listing of these names that is arranged in 3 columns, each 30 characters wide and separated by 5 blanks. Print the first name first, omit the slashes, and add spaces as appropriate and a period after any middle initial. For example, the names in the input record just given would appear in the listing as shown here:

```
JOHN DOE                           JANE S. DOE                        JILL A. DOE
MICHAEL DOE
|<---------- 30 ---------->|<- 5 ->|<---------- 30 ---------->|<- 5 ->|<---------- 30 ---------->|
```

5. Repeat Programming Problem 10 of Chapter 10 by using the TRT and EX instructions.

6. Write a program to create mailing labels from input records that appear like this:

```
John Doe<123 Circle Dr.<Bosk, RI<02800?Jill Jones<
9 Willow Way; Apt. 2<Penockquot<Vermont<90007@
```

For simplicity, call the name and address an address. A < separates the lines in each address in the input records, and a ? follows the last line. The @ follows the last address in the data set. Addresses need not appear on a single input record, and each input record can contain data for more than one address. Input records must end with <, ?, or @, possibly followed by blanks, which are ignored. Assume that the input data is error-free and specifies no more than 5 lines per label. Each label can accommodate up to 5 lines of 30 characters each; truncate any input lines that are longer than this. Assume that the labels are spaced uniformly on continuous forms. If you print a 5-line address on one label and then skip 2 lines, the next label will be in the proper position for the first line of the next address.

7. Write a portion of a word-processing program that inserts, deletes, or replaces character strings into a given text. Begin by reading the original text from input records into consecutive bytes of storage. A record that contains the characters #*$@% in its first five columns will signal the end of the text.

Each of the next input records will contain one of four commands that controls the modification of the text. Each command begins in the first column of the record and can be assumed to be error-free. Read each command and make the appropriate changes to the text, as follows:

DELETE *"string"*
This command should delete all occurrences of the character string that is represented by *string*. (Assume that *string* does not contain quotation marks.)

REPLACE *"string1"* BY *"string2"*
This command should replace every occurrence of *string1* with *string2*.

INSERT *"string1"* AFTER *"string2"*
This command inserts *string1* after each occurrence of *string2*.

STOP
This command signals the end of the command records.

After the last command has been processed, edit the blanks in the text so that there is only one blank between words and two blanks between sentences.

Print the original text, the commands read, and the final edited text.

8. A **keyword-in-context (KWIC) index** is a listing of publication titles and cross-reference numbers. Each title appears several times in the index—once for each significant, or key, word in the title. The listing prints keywords in each title in a fixed column (called the **keyword column**) in alphabetical order. A cross-reference number that is associated with each title also appears in the listing. This number points to an entry in a bibliography, which contains further information about the publication.

For example, the following titles and cross-reference numbers

```
8633 1917 SOME PROPERTIES OF BINARY COUNTERS WITH FEEDBACK.
8635 2558 A FOUR MEGACYCLE SIXTEEN-BIT CHECKED BINARY ADDER.
8523 0791 SEMIAUTOMATIC INDEXING AND ENCODING IN THE HUMANITIES.
8526 1233 BOOLEAN ALGEBRA WITH APPLICATIONS.
```

generate an index that begins with

```
8635 2558 ADDER.  A FOUR MEGACYCLE SIXTEEN-BIT CHECKED BINARY
8526 1233 ALGEBRA WITH APPLICATIONS.  BOOLEAN
8526 1233 APPLICATIONS.  BOOLEAN ALGEBRA WITH
8635 2558 BINARY ADDER.  A FOUR MEGACYCLE SIXTEEN-BIT CHECKED
```

Write a program to print a KWIC index for a given set of titles and cross-reference numbers. Adhere to the following specifications:

Input:
  Each record contains a cross-reference number in columns 1 through 9 and the corresponding title in columns 11 through 70. Each title must end with a period.

Output:
  Printed lines must not exceed 71 characters each. For testing purposes, assume that there are no more than 50 lines in the index.

9. Repeat Programming Problem 8, but change the appearance of the KWIC index so that keywords begin in column 35 of each line. This requires that some titles be wrapped around the keyword column. For example, the index for the previous titles begins as

```
                                  Keywords (Column 35)       Column 71
                                  ↓                                   ↓
8635 2558 TEEN-BIT CHECKED BINARY ADDER.     A FOUR MEGACYCLE SIX
8526 1233                 BOOLEAN ALGEBRA WITH APPLICATIONS.
8526 1233    BOOLEAN ALGEBRA WITH APPLICATIONS.
8635 2558 CLE SIXTEEN-BIT CHECKED BINARY ADDER.     A FOUR MEGACY
```

Spacing within each line of the index can differ from this example, but the wraparound section must exist.

10. Write a program that is part of a pre-registration system for a small college. Your program will read input records that contain course scheduling data, and create a data base for use in the next programming problem. Assume that there is only one section per course.

The data for each course is contained on a single input record. The fields in this record each end with a slash and are defined as follows:

Field 1: The 6-character course code; for example CSC311
Field 2: The maximum enrollment permitted (one or two digits )
Field 3: One or more single-character codes, which are written without spaces and which specify registration restrictions for the course. These codes are defined as follows:
- 1 The course is open to first-year students.
- 2 The course is open to second-year students.
- 3 The course is open to third-year students
- 4 The course is open to fourth-year students.
- M The course is open to majors only.

For example, M34 indicates that the course is open only to third- and fourth-year students who are majors.

Fields 4, 5, and 6 specify the course meeting time, the place, and the instructor, respectively. Each field will not exceed 10 characters.

For example, the following is a data record in the format just described:

```
CSC311/35/234/MWF10/28 EAST/CARRANO/
```

Create the data base in consecutive bytes of storage. Each course is represented as follows:

| | |
|---|---|
| Course code: | 6 bytes, EBCDIC |
| Current enrollment: | 1 byte, hex; initially zero |
| Maximum enrollment: | 1 byte, hex |
| Flags: | 1 byte |

Bit 0: 1 if course is open to majors only, else 0
Bits 1-4: Bit *n* is 1 if course is open to *n*th-year students, else 0
Bits 5-7: currently unused

| | |
|---|---|
| Time: | 10 bytes, EBCDIC |
| Place: | 10 bytes, EBCDIC |
| Instructor: | 10 bytes, EBCDIC |

11. Assuming the course data base as described in Programming Problem 10, write a program to read a student data base and produce class rosters. You can write this program without writing the previous one by defining the course data base with DCs, as shown here:

```
DC   C'CSC311'        COURSE CODE
DC   X'0023'          ENROLLMENTS: CURRENT = 0, MAX = 35
DC   B'00111000'      OPEN TO 2ND, 3RD, AND 4TH YEAR STUDENTS
DC   CL10'MWF10'      TIME
DC   CL10'28 EAST'    PLACE
DC   CL10'CARRANO'    INSTRUCTOR
```

The student data base is defined in input records, with one record per student, as follows:

| | |
|---|---|
| Student ID: | 9 characters |
| Student name: | 30 characters |
| Year of graduation: | 2 characters (eg. 90) |
| Curriculum code: | 3 characters (eg. CSC) |
| Requested courses: | 36 characters. This field consists of up to six 6-character course codes without separation |

A typical data record might appear as

```
000119876SMYTHE, JOHN                    90CSCMTH471CSC311ENG240
```

Assume that the student data base has been processed to remove errors and time conflicts, and that students and their requests are in order according to priority.

Process the course requests for each student. For each request, check to see if there is room in the course. Also, check the course restrictions to see if the student is permitted to register for it. If so, increment the current enrollment byte.

After you have processed all requests, produce an alphabetized class roster for each course. Label each roster with the course name, time, place, and instructor. For each student on the roster, print the ID, name, year, and curriculum code with appropriate spacing and labeling.

# 12

# Multiple Base Registers

CONTENTS



OVERVIEW

This chapter describes the rules that the assembler uses to select base registers according to the information that you supply in USING directives. The chapter begins by reviewing and extending what you know about the one base register that your programs have used so far. Then the discussion covers how to define additional base registers. This chapter demonstrates the use of multiple base registers with programs that exceed 4096 bytes in length. Using the information presented here as a foundation, the next chapter describes how to use multiple base registers to address data areas and the arguments of a subprogram.

OBJECTIVES

After studying this chapter, you should be able to:

1. Define, redefine, or delete one or more base registers as appropriate to a particular program.
2. Determine the base register that the assembler selects when it translates any given symbolic address.
3. Determine whether or not a particular base register has been correctly defined.

4. Determine whether or not any given instruction will cause an addressability error.
5. Correct any addressability errors that might occur in a program.

## Introduction

Since the displacement portion of an instruction can have a value between 0 and 4095, you can address any byte within a 4096-byte area that begins at the base address by using just one base register. However, if you try to address a field whose first byte is more than 4096 bytes beyond the base address, the assembler will give you an addressability error because the field is not **addressable**. The reason for the problem is that the required displacement exceeds 4095 and cannot be accommodated by the 12-bit displacement portion of the instruction.

As you learned in Chapter 6, an addressability error generally occurs when the assembler cannot represent a symbolic address in a base-displacement form. Although addressability errors can occur in any program, they are likely to occur in programs that exceed 4096 bytes in length. Your programs could exceed this length if you use large arrays. You can reference large arrays by using explicit operand designations in the same way that you processed character arrays in Chapter 10—thus, avoiding the addressability issue. However, your program will be easier to read if you use implicit operand designations; to do so, you may need additional base registers.

Your program could also exceed 4096 bytes in length simply because it contains many instructions. Although 4096 bytes may not sound like much, a program of this length is substantial. In fact, you probably should not write programs that long without breaking them into smaller sections, as will be discussed in the next chapter. If you do not do this, you are still faced with addressability problems. To solve these problems, you should use more than one base register.

There are other situations, which you will study in the next chapter, where multiple base registers are either necessary or desirable, so it is important to investigate how to define additional base registers and the problems that you are apt to encounter. To begin, this chapter considers the definition of a single base register and some of the subtle difficulties that can arise. Such difficulties are even more likely to occur when you define a second base register.

## One Base Register

**Distinguish between loading a base register and declaring a base register**

It is important to remember the distinction between *loading* a base register with the base address, and *declaring* both the base register and the base address to the assembler. Both steps are necessary: just loading a base register is insufficient. You must also write a USING statement that tells the assembler what base register is available and what base address to assume.

**The range of any base register is 4096 bytes in length**

As you know, you can use one base register to address 4096 bytes. These bytes are said to be within the **range** of the base register (or within the range of the USING statement). The range of any base register is always 4096 bytes in length.

The rules that the assembler uses to assign a base register and compute a displacement when it assembles any symbolic address or literal are as follows:

- The USING statement must physically precede the instruction to be assembled.
- The assembler can only use a particular base register if the resultant displacement is in the range of 0 to 4095.

---

EXAMPLE 1

**Instructions and Addresses before the Base Address**

This example answers two questions:

- Can you correctly write instructions at addresses before the base address?
- Can you branch to an address before the base address?

The answer to both questions is *yes* as long as the instructions do not require the assembler to provide a base register. Instructions that precede the base address must either be in the RR format or use explicit operands. The STM instruction and the BALR instruction in Figure 12.1 are examples of such instructions.

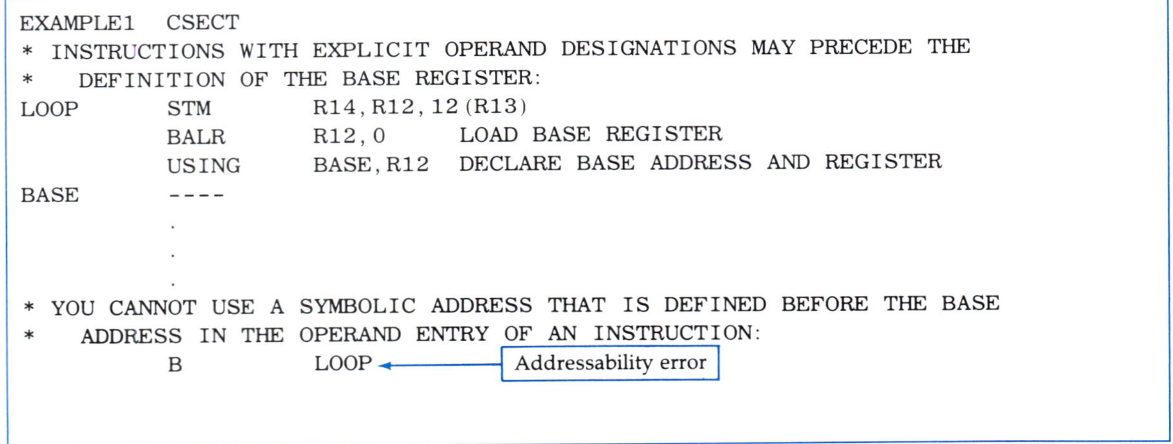

```
EXAMPLE1  CSECT
* INSTRUCTIONS WITH EXPLICIT OPERAND DESIGNATIONS MAY PRECEDE THE
*   DEFINITION OF THE BASE REGISTER:
LOOP      STM       R14,R12,12(R13)
          BALR      R12,0       LOAD BASE REGISTER
          USING     BASE,R12    DECLARE BASE ADDRESS AND REGISTER
BASE      ----
          .
          .
          .
* YOU CANNOT USE A SYMBOLIC ADDRESS THAT IS DEFINED BEFORE THE BASE
*   ADDRESS IN THE OPERAND ENTRY OF AN INSTRUCTION:
          B         LOOP
```



**Figure 12.1**
Instructions and addresses before the base address, as described in Example 1.

To branch anywhere within your program, you can write a Branch instruction either in the RR format or with explicit operand designations. However, if there is only one base register, you cannot use a symbolic address that is defined before the base address in the operand of any instruction. When translating the unconditional branch in Figure 12.1, the assembler attempts to use Register 12 as the base register. The assembler computes the displacement by subtracting the desired effective address, which is represented by LOOP, from the base address that is represented by BASE. The difference is negative and, therefore, cannot be used as a displacement. The fact that LOOP precedes the USING statement is irrelevant. However, since LOOP precedes BASE, which is the base address, there is a problem. While it is unlikely that you would want to branch to LOOP or to the BALR itself—both of which cause the same difficulty—the issue demonstrated here will occur later when you consider several base registers.

---

EXAMPLE 2

### An Incorrect Way to Define a Base Register

```
EXAMPLE2 CSECT
         STM   R14,R12,12(R13)
         LA    R12,BASE<--------Addressability error
         USING BASE,R12
BASE     ----
```

The Load Address instruction specifies a symbolic address BASE. Since a USING directive does not precede the LA instruction, the assembler cannot supply a base register or compute a displacement. Therefore, the assembler issues an addressability error message.

You may attempt to correct the error by interchanging the order of the LA and the USING instructions. However, as the next example demonstrates, this attempt is also incorrect.

---

EXAMPLE 3

### Another Incorrect Way to Define a Base Register

```
EXAMPLE3 CSECT
         STM   R14,R12,12(R13)
         USING BASE,R12
         LA    R12,BASE
BASE     ----
```

Because the error here is subtle, you may fail to detect it immediately. The assembler is able to translate the Load Address instruction since the USING directive precedes it. This USING tells the assembler to use Register 12 as the base register. The displacement is the difference between the second operand address of the LA instruction and the designated base address, both of which are represented by BASE. Obviously the displacement is zero. The resulting machine language instruction is

```
41C0C000
```

The assembler issues no error message.

At execution time, the machine language instruction just given loads bits 8 through 31 of Register 12 (assuming 24-bit addressing) with the effective address that the displacement and base register specify. This effective address is equal to

$$000 + C(\text{Register } 12)_{8-31}$$

Thus, the LA instruction sets the first byte of Register 12 to zero and does not change the rest of the register. It is most unlikely that the contents of Register 12 were already equal to the address that BASE represents, and, since the assembler used Register 12 as a base register throughout the program, execution of the program will be incorrect. If you are lucky, a program interruption will occur eventually; if you are not, you will get incorrect results without warning.

Since you can use the Load Address instruction to obtain the actual address that a symbol represents, it may seem natural to use Load Address to load a base register. The examples just given demonstrate that you cannot use the LA instruction to load the first base register. However, as you will see later, you can use it to load additional base registers.

---

EXAMPLE 4

### A Large Array

The instructions in Figure 12.2 define a 1500-fullword (6000-byte) array at ARRAY. The two Load instructions in Statements 7 and 8 are unremarkable: both N and ARRAY are well within 4095 bytes of the base address, so both instructions can use Register 12 as a base register. The Load instruction in Statement 9 uses an index register and, therefore, can address the fullword at ARRAY + 5000, even though this address is beyond BASE + 4095, which is the address of the last byte within the range of the base register. The

```
  LOC   OBJECT CODE    STMT    SOURCE  STATEMENT
000000                    1 EXAMPLE4  CSECT
000000 90EC D00C          2           STM    R14,R12,12(R13)
000004 05C0               3           BALR   R12,0
                          4           USING  BASE,R12
000006 50D0 C01E          5 BASE      ST     R13,SAVE+4
00000A 41D0 C01A          6           LA     R13,SAVE
00000E 5820 C062          7           L      R2,N
000012 5830 C066          8           L      R3,ARRAY
000016 5832 C066          9           L      R3,ARRAY(R2)
00001A 0000 0000         10           L      R3,X  <---- Addressability error
           *** ERROR ***
00001E 07FE              11           BR     R14
000020                   12 SAVE      DS     18F
000068 00001388          13 N         DC     F'5000'
00006C                   14 ARRAY     DS     1500F            (6000 BYTES)
0017DC FFFFFFFF          15 X         DC     F'-1'
```

**Figure 12.2**
Instructions that involve a large array, as described in Example 4.

important point of this third Load instruction is that the assembler computes the displacement by using the symbol ARRAY. As long as ARRAY is within the range of the base register, the index register enables you to address all of the array, regardless of its size. Review the machine language representation of these instructions and remind yourself of how the assembler computes displacements.

The Load instruction in Statement 10 causes a problem: Statement 15 defines X after the array, well beyond the range of the base register. Since the required displacement is greater than 4095, the assembler signals an addressability error. One way to avoid this error is to define X before ARRAY. However, had X been a second array of 6000 bytes, reordering these definitions would not solve the problem.

One further point: suppose you had used a literal to initialize Register 2 and had replaced Statement 7 with

```
L      R2,=F'5000'
```

Since the assembler places literal constants at the end of the program, =F'5000' would not be addressable. In long programs, you can ensure the addressability of literals by using the LTORG directive, which is described next.

---

## *The Literal Origin (LTORG) Directive*

**Use LTORG to ensure the addressability of literal constants**

You know that, as the assembler processes literals, it organizes the literal constants into a literal pool that it ordinarily places at the end of your program. However, you can indicate the location of the literal pool by writing the LTORG directive. The directive can be summarized as follows:

| Name | Operation | Operand | Instruction Name | Action |
|---|---|---|---|---|
| *symbol* or *blank* | **LTORG** | *blank* | LITERAL ORIGIN | Positions the literal pool, which was created since the beginning of the program or since the last LTORG, at the next doubleword boundary after the occurrence of the LTORG in the program. |

You can use more than one LTORG in a program to create more than one literal pool. Each literal pool that follows the first one contains only those literal constants that are generated by literals encountered since the last occurrence of LTORG.

---

EXAMPLE 5

Example 4 suggested that you could rewrite Statement 7 of Figure 12.2 with a literal. To achieve addressability of the literal constant, you can insert an LTORG before the definition of ARRAY in Statement 14. The result will look like the statements given in Figure 12.3.

---

**Figure 12.3**
The use of LTORG to ensure the addressability of literal constants, as described in Example 5.

```
EXAMPLE5 CSECT
         STM   R14,R12,12(R13)
         BALR  R12,0
         USING BASE,R12
BASE     ST    R13,SAVE+4
         LA    R13,SAVE
         L     R2,=F'5000'
         .
         .
         .
         LTORG
ARRAY    DS    1500F
```

## SELF-TEST EXERCISES

1. Indicate whether or not each of the following instruction sequences correctly defines a base register. Explain your responses.

**a.**
```
         USING BASE,R12
BASE     L     R12,ABASE
         B     AROUND
ABASE    DC    A(BASE)
AROUND   ----
```

**b.**
```
         USING BASE,R12
         BALR  R12,0
BASE     ----
```

**c.**
```
         USING BASE,R12
         L     R12,=A(BASE)
BASE     ----
```

**d.**
```
         USING *,R12
         BALR  R12,0
BASE     ----
```

**e.**
```
BASE     BALR  R12,0
         USING BASE,R12
```

2. What instructions, if any, in the following sequence will cause an addressability error? Describe the reason for each error that you find.

```
         CSECT
         STM   R14,R12,12(R13)
         BALR  R12,0
         USING BASE,R12
BASE     L     R2,N
         L     R3,=F'4000'
         L     R4,W(R3)
         B     AROUND
         LTORG
AROUND   L     R5,=F'5000'
         B     AHEAD
BACK     BR    R14
W        DC    2000F
N        DC    F'1000'
AHEAD    B     BACK
```

## Multiple Base Registers

As you have seen, there are times when one base register is insufficient and several base registers may be necessary. If BASE1 represents the first base address, then the first base register can address bytes in the range of

BASE1 to BASE1 + 4095. You can maximize the utility of a second base register by initializing it to BASE1 + 4096: its range is then BASE1 + 4096 to BASE1 + 8191, as pictured in Figure 12.4. Base register ranges can overlap, but it is common to define them without overlap unless you will use a base register solely to address a particular data area, as the next chapter will discuss.

You can load the first base register by writing a BALR instruction, and you can declare the base register as such by writing a USING directive. You can load additional base registers either by writing a Load instruction and an address constant or by writing a Load Address instruction. You then formally declare the additional registers to be base registers by writing other USING directives. As mentioned earlier, you can avoid subtle errors such as the one in Example 3 by writing the USING directive *after* the base register is loaded.

The rules that the assembler uses to select one of several possible base registers when it assembles any symbolic address or literal are a generalization of the two rules already given. The assembler will do the following:

- Choose a base register from among those that are defined by the USING directives that physically precede the instruction to be assembled.

**Figure 12.4**
The maximum ranges for two base registers.

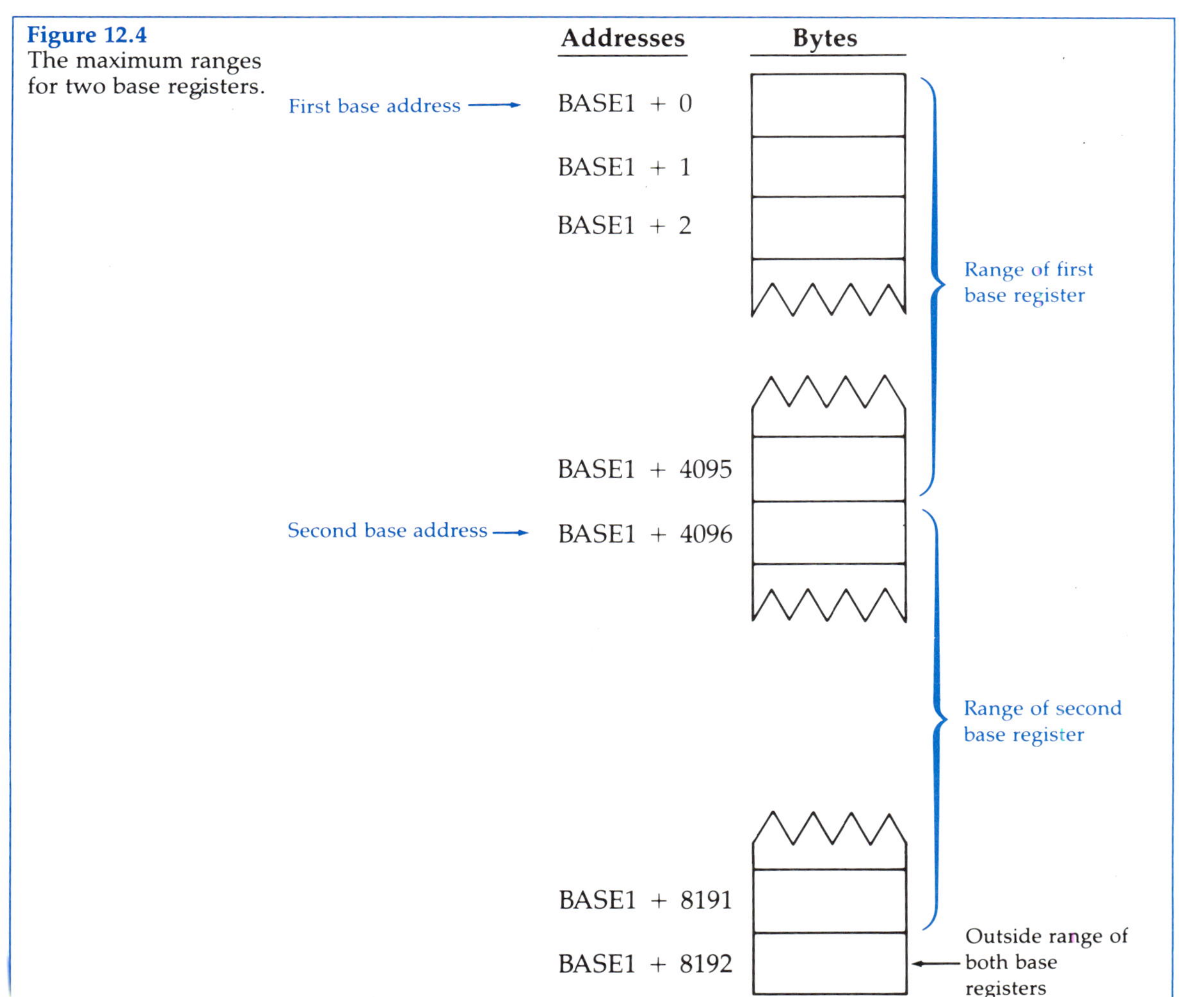

- Choose the base register that permits the smallest displacement in the range 0 to 4095. In case of a tie, the highest-numbered register is selected. (A tie implies that more than one base register contains the same value.)

The next examples illustrate the rules just given and demonstrate how to define several base registers by using a common convention that assigns base registers in descending order beginning with Register 12.

---

EXAMPLE 6

### Defining Two Base Registers

The instructions that are listed in Figure 12.5 provide an example of how to define two base registers. In Statement 3, a BALR instruction, which does not require a base register, loads the first base register. In Statement 5, a Load instruction loads the second base register with an address constant whose value is 4096 larger than the first base address BASE1. The symbolic operand designation ABASE2 in this Load instruction must be addressable by the only available base register, Register 12. Since this is the case, the Load instruction is assembled correctly.

You might be tempted to use a BALR instruction to load the second base register. To do so would require that you place the BALR immediately before the address BASE1 + 4096, branch to it, execute it, and then branch back to where you were; clearly, this is not good. (If you think you can use the Execute instruction to do this, you should see Exercise 4 at the end of this chapter.)

When translating Statement 9, the assembler has a choice of the two

```
  LOC   OBJECT CODE   STMT   SOURCE STATEMENT
000000                   1 EXAMPLE6 CSECT
000000 90EC D00C         2          STM   R14,R12,12(R13)
000004 05C0              3          BALR  R12,0          LOAD FIRST BASE REGISTER
                         4          USING BASE1,R12      DECLARE FIRST BASE REGISTER
000006 58B0 C526         5 BASE1    L     R11,ABASE2     LOAD SECOND BASE REGISTER
                         6          USING BASE1+4096,R11 DECLARE SECOND BASE REGISTER
00000A 50D0 BCA2         7          ST    R13,SAVE+4
00000E 41D0 BC9E         8          LA    R13,SAVE
000012 5820 BC9A         9 LOOP     L     R2,X
                         .          .
                         .          .
                         .          .
000124 47F0 C00C        84          B     LOOP
                         .          .
                         .          .
                         .          .
00052C 00001006        113 ABASE2   DC    A(BASE1+4096)
000530                 114 ARRAY    DS    1500F          (6000 BYTES)
001CA0 FFFFFFFF        115 X        DC    F'-1'
001CA4                 116 SAVE     DS    18F
                                    .
                                    .
                                    .
```

**Figure 12.5**
Instructions that define two base registers, as described in Example 6.

**Figure 12.6**
Instructions that define two base registers while ensuring addressability of the address constant.

```
         BALR  R12,0                LOAD FIRST BASE REGISTER
         USING BASE1,R12            DECLARE FIRST BASE REGISTER
BASE1    L     R11,ABASE2           LOAD SECOND BASE REGISTER
         USING BASE1+4096,R11       DECLARE SECOND BASE REGISTER
         B     AHEAD                BRANCH AROUND ADDRESS CONSTANT
ABASE2   DC    A(BASE1+4096)
AHEAD    ----
```

base registers that are defined by the USING statements that precede Statement 9. The assembler computes trial displacements for each one. The use of Register 12 would require a displacement that is equal to X − BASE1; this displacement is inappropriate since it exceeds 4095. Since the use of Register 11 permits a nonnegative displacement that is less than 4096, the assembler selects it as the base register.

The assembler again considers Registers 11 and 12 as base registers for the Branch instruction in Statement 84. The assembler rules out the use of Register 11 as a base register because it would require a negative displacement. However, the use of Register 12 results in a valid displacement. You should verify the displacements given in the object code for this program.

**Ensure the addressability of address constants that are used to define base registers**

To ensure the addressability of ABASE2, you can define the address constant near the Load instruction and then branch around the constant. The instructions given in Figure 12.6 demonstrate this technique.

---

EXAMPLE 7

### Using the LM Instruction to Load Several Base Registers

When you require more than two base registers, you can use a Load Multiple instruction, as demonstrated by the instructions in Figure 12.7. The second USING directive demonstrates a variation of the operand entry, which you use to declare several base registers. The assembler assumes that the first register named contains the stated address—in this case, BASE1 + 4096. Each successive register named is assumed to contain an address that is 4096 bytes larger than the address in the preceding register. Although the USING directive does not require that you choose the base registers to be consecutively numbered, if you do so, you can use the LM instruction

```
         BALR  R12,0                LOAD FIRST BASE REGISTER
         USING BASE1,R12            DECLARE FIRST BASE REGISTER
BASE1    LM    R10,R11,ABASES       LOAD 2ND AND 3RD BASE REGISTERS
         USING BASE1+4096,R11,R10   DECLARE 2ND AND 3RD BASE REGS.
*                                     (NOTE ORDER OF REGISTERS)
         B     AHEAD                BRANCH AROUND ADDRESS CONSTANTS
ABASES   DC    A(BASE1+2*4096)      3RD BASE ADDRESS
         DC    A(BASE1+4096)        2ND BASE ADDRESS
AHEAD    ----
```

**Figure 12.7**
Using the LM instruction to load several base registers, as described in Example 7.

to load them. As previously mentioned, it is customary to choose Register 12 as the first base register and to assign lower-numbered registers in descending order as additional base registers. In this example, Register 12 contains the address BASE1, Register 11 contains the address BASE1 + 4096, and Register 10 contains the address BASE1 + 2*4096. Note the order of Registers 10 and 11 in the LM and USING instructions, and the order of the address constants.

Programmers often rewrite the first four instructions given in Figure 12.7 as follows, so that the two USING instructions are combined into a single statement:

```
         BALR  R12,0
         USING BASE1,R12,R11,R10
BASE1    LM    R10,R11,ABASES
```

It is imperative that Register 12 can address ABASES (that is, ABASES must be within 4096 bytes of BASE1). If not, the assembler will use Register 10 or 11 as the base register for the LM instruction without warning. If this happens, LM will not execute correctly because Registers 10 and 11 would not as yet contain correct base addresses. The resulting errors may not be obvious. The instructions in Figure 12.7 would cause an addressability error message if Register 12 were not able to address ABASES, and, therefore, are preferable to the three instructions just discussed. Usually, you should declare a base register after it is loaded, and not before, even if it means writing several USING statements.

---

EXAMPLE 8

### An Incorrect Way to Load a Second Base Register

```
         BALR  R12,0
         USING BASE1,R12
BASE1    LA    R11,BASE1+4096 <------ Addressability error
         USING BASE1+4096,R11
```

You may be tempted to load a second base register by using the instructions in this example, but they are incorrect. The displacement required for the LA instruction is 4096, which is too large; therefore, an addressability error occurs.

---

EXAMPLE 9

### Base Registers with Overlapping Ranges

```
         BALR  R12,0                R12 = A(BASE1)
         USING BASE1,R12
BASE1    LA    R11,BASE1+4095       R11 = A(BASE1+4095)
         USING BASE1+4095,R11
```

Although you cannot address BASE1 + 4096 with the LA instruction, you can address BASE1 + 4095. As shown in Figure 12.8, the ranges of the two base registers that are defined in this example overlap by 1 byte, which is the one at BASE1 + 4095; this overlap usually is a small price to pay for

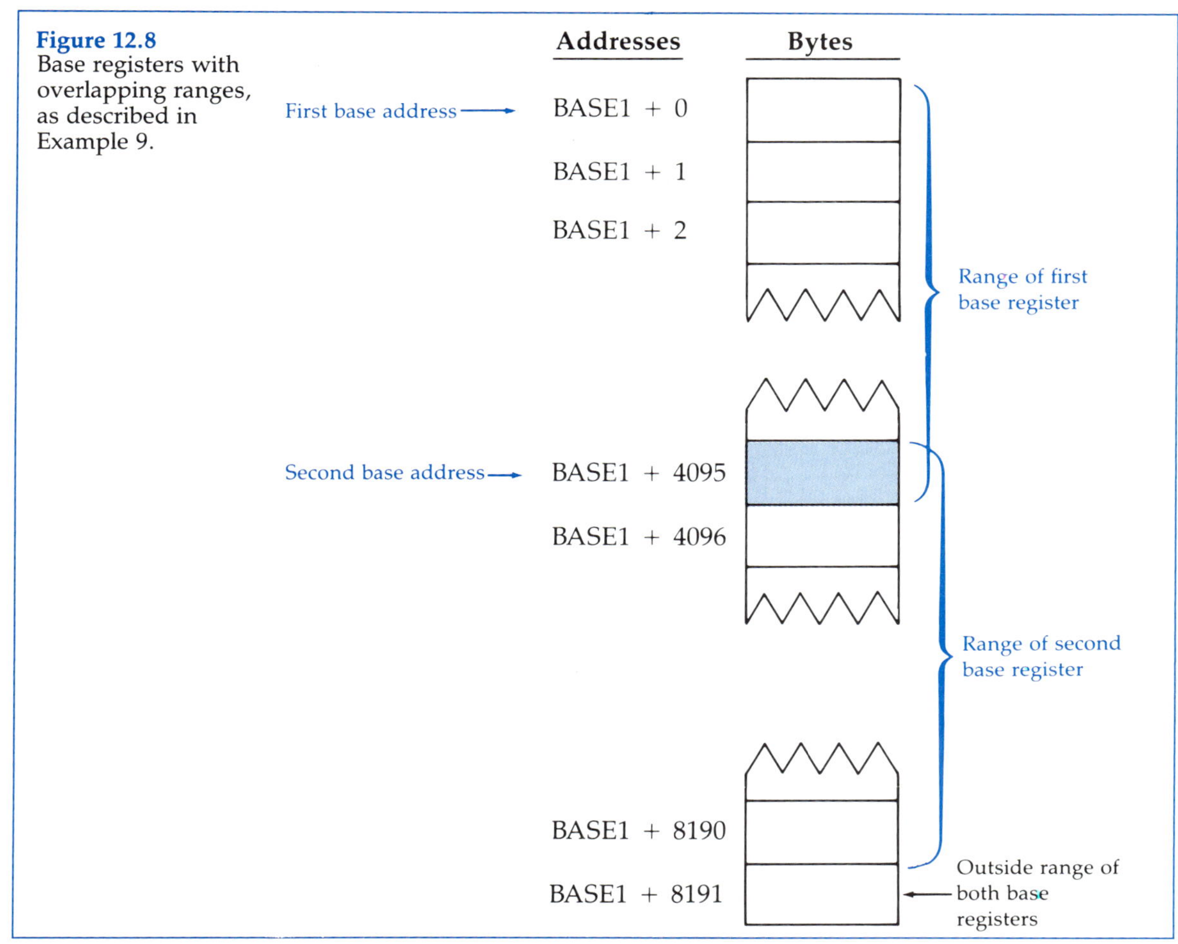


**Figure 12.8**
Base registers with overlapping ranges, as described in Example 9.

the convenience that you gain by using the LA instruction. (See the following example for a way to avoid the overlap.)

Suppose that an instruction that references the byte at BASE1 + 4095 occurs after the previously listed instructions. Which base register will the assembler select? To be more specific, suppose the instruction is

```
IC      R3,BASE1+4095
```

The assembler computes two trial displacements. With Register 12 as the base register, the displacement would be 4095, which is acceptable. If Register 11 was the base register, the displacement would be 0, which is also acceptable. However, since 0 is smaller than 4095, the assembler would select Register 11 as the base register.

---

EXAMPLE 10

**Using the LA Instruction to Load Base Registers with Addresses that Differ by 4096**

It is possible to use the LA instruction with explicit operands to define base addresses that differ by 4096 bytes. You can modify the instructions in Example 9, just given, as follows:

```
         BALR   R12,0                 R12 = A(BASE1)
         USING  BASE1,R12
BASE1    LA     R11,BASE1+4095        R11 = A(BASE1+4095)
         LA     R11,1(R11)            R11 = A(BASE1+4096)
         USING  BASE1+4096,R11
```

As another example, the following instructions load four base registers, but result in a less obvious approach than using a Load Multiple instruction with address constants:

```
         BALR   R12,0                 R12 = A(BASE1)
BASE1    LA     R9,1                   R9 = 1
         LA     R11,4095(R9,R12)      R11 = A(BASE1+4096)
         LA     R10,4095(R9,R11)      R10 = A(BASE1+2*4096)
         LA     R9,4095(R9,R10)        R9 = A(BASE1+3*4096)
         USING  BASE1,R12,R11,R10,R9
```

---

EXAMPLE 11

**Base Registers that Contain the Same Base Addresses**

```
PROG     CSECT
         STM    R14,R12,12(R13)
         USING  PROG,R15
         LR     R12,R15
         USING  PROG,R12
```

Recall that, under OS, the loader places the starting address of the program into Register 15 and that you can use this address as a base address. The instructions in this example load the starting address into Register 12, and declare both Registers 12 and 15 as base registers. The assembler will use Register 15 instead of Register 12 as the base register for subsequent instructions because 15 is a higher number than 12. While this technique may seem curious, you should remember these ideas in the context of subprograms, as you will see in the next chapter.

---

The examples just given demonstrate five possible situations that involve base registers:

1. There is one base register.
2. There are no base registers.
3. There are several base registers that have distinct ranges.
4. There are several base registers with overlapping ranges.
5. There are several base registers with the same ranges.

Figure 12.9 illustrates a program in which all of the listed situations occur. The base register represented by $B_1$ is the only base register available to address the 4096 bytes in its range. No base register in the program can address bytes that are beyond the range of $B_1$, but before the range of $B_2$. Registers $B_1$ and $B_2$ have distinct ranges; Registers $B_2$ and $B_3$ have overlapping ranges. Bytes that are within the range of $B_2$, but that are before the range of $B_3$, are addressable only by $B_2$. The assembler will select $B_3$ to address bytes within the range of $B_3$—even though some bytes may also

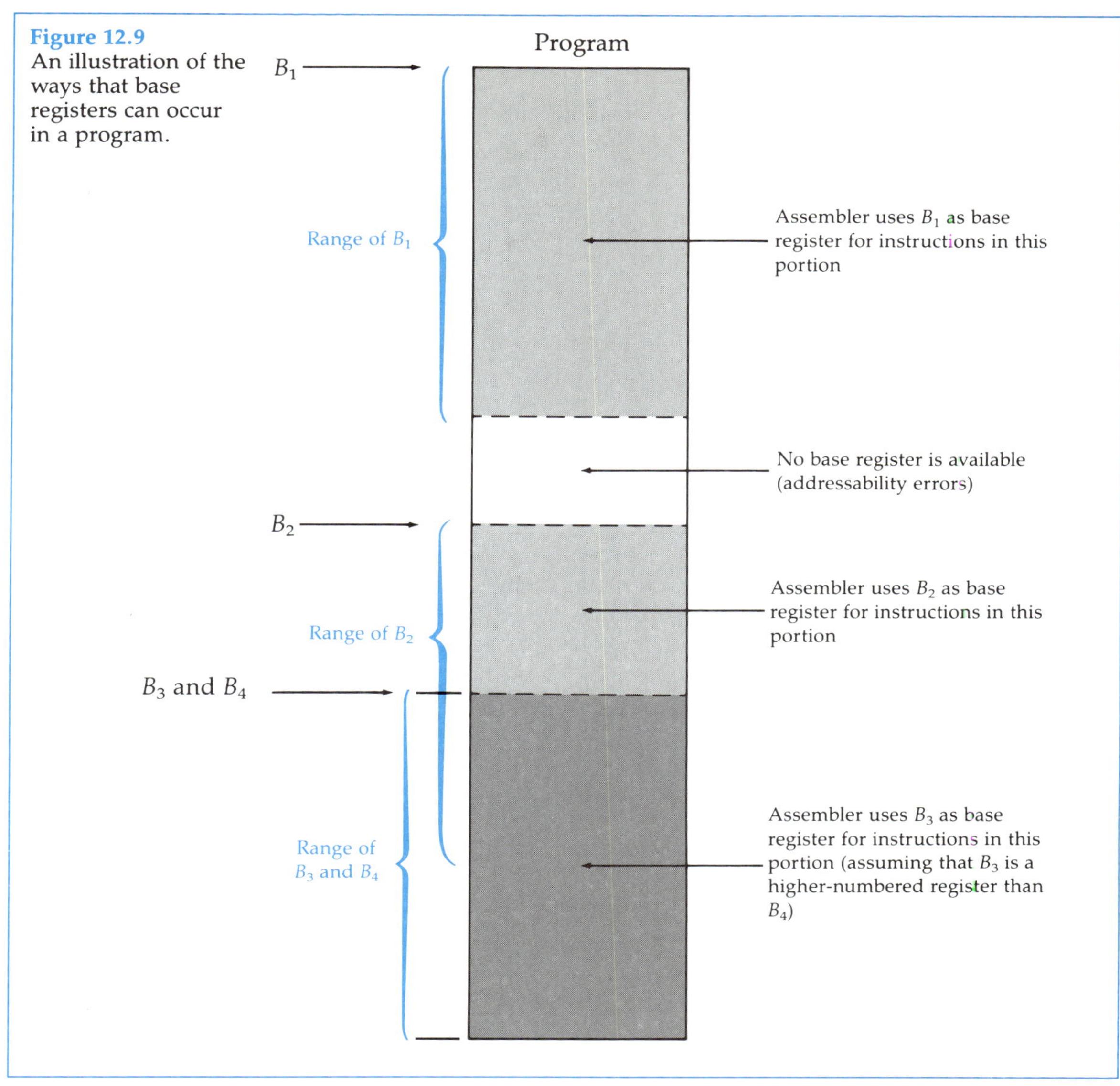


**Figure 12.9**
An illustration of the ways that base registers can occur in a program.

be within the range of $B_2$—because using $B_3$ results in a smaller displacement. The range of $B_4$ is the same as the range of $B_3$. If $B_3$ is a higher-numbered register than $B_4$, the assembler will select $B_3$ instead of $B_4$.

## *Redefining or Deleting Base Registers*

**Redefine a base register with USING**

**Delete a base register with DROP**

If you retain several base registers for the duration of the entire program, you may find that there are insufficient registers for other purposes. Instead of retaining a base register, you can redefine it by changing its value and writing a new USING directive. The assembler will assemble the instructions that appear after the new USING statement by using the information in the new USING statement, rather than that in the old USING statement.

In addition, you can remove a register from the assembler's pool of available base registers by writing a DROP directive, as described here. Instructions that appear after a DROP will not be assembled with the base registers that are listed in the DROP unless a subsequent USING declares the registers again. The DROP directive can be summarized as follows:

| Name | Operation | Operand | Instruction Name | Action |
|---|---|---|---|---|
| *blank* | **DROP** | *R1*[,*R2*,...] or *blank* | DROP BASE REGISTERS | Removes the listed registers from the pool of available base registers (or, if the operand entry is blank, removes all registers from the pool). DROP affects only those instructions that physically follow it. (Operand entries in brackets are optional.) |

To reduce the chance of error, you should DROP those registers that you no longer want to use as base registers and those that no longer contain the correct base address.

The **USING domain** for a particular base register consists of those instructions between the USING directive that declares the base register and either a later USING directive that redefines the base register, a subsequent DROP that deletes the base register, or the end of the program.

---

EXAMPLE 12

The statements listed in Figure 12.10 demonstrate the ideas just discussed. Registers 12 and 11 are defined as base registers using the technique of

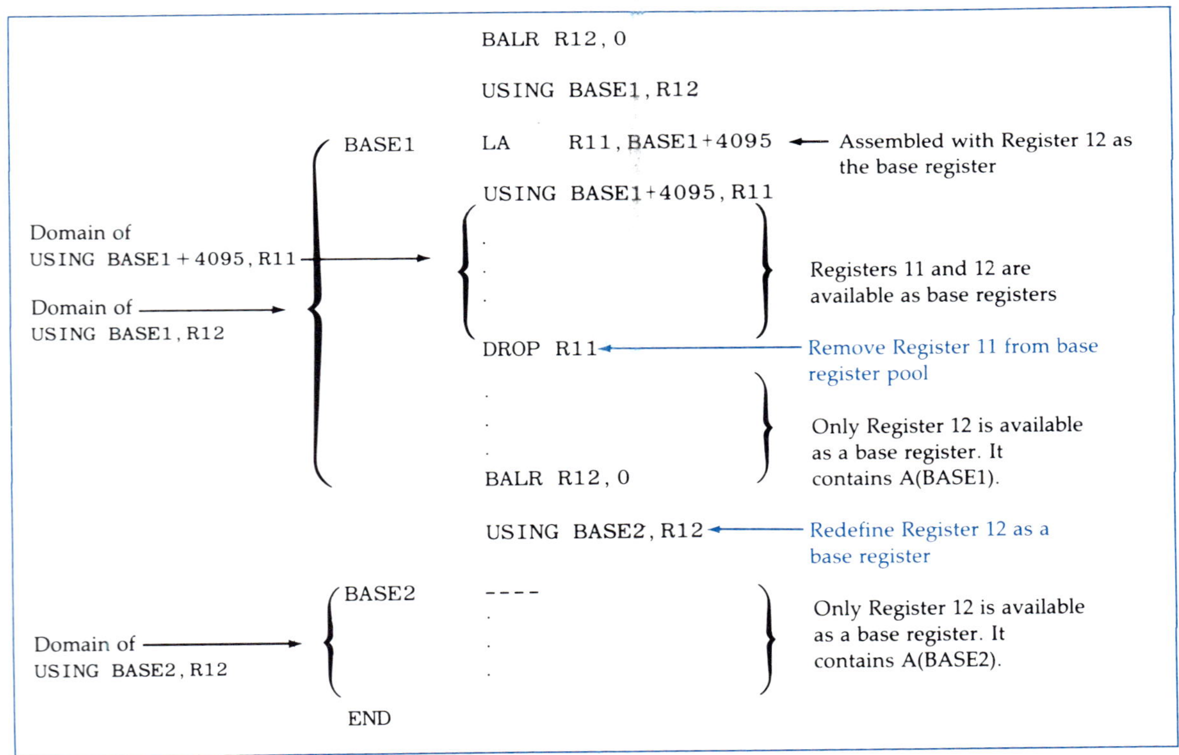


**Figure 12.10**
Instructions that demonstrate how to redefine and delete base registers, as described in Example 12.

Example 9. Both registers are available as base registers for instructions between the second USING statement and the DROP statement. After the DROP statement, only Register 12 is available. The last USING directive declares a new base address for Register 12: instructions after this USING are assembled under the assumption that Register 12 contains this new address.

The USING domains of the statements in Figure 12.10 are indicated.

---

## SELF-TEST EXERCISES

3. Rewrite the instructions in Figure 12.5, which is described in Example 6, by utilizing a literal to define the second base register. How can you ensure the addressability of the literal constant?
4. Indicate whether or not each of the following instruction sequences defines the base registers correctly. Explain your responses.

**a.**
```
PROG     CSECT
         STM   R14,R12,12(R13)
         USING PROG,R15
         USING BASE2,R12
         LA    R12,BASE2
BASE2    ----
```

**b.**
```
PROG     CSECT
         STM   R14,R12,12(R13)
         USING BASE1,R15
BASE1    L     R12,ABASE
         B     AROUND
ABASE2   DC    A(BASE2)
         USING BASE2,R12
AROUND   ----
         . . .
BASE2    ----
```

**c.**
```
         BALR  R12,0
         USING BASE1,R12
         USING BASE1+4095,R11
         USING BASE1+2*4095,R10
BASE1    LA    R11,BASE1+4095
         LA    R10,BASE1+2*4095
```

**d.**
```
         BALR  R12,0
         USING BASE1,R12
         USING BASE1+4096,R11
         USING BASE1+2*4096,R10
BASE1    LA    R11,BASE1+4095
         LA    R11,1(R11)
         LA    R10,BASE1+2*4095
         LA    R10,2(R10)
```

**e.**
```
         BALR  R12,0
         USING BASE1,R12,R11,R10
BASE1    L     R11,ABASE2
         L     R10,ABASE3
         B     AROUND
ABASE2   DC    A(BASE1+4096)
ABASE3   DC    A(BASE1+2*4096)
AROUND   ----
```

*(Continues)*

**f.**

```
         BALR  R12,0
         USING BASE1,R12
BASE1    L     R11,=A(BASE1+4096)
         USING BASE1+4096,R11
         B     AROUND
         ORG   BASE1+5000
AROUND   ----
```

**g.**

```
         BALR  R12,0
         USING BASE1,R12
         USING BASE1+4096,R11
BASE1    L     R11,=A(BASE1+4096)
         B     AROUND
         ORG   BASE1+5000
AROUND   ----
```

**5.** Indicate the base registers that are assigned when the symbolic addresses in the following segments are assembled.

**a.**

```
         BALR  R12,0
         USING BASE1,R12
BASE1    LA    R11,X
         USING X,R11
LOOP     L     R2,X
         C     R2,Y
         LA    R3,LOOP
         B     AROUND
X        DC    F'5'
Y        DC    F'6'
AROUND   ----
```

**b.**

```
         BALR  R12,0
BASE     LR    R11,R12
         USING BASE,R11
         L     R2,W
         USING BASE,R12
         L     R2,W
         B     AROUND
W        DC    F'5'
AROUND   ----
```

**c.**

```
         BALR  R12,0
BASE     LR    R11,R12
         USING BASE,R12
         L     R2,W
         USING BASE,R11
         L     R2,W
         B     AROUND
W        DC    F'5'
AROUND   ----
```

**d.**

```
         BALR  R12,0
         USING BASE1,R12
BASE1    LA    R11,BASE1+2048
         LA    R11,2048(R11)
         USING BASE1+4096,R11
         L     R10,=A(BASE1+2*4096)
         B     AWAY
         USING BASE1+2*4096,R10
         ORG   BASE1+5000
         LTORG
AWAY     B     FARAWAY
         ORG   BASE1+8500
FARAWAY  LA    R2,BASE1
         LA    R3,BASE1+8000
         L     R4,=F'5'
         BR    R14
         END
```

## Debugging Hints

1. Execution-time errors that incorrect base registers cause are usually difficult to find. In this chapter, you have seen examples of incorrectly defined base registers. However, even if you define a base register correctly, it is possible for the contents of a base register to be destroyed inadvertently. A good habit to form is to check the contents of the base registers in a dump to ensure that they are correct. This is particularly true whenever the program behaves strangely, or if the logic appears to be correct, but the results are incorrect.
2. To reduce the chance of error, use the DROP directive when you no longer want to use a particular base register or whenever a base register no longer contains the correct base address.
3. Using address constants instead of the LA instruction to load base registers offers you the advantage of being able to observe base addresses in a dump. This capability can be helpful during debugging. However, be sure that the address constants are addressable; placing them near the Load instruction, as in Figure 12.6, can be a good idea.
4. Use LTORG to ensure the addressability of literal constants—particularly when your program is long.
5. In Chapter 6, you saw an example of a program that destroyed a literal constant because an index became too large. In that example, the assembler had placed the literal pool at the end of the program after an array. When the program stored a register beyond the end of the array, the program destroyed the literal constant. To prevent the destruction of literal constants in this manner, some programmers write an LTORG directive before the program's arrays. While the LTORG does not correct the problem with the index register, the error may be easier to find if the literal constants remain intact. However, even with such a use of LTORG, it is still possible to destroy the literal constants: instructions that store into an array can address storage before the array if the index register contains a negative value. Therefore, even if the literal constants precede the arrays, they are not invulnerable.

## Stylistic Notes

1. Write the USING directive after you load the corresponding base register. This technique will help to avoid subtle errors in the definition of base registers that the assembler will not detect.
2. As your programs become longer and more complicated, the demand for registers is likely to increase. It is important that you plan your register assignments. For example, it is a good idea to use the high-numbered registers for base registers and to assign them in descending order. Usually the first base register is Register 12, the second base register is Register 11, and so on. By convention, Registers 13, 14, and 15 have special purposes that the next chapter will discuss. With the possible exception of Register 15, these registers are usually not used as base registers. This leaves the low-numbered registers for use as work registers; they are usually assigned in ascending order.

Programmers often adopt additional guidelines that they use when assigning registers. For example, you could use Registers 2 and 3 as work registers; Registers 6, 7, and 8 for BXLE or BXH loops; and Register 9 as an index register. Such guidelines will help you, but will not necessarily help someone who reads your program. When you allocate registers, keep in mind that Registers 0 and 1 are used in subprogram conventions, as discussed in the next chapter, and that the TRT instruction uses Registers 1 and 2.

3. Redefining or deleting base registers may be necessary to ensure that you have enough registers for other purposes.
4. Since the assembler aligns literal pools to a doubleword boundary, you can sometimes save a few bytes of storage by writing an LTORG statement before a data area, rather than after it.

## Summary

1. To assemble a particular symbolic address, the assembler chooses a base register from among those that are defined by the USING directives that occur before the instruction to be assembled. A USING or DROP directive that names a particular register negates the effect of an earlier USING statement on that register.
2. To assemble a particular symbolic address, the assembler chooses the base register that permits the smallest displacement in the range 0 to 4095. In case of a tie, the highest-numbered register is selected.
3. If you must change the value of a base register, declare this fact with another USING directive.
4. Remove registers from the pool of available base registers by writing a DROP directive.

## New Instruction Summary

| Name | Operation | Operand | Instruction Name | Action |
|---|---|---|---|---|
| *symbol* or *blank* | LTORG | *blank* | LITERAL ORIGIN | Positions the literal pool, which was created since the beginning of the program or since the last LTORG, at the next doubleword boundary after the occurrence of the LTORG in the program. |
| *blank* | USING | *S,R1[,R2,R3...]* | DECLARE BASE REGISTERS | Adds the listed registers to the assembler's pool of available base registers. The assembler assumes that *R1* contains the address *S*, *R2* contains the address *S* + 4096, *R3* contains the address *S* + 8192, and so on. USING changes the assumed base address of any listed registers that also appear in a previous USING directive. (Operand entries in brackets are optional.) |

| Name | Operation | Operand | Instruction Name | Action |
|---|---|---|---|---|
| *blank* | **DROP** | *R1*[,*R2*,...] or *blank* | DROP BASE REGISTERS | Removes the listed registers from the pool of available base registers (or, if the operand entry is blank, removes all registers from the pool). DROP affects only those instructions that physically follow it. (Operand entries in brackets are optional.) |

## Exercises

1. Deliberately cause some of the errors that were described in this chapter. In particular, consider the errors in Example 1 (Figure 12.1); Examples 2 and 3; Example 4 (Figure 12.2); and Example 8.
2. Indicate whether or not each of the following instruction sequences defines the base registers correctly. Explain your responses.

**a.**
```
         BALR   R12,0
BASE1    LA     R11,BASE1+4096
         USING  BASE1,R12,R11
```
**b.**
```
PROG     CSECT
         USING  *,R15
         STM    R14,R12,12(R13)
         LA     R12,BASE
         USING  BASE,R12
BASE     ----
```
**c.**
```
PROG     CSECT
         STM    R14,R12,12(R13)
         USING  PROG,R15
         USING  BASE,R12
         L      R12,ABASE
BASE     B      AROUND
ABASE    DC     A(BASE)
AROUND   ----
```
**d.**
```
PROG     CSECT
         STM    R14,R12,12(R13)
         USING  PROG,R15
         USING  BASE,R12
         L      R12,ABASE
         B      AROUND
ABASE    DC     A(BASE)
BASE     ----
AROUND   ----
```
**e.**
```
         BALR   R12,0
BASE1    LM     R9,R11,ABASES
         USING  BASE1,R12,R11,R10,R9
         B      AROUND
ABASES   DC     A(BASE1+3*4096,BASE1+2*4096,BASE1+4096)
AROUND   ----
```
**f.**
```
         BALR   R12,0
         USING  BASE1,R12
         USING  BASE1+4095,R11
BASE1    LA     R11,BASE1+4095
```

**g.**

```
        BALR  R12,0
BASE    LA    R11,4095(R12)
        LA    R10,4095(R11)
        USING BASE,R12
        USING BASE+4095,R11
        USING BASE+2*4095,R10
```

**h.**

```
        BALR  R12,0
        USING BASE1,R12
BASE1   LM    R10,R11,=A(BASE1+2*4096,BASE1+4096)
        USING BASE1+4096,R11,R10
        B     AROUND
        ORG   BASE1+6000
AROUND  ----
```

**i.**

```
        BALR  R12,0
        USING BASE1,R12
        USING BASE1+4096,R11,R10
BASE1   LM    R10,R11,=A(BASE1+2*4096,BASE1+4096)
        B     AROUND
        ORG   BASE1+6000
AROUND  ----
```

3. Indicate the base registers that are assigned when the symbolic addresses in the following segments are assembled. Indicate and explain any addressability errors that might occur.

**a.**

```
PROG    CSECT
        STM   R14,R12,12(R13)
        LA    R12,4000(R15)
        BALR  R11,0
        USING PROG+4000,R12
        USING BASE1,R11
BASE1   L     R2,X
        L     R3,N
        ST    R2,X(R3)
        L     R2,M
        BR    R14
X       DS    1000F
N       DC    F'5000'
Y       DS    1000F
M       DC    F'5'
```

**b.**

```
        BALR  R12,0
        USING BASE1,R12
BASE1   L     R11,ABASE2
        USING BASE1+4096,R11
BACK    B     AROUND
        DS    4000C
AROUND  B     NEXT
NEXT    B     AHEAD
        B     BACK
ABASE2  DC    A(BASE1+4096)
        DS    4000C
OUT     BR    R14
AHEAD   B     OUT
        B     BACK
        B     BASE1
        B     AHEAD
```

c.

```
                BALR   R12,0
                USING  *,R12
       BASE1    LA     R11,2000(R12)
                LA     R10,4000(R12)
                USING  BASE1+2000,R11
                USING  BASE1+4000,R10
                IC     R2,X
                B      AHEAD
                ORG    BASE1+2500
       X        DC     1500C'$'
       AHEAD    BALR   R11,0
                USING  *,R11
                LA     R9,BASE1
                L      R8,=F'4'
                LA     R7,X
                LA     R6,AHEAD
                DROP   R10
                LA     R5,AHEAD
```

d.

```
                BALR   R12,0
                USING  BASE1,R12
       BASE1    LM     R9,R11,ABASES
                USING  BASE1,R11,R10,R9
                B      AROUND
       ABASES   DC     A(BASE1+2*4096,BASE1+4096,BASE1)
       AROUND   L      R2,=F'-1'
                DROP   R12
                LA     R3,ABASES
                B      AHEAD
                LTORG
       AHEAD    L      R2,=F'-4'
                L      R3,=F'-1'
                B      AWAY
                ORG    BASE1+4096
                LTORG
       AWAY     LA     R3,ABASES
                USING  BASE1,R12
                LA     R3,ABASES
                L      R4,=A(ABASES)
                B      MORE
                ORG    BASE1+8500
       MORE     BR     R14
                END
```

4. Explain why the following segment is an incorrect way to establish a second base register.

```
          BALR   R12,0
          USING  BASE1,R12
BASE1     EX     0,BALR
          B      AROUND
BALR      BALR   R11,0
BASE2     EQU    *
          USING  BASE2,R11
AROUND    ----
```

# 13

# Subprograms and Data Areas

CONTENTS

**OVERVIEW**

This chapter discusses the tools that are necessary for the modular design of an assembler language program. The chapter describes source modules, control sections, external subprograms, dummy sections, common sections, and external data areas.

**OBJECTIVES**

After studying this chapter, you should be able to:

1. Describe and define the save area and the argument list for a particular subprogram.
2. Write a calling sequence for a given subprogram.
3. Write instructions within a subprogram that follow the linkage conventions to save the registers, access the arguments, restore the registers, and return to the calling program.
4. Write a function subprogram.
5. Describe and implement argument linkage whose design is either call by address or call by value.
6. Use variable-length argument lists.
7. Use the CNOP directive to write in-line subprogram calls.
8. Establish addressability throughout a source module that contains several control sections.
9. Write multiple entry subprograms.
10. Use the system macros SAVE, CALL, and RETURN.
11. Describe, define, and use control sections, dummy sections, common sections, and external data areas.
12. Describe source modules, object modules, and load modules.
13. Distinguish between external and internal subprograms.

## Introduction

When you write a subprogram in assembler language, you must be concerned with several details that involve the subprogram's relationship to and communication with the rest of the program. Adhering to a set of conventions that governs these details facilitates the programming process, particularly when several subprograms are involved. Certainly, you can design such conventions, but there are advantages to following a more universal set, such as the one that IBM defined. Among the advantages is the ability to incorporate into your program those subprograms that other programmers wrote or those that were written in high-level languages. You learned about internal subprograms in Chapter 7 and have seen several examples of their use since then. When you write an internal subprogram, you do not have to follow IBM's subprogram conventions, although there are advantages to doing so. However, with external subprograms, since they can be assembled separately from the rest of your program, you must follow the conventions. This chapter defines IBM's subprogram conventions and discusses the relevant issues to writing external subprograms in assembler language. Unless otherwise indicated, this chapter will use the term *subprogram* to refer to an external subprogram.

This chapter also considers the available techniques to define and describe data areas—thus contributing to a program's modularity. You can define a data area in one subprogram, and describe and use it in another, or several subprograms can share a data area.

## *Terminology*

Subprograms are also known as *subroutines* or *procedures* and, although the three terms may have different meanings in certain high-level languages, you can use them interchangeably here. In general, a program consists of a **main program** and several subprograms. The main program or any subprogram can **call** a subprogram; the unit that calls a subprogram is known as the **calling program** and the subprogram is sometimes referred to as the **called program**. The address of the first instruction executed in the subprogram is known as the **entry point** and the address in the calling program to which the subprogram eventually branches or *returns* is known as the **return address** or **reentry point**. Usually, subprograms operate upon input values that the calling program gives to them, and produce output values as a result. The input and output values are known as **arguments** or **parameters**.

You must establish communication between the calling program and the subprogram. Within the calling program, you must know the location of the subprogram, pass its arguments, and then branch to its entry point. Within the subprogram, you must access the arguments, pass the results back to the calling program, and eventually branch back to the point from which the subprogram was called. The instructions that perform the previous tasks constitute the **linkage** between the calling program and the subprogram, and must adhere to a set of rules known as **linkage conventions**. The instructions within the calling program that invoke the subprogram are known as the **calling sequence**.

You can divide an assembler language program into units, which are assembled at different times. Each of these units is called a **source module**. The source module is then further divided into sections: **executable control sections** and **reference control sections**. Briefly, executable control sections contain constants and executable instructions, while reference control sections describe or define data areas but do not contain actual data before execution time. Reference control sections are further classified as **dummy control sections** and **common control sections**. To simplify the terminology, this text will refer to executable control sections as **control sections**, dummy control sections as **dummy sections**, and common control sections as **common sections**. Thus, you may organize a program into several source modules, each consisting of several control sections, dummy sections, and common sections. This chapter will discuss dummy and common sections later.

### *Control Sections*

**Control sections begin with CSECT, but the first control section can begin with START.**

Until now, your programs have consisted of a single control section. However, when you write external subprograms, you will write each, as well as the main program, as a separate control section. Typically, the main program constitutes the first control section and each external subprogram is a subsequent control section. You initiate each control section within a source module with a CSECT directive but, as an option, you can begin the first control section with a START directive instead of a CSECT. The START directive can be summarized as follows:

| Name | Operation | Operand | Instruction Name | Action |
|---|---|---|---|---|
| *symbol* or *blank* | **START** | *blank* or *self-defining term* | DEFINE FIRST CONTROL SECTION | Initiates the first control section that is identified by the symbol, if any, in the name entry. |

As an option, you can specify an initial value for the location counter by writing a self-defining term in the operand entry. The START directive clearly identifies the first control section and is useful stylistically.

Each control section begins on a doubleword integral boundary and is assembled with a separate location counter—even though the locations that are printed in the source listing for a particular control section constitute a continuation of those from the preceding control section. Each control section is separately relocatable, so it must have its own base register. Since control sections within the same source module are processed during a single assembly, each section must define distinct symbols.

**Each control section must have its own base register.**

You write control sections, as well as dummy and common sections, one after another, and use the END directive to terminate the entire source module. If the source module contains a main program, then the operand entry of the END statement represents the entry point of the main program. It is possible that the source module does not contain a main program, but is assembled for later use. In this case, the END directive has no operand entry.

## Linkage Conventions for External Subprograms

As mentioned earlier, the calling program and the subprogram must perform certain tasks as part of the linkage between them. Those tasks that involve addressing arguments and branching are rather generic, but there is an additional requirement that is specified as part of IBM's conventions: the calling program assumes that the subprogram does not change the contents of the general registers. To satisfy this assumption, you must write instructions in the subprogram that immediately save the registers in an array of fullwords called the **save area**, and then restore the registers just prior to returning to the calling program.

**Each subprogram saves its registers in a save area.**

## *The Save Area*

You define the save area within the calling program, and not within the subprogram. In this way, you can use one save area for several subprograms—thereby, saving storage. The save area consists of 18 fullwords, as described in Figure 13.1. For now, do not be concerned with the third fullword of the save area. (Note that, in DOS, the save area must begin on a doubleword integral boundary.)

Register 13 contains the address of the save area.

Since the calling program and the subprogram are in different control sections and may even be in different source modules, you cannot address the save area directly from within the subprogram. Therefore, you pass the address of the save area from the calling program to the subprogram by using a register. By convention, that register is Register 13. Before you load Register 13 in the calling program with the address of the save area, you must save the prior contents of Register 13 in the second fullword of the save area. Thus, write the following instructions in the calling program:

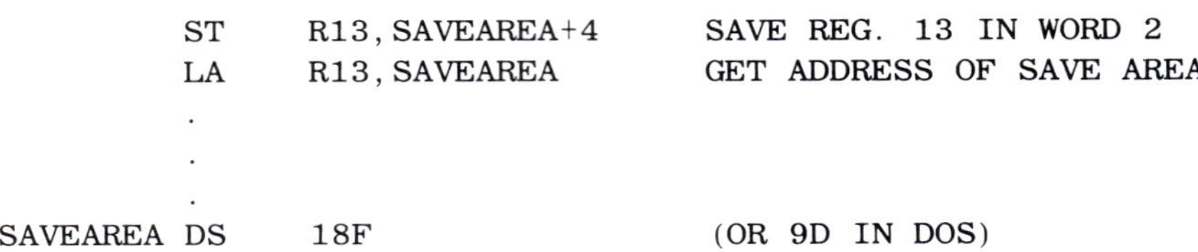

```
         ST    R13,SAVEAREA+4      SAVE REG. 13 IN WORD 2
         LA    R13,SAVEAREA        GET ADDRESS OF SAVE AREA
         .
         .
         .
SAVEAREA DS    18F                 (OR 9D IN DOS)
```

If the calling program itself is a subprogram or is a main program under OS or CMS, there are additional conventions, which will be described later.

**Figure 13.1**
The 18 fullwords in the save area, as defined in a calling program.

| Word Number | Byte Number | | |
|---|---|---|---|
| 1 | 0 | Used by certain compilers of high-level languages | |
| 2 | 4 | Contents of General Register 13 as stored by this calling program | Stored by the calling program |
| 3 | 8 | Address of another save area that is defined in the subprogram and is used to call another subprogram | Stored by the subprogram |
| 4 | 12 | Contents of General Register 14 | |
| 5 | 16 | Contents of General Register 15 | |
| 6 | 20 | Contents of General Register 0 | |
| 7 | 24 | Contents of General Register 1 | |
| 8 | 28 | Contents of General Register 2 | |
| . | . | . | |
| . | . | . | |
| . | . | . | |
| 18 | 68 | Contents of General Register 12 | |

Figure 13.1 also pictures the conventional order of registers that are stored in the save area. IBM chose this ordering with the STM instruction in mind because the instruction

```
STM   R14,R12,12(R13)
```

stores Registers 14, 15, 0, 1, and so on to 12 into consecutive fullwords, beginning with the fourth fullword of the save area. (Assume that the address of the save area is in Register 13.) Thus, this STM instruction is the one that you write in the subprogram to store all of the registers, except Register 13, in the save area that is passed to the subprogram. Think of Register 13 as the subprogram's key to the save area. Just as you would not keep the key to a safe in the safe itself, it would not make sense for you to store Register 13 into the save area whose address is in Register 13. If you accidentally destroyed the contents of Register 13, you would no longer know the address of the save area and, therefore, you would not be able to restore any of the registers. Instead, if indeed you must use Register 13 for another purpose, store Register 13 in a location within the subprogram. When a subprogram calls another subprogram, convention dictates where to store Register 13; this convention will be considered shortly.

## *The Argument List*

**Register 1 contains the address of the argument list.**

The argument list is an array of fullwords that you define in the calling program and that contains the addresses of the arguments to be passed to the subprogram. Within the calling program, load Register 1 with the address of the argument list. Note that neither the addresses of the arguments nor their values are passed directly in registers to the subprogram, but both are available within the subprogram when you use Register 1 to address the argument list. The design of the argument list allows you to define arguments of any length anywhere in the program. As straightforward as this design is, it can be very confusing when you write a subprogram. Figure 13.2 illustrates an example of the relationship between Register 1, the argument list, and the arguments, which are represented here by Z, X, and Y.

You access the arguments within the subprogram by using the address of the argument list in Register 1. For example, the instruction

```
L      R2,0(R1)        GET ADDRESS OF FIRST ARGUMENT
```

loads Register 2 with the *address* of the first argument. Since the first argument Z (in Figure 13.2) is a fullword, the instruction

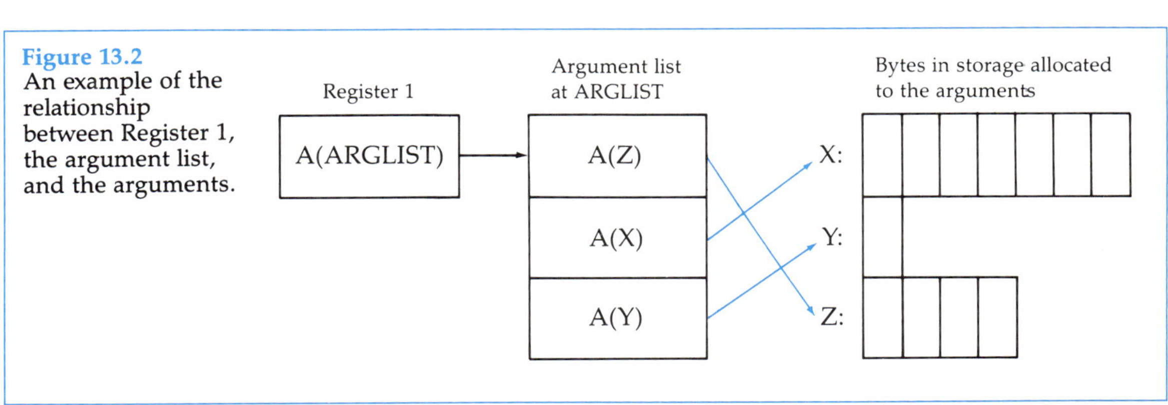


**Figure 13.2** An example of the relationship between Register 1, the argument list, and the arguments.

```
L       R5,0(R2)        GET VALUE OF FIRST ARGUMENT
```

loads Register 5 with the *value* of the first argument. If it is unnecessary to retain both the address and the value of a fullword argument, you can use one less register by writing the following instructions instead:

```
L       R2,0(R1)        GET ADDRESS OF FIRST ARGUMENT
L       R2,0(R2)        GET VALUE OF FIRST ARGUMENT
```

To access the address of the second argument X, you can write

```
L       R2,4(R1)        GET ADDRESS OF SECOND ARGUMENT
```

If you now want to copy the value of the second argument to a work area, you could write

```
MVC     WORK(7),0(R2) GET VALUE OF SECOND ARGUMENT
```

You can access and retain the addresses of all three arguments with the instruction

```
LM      R2,R4,0(R1)     GET ADDRESSES OF ARGUMENTS
```

but you should be careful when you use this method because linkage to the arguments can quickly use up the available registers. Notice that you cannot use another LM instruction to access the values of the arguments as they generally are not in consecutive fullwords in storage.

Typically, you define the arguments within the calling program. However, you can define an argument outside of the calling program and still pass the argument to the subprogram by using the argument list design just described. Note that a subprogram can change the values of the arguments that are passed to it. However, you must not pass a literal as an argument if the subprogram will change that argument.

### *The Calling Sequence*

Suppose that SUB represents the entry point of the subprogram. Since you define an external subprogram and, therefore, the symbol SUB in a control section that is distinct from the calling program, you cannot address SUB within the calling program. SUB is known as an **external symbol** and can be used only in the definition of an address constant. You can use the special constant type V within a DC statement to define **external address constants.** This use of the DC directive is summarized as follows:

| Name | Operation | Operand | Instruction Name | Action |
|---|---|---|---|---|
| *symbol* or *blank* | DC | *d*VL*n*(*symbol*) | DEFINE EXTERNAL ADDRESS CONSTANT | Defines *d* copies of a constant that is equal to the actual address represented by the stated relocatable external symbol. In the absence of an explicit length modifier L*n*, the constant occupies a fullword that is |

| | Action |
|---|---|
| | aligned to a fullword integral boundary. If present, an explicit length modifier may specify a length of 3 or 4—in which case, no boundary alignment takes place. |

You can also define V-type address constants by using literals.

**Register 15 contains the entry point of the subprogram. Register 14 contains the return address.**

By convention, you load Register 15 with the entry point of the subprogram by using a V-type address constant. In addition, you load Register 14 with the return address: you will use the return address within the subprogram to branch back to the calling program. You can load Registers 14 and 15, and branch to the subprogram by writing the following instructions:

```
L       R15,=V(SUB)
BALR    R14,R15
```

Figure 13.3 shows the instructions that are necessary to define a save area and an argument list with arguments Z, X, and Y as described in Figure 13.2, and to call the subprogram SUB.

## *Responsibilities of a Lowest-Level Subprogram*

A **lowest-level subprogram** does not call another subprogram. By implication, it does not perform I/O or request a storage dump or any other service of the operating system because these operations actually involve subprograms. Figure 13.4 shows a main program that calls the subprograms SUB1 and SUB2. SUB2, in turn, calls SUB3. SUB1 and SUB3 are examples of lowest-level subprograms.

Lowest-level subprograms must perform the following tasks:

- Save the registers.
- Establish a base register.
- Address the arguments.
- Restore the registers.
- Return to the calling program.

The instructions in a lowest-level subprogram that accomplish the tasks just listed appear in Figure 13.5. (You can call this subprogram by using the instructions given in Figure 13.3.) The STM instruction that stores the registers in the save area, which the calling program passes to the subprogram, uses explicit operand designations; therefore, this STM instruction can precede the USING directive. Thus, you can save the registers before you load the base register. An external subprogram requires its own base register because it is a separate control section and, as such, is an individual relocatable unit. The subprogram in Figure 13.5 uses Register 12 as the base register. However, since Register 15 contains a known address, which is the entry point, and since a lowest-level subprogram need not change the contents of Register 15 in order to call another subprogram, you can use Register 15 as a base register; you will see an example of how to do this later.

```
** SAVE R13; THEN LOAD R13 WITH THE ADDRESS OF THE NEW SAVE AREA:
         ST    R13,SAVEAREA+4    SAVE REG. 13 IN NEW SAVE AREA
         LA    R13,SAVEAREA      R13 = ADDRESS OF NEW SAVE AREA
         .
         .
         .
** CALL THE SUBPROGRAM SUB:
         LA    R1,ARGLIST        R1 = ADDRESS OF ARGUMENT LIST
         L     R15,=V(SUB)       R15 =  ENTRY POINT OF SUB
         BALR  R14,R15           CALL SUBPROGRAM
         .
         .
         .
** THE SAVE AREA AND THE ARGUMENT LIST:
SAVEAREA DS    18F               (OR 9D IN DOS)
ARGLIST  DC    A(Z)              ADDRESS OF FIRST ARGUMENT
         DC    A(X)              ADDRESS OF SECOND ARGUMENT
         DC    A(Y)              ADDRESS OF THIRD ARGUMENT
         .
         .
         .
** THE ARGUMENTS:
X        DS    CL7               FIRST ARGUMENT
Y        DS    X                 SECOND ARGUMENT
Z        DS    F                 THIRD ARGUMENT
         .
         .
         .
** THE SUBPROGRAM:
SUB      CSECT
         .
         .
         .
         BR    R14
         END
```

**Figure 13.3**
The necessary instructions within a calling program that call the subprogram SUB.

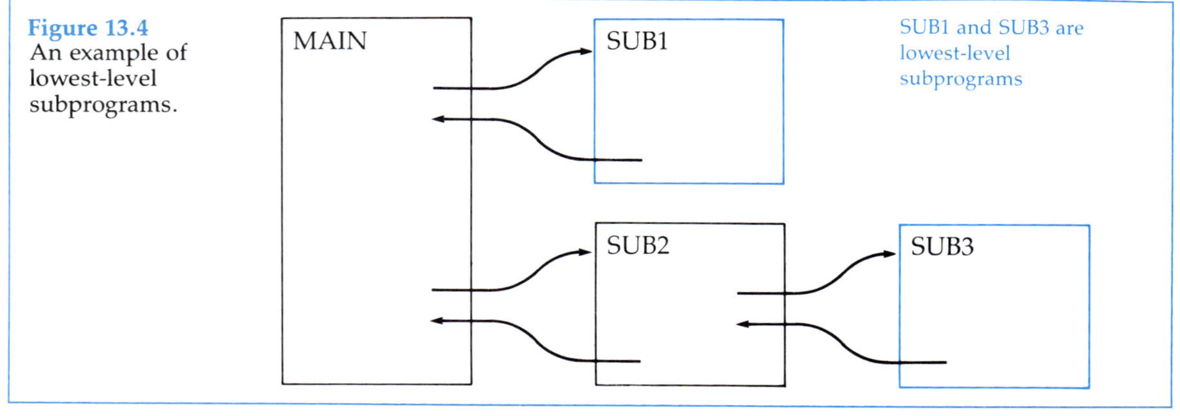


**Figure 13.4**
An example of lowest-level subprograms.

```
SUB      CSECT
         STM   R14,R12,12(R13)  SAVE REGISTERS 14, 15, 0, 1,...,12
         BALR  R12,0            LOAD BASE REGISTER
         USING BASE,R12         DECLARE BASE REGISTER
BASE     LM    R2,R4,0(R1)      GET ADDRESSES OF ARGUMENTS
         .
         .
         .
         LM    R14,R12,12(R13)  RESTORE REGISTERS 14, 15, 0, 1,...,12
         BR    R14              RETURN
         END
```

**Figure 13.5**
An example of the instructions that are necessary in a lowest-level subprogram.

While you have already seen how to address the arguments, note that the LM instruction in Figure 13.5 loads Registers 2, 3, and 4 with the addresses of the arguments for later use.

After the subprogram completes its task, it must restore the registers and return to the calling program. Since a lowest-level subprogram does not call another subprogram, you do not need to change the contents of Register 13; however, if you saved and then changed Register 13, you would restore it now. In either case, assume that Register 13 points to the save area. The following instructions restore the other registers and branch back to the calling program:

```
LM    R14,R12,12(R13)    RESTORE ALL REGISTERS EXCEPT 13
BR    R14                RETURN
```

---

EXAMPLE 1

### A Lowest-Level Subprogram to Compute the Larger of Two Fullword Integers

The subprogram in Figure 13.6 computes the larger of two fullword integers that are passed to it as arguments. A third fullword argument returns the result of this simple computation. Unlike the subprogram in Figure 13.5, this subprogram uses Register 15 as the base register. Again, this method is acceptable because the subprogram does not call another subprogram and does not need to alter the contents of Register 15. Registers 2 and 3 contain the addresses and values of the arguments, respectively.

Although this example was chosen to illustrate a subprogram that calls no other subprogram, the linkage clearly requires more instructions than the computation itself. A serious question is whether the gross inefficiency of this particular subprogram outweighs any advantages that it may have. The answer depends upon the situation and your goals. In any case, you should be conscious of the overhead that is involved in subprogram linkage.

```
MAX      CSECT
** SUBPROGRAM TO COMPUTE THE LARGER OF TWO FULLWORD INTEGERS X AND Y
** THAT ARE PASSED AS THE FIRST TWO ARGUMENTS. THE RESULT IS RETURNED
** IN THE THIRD ARGUMENT, Z.
*
*    R2 = ARGUMENT ADDRESS; R3 = ARGUMENT VALUE
*
         STM   R14,R12,12(R13)    SAVE THE REGISTERS
         USING MAX,R15            ESTABLISH BASE REGISTER
         L     R2,0(R1)           GET ADDRESS OF X
         L     R3,0(R2)           GET VALUE OF X
         L     R2,4(R1)           GET ADDRESS OF Y
         C     R3,0(R2)           COMPARE VALUES OF X AND Y
         BNL   SKIP               BRANCH IF X ≥ Y
         L     R3,0(R2)           VALUE OF Y IS LARGER
SKIP     L     R2,8(R1)           GET ADDRESS OF Z
         ST    R3,0(R2)           STORE LARGER VALUE INTO Z
         LM    R14,R12,12(R13)    RESTORE REGISTERS
         BR    R14                RETURN
         END
```

**Figure 13.6**
A lowest-level subprogram to compute the larger of two fullword integers, as described in Example 1.

---

### *Responsibilities of a Subprogram that Calls Another Subprogram*

**Additional save area conventions**

When you write a subprogram that calls another subprogram directly, or indirectly by requesting services from the operating system, you must follow all of the linkage conventions just given and you must also perform other tasks that relate to save areas. Since you are writing a subprogram, you must save all of the registers except Register 13 in the save area, which is passed to the subprogram. However, since the subprogram is also a calling program, you must define another save area for use by the subprogram to be called, and store Register 13 into the second fullword of this new save area. For cross-reference purposes, store the address of this new save area into the third fullword of the previous save area. In the event of a program interruption, the operating system uses the address in the third fullword of the save area to provide information that may help you during debugging; however, sometimes programmers omit this step to simplify the calling sequence.

Figure 13.7 pictures the two save areas. The subprogram SUB1 stores Registers 14 through 12 in the save area at SAVEM, which is defined in the main program. Next, SUB1 stores Register 13 into the second fullword of the save area at SAVE1, which is defined in the subprogram itself. Finally, SUB1 stores the address of SAVE1 in the third fullword of the save area at SAVEM in the main program. The second subprogram SUB2 stores Registers 14 through 12 in the save area at SAVE1.

Figure 13.8 lists the necessary instructions when a subprogram calls another subprogram. Since Register 15 is used in the calling sequence, it is not used as a base register here in these instructions. You can use a literal

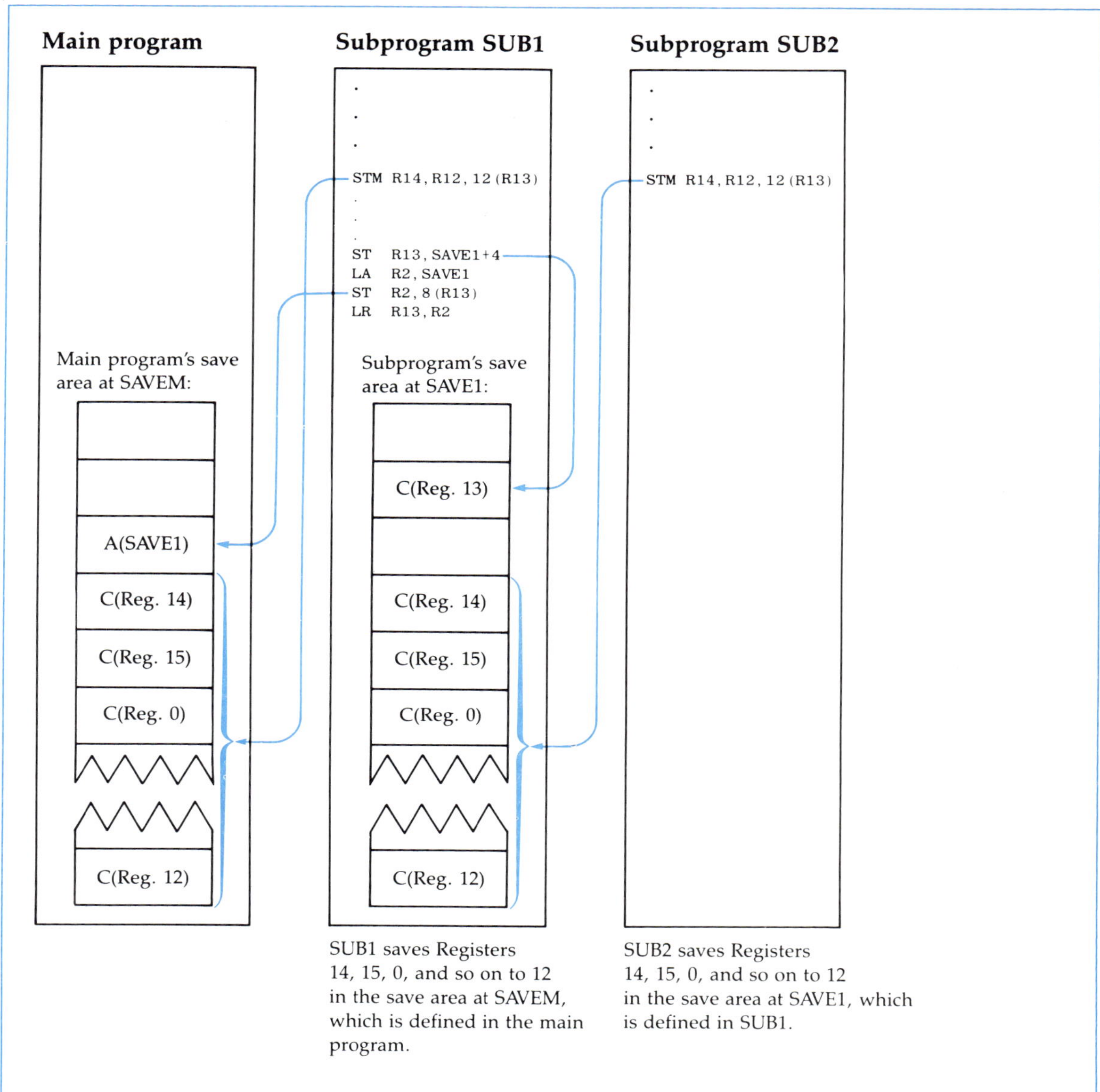


**Figure 13.7**
The save areas when a main program calls a subprogram (SUB1) that calls another subprogram (SUB2).

to define the argument list, as is done here, to make the calling sequence easier to read.

Note that a main program in OS or CMS is treated as if it was a subprogram of the operating system. As such, it follows the conventions for subprograms and would contain instructions like the ones shown in Figure 13.8.

## *Function Subprograms*

Many high-level languages permit **function subprograms** that each return a single result. You can write a function subprogram in assembler language if the result is a fullword binary integer or a floating-point number. First,

```
SUB1      CSECT
          STM    R14,R12,12(R13)   SAVE REGISTERS 14, 15, 0, 1, ..., 12
          BALR   R12,0             LOAD BASE REGISTER
          USING  BASE,R12          DECLARE BASE REGISTER
BASE      ST     R13,SAVE1+4       STORE REG. 13 IN SAVE AREA (SAVE1)
*                                    DEFINED IN THIS CONTROL SECTION
          LA     R2,SAVE1          GET ADDR. OF SAVE AREA AT SAVE1
          ST     R2,8(R13)         STORE IT IN SAVE AREA DEFINED IN
*                                    CALLING PROGRAM
          LR     R13,R2            R13 = ADDRESS OF SAVE AREA AT SAVE1
          .
          .
          .
** CALL SUBPROGRAM:
          LA     R1,=A(X,Y)        R1 = ADDRESS OF ARGUMENT LIST
          L      R15,=V(SUB2)      R15 =  ENTRY POINT
          BALR   R14,R15           CALL SUBPROGRAM
          .
          .
          .
** RETURN:
          L      R13,SAVE1+4       RESTORE R13 TO ADDRESS OF CALLING
*                                    PROGRAM'S SAVE AREA
          LM     R14,R12,12(R13)   RESTORE REGISTERS 14, 15, 0, 1, ..., 12
          BR     R14               RETURN
*
SAVE1     DS     18F               SAVE AREA
X         ----                     FIRST ARGUMENT
Y         ----                     SECOND ARGUMENT
          END
```

**Figure 13.8**
Instructions that are necessary in a subprogram (or OS or CMS main program) to call a subprogram.

**Register 0 contains the result of a function subprogram.**

consider a binary integer result. The only difference between integer functions and the subprograms just discussed is that you return an integer result from a function subprogram in Register 0. Be careful that you do not destroy the function's result in Register 0 when you restore the registers before you return to the calling program. Thus, you can write the following instructions to restore the registers

```
LM     R14,R15,12(R13)     RESTORE REGS. 14 AND 15
LM     R1,R12,24(R13)      RESTORE REGS. 1 - 12
```

or

```
ST     R0,20(R13)          SAVE RESULT IN SAVE AREA
LM     R14,R12,12(R13)     RESTORE REGISTERS
```

If the subprogram involves a floating-point computation, you return its result in Floating-Point Register 0. As there are no conventions to save floating-point registers, you do not need to do anything else. Chapter 17 discusses floating-point operations.

### *Return Codes*

You can return a code in Register 15 that signals the status of the subprogram's execution either to the calling program or to the operating system. Using a method analogous to the method that was just described for functions, you restore the registers upon return to the calling program without destroying the return code in Register 15. However, the examples in this chapter will ignore the return code.

**SELF-TEST EXERCISES**

1. Assume that you have defined two 50-character strings at S1 and S2, respectively. Write the necessary instructions to call the lowest-level subprogram SWAP, and pass to it the two character strings as arguments.
2. Using the assumptions given in Self-Test Exercise 1, write the subprogram SWAP. The subprogram should interchange the two character strings that are passed to it as arguments.
3. Rewrite the subprogram in Figure 13.6 as a function subprogram that returns the larger of two integer arguments.
4. Consider a function subprogram SUB1 with single-byte arguments called B1, B2, B3, and B4. SUB1 returns the value (B1 AND B2) OR (B3 AND B4) in the rightmost byte of Register 0. To accomplish this computation, SUB1 calls another function subprogram SUB2 that ANDs the contents of any two bytes that are passed to it. Write the two subprograms.

## Additional Information about External Subprograms

This section examines some miscellaneous but useful information about external subprograms that goes beyond the linkage conventions that were just described.

### *Variable-Length Argument Lists*

**The last fullword of a variable-length argument list contains a 1 in its first bit.**

Sometimes you may want to write a subprogram that permits an arbitrary number of arguments. For example, you can use one algorithm to compute the minimum of several values, regardless of whether there is one argument or many arguments. In such cases, you identify the last fullword of the argument list by setting its leftmost bit to 1. This causes the entire contents of the fullword to appear to be negative, but does not affect the 24-bit or 31-bit address in the fullword. The function subprogram in Figure 13.9 demonstrates this technique.

### *In-Line Argument Lists*

The argument lists in the examples given earlier have been defined within either the constant and data areas or the literal pool. Sometimes, you may want to define the argument list immediately after the BALR instruction

```
MIN      CSECT
** FUNCTION TO COMPUTE THE MINIMUM OF A VARIABLE NUMBER OF FULLWORD
** INTEGERS PASSED AS ARGUMENTS.   (ASSUME AT LEAST ONE.)
*
*     R0 = SMALLEST VALUE FOUND SO FAR; FUNCTION RESULT
*     R2 = INDEX TO ARGUMENT LIST
*     R3 = ADDRESS OF AN ARGUMENT
*
         STM   R14,R12,12(R13)   SAVE REGISTERS
         BALR  R12,0             LOAD BASE REGISTER
         USING BASE,R12          DECLARE BASE REGISTER
BASE     L     R0,=X'7FFFFFFF'   INITIALIZE TO LARGEST POSSIBLE INTEGER
         SR    R2,R2             CLEAR INDEX
* REPEAT:
LOOP     L     R3,0(R2,R1)       GET ADDRESS OF NEXT ARGUMENT
         C     R0,0(0,R3)        COMPARE SMALLEST SO FAR WITH
*                                  NEXT ARGUMENT VALUE.
         BNH   OK                IF <=, RESULT IS SMALLEST SO FAR
         L     R0,0(0,R3)        ELSE GET SMALLER VALUE
OK       LA    R2,4(R2)          INCREMENT INDEX FOR NEXT ARGUMENT
* UNTIL LAST ARGUMENT IS PROCESSED:
         LTR   R3,R3             WAS THIS THE LAST ARGUMENT?
         BNL   LOOP              IF NOT, REPEAT
* END REPEAT
         LM    R14,R15,12(R13)   ELSE RESTORE REGISTERS 14 - 15
         LM    R1,R12,24(R13)      AND 1 - 12
         BR    R14               RETURN; ANSWER IS IN REG. 0
         END
```

**Figure 13.9**
A function subprogram with a variable-length argument list.

that branches to the subprogram. Such an argument list is said to be **in-line** because it is embedded within the logical flow of the program. For example, suppose that ARG1 and ARG2 represent two arguments. The following instructions load Register 1 with the address of the argument list and then branch to the subprogram:

```
         BALR  R1,R15
         DC    A(ARG1)  ]<-- Argument list
         DC    A(ARG2)  ]
RETURN   ----
```

The instructions assume that Register 15 contains the entry point and that Register 14 contains the address RETURN. When the subprogram branches to the address in Register 14, it effectively branches around the argument list without the cost of an extra Branch instruction to branch around the argument list.

However, there is one flaw in this plan. A gap can exist between the BALR instruction and the argument list; the argument list is aligned on a fullword integral boundary, but the BALR instruction is aligned on a half-word boundary that might also be a fullword boundary, resulting in a gap. If there is a gap, you can remove it by inserting a 2-byte instruction *before* the BALR. This additional instruction should do nothing but occupy space.

Such an instruction is called a **No-Operation instruction** and is a special case of the Branch On Condition instruction. For example, the instruction

```
BCR     0,0
```

never branches for two reasons. First, the zero mask prevents a branch regardless of the condition code value and, therefore, regardless of the second operand. Second, an RR-format branch with a zero second operand never branches regardless of the mask. Although it is sufficient to specify just one operand as zero, you will usually specify both operands as zero. (Note that you can write this BCR instruction with an extended mnemonic as NOPR 0.)

CNOP forces boundary alignment of executable instructions.

It is inconvenient to decide when No-Operation instructions are indeed necessary, since predicting the integral boundary at which the assembler will align an instruction requires that you compute the relative address of the instruction. Furthermore, this relative address is likely to change as you modify the program—a probable occurrence during debugging. A better approach is to direct the assembler to decide if a No-Operation instruction is necessary by writing a **Conditional No-Operation (CNOP) instruction**. With this instruction, you can force alignment to a halfword, a fullword, or a doubleword integral boundary. The instruction can be summarized as follows:

| Name | Operation | Operand | Instruction Name | Action |
|---|---|---|---|---|
| *symbol* or *blank* | **CNOP** | *byte, group* | CONDITIONAL NO-OPERATION | Generates No-Operation instructions, if necessary, to force alignment to the byte number that is indicated by *byte* within a fullword (*group* = 4) or doubleword (*group* = 8); *byte* and *group* are absolute expressions; only *byte* values 0, 2, 4, and 6 are permitted. (In DOS, the name entry must be *blank*.) |

Figure 13.10 indicates the effects of the possible operand values for CNOP.

By using CNOP, you can align the BALR instruction to a halfword boundary so that there will be no gap between it and the argument list. Figure 13.11 gives an example of a calling sequence with an in-line argument list that specifies two arguments ARG1 and ARG2.

## *Call by Address and Call by Value*

External subprograms use call by address.

The argument list provides the subprogram with the addresses of the arguments. Thus, you can access the arguments and change their values within the subprogram. The argument list uses a concept known as **call by address**.

Another way to pass arguments to a subprogram is known as **call by value**. With this technique, you make copies of all argument values before the subprogram computation begins. Any changes that you make to the argument values in the subprogram are actually made to the copies, and not to the original definitions of the arguments. When the computation is complete, you replace the values of the original arguments by the values

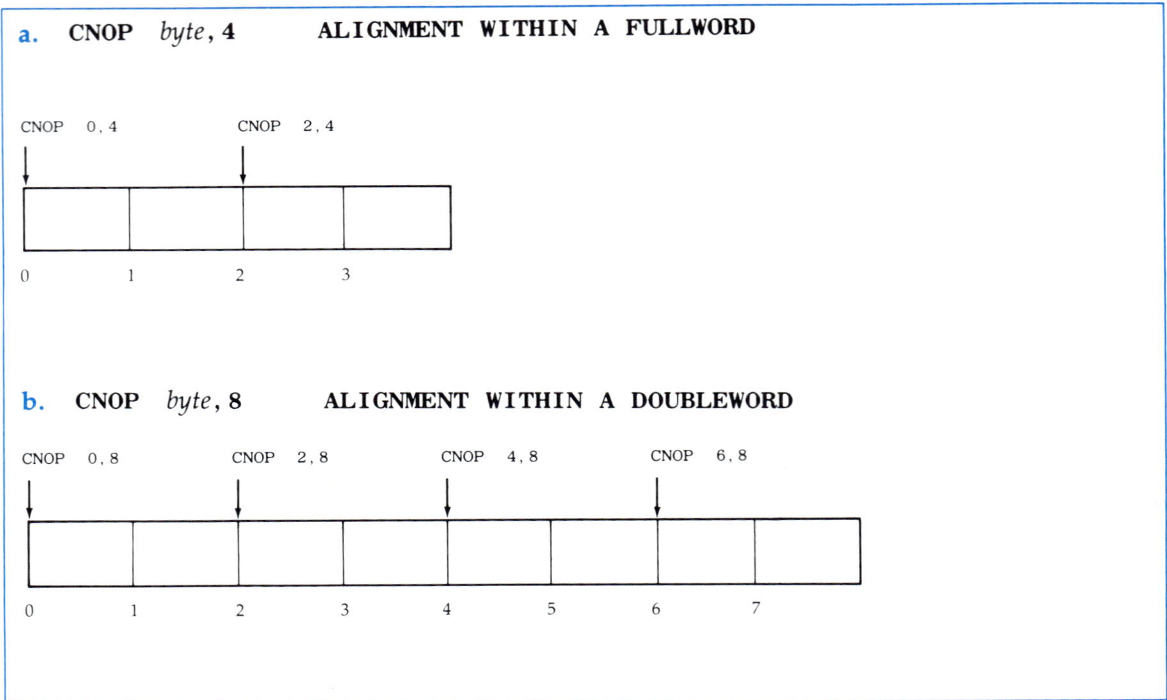


**Figure 13.10**
The boundary alignment caused by the CNOP instruction within, **a.** a fullword and, **b.** a doubleword.

```
         L      R15,=V(SUB)       R15 = ENTRY POINT
         LA     R14,RETURN        R14 = RETURN ADDRESS
         CNOP   2,4               ENSURE ALIGNMENT TO A HALFWORD BOUNDARY
*                                   THAT IS NOT A FULLWORD BOUNDARY.
         BALR   R1,R15            R1 = ADDRESS OF ARGUMENT LIST;
*                                   BRANCH TO SUBPROGRAM.
         DC     A(ARG1)           ADDRESS OF FIRST ARGUMENT
         DC     A(ARG2)           ADDRESS OF SECOND ARGUMENT
* ARG1 AND ARG2 ARE DEFINED SOMEWHERE IN THIS CONTROL SECTION
RETURN   ----
```

**Figure 13.11**
A calling sequence with an in-line argument list.

of the copies, which may have been modified. You could make the copies of the argument values within the subprogram or within the calling program. Although the outcome in either case is the same, making the copies within the subprogram is truly call by value.

It is easier to implement call by value if you do not follow the linkage conventions. For example, under certain circumstances, you could simply pass the argument value in a register. Although you do not need to follow the linkage conventions when you write an internal subprogram, you should follow them when you write an external subprogram.

```
  LOC   OBJECT CODE  STMT   SOURCE STATEMENT
000000                  1 MAIN    START
000000 90ECD00C         2         STM   R14,R12,12(R13)
000004 05C0             3         BALR  R12,0
                        4         USING BASE,R12
000006                  5 BASE    ----
   .                    .         .
   .                    .         .
   .                    .         .
000050 5830C0C6        30         L     R3,A
000054                 31         S     R3,X  <------  Addressability error
   .                    .         .
   .                    .         .
0000C8 07FE           101         BR    R14
0000CC                102 A       DS    F
   .                    .         .
   .                    .         .
   .                    .         .
000100                120 SUB     CSECT
                      121         USING SUB,R15
   .                    .         .
   .                    .         .
   .                    .         .
000142 5840C0C6       140         L     R4,A  <------  Undetected error
000146 5B40F088       141         S     R4,X
   .                    .         .
   .                    .         .
   .                    .         .
000184 07FE           160         BR    R14
000188                161 X       DS    F
                      162         END   MAIN
```

**Figure 13.12**
Some examples of incorrect references to symbols outside of a control section.

## *Addressing Concerns within Control Sections*

You must take certain addressing precautions when a source module contains several control sections. In addition to using distinct symbols within each control section as noted earlier, you may not reference the symbols of one control section within another control section. For example, consider the control sections in Figure 13.12. The reference to X in Statement 31 of the first control section is illegal because X is defined outside of the control section; the base register of the first control section cannot be used to address X. The assembler detects this error.

Unless you are careful, not all such errors are detected at assembly time. Although the reference to A in Statement 140 of the second control section is illegal because A is defined in the first control section, the instruction is assembled, without warning, with Register 12 as the base register. Both A and the base address in Register 12 are within the same control section, and the assembler incorrectly assumes that the register is still available as

```
 LOC    OBJECT CODE   STMT     SOURCE STATEMENT
000000                   1 MAIN      START
000000 90ECD00C          2           STM    R14,R12,12(R13)
000004 05C0              3           BALR   R12,0
                         4           USING  BASE,R12
000006                   5 BASE      ----
   .                     .           .
   .                     .           .
   .                     .           .
000050 5830C0C6         30           L      R3,A
000054                  31           S      R3,X   <------- Addressability error
   .                     .           .
   .                     .           .
   .                     .           .
0000C8 07FE            101           BR     R14
0000CC                 102 A         DS     F
   .                     .           .
   .                     .           .
   .                     .           .
                       119           DROP   R12
000100                 120 SUB       CSECT
                       121           USING  SUB,R15
   .                     .           .
   .                     .           .
   .                     .           .
000142                 140           L      R4,A   <------- Addressability error
000146 5B40F088        141           S      R4,X
   .                     .           .
   .                     .           .
   .                     .           .
000184 07FE            160           BR     R14
000188                 161 X         DS     F
                       162           DROP   R15
                       163           END    MAIN
```

**Figure 13.13**
Some examples of incorrect references to symbols outside of a control section that the assembler detects when DROP is used.

**DROP the base registers at the end of each control section.**

a base register. To prevent this from occurring, you should DROP the base registers at the end of each control section, as is done in Figure 13.13. This step allows the assembler to flag erroneous statements.

A second major concern is with literals. Unless the LTORG directive indicates otherwise, the assembler places all literal constants that are defined within the source module at the end of the first control section. This is true regardless of which control section first uses a particular literal. Of course, addressing problems occur when the location of the literal constant precedes the available base address, which is the case in Figure 13.14. The literal =F'5' is used only in the subprogram, but the assembler places the literal constant at the end of the main program and, thus, before the base address BASE2. Literal constants that are not positioned with LTORG are printed in the assembly listing at the end of the source module. This is true

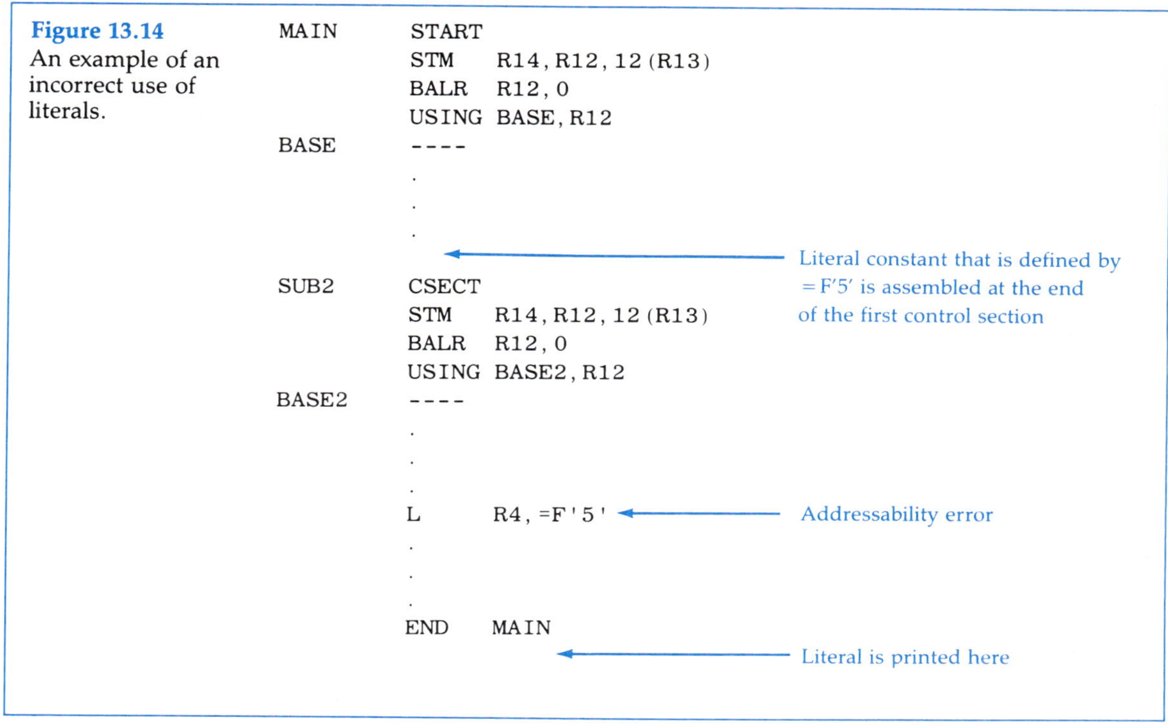


**Figure 13.14** An example of an incorrect use of literals.

in Figure 13.14, but do not be misled because the literal constant is defined at the end of the first control section. You should note the value of the location counter in the assembly listing to determine the actual location of the literal constant.

**Write LTORG at the end of each control section.**

To avoid the addressability problem in Figure 13.14, you should write an LTORG directive at the end of each control section, as is done in Figure 13.15. Notice that there are now two equal literal constants, each in a different literal pool. This phenomenon ensures addressability of the literal constants.

## *Multiple-Entry Subprograms*

So far, the symbol in the name entry of the CSECT statement has identified the entry point of a subprogram defined as a control section. In fact, this symbol is known as an **entry symbol**. However, you also can declare other symbols within the control section as entry symbols and, therefore, as entry points by listing them in an ENTRY directive. The directive can be summarized as follows:

| Name | Operation | Operand | Instruction Name | Action |
|---|---|---|---|---|
| *blank* | **ENTRY** | Relocatable symbols separated by commas | IDENTIFY ENTRY SYMBOLS | Declares the symbols listed in the operand entry to be entry symbols. |

```
MAIN     START
         STM    R14,R12,12(R13)
         BALR   R12,0
         USING  BASE,R12
BASE     ----
         L      R3,=F'5'
         .
         .
         .
         LTORG  <----------------  Literal constant that is defined by =F'5'
         DROP   R12                is assembled and printed here
SUB2     CSECT
         STM    R14,R12,12(R13)
         BALR   R12,0
         USING  BASE2,R12
BASE2    ----
         .
         .
         .
         L      R4,=F'5'
         .
         .
         .
         LTORG  <----------------  Literal constant that is defined by =F'5'
         DROP   R12                is assembled and printed here
         END    MAIN
```

**Figure 13.15**
An example in which LTORG is used to ensure the addressability of the literal constants.

**Use multiple-entry subprograms infrequently and with caution.**

Subprograms with more than one entry point are known as **multiple-entry subprograms**. They are useful when, for example, two computations are almost identical but differ somewhat initially. The next examples describe such situations. However, multiple-entry subprograms can confuse the structure of a program, so you should use them with caution.

---

EXAMPLE 2

Consider a computation that is divided into two parts, as shown in Figure 13.16. Suppose that you want to execute either the instructions in Part 1 followed immediately by the instructions in Part 2, or only the instructions in Part 2. You can do this with the multiple-entry subprogram in Figure 13.17. There are two entry points, A and B. The first entry point A is an entry symbol because it appears in the name entry of the CSECT directive; the second entry point B is also an entry symbol because it appears in the operand portion of an ENTRY statement. You can reference either entry point within the calling program by using V-type address constants. (In this example, the calling program is the main program that is defined in a separate source module.)

**Multiple-entry subprograms present challenging problems in addressability.**

Regardless of the point of entry, you must save the registers and declare a base register. (To simplify the linkage, this example assumes a lowest-level subprogram.) Maintaining addressability throughout the subprogram

**Figure 13.16**
The structure of the multiple-entry subprogram of Example 2.

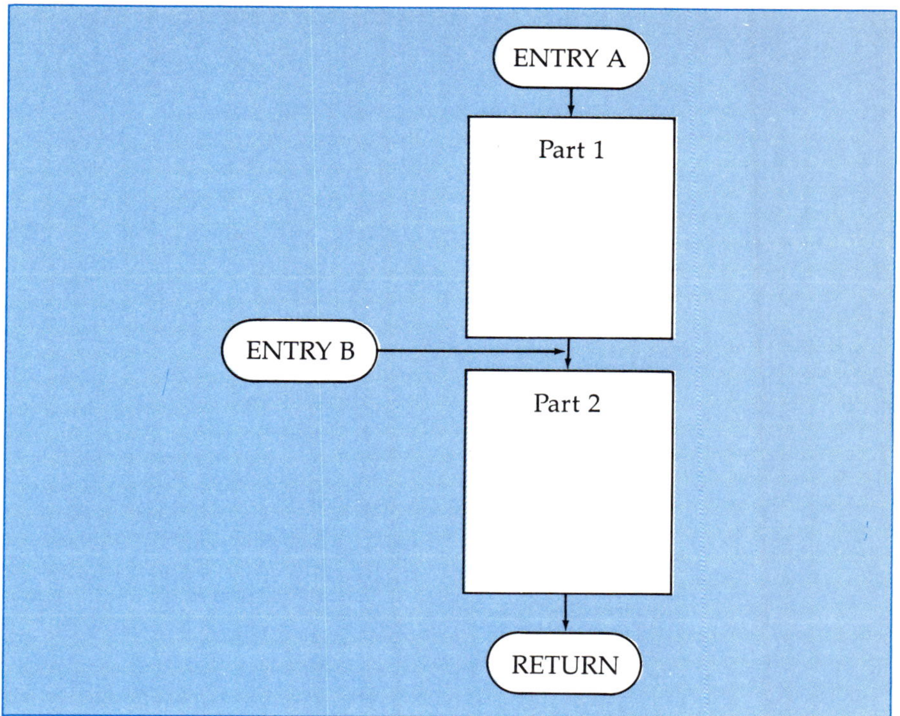


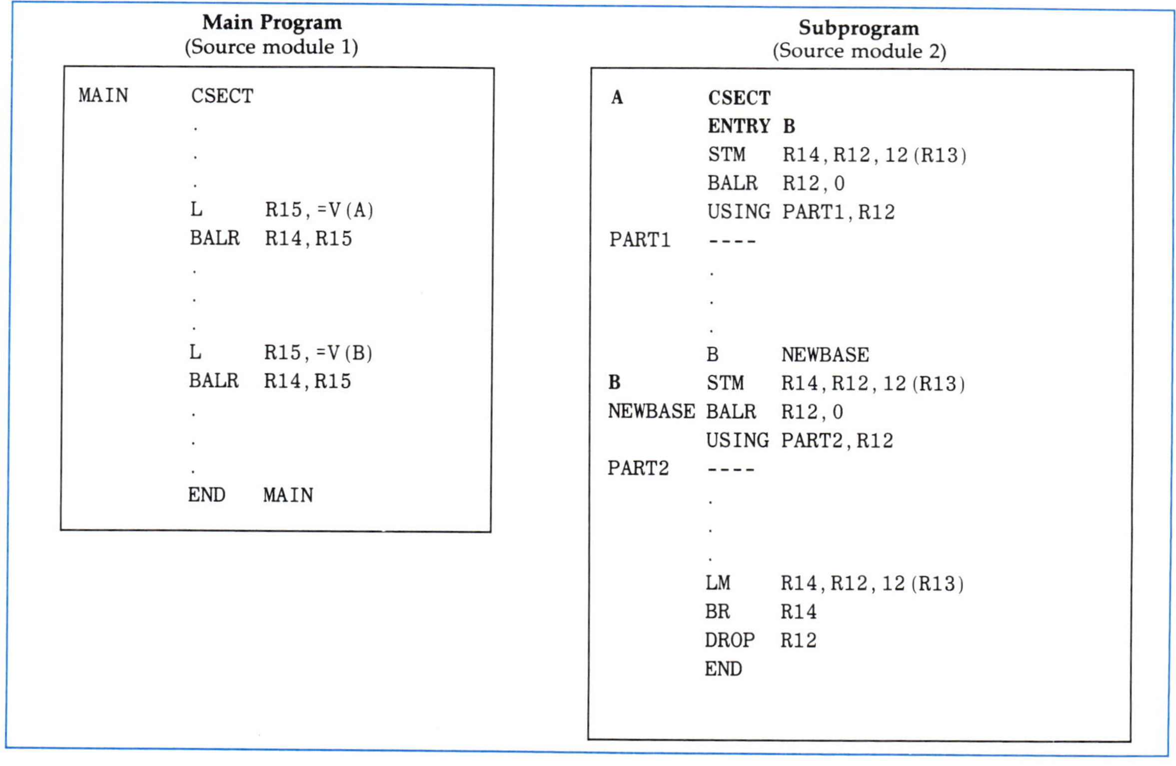


**Figure 13.17**
A multiple-entry subprogram with the structure of Figure 13.16, and its calling program, as described in Example 2.

is the primary concern when there are several entry points. After you enter at point A and execute several instructions, you cannot simply sequence into the second entry point because the registers will be saved again, which destroys the values that were already saved. Thus, you must branch around the STM instruction. Since you have already established a base register, you might be tempted to circumvent the second BALR instruction as well. However, you cannot do this because the assembler has assembled the instructions after the second entry point under the assumption that base Register 12 contains the address that PART2 represents. Unless you execute the second BALR instruction, Register 12 will contain the address PART1 instead.

---

EXAMPLE 3

Consider a computation that is divided into three parts, as pictured in Figure 13.18. Suppose that you want to execute either the instructions in Part 1 or the instructions in Part 2 and, in either case, that you next want to execute the instructions in Part 3. You can perform such a computation by using a multiple-entry subprogram with two entry points, as listed in Figure 13.19. At each entry point, save the registers and establish a base register. After you execute the first group of instructions at PART1 or PART2, either branch or sequence to the BALR instruction at NEWBASE. (To ensure correct addressability for the instructions at PART3, you must redefine the

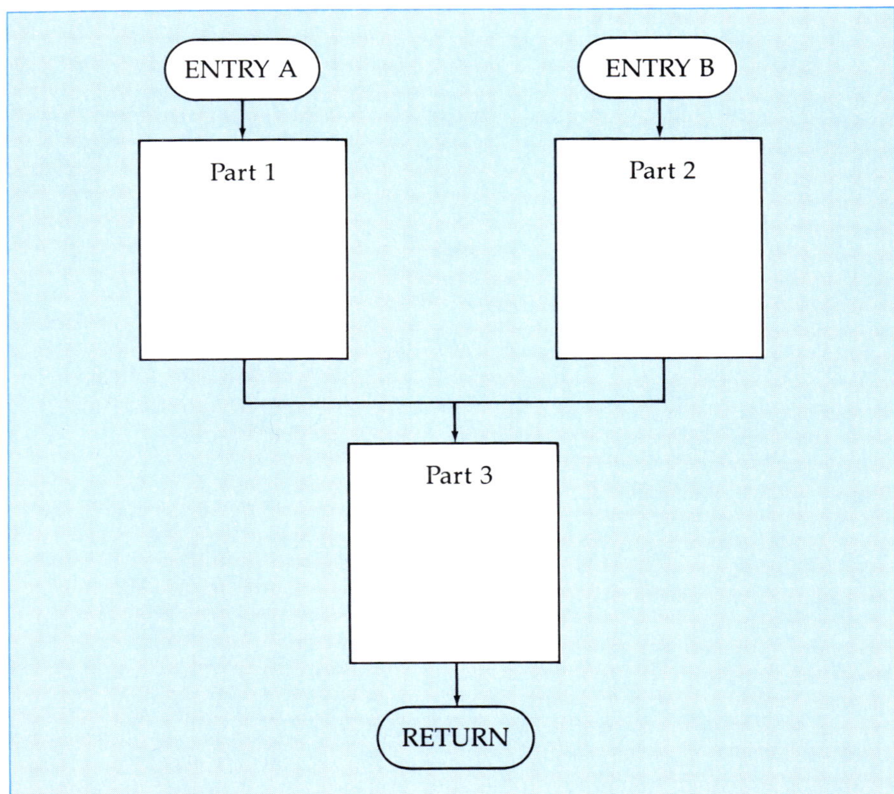


**Figure 13.18** The structure of the multiple-entry subprogram of Example 3.

**Figure 13.19**
A multiple-entry subprogram with the structure of Figure 13.18, as described in Example 3.

```
A        CSECT
         ENTRY B
         STM   R14,R12,12(R13)
         BALR  R12,0
         USING PART1,R12
PART1    ----
         .
         .
         .
         B     NEWBASE
B        STM   R14,R12,12(R13)
         BALR  R12,0
         USING PART2,R12
PART2    ----
         .
         .
         .
NEWBASE  BALR  R12,0
         USING PART3,R12
PART3    ----
         .
         .
         .
         BR    R14
         DROP  R12
         END
```

base register.) Each section then has its own base address, even though you use only one base register. However, the structure of the subprogram in Figure 13.19 does not permit certain branches. For example, you cannot branch from a point at or after PART3 to instructions that are before PART3.

## *System Macros for Subprograms*

Recall from Chapter 4 that a system macro is a predefined pattern that the assembler uses to generate a sequence of instructions, which replaces the macro instruction that you write to invoke the macro. Three system macros—SAVE, RETURN, and CALL—are available to save registers, to restore registers and return to the calling program, and to call a subprogram. Although the macros are convenient to use and can make your program easier to read, you should not use them until you have mastered the instructions that they represent. Thus, the macros are included here for your future reference.

The SAVE and RETURN macros specify a register range in the same manner as the STM and LM instructions. The macros can be summarized as follows:

| Operation | Operand | Instruction Name | Action |
|---|---|---|---|
| **SAVE** | (*R1*,*R2*)<br>or (*R1*) | SAVE REGISTERS | Stores the indicated register or registers into their proper positions in the save area, which is defined at the address in Register 13. *R1* and *R2* must be decimal integers. Has the same effect as<br>STM *R1*,*R2*,*D*(13)<br>or ST *R1*,*D*(13)<br>for an appropriate displacement *D*. |
| **RETURN** | (*R1*,*R2*)<br>or (*R1*) | RESTORE REGISTERS AND RETURN | Restores the indicated registers from the save area that is defined at the address in Register 13 and returns to the calling program. Has the same effect as<br>LM *R1*,*R2*,*D*(13)<br>or L *R1*,*D*(13)<br>followed by<br>BR 14<br>for an appropriate displacement *D*. |

The CALL macro generates an in-line calling sequence. The macro can be summarized as follows:

| Operation | Operand | Instruction Name | Action |
|---|---|---|---|
| **CALL** | *entry*,(*args*)[,VL]<br>or (15),(*args*)[,VL] | CALL A SUBPROGRAM | Calls the subprogram at the entry point that is represented by the symbol *entry* or that is contained in Register 15; *args* is a list of symbols that are separated by commas; each symbol represents a subprogram argument. VL is optional and, if present, implies that the argument list has a variable length: the first bit of the last fullword in the argument list is set to 1. (VL is unavailable under DOS.) |

Figure 13.20 shows examples of SAVE, RETURN, and CALL. (Note that under OS you can specify other parameters in the operand entries of SAVE, RETURN, and CALL; see IBM's manual *Supervisor Services and Macro Instructions*.)

## *Interrupting the Definition of a Control Section*

Interrupt the definition of a control section infrequently.

You can interrupt the definition of a control section so that you can begin the definition of another control section, dummy section, or common section. However, it usually is not a good idea to do so. Usually, your program will be easier to read if you complete each section before you begin another. Yet, sometimes, it can be useful to interrupt the definition of a control section to define a relevant dummy or common section; but even then, you must be careful not to obscure the definition of the control section. As an example of the effect of interrupting a control section, consider Figure 13.21 where the definition of control section B interrupts the definition of control section A. To continue the definition of A, another CSECT labeled A is written. (Note that, if the definition of a control section that begins with

| Macro Instruction | | Equivalent Instructions | | |
|---|---|---|---|---|
| SAVE | (R14,R12) | | STM | R14,R12,12(R13) |
| SAVE | (R0) | | ST | R0,20(R13) |
| RETURN | (R14,R12) | | LM | R14,R12,12(R13) |
| | | | BR | R14 |
| RETURN | (R1,R12) | | LM | R1,R12,24(R13) |
| | | | BR | R14 |
| CALL | SUB,(X,Y) | | L | R15,=V(SUB) |
| | | | LA | R14,RET |
| | | | CNOP | 2,4 |
| | | | BALR | R1,R15 |
| | | | DC | A(X) |
| | | | DC | A(Y) |
| | | RET | EQU | * |
| CALL | SUB,(X,Y),VL | Same as the previous CALL, but the last address constant contains a 1 in its first bit | | |
| CALL | (R15),(X,Y),VL | Same as the previous CALL, but without the first Load instruction | | |

**Figure 13.20**
Some examples of using the SAVE, RETURN, and CALL macros.

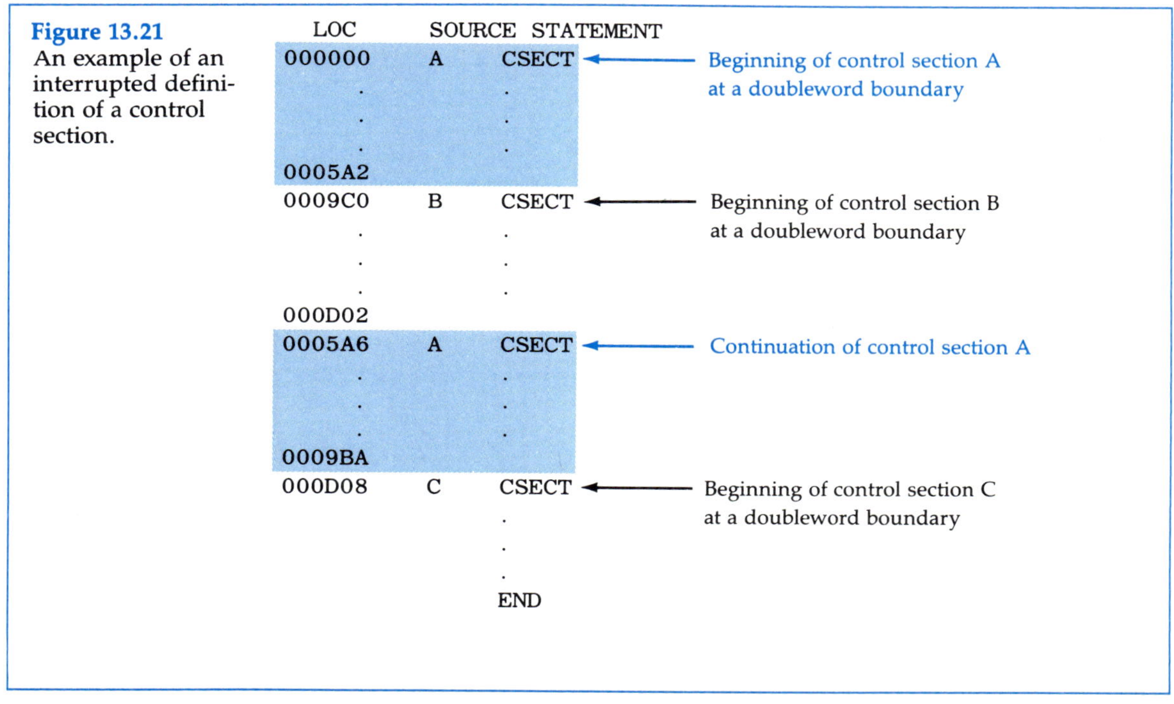


**Figure 13.21**
An example of an interrupted definition of a control section.

START is incomplete before another is begun, it is continued with a CSECT, and not another START.) Notice from the location counter values that, although the definition of control section A was interrupted, it is a contiguous unit that is followed first by B and then by C.

## SELF-TEST EXERCISES

5. Assume that you have defined fullword binary integers at A, B, C, D, E, and F. Using the subprogram MIN that was defined in Figure 13.9, write subprogram calls with in-line argument lists to compute the following:
   a. The minimum of the integers at A, C, and F. Store the result at M1.
   b. The minimum of the integers at A, B, D, E, and F. Store the result at M2.
6. Repeat Self-Test Exercise 5 to include the macro CALL.
7. Rewrite the subprogram MIN in Figure 13.9 so that it uses the SAVE and RETURN macros.
8. Consider the instructions in Figure 13.22. Identify any addressability errors that will occur, and other addressing errors that the assembler does not detect. Explain your answers.

**Figure 13.22**
The instructions for Self-Test Exercise 8.

```
SUB1     CSECT
         STM    14,12,12(13)
         BALR   12,0
         USING  BASE1,12
BASE1    L      2,=F'-1'
         A      2,CON
         ST     2,WORD
         LM     14,12,12(13)
         BR     14
WORD     DS     F
SUB2     CSECT
         STM    14,12,12(13)
         BALR   12,0
         USING  BASE2,12
BASE2    L      2,=F'-1'
         ST     2,WORD
         LM     14,12,12(13)
         BR     14
CON      DC     F'41'
         LTORG
         DROP   12
         END
```

## Data Areas

Most programs require data areas. When the program consists of several control sections that are possibly spread over more than one source module, particular organization of the data areas becomes important. You can use dummy sections, common sections, and even control sections for this purpose. A dummy section describes a data area, but does not reserve storage or define constants. A common section reserves storage that several source modules can share, but does not define constants at assembly time. A control section that is used only to reserve storage and to define constants is called an **external data area**. The fact that you can define constants at assembly time distinguishes an external data area from a common section.

## *The Dummy Section (The DSECT Directive)*

**Use the symbols that are defined in a dummy section to address a data area that is defined in another control section.**

**A dummy section describes a data area, but does not reserve storage.**

Frequently, you will define data areas in one control section and reference them in another control section. You cannot make such references symbolically with what you have learned so far because you cannot address in one control section symbols that are defined in another control section. In the past, you referenced data areas in another control section by using explicit operand designations. However, you can use symbols to address a data area that is defined in another control section by first defining the symbols in a dummy section.

A dummy section provides a symbolic description of a data area that is defined elsewhere. For example, you can write a dummy section to describe a subprogram's argument list. The assembler statements within a dummy section do not produce object code; typically, you describe a data area by using DS directives within the dummy section. To use a symbol that is defined in a dummy section, you write a USING statement that designates the symbol and a register. The register must contain the address of the actual data area that the symbol represents.

The DSECT directive initiates (or resumes) the definition of a dummy section. Its format is analogous to that of the CSECT directive. The directive can be summarized as shown:

| Name | Operation | Operand | Instruction Name | Action |
|---|---|---|---|---|
| *symbol* or *blank* | **DSECT** | None | DEFINE DUMMY SECTION | Initiates or resumes a dummy section that is identified by the symbol, if any, in the name entry. (In DOS, there must be a symbol in the name entry.) |

There may be several dummy sections within a source module. The assembler assigns to each dummy section a separate location counter that begins at zero and that is maintained in relation to the beginning of the dummy section, even if the definition of that section is interrupted and later resumed.

---

EXAMPLE 4

### A Dummy Section that Describes an Argument List

The argument list of a subprogram and the arguments themselves are good examples of data areas that are defined within one control section, but are used in another. Suppose that the calling program contains the following definitions:

```
* ARGUMENT LIST:
ARGS      DC    A(A)        ADDRESS OF FIRST ARGUMENT
          DC    A(B)        ADDRESS OF SECOND ARGUMENT
* ARGUMENT DEFINITIONS:
A         DS    CL8         FIRST FIELD OF A
          DS    CL6         SECOND FIELD OF A
B         DS    CL6
```

Even though a subprogram in another control section cannot directly address the symbols ARGS, A, and B, you can define dummy sections and use them in the subprogram to provide a symbolic description of the arguments. For example, the dummy sections defined by

```
ARGLIST  DSECT
         DS    A     ADDRESS OF X
         DS    A     ADDRESS OF Y
X        DSECT ,     FIRST ARGUMENT
X1       DS    CL8   FIRST FIELD OF X
X2       DS    CL6   SECOND FIELD OF X
Y        DSECT ,     SECOND ARGUMENT
         DS    CL6
```

describe the argument list, the arguments X and Y, and the two fields within X. However, the dummy sections do not reserve storage. These three dummy sections provide a picture of the arguments and the argument list, and define symbols that you can use in the subprogram. Thus, you can use X and Y in the subprogram to represent the **actual arguments** A and B.

To achieve addressability of the symbols ARGLIST, X, X1, X2, and Y, write the dummy section names in USING statements, as shown in Figure 13.23. The main program in the first source module contains the definition of the argument list and the arguments. Register 1, which is loaded in the main program with the address of the argument list, is declared as a base register in the subprogram that is contained in the second source module by the statement

```
USING ARGLIST,R1
```

This USING statement gives meaning to the symbol ARGLIST within the subprogram. For example, the instruction

```
LM    R9,R10,ARGLIST
```

is equivalent to

```
LM    R9,R10,0(R1)
```

This LM instruction loads Registers 9 and 10 with the addresses of the actual arguments A and B, which are defined in another control section. The symbols X and Y are then given meaning by the statements

```
USING X,R9
USING Y,R10
```

Thus, you can use X and Y to represent the actual arguments. You can also address without further effort symbols such as X1 and X2 that are defined within the dummy section. This technique makes the instruction

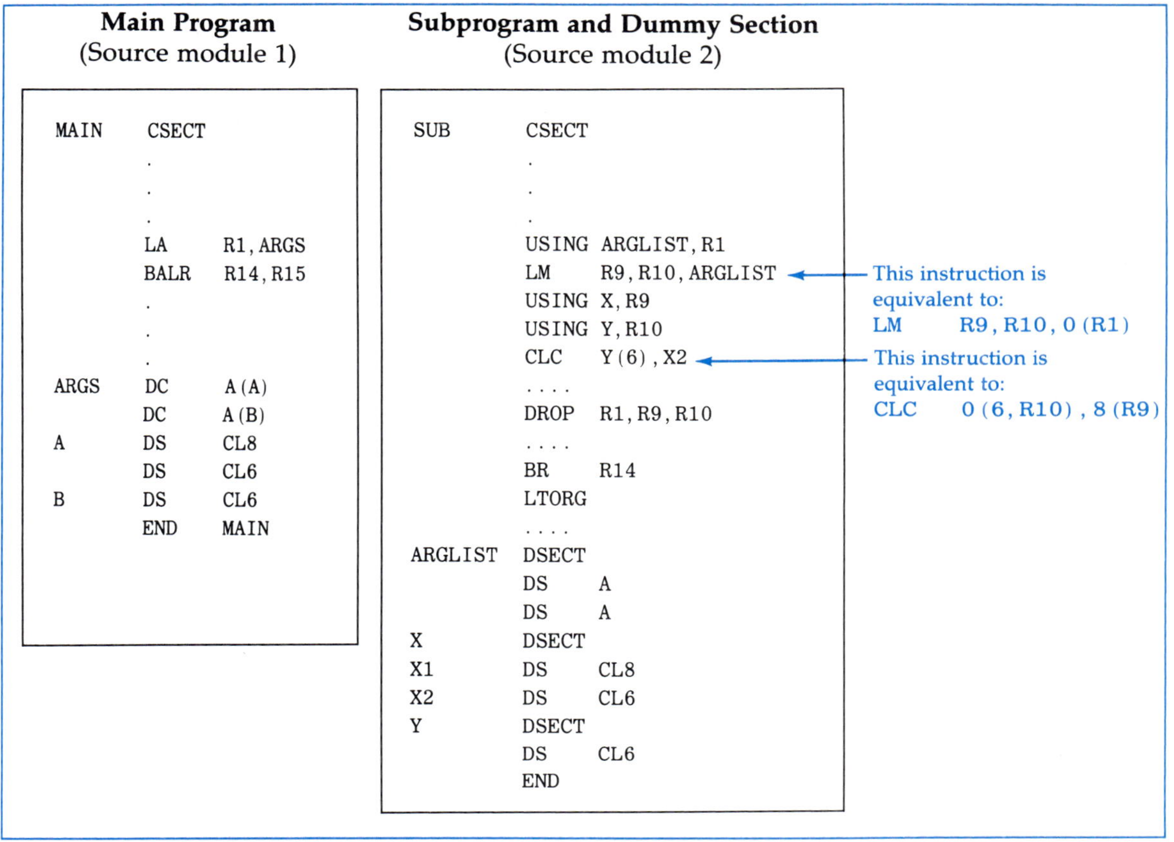


**Figure 13.23**
A dummy section that describes an argument list, as described in Example 4.

```
CLC  Y(6),X2
```

equivalent to

```
CLC  0(6,R10),8(R9)
```

Another way to address the arguments is to label each DS within the dummy section ARGLIST as follows:

```
ARGLIST  DSECT
ADX      DS    A     ADDRESS OF X
ADY      DS    A     ADDRESS OF Y
```

You can then write the following instructions to load registers with the addresses of the actual arguments A and B:

```
USING  ARGLIST,R1
L      R6,ADX        GET THE ADDRESS OF X
L      R8,ADY        GET THE ADDRESS OF Y
```

This technique is useful when you want to load the addresses of particular arguments into registers that are not numbered consecutively. The following statements allow the symbols X, X1, X2, and Y in the dummy sections defined earlier to be addressable:

```
USING X,R6
USING Y,R8
```

To reduce the chance of erroneous base register assignment, you should DROP the base registers that are associated with the symbols in a dummy section as soon as you no longer need the symbols.

You define dummy sections within the same source module as the control sections that reference them but, as Figure 13.23 demonstrated, the *actual* data need not appear in the same source module. However, you also can combine all of the sections in Figure 13.23 into one source module.

---

EXAMPLE 5

### A USING Directive that Contains a Symbol that Is Defined within a Dummy Section

The subprogram listed in Figure 13.24 is written as a function with one argument, which is an array of 50 fullword integers. The subprogram computes the sum of the integers in the array and returns the result in Register 0. A dummy section describes the array. Notice that the symbol ARRAY is defined *within* the dummy section and appears in a USING statement.

```
SUM      CSECT
** FUNCTION TO COMPUTE THE SUM OF 50 INTEGERS IN AN ARRAY PASSED
** AS AN ARGUMENT.  RETURN THE SUM IN REGISTER 0.
*     R0 = SUM OF THE INTEGERS
*     R1 = ADDRESS OF ARGUMENT LIST
*     R3 = ARRAY INDEX
*     R4 = LOOP COUNTER
*     R9 = ADDRESS OF ARRAY
         STM   R14,R12,12(R13)  SAVE REGISTERS
* INITIALIZE:
         BALR  R12,0            LOAD BASE REGISTER
         USING BASE,R12         DECLARE BASE REGISTER
         USING ARGLIST,R1       ESTABLISH ADDRESSABILITY OF ARGUMENT LIST
BASE     SR    R0,R0            CLEAR SUM ACCUMULATOR
*
****   THE NEXT INSTRUCTION IS EQUIVALENT TO: L     R9,0(R1)
         L     R9,ADDR1         GET ADDRESS OF ARRAY
         DROP  R1               DELETE R1 AS BASE REGISTER
         SR    R3,R3            CLEAR INDEX
         L     R4,N             INITIALIZE LOOP CONTROL
         USING ARRAY,R9         ESTABLISH ADDRESSABILITY OF ARRAY
* REPEAT UNTIL COUNTER = 0:
*
```

*(Continues)*

**Figure 13.24**
A function subprogram that uses a dummy section, as described in Example 5.

```
****     THE NEXT INSTRUCTION IS EQUIVALENT TO:   A      R0,0(R3,R9)
LOOP       A      R0,ARRAY(R3)      ADD NEXT INTEGER TO ACCUMULATOR
           DROP   R9                DELETE R9 AS BASE REGISTER
           LA     R3,4(R3)          INCREMENT INDEX
           BCT    R4,LOOP           REPEAT
*
* END REPEAT
           DROP   R12
           LM     R14,R15,12(R13)    RESTORE REGISTERS 14 - 15
           LM     R1,R12,24(R13)       AND 1 - 12.
           BR     R14               RETURN
*
N          DC     A((AFTER-ARRAY)/4)         NO. OF INTEGERS IN ARRAY
*
ARGLIST    DSECT                    ARGUMENT LIST
ADDR1      DS     A                 ADDRESS OF ARGUMENT
*
           DSECT
ARRAY      DS     50F               ARGUMENT
AFTER      EQU    *                 BYTE AFTER ARRAY
           END
```

**Figure 13.24**
*(Continued)*

In addition, you can use symbols that are defined within a dummy section in the definition of an address constant, but only if the symbols are paired and separated by the difference operator as is demonstrated by the definition of N. Notice that the last dummy section is an example of an unnamed dummy section. However, under DOS, you cannot write unnamed dummy sections; instead, you would write a symbol in the name entry of the DSECT instruction.

---

EXAMPLE 6

### Processing an Array of Fullwords that Are Described by a Dummy Section

Consider an array of 60 fullword binary integers that is passed as an argument to a subprogram. The subprogram replaces every third integer in the array by the sum of the preceding two integers. Figure 13.25 contains the portion of the subprogram that performs the desired computation by using a dummy section to describe the array. Since Register 1 contains the address of the argument list, the Load instruction in Statement 3 loads Register 9 with the address of the array. (You can apply the technique of Example 4 here also.) The symbol TABLE that names the dummy section in Statement 13 is associated with Register 9 in a USING statement in Statement 6. Statements 7, 8, and 9 are assembled with Register 9 as the base register and Register 4 as the index register. (Figure 13.25 notes the equivalent instructions that are written with explicit operand designations.) The DROP instruction is written as soon as Register 9 is no longer needed.

```
** ASSUME THAT REGISTER 12 IS THE BASE REGISTER AND THAT
** REGISTER 1 CONTAINS THE ADDRESS OF THE ARGUMENT LIST.
          L      R9,0(R1)          R9 = ADDRESS OF ARRAY
          L      R3,=F'20'         R3 = LOOP COUNTER
          SR     R4,R4             R4 = ARRAY INDEX
          USING  TABLE,R9
LOOP      L      R0,FIRST(R4)  ]                  [  L     R0,0(R4,R9)
          A      R0,SECOND(R4) ]<-- equivalents -->[  A     R0,4(R4,R9)
          ST     R0,SUM(R4)    ]                  [  ST    R0,8(R4,R9)
          DROP   R9
          LA     R4,LENGTH(R4)
          BCT    R3,LOOP
          .
          .
          .
TABLE     DSECT
FIRST     DS     F
SECOND    DS     F
SUM       DS     F
LENGTH    EQU    *-TABLE
```

**Figure 13.25**
Instructions to process an array of fullwords that is described by a dummy section, as explained in Example 6.

---

EXAMPLE 7

### Processing Character Strings that Are Described by a Dummy Section

Consider a data area that contains the names, identification numbers, and addresses of 50 people. In Figure 13.26, the dummy section DATA describes one entry in this data area. The instructions in Figure 13.26 search the data area for an identification number that equals the one at KEY, assuming that the address of the data area is in Register 9. The USING statement associates Register 9 with the dummy section, and makes the symbols within the dummy section addressable. However, notice that, unlike Example 6, the contents of Register 9 are changed each time through the loop by this instruction:

```
LA      R9,NEXTNAME
```

This instruction loads Register 9 with the address of the next person's name. The instruction is equivalent to

```
LA      R9,60(R9)
```

and increments Register 9 by 60 bytes, which is the length of the three fields that are associated with one person.

Be careful when you use the technique just demonstrated because you are, in fact, changing the contents of a base register. Symbols such as NEXTNAME will help you to avoid mistakes.

```
** ASSUME THAT REGISTER 12 IS THE BASE REGISTER AND THAT REGISTER 9
** CONTAINS THE ADDRESS OF THE ACTUAL DATA AREA
         L     R3,=F'50'          R3 = LOOP COUNTER
         USING DATA,R9            EST. ADDRESSABILITY OF DUMMY SECTION
LOOP     CLC   KEY,ID             COMPARE KEY WITH NEXT ID
         BE    FOUND              KEY MATCHES ID
         LA    R9,NEXTNAME        POINT TO NEXT PERSON
         DROP  R9                 DELETE R9 AS BASE REGISTER
         BCT   R3,LOOP            REPEAT
         .
         .
         .
FOUND    ----
         .
         .
         .
KEY      DS    CL9                KEY THAT IS USED IN THE SEARCH
DATA     DSECT ,                  DESCRIPTION OF DATA FOR ONE PERSON:
NAME     DS    CL21                 NAME
ID       DS    CL9                  IDENTIFICATION NUMBER
ADDRESS  DS    CL30                 ADDRESS
NEXTNAME EQU   *                  NEXT PERSON'S NAME
```

**Figure 13.26**
Instructions to process character strings that are described by a dummy section, as explained in Example 7.

---

**Dummy sections make a program easier to read and to alter.**

Dummy sections not only make a program more readable, but also make a program easier to change. In Example 7, if you change the order of the fields in the data area, you only need to change the order of the DS directives in the corresponding dummy section. Without the dummy section, you would have to change each instruction that referenced the data area.

## *The Common Section (The COM Directive)*

**A common section reserves storage that is shared by several control sections.**

Common sections enable control sections within different source modules to share data during execution. Often, you use common sections to avoid duplication of data areas when the control sections are written by different programmers. Although a common section and a dummy section are similar, they differ in one important respect: a common section reserves storage, while a dummy section describes a data area without reserving storage.

The definition of a common section is initiated or resumed with the COM directive. The directive can be summarized as follows:

| Name | Operation | Operands | Instruction Name | Action |
|---|---|---|---|---|
| *symbol* or *blank* | COM | None | DEFINE COMMON SECTION | Initiates or resumes a common section that is identified by the symbol, if any, in the name entry. (In DOS, the name entry must be *blank*.) |

**There are two types of common sections: named and unnamed.**

If a symbol appears in the name entry, the common section is called **named common** or **labeled common**; if a symbol does not appear, the section is called **unnamed common** or **blank common**. In OS and CMS, there may be one unnamed common section and several named common sections in a source module. In DOS, there may be only one unnamed common section; named common sections are not permitted.

You must define a particular common section with the COM directive in every source module that requires the common section. There must be a one-to-one correspondence between the bytes of the various definitions of the common section. Although you do not have to use the same symbols within the various definitions of a common section, it is desirable to do so.

When the linker combines several source modules—each containing a common section with the same name—it only retains the longest of these common sections. Thus, duplicate common sections do not occur.

By writing USING directives, you must establish the addressability of a common section within every control section that refers to it. The USING statements can contain the name of the common section or the symbols that are defined within it, as was just shown for dummy sections.

---

EXAMPLE 8

Figure 13.27 depicts a main program and two subprograms, each of which is assembled separately. Both subprograms reference a common section and establish its addressability by using an A-type address constant. The main program does not reference the common section so it is not defined there. Although it could have been, a good practice is to omit the definition of the common section from modules that should not reference the common section. This practice prevents unintentional changes to the common data.

This is an example of several source modules that different programmers could have written. When the modules are assembled and combined, there will be only one common section named COMMON.

---

EXAMPLE 9

The common section in Example 8 is a named common section, but DOS permits only unnamed common sections. To change the named common section to unnamed common, replace the COM statements with

```
           COM
COMMON     EQU    *
```

---

## *External Data Areas (The EXTRN Directive)*

Although common sections reserve storage, you cannot use them to define constants. However, it is sometimes useful for source modules to share a

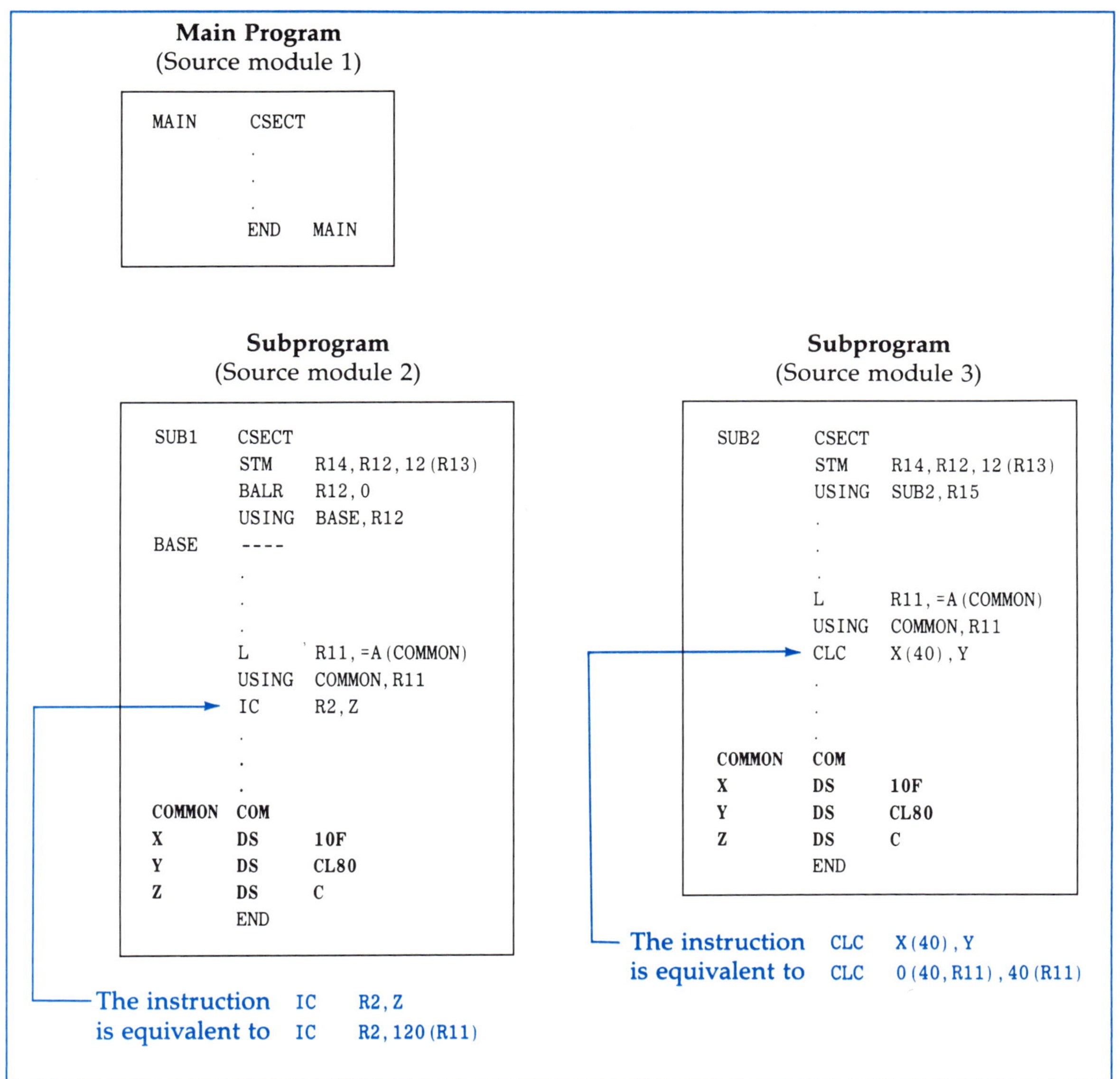


**Figure 13.27**
The use of a common section, as described in Example 8.

**An external data area defines constants that are shared by several control sections.**

single definition of several constants—particularly if the constants are numerous or lengthy. The single definition eliminates transcription errors and simplifies program maintenance. You define the constants in a separate control section within the source module, and reference them in all other source modules by using dummy sections. Such a control section, which may also reserve storage, is called an external data area. You usually establish the addressability of an external data area differently than you do for an external subprogram, even though both are control sections. You can identify the name of the external data area as an external symbol within each source module that references the data area by using an EXTRN directive. The directive can be summarized as follows:

| Name | Operation | Operand | Instruction Name | Action |
|---|---|---|---|---|
| *blank* | **EXTRN** | Relocatable symbols separated by commas | IDENTIFY EXTERNAL SYMBOLS | Declares the symbols that are listed in the operand entry to be external symbols. |

---

EXAMPLE 10

The first source module in Figure 13.28 contains the external data area DATA. The subprogram in the second source module can reference DATA by describing the external data area with a dummy section. DATA is declared as an external symbol by using the EXTRN directive, and is referenced by using an A-type address constant.

The statement

```
USING AREA,R11
```

establishes the addressability of the dummy section so that the subprogram can use the symbols of the dummy section.

You can use the technique demonstrated here in DOS to circumvent the stylistically inconvenient restriction of a single unnamed common area.

**Figure 13.28**
The use of an external data area, as described in Example 10.

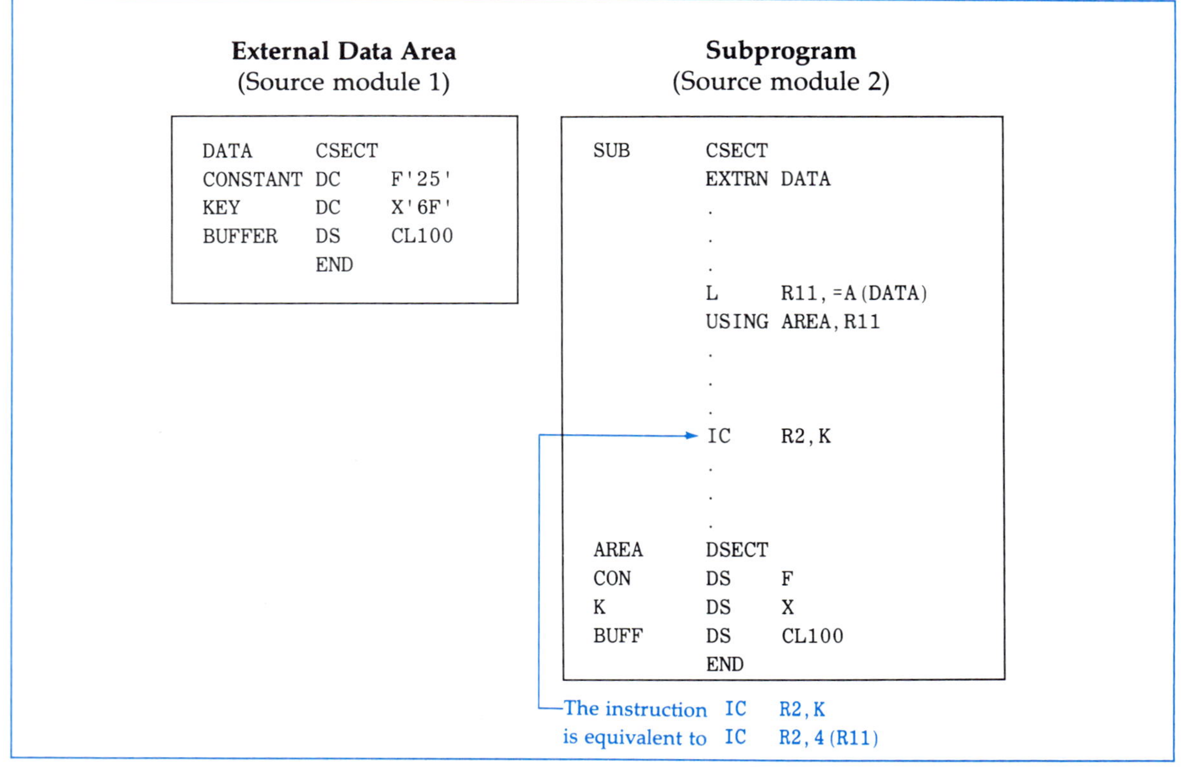

You can replace both EXTRN and the A-type address constant that you use to reference an external data area by a V-type address constant. Traditionally, V-type address constants were used only with executable control sections, but you do not need to follow this restriction.

You also can declare the name of a data field within a control section to be an entry symbol, and use the symbol within another control section, either in a V-type address constant or in an EXTRN directive. Thus, entry symbols do not need to be entry points.

## SELF-TEST EXERCISES

9. Write dummy sections to describe the arguments and the argument list that are associated with the subprogram in Figure 13.6. Using these dummy sections, rewrite the subprogram.
10. Rewrite the subprogram in Figure 13.24 so that ARRAY is not passed as an argument, but is instead defined in a common section.
11. Repeat Self-Test Exercise 10 so that the subprogram uses an external data area instead of a common section.
12. Rewrite the control sections in Figure 13.23 so that they use a common section instead of an argument list.
13. Repeat Self-Test Exercise 12 so that the control sections use an external data area instead of a common section.

# Object and Load Modules

This section briefly describes some of the steps required to transform an assembler language program into an executable form. In general, an assembler language program can consist of several source modules. In Chapter 1, you learned that the assembler translates each source module independently into a machine language segment called an object module, and that the linker combines the object modules into a load module that is finally loaded into storage.

## *The Object Module*

An object module is not in an executable form. Since the assembler does not determine the starting address of the module, the assembler generates a relative address for each instruction and each data field, and leaves incomplete any address constants that are originally defined with relocatable quantities. Such address constants are classified as **internal address constants** or **external address constants**, depending on whether the associated addresses are internal or external to the control section. An internal address constant contains a relative address after assembly; an external address constant is assembled as zero. Finally, an object module may contain references to subprograms that were not part of the source module, and are therefore missing from the object module.

The object module consists of four types of records whose format recalls the time when they were punched on cards to produce an object deck. Although this text will not describe their format, it will briefly state the purpose of each type of record here.

*The External Symbol Dictionary.* External symbol dictionary (ESD) records contain entry and external symbols, with some information about them. The records classify each symbol according to whether it is the name of a control section or a common area, it is listed in an ENTRY or an EXTRN statement, or it is referenced in a V-type address constant.

*The Relocation Dictionary.* Relocation dictionary (RLD) records contain the symbols that represent address constants defined by relocatable expressions, and indications as to whether the address constants are internal or external. Thus, this dictionary points to those constants whose definition is incomplete after the assembly process.

*The Text Records.* Text (TXT) records contain the machine language instructions and constants, with their relative addresses.

*The End Record.* This record signals the end of the object module, and contains the module's length in bytes and its entry point.

### The Load Module

To produce a load module, the linker combines the object module with any other required object modules from a previous assembly. The linker assigns an order to the control sections, and then provides all instructions, constants, and data areas with new relative addresses that are based upon the beginning of the load module. Internal address constants are appropriately modified to be consistent with these new addresses, and external address constants are redefined with a relative address; at this point, both internal and external address constants look alike.

Except for the address constants, the load module contains instructions and constants in exactly the form and order in which they will appear in storage. The load module also contains a relative entry point and a combined relocation directory.

Finally, the loader selects a starting address, and adds it to the relative entry point and all of the address constants that are named in the relocation dictionary of the load module. The loader then loads the modified load module into storage.

## Case Study

### Problem Statement

**Repeat the problem that was described in the case study of Chapter 10, but use external subprograms and dummy sections.**

The original program in Figure 10.25 read course requests for each student, printed the requests, and then printed a summary of the number of requests for each course. The program used one internal subprogram COUNT that computed the number of course requests.

## *Discussion*

The program for this case study uses the same algorithm as the one that was used in Figure 10.25, but has a different organization. A main program reads a student record and calls a subprogram AUDIT that creates an output record of the student data; AUDIT then calls a subprogram COUNT that updates the tallies of the course requests. The main program prints the record that AUDIT creates, and then calls a subprogram PRINT to print the summary of the number of course requests. The diagram in Figure 13.29 shows the relationship between the main program and the three subprograms. The pseudocode in Figure 13.30 provides an overview of the logic of each program unit; the details are the same as were used in the program in Figure 10.25.

Figure 13.31 contains the program for the case study. If you compare this program with the one in Figure 10.25, you will see some segments that are identical, and other segments that use different registers than were used in similar segments of Figure 10.25. Changes in register assignments were necessary to accommodate the linkage conventions. Notice that each subprogram call is preceded by a comments statement that contains the CALL macro instruction that you could use instead to call the subprogram. For example, Statement 86 indicates that the main program passes five arguments to the subprogram AUDIT: the input record IN, the output buffer OUT, the table TAB of unique course codes that have been detected so far, the array TAL of corresponding course tallies, and the number NUM of unique course codes that are contained in TAB. All of the data areas just listed are defined in the main program.

AUDIT fills the output buffer with data that are contained in the input record. The argument list and the output buffer are described by the dummy sections in Statements 361 through 371 that follow the subprogram. Statement 303 in AUDIT makes the argument list addressable by using the technique that was described in Example 4 (Figure 13.23), and Statement 304 loads Registers 5 through 9 with the addresses of the five arguments. The address of the output buffer in Register 6 is copied into Register 11 in Statement 307 so that the program can use one register (R11) as a base register to address the fields within the output buffer, and can alter the other register (R6) to address individual bytes within the fields. The USING

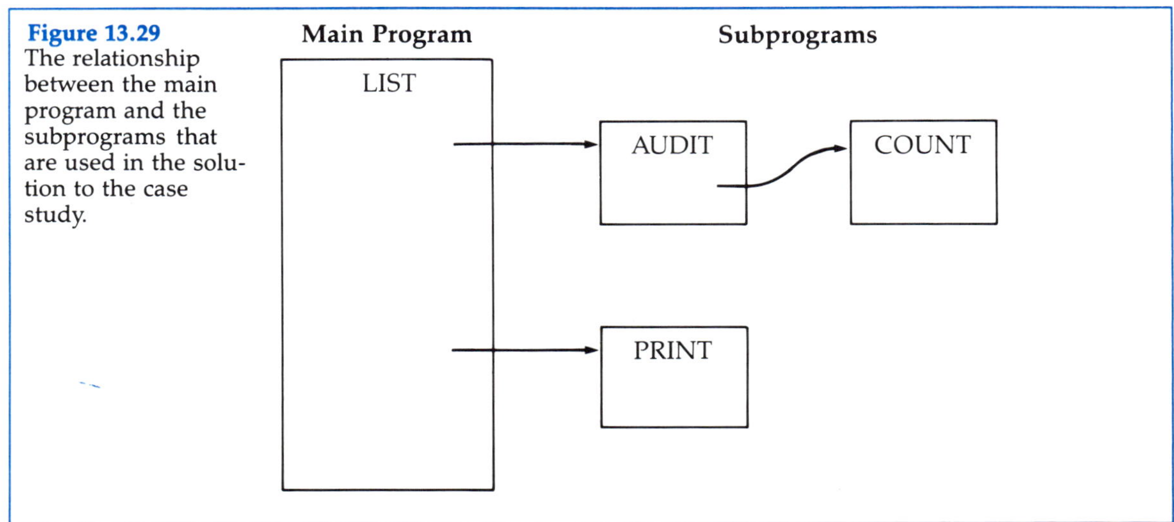


**Figure 13.29** The relationship between the main program and the subprograms that are used in the solution to the case study.

**Figure 13.30**
A pseudocode overview of the logic that is used in the case study.

**The main program LIST:**

WHILE there is data DO
    Read input record of student data
    Clear output buffer
    Call AUDIT to create line of output and update course tallies
    Print line of output for this student
END WHILE
Call PRINT to print course codes and tallies

**The subprogram AUDIT:**

Move last name, first name, and id to output buffer
REPEAT
    Move next course code to output buffer
    Call COUNT to update list of course codes and tallies
UNTIL all course codes are processed
END REPEAT

**The subprogram COUNT:**

IF course code is not in TABLE
    THEN increment N and add code to TABLE
END IF
Increment appropriate counter in TALLY

**The subprogram PRINT:**

REPEAT
    Move course code and tally to an output buffer
    Print a line of output
UNTIL all course codes in TABLE are processed
END REPEAT

instruction in Statement 308 declares Register 11 as a base register to make the fields of the output buffer addressable by using the symbols that are defined in the previously mentioned dummy section (Statements 363 through 371). Notice the references to those symbols in Statements 309, 326, 332, and 334.

AUDIT then calls the subprogram COUNT, passing it the course code and the arguments TABLE, TALLY, and N that the main program passed to AUDIT. AUDIT constructs a new argument list in Statements 339 and 340; the first address in the argument list is in Register 5 (the address of the course code), and the addresses of the remaining arguments are in Registers 7, 8, and 9. It is not always necessary to construct a new argument list. In AUDIT, if you wanted to pass the same arguments to COUNT as were passed to AUDIT by the main program, you would only ensure that Register 1 contained the same address that was passed to AUDIT.

*(Text continues on page 13.46)*

```
       PROGRAM TO LIST AND TALLY COURSE SELECTIONS

  LOC  OBJECT CODE    ADDR1 ADDR2  STMT   SOURCE STATEMENT

000000                               2 LIST     START
                                     3 ***********************************************************************
                                     4 ** LIST AND TALLY COURSE SELECTIONS
                                     5 ** INPUT:  ONE 80-BYTE RECORD PER STUDENT:
                                     6 **           BEGINNING IN COLUMN 1, NO SPACES:
                                     7 **             LAST NAME, FIRST NAME
                                     8 **             SLASH
                                     9 **             STUDENT ID NUMBER
                                    10 **             SLASH
                                    11 **             UP TO FIVE 6-CHARACTER COURSE CODES SEPARATED BY COMMAS
                                    12 **             SLASH
                                    13 **          E.G. DOE,JANE/123456789/CSC311,ART120,MTH244,ENG300,SOC202/
                                    14 **            DATA IS ASSUMED ERROR-FREE.  UP TO 100 DIFFERENT COURSES
                                    15 **            CAN BE ACCOMMODATED.
                                    16 ** OUTPUT: LISTING OF COURSE REQUESTS BY STUDENT NAME AND TOTAL NUMBER
                                    17 **            OF REQUESTS PER COURSE.
                                    18 ** SUBPROGRAMS: AUDIT, WHICH CALLS COUNT, AND PRINT.
                                    19 ***********************************************************************
                                    20          PRINT NOGEN            SUPPRESS MACRO EXPANSIONS
                                    21 ** REGISTER DEFINITIONS:
                             00001  22 R1       EQU   1                ARGUMENT LIST POINTER
                             00002  23 R2       EQU   2                WORK REGISTER   EVEN/
                             00003  24 R3       EQU   3                INDEX REGISTER        ODD PAIR
                             00004  25 R4       EQU   4                LOOP COUNTER; WORK REGISTER
                             00005  26 R5       EQU   5                INPUT RECORD POINTER
                             00006  27 R6       EQU   6                OUTPUT RECORD POINTER
                             00007  28 R7       EQU   7                COURSE TABLE POINTER
                             00008  29 R8       EQU   8                COURSE TALLY POINTER
                             00009  30 R9       EQU   9                POINTER TO NO. OF COURSE CODES
                             0000A  31 R10      EQU   10               POINTER TO PRINTER DCB
                             0000B  32 R11      EQU   11               OUTPUT RECORD POINTER
                             0000C  33 R12      EQU   12               BASE REGISTER
                             0000D  34 R13      EQU   13               SAVE AREA POINTER
                             0000E  35 R14      EQU   14               RETURN REGISTER
                             0000F  36 R15      EQU   15               ENTRY POINT REGISTER
                                    37 ** STANDARD ENTRY AND INITIALIZATION:
                                    38 *  OS:
000000 90EC D00C       0000C        39          STM   R14,R12,12(R13) SAVE REGISTERS
000004 05C0                         40          BALR  R12,0            LOAD BASE REGISTER
                             00006  41          USING BASE1,R12        DECLARE BASE ADDRESS AND REGISTER
000006 50D0 C0D2       000D8        42 BASE1    ST    R13,SAVEAREA+4   SAVE R13
00000A 4120 C0CE       000D4        43          LA    R2,SAVEAREA      GET ADDRESS OF NEW SAVE AREA
00000E 502D 0008       00008        44          ST    R2,8(R13)        STORE THIS ADDRESS IN PREVIOUS SAVE AREA
000012 18D2                         45          LR    R13,R2           R13 = ADDRESS OF NEW SAVE AREA
                                    46          OPEN  (READER,INPUT,PRINTER,OUTPUT)  PREPARE FOR I/O
                                    54 ** DOS*******
                                    55 *        BALR  R12,0            LOAD BASE REGISTER
                                    56 *        USING BASE1,R12        DECLARE BASE REGISTER
                                    57 *BASE1   LA    R13,SAVEAREA     R13 = ADDRESS OF NEW SAVE AREA
                                    58 *        OPEN  READER,PRINTER   PREPARE FOR I/O
                                    59 ******
                                    60 ** PRINT HEADINGS:
                                    61          PUT   PRINTER,HEAD1    REPORT HEADING
                                    66          PUT   PRINTER,HEAD2    COLUMN HEADINGS
                                    71          PUT   PRINTER,ULINE    UNDERLINE HEADINGS
                                    76 *
                                    77 * WHILE THERE IS DATA:
                                    78 READ     GET   READER,IN        READ STUDENT RECORD
00005A 9240 C168       0016E        83          MVI   OUT,C' '         CLEAR OUTPUT BUFFER
00005E D24E C169 C168 0016F 0016E   84          MVC   OUT+1(OPLEN-1),OUT
```

*(Continues)*

**Figure 13.31** The program for the case study.

```
                                      85 ** FILL OUTPUT BUFFER, COUNT COURSE REQUESTS FOR THIS STUDENT:
                                      86 **    CALL AUDIT,(IN,OUT,TAB,TAL,NUM)
000064 4110 C0B2        000B8         87          LA    R1,=A(IN,OUT,TAB,TAL,NUM)  R1 = ADDR. OF ARGUMENT LIST
000068 58F0 C0C6        000CC         88          L     R15,=V(AUDIT)    R15 = ENTRY POINT
00006C 05EF                           89          BALR  R14,R15          CALL AUDIT
                                      90          PUT   PRINTER,OUT      PRINT STUDENT NAME AND REQUESTS
00007C 47F0 C046        0004C         95          B     READ             CONSIDER NEXT INPUT RECORD
                                      96 * END WHILE
                                      97 ** END-OF-DATA; PRINT TALLIES FOR EACH COURSE SELECTED:
                                      98 **    CALL PRINT,(TAB,TAL,NUM,PRINTER)
000080 4110 C0A2        000A8         99 ENDDATA LA    R1,=A(TAB,TAL,NUM,PRINTER)  R1=ADDRESS OF ARGUMENT LIST
000084 58F0 C0CA        000D0        100          L     R15,=V(PRINT)    R15 = ENTRY POINT
000088 05EF                          101          BALR  R14,R15          CALL PRINT
                                     102 ** EXIT:
                                     103 *  OS:
                                     104          CLOSE (READER,,PRINTER)  I/O IS COMPLETE
00009A 58D0 C0D2        000D8        112          L     R13,SAVEAREA+4   RESTORE R13
00009E 98EC D00C        0000C        113          LM    R14,R12,12(R13)  RESTORE REMAINING REGISTERS
0000A2 07FE                          114          BR    R14              EXIT TO OS
                                     115 ** DOS*******
                                     116 *        CLOSE READER,PRINTER   I/O IS COMPLETE
                                     117 *        EOJ                    EXIT TO DOS
                                     118 ******
0000A8                               119          LTORG
0000A8 000001F30000044C              120                =A(TAB,TAL,NUM,PRINTER)
0000B8 0000011C0000016E              121                =A(IN,OUT,TAB,TAL,NUM)
0000CC 00000000                      122                =V(AUDIT)
0000D0 00000000                      123                =V(PRINT)
                                     124          DROP  R12
                                     125 *
0000D4 0000000000000000              126 SAVEAREA DC    18F'0'           MAIN SAVE AREA (9D IN DOS)
00011C                               127 IN       DS    CL80             INPUT RECORD
00016C 4040                          128          DC    2C' '            FORCED BLANKS TO END LOOP IN CASE
                                     129 *                                  COURSE CODE ENDS IN 80TH BYTE
                                     130 *                                  OF INPUT RECORD
00016E                               131 OUT      DS    0CL133           OUTPUT BUFFER FOR STUDENT DATA:
00016E 40                            132          DC    C' '               CARRIAGE CONTROL
00016F                               133          DS    CL20               LAST NAME
000183                               134          DS    X                  SPACE
000184                               135          DS    CL10               FIRST NAME
00018E                               136          DS    X                  SPACE
00018F                               137          DS    CL9                STUDENT ID NUMBER
000198                               138          DS    3X                 SPACES
00019B                               139          DS    5CL7               5 COURSE CODES SEPARATED BY BLANKS
                        00050        140 OPLEN    EQU   *-OUT              TOTAL LENGTH OF ABOVE FIELDS
0001BE 4040404040404040              141          DC    (133-OPLEN)C' '    PAD WITH BLANKS TO 133 BYTES
                                     142 *
0001F3                               143 TAB      DS    100CL6           TABLE OF UNIQUE COURSE CODES SELECTED
00044B 00
00044C 0000000000000000              144 TAL      DC    100F'0'          CORRESPONDING COUNTS OF COURSE CODES;
                                     145 *                                 INITIALLY ZERO.
0005DC 00                            146 NUM      DC    X'0'             NUMBER OF DISTINCT COURSE CODES;
                                     147 *                                 INITIALLY ZERO.
0005DD F0C3D6E4D9E2C540              148 HEAD1    DC    CL133'0COURSE SELECTION AUDIT'  REPORT HEADING
000662                               149 HEAD2    DS    0CL133           COLUMN HEADINGS AS FOLLOWS:
000662 40D3C1E2E340D5C1              150          DC    C' LAST NAME'
00066C 4040404040404040              151          DC    CL12' '
000678 C6C9D9E2E340D5C1              152          DC    C'FIRST NAME'
000682 40                            153          DC    C' '
000683 E2E3E4C4C5D5E340              154          DC    C'STUDENT ID'
00068D 4040                          155          DC    CL2' '
00068F C3D6E4D9E2C540E2              156          DC    C'COURSE SELECTIONS'
                        0003E        157 HDLEN    EQU   *-HEAD2          LENGTH OF COLUMN HEADINGS
0006A0 4040404040404040              158          DC    (133-HDLEN)C' '  PAD WITH BLANKS TO 133 BYTES
0006E7                               159 ULINE    DS    0CL133           UNDERLINE FOR HEADING
0006E7 40                            160          DC    C' '               CARRIAGE CONTROL
0006E8 6060606060606060              161          DC    (OPLEN-1)C'-'      DASHES TO UNDERLINE HEADING
000737 4040404040404040              162          DC    (133-OPLEN)C' '    PAD WITH BLANKS TO 133 BYTES
                                     163 *
```

*(Continues)*

**Figure 13.31** *(Continued)*

```
                                          164 ** DCB'S FOR I/O IN OS:
                                          165 READER    DCB    DSORG=PS,MACRF=GM,DDNAME=SYSIN,RECFM=F,LRECL=80,          X
                                                               BLKSIZE=80,EODAD=ENDDATA
                                          219 PRINTER   DCB    DSORG=PS,MACRF=PM,DDNAME=SYSPRINT,RECFM=FA,               X
                                                               LRECL=133,BLKSIZE=133
                                          273 ** DOS*******
                                          274 *READER   DTFCD  DEVADDR=SYSIPT,DEVICE=2540,IOAREA1=INBUF,WORKA=YES,       X
                                                               EOFADDR=ENDDATA,RECFORM=FIXUNB,BLKSIZE=80,TYPEFLE=INPUT
                                          275 *PRINTER  DTFPR  DEVADDR=SYSLST,DEVICE=3203,IOAREA1=OUTBUF,WORKA=YES,      X
                                                               RECFORM=FIXUNB,BLKSIZE=133,CTLCHAR=ASA
                                          276 *INBUF    DS     80C               DOS INPUT BUFFER
                                          277 *OUTBUF   DS     133C              DOS OUTPUT BUFFER
                                          278 ******
                                          279 ***********************************************************************
                                          280 ** AUDIT    SUBPROGRAM TO CREATE OUTPUT BUFFER FOR EACH STUDENT AND TO
                                          281 **             TALLY COURSE REQUESTS.
                                          282 ** INPUT:   INPUT (STUDENT RECORD), OUTPUT (OUTPUT BUFFER), TABLE
                                          283 **            (ARRAY OF UNIQUE COURSE CODES REQUESTED SO FAR), TALLY
                                          284 **            (CORRESPONDING TALLIES OF COURSE CODES), N (NUMBER OF
                                          285 **            CODES IN TABLE)
                                          286 ** OUTPUT: RETURNS OUTPUT BUFFER READY FOR PRINTING, ADDS NEW COURSE
                                          287 **            CODES TO TABLE, UPDATES N, UPDATES TALLY TO REFLECT COURSE
                                          288 **            SELECTIONS.
                                          289 ** SUBPROGRAM: COUNT
                                          290 ***********************************************************************
000830                                    291 AUDIT    CSECT
                                          292 ** MASK:
                                   00002  293 PUNC     EQU    B'0010'          CC = 2 IF SELECTED BYTE BEGINS WITH 0.
                                          294 *                                  DISTINGUISHES LETTERS FROM / OR ,
                                          295 ** INITIALIZATION:
000830 90EC D00C          0000C           296          STM    R14,R12,12(R13)  SAVE REGISTERS
000834 05C0                               297          BALR   R12,0            LOAD BASE REGISTER
                                   00836  298          USING  BASE2,R12        DECLARE BASE ADDRESS AND REGISTER
000836 50D0 C092          008C8           299 BASE2    ST     R13,AUDSAVE+4    SAVE R13 IN THIS SUBPROGRAM'S SAVE AREA
00083A 4120 C08E          008C4           300          LA     R2,AUDSAVE       GET ADDRESS OF THIS SAVE AREA
00083E 502D 0008          00008           301          ST     R2,8(R13)        STORE IN CALLING PROGRAM'S SAVE AREA
000842 18D2                               302          LR     R13,R2           R13=ADDR OF THIS SUBPROGRAM'S SAVE AREA
                                   00000  303          USING  ARGLIST,R1       ESTABLISH ADDRESSABILITY OF ARG. LIST
000844 9859 1000          00000           304          LM     R5,R9,ARGLIST    GET ADDRESSES OF ARGUMENTS
                                          305          DROP   R1               DELETE R1 FROM BASE REGISTER POOL
                                          306 *** REMINDER: R5 = INPUT POINTER, R6 = OUTPUT POINTER
000848 18B6                               307          LR     R11,R6           LOAD BASE REGISTER FOR OUTPUT
                                   00000  308          USING  OUTPUT,R11       ESTAB. ADDRESSABILITY OF OUTPUT BUFFER
00084A 4160 B001          00001           309          LA     R6,LASTNAME      POINT TO LAST NAME IN OUTPUT BUFFER
                                          310 ** MOVE LAST NAME THEN FIRST NAME TO OUTPUT BUFFER:
                                          311 * REPEAT:
                                          312 * - WHILE INPUT CHARACTER IS A LETTER (NOT "/" OR ",")
00084E BF21 5000          00000           313 LOOP     ICM    R2,B'0001',0(R5) GET NEXT INPUT CHARACTER; SET CC
000852 4720 C030          00866           314          BC     PUNC,COMSLASH    EXIT LOOP IF COMMA OR SLASH:
                                          315 *                                  (CC=2; EBCDIC CODE BEGINS WITH 0)
000856 4226 0000          00000           316          STC    R2,0(R6)         STORE LETTER IN OUTPUT LINE
00085A 4155 0001          00001           317          LA     R5,1(R5)         INCREMENT INPUT POINTER
00085E 4166 0001          00001           318          LA     R6,1(R6)         INCREMENT OUTPUT POINTER
000862 47F0 C018          0084E           319          B      LOOP             CONTINUE PROCESSING CHARACTERS
                                          320 * - END WHILE
                                          321 *
                                          322 * COMMA OR SLASH DETECTED:
000866 956B 5000          00000           323 COMSLASH CLI    0(R5),C','       COMMA IN INPUT RECORD?
00086A 4770 C044          0087A           324          BNE    SLASH            IF NOT, MUST BE SLASH
                                          325 * PREPARE TO PROCESS FIRST NAME
00086E 4160 B016          00016           326          LA     R6,FIRST         R6 = FIRST NAME ADDRESS IN OUTPUT
000872 4155 0001          00001           327          LA     R5,1(R5)         INCREMENT INPUT POINTER
000876 47F0 C018          0084E           328          B      LOOP             REPEAT
                                          329 * UNTIL SLASH ENCOUNTERED
                                          330 * END REPEAT
                                          331 ** MOVE STUDENT ID TO OUTPUT BUFFER (R5 POINTS TO PRECEDING "/"):
00087A D208 B021 5001 00021 00001         332 SLASH    MVC    ID(9),1(R5)      ID NUMBER FOLLOWS "/"; COPY TO OUTPUT
000880 4155 000B          0000B           333          LA     R5,11(R5)        ADVANCE TO FIRST COURSE CODE
```

*(Continues)*

**Figure 13.31** *(Continued)*

```
000884 4160 B02D        0002D                  LA    R6,COURSES       R6 = COURSE CODE ADDRESS IN OUTPUT
                                      ** PROCESS COURSE CODES:
                                      * REPEAT (FOR ALL COURSE CODES):
000888 D205 6000 5000 00000 00000     MORE     MVC   0(6,R6),0(R5)    COPY NEXT COURSE CODE TO OUTPUT
                                      * CALL COUNT,(CRSCOD,TABLE,TALLY,N) COUNT COURSE CODE:
00088E 5050 C0D6        0090C                  ST    R5,COUNTARG      STORE COURSE CODE ADDR. IN ARGUMENT LIST
000892 9079 C0DA        00910                  STM   R7,R9,COUNTARG+4  COMPLETE ARGUMENT LIST WITH ADDRESSES
                                      *                                   OF TABLE, TALLY, AND N
000896 4110 C0D6        0090C                  LA    R1,COUNTARG      R1 = ADDRESS OF ARGUMENT LIST
00089A 58F0 C08A        008C0                  L     R15,=V(COUNT)    R15 = ENTRY POINT
00089E 05EF                                    BALR  R14,R15          CALL COUNT
0008A0 4155 0007        00007                  LA    R5,7(R5)         POINT TO NEXT COURSE CODE IN INPUT
0008A4 4166 0007        00007                  LA    R6,7(R6)         POINT TO NEXT COURSE CODE IN OUTPUT
                                      * UNTIL BLANK ENCOUNTERED
0008A8 9540 5000        00000                  CLI   0(R5),C' '       ENDING BLANK?
0008AC 4770 C052        00888                  BNE   MORE             IF NOT, REPEAT
                                      * END REPEAT
0008B0 58D0 C092        008C8                  L     R13,AUDSAVE+4    RESTORE R13
0008B4 98EC D00C        0000C                  LM    R14,R12,12(R13)  RESTORE REMAINING REGISTERS
0008B8 07FE                                    BR    R14              RETURN TO CALLING PROGRAM
0008C0                                         LTORG
0008C0 00000000                                      =V(COUNT)
                                               DROP  R11,R12
0008C4 0000000000000000               AUDSAVE  DC    18F'0'           THIS SUBPROGRAM'S SAVE AREA (9D IN DOS)
00090C                                COUNTARG DS    4F               ARGUMENT LIST FOR COUNT
                                      *------------------------------------------------------------
                                      ** DESCRIPTIONS OF DATA AREAS FOR AUDIT SUBPROGRAM:
000000                                ARGLIST  DSECT ,                ARGUMENT LIST
000000                                         DS    5A               ADDRESSES OF 5 ARGUMENTS
000000                                OUTPUT   DSECT ,                OUTPUT BUFFER FOR STUDENT DATA:
000000                                         DS    C                  CARRIAGE CONTROL
000001                                LASTNAME DS    CL20               LAST NAME
000015                                         DS    X                  SPACE
000016                                FIRST    DS    CL10               FIRST NAME
000020                                         DS    X                  SPACE
000021                                ID       DS    CL9                STUDENT ID NUMBER
00002A                                         DS    3X                 SPACES
00002D                                COURSES  DS    5CL7               5 COURSE CODES SEPARATED BY BLANKS
                                      *
                                      ***********************************************************************
                                      ** COUNT   SUBPROGRAM TO COUNT REQUESTS FOR EACH COURSE
                                      ** INPUT:  COURSE CODE, TABLE, TALLY, N
                                      ** OUTPUT: ADDS NEW COURSE CODES ENCOUNTERED TO TABLE, UPDATES N, AND
                                      **            UPDATES TALLY FOR EACH COURSE.
                                      ***********************************************************************
000920                                COUNT    CSECT
                                      ** INITIALIZATION:
000920 90EC D00C        0000C                  STM   R14,R12,12(R13)  SAVE REGISTERS
000924 05C0                                    BALR  R12,0            LOAD BASE REGISTER
                              00926            USING BASE3,R12        DECLARE BASE ADDRESS AND REGISTER
                              00000            USING ARGLIST,R1       ESTABLISH ADDRESSABILITY OF ARG. LIST
000926 9869 1000        00000         BASE3    LM    R6,R9,ARGLIST    GET ADDRESSES OF ARGUMENTS
                                               DROP  R1               DELETE R1 FROM BASE REGISTER POOL
                              00000            USING CRSCOD,R6        ESTABLISH ADDRESSABILITY OF COURSE CODE
                              00000            USING TALLY,R8         ESTABLISH ADDRESSABILITY OF TALLY
                              00000            USING N,R9             ESTABLISH ADDRESSABILITY OF N
00092A 1827                                    LR    R2,R7            SAVE ADDRESS OF BEGINNING OF TABLE
                                      * IF COURSE CODE IS NOT IN TABLE:
00092C 1B44                                    SR    R4,R4            CLEAR R4 PRIOR TO INSERTING BYTE AT N
00092E BF41 9000        00000                  ICM   R4,B'0001',N     R4 = NUMBER OF COURSE CODES IN TABLE
000932 4780 C026        0094C                  BZ    CNULL            TABLE IS EMPTY FIRST TIME
                                      * - REPEAT N TIMES OR UNTIL CODE FOUND IN TABLE:
000936 D505 6000 7000 00000 00000     CSEARCH  CLC   CRSCOD(6),0(R7)  GIVEN COURSE CODE VS. TABLE ENTRY
00093C 4780 C034        0095A                  BE    CMATCH           EXIT LOOP IF CODE FOUND IN TABLE
000940 4177 0006        00006                  LA    R7,6(R7)         ELSE INCREMENT POINTER
000944 4640 C010        00936                  BCT   R4,CSEARCH       DECREMENT COUNTER; REPEAT IF NOT ZERO
                                      * - END REPEAT
                                      * THEN INCREMENT N AND ADD CODE TO TABLE:
```

(*Continues*)

**Figure 13.31** (*Continued*)

```
000948 4340 9000          00000        402           IC     R4,N               GET N (NO. OF TABLE ENTRIES)
00094C 4144 0001          00001        403 CNULL     LA     R4,1(R4)           R4 = N + 1
000950 4240 9000          00000        404           STC    R4,N               N = N + 1
000954 D205 7000 6000 00000 00000      405           MVC    0(6,R7),CRSCOD     INSERT COURSE CODE IN TABLE
                                       406 * END IF
                                       407 *
                                       408 ** INCREMENT TALLY (MUST SUBTRACT A(TABLE) IN R2 FROM R7, DIVIDE RESULT
                                       409 ** BY 6, AND MULTIPLY BY 4 TO GET CORRESPONDING INDEX TO TALLY ARRAY):
00095A 1B72                            410 CMATCH    SR     R7,R2              R7 = INDEX TO COURSE CODE TABLE
                                       411 *                                      = 0, 6, 12, ...
00095C 1827                            412           LR     R2,R7              COPY R7 TO EVEN REG. OF EVEN/ODD PAIR
00095E 8E20 0020          00020        413           SRDA   R2,32              PREPARE FOR DIVISION
000962 5D20 C05A          00980        414           D      R2,=F'6'           R3 = 0, 1, 2, ...
000966 8B30 0002          00002        415           SLA    R3,2               R3 = 0, 4, 8, ...
00096A 5843 8000          00000        416           L      R4,TALLY(R3)       R4 = # OF REQUESTS FOR COURSE SO FAR
00096E 5A40 C05E          00984        417           A      R4,=F'1'           INCREMENT TALLY (# OF REQUESTS)
000972 5043 8000          00000        418           ST     R4,TALLY(R3)       STORE UPDATED TALLY
000976 98EC D00C          0000C        419           LM     R14,R12,12(R13)    RESTORE REGISTERS
00097A 07FE                            420           BR     R14                RETURN TO CALLING PROGRAM
000980                                 421           LTORG
000980 00000006                        422                  =F'6'
000984 00000001                        423                  =F'1'
                                       424           DROP   R6,R8,R9,R12
                                       425 *-----------------------------------------------------------
                                       426 ** DESCRIPTIONS OF ARGUMENTS FOR COUNT SUBPROGRAM:
000000                                 427 CRSCOD    DSECT
000000                                 428           DS     CL6                COURSE CODE
000000                                 429 TABLE     DSECT
000000                                 430           DS     100CL6             TABLE OF UNIQUE COURSE CODES SELECTED
000000                                 431 TALLY     DSECT
000000                                 432           DS     100F               CORRESPONDING COUNTS OF COURSE CODES
000000                                 433 N         DSECT
000000                                 434           DS     X                  NUMBER OF DISTINCT COURSE CODES
                                       435 *
                                       436 *******************************************************************=******
                                       437 ** PRINT   SUBPROGRAM TO PRINT TALLIES FOR EACH COURSE
                                       438 ** INPUT:  TABLE, TALLY, N, DCB FOR PRINTER
                                       439 ** OUTPUT: PRINTS CHART OF COURSE CODES AND NO. OF REQUESTS PER COURSE
                                       440 **************************************************************************
000988                                 441 PRINT     CSECT
                                       442 ** INITIALIZATION:
000988 90EC D00C          0000C        443           STM    R14,R12,12(R13)    SAVE REGISTERS
00098C 05C0                            444           BALR   R12,0              LOAD BASE REGISTER
                                0098E  445           USING  BASE4,R12          DECLARE BASE ADDRESS AND REGISTER
00098E 50D0 C186          00B14        446 BASE4     ST     R13,PRTSAVE+4      SAVE R13 IN THIS SUBPROGRAM'S SAVE AREA
000992 4120 C182          00B10        447           LA     R2,PRTSAVE         GET ADDRESS OF NEW SAVE AREA
000996 502D 0008          00008        448           ST     R2,8(R13)          STORE IN CALLING PROGRAM'S SAVE AREA
00099A 18D2                            449           LR     R13,R2             R13 = ADDR. OF THIS PROGRAM'S SAVE AREA
                                00000  450           USING  ARGLIST,R1         ESTABLISH ADDRESSABILITY OF ARG. LIST
00099C 987A 1000          00000        451           LM     R7,R10,ARGLIST     GET ADDRESSES OF ARGUMENTS
                                       452           DROP   R1                 DELETE R1 FROM BASE REGISTER POOL
                                00000  453           USING  TABLE,R7           ESTABLISH ADDRESSABILITY OF TABLE
                                00000  454           USING  TALLY,R8           ESTABLISH ADDRESSABILITY OF TALLY
                                00000  455           USING  N,R9               ESTABLISH ADDRESSABILITY OF N
                                00000  456           USING  PRT,R10            ESTABLISH ADDRESSABILITY OF PRINTER DCB
                                       457           PUT    PRT,HEAD3          PRINT TALLY HEADING
0009AE 1B44                            462           SR     R4,R4              CLEAR R4 PRIOR TO INSERTING BYTE AT N
0009B0 4340 9000          00000        463           IC     R4,N               R4 = N = NO. OF DISTINCT COURSES
0009B4 1B33                            464           SR     R3,R3              R3 = TALLY INDEX
                                       465 * REPEAT:
0009B6 D205 C06B 7000 009F9 00000      466 TLOOP     MVC    CODE(6),TABLE      MOVE NEXT COURSE CODE FROM TABLE TO
                                       467 *                                     TEMPORARY ARRAY CALLED LINE
0009BC 5823 8000          00000        468           L      R2,TALLY(R3)       GET NO. OF REQUESTS FOR THIS COURSE
0009C0 4E20 C0F2          00A80        469           CVD    R2,TEMP            CONVERT
0009C4 960F C0F9          00A87        470           OI     TEMP+7,X'0F'         TO EBCDIC AND
0009C8 F397 C074 C0F2 00A02 00A80      471           UNPK   TOTAL(10),TEMP(8)    STORE IN LINE
                                       472           PUT    PRT,LINE           PRINT COURSE CODE AND NO. OF REQUESTS
0009DC 4133 0004          00004        477           LA     R3,4(R3)           INCREMENT TALLY INDEX
0009E0 4177 0006          00006        478           LA     R7,6(R7)           INCREMENT TABLE POINTER
```

*(Continues)*

**Figure 13.31** *(Continued)*

```
                                     479 * UNTIL ALL COURSE CODES ARE PROCESSED
0009E4 4640 C028      009B6          480          BCT   R4,TLOOP          DECREMENT COUNTER; REPEAT IF NOT ZERO
                                     481 * END REPEAT
0009E8 58D0 C186      00B14          482          L     R13,PRTSAVE+4     RESTORE R13
0009EC 98EC D00C      0000C          483          LM    R14,R12,12(R13)   RESTORE REMAINING REGISTERS
0009F0 07FE                          484          BR    R14               RETURN TO CALLING PROGRAM
0009F8                               485          LTORG
                                     486          DROP  R7,R8,R9,R10,R12
                                     487 *
0009F8                               488 LINE     DS    0CL133            OUTPUT BUFFER FOR TALLY LINE:
0009F8 40                            489          DC    C' '                CARRIAGE CONTROL
0009F9                               490 CODE     DS    CL6                 COURSE CODE
0009FF 407E40                        491          DC    C' = '
000A02                               492 TOTAL    DS    CL10                NUMBER OF REQUESTS
                            00014    493 LLEN     EQU   *-LINE              TOTAL LENGTH OF ABOVE FIELDS
000A0C 4040404040404040              494          DC    (133-LLEN)C' '      PAD WITH BLANKS TO 133 BYTES
000A80                               495 TEMP     DS    D                 WORK AREA FOR EBCDIC CONVERSIONS
                                     496 *
000A88 F0E3D6E3C1D340D5              497 HEAD3    DC    CL133'0TOTAL NUMBER OF REQUESTS BY COURSE:'
000B0D 000000
000B10 0000000000000000              498 PRTSAVE  DC    18F'0'            THIS SUBPROGRAM'S SAVE AREA (9D IN DOS)
                                     499 *-------------------------------------------------------------
                                     500 ** DESCRIPTIONS OF ARGUMENTS FOR PRINT SUBPROGRAM:
                                     501 * TABLE, TALLY, AND N ARE AS FOR COUNT (DEFINED ABOVE)
000000                               502 PRT      DSECT                   PRINTER DCB
000000                               503          END   LIST
```

```
COURSE SELECTION AUDIT
LAST NAME                 FIRST NAME STUDENT ID  COURSE SELECTIONS
------------------------------------------------------------------------------
DOE                       JANE       123456789   CSC311 ART120 MTH244 ENG300 SOC202
BROWN                     JACK       987654321   ART120 CSC311 ECN125
GREEN                     MARK       555555555   ECN125 ART208 MTH244 CSC311

TOTAL NUMBER OF REQUESTS BY COURSE:
CSC311 = 0000000003
ART120 = 0000000002
MTH244 = 0000000002
ENG300 = 0000000001
SOC202 = 0000000001
ECN125 = 0000000002
ART208 = 0000000001
```

Output from program

**Figure 13.31** *(Continued)*

The dummy sections in Statements 427 through 434 describe COUNT's arguments. Statement 385 loads Registers 6 through 9 with the addresses of the arguments. Notice that ARGLIST, which was defined by a previous dummy section, is used here to represent this subprogram's argument list also. Statements 387 through 389 permit symbolic references of three of the arguments within the instructions of COUNT. These symbolic references occur in Statements 393, 396, 402, 404, 405, 416, and 418. Notice that, although TABLE is not referenced symbolically within COUNT, TABLE is referenced symbolically within the subprogram PRINT and, therefore, is defined in a dummy section.

Both the main program and the subprogram PRINT perform I/O. Here, the main program defines the DCBs (or, in DOS, the DTF tables) that it requires, and makes the one at PRINTER available to the subprogram by passing PRINTER as an argument. Statements 450 through 456 make addressable the four arguments, which the main program passes in Statement 99 to the subprogram PRINT. Statements 450 through 456 use the symbols ARGLIST, TABLE, TALLY, and N, all of which previous dummy sections define, and the symbol PRT, which the DSECT in Statement 502 defines. References to these symbols occur within the subprogram in Statements 451, 457, 463, 466, 468, and 472.

Notice the DROP instruction in Statement 452, which deletes Register 1 from the assembler's pool of available base registers. This instruction is necessary because the subsequent PUT instruction in Statement 457 alters the contents of Register 1. Although not required in the subprograms AUDIT and COUNT, similar DROP instructions occur in Statements 305 and 386 as precautions. Finally, notice the LTORG and DROP instructions at the end of each control section (Statements 119, 124, 354, 356, 421, 424, 485, and 486).

## Debugging Hints

1. The major source of error in writing subprograms is establishing addressability of the arguments, the instructions, the literals, and the data areas. Base register issues that were raised in Chapter 12 are relevant here and you should review them if necessary.

   Confusion between the address and value of an argument is a common difficulty. A correctly used dummy section will help, but errors introduced in doing so will complicate debugging. In such cases, you may find it useful to examine the object code to see if there is a discrepancy between your intention and the actual instructions. You can use intermediate dumps to verify the linkage to the arguments before you perform any computations.
2. Define save areas with DCs instead of DSs so that you can initialize them to zeros or some other distinctive constant. If you must examine a save area in a dump at a later time, then any unchanged portions of the save area will be obvious.

## Stylistic Notes

1. Modular and top-down design strategies give rise to subprograms. You should use these strategies when writing assembler language programs.
2. Every subprogram should begin with a prologue that describes its arguments and calling sequence, as well as its purpose and the algorithm used.
3. Write the control sections in a source module so that the main program, if any, is first. Write the subprograms in order so that each calls only those subprograms that appear somewhere after it.
4. Use common sections and external data areas to categorize data. When a common section is defined in more than one source module, use the same symbols in each definition.
5. Initiate the first control section of a source module with the START directive. Try to avoid interrupting the definition of control sections; if you decide to interrupt the definition, do so only to define relevant data areas.

6. When you must perform a short computation at various points in a control section, you may find it advantageous to isolate the computation as an internal subprogram, and then branch to it each time that you need it. You write internal subprograms as part of a control section, instead of as a separate control section. Since it is unnecessary to follow linkage conventions, you can avoid the situations where the subprogram linkage exceeds the length and complexity of the computation itself. You usually do not have to save the registers in a save area; since you can use the BAL instruction instead of the BALR instruction to call the subprogram, you do not have to worry about Register 15. However, do not think that you can ignore all linkage conventions. For example, it is generally a good idea to use Register 14 for the return address.

   An internal subprogram has direct access to all storage that is defined in the control section, so it is often unnecessary to use a formal argument list. Instead, you can pass the value of an argument in a register or a storage location. This is a simple implementation of call by value. When using linkage of your own design, you must document it clearly in the comments statements of the subprogram. If there are several arguments, it can be a good idea to use argument list conventions. This is particularly true for a lengthy or complex subprogram because you may find later that you should have written it as an external subprogram, instead of as an internal subprogram. Conversion from one form to another is easier if you have followed convention. If you reserve internal subprograms for short, simple computations, the need to convert to an external form is less likely to occur.

## Summary

1. The save area is an 18-fullword array that you define within the calling program. Load the address of the save area into Register 13. Within the subprogram, save the contents of all registers except Register 13 in the save area that you defined in the calling program and passed to the subprogram.
2. If a subprogram calls another subprogram, you must define another save area within the first subprogram, and then store Register 13 into the second fullword of this save area.
3. The argument list is an array of fullwords that contain the addresses of the arguments. Within the calling program, load the address of the argument list into Register 1.
4. Use a V-type address constant within the calling program to define the entry point of the subprogram.
5. Within the calling program, load Register 15 with the entry point of the subprogram, and Register 14 with the return address.
6. Write each external subprogram as a separate control section. Each control section and, therefore, each external subprogram requires its own base register.
7. Use General Register 0 to return binary integer results for function subprograms; use Floating-Point Register 0 to return a floating-point result.
8. You can define a variable-length argument list by setting the leftmost bit of the last fullword in the argument list to 1.
9. The CNOP instruction forces boundary alignment by inserting No-Operation instructions as required. Use CNOP when writing calling sequences with in-line argument lists.
10. You can pass arguments by using a call by address technique or a call by value technique. Call by address means that you pass the addresses of the arguments to the subprogram; call by value means that you pass the actual values of the arguments. By convention, you do not use call by value with external subprograms.
11. Initiate or resume the definition of a control section with the CSECT directive. As an option,

you can initiate the first control section with the START directive.

12. DROP the base registers at the end of each control section to avoid addressing errors that the assembler may not detect at assembly time.
13. Use LTORG at the end of each control section to ensure addressability of its literals.
14. You can use the system macros SAVE, RETURN, and CALL to save and restore registers, and to call subprograms.
15. A subprogram may contain several entry points. The first entry point is represented by the symbol in the name entry of the CSECT (or START) directive. You can define additional entry points with the ENTRY directive. A subprogram with several entry points is called a multiple-entry subprogram.
16. Use dummy sections to describe symbolically data areas that are defined elsewhere. Initiate or resume a dummy section with the DSECT directive. Dummy sections do not reserve storage; in fact, instructions within a dummy section do not produce object code.
17. Use common sections to reserve storage that control sections in different source modules will share. Initiate or resume a common section with the COM directive. Two types of common sections are possible in OS: named and unnamed. Only unnamed common sections are possible in DOS.
18. The source module consists of the assembler language statements that are presented to the assembler. It may contain one or more control sections, common sections, and dummy sections. The result of such an assembly is called the object module. The linker transforms one or more object modules into a single load module, which is loaded into storage for execution.
19. An internal subprogram is written as part of the control section that uses it.

## New Instruction Summary

### New Directives

| Name | Operation | Operand | Instruction Name | Action |
|---|---|---|---|---|
| *symbol* or *blank* | **START** | *blank* or *self-defining term* | DEFINE FIRST CONTROL SECTION | Initiates the first control section that is identified by the symbol, if any, in the name entry. |
| *symbol* or *blank* | **DC** | *d*VL*n*(*symbol*) | DEFINE EXTERNAL ADDRESS CONSTANT | Defines *d* copies of a constant that is equal to the actual address represented by the stated relocatable external symbol. In the absence of an explicit length modifier L*n*, the constant occupies a fullword that is aligned to a fullword integral boundary. If present, an explicit length modifier may specify a length of 3 or 4—in which case, no boundary alignment takes place. |

| Name | Operation | Operand | Instruction Name | Action |
|---|---|---|---|---|
| *symbol* or *blank* | **CNOP** | *byte,group* | CONDITIONAL NO-OPERATION | Generates No-Operation instructions, if necessary, to force alignment to the byte number that is indicated by *byte* within a fullword (*group* = 4) or doubleword (*group* = 8); *byte* and *group* are absolute expressions; only *byte* values 0, 2, 4, and 6 are permitted. (In DOS, the name entry must be *blank*.) |
| *blank* | **ENTRY** | Relocatable symbols separated by commas | IDENTIFY ENTRY SYMBOLS | Declares the symbols listed in the operand entry to be entry symbols. |
| *symbol* or *blank* | **DSECT** | None | DEFINE DUMMY SECTION | Initiates or resumes a dummy section that is identified by the symbol, if any, in the name entry. (In DOS, there must be a symbol in the name entry.) |
| *symbol* or *blank* | **COM** | None | DEFINE COMMON SECTION | Initiates or resumes a common section that is identified by the symbol, if any, in the name entry. (In DOS, the name entry must be *blank*.) |
| *blank* | **EXTRN** | Relocatable symbols separated by commas | IDENTIFY EXTERNAL SYMBOLS | Declares the symbols that are listed in the operand entry to be external symbols. |

## New System Macros

| Operation | Operand | Instruction Name | Action |
|---|---|---|---|
| **SAVE** | (*R1*,*R2*) or (*R1*) | SAVE REGISTERS | Stores the indicated register or registers into their proper positions in the save area, which is defined at the address in Register 13. *R1* and *R2* must be decimal integers. Has the same effect as<br>STM *R1*,*R2*,*D*(13)<br>or ST *R1*,*D*(13)<br>for an appropriate displacement *D*. |

| Operation | Operand | Instruction Name | Action |
|---|---|---|---|
| RETURN | (*R1*,*R2*) or (*R1*) | RESTORE REGISTERS AND RETURN | Restores the indicated registers from the save area that is defined at the address in Register 13 and returns to the calling program. Has the same effect as LM *R1*,*R2*,*D*(13) or L *R1*,*D*(13) followed by BR 14 |
| CALL | *entry*,(*args*)[,VL] or (15),(*args*)[,VL] | CALL A SUBPROGRAM | Calls the subprogram at the entry point that is represented by the symbol *entry* or that is contained in Register 15; *args* is a list of symbols that are separated by commas; each symbol represents a subprogram argument. VL is optional and, if present, implies that the argument list has a variable length: the first bit of the last fullword in the argument list is set to 1. (VL is unavailable under DOS.) |

## Exercises

1. Consider a subprogram SUB1 with single-byte arguments called B1, B2, B3, and B4 that computes B2 AND B3 AND B4 and stores the result in B1. Write the necessary instructions to call SUB1, and then write SUB1 itself.
2. Write a function subprogram SUB2 with single-byte arguments called B1, B2, B3, and B4 that concatenates the four argument bytes to form a 32-bit quantity in Register 0.
3. Write a subprogram SUB3 with single-byte arguments called B1, B2, B3, and B4 that calls another subprogram SUB4 with two arguments that equal B1 AND B2 and B3 OR B4. Do not be concerned with the purpose of SUB3 or SUB4.
4. Consider a subprogram that is called with the arguments W, X, Y, and Z in this order. Write instructions within the subprogram to call another subprogram and pass to it X and Z as arguments.
5. Write instructions in a main program to pass an array to a subprogram. Write the instructions within the subprogram to pass the same array to another subprogram.
6. Consider a main program that defines a table that contains data about 100 students. The following dummy section describes the entry for each student in the table:

```
STUDENT  DSECT
NAME     DS     CL20
ID       DS     CL9
YEAR     DS     CL2
ADDRESS  DS     CL40
NEXTNAME EQU    *
LENGTH   EQU    *-STUDENT
```

   Assume that the main program passes the table to a subprogram. This subprogram prints each student's name and, immediately on the next line, the student's address. Write the subprogram using the given dummy section.
7. Repeat Exercise 6, assuming that the table of data is defined in a common section, instead of in the main program.
8. Repeat Exercise 6, assuming that the table of data is defined in an external data area, instead of the main program.
9. What revisions are necessary to the program in Figure 11.21 (the case study of Chapter 11) to change the output buffer at OUTPUT into a common section?
10. It is possible to define an in-line save area in a way that is similar to the way that you defined an in-line argument list. The advantage is that you can use Register 13 as a base register and leave Register 12 for another purpose. Rewrite the instructions that usually begin a control section to use an in-line save area and Register 13 as the base register.

## Programming Problems

1. Many problems in previous chapters asked you to write an internal subprogram. Repeat the following Programming Problems from Chapter 8 so that you write external, instead of internal, subprograms and appropriate main programs to call the subprograms:
   **a.** Programming Problem 4
   **b.** Programming Problem 5
   **c.** Programming Problem 6
   **d.** Programming Problem 7
   **e.** Programming Problem 8
2. Repeat Programming Problem 6 of Chapter 10 so that you use three external subprograms: one to perform the input, one to alphabetize the strings, and one to perform the output.
3. Repeat Programming Problem 7 of Chapter 10 so that you use three external subprograms: one to perform the input, one to merge the arrays, and one to perform the output.
4. Repeat Programming Problem 3 so that the arrays are defined in a common area.
5. Repeat Programming Problem 3 so that the arrays are defined in an external data area.
6. Repeat Programming Problem 11 of Chapter 10 so that you use an external data area for the vocabulary and a subprogram to generate random integers.
7. Repeat Programming Problem 14 of Chapter 10 so that you define the linked list in an external data area.
8. Repeat Programming Problem 6 of Chapter 11. Use a subprogram that returns the next line of an address and the number of characters in the line. The subprogram should indicate to the calling program when a line is the last line in the address, and should read input records as necessary.
9. Repeat Programming Problem 7 of Chapter 11 so that you implement each command with a subprogram. Assume that the text is in a common area.
10. Repeat Programming Problem 8 or 9 of Chapter 11 so that you use subprograms when appropriate.

# 14

# Decimal Representations and Conversions

CONTENTS

**OVERVIEW**

This chapter begins a two-chapter discussion of decimal numbers by describing the two formats that represent decimal numbers on the IBM System/370. You will learn about the relationship between decimal numbers, binary numbers, and EBCDIC notation, and the instructions that convert between the two decimal forms and between decimal and binary numbers. In addition, you will learn powerful instructions that prepare a decimal field for output. An important application of the instructions in this chapter is the conversion between an EBCDIC field that represents a numeric quantity and the internal form that is required for binary or decimal arithmetic. Decimal arithmetic is the subject of the next chapter.

**OBJECTIVES**

After studying this chapter, you should be able to:

1. Use P and Z constant types with DC and DS directives to define packed-decimal and zoned-decimal fields.
2. Write the internal representation in hexadecimal of any packed-decimal or zoned-decimal constant.
3. Use the instructions PACK and UNPK to convert between packed-decimal and zoned-decimal formats.
4. Use the instructions CVB and CVD to convert between packed-decimal numbers and binary integers.
5. Describe the circumstances under which a data exception occurs.
6. Use the instructions ED and EDMK to convert packed-decimal numbers to a form suitable for output.

## Introduction

So far, all arithmetic instructions have involved binary numbers. However, it is sometimes preferable to perform arithmetic with decimal numbers. For example, programmers usually perform financial computations with decimal numbers. The IBM System/370 makes this possible by providing representations for decimal numbers and instructions to operate upon them.

The IBM System/370 represents decimal numbers in two different ways for two separate purposes. **Zoned-decimal numbers** are associated with input and output operations; **packed-decimal numbers** are used for decimal arithmetic. There are instructions to convert between packed-decimal and zoned-decimal numbers, and between packed-decimal and binary numbers. There are also instructions that transform a packed-decimal number into an EBCDIC field that is suitable for output, and that rapidly perform such tasks as the insertion of commas and decimal points, and the replacement of leading zeros by blanks. In this chapter, you will learn about the decimal representations and the various conversion instructions just mentioned; you will learn about decimal arithmetic in the next chapter.

The instructions in this chapter are also important for nondecimal computations. The results of most input and output operations are in character form, and most numeric fields that exist outside of the computer are decimal. Thus, even if the planned computations are binary or floating-point, you need the instructions presented here to convert between external numbers and internal representations.

## The Representation of Decimal Numbers

**Hex digits A, C, E, and F are plus signs; B and D are minus signs; of these, C and D are preferred signs.**

A decimal number is represented by a sign-magnitude integer notation that occupies from 1 to 16 bytes of storage. The length of the number is not part of its internal representation, but is indicated within the instructions that use it. Each decimal digit is represented by its 4-bit binary equivalent; this is called a **digit code**. The sign of the number is represented by a 4-bit **sign code** that appears in the rightmost byte of the number; its position within the byte depends upon whether the number is zoned-decimal or packed-decimal, as you shall see later. A plus sign can be any of the hexadecimal digits A, C, E, or F; a minus sign can be B or D. Although the computer recognizes any of the sign codes as valid, if the assembler generates a sign code, or if a packed-decimal number is the result of an arithmetic operation, the computer will use only two sign codes: $C_{16}$ for plus and $D_{16}$ for minus. C and D are called **preferred signs**. Figure 14.1 summarizes the codes used in decimal representations.

Figure 14.1
Codes that are used in decimal representations.

| Decimal digit | Digit code in binary |
|---|---|
| 0 | 0000 |
| 1 | 0001 |
| 2 | 0010 |
| 3 | 0011 |
| 4 | 0100 |
| 5 | 0101 |
| 6 | 0110 |
| 7 | 0111 |
| 8 | 1000 |
| 9 | 1001 |

| Sign | Sign code binary | Sign code hex | |
|---|---|---|---|
| + | 1010 | A | |
| | 1100 | C | ← Preferred |
| | 1110 | E | |
| | 1111 | F | |
| – | 1011 | B | |
| | 1101 | D | ← Preferred |

| Zone code binary | Zone code hex |
|---|---|
| 1111 | F |

## THE HISTORY OF SIGN CODES IN DECIMAL NUMBERS

The preferred signs C and D have their origins in conventions that are used with punched cards. Punched cards contain 12 rows: the first 2 rows are called the 12-zone and the 11-zone; the remaining rows represent the digits 0 to 9. It was standard practice in the past—particularly in commercial data processing applications—to punch the sign of a number in the same column as its rightmost digit. In BCDIC (the predecessor of EBCDIC), the character "+" was represented by a punch in the 12-zone and the character "−" was represented by a punch in the 11-zone. When a punch in a 12-zone or 11-zone was made in a column that already contained a digit punch, the resulting punched code represented a character whose BCDIC code began with a hexadecimal C or D. For example, if a minus sign were punched over the 4 in 1234, the result of reading this field would be F1F2F3D4 (in hex). Similarly, if a plus sign were punched over the 4 in 1234, the result of reading the field would be F1F2F3C4. If nothing were punched over the 4, the field would be read as F1F2F3F4. F1F2F3D4, F1F2F3C4, and F1F2F3F4 are examples of what are now called zoned-decimal numbers. The designers of the IBM System/360 chose the hex digits C and D to represent plus and minus signs in order to be consistent with the standard practice of that time.

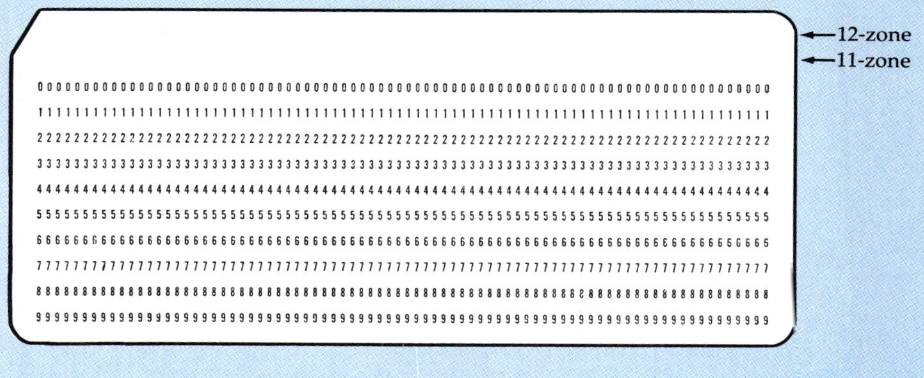


Although the representation of decimal numbers uses an integer notation, you may *assume* that there is a decimal point anywhere within the number; however, there is no internal indication of the decimal point.

The comments just given apply to both zoned-decimal and packed-decimal numbers. Now, consider the general formats of and distinctions between the two decimal representations.

### *Zoned-Decimal Numbers*

Each byte in a zoned-decimal number consists of two portions. The leftmost 4 bits are called the **zone bits**; the rightmost 4 bits are the **numeric bits**. As shown in Figure 14.2, the numeric bits of every byte contain a digit code. The sign code is in the zone bits of the rightmost byte. For all other bytes, the zone bits contain $1111_2$ (or $F_{16}$), which is known as the **zone code**.

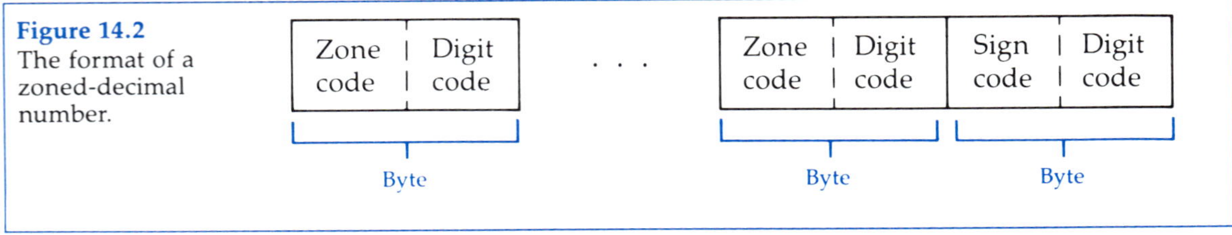


**Figure 14.2** The format of a zoned-decimal number.

Since a zoned-decimal number is a maximum of 16 bytes long, and since each byte represents one decimal digit, the decimal integer that it represents can be a maximum of 16 digits long.

---

EXAMPLE 1

The following are some examples of zoned-decimal numbers:

| Zoned-decimal number (in hex) | Decimal equivalent |
|---|---|
| F1F2C3 (with preferred sign) | +123 |
| F1F2F3 | +123 |
| F1F2D3 (with preferred sign) | −123 |
| F1F2B3 | −123 |

Notice that the second form of +123 is simply the EBCDIC for 123.

---

**Use zoned-decimal numbers with I/O.**

You cannot use zoned-decimal numbers with decimal arithmetic instructions, but they are an intermediate form between the EBCDIC characters that are associated with input and output operations and the packed-decimal form that is required for arithmetic. In fact, zoned-decimal notation is similar to the EBCDIC representation of a decimal number. If the computer reads the unsigned decimal integer 1234, its internal EBCDIC representation will be F1F2F3F4. This representation is a valid zoned-decimal number since F is a valid plus sign. However, −1234 is represented by 60F1F2F3F4 in EBCDIC, but by F1F2F3D4 in zoned-decimal notation. In this case, you will need several instructions to convert the EBCDIC characters to the required zoned-decimal form.

## *Packed-Decimal Numbers*

**Use packed-decimal numbers for arithmetic.**

Zone codes are not used in packed-decimal notation in order to allow a more compact representation than zoned-decimal. As shown in Figure 14.3, each byte except for the rightmost one contains two digit codes; the rightmost byte consists of a digit code that is followed by a sign code. Compare the rightmost bytes of the packed-decimal and zoned-decimal formats: you will see that the sign and digit codes are in reverse order.

Since a packed-decimal number can occupy a maximum of 16 bytes, it can represent a maximum of 31 decimal digits.

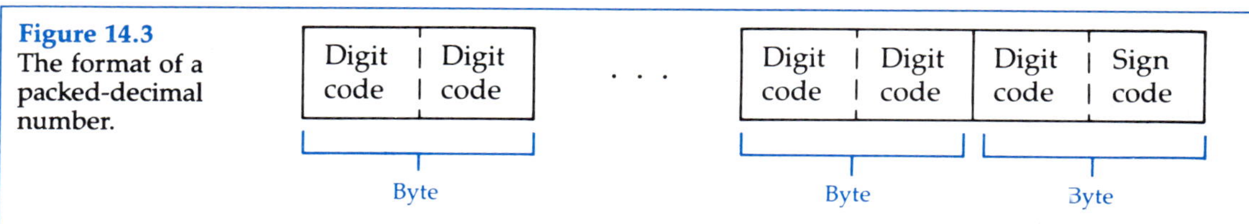


**Figure 14.3** The format of a packed-decimal number.

EXAMPLE 2

The following are examples of packed-decimal numbers:

| Packed-decimal number (in hex) | Decimal equivalent |
|---|---|
| 123C (with preferred sign) | +123 |
| 123F | +123 |
| 123D (with preferred sign) | −123 |
| 00123B | −123 |

## *Additional Constant Types for DC and DS*

**Constant types P (packed) and Z (zoned)**

Two constant types are available to define decimal fields: P for packed-decimal numbers and Z for zoned-decimal numbers. P and Z do not cause boundary alignment. If you write a constant without using an explicit length modifier, the assembler defines the minimum number of bytes necessary to represent the constant, and assigns this number as the length attribute of the symbol, if any, in the name entry. You may write decimal points for your own information in the constant without affecting the internal representation or the number of bytes reserved.

Some of the examples in this chapter require that you reserve doublewords. Recall that you can do this by using a D-type constant in the DS directive.

*DC.* When you use constant types P and Z in the DC directive, if either padding or truncation occurs, it will be on the left of the number. The assembler pads packed-decimal numbers with binary zeros, and pads zoned-decimal numbers with EBCDIC zeros ($F0_{16}$). The assembler always generates preferred signs. As with any other constant, you also may define decimal constants with literals.

EXAMPLE 3

The following are examples of constants that are defined with the DC directive.

| Operand | Assembled Constant | Remark |
|---|---|---|
| `P'123'` | 123C | Plus sign assumed |
| `P'-12'` | 012D | Padded with a zero on the left |

| Operand | Assembled Constant | Remark |
|---|---|---|
| `PL3'+12.3'` | 00123C | Padded with zeros; decimal point ignored |
| `PL2'1234'` | 234C | Truncation occurs on the left |
| `Z'+123'` | F1F2C3 | One byte per digit |
| `ZL3'-1.2'` | F0F1D2 | Padded with F0; decimal point ignored |
| `ZL2'123'` | F2C3 | Truncation occurs on the left |

---

EXAMPLE 4

Notice the difference between the constant described by Z′+123′, which is assembled as F1F2C3, and that described by C′+123′, which is assembled as 4EF1F2F3.

---

*DS.* When used in the DS directive, P and Z are analogous to C, X, or B. When both a constant and an explicit length modifier are absent, the length attribute of a symbol in the name entry is 1. If you write a constant, the assembler uses the constant to determine the number of bytes to reserve just as it would for the DC directive, but it does not define the constant.

---

EXAMPLE 5

Each of the following reserves the next three bytes:

```
A     DS     3P          L'A = 1
B     DS     PL3         L'B = 3
C     DS     Z'123'      L'C = 3
D     DS     Z'1.23'     L'D = 3
```

The length attribute of A is 1; it is 3 for B, C, and D. Note that the constants written for C and D are not assembled.

---

## SELF-TEST EXERCISES

1. What hex constant is defined by each of the following when it is written as the operand entry for a DC directive?
   - **a.** `P'908'`
   - **b.** `P'1.2'`
   - **c.** `PL4'0.0'`
   - **d.** `PL4'-7.408'`
   - **e.** `PL2'-7.408'`
   - **f.** `Z'-123'`
   - **g.** `ZL4'-1.98'`
   - **h.** `2Z'7'`
   - **i.** `ZL2'2.419'`
   - **j.** `ZL3'0'`
2. Assume that a DS directive defines DEC. For each of the following operand entries, indicate the number of reserved bytes and the length attribute of DEC.
   - **a.** `2Z`
   - **b.** `ZL4`
   - **c.** `3PL2`
   - **d.** `Z'-987'`
   - **e.** `P'-987'`

# Conversions

Since the results of an input operation and the fields used in an output operation are typically in character form, programs that perform both I/O operations and arithmetic computations must convert between EBCDIC representations and the proper internal form that is required for the type of arithmetic desired. This section describes four instructions that facilitate some of these conversions. The Pack and Unpack instructions perform conversions between zoned-decimal and packed-decimal numbers. The format of these two instructions is a variation of the SS format and is described next. The Convert to Binary instruction and the Convert to Decimal instruction perform conversions between packed-decimal and binary numbers. These two instructions are RX instructions, and serve as a bridge between the binary-related instructions that you know and the decimal instructions that you will study later.

## *A Variation of the SS Format*

Recall that SS instructions specify two fields in storage. For the SS instructions that have been introduced so far, the two fields are of the same length, but for many of the decimal instructions that will be introduced, the two fields may differ in length. In such cases, the second byte of the instruction represents two field lengths instead of just one, as shown:

| Op code | *L1* − 1 | *L2* − 1 | *B1* | *D1* | *B2* | *D2* |
|---|---|---|---|---|---|---|
| 0 7 | 8 11 | 12 15 | 16 19 | 20 31 | 32 35 | 36 47 |

The first operand at effective address *E1* (which is represented by the base register *B1* and the displacement *D1*) is *L1* bytes in length; the second operand at effective address *E2* is of length *L2*. As you learned earlier, each internal length code is 1 less than the actual length of the operand. Here, each length code occupies 4 bits and has a value of 0 to 15, which can represent 1 to 16 bytes, respectively. By design, the length of decimal numbers falls into this range.

You can designate either one or both operands in assembler language explicitly or implicitly. If both operands are written explicitly, they appear as

*D1*(*L1*,*B1*),*D2*(*L2*,*B2*)

and if both are written implicitly, they appear as

*S1*(*L1*),*S2*(*L2*)

To save space in the text, only these two operand entries will appear when new instructions are introduced. However, you can designate either operand explicitly or implicitly. You also can omit the length specification when you designate an operand implicitly—in which case, the assembler uses the length attribute of the appropriate operand instead. Thus, if you assume

```
X     DC     Z'123'      (F1F2F3)
```

and

```
Y     DC     P'-123'     (123D)
```

the operand entry

```
X,Y
```

is equivalent to

```
X(3),Y(2)
```

This text uses $SS_2$ to denote the variation of the SS format described here; this suggests the existence of two length specifications instead of just one. The text uses $SS_1$ to denote the previously encountered SS format.

### *Conversion from Zoned to Packed Formats: The Pack (PACK) Instruction*

**PACK converts to packed-decimal form.**

The PACK instruction converts decimal numbers from a zoned form into a packed form. The instruction can be summarized as follows:

| Operation | Operand | Format | Instruction Name | Action |
|---|---|---|---|---|
| **PACK** | *S1*(*L1*),*S2*(*L2*) or *D1*(*L1*,*B1*),*D2*(*L2*,*B2*) | $SS_2$ | PACK | $C(E1)_{L1} \leftarrow$ Packed version of $C(E2)_{L2}$ |

The PACK instruction treats the *L2* bytes of the second operand as if they represented a zoned-decimal number and, without checking for validity, converts them to a packed-decimal format. The result is right-justified and replaces the *L1* bytes of the first operand. The instruction does not change the second operand.

If *L1* is larger than necessary, the result is padded on the left with binary zeros. However, if *L1* is too small, the instruction truncates the result and ignores the extra bytes of the second operand without indicating that it is doing so.

You can predict the result as follows. Consider the bytes in each operand right to left. Interchange the sign and digit codes of the rightmost byte of the second operand, and store them into the rightmost byte of the first operand *without modification*. Proceeding to the left, consider subsequent bytes of the second operand 2 at a time; discard the zones and store the resulting 2 digit codes—without change—into the next byte of the first operand. This process is illustrated in Figure 14.4.

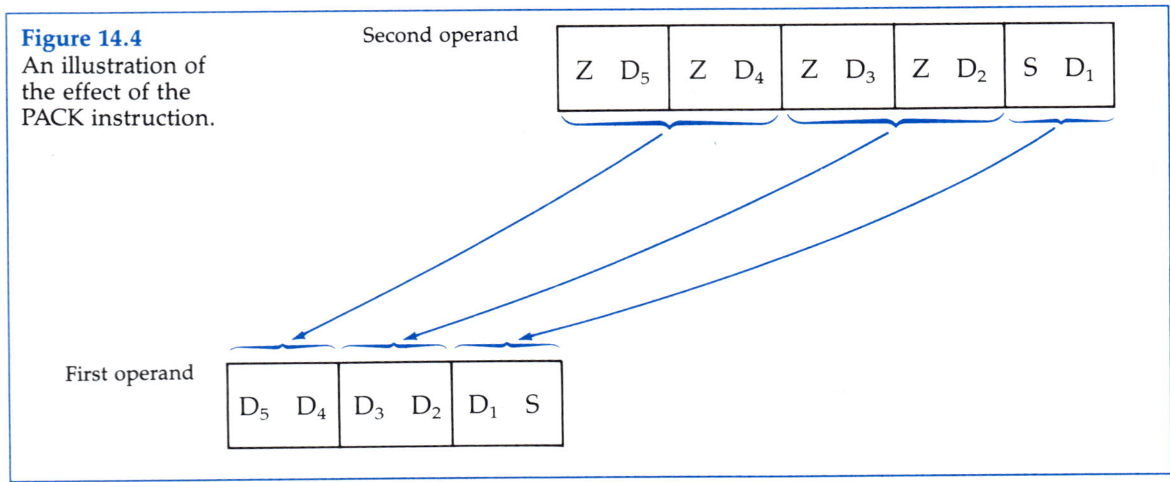


**Figure 14.4**
An illustration of the effect of the PACK instruction.

**PACK does not check for valid decimal codes.**

Since the instruction does not check to see if the second operand contains a valid zoned-decimal number, you can use PACK for applications other than those that are associated with decimal numbers. You should interpret a reference to a zone code, digit code, or sign code as a reference to the 4-bit quantity that occurs in the zone position, digit position, or sign position within a byte.

---

EXAMPLE 6

```
PACK   P(3),Z(4)
```

| | The bytes at P | The bytes at Z |
|---|---|---|
| Before execution: | ?? ?? ?? | F5 F4 F3 D2 |
| | Pad | |
| After execution: | 05 43 2D | F5 F4 F3 D2 |

The instruction converts the 4-byte zoned-decimal number at Z to packed-decimal format, and stores the result right-justified into the 3 bytes at P. Since there is room for another digit in P, a zero is stored on the left.

---

EXAMPLE 7

```
PACK   P(4),Z(4)
```

| | The bytes at P | The bytes at Z |
|---|---|---|
| Before execution: | ?? ?? ?? ?? | F5 F4 F3 F2 |
| | Pad | |
| After execution: | 00 05 43 2F | F5 F4 F3 F2 |

This example is similar to Example 6, but here the field at P is longer. The result is right-justified and padded on the left with zeros. Notice that the sign code (F) is *not* changed to the preferred sign.

---

EXAMPLE 8

```
PACK   P(2),Z(4)
```

| | The bytes at P | The bytes at Z |
|---|---|---|
| Before execution: | ?? ?? | F5 F4 F3 C2 |
| | Ignored | |
| After execution: | 43 2C | F5 F4 F3 C2 |

In this example, the field at P is too short to accommodate the result; the instruction truncates the result on the left without warning.

---

**Try to avoid field overlap.**

*Field Overlap.* The fields that contain the first and second operands of the PACK instruction may, in fact, overlap—although you usually should try to avoid this. Be careful if you do use overlapping fields, because there is no warning when the results are incorrect. You obtain correct results when the rightmost byte of the first operand coincides with or is to the right of the rightmost byte of the second operand. To predict the outcome when the fields overlap, store the result byte into the first operand as soon as it has been computed.

Examples 9 and 10 demonstrate correct field overlap, but Example 11 shows results that are incorrect.

---

EXAMPLE 9

```
PACK    X(3),X(3)
```

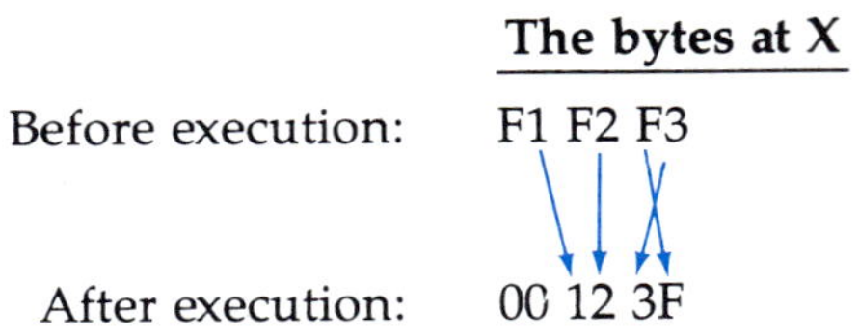

| | **The bytes at X** |
|---|---|
| Before execution: | F1 F2 F3 |
| After execution: | 00 12 3F |

This example demonstrates that it is possible to PACK a field onto itself. The instruction interchanges the hexadecimal digits in the rightmost byte of the field at X. The instruction then discards the zones of the other 2 bytes and the resultant digit codes replace the second byte. Finally, the result is padded on the left with zeros.

---

EXAMPLE 10

```
PACK    X+2(3),X(3)
```

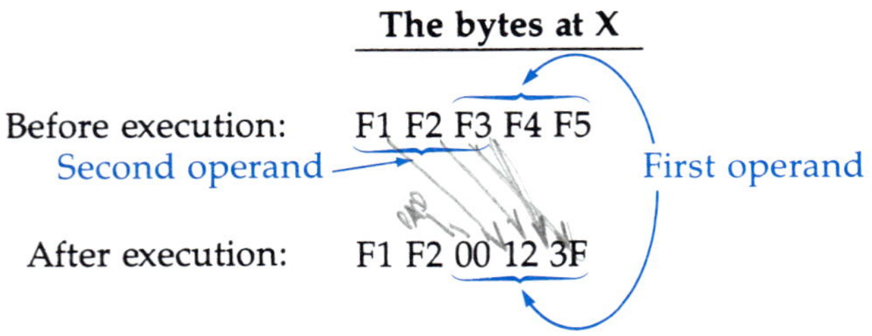

| | **The bytes at X** |
|---|---|
| Before execution: | F1 F2 F3 F4 F5 |
| After execution: | F1 F2 00 12 3F |

Second operand

First operand

The operand fields overlap by 1 byte but, since the first operand field extends to the right of the second, the results are correct. The overlap occurs at the third byte of X; this byte is both the first byte of the first operand and the last byte of the second operand. The instruction processes the original contents of this byte before a portion of the result destroys them.

---

EXAMPLE 11

**PACK Y(2),Y(3)**

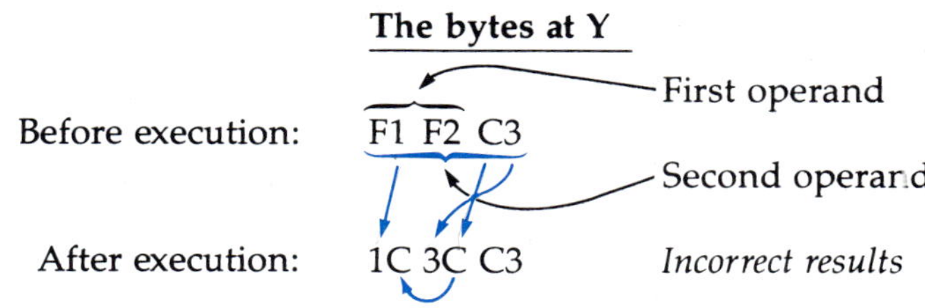


The instruction interchanges the hexadecimal digits in the third byte at Y and stores them into the second byte at Y. The first two bytes at Y then contain F13C; the digit portions—the 1 and the C—are stored into the first byte at Y. The results are incorrect.

EXAMPLE 12

**PACK B(1),B(1)**

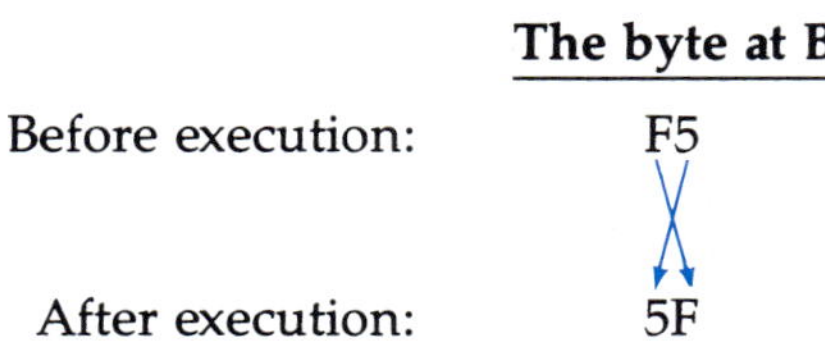


You can use the PACK instruction to interchange the hexadecimal digits of a byte.

EXAMPLE 13

**Remove the Zone Codes and the Sign Code**

Suppose that you want to extract the digit codes from a zoned-decimal number by removing its sign and zone codes. The PACK instruction will remove the zone codes for all but the rightmost byte; the instruction interchanges the digit and sign codes of the rightmost byte without modification; for example,

```
PACK    P(3),Z(3)
```

| | The bytes at P | The bytes at Z |
|---|---|---|
| Before execution: | ?? ?? ?? | F1 F2 F3 |
| After execution: | 00 12 3F | F1 F2 F3 |

Although this instruction may appear to have accomplished your goal, it is rather inconvenient to isolate the desired result 00123 since the 3 is adjacent to the F within the same byte. The solution is to change the instruction by padding the field at Z on the right with a dummy byte, and by then increasing the *L2* specification by 1. PACK will treat this byte as if it contained a digit and a sign code, and will remove the zones from the rest of the field. You can then ignore the rightmost byte of the result. Thus,

```
PACK   P(3),Z(4)
```

| | The bytes at P | The bytes at Z |
|---|---|---|
| Before execution: | ?? ?? ?? | F1 F2 F3 *xy* (Dummy) |
| After execution: | 01 23 *yx* (Result: 01 23; Ignored: *yx*) | F1 F2 F3 *xy* |

The first 2 bytes at P contain the desired result.

---

## *Conversion from Packed to Zoned Formats: The Unpack (UNPK) Instruction*

**UNPK converts to zoned-decimal (unpacked) form.**

The UNPK instruction is analogous to PACK, and is used to convert a packed-decimal number to a zoned-decimal form. It is sometimes confusing to distinguish between PACK and UNPK because of their names. The result of the PACK instruction is in packed form. Generally, a packed number occupies less space than its zoned version, so PACK can also suggest the conversion to a more compact form. In contrast, UNPK suggests an expansion: that is, the conversion from a packed form to the more expansive zoned form. It may help you to think of the zoned form as an "unpacked" form.The UNPK instruction can be summarized as follows:

| Operation | Operand | Format | Instruction Name | Action |
|---|---|---|---|---|
| UNPK | *S1(L1),S2(L2)* or *D1(L1,B1),D2(L2,B2)* | $SS_2$ | UNPACK | $C(E1)_{L1} \leftarrow$ Zoned version of $C(E2)_{L2}$ |

The UNPK instruction treats the *L2* bytes of the second operand as if they represented a packed-decimal number and, without checking for validity, converts them into a zoned-decimal form. The result is right-justified and replaces the *L1* bytes of the first operand. The instruction leaves the second operand unchanged. If *L1* is larger than necessary, the instruction pads the result on the left with EBCDIC zeros ($F0_{16}$). However, if *L1* is too small, the instruction truncates the result and ignores the extra digit codes of the second operand without indication.

You can predict the result as follows. Consider the bytes in each operand from right to left. Interchange the digit code and the sign code in the rightmost byte of the second operand, and store them into the rightmost byte of the first operand without modification. Proceeding to the left, consider subsequent bytes of the second operand one at a time. Insert zones before the digit codes so that each byte produces two result bytes. As you compute the result bytes, store them into the first operand. This process is illustrated in Figure 14.5.

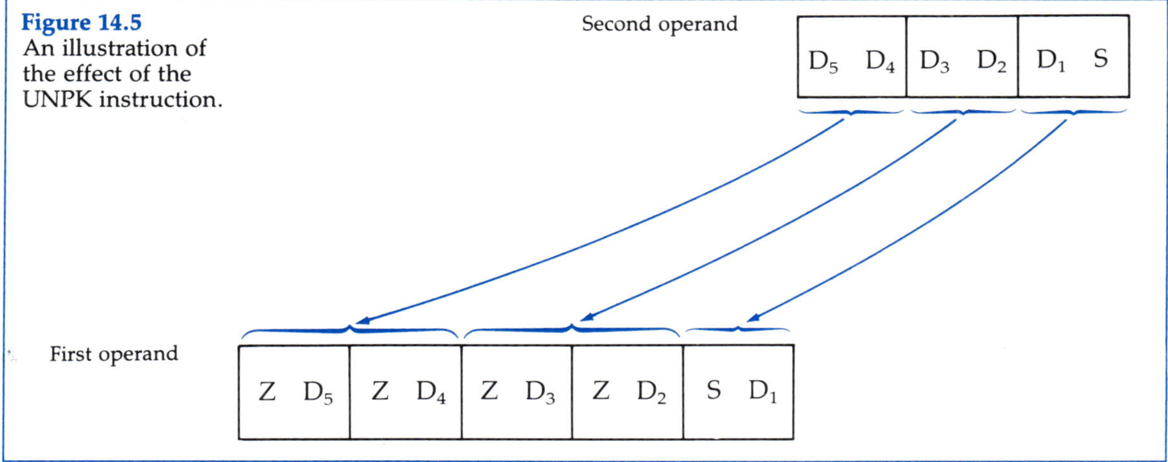


**Figure 14.5**
An illustration of the effect of the UNPK instruction.

**UNPK does not check for valid decimal codes.**

UNPK does not check for valid zone codes, digit codes, or a valid sign code; like PACK, you can use it for applications that are not associated with decimal numbers.

---

EXAMPLE 14

```
UNPK    Z(5),P(3)
```

| | The bytes at Z | The bytes at P |
|---|---|---|
| Before execution: | ?? ?? ?? ?? ?? | 12 34 5C |
| After execution: | F1 F2 F3 F4 C5 | 12 34 5C |

The instruction interchanges the sign and digit codes in the rightmost byte of P and stores them into the rightmost byte of Z. Each of the digit codes in the remaining bytes of P is preceded by the zone code ($F_{16}$) and stored into Z.

---

EXAMPLE 15

```
UNPK    Z(4),P(2)
```

| | The bytes at Z | The bytes at P |
|---|---|---|
| Before execution: | ?? ?? ?? ?? | 12 3F |
| After execution: | F0 F1 F2 F3 (Pad: F0) | 12 3F |

The field at Z is longer than necessary so the instruction pads the result on the left with an EBCDIC zero. The sign code is not changed; UNPK, like PACK, does not insist upon preferred signs.

---

EXAMPLE 16

```
UNPK   Z(2),P(2)
```

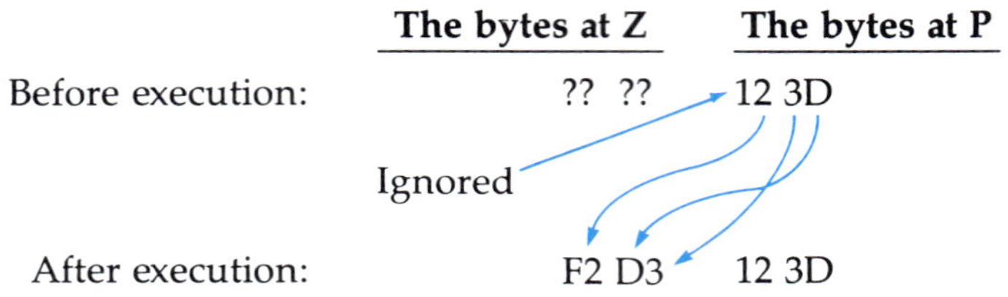

| | The bytes at Z | The bytes at P |
|---|---|---|
| Before execution: | ?? ?? | 12 3D |
| | Ignored | |
| After execution: | F2 D3 | 12 3D |

The field at Z is too short; the instruction truncates the result on the left without warning.

**Try to avoid field overlap.**

*Field Overlap.* As with PACK, the fields that contain the first and second operands of the UNPK instruction can overlap, but again you must take care so that the results are correct. To predict the outcome when the fields overlap, store the result bytes as soon as they have been computed.

The rules for correct field overlap are as follows:

1. A single-byte field can be unpacked onto itself.
2. For fields that begin at the same address, the rightmost byte of the first operand must extend to the right of the rightmost byte of the second operand by at least $L2 - 1$ bytes: that is, $L1 \geqslant 2 * L2 - 1$. (See part **a** of Figure 14.6.)
3. If the fields do not begin at the same address, the extension mentioned in Rule 2 of the first operand over the second operand only needs to be $L2 - 2$ bytes. (See part **b** of Figure 14.6.)

EXAMPLE 17

**Rule 1**

```
UNPK   X(1),X(1)
```

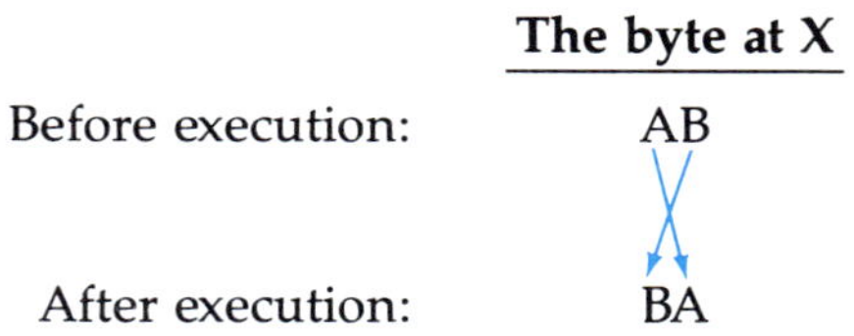

| | The byte at X |
|---|---|
| Before execution: | AB |
| After execution: | BA |

This instruction produces the same result as if you had used the PACK instruction; the two hexadecimal digits at X are interchanged.

EXAMPLE 18

**Rule 2**

```
UNPK   X(5),X(3)
```

**The bytes at X**

| | |
|---|---|
| Before execution: | 12 34 5C ?? ?? (First operand: 12 34 5C ?? ??; Second operand: 12 34 5C) |
| After execution: | F1 F2 F3 F4 C5 |

Notice that since *L1* is 5 and *L2* is 3, then

$L1 = 2 * L2 - 1$

Equivalently, the first operand extends to the right of the second operand by $L2 - 1$, which is 2, bytes.

---

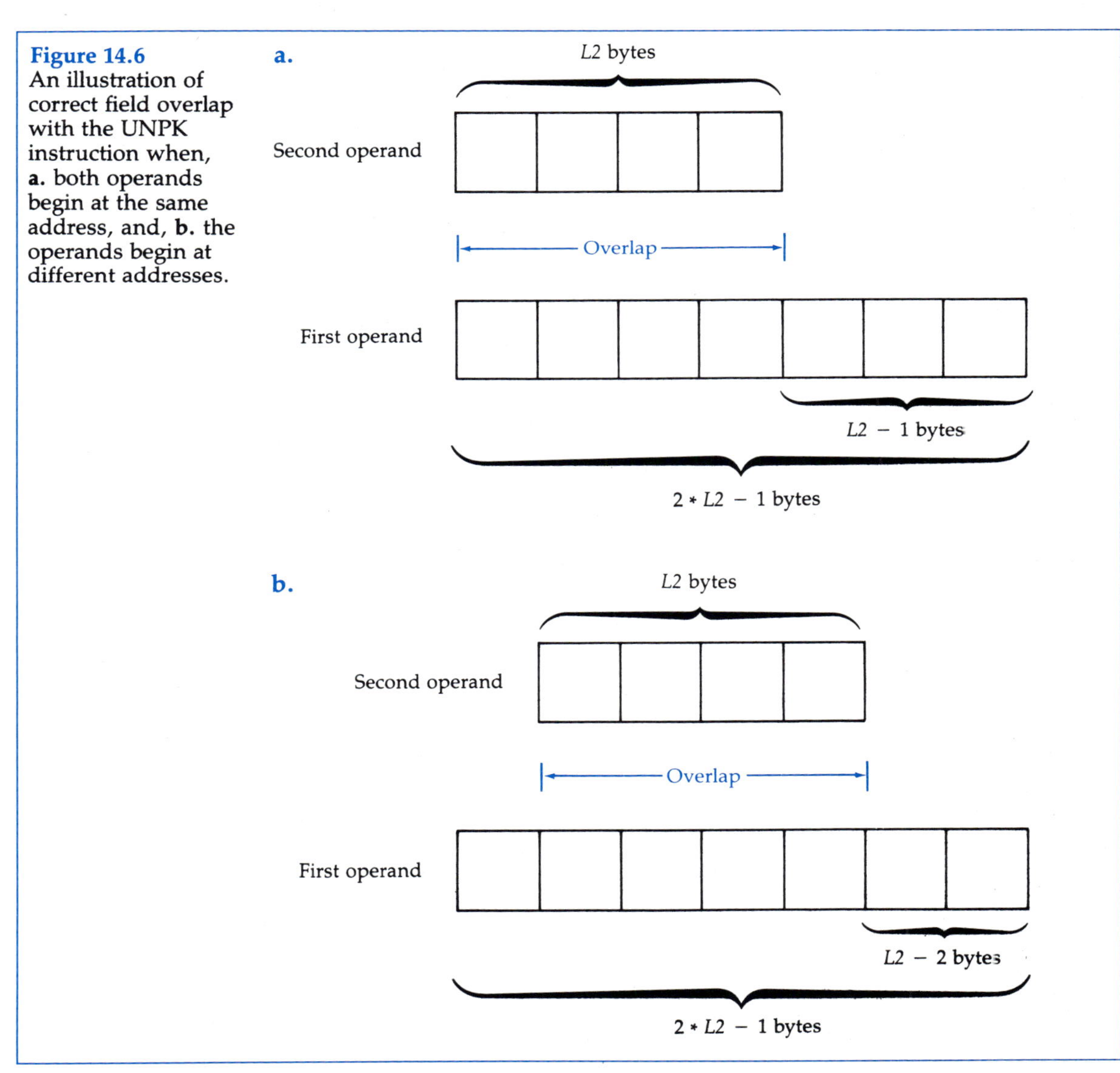


**Figure 14.6** An illustration of correct field overlap with the UNPK instruction when, **a.** both operands begin at the same address, and, **b.** the operands begin at different addresses.

EXAMPLE 19

**Rule 3**

```
UNPK   X-1(5),X(3)
```

**The bytes at X − 1**

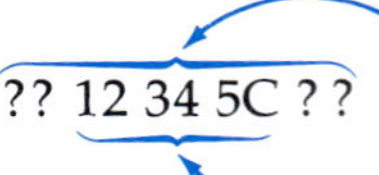

| | | |
|---|---|---|
| Before execution: | ?? 12 34 5C ? ? | First operand / Second operand |
| After execution: | F1 F2 F3 F4 C5 | |

The first operand extends to the right of the second operand by *L2* − 2, or 1, byte and the results are correct.

---

EXAMPLE 20

```
UNPK   X(4),X(3)
```

**The bytes at X**

| | | |
|---|---|---|
| Before execution: | 12 34 5C ?? | First operand / Second operand |
| After execution: | F2 F3 F4 C5 | *Incorrect results* |

Although both operands begin at the same address, the first operand extends to the right of the second operand by only *L2* − 2, or 1, byte. The result is incorrect because the first operand is insufficiently long.

---

EXAMPLE 21

```
UNPK   X(3),X(3)
```

**The bytes at X**

| | |
|---|---|
| Before execution: | 00 12 3C (Ignored: 00) |
| After execution: | F1 F2 C3 |

Even though the overlap violates the rules given earlier, the result is correct because the ignored bytes are zero. This is not always true, as in the following:

**The bytes at X**

| | | |
|---|---|---|
| Before execution: | 12 34 5C (Ignored: 12) | |
| After execution: | F3 F4 C5 | *Incorrect results* |

Here, the truncated result is incorrect and, in general, you should avoid this type of overlap.

---

## SELF-TEST EXERCISES

3. What are the results in hexadecimal after each of the following PACK instructions is executed? Assume A and B are defined by

```
A     DS    PL5
B     DC    Z'12345'
```

   a. `PACK  A(3),B(5)`
   b. `PACK  A(5),B(5)`
   c. `PACK  A(2),B(5)`
   d. `PACK  B(5),B(5)`

4. What are the results in hexadecimal after each of the following UNPK instructions is executed? Assume A and B are defined by

```
A     DS    ZL6
B     DC    P'+12345'
      DS    3X
```

   a. `UNPK  A(5),B(3)`
   b. `UNPK  A(3),B(3)`
   c. `UNPK  A(6),B(3)`
   d. `UNPK  B(6),B(3)`
   e. `UNPK  B-2(5),B(3)`

5. Describe the conditions under which the first operand of a PACK instruction is too small to contain the correct packed-decimal result. Next, describe the conditions under which the first operand of an UNPK instruction is too small to contain the correct zoned-decimal result.

### *Conversions between Packed-Decimal and Binary: The CVB and CVD Instructions*

The Convert to Binary (CVB) instruction and the Convert to Decimal (CVD) instruction provide a link between two's complement binary integers and packed-decimal numbers. This is important for a number of reasons. First, if a loop parameter that is associated with a decimal computation is itself a packed-decimal number, you can convert its value to binary so that you can control the loop with such instructions as BCT. Usually, such a move will save execution time. Second, if the computation involves only binary arithmetic, you usually must make several conversions before you can perform the binary computation: for example, you must convert a decimal integer that is read in EBCDIC, first to packed-decimal form and then to binary. Conversely, you must convert the result of a binary computation to packed-decimal and then to EBCDIC prior to printing.

*Convert to Binary.* The CVB instruction can be summarized as follows:

| Operation | Operand | Format | Instruction Name | Action |
|---|---|---|---|---|
| **CVB** | *R1,S2*<br>or *R1,S2(X2)*<br>or *R1,D2(X2,B2)* | RX | CONVERT TO BINARY | C(*R1*) ← The two's complement binary equivalent of $C(E2)_{0-63}$ |

The second operand of the CVB instruction must be an 8-byte field.

The CVB instruction converts the packed-decimal number in the 8-byte field at the effective address *E2* to an integer in the two's complement binary number system. The binary integer then replaces the contents of *R1*. The instruction checks both the sign code and the digit codes of the packed-decimal number for validity; if any codes are invalid, a **data exception** occurs, which is followed by a program interruption. (The interruption code is 0007.)

Data exceptions and fixed-point divide exceptions can occur when you use the CVB instruction.

The value of the decimal number can be outside of the range of binary integers ($-2^{31}$ to $2^{31}-1$, or $-2{,}147{,}483{,}648$ to $+2{,}147{,}483{,}647$) since an 8-byte packed-decimal number can represent up to 15 decimal digits. If this is the case, the rightmost 32 bits of the binary equivalent replace the contents of *R1* and a fixed-point divide exception occurs. (This is the same exception that can occur during a binary division. The interruption code is 0009.) The condition code remains unchanged.

Normally, you should align the second operand at a doubleword integral boundary.

---

EXAMPLE 22

```
         CVB   3,P
          .
          .
          .
P        DS    0D
         DC    PL8'123'
```

| | Reg. 3 | The bytes at P |
|---|---|---|
| Before execution: | ???????? | 00 00 00 00 00 00 12 3C |
| After execution: | 0000007B | 00 00 00 00 00 00 12 3C |

---

EXAMPLE 23

**Convert a Two-Digit Decimal Integer from Character Form to Binary**

Assume that the EBCDIC form of a decimal integer is contained in the 2 bytes at X, and that D represents a doubleword in storage. The following traces the conversion of a 2-digit decimal integer from character form to binary:

| | Reg. 3 | The bytes at D | The bytes at X |
|---|---|---|---|
| | ???????? | ?? ?? ?? ?? ?? ?? ?? ?? | F4 F2 |
| PACK D(8),X(2) | ???????? | 00 00 00 00 00 00 04 2F | F4 F2 |
| CVB 3,D | 0000002A | 00 00 00 00 00 00 04 2F | F4 F2 |

Since the bytes at X contain a valid zoned-decimal number, the result at D is a valid packed-decimal number. Notice that the PACK instruction does more than simply perform this conversion: it places the packed-decimal result right-justified into the doubleword at D. You should use this data-movement capability of the PACK instruction to your advantage. Do not attempt to PACK X on top of itself and then move the result to D by using an MVC instruction. (Exercise 4 at the end of this chapter asks you to describe the problems that you will encounter if you try this.) Also, do not succumb to an easy pitfall by writing the instruction `CVB 3,D(8)`. Since CVB is an RX instruction, the 8 designates an index register, and not a length.

The instructions in this example assume that the given integer is unsigned. Notice that the CVB instruction treats the F-zone of EBCDIC notation as a valid plus sign. Exercises 7 and 8 at the end of this chapter consider signed integers.

---

EXAMPLE 24

**Convert an L-Digit Decimal Integer from Character Form to Binary**

This example is similar to Example 23, but it assumes that the number of EBCDIC characters at X is stored in Register 3 as a binary integer and does not exceed nine. As with other SS instructions that you have studied, you can specify field lengths that are not known until execution time using an EX instruction. However, unlike your previous experiences, there are two length specifications in the second byte of the PACK instruction; in this example, only the second length must be changed. In the instructions listed in Figure 14.7, the second byte of the PACK instruction contains $70_{16}$. At the time that EX is executed, if the last byte of Register 3 contains $05_{16}$, for example, then the result of Execute's OR operation will be $75_{16}$. This result is used as the second byte of the PACK instruction and implies that the length of the first operand is 8 and that of the second is 6.

Altering the length of the first field or of both fields, as required by Exercises 2 and 3 at the end of this chapter, is slightly more complicated.

```
** CONVERT A DECIMAL INTEGER IN EBCDIC TO BINARY.
** ASSUME UP TO 9 EBCDIC DIGITS ARE STORED AT X.  THE NUMBER OF
** DIGITS IS IN REGISTER 3 AS A BINARY INTEGER.
          S     R3,=F'1'         R3 = INTERNAL LENGTH
          EX    R3,PACK          CONVERT TO PACKED-DECIMAL; RESULT IN D
          B     AROUND           SKIP TARGET INSTRUCTION
PACK      PACK  D(8),X(0)        CONVERT ZONED X INTO PACKED DOUBLEWORD
AROUND    CVB   R4,D             R4 = BINARY EQUIVALENT
          .
          .
          .
X         DS    CL9              GIVEN EBCDIC FIELD
D         DS    D                DOUBLEWORD FOR CVB
```

**Figure 14.7**
Instructions to convert a decimal integer from character form to binary, as described in Example 24.

*Convert to Decimal.* The CVD instruction can be summarized as follows:

| Operation | Operand | Format | Instruction Name | Action |
|---|---|---|---|---|
| CVD | *R1*,*S2*<br>or *R1*,*S2*(*X2*)<br>or *R1*,*D2*(*X2*,*B2*) | RX | CONVERT<br>TO<br>DECIMAL | $C(E2)_{0\text{-}63} \leftarrow$ The packed-decimal equivalent of C(*R1*) |

The CVD instruction converts the integer in register *R1*, which is assumed to be an integer in the two's complement binary number system, to packed-decimal form and stores the result into the 8-byte field at the effective address *E2*. The instruction uses preferred signs. An overflow cannot occur since the decimal equivalent of a 32-bit binary integer requires at most 10 digits and an 8-byte field provides space for 15 digits. Therefore, the instruction pads the result on the left with zeros. The condition code remains unchanged.

**The result of a CVD instruction is in the second operand.**

Notice that this instruction is one of the few instructions in which the result replaces the second operand, instead of the first operand. As with the CVB instruction, you normally should align the second operand at a doubleword integral boundary.

---

EXAMPLE 25

```
        CVD    3,Z
         .
         .
         .
Z       DS     D
```

| | Reg. 3 | The bytes at Z |
|---|---|---|
| Before execution: | FFFFFFFE | ?? ?? ?? ?? ?? ?? ?? ?? |
| After execution: | FFFFFFFE | 00 00 00 00 00 00 00 2D |

---

EXAMPLE 26

**Convert a Binary Integer to Decimal in a Form Suitable for Printing**

Assume that Register 3 contains a two's complement binary integer. The instructions in Figure 14.8 convert the integer to base 10, and represent it in EBCDIC preceded by an appropriate sign. The CVD instruction performs the conversion from binary form to packed-decimal form. The UNPK instruction then converts the result to zoned-decimal form. At this point, the rightmost byte of the result contains a preferred sign—hexadecimal C or D—as generated by the CVD instruction. If left as is, this byte will not print as a digit and, therefore, the sign code must be changed to $F_{16}$. Finally, a + character or a − character is moved to the left of the result. Notice how this is done: the sign is arbitrarily set to plus and changed to minus if necessary. Testing Register 3 before setting the sign is awkward due to the additional Branch instruction that would be required.

```
** CONVERT A BINARY INTEGER IN REGISTER 3 INTO A DECIMAL PRINTABLE
** FORM WITH SIGN.
         CVD    R3,PDN           PDN = PACKED-DECIMAL RESULT
         UNPK   ZDN(10),PDN(8)   ZDN = ZONED-DECIMAL RESULT
         OI     ZDN+9,X'F0'      CHANGE SIGN CODE TO ZONE CODE
         MVI    SIGN,C'+'        INITIALIZE EBCDIC SIGN
         LTR    R3,R3            TEST SIGN OF BINARY INTEGER
         BNM    DONE             IF NONNEGATIVE, FINISHED
         MVI    SIGN,C'-'        ELSE MOVE IN MINUS SIGN
DONE     ---                     RESULT IS AT OUTPUT
         .
         .
         .
PDN      DS     D                DOUBLEWORD FOR CVD
OUTPUT   DS     0CL11            OUTPUT BUFFER WITH FIELDS AS FOLLOWS:
SIGN     DS     C                  EBCDIC SIGN OF RESULT
ZDN      DS     ZL10               ZONED/EBCDIC FORM OF INTEGER
```

**Figure 14.8**
Instructions to convert a binary integer to decimal in a form suitable for printing, as described in Example 26.

The 11 bytes at OUTPUT are now ready for printing. However, observe that leading zeros will be printed. A more sophisticated approach to this problem is possible with the Edit instruction, which is discussed later in this chapter: this instruction allows you to replace leading zeros by blanks.

---

## SELF-TEST EXERCISE

6. Assume the following hexadecimal status of Registers 2, 3, and 4, and the doublewords at X, Y, and Z:

   Reg. 2 = 0000005B
   Reg. 3 = FFFFFFFC
   Reg. 4 = FFFFFFFF
   X = 00000000 0000254D
   Y = 00000000 0000042C
   Z = 00000000 00000000

   Indicate the effect that each of the following instructions has upon this status:

   **a.** CVB 2,X
   **b.** CVB 3,Y
   **c.** CVB 4,Z
   **d.** CVD 2,X
   **e.** CVD 3,Y
   **f.** CVD 4,Z

## *The Steps between I/O and Decimal or Binary Arithmetic*

In the previous section, an underlying theme was the relationship between input/output operations, EBCDIC, and decimal numbers. Figure 14.9 traces the steps that a program must take to read a decimal number, use it in a decimal or binary computation, and finally print the results. Input data is represented in EBCDIC after a read operation. Before you can perform decimal arithmetic, you must transform the sign character and the digit characters into a zoned-decimal number, and then convert the zoned-decimal number into a packed-decimal number. If the input field is unsigned, its EBCDIC representation is already a valid zoned-decimal form, so you can convert it directly to a packed-decimal number. The result of decimal arithmetic is another packed-decimal number; since it is not in printable form, you must convert it first to zoned-decimal and then to an EBCDIC field that contains the proper sign character and other desired punctuation or labels.

If binary arithmetic is your goal, you proceed from input to a packed-decimal number. You must convert the packed-decimal number to binary before you perform the arithmetic; you must convert the result of the arithmetic to a packed-decimal number and then ultimately to an EBCDIC field before printing.

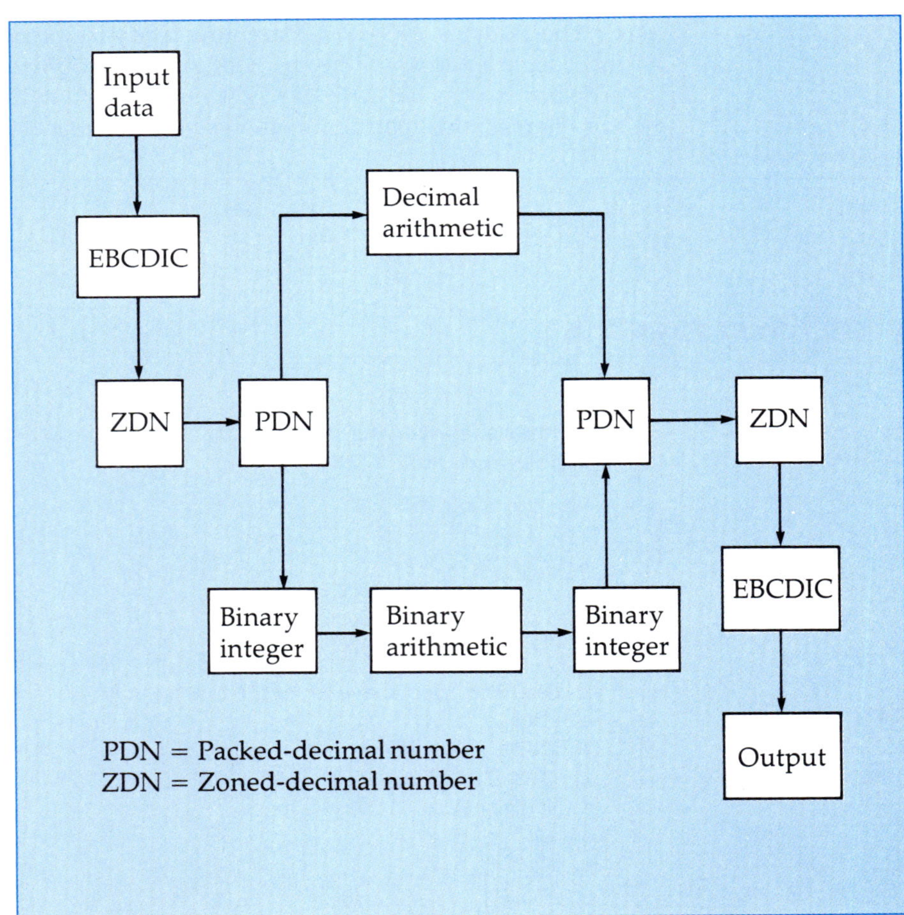


**Figure 14.9**
The conversion path from input to output for a program that involves arithmetic.

# Editing for Output

Creating a printable field from a packed-decimal number can be a tedious task. After you convert the number to a zoned format, you must change the sign code to a zone, move the sign as a character into place, and possibly insert other punctuation, such as decimal points or commas. The Edit (ED) instruction and its companion the Edit and Mark (EDMK) instruction permit an efficient way to accomplish these tasks.

A pattern that you construct from special codes controls the editing process. The pattern serves as a template for the output field, and specifies the placement of digits and any other characters. The Edit instructions convert digits in a packed-decimal number to zoned form as they are processed; you do not use a separate UNPK instruction. This should not imply that you will no longer have a need for UNPK. Unlike UNPK, ED and EDMK cause a data exception if they detect invalid digit or sign codes and, thus, are restricted to processing *only* packed-decimal fields. You will find many other uses for UNPK.

ED and EDMK are similar: EDMK does everything that ED does, but it also places an address into Register 1, which you can use, for example, to position a sign or dollar sign immediately before the edited number or to determine the length of the edited number.

The description of these instructions is more involved than any description discussed so far in this text. Do not become so overwhelmed with the details that you lose sight of what editing accomplishes.

## *The Edit (ED) Instruction*

The ED instruction can be summarized as follows:

| Operation | Operand | Format | Instruction Name | Action |
|---|---|---|---|---|
| **ED** | *S1*(*L1*),*S2* or *D1*(*L1*,*B1*),*D2*(*B2*) | $SS_1$ | EDIT | $C(E1)_{L1} \leftarrow$ Zoned and edited packed-decimal field, or fields, at *E2*. Sets the condition code as described later in this section. |

**ED converts a packed-decimal source field to printable form by using a pattern.**

Edit is an SS instruction with only one length specification. Its second operand is called the **source field**, and contains one or more contiguous packed-decimal numbers that will be converted to printable form. The digit codes in these packed-decimal numbers are called **source digits**. The first operand is an array of *L1* single-byte codes and EBCDIC characters that are used as a **pattern** to describe the output field. The result of the editing process replaces the pattern. The result is computed as if the fields were processed left to right, one byte at a time. Although you do not state the length of the second operand explicitly within the instruction, the source bytes must contain exactly the correct number of decimal digits as implied by the contents of the pattern.

The first byte of the pattern, regardless of its contents, is called the **fill character**. Other bytes of the pattern are either:

- Replaced by the fill character.
- Replaced by a source digit in zoned form.
- Left unchanged.

You can use the fill character, which is often a blank, to replace the leading zeros in a field.

You can also write any EBCDIC characters, such as punctuation or labels, in a pattern. Such characters are called **message characters**. In addition, you will use three nonprintable hexadecimal codes when you construct a pattern. The codes are as follows:

**Pattern characters**

| Name | Hex Code | Notation |
|---|---|---|
| Digit Selector | 20 | *d* |
| Significance Starter | 21 | *[* |
| Field Separator | 22 | *]* |

The notation will help to clarify the examples, but remember that the codes 20, 21, and 22 do *not* represent the characters *d*, *[*, and *]* in EBCDIC; they do not represent any characters. The contents of any pattern byte are called the **pattern character** in the sequel even though it may very well be a nonprintable code such as the Digit Selector.

The Edit instructions replace or leave a pattern character according to all of the following conditions:

**Factors that determine whether a pattern character is replaced or left alone**

- The type of pattern character.
- Whether or not the next source digit from the left is zero.
- The state of the **Significance Indicator**.

**ED sets its own indicator, which is called the Significance Indicator.**

The Significance Indicator is simply an on/off switch that indicates the significance of subsequent source digits or message characters. Only those digits and message characters that are defined as significant by the Significance Indicator become part of the result. The Significance Indicator is always off at the start of an Edit instruction, but its status can change each time that a pattern character is processed.

Although any of several conditions can affect the status of the Significance Indicator, one condition is considered now. Certain pattern characters indicate whether the Edit instruction will examine a source digit. The instruction extracts source digits from the source bytes as needed. If the digit code is in the leftmost 4 bits of a byte, the instruction immediately examines the rightmost 4 bits for a sign code. If a plus sign is detected at this point, the instruction turns the Significance Indicator off after processing the digit; otherwise the status of the Significance Indicator is unchanged.

**ED sets the condition code according to the status of the Significance Indicator.**

At the conclusion of the instruction, the condition code is set. When the source field is nonzero, the condition code reflects the final status of the Significance Indicator. From this, the program can deduce the sign of the field. Later, the status of the condition code will be described fully.

You now have learned sufficient terminology to understand the effect of the various pattern characters.

**Digit Selectors process the next available source digit.**

*The Digit Selector (X'20').* You use the Digit Selector to process the next available digit code in the source field. The Edit instruction replaces the Digit Selector with either the fill character or a zoned version of the source digit. This is done according to whether the digit is significant or not. If the Significance Indicator is off and the source digit is zero, the fill character

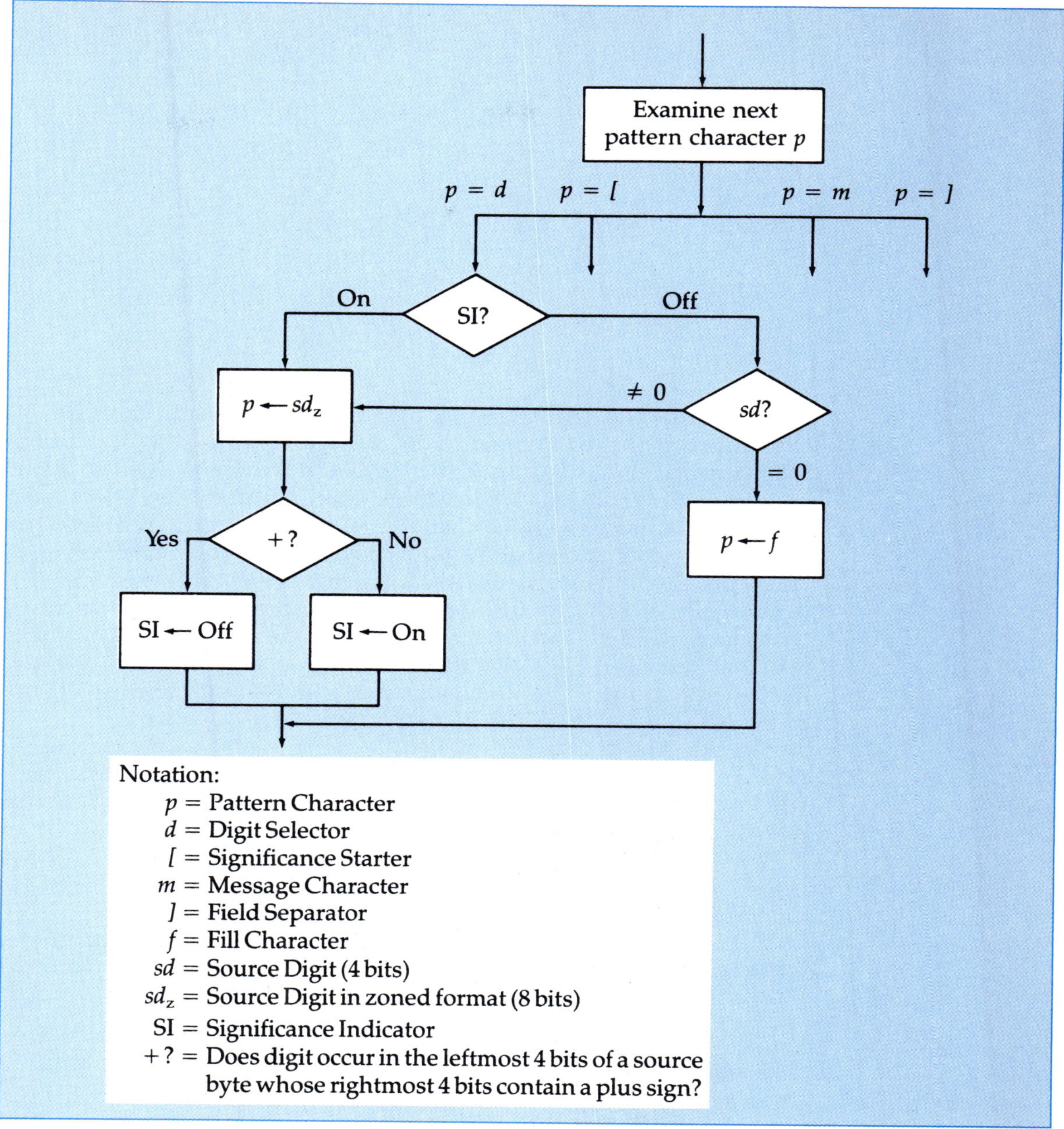


**Figure 14.10**
The effect of the Digit Selector.

replaces the Digit Selector in the pattern and the instruction considers the next pattern character. However, if the source digit is not zero, or if the Significance Indicator is on, the source digit, when converted to a zoned form, replaces the pattern character. If the digit occurred in the leftmost 4 bits of the source byte and if the rightmost 4 bits of the source byte contain a plus sign, the Significance Indicator is turned off; otherwise, it is turned on. The effect of the Digit Selector is summarized in Figure 14.10.

In the following examples, the status of the Significance Indicator (SI) is given both at the start of the instruction and when its value changes.

EXAMPLE 27

**ED P(6),S**

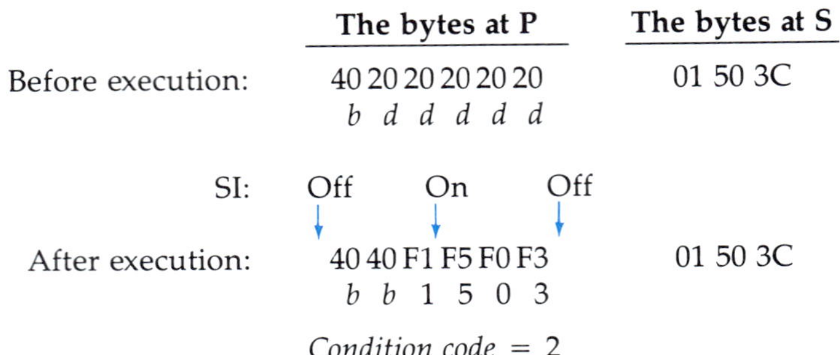


The fill character in the first byte of the pattern is a blank. There are five Digit Selectors that correspond to the five source digits 0, 1, 5, 0, and 3. When the first zero is processed, the Significance Indicator is off so the fill character replaces the first Digit Selector. Since the next Digit Selector corresponds to a nonzero source digit (the 1), the source digit in zoned form replaces the pattern character. As this is the first nonzero digit encountered, the Significance Indicator is turned on. The instruction converts subsequent digits—including the 0 since the Significance Indicator is on—to zoned form and replaces the pattern characters with these zoned digits. The source byte that contains the last digit (the 3) also contains a plus sign in its rightmost 4 bits so the Significance Indicator is turned off after the digit is processed.

Since the Significance Indicator is off when the edit is complete and the field is nonzero, the condition code is set to 2. (The condition code settings will be discussed in detail later. They are included here for subsequent reference.)

If the field at S is negative instead of positive, the Significance Indicator is left on at the conclusion of the edit and the condition code is set to 1. The result at P is exactly the same as before.

If the source field at S contains more decimal digits than the pattern can accommodate, the results will be incorrect, as shown:

| | The bytes at P | The bytes at S |
|---|---|---|
| Before execution: | 40 20 20 20 20 20<br>*b d d d d d* | 89 71 64 2C |
| SI: | Off ↓ On ↓ | |
| After execution: | 40 F8 F9 F7 F1 F6<br>*b* 8 9 7 1 6 | 89 71 64 2C |

*Condition code* = 1, *Incorrect results*

The Edit instruction does not process all of S, so the result is incorrect, but there is no warning of this fact.

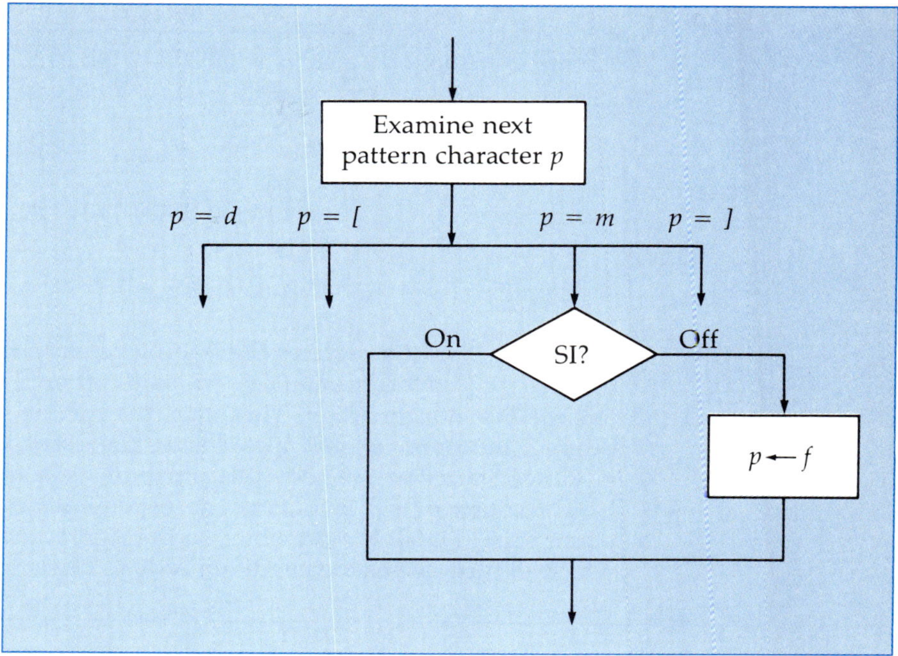


**Figure 14.11**
The effect of a message character.

**Message characters are left unchanged or are replaced by the fill character, according to the Significance Indicator.**

*Message Characters.* You can insert characters anywhere within the pattern to punctuate or label the output field. When the Edit instruction encounters a message character in the pattern, the character is either left unchanged if the Significance Indicator is on, or it is replaced by the fill character. Figure 14.11 shows the effect of a message character.

The next example demonstrates how to insert a comma into a 5-digit numeric field and how to omit it when the field contains only 3 or fewer digits.

---

EXAMPLE 28

```
ED      P(10),S
```

| | The bytes at P | The bytes at S |
|---|---|---|
| Before execution: | 40 20 20 6B 20 20 20 4B 20 20<br>*b d d , d d d . d d* | 01 23 00 4F |
| SI: | Off ↓ (at 40) On ↓ (at 20 → F1) Off ↓ (at F4) | |
| After execution: | 40 40 F1 6B F2 F3 F0 4B F0 F4<br>*b b* 1 , 2 3 0 . 0 4 | 01 23 00 4F |

*Condition code* = 2

After this Edit instruction processes the first significant digit (the 1), the Significance Indicator is turned on. All subsequent digits and message characters are then significant and appear in the result. When the last digit (the 4) is selected, its byte contains a plus sign in the rightmost 4 bits, so the Significance Indicator is turned off; this in turn causes the condition code to be set to 2.

Now consider a negative source field with several leading zeros.

| | The bytes at P | The bytes at S |
|---|---|---|
| Before execution: | 40 20 20 6B 20 20 20 4B 20 20 | 00 00 01 2D |
| | *b d d , d d d . d d* | |
| SI: | Off ↓ … On ↓ | |
| After execution: | 40 40 40 40 40 40 40 40 F1 F2 | 00 00 01 2D |
| | *b b b b b b b b* 1 2 | |
| | *Condition code* = 1 | |

The fill character replaces the leading zeros and the message characters because the Significance Indicator remains off until the instruction encounters the first nonzero digit. This omits the comma from the output field as desired, but unfortunately also deletes the decimal point. Use of the Significance Starter will remedy this situation, as described next.

The source byte that contains the last digit selected (the 2) does not have a plus sign in its rightmost 4 bits, so the Significance Indicator remains on, which in turn causes the condition code to be set to 1.

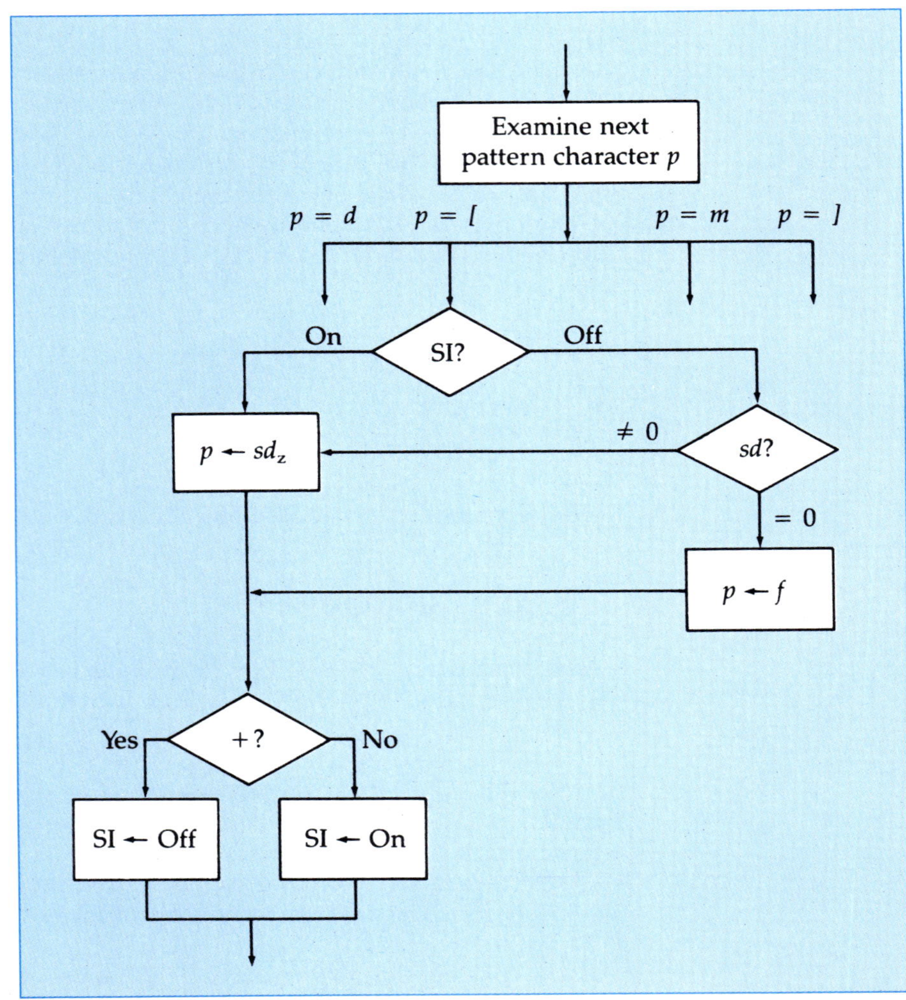


**Figure 14.12**
The effect of the Significance Starter.

**The Significance Starter performs the same function as a Digit Selector, but also forces the significance of leading zeros or message characters.**

*The Significance Starter (X'21').* You use the Significance Starter to forc significance of leading zeros and message characters. The next avai... source digit affects the Significance Starter in almost the same manner as the Digit Selector. The only difference is that, when the fill character replaces the Significance Starter a determination is made as to whether the corresponding source digit (which must be zero) occurs in the leftmost 4 bits of a source byte that contains a plus sign in its rightmost 4 bits. If it does not, the Significance Indicator is turned on; if it does, the Significance Starter is left off. Figure 14.12 shows the effect of the Significance Starter. In contrast, when the fill character replaces a Digit Selector, the Significance Indicator is left unchanged and processing continues with the next pattern character.

---

EXAMPLE 29

```
ED      P(11),S
```

| | The bytes at P | The bytes at S |
|---|---|---|
| Before execution: | 40 20 20 6B 20 20 21 4B 20 20 60 | 00 00 01 2D |
| | b d d , d d [ . d d – | |
| SI: | Off ↓ ... On ↓ | |
| After execution: | 40 40 40 40 40 40 40 4B F1 F2 60 | 00 00 01 2D |
| | b b b b b b b . 1 2 – | |
| | *Condition code* = 1 | |

The fill character (the blank) replaces each of the pattern characters before the Significance Starter. The Significance Starter then selects the fifth 0 in S. Since the Significance Indicator is off, the fill character replaces the Significance Starter. Since the source byte that contains this 0 does not contain a plus sign in its rightmost 4 bits (these bits contain the next digit, 1), the Significance Indicator is then turned on. This action makes the next message character, the decimal point, significant, so it is retained in the result.

After the instruction processes the last Digit Selector, the Significance Indicator is left on because of the absence of a plus sign in the last source byte considered. Therefore, the last message character, the minus sign, is retained in the result. The effect is that a trailing minus sign flags a negative value in the output field, a common practice in financial statements. The condition code is set to 1 since the Significance Indicator is on at the conclusion of the instruction.

Note that if S had contained a positive number, the Significance Indicator would have been turned off after the selection of the last digit. This would cause the fill character to replace the last message character, which is the minus sign, and the condition code to be set to 2.

Notice that a 0 does not appear to the left of the decimal point. Often, it is desirable to print such a 0; to do this, you must move the Significance Starter one byte to the left, as demonstrated next.

---

```
ED      P(11),S
```

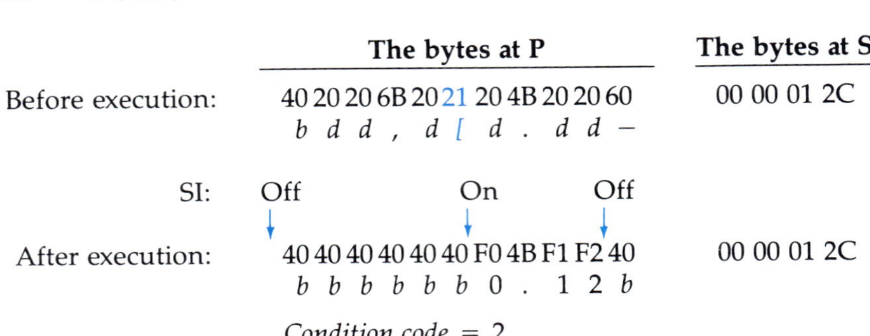


Here, the Significance Starter is positioned 1 byte before its position in the pattern of Example 29. As a result, the Significance Indicator is turned on prior to the rightmost leading zero, which makes this zero significant.

The Significance Indicator is turned off after the last digit is processed because of the plus sign. Therefore, the fill character replaces the final message character, which is the minus sign. The condition code is set to 2.

---

**The Field Separator allows you to process several fields with one Edit instruction.**

*The Field Separator (X'22').* A single Edit instruction can process several packed-decimal fields that are defined in contiguous bytes of storage. The edit pattern must consist of several subpatterns—one per packed-decimal field—that are separated by Field Separator codes (X'22'). The Edit instruction always replaces each Field Separator with the fill character and then turns the Significance Indicator off. Figure 14.13 shows the effect of the Field Separator. When you use a single Edit instruction to process several fields, the condition code reflects the status of only the last field.

**Figure 14.13**
The effect of the Field Separator.

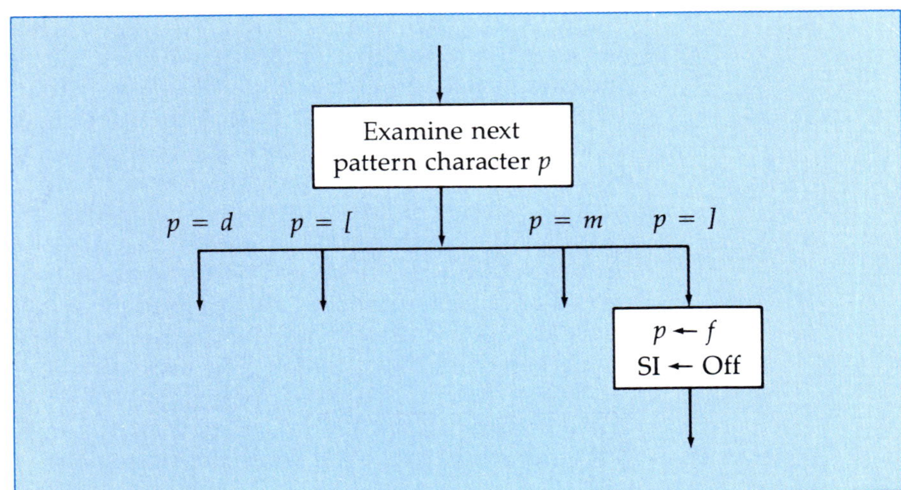

EXAMPLE 31 **ED P(11),S**

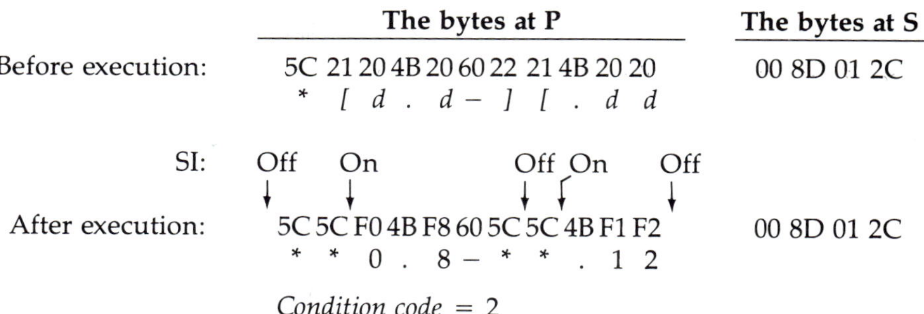

| | The bytes at P | The bytes at S |
|---|---|---|
| Before execution: | 5C 21 20 4B 20 60 22 21 4B 20 20<br>* [ d . d – ] [ . d d | 00 8D 01 2C |
| SI: | Off On Off On Off | |
| After execution: | 5C 5C F0 4B F8 60 5C 5C 4B F1 F2<br>* * 0 . 8 – * * . 1 2 | 00 8D 01 2C |

*Condition code* = 2

There are two packed-decimal fields at S, and two subpatterns, which are separated by a Field Separator, at P. The fill character, which is an asterisk, applies to both fields; that is, the second subpattern does not start with its own fill character. The fill character replaces the first Significance Starter since a leading zero was selected when the Significance Indicator was off; the Significance Indicator is then turned on. Because the Significance Indicator is on, the zero that is selected by the next Digit Selector is retained as are the decimal point, the next digit, and the trailing minus sign. The Significance Indicator is still on at this point because the instruction has not detected a plus sign. The fill character replaces the Field Separator and the Significance Indicator is turned off. The first packed-decimal field has now been processed.

The fill character then replaces the next Significance Starter since the Significance Indicator is off and the corresponding source digit is zero. The Significance Indicator is then turned on; this causes the decimal point to be retained in the result. When the plus sign is encountered, the Significance Indicator is turned off and the condition code is set to 2, which reflects the status of the last field.

*The Condition Code.* The condition code reflects the status of the last or only packed-decimal field edited; it is set to one of the following:

0 if the last field edited is zero or if no Digit Selector or Significance Starter codes are encountered.
1 if the last field edited is nonzero and the Significance Indicator is on at the conclusion of the instruction.
2 if the last field edited is nonzero and the Significance Indicator is off at the conclusion of the instruction.

As long as the last source byte that is edited contains a sign code in its rightmost 4 bits, the Significance Indicator and, therefore, the condition code reflect the sign of the last field. This is the typical case.

## SELF-TEST EXERCISES

7. Indicate the results—the edited field, the condition code, and the changes to the Significance Indicator—of editing each of the following source fields with the given pattern. Continue to use the same pattern until a new one is listed.

| | Pattern | Source |
|---|---|---|
| a. | 40 20 20 20 20 20 | 98765D |
| b. | | 00802C |
| c. | 40 20 20 6B 20 20 20 4B 20 20 | 0109807D |
| d. | | 0000100C |
| e. | | 6000000D |
| f. | | 0000004C |
| g. | 40 20 20 6B 20 20 21 4B 20 20 60 | 9000008D |
| h. | | 0050042C |
| i. | | 0012305D |
| j. | | 0004600C |
| k. | | 0000199D |
| l. | | 0000002C |
| m. | 40 20 20 6B 20 21 20 4B 20 20 60 | 9000008D |
| n. | | 0050042C |
| o. | | 0012305D |
| p. | | 0004600C |
| q. | | 0000199D |
| r. | | 0000002C |
| s. | 5C 21 20 4B 20 60 22 21 4B 20 20 | 091C500D |
| t. | | 123D001C |
| u. | | 000C090D |

8. The following are EBCDIC results that you can create when the packed-decimal number =X'00123C' is edited with the ED instruction. What pattern is necessary in each case?

| | Character Form | Hexadecimal Form |
|---|---|---|
| a. | *bbb*123 | 404040F1F2F3 |
| b. | *bbb*.123 | 4040404BF1F2F3 |
| c. | *bb*0.123 | 4040F04BF1F2F3 |
| d. | *bbb*1.23 | 404040F14BF2F3 |
| e. | *bbb*12.3 | 404040F1F24BF3 |
| f. | *bbb*123. | 404040F1F2F34B |

### *The Edit and Mark (EDMK) Instruction*

Assume that the results of an Edit instruction appear at P as

*b b b b b* 1 2 . 3 4

Suppose that you want to insert a dollar sign into this field. Without examining each byte, you have no way of knowing how many leading blanks, if any, exist in the field. Therefore, the best that you can do in general is to place the dollar sign in the leftmost byte of the field by using

```
MVI   P,C'$'
```

The result is then

$bbbb12.34

The blanks between the dollar sign and the first digit are a problem. To avoid them, you could change the fill character to an asterisk and obtain

$****12.34

A better alternative is possible with the Edit and Mark instruction because it can determine the address of the leftmost significant digit. Using this instruction, you can easily move the dollar sign into the preceding position. The instruction can be summarized as follows:

| Operation | Operand | Format | Instruction Name |
|---|---|---|---|
| **EDMK** | *S1(L1),S2* or *D1(L1,B1),D2(B2)* | $SS_1$ | EDIT AND MARK |

**Action**

$C(E1)_{L1}$ ← Zoned and edited packed-decimal field, or fields, at *E2*.
C(Register $1)_{8\text{-}31}$ ← Address of the first nonzero digit selected unless a previous Significance Starter forced the digit's significance. (In 31-bit addressing, bits 1 through 31 contain the address, and bit 0 is set to 0.)
The pattern characters and the condition code settings are the same as for the ED instruction.

**EDMK can affect Register 1.**

EDMK performs all of the functions of the ED instruction and also places the address of the leftmost nonzero digit of the result into Register 1, unless an earlier Significance Starter turned the Significance Indicator on, which would force significance of this digit. In other words, if the Significance Indicator is off and a zoned digit (which will be nonzero) replaces the pattern character, the address of the pattern character is placed into Register 1. Such pattern characters will only be a Digit Selector or a Significance Starter since only they select source digits. The portion of each flowchart in Figures 14.10 and 14.12 that relates to these two pattern characters is redrawn in Figure 14.14 to indicate exactly when EDMK affects Register 1.

Unfortunately, the EDMK instruction does not always affect Register 1. In such cases, the first significant digit or message character will be in the byte after the Significance Starter. Prior to execution of EDMK, you should

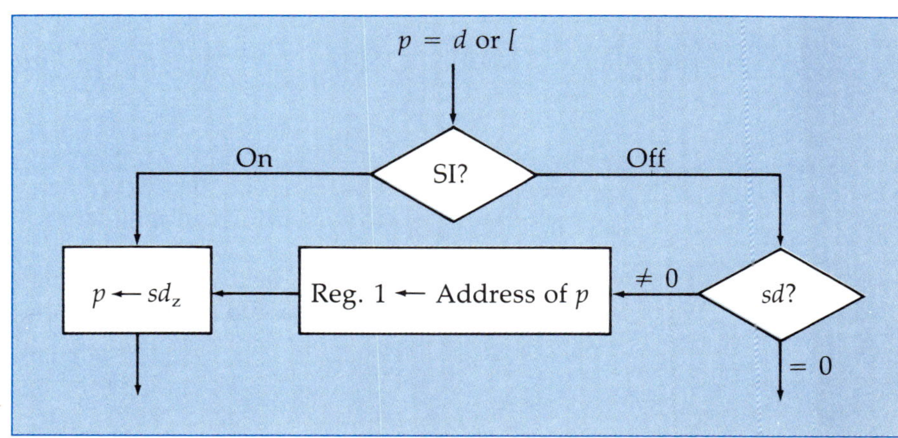


**Figure 14.14** The effect of the EDMK instruction on Register 1.

initialize Register 1 to the address of this byte so that, following execution, the register will always point to the first significant digit in the result. This is demonstrated later in Example 33.

---

EXAMPLE 32

```
EDMK    P(9),S
```

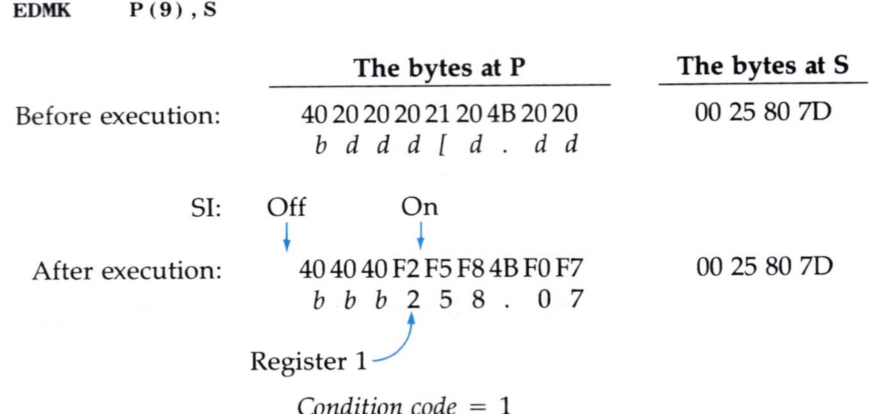


The fill character replaces the first two Digit Selectors since they correspond to zeros and since the Significance Indicator is off. The digit 2 in zoned form replaces the third Digit Selector and, since this is a nonzero digit, the Significance Indicator is turned on. The address of this result byte is placed into Register 1. If P represents the address 05A407, then Register 1 contains the address 05A40A. The Significance Indicator remains on because the source field is negative.

In this example, the first nonzero digit corresponds to the Digit Selector to the left of the Significance Starter. Now, suppose that it corresponds to the Significance Starter itself, as in the following:

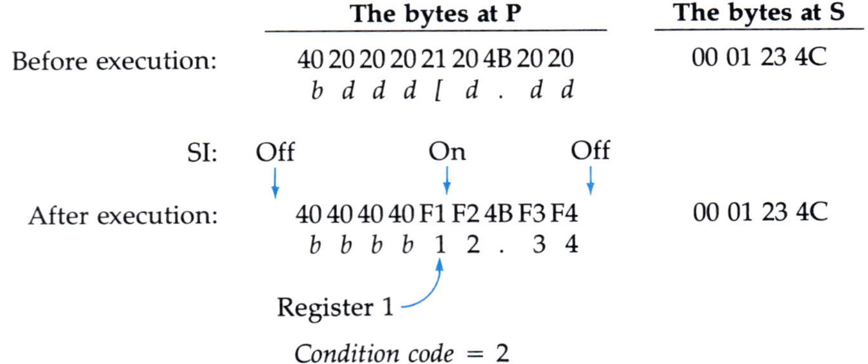


The Significance Starter selects the first nonzero digit; since the Significance Indicator is off, the address of this pattern character is placed into Register 1 and the Significance Indicator is turned on.

Finally, consider a source field whose first nonzero digit corresponds to a Digit Selector to the right of the Significance Starter.

| | The bytes at P | The bytes at S |
|---|---|---|
| Before execution: | 40 20 20 20 21 20 4B 20 20<br>*b d d d [ d . d d* | 00 00 00 7D |
| SI: | Off ↓ On ↓ | |
| After execution: | 40 40 40 40 40 F0 4B F0 F7<br>*b b b b b* 0 . 0 7 | 00 00 00 7D |

Register 1 is unchanged.

*Condition code* = 1

Register 1 remains unchanged since the Significance Indicator is on at the time a zoned source digit first replaces a pattern character. Notice that this source digit is zero and an earlier Significance Starter forced its significance.

---

EXAMPLE 33

**Insert a Dollar Sign Adjacent to the Leftmost Digit**

The sequence of instructions in Figure 14.15 inserts a dollar sign immediately to the left of the first digit of the result. The address of this digit will always be in Register 1 either by default or through the action of the EDMK instruction. The MVI instruction moves the dollar sign into the byte at the preceding address.

The reference to DEFAULT, which is the default value of Register 1 (the address of the byte after the Significance Starter), is prone to error since the pattern may change during program development. Since this example involves money, the rightmost portion of the pattern is less likely to change than the leftmost portion; therefore, the reference *−4 was used instead of RESULT+5. (Another approach is taken in the next example.)

It is a good idea to use a copy of the pattern when you edit a field, as is done here, so that you can reuse the original pattern later in the program.

**Figure 14.15** Instructions to insert a dollar sign adjacent to the leftmost digit, as described in Example 33.

```
** EDIT FIELD AND INSERT DOLLAR SIGN
          LA    R1,DEFAULT          POINT TO POSITION LEFT OF POINT
          MVC   RESULT,PATT         COPY PATTERN
          EDMK  RESULT,SOURCE       EDIT SOURCE; MARK FIRST SIG. DIGIT
          BCTR  R1,0                POINT TO LEFT OF FIRST SIG. DIGIT
          MVI   0(R1),C'$'          MOVE IN DOLLAR SIGN
          .
          .
          .
SOURCE    DS    PL4                 PACKED-DECIMAL SOURCE FIELD
PATT      DC    X'4020202021204B2020' PATTERN: BDDD[D.DD
RESULT    DS    CL9                 THE EBCDIC RESULT
DEFAULT   EQU   *-4                 POSITION OF DEFAULT SIG. DIGIT
```

EXAMPLE 34

**Insert a Minus Sign Adjacent to the Leftmost Digit of a Negative Number**

The sequence of instructions in Figure 14.16 inserts a minus sign to the immediate left of the first significant digit of a negative result. This example is similar to Example 33: in fact, it uses the same pattern but defines it differently so that each portion can be identified. By giving a name to the default address for Register 1, you are less likely to make a mistake if you subsequently change the pattern. As you become more experienced in pattern construction, you may find this technique tedious, but it can help you now.

Notice how the condition code is used to determine the sign of the result. Negative numbers will be preceded with a minus sign; positive numbers are left unsigned.

```
** EDIT FIELD AND INSERT MINUS SIGN IF NEGATIVE
         LA     R1,SIGDIG             POINT TO POSITION LEFT OF POINT
         MVC    RESULT,PATT           COPY PATTERN
         EDMK   RESULT,SOURCE         EDIT SOURCE; MARK FIRST SIG. DIGIT
         BNM    DONE                  IF POSITIVE, FINISHED;
         BCTR   R1,0                  ELSE POINT LEFT OF FIRST SIG. DIGIT
         MVI    0(R1),C'-'            MOVE IN MINUS SIGN
DONE     ---
         .
         .
         .
SOURCE   DS     PL4                   PACKED-DECIMAL SOURCE FIELD
PATT     DS     0X                    PATTERN: BDDD[D.DD
         DC     C' '                    FILL CHARACTER
         DC     X'202020'               3 DIGIT SELECTORS
         DC     X'21'                   SIGNIF. STARTER
SIGDIG   DC     X'20'                   DEFAULT SIGNIF. DIGIT
         DC     C'.'                    DECIMAL POINT
         DC     X'2020'                 2 DIGIT SELECTORS
RESULT   DS     CL9                   THE EBCDIC RESULT
```

**Figure 14.16**
Instructions to insert a minus sign adjacent to the leftmost digit of a negative number, as described in Example 34.

EXAMPLE 35

**Determine the Length of an Edited Result**

In Example 33 and Example 34, you can readily determine the address of the rightmost byte of the result. (It is represented by RESULT+8.) Since Register 1 contains the address of the first nonblank character in the result, you can compute the length of the result, and use the MVC and EX instructions to move the result to another location. This is particularly useful when you must insert the edited result without using extra spaces into several places in a text. (Exercise 15 at the end of the chapter considers this further.)

## SELF-TEST EXERCISES

9. Indicate the results of

```
MVC    P(10),=X'5C2020206B2020214B20'
EDMK   P(10),S
```

when S contains the following:

a. 9876543C  c. 0005028D
b. 0010000C  d. 0000002D

10. Indicate the results of the instructions in Figure 14.15 when SOURCE contains the following:

a. PL4'1234567'  c. PL4'123'
b. PL4'1234'  d. PL4'12'

Repeat with the instructions in Figure 14.16.

11. The following are EBCDIC results that can be created after you edit the packed-decimal number =X'01234D' with the EDMK instruction. What pattern is necessary in each case?

| | Character Form | Hexadecimal Form |
|---|---|---|
| a. | *bb*−1,234 | 404060F16BF2F3F4 |
| b. | *b*−1,234. | 4060F16BF2F3F44B |
| c. | *bb*−123.4 | 404060F1F2F34BF4 |
| d. | *bb*.1234− | 40404BF1F2F3F460 |

12. Write instructions that include EDMK to convert a 32-bit binary integer to decimal in a form that is suitable for printing. Compare your answer with the instructions in Figure 14.8 (Example 26).

13. Formulate rules that predict the contents of Register 1 when you use one EDMK instruction to edit multiple packed-decimal fields.

### *Creating the Pattern*

The ability to predict the results of ED or EDMK given a pattern is usually not sufficient to avoid the pitfalls that you encounter when you write your own patterns. The observations and suggestions made here should facilitate your task and help you to avoid errors.

**The total number of Digit Selector codes and Significance Starter codes in an edit pattern must be odd.**

First, observe that the total number of Digit Selector codes and Significance Starter codes in the pattern must equal the maximum possible number of digits that can be represented in the packed-decimal field. This is true because only those codes select digits, and the ED or EDMK instruction must select all digits if the field is to be properly edited. Now, if you count leading zeros, a packed-decimal number always represents an odd number of digits since all but the last byte contain 2 digits each; the last byte contains just 1 digit. Thus, an $L$-byte field represents $2 * L - 1$ digits, and therefore the total number of Digit Selector codes and Significance Starter codes in a pattern must be odd. You should check each pattern to ensure that this is true.

You should define the source field with an explicit length modifier and some indication of the assumed number of digits to the right of the decimal point. For example, you might write

```
SOURCE    DS    PL6    000000000.00
```

or

```
SOURCE      DC     PL6'.00'
```

As demonstrated in Examples 33 and 34, you should define the pattern separately from the result field, and then copy the pattern into the result field prior to each edit. The pattern and the result field are of the same length. To help you construct a pattern, first reserve space for the result field by using the DS or DC directive and a picture of the intended output. Since the result is a character field, use a C-type constant. The result should begin with the fill character since the pattern does. There should be one character for each digit in the source field, as well as room for desired punctuation or labels. Decide if and where a significant digit must occur, and mark it with an X; designate other digits with zeros. The following statements define two identical result fields where PATT represents the address of the pattern:

```
RESULT1    DC     CL(L'PATT)' 000,000,00X.00'
```

or

```
RESULT2    DS     CL(L'PATT)          ' 000,000,00X.00'
```

A DC and a constant define RESULT1; a DS and a remark define and describe RESULT2. During early versions of the program, RESULT1 has the advantage that you can use it for output as is.

The definitions of RESULT1 and RESULT2 use an explicit length that equals the length of the pattern. Even if this length is in error, when you copy the pattern into the result field, at least the lengths of the two fields will match. Note that you must write the definition of PATT before you use L'PATT as an explicit length modifier—this is a slight inconvenience because you will design the pattern last.

Finally, define the pattern as a hexadecimal constant by using the picture of the results that you have already written. Each pattern byte corresponds to one character in the result. Copy the fill character and the message characters from the result field into the pattern. If there is an X in the result field, write a Significance Starter (X'21') in the pattern byte that corresponds to the 0 that is immediately before the X. Write a Digit Selector (X'20') for the X and all other zeros. If the result field does not contain an X, simply write Digit Selectors in the pattern to correspond to each 0 in the result. Thus, the required pattern for the previous result field at RESULT1 is defined by

```
PATT DC    X'402020206B2020206B2021204B2020'   'bddd,ddd,d[d.dd'
```

It may help you to memorize the more common EBCDIC codes that are used in patterns, such as those listed here:

| Character: | Blank | . | * | – | , |
|---|---|---|---|---|---|
| Hex code: | 40 | 4B | 5C | 60 | 6B |

Use the source, result, and pattern fields just defined as follows:

```
MVC    RESULT1,PATT          COPY PATTERN
ED     RESULT1,SOURCE        EDIT SOURCE FIELD
```

Do not specify a length in either instruction. The assembler will define the *L1* field in both instructions to be L'RESULT1, which by design is equal to L'PATT.

A similar but inferior approach is to define the following:

```
RESULT   DC    C' 000,000,00X.00'
PATT     DC    XL(L'RESULT)'402020206B2020206B2021204B2020'
```

As long as both fields are errorfree, this approach is acceptable; however, if RESULT is shorter than necessary, the assembler will truncate PATT on the left without warning and, therefore, the pattern will be incorrect.

The following guidelines summarize the steps that you should take to prepare for an editing operation. For simplicity, one packed-decimal field is assumed; however, if a single instruction edits several such fields, the following apply to each subpattern that corresponds to a packed-decimal field:

**Guidelines for pattern construction**

1. Use an explicit length modifier when you define the source field. Indicate the assumed number of places to the right of the decimal point.
2. Define the result field with a C-type constant by using characters that picture the desired output. Leave room for the fill character, the digits, and any required punctuation or labels. Decide if you want to force a significant digit and, if so, indicate this digit with an X; indicate the other digits with a zero. Use an explicit and symbolic length modifier that equals the length of the pattern. This requires that the result field follow the definition of the pattern.
3. Define the pattern with hexadecimal constants by using the result field as a guide. Each digit in the result must correspond to a Digit Selector or, in at most one case, a Significance Starter. Do not use an explicit length modifier.
4. The total number of Digit Selector and Significance Starter codes in the pattern must equal the number of source digits. This number is always *odd*.
5. Before each edit, copy the pattern into the result field. Omit length specifications in both the Move instruction and the Edit instruction.

## Debugging Hints

1. PACK and UNPK are the only instructions in this chapter that are in the $SS_2$ format. Remember that $SS_2$ instructions contain two lengths internally and, if you omit one or both lengths when you designate the operands, the assembler will use the length attribute of each relevant operand. This may or may not be what you intended. When in doubt, check the object code.
2. Two exceptions that cause program interruptions are common when you use the CVB instruction. A data exception indicates an invalid digit code or an invalid sign code in the second operand. This is likely to occur if the second operand is not 8 bytes long. A fixed-point divide exception signals an overflow; the magnitude of the packed-decimal number is larger than a 32-bit binary integer can represent.
3. Despite the fact that ED and EDMK process packed-decimal fields, each requires only one length specification and processes the fields left to right. In this respect, they differ from PACK, UNPK, and the

remaining decimal instructions that you will encounter in the next chapter. In this chapter, the section called "Creating the Pattern" included debugging hints, preventative measures, and stylistic comments that are relevant to these instructions. Keep them in mind.

4. The EDMK instruction does not always affect Register 1. To compensate, be sure that you have initialized Register 1 before you execute EDMK.

## Stylistic Notes

1. Try to avoid all but the simplest of field overlaps when you use PACK and UNPK. If you do overlap fields, start both fields at the same address, if possible. Specify the field lengths explicitly in cases of field overlap.
2. Use the data movement property of the PACK and UNPK instructions to your advantage. For example, do not PACK a zoned field on top of itself and then move the result to another area. Instead, specify the ultimate destination as the first operand of the PACK instruction. Although the ZAP instruction, which is described in the next chapter, provides a convenient way to move a packed-decimal field to a longer or shorter area (unlike the MVC instruction), using it after a PACK or UNPK instruction adds an unnecessary step.

## Summary

1. A zoned-decimal number occupies a maximum of 16 bytes in storage, and can represent a maximum of 16 decimal digits. Except for the rightmost byte, each byte consists of a zone code and a digit code; the rightmost byte contains a sign code and a digit code.
2. A packed-decimal number occupies a maximum of 16 bytes in storage, and can represent a maximum of 31 decimal digits. Except for the rightmost byte, each byte consists of two digit codes; the rightmost byte contains a digit code and a sign code. Each packed-decimal field represents an odd number of digits. If the field is $L$ bytes long, then you can represent $2 * L - 1$ digits.
3. You can perform decimal arithmetic with packed-decimal numbers (as you will see in the next chapter), but not with zoned-decimal numbers. Zoned-decimal numbers are an intermediate form between packed-decimal numbers and EBCDIC characters, and are associated with input and output operations.
4. The computer recognizes the hexadecimal digits A, C, E, and F as valid plus signs, and B and D as valid minus signs. The preferred signs C and D are generated when decimal constants are assembled or when the CVD instruction is executed.
5. The PACK instruction converts decimal numbers from zoned-decimal form to packed-decimal form. The UNPK instruction converts decimal numbers from packed-decimal form to zoned-decimal form. Neither instruction checks the validity of any code and, therefore, these instructions can be used with any data.
6. The CVB instruction converts a packed-decimal number to a two's complement binary number. The CVD instruction converts a two's complement binary number to a packed-decimal number. Both instructions use a register and an 8-byte field in storage.
7. If the CVB instruction detects an illegal digit or sign code in its packed-decimal operand, a data exception will occur. If there is an overflow during the conversion to binary, a fixed-point divide exception will occur.
8. The ED instruction converts a packed-decimal number into an EBCDIC field suitable for output. In addition, the EDMK instruction loads Register 1 with the address of the first nonzero digit unless an earlier Significance Starter forced the digit's significance. You can use this address to position a sign or a dollar sign, or to determine the length of the result.
9. The total number of Digit Selector codes or Significance Starter codes that appear in an Edit pattern must be odd.

## New Instruction Summary

| Operation | Operand | Format | Instruction Name | Action |
|---|---|---|---|---|
| **PACK** | *S1*(*L1*),*S2*(*L2*) or *D1*(*L1*,*B1*),*D2*(*L2*,*B2*) | $SS_2$ | PACK | $C(E1)_{L1} \leftarrow$ Packed version of $C(E2)_{L2}$ |
| **UNPK** | *S1*(*L1*),*S2*(*L2*) or *D1*(*L1*,*B1*),*D2*(*L2*,*B2*) | $SS_2$ | UNPACK | $C(E1)_{L1} \leftarrow$ Zoned version of $C(E2)_{L2}$ |
| **CVB** | *R1*,*S2* or *R1*,*S2*(*X2*) or *R1*,*D2*(*X2*,*B2*) | RX | CONVERT TO BINARY | $C(R1) \leftarrow$ The two's complement binary equivalent of $C(E2)_{0\text{-}63}$ |
| **CVD** | *R1*,*S2* or *R1*,*S2*(*X2*) or *R1*,*D2*(*X2*,*B2*) | RX | CONVERT TO DECIMAL | $C(E2)_{0\text{-}63} \leftarrow$ The packed-decimal equivalent of $C(R1)$ |
| **ED** | *S1*(*L1*),*S2* or *D1*(*L1*,*B1*),*D2*(*B2*) | $SS_1$ | EDIT | $C(E1)_{L1} \leftarrow$ Zoned and edited packed-decimal field, or fields, at *E2* |

Pattern characters:

Digit Selector = X'20'
Significance Starter = X'21'
Field Separator = X'22'

Condition code =
- 0 if the last field edited is zero or if no Digit Selector or Significance Starter codes are encountered while editing the last field
- 1 if the last field edited is nonzero and the Significance Indicator is on at the conclusion of the instruction
- 2 if the last field edited is nonzero and the Significance Indicator is off at the conclusion of the instruction

| Operation | Operand | Format | Instruction Name | Action |
|---|---|---|---|---|
| **EDMK** | *S1*(*L1*),*S2* or *D1*(*L1*,*B1*),*D2*(*B2*) | $SS_1$ | EDIT AND MARK | $C(E1)_{L1} \leftarrow$ Zoned and edited packed-decimal field(s) at *E2* $C(\text{Register } 1)_{8\text{-}31} \leftarrow$ Address of the first nonzero digit selected unless a previous Significance Starter forced the digit's significance. (In 31-bit addressing, bits 1 through 31 contain the address, and bit 0 is set to 0.) The pattern characters and the condition code settings are the same as for the ED instruction. |

## New Constant Types with DC or DS Directives

| Name | Operation | Operand | Action |
|---|---|---|---|
| *symbol* or *blank* | DC | *d*PL*n*'*c*' | Defines *d* copies of an *n*-byte packed-decimal number whose value is *c*. Padding with 0's or truncation occurs on the left, as necessary. When L*n* is omitted, chooses *n* to accommodate *c*. |
| *symbol* or *blank* | DC | *d*ZL*n*'*c*' | Defines *d* copies of an *n*-byte zoned-decimal number whose value is *c*. Padding with F0's or truncation occurs on the left, as necessary. When L*n* is omitted, chooses *n* to accommodate *c*. |
| *symbol* or *blank* | DS | *d*PL*n*'*c*' or *d*ZL*n*'*c*' | Reserves *d***n* bytes whether or not '*c*' is written. When L*n* is omitted, chooses *n* to accommodate *c*, but does not define a constant. When both L*n* and '*c*' are omitted, reserves *d* bytes. |

## Exercises

1. If you UNPK a field and then PACK the result, how does what you have differ from the original field?
2. Assume that an *L*-byte zoned-decimal field begins at Z and that Register 3 contains the value of *L* as a binary integer. Write instructions that will convert the field to packed-decimal form, and will store it into the *L* bytes at Z; that is, PACK the field onto itself.
3. Assume that the 5-byte packed-decimal number at P contains *L* digits where *L* is in Register 3. Write instructions to convert the contents of P to zoned-decimal form and to store the result in the *L* bytes at Z.
4. Consider the following:

```
         PACK  X,X
         . . .
X        DS    ZL2
D        DS    D
```

What problems will you encounter if, after the PACK instruction, you try to move (by using an MVC instruction) the packed field at X to the field at D, in preparation for a CVB instruction?

5. Write instructions that include the UNPK and TR instructions to print, in hexadecimal, the contents of the 20-byte field at X.
6. Assume that your program has read an input record that contains an unsigned decimal integer right-justified in the first 9 columns. The integer may contain leading zeros or blanks. Write instructions to convert the integer into a 32-bit two's complement binary form.
7. Repeat Exercise 6, but assume that the record contains a plus sign or a minus sign in the first column, and that it is followed by a 9-digit decimal integer without blanks.
8. Repeat Exercise 7, but assume that the record contains an optionally signed decimal integer that is right-justified in a field of 10.
9. For each of the following character strings, write instructions that create the string from the packed-decimal number =P'−12345'.
   - **a.** 123.45
   - **b.** 12.345−
   - **c.** −12345
   - **d.** 1,234.5−
   - **e.** \$123.45−
   - **f.** \$12345.00
   - **g.** 12:34.5
10. Assume that the field at PDN contains a 9-digit packed-decimal number. Edit the field by using the ED instruction so that the result has all of the following properties: a decimal point is positioned with 2 digits to its right and at least 1 digit (possibly 0) to its left; there are no commas; and, if negative, the number is followed by CR.
11. Use the pattern that was defined in Example 30 with the EDMK instruction. After you edit the field, modify it so that any minus sign is to the

immediate left of the first nonblank character, instead of at the end of the field. Do this without testing the condition code. How does your answer compare with the approach used in Figure 14.16 of Example 34?

12. Assume that the 3-byte field at TEMP contains a packed-decimal number that represents a temperature in Celsius within the range of −999.9 to +999.9. Write instructions to print lines such as

```
THE TEMPERATURE IS -13.2 DEGREES CELSIUS.
```

or

```
THE TEMPERATURE IS 0.1 DEGREES CELSIUS.
```

Do not allow extra spaces in these lines.

13. Assume that the 5-byte field at BALANCE contains a packed-decimal number that represents a credit card balance. A positive value represents the amount owed; a negative value indicates a credit. Write instructions to print lines such as

```
YOU OWE $1,234.56 AS OF TODAY.
```

or

```
YOU HAVE A CREDIT OF $0.98 AS OF TODAY.
```

Do not allow extra spaces in these lines.

14. Under the same assumptions as given in Exercise 13, write instructions that will print negative balances enclosed in parentheses. Thus, $(0.98) represents a credit, while $1,234.56 is a balance due.

15. Assume two 2-byte fields at DIM1 and DIM2 that represent the dimensions of a room in feet. Write instructions to create a character string, such as

21′ BY 24′

Move the string to each of the fields whose beginning addresses are in Registers 7 and 10, respectively.

## Programming Problems

1. Write a subprogram to convert an unsigned hexadecimal number from an EBCDIC representation to a 32-bit binary representation.
2. Write a subprogram to convert an unsigned 32-bit binary integer to an 8-digit hexadecimal integer that is represented in EBCDIC.
3. Repeat Programming Problem 2 to allow the binary integer to be signed. The subprogram should produce a plus sign or a minus sign in its result.
4. Write a subprogram to print a signed 32-bit binary integer as a decimal integer that is right-justified in a field of 11 characters. Do not print leading zeros or a plus sign.
5. Write a subprogram that reads an optionally signed decimal integer from anywhere in an 80-byte data record, and that converts it to a 16-byte packed-decimal number. The subprogram should detect invalid characters or integers that are too large to be represented in packed-decimal form.
6. Repeat Programming Problem 5, but convert the input to a 32-bit signed binary integer.
7. Write a subprogram to convert an $n$-byte packed-decimal number to an $m$-byte EBCDIC field. The result should be right-justified in the $m$-byte field with blanks substituted for any leading zeros. Positive numbers should be unsigned, but negative numbers should have their sign adjacent to the leftmost digit. Insert commas into the result as appropriate. Assume that the addresses and lengths of the packed-decimal fields and the EBCDIC fields are arguments of the subprogram. If $m$ bytes are too few to contain the result, place $m$ asterisks in the EBCDIC field.
8. Write a subprogram that takes an array of five 8-byte packed-decimal numbers and prints the numbers on one line. Assume that the first number in the array is an unsigned integer, and that each of the remaining numbers has two decimal places and represents a monetary amount. Print dollar signs and decimal points as appropriate. Follow negative numbers with an asterisk.
9. Repeat Programming Problem 8, but assume that variable-length packed-decimal numbers are passed as arguments. The arguments are arranged in pairs: the first argument in the pair represents the packed-decimal number, and the second argument in the pair represents a 1-byte length of the number.

# 15

# Decimal Arithmetic

CONTENTS



OVERVIEW

This chapter continues the discussion of decimal numbers by presenting the instructions to perform decimal arithmetic. Because you can treat a packed-decimal number as an integer or assume a decimal point in a fixed position, you can perform either integral or nonintegral decimal computations. Nonintegral computations are common among the applications of decimal arithmetic.

**OBJECTIVES**

After studying this chapter, you should be able to:

1. Use the decimal instructions AP, SP, MP, DP, CP, and ZAP to add, subtract, multiply, divide, compare, and move decimal integers in packed-decimal form.
2. Use the instruction SRP or the instructions MVO and MVN to shift packed-decimal numbers to the right with optional rounding or to the left.
3. Perform decimal arithmetic with nonintegral data.
4. Describe the cause of a data exception, a decimal overflow exception, and a decimal divide exception in given situations.

## Introduction

Chapter 14 discussed the representations of decimal numbers. This chapter considers the details of decimal arithmetic, and defines instructions to add, subtract, multiply, divide, compare, move, and shift packed-decimal numbers. Although the decimal instructions perform integer arithmetic, most applications deal with nonintegral data. In such cases, you must keep track of the position of an *assumed* decimal point—possibly shifting the decimal number to align, or otherwise adjust, the position of the imaginary decimal point.

Typically, you use decimal arithmetic only in particular situations. Decimal arithmetic is an appropriate choice when you need exact decimal fractions as when money is involved. When you need only a few arithmetic calculations, it is usually easier to perform them with the decimal instructions than to convert the numbers to binary so that you can use the binary arithmetic instructions. Decimal arithmetic allows more precision than binary arithmetic, although double-precision floating-point arithmetic, which will be described in Chapter 17, may be better than either decimal or binary arithmetic. Finally, you may want to link an assembler language program with a COBOL program by using decimal representations in both programs.

## The Decimal Arithmetic Instructions

**You must use packed-decimal numbers to perform decimal arithmetic.**

This section introduces six instructions: Add Packed (AP), Subtract Packed (SP), Zero and Add Packed (ZAP), Compare Packed (CP), Multiply Packed (MP), and Divide Packed (DP). All six instructions require valid packed-decimal operands, and all six perform sign-magnitude arithmetic. Computed results always have a preferred sign, even though the operands can contain any valid sign. Operands may differ in length and may overlap if their rightmost bytes are coincident. If the CPU detects an invalid sign or digit code, or an invalid operand overlap, a data exception (and a program interruption) will occur.

### *The Add Packed (AP) Instruction*

The Add Packed instruction adds two packed-decimal numbers; the sum, also in packed-decimal form, replaces the first operand. The condition code is set to reflect the sign of the result or to indicate an overflow. The instruction can be summarized as follows:

| Operation | Operand | Format | Instruction Name | Action |
|---|---|---|---|---|
| **AP** | *S1*(*L1*),*S2*(*L2*) or *D1*(*L1*,*B1*),*D2*(*L2*,*B2*) | $SS_2$ | ADD PACKED | $C(E1)_{L1} \leftarrow C(E1)_{L1} + C(E2)_{L2}$ |

$$\text{Condition code} = \begin{cases} 0 \text{ if the sum is zero} \\ 1 \text{ if the sum is negative} \\ 2 \text{ if the sum is positive} \\ 3 \text{ if an overflow occurs} \end{cases}$$

**A decimal overflow exception can be masked off.**

In case *L1* is too small to accommodate the sum, an overflow occurs; the leftmost digits of the sum are lost. However, the digits that can be accommodated and the sign are correct and are stored at *E1*. The condition code is set to 3 and a **decimal overflow exception** occurs. A program interruption will also occur if the second bit of the program mask is 1. (The interruption code will be $000A_{16}$.) If the second bit of the program mask is 0, the exception is ignored and no interruption takes place. Decimal overflow is analogous to a fixed-point overflow that you may encounter during a binary addition.

It is possible for a negative zero to occur as a result of overflow; however, correct zero results are always positive.

---

EXAMPLE 1

```
AP    X(2),Y(1)
```

| | The bytes at X | The byte at Y |
|---|---|---|
| Before execution: | 12 3C | 1D |
| After execution: | 12 2C | 1D |
| | *Condition code* = 2 | |

The instruction performs the computation +123 + (−1) = +122.

---

---

EXAMPLE 2

```
AP      X(2),Y(3)
```

| | The bytes at X | The bytes at Y |
|---|---|---|
| Before execution: | 12 3B | 00 02 3C |
| After execution: | 10 0D | 00 02 3C |
| | *Condition code* = 1 | |

The instruction computes −123 + 23 = −100. Notice that, while the first operand contains an alternate minus sign, the result uses the preferred sign. Also, notice that, even though $L2 > L1$, an overflow does not occur and, in general, you cannot predict an overflow from the operand lengths.

---

EXAMPLE 3

```
AP      X(3),Y(3)
```

| | The bytes at X | The bytes at Y |
|---|---|---|
| Before execution: | 01 23 4D | 01 23 4C |
| After execution: | 00 00 0C | 01 23 4C |
| | *Condition code* = 0 | |

A valid zero result is always positive.

---

EXAMPLE 4

```
AP      X(2),Y(3)
```

| | The bytes at X | The bytes at Y |
|---|---|---|
| Before execution: | 23 4C | 01 23 4D |
| After execution: | 00 0D | 01 23 4D |
| | *Decimal overflow, Condition code* = 3 | |

The instruction computes +234 + (−1234) = −1000, but the result does not fit into 2 bytes. The rightmost 3 digits and the sign of the sum are stored at X, and are correct. The condition code is set to 3 and a decimal overflow exception occurs. A negative zero is the result of this particular overflow.

---

EXAMPLE 5

```
AP      X(2),X(2)
```

| | The bytes at X |
|---|---|
| Before execution: | 12 3D |
| After execution: | 24 6D |
| | *Condition code* = 1 |

Field overlap is permissible when the rightmost bytes of the fields are coincident. In this example, the operands are identical and X is added to itself.

---

### *The Subtract Packed (SP) Instruction*

Decimal subtraction is analogous to decimal addition. The Subtract Packed instruction computes the difference by changing the sign of a copy of the second operand and adding it to the first operand. The instruction can be summarized as follows:

| Operation | Operand | Format | Instruction Name | Action |
|---|---|---|---|---|
| **SP** | *S1*(*L1*),*S2*(*L2*)<br>or *D1*(*L1*,*B1*),*D2*(*L2*,*B2*) | $SS_2$ | SUBTRACT PACKED | $C(E1)_{L1} \leftarrow C(E1)_{L1} - C(E2)_{L2}$<br>The condition code is set just as for AP. |

---

EXAMPLE 6

```
SP    X(2),Y(1)
```

| | The bytes at X | The byte at Y |
|---|---|---|
| Before execution: | 12 3C | 1D |
| After execution: | 12 4C | 1D |
| | *Condition code* = 2 | |

The instruction computes $+123 - (-1) = +124$.

---

EXAMPLE 7

```
SP    X(2),Y(3)
```

| | The bytes at X | The bytes at Y |
|---|---|---|
| Before execution: | 12 3C | 00 45 6C |
| After execution: | 33 3D | 00 45 6C |
| | *Condition code* = 1 | |

The instruction computes $+123 - (+456) = -333$.

---

EXAMPLE 8

```
SP    X(2),Y(3)
```

| | The bytes at X | The bytes at Y |
|---|---|---|
| Before execution: | 23 4C | 01 23 4D |
| After execution: | 46 8C | 01 23 4D |
| | *Decimal overflow, Condition code* = 3 | |

The instruction computes $+234 - (-1234) = +1468$, but the result does not fit into 2 bytes. The rightmost 3 digits and the sign are stored at X, and are correct. The condition code is set to 3 and a decimal overflow exception occurs.

---

EXAMPLE 9

```
SP      X(3),X(3)
```

| | The bytes at X |
|---|---|
| Before execution: | 01 23 4D |
| After execution: | 00 00 0C |
| | *Condition code* = 0 |

X is subtracted from itself. As shown previously, notice that a valid zero result is positive.

You can use the SP instruction to set a field to decimal zero as long as the field already contains a valid packed-decimal number. Because of this restriction, it is often more convenient to use instead the ZAP instruction, which is described next.

### *The Zero and Add Packed (ZAP) Instruction*

**Use ZAP to move a packed-decimal number.**

Often, during the course of a decimal computation, you must move a packed-decimal number from one storage location to another, either for initialization purposes or to alter the length of the number's representation. The MVC instruction is inadequate for this purpose since both of its operands must be of the same length. ZAP makes moving a packed-decimal number simple.

Zero and Add Packed is technically an arithmetic instruction, but it may help to think of it as a load operation. The instruction replaces the contents of the first operand field with a copy of the packed-decimal number in the second operand field, which is adjusted appropriately to match the length *L1* of the first field. If necessary, the left side of the number is either padded with zeros or truncated. The result of the ZAP instruction is equivalent to that obtained by adding the second operand to a zeroed first operand. The instruction can be summarized as follows:

| Operation | Operand | Format | Instruction Name | Action |
|---|---|---|---|---|
| **ZAP** | *S1*(*L1*),*S2*(*L2*)<br>or *D1*(*L1*,*B1*),*D2*(*L2*,*B2*) | $SS_2$ | ZERO AND ADD PACKED | $C(E1)_{L1} \leftarrow 0 + C(E2)_{L2}$ |

Condition code = 0 if the result is zero; 1 if the result is negative; 2 if the result is positive; 3 if an overflow occurs

Here, condition code settings, exceptions, and comments that are relevant to the AP instruction apply with the following modification. Operand fields may overlap if the rightmost byte of the first operand is coincident with *or to the right of* the rightmost byte of the second operand, as illustrated in Figure 15.1.

It is important to realize that the first operand can contain anything initially; the operand does not need to be a valid packed-decimal number.

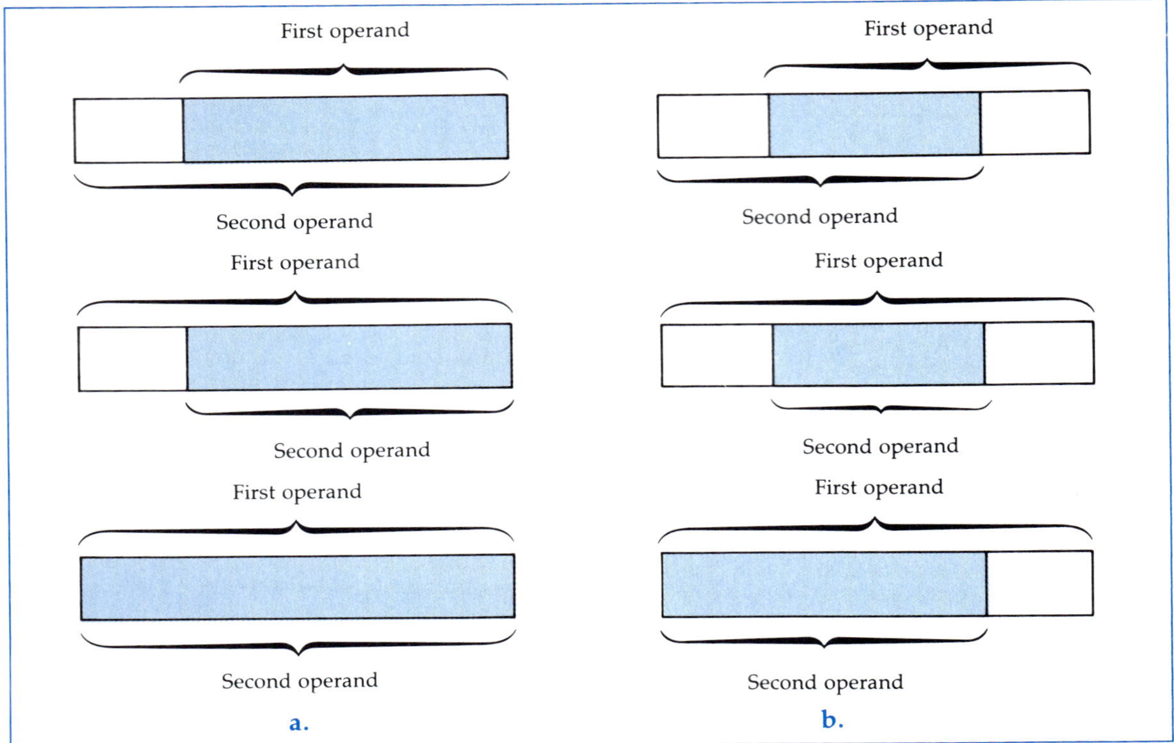


**Figure 15.1**
The possible ways that operands can overlap with the ZAP instruction: **a.** when the rightmost bytes are coincident; and, **b.** when the rightmost byte of the first operand is to the right of the rightmost byte of the second operand.

---

EXAMPLE 10

```
ZAP      X(4),Y(2)
```

| | **The bytes at X** | **The bytes at Y** |
|---|---|---|
| Before execution: | 45 67 89 0C | 12 3D |
| After execution: | 00 00 12 3D | 12 3D |
| | *Condition code* = 1 | |

The instruction replaces the field at X with a copy of the number at Y, which is padded on the left with zeros. Since the result at X is negative, the condition code is set to 1.

---

EXAMPLE 11

```
ZAP      X(2),Y(4)
```

| | **The bytes at X** | **The bytes at Y** |
|---|---|---|
| Before execution: | ?? ?? | 00 00 12 3F |
| After execution: | 12 3C | 00 00 12 3F |
| | *Condition code* = 2 | |

Even though the field at Y is longer than the field at X, the discarded digits are zeros, so the value of the result is correct. Note that the preferred sign is generated. Also, notice that the prior contents of X are irrelevant: they do not need to be a valid packed-decimal number.

---

EXAMPLE 12

```
ZAP     X(2),Y(4)
```

| | The bytes at X | The bytes at Y |
|---|---|---|
| Before execution: | ?? ?? | 12 34 56 7D |
| After execution: | 56 7D | 12 34 56 7D |

*Decimal overflow, Condition code* = 3

The contents of Y do not fit into the field at X. The leftmost digits are lost, the condition code is set to 3, and a decimal overflow exception occurs.

---

EXAMPLE 13

```
ZAP     X(5),=P'0'
```

| | The bytes at X | =P'0' |
|---|---|---|
| Before execution: | ?? ?? ?? ?? ?? | 0C |
| After execution: | 00 00 00 00 0C | 0C |

*Condition code* = 0

**Use ZAP to initialize a field to packed-decimal zero.**

This example demonstrates a convenient way to set a field to decimal zero. Although you need a constant in storage, the fact that the prior contents of the field X do not need to be a valid packed-decimal number usually makes this approach preferable to using the SP instruction, as was demonstrated in Example 9.

Notice that the length of the second operand is not stated explicitly, but the literal implies it to be 1.

---

EXAMPLE 14

```
ZAP     X(6),X(4)
```

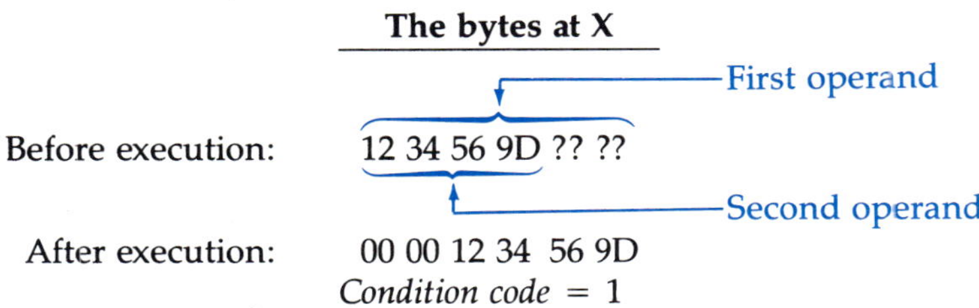


This is an example of correct field overlap: the rightmost byte of the first operand (at address X+5) is to the right of the rightmost byte of the second operand (at X+3).

---

EXAMPLE 15

**Compute the Sum of Several Packed-Decimal Numbers**

Consider an array of N packed-decimal numbers. Assume that N represents a fullword binary integer. The instructions in Figure 15.2 accumulate the sum of the numbers in this array.

Since each packed-decimal number is 3 bytes long, each contains at most 5 decimal digits. If you knew the nature of the numbers and the maximum value of N, you could estimate the number of digits that is necessary for the sum. However, you could just compute the sum in a 16-byte field, as shown in this example, since this would permit the largest possible packed-decimal result. Although 16 bytes may not be sufficient, it is the best that you can do without much more work.

```
** COMPUTE THE SUM OF THE N DECIMAL INTEGERS IN THE ARRAY AT NUMBERS.
** ASSUME N IS A FULLWORD BINARY INTEGER; N ≥ 1
*
* INITIALIZE:
          L     R3,N                R3 = LOOP COUNTER = NO. OF
*                                     INTEGERS
          SR    R4,R4               R4 = INDEX REGISTER = 0
          ZAP   SUM,=P'0'           CLEAR SUM AREA
* REPEAT:
LOOP      LA    R5,NUMBERS(R4)      R5 = ADDRESS OF NEXT INTEGER IN
*                                     ARRAY
          AP    SUM,0(L'NUMBERS,R5) ADD NEXT INTEGER TO SUM
          LA    R4,L'NUMBERS(R4)    INCREMENT INDEX BY LENGTH
*                                     OF INTEGER
* UNTIL COUNTER = 0
          BCT   R3,LOOP             DECREMENT COUNTER; REPEAT IF
*                                     NONZERO
* END REPEAT
          .
          .
          .
N         DS    F                   NO. OF INTEGERS IN THE ARRAY
NUMBERS   DS    50PL3               ARRAY OF 5-DIGIT INTEGERS
SUM       DS    PL16                SUM OF THE INTEGERS (31 DIGITS)
```

Figure 15.2
Instructions to compute the sum of several packed-decimal numbers, as described in Example 15.

## *The Compare Packed (CP) Instruction*

The Compare Packed instruction algebraically compares the values of two packed-decimal operands and sets the condition code accordingly. The instruction can be summarized as follows:

| Operation | Operand | Format | Instruction Name | Action |
|---|---|---|---|---|
| **CP** | $S1(L1),S2(L2)$ or $D1(L1,B1),D2(L2,B2)$ | $SS_2$ | COMPARE PACKED | Compares $C(E1)_{L1}$ with $C(E2)_{L2}$ |

$$\text{Condition code} = \begin{cases} 0 \text{ if } C(E1)_{L1} = C(E2)_{L2} \\ 1 \text{ if } C(E1)_{L1} < C(E2)_{L2} \\ 2 \text{ if } C(E1)_{L1} > C(E2)_{L2} \end{cases}$$

**All plus signs are equal; both minus signs are equal.**

CP differs from the Compare instructions that you already know because an "equal" comparison here does not imply that the operands have identical bit patterns or that they are of equal length; rather, the operands represent the same decimal values. CP considers all valid plus signs to be equal and all valid minus signs to be equal. It also considers two zero-valued operands to be equal, even if they have opposite signs.

---

EXAMPLE 16

```
CP      X(2),Y(4)
```

| | The bytes at X | The bytes at Y |
|---|---|---|
| Before execution: | 12 3C | 45 67 89 0D |
| After execution: | 12 3C | 45 67 89 0D |
| | *Condition code* = 2 | |

Here, +123 is greater than −4567890.

---

EXAMPLE 17

```
CP      X(3),Y(4)
```

| | The bytes at X | The bytes at Y |
|---|---|---|
| Before execution: | 12 34 5C | 00 12 34 5F |
| After execution: | 12 34 5C | 00 12 34 5F |
| | *Condition code* = 0 | |

The operands have equal values, even though their representations differ in length and use different plus signs.

---

EXAMPLE 18

```
CP      X(3),=P'0'
```

| | The bytes at X | =P'0' |
|---|---|---|
| Before execution: | 00 00 0D | 0C |
| After execution: | 00 00 0D | 0C |
| | *Condition code* = 0 | |

A positive zero and a negative zero are equal.

---

## SELF-TEST EXERCISE

1. Assume that the field at A contains 1234567F and that the field at B contains 067C. What effect does each of the following instructions have on A, B, and the condition code?

   **a.** `AP A(4),B(2)`
   **b.** `AP A+2(2),B(2)`
   **c.** `AP B+1(1),A+3(1)`
   **d.** `AP A+1(3),=P'-40000'`
   **e.** `SP B(2),A(4)`
   **f.** `SP A+3(1),B+1(1)`
   **g.** `SP B(2),A+2(2)`
   **h.** `SP B(2),=P'-100'`
   **i.** `CP A+3(1),B+1(1)`
   **j.** `CP A+2(2),B(2)`
   **k.** `CP B(2),A(4)`
   **l.** `CP A(4),=P'0'`
   **m.** `ZAP A(4),B(2)`
   **n.** `ZAP A(2),B(2)`
   **o.** `ZAP B(2),A+2(2)`
   **p.** `ZAP B(2),A+3(1)`
   **q.** `ZAP A(4),A+1(3)`
   **r.** `ZAP A+1(3),=P'0'`
   **s.** `ZAP A(4),A(4)`

### *The Multiply Packed (MP) Instruction*

The Multiply Packed instruction forms the product of two packed-decimal numbers—the multiplicand and the multiplier—that are specified as the first and second operands, respectively. The product replaces the first operand field, as illustrated in Figure 15.3. The condition code remains unchanged. The instruction can be summarized as follows:

| Operation | Operand | Format | Instruction Name | Action |
|---|---|---|---|---|
| MP | *S1(L1),S2(L2)* or *D1(L1,B1),D2(L2,B2)* | $SS_2$ | MULTIPLY PACKED | $C(E1)_{L1} \leftarrow C(E1)_{L1} * C(E2)_{L2}$ |

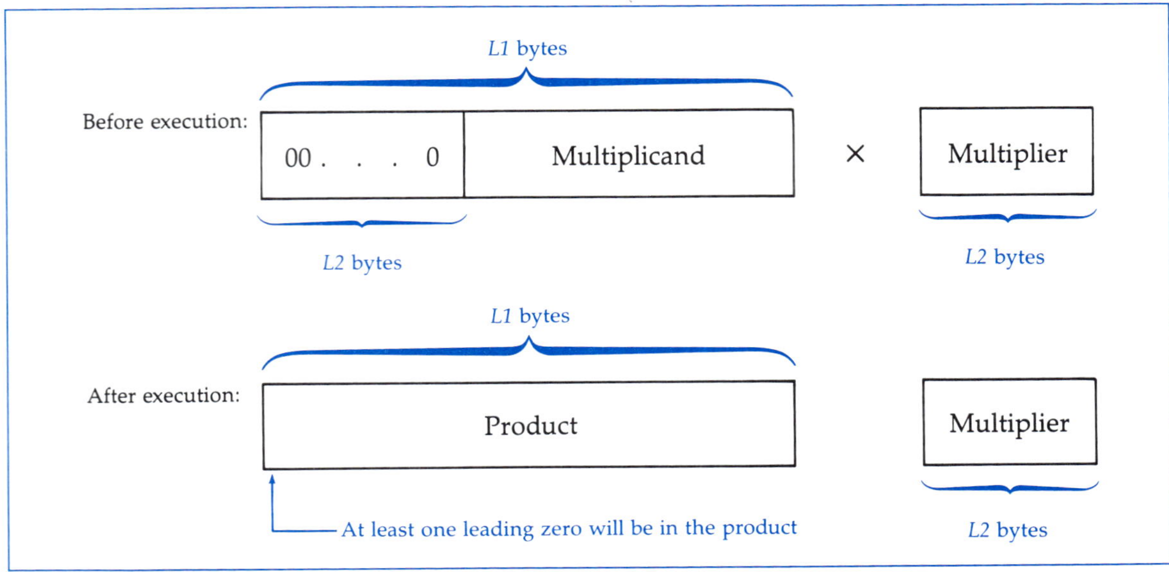


**Figure 15.3**
The effect of the MP instruction.

If you ignore leading zeros, the number of digits in a decimal integer product cannot exceed the sum of the number of digits in the two operands. To ensure that the product will fit into the *L1* bytes of the first operand field, the MP instruction restricts the operands as follows:

**The multiplicand and multiplier must satisfy certain restrictions.**

- $L2 \leqslant 8$ and $L2 < L1$. (Violation of these restrictions will result in a specification exception.)
- The first operand must contain at least *L2* bytes of leading zeros. (Violation of this restriction will result in a data exception.)

The restrictions just listed make overflow impossible and, in addition, guarantee that the product will always contain at least one leading zero.

The sign of the product is determined from the signs of the operands by using the rules of algebra, even if the product is zero. Thus, a negative zero is a possible result.

---

EXAMPLE 19

```
MP      X(4),Y(2)
```

| | The bytes at X | The bytes at Y |
|---|---|---|
| Before execution: | 00 00 12 3C | 10 0D |
| After execution: | 00 12 30 0D | 10 0D |

The instruction computes $+123 * (-100) = -12300$.

---

EXAMPLE 20

```
MP      X(4),Y(2)
```

| | The bytes at X | The bytes at Y | |
|---|---|---|---|
| Before execution: | 00 01 23 4C | 56 7D | |
| After execution: | 00 01 23 4C | 56 7D | *Data exception* |

The first operand does not contain 2 (*L2*) bytes of leading zeros, so a data exception will occur; the multiplication does not take place.

---

EXAMPLE 21

**Preparing the First Operand for Multiplication**

If the multiplicand does not contain a sufficient number of leading zeros, or if it is not longer than the multiplier, you must copy the multiplicand into a longer field before the multiplication can take place. You can use the ZAP instruction to make the copy.

For example, suppose that you have a field defined by

```
X      DC      P'-605'
```

($605D_{16}$)

and that you want to compute X * X. The instruction

```
MP      X(2),X(2)
```

will cause a specification exception because *L2* is not less than *L1*. You can copy X into a longer field so that the result will have *L2*, or 2, bytes of leading zeros. The following traces the execution of the sequence of instructions that will square X:

| | The bytes at W | The bytes at X |
|---|---|---|
| | ?? ?? ?? ?? | 60 5D |
| `ZAP W(4),X(2)` | 00 00 60 5D | 60 5D |
| `MP W(4),X(2)` | 03 66 02 5C | 60 5D |

```
        .
        .
        .
W       DS      PL4
```

## *The Divide Packed (DP) Instruction*

The Divide Packed instruction divides two packed-decimal numbers—the dividend and the divisor—that are specified as the first and second operands, respectively. The quotient and the remainder replace the first operand field, as pictured in Figure 15.4. The condition code is unchanged. The instruction can be summarized as follows:

| Operation | Operand | Format | Instruction Name |
|---|---|---|---|
| **DP** | *S1(L1),S2(L2)* or *D1(L1,B1),D2(L2,B2)* | $SS_2$ | DIVIDE PACKED |

**Action**

$C(E1)_{L1-L2} \leftarrow$ Quotient of $C(E1)_{L1} \div C(E2)_{L2}$
$C(E1 + L1 - L2)_{L2} \leftarrow$ Remainder of $C(E1)_{L1} \div C(E2)_{L2}$

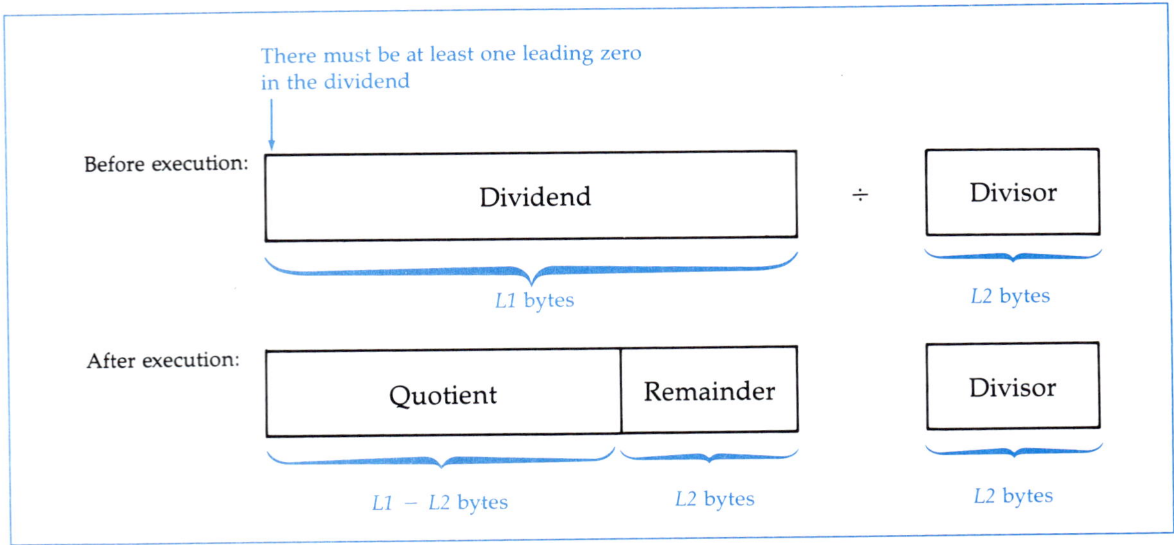


**Figure 15.4**
The effect of the DP instruction.

There is always a remainder even if its value is zero; it is placed immediately adjacent to and to the right of the quotient. The largest possible absolute value of a remainder in an integer division is 1 less than the divisor. For example, 129 ÷ 26 is 4 with a remainder of 25. Therefore, the remainder can occupy as many bytes as the divisor, so the DP instruction always uses *L2* bytes for the remainder. This leaves *L1* − *L2* bytes for the quotient.

The sign of the quotient is determined from the signs of the operands by using the rules of algebra; the sign of the remainder is the sign of the dividend. The rules to determine the signs of the quotient and the remainder are followed even if the quotient or the remainder is zero; thus, negative zeros are possible.

The operands are restricted as follows:

**The dividend and the divisor must satisfy certain restrictions.**

- *L2* ≤ 8 and *L2* < *L1*. (If you do not observe this rule, a specification exception will occur.)
- The leftmost digit of the first operand must be zero. (If you do not observe this rule, a **decimal divide exception** will occur. This exception causes a program interruption. The interruption code is $000B_{16}$.)

The length restrictions on the operands are the same as for multiplication. However, the first operand does not need to contain *L2* bytes of leading zeros prior to the division, as was the case for multiplication—although this is often desirable, as you will see later.

**A decimal divide exception occurs if the dividend does not contain at least one leading zero, if the divisor is zero, or if the quotient is too large.**

A decimal divide exception will also occur if the divisor is zero or if the quotient is too large to fit into the designated *L1* − *L2* bytes. Although a quotient that is too large is a case of overflow, a decimal overflow exception does *not* occur. As with all of the decimal arithmetic instructions given earlier, invalid digit codes or sign codes cause a data exception, which takes precedence over a decimal divide exception.

---

EXAMPLE 22

```
DP      X(5),Y(2)
```

| | The bytes at X | The bytes at Y |
|---|---|---|
| Before execution: | 00 00 48 48 4D | 00 4D |
| After execution: | 12 12 1C 00 0D | 00 4D |

Quotient: 12 12 1C; Remainder: 00 0D

The computation −48484 ÷ (−4) results in a quotient of +12121 and a remainder of −0. The quotient is positive because X and Y have the same signs; the remainder has the same sign as the first operand X and is, therefore, negative—even though it is zero. The remainder occupies 2 bytes (*L2* is 2); the quotient occupies the remaining bytes of the first operand.

---

EXAMPLE 23

```
DP      X(2),Y(1)
```

| | The bytes at X | The byte at Y |
|---|---|---|
| Before execution: | 07 8C | 9D |
| After execution: | 8D 6C | |

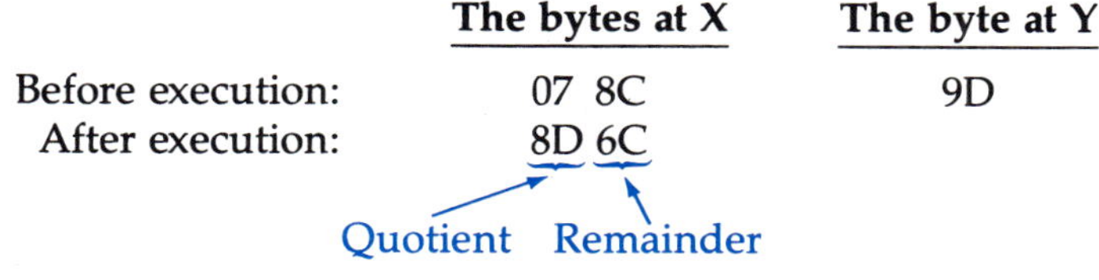

The computation +78 ÷ (−9) results in a quotient of −8 and a remainder of +6. The quotient is negative because X and Y are of opposite signs; the remainder is positive because X is positive. Note that the dividend X had only one leading zero prior to the division.

---

EXAMPLE 24

```
DP      X(2),Y(1)
```

| | The bytes at X | The byte at Y |
|---|---|---|
| Before execution: | 09 9C | 9D |
| After execution: | 09 9C | 9D |
| | *Decimal divide exception* | |

The instruction attempts to compute + 99 ÷ (−9), but a decimal divide exception occurs because the quotient 011C will not fit into the 1 byte available for it (*L1* − *L2* is 1). Even though the remainder of this division is zero, it is not discarded, and you must allow room for it in the rightmost portion of the first operand. (Due to the exception, the remainder is not represented.) Notice that the fact that the dividend contains one leading zero as required does not guarantee a correct division.

---

You may not always be able to predict when a division will produce a quotient that is too large and, therefore, when it will cause a decimal divide exception. As mentioned earlier, a decimal divide exception will occur when the dividend does not contain at least one leading zero, but the existence of a zero does not ensure that the exception will not occur. However, either of the following rules will guarantee enough room for the quotient:

**Either Rule 1 or Rule 2 guarantees enough room for the quotient.**

Rule 1. The dividend (the first operand) must have at least two more leading zeros than the divisor (the second operand).

Rule 2. The dividend must have one more leading zero than the divisor, and the first nonzero digit of the dividend must be less than the first nonzero digit of the divisor.

Reconsider the three examples given earlier: Example 22 demonstrates Rule 1 because X contains two more leading zeros than Y. Example 23 demonstrates Rule 2 because X has one more leading zero than Y, and because the first nonzero digit of X, which is the 7, is less than the first nonzero digit of Y, which is the 9. Example 24 violates both rules and a decimal divide exception occurs.

Although Rule 1 and Rule 2 are difficult to apply in general, you can use them when you want the first operand to be as short as possible. Making the first operand as short as possible not only saves space, but also saves execution time since, for SS instructions, execution time depends on the operand lengths. However, the savings are usually negligible because leading zeros are processed more rapidly than nonzeros during decimal arithmetic. Thus, you often can use the following simpler approach instead of using Rule 1 and Rule 2.

The quotient can never exceed the dividend in value and, therefore, in length, and the remainder always occupies *L2* bytes, which is the length of the divisor. Therefore, if the dividend contains *L2* bytes of leading zeros or, alternatively, if you extend the dividend field on the left by *L2* bytes of zeros, there will be enough room in the first operand to accommodate both the quotient and the remainder. To extend the dividend, copy it into a work area whose length is the sum of the lengths of the original dividend and divisor. Since the length of the work area cannot exceed 16 bytes, which is the length of the largest packed-decimal number, a convenient simplification is to use a 16-byte work area. The procedure just described covers all divisions that are feasible when you use the DP instruction.

---

EXAMPLE 25

**Preparing the First Operand for Division**

Suppose that you want to compute Z = X ÷ Y, where X, Y, and Z are defined as follows:

```
X      DC    P'-12345678'       (Assembles as 01 23 45 67 8D)
Y      DC    P'+1234567'        (Assembles as 12 34 56 7C)
Z      DS    PL5
```

**Figure 15.5** Instructions to perform a decimal division using, **a.** one work area that includes both the quotient and the remainder; and, **b.** separate definitions for the quotient and the remainder, as described in Example 25.

From the internal hexadecimal equivalents noted here, you can see that X is a 5-byte field and Y is a 4-byte field. The quotient cannot exceed the dividend in length, so Z is defined as a 5-byte field. The remainder will occupy 4 bytes, which is the length of the divisor Y. If you knew only the lengths of X and Y, then the best that you could do would be to use a 9-byte work area for the first operand.

The instructions in part **a** of Figure 15.5 use the 9-byte work area at TEMP. After the division, TEMP contains both the quotient and the remainder. TEMP represents the address of the quotient, but, since the length attribute of TEMP is larger than the length of the quotient (5), you need an

**a.**

```
          ZAP   TEMP,X          COPY X TO A LONGER WORK AREA
          DP    TEMP,Y          COMPUTE X/Y
          ZAP   Z,TEMP(5)       Z = QUOTIENT
           .
           .
           .
X         DC    P'-12345678'    DIVIDEND
Y         DC    P'+1234567'     DIVISOR
Z         DS    PL5             RESULT
TEMP      DS    PL9             WORK AREA FOR DIVISION
*                                  (L'TEMP = L'X + L'Y)
```

**b.**

```
          ZAP   TEMP,X          COPY X TO A LONGER WORK AREA
          DP    TEMP,Y          COMPUTE X/Y
          ZAP   Z,QUOTIENT      Z = QUOTIENT
           .
           .
           .
X         DC    P'-12345678'    DIVIDEND
Y         DC    P'+1234567'     DIVISOR
Z         DS    PL5             RESULT
TEMP      DS    0PL(L'X+L'Y)    WORK AREA FOR DIVISION (TWO FIELDS):
QUOTIENT  DS    PL(L'X)           QUOTIENT HAS LENGTH OF X
REMAIN    DS    PL(L'Y)           REMAINDER HAS LENGTH OF Y
```

explicit length entry in the last ZAP instruction that moves the quotient to Z. It is preferable to define the quotient and remainder fields separately by using symbolic lengths, as shown in part **b** of Figure 15.5.

In this example, you know the specific values of X and Y, so you can make some further observations. X and Y violate both Rules 1 and 2; however, if you extended X on the left by 1 byte, Rule 1 would be satisfied. Thus, a 6-byte first operand would be sufficient. Notice that the quotient is $-10$ and requires 2 bytes for its internal hexadecimal representation of 01 0D. This 2-byte quotient and the 4-byte remainder also indicate that the first operand must be a minimum of 6 bytes long. Finally, notice that, while Z is too short to be the first operand, it is really longer than necessary to accommodate the quotient. An analysis such as the one just done is usually impractical; it is easier to use a first operand that is longer than necessary.

---

EXAMPLE 26

## Compute the Rounded Average of the Squares of the Positive Integers in an Array

Consider an array of a maximum of fifty 9-digit packed-decimal integers at the address DATA. The actual number of integers is stored in the packed-decimal field at N. The program segment in Figure 15.6 computes the rounded average of the squares of the positive integers in this array.

To reduce execution time, a BCT instruction controls the loop that examines each integer in the array. This necessitates the conversion of N to binary. As each positive integer is encountered, it must be counted so that the average can be computed later. The example uses decimal arithmetic to perform this count, although it could have used binary arithmetic instead.

To estimate the size of the sum, note that the product of two 9-digit integers will not exceed 18 digits in length; the sum of a maximum of 50 such integers will not exceed 20 digits in length. (When an 18-digit number is multiplied by 50, a 2-digit number, the result contains a maximum of 20 digits.) Since the number of digits in a packed-decimal number is always odd, reserve enough space for 21 digits.

The result of the division is rounded by adding 1 to the quotient when the remainder is at least one-half of N, in which case, the following is true:

$$REM \geq N/2$$

This inequality is equivalent to the next one, which is more convenient:

$$2 * \text{REM} \geq \text{N}$$

You can compute 2 * REM by adding the remainder to itself as long as the field reserved for the remainder is sufficiently long to accommodate the sum. To see that it is, observe that the remainder (REM) is less than the divisor (NPOS), and that the following relationship is true:

$$\text{NPOS} \leq \text{N} \leq 50$$

It follows that

$$\text{REM} \leq 49$$

so

$$2 * \text{REM} \leq 98$$

Thus, the remainder and twice its value do not exceed 2 digits in length.

---

```
** COMPUTE THE ROUNDED AVERAGE OF THE SQUARES OF THE POSITIVE
** PACKED-DECIMAL INTEGERS IN THE ARRAY AT DATA.  ASSUME THAT
** THERE ARE N 9-DIGIT INTEGERS WHERE N IS A PACKED-DECIMAL INTEGER
** 1 <= N <= 50
*
* INITIALIZE:
         ZAP   TEMP,N               PREPARE FOR CVB; PLACE N IN
*                                     DOUBLEWORD
         CVB   R2,TEMP              R2 = LOOP COUNTER = N
         ZAP   NPOS,=P'0'           CLEAR COUNTER OF POSITIVE NUMBERS
         ZAP   SUM,=P'0'            CLEAR SUM AREA
         SR    R3,R3                R3 = INDEX REGISTER = 0
* COMPUTE SUM OF SQUARES OF POSITIVE INTEGERS:
* REPEAT:
LOOP     LA    R4,DATA(R3)          R4 = ADDRESS OF NEXT ARRAY ITEM
* - IF ARRAY ITEM IS POSITIVE:
         CP    0(L'DATA,R4),=P'0'   IS ITEM POSITIVE?
         BNP   CONTINUE             NO; SKIP TO LOOP CONTROL
* - - THEN SQUARE IT AND ADD TO SUM:
         ZAP   SQUARE,0(L'DATA,R4)  EXTEND MULTIPLICAND
         MP    SQUARE,0(L'DATA,R4)  MULTIPLY NUMBER BY ITSELF
         AP    SUM,SQUARE           ADD SQUARE TO SUM AREA
         AP    NPOS,=P'1'           COUNT IT
* - END IF
* UNTIL COUNT = 0
CONTINUE LA    R3,L'DATA(R3)        INCREMENT INDEX BY INTEGER LENGTH
         BCT   R2,LOOP              DECREMENT COUNTER; REPEAT IF NOT 0
* END REPEAT
* COMPUTE ROUNDED AVERAGE:
         ZAP   WORK,SUM             PREPARE SUM FOR DIVISION
         DP    WORK,NPOS            DIVIDE BY NO. OF ITEMS ADDED
         AP    REM,REM              DOUBLE REMAINDER
         CP    REM,N                COMPARE 2*REM WITH N (SAME AS
*                                     COMPARING REM WITH N/2)
         BL    DONE                 IF LESS THAN, IGNORE REMAINDER
         AP    AVERAGE,=P'1'        ELSE ROUND BY ADDING 1 TO AVERAGE
DONE     ---
* RESULT IS AT AVERAGE
         .
         .
         .
N        DS    PL2                  NO. OF ITEMS IN ARRAY AT DATA
DATA     DS    50PL5                ARRAY OF 9-DIGIT DECIMAL INTEGERS
NPOS     DS    PL(L'N)              COUNTS NO. OF POSITIVE ITEMS IN ARRAY
TEMP     DS    D                    DOUBLEWORD FOR CVB
SQUARE   DS    PL(2*L'DATA)         9 DIGITS TIMES 9 DIGITS = 18 DIGITS
*                                     (ROOM FOR 19 DIGITS)
SUM      DS    PL(L'SQUARE+1)       ACCUMULATOR OF SUM: ASSUME 20 DIGITS
*                                     (18 DIGITS TIMES 50 = 20 DIGITS;
*                                     ROOM FOR 21 DIGITS)
WORK     DS    0PL16                WORK AREA FOR DIVISION; 2 FIELDS ARE:
AVERAGE  DS    PL(16-L'NPOS)          QUOTIENT OF DIVISION (THE RESULT)
REM      DS    PL(L'NPOS)             REMAINDER OF DIVISION
```

**Figure 15.6**

A program segment to compute the rounded average of the squares of the positive integers in an array, as described in Example 26.

**SELF-TEST EXERCISES**

2. Assume that the field at U contains 0000040C and that the field at W contains 012D. What effect does each of the following instructions have on U and W? Indicate any exceptions that occur.

| | | | | | |
|---|---|---|---|---|---|
| **a.** | MP | U(4),W(2) | **h.** | DP | U(4),W(2) |
| **b.** | MP | U(2),W+1(1) | **i.** | DP | W(2),U(4) |
| **c.** | MP | U+1(3),W+1(1) | **j.** | DP | W(2),U+3(1) |
| **d.** | MP | U(4),U+2(2) | **k.** | DP | W(2),U+2(2) |
| **e.** | MP | U+1(3),W(2) | **l.** | DP | U(4),W+1(1) |
| **f.** | MP | W(2),U(4) | **m.** | DP | U(4),=P'-12345' |
| **g.** | MP | U(4),=Z'-2' | **n.** | DP | W(2),=P'-1' |

3. Write instructions that compute the following by using the shortest possible work area in each case. Define the required constants by using P-type literals.
   **a.** 10 * 198
   **b.** (−2) * 12345678912345678
   **c.** 501 ÷ (−50)
   **d.** 4591 ÷ 123456789

## Shifting Decimal Fields

The beginning of this chapter noted that decimal arithmetic applications often involve nonintegral data. Arithmetic with such data requires that you adjust the position of an assumed decimal point by shifting the contents of a decimal field to the left or to the right. This section defines the instructions that make shifting possible, and begins by examining an example where shifting is necessary.

The following statements define four identical hexadecimal constants, with each constant equal to 123C:

```
A        DC      P'123'
B        DC      P'12.3'
C        DC      P'1.23'
D        DC      P'.123'
```

If you use the AP instruction to compute B + C, you will get the following result:

$$\begin{array}{r} 12\ 3C \\ +\ \underline{12\ 3C} \\ 24\ 6C \end{array}$$

This result does not represent the correct sum:

$$\begin{array}{r} 12.3 \\ +\ \underline{1.23} \\ 13.53 \end{array}$$

As you know, you must align the decimal points prior to an addition. A correct packed-decimal computation would appear as follows:

```
  01 23 0C
+    12 3C
  --------
  01 35 3C
```

One way to obtain 01230C as the value of B is to define B with 2 places to the right of the decimal point, so that it matches C:

```
B       DC      P'12.30'      (Assembles as 01 23 0C)
```

Another way to do this is to take the original value of B, which is 123C, and shift it to the left by one decimal place. Both ways achieve the required decimal alignment. (Notice that you can also achieve decimal alignment by shifting C to the right by one place, but this is unwise because you would lose a digit.)

Now consider the computation B * C written as it would appear when performed by the MP instruction and by hand:

```
Using the MP instruction      By hand
      00 00 12 3C               12.3
  ×         12 3C            ×  1.23
      -----------            -------
      00 15 12 9C             15.129
```

Except for possibly extending one operand on the left with zeros, as was necessary here, the MP instruction produces the correct result without first shifting the operand. The number of decimal places—those places to the right of the decimal point—in the product is the sum of those in the operands. Typically, you will not want to retain all of the decimal places—particularly if you will use the product in yet another multiplication. Suppose that you decide that 2 decimal places are sufficient in the previous product. You can truncate the result to 15.12 or round it to 15.13. You can truncate the packed-decimal result by using a right decimal shift of one place to yield 00 01 51 2C. You can round the result by first adding 5 to the 9, and then shifting the sum to the right as follows:

```
  00 15 12 9C
+          5C
  -----------
  00 15 13 4C   →   00 01 51 3C
```

You can shift decimal fields readily with the Shift and Round Packed (SRP) instruction. SRP was not available on the IBM System/360, so shifting was performed with a sequence of several instructions. Both techniques are described in this chapter.

## *Shifting on the IBM System/370: The SRP Instruction*

The Shift and Round Packed instruction shifts the digits in a packed-decimal field to the right or to the left by a specified number of places. The sign of the second operand indicates the direction of the shift. If desired, you can round the result during a right shift.

The instruction has a format that is a variation of $SS_2$, and can be summarized as follows:

| Operation | Operand | Format | Instruction Name |
|---|---|---|---|
| **SRP** | *S1(L1),D2(B2),I3* or *D1(L1,B1),D2(B2),I3* | $SS_2$ | SHIFT AND ROUND PACKED |

*D1(L1,B1)* — Address and length of field to be shifted
*D2(B2)* — Direction and amount of shift
*I3* — Rounding digit

**Action**

Shifts $C(E1)_{L1}$ by $|n|$ places where $n = E2 \pmod{64}$ represents a signed value. The shift is to the left if $n$ is positive, and to the right if $n$ is negative. *I3* is the rounding digit for right shifts.

Condition code = 
- 0 if the result is zero
- 1 if the result is negative
- 2 if the result is positive
- 3 if an overflow occurs

The first operand is the packed-decimal number to be shifted and is replaced by the results of the shift. During the operation, the sign code remains fixed in place and only the digit codes are shifted. Digits shifted out of one end of the number are discarded, and vacancies introduced on the other end are filled in with zeros. If significant digits are lost during a left shift, a decimal overflow exception occurs; this causes a program interruption if the second bit of the program mask is 1.

**Use a positive shift value to shift left; use a negative shift value to shift right.**

The second operand designates the shift amount and direction by using a base-displacement specification. As was true for the binary shift instructions, you should designate the second operand explicitly. The rightmost 6 bits of the effective address *E2* represent a signed value, which is called the **shift value**, by using a two's complement binary notation. The magnitude of the shift value is the shift amount; its sign specifies the direction of the shift. Positive values indicate a shift to the left; negative values indicate a shift to the right.

**Use a rounding digit of 0 for truncation; use a rounding digit of 5 for ordinary rounding.**

Since there is only one packed-decimal field, you only need one length specification, *L1*. Instead of an *L2* specification, bits 12 through 15 of the instruction contain a digit code called the **rounding digit**: it is written as the third operand and is denoted by *I3*. During a right shift, the instruction adds the rounding digit to the last digit to be shifted out while ignoring signs, and propagates any carry to the left. A rounding digit of 5 causes ordinary rounding, as you saw earlier. A rounding digit of 0 produces truncation; a rounding digit of 9 rounds the result up. Even though the rounding digit is not used during a left shift, you must always write *I3*. Note that *I3* is an absolute quantity; it is a digit code, and not a packed-decimal number.

The CPU checks the digit codes, the sign codes, and the rounding digit for validity before the shift takes place. Invalid codes cause a data exception even if the shift amount is zero; an invalid rounding digit will cause a data exception even if it is not used. Preferred signs are produced in the result.

EXAMPLE 27

**The Shift Value**

Figure 15.7 gives some examples of the shift value as designated by the second operand of the SRP instruction. Notice that 64 − 3 specifies a right shift of 3 places. Recall from the discussion of number systems in Chapter 2 that 64 − 3, or $2^6 - 3$, is the two's complement of 3 and represents −3. This indicates a shift to the right of 3 places. Although some assemblers will accept −3 as an operand, some will not. Since 64 − 3 always works, use it. For the sake of consistency, if you prefer you may also specify positive shift amounts in this form. Thus, 64 + 3 specifies a shift value of +3.

Notice that, due to the nature of two's complement notation, left shifts can range from 0 to 31, and right shifts can range from 0 to 32. Since there are a maximum of 31 digits in a packed-decimal number, this range is sufficient.

**Figure 15.7** Some examples of the shift value in the SRP instruction, as described in Example 27.

| Second operand | Rightmost 6 bits of *E2* | Shift value | Shift amount | Shift direction |
|---|---|---|---|---|
| 3 | 000011 | 3 | 3 | Left |
| 64 − 3 | 111101 | −3 | 3 | Right |
| 64 + 3 | 000011 | 3 | 3 | Left |
| 31 | 011111 | 31 | 31 | Left |
| 64 − 31 | 100001 | −31 | 31 | Right |
| 64 − 32 | 100000 | −32 | 32 | Right |

EXAMPLE 28

```
SRP    X(4),3,0    SHIFT LEFT 3 PLACES
```

| | The bytes at X |
|---|---|
| Before execution: | 00 00 12 3C |
| After execution: | 01 23 00 0C |
| | *Condition code* = 2 |

The positive shift value 3 indicates a left shift. Notice that, even though rounding is irrelevant during a left shift, you must write a valid rounding digit; it will be ignored even if it is nonzero.

EXAMPLE 29

```
SRP    X(4),6,5    SHIFT LEFT 6 PLACES
```

| | The bytes at X | |
|---|---|---|
| Before execution: | 12 34 98 7C | |
| After execution: | 70 00 00 0C | *Decimal overflow, Condition code* = 3 |

Since significant digits are lost on the left, a decimal overflow exception occurs and the condition code is set to 3. Depending upon the decimal-overflow (second) bit in the program mask, a program interruption may occur.

The rounding digit is ignored.

---

EXAMPLE 30

```
SRP     X(4),64-3,5     SHIFT RIGHT 3 AND ROUND
```

| | The bytes at X |
|---|---|
| Before execution: | 09 87 61 2D |
| After execution: | 00 00 98 8D |
| | *Condition code* = 1 |

The instruction adds the rounding digit 5 to the digit 6, which is the last one to be shifted out of X, as if X were positive. The carry is propagated to the left. The net effect is ordinary rounding.

---

EXAMPLE 31

```
SRP     X(4),64-1,5     SHIFT RIGHT 1 AND ROUND
```

| | The bytes at X |
|---|---|
| Before execution: | 00 01 23 4B |
| After execution: | 00 00 12 3**D** |
| | *Condition code* = 1 |

When the instruction adds the rounding digit to the 4 in X, no carry occurs. Notice that the sign of X is changed to a preferred sign.

---

EXAMPLE 32

```
SRP     X(4),0(1),9     SHIFT RIGHT 2 AND ROUND UP
```

| | The bytes at X | Reg. 1 |
|---|---|---|
| Before execution: | 82 34 91 7C | FFFFFFFE |
| After execution: | 00 82 35 0C | FFFFFFFE |
| | *Condition code* = 2 | |

In this example, the shift value is specified at execution time by using Register 1. The rightmost 6 bits of the effective address *E2* are $111110_2$, which represents $-2$. Thus, X is shifted 2 places to the right. The rounding digit, 9, is added to the 1 in X; the carry is propagated to the left and, in this case, its effect goes beyond the adjacent digit.

---

EXAMPLE 33

```
SRP     X(4),64-3,0     SHIFT RIGHT 3 AND TRUNCATE
```

| | The bytes at X |
|---|---|
| Before execution: | 00 98 76 5D |
| After execution: | 00 00 09 8D |
| | *Condition code* = 1 |

No rounding occurs because the rounding digit is zero and adding zero clearly has no effect.

---

## *Shifting on the IBM System/360: The MVO, MVN, and MVZ Instructions*

**Use MVO and MVN to shift when SRP is not available.**

You must write several instructions to shift a packed-decimal field when the SRP instruction is not available. Two new instructions, MVO and MVN, are required for this task. Another instruction, MVZ, is similar to MVN so it is introduced here, even though you do not use it to shift fields.

*The Move with Offset (MVO) Instruction.* The Move with Offset instruction is an $SS_2$ instruction that involves two fields, which do not necessarily have to be of the same length. The instruction can be summarized as follows:

| Operation | Operand | Format | Instruction Name | Action |
|---|---|---|---|---|
| MVO | $S1(L1),S2(L2)$ or $D1(L1,B1),D2(L2,B2)$ | $SS_2$ | MOVE WITH OFFSET | $C(E1)_{0\,-\,(8\,*\,L1\,-\,5)} \leftarrow C(E2)_{L2}$ |

The rightmost 4 bits of the first operand remain fixed and unchanged. The rest of the first operand field is replaced by the second operand. Thus, the second operand is *offset* to the left by 4 bits and stored into the first operand field. If the first field is longer than necessary, the instruction pads the result on the left with zeros. Conversely, if the first field is too short, the instruction truncates the result on the left, and ignores the excess portion of the second operand without warning.

You can predict the results by assuming that the fields are processed right to left, one byte at a time. To determine the results when the fields overlap, store each result byte as soon as it is computed. Although the fields typically contain packed-decimal numbers, they do not have to, as there is no check for validity of the sign or digit codes.

**MVO does not check for valid digit codes or sign codes.**

---

EXAMPLE 34

```
MVO    X(3),Y(2)
```

| | The bytes at X | The bytes at Y |
|---|---|---|
| Before execution: | 12 34 5D | 67 89 |
| After execution: | 06 78 9D | 67 89 |



---

EXAMPLE 35

```
MVO    X(3),Y(5)
```

| | The bytes at X | The bytes at Y |
|---|---|---|
| Before execution: | 00 00 0F | 12 34 56 78 9D |
| After execution: | 67 89 DF | |

The excess digits of Y are discarded without indication. The result is not a packed-decimal number.

EXAMPLE 36

```
MVO     X(4),X(2)
```

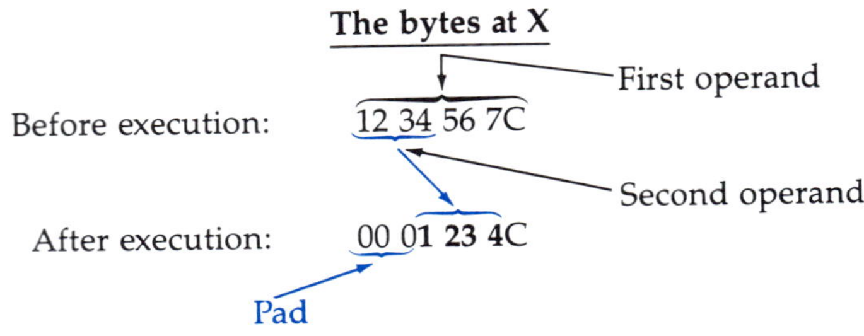


The fields in this example overlap.

---

MVN and MVZ are analogous to MVC.

*The Move Numerics (MVN) and Move Zones (MVZ) Instructions.* The Move Numerics instruction and the Move Zones instruction are $SS_1$ format instructions that are analogous to the MVC instruction. They specify one length, which is the length of each of the two operands. The MVN instruction moves the rightmost 4 bits (the numeric bits) of each byte in the second operand field to the corresponding bits of the first operand field. The MVZ instruction moves the leftmost 4 bits (the zone bits) instead. You can predict the results by assuming that the bytes are processed left to right, one byte at a time. The operand fields may contain anything, and are not restricted to packed-decimal numbers. Fields may overlap and the results are computed in the same manner as for the MVC instruction.

The instructions can be summarized as follows:

| Operation | Operand | Format | Instruction Name | Action |
|---|---|---|---|---|
| MVN | *S1(L),S2* or *D1(L,B1),D2(B2)* | $SS_1$ | MOVE NUMERICS | Numerics of $C(E1)_L \leftarrow$ Numerics of $C(E2)_L$ |
| MVZ | *S1(L),S2* or *D1(L,B1),D2(B2)* | $SS_1$ | MOVE ZONES | Zones of $C(E1)_L \leftarrow$ Zones of $C(E2)_L$ |

---

EXAMPLE 37

```
MVN     X(3),Y
```

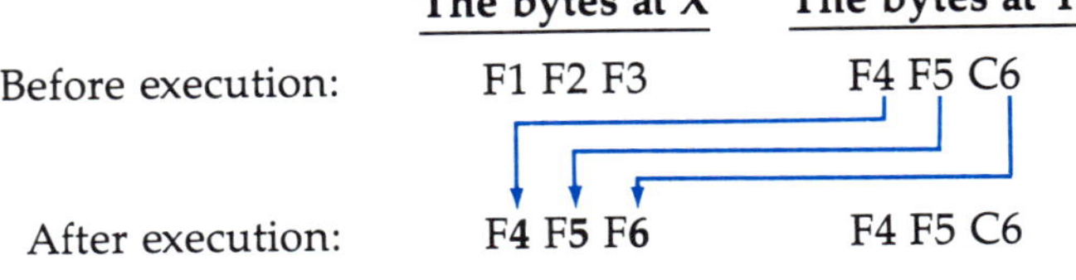

EXAMPLE 38

```
MVN    X+2(1),=P'-1'
```

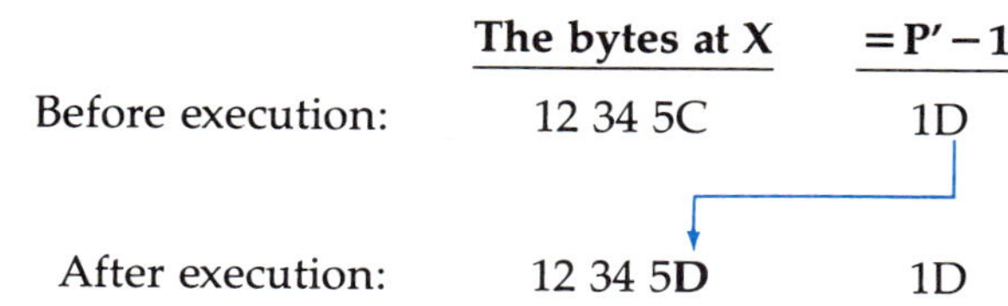


You can use the MVN instruction to change the sign of a packed-decimal number.

---

EXAMPLE 39

```
MVZ    X+2(1),Y
```

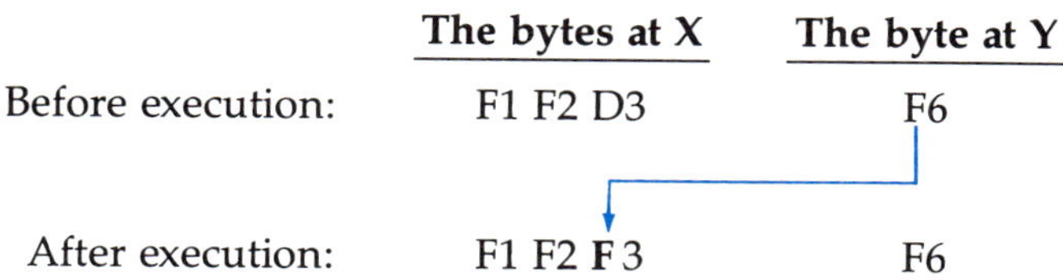


You can use the MVZ instruction to change the sign of a zoned-decimal number.

---

*Shifting Decimal Fields.* Figure 15.8 gives examples of right shifts both with and without rounding, and of left shifts. These examples consider specific shift amounts and the general case of shifting N digits. (Assume that N is an absolute symbol equated to the shift amount.) Notice that you need different instruction sequences for even and odd shift amounts; clearly, the SRP instruction is much simpler to use.

Although not considered here, you can cause left shifts of up to 14 places by using the MP instruction.

## SELF-TEST EXERCISES

**4.** Assume that the field at W contains 123456789D and that the field at Z contains 9876543F. What effect does each of the following instructions have on W, Z, and the condition code?

**a.** `SRP    W(5),2,5`
**b.** `SRP    W(5),64+1,0`
**c.** `SRP    W(5),64-2,0`
**d.** `SRP    W(5),64-3,5`
**e.** `SRP    Z(4),64-1,5`
**f.** `SRP    Z(4),64-2,9`
**g.** `SRP    Z(4),65,9`

*(Continues)*

5. Assume that W and Z have the same values as given in Self-Test Exercise 4. What effect does each of the following instructions have on W and Z?

   a. `MVO W(5),Z(4)`
   b. `MVO Z(4),W(5)`
   c. `MVO W(5),W(3)`
   d. `MVO W(3),W(5)`
   e. `MVN Z(4),W`
   f. `MVN W+1(4),W`
   g. `MVN Z+3(1),=P'0'`
   h. `MVZ Z(4),W`
   i. `MVZ W+1(4),W`
   j. `MVZ Z+3(1),=P'0'`

6. Write SRP instructions to shift the 4-byte packed-decimal number at Y as follows:
   a. Right by 5 places without rounding.
   b. Right by 6 places without rounding.
   c. Right by 1 place with rounding.
   d. Right by 2 places with rounding.
   e. Left by 1 place.
   f. Left by 6 places.

7. Repeat Self-Test Exercise 6, but perform the shifts without the SRP instruction.

*Right shift by an odd number of places without rounding*

```
* RIGHT SHIFT BY N
          MVO    Y,Y(L'Y-(N+1)/2)

* RIGHT SHIFT BY 3                                   Y = 12 34 56 7D
          MVO    Y(4),Y(2)                               00 01 23 4D
```

*Right shift by an odd number of places with rounding*

```
* RIGHT SHIFT BY N AND ROUND
                              N-1 0's
          ZAP    TEMP,=P'50...0'       GET ROUNDING DIGIT
          MVN    TEMP+15(1),Y+L'Y-1    MAKE ITS SIGN SAME AS Y'S
          AP     TEMP,Y                ADD ROUNDING DIGIT
          MVO    Y,TEMP(16-(N+1)/2     SHIFT AND REPLACE Y
          . . .
TEMP      DS     PL16

* RIGHT SHIFT BY 3 AND ROUND                                    Y = 12 34 56 7D
          ZAP    TEMP,=P'500'      GET ROUNDING DIGIT       TEMP = 0 . . . 50 0C
          MVN    TEMP+15(1),Y+3    MAKE ITS SIGN SAME AS Y'S       0 . . . 50 0D
          AP     TEMP,Y            ADD ROUNDING DIGIT              0 ...00 12 35 06 7D
          MVO    Y,TEMP(14)        SHIFT AND REPLACE Y          Y = 00 01 23 5D
          . . .
TEMP      DS     PL16
```

*Right shift by an even number of places without rounding*

```
* RIGHT SHIFT BY N
          MVO    Y,Y(L'Y-1)        SHIFT 1
          MVO    Y,Y(L'Y-N/2)      SHIFT N-1

* RIGHT SHIFT BY 4                              Y = 12 34 56 7D
          MVO    Y(4),Y(3)         SHIFT 1          01 23 45 6D
          MVO    Y(4),Y(2)         SHIFT 3          00 00 12 3D
```

(Continues)

**Figure 15.8**
Examples of decimal shifting on the IBM System/360.

*Right shift by an even number of places with rounding*

```
* RIGHT SHIFT BY N AND ROUND
                       N-1 0's
         ZAP   TEMP,=P'50...0'     GET ROUNDING DIGIT
         MVN   TEMP+15(1),Y+L'Y-1  MAKE ITS SIGN SAME AS Y'S
         AP    TEMP,Y              ADD ROUNDING DIGIT
         MVO   TEMP,TEMP(15)       SHIFT 1
         MVO   Y,TEMP(16-N/2)      SHIFT N-1 AND REPLACE Y
         . . .
TEMP     DS    PL16
```

```
* RIGHT SHIFT BY 4 AND ROUND                               Y = 12 34 56 7D
         ZAP   TEMP,=P'5000'   GET ROUNDING DIGIT       TEMP = 0 . . . 05 00 0C
         MVN   TEMP+15(1),Y+3  MAKE ITS SIGN SAME AS Y'S       0 . . . 05 00 0D
         AP    TEMP,Y          ADD ROUNDING DIGIT              0 ...00 12 39 56 7D
         MVO   TEMP,TEMP(15)   SHIFT 1                         0 ...00 01 23 95 6D
         MVO   Y,TEMP(14)      SHIFT 3 AND REPLACE Y       Y = 00 00 12 3D
         . . .
TEMP     DS    PL16
```

*Left shift by an odd number of places*

```
* LEFT SHIFT BY N
         ZAP   TEMP,Y              PLACE 32 0'S TO RIGHT OF Y
         NI    TEMP+15,X'F0'       CHANGE SIGN CODE TO 0
         MVO   Y,TEMP+(N-1)/2(16)  MOVE RESULT NEXT TO Y'S SIGN
         . . .
TEMP     DS    PL16
         DC    XL16'0'
```

```
* LEFT SHIFT BY 3                    Y = 00 00 12 34 56 7D
         ZAP   TEMP,Y             TEMP = 0 ...0 12 34 56 7D 00 ... 0
         NI    TEMP+15,X'F0'             0 ...0 12 34 56 70  00 ... 0
         MVO   Y,TEMP+1(16)          Y = 01 23 45 67 00 0D
         . . .
TEMP     DS    PL16
         DC    XL16'0'
```

*Left shift by an even number of places*

```
* LEFT SHIFT BY N
         MVO   TEMP,Y              ANY DIGIT AND 32 0'S PLACED TO RIGHT OF Y
         MVI   TEMP+15,X'00'       CHANGE SIGN CODE AND NEXT POSITION TO 0'S
         MVO   Y,TEMP+N/2-1(16)    MOVE RESULT NEXT TO Y'S SIGN
         . . .
TEMP     DS    PL16
         DC    XL16'0'
```

```
* LEFT SHIFT BY 4                    Y = 00  00 12 34 56 7D
         MVO   TEMP,Y             TEMP = 0 ...01 23 45 67 D? 00 ... 0
         MVI   TEMP+15,X'00'             0 ...01 23 45 67 00  00 ... 0
         MVO   Y,TEMP+1(16)          Y = 12  34 56 70 00 0D
         . . .
TEMP     DS    PL16
         DC    XL16'0'
```

**Figure 15.8**
***(Continued)***

# Decimal Arithmetic with Nonintegral Data

You have seen the need for decimal shifting and the instructions to accomplish it. This section builds upon your knowledge to investigate the details of decimal arithmetic with nonintegral data. Note that you can apply ideas that are analogous to those in this section to binary arithmetic.

## *Planning Space Requirements*

Before performing decimal arithmetic, you must examine the data to determine the number of places to the right and the number of places to the left of the decimal point, and decide how many places to carry in the computation. If possible, arrange for all of your data to contain the same number of places to the right of the decimal point. You could simplify much of what follows if you do this.

Chapter 10 defined the length attribute of a symbol. Later when Chapter 18 discusses macros, you will encounter two additional symbol attributes that will be helpful here: the **scaling attribute** and the **integer attribute**. When applied to symbols that represent packed-decimal fields, the scaling attribute is the number of digits to the right of the decimal point. The integer attribute is the number of digits, including leading zeros, to the left of the decimal point. For example, consider the following definition:

```
X       DC      P'12.3456'      (Assembles as 01 23 45 6C)
```

The scaling attribute of X is 4. The integer attribute of X is 3 since there is room for a leading zero internally. The length attribute of X is 4 since the constant P'12.3456' requires 4 bytes. Recall that the length attribute reference is L'X. Unfortunately, you cannot reference the scaling and integer attributes outside of a macro definition as you can reference the length attribute. The scaling and integer attributes are introduced here to provide some terminology; for now, the scaling and integer attributes of the field X will be denoted by $S_X$ and $I_X$, respectively.

The total number of digits that are represented in a packed-decimal field X is the sum of the field's scaling and integer attributes: $S_X + I_X$. In Chapter 14, you saw that the total number of digits is also equal to $2 * L_X - 1$, where $L_X$ is the number of bytes in the field.[†] (Recall that each byte of a packed-decimal field, except for the rightmost byte, represents 2 digits.) Therefore, the following relationship is true:

$$2 * L_X - 1 = S_X + I_X$$

You will find this relationship to be helpful when you plan the space requirements for a computation, as you will see in later examples.

[†]The number of bytes in a particular packed-decimal field is not always equal to the length attribute of the symbol that represents the address of the field. Therefore, $L_X$ is used here, instead of L'X.

### *Matching the Scaling Attribute of a Field*

You know that shifting is necessary when you perform arithmetic with nonintegral data either to align the decimal points of certain operands or to eliminate excess decimal places in a result. In both cases, you take one number and, by shifting it, make its scaling attribute match the scaling attribute of another number.

Consider two packed-decimal fields, X and Y, that represent numbers in the following form:

| | | |
|---|---|---|
| X: | *xxx.xx* | ( $S_X = 2$ ) |
| Y: | *yy.yyyyyy* | ( $S_Y = 6$ ) |

X has fewer decimal places than Y has; equivalently, the scaling attribute of X is less than the scaling attribute of Y. To make the scaling attribute of X match that of Y—that is, to make X look as if it had 6 places to the right of the decimal point—you would shift X to the left by 4 places, or in general by $S_Y - S_X$ places. X would then look like this:

*xxx.xx*0000

(Note that you cannot actually change the scaling attribute of a symbol during execution since the scaling attribute is an assembly-time concept.)

Now suppose that X and Y appear as follows:

| | | |
|---|---|---|
| X: | *xx.xxxx* | ( $S_X = 4$ ) |
| Y: | *y.y* | ( $S_Y = 1$ ) |

X has more decimal places than Y has. To make the scaling attribute of X match the scaling attribute of Y, you would shift X to the right by 3 places, or in general by $S_X - S_Y$ places. Notice that $S_Y - S_X$ is $-3$ in this case and, when used as the shift value in an SRP instruction, causes a right shift.

**Matching the scaling attribute of X to that of Y**

Therefore, to make the scaling attribute of the field X match the scaling attribute of the field Y, shift X by $S_Y - S_X$ places by using the SRP instruction.

### *The Four Arithmetic Operations*

Consider each of the four arithmetic operations as applied to nonintegral data. Assume that X and Y are two packed-decimal fields that do not necessarily have the same scaling attributes or the same integer attributes. This section will demonstrate how to add, subtract, multiply, and divide X and Y, storing the result in another field, Z.

**Shift the number with the smaller scaling attribute prior to the addition.**

*Addition: Compute Z = X + Y.* Earlier, when you tried to add 12.3 and 1.23, you found that you had to shift 12.3 to the left by 1 place before adding. In general, you must shift the number with the smaller scaling attribute. Without loss of generality, assume that X has the smaller scaling attribute and shift X to the left by $S_Y - S_X$ places. You can shift X in place if it has a sufficient number of leading zeros to avoid an overflow, or you can first copy X to a larger work area by using a ZAP instruction. Copying X into a work area before shifting is the more general approach.

You can determine the integer attribute and the scaling attribute of the sum X + Y from those of X and Y. The integer attribute of the sum can exceed by 1 the larger of the integer attributes of X and Y because a carry can occur on the left, as it does in the following addition:

```
    2.6
+  98.76543
  101.36543
```

Thus, the integer attribute of this sum is equal to Max(1,2) + 1, which is 3. In general, the integer attribute of the sum X + Y satisfies the following equation:

$$I_{Sum} = Max(I_X, I_Y) + 1$$

The scaling attribute of the sum is simply the larger of the scaling attributes of X and Y. The scaling attribute of the previous sum 101.36543 is 5, which is the scaling attribute of Y. In general, the following equation is true:

$$S_{Sum} = Max(S_X, S_Y)$$

To compute X + Y, the first operand field of the AP instruction must be large enough to accommodate $I_{Sum}$ digits to the left of the decimal point and $S_{Sum}$ digits to the right of the decimal point, but it could be larger. You can determine the minimum required length of the first operand field from the relationship

$$2 * L_{Sum} - 1 = I_{Sum} + S_{Sum}$$

For the previous addition (2.6 + 98.76543 = 101.36543), $I_{Sum} + S_{Sum}$ is equal to 3 + 5, which is 8. Therefore, $L_{Sum}$ is 9/2, or 5, when you round up to the next higher integer. Thus, you need at least a 5-byte work area to compute this particular sum. As an alternative to the analysis just given, you can define a 16-byte work area since it can contain the largest valid packed-decimal number and hence it permits you to compute the best sum possible. (Once again, note that extra leading zeros do not cost much in added execution time.) If one of the fields X, Y, or Z is long enough, you could use it as the work area.

After the addition, you may choose not to retain all of the digits in the result that are to the right of the decimal point; that is, the scaling attribute of Z does not need to be the same as the scaling attribute of the sum. Suppose that you retain only 4 of the 5 available decimal places in the previous sum 101.36543. To determine the minimum length required for Z, you proceed as you did for the sum:

$$\begin{aligned} 2 * L_Z - 1 &= I_Z + S_Z \\ &= 3 + 4 \\ &= 7 \end{aligned}$$

Therefore,

$$\begin{aligned} L_Z &= 8/2 \\ &= 4 \end{aligned}$$

which shows that only 4 bytes are required for Z. Shift the sum so that its scaling attribute matches the scaling attribute that you want and copy the result into Z.

```
** COMPUTE Z = X + Y.  ASSUME X HAS THE SMALLER SCALING ATTRIBUTE.
** USE A 16-BYTE WORK AREA TO ACCUMULATE THE SUM.
SX          EQU   1                 SCALING ATTRIBUTE OF X
SY          EQU   5                 SCALING ATTRIBUTE OF Y
SZ          EQU   4                 SCALING ATTRIBUTE OF Z
            .
            .
            .
            ZAP   WORK,X            GET VALUE WITH SMALLER SCALING ATTR.
            SRP   WORK,SY-SX,0      ALIGN DEC. POINTS (MATCH SCALING ATTR. OF Y)
            AP    WORK,Y            X + Y
            SRP   WORK,SZ-SY,5      MATCH SUM TO SCALING ATTR. OF Z
*                                      (SCALING ATTR. OF SUM IS SY)
            ZAP   Z,WORK            PLACE SUM IN Z
            .
            .
            .
X           DC    P'2.6'            (02 6C)
Y           DC    P'98.76543'       (98 76 54 3C)
Z           DC    P'000.0000'       (RESERVES 4 BYTES)
WORK        DS    PL16              WORK AREA
```

**Figure 15.9**
Instructions to compute Z = X + Y, where X has the smaller scaling attribute.

The instructions that compute the sum of 2.6 and 98.76543 by using the previous analysis are listed in Figure 15.9. The instructions use a 16-byte work area for shifting X, computing the sum, and shifting the sum to match the scaling attribute of Z. Instead of defining Z with an explicit length modifier of 4, you can let the assembler determine the required length of Z by using a DC directive with an operand entry of P'000.0000', as in Figure 15.9. Notice that the assembler also computes the lengths of X and Y and, since a 16-byte work area is used, you need not specify the lengths in the arithmetic instructions.

*Subtraction: Compute Z = X − Y.* The only difference between subtraction and addition is that you must consider two cases: $S_X \leq S_Y$ and $S_X > S_Y$. The instructions to compute X − Y when $S_X \leq S_Y$ are the same as those in Figure 15.9, except that SP replaces AP. You can transform the case when $S_X > S_Y$ into the case when $S_X \leq S_Y$ by first computing Y − X and then changing the sign of the result, as demonstrated in Figure 15.10. To change the sign of the result, notice that the preferred signs C and D differ only in their rightmost bits; you can invert this bit value by using an Exclusive Or instruction.

*Multiplication: Compute Z = X * Y.* When you compute a product, your first concern should be with the MP instruction and not with the number of decimal places in the data. The second operand of MP cannot exceed 8 bytes in length, so choose it to be the shorter of X or Y; without loss of generality, assume that Y is the shorter operand. (If both X and Y exceed 8 bytes in length, you cannot continue.) Place X into a 16-byte first operand field; the first operand is then longer than the second operand as required. Now, recall that the first operand must contain the same number of bytes of leading zeros as there are bytes in the second operand, which is Y. Since

```
** COMPUTE Z = X - Y.  ASSUME Y HAS THE SMALLER SCALING ATTRIBUTE.
** USE A 16-BYTE WORK AREA TO COMPUTE THE DIFFERENCE.
SX          EQU   3               SCALING ATTRIBUTE OF X
SY          EQU   1               SCALING ATTRIBUTE OF Y
SZ          EQU   2               SCALING ATTRIBUTE OF Z
            .
            .
            .
            ZAP   WORK,Y          GET VALUE WITH SMALLER SCALING ATTR.
            SRP   WORK,SX-SY,0    ALIGN DEC. POINTS (MATCH SCALING ATTR. OF X)
            SP    WORK,X          COMPUTE Y - X
            XI    WORK+15,X'01'   CHANGE SIGN TO GET X - Y
            SRP   WORK,SZ-SX,5    MATCH RESULT TO SCALING ATTR. OF Z
*                                    (SCALING ATTR. OF DIFFERENCE IS SX)
            ZAP   Z,WORK          MOVE RESULT TO Z
            .
            .
            .
X           DC    P'4.567'        (04 56 7C)
Y           DC    P'12.3'         (12 3C)
Z           DC    P'000.00'       (RESERVES 3 BYTES)
WORK        DS    PL16            WORK AREA
```

**Figure 15.10**
Instructions to compute Z = X − Y, where Y has the smaller scaling attribute.

X might not have any leading zeros, you cannot proceed unless the following inequalities are true:

$$L_Y \leq 8$$
$$L_X \leq 16 - L_Y$$

The number of digits to the right of the decimal point in the product is the sum of the scaling attributes of the operands, as indicated by the following equation:

$$S_{Product} = S_X + S_Y$$

If you do not want to retain all of the decimal places in the product, shift the product to the right. The instructions in Figure 15.11 perform the computation just described.

*Division: Compute Z = X ÷ Y.* Consider an example of division by hand so that you can study the position of the decimal point. Prior to a division, you move the decimal point of the divisor (Y) to the right of its rightmost digit. You then move the decimal point of the dividend (X) to the right by the same number of places. Next, you decide how many digits that you want to the right of the decimal point in the quotient (Z). If the dividend has fewer than this number of places to the right of the newly positioned decimal point, you must write a sufficient number of additional low-order zeros. Conversely, if there are too many digits, you must truncate, or round, the dividend. For example, consider the following division:

$$4.567 \div 0.0123$$

```
** COMPUTE Z = X * Y; ASSUME L'Y < L'X
SX       EQU    3               SCALING ATTRIBUTE OF X
SY       EQU    2               SCALING ATTRIBUTE OF Y
SZ       EQU    4               SCALING ATTRIBUTE OF Z
         .
         .
         .
         ZAP    WORK,X          GET LONGER OPERAND; PRECEDE WITH 0'S
         MP     WORK,Y          X * Y
         SRP    WORK,SZ-(SX+SY),5  MATCH PRODUCT TO SCALING ATTR. OF Z
*                                  (SCALING ATTR. OF PRODUCT IS SX + SY)
         ZAP    Z,WORK          MOVE PRODUCT TO Z
         .
         .
         .
X        DC     P'-12.345'      (12 34 5D)
Y        DC     P'6.78'         (67 8C)
Z        DC     P'000.0000'     (RESERVES 4 BYTES)
WORK     DS     PL16            WORK AREA
```

**Figure 15.11** Instructions to compute Z = X * Y, where Y is the shorter operand.

First, move the decimal point 4 places to the right in both the divisor and the dividend. Suppose that you want 3 decimal places in the quotient. You then must write 3 more zeros in the dividend, as shown:

0.0123 )4.567 0 000

You have written a total of 4 zeros to the right of the original dividend. You can accomplish this by using a left shift of 4 places.

In general, if $S_Z$ is the desired scaling attribute of the quotient, you must shift the dividend by

$$S_Z + S_Y - S_X$$

places before you can do the division. Study the examples in Figure 15.12 and observe that sometimes the shift amount is negative. In such cases, there are too many places in the dividend; you must then shift it to the right. This is exactly what the SRP instruction does when its shift value is negative. The instructions in Figure 15.13 perform the division of X by Y using the ideas just discussed.

Instead of shifting the dividend, you could divide first and then shift the quotient to match the desired scaling attribute. This would be analogous to the procedures described earlier for addition, subtraction, and multiplication. Shifting the dividend saves time because the DP instruction is faster when there are fewer significant digits involved; however, shifting the quotient can be more accurate. You can decide to shift the dividend since, if accuracy becomes a problem, you can go back and increase $S_Z$.

**Figure 15.12**
Examples of the shift amount that is necessary to adjust the decimal point in the dividend of the division 4.567 ÷ 0.0123.

| Y )X | *Shift Amount* $S_Z + S_Y - S_X$ (Assume $S_Z = 3$) |
|---|---|
| .0123 )4.5670,000 | 3 + 4 − 3 = 4 |
| .0123 )4567.0000,000 | 3 + 4 − 0 = 7 |
| .0123 ).4567,000 | 3 + 4 − 4 = 3 |
| .0123 ).0456,700 | 3 + 4 − 5 = 2 |
| .0123 ).0000,4567 | 3 + 4 − 8 = −1 |
| 123 )4.567 | 3 + 0 − 3 = 0 |
| 123 )4567.000 | 3 + 0 − 0 = 3 |
| 123 ).4567 | 3 + 0 − 4 = −1 |
| 123 ).04567 | 3 + 0 − 5 = −2 |

```
** COMPUTE Z = X/Y
SX        EQU  3                   SCALING ATTRIBUTE OF X
SY        EQU  4                   SCALING ATTRIBUTE OF Y
SZ        EQU  3                   SCALING ATTRIBUTE OF Z
          .
          .
          .
          ZAP  WORK,X              COPY DIVIDEND TO WORK AREA
          SRP  WORK,SZ+SY-SX,5     ADJUST ACCORDING TO EXISTING AND
*                                    DESIRED SCALING ATTRIBUTES.
          DP   WORK,Y              X/Y
          ZAP  Z,QUOTIENT          MOVE QUOTIENT TO Z
          .
          .
          .
X         DC   P'4.567'            (04 56 7C)
Y         DC   P'.0123'            (12 3C)
Z         DC   P'000.000'          (4 BYTES)
WORK      DS   0PL16               WORK AREA FOR DIVISION; 2 FIELDS:
QUOTIENT  DS   PL(16-L'Y)            THE QUOTIENT
REMAIN    DS   PL(L'Y)               THE REMAINDER
```

**Figure 15.13**
Instructions to compute Z = X ÷ Y.

EXAMPLE 40

### A Decimal Computation with Nonintegral Data

To see a decimal computation with nonintegral data, suppose that you want to evaluate the following expression to 2 decimal places, where the integer and scaling attributes of the variables are as indicated:

$$\frac{A(B + C)^E}{D}$$

A = *xxxxx.*
B = *x.x*
C = *.xxx*
D = *xx.xx*
E = *x*

The program segment in Figure 15.14 demonstrates some of the concerns that you must have when you perform a decimal computation with nonintegral data. The segment defines specific values for A, B, C, D, and E; a trace of the instructions is provided in Figure 15.15.

**Figure 15.14** Instructions to perform a decimal computation with nonintegral data, as described in Example 40.

```
** COMPUTE (A * (B + C) ** E) / D
** ASSUME A, B, C, D, AND E ARE PACKED-DECIMAL NUMBERS.
** ALSO ASSUME D IS NOT 0 AND E >= 2.
         ZAP    DOUBLE,E        MOVE E TO A DOUBLEWORD PRIOR TO CVB
         CVB    R6,DOUBLE       CONVERT EXPONENT TO BINARY
         SH     R6,=H'1'        R6 = E-1 FOR LOOP CONTROL
         ZAP    SUM,B           MOVE B TO SUM AREA
         SRP    SUM,2,0         SHIFT LEFT 2 TO MATCH SCALE OF C
         AP     SUM,C           B + C
         ZAP    PROD,SUM        MOVE SUM TO PRODUCT WORK AREA
         SRP    PROD,2,0        SHIFT LEFT 2 TO INCREASE PRECISION
* REPEAT E-1 TIMES:
LOOP     MP     PROD,SUM        MULTIPLY BY (B + C)
         SRP    PROD,64-3,5     SHIFT RIGHT 3 (ROUND TO 5 PLACES)
         BCT    R6,LOOP         REPEAT
* END REPEAT
         MP     PROD,A          A * (B + C) ** E
         DP     PROD,D          (A * (B + C) ** E) / D
         SRP    PROD(13),64-1,5   ROUND TO 2 DECIMAL PLACES
         ZAP    RESULT,PROD(13)   SAVE RESULT
         .
         .
         .
SUM      DS     PL3             AREA TO COMPUTE B + C
PROD     DS     PL16            AREA TO COMPUTE PRODUCT
DOUBLE   DS     D               DOUBLEWORD FOR CVB
RESULT   DS     PL16            THE COMPUTED RESULT
A        DC     P'12345'        (12 34 5C)
B        DC     P'6.4'          (06 4C)
C        DC     P'.123'         (12 3C)
D        DC     P'81.09'        (08 10 9C)
E        DC     P'3'            (3C)
```

**Figure 15.15**
A trace of the instructions that are in Figure 15.14.

| | | | SUM |
|---|---|---|---|
| 1 | ZAP | SUM, B | 00 06 4C |
| 2 | SRP | SUM, 2, 0 | 06 40 0C |
| 3 | AP | SUM, C | 06 52 3C |
| | | | **PROD** |
| 4 | ZAP | PROD, SUM | 00 ... 00 00 00 00 00 00 06 52 3C |
| 5 | SRP | PROD, 2, 0 | 00 ... 00 00 00 00 00 06 52 30 0C |
| 6 | MP | PROD, SUM | 00 ... 00 00 00 04 25 49 52 90 0C |
| 7 | SRP | PROD, 64-3, 5 | 00 ... 00 00 00 00 00 42 54 95 3C |
| 8 | MP | PROD, SUM | 00 ... 00 00 00 27 75 50 58 41 9C |
| 9 | SRP | PROD, 64-3, 5 | 00 ... 00 00 00 00 02 77 55 05 8C |
| 10 | MP | PROD, A | 00 ... 00 00 03 42 63 61 91 01 0C |
| 11 | DP | PROD, D | 00 ... 00 04 22 53 81 5C 05 17 5C |
| 12 | SRP | PROD(13), 64-1, 5 | 00 ... 00 00 42 25 38 2C 05 17 5C |
| | | | **RESULT** |
| 13 | ZAP | RESULT, PROD(13) | 00 ... 00 00 00 00 00 42 25 38 2C |

The calculation begins by computing B + C to 3 decimal places in the 3-byte field at SUM. The result is 6.523 (as shown in Line 3 of Figure 15.15). Generally, you cannot raise 6.523 to a power without first deciding how many decimal places to retain after each multiplication. Here, although the 16-byte work area at PROD is long enough to accommodate the result of exponentiation because the exponent is only 3, a bigger exponent would cause the product to become too large to participate in another multiplication. Your decision about the number of decimal places to retain at any step in the computation affects the accuracy of the final result. Although a complete analysis of the number of decimal places that you should carry to preserve accuracy is beyond the scope of this text, the simple decisions made here demonstrate how to use the decimal instructions.

Suppose that, since you want to compute the result to 2 decimal places, you first compute the quotient to 3 decimal places and then round. Given a divisor with 2 decimal places, to compute a quotient with 3 decimal places requires a dividend that is computed to 5 decimal places. Therefore, the instructions in Figure 15.14 compute the product to 5 decimal places. First, as shown in Lines 4 and 5 of Figure 15.15, SUM is moved to the work area PROD and the result is shifted left 2 places to increase the number of decimal places to 5. After the multiplication, the product contains 8 decimal places, as shown in Line 6, and is rounded to 5 decimal places by a right shift of 3 places, as shown in Line 7. When the exponentiation is complete, PROD contains $(B + C)^E$ to 5 decimal places (Line 9). The value in PROD is then multiplied by A and the product is divided by D. The quotient is in the first 13 bytes of PROD and contains 3 decimal places, as shown in Line 11. The quotient is rounded to 2 decimal places by shifting it right by 1 place (Line 12) and is then copied to the field at RESULT (Line 13).

## SELF-TEST EXERCISES

8. Write instructions to compute Z = 2.6 + 98.76543 by using Z to accumulate the sum, instead of using a separate work area. Make the scaling attribute of Z equal 4. (Hint: In the previous section, you saw that the minimum length of the sum is 5 bytes; but if the scaling attribute of Z is 4, then Z need only be 4 bytes long. Therefore, you must define Z differently than in Figure 15.9.)
9. Assume the following definitions:

```
W        DC    P'12.38'
X        DC    P'1.92'
Y        DC    P'3.4'
```

Write instructions to perform the following computations by using Z instead of a separate work area. In each case, define Z to be as short as possible. Retain the indicated number of decimal places in the result.

**a.** Z = X + Y, truncated to 2 decimal places.
**b.** Z = W − Y, rounded to 1 decimal place.
**c.** Z = W * X, rounded to 2 decimal places.
**d.** Z = W ÷ Y, rounded to 3 decimal places.

# Case Study

## *Problem Statement*

**Print a table of monthly payments on a loan.**

For each payment, indicate the monthly interest charge and the amount applied toward payment of the principal.

## *Discussion*

Suppose that you borrow $1000 to be paid back in 12 monthly payments, which include a total interest charge of $150. The total amount to be paid is $1150. The desired table of payments appears as follows:

| Number | Payment | Interest | Principal |
|---|---|---|---|
| 1 | $95.83 | $23.08 | $72.75 |
| 2 | 95.83 | 21.15 | 74.68 |
| . | . | . | . |
| . | . | . | . |
| . | . | . | . |
| 12 | 95.87 | 1.92 | 93.95 |
| **Totals:** | $1150.00 | $150.00 | $1000.00 |

Although each of the first 11 payments is equal to 1/12 of $1150, or $95.83, the last payment may differ because of rounding errors that the computation introduces, as it does here. The last payment is computed as follows:

1150. − 11 * 95.83 = 95.87

Typically, the interest charge on an installment loan is not evenly divided among the total number of payments. Instead, the interest portion of each payment is at a maximum during the first month, and then decreases with each successive month. One widely used method to apportion the total interest charge among the monthly payments is called the *Rule of 78's*[†]. To apply the Rule of 78's, you first compute the sum of the digits from 1 to $n$, where $n$ is the number of payments. This sum is equal to $n * ( n + 1 ) / 2$. The sum of the digits from 1 to 12 is 78, which explains the rule's name. During the first month of the 12-month loan just described, you have the use of 12 parts (that is, all) of the amount borrowed; therefore, you pay 12/78 of the total interest charge in the first payment. During the second month, you have the use of 11 parts of the amount that you borrowed, so you pay 11/78 of the total interest charge in the second payment. This process continues in like manner for the rest of the months.

Although you should pay 1/78 of the total interest charge in the last payment, the actual interest charge may differ because of rounding errors that were introduced in the calculations of the earlier interest charges. The interest charge in the last payment is equal to the difference between the total interest charge and the interest that was included in earlier payments.

The program that prints the desired table is organized into three control sections: MAIN, LOAN, and PRINT. MAIN calls an external subprogram LOAN that performs the necessary computations. LOAN calls another external subprogram PRINT to print a line in the table. Figure 15.16 shows the relationship between the control sections. The pseudocode in Figure 15.17 and the flowchart in Figure 15.18 describe the logic details. Figure 15.19 contains a listing of the program.

The main program reads three data items: the principal borrowed, the total interest charge, and the number of payments. The principal is a dollar amount that is given in 6 or fewer digits. The total interest charge is given in dollars and cents with a decimal point, and does not exceed the principal. The number of payments does not exceed 999. The main program converts the data to packed-decimal form, and then stores the results in the three fields that are defined by the following statements (which are Statements 97, 98, and 99 in the program):

```
P          DC      P'000000.'      PRINCIPAL BORROWED
I          DC      P'000000.00'    TOTAL INTEREST CHARGE
NP         DC      P'000'          NUMBER OF PAYMENTS
```

The assembler reserves the minimum space that is required for the fields at P, I, and NP by using the lengths that the specified constants imply.

[†]Department of Consumer Affairs. "The Rule of 78's or What May Happen When You Pay Off a Loan Early." Philadelphia: Federal Reserve Bank of Philadelphia, 1986.

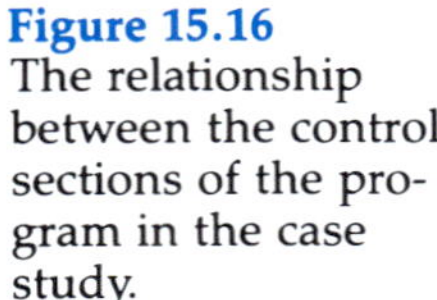

**Figure 15.16**
The relationship between the control sections of the program in the case study.

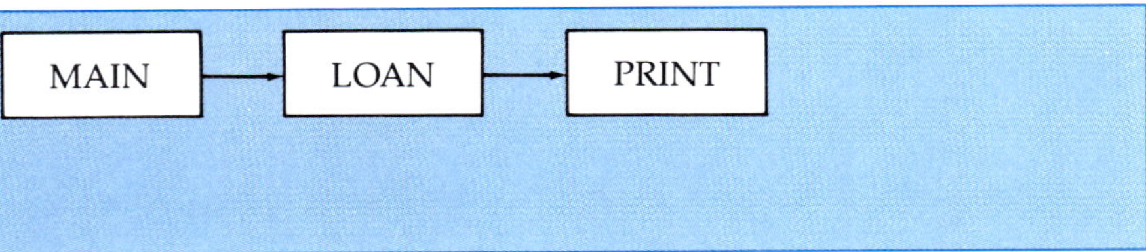

**Figure 15.17**
A pseudocode solution for the case study.

**Notation:**

*PRINCIPAL* - the amount borrowed
*INTEREST* - the total interest charge
*N* - the number of payments
} Input to program

*TOTALDUE* - the principal plus the total interest charge
*PAYMENT* - the monthly payment
*LASTPAY* - the last monthly payment
*S* - the sum of the first *N* integers
*INTPAID* - the total interest in the first *N*-1 payments
*INTPAY* - the interest portion of the payment
*PRINPAY* - the principal portion of the payment
*PAYNO* - the payment number

**The main program:**

```
Read input record
Convert input fields from EBCDIC to packed-decimal form
Print table heading
Call LOAN passing PRINCIPAL, INTEREST, and N
```

**The subprogram LOAN:**

```
TOTALDUE := PRINCIPAL + INTEREST
PAYMENT := TOTALDUE / N
LASTPAY := TOTALDUE − (N − 1) * PAYMENT
S := N * ( N + 1) / 2
INTPAID := 0
PAYNO := 1
FOR J := N , N − 1, . . . , 2
      INTPAY := (J / S) * INTEREST
      INTPAID := INTPAID + INTPAY
      PRINPAY := PAYMENT − INTPAY
      Call PRINT passing PAYNO, PAYMENT, INTPAY, and PRINPAY
      PAYNO := PAYNO + 1
END FOR
INTPAY := INTEREST − INTPAID
PRINPAY := LASTPAY − INTPAY
Call PRINT passing PAYNO, LASTPAY, INTPAY, and PRINPAY
PAYNO := 0
Call PRINT passing PAYNO, TOTALDUE, INTEREST, and PRINCIPAL
```

**The subprogram PRINT:**

```
IF PAYNO is 0 or 1
     THEN precede dollar amounts with dollar signs
END IF
IF PAYNO is 0
     THEN PAYNO := "TOTALS"
END IF
Print PAYNO, PAYMENT, INTPAY, and PRINPAY
```

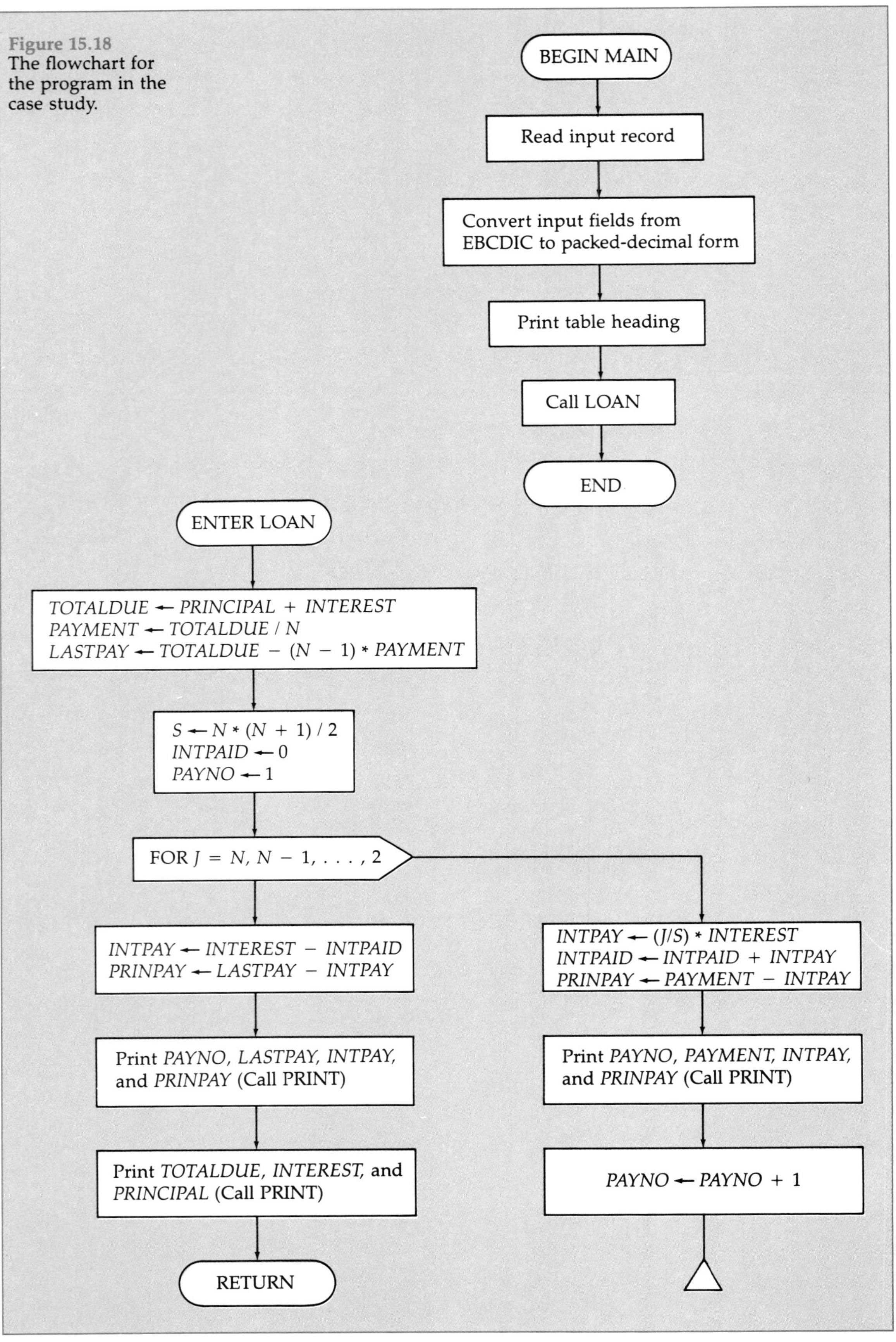


**Figure 15.18**
The flowchart for the program in the case study.

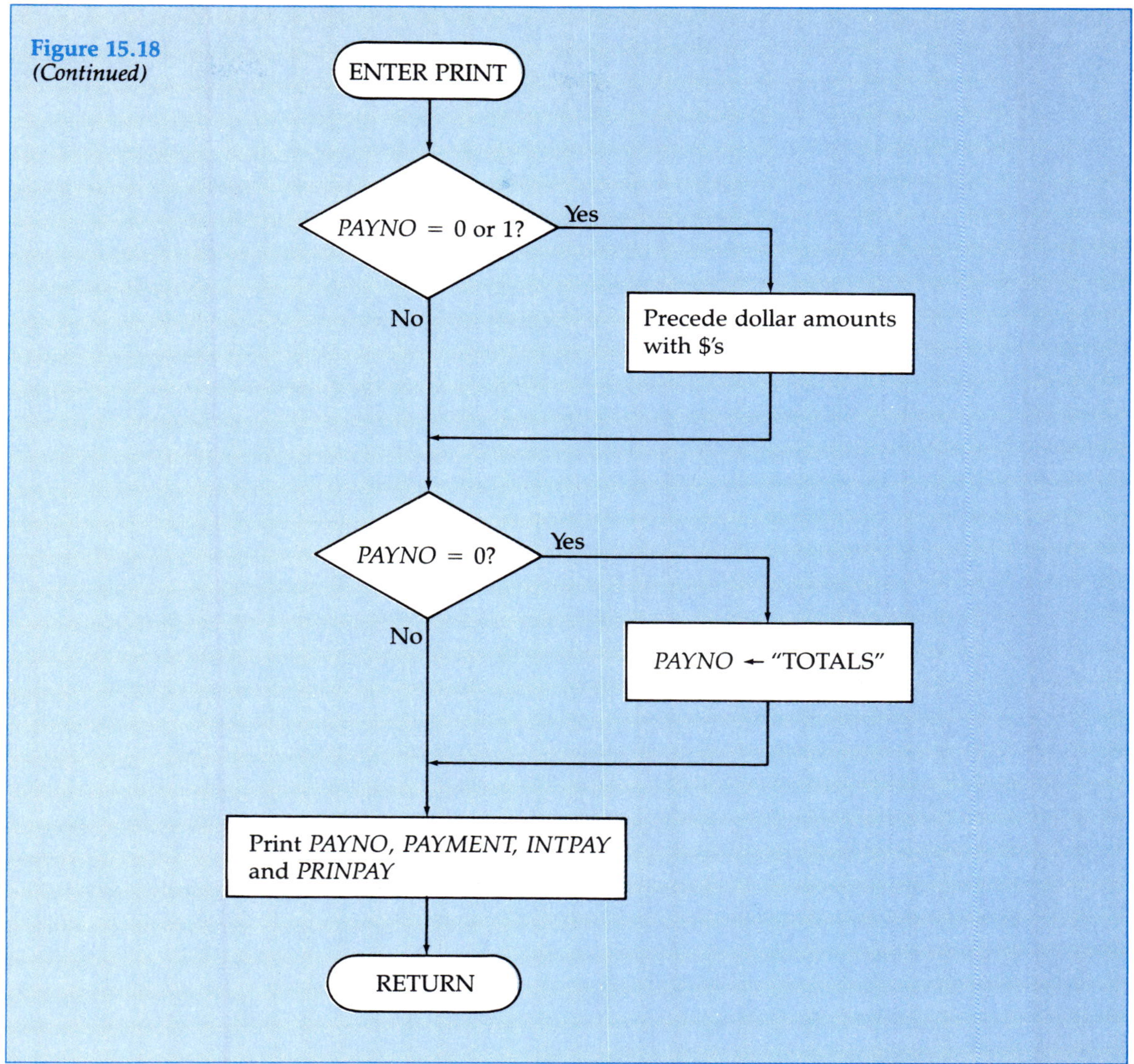


**Figure 15.18**
*(Continued)*

Implied lengths are used in many of the other definitions throughout the program, including the dummy sections. Implied lengths are convenient and can help you to avoid errors, but you must be careful: you cannot completely ignore the actual lengths of packed-decimal numbers when you perform arithmetic—particularly when multiplication or division is involved. There are several instances in the program where an explicit length must be written; for example, in Statements 260, 261, 267, 274, 285, 287, 288, 291, 292, and 293.

The logic of the program is straightforward and the arithmetic details are similar to those that you already encountered in earlier discussions. However, there are a few points that you should see. The principal is given in dollars, but it must be scaled to include cents, as done in Statement 254, before it is used in computations. In addition, the scaled value is saved in PRINADJ by Statement 255 and used in Statement 316 when the column totals are printed. In the subprogram PRINT, the edit pattern at PATT234 in Statement 441 can accommodate dollar amounts of up to 7 digits, even

```
        PRINT TABLE OF MONTHLY LOAN PAYMENTS


   LOC  OBJECT CODE    ADDR1 ADDR2  STMT   SOURCE STATEMENT

000000                                 2 MAIN     START
                                       3 ***********************************************************************
                                       4 ** INPUT: (ALL VALUES ARE RIGHT-JUSTIFIED IN THEIR FIELDS)
                                       5 **        COLS 1 -  6: PRINCIPAL IN DOLLARS, NO DECIMAL POINT,
                                       6 **                          RIGHT-JUSTIFIED
                                       7 **             8 - 16: INTEREST CHARGE IN DOLLARS AND CENTS WITH
                                       8 **                          DECIMAL POINT
                                       9 **            18 - 20: NUMBER OF PAYMENTS, 3-DIGIT INTEGER
                                      10 ** OUTPUT: TABLE OF MONTHLY LOAN PAYMENTS
                                      11 ** SUBPROGRAM: LOAN (LOAN CALLS PRINT)
                                      12 ***********************************************************************
                                      13          PRINT NOGEN           SUPPRESS MACRO EXPANSIONS
                                      14          ENTRY PRINTER         MAKE PRINTER DCB AVAILABLE TO SUBPROG.
                                      15 ** REGISTER DEFINITIONS:
                               00001  16 R1       EQU   1               ADDRESS OF ARGUMENT LIST, EDMK POINTER
                               00007  17 R7       EQU   7               DCB POINTER
                               00008  18 R8       EQU   8               ARGUMENT POINTER
                               00009  19 R9       EQU   9               ARGUMENT POINTER
                               0000A  20 R10      EQU   10              ARGUMENT POINTER
                               0000B  21 R11      EQU   11              ARGUMENT POINTER
                               0000C  22 R12      EQU   12              BASE REGISTER
                               0000D  23 R13      EQU   13              SAVE AREA ADDRESS
                               0000E  24 R14      EQU   14              RETURN REGISTER
                               0000F  25 R15      EQU   15              ENTRY POINT
                                      26 ** INITIALIZE:
                                      27 *  OS:
000000 90EC D00C         0000C        28          STM   R14,R12,12(R13) SAVE REGISTERS
000004 05C0                           29          BALR  R12,0           LOAD BASE REGISTER
                               00006  30          USING BASEM,R12       DECLARE BASE REGISTER
000006 50D0 C1FE         00204        31 BASEM    ST    R13,SAVEM+4     SAVE R13
00000A 41E0 C1FA         00200        32          LA    R14,SAVEM       GET ADDRESS OF NEW SAVE AREA
00000E 50ED 0008         00008        33          ST    R14,8(R13)      STORE IT IN PREVIOUS SAVE AREA
000012 18DE                           34          LR    R13,R14         R13 = ADDRESS OF NEW SAVE AREA
                                      35          OPEN  (READER,INPUT,PRINTER,OUTPUT)  PREPARE FOR I/O
                                      43 ** DOS*******
                                      44 *        BALR  R12,0           LOAD BASE REGISTER
                                      45 *        USING BASEM,R12       DECLARE BASE REGISTER
                                      46 *BASEM   LA    R13,SAVEM       R13 = ADDRESS OF NEW SAVE AREA
                                      47 *        OPEN  READER,PRINTER  PREPARE FOR I/O
                                      48 ******
                                      49 ** READ DATA AND CONVERT TO PACKED-DECIMAL FORM:
                                      50          GET   READER,INPUT    READ INPUT RECORD
000030 F235 C092 C09D 00098 000A3     55          PACK  P,INFLD1        CONVERT PRINCIPAL TO PACKED FORM
000036 D201 C0AA C0AB 000B0 000B1     56          MVC   INFLD2PT(2),INFLD2PT+1 REMOVE DECIMAL POINT IN 2ND
                                      57 *                                     FIELD BY SHIFTING DECIMAL
                                      58 *                                     PLACES TO THE LEFT
00003C F247 C096 C0A4 0009C 000AA     59          PACK  I,INFLD2(L'INFLD2-1)  CONVERT INTEREST TO PACKED
000042 F212 C09B C0AE 000A1 000B4     60          PACK  NP,INFLD3       CONVERT NUMBER OF PAYMENTS TO PACKED
                                      61 *
                                      62          PUT   PRINTER,HEADING PRINT TABLE HEADING
                                      67          PUT   PRINTER,ULINE   PRINT UNDERLINE
                                      72 ** CALL LOAN, (P,I,NP)
000064 58F0 C082         00088        73          L     R15,=V(LOAN)    R15 = ENTRY POINT
000068 4110 C086         0008C        74          LA    R1,=A(P,I,NP)   R1 = ADDRESS OF ARGUMENT LIST
00006C 05EF                           75          BALR  R14,R15         CALL LOAN
                                      76 *  OS:
                                      77          CLOSE (READER,,PRINTER)  I/O IS COMPLETE
00007E 58D0 C1FE         00204        85          L     R13,SAVEM+4     RESTORE R13
000082 98EC D00C         0000C        86          LM    R14,R12,12(R13) RESTORE REMAINING REGISTERS
000086 07FE                           87          BR    R14             EXIT TO OS
```

*(Continues)*

**Figure 15.19**
The program for the case study.

```
                                        88 ** DOS*******
                                        89 *         CLOSE READER,PRINTER   I/O IS COMPLETE
                                        90 *         EOJ                    EXIT TO DOS
                                        91 ******
000088                                  92           LTORG
000088 00000000                         93                 =V(LOAN)
00008C 000000980000009C                 94                 =A(P,I,NP)
                                        95           DROP  R12
                                        96 *
000098 0000000C                         97 P         DC    P'000000.'       PRINCIPAL BORROWED
00009C 000000000C                       98 I         DC    P'000000.00'     TOTAL INTEREST CHARGE
0000A1 000C                             99 NP        DC    P'000'           NUMBER OF PAYMENTS
0000A3                                 100 INPUT     DS    CL80             INPUT BUFFER WITH THE FOLLOWING FIELDS:
0000F3                       000A3     101           ORG   INPUT
0000A3                                 102 INFLD1    DS    CL6                PRINCIPAL  XXXXXX  (COLS. 1-6)
0000A9                                 103           DS    X                  SPACE
0000AA                                 104 INFLD2    DS    CL9                INTEREST CHARGE XXXXXX.XX (COLS. 8-16)
                             000B0     105 INFLD2PT  EQU   *-3                DECIMAL POINT IN INTEREST CHARGE
0000B3                                 106           DS    X                  SPACE
0000B4                                 107 INFLD3    DS    CL3                NUMBER OF PAYMENTS  XXX  (COLS. 18-20)
0000B7                       000F3     108           ORG
0000F3 F0D5E4D4C2C5D940                109 HEADING   DC    CL16'0NUMBER',CL15'PAYMENT',CL15'INTEREST'
000121 D7D9C9D5C3C9D7C1                110           DC    CL15'PRINCIPAL'
                             0003D     111 LHEAD     EQU   *-HEADING          LENGTH OF HEADINGS
000130 4040404040404040                112           DC    (133-LHEAD)C' '    PAD WITH BLANKS TO 133 BYTES
000178 4060606060606060                113 ULINE     DC    C' ',(LHEAD-1)C'-',(133-LHEAD)C' '  UNDERLINE
000200                                 114 SAVEM     DS    18F              SAVE AREA (9D IN DOS)
                                       115 ** DCB'S FOR I/O IN OS:
                                       116 READER    DCB   DSORG=PS,MACRF=GM,DDNAME=SYSIN,RECFM=F,LRECL=80,           X
                                                           BLKSIZE=80
                                       170 PRINTER   DCB   DSORG=PS,MACRF=PM,DDNAME=SYSPRINT,RECFM=FA,                X
                                                           LRECL=133,BLKSIZE=133
                                       224 ** DOS*******
                                       225 *READER   DTFCD DEVADDR=SYSIPT,DEVICE=2540,IOAREA1=INBUF,                  X
                                                           RECFORM=FIXUNB,BLKSIZE=80,TYPEFLE=INPUT,WORKA=YES
                                       226 *PRINTER  DTFPR DEVADDR=SYSLST,DEVICE=3203,IOAREA1=OUTBUF,WORKA=YES,       X
                                                           RECFORM=FIXUNB,BLKSIZE=133,CTLCHAR=ASA
                                       227 *INBUF    DS    80C              DOS INPUT BUFFER
                                       228 *OUTBUF   DS    133C             DOS OUTPUT BUFFER
                                       229 ***********************************************************************
                                       230 ** LOAN    SUBPROGRAM TO COMPUTE AND PRINT MONTHLY PAYMENTS, DIVIDED
                                       231 **         INTO INTEREST AND PRINCIPAL, FOR AN INSTALLMENT LOAN.
                                       232 ** INPUT:  PRINCIPAL, TOTAL INTEREST CHARGE, AND NUMBER OF PAYMENTS,
                                       233 **           ALL IN PACKED-DECIMAL FORM
                                       234 ** OUTPUT: A TABLE OF MONTHLY INTEREST AND PRINCIPAL PAYMENTS.
                                       235 ** SUBPROGRAM: PRINT
                                       236 ***********************************************************************
000308                                 237 LOAN      CSECT
                                       238 ** INITIALIZE:
000308 90EC D00C        0000C          239           STM   R14,R12,12(R13)  SAVE REGISTERS
00030C 05C0                            240           BALR  R12,0            LOAD BASE REGISTER
                             0030E     241           USING BASEL,R12        DECLARE BASE REGISTER
00030E 50D0 C1B2        004C0          242 BASEL     ST    R13,SAVEL+4      SAVE R13
000312 41E0 C1AE        004BC          243           LA    R14,SAVEL        GET ADDRESS OF NEW SAVE AREA
000316 50ED 0008        00008          244           ST    R14,8(R13)       STORE IT IN PREVIOUS SAVE AREA
00031A 18DE                            245           LR    R13,R14          R13 = ADDRESS OF NEW SAVE AREA
                             00000     246           USING ARGLIST,R1       ESTABLISH ADDRESSABILITY OF ARGLIST
00031C 989B 1000        00000          247           LM    R9,R11,ARGLIST   GET ADDRESSES OF ARGUMENTS
                                       248           DROP  R1               DELETE R1 FROM BASE REGISTER POOL
                             00000     249           USING PRIN,R9          ESTABLISH ADDRESSABILITY OF PRIN
                             00000     250           USING INTEREST,R10     ESTABLISH ADDRESSABILITY OF INTEREST
                             00000     251           USING N,R11            ESTABLISH ADDRESSABILITY OF N
```

*(Continues)*

**Figure 15.19**
*(Continued)*

```
                                      ** COMPUTE MONTHLY PAYMENTS:
000320 F8F3 C19C 9000 004AA 00000     BASE3    ZAP   WORK,PRIN        GET PRINCIPAL (DOLLARS)
000326 F0F0 C19C 0002 004AA 00002              SRP   WORK,2,0         ADJUST FOR CENTS PORTION
00032C F84F C175 C19C 00483 004AA              ZAP   PRINADJ,WORK     SAVE ADJUSTED PRINCIPAL FOR OUTPUT LATER
000332 FAF4 C19C A000 004AA 00000              AP    WORK,INTEREST    TOTAL AMOUNT DUE = PRINCIPAL + INTEREST
000338 F84F C17A C19C 00488 004AA              ZAP   TOTALDUE,WORK    SAVE TOTAL DUE
00033E F0F0 C19C 0001 004AA 00001              SRP   WORK,1,0         SHIFT LEFT TO GET 1 MORE DECIMAL PLACE
000344 FDF1 C19C B000 004AA 00000              DP    WORK,N           COMPUTE MONTHLY PAYMENT
00034A F0D5 C19C 003F 004AA 0003F              SRP   WORK(14),64-1,5  ROUND TO 2 DECIMAL PLACES
000350 F84D C17F C19C 0048D 004AA              ZAP   PAYMENT,WORK(14) SAVE ROUNDED MONTHLY PAYMENT
                                      ** COMPUTE LAST PAYMENT = TOTAL DUE - (N-1) * MONTHLY PAYMENT:
000356 F8F1 C19C B000 004AA 00000              ZAP   WORK,N           GET N
00035C FBF0 C19C C16E 004AA 0047C              SP    WORK,=P'1'       N - 1
000362 FCF4 C19C C17F 004AA 0048D              MP    WORK,PAYMENT     (N - 1) * MONTHLY PAYMENT
000368 FBF4 C19C C17A 004AA 00488              SP    WORK,TOTALDUE    NEGATIVE OF LAST PAYMENT
00036E D100 C1AB C16F 004B9 0047D              MVN   WORK+15(1),=P'0' MAKE SIGN +
000374 F84F C184 C19C 00492 004AA              ZAP   LASTPAY,WORK     SAVE LAST PAYMENT
                                      ** COMPUTE S = N * (N + 1) / 2:
00037A F8F1 C19C B000 004AA 00000              ZAP   WORK,N           GET N
000380 FAF0 C19C C16E 004AA 0047C              AP    WORK,=P'1'       N + 1
000386 FCF1 C19C B000 004AA 00000              MP    WORK,N           N * (N + 1)
00038C FDF0 C19C C170 004AA 0047E              DP    WORK,=PL1'2'     N * (N + 1) / 2 (1 BYTE REMAINDER = 0)
000392 F83E C171 C19C 0047F 004AA              ZAP   S,WORK(15)       SAVE S
                                      ** COMPUTE AND PRINT MONTHLY INTEREST AND PRINCIPAL PAYMENTS:
000398 F840 C193 C16F 004A1 0047D              ZAP   INTPAID,=P'0'    SET TOTAL INTEREST PAID TO 0
00039E F810 C198 C16E 004A6 0047C              ZAP   PAYNO,=P'1'      INITIALIZE PAYMENT NUMBER
0003A4 F811 C19A B000 004A8 00000              ZAP   J,N              INITIALIZE J FOR NEXT LOOP
                                      * FOR J = N, N - 1,..., 2 DO:
                                      * COMPUTE J / S TO 5 DECIMAL PLACES:
0003AA F8F1 C19C C19A 004AA 004A8     LOOP     ZAP   WORK,J           GET J
0003B0 F0F0 C19C 0005 004AA 00005              SRP   WORK,5,0         SHIFT LEFT 5 PLACES
0003B6 FDF3 C19C C171 004AA 0047F              DP    WORK,S           J / S IN FIRST 12 BYTES
                                      * INTEREST FOR THIS PAYMENT = (J / S) * TOTAL INTEREST:
0003BC FCB4 C19C A000 004AA 00000              MP    WORK(12),INTEREST   COMPUTE INTEREST FOR THIS PAYMENT -
                                      *                                     PRODUCT HAS 7 DECIMAL PLACES
0003C2 F0B5 C19C 003B 004AA 0003B              SRP   WORK(12),64-5,5 ROUND TO 2 DECIMAL PLACES
0003C8 F84B C189 C19C 00497 004AA              ZAP   INTPAY,WORK(12) SAVE INTEREST PAYMENT FOR THIS MONTH
0003CE FA44 C193 C189 004A1 00497              AP    INTPAID,INTPAY  UPDATE INTEREST PAID TO DATE
                                      * PRINCIPAL FOR THIS PAYMENT = MONTHLY PAYMENT - INTEREST FOR MONTH:
0003D4 FBB4 C19C C17F 004AA 0048D              SP    WORK(12),PAYMENT  INTEREST - MONTHLY PAYMENT
0003DA D100 C1A7 C16F 004B5 0047D              MVN   WORK+11(1),=P'0'  CHANGE SIGN TO +
0003E0 F84B C18E C19C 0049C 004AA              ZAP   PRINPAY,WORK(12)  SAVE PRINCIPAL PAYMENT FOR THIS MONTH
                                      * PRINT LINE OF OUTPUT:
0003E6 4110 C13A      00448                    LA    R1,=A(PAYNO,PAYMENT,INTPAY,PRINPAY)  R1 = A(ARG. LIST)
0003EA 58F0 C16A      00478                    L     R15,=V(PRINT)    R15 = ENTRY POINT
0003EE 05EF                                    BALR  R14,R15          CALL PRINT FOR NEXT PAYMENT
                                      *
0003F0 FA10 C198 C16E 004A6 0047C              AP    PAYNO,=P'1'      INCREMENT PAYMENT NUMBER
0003F6 FB10 C19A C16E 004A8 0047C              SP    J,=P'1'          DECREMENT J
0003FC F910 C19A C16E 004A8 0047C              CP    J,=P'1'          IS J = 1?
000402 4720 C09C      003AA                    BH    LOOP             REPEAT IF J > 1
                                      * END FOR
                                      ** COMPUTE AND PRINT LAST PAYMENT:
000406 F844 C189 A000 00497 00000              ZAP   INTPAY,INTEREST GET TOTAL INTEREST TO BE PAID
00040C FB44 C189 C193 00497 004A1              SP    INTPAY,INTPAID  SUBTRACT INTEREST ALREADY PAID TO GET
                                      *                                LAST INTEREST PAYMENT
000412 F844 C18E C184 0049C 00492              ZAP   PRINPAY,LASTPAY GET LAST PAYMENT
000418 FB44 C18E C189 0049C 00497              SP    PRINPAY,INTPAY  SUBTRACT LAST INTEREST PAYMENT TO GET
                                      *                                LAST PRINCIPAL PAYMENT
00041E 4110 C14A      00458                    LA    R1,=A(PAYNO,LASTPAY,INTPAY,PRINPAY)  R1 = A(ARG. LIST)
000422 58F0 C16A      00478                    L     R15,=V(PRINT)   R15 = ENTRY POINT
000426 05EF                                    BALR  R14,R15         CALL PRINT FOR LAST PAYMENT
                                      ** PRINT COLUMN TOTALS:
000428 F844 C189 A000 00497 00000              ZAP   INTPAY,INTEREST COPY TOTAL INTEREST DUE FOR PRINT
00042E 4110 C15A      00468                    LA    R1,=A(ZERO,TOTALDUE,INTPAY,PRINADJ)  R1 = A(ARG. LIST);
                                      *                                  ZERO INDICATES LINE IS FOR TOTALS
000432 58F0 C16A      00478                    L     R15,=V(PRINT)   R15 = ENTRY POINT
000436 05EF                                    BALR  R14,R15         CALL PRINT FOR TOTALS
```

(Continues)

**Figure 15.19** *(Continued)*

```
                                          ** RETURN:
000438 58D0 C1B2      004C0                        L     R13,SAVEL+4      RESTORE R13
00043C 98EC D00C      0000C                        LM    R14,R12,12(R13)  RESTORE REMAINING REGISTERS
000440 07FE                                        BR    R14              RETURN TO CALLING PROGRAM
000448                                             LTORG
000448 000004A60000048D                                  =A(PAYNO,PAYMENT,INTPAY,PRINPAY)
000458 000004A600000492                                  =A(PAYNO,LASTPAY,INTPAY,PRINPAY)
000468 000004BA00000488                                  =A(ZERO,TOTALDUE,INTPAY,PRINADJ)
000478 00000000                                          =V(PRINT)
00047C 1C                                                =P'1'
00047D 0C                                                =P'0'
00047E 2C                                                =PL1'2'
                                                   DROP  R9,R10,R11,R12
00047F 0000000C                           S        DC    P'000000'        S = N * (N + 1) / 2
000483 000000000C                         PRINADJ  DC    P'000000.00'     PRINCIPAL WITH CENTS FOR OUTPUT
000488 000000000C                         TOTALDUE DC    P'000000.00'     PRINCIPAL PLUS TOTAL INTEREST
00048D 000000000C                         PAYMENT  DC    P'000000.00'     MONTHLY PAYMENT
000492 000000000C                         LASTPAY  DC    P'000000.00'     LAST PAYMENT
000497 000000000C                         INTPAY   DC    P'000000.00'     INTEREST PAID IN A PAYMENT
00049C 000000000C                         PRINPAY  DC    P'000000.00'     PRINCIPAL PAID IN A PAYMENT
0004A1 000000000C                         INTPAID  DC    P'000000.00'     TOTAL INTEREST PAID SO FAR
0004A6 000C                               PAYNO    DC    P'000'           PAYMENT NUMBER
0004A8 000C                               J        DC    P'000'           COUNTS N, N-1, ...
0004AA                                    WORK     DS    PL16             WORK AREA
0004BA 000C                               ZERO     DC    P'000'           USED TO SIGNAL TOTALS LINE IN PRINT
0004BC                                    SAVEL    DS    18F              SAVE AREA (9D IN DOS)
                                          ** DUMMY SECTIONS FOR LOAN:
000000                                    ARGLIST  DSECT ,                ARGUMENT LIST
000000                                             DS    4A
000000                                    DUM1     DSECT
000000                                    PRIN     DS    P'000000.'       PRINCIPAL BORROWED
000000                                    DUM2     DSECT
000000                                    INTEREST DS    P'000000.00'     TOTAL INTEREST CHARGE
000000                                    DUM3     DSECT
000000                                    N        DS    P'000'           NUMBER OF PAYMENTS
                                          *******************************************************************
                                          ** PRINT   SUBPROGRAM TO CREATE AND PRINT A LINE IN THE TABLE.
                                          ** INPUT:  PAYMENT NUMBER, PAYMENT, INTEREST PAYMENT, PRINCIPAL
                                          **            PAYMENT, ALL IN PACKED-DECIMAL FORM
                                          ** OUTPUT: ONE LINE OF PRINT
                                          ** CASES:  IF PAYMENT NUMBER IS
                                          **            > 1, THEN PRINTS NUMBERS WITHOUT A $
                                          **            = 1, THEN PRINTS NUMBERS WITH A $
                                          **            = 0, THEN SKIPS A LINE, PRINTS "TOTALS" INSTEAD OF A
                                          **                 PAYMENT NUMBER, AND PRINTS NUMBERS WITH A $
                                          *******************************************************************
000508                                    PRINT    CSECT
                                          ** INITIALIZE:
000508 90EC D00C      0000C                        STM   R14,R12,12(R13)  SAVE REGISTERS
00050C 05C0                                        BALR  R12,0            LOAD BASE REGISTER
                              0050E                USING BASEP,R12        DECLARE BASE REGISTER
00050E 50D0 C0C6      005D4               BASEP    ST    R13,SAVEP+4      SAVE R13
000512 41E0 C0C2      005D0                        LA    R14,SAVEP        GET ADDRESS OF NEW SAVE AREA
000516 50ED 0008      00008                        ST    R14,8(R13)       STORE IT IN PREVIOUS SAVE AREA
00051A 18DE                                        LR    R13,R14          R13 = ADDRESS OF NEW SAVE AREA
                              00000                USING ARGLIST,R1       ESTAB. ADDRESSABILITY OF ARGUMENT LIST
00051C 988B 1000      00000                        LM    R8,R11,ARGLIST   GET ADDRESSES OF ARGUMENTS
                                                   DROP  R1               DELETE R1 FROM BASE REGISTER POOL
                                          ** ESTABLISH ADDRESSABILITY OF ARGUMENTS; GET ADDRESS OF PRINTER DCB:
                              00000                USING PN,R8            PN  = PAYMENT NUMBER
                              00000                USING PAY,R9           PAY = MONTHLY PAYMENT
                              00000                USING IP,R10           IP  = INTEREST PAYMENT
                              00000                USING PP,R11           PP  = PRINCIPAL PAYMENT
000520 5870 C0B2      005C0                        L     R7,=V(PRINTER)   R7  = ADDRESS OF PRINTER DCB
```

*(Continues)*

**Figure 15.19** *(Continued)*

```
                                           ** COPY PATTERNS INTO OUTPUT FIELDS:
000524 D203 C11C C10A 0062A 00618                   MVC   FLD1,PATT1
00052A D20A C125 C10E 00633 0061C                   MVC   FLD2,PATT234
000530 D20A C135 C10E 00643 0061C                   MVC   FLD3,PATT234
000536 D20A C145 C10E 00653 0061C                   MVC   FLD4,PATT234
                                           ** EDIT FIELDS:
00053C DE03 C11C 8000 0062A 00000                   ED    FLD1,PN          PREPARE PAYMENT NUMBER FOR OUTPUT
                                           * IF PAYMENT NUMBER IS 0 OR 1:
000542 F910 8000 C0B6 00000 005C4                   CP    PN,=P'1'         COMPARE PAYMENT NUMBER WITH 1
000548 4720 C088       00596                        BH    NO$              IF GREATER THEN, SKIP NEXT SECTION
                                           * - THEN EDIT FIELDS 2, 3, AND 4, AND PRECEDE WITH $'S:
00054C 4110 C12C       0063A                        LA    R1,SIGDIG2       SET DEFAULT VALUE FOR EDMK
000550 DF0A C125 9000 00633 00000                   EDMK  FLD2,PAY         PREPARE PAYMENT FOR OUTPUT
000556 0610                                         BCTR  R1,0             POINT TO POSITION TO RECEIVE $
000558 925B 1000       00000                        MVI   0(R1),C'$'       MOVE IN $
00055C 4110 C13C       0064A                        LA    R1,SIGDIG3       SET DEFAULT VALUE FOR EDMK
000560 DF0A C135 A000 00643 00000                   EDMK  FLD3,IP          PREPARE INTEREST PAYMENT FOR OUTPUT
000566 0610                                         BCTR  R1,0             POINT TO POSITION TO RECEIVE $
000568 925B 1000       00000                        MVI   0(R1),C'$'       MOVE IN $
00056C 4110 C14C       0065A                        LA    R1,SIGDIG4       SET DEFAULT VALUE FOR EDMK
000570 DF0A C145 B000 00653 00000                   EDMK  FLD4,PP          PREPARE PRINCIPAL PAYMENT FOR OUTPUT
000576 0610                                         BCTR  R1,0             POINT TO POSITION TO RECEIVE $
000578 925B 1000       00000                        MVI   0(R1),C'$'       MOVE IN $
                                           * END IF
                                           * IF PAYMENT NUMBER IS 0:
00057C F910 8000 C0B7 00000 005C5                   CP    PN,=P'0'         COMPARE PAYMENT NUMBER WITH 0
000582 4720 C09A       005A8                        BH    PRT              IF NOT 0, BRANCH TO PRINT OUTPUT
                                           * - THEN REPLACE CARRIAGE CONTROL (SKIP A LINE), AND REPLACE FIRST
                                           *     FIELD WITH THE LABEL "TOTALS":
000586 D200 C119 C0B8 00627 005C6                   MVC   OUTPUT(1),=C'0' REPLACE CARRIAGE CONTROL
00058C D206 C11C C0B9 0062A 005C7                   MVC   FLD1(7),=C'TOTALS:'
                                           * END IF
000592 47F0 C09A       005A8                        B     PRT              BRANCH TO PRINT AND EXIT
                                           ** PAYMENT NUMBER IS > 1:  EDIT FIELDS 2, 3, AND 4 WITHOUT $'S:
000596 DE0A C125 9000 00633 00000          NO$      ED    FLD2,PAY         PREPARE PAYMENT FOR OUTPUT
00059C DE0A C135 A000 00643 00000                   ED    FLD3,IP          PREPARE INTEREST PAYMENT FOR OUTPUT
0005A2 DE0A C145 B000 00653 00000                   ED    FLD4,PP          PREPARE PRINCIPAL PAYMENT FOR OUTPUT
                                           ** PRINT LINE OF OUTPUT:
                                           PRT      PUT   0(R7),OUTPUT     PRINT OUTPUT BUFFER
                                           ** EXIT
0005B6 58D0 C0C6       005D4                        L     R13,SAVEP+4      RESTORE R13
0005BA 98EC D00C       0000C                        LM    R14,R12,12(R13) RESTORE REMAINING REGISTERS
0005BE 07FE                                         BR    R14              RETURN TO CALLING PROGRAM
0005C0                                              LTORG
0005C0 00000000                                           =V(PRINTER)
0005C4 1C                                                 =P'1'
0005C5 0C                                                 =P'0'
0005C6 F0                                                 =C'0'
0005C7 E3D6E3C1D3E27A                                     =C'TOTALS:'
                                                    DROP  R8,R9,R10,R11,R12
0005D0                                     SAVEP    DS    18F              SAVE AREA (9D IN DOS)
                                           ** EDIT PATTERNS:
000618 40202020                            PATT1    DC    X'40202020'             BDDD         FIRST FIELD
00061C 4020202020202120                    PATT234  DC    X'402020202020212048202020' BDDDDD[D.DD  FIELDS 2, 3, 4
```

(Continues)

Figure 15.19
*(Continued)*

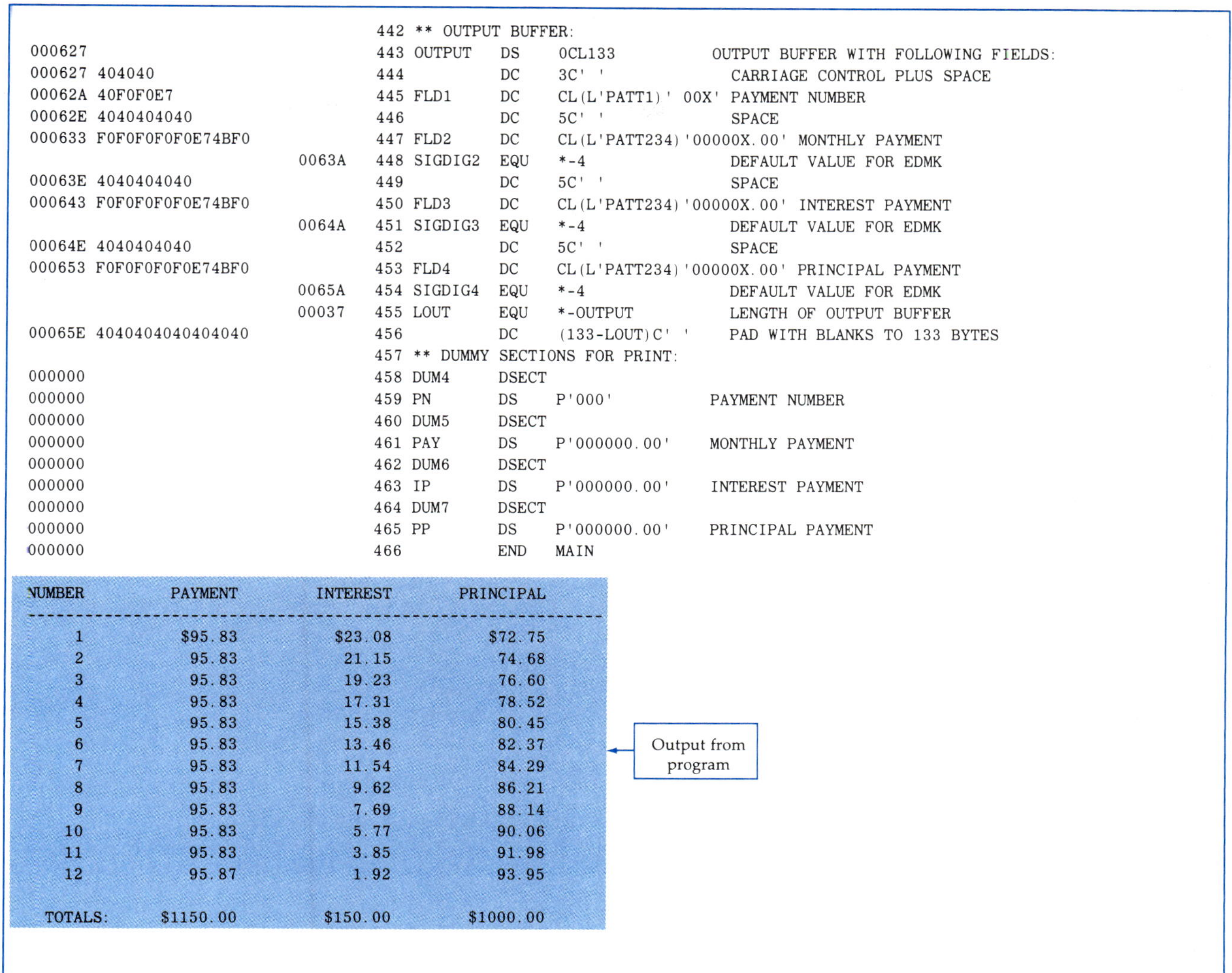

```
                                  ** OUTPUT BUFFER:
000627                            OUTPUT   DS    0CL133           OUTPUT BUFFER WITH FOLLOWING FIELDS:
000627 404040                              DC    3C' '              CARRIAGE CONTROL PLUS SPACE
00062A 40F0F0E7                   FLD1     DC    CL(L'PATT1)' 00X'  PAYMENT NUMBER
00062E 4040404040                          DC    5C' '              SPACE
000633 F0F0F0F0F0E74BF0           FLD2     DC    CL(L'PATT234)'00000X.00' MONTHLY PAYMENT
                          0063A   SIGDIG2  EQU   *-4                DEFAULT VALUE FOR EDMK
00063E 4040404040                          DC    5C' '              SPACE
000643 F0F0F0F0F0E74BF0           FLD3     DC    CL(L'PATT234)'00000X.00' INTEREST PAYMENT
                          0064A   SIGDIG3  EQU   *-4                DEFAULT VALUE FOR EDMK
00064E 4040404040                          DC    5C' '              SPACE
000653 F0F0F0F0F0E74BF0           FLD4     DC    CL(L'PATT234)'00000X.00' PRINCIPAL PAYMENT
                          0065A   SIGDIG4  EQU   *-4                DEFAULT VALUE FOR EDMK
                          00037   LOUT     EQU   *-OUTPUT           LENGTH OF OUTPUT BUFFER
00065E 4040404040404040                    DC    (133-LOUT)C' '     PAD WITH BLANKS TO 133 BYTES
                                  ** DUMMY SECTIONS FOR PRINT:
000000                            DUM4     DSECT
000000                            PN       DS    P'000'           PAYMENT NUMBER
000000                            DUM5     DSECT
000000                            PAY      DS    P'000000.00'     MONTHLY PAYMENT
000000                            DUM6     DSECT
000000                            IP       DS    P'000000.00'     INTEREST PAYMENT
000000                            DUM7     DSECT
000000                            PP       DS    P'000000.00'     PRINCIPAL PAYMENT
000000                                     END   MAIN
```

| NUMBER | PAYMENT | INTEREST | PRINCIPAL |
|---|---|---|---|
| 1 | $95.83 | $23.08 | $72.75 |
| 2 | 95.83 | 21.15 | 74.68 |
| 3 | 95.83 | 19.23 | 76.60 |
| 4 | 95.83 | 17.31 | 78.52 |
| 5 | 95.83 | 15.38 | 80.45 |
| 6 | 95.83 | 13.46 | 82.37 |
| 7 | 95.83 | 11.54 | 84.29 |
| 8 | 95.83 | 9.62 | 86.21 |
| 9 | 95.83 | 7.69 | 88.14 |
| 10 | 95.83 | 5.77 | 90.06 |
| 11 | 95.83 | 3.85 | 91.98 |
| 12 | 95.87 | 1.92 | 93.95 |
| TOTALS: | $1150.00 | $150.00 | $1000.00 |



**Figure 15.19**
*(Continued)*

though the principal is a maximum of 6 digits. (The pattern actually specifies 9 digits to include 2 for the cents portion.) An edit pattern must accommodate an odd number of digits because a packed-decimal number always represents an odd number of digits. If you are not careful, the discrepancy between the maximum number of digits that is provided in the input data set and the number of digits that is represented internally can lead to an error. If possible, avoid this discrepancy by redefining the program's input specifications to involve an odd number of digits. If you cannot alter the design of the input data set, as is assumed in this program, remember to accommodate the odd number when you design edit patterns.

There is one more aspect of this program that you should note. As you saw in Chapter 13, the main program defines DCBs (or in DOS, the DTF tables), which it uses for I/O. However, the subprogram PRINT also requires the DCB or the DTF table at PRINTER. You can pass PRINTER as an argument to PRINT, but doing so requires that you pass it from the main program to the subprogram LOAN, and then from LOAN to the subprogram PRINT. This process is awkward and, since the subprogram LOAN does not use PRINTER, the following technique can be desirable. You can make the DCB or the DTF table available to the subprogram PRINT first by declaring PRINTER as an entry symbol in the main program (Statement 14), and then by using a V-type address constant, which defines the address that PRINTER represents, within the subprogram. Thus, you can load a register with the address of the DCB or the DTF table, and use that register to designate the address in a PUT instruction. Observe that Statements 383 and 422 do just this.

## Debugging Hints

The cause of program exceptions that occur with decimal instructions is not always obvious. The following summary should help you to discover the source of your error. For completeness, the CVB, ED, and EDMK instructions are included from Chapter 14.

*Data exceptions* are caused by any of the following situations:

- Invalid digit or sign codes in the fields that are specified by either operand of AP, SP, MP, DP, or CP; the first operand of SRP, ED, or EDMK; or the second operand of ZAP or CVB.
- An invalid rounding digit in SRP, even if it is not used.
- Improper field overlap in AP, SP, MP, DP, CP, or ZAP.
- The MP instruction when its first operand field does not contain *L2* bytes of leading zeros.

*Decimal overflow exceptions* are caused when the results of the AP, SP, ZAP, or SRP instructions cannot be correctly represented in the first operand field.

*Decimal divide exceptions* are caused by the DP instruction when any of the following is true:

- The quotient is too large to be correctly represented in $L1 - L2$ bytes. (Note that this is not decimal overflow.)
- The divisor is zero.
- The leftmost digit of the dividend is not zero.

*Specification exceptions* are caused by the MP and DP instructions when $L2 > 8$ or $L2 \geq L1$.

## Stylistic Notes

1. When defining packed-decimal fields with the DC and DS directives, be sure that the length attribute of each defined symbol is equal to the intended length of the field. You can accomplish this by specifying either a length modifier or a constant; do not use a duplication factor instead of a length modifier. Thus, for example, to reserve 3 bytes, write

```
X        DC      P'00.000'
```

or

```
X          DS     PL3
```

but not

```
X          DS     3P
```

In particular, define separate fields with correct length attributes for the quotient and the remainder of a division.

2. Recall that you can write a constant in the operand entry of a DS directive. Some programmers do this when they want the assembler to compute the required length of the field, as described in Stylistic Note 1. However, remember that, if you use DS with a constant, the constant is not assembled.
3. Defining a field with an implied length can prevent errors since the assembler will compute the field length for you. For example, the following definition for N specifies the number of digits to the left and the number of digits to the right of the decimal point:

```
N          DC     P'00000.00'
```

However, if you know the number of required bytes, specify an explicit length modifier in the DC or DS directive.
4. When fields are defined with symbols that have the correct length attribute, as described in Stylistic Note 1, you can often omit explicit lengths in the operand entries of SS instructions that reference such fields. Many programmers find it convenient to do so—particularly when working with decimal fields. However, when you omit explicit field lengths, it is easy to become careless and to make errors. Remain aware of field lengths, whether or not you write them explicitly.
5. Try to avoid field overlap whenever possible—unless both operands specify the same field. If you must have field overlap, use explicit length entries.

## Summary

1. You must use valid packed-decimal numbers with the decimal arithmetic instructions.
2. The instructions AP, SP, MP, DP, and CP are used to add, subtract, multiply, divide, and compare two packed-decimal fields.
3. The MP and DP instructions require that $L2 \leq 8$ and $L2 < L1$. MP also requires that the first operand contain *L2* bytes of leading zeros. While the DP instruction is not as restrictive, if you follow this rule, you will have sufficient space for the division.
4. You can move a packed-decimal number to another field, which is possibly shorter or longer than the present one, with the ZAP instruction.
5. Only the second operand of the ZAP instruction needs to be a valid packed-decimal number. Therefore, it is convenient to use ZAP to set a decimal field to zero.
6. The SRP instruction will shift a decimal field either to the right with optional rounding or to the left.
7. You can use sequences of instructions that include the MVO and MVN instructions to shift decimal fields when the SRP instruction is not available.
8. To make the field X match the scaling attribute of the field Y, shift X by $S_Y - S_X$ places by using the SRP instruction.

## New Instruction Summary

| Operation | Operand | Format | Instruction Name | Action |
|---|---|---|---|---|
| **AP** | $S1(L1),S2(L2)$ or $D1(L1,B1),D2(L2,B2)$ | $SS_2$ | ADD PACKED | $C(E1)_{L1} \leftarrow C(E1)_{L1} + C(E2)_{L2}$<br>Condition code = $\begin{cases} 0 \text{ if the sum is zero} \\ 1 \text{ if the sum is negative} \\ 2 \text{ if the sum is positive} \\ 3 \text{ if an overflow occurs} \end{cases}$ |
| **SP** | $S1(L1),S2(L2)$ or $D1(L1,B1),D2(L2,B2)$ | $SS_2$ | SUBTRACT PACKED | $C(E1)_{L1} \leftarrow C(E1)_{L1} - C(E2)_{L2}$<br>The condition code is set just as for AP. |
| **ZAP** | $S1(L1),S2(L2)$ or $D1(L1,B1),D2(L2,B2)$ | $SS_2$ | ZERO AND ADD PACKED | $C(E1)_{L1} \leftarrow 0 + C(E2)_{L2}$<br>The condition code is set just as for AP. |
| **CP** | $S1(L1),S2(L2)$ or $D1(L1,B1),D2(L2,B2)$ | $SS_2$ | COMPARE PACKED | Compare $C(E1)_{L1}$ with $C(E2)_{L2}$<br>Condition code = $\begin{cases} 0 \text{ if } C(E1)_{L1} = C(E2)_{L2} \\ 1 \text{ if } C(E1)_{L1} < C(E2)_{L2} \\ 2 \text{ if } C(E1)_{L1} > C(E2)_{L2} \end{cases}$ |
| **MP** | $S1(L1),S2(L2)$ or $D1(L1,B1),D2(L2,B2)$ | $SS_2$ | MULTIPLY PACKED | $C(E1)_{L1} \leftarrow C(E1)_{L1} * C(E2)_{L2}$ |
| **DP** | $S1(L1),S2(L2)$ or $D1(L1,B1),D2(L2,B2)$ | $SS_2$ | DIVIDE PACKED | $C(E1)_{L1-L2} \leftarrow$ Quotient of $C(E1)_{L1} \div C(E2)_{L2}$<br>$C(E1 + L1 - L2)_{L2} \leftarrow$ Remainder of $C(E1)_{L1} \div C(E2)_{L2}$ |
| **SRP** | $S1(L1),D2(B2),I3$ or $D1(L1,B1),D2(B2),I3$ | $SS_2$ | SHIFT AND ROUND PACKED | Shifts $C(E1)_{L1}$ by $\|n\|$ places where $n = E2 \pmod{64}$ represents a signed value. The shift is to the left if $n$ is positive, and to the right if $n$ is negative. $I3$ is the rounding digit for right shifts.<br>Condition code = $\begin{cases} 0 \text{ if the result is zero} \\ 1 \text{ if the result is negative} \\ 2 \text{ if the result is positive} \\ 3 \text{ if an overflow occurs} \end{cases}$ |
| **MVO** | $S1(L1),S2(L2)$ or $D1(L1,B1),D2(L2,B2)$ | $SS_2$ | MOVE WITH OFFSET | $C(E1)_{0-(8*L1-5)} \leftarrow C(E2)_{L2}$ |
| **MVN** | $S1(L),S2$ or $D1(L,B1),D2(B2)$ | $SS_1$ | MOVE NUMERICS | Numerics of $C(E1)_L \leftarrow$ Numerics of $C(E2)_L$ |
| **MVZ** | $S1(L),S2$ or $D1(L,B1),D2(B2)$ | $SS_1$ | MOVE ZONES | Zones of $C(E1)_L \leftarrow$ Zones of $C(E2)_L$ |

## Exercises

1. Assume the following definitions:

```
W    DS    PL2
Y    DS    PL4
Q    DS    PL16
```

Indicate what exception, if any, occurs when each of the following pairs of instructions is executed.

```
a. ZAP   W,=P'1234'
   AP    W,=P'9'
b. ZAP   W,=P'-71'
   SP    W,=P'950'
c. ZAP   Y,=P'-9648'
   MP    Y,=P'20'
d. ZAP   Y,=P'-9'
   MP    Y(2),=P'4'
e. ZAP   Q,=P'12'
   MP    Q,=PL9'-801476'
f. ZAP   Y,=P'-9'
   DP    Y,=P'2'
g. ZAP   W,=P'1'
   DP    W,=P'500'
h. ZAP   W,=P'123'
   DP    W,=P'9'
i. ZAP   Y,=P'-9648'
   SRP   Y,4,5
```

2. Write instructions that alter the sign of a packed-decimal number, as follows:
   a. Make the sign plus.
   b. Make the sign minus.
   c. Change the sign—if it is plus, make it minus and, if it is minus, make it plus.
3. Given a positive integer $n$, write instructions to compute $7.19^n$ and retain all digits to the right of the decimal point. Is there a limit on the magnitude of $n$ that makes this possible?
4. Repeat Exercise 3, but round each product to 3 decimal places and the final product to 2 decimal places.
5. Write instructions to shift a given packed-decimal number to the left by using multiplication. What limits, if any, are necessary on the original packed-decimal number and the shift amount?
6. Assume:

```
X    DC    P'31.9086'
Y    DC    P'5.1'
```

Write instructions to perform the following computations:
   a. Replace X by the sum of X and Y (add Y to X).
   b. Replace X by X * Y, which is rounded to 1 place after the decimal point.
   c. Compute X ÷ Y and Y ÷ X. Truncate each quotient to 6 decimal places.
7. For each of the following, write instructions to perform the indicated computations:
   a. Compute the area of a circle ($\pi r^2$).
   b. Compute the area of a trapezoid ($h(b_1 + b_2)/2$).
   c. Convert a given temperature from Fahrenheit to Celsius and from Celsius to Fahrenheit, by using the relationship $C = (F - 32) * 5/9$.
8. Write a program segment to compute the sum of the packed-decimal integers in the array at PDN. Each integer is 10 bytes long. The value of the last integer in the array is zero; use this value to terminate the loop.
9. Repeat Exercise 8, but assume that each integer has a length of L bytes, where L is stored in a halfword.
10. Write a program segment to determine the smallest and largest packed-decimal number in an array of N numbers. Each number has a length of L bytes. Assume that N and L are stored in fullwords.
11. Write instructions to perform the following right shifts without using the SRP instruction:
    a. 1 place without rounding.
    b. 2 places without rounding.
    c. 5 places with rounding.
    d. 6 places with rounding.
    e. 4 places without rounding and without the MVO instruction.
12. Write instructions to perform the following left shifts without using the SRP instruction:
    a. 5 places.
    b. 2 places.
    c. 4 places by shifting left 5 places and then shifting right by 1 place.
    d. 4 places without the MVO instruction.

## Programming Problems

1. Write a subprogram to determine the day of the week of any given date by using Zeller's congruence and decimal arithmetic. (Refer to the case study in Chapter 5 for more information about Zeller's congruence.)
2. Write a subprogram that reads a clock time, such as 10:04 A.M. or 2:53 P.M., and represents it as a packed-decimal number that uses a 24-hour notation. Thus, 10:04 A.M. is represented by =P'1004' and 2:53 P.M. by =P'1453'.

3. Write a subprogram to compute the difference between two clock times that are less than 24 hours apart. Assume that the second time given is later in the day than the first time. For example, the difference between 3:07 P.M. and 3:04 A.M. the next day is 11 hours, 57 minutes. Assume the times are available in 24-hour notation as packed-decimal integers. (See Programming Problem 2 for an example of this notation.) Return the difference as a single packed-decimal number: for example, 11 hours and 57 minutes are represented by =P'1157'.

4. Modify Programming Problem 1 of Chapter 11 to include a subprogram that computes the sales tax and the total sale. Assume that the sales tax is given as a percentage.

5. Write a subprogram to evaluate the expression that is given in Example 40 to 4 decimal places. Assume that the variables have the following formats:

   A = *xxxx.x*
   B = *x.xx*
   C = *.x*
   D = *x.xxx*
   E = *x*

6. Write a program to compute the grade point average for every student in an input data set. The data records for each student are as follows.

   Record 1: ID number (9 digits) and student name.
   Record 2: Course code, credit hours, and grade received for up to 6 courses in the format demonstrated by the following example:

   CSC311/3,A/CSC401/3,B+/ART100/4,A−/

   Letter grades have the following values:
   A = 4.0
   A− = 3.8
   B+ = 3.2
   B = 3.0
   B− = 2.8
   C+ = 2.2
   C = 2.0
   C− = 1.8
   D+ = 1.2
   D = 1.0
   F = 0.0

   For each student, print a grade report that lists the student's name and ID number, the courses taken with credits hours and grades received, the total number of credits taken, and the grade point average.

7. Write a subprogram to compute the monthly mortgage payment $M$ on an $n$-year loan of $P$ dollars at a fixed interest rate of $i$ percent. Assume that $n$ and $P$ are integers, that $i$ is given to 2 decimal places, and that all three values are in packed-decimal form. $M$ is given by the following equation:

$$M = \frac{P(i/1200)(1 + i/1200)^{12n}}{(1 + i/1200)^{12n} - 1}$$

8. Write a program to compute and print an amortization table for the mortgage that was described in Programming Problem 7. Monthly interest is $i/1200$ times the present loan balance; the amount applied towards the principal is the difference between the monthly payment and the monthly interest. The table should contain the payment number, the amount of the payment, the amount of interest for the month, the total interest paid to date, the amount applied toward the principal, and the principal outstanding after this payment. (The last monthly payment may differ from other payments.)

9. Write a subprogram to compute the square root of a decimal number $x$ by using the algorithm described in Programming Problem 10 of Chapter 8. Specify as subprogram arguments the number of decimal places in $x$ and the desired number of decimal places in the square root of $x$.

# 16

# Input and Output under OS and DOS

CONTENTS

## OVERVIEW

So far you have used certain macro instructions to perform specific, simple input and output operations. This chapter will expand your knowledge of I/O under OS and DOS by defining more completely the macro instructions that you know and by introducing new macro instructions. The chapter also examines the organization and manipulation of data sets—particularly those that are defined on magnetic disks and tapes.

## OBJECTIVES

After studying this chapter, you should be able to:

1. Describe briefly sequential, partitioned, indexed-sequential, direct, and virtual data sets.
2. Distinguish between logical and physical records, fixed-length and variable-length records, and blocked and unblocked records.
3. Compute an appropriate block size for tape data sets and disk data sets when you are given the necessary physical specifications of the device.
4. Create, read, or update sequential data sets by using either the queued-sequential access method (QSAM) under OS, the sequential access method (SAM) under DOS, or the basic-sequential access method (BSAM) under OS.

## Introduction

A **data set** or **file** is a collection of related data that can be input to or output from a program. For example, an input data set might consist of the raw data that was derived from a survey questionnaire or a scientific experiment. An input data set might also consist of facts or other data that is relatively static in nature; such a data set can be called a **master file**. For example, in an airline reservation system, the various dates and times of possible flights constitute a master file. It can change, but it will not change frequently. Another type of input data set is one that does change frequently; it is called a **dynamic file**. Thus, in an airline reservation system, the passenger reservations on particular flights form a dynamic file.

There are several kinds of output data sets. When you create a master file, it is an output data set. When you modify a dynamic file, it is an output data set. For example, the previous reservations file is modified when a passenger reserves or cancels a particular flight. Printed reports are also output data sets: with the dynamic file, you can print passenger lists or compute and print statistics about the flights.

In addition to examining the ways in which you can organize and process data sets, this chapter covers the details of input and output operations under OS and DOS. User programs cannot communicate directly with the I/O devices, but must request the operating system to perform any necessary I/O operation. You make such requests by writing **data management macro instructions**, the use of which is a major subject in this chapter. Recall that the assembler can replace a macro instruction with many instructions that ordinarily appear in the assembly listing. The instructions that the I/O macro instructions generate can obscure the assembly listing, so you may want to tell the assembler to suppress them. As you know, you can do this by writing

```
PRINT NOGEN
```

Although a presentation of I/O operations in their entirety is beyond the scope of this text, this chapter outlines available techniques, and examines three important approaches—QSAM, SAM, and BSAM—in detail. This chapter should serve as a basis for future study.

## Secondary Storage

You can store large amounts of data on magnetic media, which are collectively known as **secondary storage**. Two popular storage devices are magnetic tapes and magnetic disks. The macros necessary to perform I/O operations with tapes and disks are the same as those required to read the data entered at a keyboard or to write data on either a display or a line printer. While there are certainly details that depend upon the type of device, at a broad level, many I/O concepts do not depend upon the type of device. In addition, data set organizations, although conceptual, are based upon the physical characteristics of the I/O devices. For these reasons, you should be familiar with the physical characteristics of I/O devices, especially tapes and disks.

## *Magnetic Tapes*

**Data is organized sequentially on tapes.**

Computers can record data on magnetic tapes, which have conceptual similarities to the audio and video tapes that you are familiar with. Data is recorded magnetically and organized sequentially; to access something that is recorded in the middle of the tape, you must pass everything that precedes it. While *reading* (playing) or *writing* (recording), the tape must move past a **read/write head** at a fixed, predefined speed. Both the tape speed and the **recording density** affect the rate at which data is transmitted. This transmission rate is much slower for audio and video tapes than for computer tapes, where data is transmitted as rapidly as possible. Recording densities for magnetic tapes range from 800 bytes per inch (bpi) to 6250 bpi, and tape transport speeds are around 200 inches per second (ips).

Consider a computer tape that is at rest and about to be read. The tape cannot reach the high velocity that is used for data transmission instantaneously. During the time that the tape is accelerating to its proper speed, any bytes that pass the read/write head are lost. The solution to this problem is to leave this portion of the tape blank. However, it is insufficient to leave only a blank portion at the beginning of the tape; unlike audio and video tapes that usually play for an extended period, data is often transmitted to and from computer tapes over several short, distinct periods, between which the tape is at rest. For this reason, bytes that are written on a computer tape are grouped into units called **blocks**. The blocks are separated by gaps of about one-half inch called **interrecord gaps**. When the tape is at rest, the gap is positioned at the read/write head. The tape accelerates to its proper speed (or decelerates to a stop) while the gap passes the head. After the tape reaches the correct speed, data is transmitted one block at a time. Although a tape unit may transmit several blocks without stopping, it cannot read a portion of a block now and the rest later; it can only read an entire block. A diagram of a tape unit appears in Figure 16.1. Figure 16.2 contains photographs that compare two types of IBM tape units.

**Data is written on tapes in blocks that are separated by gaps.**

The capacity in bytes of a given length of tape that is recorded at a particular density depends upon the amount of tape that is devoted to interrecord gaps. This amount of tape depends on the number of blocks on the tape; the number of blocks, in turn, depends on the length of the blocks. The longer the blocks, the fewer their number and the fewer the number of interrecord gaps. Figure 16.3 and Figure 16.4 show the effect of block length on the total capacity of a 2400-foot tape that is recorded on an IBM 3420 Model 8 tape unit at 6250 bpi with 0.3-inch gaps. Block length is usually measured in bytes, instead of inches, and is called the **block size**. As you probably expect, the total capacity of a tape increases with the block size.

The time that is required to read or write the next block on a tape, which is initially at rest, depends upon the data transmission rate and the **access time**. Access time is the time that the tape unit needs to accelerate the tape to its proper speed and to reach the end of the interrecord gap. For the IBM 3420 Model 8 tape unit, the access time is 1.1 milliseconds (ms) for reading and 0.95 ms for writing; the data transmission rate is 1,250,000 bytes per second, or 1 byte per 0.8 microseconds ($\mu$s). Remember that 1 ms equals $10^{-3}$ seconds and that 1 $\mu$s equals $10^{-6}$ seconds. At this data transmission rate, the tape unit would need 0.5 ms to transmit a 625-byte block after it was accessed. The access time is clearly greater than the transmission time in this case. You could argue that after you spend the time getting the tape up to speed, you might as well transmit as much data as possible; that is, you should use a large block size. Although you can obtain the best time

**Figure 16.1**
A diagram of a magnetic tape unit.

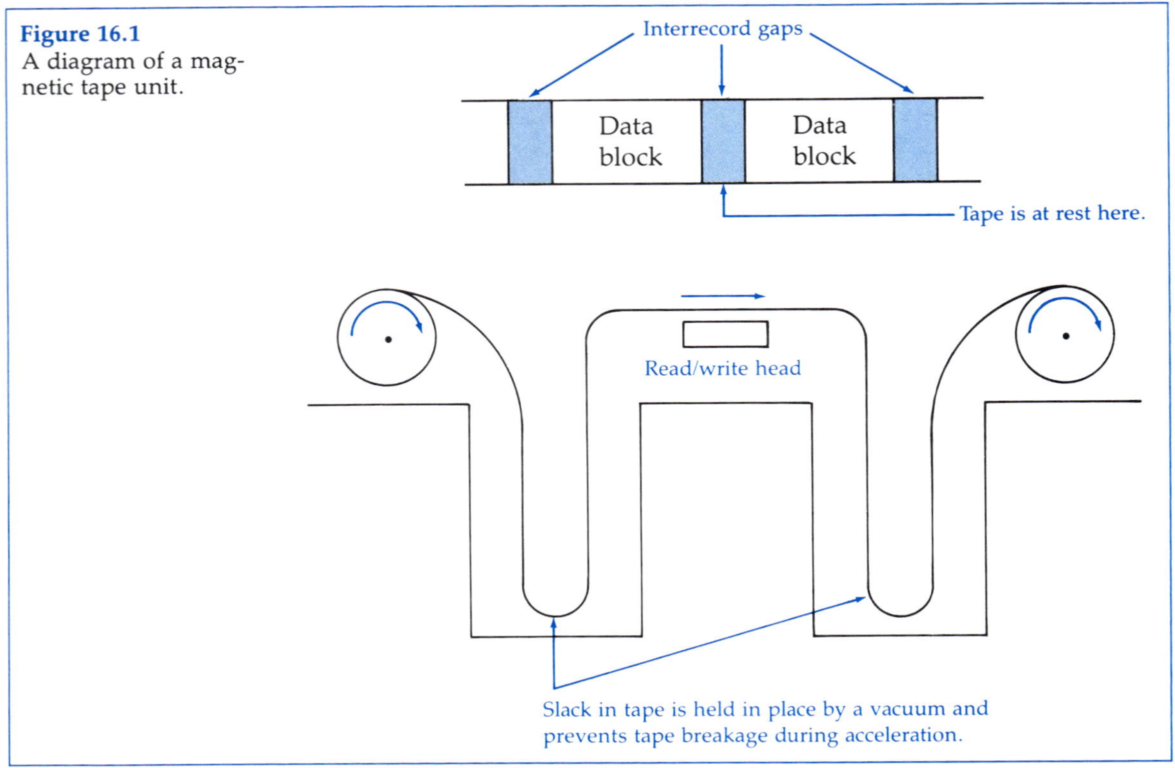


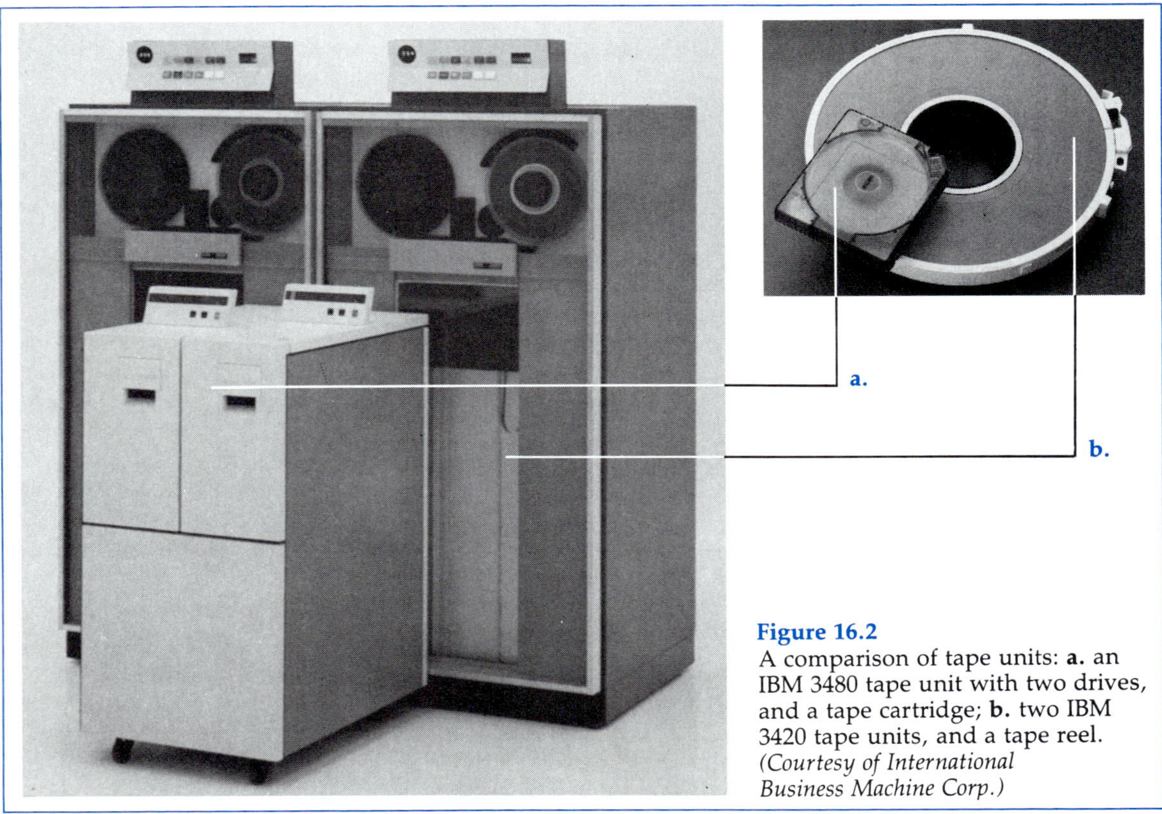


**Figure 16.2**
A comparison of tape units: **a.** an IBM 3480 tape unit with two drives, and a tape cartridge; **b.** two IBM 3420 tape units, and a tape reel. *(Courtesy of International Business Machine Corp.)*

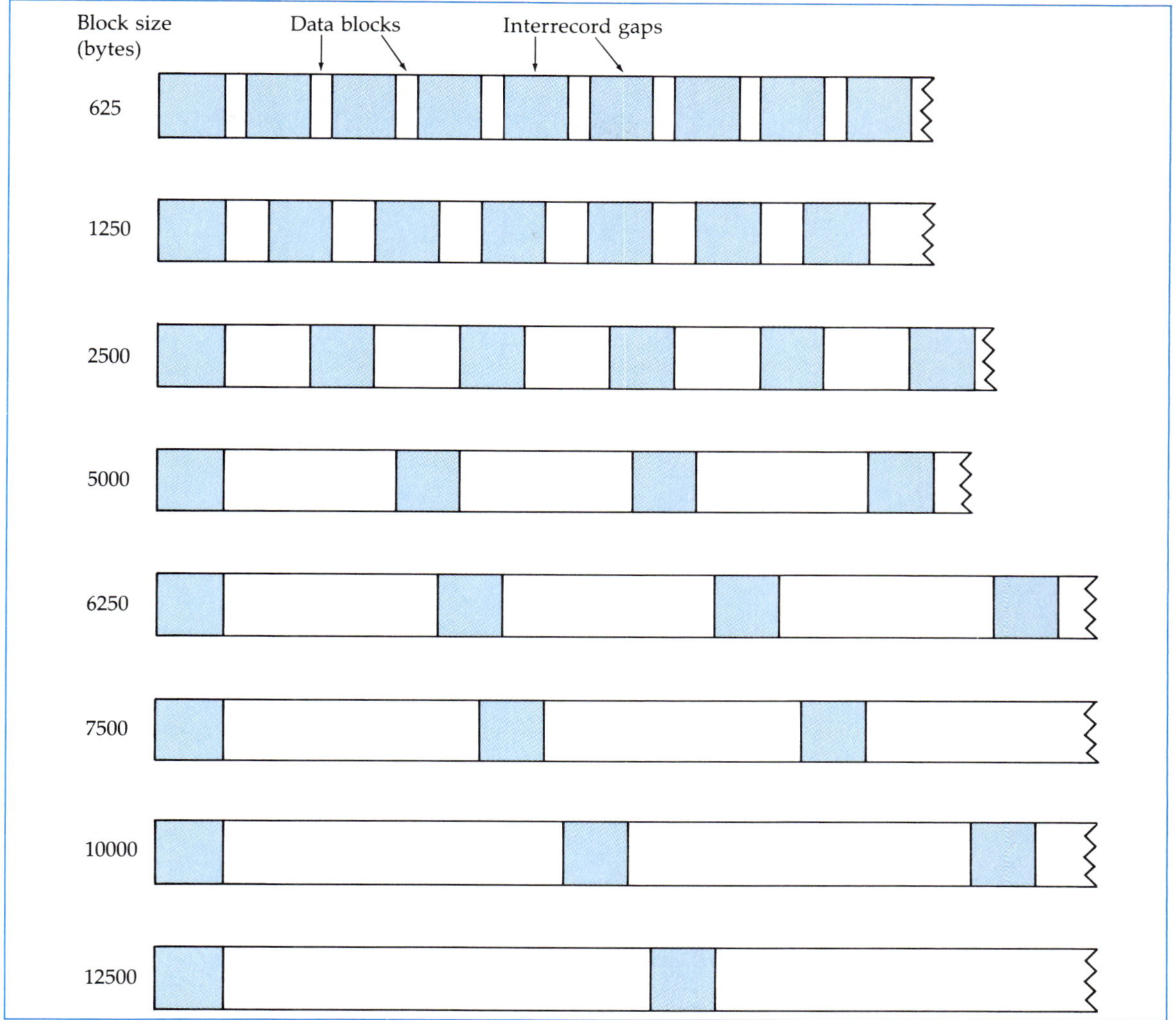


**Figure 16.3**
Data blocks on a magnetic tape that is recorded at 6250 bpi with 0.3-inch interrecord gaps.

efficiency by organizing all of your data into a single block, transmitting such a block uses a great deal of main storage. The nature of the application at hand usually affects your choice of block size and, typically, you must make a compromise between time and storage efficiencies.

Suppose that you want to read a block that is near the middle of a tape, which is positioned at its beginning. At 200 ips, the tape unit will need 1 minute to traverse 1000 feet of tape. This excessive delay is a significant disadvantage of magnetic tapes and is one that you can avoid by using magnetic disks.

## *Magnetic Disks*

A magnetic disk is composed of one or more circular plates, with one or both surfaces containing data that has been recorded magnetically in concentric circles called **tracks**. While the plates rotate, one of several read/write heads transmits the data. The read/write heads are either in a fixed position, one per track, or—as assumed here—on a movable arm so that there is one head per surface. The arm then moves to position the head at the desired track. Several configurations of plates are possible. For example,

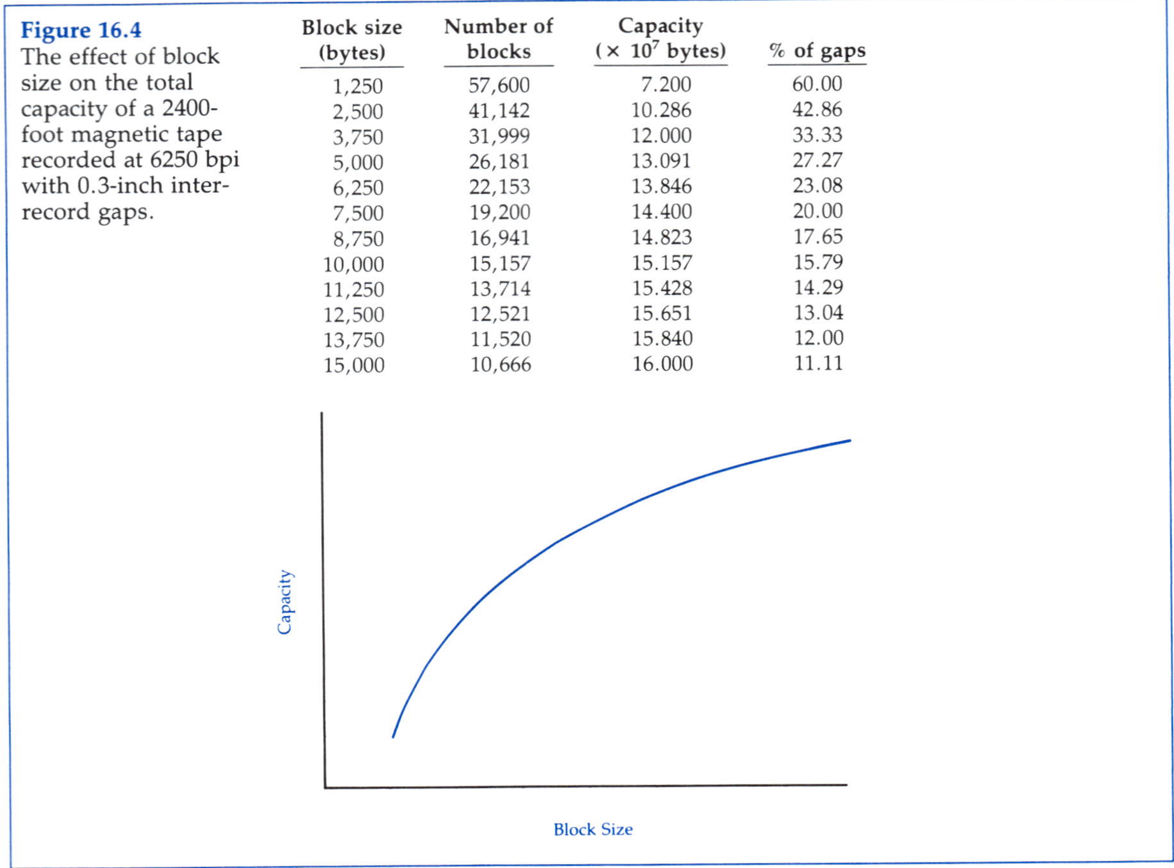

| Block size (bytes) | Number of blocks | Capacity ($\times 10^7$ bytes) | % of gaps |
|---|---|---|---|
| 1,250 | 57,600 | 7.200 | 60.00 |
| 2,500 | 41,142 | 10.286 | 42.86 |
| 3,750 | 31,999 | 12.000 | 33.33 |
| 5,000 | 26,181 | 13.091 | 27.27 |
| 6,250 | 22,153 | 13.846 | 23.08 |
| 7,500 | 19,200 | 14.400 | 20.00 |
| 8,750 | 16,941 | 14.823 | 17.65 |
| 10,000 | 15,157 | 15.157 | 15.79 |
| 11,250 | 13,714 | 15.428 | 14.29 |
| 12,500 | 12,521 | 15.651 | 13.04 |
| 13,750 | 11,520 | 15.840 | 12.00 |
| 15,000 | 10,666 | 16.000 | 11.11 |



**Figure 16.4**
The effect of block size on the total capacity of a 2400-foot magnetic tape recorded at 6250 bpi with 0.3-inch inter-record gaps.

microcomputers use diskettes that are single plates. In the larger storage devices that the IBM 370 uses, plates are stacked on a common spindle with separations between the plates to accommodate the read/write heads. The arms either can move the read/write heads independently of one another or can be connected so that all heads move in unison. The stack of plates can be either permanently mounted within the I/O device or removable.

As Figure 16.5 shows, there is one read/write head per surface, and the heads are positioned one over the other. The arms and heads move as a unit until the desired track is aligned with its read/write head. The disks are in constant rotation at a fixed speed. The head at the desired track only needs to be activated electronically for the data transmission to take place. Only one head at a time can transmit data.

**You can access tracks on a disk directly and data on a track sequentially. Data is written on disk tracks in blocks that are separated by gaps.**

Each track is directly accessible without having to read the other tracks. For this reason, a magnetic disk is called a **direct-access device**. Even though the arm can go directly to the desired track, you must process the data on that track sequentially because the data is organized into blocks and gaps much like the data on magnetic tapes. Although tracks are concentric circles, they have a beginning and an end. Imagine a radius that is drawn on the surface of the disk. Each track on the surface begins and ends at the point where the track crosses the radius. A physical mark called the **index marker** on the disk indicates where this radius is and, hence, where the beginning of each track is.

The time that the arm takes to move into its proper position is called the **seek time**. For the IBM 3380 disk storage system, the seek time can

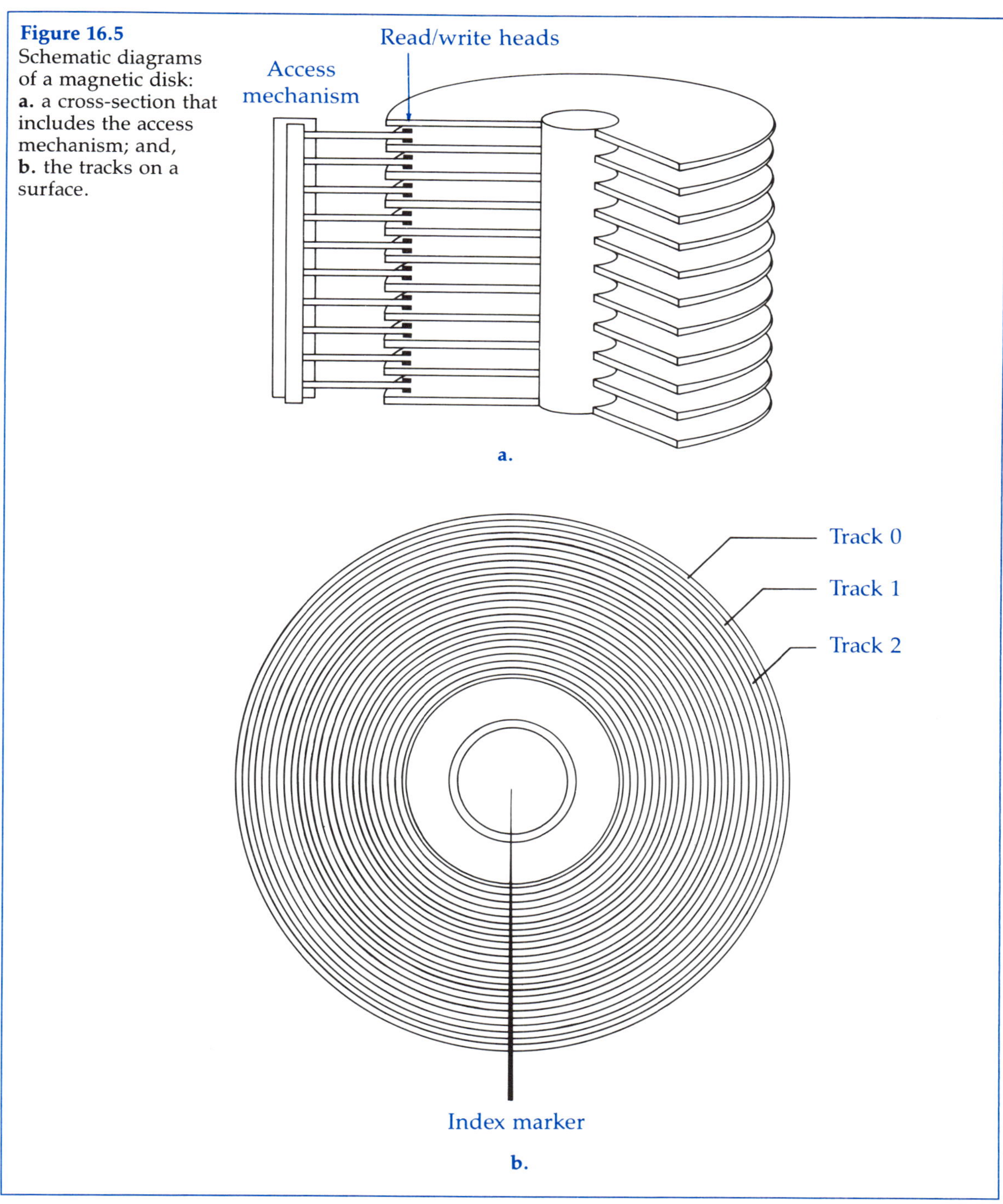


**Figure 16.5** Schematic diagrams of a magnetic disk: **a.** a cross-section that includes the access mechanism; and, **b.** the tracks on a surface.

range from 0 ms, if the arm is already in position, to 31 ms, if the arm must travel its full range. Moving the arm to the next track takes 3 ms, and the average seek time is 15 ms to 17 ms, depending upon the particular model of the IBM 3380. After the arm is positioned at the required track, the time that the desired data block needs to reach the read/write head is called the **rotational delay**. For the IBM 3380, a full rotation of the disk takes 16.7 ms so that the rotational delay can range from 0 ms to 16.7 ms. The average

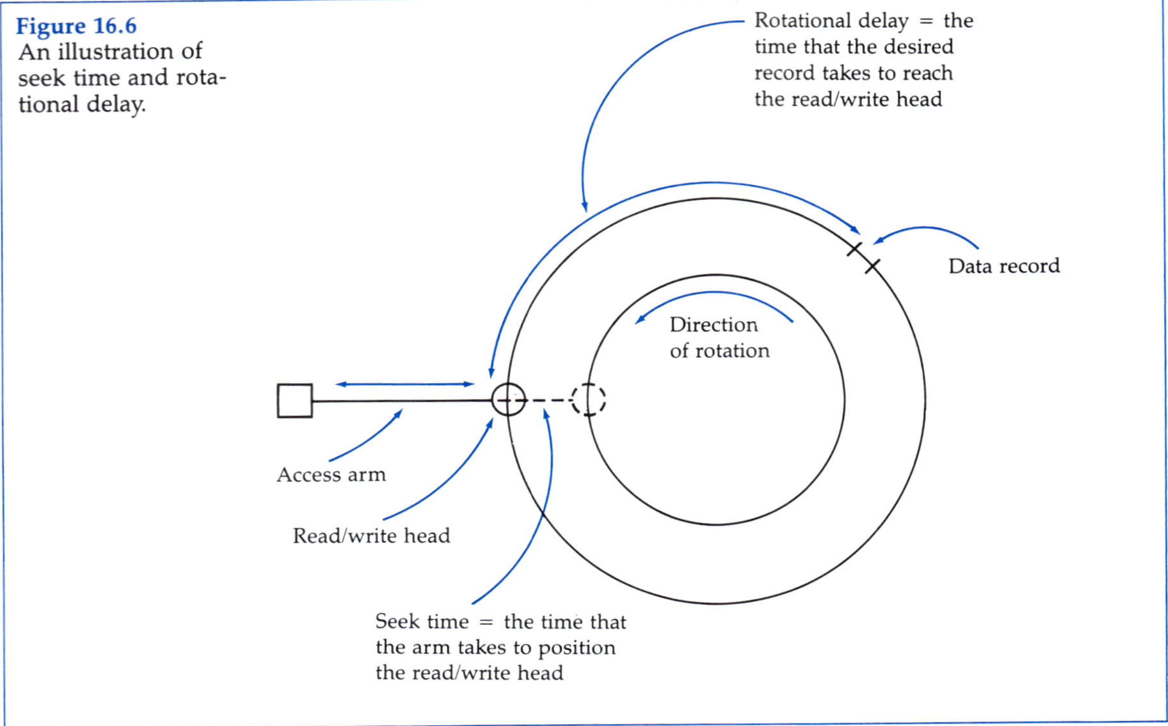


**Figure 16.6**
An illustration of seek time and rotational delay.

rotational delay is taken as one-half of the time for a full rotation, or approximately 8.3 ms. In the worst case, the access time includes a 31-ms seek time and a 16.7-ms rotational delay, which is a total of 47.7 ms. Compare this time with the several minutes necessary to access a block near the end of a magnetic tape. Figure 16.6 illustrates seek time and rotational delay. After the data is located, it is transmitted at the rate of 3 megabytes (Mb) per second. (1 Mb equals 1 million bytes.)

The group of tracks that lie on an imaginary cylinder that passes through the disks is called a **cylinder**. With one positioning of the arm, all tracks in the cylinder are aligned with the read/write heads, and can be accessed without further arm movement. Therefore, organizing a data set into cylinders reduces the access time for the data set. Cylinders are also used to identify tracks. Each track has a numeric address that indicates its associated cylinder and read/write head.

All tracks are written in a standard format. Beginning at the index marker, there is a **home address** and a **track descriptor record**. Each contains track status information and a track address in the form *CCHH*, where *CC* is a cylinder number and *HH* is a head number. Next are **data records**, or blocks, that are written in one of two formats: **count-key-data format** or **count-data format**. In count-key-data format, each data record contains a **key area** of a maximum of 255 bytes. The key area can contain any character string that is relevant to the data, such as an account number or Social Security number, and is used to locate the desired data record. The data record also contains a **count area** that includes an 8-byte field of the form *CCHHRKDD*, where *CC* is the cylinder number, *HH* is the head number, *R* is the record number, *K* is the key length, and *DD* is the data length. The key area and count area are separated from each other and from the data area by gaps. In count-data format, there is no key area and *K* in the count area is 0. All data

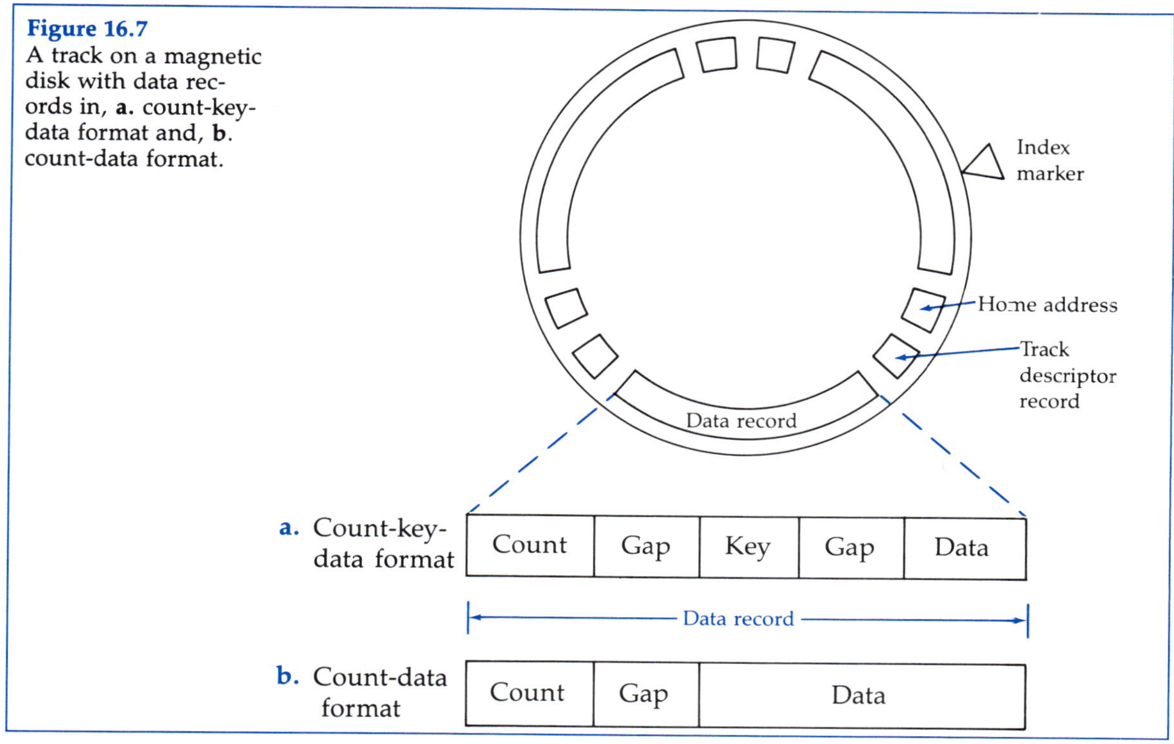


**Figure 16.7**
A track on a magnetic disk with data records in, **a.** count-key-data format and, **b.** count-data format.

**Each track has the same byte capacity.**

records in a particular data set must be in the same format Figure 16.7 illustrates data record formats and the track format.

Although the tracks on a disk vary in circumference, each track has the same capacity in bytes because the density at which data is recorded differs from track to track. Even with this difference, the number of bytes that pass the read/write heads per unit time is the same for each track. However, track capacity does vary according to the particular device and the data format used. For example, the IBM 3380 can store a maximum of 47,476 bytes[†] of data per track with count-data format. Since each data record has a count area, the number of data bytes that are recorded per track decreases as the records per track increase. The number of data records per track depends upon the block size. The table[‡] in Figure 16.8 indicates, for various maximum block sizes ($B$), the number ($N$) of blocks that fit on a track and achieve maximum track capacity. These figures satisfy the equation

$$N = \left\lfloor \frac{1499}{15 + \left\lceil \dfrac{B + 12}{32} \right\rceil} \right\rfloor$$

where $\lceil\ \rceil$ indicates rounding up to the next higher integer and $\lfloor\ \rfloor$ indicates discarding the fractional portion of the quotient.

[†]The IBM publication *Data Management Services Guide* provides these figures for several disk units.

[‡]A more complete table, as well as a table for count-key-data format, appears in the manual entitled *IBM 3380 Direct Access Storage: Planning and Use*. Information for other direct access devices is available in similar IBM publications.

**Figure 16.8**
The relationship between block size and track capacity for an IBM 3380 disk storage system that uses count-data format.

| Maximum block size ($B$) (bytes) | Track Capacity: Number of blocks per track ($N$) | Track Capacity: Maximum bytes per track ($N*B$) | Track Capacity: Utilization (%) ($N*B*100$)/47476 |
|---|---|---|---|
| 47,476 | 1 | 47,476 | 100.00 |
| 23,476 | 2 | 46,952 | 98.90 |
| 15,476 | 3 | 46,428 | 97.79 |
| 11,476 | 4 | 45,904 | 96.69 |
| 9,076 | 5 | 45,380 | 95.59 |
| 7,476 | 6 | 44,856 | 94.48 |
| 6,356 | 7 | 44,492 | 93.71 |
| 5,492 | 8 | 43,936 | 92.54 |
| 4,820 | 9 | 43,380 | 91.37 |
| 4,276 | 10 | 42,760 | 90.07 |
| 3,860 | 11 | 42,460 | 89.43 |
| 3,476 | 12 | 41,712 | 87.86 |
| 3,188 | 13 | 41,444 | 87.29 |
| 2,932 | 14 | 41,048 | 86.46 |
| 2,676 | 15 | 40,140 | 84.55 |
| 1,876 | 20 | 37,520 | 79.03 |
| 1,396 | 25 | 34,900 | 73.51 |
| 1,076 | 30 | 32,280 | 67.99 |

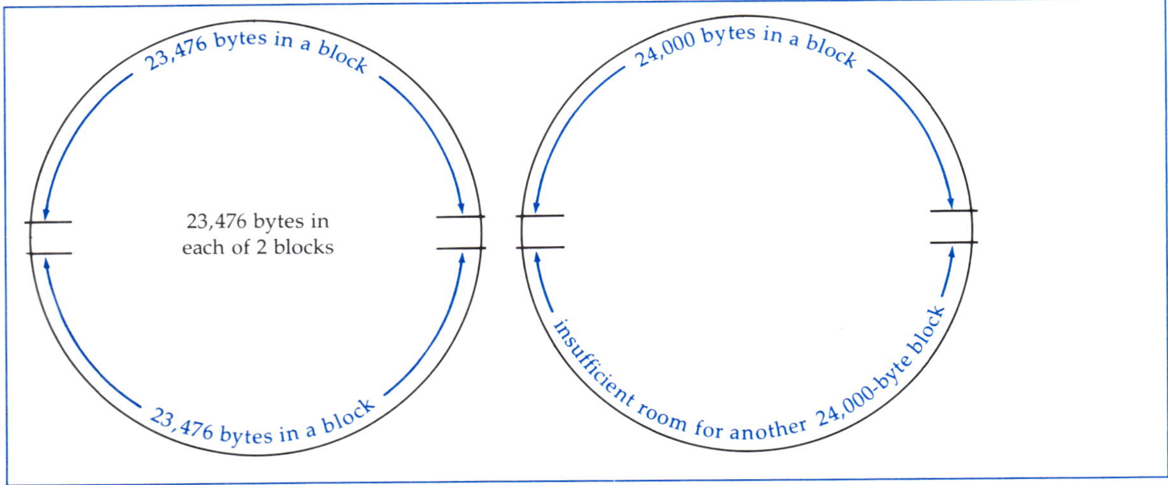


**Figure 16.9**
The effect of block size on track utilization for an IBM 3380 disk storage system.

You can use the space on an IBM 3380 track most efficiently by choosing a block size of 47,476. However, the standard I/O techniques that are described in this chapter limit the block size to a maximum of 32,760. The next best choice is a block size of 23,476. Two blocks of this size will fit on one track for a total capacity of 46,952 bytes, or a 98.90% utilization. The space that remains on the track is insufficient to accommodate another block and, since you cannot store part of a block on a track, this space is wasted. Note that the amount of wasted space increases as the number of blocks per track increases. The equation just given and the table that was given in Figure 16.8 will help you to choose an efficient block size, as you will see later. Figure 16.9 illustrates the effect of block size on track utilization.

Large block sizes not only save disk storage space, but also they can save execution time. The computing system can transfer more data per unit time between an I/O device and main storage if the block size is large than if the block size is small. However, since the I/O device and channel are unavailable for other operations during data transmission, transmitting a long data block can be undesirable in certain situations. Yet the speed of the IBM 3380 makes this less of a problem than with other disk storage systems that you might use. As with tape data sets, your particular application also affects your choice of block size. For example, a block size that does not exceed 4096 can be a good choice because the operating system allocates main storage in units of 4096 bytes.

## Data Sets

This section describes the nature of data sets and their various organizations. This information affects the way in which you perform I/O operations.

### *Records and Blocks*

**A physical record or block consists of logical records.**

A data set contains units called **logical records** whose size and content are related to the logic of the program. For example, if a program processes a list of names, each name could be a logical record. A **physical record** consists of one or more logical records that are placed end to end without distinction or separation. The physical record appears on an I/O medium as a block. Although the program deals with logical records, the I/O device can only transmit physical records. Either your program or the operating system must extract the logical records from the physical records. (Note that this chapter often uses the word *record* instead of logical record and the word *block* instead of physical record.)

**Records can be blocked or unblocked, fixed-length or variable-length.**

When each physical record contains more than one logical record, the data set is **blocked**; if the physical record contains only one logical record, the data set is **unblocked**. Logical records and, therefore, physical records, may be of a fixed or variable length. Figure 16.10 illustrates fixed-length blocked records.

Each variable-length logical record and each variable-length block begins with a 4-byte field. The field in a record is called the **record descriptor word (RDW)**, and the field in a block is called the **block descriptor word (BDW)**. A descriptor word contains, in its first 2 bytes, the length of the record or block, including the length of the descriptor word itself. The second 2 bytes of an RDW or BDW must be zero. You can see the RDW and the BDW in the variable-length blocked records that are shown in Figure 16.11. Data sets cannot contain both fixed-length records and variable-length records.

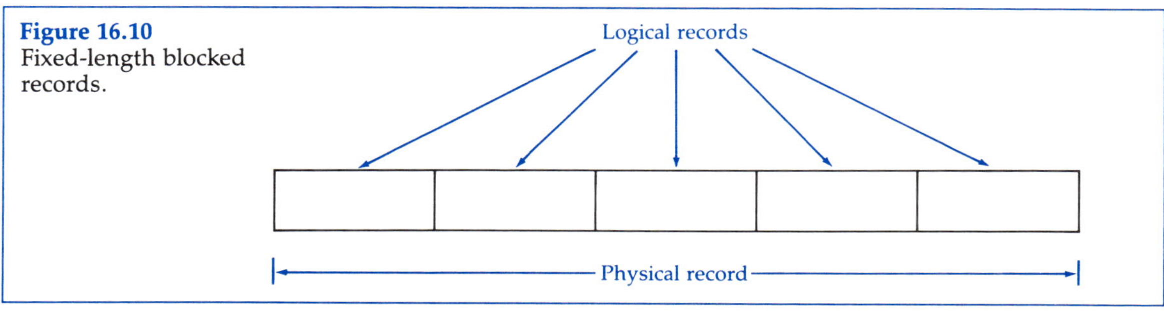


**Figure 16.10**
Fixed-length blocked records.

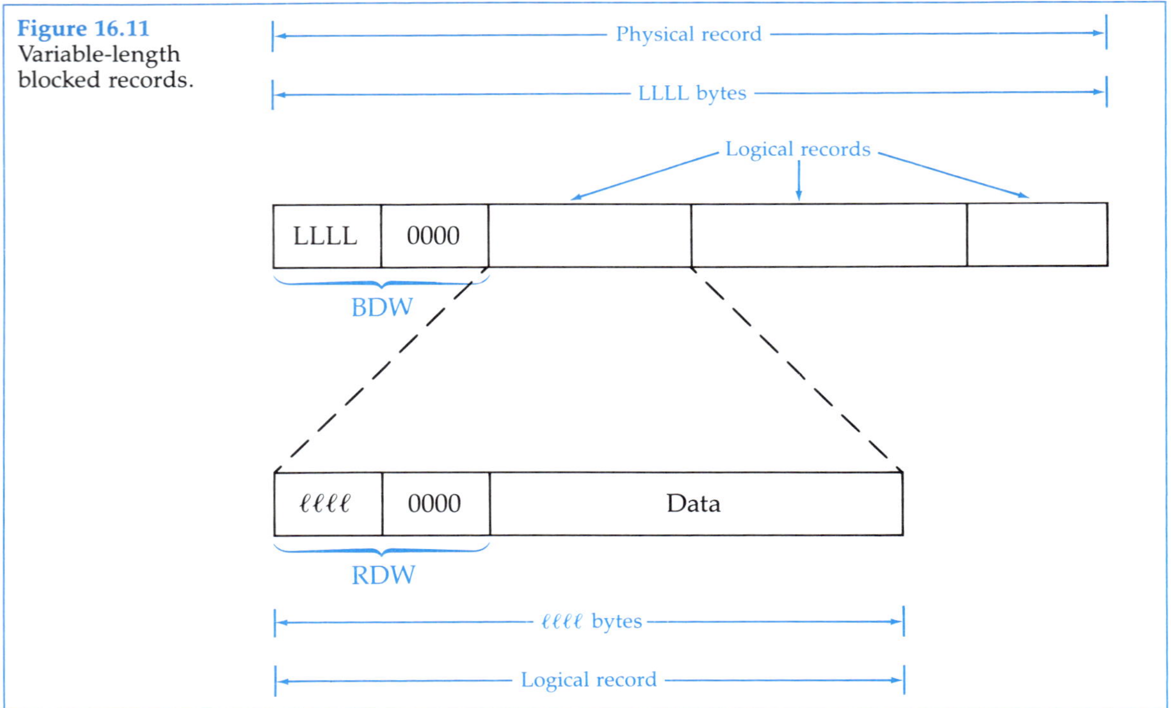


**Figure 16.11** Variable-length blocked records.

The nature of a data set's records (whether blocked or unblocked, or fixed-length or variable-length) is called its **record format**.

## *Data Set Organizations*

You can organize data sets in several ways. As mentioned earlier, data set organizations are based upon the physical devices that are available for input and output. For example, the idea of a **sequential data set** is based on the nature of magnetic tape, although you may also define a sequential data set on a direct-access device. To read a record from a sequential data set, you must first read through all of the records that precede it. Although you may add records to the end of the data set, other insertions or deletions require that you rewrite the data set. Data sets that are associated with keyboards, card readers, displays, and line printers are also sequential, again due to the nature of the devices.

All other System/370 data set organizations are based upon direct-access devices. A **partitioned data set (PDS)** is a collection of sequential data sets called **members**, with each member having a unique name. Within the PDS exists a **directory** of names and relative addresses that point to the corresponding members. Searching the directory permits you to access a member without searching the entire partitioned data set. After the member is located, you process the member sequentially. You can use partitioned data sets to establish libraries of programs, such as assemblers, compilers, linkers, or mathematical subprograms in source module, object module, or load module form.

You can process an **indexed sequential data set** sequentially or in any order that you desire. Each logical record contains a key; the keys are in an ascending order that corresponds to the sequential order of the records. Data blocks are stored in count-key-data format, where the key is the key of the last logical record in the block. To access any particular logical record, you specify the appropriate key. The operating system then locates the desired record by using an index of tracks and cylinders.

A **direct data set** allows you to access records directly without having to search through either the other records, a directory, or an index. This access requires that you know the cylinder number and the track number of the desired data records. For example, you can define a relationship between a key and the location of the corresponding physical record.

**Virtual Storage Access Method (VSAM) data sets** are also available as a more efficient substitute for some of the organizations described earlier. There are three types of VSAM data sets. An **entry-sequenced data set** has fixed-length or variable-length records that appear in the order in which you enter them. This type of data set is analogous to and can be used instead of a sequential data set. A **key-sequenced data set** has fixed-length or variable-length records that are in ascending collating order by key fields. You can access a record by its key. Key-sequenced data sets were designed to replace the indexed sequential organization. A **relative-record data set** contains fixed-length slots that are numbered with consecutive integers from 1 to *n*. Each slot can contain one logical record. You can place a record into any slot or retrieve a record from any slot by specifying the record number. Note that the record does not have to contain the record number.

### *Data Set Labels*

A particular magnetic tape or disk is called a **volume** and is identified by a **volume serial number**. A description of each data set on a volume—including the data set's name, organization, record format, and block size—can appear with the volume serial number on the volume itself. The data sets on such a volume are said to have a **label**. Labels are mandatory for disk data sets, but optional (although desirable) for tape data sets. The operating system writes labels in a standard way, although you could define and use nonstandard labels. All examples in this chapter assume standard labels.

## General Software Concepts

This section summarizes the ways that you can process data sets, and defines buffering, data control blocks under OS, and DTF tables under DOS.

### *Access Methods*

The various data set organizations necessitate different processing methods called **access methods**. They include the **sequential**, **partitioned**, **indexed-sequential**, **direct**, and **virtual storage** access methods. For non-VSAM data sets under OS, there are two general approaches: **queued access** and **basic access**. When you use queued access methods, the operating system handles the details of the I/O operation automatically, whereas you must handle many of these details yourself when you use basic access methods. Basic access methods are available under OS for all non-VSAM data sets, but you may process only sequential and indexed-sequential data sets with queued techniques. Figure 16.12 summarizes the possible access methods. VSAM was designed to replace the indexed-sequential methods BISAM, QISAM,

**Figure 16.12**
Available access methods, which are listed according to data set organization and operating system.

| Data set organization | Access Methods: Under OS, basic | Under OS, queued | Under DOS |
|---|---|---|---|
| Sequential | BSAM | QSAM | SAM |
| Partitioned | BPAM | — | — |
| Indexed-Sequential | BISAM | QISAM | ISAM |
| Direct | BDAM | — | DAM |
| Virtual | VSAM | | VSAM |

and ISAM; you can also use it instead of the sequential methods BSAM, QSAM, and SAM.

This chapter considers only QSAM, SAM, and BSAM in detail. You will find descriptions of the other access methods in the following IBM publications: *Data Management Services Guide, Data Management Macro Instructions*, and *Virtual Storage Access Method (VSAM) Programmer's Guide*. (See Appendix B for the complete information about these publications.)

## *Buffering*

When the operating system reads a data set, the input device transmits a physical record and the channel places the record into an area of main storage called a **buffer**. When you use QSAM or SAM to request a logical record for your program, the operating system locates the record within the buffer and makes it available to you. Conversely, when your program writes a logical record, the operating system places the data into a buffer. When the buffer is full, the operating system initiates the transmission of the contents of the buffer as a physical record to the output device. When you use BSAM, you must locate input records within the buffer and place output records into another buffer. Thus, regardless of access method, buffers enable the **blocking** and **deblocking** of records.

**Buffers are used to block and deblock records.**

Buffers offer another advantage. After the operating system initiates an I/O operation, the channel controls the details of the data transmission. This step frees the CPU for other processing and, in particular, enables the user program to continue execution. One way to take advantage of this capability is to use more than one buffer. For example, for sequential tape and disk files, there are typically two buffers. During output, after the user program has filled one buffer with records, the operating system writes the resulting block to an output device. Meanwhile, the user program writes records to the second buffer. During input, the operating system fills one buffer while the user program processes records in the second buffer.

**Buffers enable programs to execute more efficiently.**

Buffers are organized into a **buffer pool**. The operating system or your program allocates and controls them in several ways. You will see how to handle buffers later in this chapter.

## *The Data Control Block and the DTF Table*

**Every data set must be described by a DCB in OS or a DTF table in DOS.**

You must describe the characteristics of each non-VSAM data set that you use in a program by using several fields in storage, which are collectively known in OS as the **data control block (DCB)** or in DOS as the **Define The**

**File (DTF) table**. Although many such characteristics are possible, the following are common to most data set organizations and access methods:

- Data set organization
- Record format
- Logical record length
- Block size

You can specify these and other characteristics in one of four ways. First, you can use a declarative macro (DCB in OS or DTF*xx* in DOS) to reserve storage for a data control block or DTF table, and to define whatever characteristics that you desire at assembly time. Second, since it is often desirable to postpone the specification of certain characteristics until execution time, you can specify the characteristics in the job control statements that are required for every data set. (These statements are the DD statements in OS or the EXTENT and DLBL statements in DOS.) In the job control statements, you can specify the device type, the volume serial number, the format and size of the records and blocks, and so on. Where possible, the operating system fills in missing fields in the data control block or DTF table. In cases where you have specified a characteristic in both the declarative macro and the job control statements, the macro has precedence. Third, for input data sets, there is another source of information, which is also available at execution time: the data set label. Information that you specify in a declarative macro or job control statement has precedence over the information in the data set label. Fourth, you can supplement or replace any field in the data control block or DTF table at appropriate times during program execution; you will see an example of this, which uses BSAM processing, later in this chapter.

## QSAM under OS

This section describes the syntax and purpose of six of the approximately two dozen macro instructions that are available for QSAM I/O. The names and functions of the six macros are as follows:

| Name | Function |
|---|---|
| OPEN | Logically connect a data set |
| CLOSE | Logically disconnect a data set |
| GET | Read the next logical record |
| PUT | Write the next logical record |
| PUTX | Rewrite a logical record on an existing data set |
| DCB | Construct a data control block |

All macros but DCB generate executable instructions that branch to system subprograms; therefore, you must define a save area and load its address into Register 13 if you have not already done so. The I/O routines destroy the contents of Registers 0, 1, 14, and 15; you are responsible for saving their contents. A name entry is required for the DCB macro, but is optional for the others.

If you want to reference the fields of a data control block, you can use the DCBD macro to define a dummy section that describes the DCB. Although DCBD is available under both QSAM and BSAM processing, this chapter will not describe it until the BSAM section given later.

## *The OPEN Macro*

**You must open a data set before you can process it.**

Several preparatory steps are necessary before you can access a data set. However, the OPEN macro performs all of these steps and is said to **open** the data set. This process completes the relevant data control block, loads the necessary access routines, locates the data set, and processes the data set label. (The data set label is either read for verification or written, according to whether the data set already exists or is new.) The OPEN macro can be summarized as follows:

| Operation | Operand | Instruction Name | Action |
|---|---|---|---|
| OPEN | (*dcbaddress*,*option*, . . .) | LOGICALLY CONNECT A DATA SET | Opens each data set whose DCB is at *dcbaddress*. |

The *dcbaddress* specifies the address of the data control block that is associated with the data set. Usually, *dcbaddress* is the symbol in the name entry of the DCB macro instruction that constructs the data control block; however, *dcbaddress* could be anything that you can use to specify an A-type constant. You can also load one of Registers 2 through 12 with the address of the data control block, and write the register name in parentheses in the *dcbaddress* entry. The *option* indicates how you will use the data set. Some possibilities for *option* and their meanings are as follows:

| *Option* | Meaning |
|---|---|
| INPUT | An input data set |
| OUTPUT | An output data set |
| EXTEND | Records to be written at the end of an output data set |
| UPDAT | A direct-access data set whose records are to be updated in place |

You can omit *option* and, if you do, INPUT is assumed; however, your intent will be less clear to others who read your program.

A second option that positions a tape volume is possible; in this case, you write *option* as (*option1*,*option2*). However, this text will not discuss this possibility further.

---

EXAMPLE 1

The following are some examples of OPEN macro instructions:

| | |
|---|---|
| `OPEN (DCB1,INPUT)` | The data set that the data control block at DCB1 describes is opened for input. |
| `OPEN ((3),OUTPUT)` | The data set that is described by the data control block whose address is in Register 3 is opened for output. |

| | | |
|---|---|---|
| OPEN | (DCB1, INPUT, DCB2, OUTPUT) | The data set that the data control block at DCB1 describes is opened for input, and the data set that the data control block at DCB2 describes is opened for output. |

## *The CLOSE Macro*

**You must close a data set when you are finished with it.**

After your program has processed a data set, you must **close** it. The CLOSE macro first disassociates the data set from the program. CLOSE then restores the data control block to the status that it had before the data set was opened so that you can reuse the data control block easily in another OPEN macro instruction. For output data sets on tapes or disks, CLOSE causes any logical records that remain in the output buffer to be written and then follows the records by an **end-of-file marker**, which is a special code that signals the end of a data set. The CLOSE macro can be summarized as follows:

| Operation | Operand | Instruction Name | Action |
|---|---|---|---|
| **CLOSE** | (*dcbaddress*,[*option*], . . .) | LOGICALLY DISCONNECT A DATA SET | Closes each data set whose DCB is at *dcbaddress*. |

The *dcbaddress* has the same meaning as for OPEN. Although you can specify an *option* in the CLOSE macro to position a tape volume after it is processed, this text will not describe this possibility. If you omit *option*, you must write its comma when another *dcbaddress* follows it. If you close only one data set, you can omit the parentheses.

EXAMPLE 2

The following are some examples of CLOSE macro instructions:

| | | |
|---|---|---|
| CLOSE | (DCB1,,DCB2) | The two data sets that the data control blocks at DCB1 and DCB2 describe are closed. |
| CLOSE | ((3),,INDCB) | The two data sets that the data control blocks at the address in Register 3 and at INDCB describe are closed. |
| CLOSE | DATA1 | The data set that the data control block at DATA1 describes is closed. |

### *The GET Macro*

GET obtains the next logical record.

The GET macro obtains the next logical record from the input buffer. An actual read from the input data set probably will not occur when GET is executed because the operating system should have already done this automatically. The operating system can process the records of a particular input data set in one of four modes. These modes affect how the operating system makes the next logical record available to your program. Although you specify the mode within the DCB macro (as you will see later), the mode affects how you write the GET macro. In **move mode**, the GET macro must specify the address of a work area within your program. The operating system will move the next logical record into this work area. In **locate mode**, the operating system places the address of the next logical record into Register 1. Then you can either process the logical record in its present location within the buffer or move the record to an area within your program. The **substitute mode** and **data mode** are also available, but this text will not discuss them. At any one time, you may open a data set for processing under only one mode.

The GET macro can be summarized as follows:

| Operation | Operand | Instruction Name | Action |
|---|---|---|---|
| GET | *dcbaddress*[,*work area address*] | READ NEXT LOGICAL RECORD | Obtains the next logical record in the data set that the DCB at *dcbaddress* describes; in move mode, places the record into the work area at the address that *work area address* specifies; in locate mode, places the address of the record into Register 1. |

The first operand entry specifies the address of the data control block that describes the input data set. The *dcbaddress* can be either anything that is valid as the operand entry of an RX instruction, or a register name, which is in parentheses, that you select from 1 through 12. Typically, *dcbaddress* is the symbol in the name entry of the associated DCB macro. In move mode, you can either write *work area address* as you would an RX operand entry, or load either Register 0 or one of Registers 2 through 12 with the work area address and write the register's name in parentheses as the second operand entry. In locate mode, you omit the second operand entry. If you omit the second operand entry in move mode, GET assumes that Register 0 contains the work area address.

If the end of the data set is encountered during the execution of a GET, program execution either will be terminated or will continue at the address that the EODAD parameter of the DCB macro specifies.

---

EXAMPLE 3

The following are some examples of GET macro instructions. In each example, INDCB represents the address of the DCB macro that describes the input data set.

```
GET INDCB
```
Assuming locate mode, this instruction loads Register 1 with the address of the input record.

| | | |
|---|---|---|
| GET | INDCB,WORK | Assuming move mode, this instruction moves the input record to the area at WORK. |
| GET | INDCB,(4) | Assuming move mode, this instruction moves the input record to the address in Register 4. |

---

## *The PUT Macro*

**PUT writes the next logical record.**

The PUT macro places a logical record into the output buffer. The operating system might not write to the output data set at this time, but it will do so when the output buffer is full. The same processing modes and operand entries that were described earlier for GET are valid for PUT. The macro can be summarized as follows:

| Operation | Operand | Instruction Name | Action |
|---|---|---|---|
| **PUT** | *dcbaddress*[,*work area address*] | WRITE NEXT LOGICAL RECORD | Writes the next logical record onto the data set that the DCB at *dcbaddress* describes; in move mode, the record is assumed to be at the address that *work area address* specifies; in locate mode, loads Register 1 with the address of an area within the output buffer. |

In move mode, PUT moves the logical record at the work area address to the output buffer. In locate mode, PUT loads Register 1 with the address of the next available area within the output buffer. You then must place the logical record at this address.

## *Illustrations of Move-mode Processing and Locate-mode Processing*

Processing data sets frequently involves reading a record from one data set and writing it on another. The required GET and PUT macro instructions do not need to use the same processing modes. All of the possible mode combinations are considered here.

*GET-move, PUT-move.* In move-mode processing, the operating system moves the records between the buffers and a work area that you specify in your program. GET moves the record from the input buffer to the work area; PUT moves it from the work area to the output buffer. Figure 16.13 illustrates this process.

*GET-locate, PUT-move.* A locate-mode GET returns the address of the next input record in Register 1. A move-mode PUT can specify this address as the work area address. The operating system then moves the record directly from the input buffer to the output buffer. Figure 16.14 illustrates this process. You must copy the address in Register 1 to another register because you cannot use Register 1 to specify the second operand of the PUT macro.

*GET-locate, PUT-locate.* In locate-mode processing, the user program must move the record from the input buffer to the output buffer. GET returns the address of the next logical record in Register 1. You must copy this

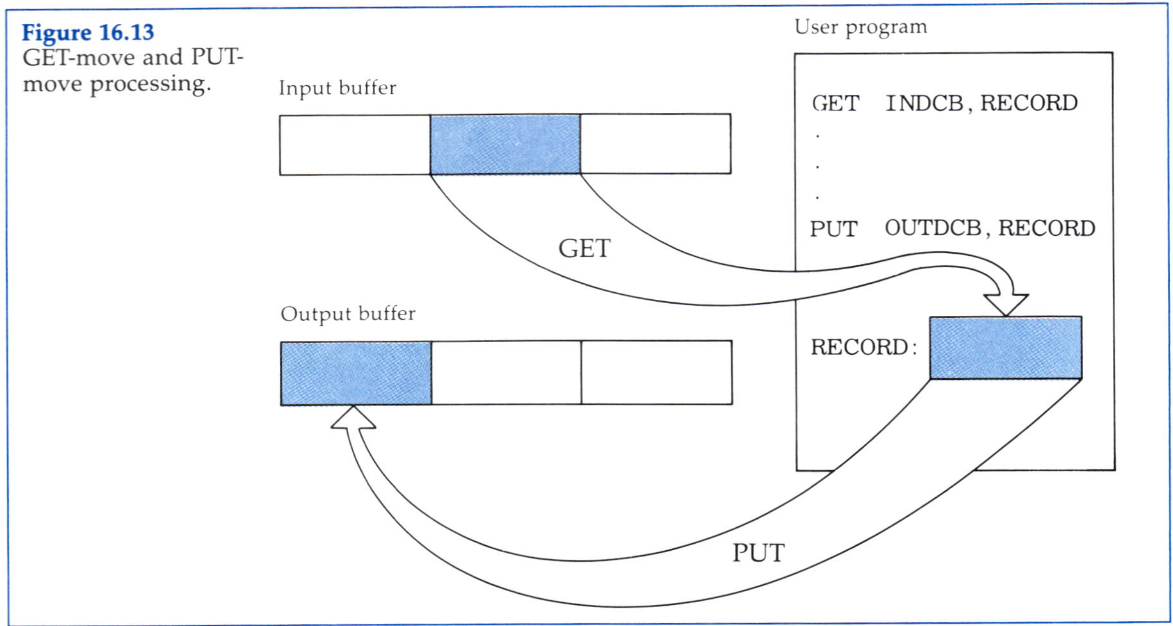


**Figure 16.13**
GET-move and PUT-move processing.

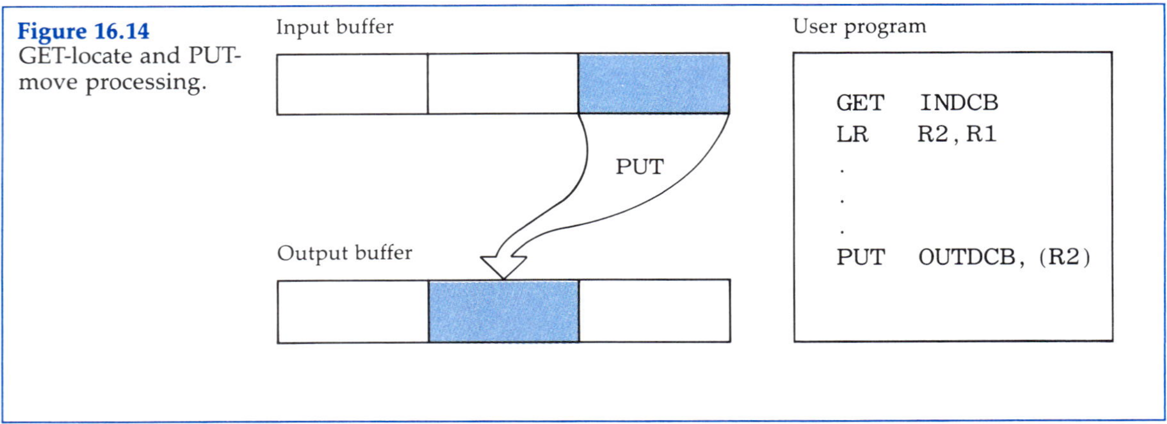


**Figure 16.14**
GET-locate and PUT-move processing.

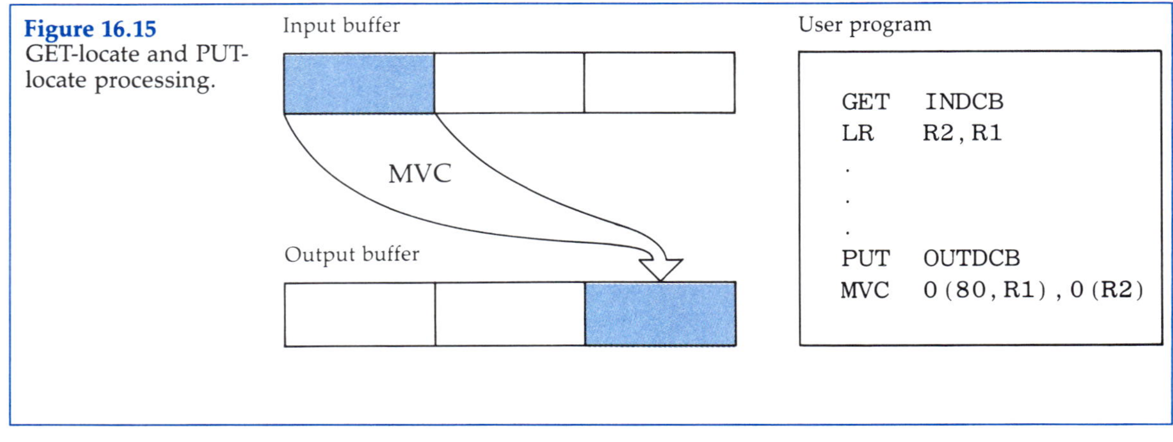


**Figure 15.15**
GET-locate and PUT-locate processing.

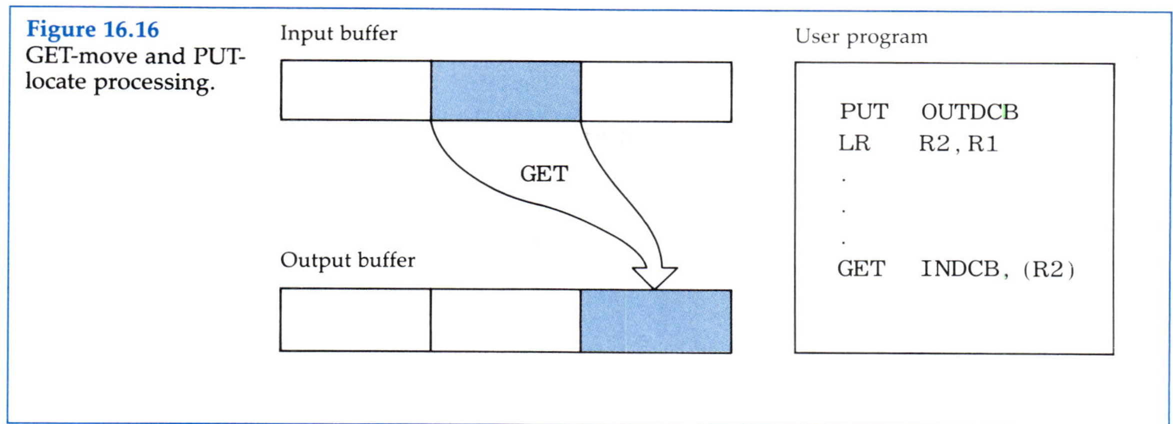


**Figure 16.16** GET-move and PUT-locate processing.

address to another register since the subsequent PUT loads Register 1 with the address of the next available space in the output buffer. You can use these two addresses to move the data. Figure 16.15 illustrates this process.

*GET-move, PUT-locate.* With a move-mode GET and a locate-mode PUT, you must first locate the address of the next available space in the output buffer by using PUT, which places this address into Register 1. You then must copy the address in Register 1 to another register, which you specify in the move-mode GET. GET moves the data from the input buffer to the output buffer. Figure 16.16 illustrates this process.

## *The PUTX Macro*

**PUTX updates a record.**

Executing PUTX writes the last logical record that was read from an existing direct-access data set. If you open such a data set for update (UPDAT), you can read a record with a locate-mode GET, modify the record, and write it on top of the original record in the data set by using PUTX in move mode. In this case, PUTX can be summarized as follows:

| Operation | Operand | Instruction Name | Action |
|---|---|---|---|
| **PUTX** | *dcbaddress* | WRITE RECORD ON AN EXIST-ING DATA SET | In update mode, rewrites the record just read from an existing data set that the DCB at *dcbaddress* describes. |

## *The DCB Macro*

**The DCB macro defines the data control block that is required of every data set.**

You use the DCB macro to construct a data control block for a particular data set. The macro instruction is nonexecutable, and you must place it accordingly in the program. A symbol must appear in the name entry of the instruction; this is the same symbol that you can use to specify *dcbaddress* in the macros described earlier. The operands are in a **keyword format**, which means they are of the form

*keyword = option*

For example, BLKSIZE=800 specifies a block size of 800 bytes. You do not have to specify every possible keyword operand; those that you do specify may be written in any order. The DCB macro can be summarized as follows:

| Name | Operation | Operand | Instruction Name | Action |
|---|---|---|---|---|
| *symbol* | **DCB** | *keyword*=*option*, . . . | DEFINE DATA CONTROL BLOCK | Constructs a data control block at the address that the symbol in the name entry represents. |

The most common DCB keywords and their meanings are as follows:

| Keyword | Meaning |
|---|---|
| DSORG | Data set organization |
| MACRF | Macro form |
| DDNAME | Data definition (DD) name |
| RECFM | Record format |
| LRECL | Logical record length |
| BLKSIZE | Block size |
| EODAD | End-of-data address |

The following describes how to write these keywords in a DCB macro instruction:

- DSORG=PS or PSU specifies that the data is sequential. (PS stands for *physical sequential*.) If the file contains absolute addresses as part of its data, it is said to be *unmovable*; the U of PSU indicates this.
- MACRF= specifies the processing mode and whether GET or PUT macros are used. Thus, you can write one of the following:

  MACRF=GM to specify GET in move mode.
  MACRF=GL to specify GET in locate mode.
  MACRF=PM to specify PUT in move mode.
  MACRF=PL to specify PUT in locate mode.

  When you open a data set in update mode, you use both GET and PUTX with the same data set, and write

  MACRF=(GL,PM)

- DDNAME=*symbol* specifies the symbol in the name entry of the relevant DD statement in the JCL that is associated with the program.
- RECFM= specifies the format of the logical records. For the record formats discussed earlier, the following are possible:

  RECFM=F to specify fixed-length unblocked records.
  RECFM=FB to specify fixed-length blocked records.
  RECFM=V to specify variable-length unblocked records.
  RECFM=VB to specify variable-length blocked records.

  If you print the data set, and if the first character of each logical record is an ANSI carriage-control character, then you add an A to the record format code; for example, FBA. All examples of printed output that appeared in previous chapters assumed ANSI carriage control. However, you can omit carriage control, as you will see later.
- LRECL=*n* specifies the length *n* in bytes of either a fixed-length logical record or the longest variable-length record. The length of the longest variable-length record includes 4 bytes for the record descriptor word.

- BLKSIZE=$n$ specifies the number $n$ of bytes in a block, or physical record. For fixed-length unblocked records, $n$ is equal to the logical record length. For fixed-length blocked records, $n$ is a multiple of the logical record length. If the records are variable-length and unblocked, $n$ must be at least 4 bytes greater than the logical record length to accommodate the block descriptor word. For variable-length blocked records, $n$ is at least 4 bytes greater than a multiple of the logical record length.
- EODAD= specifies a symbolic address to which the operating system branches if a GET instruction tries to read beyond the end of the data set. If you omit EODAD and an end-of-data condition occurs, the operating system will terminate program execution.

Two keywords that you must write in every DCB macro instruction are DSORG and MACRF. If the program does not alter the fields of the data control block, as is assumed here, then you must also write the keyword DDNAME in the DCB macro instruction. You can specify the RECFM, LRECL, and BLKSIZE parameters in either the DCB macro instruction or the DD statement of the JCL. You may also include these parameters in the data set label of an input data set; if these parameters appear in more than one place, the operating system assumes that specifications in the DCB have precedence over those in the DD statement, which have precedence over the data set label.

**Continuation lines**

DCB macro instructions are often lengthy, requiring more than one line. You can continue any macro instruction onto any number of lines by using the rules that you already know: write a continuation character in column 72 and continue the operand entry on the next line by beginning in column 16. However, you can write the operand entry in one or both of the following ways. You can extend the entry through column 71 without blanks—as for any other instruction—or you can interrupt the entry at a comma and follow the comma with at least one blank; as an option, you can follow this blank with a remark. The next examples and Figure 16.18 demonstrate these new techniques.

---

EXAMPLE 4

The DCB macro instruction for an input sequential data set on magnetic tape or disk that is read in locate mode could appear as follows:

```
INDATA   DCB   DSORG=PS,MACRF=GL,DDNAME=DD1,RECFM=FB,LRECL=100,         X
               BLKSIZE=4000,EODAD=ENDINPUT
```

---

EXAMPLE 5

The DCB macro instruction for an output sequential data set on magnetic tape or disk that is written in locate mode could appear as follows:

```
OUTDATA  DCB   DSORG=PS,MACRF=PL,DDNAME=DD2,RECFM=VB,LRECL=104,         X
               BLKSIZE=4164
```

Each variable-length logical record contains a maximum of 100 bytes of data and a 4-byte record descriptor word. Each physical record can accommodate up to 40 maximum size logical records, as well as a 4-byte block descriptor word ($40 \times 104 + 4 = 4164$).

---

EXAMPLE 6

The DCB macro instruction for an output sequential data set that is to be printed in move mode could appear as follows:

```
PRINT    DCB    DSORG=PS,MACRF=PM,DDNAME=LISTING,RECFM=FA,LRECL=133,        X
                BLKSIZE=133
```

This instruction assumes that the first byte of each logical record contains an ANSI carriage control character.

---

## *The DD Statement in OS JCL*

**You must write a DD statement for every data set that you use.**

You must describe every data set—new or old—by using a Data Definition (DD) statement. For example, it is in a DD statement that a new data set is assigned to a type of I/O device, given a name, allocated space if it is on a direct-access device, and identified as either a temporary data set or a data set that should be retained. You can request that the operating system enter the names of permanent data sets into its **catalog** to facilitate future use of the data set.

A DD statement has the following form:

*//ddname* DD *keyword=option, . . .*

The entry *ddname* is required. It is a symbol that the DDNAME keyword in the DCB macro references as previously described. The more important DD keywords and their meanings are as follows:

| Keyword | Meaning |
|---|---|
| DSNAME | Data set name |
| DISP | Present status and future disposition |
| UNIT | Device type |
| VOL=SER | Volume serial number |
| DCB | Data control block fields |
| SPACE | Space allocation |
| LABEL | Tape data set sequence number |

The following describes how to write these keywords in a DD statement:

- DSNAME=*symbol* provides a name for a new data set or identifies an existing one. If an existing data set is cataloged, you can use this name to locate the data set and identify its characteristics. In this case, the only other keyword that you should specify is DISP.
- DISP=(*present status,normal disposition*[*,abnormal disposition*]) specifies the present status and final disposition of the data set. The *present status* can be one of the following:

  NEW if the program will create the data set.
  SHR if the data set already exists and can be shared with other programs in a multiprogramming environment.
  OLD if the data set already exists, but is to be used exclusively by the program.
  MOD if either the data set already exists, is sequential, and is to be extended or modified; or the data set does not exist and will be created by the program. When the data set is opened, the device is positioned either after the last data block, if the data set exists,

or at the beginning, if the data set will be created. If the data set does not exist, you must omit the VOL=SER parameter.

The *normal disposition* indicates what will happen to the data set after the program terminates successfully, whereas *abnormal disposition* specifies what will happen if the program terminates abnormally. Each disposition designation can have one of the following values:

KEEP if you want to retain the data set.
CATLG if you want to retain the data set and add its name to the catalog.
UNCATLG if you want to retain the data set, but remove its name from the catalog.
DELETE if you do not want to retain the data set. In this case, you can use its space for future data sets. If you omit the VOL=SER parameter, then DELETE also removes a cataloged data set from the catalog.
PASS if you want to make the data set available to a subsequent job step. You can specify the final disposition in another DD statement that is associated with that job step.

If you omit *normal disposition*, new data sets are deleted and existing data sets are retained. If you omit *abnormal disposition*, then the value of *normal disposition* is used unless it is PASS; in that case, new data sets are deleted and existing ones are retained. Omitting the DISP parameter entirely has the same effect as DISP=(NEW,DELETE,DELETE).

- UNIT= specifies the model number or the symbolic name of the desired I/O device. For example, 3380 specifies any Model 3380 disk storage unit, SYSDA specifies any direct-access storage device, and TAPE specifies any magnetic tape unit. (Note that symbolic names such as SYSDA and TAPE depend on the computer installation that you have.) The operating system has more flexibility in allocating new data sets when you use symbolic names rather than model numbers.
- VOL=SER= specifies the volume serial number of a particular disk or tape. You only need to use the volume serial number for existing uncataloged data sets. If you specify this parameter for existing data sets, the operating system will not access the catalog; if you omit this parameter for new data sets, the operating system will allocate space on any available volume. The volume serial number specification tends to depend upon the local requirements of your computer installation.
- DCB=(RECFM=*record format*,LRECL=*logical record length*,BLKSIZE=*block size*) specifies the record format, logical record length, and block size as described earlier. If you have already specified this information in a DCB macro instruction, you can omit it from the DD statement because it will be ignored anyway. However, the DD statement has precedence over similar information that may appear in the data set label of an existing data set.
- SPACE=(*unit*,(*primary amount*,*increment*)[,RLSE]) allocates space for new data sets on direct-access devices; do not use it for tape data sets. You can request space in one of three units by using the first operand entry, as follows:

TRK requests tracks.
CYL requests cylinders.
*nnn* requests blocks of *nnn* bytes each.

The second operand entry indicates the number of units that you request initially; should this number prove to be insufficient, the operating system will allocate a number of additional units of space according to what the third operand entry specifies. For example,

SPACE=(TRK,(3,2))

allocates 3 tracks initially and, if necessary, allocates additional increments of 2 tracks each. A maximum of 16 additional increments is possible. When you request space in blocks of *nnn* bytes, the operating system allocates entire tracks, even though your request may be only for a partial track. RLSE is optional: when specified, unused tracks will be *released* for use in another data set.

- LABEL=*n* specifies the **data set sequence number**, which indicates the order that a data set occurs on a magnetic tape. Omit the LABEL parameter for cataloged data sets. You also can use the LABEL parameter to specify whether or not the data set contains labels other than standard ones, or whether or not to skip the label. In addition, you can specify password protection and a retention or expiration date for the data set; however, this text will not discuss these features of the LABEL parameter.

DD statements are often long: you can continue a DD statement onto a subsequent line by ending a specification at a comma, and beginning the continuation line with two slashes and at least one blank. The specifications on a continued line must begin between columns 4 to 16, inclusive.

---

EXAMPLE 7

```
//INPUTDD   DD   DSNAME=MYDATA,DISP=(OLD,KEEP)
```

The data set MYDATA exists and is to be retained regardless of whether the program terminates normally or abnormally. You use this DD statement when the data set either is already cataloged or has been passed from a previous job step. This statement does not indicate whether the data set resides on a tape or a disk; this information is contained in the catalog.

---

EXAMPLE 8

```
//OUTPUTDD DD UNIT=SYSDA,SPACE=(TRK,(4,2),RLSE),
//             DSNAME=DATA,DISP=(NEW,CATLG,DELETE)
```

This instruction defines a new data set on any available direct-access device. Initially, 4 tracks are allocated, but 2-track increments will supplement these tracks, if necessary. Unused tracks will be released. If the program terminates normally, the data set will be cataloged; if the program terminates abnormally, the data set will be deleted.

---

EXAMPLE 9

```
//IN DD UNIT=TAPE,VOL=SER=TP012,DSNAME=SURVEY,
//        DISP=(OLD,KEEP),LABEL=2
```

The existing data set named SURVEY is the second data set on the magnetic tape volume TP012. Since VOL=SER appears, the operating system will not access the catalog. The data set is retained when the program terminates.

*The System Input and Output Data Sets.* The **system input (SYSIN) data set** consists of EBCDIC records that are included with the job control statements associated with the user program, and that are preceded by

```
//GO.SYSIN    DD    *
```

Assume here that GO is the name of the execution step in a cataloged procedure. The **system output (SYSOUT) data set** contains EBCDIC records that are produced by the user program and that will be printed. The associated DD statement is named SYSPRINT and appears† as

```
//GO.SYSPRINT   DD   SYSOUT=A
```

You can process SYSIN and SYSOUT data sets just like any other data sets by using QSAM or BSAM macro instructions.

†This SYSPRINT statement assumes that values for the RECFM, LRECL, and BLKSIZE parameters are provided by the operating system and, therefore, may be omitted. However, this may not be the case for your computer installation, so check for local variations in the given JCL.

## SELF-TEST EXERCISES

1. Write a DCB macro instruction for an input sequential data set that contains fixed-length logical records of length 80, which are blocked at 20 records per block. Assume move-mode processing.
2. Write the OPEN and CLOSE macro instructions for the data set that was described in Self-Test Exercise 1.
3. Write instructions that read a record from the data set that was described in Self-Test Exercise 1. Then, by using move-mode processing, write the record on the data set that the DCB at OUT describes.
4. Repeat Self-Test Exercise 3 and use locate-mode processing to write the record.
5. Write a DD statement for an uncataloged data set like the one that was described in Self-Test Exercise 1. Assume that the data set resides on a magnetic tape.
6. Repeat Self-Test Exercise 5 but assume that the data set resides on a disk.
7. Write a DCB macro instruction and a DD statement to define a temporary sequential disk data set that you will use for output during program execution, but will not retain after execution is complete.

## SAM under DOS

Processing sequential files under DOS is conceptually similar to what the previous section has just presented for OS. The names and functions of the important macros that you need to perform I/O using SAM are as follows:

| Name | Function |
|---|---|
| OPEN | Logically connect a file |
| CLOSE | Logically disconnect a file |
| GET | Read the next logical record |
| PUT | Write the next logical record |
| DTF*xx* | Construct a DTF table |

Twelve DTF*xx* macros are available according to the I/O device used, but this section only considers the following five:

DTFSD for sequential files on a direct-access device.
DTFMT for files on magnetic tape.
DTFPR for printer files.
DTFCD for card reader files.
DTFDI for device-independent files.

Except for the DTF*xx* macros, the SAM macros given in this section generate executable instructions that branch to system subprograms. Therefore, you must define a save area and load its address into Register 13 if you have not already done so. The I/O routines destroy the contents of Registers 14 and 15, and possibly the contents of Registers 0 and 1. You are responsible for saving their contents. A name entry is required for the DTF*xx* macros, but is optional for the other I/O macros.

### *The OPEN and CLOSE Macros*

**You must open a data set before you can process it.**

Before you access a file, you must open it with an OPEN macro instruction. Unlike OS, the DOS OPEN macro does not specify whether the file will be used for input or output; you make this specification in the DTF*xx* macro instruction. To open a file, the operating system completes the relevant DTF table as described earlier, loads the necessary access routines, and locates the data set. The OPEN macro can be summarized as follows:

| Operation | Operand | Instruction Name | Action |
|---|---|---|---|
| OPEN | *dtfaddress*, . . . | LOGICALLY CONNECT A DATA SET | Opens each data set whose DTF table is at *dtfaddress*. |

The *dtfaddress* specifies the address of the DTF table that is associated with the data set. Usually, *dtfaddress* is the symbol in the name entry of a DTF*xx* macro instruction, but it also could be a register name that is in parentheses if the register contains the address of the DTF table. You can use any register except Register 1 for this purpose; however, IBM suggests that you use only Registers 2 through 12.

The CLOSE macro logically disconnects the file from the program, but does not restore the DTF table to the status that it had before it was opened, as is done under OS. The CLOSE macro can be summarized as follows, where *dtfaddress* has the same meaning as for OPEN:

**You must close a data set when you are finished with it.**

| Operation | Operand | Instruction Name | Action |
|---|---|---|---|
| **CLOSE** | *dtfaddress, . . .* | LOGICALLY DISCONNECT A DATA SET | Closes each data set whose DTF table is at *dtfaddress*. |

## *The GET and PUT Macros*

**GET obtains the next logical record.**

**PUT writes the next logical record.**

You use the GET macro to obtain the next logical record from the input buffer, and the PUT macro to place a logical record into the output buffer. The format and processing modes for GET and PUT are the same for both DOS and OS. GET and PUT can be summarized as follows:

| Operation | Operand | Instruction Name | Action |
|---|---|---|---|
| **GET** | *dtfaddress*[,*work area address*] | READ NEXT LOGICAL RECORD | Obtains the next logical record in the data set that the DTF table at *dtfaddress* describes; in move mode, places the record into the work area at the address that *work area address* specifies; in locate mode, places the address of the record into the register that is specified by the IOREG parameter of the corresponding DTF*xx* macro instruction. |
| **PUT** | *dtfaddress*[,*work area address*] | WRITE NEXT LOGICAL RECORD | Writes the next logical record in the data set that the DTF table at *dtfaddress* describes; in move mode, the record must be at the address that *work area address* specifies; in locate mode, places the address of an area within the output buffer into the register that is specified by the IOREG parameter of the corresponding DTF*xx* macro instruction. |

The *dtfaddress* has the same meaning for GET and PUT as it does for OPEN and CLOSE, except that you can use one of Registers 1 through 12 to specify the address of the DTF table. You specify *work area address* for move mode, but not for locate mode. The *work area address* is either a symbol that represents the address of the record in storage or a register name that is enclosed in parentheses. You can use either Register 0 or one of Registers 2 through 12 for this purpose. If you specify either operand entry with a register, you can save execution time and storage space by using Register 1 for *dtfaddress* and Register 0 for *work area address*.

When you use locate mode with GET, the operating system places the address of the desired logical record into the register that you specify with the IOREG parameter of the DTF*xx* macro. When you use locate mode with PUT, the operating system places the address of an area within the output buffer into the register that you specify with the IOREG parameter of the

DTF*xx* macro. You can use only Registers 2 through 12 for this purpose, and not Register 1 as you can under OS.

If the operating system encounters the end of the data set during the execution of a GET, program execution will either be terminated or will continue at the address that the EOFADDR parameter of the DTF*xx* macro specifies.

Notice that there is no PUTX macro in DOS; you can use PUT instead to update a file.

### The DTFxx Macros

**A DTF*xx* macro defines the DTF table that is required of every file.**

You use one of the DTF*xx* (Define The File) macros to construct a DTF table for a particular data set on a specific type of I/O device. Like the DCB macro, these macros produce nonexecutable instructions, so you must place them accordingly in the program. A symbol must appear in the name entry; this symbol is restricted to seven characters. This is the same symbol that you can use to specify *dtfaddress* in the macros described earlier. The DTF*xx* macros can be summarized as follows:

| Name | Operation | Operand | Instruction Name | Action |
|---|---|---|---|---|
| *symbol* | **DTFxx** | *keyword = option, . . .* | CONSTRUCT A DTF TABLE | Constructs a DTF table at the address that the symbol in the name entry represents. |

DTF*xx* is DTFSD (sequential disk file), DTFMT (magnetic tape file), DTFPR (printer file), DTFCD (card reader file), or DTFDI (device-independent file). Operand entries are in a keyword format and, although many keywords are possible, you do not need to specify all of them. The most important keywords and their meanings are as follows:

| Keyword | Meaning | Keyword | Meaning |
|---|---|---|---|
| DEVADDR | Device address | WORKA = YES | Move mode |
| DEVICE | Device unit number | IOREG | Locate mode |
| IOAREA1 | First buffer address | UPDATE = YES | Update mode |
| IOAREA2 | Second buffer address | EOFADDR | End-of-file address |
| RECFORM | Record format | ERROPT | Error option |
| RECSIZE | Logical record size | CTLCHR = ASA | Carriage control (ANSI) |
| BLKSIZE | Block size | FILABL | File label |
| TYPEFLE | File type | | |

The following describes how to write these keywords in a DTF*xx* macro instruction:

- DEVADDR= specifies a **symbolic unit** that represents a class of devices. For example, SYSIPT is the primary input unit, SYSLST is the primary unit for printed output, and SYS*nnn* represents the program's data sets.
- DEVICE= specifies the model number of the desired I/O device. You omit this parameter for tape files and disk files.
- IOAREA1= specifies the address of the first buffer. DOS requires that you define a buffer area and specify its address with this parameter.

The buffer length must be the same as the block size that you specify in the BLKSIZE parameter.

- IOAREA2= specifies the address of a second buffer. Although this parameter is optional, you will probably increase efficiency if you specify it. A maximum of two buffers is possible under DOS.
- RECFORM= specifies the format of the logical records. For the record formats discussed here, the following are possibilities:

  RECFORM=FIXUNB for fixed-length unblocked records.
  RECFORM=FIXBLK for fixed-length blocked records.
  RECFORM=VARUNB for variable-length unblocked records.
  RECFORM=VARBLK for variable-length blocked records.

  Card reader files and printer files are either FIXUNB or VARUNB.
- RECSIZE=*n* specifies the logical record size *n* for fixed-length blocked (FIXBLK) records only.
- BLKSIZE=*n* specifies the block size *n*. For output sequential disk files, the block size should include 8 extra bytes to accommodate a count field that the operating system requires.
- TYPEFLE= specifies whether you will use the file for INPUT or for OUTPUT. Omit this parameter for printer files.
- WORKA=YES indicates that processing will use the move mode. If you specify this, do not specify IOREG.
- IOREG=(*register*) indicates one of Registers 2 through 12 that GET or PUT will use in locate mode. When you write this parameter, do not write WORKA.
- UPDATE=YES indicates that a sequential disk file may be updated.
- EOFADDR= specifies a symbolic address to which the operating system will branch if a GET instruction tries to read beyond the end of the data set. If you omit EOFADDR and an end-of-file condition occurs, the operating system terminates program execution.
- ERROPT= specifies an option to be followed or the address of an error-processing routine in case an input/output error occurs. The options are IGNORE or SKIP.
- CTLCHR=ASA indicates that a printer file contains ANSI carriage-control characters.
- FILABL= indicates whether a tape file contains a standard label (STD) or no label (NO).

Figure 16.17 indicates which of the keywords just given are required with the five DTF*xx* macros, and which are applicable in the context of the features that are discussed in this section.

**Continuation lines**

DTF*xx* macro instructions are often lengthy, requiring more than one line. You can continue any macro instruction onto any number of lines by using the rules that you already know: write a continuation character in column 72 and continue the operand entry on the next line by beginning in column 16. However, you can write the operand entry in one or both of the following ways. You can extend the entry through column 71 without blanks—as for any other instruction—or you can interrupt the entry at a comma and follow the comma with at least one blank; as an option, you can follow this blank with a remark. The next examples and Figure 16.19 demonstrate these new techniques.

| Keyword | DTFCD | DTFPR | DTFSD | DTFMT | DTFDI |
|---|---|---|---|---|---|
| DEVADDR | * | * | √ | * | * |
| DEVICE | √ | √ | — | — | — |
| IOAREA1 | * | * | √ | √ | * |
| IOAREA2 | √ | √ | √ | √ | √ |
| RECFORM | √ | √ | √ | √ | — |
| RECSIZE | — | — | √ | √ | √ |
| BLKSIZE | √ | √ | * | * | — |
| TYPEFLE | √ | — | √ | √ | — |
| WORKA | √ | √ | √ | √ | — |
| IOREG | √ | √ | √ | √ | √ |
| UPDATE | — | — | √ | — | — |
| EOFADDR | √ | — | * (input) | * (input) | √ |
| ERROPT | √ | √ | √ | √ | √ (input) |
| CTLCHR | — | √ | — | — | — |
| FILABL | — | — | — | * | — |

(Columns DTFCD through DTFDI are grouped under the heading "DTF*xx* Macros".)

* = required operand
√ = permitted operand
— = not applicable

**Figure 16.17**
A partial list of applicable keywords for the DTF*xx* macros.

---

EXAMPLE 10

The DTFMT macro instruction for an input tape file that will be processed in locate mode could appear as follows:

```
INDATA   DTFMT DEVADDR=SYS001,IOAREA1=BUFFER1,RECFORM=FIXBLK,          X
               RECSIZE=100,BLKSIZE=4000,TYPEFLE=INPUT,IOREG=(2),       X
               EOFADDR=ENDIN,FILABL=STD
```

---

EXAMPLE 11

The DTFSD macro instruction for a sequential output disk file that is processed in locate mode could appear as follows:

```
OUTDATA  DTFSD DEVADDR=SYS002,IOAREA1=BUFFER1,RECFORM=VARBLK,          X
               BLKSIZE=4172,TYPEFLE=OUTPUT,IOREG=(2)
```

Assume that each logical record contains a maximum of 100 bytes of data and a 4-byte record descriptor word. Each physical record can accommodate up to 40 maximum-size logical records, a 4-byte block descriptor record, and an 8-byte system count field that is required of DOS disk output files; thus, $40 \times 104 + 4 + 8 = 4172$.

Note that you do not specify RECSIZE for variable-length records.

---

EXAMPLE 12

The DTFPR macro instruction for a printer file that is processed in move mode could appear as follows:

```
OUTPRNT  DTFPR DEVADDR=SYSLST,DEVICE=3203,IOAREA1=BUFFER1,          X
               RECFORM=FIXUNB,BLKSIZE=133,WORKA=YES,CTLCHR=ASA
```

Note that you omit TYPEFLE for printer files.

## *DOS JCL Statements for Disk and Tape Files*

The ASSGN statement follows the OPTION statement and assigns physical devices to logical units. For disk and tape files, it has the following form:

// ASSGN SYS*nnn*,*unit*,VOL=*vol-ser*

Here, SYS*nnn* is the symbolic unit, *unit* is the device address, and *vol-ser* is the volume serial number of the disk or tape. For example, the following statement assigns the 3380 disk volume named DATA2 to the symbolic unit SYS001:

```
//  ASSGN  SYS001,3380,VOL=DATA2
```

*Disk Files.* You use the DLBL and EXTENT statements to define a disk file. You write a DLBL statement for each disk file as follows:

// DLBL *dtfname,'file-id',retention,type-code*

The *dtfname* is the name of the DTF table that describes the file. Typically, *dtfname* is the symbol in the name entry of the associated DTFSD macro instruction. The *file-id* is a filename of a maximum of 44 characters. The *retention* specifies either the retention period of the file in days or an expiration date in the form *yy/ddd*. For example, 99/032 is Feb. 1, 1999. The *type-code* is a file type code. For example, SD specifies a sequential disk file.

Usually, each disk file also requires one or more EXTENT statements in the following form:

// EXTENT SYS*nnn*,*vol-ser*,*type*,*seq-no.*,*rel-track*,*no.-of-tracks*

Here, SYS*nnn* is the symbolic unit, *vol-ser* is the volume serial number, and *type* is a number that classifies the type of file. An ordinary data file is type 1. The *seq-no.* is a sequence number for a file with more than one extent. You omit this parameter for SAM files. The *rel-track* is a track number at which the data set should begin. (0 is the first track.) You must specify this parameter for new data sets, but you can omit it for SAM input files. The *no.-of-tracks* parameter indicates the number of tracks to be allocated to the file. If you specify a relative track number, then you must specify the number of tracks; if you omit the relative track number, you must also omit the number of tracks. You can omit the EXTENT statement for an input file that resides on a single disk pack if you have specified the DEVADDR parameter in the DTF table.

The DLBL and EXTENT statements appear after the statement

```
//  EXEC  LNKEDT
```

with each DLBL statement immediately before its corresponding EXTENT statements, as shown:

```
//  EXEC  LNKEDT
//  DLBL  OUTDTF,'DATA',99/032,SD
//  EXTENT  SYS002,DISK1,1,,65,12
//  EXEC
```

*Tape Files.* The TLBL statement that is necessary to define a tape file appears as follows:

// TLBL *dtfname,'file-id',retention,vol-ser*

The operand entries are the same as described for disk files, except that *file-id* can be a maximum of 17 characters.

The following is an example of how to use the TLBL statement; the LBLTYP statement indicates that tape labels exist:

```
//  LBLTYP  TAPE
//  EXEC  LNKEDT
//  TLBL  INDTF,'DATAFILE',90,TAPE4
//  EXEC
```

*The System Input and Output Files.* A program that is run under DOS may read from the system input file SYSIPT, which is normally associated with a card reader. The operating system writes records that will be printed on the system output file SYSLST. No special JCL statements are necessary.

## SELF-TEST EXERCISES

8. Write a DTFSD macro instruction for an input sequential file that contains fixed-length logical records of length 80, which are blocked at 20 records per block. Assume move-mode processing.
9. Write the OPEN and CLOSE macro instructions for the file that was described in Self-Test Exercise 8.
10. Write instructions that read a record from the file that was described in Self-Test Exercise 8. Then, by using move-mode processing, write the record on the file that the DTF table at OUT describes.
11. Repeat Self-Test Exercise 10 and use locate-mode processing to write the record.
12. Write a TLBL statement for a file like the one that was described in Self-Test Exercise 8. Assume that the file resides on a magnetic tape.
13. Write a DLBL statement for a file like the one that was described in Self-Test Exercise 8. Assume that the file resides on a magnetic disk.
14. Write a DTF*xx* macro instruction and the necessary JCL to define a temporary sequential disk data set that you will use for output during program execution, but will not retain after execution is complete.

## Processing Sequential Data Sets Using QSAM (OS) and SAM (DOS)

This section illustrates the material presented so far by using simple examples that define and process sequential data sets with QSAM under OS and SAM under DOS. It also defines the extend and update modes that you can use to revise a data set. The first example is written as a complete control section to emphasize that you must follow the standard linkage conventions when you use I/O macros. For the sake of brevity, subsequent examples are written as program segments.

### *Creating, Copying, and Printing Data Sets Using the Move and Locate Modes*

The first three examples involve fixed-length records. In Example 13, you create a sequential disk data set with records that you will read from the system input data set. The example demonstrates move-mode processing for both input and output operations. In Example 14, you print and make a copy of the data set that you created in Example 13. Example 14 demonstrates input in locate mode and output in move mode. In Example 15, you make another copy of the data set by using locate mode for both input and output.

---

EXAMPLE 13

**Read fixed-length unblocked records and create a blocked data set.**

#### Creating a Sequential Data Set Using Move Mode Processing

Assume that each record that is read from the system input data set (SYSIN in OS or SYSIPT in DOS) is 80 bytes long and is unblocked. (Whether these records are blocked or not depends on your computer installation.) The problem is to create a sequential disk data set with blocked records in count-data format. Thus, one of your first tasks is to choose the block size. The block size must be an integral multiple of the logical record length, which is 80 in this case. Suppose that you want a block size that is as large as possible without exceeding 4096 but that wastes little space when several blocks are written on a track. Consider a block size of 4080, which is the largest multiple of 80 that is less than 4096. From the chart for the IBM 3380 that was given in Figure 16.8, you can see that 4080 lies between 4276 and 3860; so ten 4080-byte blocks will fit on a track. Alternatively, you could evaluate

$$1499/(15 + \lceil(B + 12)/32\rceil)$$

for $B$ = 4080. After you discard the fraction, the result is 10. Now 10 $\times$ 4080 = 40,800 bytes, which is 85.94% of the maximum track capacity of 47,476. For 11 blocks per track, Figure 16.8 indicates that the block size should be as close to 3860 as possible. In particular, 3840 is the largest multiple of 80 that does not exceed 3860. One track will accommodate 11 such data blocks for a total of 42,240 bytes, which is 88.97% of the maximum track capacity. By continuing this computation, you will find that this result is the best that you can produce. Although you wanted a maximum block size of 4096, a block size of 3840 provides a more efficient track utilization. You must make a choice; this example uses a compromise value of 4080.

```
** CREATE A SEQUENTIAL DATA SET BY USING MOVE MODE PROCESSING IN QSAM
EX13     CSECT
R12      EQU   12
R13      EQU   13
R14      EQU   14
** STANDARD ENTRY:
         STM   R14,R12,12(R13)
         BALR  R12,0
         USING *,R12
         ST    R13,SAVE+4
         LA    R14,SAVE
         ST    R14,8(R13)
         LR    R13,R14
*
         OPEN  (INFILE,INPUT,OUTFILE,OUTPUT) OPEN DATA SETS
* WHILE NOT END-OF-INFILE:
LOOP     GET   INFILE,RECORD      READ A RECORD FROM SYSIN
         PUT   OUTFILE,RECORD     WRITE THE RECORD
         B     LOOP               REPEAT
* END WHILE
** END-OF-DATA EXIT; CLOSE DATA SETS AND EXIT:
ENDDATA  CLOSE INFILE
         CLOSE OUTFILE
         L     R13,SAVE+4
         LM    R14,R12,12(R13)
         BR    R14
*
INFILE   DCB   DSORG=PS,          PHYSICAL SEQUENTIAL DATA SET         X
               MACRF=GM,          USES GET IN MOVE MODE                X
               DDNAME=SYSIN,      STANDARD INPUT DATA SET              X
               RECFM=F,           FIXED, UNBLOCKED RECORDS             X
               LRECL=80,          LOGICAL RECORD LENGTH                X
               BLKSIZE=80,        BLOCK SIZE                           X
               EODAD=ENDDATA      END-OF-DATA ADDRESS
*
OUTFILE  DCB   DSORG=PS,          PHYSICAL SEQUENTIAL DATA SET         X
               MACRF=PM,          USES PUT IN MOVE MODE                X
               DDNAME=OUTPUT,     DATA SET DEFINED BY DD NAMED OUTPUT  X
               RECFM=FB,          FIXED, BLOCKED RECORDS               X
               LRECL=80,BLKSIZE=4080 LOGICAL RECORD AND BLOCK SIZES
*
RECORD   DS    CL80               WORK AREA
SAVE     DS    18F                SAVE AREA
         END   EX13
/*
//GO.OUTPUT DD UNIT=SYSDA,VOL=SER=ABC002,SPACE=(TRK,(4,1)),
//             DSNAME=MYDATA,DISP=(NEW,CATLG)
//GO.SYSIN  DD *
  (input data set)
/*
```

**Figure 16.18**
The OS version of the instructions that are described in Example 13.

The required instructions for this problem and the required JCL to define the data sets are listed in Figure 16.18 for OS and Figure 16.19 for DOS. In OS, you do not specify the actual output device within the program; instead you make this specification in the JCL. In fact, you could use a magnetic tape here instead of a disk by modifying the JCL, without making a change to the program. However, this is not the case for the DOS program because

```
** CREATE A SEQUENTIAL FILE BY USING MOVE MODE PROCESSING IN SAM
EX13     CSECT
R12      EQU   12
R13      EQU   13
** STANDARD ENTRY:
         BALR  R12,0
         USING *,R12
         LA    R13,SAVE
*
         OPEN  INFILE,OUTFILE     OPEN FILES
* WHILE NOT END-OF-INFILE:
LOOP     GET   INFILE,RECORD      READ A RECORD FROM SYSIPT
         PUT   OUTFILE,RECORD     WRITE THE RECORD TO SYS001
         B     LOOP               REPEAT
* END WHILE
** END-OF-FILE EXIT; CLOSE FILES AND EXIT:
ENDDATA  CLOSE INFILE,OUTFILE
         EOJ   ,                  RETURN TO OPERATING SYSTEM
*
INFILE   DTFCD DEVADDR=SYSIPT,    STANDARD INPUT FILE                 X
               DEVICE=2540,       CARD READER MODEL                   X
               IOAREA1=INBUF1,    INPUT BUFFER                        X
               RECFORM=FIXUNB,    FIXED, UNBLOCKED RECORDS            X
               BLKSIZE=80,        BLOCK SIZE                          X
               TYPEFLE=INPUT,     INPUT FILE                          X
               WORKA=YES,         MOVE MODE                           X
               EOFADDR=ENDDATA    END-OF-FILE ADDRESS
*
OUTFILE  DTFSD DEVADDR=SYS001,    SEQUENTIAL DISK FILE                X
               IOAREA1=OUTBUF1,   OUTPUT BUFFER                       X
               RECFORM=FIXBLK,    FIXED, BLOCKED RECORDS              X
               RECSIZE=80,        LOGICAL RECORD SIZE                 X
               BLKSIZE=4088,      BLOCK SIZE (51 x 80 + 8)            X
               TYPEFLE=OUTPUT,    OUTPUT FILE                         X
               WORKA=YES          MOVE MODE
*
RECORD   DS    CL80               WORK AREA
SAVE     DS    9D                 SAVE AREA
         LTORG ,                  ENSURE LITERAL ADDRESSABILITY
INBUF1   DS    CL80               INPUT BUFFER
OUTBUF1  DS    CL4088             OUTPUT BUFFER
         END   EX13
/*
// EXEC LNKEDT
// DLBL OUTFILE,'MYDATA',50,SD
// EXTENT SYS001,ABC002,1,,60,4
// EXEC
   (input data set)
/*
/&
```

**Figure 16.19**
The DOS version of the instructions that are described in Example 13.

the DTFSD macro specifies a sequential direct-access file. Yet, you can use the DTFDI macro to gain a measure of device independence. For example, you can replace the DTFCD macro instruction in Figure 16.19 by the following:

```
INFILE   DTFDI DEVADDR=SYSIPT,IOAREA1=INBUF1,EOFADDR=ENDDATA
```

You should note two other important aspects of the DOS program: First, the block size of the disk data set is 4088—not 4080—since the operating system requires an 8-byte count field for output sequential disk files. Second, you define input/output buffers within the program. Since these buffers are usually long, define them at the end of the program and precede the definitions by LTORG to ensure that any literals will be addressable (however, there are no literals in this program).

---

EXAMPLE 14

**Copy and print a data set of fixed-length blocked records.**

## Copying and Printing a Sequential Data Set Using Locate Mode for Input and Move Mode for Output

Suppose that you now want to make a backup copy and print a listing of the data set that you created in Example 13. Although printing does not have to involve carriage-control characters, it often does. This example demonstrates this case.

To read the data set in the locate mode, you would write MACRF = GL in the DCB macro instruction in OS, and IOREG instead of WORKA in the

**Figure 16.20**
The OS version of the instructions that are described in Example 14.

```
** COPY AND PRINT A SEQUENTIAL DATA SET BY USING GET-LOCATE
** AND PUT-MOVE PROCESSING IN QSAM.
         OPEN   (INFILE,INPUT,OUTFILE,OUTPUT,PRTFILE,OUTPUT)
* WHILE NOT END-OF-INFILE:
LOOP     GET    INFILE            R1 = INPUT RECORD ADDRESS
         MVC    LINE+1(80),0(R1)  MOVE INPUT RECORD TO PRINT AREA
         PUT    OUTFILE,LINE+1    COPY INPUT RECORD TO NEW FILE
         PUT    PRTFILE,LINE      PRINT INPUT RECORD
         B      LOOP              REPEAT
* END WHILE
** END-OF-DATA EXIT:
ENDDATA  CLOSE  (INFILE,,OUTFILE,,PRTFILE)
         .
         .
         .
INFILE   DCB    DSORG=PS,MACRF=GL,         USES GET IN LOCATE MODE      X
                DDNAME=DATA,RECFM=FB,LRECL=80,BLKSIZE=4080,EODAD=ENDDATA
*
OUTFILE  DCB    DSORG=PS,MACRF=PM,DDNAME=COPY,RECFM=FB,LRECL=80,        X
                BLKSIZE=4080
*
PRTFILE  DCB    DSORG=PS,MACRF=PM,                                      X
                DDNAME=SYSPRINT,           STANDARD OUTPUT FILE         X
                RECFM=FA,                  ANSI CARRIAGE CONTROL        X
                LRECL=81,BLKSIZE=81        INCLUDE CARR. CONTROL IN COUNT
*
LINE     DS     0CL81             PRINT AREA:
         DC     C'0'                CARRIAGE CONTROL
         DS     CL80                DATA AREA
         END    EX14
/*
//GO.DATA   DD  DSNAME=MYDATA,DISP=(OLD,KEEP)
//GO.COPY   DD  UNIT=SYSDA,VOL=SER=ABC003,SPACE=(TRK,(4,1)),
//              DSNAME=BACKUP,DISP=(NEW,KEEP)
//GO.SYSPRINT   DD SYSOUT=A
/*
```

```
** COPY AND PRINT A SEQUENTIAL FILE BY USING GET-LOCATE
** AND PUT-MOVE PROCESSING IN SAM.
         OPEN  INFILE,OUTFILE,PRTFILE  OPEN FILES
* WHILE NOT END-OF-INFILE:
LOOP     GET   INFILE              R2 = INPUT RECORD ADDRESS
         MVC   LINE+1(80),0(R2)    MOVE INPUT RECORD TO PRINT AREA
         PUT   OUTFILE,LINE+1      COPY INPUT RECORD TO NEW FILE
         PUT   PRTFILE,LINE        PRINT INPUT RECORD
         B     LOOP                REPEAT
* END WHILE
** END-OF-FILE EXIT:
ENDDATA  CLOSE INFILE,OUTFILE,PRTFILE  CLOSE FILES
         .
         .
         .
INFILE   DTFSD DEVADDR=SYS001,IOAREA1=INBUF1,IOAREA2=INBUF2,             X
               RECFORM=FIXBLK,RECSIZE=80,BLKSIZE=4080,TYPEFLE=INPUT,     X
               IOREG=(R2),         LOCATE MODE                           X
               EOFADDR=ENDDATA
*
OUTFILE  DTFSD DEVADDR=SYS002,IOAREA1=OUTBUF1,IOAREA2=OUTBUF2,           X
               RECFORM=FIXBLK,RECSIZE=80,BLKSIZE=4088,TYPEFLE=OUTPUT,    X
               WORKA=YES           MOVE MODE
*
PRTFILE  DTFPR DEVADDR=SYSLST,     STANDARD OUTPUT FILE                  X
               DEVICE=3203,IOAREA1=PRTBUF1,IOAREA2=PRTBUF2,              X
               RECFORM=FIXUNB,BLKSIZE=81,WORKA=YES,                      X
               CTLCHAR=ASA         ANSI CARRIAGE CONTROL
*
LINE     DS    0CL81               PRINT AREA:
         DC    C'0'                  CARRIAGE CONTROL
         DS    CL80                  DATA AREA
         LTORG ,                   ENSURE LITERAL ADDRESSABILITY
INBUF1   DS    CL4080              FIRST INPUT BUFFER
INBUF2   DS    CL4080              SECOND INPUT BUFFER
OUTBUF1  DS    CL4088              FIRST OUTPUT BUFFER
OUTBUF2  DS    CL4088              SECOND OUTPUT BUFFER
PRTBUF1  DS    CL81                FIRST PRINT BUFFER
PRTBUF2  DS    CL81                SECOND PRINT BUFFER
         END   EX14
/*
// EXEC LNKEDT
// DLBL INFILE,'MYDATA',50,SD
// DLBL OUTFILE,'BACKUP',50,SD
// EXTENT SYS002,ABC003,1,,190,4
// EXEC
/*
/&
```

**Figure 16.21**
The DOS version of the instructions that are described in Example 14.

DTF*xx* macro instruction in DOS. OS always uses Register 1 to return the address of the next logical record, while DOS uses the register that you specify with the IOREG parameter. (The DOS example uses Register 2.) Look for these aspects in the program segments in Figure 16.20 and Figure 16.21.

To print each record that you read, you must move it to a work area that is preceded by a carriage-control character. In OS, you make this move immediately after the GET because the next PUT destroys Register 1. While

DOS also destroys Register 1, in this example, since Register 2 contains the address of the input record, it is not critical for MVC to precede PUT.

In OS, the instruction

```
PUT    OUTFILE,LINE+1
```

moves the input record to the disk's output buffer. However, if you were not printing the record, you would have no need for the field at LINE. Therefore, you could have copied the record directly from the input buffer by writing instead

```
LR     R2,R1
PUT    OUTFILE,(R2)
```

Similar comments are true in DOS.

---

EXAMPLE 15

## Copying a Sequential Data Set Using Locate Mode for Both Input and Output

Copy a data set of fixed-length blocked records.

The program segments in Figure 16.22 and Figure 16.23 create a duplicate of a given sequential data set by using locate-mode processing. When GET is executed in locate mode, the operating system places the address of the next logical record into a register (Register 1 in OS or the register that IOREG specifies in DOS). In OS, you must save the contents of Register 1 since it will be destroyed by the subsequent locate-mode PUT, which obtains the address of the next available space in the output buffer. However, in DOS, you can specify different registers for GET and PUT so that PUT does not

**Figure 16.22**
The OS version of the instructions that are described in Example 15.

```
** COPY A SEQUENTIAL DATA SET BY USING LOCATE MODE PROCESSING IN QSAM.
         OPEN   (INFILE,INPUT,OUTFILE,OUTPUT)   OPEN DATA SETS
* WHILE NOT END-OF-INFILE:
LOOP     GET    INFILE             R1 = ADDRESS OF NEXT LOGICAL INPUT
*                                       RECORD.
         LR     R2,R1              SAVE IT; R1 WILL BE DESTROYED BY PUT.
         PUT    OUTFILE            R1 = ADDRESS FOR NEXT LOGICAL RECORD IN
*                                       OUTPUT BUFFER.
         MVC    0(80,R1),0(R2)     MOVE RECORD FROM INPUT TO OUTPUT BUFFER
         B      LOOP               REPEAT
* END WHILE
** END-OF-DATA EXIT:
ENDDATA  CLOSE  (INFILE,,OUTFILE)   CLOSE DATA SETS
         .
         .
         .
INFILE   DCB    DSORG=PS,MACRF=GL,DDNAME=DATA,RECFM=FB,LRECL=80,        X
                BLKSIZE=4080,EODAD=ENDDATA                              X
*
OUTFILE  DCB    DSORG=PS,MACRF=PL,DDNAME=COPY,RECFM=FB,LRECL=80,        X
                BLKSIZE=4080
```

```
** COPY A SEQUENTIAL FILE BY USING LOCATE MODE PROCESSING IN SAM.
         OPEN   INFILE,OUTFILE      OPEN FILES
* WHILE NOT END-OF-INFILE:
LOOP     GET    INFILE              R2 = ADDRESS OF NEXT LOGICAL INPUT
*                                        RECORD.
         PUT    OUTFILE             R3 = ADDRESS FOR NEXT LOGICAL RECORD IN
*                                        OUTPUT BUFFER.
         MVC    0(80,R3),0(R2)      MOVE RECORD FROM INPUT TO OUTPUT BUFFER
         B      LOOP                REPEAT
* END WHILE
** END-OF-FILE EXIT:
ENDDATA  CLOSE  INFILE,OUTFILE      CLOSE FILES
         .
         .
         .
INFILE   DTFSD  DEVADDR=SYS001,IOAREA1=INBUF1,IOAREA2=INBUF2,            X
                RECFORM=FIXBLK,RECSIZE=80,BLKSIZE=4080,                  X
                TYPEFLE=INPUT,IOREG=(R2),EOFADDR=ENDDATA
*
OUTFILE  DTFSD  DEVADDR=SYS002,IOAREA1=OUTBUF1,IOAREA2=OUTBUF2,          X
                RECFORM=FIXBLK,RECSIZE=80,BLKSIZE=4088,                  X
                TYPEFLE=OUTPUT,IOREG=(R3)
*
         LTORG  ,                   ENSURE LITERAL ADDRESSABILITY
INBUF1   DS     CL4080              FIRST INPUT BUFFER
INBUF2   DS     CL4080              SECOND INPUT BUFFER
OUTBUF1  DS     CL4088              FIRST OUTPUT BUFFER
OUTBUF2  DS     CL4088              SECOND OUTPUT BUFFER
```

**Figure 16.23**
The DOS version of the instructions that are described in Example 15.

destroy the address that GET obtained. Using these addresses, you can move the input record directly from the input buffer to the output buffer; you do not need to define a work area for the records.

If the input and output disk data sets are the same as the ones in Example 14, then the JCL statements to define them are the same as the ones given in Figure 16.20 and Figure 16.21.

---

The next examples demonstrate how to process data sets that have variable-length records. Recall that such records begin with a 4-byte record descriptor word (RDW) that contains a length field in its first 2 bytes. Before you can write a variable-length record, you must create an RDW. When the operating system reads a variable-length record, it uses the RDW to determine the length of the data. In Example 16, you read fixed-length EBCDIC records from the system input data set, delete the rightmost blanks to obtain variable-length records, and write the results to a disk data set. In Example 17, you print a data set that has variable-length records. Both examples use the move mode to simplify the logic. The program segments in both cases are for OS, but there are comments that note the modifications required for DOS.

EXAMPLE 16

**Creating a Sequential Data Set of Variable-Length Records Using Move Mode Processing**

**Read fixed-length unblocked records and create a blocked data set of variable-length records.**

Each fixed-length record that is read from the system input data set is scanned from the right to determine its rightmost nonblank character. (Assume that no record consists only of blanks.) This character and the ones that precede it in the input record constitute a variable-length data field whose length plus 4 must appear in the first 2 bytes of the RDW of the output record. Since each input record is 80 bytes long, the logical record length of each output record is 84—which is the maximum data length (80) plus the length of the RDW (4). The block size of the output data set includes 4 extra bytes for the block descriptor record; in DOS, the block size includes 8 more bytes for a count field. Figure 16.24 lists the program segment.

---

EXAMPLE 17

**Printing a Sequential Data Set of Variable-Length Records Using Move Mode Processing**

**Read and print variable-length blocked records.**

Suppose that you want to read and print the data set that you created in Example 16. This input data set has blocked variable-length records. To create fixed-length records that you can print, define a work area that is initialized to blanks and that is preceded by a carriage-control character. Move the variable-length data from the input record to this work area prior to printing. The instructions in Figure 16.25 use an EX instruction to perform this move. Since the length in the RDW is 4 more than the length of the data field, subtracting 5 from the RDW results in the length of the data field minus 1, as the EX instruction requires.

---

## *Revising a Sequential Data Set*

Existing data sets seldom remain unchanged; you need to make modifications in order to correct errors or to keep data current. In the airline reservation example described in the introduction of this chapter, both the master flight schedule and the dynamic reservations file require revision at some point. Although the master file requires modification less often than the dynamic file, there is no difference in the nature of the revision process that you should use. In general, a sequential data set may require the following revisions to its logical records:

- Add records to the end of the data set.
- Modify data within a record without changing its length.
- Delete entire records.
- Insert records between existing records.
- Change the length of a record by adding or deleting data within the record.

The first two revisions in this list are special cases that, unlike the other revisions, do not require you to rewrite the data set. Instead, you can use the extend and update modes of processing, which are considered next.

```
** CREATE A SEQUENTIAL DATA SET WITH VARIABLE-LENGTH RECORDS BY USING
** MOVE MODE PROCESSING.  ASSUME INPUT RECORDS ARE NONBLANK.
         OPEN  (INFILE,INPUT,OUTFILE,OUTPUT)  OPEN DATA SETS
*        OPEN  INFILE,OUTFILE    DOS
* WHILE NOT END-OF-INFILE:
LOOP     GET   INFILE,RECORD     GET INPUT RECORD
         LA    R2,RECORD+80      POINT TO BYTE AFTER RECORD
* REMOVE BLANKS FROM RIGHT OF RECORD:
* - WHILE BYTE ON RIGHT IS BLANK:
BLANK    BCTR  R2,0              DECREMENT POINTER
         CLI   0(R2),C' '        DOES BYTE CONTAIN BLANK?
         BE    BLANK             YES; IGNORE IT
* - END WHILE (NONBLANK FOUND)
         S     R2,=A(RDW-1)      LENGTH OF NONBLANK FIELD PLUS 4 (RDW)
         STH   R2,RDW            STORE IN RDW FOR OUTPUT RECORD
         PUT   OUTFILE,RDW       MOVE RECORD TO OUTPUT BUFFER
         B     LOOP              REPEAT FOR ALL RECORDS
* END WHILE
** END-OF-DATA EXIT:
ENDDATA  CLOSE (INFILE,,OUTFILE)   CLOSE DATA SETS
*ENDDATA CLOSE INFILE,OUTFILE      DOS
         .
         .
         .
INFILE   DCB   DSORG=PS,MACRF=GM,DDNAME=SYSIN,RECFM=F,LRECL=80,         X
               BLKSIZE=80,EODAD=ENDDATA
*
OUTFILE  DCB   DSORG=PS,MACRF=PM,DDNAME=OUTPUT,                         X
               RECFM=VB,         VARIABLE BLOCKED RECORDS               X
               LRECL=84,         MAXIMUM DATA LENGTH PLUS 4 FOR RDW     X
               BLKSIZE=4036      48 X 84 + 4 FOR BDW
* DOS DTF'S:
*INFILE  DTFCD DEVADDR=SYSIPT,DEVICE=2540,IOAREA1=INBUF1,               X
               IOAREA2=INBUF2,RECFORM=FIXUNB,BLKSIZE=80,TYPEFLE=INPUT,  X
               WORKA=YES,EOFADDR=ENDDATA
*
*OUTFILE DTFSD DEVADDR=SYS001,IOAREA1=OUTBUF1,IOAREA2=OUTBUF2,          X
               RECFORM=VARBLK,   VARIABLE BLOCKED RECORDS               X
               BLKSIZE=4044,     (48 x 84 + 4 + 8)                      X
               TYPEFLE=OUTPUT,WORKA=YES
*
RDW      DS    H                 RECORD LENGTH
         DC    H'0'              RIGHT HALF OF RDW; ALWAYS ZERO
RECORD   DS    CL80              DATA AREA
*        LTORG ,                 ENSURE ADDRESSABILITY OF LITERALS (DOS)
*INBUF1  DS    CL80              FIRST DOS INPUT BUFFER
*INBUF2  DS    CL80              SECOND DOS INPUT BUFFER
*OUTBUF1 DS    CL4044            FIRST DOS OUTPUT BUFFER
*OUTBUF2 DS    CL4044            SECOND DOS OUTPUT BUFFER
```

**Figure 16.24**
The instructions that are described in Example 16.

The remaining operations are considered in Programming Problems 1 and 2 of this chapter.

**Adding records to the end of a data set**

*The Extend Mode (OS Only).* EXTEND is an option of the OPEN macro in OS. EXTEND allows you to add records to the end of an existing sequential data set. For example, the following instruction opens the data set that is

```
** PRINT A SEQUENTIAL DATA SET OF VARIABLE-LENGTH RECORDS BY USING
** MOVE MODE PROCESSING.
         OPEN  (INFILE,INPUT,PRTFILE,OUTPUT)  OPEN DATA SETS
*        OPEN  INFILE,PRTFILE     DOS
* WHILE NOT END-OF-INFILE:
LOOP     GET   INFILE,RECORD      GET INPUT RECORD
         MVC   LINE+1(80),LINE    CLEAR PRINT AREA
         LH    R2,RDW             R2 = RECORD LENGTH
         SH    R2,=H'5'           R2 = DATA LENGTH LESS 1
         EX    R2,MOVE            MOVE DATA FIELD TO PRINT AREA
         PUT   PRTFILE,LINE       PRINT DATA
         B     LOOP               REPEAT
* END WHILE
*-------------------------------------------------------------
MOVE     MVC   LINE+1(0),DATA     TARGET INSTRUCTION FOR EX
*-------------------------------------------------------------
** END-OF-DATA EXIT:
ENDDATA  CLOSE (INFILE,,PRTFILE)  CLOSE DATA SETS
*ENDDATA CLOSE INFILE,PRTFILE     DOS
         .
         .
         .
INFILE   DCB   DSORG=PS,MACRF=GM,DDNAME=DATA,RECFM=VB,LRECL=84,        X
               BLKSIZE=4036,EODAD=ENDDATA
*
PRTFILE  DCB   DSORG=PS,MACRF=PM,DDNAME=SYSPRINT,RECFM=FA,LRECL=81,    X
               BLKSIZE=81
* DOS DTF'S:
*INFILE  DTFSD DEVADDR=SYS001,IOAREA1=INBUF1,IOAREA2=INBUF2,           X
               RECFORM=VARBLK,BLKSIZE=4036,TYPEFLE=INPUT,              X
               WORKA=YES,EOFADDR=ENDDATA
*
*PRTFILE DTFPR DEVADDR=SYSLST,DEVICE=3203,IOAREA1=PRTBUF1,             X
               IOAREA2=PRTBUF2,RECFORM=FIXUNB,BLKSIZE=81,WORKA=YES,    X
               CTLCHAR=ASA
*
         DS    0H                 ALIGN RDW
RECORD   DS    0CL84              INPUT WORK AREA:
RDW      DS    CL4                  RECORD DESCRIPTOR WORD
DATA     DS    CL80                 DATA AREA
*
LINE     DC    C' '               CARRIAGE CONTROL
         DS    CL80               PRINT AREA
*        LTORG ,                  ENSURE LITERAL ADDRESSABILITY (DOS)
*INBUF1  DS    CL4036             FIRST DOS INPUT BUFFER
*INBUF2  DS    CL4036             SECOND DOS INPUT BUFFER
*PRTBUF1 DS    CL81               FIRST DOS PRINT BUFFER
*PRTBUF2 DS    CL81               SECOND DOS PRINT BUFFER
```

**Figure 16.25**
The instructions that are described in Example 17.

associated with the DCB macro instruction named DATASET in the extend mode:

```
OPEN    (DATASET,EXTEND)
```

As you write records, the operating system adds them to the end of the data set. Except for the OPEN macro instruction, the instructions required to extend a data set are the same as the ones that you use to create it. Records may have either a fixed length or a variable length; processing may use either the move mode or the locate mode.

Extend mode does not exist in DOS. There is no distinction between adding records to the end of a DOS file and inserting records elsewhere in the file: both operations require that you rewrite the file.

**Modifying a record in a data set without changing its length**

*The Update Mode.* The update mode applies only to data sets on direct-access devices. It permits you to read a record, modify it, and rewrite it before you read another record from the data set. Thus, you can change the record in its original position in the data set. When you read a record that does not require change, you simply ignore it and do not rewrite it. Note that you cannot alter the length of a record even if the data set contains variable-length records.

In OS, you open a data set in update mode by specifying UPDAT as the option in the OPEN instruction, as in the following example:

```
OPEN      (DATASET, UPDAT)
```

Use a locate-mode GET to read a record, and PUTX to rewrite it before another GET is executed for the same data set. The DCB macro instruction that describes the data set must contain

MACRF=(GL,PM)

In DOS, you write UPDATE=YES and TYPEFLE=INPUT in the DTF*xx* macro. Use GET and PUT to read and write the records; remember that PUTX does not exist in DOS.

---

EXAMPLE 18

**Updating a Mailing List**

Consider a sequential disk data set of names and addresses with fixed-length logical records in the following form:

| Name (30 characters) | Address (50 characters) |
|---|---|

Now, suppose that you must make a number of address changes. Each change will appear on a record in the system input data set; this record has the same form as the mailing list records. You can use the name on a change record to locate the record that is to be revised in the mailing list. After you locate the address in the mailing list, replace it with the address on the change record. For simplicity, assume that all records are error-free, that change records appear in the same order that the corresponding records in the mailing list appear in, that there is at most one address change per person, that a change is not requested for someone who is not on the mailing list, and that the names on the mailing list are unique. Figure 16.26 lists the required instructions.

```
** SIMPLIFIED MAILING LIST MAINTENANCE PROGRAM
R         EQU    1                    OS
*R        EQU    2                    DOS
          OPEN   (CHANGES,INPUT,MAILIST,UPDAT)  OPEN DATA SETS
*         OPEN   CHANGES,MAILIST      DOS
* WHILE NOT END-OF-CHANGES:
CLOOP     GET    CHANGES,RECORD       GET NEXT CHANGE
* - REPEAT UNTIL RECORD IS LOCATED:
MLOOP     GET    MAILIST              GET NEXT RECORD IN MAILING LIST
          CLC    NAME,0(R)            COMPARE THE TWO NAMES
          BNE    MLOOP                IF UNEQUAL, CONTINUE SEARCH OF LIST
* - END REPEAT (RECORD IS FOUND)
          MVC    30(50,R),ADDRESS IF EQUAL, REPLACE ADDRESS
          PUTX   MAILIST              REWRITE RECORD
*         PUT    MAILIST              DOS
          B      CLOOP                REPEAT FOR NEXT CHANGE
* END WHILE
** END-OF-DATA EXIT:
END       CLOSE  (CHANGES,,MAILIST)   CLOSE DATA SETS
*END      CLOSE  CHANGES,MAILIST      DOS
          .
          .
          .
CHANGES   DCB    DSORG=PS,MACRF=GM,DDNAME=SYSIN,RECFM=F,LRECL=80,          X
                 BLKSIZE=80,EODAD=END
*
MAILIST   DCB    DSORG=PS,MACRF=(GL,PM),DDNAME=LIST,RECFM=FB,LRECL=80,     X
                 BLKSIZE=4080
* DOS DTF'S:
*CHANGES DTFCD DEVADDR=SYSIPT,DEVICE=2540,IOAREA1=CBUF1,IOAREA2=CBUF2,     X
                 RECFORM=FIXUNB,BLKSIZE=80,TYPEFLE=INPUT,WORKA=YES,        X
                 EOFADDR=END
*
*MAILIST DTFSD DEVADDR=SYS001,IOAREA1=MBUF1,IOAREA2=MBUF2,                 X
                 RECFORM=FIXBLK,RECSIZE=80,BLKSIZE=4080,TYPEFLE=INPUT,     X
                 IOREG=(R),UPDATE=YES
RECORD    DS     0CL80                CHANGE RECORD WITH FIELDS AS FOLLOWS:
NAME      DS     CL30                   NAME
ADDRESS   DS     CL50                   ADDRESS
*         LTORG  ,                    ENSURE LITERAL ADDRESSABILITY IN DOS
*CBUF1    DS     CL80                 FIRST CHANGES BUFFER (DOS)
*CBUF2    DS     CL80                 SECOND CHANGES BUFFER (DOS)
*MBUF1    DS     CL4080               FIRST MAILING LIST BUFFER (DOS)
*MBUF2    DS     CL4080               SECOND MAILING LIST BUFFER (DOS)
```

**Figure 16.26**
The instructions that are described in Example 18.

**SELF-TEST EXERCISES**

15. Write the DD statement that is required in OS to define on a magnetic tape the output data set of Example 13 (Figure 16.18).
16. Revise the instructions in Figure 16.19 (Example 13) and write the JCL statements that are required in DOS to define the output data set on a magnetic tape.
17. Revise the instructions in Figure 16.18 or Figure 16.19 (Example 13) to use locate mode processing.
18. Revise the instructions in Figure 16.22 or Figure 16.23 (Example 15) to use move mode for input and locate mode for output.
19. Revise the instructions in Figure 16.26 (Example 18) so that, in addition to updating the mailing list, they print the name and the new address.

## BSAM under OS

There are several differences between the queued and the basic sequential access methods—most notably in the areas of buffering, blocking, and synchronization. This section describes those differences and introduces several of the macros that are available for I/O operations under BSAM.

**You must define buffers or ask the operating system to do so.**

Under QSAM, the operating system automatically defines two buffers for almost all data sets. However, you can request *n* buffers by writing BUFNO=*n* either in the DCB macro or as a subparameter of the DCB keyword of the DD statement. Under BSAM, you must either provide the buffers or specifically request that the operating system allocate them.

**You must perform blocking and deblocking, and initiate reading and writing blocks.**

In addition, the operating system under QSAM performs all blocking and deblocking for you. While automatically reading and writing blocks (physical records), the operating system provides a single record when GET is executed and accepts a single record when PUT is executed. With BSAM, you must perform blocking and deblocking, and initiate the reading and writing of blocks. If you must write or read a short block—a block that contains fewer than the maximum number of records—such as the one that might exist at the end of a data set, you must provide for this special case. For data sets with variable-length blocked (VB) records, you must provide the block descriptor word (BDW).

**You must verify the successful completion of an I/O operation.**

When you use QSAM to perform a read or write operation, the operating system does not return control to your program until the operation is completed successfully. With BSAM, the operating system may return control to your program before the I/O operation is complete. This allows your program to continue execution without delay, but the program must not do anything that depends upon the successful completion of the I/O operation until you verify that successful completion actually has occurred. This process is called **synchronization** and will be demonstrated later in this chapter.

The names and functions of the most important macros that are available for BSAM processing are as follows:

| Name | Function |
|---|---|
| OPEN | Logically connect a data set |
| CLOSE | Logically disconnect a data set |
| READ | Read the next physical record (block) |
| WRITE | Write the next physical record (block) |
| CHECK | Wait for and test the completion of a READ or WRITE |
| DCB | Construct a data control block |
| DCBD | Construct a dummy section that describes a data control block |
| GETBUF | Obtain the address of a buffer from a buffer pool |
| FREEBUF | Return a buffer to the buffer pool |
| FREEPOOL | Free the space acquired for a buffer pool |

The OPEN and CLOSE macros are the same for BSAM as they are for QSAM.

### *The READ Macro*

READ gets the next physical record (block).

The READ macro retrieves the next block from an input data set and places it into storage at a specified location. The READ macro generates a **data event control block (DECB)**, which, among other things, indicates whether or not the input operation was performed successfully. Since the operating system might return control to your program before reading is complete, you must check the DECB by using the CHECK macro to ensure a successful read before you use the block that was read and before you reuse the DECB. The READ macro can be summarized as follows:

| Operation | Operand | Instruction Name | Action |
|---|---|---|---|
| **READ** | *decbname,type,dcbaddress, work area address* | READ NEXT BLOCK | Reads into storage at *work area address* the next block from the data set that the DCB at *dcbaddress* describes; creates a DECB at the address that the symbol *decbname* represents. The *type* is either SF or SB. |

You must write a unique symbol for *decbname* so that READ can assign the symbol as the name of the DECB that it creates. The *type* is almost always SF (sequential forward retrieval), but SB (sequential backward retrieval) is possible for magnetic tape. The *dcbaddress* has the same meaning as for the OPEN macro: it can be an A-type address or a register name, which is in parentheses, that you select from 2 through 12. READ places the input block into storage at the address specified by *work area address*, which has the same form as *dcbaddress*.

---

EXAMPLE 19

The following are examples of READ macro instructions:

| | |
|---|---|
| `READ  D1,SF,INDCB,WORK` | Reads a block from the data set that the DCB at INDCB describes, and places the block into storage at the address WORK. Assigns the name D1 to the DECB. |

| | |
|---|---|
| `READ X,SF,(5),(3)` | Reads a block from the data set that the DCB located at the address in Register 5 describes, and places the block into storage at the address in Register 3. Assigns the name X to the DECB. |

## *The WRITE Macro*

**WRITE writes the next physical record (block).**

The WRITE macro writes onto an output data set a block that is at a specified storage address. You may also use WRITE to return an updated block to a data set that you opened in UPDAT mode. The WRITE macro creates a DECB; since the operating system might return control to your program before writing is complete, you must use the CHECK macro to check the DECB for successful completion of the write operation before you reuse the DECB. The WRITE macro can be summarized as follows:

| Operation | Operand | Instruction Name | Action |
|---|---|---|---|
| **WRITE** | *decbname*,SF,*dcbaddress*, *work area address* | WRITE NEXT BLOCK | Writes the block at *work area address* onto the data set that the DCB at *dcbaddress* describes; creates a DECB at the address that the symbol *decbname* represents. |

Here, *decbname*, *dcbaddress*, and *work area address* are defined as for READ. You always specify SF.

## *The CHECK Macro*

**CHECK waits for a READ or WRITE to finish.**

You use the CHECK macro after a READ or WRITE to test for the completion of the I/O operation. If necessary, CHECK delays execution of your program until the I/O operation is complete. If there are no errors or exceptional conditions that are associated with the I/O operation, then the operating system returns control to the instruction after CHECK. In the absence of a routine to analyze I/O errors, as is assumed here, I/O errors cause your program to terminate. If a READ operation has read all blocks, CHECK branches to the end-of-data address that EODAD in the DCB macro specifies. The CHECK macro can be summarized as follows:

| Operation | Operand | Instruction Name | Action |
|---|---|---|---|
| **CHECK** | *decbaddress* | CHECK COMPLETION OF READ/WRITE | Tests and waits for the completion of the READ/WRITE operation that is associated with the DECB at *decbaddress*. |

Here, *decbaddress* specifies the address of the DECB that the READ or WRITE macro created. You can designate *decbaddress* either as you would designate the operand of an RX instruction or as a register name, which is in parentheses, that you select from 1 through 12. Usually, you designate *decbaddress* by writing the name of the DECB that you wrote in the READ or WRITE macro instruction.

You must write a CHECK macro instruction for each read and write operation. For a particular data set, you must write the CHECK instructions in the same order that the associated READ and WRITE instructions are executed.

### The DCB Macro

You can use the DCB macro in BSAM to construct a data control block in the same way that you would in QSAM. All of the operand entries described earlier for QSAM are valid, except that the options for MACRF are R for READ and W for WRITE. To specify both R and W, write

MACRF=(R,W)

Two other keywords are important for BSAM processing:

NCP=*absolute expression* specifies the maximum number (which must be less than or equal to 99) of READ and WRITE macro instructions that will be executed before the first CHECK instruction is executed. A default value of 1 is assumed if you do not specify NCP.

BUFNO=*absolute expression* specifies the number of buffers that the operating system creates automatically. If you would rather define and control the buffers yourself, you should omit BUFNO.

---

EXAMPLE 20

```
DISK     DCB   DSORG=PS,MACRF=W,DDNAME=DK1,RECFM=FB,LRECL=30,             X
               BLKSIZE=180,BUFNO=2,NCP=2
```

This DCB macro instruction causes the operating system to create two buffers automatically and specifies that two WRITE instructions precede the first CHECK instruction in the program.

---

### The DCBD Macro

**DCBD defines a dummy section to describe a DCB.**

You sometimes will have to access specific fields in a data control block. To facilitate this task, you can use the DCBD macro to generate a dummy section that provides symbolic names for each field in the data control block. Each symbolic name consists of the letters DCB and the appropriate keyword, which is truncated, if necessary, to five letters. For example, DCBBLKSI is the name of the field that contains the block size. The dummy section itself is named IHADCB. For a sequential data set, the DCBD macro instruction is summarized as follows:

| Operation | Operand | Instruction Name | Action |
|---|---|---|---|
| DCBD | DSORG=PS | DEFINE DUMMY SECTION FOR DCB | Defines a dummy control section named IHADCB that you can use to reference a data control block. |

This form of the DCBD macro is valid for both QSAM and BSAM. Write the DCBD macro instruction anywhere that you would place a dummy section.

## *The GETBUF Macro*

**GETBUF gets a buffer.**

If you write the BUFNO keyword in the DCB macro, thereby specifying that the operating system is to create buffers automatically for you, then you must also determine the location of these buffers before you can use the READ and WRITE macros. You use the GETBUF macro to make this determination. GETBUF obtains a buffer from the buffer pool that is associated with the designated data control block, and returns the address of that buffer. The GETBUF macro can be summarized as follows:

| Operation | Operand | Instruction Name | Action |
|---|---|---|---|
| **GETBUF** | *dcbaddress,(register)* | OBTAIN A BUFFER | Obtains a buffer from the buffer pool that is associated with the DCB at *dcbaddress*, and places the buffer address into the register that *register* designates. |

The *dcbaddress* specifies the address of the relevant DCB that contains the address of the buffer pool. You designate *dcbaddress* with either an RX operand or a register name, which is in parentheses, that you select from 1 through 12. GETBUF places the address of the buffer into one of Registers 2 through 12, as *register* designates. If no buffer is available, GETBUF sets the contents of this register to zero. You must write an OPEN instruction before you use GETBUF.

---

EXAMPLE 21

```
GETBUF DCB1,(4)
```

This instruction gets a buffer from the buffer pool that is associated with the DCB at DCB1, and places its address into Register 4.

---

## *The FREEBUF and FREEPOOL Macros*

**Use FREEBUF and FREEPOOL when you are finished using buffers.**

After you use a buffer that you acquired with the GETBUF macro, you can return it to the buffer pool by using the FREEBUF macro, which can be summarized as follows:

| Operation | Operand | Instruction Name | Action |
|---|---|---|---|
| **FREEBUF** | *dcbaddress,(register)* | RETURN BUFFER TO POOL | Returns the buffer whose address is in the register that *register* designates to the buffer pool, which is associated with the DCB at *dcbaddress*. |

The operand entries are the same as for GETBUF, except that the specified register must contain the address of the buffer that will be returned to the buffer pool.

The FREEPOOL macro releases the storage area that was assigned as a buffer pool for a specified DCB. FREEPOOL can be summarized as follows:

| Operation | Operand | Instruction Name | Action |
|---|---|---|---|
| FREEPOOL | *dcbaddress* | RELEASE BUFFER POOL | Releases the storage that the operating system assigned to the buffer pool, which is associated with the DCB at *dcbaddress*. |

You specify *dcbaddress* as you did for FREEBUF.

**SELF-TEST EXERCISE**

20. Write BSAM macro instructions for each of the following tasks:
    - **a.** Read into the storage area at B1 the block from the data set that the DCB at D1 describes.
    - **b.** Write the block at the address that is in Register 8 onto the data set that is described by the DCB whose address is in Register 5.
    - **c.** Test for the completion of the write operation in part **b** just given.
    - **d.** Request the operating system to define three buffers and to load Register 4 with the address of one of them.

## Processing Sequential Data Sets Using BSAM (OS)

The simple examples given in this section demonstrate how you can use the I/O macros with BSAM to create, print, and revise sequential data sets. You will encounter fixed-length records and variable-length records, as well as blocked and unblocked records. The examples also demonstrate how you can handle buffering and synchronization. Each example provides JCL that is appropriate for the execution of the program segment. As in an earlier section of this chapter, the first example is written as a complete control section to emphasize that you must follow the standard linkage conventions when you use I/O macros. For the sake of brevity, subsequent examples are written as program segments.

### *Creating and Printing Data Sets with Unblocked Records*

The first two examples in this section involve data sets with unblocked fixed-length records. In Example 22, you use records from the system input data set to create a sequential disk data set. In Example 23, you print the data set that you created in Example 22. The examples also demonstrate how to use buffers that you define in your program and those buffers that the operating system defines.

EXAMPLE 22

## Creating an Unblocked Sequential Data Set Using Buffers That You Define

**Read fixed-length unblocked records and create an unblocked data set.**

Assume that each record from the system input data set is 80 bytes long and is unblocked. The instructions in Figure 16.27 read these records and write them to a sequential disk data set as unblocked records. To provide your own I/O buffer, define an 80-byte area at BUF, and designate it as an operand in the READ and WRITE macro instructions. Since the output records are unblocked, you can write them as soon as they are read. Therefore, you simply test and wait for the completion of each read and write operation by using a CHECK macro instruction. Note that, by default, the DCB macro instructions imply that NCP = 1.

**Figure 16.27** The instructions that are described in Example 22.

```
** CREATE AN UNBLOCKED SEQUENTIAL DATA SET WITH FIXED-LENGTH
** RECORDS BY USING BSAM.  USE BUFFERS DEFINED IN THE PROGRAM.
EX22     CSECT
R12      EQU   12
R13      EQU   13
R14      EQU   14
** STANDARD ENTRY
         STM   R14,R12,12(R13)
         BALR  R12,0
         USING *,R12
         ST    R13,SAVE+4
         LA    R14,SAVE
         ST    R14,8(R13)
         LR    R13,R14
*
         OPEN  (INFILE,INPUT,OUTFILE,OUTPUT)   OPEN DATA SETS
* WHILE NOT END-OF-INFILE:
LOOP     READ  DECB1,SF,INFILE,BUF        READ INPUT RECORD
         CHECK DECB1                      WAIT FOR READ TO FINISH
         WRITE DECB2,SF,OUTFILE,BUF       WRITE THE RECORD JUST READ
         CHECK DECB2                      WAIT FOR WRITE TO FINISH
         B     LOOP                       REPEAT
* END WHILE
** END-OF-DATA EXIT; CLOSE DATA SETS AND RETURN:
ENDDATA  CLOSE (INFILE,,OUTFILE)          CLOSE DATA SETS
         L     R13,SAVE+4
         LM    R14,R12,12(R13)
         BR    R14
*
INFILE   DCB   DSORG=PS,MACRF=R,DDNAME=SYSIN,RECFM=F,LRECL=80,          X
               BLKSIZE=80,EODAD=ENDDATA
OUTFILE  DCB   DSORG=PS,MACRF=W,DDNAME=DS1,RECFM=F,LRECL=80,BLKSIZE=80
*
BUF      DS    CL80                       BUFFER
SAVE     DS    18F                        SAVE AREA
         END   EX22
/*
//GO.DS1     DD  UNIT=SYSDA,VOL=SER=ABC002,SPACE=(TRK,(1,1)),
//               DSNAME=DATA1,DISP=(NEW,KEEP)
//GO.SYSIN DD    *
   (input data set)
/*
```

EXAMPLE 23

## Printing an Unblocked Sequential Data Set Using Buffers That the Operating System Defines

**Read and print fixed-length unblocked records.**

Suppose that you want to print the data set that you created in Example 22. The instructions in Figure 16.28 print this data set. In addition, they demonstrate how to use the GETBUF, FREEBUF, and FREEPOOL macros to provide buffers, and the CHECK macro to achieve some overlap between the input and output operations.

The two GETBUF macro instructions acquire two buffers from the operating system so that the loop can process two records at a time as follows: You can read two records into separate buffers by writing two READ instructions. The first CHECK instruction waits for the first read operation to finish—at which time, you make a request to print the input record. (Note that this example does not use carriage control.) The second CHECK instruction waits for the second read operation to finish—at which time, you make a request to print that input record. The next two CHECK instructions then wait for printing to finish before allowing the loop to repeat.

When the end of the data set is detected, you can return the buffers to the buffer pool by using the FREEBUF macro, and you can free the buffer pool by using the FREEPOOL macro.

**Figure 16.28**
The instructions that are described in Example 23.

```
** READ AND PRINT AN UNBLOCKED SEQUENTIAL DATA SET WITH FIXED-LENGTH
** RECORDS USING BSAM AND BUFFERS SUPPLIED BY THE OPERATING SYSTEM.
** I/O OPERATIONS OVERLAP AND THE PROGRAM PERFORMS SYNCHRONIZATION.
         OPEN   (DISK,INPUT,PRINT,OUTPUT) OPEN DATA SETS
         GETBUF DISK,(R2)                 R2 = ADDR. OF FIRST BUFFER
         GETBUF DISK,(R3)                 R3 = ADDR. OF SECOND BUFFER
* WHILE NOT END-OF-DISK:
LOOP     READ   DECB1,SF,DISK,(R2)        START FIRST READ
         READ   DECB2,SF,DISK,(R3)        START SECOND READ
         CHECK  DECB1                     WAIT FOR FIRST READ TO FINISH
         WRITE  DECB3,SF,PRINT,(R2)       START FIRST WRITE
         CHECK  DECB2                     WAIT FOR SECOND READ TO FINISH
         WRITE  DECB4,SF,PRINT,(R3)       START SECOND WRITE
         CHECK  DECB3                     WAIT FOR FIRST WRITE TO FINISH
         CHECK  DECB4                     WAIT FOR SECOND WRITE TO FINISH
         B      LOOP                      REPEAT
* END WHILE
** END-OF-DATA EXIT:
ENDDATA  FREEBUF  DISK,(R2)               FREE FIRST BUFFER
         FREEBUF  DISK,(R3)               FREE SECOND BUFFER
         CLOSE    (DISK,,PRINT)           CLOSE DATA SETS
         FREEPOOL DISK                    FREE BUFFER POOL
         .
         .
         .
DISK     DCB    DSORG=PS,MACRF=R,DDNAME=DS2,RECFM=F,LRECL=80,          X
               BLKSIZE=80,EODAD=ENDDATA,BUFNO=2,NCP=2
PRINT    DCB    DSORG=PS,MACRF=W,DDNAME=SYSPRINT,RECFM=F,LRECL=80,     X
               BLKSIZE=80,NCP=2
         END    EX23
/*
//GO.DS2    DD  UNIT=SYSDA,VOL=SER=ABC002,DSNAME=DATA1,DISP=(OLD,KEEP)
//GO.SYSPRINT  DD  SYSOUT=A
/*
```

## *Creating and Printing Data Sets with Blocked Records*

The next three examples use blocked records. Example 24 and Example 25 are similar to Example 22 and Example 23: you use records from the system input data set to create a sequential disk data set with fixed-length blocked records, and then you print the data set that you created. Example 26 creates a data set with variable-length blocked records. All three examples use buffers that you define in your program.

---

EXAMPLE 24

### Create a Blocked Sequential Data Set with Fixed-Length Records

**Read fixed-length unblocked records and create a blocked data set.**

When you use BSAM to create a data set with blocked records, you must form the blocks from the logical records and write each block as you complete it. In addition, you sometimes must write blocks that are shorter than the block size specified in the data control block.

The instructions in Figure 16.29 create a sequential data set that has blocks, each of which contains three 80-byte records. You fill a 240-byte buffer with the next three logical records that are read, and then write the buffer on the data set. When the end of the input data set is detected, you must determine if the buffer is partially full and, if so, you must write it on the data set. Before writing a partially filled buffer, you must alter the block size field in the DCB. You could locate this field by examining the expansion of the DCB macro instruction, but it is more convenient to use the DCBD macro to define a dummy section that describes the data control block. As you learned in Chapter 13, you establish addressability of the dummy section by declaring its name IHADCB to be a base address. You can then use the symbol DCBBKLSI to reference the block size field, which is a halfword, and replace the field with the length of the block.

---

EXAMPLE 25

### Reading and Printing a Blocked Sequential Data Set

**Read and print fixed-length blocked records.**

When you use BSAM to read a blocked sequential data set with fixed-length records, the operating system gives you a block, from which you must obtain the logical records. The data set can contain blocks that consist of fewer than the maximum number of records and, therefore, that are shorter than the block size specified in the DCB. You must detect these short blocks when they are read so that you do not process meaningless bytes at the end of the buffer. To do so, you can examine the **input/output block (IOB)** that is associated with every open data set. The IOB contains information about the processing of the data set, including the difference between the block size and the number of bytes that were actually read. The operating system stores this difference in the halfword that is 14 bytes beyond the IOB address. The IOB address itself is in the fullword that is 16 bytes beyond the beginning of the DECB, which the READ instruction generated. Check the IOB for any block that might be short, including the last block of a data set.

The program segment in Figure 16.30 reads the blocks in a sequential data set that has fixed-length logical records, such as the one that was created in Example 24, and uses the IOB for each block read. The segment prints each record by using the PUT macro of QSAM to demonstrate that you can use both BSAM and QSAM within the same program.

```
** CREATE A BLOCKED SEQUENTIAL DATA SET WITH FIXED-LENGTH RECORDS
** USING BSAM.  THERE ARE 3 RECORDS PER FULL BLOCK.
         OPEN   (INFILE,INPUT,DISK,OUTPUT)  OPEN DATA SETS
* WHILE NOT END-OF-INFILE:
OUTLOOP  LA     R5,3                   R5 = NO. OF RECORDS PER BLOCK
         LA     R4,BUF                 R4 = ADDR. FOR FIRST RECORD IN BLOCK
* - REPEAT 3 TIMES:
INLOOP   READ   DECB1,SF,INFILE,(R4)   READ INPUT RECORD INTO BLOCK
         CHECK  DECB1                  WAIT FOR READ TO FINISH
         LA     R4,80(R4)              R4 = ADDR. FOR NEXT RECORD IN BLOCK
         BCT    R5,INLOOP              DECREMENT R5; REPEAT IF NOT 0
* - END REPEAT
         WRITE  DECB2,SF,DISK,BUF      WRITE A FULL BLOCK
         CHECK  DECB2                  WAIT FOR WRITE TO FINISH
         B      OUTLOOP                REPEAT FOR NEXT BLOCK
* END WHILE
** END-OF-DATA EXIT:
ENDDATA  C      R5,=F'3'               IS CURRENT BLOCK EMPTY?
         BE     DONE                   YES; ALL DONE
         LA     R11,DISK               NO; ESTABLISH ADDRESSABILITY OF
         USING  IHADCB,R11                DUMMY SECTION FOR DCB
         S      R4,=A(BUF)             R4 = LENGTH OF CURRENT SHORT BLOCK
         STH    R4,DCBBLKSI            STORE LENGTH IN BLKSIZE FIELD OF DCB
         WRITE  DECB3,SF,DISK,BUF      WRITE SHORT BLOCK USING NEW LENGTH
         CHECK  DECB3                  WAIT FOR WRITE TO FINISH
DONE     CLOSE  (INFILE,,DISK)         CLOSE DATA SETS
         .
         .
         .
         LTORG
INFILE   DCB    DSORG=PS,MACRF=R,DDNAME=SYSIN,RECFM=F,LRECL=80,          X
                BLKSIZE=80,EODAD=ENDDATA
DISK     DCB    DSORG=PS,MACRF=W,RECFM=FB,LRECL=80,BLKSIZE=240,          X
                DDNAME=DS3
BUF      DS     CL240                  BUFFER (THREE 80-BYTE RECORDS)
         DCBD   DSORG=PS               CREATE DSECT TO DESCRIBE DCB
         END    EX24
/*
//GO.DS3    DD  UNIT=SYSDA,VOL=SER=ABC002,SPACE=(TRK,(1,1)),
//              DSNAME=DATA2,DISP=(NEW,KEEP)
//GO.SYSIN DD   *
    (input data set)
/*
```

**Figure 16.29**
The instructions that are described in Example 24.

---

EXAMPLE 26

**Read fixed-length unblocked records and create a data set with variable-length records.**

**Create a Sequential Data Set with Variable-Length Blocked Records**

When you write variable-length records in BSAM, you must create an RDW for each record in exactly the same way that you do in QSAM. If the data set is blocked, you must also perform the blocking and create a BDW for each block. (Refer back to Figure 16.11 for a picture of variable-length blocked records.)

The program segment in Figure 16.31 creates a blocked sequential data

```
** READ AND PRINT A BLOCKED SEQUENTIAL DATA SET WITH FIXED-LENGTH
** RECORDS.  USE BSAM FOR INPUT AND QSAM FOR OUTPUT.
         OPEN   (DISK,INPUT,PRINT,OUTPUT)  OPEN DATA SETS
* WHILE NOT END-OF-DISK:
OUTLOOP  READ   DECB1,SF,DISK,BUF       READ A RECORD FROM DISK
         CHECK  DECB1                   WAIT FOR READ TO FINISH
         L      R6,DECB1+16             R6 = ADDR. OF IOB
         LA     R5,L'BUF                R5 = BLOCK SIZE
         SH     R5,14(R6)               SUBTRACT NO. OF BYTES NOT READ
*                                       R5 = NO. OF BYTES OF DATA READ
         LA     R2,BUF                  R2 = ADDR. OF BUFFER
         LA     R3,0(R5,R2)             R3 = ADDR. OF FIRST BYTE AFTER DATA
* - REPEAT UNTIL ALL RECORDS IN BLOCK ARE PRINTED:
INLOOP   PUT    PRINT,(R2)              PRINT RECORD
         LA     R2,80(R2)               POINT TO NEXT RECORD IN BUFFER
         CR     R2,R3                   BEYOND LAST RECORD?
         BL     INLOOP                  NO; GO PRINT IT
* - END REPEAT
         B      OUTLOOP                 YES; GET NEXT BLOCK
* END WHILE
** END -OF-DATA EXIT:
ENDDATA  CLOSE  (DISK,,PRINT)           CLOSE DATA SETS
         .
         .
         .
DISK     DCB    DSORG=PS,MACRF=R,DDNAME=DS4,RECFM=FB,LRECL=80,         X
                BLKSIZE=240,EODAD=ENDDATA
PRINT    DCB    DSORG=PS,MACRF=PM,RECFM=F,LRECL=80,BLKSIZE=80,         X
                DDNAME=SYSPRINT
BUF      DS     CL240                   BUFFER (THREE 80-BYTE RECORDS)
         END    EX25
/*
//GO.DS4  DD    UNIT=SYSDA,VOL=SER=ABC002,DSNAME=DATA2,DISP=(OLD,KEEP)
//GO.SYSPRINT DD SYSOUT=A
/*
```

**Figure 16.30**
The instructions that are described in Example 25.

set that has variable-length records, which are derived from the fixed-length records in the system input data set. Although BSAM is used for writing the new data set, this example uses QSAM to read the input data set for the sake of demonstration. You read an 80-byte input record and place it either 8 bytes beyond the beginning of the buffer or 4 bytes beyond the end of the previous record that is already in the buffer. You do this so that you can insert a BDW at the beginning of the block and an RDW before each data record that is read. By examining the input record from the right, you can ignore trailing blanks and determine the end of the data in the record, which is also the end of the resulting variable-length record. With this information, you can compute the length of the new record and store the length into the record's RDW. When the buffer cannot accommodate the next input record, compute the length of the block in the buffer and store it in the BDW at the beginning of the buffer. Then write the block on the output data set. Continue filling the buffer and writing blocks until the GET instruction detects the end of the input data set. At that time, write the last—possibly short—block.

```
** CREATE A SEQUENTIAL DATA SET WITH VARIABLE-LENGTH BLOCKED RECORDS.
** USE QSAM FOR INPUT AND BSAM FOR OUTPUT.
** ASSUME INPUT RECORDS ARE NOT BLANK.
          OPEN   (INFILE,INPUT,OUTFILE,OUTPUT)  OPEN DATA SETS
          LA     R5,L'BUF-4            R5 = BLKSIZE-4 = BLKSIZE MINUS LENGTH
*                                         OF BDW = TOTAL SPACE FOR RECORDS
          LA     R4,BUF+4              R4 = ADDR. FOR FIRST RECORD IN BLOCK
LOOP1     GET    INFILE,4(R4)          READ DATA RECORD LEAVING ROOM FOR RDW
* REMOVE TRAILING BLANKS FROM RECORD:
          LA     R2,84(R4)             R2 = ADDR. AFTER RECORD
BLANK     BCTR   R2,0                  DECREMENT R2
          CLI    0(R2),C' '            BLANK?
          BE     BLANK                 YES; REPEAT
*
          LA     R2,1(R2)              END OF DATA FOUND; R2 = ADDR. OF
*                                        BYTE AFTER NEW RECORD
          SR     R2,R4                 R2 = RECORD LENGTH
          CR     R2,R5                 WILL RECORD FIT IN REST OF BLOCK?
          BNH    LOOP2                 YES; BRANCH AHEAD
NOSPACE   BAL    R6,WRTBLK             NO; GO PRINT CURRENT BLOCK
          EX     R2,MOVE               MOVE NEXT RECORD INTO START OF BUFFER
*                    (EX MOVES 1 EXTRA BYTE)
          B      AROUND                SKIP TARGET INSTRUCTION
MOVE      MVC    BUF+8(0),4(R4)        TARGET FOR EX
AROUND    LA     R5,L'BUF-4            RESET COUNTER
          LA     R4,BUF+4              RESET POINTER
LOOP2     STH    R2,0(R4)              STORE RECORD LENGTH IN RDW
          XC     2(2,R4),2(R4)         ZERO REST OF RDW
          AR     R4,R2                 R4 = ADDR. FOR NEXT RECORD IN BLOCK
          SR     R5,R2                 R5 = NO. OF BYTES REMAINING IN BUFFER
          B      LOOP1                 GO GET ANOTHER INPUT RECORD
** END-OF-DATA EXIT:
ENDDATA   BAL    R6,WRTBLK             WRITE LAST BLOCK
          CLOSE  (INFILE,,OUTFILE)     CLOSE DATA SETS
          B      EXIT                  BRANCH TO STANDARD EXIT
** INTERNAL SUBPROGRAM TO STORE BDW AND TO WRITE BLOCK:
WRTBLK    S      R5,=A(L'BUF)          COMPUTE
          LPR    R5,R5                   LENGTH OF BLOCK
          STH    R5,BUF                STORE LENGTH IN BDW
          XC     BUF+2(2),BUF+2        ZERO REST OF BDW
          WRITE  DECB1,SF,OUTFILE,BUF  WRITE BLOCK
          CHECK  DECB1                 WAIT FOR WRITE TO FINISH
          BR     R6                    RETURN TO PROGRAM
*
EXIT      ----                         STANDARD EXIT
           .
           .
           .
          LTORG
BUF       DS     CL256                 BUFFER (3 x 84 + 4 = 256)
          DS     CL80                  SPACE FOR RECORD READ THAT DOES NOT
*                                        FIT INTO BUFFER
INFILE    DCB    DSORG=PS,MACRF=GM,DDNAME=SYSIN,RECFM=F,LRECL=80,          X
                 BLKSIZE=80,EODAD=ENDDATA
OUTFILE   DCB    DSORG=PS,MACRF=W,DDNAME=DS5,RECFM=VB,LRECL=84,            X
                 BLKSIZE=256
          END    EX26
/*
//GO.DS5     DD  UNIT=SYSDA,VOL=SER=ABC002,SPACE=(TRK,(1,1)),
//               DSNAME=DATA3,DISP=(NEW,KEEP)
//GO.SYSIN DD    *
 (input data set)
/*
```

**Figure 16.31** The instructions that are described in Example 26.

## *Updating a Sequential Data Set*

Use the list form and the execute form of READ and WRITE to update a data set.

In BSAM, as in QSAM, you can specify UPDAT in an OPEN macro instruction whenever you want to modify a record without changing its length. In BSAM, both the READ macro instruction and the WRITE macro instruction must use the same DECB; but each READ and WRITE instruction, in the form that you have seen so far, creates a separate DECB. However, there are two other forms of these instructions: the **list form**, which creates a DECB, but does not read or write; and the **execute form**, which uses a previously created DECB when it performs the I/O operation. You must use both forms so that the READ and WRITE instructions can share one DECB.

The keyword MF specifies the form of the READ and WRITE instructions: you indicate list form by writing MF=L in the operand entry of the READ or WRITE instruction, and execute form by writing MF=E. You must specify *decbaddress* and *type* in both the list form and the execute form of the instructions, but you can specify *dcbaddress* and *work area address* in either form. If you specify *dcbaddress* or *work area address* in both forms, the instructions use the specifications in the execute form. The list forms of READ and WRITE do not generate executable instructions. Therefore, you must position them in your program in the same way that you would position a DCB macro instruction.

---

EXAMPLE 27

Consider updating an unblocked sequential data set that has fixed-length records, such as the one that was created in Example 22. For each record whose first character contains a 1 in its seventh bit, insert the character W into the record's sixth byte. Figure 16.32 lists the required instructions. The list-form READ instruction at the end of the segment creates the DECB,

**Figure 16.32**
The instructions that are described in Example 27.

```
** UPDATE A SEQUENTIAL DATA SET USING BSAM
         OPEN  (DISK,UPDAT)          OPEN DATA SET
* WHILE NOT END-OF-DISK:
LOOP     READ  DECB1,SF,DISK,BUF,MF=E   READ A RECORD
         CHECK DECB1                 WAIT FOR READ TO FINISH
         TM    BUF,X'02'             UPDATE THIS RECORD? (TEST 7TH BIT)
         BZ    LOOP                  NO; GO BACK FOR NEXT RECORD
         MVI   BUF+5,C'W'            YES; PERFORM UPDATE
         WRITE DECB1,SF,DISK,BUF,MF=E   REWRITE UPDATED RECORD
         CHECK DECB1                 WAIT FOR WRITE TO FINISH
         B     LOOP                  REPEAT
* END WHILE
** END-OF-DATA EXIT:
ENDDATA  CLOSE DISK                  CLOSE DATA SET
         .
         .
         .
BUF      DS    CL80                  BUFFER
DISK     DCB   DSORG=PS,MACRF=(R,W),DDNAME=DS6,RECFM=F,LRECL=80,          X
               BLKSIZE=80,EODAD=ENDDATA
         READ  DECB1,SF,DISK,BUF,MF=L   CREATE DECB
         END   EX27
/*
//GO.DS6    DD   UNIT=SYSDA,VOL=SER=ABC002,DSNAME=DATA1,DISP=(OLD,KEEP)
/*
```

and specifies the addresses of the buffer and the associated DCB. Each of the execute-form READ and WRITE instructions in the segment specifies the same DECB as the one that the list-form READ created.

---

**SELF-TEST EXERCISES**

21. Revise the instructions in Figure 16.27 to use two buffers that you define in the program. Perform some overlap of I/O operations.
22. Revise the instructions in Figure 16.28 so that the program, and not the operating system, defines the two buffers.
23. Revise the instructions in Figure 16.30 to use a buffer that the operating system, and not the program, defines.
24. Replace both PUT in Figure 16.30 and GET in Figure 16.31 with appropriate BSAM macro instructions.

## Debugging Hints

1. Failure to open or close a data set is a common error. You must reference each data set with an OPEN macro instruction and a CLOSE macro instruction, and define a DCB in OS or a DTF table in DOS. Establish a check list for each data set, and verify that you have taken all steps and specified all necessary operands in the DCB or DTF*xx* macro instructions.
2. When you read an existing data set, problems can arise if there is a conflict between its block size and the block size that is specified either in the DCB or DTF*xx* macro instructions, or in the JCL. Often, it is good practice to depend upon the data set label for this information and omit it from the program.

## Stylistic Notes

1. If you open or close more than one data set at a particular point in a program, it is more efficient to use one OPEN or CLOSE instruction instead of several. For example, fewer instructions are executed when you use one OPEN instruction to open two data sets than when you use two OPEN instructions.

## Summary

1. Magnetic tapes can only contain sequential data sets. Magnetic disks can contain sequential data sets and other kinds of data sets that take advantage of a disk's direct-access characteristics.
2. Disks and tapes contain blocks of data that are called physical records. Each physical record contains at least one logical record of a fixed or variable length. If a physical record contains several logical records, it is said to be blocked; if it does not, it is said to be unblocked.
3. Large block sizes allow more efficient utilization of the space on a tape or disk. A block size close to, but not exceeding, 4096 is a good choice because of the way that the operating system

allocates storage; but since a track on a disk cannot contain partial blocks, you must also consider the track capacity of the particular device to avoid significantly wasting space.

4. Buffers enable the blocking and deblocking of records. Using buffers also takes advantage of the computer's ability to perform I/O while the user program continues execution.
5. You must open a data set before you can access it, and you must close the data set after you process it. The OPEN and CLOSE macros are available for this purpose.
6. For each data set, you must define either a data control block under OS or a DTF table under DOS by using the DCB and DTF*xx* macros, respectively.
7. With QSAM or SAM, you can use GET and PUT to read and write logical records in move mode or locate mode. In move mode, the operating system moves a record between the buffer and a work area that is specified by the program. In locate mode, the operating system does not move records. Instead, it returns the address of either the next input record or the next available space in the output buffer.
8. With QSAM or SAM, you can use the update mode and either PUTX under OS or PUT under DOS to revise a sequential data set on a direct-access device. Doing this causes the most recent input record to be rewritten in place.
9. With BSAM, you must arrange for buffers, perform blocking and deblocking of records, and be concerned with synchronization. You use the READ and WRITE macros to read and write physical records.
10. With BSAM, you can use the update mode to revise a sequential data set on a direct-access device. You use the execute form of the READ and WRITE macro instructions, which must reference the same DECB. You create this DECB by using a list-form READ or WRITE.

## New Instruction Summary

### I/O Macro Instructions under OS

| Operation | Operand | Instruction Name | Action |
|---|---|---|---|
| **OPEN** | (*dcbaddress*,*option*, . . .) where *option* = INPUT, OUTPUT, EXTEND, or UPDAT | LOGICALLY CONNECT A DATA SET | Opens each data set whose DCB is at *dcbaddress*. |
| **CLOSE** | (*dcbaddress*,[*option*], . . .) | LOGICALLY DISCONNECT A DATA SET | Closes each data set whose DCB is at *dcbaddress*. |
| **GET** | *dcbaddress*[,*work area address*] | READ NEXT LOGICAL RECORD | Obtains the next logical record in the data set that the DCB at *dcbaddress* describes; in move mode, places the record into the work area at the address that *work area address* specifies; in locate mode, places the address of the record into Register 1. |
| **PUT** | *dcbaddress*[,*work area address*] | WRITE NEXT LOGICAL RECORD | Writes the next logical record onto the data set that the DCB at *dcbaddress* describes; in move mode, the record is assumed to be at the address that *work area address* specifies; in locate mode, loads Register 1 with the address of an area within the output buffer. |

| Operation | Operand | Instruction Name | Action |
|---|---|---|---|
| **PUTX** | *dcbaddress* | WRITE RECORD ON AN EXISTING DATA SET | In update mode, rewrites the record just read from an existing data set that the DCB at *dcbaddress* describes. |
| **READ** | *decbname, type, dcbaddress, work area address*[,MF=E\|L] | READ NEXT BLOCK | Reads into storage at *work area address* the next block from the data set that the DCB at *dcbaddress* describes; creates a DECB at the address that the symbol *decbname* represents. *Type* is either SF (sequential forward) or SB (sequential backward). In execute form (MF=E), reads by using the DECB at *decbname*, but does not create a DECB; in list form (MF=L), creates a DECB, but does not read. |
| **WRITE** | *decbname*, SF, *dcbaddress, work area address* [,MF=E\|L] | WRITE NEXT BLOCK | Writes the block at *work area address* onto the data set that the DCB at *dcbaddress* describes; creates a DECB at the address that the symbol *decbname* represents; in execute form (MF=E), writes by using the DECB at *decbname*, but does not create a DECB; in list form (MF=L), creates a DECB, but does not write. |
| **CHECK** | *decbaddress* | CHECK COMPLETION OF READ/WRITE | Tests and waits for the completion of the READ/WRITE operation that is associated with the DECB at *decbaddress*. |
| **DCB** | *keyword=option, . . .* | DEFINE DATA CONTROL BLOCK | Constructs a data control block at the address that the symbol in the name entry represents. |

Some possible keywords are as follows: DSORG= *data set organization*; MACRF= *macro form*; DDNAME= *data definition (DD) name*; RECFM= *record format*; LRECL= *logical record length*; BLKSIZE= *block size*; EODAD= *end-of-data address*; NCP = *number of READ/WRITE instructions before first CHECK*; BUFNO= *number of buffers that the operating system creates.*

| Operation | Operand | Instruction Name | Action |
|---|---|---|---|
| **DCBD** | DSORG=PS | DEFINE DUMMY SECTION FOR DCB | Defines a dummy control section named IHADCB that you can use to reference a data control block. |
| **GETBUF** | *dcbaddress,(register)* | OBTAIN A BUFFER | Obtains a buffer from the buffer pool that is associated with the DCB at *dcbaddress*, |

| Operation | Operand | Instruction Name | Action |
|---|---|---|---|
| | | | and places the buffer address into the register that *register* designates. |
| **FREEBUF** | *dcbaddress*,(*register*) | RETURN BUFFER TO POOL | Returns the buffer whose address is in the register that *register* designates to the buffer pool, which is associated with the DCB at *dcbaddress*. |
| **FREEPOOL** | *dcbaddress* | RELEASE BUFFER POOL | Releases the storage that the operating system assigned to the buffer pool, which is associated with the DCB at *dcbaddress*. |

## I/O Macro Instructions under DOS

| Operation | Operand | Instruction Name | Action |
|---|---|---|---|
| **OPEN** | *dtfaddress*, . . . | LOGICALLY CONNECT A DATA SET | Opens each data set whose DTF table is at *dtfaddress*. |
| **CLOSE** | *dtfaddress*, . . . | LOGICALLY DISCONNECT A DATA SET | Closes each data set whose DTF table is at *dtfaddress*. |
| **GET** | *dtfaddress*[,*work area address*] | READ NEXT LOGICAL RECORD | Obtains the next logical record in the data set that the DTF table at *dtfaddress* describes; in move mode, places the record into the work area at the address that *work area address* specifies; in locate mode, places the address of the record into the register that is specified by the IOREG parameter of the corresponding DTF*xx* macro instruction. |
| **PUT** | *dtfaddress*[,*work area address*] | WRITE NEXT LOGICAL RECORD | Writes the next logical record in the data set that the DTF table at *dtfaddress* describes; in move mode, the record must be at the address that *work area address* specifies; in locate mode, places the address of an area within the output buffer into the register that is specified by the IOREG parameter of the corresponding DTF*xx* macro instruction. |

| Operation | Operand | Instruction Name | Action |
|---|---|---|---|
| **DTFxx** | *keyword = option, . . .* | CONSTRUCT A DTF TABLE | Constructs a DTF table at the address that the symbol in the name entry represents. Some possibilities for DTF*xx* are DTFSD (sequential disk), DTFMT (magnetic tape), DTFPR (printer), DTFCD (card reader), and DTFDI (device independent). |

Some possible keywords are as follows: DEVADDR = *device address*; DEVICE = *device unit number*; IOAREA1 = *first buffer address*; IOAREA2 = *second buffer address*; RECFORM = *record format*; RECSIZE = *logical record size*; BLKSIZE = *block size*; TYPEFLE = *file type*; WORKA = YES move mode; IOREG = (*register*) locate mode; UPDATE = YES update mode; EOFADDR = *end-of-file address*; ERROPT = *error option*; CTLCHR = ASA carriage control (ANSI); FILABL = *file label*.

## Exercises

1. Recompute the data in Figure 16.4. Assume interrecord gaps of 0.6 inches and a recording density of 1600 bpi. Use block sizes that range from 400 to 4800 at intervals of 400 bytes.
2. For each of the following cases, determine the largest block size that does not exceed 4096 for a sequential data set on magnetic tape, assuming an IBM 3420 model 8 tape drive.
   a. Fixed-length unblocked records of length 200.
   b. Fixed-length blocked records of length 200.
   c. Variable-length unblocked records of maximum length 500.
   d. Variable-length blocked records of maximum length 500.
3. Repeat Exercise 2 and assume that the data set is stored on an IBM 3380 magnetic disk storage system.
4. Consider a sequential data set that is stored on an IBM 3380 magnetic disk storage system and that contains a maximum of 8000 fixed-length logical records.
   a. What is the largest block size, not exceeding 4096, that you would use if the logical record length is 80?
   b. How many tracks does this data set require?
   c. Write the SPACE parameter of a DD statement that is necessary for this data set.
5. Repeat Exercise 4 and assume a logical record length of 100.
6. Repeat Exercise 4 and assume a logical record length of 133.
7. Repeat Exercises 4, 5, and 6; assume that the data set contains variable-length records and that the logical record lengths given are maximum lengths.
8. Revise the instructions in Figure 16.14 so that they have the same effect on the input and output buffers but use only Register 1.
9. Write instructions that have the same effect as the ones in Figure 16.16, in which a GET in move mode precedes a PUT in locate mode.
10. What would happen if you used Register 15 as the base register of a subprogram that uses the I/O macros?
11. Write a DCB macro instruction for an output data set whose records will be of variable lengths. Assume that each record contains not more than 100 bytes of data, and that the records are blocked at 40 records per block. Also assume locate-mode processing under QSAM.
12. Repeat Exercise 11, but write a DTF*xx* macro instruction and assume processing under SAM.
13. Repeat Exercise 11 and assume BSAM with 2 buffers that you will define.
14. Write OPEN and CLOSE macro instructions for the data set that was described in Exercise 11 or Exercise 12.
15. Write JCL statements that describe the data set that was defined in Exercise 11 or Exercise 12, and assume that it resides on magnetic tape.
16. Repeat Exercise 15 and assume that the data set resides on magnetic disk.

17. Write instructions that read a record from the sequential data set that the DCB at IN describes. Write the record without trailing blanks on the data set that was described in Exercise 11. Use locate-mode processing under QSAM for both the input operation and the output operation.

18. Write instructions that read a record from the data set that the DTF at IN describes. Write the record without trailing blanks on the data set that was described in Exercise 12. Use locate-mode processing under SAM for both the input operation and the output operation.

19. Repeat either Exercise 17 or Exercise 18, but perform the read by using move-mode processing.

20. Write instructions that read a record from the sequential data set that the DCB at IN describes. Write the record without trailing blanks on the data set that was described in Exercise 13. Use BSAM processing.

## Programming Problems

*You can do each of the following problems by using QSAM, SAM, or BSAM. If you use OS, solve each problem under QSAM and then again under BSAM.*

1. Write subprograms that modify the mailing list data set that was described in Example 18 by deleting or inserting records according to change records of your design, which you read from the system input data set.

2. Create a blocked sequential data set of names and addresses that are available in alphabetic order by name on the system input data set. Represent each name/address pair with two sequential variable-length records. Write subprograms that modify the data set by doing the following:
   - Add a name/address pair to the end of the data set.
   - Correct typographical errors within a record without changing the length of the record.
   - Delete a name/address pair.
   - Insert a name/address pair in its proper order within the data set.
   - Change a person's address, possibly modifying the length of a record.

3. Consider two sequential data sets with fixed-length blocked records. Each record consists of a 25-character string; the records in each data set are in alphabetical order. Merge the two data sets into a third data set that is also in alphabetical order but contains distinct records.

4. Repeat Programming Problem 10 in Chapter 10 to generate a source listing in standard form from another source listing that is on a sequential disk data set in free format. Write the revised listing on another disk data set. Under what circumstances could you use update mode to revise the given data set, instead of creating a new one?

5. Write the subprogram IO that was described in the case study of Chapter 11. Use blocked fixed-length records. Is it possible to change the block size without changing the rest of the program in Figure 11.21?

6. Consider textual data that is in a sequential disk data set. Revise the text according to the commands that are described in Programming Problem 7 of Chapter 11 and that are contained in the system input data set. Assume that the text is too long to reside in its entirety in main storage.

7. Repeat either Programming Problem 8 or Programming Problem 9 of Chapter 11 to create a keyword-in-context index for the titles that are in a sequential tape data set of your design. Write the KWIC index on a sequential disk data set before you print it.

8. Repeat Programming Problem 10 and Programming Problem 11 of Chapter 11, and use sequential disk data sets. Create a data base of course information given input records; these input records are in the system input data set in alphabetical order by course code. Similarly, create a data base of student records, assuming that input records are in order according to ID number. Assuming that the course requests appear on another sequential data set, produce class rosters as described in these problems. Store the rosters on a disk and then print them.

9. Write subprograms to revise the course and student data bases that you created in Programming Problem 8. Your subprograms should change data about a particular course or student, add courses or students, and delete courses or students.

10. Print a listing of courses given the data base that you created in Programming Problem 8. The output should be in a readable format that is suitable for students to use during course registration.

17

# Floating-Point Operations

CONTENTS

## OVERVIEW

The floating-point instructions provide an important alternative to the integer (fixed-point) arithmetic instructions that you already know. Because of the greater range and a choice of precisions, floating-point arithmetic is extremely important for scientific computations. This chapter describes the floating-point instructions that are available on the IBM 370, and demonstrates such issues as precision and rounding that arise when you use these instructions in a program. The chapter also explains how to convert between floating-point, binary integer, and EBCDIC representations.

## OBJECTIVES

After studying this chapter, you should be able to:

1. Represent a given decimal number in short-form, long-form, or extended-form floating-point notation for the IBM System/370.
2. Compute the sum, difference, product, and quotient of any given numbers that are represented by floating-point notation.
3. Describe the results of any floating-point instructions under given conditions.
4. Use the floating-point instructions within a program.
5. Define the exceptions that can occur during the execution of a floating-point instruction, and describe their possible causes.

6. Determine the cause of a particular program interruption within a given program, and suggest a way to prevent it.
7. Write instructions to convert between floating-point numbers and binary integers, and between floating-point numbers and character strings that are suitable for I/O.

## Introduction

There are three general classes of arithmetic instructions that are available on the IBM 370: binary integer, decimal integer, and floating-point. This text has examined binary integer arithmetic that uses the two's complement binary number system, and decimal integer arithmetic that uses packed-decimal numbers. Although the binary arithmetic instructions and the decimal arithmetic instructions operate upon integers, it is possible to assume and keep track of the position of either a decimal point within a packed-decimal number, as has been discussed, or a binary point within a binary number. However, you can avoid the tedious detail that characterizes such *fixed-point arithmetic* by using **floating-point arithmetic**, since the floating-point notation enables the instructions to keep track of the point for you. Furthermore, a much greater range of numbers is possible with floating-point notation than with integer notations; this is one reason why most scientific computations are performed by using floating-point arithmetic. In fact, when Pascal and FORTRAN programs use *real* arithmetic, they are actually using floating-point instructions. Various precisions are also available: the IBM 370 can perform floating-point computations in either single, double, or quadruple precisions. IBM refers to quadruple precision as **extended precision**.

The instructions that use extended-precision operands and an instruction that rounds from double precision to single precision compose the **extended-precision instruction set**. These instructions were not defined for the IBM 360, but are now available as an option. In fact, the remaining floating-point instructions are also optional and do not need to be installed on every System/370 computer. Attempting to execute an unavailable instruction will cause an operation exception. In some operating systems, such an exception causes a branch to a subprogram that simulates the missing instruction, rather than causing the termination of the program. If this is the case with your computer system, you may not even be aware that the floating-point hardware is not installed.

## Floating-Point Numbers

Floating-point representations are similar to scientific notation, in which each decimal number is expressed with a power of 10 multiplier, such as in

$$.12345 \times 10^2$$

and

$$.12345 \times 10^{-3}$$

The fractional portion of the number (the .12345 in this case) is called the **mantissa**, or simply the **fraction**. The fraction is said to be **normalized** when the first digit to the right of the decimal point is nonzero, as in the previous examples. Sometimes you do not need to insist upon normalization. For example, you could write 12.345 in an **unnormalized** form as $.0012345 \times 10^4$. Clearly, the following equality is true:

$$.0012345 \times 10^4 = .12345 \times 10^2$$

As you move the decimal point, you must adjust the exponent of 10 accordingly. Normalization is important in those situations where you can retain only a finite number of digits; for example, when you use computers, you normalize the fractions so that digit positions are not wasted on leading zeros.

The concepts just described are not restricted to decimal numbers. Since the IBM System/370 floating-point representation uses the hexadecimal number system, you will want to write hexadecimal numbers in a scientific notation. For example, you can write $A2F.4_{16}$ as follows†:

$$.A2F4_{16} \times 16^3$$

This is also equal to the following unnormalized form:

$$.0A2F4_{16} \times 16^4$$

You must adjust the exponent of 16 by 1 for each position that you move the hexadecimal point.

### *Conversions between Decimal, Binary, and Hexadecimal Fractions*

While you study floating-point notation, you will find it useful to be able to convert between decimal, binary, and hexadecimal numbers. Chapter 2 discussed these conversions for integers; this section briefly examines the techniques necessary for fractions.

*Decimal to Binary.* You can convert a decimal fraction to another base by performing decimal multiplication by that base repeatedly. To convert a decimal fraction to binary, you first multiply the fraction by 2. You then note the integral portion of the result, which must be either 0 or 1, and multiply the fractional portion of the result by 2. By repeating the process, the integral portions that you note form the bits of the binary equivalent. Continue until the fractional portion is zero—in which case the representation is exact—or until you generate a sufficient number of bits of an infinite fraction. (Notice that finite decimal fractions do not always correspond to a finite fraction in another base, and vice versa.)

†For clarity, the fraction has been written in hexadecimal, but the base and exponent are in decimal. Technically, the entire number should be written in hexadecimal as $.A2F4 \times 10^3$. However, the base of any number system, when written in that number system, is 10, which looks like ten and can get confusing.

---

EXAMPLE 1

**Convert .25 to Binary**

The computation to convert .25 to binary appears as follows:

$$.25 \times 2 = 0.50 \quad 0$$
$$.50 \times 2 = 1.00 \quad 1$$

The result is read from top to bottom

Zeros indicate termination of the process

Therefore, $.25_{10}$ is equal to $.01_2$

EXAMPLE 2

**Convert .3 to Binary**

The computation to convert .3 to binary proceeds as in Example 1, but does not terminate because the binary equivalent of .3 is an infinite fraction, as shown:

| | | |
|---|---|---|
| | $.3 \times 2 = 0.6$ | 0 |
| | $.6 \times 2 = 1.2$ | 1 |
| | $.2 \times 2 = 0.4$ | 0 |
| | $.4 \times 2 = 0.8$ | 0 |
| | $.8 \times 2 = 1.6$ | 1 |
| Repetition begins here | $.6 \times 2 = 1.2$ | 1 |
| | $.2 \times 2 = 0.4$ | 0 |
| | $.4 \times 2 = 0.8$ | 0 |
| | . . . | |

The computations, as well as the generated bits; are repetitive. You should stop as soon as you can determine a pattern in the results. By reading the bits from top to bottom, you obtain the desired binary equivalent, as shown here:

$$.3_{10} = .010011001\ldots_2$$
$$= .0\overline{1001}_2$$

Here, the repeated portion is denoted by overscoring it.

---

*Decimal to Hexadecimal.* You can convert a decimal fraction to hexadecimal by using a process that is analogous to the one just described for conversions to binary. You multiply the fractions by 16, converting the integral portion of each product to hexadecimal and noting the result.

---

EXAMPLE 3

**Convert .640625 to Hexadecimal**

The computation to convert .640625 to hexadecimal is finite and appears as follows:

| | | |
|---|---|---|
| $.640625 \times 16 = 10.25$ | $10 \rightarrow A$ |
| $.25 \times 16 = 4.00$ | $4 \rightarrow 4$ |

The integral portion of each product is converted to hexadecimal; the resulting hex digits are read from top to bottom; thus, $.640625_{10}$ is equal to $.A4_{16}$.

EXAMPLE 4

**Convert .9 to Hexadecimal**

The computation to convert .9 to hexadecimal does not terminate, as shown here:

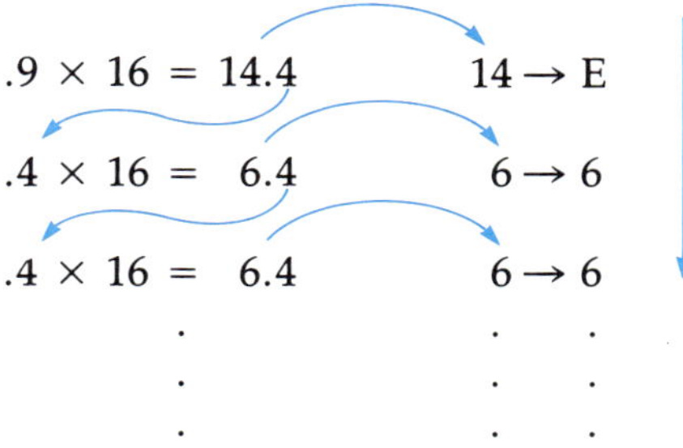


Therefore, $.9_{10}$ is equal to $.E66\ldots_{16}$, or $.E\overline{6}_{16}$.

---

*Conversions between Binary and Hexadecimal.* You can convert between binary and hexadecimal fractions by using the same technique that you used for integers. You convert a hexadecimal fraction to binary by replacing each digit with its 4-bit equivalent. You convert a binary fraction to hexadecimal by forming groups of 4 bits, beginning at the binary point and working to the right. Be sure that the rightmost group contains 4 bits by padding the fraction on the right with zeros, if necessary. You then convert each group to its hexadecimal equivalent as in this example:

$$\begin{aligned} .0100111011_2 &= .\underbrace{0100}_{4}\ \underbrace{1110}_{E}\ \underbrace{1100_2}_{C_{16}} \\ &= .\ 4\ \ E\ \ C_{16} \end{aligned}$$

## *The IBM System/370 Floating-Point Notation*

A floating-point notation must represent the various portions of a number that is written in scientific notation. These portions include the fraction, the exponent, the sign of the fraction, and the sign of the exponent; however, the base of the number system is assumed and does not appear explicitly within the notation. Different computers use various ways to represent these quantities: some computers use the same base to represent the fraction and the exponent; some computers use the same type of number system—such as sign-magnitude or two's complement binary—to represent the fraction and the exponent. Despite such differences, there are conceptual similarities between the various floating-point representations that computers use today. Although this chapter examines only the IBM System/370 notation, after you have learned that notation, it will be much easier to understand the floating-point notation that other computers use.

There are three forms of floating-point numbers.

The System/370 uses a floating-point representation that is in base 16. The fraction is in a sign-magnitude notation, and the exponent and its sign are represented by an *excess notation* to be defined. Three forms of the notation, which are pictured in Figure 17.1, permit three different precisions. **Short-form**, or single-precision, numbers occupy 4 bytes; **long-form**,

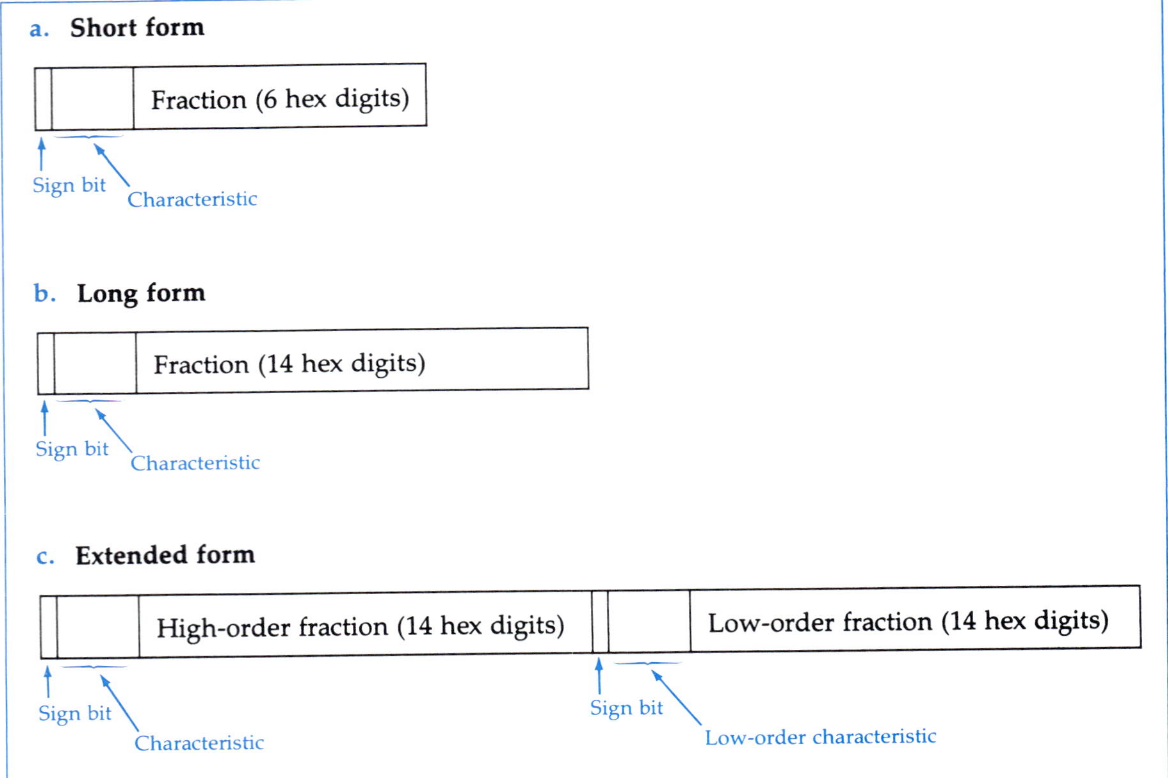


**Figure 17.1**
The three forms of floating-point numbers: **a.** short form; **b.** long form; and, **c.** extended form.

or double-precision, numbers occupy 8 bytes; and **extended-form**, or extended-precision, numbers occupy 16 bytes.

**The characteristic represents the exponent with its sign.**

The first byte of each of these formats is the same. The first bit represents the sign of the number: 0 is plus and 1 is minus. The remaining 7 bits are called the **characteristic** and represent the value of the exponent, including its sign. This 7-bit binary integer can range from 0 to 127 in value, and represents one of 128 signed exponents. To permit approximately the same number of negative exponents as positive ones, 64—which is one-half of 128—was chosen to represent an exponent of zero. Characteristics that are less than 64 represent negative exponents, and characteristics that are greater than 64 represent positive exponents. The following equation relates the characteristic and the exponent:

$$\textit{Characteristic} = 64 + \textit{Exponent}$$

This notation is called an **excess-64 notation**. Characteristics from 0 to 127 represent exponents from $-64$ to $+63$, as indicated in Figure 17.2.

An extended-form number contains a second sign and characteristic in its ninth byte. The sign is the same as the sign of the number and, except when certain program interruptions occur, the characteristic is 14 less than the characteristic in the first byte. This second characteristic is called the **low-order characteristic** since it appears in the second doubleword, or low-order portion, of the number. Although the ninth byte is ignored when you use an extended-form number in an arithmetic operation, an extended-form result will contain a properly computed low-order sign and characteristic.

The fraction of any floating-point number occupies its remaining bytes. In short form, 3 bytes are available; the fraction represents 6 hexadecimal

## THE HISTORY OF FLOATING-POINT NOTATION

Computer designers often make use of mathematical principles that were discovered long ago. One of the oldest is floating-point arithmetic, which is an idea that was developed in ancient Babylon, by one of the earth's first recorded civilizations.

During the eighteenth century B.C., the Babylonians used a base-60 floating-point representation for certain types of computations. However, their notation did not include an exponent. For example, their symbol for five could mean $5 \times 60^2$, or $5 \times 60^{-1}$, or 5 times any other power of 60. When Babylonians saw a floating-point number, they somehow knew how big a number it represented from the number's real-life context.

The concepts that surround floating-point representations did not make a significant appearance again until the 1600s, when logarithms and the slide rule were invented. In 1936, Konrad Zuse, a young German engineer, began to build computing machines that used a binary floating-point arithmetic. His third machine, the Z3, was completed in 1941. It used 22 relays—one relay per bit—to store the fraction, sign, and exponent of 2 for each floating-point number. For example, the decimal number 234 is 11101010, or $1.110101 \times 10^{111}$, in binary. Normalization in this notation meant that every number was written with a 1 before the binary point. To save space, this 1 was not stored since it was identical in all numbers. The Z3 used 7 relays for the exponent, 1 relay for the number's sign (1 meant +), and 14 relays for the portion of the fraction that was to the right of the binary point. Thus, to the Z3, $234_{10}$ was 0000111 1 11010100000000.

The bombs of World War II destroyed the Z3 and its predecessors. Although the war prevented virtually all contact between German and American scientists, George Stibitz, a mathematician at New Jersey's Bell Laboratories, independently designed a floating-point arithmetic at about the same time as Zuse. As a result, the Bell Labs Model V and the Harvard Mark II, both designed in 1944, were the first American computers to use built-in floating-point arithmetic.

Floating-point representation is convenient when you use the wide range of numbers that occur in scientific calculations, in comparison to the more uniform and predictable range of numbers that are used in commercial data processing. Today, computer programmers choose floating-point arithmetic for scientific applications and other notations for business applications. The ancient Babylonians did the same: they used floating-point notation only for complicated mathematics, while they used a separate arithmetic for day-to-day commerce. Zuse and Stibitz might not have known it, but their "new" idea was already 37 centuries old when it made its contribution to computer design.

digits, or approximately 7 decimal digits. In long form, the fraction occupies 7 bytes and contains 14 hexadecimal, or approximately 16 decimal, digits. Since extended-form numbers have 2 characteristics, only 14 bytes are available for the fraction. This fraction represents 28 hexadecimal, or approximately 33 decimal, digits. Fractions can be either normalized or unnormalized. Typically, you should perform floating-point computations with

**Figure 17.2**
Excess-64 characteristics—given in decimal, hexadecimal, and binary—and the exponents that they represent.

| Exponent | Characteristic Decimal | Characteristic Hex | Characteristic Binary |
|---|---|---|---|
| +63 | 127 | 7F | 1111111 |
| +62 | 126 | 7E | 1111110 |
| . | . | . | . |
| . | . | . | . |
| . | . | . | . |
| +2 | 66 | 42 | 1000010 |
| +1 | 65 | 41 | 1000001 |
| 0 | 64 | 40 | 1000000 |
| −1 | 63 | 3F | 0111111 |
| −2 | 62 | 3E | 0111110 |
| . | . | . | . |
| . | . | . | . |
| . | . | . | . |
| −63 | 1 | 01 | 0000001 |
| −64 | 0 | 00 | 0000000 |

normalized operands to maximize accuracy. However, there are some special applications for which you should use unnormalized operands; this chapter presents an example of one later when conversions from floating-point to integer representation are discussed.

---

EXAMPLE 5

Figure 17.3 gives several instances of floating-point numbers. Consider two of these in detail now. The decimal number 12.9 is equivalent to the hexadecimal number C.E66. . . , which you can write in scientific notation as

$$.CE66...{}_{16} \times 16^1$$

Since the number is positive, the sign bit is 0; since the exponent is 1, the characteristic is $1000001_2$. Thus, the first byte of the floating-point representation appears in binary as follows:

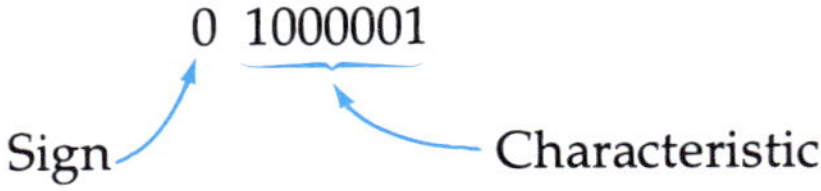


When taken together, the sign and the characteristic are represented by 41 in hexadecimal. The short-form representation for 12.9 then appears in binary and hexadecimal as follows:

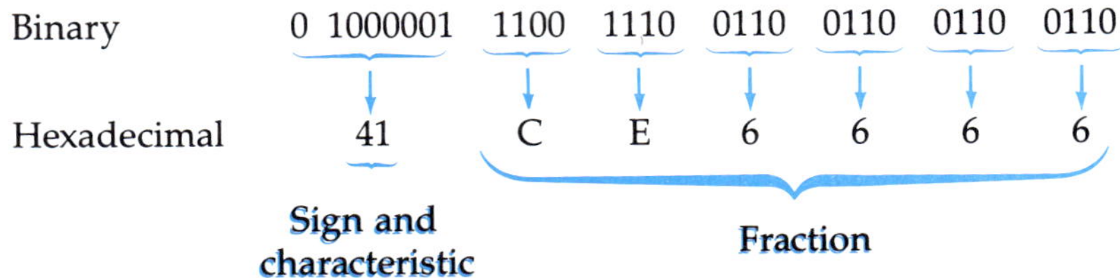


The long-form representation of 12.9 has a first byte that is identical to the first byte of the short-form number, and has a fraction that is 4 bytes longer

| Scientific notation (fraction is in hex) | Floating-Point (Hexadecimal) Short | Long | Extended | Approximate decimal equivalent |
|---|---|---|---|---|
| $0.CE66... \times 16^1$ | 41CE6666 | 41CE6666 66666666 | 41CE6666 66666666 33666666 66666666 | 12.9 |
| $-0.CE66... \times 16^1$ | C1CE6666 | C1CE6666 66666666 | C1CE6666 66666666 B3666666 66666666 | −12.9 |
| $0.1466... \times 16^2$ | 42146666 | 42146666 66666666 | 42146666 66666666 34666666 66666666 | 20.4 |
| $-0.1466... \times 16^2$ | C2146666 | C2146666 66666666 | C2146666 66666666 B4666666 66666666 | −20.4 |
| $0.1999... \times 16^0$ | 40199999 | 40199999 99999999 | 40199999 99999999 32999999 99999999 | 0.1 |
| $-0.1999... \times 16^0$ | C0199999 | C0199999 99999999 | C0199999 99999999 B2999999 99999999 | −0.1 |
| $0.1000000 \times 16^4$ | 44100000 | 44100000 00000000 | 44100000 00000000 36000000 00000000 | 4096. |
| $-0.1000000 \times 16^4$ | C4100000 | C4100000 00000000 | C4100000 00000000 B6000000 00000000 | −4096. |
| $0.CCC... \times 16^{-3}$ | 3DCCCCCC | 3DCCCCCC CCCCCCCC | 3DCCCCCC CCCCCCCC 2FCCCCCC CCCCCCCC | 0.0001953125 |
| $-0.CCC... \times 16^{-3}$ | BDCCCCCC | BDCCCCCC CCCCCCCC | BDCCCCCC CCCCCCCC AFCCCCCC CCCCCCCC | −0.0001953125 |

**Figure 17.3**
Some floating-point numbers.

than the short-form fraction. In hexadecimal, the long-form representation of 12.9 appears as

41 CE6666 66666666

Sign and characteristic — Fraction

The first byte of the extended-form representation of 12.9 is also identical to the first byte of the short-form number. The ninth byte contains both a copy of the sign bit and a low-order characteristic of $0110011_2$, which is 14 less than the number's characteristic, $1000001_2$. In hexadecimal, the extended-form representation appears as

41 CE6666 66666666 33 666666 66666666

Sign and characteristic — High-order fraction — Sign and low-order characteristic — Low-order fraction

The representation of −12.9 is the same as that for 12.9, except that the sign bit is 1 instead of 0. The first byte of the short form, the long form, and the extended form of −12.9 appears in binary as

1 1000001

Sign — Characteristic

or C1 in hexadecimal. The ninth byte of the extended form appears in binary as

or B3 in hexadecimal.

---

Unless the text notes otherwise, assume that floating-point representations in this chapter are in hexadecimal.

## *The Range of Floating-Point Numbers*

The largest positive short-form normalized floating-point number is 7FFFFFFF, which represents $.FFFFFF_{16} \times 16^{63}$, or approximately $.7 \times 10^{76}$ in decimal. The smallest positive short-form normalized floating-point number is 00100000, which represents $.1_{16} \times 16^{-64}$, or approximately $.5 \times 10^{-78}$ in decimal. Thus, the magnitudes of short-form normalized floating-point numbers lie in the approximate range

$.5 \times 10^{-78}$ to $.7 \times 10^{76}$

The order of magnitude of a number that is represented in this floating-point notation depends primarily on its characteristic, so that the ranges for long-form and extended-form numbers are about the same as for short-form numbers. The range of unnormalized numbers differs somewhat from the range of normalized numbers. At the end of this section, Self-Test Exercise 13 considers this range.

**Using base 16 rather than base 2 for a floating-point number system permits a greater range.**

You should understand clearly that this floating-point number system is truly a base-16 number system, since exponents are exponents of 16 and not of 2. Using a hexadecimal number system rather than a binary number system permits a greater range of magnitudes when given a particular exponent size. In this case, the range is approximately $16^{-65}$ to $16^{63}$, instead of $2^{-65}$ to $2^{63}$. You must allocate 3 more bits to the characteristic portion of a base-2 floating-point number to represent the range of numbers that is possible in the hexadecimal system. (Can you show that this is true?)

## *The Precision of Floating-Point Numbers*

**Numbers that are normalized in hexadecimal are not necessarily normalized in binary as well.**

In addition to affecting the range of magnitudes, the choice of base affects the number of significant bits in the fraction of certain normalized numbers. For example, the hexadecimal fraction .199999 is normalized in hexadecimal, but is unnormalized in binary, as shown here:

$$.199999_{16} = .0001\ 1001\ 1001\ 1001\ 1001\ 1001_2$$

Normalized in hex (↑ under the first digit of $.199999_{16}$) — Unnormalized in binary (↑ under the first digit of the binary fraction)

The first 3 bits of the binary representation are wasted because they contain zeros that are just place holders. If you use a binary floating-point notation, these zeros would not exist since normalization would occur in binary. Notice that the 3 bits that are gained in the fraction by using a binary notation are given up to the exponent to increase the range, as was previously noted. The example given here is a worst case: not all fractions begin with 3 bits that are zero. On the average, the base 16 notation allows slightly more precision than a base 2 notation, and permits the characteristic to fit into 1 byte.

It is important to realize that, due to its finite nature, any floating-point number system cannot represent every real number that lies within its range. There are only a finite number of digits in each fraction and, therefore, only a finite number of floating-point numbers within the range. However, within this same range, there are infinitely many real numbers. For example, you have seen that the short-form floating-point representation of 12.9 is 41CE6666. This representation, with its finite fraction, cannot represent 12.9 exactly since .9 is equal to an infinite hexadecimal fraction. Note that 41CE6666 and 41CE6667 are consecutive floating-point numbers, but the hexadecimal numbers CE.6666 and CE.6667, which they represent, have many numbers between them. Two such numbers are CE.66661 and CE.66662 and, therefore, cannot be represented as short-form floating-point numbers.

## *Additional Constant Types for DC and DS: E, D, and L*

You can have the assembler convert decimal numbers into normalized floating-point numbers by using the following constant types either with the DC directive or with a literal:

E (Short form)
D (Long form)
L (Extended form)

You write each constant in base 10 with an optional decimal point, sign, or exponent. The exponent is similar to the exponent that is used in Pascal or FORTRAN to define real constants: you write the exponent as E*n*, where *n* can range from −85 to +75. The assembler aligns short-form constants to a fullword integral boundary; the assembler aligns long-form and extended-form constants to a doubleword integral boundary.

The assembler creates normalized floating-point constants, even if the decimal constants that you write are not normalized. The assembler also rounds the floating-point constant to fit into the space that it reserves. You can define unnormalized constants by writing a **scale modifier** but, since unnormalized constants are rarely used, this chapter will not discuss scale modifiers. You can specify an explicit length modifier, which prevents alignment of the constant to the integral boundaries that were mentioned earlier. Almost in all cases, using an explicit length modifier with floating-point constants is a poor idea.

When used with the DS directive, E reserves a fullword, D reserves a doubleword (as you already know), and L reserves two doublewords. Comments that relate to specified constants and length modifiers are the same as for DC. Figure 17.4 gives examples of E, D, and L constant types in the DC and DS directives.

**Figure 17.4**
Examples of E, D, and L constant types in the DC and DS directives.

| Statement | | Constant defined or storage reserved |
|---|---|---|
| DC | `E'12.9'` | 41CE6666 |
| DC | `D'12.9'` | 41CE6666 66666666 |
| DC | `D'1.29E1'` | 41CE6666 66666666 |
| DC | `L'12.9'` | 41CE6666 66666666 33666666 66666666 |
| DC | `E'.1953125E-3'` | 3DCCCCCD (Note rounding in hex.) |
| DS | E | The next fullword |
| DS | D | The next doubleword |
| DS | L | The next two doublewords |
| DS | 3E | The next three fullwords |

## SELF-TEST EXERCISES

1. Convert the following decimal numbers to binary and to hexadecimal:
   **a.** 0.3
   **b.** 0.75
   **c.** 27.71
   **d.** 16.6
2. Convert the following binary numbers to hexadecimal:
   **a.** 0.0000011000011
   **b.** 11.01
3. Convert the following hexadecimal numbers to binary:
   **a.** A4.10F
   **b.** 0.2C
4. Write the hexadecimal short-form floating-point representations for the following hexadecimal numbers:
   **a.** 0.F98765
   **b.** 100.ABF
   **c.** −AB.CDEF
   **d.** 0.000F160E
   **e.** −0.0000012A
5. Write the hexadecimal long-form floating-point representations for the hexadecimal numbers in parts **d** and **e** of Self-Test Exercise 4.
6. Write the hexadecimal extended-form floating-point representations for the hexadecimal numbers in parts **d** and **e** of Self-Test Exercise 4.
7. Write the hexadecimal short-form floating-point representations for the following decimal numbers. (You converted some of these numbers to hexadecimal in Self-Test Exercise 1.)
   **a.** −0.75
   **b.** 27.71
   **c.** −0.3
   **d.** $0.5 \times 16^{-2}$
   **e.** $-0.004 \times 10^{2}$
8. Repeat Self-Test Exercise 7, but write long-form representations instead.
9. Repeat Self-Test Exercise 7, but write extended-form representations instead.
10. What decimal numbers do the following floating-point numbers represent?
    **a.** 42900000
    **b.** C1180000
    **c.** BF500000
    **d.** 3DC00000
    **e.** 81100000
    (Write your answer to part **e** with a factor that is a power of 16.)
11. What hexadecimal constants are defined when the following are operands of the DC directive?
    **a.** D'−0.26'
    **b.** E'1.19E1'
    **c.** L'10000.E−5'
12. Write the normalized form of the following unnormalized floating-point numbers:
    **a.** 4800002F
    **b.** 830012AB
    **c.** 3000F400
    **d.** B1000ABC
13. What is the approximate range of positive short-form floating-point numbers if normalization is permitted but not required?

## Characteristics of the Instruction Set

There are 52 floating-point instructions. Eight of these instructions compose the extended-precision instruction set, which includes 7 instructions that involve extended-precision computations, and 1 rounding instruction that does not. The remaining floating-point instructions are almost equally divided between short-form and long-form operations.

All but one of the floating-point instructions are in either the RR format or the RX format and, as usual, mnemonics for the RR instructions end in R. All mnemonics utilize the following letters to designate the floating-point form of the operands:

- E for normalized short form.
- D for normalized long form.
- X for normalized extended form.
- U for unnormalized short form.
- W for unnormalized long form†.

**There are four 64-bit floating-point registers.**

Floating-point operations involve four 64-bit floating-point registers that are named 0, 2, 4, and 6. These registers are completely distinct from the general registers, and you cannot use them as index or base registers; index or base registers must be general registers. Since there are general registers with the same names as floating-point registers, it is entirely possible that you will use both types of registers in the same instruction. Therefore, you must be careful when you designate register operands. Although the computer can distinguish various register types by the context in which the register is used, you should choose symbolic register names to differentiate between the register types. For example, you can use the symbols F0, F2, F4, and F6 to denote the floating-point registers.

Only the high-order 32 bits of a floating-point register are used to represent a short-form operand; the rest of the register is ignored and unchanged. Long-form operands use the entire register, and extended-form operands use a pair of registers. These pairs can only be Register 0 and Register 2 (denoted by 0), or Register 4 and Register 6 (denoted by 4). Specifying a register pair by a value other than 0 or 4 will result in an assembly error or a specification exception, as will specifying any floating-point register by a value other than 0, 2, 4, or 6.

In the instruction definitions that follow, *FPR1* denotes a floating-point register that is used as a first operand, and *FPR2* denotes a floating-point register that is used as a second operand. A register pair will be denoted by *FPR1*,*FPR1*+2 or *FPR2*,*FPR2*+2.

## The Load and Store Instructions (LER, LE, LDR, LD, STE, and STD)

The Load and Store instructions transfer data between storage and the floating-point registers. The numbers that are involved are presumed to be floating-point numbers, but there is no check for validity. Indeed, a validity check is not possible since any bit pattern of an appropriate length can have meaning as a floating-point number. Furthermore, the instructions do not distinguish between normalized operands and unnormalized operands.

†"W" (*double U*) is a pun that suggests a double-precision unnormalized operation.

As with all other load and store instructions, the second operand of the floating-point Load instructions and the first operand of the floating-point Store instructions are unchanged, as is the condition code. The instructions can be summarized as follows:

| Operation | Operand | Format | Instruction Name | Action |
|---|---|---|---|---|
| **LER** | *FPR1,FPR2* | RR | LOAD SHORT REGISTER | $C(FPR1)_{0-31} \leftarrow C(FPR2)_{0-31}$ Replaces the high-order 32 bits of the first register operand with a copy of the corresponding bits of the second register operand. The low-order portion of the first register operand is unchanged. |
| **LE** | *FPR1,S2(X2)* or *FPR1,D2(X2,B2)* | RX | LOAD SHORT | $C(FPR1)_{0-31} \leftarrow C(E2)_{0-31}$ Replaces the high-order 32 bits of the first register operand with a copy of the contents of the 4 bytes in storage that are designated as the second operand. The low-order portion of the register operand is unchanged. |
| **LDR** | *FPR1,FPR2* | RR | LOAD DOUBLE REGISTER | $C(FPR1)_{0-63} \leftarrow C(FPR2)_{0-63}$ Replaces the first register operand with a copy of the second register operand. |
| **LD** | *FPR1,S2(X2)* or *FPR1,D2(X2,B2)* | RX | LOAD DOUBLE | $C(FPR1)_{0-63} \leftarrow C(E2)_{0-63}$ Replaces the first register operand with a copy of the contents of the 8 bytes in storage that are designated as the second operand. |
| **STE** | *FPR1,S2(X2)* or *FPR1,D2(X2,B2)* | RX | STORE SHORT | $C(E2)_{0-31} \leftarrow C(FPR1)_{0-31}$ Stores the high-order 32 bits of the first register operand into the 4 bytes at the effective address *E2*. The low-order portion of the register is ignored. |
| **STD** | *FPR1,S2(X2)* or *FPR1,D2(X2,B2)* | RX | STORE DOUBLE | $C(E2)_{0-63} \leftarrow C(FPR1)_{0-63}$ Stores the first register operand into the 8 bytes at the effective address *E2*. |

There are no instructions to load or store extended-precision numbers. You must load or store a pair of registers by using two Load Double or two Store Double instructions.

EXAMPLE 6

```
1        LD    F4,X        F4 = C1CE6666 66666666
2        STE   F4,Z        Z  = C1CE6666
3        LE    F4,Y        F4 = 43100000 66666666
4        LDR   F6,F4       F6 = 43100000 66666666
5        LA    R6,4        R6 = 00000004
6        LE    F6,X(R6)    F6 = 66666666 66666666
         .
         .
         .
    X    DC    D'-12.9'    C1CE6666 66666666
    Y    DC    E'256.'     43100000
    Z    DS    E
```

This sequence of instructions demonstrates the behavior of the floating-point Load and Store instructions. The first instruction loads Floating-Point Register 4 (F4) with the contents of the doubleword at X. The second instruction stores the high-order portion of F4 into the fullword at Z. The third instruction replaces the high-order portion of F4 with the contents of the fullword at Y, but does not affect the low-order portion of F4. The fourth instruction replaces the contents of F6 with the contents of F4. The fifth instruction loads General Register 6 with the integer 4. Finally, the sixth instruction loads the high-order portion of F6 with the contents of the fullword at X+4.

Notice how the choice of symbols distinguishes the floating-point and general registers—particularly in the sixth instruction. The sixth instruction is equivalent to

```
LE    6,X(6)
```

which does not confuse the computer, but is more confusing than the symbolic form to humans.

## SELF-TEST EXERCISE

**14.** What effect does each of these instructions have upon the contents of the following floating-point and general registers and the bytes at X?

Flt. Pt. Reg. 2 = 12345678 9ABCDEF0
Flt. Pt. Reg. 6 = 41F00000 666 66666
Reg. 2 = 00000004
The bytes at X = 3E111111 22222222

**a.** LE 2,X
**b.** LER 2,6
**c.** LD 6,X
**d.** LDR 6,2
**e.** STE 2,X
**f.** STE 2,X(2)
**g.** STD 6,X

## Normalized Addition and Subtraction

The instructions that perform normalized addition and subtraction generate normalized results from operands that are either normalized or unnormalized. This section examines the mathematical details of the addition and subtraction of floating-point numbers, and defines the instructions that perform such arithmetic.

### *The Mechanics of Addition*

The addition of floating-point numbers involves the same steps that are necessary to add numbers in a scientific notation. Consider the following decimal addition in two forms:

An addition in decimal scientific notation

$$\begin{array}{r} 0.100 \times 10^0 \\ +\ 0.204 \times 10^2 \\ \hline \end{array} \quad \text{or} \quad \begin{array}{r} 0.1 \\ +\ 20.4 \\ \hline \end{array}$$

Of course, you must align the decimal points before adding these numbers. To align the decimal points in scientific notation, you shift the fraction of the operand that has the smaller exponent to the right by a number of places equal to the difference between the exponents; you adjust the exponent of that operand accordingly. After the shift, both operands have the same exponent, so you can add them as shown here:

$$\begin{array}{r} 0.001 \times 10^2 \\ +\ 0.204 \times 10^2 \\ \hline 0.205 \times 10^2 \end{array} \qquad \begin{array}{r} 0.1 \\ +\ 20.4 \\ \hline 20.5 \end{array}$$

You can use a similar procedure for hexadecimal numbers.

Now, consider an example that demonstrates the steps that are necessary to add two floating-point numbers. Although this example uses short form operands, the procedures are the same for long and extended operands. Consider the sum of 0.1 + 20.4 again. As you saw in Figure 17.3, the floating-point representations for 0.1 and 20.4 are 40199999 and 42146666, respectively. The following computations are written both in floating-point notation and in scientific notation:

| Floating-point | Scientific Notation |
|---|---|
| 40 199999 | $.199999_{16} \times 16^0$ |
| + 42 146666 | $+\ .146666_{16} \times 16^2$ |

A summary of the necessary steps follows.

*Step 1. Shift the fraction of the operand with the smaller characteristic to the right by* n *hexadecimal places.* Here, *n* is the difference between the characteristics. Internally, each shift of a hexadecimal digit is actually a shift of 4 bits. To help reduce the impact of lost digits that this shift causes, each fraction is temporarily augmented on the right by one hex digit called the **guard digit**. Initially, the guard digits are zero but, if a right shift is necessary, the last hex digit shifted out is retained in the guard digit position. The characteristic of the shifted operand is adjusted accordingly, so that, after the shift, both characteristics are equal. The following illustrates these ideas:

The guard digit retains the last hex digit that is shifted out of the fraction.

Guard digits

$$\begin{array}{rr} 42\ 001999\ 9 & .001999\ 9_{16} \times 16^2 \\ +\ 42\ 146666\ 0 & +\ .146666\ 0_{16} \times 16^2 \\ \hline \end{array}$$

*Step 2. Add the fractions.* Include the guard digits and use the rules for sign-magnitude addition. The sum has both the common characteristic of the operands and the sign of the operand with the larger magnitude. The result is called the **intermediate sum,** which is shown here:

**This intermediate sum is normalized, but some are not.**

Guard digits

$$\begin{array}{rr} 42\ 001999\ 9 & .001999\ 9_{16} \times 16^2 \\ +\ 42\ 146666\ 0 & +\ .146666\ 0_{16} \times 16^2 \\ \hline 42\ 147FFF\ 9 & .147FFF\ 9_{16} \times 16^2 \end{array}$$

*Step 3. Normalize the intermediate sum if necessary.* Drop the guard digit to form the final sum. In the addition above, the intermediate sum is already normalized, so the final sum is simply 42147FFF. Notice that the guard digit is not used to round the result; truncation occurs. Now consider the following addition, in which the intermediate sum is unnormalized:

```
  41 119999
+ C0 199999
-----------
```

You must examine the first byte of each operand in binary to determine the signs and characteristics, as follows:

$41_{16} = 0\ 1000001_2$
$C0_{16} = 1\ 1000000_2$

Signs — Characteristics

Here, the second operand has the smaller characteristic, so its fraction must be shifted to the right. Since the signs differ, the adjusted fractions will be subtracted; as shown here, the difference will be positive because the operand that has the larger magnitude is positive:

**This intermediate sum requires normalization.**

```
                        Guard digits
41 119999  --->    41 119999 0
C0 199999        + C1 019999 9
                 -------------
                   41 0FFFFF 7 ---> 40 FFFFF7
                Intermediate sum    Final sum
```

The intermediate sum is unnormalized, so its fraction with the guard digit is shifted to the left until its leftmost digit is nonzero. The characteristic is decreased by the number of places shifted. The final sum does not contain a guard digit.

Another type of normalization may be necessary instead of the type just described. During the addition of the fractions, a carry may occur out of the leftmost position, as is shown here:

This intermediate sum requires a different type of normalization.

```
                       Guard digits
                              ↓
  43 FFF000        43 FFF000 0
+ 42 116666  →   + 43 011666 6
                 43¹010666 6  → 44 101066
```

To make room for the carry, the fraction is shifted to the right. The characteristic is increased to compensate for this shift, and the guard digit is dropped to form the final sum. Notice that this carry by itself is not an overflow. However, an overflow can only occur in this type of situation, as you will see later.

Normalized addition implies that the sum will be normalized, but it is possible for one or both operands to be unnormalized, as is demonstrated by the following:

Unnormalized operands are possible.

```
                         Guard digits
                              ↓
  42 01F111         42 01F111 0
+ C0 F1119B  →    + C2 00F111 9
                    42 00FFFF 7  → 40 FFFF70
```

This addition also emphasizes the function of the guard digit. As stated previously, only the last digit that is shifted out of an operand is retained in the guard position; in this case, the B is lost. During normalization of the intermediate sum, the fraction is shifted two places to the left. The guard digit and a zero are shifted into the fraction.

It is important to realize that the guard digits only exist during the addition, and are made possible by the floating-point hardware. Guard digits are not part of floating-point numbers; they do not appear in storage or in registers.

**SELF-TEST EXERCISE**

**15.** Perform the following decimal additions using short-form, long-form, and extended-form floating-point representations:

**a.** −20.1 + 0.4

**b.** −22.4 + (−244.1)

**c.** −16.4 + 1.4

## *True Zero*

The sum of two floating-point numbers that have the same magnitudes but opposite signs should be zero, as in the following:

```
       Guard digits
          ↓
  49 100000 0
+ C9 100000 0
  49 000000 0
  Intermediate sum
```

The intermediate sum cannot be normalized because its fraction is zero.

However, consider what happens if 49000000, which has a value of zero, is added to another number, such as 41100000:

```
41 100000  -->  49 000000 0  <-- All significant digits are lost
49 000000       49 000000 0
                -----------
                49 000000 0
```

The digits in the fraction of the given number 41100000 are shifted out and lost. Thus, 49000000 does not behave like a zero, since the addition of zero to a number should not change that number.

What, then, should zero look like? Consider adding 00000000 to a number:

```
41 100000  -->  41 000000 0
00 000000       41 000000 0
                -----------
                41 100000 0  -->  41 100000
```

This example demonstrates that 00000000 behaves as a zero should; 00000000 is called **true zero**. Since the characteristic of true zero cannot exceed that of any other floating-point number, its fraction—and not the fraction of the other operand—will be shifted during an addition.

### *The Normalized Add Instructions (AER, AE, ADR, AD, and AXR)*

The normalized Add instructions perform normalized floating-point addition as just described. The sum replaces the first operand, and the second operand is unchanged. The instructions can be summarized as follows:

| Operation | Operand | Format | Instruction Name | Action |
|---|---|---|---|---|
| **AER** | *FPR1,FPR2* | RR | ADD SHORT REGISTERS | $C(FPR1)_{0-31} \leftarrow C(FPR1)_{0-31} + C(FPR2)_{0-31}$ Adds the short-form floating-point numbers in the high-order portions of the designated registers. The sum replaces the high-order portion of the first register operand; the low-order portion of this register is ignored and unchanged. |
| **AE** | *FPR1,S2(X2)* or *FPR1,D2(X2,B2)* | RX | ADD SHORT | $C(FPR1)_{0-31} \leftarrow C(FPR1)_{0-31} + C(E2)_{0-31}$ Adds the short-form floating-point number in storage that is designated as the second operand to the short-form floating-point number in the high-order portion of the first register operand. The sum replaces the high-order portion of the register; the low-order portion of this register is ignored and unchanged. |

| Operation | Operand | Format | Instruction Name | Action |
|---|---|---|---|---|
| **ADR** | *FPR1,FPR2* | RR | ADD DOUBLE REGISTERS | $C(FPR1)_{0-63} \leftarrow C(FPR1)_{0-63} + C(FPR2)_{0-63}$ Adds the long-form floating-point numbers in the designated registers. The sum replaces the first register operand. |
| **AD** | *FPR1,S2(X2)* or *FPR1,D2(X2,B2)* | RX | ADD DOUBLE | $C(FPR1)_{0-63} \leftarrow C(FPR1)_{0-63} + C(E2)_{0-63}$ Adds the long-form floating-point number in storage that is designated as the second operand to the long-form floating-point number that is the first register operand. The sum replaces the first register operand. |
| **AXR** | *FPR1,FPR2* | RR | ADD EXTENDED REGISTERS | $C(FPR1,FPR1+2) \leftarrow C(FPR1,FPR1+2) + C(FPR2,FPR2+2)$ Adds the extended-form floating-point numbers in the designated register pairs, and replaces the register pair that is designated as the first operand with the sum. Although the low-order characteristic and sign of each operand are ignored, they are defined in the result. |

The condition code is set as follows for all of the normalized Add instructions:

$$\text{Condition Code} = \begin{cases} 0 \text{ if the fraction of the sum is zero} \\ 1 \text{ if the sum is negative} \\ 2 \text{ if the sum is positive} \end{cases}$$

Unlike their binary integer counterparts, these instructions do not set the condition code to 3 in the case of an overflow.

---

EXAMPLE 7

This example compares short-form, long-form, and extended-form additions that use RR instructions. Assume the same register status before the execution of each instruction.

| | Flt. Pt. Reg. 4 | Flt. Pt. Reg. 6 |
|---|---|---|
| Before execution: | 42146666 66666666 | 40122222 22222222 |
| After execution of: | | |
| AER 4,6 | 42147888 66666666 | 40122222 22222222 |
| ADR 4,6 | 42147888 88888888 | 40122222 22222222 |
| AER 4,4 | 4228CCCC 66666666 | 40122222 22222222 |
| ADR 4,4 | 4228CCCC CCCCCCCC | 40122222 22222222 |
| AXR 4,4 | 4228CCCC CCCCCCCC | 34244444 44444444 |

In each case, the condition code is set to 2 because the result is positive.

The AXR instruction ignores the first byte of Register 6 during the addition, but replaces that byte by both the sign and low-order characteristic of the sum. The low-order characteristic is $E_{16}$ less than the characteristic in the first byte of the result.

---

## *Exceptions*

**Addition and subtraction can cause significance exceptions, exponent overflow exceptions, or exponent underflow exceptions.**

Four exceptions that can cause program interruptions are peculiar to floating-point operations. Three of them are relevant to addition and subtraction, and are described in this section. The fourth can occur only during a division, and is described later in this chapter.

**You can mask off significance exceptions.**

*Significance.* A **significance exception** occurs whenever the intermediate sum has a zero fraction and a zero guard digit. You can mask off this exception: if you set the fourth bit of the program mask to 0 by using the SPM instruction, the exception will be ignored and the final sum will be true zero. However, if you set the mask bit to 1, the intermediate sum becomes the final sum and a program interruption takes place. (The interruption code is 000E.)

Significance exceptions prevent the existence of numbers with both zero fractions and nonzero characteristics. In a typical floating-point computation, you should mask off significance exceptions.

---

EXAMPLE 8

```
AE      0,=E'16.0'
```

| | Flt. Pt. Reg. 0 | =E'16.0' |
|---|---|---|
| Before execution: | C2 100000 ???????? | 42 100000 |
| After execution: | 00 000000 ???????? | 42 100000 |
| | *Significance exception (masked off)* | |
| | *Condition code* = 0 | |

The intermediate sum is 42000000 and a significance exception occurs. If the exception is masked off, as is assumed here, the final sum is true zero and the condition code is set to 0.

---

EXAMPLE 9

```
AE      2,=E'1.'
```

| | Flt. Pt. Reg. 2 | =E'1.0' |
|---|---|---|
| Before execution: | 49 100000 ???????? | 41 100000 |
| After execution: | 49 100000 ???????? | 41 100000 |
| | *Condition code* = 2 | |

When the fraction of the second operand is shifted to the right, all significant digits are lost. Therefore, the first operand is unchanged. This is *not* an example of a significance exception.

---

**An exponent overflow exception always causes a program interruption.**

*Exponent Overflow.* Recall that, when there is a carry out of the leftmost digit of the fraction of the intermediate sum, the intermediate characteristic is incremented by one. If the characteristic exceeds its maximum possible value of 127, both an **exponent overflow exception** and a program interruption occur. (The interruption code is 000C.) The final sum has a characteristic that is 128 smaller than it should be—although its fraction and sign are correct. The low-order characteristic of an extended-form result is also correct. Exponent overflow is not recognized if the fraction of the sum is zero; a significance exception will occur instead.

Operand adjustment prior to the actual addition increases the characteristic, but cannot cause an exponent overflow. (Can you explain why this is so?)

---

EXAMPLE 10

```
ADR     6,6
```

| | Flt. Pt. Reg. 6 | |
|---|---|---|
| Before execution: | 7FA00000 00000000 | |
| After execution: | 00140000 00000000 | *Exponent overflow* |

The intermediate sum is

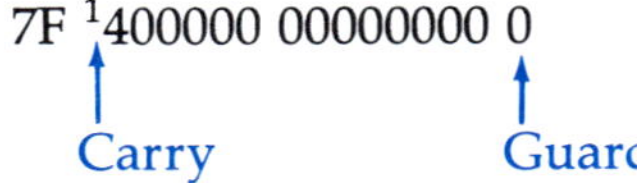


When the fraction is shifted to the right to accommodate the carry, the characteristic is increased by 1, which causes an overflow.

The following demonstrates the same situation with a negative number:

| | | |
|---|---|---|
| Before execution: | FFA00000 00000000 | |
| After execution: | 80140000 00000000 | *Exponent overflow* |

The intermediate sum is

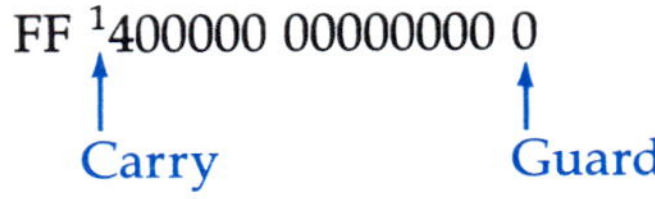


The two examples differ only in sign. Notice that overflow does not affect the sign bit.

---

**You can mask off an exponent underflow exception.**

*Exponent Underflow.* When the intermediate fraction contains leading zeros, the characteristic will be decreased during normalization. If the characteristic falls below zero, which is its minimum possible value, an **exponent underflow exception** occurs. When the third bit of the program mask is 0, this exception is masked off and ignored, and the final result is true zero. When the mask bit is 1, a program interruption occurs (the interruption code is 000D), and the final sum has a characteristic that is 128 larger than it should be—although its fraction and sign are correct. Underflow of a low-order characteristic in an extended-form result is ignored.

Sometimes, a result will be so small that it might as well be zero in subsequent computations. In such cases, you should mask off exponent underflow exceptions.

---

EXAMPLE 11

**ADR 2,6**

| | Flt. Pt. Reg. 2 | Flt. Pt. Reg. 6 |
|---|---|---|
| Before execution: | 00 180000 00000000 | 80 1000000 00000000 |
| After execution: | 7F 800000 00000000 | 80 1000000 00000000 |
| | *Exponent underflow (not masked off)* | |

The intermediate sum is

00 080000 00000000 0
↑
Guard

Normalization causes the characteristic to be decreased by 1, and 7F is the result. If the exception had been masked off, the result would have been true zero.

---

### *The Normalized Subtract Instructions (SER, SE, SDR, SD, and SXR)*

**The normalized Subtract instructions are analogous to the normalized Add instructions.**

The subtract instructions invert the sign of a copy of the second operand and add the result to the first operand. Except for this change of sign, the Subtract instructions are the same as the Add instructions in all other respects.

You can use the RR Subtract instructions to initialize a floating-point register to true zero, just as you used the SR instruction to clear a general register. However, when a floating-point number is subtracted from itself, a significance exception occurs and must be masked off if subtraction is to be a viable approach for register initialization. If masking off the significance exception is inappropriate to the computation that you have planned, then you should initialize registers by using the Load instructions.

The normalized Subtract instructions can be summarized as follows:

| Operation | Operand | Format | Instruction Name | Action |
|---|---|---|---|---|
| **SER** | *FPR1,FPR2* | RR | SUBTRACT SHORT REGISTERS | $C(FPR1)_{0-31} \leftarrow C(FPR1)_{0-31} - C(FPR2)_{0-31}$ |
| **SE** | *FPR1,S2(X2)* or *FPR1,D2(X2,B2)* | RX | SUBTRACT SHORT | $C(FPR1)_{0-31} \leftarrow C(FPR1)_{0-31} - C(E2)_{0-31}$ |
| **SDR** | *FPR1,FPR2* | RR | SUBTRACT DOUBLE REGISTERS | $C(FPR1)_{0-63} \leftarrow C(FPR1)_{0-63} - C(FPR2)_{0-63}$ |

| Operation | Operand | Format | Instruction Name | Action |
|---|---|---|---|---|
| SD | *FPR1,S2(X2)* or *FPR1,D2(X2,B2)* | RX | SUBTRACT DOUBLE | $C(FPR1)_{0-63} \leftarrow C(FPR1)_{0-63} - C(E2)_{0-63}$ |
| SXR | *FPR1,FPR2* | RR | SUBTRACT EXTENDED REGISTERS | $C(FPR1,FPR1+2) \leftarrow C(FPR1,FPR1+2) - C(FPR2,FPR2+2)$ |

The condition code settings for the Subtract instructions are the same as those settings for the Add instructions.

**SELF-TEST EXERCISE**

16. What effect does each of these instructions have upon the condition code, the contents of the following floating-point and general registers, and the bytes at X and Y? Indicate the exceptions, if any, that occur.

```
Flt. Pt. Reg. 0   = 42146666 66666666
Flt. Pt. Reg. 2   = 34666666 66666666
Flt. Pt. Reg. 4   = C3104766 66666666
Flt. Pt. Reg. 6   = FF800000 00000000
The bytes at X = 3D2F0000 FFFFFFFF
The bytes at Y = 00FFFFFF
```

| | | | | | |
|---|---|---|---|---|---|
| **a.** | AE | 0,X | **h.** | SER | 6,6 |
| **b.** | AD | 0,X | **i.** | SD | 0,X |
| **c.** | AER | 0,4 | **j.** | SER | 4,0 |
| **d.** | ADR | 4,0 | **k.** | SDR | 4,0 |
| **e.** | AER | 6,6 | **l.** | SE | 6,Y |
| **f.** | AXR | 0,4 | **m.** | SXR | 0,4 |
| **g.** | SE | 0,X | | | |

# Multiplication, Division, and Halving

There are seven instructions for multiplication that involve short-form, long-form, or extended-form operands. Four instructions perform division of short-form or long-form operands, and one instruction, which is available only with the extended (370-XA) architecture, divides extended-form operands. There are also two Halve instructions that divide a floating-point number by two. All of these instructions operate upon normalized or unnormalized floating-point numbers, but always produce a normalized result.

## *The Multiply Instructions (MER, ME, MDR, MD, MXDR, MXD, and MXR)*

**The Multiply instructions produce normalized products.**

The Multiply instructions first examine their floating-point operands and, if necessary, normalize them. The instructions then multiply the normalized fractions to form the fraction of the intermediate product; the characteristic of the intermediate product is equal to the sum of the operand characteristics minus 64. Since the product's fraction can contain one leading zero, the instructions then normalize the intermediate product, if necessary.

The MER and ME instructions multiply short-form operands and produce an exact long-form product, which replaces the entire first register operand. Each operand fraction contains 6 hex digits, and the product's fraction contains 14 hex digits, of which the rightmost two are zeros.

The MDR and MD instructions multiply long-form operands to form a normalized product, which the instructions then truncate to long form.

The MXDR and MXD instructions multiply long-form operands, and form an exact extended-form product in a pair of floating-point registers. Each operand fraction contains 14 hex digits, and the product fraction contains 28 hex digits.

The MXR instruction uses extended-form operands to compute an extended-form product. Each operand fraction contains 28 hex digits; the instruction normalizes the product fraction and then truncates it to 28-digits. Extended-form products also contain a low-order sign and a low-order characteristic.

The sign of a product is plus either if the product is true zero or if both operands have the same sign; otherwise, the sign is minus. These instructions do not affect the condition code.

The Multiply instructions can be summarized as follows:

| Operation | Operand | Format | Instruction Name | Action |
|---|---|---|---|---|
| **MER** | *FPR1,FPR2* | RR | MULTIPLY SHORT REGISTERS | $C(FPR1)_{0-63} \leftarrow C(FPR1)_{0-31} * C(FPR2)_{0-31}$ Multiplies the short-form floating-point numbers in the high-order portions of the designated registers. The long-form product replaces the entire first register operand. |
| **ME** | *FPR1,S2(X2)* or *FPR1,D2(X2,B2)* | RX | MULTIPLY SHORT | $C(FPR1)_{0-63} \leftarrow C(FPR1)_{0-31} * C(E2)_{0-31}$ Multiplies the short-form floating-point number in storage that is designated as the second operand by the short-form floating-point number in the high-order portion of the first register operand. The long-form product replaces the entire first register operand. |
| **MDR** | *FPR1,FPR2* | RR | MULTIPLY DOUBLE REGISTERS | $C(FPR1)_{0-63} \leftarrow C(FPR1)_{0-63} * C(FPR2)_{0-63}$ Multiplies the long-form floating-point numbers in the designated registers. The long-form product replaces the first register operand. |

| Operation | Operand | Format | Instruction Name | Action |
|---|---|---|---|---|
| MD | *FPR1,S2(X2)* or *FPR1,D2(X2,B2)* | RX | MULTIPLY DOUBLE | $C(FPR1)_{0-63} \leftarrow C(FPR1)_{0-63} * C(E2)_{0-63}$ Multiplies the long-form floating-point number in storage that is designated as the second operand by the long-form floating-point number that is the first register operand. The long-form product replaces the first register operand. |
| MXDR | *FPR1,FPR2* | RR | MULTIPLY EXTENDED FROM DOUBLE REGISTERS | $C(FPR1,FPR1+2) \leftarrow C(FPR1)_{0-63} * C(FPR2)_{0-63}$ Multiplies the long-form floating-point numbers in the designated registers. The extended-form product replaces the contents of the register pair that the first operand entry designates. |
| MXD | *FPR1,S2(X2)* or *FPR1,D2(X2,B2)* | RX | MULTIPLY EXTENDED FROM DOUBLE | $C(FPR1,FPR1+2) \leftarrow C(FPR1)_{0-63} * C(E2)_{0-63}$ Multiplies the long-form floating-point number in storage that is designated as the second operand by the long-form floating-point number that is the first register operand. The extended-form product replaces the contents of the register pair that the first operand entry designates. |
| MXR | *FPR1,FPR2* | RR | MULTIPLY EXTENDED REGISTERS | $C(FPR1,FPR1+2) \leftarrow C(FPR1,FPR1+2) * C(FPR2,FPR2+2)$ Multiplies the extended-form floating-point numbers in the designated register pairs, and replaces the register pair, which the first operand entry designates, with the product. |

EXAMPLE 12

```
ME    4,=E'0.5'
```

| | Flt. Pt. Reg. 4 | =E'0.5' |
|---|---|---|
| Before execution: | C2 155555 ???????? | 40 800000 |
| After execution: | C1 AAAAA8 00000000 | 40 800000 |

EXAMPLE 13

```
MD      4,=D'0.5'
```

| | Flt. Pt. Reg. 4 | =D'0.5' |
|---|---|---|
| Before execution: | C2 155555 55555555 | 40 800000 00000000 |
| After execution: | C1 AAAAAA AAAAAAA8 | 40 800000 00000000 |

EXAMPLE 14

```
MER     0,0
```

| | Flt. Pt. Reg. 0 |
|---|---|
| Before execution: | C0 111111 ???????? |
| After execution: | 3F 123456 54321000 |

Here, the square of the hexadecimal number −0.111111 is +0.0123456 54321.

EXAMPLE 15

```
MDR     0,0
```

| | Flt. Pt. Reg. 0 |
|---|---|
| Before execution: | C0 111111 11111111 |
| After execution: | 3F 123456 789ABCDE |

The square of the hexadecimal number −0.111111 11111111 is +0.0123456 789ABCDE DCBA9876 54321. This result is truncated to fit into Floating-Point Register 0.

EXAMPLE 16

```
MXDR    0,0
```

| | Flt. Pt. Reg. 0 | Flt. Pt. Reg. 2 |
|---|---|---|
| Before execution: | C0 111111 11111111 | ?? ?????? ???????? |
| After execution: | 3F 123456 789ABCDE | 31 DCBA98 76543210 |

Sign and low-order characteristic (the 31 in Flt. Pt. Reg. 2)

The square of the hexadecimal number −0.111111 11111111 was given in Example 15. Here, Floating-Point Register 0 and Floating-Point Register 2 contain the product exactly. The low-order characteristic of the product is $E_{16}$ less than the characteristic in the first byte of the product.

EXAMPLE 17

```
MXR     0,0
```

| | Flt. Pt. Reg. 0 | Flt. Pt. Reg. 2 |
|---|---|---|
| Before execution: | C0 111111 11111111 | B2 111111 11111111 (B2 Ignored) |
| After execution: | 3F 123456 789ABCDF | 31 012345 6789ABCD |

This instruction squares the extended-form number in the register pair 0,2.

*Exceptions.* It is possible to have exponent overflow and exponent underflow exceptions as described earlier for addition. The only difference occurs during an overflow of an extended-form product. Unlike the AXR instruction, the MXDR, MXD, and MXR instructions can generate an overflow in the low-order characteristic of the result—in which case, it becomes 128 too small. Exponent overflows and exponent underflows are more likely to occur during multiplication than during either addition or subtraction.

A significance exception never occurs during a multiplication. If either operand fraction is zero, the product is always true zero.

## *The Divide Instructions (DER, DE, DDR, DD, and DXR)*

**The Divide instructions produce normalized quotients.**

Unlike integer division, a floating-point division results in only a quotient. There is no remainder. The dividend and the divisor are floating-point numbers that you specify as the first operand and the second operand, respectively. Each Divide instruction examines the dividend and divisor, and normalizes them if necessary. The instruction then computes the fraction of the intermediate quotient by dividing the normalized fraction of the first operand by that of the second. The characteristic of the intermediate quotient is equal to 64 plus the difference between the characteristics of the dividend and divisor. The quotient fraction does not contain leading zeros, but the instruction may need to shift it to the right by one hex digit to normalize it. If so, the quotient characteristic is incremented by one.

The sign of the quotient is plus either if the quotient is true zero or if the signs of the operands are the same; otherwise, the sign of the quotient is minus.

The DER and DE instructions divide short-form numbers and produce a short-form quotient. Unlike the instructions MER and ME, DER and DE ignore and do not change the low-order portions of the registers. The DDR and DD instructions divide long-form numbers, and produce a long-form quotient. The DXR instruction, which is available only with the extended architecture, divides extended-form numbers and produces an extended-form quotient. The DXR instruction is in an RRE format: DXR uses 2 bytes for its op code, instead of 1 byte.

The Divide instructions can be summarized as follows:

| Operation | Operand | Format | Instruction Name | Action |
|---|---|---|---|---|
| **DER** | *FPR1,FPR2* | RR | DIVIDE SHORT REGISTERS | $C(FPR1)_{0-31} \leftarrow C(FPR1)_{0-31} \div C(FPR2)_{0-31}$ Divides the short-form floating-point numbers in the high-order portions of the first and second register operands. The short-form quotient replaces the high-order portion of the first register operand. |
| **DE** | *FPR1,S2(X2)* or *FPR1,D2(X2,B2)* | RX | DIVIDE SHORT | $C(FPR1)_{0-31} \leftarrow C(FPR1)_{0-31} \div C(E2)_{0-31}$ Divides the short-form floating-point number in the high-order portion of the first register operand by the short-form floating-point number in storage that is designated as the second operand. The short-form quotient replaces the high-order portion of the first register operand. |
| **DDR** | *FPR1,FPR2* | RR | DIVIDE DOUBLE REGISTERS | $C(FPR1)_{0-63} \leftarrow C(FPR1)_{0-63} \div C(FPR2)_{0-63}$ Divides the long-form floating-point numbers that are the first and second register operands. The long-form quotient replaces the first register operand. |
| **DD** | *FPR1,S2(X2)* or *FPR1,D2(X2,B2)* | RX | DIVIDE DOUBLE | $C(FPR1)_{0-63} \leftarrow C(FPR1)_{0-63} \div C(E2)_{0-63}$ Divides the long-form floating-point number that is the first register operand by the long-form floating-point number in storage that is designated as the second operand. The long-form quotient replaces the first register operand. |
| **DXR** *(370-XA only)* | *FPR1,FPR2* | RRE | DIVIDE EXTENDED REGISTERS | $C(FPR1,FPR1+2) \leftarrow C(FPR1,FPR1+2) \div C(FPR2,FPR2+2)$ Divides the extended-form floating-point numbers in the designated register pairs, and replaces the register pair, which the first operand entry designates, with the quotient. |

EXAMPLE 18

**DER 4,0**

| | Flt. Pt. Reg. 4 | Flt. Pt. Reg. 0 |
|---|---|---|
| Before execution: | C2 155555 ???????? | 41 200000 ???????? |
| After execution: | C1 AAAAA8 ???????? | 41 200000 ???????? |

Compare the results of this instruction with the results of the ME instruction in Example 12, and notice the difference between the low-order portions of the register in each case.

EXAMPLE 19

**DDR 4,0**

| | Flt. Pt. Reg. 4 | Flt. Pt. Reg. 0 |
|---|---|---|
| Before execution: | C2 155555 55555555 | 41 200000 00000000 |
| After execution: | C1 AAAAAA AAAAAAA8 | 41 200000 00000000 |

The results of this instruction are the same as the results of the MD instruction in Example 13.

EXAMPLE 20

**DXR 4,0**

| | Flt. Pt. Reg. 4 | Flt. Pt. Reg. 6 |
|---|---|---|
| Before execution: | C2 155555 55555555 | B4 555555 55555555 |
| | **Flt. Pt. Reg. 0** | **Flt. Pt. Reg. 2** |
| | 41 200000 00000000 | 33 000000 00000000 |

| | Flt. Pt. Reg. 4 | Flt. Pt. Reg. 6 |
|---|---|---|
| After execution: | C1 AAAAAA AAAAAAAA | B3 AAAAAA AAAAAAA8 |
| | **Flt. Pt. Reg. 0** | **Flt. Pt. Reg. 2** |
| | 41 200000 00000000 | 33 000000 00000000 |

*Exceptions.* Exponent overflow exceptions and exponent underflow exceptions—such as those that were described for multiplication—are possible, and are more likely to occur than during an addition or a subtraction. A significance exception cannot occur during a division: if the fraction of the dividend is zero and the fraction of the divisor is nonzero, the quotient is true zero. If the fraction of the divisor is zero, the division does not take place and a **floating-point divide exception**, which causes a program interruption, occurs. (The interruption code is 000F.)

### *The Halve Instructions (HER and HDR)*

The Halve instructions provide a convenient way to divide a floating-point number in half. In fact, they produce results that are identical to the results that the Divide instructions produce with a divisor of two. Each Halve instruction assumes that the short-form or long-form number that will be halved is the second register operand, and replaces the first register operand with the result. HER uses short-form operands; it ignores and does not change the low-order portions of the registers. Thus, HER is not equivalent to multiplication by one-half since no Multiply instruction produces a short-form result. However, HDR uses long-form operands and produces the same result as the MD instruction or the MDR instruction with a multiplier of one-half.

The Halve instructions shift the fraction and the guard digit to the right by one bit. The instructions then normalize the intermediate result, if necessary, and truncate it to the desired length. An exponent underflow exception is possible, but an exponent overflow exception and a significance exception are not.

The Halve instructions can be summarized as follows:

| Operation | Operand | Format | Instruction Name | Action |
|---|---|---|---|---|
| **HER** | *FPR1,FPR2* | RR | HALVE SHORT REGISTER | $C(FPR1)_{0-31} \leftarrow C(FPR2)_{0-31} \div 2$ Replaces the high-order portion of the first register operand with one-half of the short-form number that is designated as the second register operand. |
| **HDR** | *FPR1,FPR2* | RR | HALVE DOUBLE REGISTER | $C(FPR1)_{0-63} \leftarrow C(FPR2)_{0-63} \div 2$ Replaces the contents of the first register operand with one-half of the long-form number that is designated as the second register operand. |

---

EXAMPLE 21

```
HER     4,4
```

| | Flt. Pt. Reg. 4 |
|---|---|
| Before execution: | `C2 155555 ????????` |
| After execution: | `C1 AAAAA8 ????????` |

This instruction produces results that are the same as those of the DER instruction in Example 18. Compare the results with the results of the ME instruction in Example 12, and notice the difference between the low-order portions of the register in each case.

---

## SELF-TEST EXERCISES

**17.** What effect does each of these instructions have upon the contents of the following floating-point registers? Indicate any exceptions that might occur.

Flt. Pt. Reg. 0 = 40 111111 11111111
Flt. Pt. Reg. 2 = 32 111111 11111111
Flt. Pt. Reg. 4 = C1 222222 22222222
Flt. Pt. Reg. 6 = B3 000000 00000000

| | | | | | |
|---|---|---|---|---|---|
| **a.** | ME | 4,=E'.25' | **e.** | MXDR | 4,0 |
| **b.** | MD | 4,=D'-.25' | **f.** | MXD | 4,=D'.25' |
| **c.** | MER | 0,4 | **g.** | MXD | 4,=D'0' |
| **d.** | MDR | 4,0 | **h.** | MXR | 0,4 |

**18.** What effect does each of these instructions have upon the contents of the following floating-point registers? Indicate any exceptions that might occur.

Flt. Pt. Reg. 0 = 41 400000 00000000
Flt. Pt. Reg. 2 = 32 000000 00000000
Flt. Pt. Reg. 4 = C1 222222 22222222
Flt. Pt. Reg. 6 = B3 000000 00000000

| | | | | | |
|---|---|---|---|---|---|
| **a.** | DE | 4,=E'4' | **e.** | DER | 4,0 |
| **b.** | DD | 4,=D'-4' | **f.** | DXR | 4,0 |
| **c.** | DD | 4,=D'0' | **g.** | HER | 6,4 |
| **d.** | DDR | 6,4 | **h.** | HDR | 6,4 |

---

EXAMPLE 22

```
HDR      4,6
```

| | Flt. Pt. Reg. 4 | Flt. Pt. Reg. 6 |
|---|---|---|
| Before execution: | ?? ?????? ???????? | C2 155555 55555555 |
| After execution: | C1 AAAAAA AAAAAAA8 | C2 155555 55555555 |

This instruction produces results that are the same as those of the DDR instruction in Example 19 and the MD instruction in Example 13.

---

You can double the floating-point number in a register or register pair by using either AER, ADR, or AXR.

## Rounding: the LRER and LRDR Instructions

**The Rounding instructions are the only instructions that round floating-point numbers.**

Generally it is better to round, rather than to truncate, the results of a computation—particularly when the computation is long or sensitive to error accumulation. Even so, the intermediate results of the floating-point arithmetic instructions that have been presented so far are truncated instead of rounded when there are more digits than required for the final form.

The Load Rounded instructions, LRER and LRDR, provide the only hardware rounding that is available for floating-point numbers. Both instructions are part of the extended-precision instruction set and, therefore, are not available on all models of the System/370.

LRER rounds its long-form second operand to a short form, and places the result into the high-order portion of the first register operand. LRDR rounds the extended-form number in the register pair that is designated as the second operand to a long form, which replaces the first register operand. These instructions can be summarized as follows:

| Operation | Operand | Format | Instruction Name | Action |
|---|---|---|---|---|
| **LRER** | *FPR1,FPR2* | RR | LOAD ROUNDED SHORT REGISTER | $C(FPR1)_{0-31} \leftarrow C(FPR2)_{0-63}$ rounded |
| **LRDR** | *FPR1,FPR2* | RR | LOAD ROUNDED DOUBLE REGISTER | $C(FPR1)_{0-63} \leftarrow C(FPR2,FPR2+2)_{0-127}$ rounded |

The instructions perform rounding by adding 8 to the first hexadecimal digit of the low-order portion of the second operand fraction, while ignoring its sign, and then by propagating any carries to the left. If a carry occurs out of the leftmost digit of the fraction, it is retained, and the fraction and characteristic are adjusted accordingly, as was described for addition. The instructions then truncate the result to short form or long form, as appropriate. An exponent overflow exception is possible, but an exponent underflow exception and a significance exception are not.

---

EXAMPLE 23 **LRER 2,4**

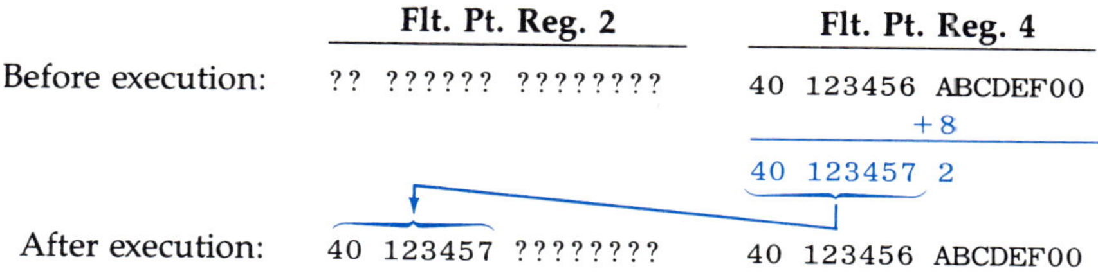


The addition causes a carry into the high-order portion of Register 4.

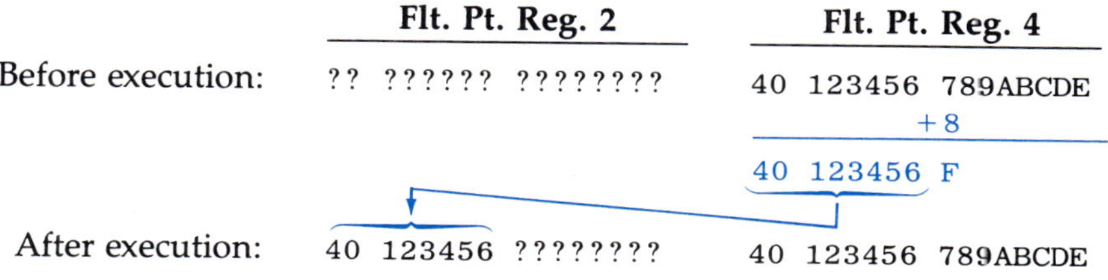


There is no carry as a result of the addition.

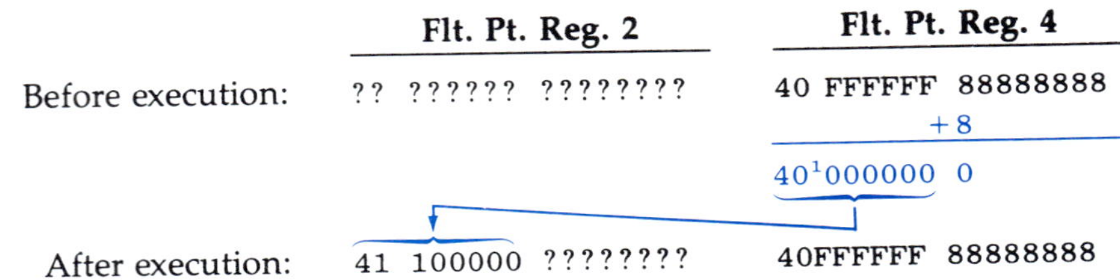


The addition causes a carry that is propagated throughout the high-order portion of the fraction. The carry out of the leftmost position of the fraction causes the fraction to be shifted to the right, and the characteristic to be increased by one.

---

EXAMPLE 24 **LRDR 2,4**

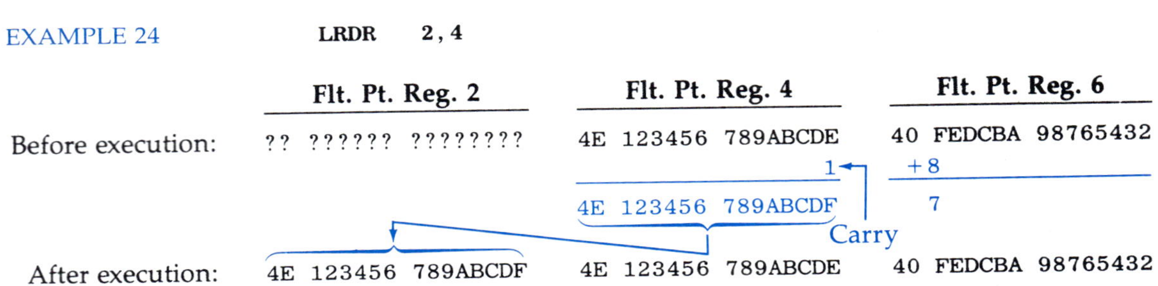


The hex digit 8 is added to the F, which is the first digit of the low-order fraction; a carry is propagated to the next fraction digit to the left (the E). Notice that the instruction ignores the low-order characteristic and sign in Register 6, and does not affect the contents of Register 4 and Register 6.

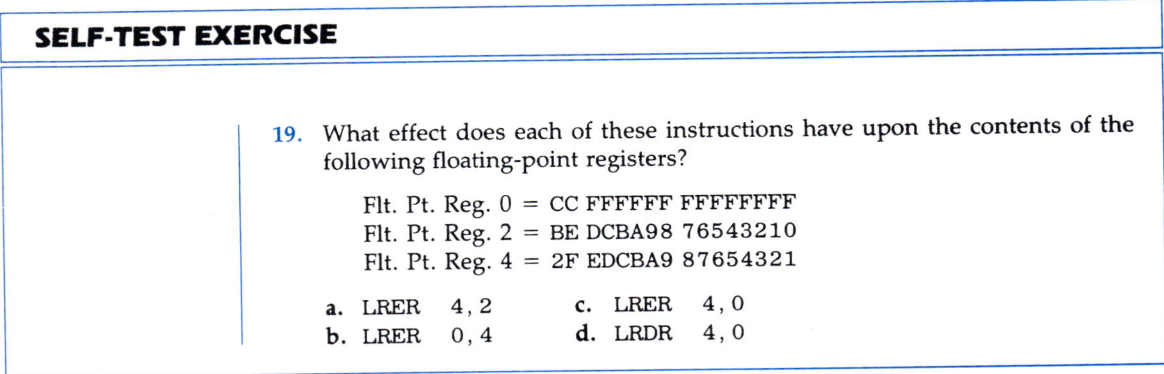

**SELF-TEST EXERCISE**

19. What effect does each of these instructions have upon the contents of the following floating-point registers?

    Flt. Pt. Reg. 0 = CC FFFFFF FFFFFFFF
    Flt. Pt. Reg. 2 = BE DCBA98 76543210
    Flt. Pt. Reg. 4 = 2F EDCBA9 87654321

    **a.** LRER 4,2 **c.** LRER 4,0
    **b.** LRER 0,4 **d.** LRDR 4,0

## Comparisons and Sign Changes

This section describes the instructions that compare floating-point numbers, and the instructions that test or alter the sign of a floating-point number.

### *The Compare Instructions (CER, CE, CDR, and CD)*

The Compare instructions algebraically compare two short-form numbers or two long-form numbers, and set the condition code. A temporary normalized subtraction determines the comparison; but the operands are unchanged and exponent overflow, exponent underflow, and significance exceptions cannot occur. The Compare instructions can be summarized as follows:

| Operation | Operand | Format | Instruction Name | Action |
|---|---|---|---|---|
| **CER** | *FPR1,FPR2* | RR | COMPARE SHORT REGISTERS | Compares $C(FPR1)_{0-31}$ with $C(FPR2)_{0-31}$ |
| **CE** | *FPR1,S2(X2)* or *FPR1,D2(X2,B2)* | RX | COMPARE SHORT | Compares $C(FPR1)_{0-31}$ with $C(E2)_{0-31}$ |
| **CDR** | *FPR1,FPR2* | RR | COMPARE DOUBLE REGISTERS | Compares $C(FPR1)_{0-63}$ with $C(FPR2)_{0-63}$ |
| **CD** | *FPR1,S2(X2)* or *FPR1,D2(X2,B2)* | RX | COMPARE DOUBLE | Compares $C(FPR1)_{0-63}$ with $C(E2)_{0-63}$ |

These four floating-point Compare instructions set the condition code in the same way as the other Compare instructions that you know:

$$\text{Condition code} = \begin{cases} 0 \text{ if the operands are equal} \\ 1 \text{ if the first operand is less than the second operand} \\ 2 \text{ if the first operand is greater than the second operand} \end{cases}$$

---

EXAMPLE 25

This example demonstrates short-form and long-form comparisons. The same register status is assumed before the execution of each Compare instruction.

| | Flt. Pt. Reg. 2 | Flt. Pt. Reg. 6 |
|---|---|---|
| Before execution: | C8 123400 5678ABCD | C8 123400 00000000 |

After execution of:

| | |
|---|---|
| `CER 2,6` | Condition code = 0. The high-order portions of the registers are equal. |
| `CDR 2,6` | Condition code = 1. The entire contents of both registers are compared. Although the magnitude of the first number is greater than that of the second, the numbers are negative, so the comparison is less than. |
| `CE 2,=X'C9012340'` | Condition code = 0. The literal defines an unnormalized number that has the same value as the value in the high-order portion of Floating-Point Register 2. This instruction demonstrates that equal operands do not necessarily have identical bit patterns. |

---

### *Instructions That Test or Change Signs: LTER, LTDR, LPER, LPDR, LNER, LNDR, LCER, and LCDR*

The special Load instructions in this section are similar to the binary integer instructions that test and alter the signs of the general registers. LTER and LTDR perform a load operation as LER and LDR do, but also set the condition code to reflect the value of the register contents. LPER and LPDR change the sign bit to 0; LNER and LNDR change the sign bit to 1, even if the fraction is zero; and LCER and LCDR invert the sign bit, even if the fraction is zero. Unlike their binary integer counterparts, these instructions do not leave zero invariant.

The instructions can be summarized as follows:

| Operation | Operand | Format | Instruction Name | Action |
|---|---|---|---|---|
| **LTER** | *FPR1,FPR2* | RR | LOAD AND TEST SHORT REGISTER | $C(FPR1)_{0-31} \leftarrow C(FPR2)_{0-31}$ |
| **LTDR** | *FPR1,FPR2* | RR | LOAD AND TEST DOUBLE REGISTER | $C(FPR1)_{0-63} \leftarrow C(FPR2)_{0-63}$ |
| **LPER** | *FPR1,FPR2* | RR | LOAD POSITIVE SHORT REGISTER | $C(FPR1)_{0-31} \leftarrow \lvert C(FPR2)_{0-31}\rvert$ |
| **LPDR** | *FPR1,FPR2* | RR | LOAD POSITIVE DOUBLE REGISTER | $C(FPR1)_{0-63} \leftarrow \lvert C(FPR2)_{0-63}\rvert$ |
| **LNER** | *FPR1,FPR2* | RR | LOAD NEGATIVE SHORT REGISTER | $C(FPR1)_{0-31} \leftarrow -\lvert C(FPR2)_{0-31}\rvert$ |
| **LNDR** | *FPR1,FPR2* | RR | LOAD NEGATIVE DOUBLE REGISTER | $C(FPR1)_{0-63} \leftarrow -\lvert C(FPR2)_{0-63}\rvert$ |
| **LCER** | *FPR1,FPR2* | RR | LOAD COMPLEMENT SHORT REGISTER | $C(FPR1)_{0-31} \leftarrow -C(FPR2)_{0-31}$ |
| **LCDR** | *FPR1,FPR2* | RR | LOAD COMPLEMENT DOUBLE REGISTER | $C(FPR1)_{0-63} \leftarrow -C(FPR2)_{0-63}$ |

All of the instructions just given set the condition code to reflect the status of the results. Obviously, not all settings are possible for several of the instructions. The condition code is set as follows:

$$\text{Condition code} = \begin{cases} 0 \text{ if the result has a zero fraction} \\ 1 \text{ if the result is negative} \\ 2 \text{ if the result is positive} \end{cases}$$

Even though the instructions can produce a negative zero, they do not distinguish between positive and negative zeros in the setting of the condition code. Notice that the instructions never set the condition code to 3. In addition, since only the sign bit is affected, exponent overflow, exponent underflow, and significance exceptions cannot occur.

You can alter the signs of floating-point numbers in storage directly by using the Boolean instructions. Exercise 14 at the end of this chapter considers this situation.

**SELF-TEST EXERCISE**

20. What effect does each of these instructions have upon the condition code and the contents of the following floating-point registers?

    Flt. Pt. Reg. 0 = 80 FEDCBA 98765432
    Flt. Pt. Reg. 4 = 42 300000 00000000
    Flt. Pt. Reg. 6 = 80 FEDCBA 98888888

    a. CER 0,6
    b. CDR 0,6
    c. CE 4,=E'3'
    d. CD 4,=D'3'
    e. CE 4,=X'47000003'
    f. LTER 0,4
    g. LTDR 0,4
    h. LPER 4,6
    i. LPDR 4,6
    j. LNER 4,6
    k. LNDR 6,4
    l. LCER 0,4
    m. LCDR 0,6

---

EXAMPLE 26

| | Flt. Pt. Reg. 0 | Flt. Pt. Reg. 2 | Condition code |
|---|---|---|---|
| Before execution: | ?? ?????? ???????? | C8 123456 789ABCDE | |
| After execution of: | | | |
| LTER 0,2 | C8 123456 ???????? | Unchanged | 1 |
| LNER 0,2 | C8 123456 ???????? | Unchanged | 1 |
| LPDR 0,2 | 48 123456 789ABCDE | Unchanged | 2 |
| LCDR 0,2 | 48 123456 789ABCDE | Unchanged | 2 |

---

EXAMPLE 27

**LCER 4,4**

| | Flt. Pt. Reg. 4 |
|---|---|
| Before execution: | 00 000000 00000000 |
| After execution: | 80 000000 00000000 |
| | *Condition code* = 0 |

The LCER, LCDR, LNER, and LNDR instructions can produce negative zeros, but they do not detect them. Notice that the condition code is 0 to indicate a zero fraction; in this case, the condition code does not reflect the sign.

---

## Sample Floating-Point Computations

The examples in this section illustrate how you can use the instructions that you have learned in this chapter to evaluate some common mathematical formulas. The program segments perform the computations with various precisions and demonstrate how you can apply the rounding instructions.

EXAMPLE 28

## Compute the Area of a Trapezoid

**A comparison of long-form and extended-form arithmetic**

The area of a trapezoid is equal to the sum of its bases multiplied by one-half of its height. This fact is represented by the following equation:

$$A = (B_1 + B_2) * H / 2$$

Assuming that the height and the bases are given as floating-point numbers, the two segments in Figure 17.5 compute the desired area, but differ in the precisions that they use. Although the first segment uses long-form arithmetic and the second uses extended precision, both segments compute long-form results. The second segment rounds the extended-form product to long form before it halves it because the Halve instructions are not available in extended form; it also does this to demonstrate how you can proceed without the DXR instruction, since DXR is only available with the extended architecture. Notice how awkward it is to use the extended-precision instructions; since they are not available in RX format, you must load both operands into register pairs, and you must use two Load instructions for each register pair.

**Figure 17.5**
The instructions to compute the area of a trapezoid by using, **a.** double-precision arithmetic and, **b.** extended-precision arithmetic, as described in Example 28.

**a.**

```
** COMPUTE THE AREA OF A TRAPEZOID USING DOUBLE-PRECISION ARITHMETIC
** AREA = (BASE1 + BASE2) * HEIGHT/2
         LD    F0,BASE1         F0 = FIRST BASE
         AD    F0,BASE2         ADD SECOND BASE
         MD    F0,HEIGHT        (BASE1 + BASE2) * HEIGHT
         HDR   F0,F0            DIVIDE BY 2
         STD   F0,AREA          SAVE RESULT
         .
         .
         .
BASE1    DS    D
BASE2    DS    D
HEIGHT   DS    D
AREA     DS    D
```

**b.**

```
** COMPUTE THE AREA OF A TRAPEZOID USING EXTENDED-PRECISION ARITHMETIC
** AREA = (BASE1 + BASE2) * HEIGHT/2
         LD    F0,BASE1         F0 = HIGH-ORDER PART OF BASE1
         LD    F2,BASE1+8       F2 = LOW-ORDER PART OF BASE1
         LD    F4,BASE2         F4 = HIGH-ORDER PART OF BASE2
         LD    F6,BASE2+8       F6 = LOW-ORDER PART OF BASE2
         AXR   F0,F4            (BASE1 + BASE2)
         LD    F4,HEIGHT        F4 = HIGH-ORDER PART OF HEIGHT
         LD    F6,HEIGHT+8      F6 = LOW-ORDER PART OF HEIGHT
         MXR   F0,F4            (BASE1 + BASE2) * HEIGHT
         LRDR  F0,F0            ROUND TO LONG FORM
         HDR   F0,F0            DIVIDE BY 2
         STD   F0,AREA          SAVE RESULT
         .
         .
         .
BASE1    DS    L
BASE2    DS    L
HEIGHT   DS    L
AREA     DS    D
```

EXAMPLE 29

## Compute the Volume of a Sphere

The formula for the volume of a sphere of diameter $D$ is

$$V = \frac{\pi * D^3}{6}$$

Assuming that the diameter is available as a floating-point number, the two segments in Figure 17.6 compute the desired volume by using short-form arithmetic.

The ME instruction produces a long-form product. You can ignore its low-order portion or, as is done in Figure 17.6, you can round each product to short form before you use it in another short-form operation.

**Two approaches to rounding**

The two segments in Figure 17.6 differ after the third multiplication. The first segment rounds the product to short form and then divides it. The second segment divides the product by using a long-form Divide instruction and then rounds the quotient to short form. Although a difference, if any, in the two computed volumes will be small, you must be careful with precision and rounding when the computations are longer or are numerically sensitive. (Further discussion of numerical accuracy is beyond the scope of this book.)

**Figure 17.6** The instructions to compute the volume of a sphere by using single-precision arithmetic with rounding where, **a.** rounding occurs before division and where, **b.** rounding occurs after division, as described in Example 29.

**a.**

```
** COMPUTE THE VOLUME OF A SPHERE USING SINGLE-PRECISION ARITHMETIC
** VOLUME = (PI * DIAMETER ** 3)/6
** ROUND BEFORE THE DIVISION
         LE    F0,PI              F0 = ACCUMULATOR = PI
         ME    F0,DIAMETER        PI * DIAMETER
         LRER  F0,F0              ROUND LONG PRODUCT TO SHORT FORM
         ME    F0,DIAMETER        PI * DIAMETER ** 2
         LRER  F0,F0              ROUND LONG PRODUCT TO SHORT FORM
         ME    F0,DIAMETER        PI * DIAMETER ** 3
         LRER  F0,F0              ROUND LONG PRODUCT TO SHORT FORM
         DE    F0,=E'6.'          DIVIDE SHORT PRODUCT
         STE   F0,VOLUME          STORE SHORT RESULT
         .
         .
         .
DIAMETER DS    E
VOLUME   DS    E
PI       DC    E'3.141593'
```

**b.**

```
** COMPUTE THE VOLUME OF A SPHERE USING SINGLE-PRECISION ARITHMETIC
** VOLUME = (PI * DIAMETER ** 3)/6
** ROUND AFTER THE DIVISION
         LE    F0,PI              F0 = ACCUMULATOR = PI
         ME    F0,DIAMETER        PI * DIAMETER
         LRER  F0,F0              ROUND LONG PRODUCT TO SHORT FORM
         ME    F0,DIAMETER        PI * DIAMETER ** 2
         LRER  F0,F0              ROUND LONG PRODUCT TO SHORT FORM
         ME    F0,DIAMETER        PI * DIAMETER ** 3
         DD    F0,=D'6.'          DIVIDE LONG PRODUCT
         LRER  F0,F0              ROUND LONG QUOTIENT TO SHORT FORM
         STE   F0,VOLUME          STORE SHORT RESULT
         .
         .
         .
DIAMETER DS    E
VOLUME   DS    E
PI       DC    E'3.141593'
```

**SELF-TEST EXERCISES**

21. Given a long-form number $x$ in Floating-Point Register 4, compute $(x^4 - 1)/7$ in double precision. Store the result at Z.
22. Given a short-form number $n$ in a fullword of storage, compute $n^2$ and store the rounded short-form result at NSQ.
23. Given the short-form numbers $x$ and $y$ that are stored as fullwords, compute $3 * (x^2 + y^2)/4$ in double precision. Store the rounded result in the fullword at W.

## Unnormalized Addition and Subtraction

The unnormalized Add and Subtract instructions do not normalize the intermediate result.

As noted earlier, you would typically use normalized arithmetic for floating-point computations. However, in certain circumstances—notably in conversions that involve floating-point numbers—the unnormalized addition and subtraction instructions are useful. Like the normalized arithmetic instructions, the unnormalized addition and subtraction instructions operate upon operands that can be either normalized or unnormalized. The intermediate result of an unnormalized add operation or an unnormalized subtract operation is the same as the intermediate result that a normalized operation produces. However, the intermediate result is also the final result; no normalization takes place. It follows that exponent underflow is impossible. Furthermore, when the unnormalized instructions test for a zero fraction in the result, they ignore the guard digit. Except for these differences, the unnormalized instructions are the same as their normalized counterparts, but are not available for extended-form operands.

The unnormalized Add and Subtract instructions can be summarized as follows:

| Operation | Operand | Format | Instruction Name | Action |
|---|---|---|---|---|
| **AUR** | *FPR1,FPR2* | RR | ADD UNNORMALIZED SHORT REGISTERS | $C(FPR1)_{0-31} \leftarrow C(FPR1)_{0-31} + C(FPR2)_{0-31}$ |
| **AU** | *FPR1,S2(X2)* or *FPR1,D2(X2,B2)* | RX | ADD UNNORMALIZED SHORT | $C(FPR1)_{0-31} \leftarrow C(FPR1)_{0-31} + C(E2)_{0-31}$ |
| **AWR** | *FPR1,FPR2* | RR | ADD UNNORMALIZED DOUBLE REGISTERS | $C(FPR1)_{0-63} \leftarrow C(FPR1)_{0-63} + C(FPR2)_{0-63}$ |
| **AW** | *FPR1,S2(X2)* or *FPR1,D2(X2,B2)* | RX | ADD UNNORMALIZED DOUBLE | $C(FPR1)_{0-63} \leftarrow C(FPR1)_{0-63} + C(E2)_{0-63}$ |
| **SUR** | *FPR1,FPR2* | RR | SUBTRACT UNNORMALIZED SHORT REGISTERS | $C(FPR1)_{0-31} \leftarrow C(FPR1)_{0-31} - C(FPR2)_{0-31}$ |
| **SU** | *FPR1,S2(X2)* or *FPR1,D2(X2,B2)* | RX | SUBTRACT UNNORMALIZED SHORT | $C(FPR1)_{0-31} \leftarrow C(FPR1)_{0-31} - C(E2)_{0-31}$ |

| Operation | Operand | Format | Instruction Name | Action |
|---|---|---|---|---|
| **SWR** | *FPR1,FPR2* | RR | SUBTRACT UNNORMALIZED DOUBLE REGISTERS | $C(FPR1)_{0-63} \leftarrow C(FPR1)_{0-63} - C(FPR2)_{0-63}$ |
| **SW** | *FPR1,S2(X2)* or *FPR1,D2(X2,B2)* | RX | SUBTRACT UNNORMALIZED DOUBLE | $C(FPR1)_{0-63} \leftarrow C(FPR1)_{0-63} - C(E2)_{0-63}$ |

The condition code settings are the same as those settings for the normalized operations.

---

EXAMPLE 30

```
SUR     4,2
```

| | Flt. Pt. Reg. 4 | Flt. Pt. Reg. 2 |
|---|---|---|
| Before execution: | 41 119999 ???????? | 40 199999 ???????? |
| After execution: | 41 0FFFFF ???????? | 40 199999 ???????? |
| | *Condition code* = 2 | |

---

EXAMPLE 31

```
AW      4,=D'17.4'
```

| | Flt. Pt. Reg. 4 | =D'17.4' |
|---|---|---|
| Before execution: | 43 FFF000 00000000 | 42 116666 66666666 |
| After execution: | 44 101066 66666666 | 42 116666 66666666 |
| | *Condition code* = 2 | |

Here, the results of the instruction are no different than if a normalized Add instruction had been executed.

---

## SELF-TEST EXERCISE

**24.** What effect does each of these instructions have upon the condition code and the contents of the following floating-point registers? Indicate the type of exceptions, if any, that occur.

Flt. Pt. Reg. 2 = 31 000007 20000000
Flt. Pt. Reg. 4 = 31 001122 9988FFFF
Flt. Pt. Reg. 6 = 2F 112299 FFFFFFFF

**a.** AUR 4,6
**b.** AWR 2,4
**c.** AU 4,=X'B0011229'
**d.** SUR 6,4
**e.** SWR 6,4
**f.** SU 6,=X'2F112200'
**g.** SW 2,=D'.5'

## Conversions to and from Floating-Point

You must write a sequence of instructions that convert to and from floating-point notation.

When you perform floating-point computations in an assembler language program, you will frequently have a binary integer, such as a loop counter, whose value you will also need in the floating-point computation. In such an instance, you must convert the binary integer to a floating-point representation. Conversely, you may want to discard the fractional portion of a floating-point number, and represent the integral portion as a binary integer. If you also perform input/output operations, you may have to convert between floating-point representations and character strings that are used with I/O operations. Special instructions do not exist to perform the conversions that are described here; instead, you must use a sequence of instructions that are discussed in this section.

### *Conversion from Binary Integer to Floating-Point*

You can convert a binary integer to a short-form floating-point number by using an algorithm that is based upon the following observation: an unnormalized long-form floating-point representation of the hexadecimal integer $h_1h_2h_3h_4h_5h_6h_7h_8$ appears as

$$4\ E\ 0\ 0\ 0\ 0\ 0\ 0\ h_1h_2h_3h_4h_5h_6h_7h_8$$

You can verify that this floating-point number does, indeed, represent the given integer by writing the value of the floating-point number in scientific notation, as shown.

$$(\,.\,0\ 0\ 0\ 0\ 0\ 0\ h_1h_2h_3h_4h_5h_6h_7h_8)_{16} \times 16^{14}$$

For example, the floating-point number 4E000000 0000000A represents the hexadecimal integer 0000000A. You can normalize 4E000000 0000000A by adding it to true zero with a normalized Add instruction.

The instructions in Figure 17.7 convert the binary integer in the fullword at INTEGER into a short-form floating-point number at FLOAT. The following traces the conversion process that this program segment performs for three different values of INTEGER:

**Figure 17.7**
The instructions to convert a binary integer to floating-point notation.

```
** CONVERT A BINARY INTEGER TO FLOATING-POINT NOTATION
          L     R2,INTEGER       R2 = BINARY INTEGER
          LPR   R3,R2            R3 = ITS MAGNITUDE
          ST    R3,UNLOW         PLACE IN LOW-ORDER PART OF UNNORM
          LD    F0,UNNORM        F0 = UNNORMALIZED VERSION OF
*                                     FLT-PT RESULT
          AD    F0,=D'0'         NORMALIZE RESULT
          LTR   R2,R2            TEST SIGN OF ORIGINAL INTEGER
          BNM   CONTINUE         IF NON-NEG., SIGN IS ALREADY PLUS
          LNDR  F0,F0            MAKE SIGN MINUS
CONTINUE  LRER  F0,F0            ROUND TO SHORT FORM
          STE   F0,FLOAT         STORE RESULT
          .
          .
          .
INTEGER   DS    F                BINARY INTEGER
UNNORM    DS    0D               4E000000 HHHHHHHH
          DC    X'4E000000'        HIGH-ORDER PORTION
UNLOW     DC    X'00000000'        LOW-ORDER PORTION
FLOAT     DS    E                FLOATING-POINT RESULT
```

| INTEGER | UNNORM | Flt. Pt. Reg. 0 after the addition | FLOAT |
|---|---|---|---|
| 0000000A | 4E000000 0000000A | 41A00000 00000000 | 41A00000 |
| FFFFFFFF | 4E000000 00000001 | 41100000 00000000 | C1100000 |
| 12345678 | 4E000000 12345678 | 48123456 78000000 | 48123456 |

Notice that there is insufficient room in a short-form number to retain all of the digits that are available in the last integer 12345678: you could either use the long-form result in Floating-Point Register 0, or round the result to short form, as is done here.

## *Conversion from Floating-Point to Binary Integer*

You can convert a short-form floating-point number to a fullword binary integer by using an algorithm that is illustrated here. If you have the floating-point number 41280000 (which is $2.5_{10}$), the desired integer is 00000002 in hexadecimal. To achieve this, first extend the floating-point number on the right with zeros to convert it to long form. If you add the long-form result to a number that has a characteristic of 4E, the fraction will be shifted out. In particular, an unnormalized Add produces the following:

```
  4E000000 00000000 ← Number with a characteristic of 4E
+ 41280000 00000000 ← Long-form version of the given number
  4E000000 00000002 ← Unnormalized sum
           ↑
      Integer result
```

The integral portion of the given floating-point number is the low-order half of the sum, and constitutes the desired result.

When you convert a negative number to an integer, it is usually rounded down. Since the number is negative, you must also compute the two's complement of the integral result. You can accomplish these steps by replacing 4E000000 00000000 by 4E000001 00000000 in the computation just given. For example, the conversion of −2.5 to integer appears as follows:

**Converting a negative floating-point number to integer form**

```
4E000001 00000000 ← Number with a characteristic of 4E
C1280000 00000000 ← Long-form version of the given number
4E000000 FFFFFFFD ← Unnormalized sum
         ↑
    Integer result
```

The low-order portion contains the two's complement of 3 as required. Notice that 4E000001 00000000 has a decimal value of $2^{32}$. The integral result FFFFFFFD represents the decimal quantity $2^{32} - 3$, which is the two's complement of 3.

You can use 4E000001 00000000 even if the given number is positive, since the result of the addition is correct regardless of the sign of the original number. For example, the computation to convert 2.5, which was given earlier, appears as follows:

**Converting a positive floating-point number to integer form**

```
  4E000001 00000000
+ 41280000 00000000
  4E000001 00000002
           ↑
      Integer result
```

```
** CONVERT A FLOATING-POINT NUMBER TO BINARY INTEGER NOTATION
** ASSUME FLOAT IS SHORT FORM WITH VALUE IN RANGE -2**31 TO 2**31 - 1
         LD    F0,=D'0'          LOW-ORDER PORTION OF F0 = 0
         LE    F0,FLOAT          LOAD HIGH-ORDER PORTION
         AW    F0,=X'4E00000100000000'  SHIFT OUT FRACTION AND
*                                       COMPLEMENT IF NEGATIVE
         STD   F0,TEMP           STORE TO ACCESS LOW-ORDER PART
         MVC   INTEGER,TEMP+4    GET INTEGER RESULT
         .
         .
         .
FLOAT    DS    E                 FLOATING-POINT NUMBER
TEMP     DS    D                 TEMPORARY STORAGE
INTEGER  DS    F                 BINARY INTEGER RESULT
```

**Figure 17.8**
The instructions to convert a floating-point number to binary notation.

The integral result is still in the low-order portion. Therefore, you do not need to distinguish between positive and negative numbers. This approach reduces the number of instructions that are required for the conversion.

The instructions in Figure 17.8 convert the short-form floating-point number at FLOAT into a binary integer stored at INTEGER. The instructions assume that the given floating-point number has a value within the range of binary integers. The following traces the conversion process that this program segment performs for four different values of FLOAT:

| FLOAT | Flt. Pt. Reg. 0 before the addition | Flt. Pt. Reg. 0 after the addition (TEMP) | INTEGER |
|---|---|---|---|
| 41280000 | 41280000 00000000 | 4E000001 00000002 | 00000002 |
| C1280000 | C1280000 00000000 | 4E000000 FFFFFFFD | FFFFFFFD |
| 487FFFFF | 487FFFFF 00000000 | 4E000001 7FFFFF00 | 7FFFFF00 |
| C87FFFFF | C87FFFFF 00000000 | 4E000000 80000100 | 80000100 |

## *Conversion from Floating-Point to EBCDIC Characters*

**Printing floating-point numbers**

The goal in this section is to produce a character string that is suitable for printing a floating-point number. Suppose that Floating-Point Register 0 contains a short-form floating-point number, and that you want to convert it into a character string with the following form:

0.*xxxxxxx*E *xx*

The printed number will always be normalized, contain 7 digits, and appear with an exponent. A minus sign will precede each negative number and each negative exponent.

There are many ways to convert a floating-point number to printable form, and the details of each way depend upon the desired form of the output. The algorithm that the instructions in Figure 17.9 use considers two cases: in the first case, the listed instructions convert numbers whose magnitudes are greater than 1; Programming Problem 1 at the end of this chapter considers the other case of converting numbers whose magnitudes are less than or equal to 1.

```
** CONVERT A SHORT-FORM FLOATING-POINT NUMBER IN F0 TO PRINTABLE FORM
FE       LD     F2,=D'0'           CLEAR F2 SO LOW-ORDER PART IS 0
         LPER   F2,F0              F2 = ABSOLUTE VALUE OF GIVEN NUMBER
*                                       IN LONG FORM
         BZ     ZERO               MAGNITUDE IS ZERO; SPECIAL CASE
         LDR    F4,F2              F4 = COPY OF F2 FOR LATER
* IF MAGNITUDE OF NUMBER IS > 1.0:
         CE     F2,=E'1'           COMPARE MAGNITUDE WITH FLT. PT. 1.0
         BNH    LTEONE             BRANCH AHEAD IF <= 1.0
* - THEN:
         MVI    SIGNEXP,C' '       SET SIGN OF EXPONENT (+)
         L      R3,=F'1'           R3 = EXPONENT = 1
         SR     R5,R5              R5 = INDEX TO POWERS OF 10 = 0
** FIND N SUCH THAT 10**(N-1) <= NUMBER < 10**N
* - - FOR J = 10, 20, ..., 80:
LOOP1    CD     F2,GTAB2+8(R5)     COMPARE WITH 10**J, J= 10, 20,..., 80
         BL     OUT1               IF <, EXIT LOOP
         LA     R5,8(R5)           POINT TO NEXT POWER OF 10
         LA     R3,10(R3)          INCREMENT EXPONENT
         B      LOOP1              REPEAT
* - - END FOR
OUT1     LD     F6,GTAB2(R5)       GET 10**A. (A= J-10)
         DDR    F2,F6              DIVIDE BY 10**A
* - - FOR B = 1, 2, ..., 10:
         SR     R5,R5              R5 = INDEX = 0
LOOP2    CD     F2,GTAB1(R5)       COMPARE WITH 10**B, B= 1, 2, ..., 10
         BL     OUT2               IF <, EXIT LOOP
         LA     R5,8(R5)           POINT TO NEXT POWER OF 10
         LA     R3,1(R3)           INCREMENT EXPONENT
         B      LOOP2              REPEAT
* - - END FOR
OUT2     MD     F6,GTAB1(R5)       F6 = (10**A)*(10**B) = 10**N
SCALE    DDR    F4,F6              DIVIDE ORIGINAL LONG-FORM MAGNITUDE
*                                    BY 10**N
         MD     F4,=D'1E7'         SCALE: INTEGRAL PORTION IS FIRST 7
*                                    DIGITS OF ORIGINAL NUMBER
         AW     F4,=X'4E00000000000000' ISOLATE FIRST 7 DIGITS
         STD    F4,TEMP            STORE MOMENTARILY
         L      R5,TEMP+4          GET INTEGER FORM OF FIRST 7 DIGITS
         CVD    R5,DOUBLE          CONVERT INTEGER TO PACKED-DECIMAL FORM
         OI     DOUBLE+7,X'0F'     CHANGE SIGN CODE TO ZONE CODE
         UNPK   FRAC,DOUBLE        CONVERT TO EBCDIC
         CVD    R3,DOUBLE          CONVERT EXPONENT TO PACKED-DECIMAL FORM
         OI     DOUBLE+7,X'0F'     CHANGE SIGN CODE TO ZONE CODE
         UNPK   EXP,DOUBLE         CONVERT TO EBCDIC
         MVI    SIGN,C' '          INITIALIZE SIGN PORTION IN OUTPUT
         LTER   F0,F0              TEST SIGN OF ORIGINAL NUMBER
         BNL    DONE               IF NOT NEGATIVE, FINISHED
         MVI    SIGN,C'-'          ELSE SET SIGN TO MINUS
         B      DONE               FINISHED
* - ELSE:
LTEONE   ----                      MAGNITUDE IS <= 1.0
         .
         .
         .
         B      DONE
```

(Continues)

**Figure 17.9**
The instructions that convert a floating-point number to an EBCDIC character string.

```
* END IF
ZERO      ----                         MAGNITUDE IS ZERO
          .
          .
          .
DONE      ----                         CONVERSION IS COMPLETE
          .
          .
          .
GTAB1     DC     D'1E1,1E2,1E3,1E4,1E5,1E6,1E7,1E8,1E9,1E10'
GTAB2     DC     D'1,1E10,1E20,1E30,1E40,1E50,1E60,1E70,1E80'
          DC     X'7FFFFFFFFFFFFFFF' LARGEST NUMBER
TEMP      DS     D                     TEMPORARY STORAGE
DOUBLE    DS     D                     DOUBLEWORD FOR CVD
OUTPUT    DS     0CL14                 EBCDIC RESULT:
SIGN      DS     C                       SIGN OF NUMBER
          DC     C'0.'
FRAC      DS     CL7                     7-DIGIT FRACTION
          DC     C'E'
SIGNEXP   DS     C                       SIGN OF EXPONENT
EXP       DS     CL2                     2-DIGIT EXPONENT
```

**Figure 17.9**
*(Continued)*

The integral exponent $n$ of 10 that is required in the printed number satisfies the following inequality, where $f$ is the value of the floating-point number:

$$10^{n-1} \leq |f| < 10^{n}$$

To determine $n$, first divide $|f|$ by the largest value that does not exceed $|f|$ and is of the form $10^a$, where $a$ is either zero or a multiple of 10. Then determine the smallest value $10^b$ that exceeds the quotient just computed, where $b$ is an integer. Thus, $10^n = 10^a * 10^b$, where $a$ is either zero or a multiple of 10, and where $b$ is between 1 and 10.

The fraction in the printed number must be greater than or equal to .1, but less than 1; the fraction is equal to $|f| \div 10^a$, which was computed previously, divided by $10^b$. However, instead of performing this division, you can reduce inaccuracy due to rounding by dividing the original value of $|f|$ by $10^n$. To obtain the 7 digits of the fraction for the printed form, multiply the quotient that you just calculated by $10^7$ and truncate the result to an integer. Convert the 7 digits and the exponent to EBCDIC, and punctuate the result as necessary.

## *Conversion from EBCDIC Characters to Floating-Point*

**Reading floating-point numbers**

You can read numbers and then convert them to floating-point form by using the ideas in this section. As with floating-point numbers that you print, the format of the input data determines the details of the conversion algorithm. For example, input data can appear with a fixed or variable number of digits, with or without an exponent, and with or without a decimal point. As a preliminary step, you must process the input character string to determine the number's integral portion, fractional portion, and exponent, if one is specified. (The necessary techniques were discussed in Chapters 10 and 11; they will not be repeated here.)

The instructions in Figure 17.10 are part of a subprogram that performs the conversion to floating-point representation. Assume that the number

```
** CONVERT AN INPUT DATA VALUE TO FLOATING-POINT FORM.
** ASSUME R7 = ADDRESS OF INTEGRAL PORTION, R8 = ADDRESS OF FRACTIONAL
** PORTION, AND R9 = ADDRESS OF EXPONENT.
         ZAP   DOUBLE,0(4,R7)    MOVE INTEGRAL PORTION TO DOUBLEWORD
         BAL   R14,FLT           CONVERT IT TO FLOATING-POINT (IN F0)
         STD   F0,TEMP           SAVE INTEGER PORTION FOR LATER
         ZAP   DOUBLE,0(4,R8)    MOVE FRACTIONAL PORTION TO DOUBLEWORD
         BAL   R14,FLT           CONVERT IT TO FLOATING-POINT (IN F0)
         DD    F0,=D'1.E7'       SCALE FRACTIONAL PORTION
         AD    F0,TEMP           ADD SCALED FRACTION TO INTEGRAL PORTION
         ZAP   DOUBLE,0(2,R9)    MOVE EXPONENT TO DOUBLEWORD
         CVB   R2,DOUBLE         CONVERT EXPONENT TO BINARY
         LTR   R2,R2             TEST SIGN OF EXPONENT
         BZ    DONE              CONVERSION IS COMPLETE IF EXPONENT IS 0
* COMPUTE POWER OF 10 SCALE FACTOR IN TWO PARTS: (10**A)*(10**B) WHERE
*   0 <= A <= 7 AND B IS A MULTIPLE OF 8
         LA    R4,PTAB           R4 = ADDR. OF POSITIVE EXPONENTS TABLE
         BP    GETPOWER          SKIP AHEAD IF EXPONENT IS POSITIVE
         LA    R4,NTAB           R4 = ADDR. OF NEGATIVE EXPONENTS TABLE
         LPR   R2,R2             GET ABSOLUTE VALUE OF EXPONENT
GETPOWER SRDA  R2,3              R2 = EXPONENT DIVIDED BY 2**3 = 8
         SRL   R3,29             R3 = REMAINDER OF DIVISION
         SLL   R3,3              R3 = INDEX TO POWERS 10**J, J = 0,...,7
         LD    F2,0(R3,R4)       F2 = 10**A
         SLA   R2,3              R2 = 8 + INDEX TO POWERS 10**J,
**                               J = 8,16,...
         BZ    CONTINUE          SKIP AHEAD IF R2 = 0
         LA    R4,64(R4)         POINT TO 2ND PART OF POWERS TABLE
         MD    F2,56(R2,R4)      MULTIPLY 10**A BY 10**B
CONTINUE MDR   F0,F2             MULTIPLY NUMBER BY SCALE FACTOR
DONE     LRER  F0,F0             ROUND RESULT TO SHORT FORM
         LM    R14,R12,12(R13)   RESTORE REGISTERS
         BR    R14               RETURN
** INTERNAL SUBPROGRAM TO CONVERT A PACKED-DECIMAL INTEGER TO
**   FLOATING-POINT.
**   INPUT: DOUBLE=DEC.INTEGER; OUTPUT: F0 = FLOATING-POINT RESULT
FLT      CVB   R2,DOUBLE         CONVERT PACKED-DECIMAL INTEGER TO BINARY
         LPR   R3,R2             R3 = ABSOLUTE VALUE OF GIVEN INTEGER
         ST    R3,UNLOW          STORE AS LOW-ORDER PART OF UNNORMALIZED
*                                  FLOATING-POINT EQUIVALENT
         LD    F0,UNNORM         F0 = UNNORMALIZED FLOATING-POINT EQUIV.
         AD    F0,=D'0'          NORMALIZE F0
         LTR   R2,R2             TEST SIGN OF ORIGINAL INTEGER
         BNM   RETURN            IF INTEGER IS NOT NEGATIVE, DONE
         LNDR  F0,F0             IF INTEGER IS NEGATIVE, MAKE F0 NEGATIVE
RETURN   BR    R14               RETURN
UNNORM   DS    0D                UNNORMALIZED FLOATING-POINT EQUIVALENT:
         DC    X'4E000000'         HIGH-ORDER PART
UNLOW    DC    X'00000000'         LOW-ORDER PART
*
TEMP     DS    D                 TEMPORARY STORAGE
DOUBLE   DS    D                 DOUBLEWORD FOR CVB
* TABLE OF POSITIVE POWERS OF 10:
PTAB     DC    D'1,1E1,1E2,1E3,1E4,1E5,1E6,1E7'
         DC    D'1E8,1E16,1E24,1E32,1E40,1E48,1E56,1E64,1E72'
* TABLE OF NEGATIVE POWERS OF 10:
NTAB     DC    D'1,1E-1,1E-2,1E-3,1E-4,1E-5,1E-6,1E-7'
         DC    D'1E-8,1E-16,1E-24,1E-32,1E-40,1E-48,1E-56,1E-64,1E-72'
```

**Figure 17.10**
The instructions that convert a character string to floating-point representation.

read has been processed so that its integral portion, fractional portion, and exponent are available as packed-decimal integers at the addresses in Registers 7, 8, and 9, respectively. Also assume that the fractional portion is represented as a 7-digit integer, which is padded with zeros on the right if necessary. Thus, you can represent the fractional portion in 4 bytes. The instructions assume that the integral portion occupies 4 bytes, and that the exponent occupies 2 bytes.

You can convert the integral portion and the fractional portion to floating-point by using the internal subprogram at FLT, whose instructions are similar to those in Figure 17.7. You must scale the floating-point equivalent of the fraction by dividing it by $10^7$. Add this quotient to the floating-point representation of the integral portion. If there is an exponent portion with a value of $n$, you must multiply the previous sum by $10^n$. To do this, write $n$ as $a + b$, where $a$ is between 0 and 7, and $b$ is a multiple of 8. Here, 8 is chosen because it is simple to divide the exponent by 8 with a Shift instruction. To compute $10^n$, the algorithm here uses two tables—each table in two parts. For example, the table for positive exponents contains long-form values of $10^0$, $10^1$, and so on to $10^7$; and long-form values of $10^8$, $10^{16}$, and so on to $10^{72}$ in increments of $10^8$. If you divide the exponent by 8 and multiply the remainder of this division by 8, you obtain the index value that is necessary to address $10^a$. If you multiply the quotient by 8, you obtain a value that is 8 more than the index value that is necessary to address $10^b$. The product of $10^a$ and $10^b$ is $10^n$.

To preserve accuracy, the computations are performed in double precision, and the result is rounded to single precision.

## Case Study

### *Problem Statement*

**Write a subprogram that computes a real root of the polynomial equation**

$$a_0x^n + a_1x^{n-1} + \cdots + a_{n-1}x + a_n = 0$$

**by using the Newton-Raphson method.**

### *Discussion*

The Newton-Raphson method starts with an initial guess of $x_0$ at a real root of the equation, and generates a sequence $\{x_k\}$ of approximations that will converge to the root if the guess was sufficiently close to the root. The sequence $\{x_k\}$ is defined as follows:

$$x_{k+1} = x_k - \mathrm{P}(x_k) \,/\, \mathrm{P}'(x_k)$$

$\mathrm{P}(x)$ is the polynomial and $\mathrm{P}'(x)$ is its first derivative. You can evaluate the polynomial and its first derivative at any point $z$ by using Horner's method, as follows.

If you compute

$$b_0 = a_0$$
$$b_j = a_j + z * b_{j-1} \text{ for } j = 1, 2, \cdots, n$$

**Figure 17.11**
A pseudocode solution for the case study.

**The main program:**

```
Read and print the degree
Read the coefficients into an array and print them
Read and print the initial guess
Call the subprogram NEWTON
IF error flag is set
    THEN print an error message
    ELSE print the root
END IF
```

**The subprogram NEWTON:**

```
xnew := guess
count := 25
REPEAT
    xold := xnew
    b0 := a0
    c0 := a0
    FOR j = 1 TO n - 1
        bj := aj + xold * bj-1
        cj := bj + xold * cj-1
    END FOR
    bn := an + xold * bn-1
    xnew := xold - bn / cn-1
    count := count - 1
UNTIL |xold - xnew| < 0.5 × 10^-5 or count = 0
END REPEAT
IF count = 0
    THEN set error flag to indicate failure
    ELSE root := xnew
END IF
```

$$c_0 = a_0$$
$$c_j = b_j + z * c_{j-1} \text{ for } j = 1, 2, \cdots, n-1$$

then P(z) is equal to $b_n$ and P′(z) is equal to $c_{n-1}$.

Compute approximations until either

$$|x_k - x_{k+1}| < 0.5 \times 10^{-5}$$

in which case, take $x_{k+1}$ as the root; or 25 approximations are calculated—in which case, the method fails.

The pseudocode solution in Figure 17.11 and the flowchart in Figure 17.12 describe the required computation. Notice that you do not have to retain the entire sequence of approximations. It is sufficient to retain the previous approximation *xold* and the new approximation *xnew.*

The program in Figure 17.13 assumes that two subprograms CONVIN and CONVOUT are available to perform the necessary conversions for reading and printing floating-point numbers. Although both sequences $\{b_j\}$ and $\{c_j\}$ are indicated in the pseudocode and flowchart, the subprogram NEWTON does not implement them as arrays; instead, only the latest elements are retained in the Floating-Point Registers F4 and F6.

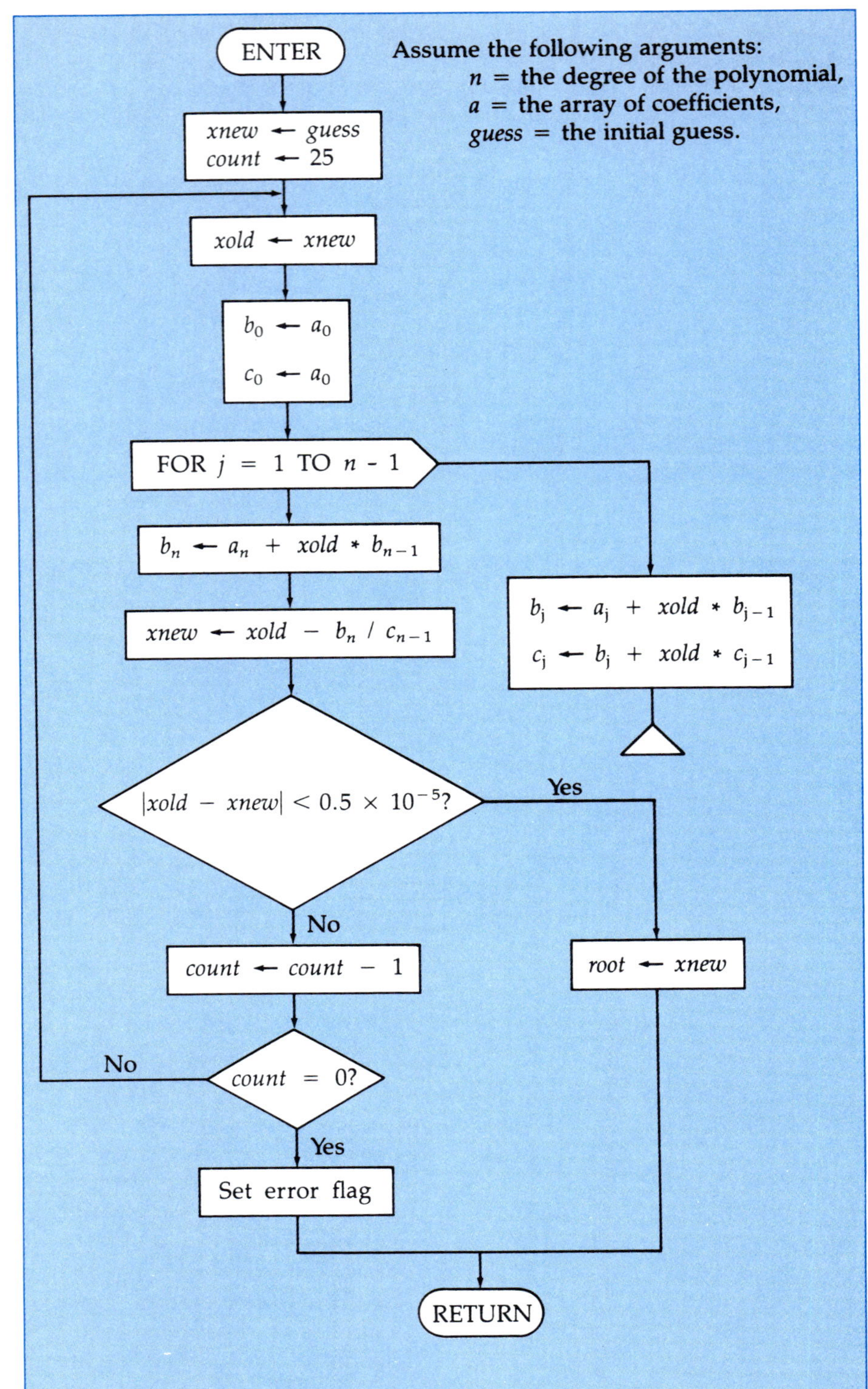


**Figure 17.12**
The flowchart for the subprogram NEWTON.

```
        REAL ROOTS OF POLYNOMIAL EQUATIONS

  LOC  OBJECT CODE    ADDR1 ADDR2  STMT   SOURCE STATEMENT

000000                                2 MAIN      CSECT
                                      3 **********************************************************************
                                      4 ** PURPOSE:  COMPUTES A REAL ROOT OF A POLYNOMIAL EQUATION USING THE
                                      5 **           NEWTON-RAPHSON METHOD
                                      6 ** INPUT:    DEGREE OF POLYNOMIAL IN COLUMNS 1 AND 2 OF FIRST RECORD.
                                      7 **           POLYNOMIAL COEFFICIENTS IN ORDER OF DECREASING POWERS OF X,
                                      8 **             IN SUBSEQUENT RECORDS.  EACH COEFFICIENT IS
                                      9 **             RIGHT-JUSTIFIED IN FIELDS OF 10, 8 FIELDS PER RECORD, AND
                                     10 **             APPEARS WITH A DECIMAL POINT, AN OPTIONAL SIGN, NO
                                     11 **             EXPONENT, AND AT MOST 7 SIGNIFICANT DIGITS.
                                     12 **           GUESS AT THE ROOT, IN THE SAME FORMAT AS A COEFFICIENT, IN
                                     13 **           THE LAST RECORD.
                                     14 ** OUTPUT:   PRINTS THE DEGREE, COEFFICIENTS, INITIAL GUESS, AND EITHER
                                     15 **           THE ROOT OR, IF THE METHOD FAILS, AN ERROR MESSAGE.
                                     16 ** SUBPROGRAMS:
                                     17 **           CONVIN:  CONVERTS ONE INPUT FIELD INTO SHORT-FORM FLT. PT.
                                     18 **           CONVOUT: CONVERTS ONE SHORT-FORM FLT. PT. NO. INTO A
                                     19 **                    STRING OF 15 EBCDIC CHARACTERS.
                                     20 **           NEWTON:  FINDS ROOT USING THE NEWTON-RAPHSON METHOD.
                                     21 **********************************************************************
                                     22           PRINT NOGEN               SUPPRESS MACRO EXPANSIONS
                                     23 ** REGISTER DEFINITIONS:
                        00001        24 R1        EQU   1                   ARGUMENT LIST POINTER
                        00002        25 R2        EQU   2                   COUNTER
                        00003        26 R3        EQU   3                   COUNTER
                        00004        27 R4        EQU   4                   INDEX TO INPUT RECORD
                        00005        28 R5        EQU   5                   INDEX TO ARRAY OF COEFFICIENTS
                        00006        29 R6        EQU   6                   WORK REGISTER
                        00007        30 R7        EQU   7                   DEFINED IN NEWTON SUBPROGRAM
                        00008        31 R8        EQU   8                   DEFINED IN NEWTON SUBPROGRAM
                        0000C        32 R12       EQU   12                  BASE REGISTER
                        0000D        33 R13       EQU   13                  SAVE AREA POINTER
                        0000E        34 R14       EQU   14                  RETURN REGISTER
                        0000F        35 R15       EQU   15                  ENTRY POINT REGISTER
                        00000        36 F0        EQU   0                   FLT. PT. REG. 0; SUBPROGRAM RESULT
                        00002        37 F2        EQU   2                   DEFINED IN NEWTON SUBPROGRAM
                        00004        38 F4        EQU   4                   DEFINED IN NEWTON SUBPROGRAM
                        00006        39 F6        EQU   6                   DEFINED IN NEWTON SUBPROGRAM
                                     40 ** INITIALIZATION:
                                     41 *  OS:
000000 90EC D00C    0000C            42           STM   R14,R12,12(R13)     SAVE REGISTERS
000004 05C0                          43           BALR  R12,0               LOAD BASE REGISTER
                        00006        44           USING BASE,R12            DECLARE BASE REGISTER
000006 50D0 C352    00358            45 BASE      ST    R13,SAVE+4          SAVE R13
00000A 41E0 C34E    00354            46           LA    R14,SAVE            GET ADDRESS OF NEW SAVE AREA
00000E 50ED 0008    00008            47           ST    R14,8(R13)          STORE THIS ADDR. IN OLD SAVE AREA
000012 18DE                          48           LR    R13,R14             R13 = ADDR. OF NEW SAVE AREA
                                     49           OPEN  (READER,INPUT,PRINTER,OUTPUT)    PREPARE FOR I/O
                                     57 ** DOS*******
                                     58 *         BALR  R12,0               LOAD BASE REGISTER
                                     59 *         USING BASE,R12            DECLARE BASE REGISTER
                                     60 *BASE     LA    R13,SAVE            R13 = ADDR. OF NEW SAVE AREA
                                     61 *         OPEN  READER,PRINTER      PREPARE FOR I/O
                                     62 ******
                                     63 ** READ, PRINT, AND CONVERT DEGREE:
                                     64           GET   READER,RECORD       READ DEGREE
000030 D208 C146 C472 0014C 00478    69           MVC   LABEL,=CL9'0DEGREE ='  LABEL FOR OUTPUT
                                     70           PUT   PRINTER,LABEL       PRINT DEGREE
000044 F271 C342 C150 00348 00156    75           PACK  DOUBLE,RECORD(2)    CONVERT DEGREE TO PACKED-DECIMAL FORM
00004A 4F20 C342    00348            76           CVB   R2,DOUBLE           CONVERT DEGREE TO BINARY
00004E 5020 C1AA    001B0            77           ST    R2,N                SAVE DEGREE IN N
000052 4122 0001    00001            78           LA    R2,1(R2)            R2 = NO. OF COEFFICIENTS = N + 1
```

*(Continues)*

**Figure 17.13** The program for the case study.

```
                                          79 ** READ, PRINT, AND CONVERT N+1 COEFFICIENTS, 8 PER RECORD
                                          80          PUT    PRINTER,=CL90'0COEFFICIENTS:'  PRINT HEADING
000064 1B55                               85          SR     R5,R5             CLEAR INDEX TO COEFFICIENT ARRAY
                                          86 * REPEAT FOR ALL RECORDS:
000066 1B44                               87 OUTLOOP  SR     R4,R4             CLEAR INDEX TO INPUT RECORD
                                          88 * (COMPUTE R3 = MIN(8,R2) AND THEN R2 = R2 - R3):
000068 4130 0008       00008              89          LA     R3,8              R3 COUNTS 8 FIELDS PER RECORD
00006C 1923                               90          CR     R2,R3             COMPARE R2 WITH 8
00006E 47B0 C06E       00074              91          BNL    SKIP              IF R2>=8, LEAVE R3=8 AND SKIP AHEAD
000072 1832                               92          LR     R3,R2             ELSE R3=R2, WHICH IS < 8
000074 1B23                               93 SKIP     SR     R2,R3             R2 = R2-R3 = # OF COEFFS LEFT TO READ
                                          94 *                                   AFTER NEXT GET
                                          95          GET    READER,RECORD     READ NEXT RECORD OF COEFFICIENTS
                                         100          PUT    PRINTER,RECORD-1  PRINT RECORD
000092 4110 C396       0039C             105          LA     R1,ARG1           R1 = ADDRESS OF ARGUMENT LIST
                                         106 * - REPEAT FOR UP TO 8 FIELDS PER RECORD:
000096 4164 C150       00156             107 INLOOP   LA     R6,RECORD(R4)     R6 = ADDR. OF NEXT FIELD IN INPUT RECD.
00009A 5060 C396       0039C             108          ST     R6,ARG1           STORE ADDR. INTO ARGUMENT LIST
00009E 58F0 C3B2       003B8             109          L      R15,=V(CONVIN)    R15 = ENTRY POINT
0000A2 05EF                              110          BALR   R14,R15           CONVERT COEFFICIENT TO FLT. PT.
0000A4 7005 C1AE       001B4             111          STE    F0,A(R5)          STORE COEFFICIENT IN ARRAY
0000A8 4144 000A       0000A             112          LA     R4,10(R4)         POINT TO NEXT FIELD IN INPUT RECORD
0000AC 4155 0004       00004             113          LA     R5,4(R5)          POINT TO NEXT WORD IN COEFFICIENT ARRAY
0000B0 4630 C090       00096             114          BCT    R3,INLOOP         DECREMENT R3, REPEAT IF NOT 0
                                         115 * - END REPEAT
                                         116 * UNTIL ALL COEFFICIENTS ARE READ
0000B4 1222                              117          LTR    R2,R2             MORE COEFFICIENTS LEFT TO READ?
0000B6 4720 C060       00066             118          BP     OUTLOOP           YES; REPEAT
                                         119 * END REPEAT
                                         120 ** READ, PRINT, AND CONVERT INITIAL GUESS:
                                         121 OUT      GET    READER,RECORD     READ GUESS
0000C8 D208 C146 C47B 0014C 00481        126          MVC    LABEL,=CL9'0GUESS ='  LABEL FOR OUTPUT
                                         127          PUT    PRINTER,LABEL     PRINT GUESS
0000DC 4110 C396       0039C             132          LA     R1,ARG1           R1 = ADDRESS OF ARGUMENT LIST
0000E0 4160 C150       00156             133          LA     R6,RECORD         R6 = ADDRESS OF GUESS
0000E4 5060 C396       0039C             134          ST     R6,ARG1           STORE ADDRESS IN ARGUMENT LIST
0000E8 58F0 C3B2       003B8             135          L      R15,=V(CONVIN)    R15 = ENTRY POINT
0000EC 05EF                              136          BALR   R14,R15           CONVERT GUESS TO FLT. PT.
0000EE 7000 C33E       00344             137          STE    F0,GUESS          SAVE GUESS
                                         138 ** COMPUTE AND PRINT ROOT:
0000F2 4110 C39A       003A0             139          LA     R1,ARG2           R1 = ADDRESS OF ARGUMENT LIST
                                         140 *                                   (COEFFICIENTS, DEGREE, GUESS)
0000F6 58F0 C3B6       003BC             141          L      R15,=V(NEWTON)    R15 = ENTRY POINT
0000FA 05EF                              142          BALR   R14,R15           FIND ROOT
0000FC 4710 C120       00126             143          BO     ERROR             METHOD FAILED IF COND. CODE = 3
000100 7000 C34A       00350             144          STE    F0,ROOT           SAVE ROOT
000104 4110 C3A6       003AC             145          LA     R1,ARG3           R1 = ADDRESS OF ARGUMENT LIST
000108 58F0 C3BA       003C0             146          L      R15,=V(CONVOUT)   R15 = ENTRY POINT
00010C 05EF                              147          BALR   R14,R15           CONVERT ROOT TO EBCDIC; STORE IN RECORD
00010E D208 C146 C484 0014C 0048A        148          MVC    LABEL,=CL9'0ROOT ='  LABEL FOR OUTPUT
                                         149          PUT    PRINTER,LABEL     PRINT ROOT
000122 47F0 C12E       00134             154          B      FIN               FINISHED
                                         155 ** EXITS:
                                         156 ERROR    PUT    PRINTER,=CL90' METHOD FAILED'   ERROR MESSAGE
                                         161 *  OS:
                                         162 FIN      CLOSE  (READER,,PRINTER)  I/O IS COMPLETE
000142 58D0 C352       00358             170          L      R13,SAVE+4        RESTORE R13
000146 98EC D00C       0000C             171          LM     R14,R12,12(R13)   RESTORE REMAINING REGISTERS
00014A 07FE                              172          BR     R14               RETURN TO OS
                                         173 ** DOS*******
                                         174 *FIN     CLOSE READER,PRINTER     I/O IS COMPLETE
                                         175 *        EOJ                      RETURN TO DOS
```

*(Continues)*

**Figure 17.13** *(Continued)*

```
                                   ******
00014C                             LABEL    DS    CL9            LABEL FIELD
000155 40                                   DC    C' '           CARRIAGE CONTROL/SPACE
000156                             RECORD   DS    CL80           INPUT RECORD/ OUTPUT BUFFER
0001A6 4040404040404040                     DC    CL9' '         PAD OUTPUT BUFFER TO 89 CHARACTERS
0001B0                             N        DS    F              DEGREE
0001B4                             A        DS    100E           COEFFICIENTS
000344                             GUESS    DS    E              INITIAL GUESS
000348                             DOUBLE   DS    D              DOUBLEWORD FOR CVB
000350                             ROOT     DS    E              THE COMPUTED ROOT
000354                             SAVE     DS    18F            SAVE AREA (9D IN DOS)
                                   * ARGUMENT LIST FOR CONVIN:
00039C                             ARG1     DS    F              ARGUMENT ADDR. COMPUTED BY PROGRAM
                                   * ARGUMENT LIST FOR NEWTON:
0003A0 000001B4                    ARG2     DC    A(A)           ADDR. OF COEFFICIENT ARRAY
0003A4 000001B0                             DC    A(N)           ADDR. OF DEGREE
0003A8 00000344                             DC    A(GUESS)       ADDR. OF GUESS
                                   * ARGUMENT LIST FOR CONVOUT:
0003AC 00000350                    ARG3     DC    A(ROOT)        ADDR. OF ROOT
0003B0 00000156                             DC    A(RECORD)      ADDR. OF EBCDIC RESULT
0003B8                                      LTORG
0003B8 00000000                                   =V(CONVIN)
0003BC 00000000                                   =V(NEWTON)
0003C0 00000000                                   =V(CONVOUT)
0003C4 F0C3D6C5C6C6C9C3                           =CL90'0COEFFICIENTS:'
00041E 40D4C5E3C8D6C440                           =CL90' METHOD FAILED'
000478 F0C4C5C7D9C5C540                           =CL9'0DEGREE ='
000481 F0C7E4C5E2E2407E                           =CL9'0GUESS ='
00048A F0D9D6D6E3407E40                           =CL9'0ROOT ='
                                            DROP  R12
                                   ** DCB'S FOR I/O IN OS:
                                   READER   DCB   DSORG=PS,MACRF=GM,DDNAME=SYSIN,RECFM=F,LRECL=80,          X
                                                  BLKSIZE=80
                                   PRINTER  DCB   DSORG=PS,MACRF=PM,DDNAME=SYSPRINT,RECFM=FA,LRECL=90,      X
                                                  BLKSIZE=90
                                   ** DOS*******
                                   *READER  DTFCD DEVADDR=SYSIPT,DEVICE=2540,IOAREA1=INBUF,                 X
                                                  RECFORM=FIXUNB,BLKSIZE=80,TYPEFLE=INPUT,WORKA=YES
                                   *PRINTER DTFPR DEVADDR=SYSLST,DEVICE=3203,IOAREA1=OUTBUF,WORKA=YES,      X
                                                  RECFORM=FIXUNB,BLKSIZE=90,CTLCHAR=ASA
                                   *INBUF   DS    80C            DOS INPUT BUFFER
                                   *OUTBUF  DS    90C            DOS OUTPUT BUFFER
                                   ***********************************************************************
                                   ** SUBPROGRAM TO COMPUTE A REAL ROOT OF A POLYNOMIAL EQUATION USING
                                   ** THE NEWTON-RAPHSON METHOD.  THE POLYNOMIAL IS:
                                   **     A(0)*X**N + A(1)*X**(N-1) + ... + A(N-1)*X + A(N)
                                   ** ARGUMENTS: ARRAY OF SHORT-FORM FLT. PT. COEFFICIENTS,
                                   **            DEGREE OF POLYNOMIAL (FULLWORD BINARY),
                                   **            INITIAL GUESS (SHORT-FORM FLT. PT.).
                                   ** OUTPUT:    RETURNS ROOT IN FLT. PT. REG. 0.  SETS CONDITION CODE TO
                                   **              3 IF METHOD FAILS AFTER 25 ITERATIONS.
                                   ***********************************************************************
000558                             NEWTON   CSECT
                                   ** REGISTER ASSIGNMENTS (OTHER THAN R1, R12, R13, R14, R15):
                                   *R2                           LOOP COUNTER
                                   *R3                           LOOP COUNTER
                                   *R5                           INDEX TO COEFFICIENT ARRAY A
                                   *R6                           ADDRESS OF COEFFICIENT ARRAY A
                                   *R7                           ADDRESS OF DEGREE OF POLYNOMIAL
                                   *R8                           ADDRESS OF INITIAL GUESS
                                   ** FLOATING-POINT REGISTER ASSIGNMENTS:
                                   *F0                           XNEW AND ROOT
                                   *F2                           XOLD
                                   *F4                           B(J)
                                   *F6                           C(J)
```

*(Continues)*

**Figure 17.13** *(Continued)*

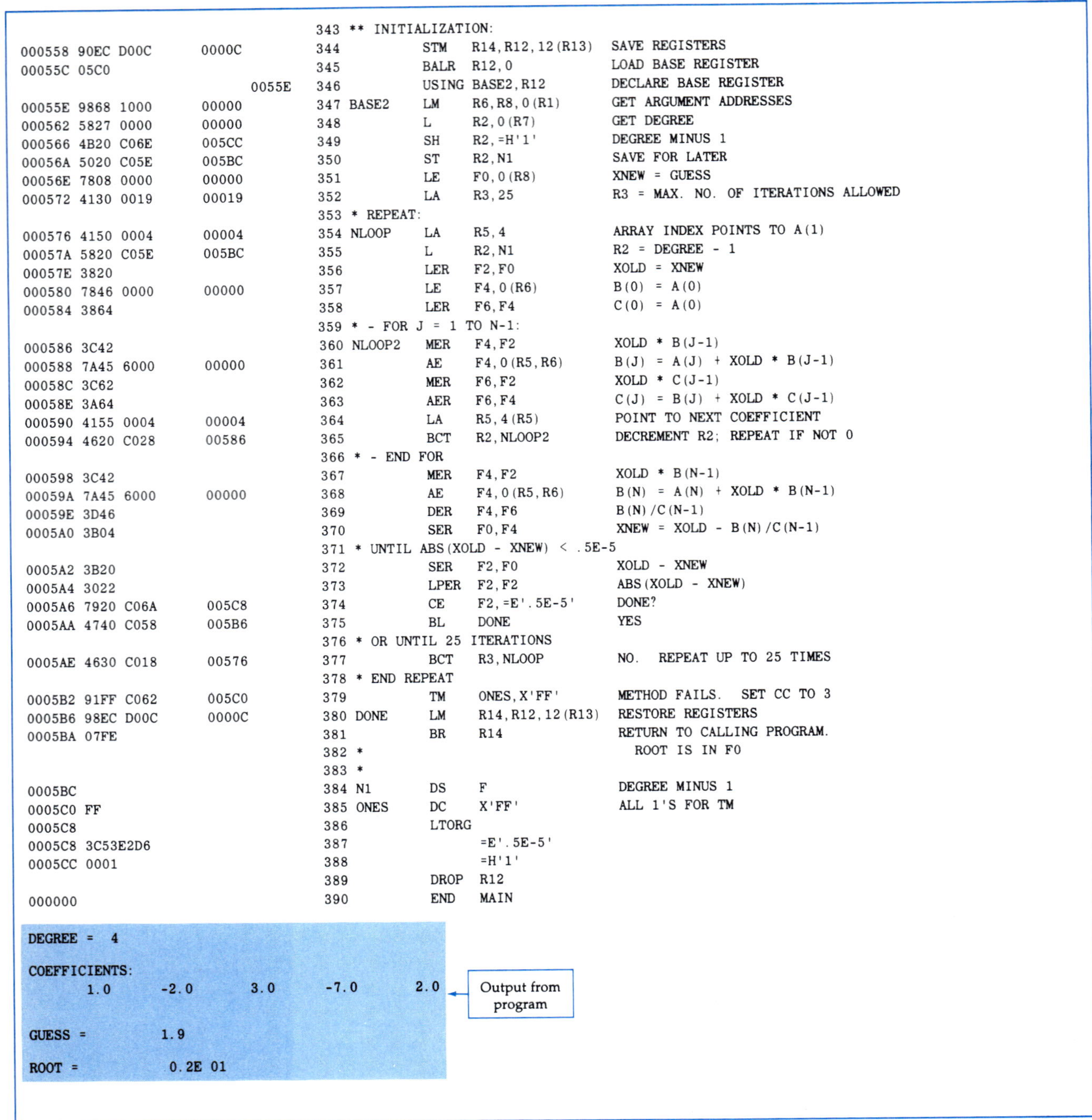

```
                                     ** INITIALIZATION:
000558 90EC D00C      0000C                    STM   R14,R12,12(R13)   SAVE REGISTERS
00055C 05C0                                    BALR  R12,0             LOAD BASE REGISTER
                              0055E            USING BASE2,R12         DECLARE BASE REGISTER
00055E 9868 1000      00000          BASE2     LM    R6,R8,0(R1)       GET ARGUMENT ADDRESSES
000562 5827 0000      00000                    L     R2,0(R7)          GET DEGREE
000566 4B20 C06E      005CC                    SH    R2,=H'1'          DEGREE MINUS 1
00056A 5020 C05E      005BC                    ST    R2,N1             SAVE FOR LATER
00056E 7808 0000      00000                    LE    F0,0(R8)          XNEW = GUESS
000572 4130 0019      00019                    LA    R3,25             R3 = MAX. NO. OF ITERATIONS ALLOWED
                                     * REPEAT:
000576 4150 0004      00004          NLOOP     LA    R5,4              ARRAY INDEX POINTS TO A(1)
00057A 5820 C05E      005BC                    L     R2,N1             R2 = DEGREE - 1
00057E 3820                                    LER   F2,F0             XOLD = XNEW
000580 7846 0000      00000                    LE    F4,0(R6)          B(0) = A(0)
000584 3864                                    LER   F6,F4             C(0) = A(0)
                                     * - FOR J = 1 TO N-1:
000586 3C42                          NLOOP2    MER   F4,F2             XOLD * B(J-1)
000588 7A45 6000      00000                    AE    F4,0(R5,R6)       B(J) = A(J) + XOLD * B(J-1)
00058C 3C62                                    MER   F6,F2             XOLD * C(J-1)
00058E 3A64                                    AER   F6,F4             C(J) = B(J) + XOLD * C(J-1)
000590 4155 0004      00004                    LA    R5,4(R5)          POINT TO NEXT COEFFICIENT
000594 4620 C028      00586                    BCT   R2,NLOOP2         DECREMENT R2; REPEAT IF NOT 0
                                     * - END FOR
000598 3C42                                    MER   F4,F2             XOLD * B(N-1)
00059A 7A45 6000      00000                    AE    F4,0(R5,R6)       B(N) = A(N) + XOLD * B(N-1)
00059E 3D46                                    DER   F4,F6             B(N)/C(N-1)
0005A0 3B04                                    SER   F0,F4             XNEW = XOLD - B(N)/C(N-1)
                                     * UNTIL ABS(XOLD - XNEW) < .5E-5
0005A2 3B20                                    SER   F2,F0             XOLD - XNEW
0005A4 3022                                    LPER  F2,F2             ABS(XOLD - XNEW)
0005A6 7920 C06A      005C8                    CE    F2,=E'.5E-5'      DONE?
0005AA 4740 C058      005B6                    BL    DONE              YES
                                     * OR UNTIL 25 ITERATIONS
0005AE 4630 C018      00576                    BCT   R3,NLOOP          NO.  REPEAT UP TO 25 TIMES
                                     * END REPEAT
0005B2 91FF C062      005C0                    TM    ONES,X'FF'        METHOD FAILS.  SET CC TO 3
0005B6 98EC D00C      0000C          DONE      LM    R14,R12,12(R13)   RESTORE REGISTERS
0005BA 07FE                                    BR    R14               RETURN TO CALLING PROGRAM.
                                     *                                   ROOT IS IN F0
                                     *
0005BC                               N1        DS    F                 DEGREE MINUS 1
0005C0 FF                            ONES      DC    X'FF'             ALL 1'S FOR TM
0005C8                                         LTORG
0005C8 3C53E2D6                                      =E'.5E-5'
0005CC 0001                                          =H'1'
                                               DROP  R12
000000                                         END   MAIN
```

```
DEGREE =  4

COEFFICIENTS:
        1.0       -2.0        3.0       -7.0        2.0

GUESS =           1.9

ROOT =             0.2E 01
```



**Figure 17.13**
(*Continued*)

## Debugging Hints

1. The following is a summary of the exceptions that can occur during a floating-point computation.

   - *Operation*. This exception occurs when the hardware to support the floating-point or extended-precision instruction sets is not installed.

- *Specification.* This exception occurs either when a register other than 0, 2, 4, or 6 has been specified as a floating-point register operand, or when a register other than 0 or 4 has been specified as an extended-precision register operand.
- *Exponent Overflow.* This exception can occur during the execution of these floating-point instructions: normalized or unnormalized Add or Subtract, Multiply, Divide, or Round. The correct characteristic exceeds $7F_{16}$, but the characteristic in the result is 128 too small.
- *Exponent Underflow.* This exception can occur during the execution of these floating-point instructions: normalized Add or Subtract, Multiply, Divide, or Halve. The correct characteristic is less than zero; however if this exception is not masked off, the characteristic in the result is 128 too large. If the exception is masked off, the result is true zero.
- *Significance.* This exception can occur only during normalized or unnormalized Add or Subtract instructions. The fraction of the result is zero. If the exception is masked off, the final result is true zero.
- *Floating-Point Divide.* This exception can occur during the execution of a floating-point Divide instruction. The exception occurs because the divisor has a zero fraction.

2. Frequently, an exponent overflow exception, an exponent underflow exception, a significance exception, or a floating-point divide exception occurs because an operand is specified incorrectly. For example, an operand might be a binary integer instead of a floating-point number: you may have omitted a conversion, or the effective address may be incorrect because the base or index register is incorrect.
3. If one of the four exceptions named in Debugging Hint 2 is due to the inherent nature of a correctly specified floating-point computation, then a new algorithm design may be necessary, just as it would be if you had used a high-level language. If the result has become too large, you can use a procedure known as **scaling**. By factoring out a power of 16, you can reduce the magnitude of the result without introducing a change in its fraction. You will only alter the characteristic, and you can accommodate this change when you interpret the results. Similarly, multiplying a computation by a power of 16 can eliminate an exponent underflow. However, underflows often can be ignored and masked off to prevent an interruption.

## Stylistic Notes

1. Differentiate between the general and floating-point registers by defining them symbolically. This is a particularly important step when the operand entry of an instruction designates both types of registers.

## Summary

1. The floating-point notation for the IBM 370 uses a sign-magnitude hexadecimal representation. Three forms are available to represent floating-point numbers: short, long, and extended. The first byte of each form contains both the sign of the number and the characteristic, which represents the exponent in an excess-64 notation.
2. You can use the constant types E, D, and L with the DC or DS directives to define short-form, long-form, and extended-form floating-point fields.
3. Most floating-point instructions produce results whose forms are the same as the forms of the instructions' operands. Only six instructions,

| Mnemonic | Form of operand | Form of result |
|---|---|---|
| MER | Short | Long |
| ME | Short | Long |
| MXDR | Long | Extended |
| MXD | Long | Extended |
| LRDR | Extended | Long |
| LRER | Long | Short |

**Figure 17.14**
The six instructions whose results differ in form from that of their operands.

which are listed in Figure 17.14, have results that differ in form from that of their operands. MER and ME produce long-form products from short-form operands; MXDR and MXD produce extended-form products from long-form operands; and LRDR and LRER round extended and long operands, respectively, to the next shortest form.

4. All floating-point arithmetic instructions can have operands that are either normalized or unnormalized. Most of these instructions produce normalized results. Only the Add and Subtract instructions are available in unnormalized versions that do not remove leading zeros from the fraction of the result. You use these instructions for special purposes, but not for most computations.
5. Most floating-point instructions are available for both short-form and long-form operands. Seven optional instructions involve extended-form operands: they perform normalized addition and subtraction, multiplication, rounding, and, with the extended architecture, division. The only instructions that produce extended-form results from extended-form operands use register operands, and are in RR format or RRE format.
6. Floating-point instructions use a guard digit during arithmetic in an attempt to increase the accuracy of the result.
7. All arithmetic results are truncated—and not rounded—to the required length. Two optional instructions are available to round from extended form to long form, or from long form to short form.
8. Four exceptions, which are peculiar to floating-point arithmetic, are possible: exponent overflow, exponent underflow, significance, and floating-point divide. You can mask off exponent underflow and significance exceptions so that they do not cause a program interruption.
9. There are no special instructions that convert between either floating-point numbers and binary integers, or floating-point numbers and EBCDIC character strings.

## New Instruction Summary

| Operation | Operand | Format | Instruction Name | Action |
|---|---|---|---|---|
| **LER** | *FPR1,FPR2* | RR | LOAD SHORT REGISTER | $C(FPR1)_{0-31} \leftarrow C(FPR2)_{0-31}$ |
| **LE** | *FPR1,S2(X2)* or *FPR1,D2(X2,B2)* | RX | LOAD SHORT | $C(FPR1)_{0-31} \leftarrow C(E2)_{0-31}$ |
| **LDR** | *FPR1,FPR2* | RR | LOAD DOUBLE REGISTER | $C(FPR1)_{0-63} \leftarrow C(FPR2)_{0-63}$ |
| **LD** | *FPR1,S2(X2)* or *FPR1,D2(X2,B2)* | RX | LOAD DOUBLE | $C(FPR1)_{0-63} \leftarrow C(E2)_{0-63}$ |
| **STE** | *FPR1,S2(X2)* or *FPR1,D2(X2,B2)* | RX | STORE SHORT | $C(E2)_{0-31} \leftarrow C(FPR1)_{0-31}$ |
| **STD** | *FPR1,S2(X2)* or *FPR1,D2(X2,B2)* | RX | STORE DOUBLE | $C(E2)_{0-63} \leftarrow C(FPR1)_{0-63}$ |
| **AER** | *FPR1,FPR2* | RR | ADD SHORT REGISTERS | $C(FPR1)_{0-31} \leftarrow C(FPR1)_{0-31} + C(FPR2)_{0-31}$ |

| Operation | Operand | Format | Instruction Name | Action |
|---|---|---|---|---|
| **AE** | *FPR1,S2(X2)* or *FPR1,D2(X2,B2)* | RX | ADD SHORT | $C(FPR1)_{0-31} \leftarrow C(FPR1)_{0-31} + C(E2)_{0-31}$ |
| **ADR** | *FPR1,FPR2* | RR | ADD DOUBLE REGISTERS | $C(FPR1)_{0-63} \leftarrow C(FPR1)_{0-63} + C(FPR2)_{0-63}$ |
| **AD** | *FPR1,S2(X2)* or *FPR1,D2(X2,B2)* | RX | ADD DOUBLE | $C(FPR1)_{0-63} \leftarrow C(FPR1)_{0-63} + C(E2)_{0-63}$ |
| **AXR** | *FPR1,FPR2* | RR | ADD EXTENDED REGISTERS | $C(FPR1,\ FPR1+2) \leftarrow C(FPR1,\ FPR1+2) + C(FPR2,FPR2+2)$ |

*The condition code is set as follows for all of the normalized Add instructions just given:*

$$\text{Condition Code} = \begin{cases} 0 \text{ if the fraction of the sum is zero} \\ 1 \text{ if the sum is negative} \\ 2 \text{ if the sum is positive} \end{cases}$$

| Operation | Operand | Format | Instruction Name | Action |
|---|---|---|---|---|
| **SER** | *FPR1,FPR2* | RR | SUBTRACT SHORT REGISTERS | $C(FPR1)_{0-31} \leftarrow C(FPR1)_{0-31} - C(FPR2)_{0-31}$ |
| **SE** | *FPR1,S2(X2)* or *FPR1,D2(X2,B2)* | RX | SUBTRACT SHORT | $C(FPR1)_{0-31} \leftarrow C(FPR1)_{0-31} - C(E2)_{0-31}$ |
| **SDR** | *FPR1,FPR2* | RR | SUBTRACT DOUBLE REGISTERS | $C(FPR1)_{0-63} \leftarrow C(FPR1)_{0-63} - C(FPR2)_{0-63}$ |
| **SD** | *FPR1,S2(X2)* or *FPR1,D2(X2,B2)* | RX | SUBTRACT DOUBLE | $C(FPR1)_{0-63} \leftarrow C(FPR1)_{0-63} - C(E2)_{0-63}$ |
| **SXR** | *FPR1,FPR2* | RR | SUBTRACT EXTENDED REGISTERS | $C(FPR1,FPR1+2) \leftarrow C(FPR1,FPR1+2) - C(FPR2,FPR2+2)$ |

*The condition code for all of the normalized Subtract instructions is set as for addition.*

| Operation | Operand | Format | Instruction Name | Action |
|---|---|---|---|---|
| **MER** | *FPR1,FPR2* | RR | MULTIPLY SHORT REGISTERS | $C(FPR1)_{0-63} \leftarrow C(FPR1)_{0-31} * C(FPR2)_{0-31}$ |
| **ME** | *FPR1,S2(X2)* or *FPR1,D2(X2,B2)* | RX | MULTIPLY SHORT | $C(FPR1)_{0-63} \leftarrow C(FPR1)_{0-31} * C(E2)_{0-31}$ |
| **MDR** | *FPR1,FPR2* | RR | MULTIPLY DOUBLE REGISTERS | $C(FPR1)_{0-63} \leftarrow C(FPR1)_{0-63} * C(FPR2)_{0-63}$ |
| **MD** | *FPR1,S2(X2)* or *FPR1,D2(X2,B2)* | RX | MULTIPLY DOUBLE | $C(FPR1)_{0-63} \leftarrow C(FPR1)_{0-63} * C(E2)_{0-63}$ |

| Operation | Operand | Format | Instruction Name | Action |
|---|---|---|---|---|
| **MXDR** | *FPR1,FPR2* | RR | MULTIPLY EXTENDED FROM DOUBLE REGISTERS | $C(FPR1,FPR1+2) \leftarrow C(FPR1)_{0-63} * C(FPR2)_{0-63}$ |
| **MXD** | *FPR1,S2(X2)* or *FPR1,D2(X2,B2)* | RX | MULTIPLY EXTENDED FROM DOUBLE | $C(FPR1,FPR1+2) \leftarrow C(FPR1)_{0-63} * C(E2)_{0-63}$ |
| **MXR** | *FPR1,FPR2* | RR | MULTIPLY EXTENDED REGISTERS | $C(FPR1,FPR1+2) \leftarrow C(FPR1,FPR1+2) * C(FPR2,FPR2+2)$ |
| **DER** | *FPR1,FPR2* | RR | DIVIDE SHORT REGISTERS | $C(FPR1)_{0-31} \leftarrow C(FPR1)_{0-31} \div C(FPR2)_{0-31}$ |
| **DE** | *FPR1,S2(X2)* or *FPR1,D2(X2,B2)* | RX | DIVIDE SHORT | $C(FPR1)_{0-31} \leftarrow C(FPR1)_{0-31} \div C(E2)_{0-31}$ |
| **DDR** | *FPR1,FPR2* | RR | DIVIDE DOUBLE REGISTERS | $C(FPR1)_{0-63} \leftarrow C(FPR1)_{0-63} \div C(FPR2)_{0-63}$ |
| **DD** | *FPR1,S2(X2)* or *FPR1,D2(X2,B2)* | RX | DIVIDE DOUBLE | $C(FPR1)_{0-63} \leftarrow C(FPR1)_{0-63} \div C(E2)_{0-63}$ |
| **DXR** *(370-XA only)* | *FPR1,FPR2* | RRE | DIVIDE EXTENDED REGISTERS | $C(FPR1,FPR1+2) \leftarrow C(FPR1,FPR1+2) \div C(FPR2,FPR2+2)$ |
| **HER** | *FPR1,FPR2* | RR | HALVE SHORT REGISTER | $C(FPR1)_{0-31} \leftarrow C(FPR2)_{0-31} \div 2$ |
| **HDR** | *FPR1,FPR2* | RR | HALVE DOUBLE REGISTER | $C(FPR1)_{0-63} \leftarrow C(FPR2)_{0-63} \div 2$ |
| **LRER** | *FPR1,FPR2* | RR | LOAD ROUNDED SHORT REGISTER | $C(FPR1)_{0-31} \leftarrow C(FPR2)_{0-63}$ rounded |
| **LRDR** | *FPR1,FPR2* | RR | LOAD ROUNDED DOUBLE REGISTER | $C(FPR1)_{0-63} \leftarrow C(FPR2,FPR2+2)_{0-127}$ rounded |
| **CER** | *FPR1,FPR2* | RR | COMPARE SHORT REGISTERS | Compares $C(FPR1)_{0-31}$ with $C(FPR2)_{0-31}$ |

| Operation | Operand | Format | Instruction Name | Action |
|---|---|---|---|---|
| **CE** | *FPR1,S2(X2)* or *FPR1,D2(X2,B2)* | RX | COMPARE SHORT | Compares $C(FPR1)_{0-31}$ with $C(E2)_{0-31}$ |
| **CDR** | *FPR1,FPR2* | RR | COMPARE DOUBLE REGISTERS | Compares $C(FPR1)_{0-63}$ with $C(FPR2)_{0-63}$ |
| **CD** | *FPR1,S2(X2)* or *FPR1,D2(X2,B2)* | RX | COMPARE DOUBLE | Compares $C(FPR1)_{0-63}$ with $C(E2)_{0-63}$ |

*The condition code is set as follows for the Compare instructions just given:*

$$\text{Condition code} = \begin{cases} 0 \text{ if the operands are equal} \\ 1 \text{ if the first operand is less than the second operand} \\ 2 \text{ if the first operand is greater than the second operand} \end{cases}$$

| Operation | Operand | Format | Instruction Name | Action |
|---|---|---|---|---|
| **LTER** | *FPR1,FPR2* | RR | LOAD AND TEST SHORT REGISTER | $C(FPR1)_{0-31} \leftarrow C(FPR2)_{0-31}$ |
| **LTDR** | *FPR1,FPR2* | RR | LOAD AND TEST DOUBLE REGISTER | $C(FPR1)_{0-63} \leftarrow C(FPR2)_{0-63}$ |
| **LPER** | *FPR1,FPR2* | RR | LOAD POSITIVE SHORT REGISTER | $C(FPR1)_{0-31} \leftarrow \lvert C(FPR2)_{0-31}\rvert$ |
| **LPDR** | *FPR1,FPR2* | RR | LOAD POSITIVE DOUBLE REGISTER | $C(FPR1)_{0-63} \leftarrow \lvert C(FPR2)_{0-63}\rvert$ |
| **LNER** | *FPR1,FPR2* | RR | LOAD NEGATIVE SHORT REGISTER | $C(FPR1)_{0-31} \leftarrow -\ \lvert C(FPR2)_{0-31}\rvert$ |
| **LNDR** | *FPR1,FPR2* | RR | LOAD NEGATIVE DOUBLE REGISTER | $C(FPR1)_{0-63} \leftarrow -\ \lvert C(FPR2)_{0-63}\rvert$ |
| **LCER** | *FPR1,FPR2* | RR | LOAD COMPLE-MENT SHORT REGISTER | $C(FPR1)_{0-31} \leftarrow -\ C(FPR2)_{0-31}$ |
| **LCDR** | *FPR1,FPR2* | RR | LOAD COMPLE-MENT DOUBLE REGISTER | $C(FPR1)_{0-63} \leftarrow -\ C(FPR2)_{0-63}$ |

| Operation | Operand | Format | Instruction Name | Action |
|---|---|---|---|---|

*The condition code is set for the Load Register instructions just given to reflect the status of the results:*

$$\text{Condition code} = \begin{cases} 0 \text{ if the result has a zero fraction} \\ 1 \text{ if the result is negative} \\ 2 \text{ if the result is positive} \end{cases}$$

| Operation | Operand | Format | Instruction Name | Action |
|---|---|---|---|---|
| **AUR** | *FPR1,FPR2* | RR | ADD UNNORMALIZED SHORT REGISTERS | $C(FPR1)_{0-31} \leftarrow C(FPR1)_{0-31} + C(FPR2)_{0-31}$ |
| **AU** | *FPR1,S2(X2)* or *FPR1,D2(X2,B2)* | RX | ADD UNNORMALIZED SHORT | $C(FPR1)_{0-31} \leftarrow C(FPR1)_{0-31} + C(E2)_{0-31}$ |
| **AWR** | *FPR1,FPR2* | RR | ADD UNNORMALIZED DOUBLE REGISTERS | $C(FPR1)_{0-63} \leftarrow C(FPR1)_{0-63} + C(FPR2)_{0-63}$ |
| **AW** | *FPR1,S2(X2)* or *FPR1,D2(X2,B2)* | RX | ADD UNNORMALIZED DOUBLE | $C(FPR1)_{0-63} \leftarrow C(FPR1)_{0-63} + C(E2)_{0-63}$ |
| **SUR** | *FPR1,FPR2* | RR | SUBTRACT UNNORMALIZED SHORT REGISTERS | $C(FPR1)_{0-31} \leftarrow C(FPR1)_{0-31} - C(FPR2)_{0-31}$ |
| **SU** | *FPR1,S2(X2)* or *FPR1,D2(X2,B2)* | RX | SUBTRACT UNNORMALIZED SHORT | $C(FPR1)_{0-31} \leftarrow C(FPR1)_{0-31} - C(E2)_{0-31}$ |
| **SWR** | *FPR1,FPR2* | RR | SUBTRACT UNNORMALIZED DOUBLE REGISTERS | $C(FPR1)_{0-63} \leftarrow C(FPR1)_{0-63} - C(FPR2)_{0-63}$ |
| **SW** | *FPR1,S2(X2)* or *FPR1,D2(X2,B2)* | RX | SUBTRACT UNNORMALIZED DOUBLE | $C(FPR1)_{0-63} \leftarrow C(FPR1)_{0-63} - C(E2)_{0-63}$ |

*The condition code settings for the unnormalized instructions are the same as those for the normalized instructions.*

## New Constant Types with DC or DS Directives

| Name | Operation | Operand | Action |
|---|---|---|---|
| *symbol* or *blank* | DC | *dt'c'* | Defines *d* short-form ($t$ = E), long-form ($t$ = D), or extended-form ($t$ = L) floating-point numbers, each with a value equal to the decimal constant *c*. |
| *symbol* or *blank* | DS | *dt* | Reserves *d* fullwords ($t$ = E), *d* doublewords ($t$ = D), or 2∗*d* doublewords ($t$ = L). |

## Exercises

**1.** Verify that the range for short-form floating-point numbers is approximately from $.5 \times 10^{-78}$ to $.7 \times 10^{76}$.

**2.** Explain why the LPER instruction, unlike the LPR instruction, cannot cause an overflow.

**3.** Indicate the effect that these C and CE instructions have upon the condition code for each of the listed definitions of X and Y:

```
L     2,X
C     2,Y
LE    2,X
CE    2,Y
```

**a.**
```
X     DC     E'-5.1'
Y     DC     E'-12'
```

**b.**
```
X     DC     E'10'
Y     DC     E'-10'
```

**c.**
```
X     DC     E'5.1'
Y     DC     E'10'
```

**d.**
```
X     DC     E'-12'
Y     DC     E'-12'
```

**4.** What effect does each of these instructions have upon the condition code and the relevant register operands? Assume that significance exceptions and exponent underflow exceptions are masked off.

**a.**
```
LD     6,=D'123.7'
AD     6,=D'-123.7'
```

**b.**
```
LE     4,=E'1E-64'
DE     4,=E'1E64'
```

**c.**
```
LE     2,=E'-2E-50'
ME     2,=E'-3E-40'
```

**5.** For each of these mnemonics, write instructions that perform the analogous operation for extended-form numbers.

**a.** LER
**b.** LE
**c.** STE
**d.** CER
**e.** CE
**f.** LTER
**g.** LPER
**h.** LNER
**i.** LCER

**6.** Write floating-point instructions that accomplish each of these tasks, assuming that A, B, C, D, and E are defined as follows:

```
A     DC     E'-4.3'
B     DC     D'1.7E2'
C     DC     L'9.1'
D     DS     D
E     DS     E
```

**a.** Subtract $-4.3$ from the number at E and store the result at E.

**b.** Divide the number at D by the number at B and store the result at D.

**c.** Square the number at A, round the product to short form, and store the result at E.

**d.** Square the number at C, round the product to long form, and store the result at D.

**e.** Add the numbers at A and B, and store the long-form result at D.

**f.** Replace the number at B by one-half of its present value.

**g.** Store zero at E if the number at D is less than 5.1.

h. Change the sign of the number at D by using a Load instruction.
i. Change the sign of the number at D by using a Boolean operation.

7. What exceptions occur or are possible during the execution of each of these instructions?
 a. `ADR 2,2`
 b. `SER 6,6`
 c. `MER 4,4`
 d. `DDR 2,4`
 e. `LRER 0,6`
 f. `LCDR 2,0`
 g. `ME 4,=E'0'`
 h. `SD 2,=D'12.1'`
 i. `SW 2,=D'1.1'`
 j. `HER 2,4`

8. Write instructions that set the program mask as follows:
 a. Allow a program interruption due to a significance exception.
 b. Allow a program interruption due to an exponent underflow exception, but not due to a significance exception.
 c. Prevent program interruptions due to significance exceptions and exponent underflow exceptions.

9. Given the long-form numbers $x$, $y$, and $z$, which are stored as doublewords, write instructions that evaluate these expressions in double precision.
 a. $(x - y) / z$
 b. $(x / 2 + z / 5.1) * (y + 1)$
 c. $y^3 / (z^2 + x)$

10. Write instructions that convert a long-form floating-point number to 32-bit integer form.

11. Write instructions that convert a 32-bit integer to long-form floating-point notation.

12. Write instructions that compute the average of the 50 long-form numbers in the array at F. Round the result to short-form, and store it in the fullword at AVG.

13. Write instructions that compute the long-form sum of the squares of the 50 short-form numbers in the array at G. Store the result in the doubleword at SUMSQ.

14. Write Boolean instructions that alter the sign of a floating-point number in storage, as follows:
 a. Make the sign plus.
 b. Make the sign minus.
 c. Invert the sign.

## Programming Problems

1. Complete the instructions in Figure 17.9 that convert a floating-point number to a printable form. Consider three cases: the number is 0; the magnitude of the number is 1; and the magnitude of the number is less than 1.

2. Write a subprogram that converts a short-form floating-point number to an EBCDIC character string without an exponent. The string should be suitable for printing. For example, the floating-point number C1A80000 would appear as −10.5. The character string should contain *w* characters with *d* digits to the right of the decimal point. Let *w* and *d* be arguments of the subprogram. If the number is too large to be accommodated by *w* characters, produce *w* asterisks.

3. Write a subprogram to compute $e^x$ in double precision by using this Taylor series:

$$e^x = 1 + x + x^2/2! + x^3/3! + \ldots$$

You can compute each term $x^k/k!$ recursively from the term that precedes it by using the following equations:

$$t_1 = 1$$
$$t_{k+1} = x * t_k / k$$

where $k$ is equal to 1, 2, and so on. Terminate the computation when either the magnitude of the ratio of the next term to the sum of the preceding terms is less than $0.5 \times 10^{-5}$; or 25 terms have been computed. Signal the calling program in case the first criterion is not satisfied within 25 terms. Test your subprogram with the following values of $x$: 0.1, 0.25, 0.8, 1.0, 5.0, and 15.5.

4. Write a subprogram that computes the value of the definite integral $\int_a^b f(x)\,dx$ by using Simpson's Rule, which is described as follows: let

$$h_n = (b - a)/n$$

for an even integer $n$, and

$$x_0 = a$$
$$x_k = x_{k-1} + h_n$$

where $k$ is equal to 1, 2, and so on, to $n$. The following is an approximation to the definite integral:

$$I_n = h_n\{f(a) + 4[f(x_1) + f(x_3) + \ldots + f(x_{n-1})] + 2[f(x_2) + f(x_4) + \ldots + f(x_{n-2})] + f(b)\}$$

Compute a sequence of single-precision approximations $I_n$ for $n = 2, 4$, and so on. Stop the computation when

$$|I_{n+2} - I_n| < 0.5 \times 10^{-5}$$

and return $I_{n+2}$ as the value of the integral. Your subprogram should call a function subprogram to evaluate $f(x)$ for any given $x$.

5. Write a subprogram that computes the square root of the long-form number $z$ by using this recursion relation, which is obtained by applying the Newton-Raphson method to the equation $x^2 - z = 0$:

$$x_0 = \text{initial guess at } \sqrt{z}$$
$$x_{k+1} = (x_k + z/x_k)/2$$

where $k$ is equal to 0, 1, 2, and so on.
Terminate the computation when

$$|x_{k+1} - x_k| < 0.5 \times 10^{-5}\,|x_{k+1}|$$

Use $z/2$ as the value of $x_0$. Test your subprogram with the following values of $z$: 2, 64, 100, and 999.1. Print $z$, $x_0$, the computed value of $\sqrt{z}$, and the number of iterations that are required for the computation.

# 18

# Macro Definitions and the Conditional Assembly Language

CONTENTS

## OVERVIEW

Since each macro instruction can represent many assembler language statements, macro instructions simplify writing and organizing a program. This chapter describes how you can write your own macro definitions. Macro definitions often include statements—collectively known as the conditional assembly language—that affect the source program before it is translated into machine language, and therefore greatly enhance the capability of macros. You can also use the conditional assembly language outside of macro definitions, but that use is not its primary application.

## OBJECTIVES

After studying this chapter, you should be able to:

1. Differentiate between preassembly time, assembly time, and execution time.
2. Write macro definitions that use positional or keyword parameters.
3. Write preassembly-time loops.
4. Define and use attributes.
5. Use the system variable symbols &SYSNDX, &SYSLIST, &SYSDATE, &SYSTIME, &SYSECT, and &SYSPARM.
6. Use sublists, substrings, and subscripted SET symbols.
7. Use nested macro instructions.
8. Use the conditional assembly language inside and outside of macro definitions.

# Introduction

Typically, a **macro instruction** represents at least several assembler language statements; the assembler replaces the macro instruction with these statements.† As such, macro instructions simplify the programming process because you write only one statement to perform an operation that is equivalent to possibly many complex statements. Thus, using macro instructions can improve the organization of a program and make it easier to read.

The assembler generates statements from a macro instruction according to a predefined pattern called a **macro definition** or, loosely, a **macro.** The macro instruction is said to **invoke** or **call** the macro definition. In previous chapters, you were introduced to several macros, such as SAVE, RETURN, OPEN, CLOSE, GET, and PUT. These macros are examples of **library macro definitions** that are already defined for you. However, you can write your own macro definitions within your source program. Such definitions are called **source macro definitions** and are discussed in this chapter.

## *An Overview of Fundamental Concepts and Terminology*

All source macro definitions must precede the first control section of your source program. Statements that begin with the first CSECT or START directive are known as the **open code.** Within the open code, you write macro instructions that invoke the macro definitions. The assembler processes the macro instructions and, during a **preassembly phase,** typically replaces each of them with assembler language statements that are called the **macro expansion.** In the assembly listing, a plus sign identifies each statement in the macro expansions.

Figure 18.1 gives a simple example of a source macro definition. The **header statement** MACRO and the **trailer statement** MEND delineate the definition. Immediately following the header statement is the **prototype statement.** It defines the macro name and, in general, lists the operand entries that can appear in the macro instruction. (However, this example has no operand entries.) The rest of the definition is the **body** of the macro. It includes **model statements,** from which the assembler generates the assembler language statements that constitute the macro expansion. For example, the BASE macro generates BALR and USING instructions that establish Register 12 as a base register.

BASE is an atypical macro instruction because its expansion is the same each time that you write it. Most macro instructions specify operands that affect the expansion. You represent such operands in the prototype statement by using **symbolic parameters.** For instance, the macro definition for BASE is rewritten in Figure 18.2 so that you can specify the desired base register as an operand in the macro instruction. In this case, ® is a symbolic parameter that corresponds to a particular value when you invoke the macro. That value—which is 10 here—replaces each occurrence of ® in the macro body.

Macro definitions can also contain statements that affect the macro expansion. These statements, collectively known as the **conditional assembly language,** are like the statements in a high-level language. For instance, you can write branching instructions that alter the sequence in which the

†It is possible, though not usual, that a macro instruction will not represent any assembler language statements.

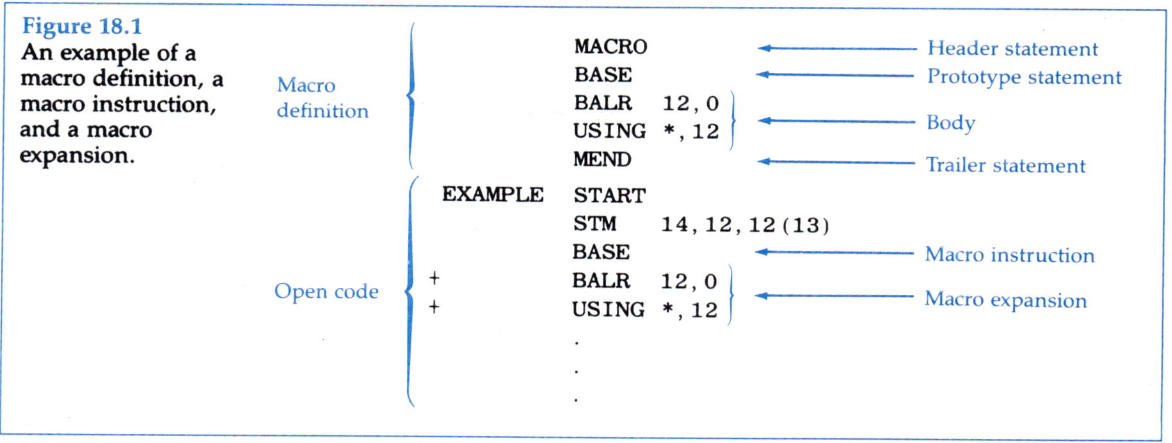


**Figure 18.1** An example of a macro definition, a macro instruction, and a macro expansion.

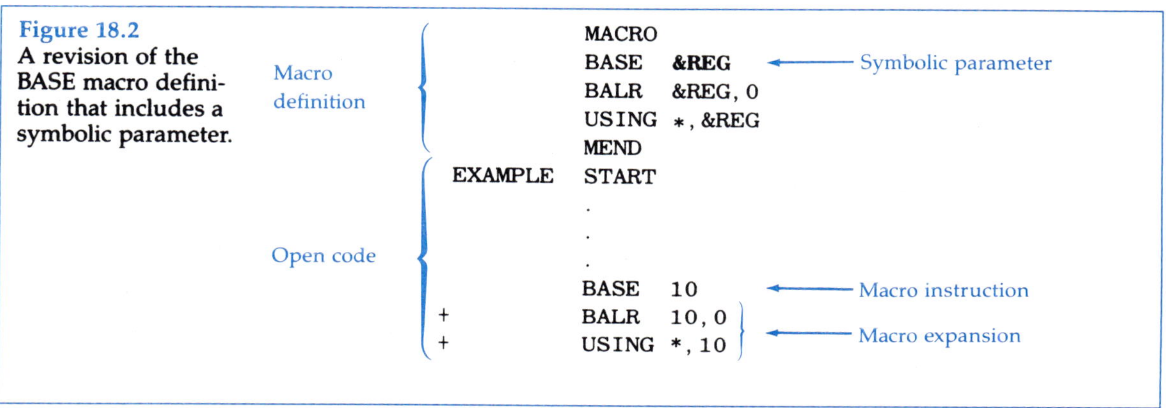


**Figure 18.2** A revision of the BASE macro definition that includes a symbolic parameter.

assembler processes model statements. You should realize that the conditional assembly language affects the source program before the assembler translates it into machine language. Thus, the preassembly phase of the assembler processes model statements and conditional assembly language statements in order to produce macro expansions. A second phase of the assembler then translates the macro expansions and the rest of the source program into machine language. Figure 18.3 illustrates this process. Although the major application of the conditional assembly language is within macro definitions, you can also use it within the open code.

You can use several kinds of symbols within a macro definition; they are classified as **ordinary symbols, variable symbols,** and **sequence symbols.** *Ordinary symbols* are simply those symbols that you have encountered in earlier chapters.

*Variable symbols* consist of an ampersand (&) and 1 to 7 alphanumeric characters, the first of which must be alphabetic. For example, these are variable symbols:

&X
&DATA123
&$22A

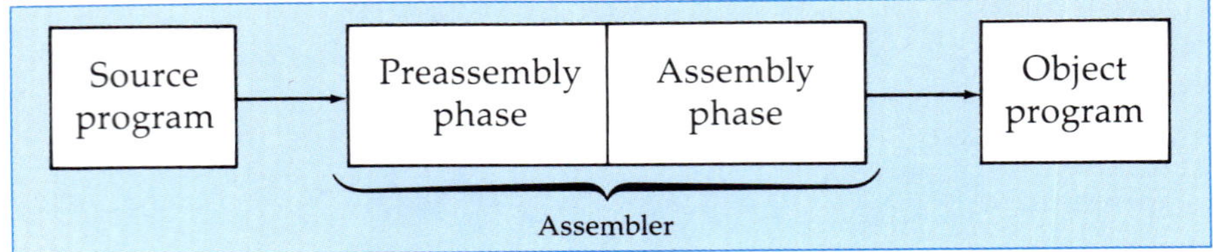


**Figure 18.3**
The preassembly and assembly phases of the assembler.

You write variable symbols in model statements to represent specific values. The assembler replaces the variable symbols with their values in the machine and assembler instructions that it generates from the model statements. You also can use variable symbols in conditional assembly language statements to affect the macro expansion. There are three types of variable symbols: **symbolic parameters, SET symbols,** and **system variable symbols.** You saw an example of a *symbolic parameter* (®) in Figure 18.2. *SET symbols* are a part of the conditional assembly language and, as shown later, you use them much like the variables in a high-level programming language. Note that there is no visible distinction between symbolic parameters and SET symbols; the ways that they are used differentiate them. Also note that there are 6 built-in *system variable symbols*—each beginning with &SYS—whose values are predefined for you. For example, &SYSNDX is a 4-digit counter that the assembler increments by 1 each time that it processes a macro instruction. The other system variable symbols are &SYSLIST, &SYSDATE, &SYSTIME, &SYSECT, and &SYSPARM.

Although *sequence symbols* begin with a period instead of an ampersand, they are formed like variable symbols. You use sequence symbols to label statements so that you can reference them by other conditional assembly language statements. Like symbolic parameters and system variable symbols, sequence symbols have meaning only during preassembly time.

The similarity of name and physical appearance of these symbols can cause confusion—particularly at first—so be careful.

## Writing Macro Definitions

This section describes the basic features that you need to write your own macro definitions. With few exceptions, you can use these features only within macro definitions, and not within the open code.

### *The Prototype Statement*

As indicated earlier in this chapter, you begin a macro definition with the MACRO instruction, and end it with the MEND instruction. Immediately after the MACRO instruction is the prototype statement, which describes the format of the macro instruction that you will use to call the macro. The prototype statement has an ordinary symbol in its operation entry; this symbol names the macro. The operand entry of the prototype statement contains symbolic parameters that represent input arguments to the macro. Symbolic parameters in the operand entry are classified as either **positional parameters** or **keyword parameters.** Optionally, you can write a symbolic parameter, which is called the **name field parameter,** in the name entry of the prototype statement. It represents the name entry, if any, of the macro instruction. To be effective, the name field parameter should also appear within the macro body—normally in the name entry of a model statement. The prototype statement can be summarized as follows:

The prototype statement

| Name | Operation | Operand |
|---|---|---|
| *variable symbol* or *blank* | *macro name* | *positional or keyword parameters separated by commas* |

*Positional Parameters.* Positional parameters are variable symbols that you write in a list in the operand entry of the prototype statement. The positional parameters are separated by commas. The operands that you write in the macro instruction to correspond to positional parameters are called **positional operands.** Such operands must appear in the same order as the corresponding positional parameters of the prototype statement. Although you can omit a positional operand from the macro instruction, you must write its trailing comma if another operand follows.

---

EXAMPLE 1

The DOUBLE macro, as defined in Figure 18.4, doubles the binary integer in the fullword that the symbolic parameter &NUMBER represents. DOUBLE then stores the result into the fullword that &RESULT represents. When you invoke the macro with the instruction

```
LOOP     DOUBLE  X,TWICEX
```

the assembler makes the following correspondence between the symbolic parameters of the prototype statement and the operands of the macro instruction:

&LABEL ↔ LOOP
&NUMBER ↔ X
&RESULT ↔ TWICEX

The resulting macro expansion appears in part **a** of Figure 18.5. Assume that X and TWICEX represent fullwords in storage.

If you omit the name entry from the macro instruction, as shown in part **b** of Figure 18.5, the name entry is omitted from the expansion because &LABEL in the macro definition (Figure 18.4) is null. Notice also that &RESULT in the macro definition corresponds to 0(R5) in the macro instruction, where it is assumed both that R5 is equated to 5 elsewhere in the program, and that Register 5 contains the address of a fullword in storage.

The accuracy of a macro expansion depends upon the macro instruction that you use to invoke the macro. For example, you must write the operands for the DOUBLE macro in the correct order and you cannot omit any. The

**Figure 18.4**
The definition of the DOUBLE macro, as described in Example 1.

```
        MACRO
&LABEL  DOUBLE  &NUMBER,&RESULT
&LABEL  L       2,&NUMBER           LOAD THE NUMBER
        AR      2,2                 DOUBLE IT
        ST      2,&RESULT           SAVE THE RESULT
        MEND
```

**Figure 18.5**
Some expansions of the DOUBLE macro, which was defined in Figure 18.4, that illustrate what happens when the macro instruction contains, **a.** a symbol in the name entry; **b.** no symbol in the name entry; and **c.** an incorrect number of operands.

**a.**

```
 LOOP     DOUBLE  X,TWICEX
+LOOP     L       2,X                    LOAD THE NUMBER
+         AR      2,2                    DOUBLE IT
+         ST      2,TWICEX               SAVE THE RESULT
```

**b.**

```
          DOUBLE  DATA,0(R5)
+         L       2,DATA                 LOAD THE NUMBER
+         AR      2,2                    DOUBLE IT
+         ST      2,0(R5)                SAVE THE RESULT
```

**c.**

```
          DOUBLE  DATA
+         L       2,DATA                 LOAD THE NUMBER
+         AR      2,2                    DOUBLE IT
+         ST      2,                     SAVE THE RESULT
```

Error: missing operand

macro instruction in part **c** of Figure 18.5 has only one operand, so the resulting Store instruction is incorrect. This error is not detected at preassembly time unless you write instructions within the macro definition to do so, but it is recognized when the assembler attempts to translate the macro expansion into machine language. The preassembly phase is merely a text-editing step: symbolic parameters are replaced by character strings to produce assembler language statements.

**The assembler replaces symbolic parameters with character strings.**

---

*Keyword Parameters.* You write a keyword parameter in the prototype statement as

&*keyword* = [*default*]

where &*keyword* is a variable symbol, and where *default* is an optional default value that the assembler assigns to the symbolic parameter &*keyword* if you omit the corresponding **keyword operand** from the macro instruction. A keyword operand has the following form:

*keyword* = *value*

Note that you do not write the ampersand here. This operand assigns *value* to the symbolic parameter &*keyword*. You write keyword operands in the macro instruction, separating them with commas and putting them in any order; their order does not have to follow the order of the keyword parameters in the prototype statement. If you omit keyword operands that do not have a default value, each of the corresponding symbolic parameters is replaced by the null string in the macro expansion.

---

EXAMPLE 2

You can revise the definition of the DOUBLE macro in Figure 18.4 to use keyword parameters, as shown in Figure 18.6, instead of using positional parameters. The macro definition specifies a default value for ® that the assembler uses if you omit this keyword from the macro instruction.

**Figure 18.6**
A revision of the DOUBLE macro that uses keyword parameters, as described in Example 2.

```
         MACRO
&LABEL   DOUBLE  &NUMBER=,&RESULT=,&REG=2
         L       &REG,&NUMBER          LOAD THE NUMBER
         AR      &REG,&REG             DOUBLE IT
         ST      &REG,&RESULT          SAVE THE RESULT
         MEND
```

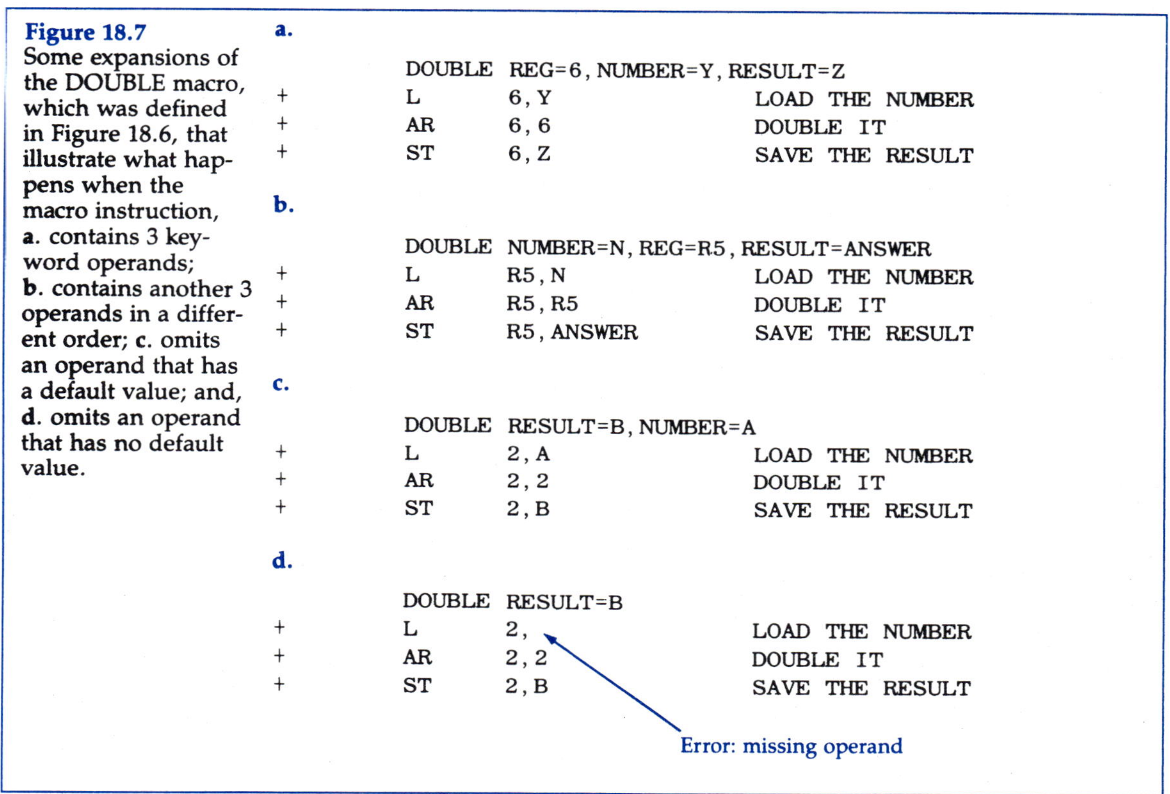

**Figure 18.7**
Some expansions of the DOUBLE macro, which was defined in Figure 18.6, that illustrate what happens when the macro instruction, **a**. contains 3 keyword operands; **b**. contains another 3 operands in a different order; **c**. omits an operand that has a default value; and, **d**. omits an operand that has no default value.

**a.**

```
         DOUBLE  REG=6,NUMBER=Y,RESULT=Z
+        L       6,Y                   LOAD THE NUMBER
+        AR      6,6                   DOUBLE IT
+        ST      6,Z                   SAVE THE RESULT
```

**b.**

```
         DOUBLE  NUMBER=N,REG=R5,RESULT=ANSWER
+        L       R5,N                  LOAD THE NUMBER
+        AR      R5,R5                 DOUBLE IT
+        ST      R5,ANSWER             SAVE THE RESULT
```

**c.**

```
         DOUBLE  RESULT=B,NUMBER=A
+        L       2,A                   LOAD THE NUMBER
+        AR      2,2                   DOUBLE IT
+        ST      2,B                   SAVE THE RESULT
```

**d.**

```
         DOUBLE  RESULT=B
+        L       2,                    LOAD THE NUMBER
+        AR      2,2                   DOUBLE IT
+        ST      2,B                   SAVE THE RESULT
```



Figure 18.7 lists some sample macro instructions that invoke DOUBLE. Each of the two instructions in parts **a** and **b** of Figure 18.7 specifies all three operands, but in different orders. Notice that REG is specified as 6 in the first macro instruction and is specified as R5 in the second macro instruction. In part **c** of Figure 18.7, the keyword REG is omitted; in the expansion, the assembler uses the default value of 2, as specified in the macro definition. Lastly, the expansion in part **d** of Figure 18.7 is incorrect because the keyword NUMBER is omitted from the macro instruction, and the macro definition does not specify a default value.

---

**Keyword vs. positional parameters**

Keyword parameters offer reminders of their meanings and, therefore, are particularly advantageous when you are using many parameters. They are convenient to use because you can write the corresponding keyword operands in any order. When operand values change infrequently, the keyword form is appropriate because you can specify a default value in the prototype and omit the keyword operand from the macro instruction. However, positional parameters are appropriate when the specified values change frequently, which makes default values impractical. You can intermix positional and keyword parameters, choosing the better format for each parameter. Any desired ordering of symbolic parameters is possible in the prototype. (However, under DOS, you must write all positional parameters first.) In the corresponding macro instruction, the positional operands must appear in the same order as the corresponding parameters of the prototype, but keyword operands may appear anywhere and in any order, as shown in the next example.

---

EXAMPLE 3

Assume the following macro prototype statement:

```
DEMO    &A, &B, &KEY1= , &C, &KEY2=10, &KEY3= , &D, &KEY4=
```

The macro instruction

```
DEMO    X, , Y, KEY3=8, Z, KEY1=42
```

produces the following correspondence between symbolic parameters and operands:

&A ↔ X
&B ↔ null
&C ↔ Y
&D ↔ Z
&KEY1 ↔ 42
&KEY2 ↔ 10
&KEY3 ↔ 8
&KEY4 ↔ null

The macro instruction

```
DEMO    X, KEY3=8, KEY1=42, , Y, Z
```

produces the same correspondence.

---

## SELF-TEST EXERCISES

1. The definition of the DOUBLE macro in Figure 18.4 always uses Register 2. Revise the macro definition to use a third positional parameter so that you can specify in the macro instruction a register that will be used to compute the sum.
2. Repeat Self-Test Exercise 1 and use a keyword parameter to specify the register. Use Register 2 as the default value.
3. List the correspondence between symbolic parameters and macro instruction operands when the DEMO macro of Example 3 is invoked with the following instruction:

```
DEMO    , X, KEY2=3, , KEY3=0, KEY4=8, Y
```

## *Concatenation*

In a model statement such as

```
ST    2,&RESULT
```

the variable symbol &RESULT is concatenated with the characters 2 and the comma. In general, you can concatenate any variable symbol with other variable symbols or characters. For instance, X&INPUT&B is one such concatenation. If you assume the following correspondence between variable symbols and values

&INPUT ↔ DATA
&B ↔ 2

then X&INPUT&B represents XDATA2. This particular concatenation is unambiguous, as were the ones in the macro definitions given earlier. However, if you want to follow &INPUT with X, you cannot write &INPUTX because it looks like another variable symbol. Instead, you must separate &INPUT and X with a period to indicate concatenation; the period, which is the **concatenation character,** does not appear in the expansion. Thus, if &INPUT has the value DATA, then &INPUT.X represents DATAX in the macro expansion. You must write a period whenever a variable symbol is followed by either an alphanumeric character, a period that will appear in the macro expansion, or a left parenthesis that is not part of a subscript notation, which is discussed later. The period is optional when the variable symbol is either followed by any other character, or preceded by characters or variable symbols. You can use concatenation to affect any part of an assembler language statement.

---

EXAMPLE 4

Assume the following correspondence between variable symbols and values:

&X ↔ DATA
&Y ↔ R3

These are some sample concatenations that you can use within model statements:

Examples of concatenation

| Portion of model statement | Result of expansion | Notes |
|---|---|---|
| =A(&X) | =A(DATA) | A period is unnecessary. |
| &X.(&Y) | DATA(R3) | The period is necessary because a variable symbol precedes a left parenthesis. |
| &X&Y | DATAR3 | A period is unnecessary. |
| &X.2 | DATA2 | The period is necessary to distinguish between the variable symbol &X2 and concatenation. |

---

## *The System Variable Symbol &SYSNDX*

Use &SYSNDX to generate unique symbols.

&SYSNDX is a 4-digit counter that the assembler increments by 1 each time that it encounters a macro instruction in your program. &SYSNDX has a value of 0001 for the first macro instruction that is encountered. You can use &SYSNDX within a macro definition to construct symbols that will be unique when the macro is expanded. For example, consider a macro definition that contains a loop:

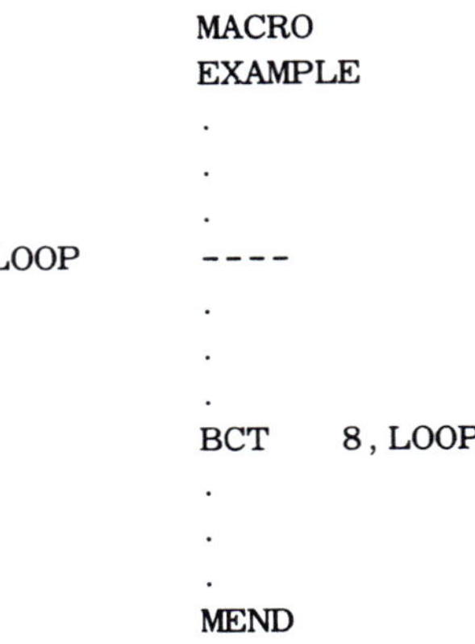

```
         MACRO
         EXAMPLE
         .
         .
         .
LOOP     ----
         .
         .
         .
         BCT    8,LOOP
         .
         .
         .
         MEND
```

If you invoke this macro more than once, several instructions in the program will be labeled LOOP—which is an obvious error. Instead, you can write

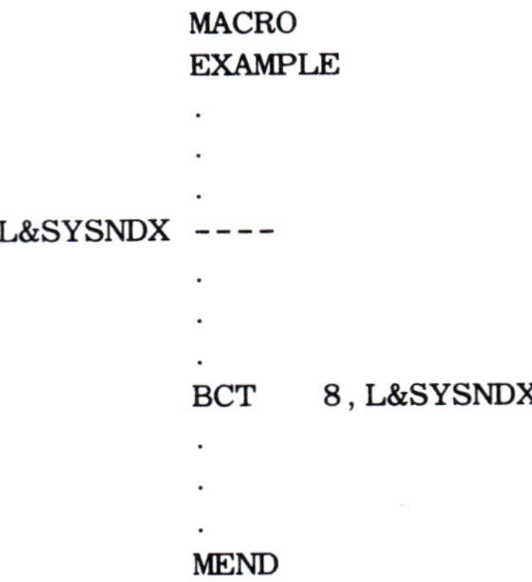

```
         MACRO
         EXAMPLE
         .
         .
         .
L&SYSNDX ----
         .
         .
         .
         BCT    8,L&SYSNDX
         .
         .
         .
         MEND
```

If the fifth macro instruction that the assembler encounters is EXAMPLE, L&SYSNDX will be L0005. If the sixth macro instruction also is EXAMPLE, L&SYSNDX will be L0006. Within a single expansion, &SYSNDX has the same value; thus, if you require several different labels within a macro definition, you must precede &SYSNDX with different characters. Since the value of &SYSNDX is always 4 characters long, you can concatenate it with a maximum of 4 characters to produce a valid symbol.

## *Comments within Macro Definitions*

Two types of comments statements may appear within the body of a macro definition. Ordinary comments statements that begin with an asterisk become part of the macro expansion. **Internal macro comments statements** begin with . * and do not appear in the expansion; you can only use such comments to document the macro definition.

Neither type of comments statement may appear before the prototype statement. Variable symbols that appear in either type of comments statement are not replaced by their values when the macro is expanded.

---

EXAMPLE 5

The macro definition in Figure 18.8 computes the sum of the binary integers in an array of fullwords. Notice the use of &SYSNDX, concatenation, and both types of comments statements. The Add instruction contains the only necessary concatenation character.

The sample expansion in Figure 18.9 is the result of the fifteenth macro instruction in the program, although this might be the first time that SUM has been invoked. Notice that only one comments statement appears in the expansion, and that the assembler assigns the default value 0 to &ACCUM since the keyword ACCUM is omitted from the macro instruction.

```
         MACRO
&L       SUM    &ARRAY,&N,&ACCUM=0,&INDEX=1
.** THIS MACRO COMPUTES THE SUM OF THE BINARY INTEGERS IN AN ARRAY
.** OF FULLWORDS.
.** &ARRAY = ADDRESS OF THE ARRAY
.** &N = REGISTER CONTAINING THE NUMBER OF FULLWORDS IN THE ARRAY
.** &ACCUM = REGISTER USED AS AN ACCUMULATOR; (DEFAULT IS REG. 0)
.** &INDEX = REGISTER USED AS AN INDEX; (DEFAULT IS REG. 1)
.*
.* THE NEXT STATEMENT IS A GENERATED COMMENTS STATEMENT:
** COMPUTE SUM OF THE ARRAY:
.* INITIALIZE:
         SR     &INDEX,&INDEX              CLEAR INDEX
         SR     &ACCUM,&ACCUM              CLEAR ACCUMULATOR
.* REPEAT &N TIMES:
L&SYSNDX A      &ACCUM,&ARRAY.(&INDEX)     ADD NEXT ELEMENT
         LA     &INDEX,4(&INDEX)           INCREMENT INDEX
         BCT    &N,L&SYSNDX                LOOP CONTROL
.* END REPEAT
         MEND
```

**Figure 18.8**
The definition of the SUM macro, as described in Example 5.

**Figure 18.9**
A sample expansion of the SUM macro that was defined in Figure 18.8.

```
                 SUM    X,5,INDEX=8
+** COMPUTE SUM OF THE ARRAY:
+                SR     8,8                   CLEAR INDEX
+                SR     0,0                   CLEAR ACCUMULATOR
+L0015           A      0,X(8)                ADD NEXT ELEMENT
+                LA     8,4(8)                INCREMENT INDEX
+                BCT    5,L0015               LOOP CONTROL
```

---

## *Sublists*

A **sublist** consists of one or more items that are separated by commas and enclosed in parentheses. For instance, the quantity (X,2,Y) is a sublist. You can write a sublist as an operand in a macro instruction to specify several values. In the prototype statement, a symbolic parameter that corresponds to a sublist in a macro instruction represents the entire sublist within the macro definition. You can reference individual entries in the sublist by using a **subscripted parameter,** which consists of a subscript that is attached to a symbolic parameter—similar to the way that array elements are referenced in a high-level language. The subscript, which is enclosed in parentheses, must have a value greater than or equal to 1, and indicates the position of the desired entry in the sublist. For instance, if the sublist (W,15) corresponds to the symbolic parameter &ABC, then the following correspondence between subscripted parameters and values is true:

&ABC(1) ↔ W
&ABC(2) ↔ 15

Compare &ABC(1) with &ABC.(1): &ABC.(1) denotes concatenation and has the value (W,15)(1).

If the subscript is greater than the number of entries in the sublist, or if the subscripted parameter references a missing sublist entry, then the value of the subscripted parameter is the null string. If a subscripted parameter references an operand that is not a sublist, the operand is treated as if it were a sublist with one entry.

Subscripts can be arithmetic expressions as defined later when this chapter discusses SETA symbols.

---

EXAMPLE 6

Consider various operands in a macro instruction that correspond to the symbolic parameter &ABC. The following shows the values that the assembler, given these operands, uses to substitute for the symbolic parameters and subscripted parameters within the model statements of the macro definition:

| Operand in macro instruction that corresponds to &ABC | Parameter in model statement | Value used in macro expansion |
|---|---|---|
| (W,,X,YZ) | &ABC | (W,,X,YZ) |
| (W,,X,YZ) | &ABC(4) | YZ |
| (W,,X,YZ) | &ABC(2) | null |
| (W,,X,YZ) | &ABC(5) | null |
| (S) | &ABC | (S) |
| (S) | &ABC(1) | S |
| (S) | &ABC(2) | null |
| S | &ABC | S |
| S | &ABC(1) | S |
| S | &ABC(2) | null |

These examples are valid regardless of whether &ABC is a positional parameter or a keyword parameter. If &ABC is a keyword parameter whose keyword operand is omitted, assume that the first column is a list of default values.

---

EXAMPLE 7

Figure 18.10 shows the definition and a sample expansion of the ADD macro that computes the sum of the three entries in a sublist. This macro definition demonstrates the use—but not the power—of sublists. In the present context, the sublist has a fixed length. After you have learned the conditional assembly language, you can use sublists that have a variable length.

```
         MACRO
&L       ADD    &LIST,&REG,&RESULT
.** COMPUTES THE SUM OF FULLWORD BINARY INTEGERS IN
.** THE SUBLIST &LIST.
.** &REG = A WORK REGISTER
.** &RESULT = A FULLWORD IN STORAGE.
&L       L      &REG,&LIST(1)      LOAD FIRST ENTRY
         A      &REG,&LIST(2)      ADD SECOND ENTRY
         A      &REG,&LIST(3)      ADD THIRD ENTRY
         ST     &REG,&RESULT       STORE SUM
         MEND
         .
         .
         .
         ADD    (X,Y,=F'16'),R0,ANSWER
+        L      R0,X               LOAD FIRST ENTRY
+        A      R0,Y               ADD SECOND ENTRY
+        A      R0,=F'16'          ADD THIRD ENTRY
+        ST     R0,ANSWER          STORE SUM
```



**Figure 18.10**
The definition of the ADD macro and a sample expansion, as described in Example 7.

EXAMPLE 8

You can use the CALL macro that is defined in Figure 18.11 to call a subprogram. The following macro instruction calls the subprogram SUB with the arguments X, Y, and Z:

```
CALL   SUB,(X,Y,Z)
```

```
          MACRO
&LABEL    CALL   &ENTRY,&ARGS
.** CALLS THE SUBPROGRAM AT &ENTRY.  DEFINES AND PASSES AN ARGUMENT
.** LIST MADE UP OF THE ARGUMENTS THAT ARE DESIGNATED BY &ARGS.
&LABEL    L      15,=V(&ENTRY)      LOAD ENTRY POINT
          LA     14,R&SYSNDX        LOAD RETURN ADDRESS
          CNOP   2,4                ALIGN TO HALFWORD BOUNDARY
          BALR   1,15               GET ADDRESS OF ARGUMENT LIST;
*                                     CALL SUBPROGRAM
          DC     A&ARGS             ARGUMENT LIST
R&SYSNDX  EQU    *                  RETURN POINT
          MEND
```

**Figure 18.11**
The definition of the CALL macro, as described in Example 8.

```
 CONTINUE CALL  SUB, (X,Y,Z)
+CONTINUE L     15,=V(SUB)         LOAD ENTRY POINT
+         LA    14,R0007           LOAD RETURN ADDRESS
+         CNOP  2,4                ALIGN TO HALFWORD BOUNDARY
+         BALR  1,15               GET ADDRESS OF ARGUMENT LIST;
+*                                   CALL SUBPROGRAM
+         DC    A(X,Y,Z)           ARGUMENT LIST
+R0007    EQU   *                  RETURN POINT
```

**Figure 18.12**
A sample expansion of the CALL macro that was defined in Figure 18.11.

The resulting macro expansion in Figure 18.12 assumes that the macro instruction is the seventh macro instruction in the source program.

Notice that the second operand (X,Y,Z) is a sublist, and that the symbolic parameter &ARGS represents the entire sublist.

---

## *The System Variable Symbol &SYSLIST*

You can use &SYSLIST to reference symbolic parameters.

You can use &SYSLIST(*n*) and &SYSLIST(*n*,*m*) within the model statements of a macro definition instead of using symbolic parameters to reference the positional operands of an associated macro instruction. &SYSLIST(*n*) represents the *n*th positional operand; keyword operands may not be referenced with this notation, and are ignored when the relative position of a positional operand is determined. The special case &SYSLIST(0) represents the symbol, if any, in the name entry of the macro instruction. If the *n*th positional operand is a sublist, you can use &SYSLIST(*n*,*m*) to reference the sublist's *m*th entry. (If the operand is not a sublist, &SYSLIST(*n*,1) has the same meaning as &SYSLIST(*n*).) If a &SYSLIST reference corresponds to an omitted or nonexistent operand or sublist entry, the reference is assigned a null value.

&SYSLIST(*n*) and &SYSLIST(*n*,*m*) enable you to write both macro prototype statements that have no symbolic parameters, and macro instructions that have an arbitrary number of positional operands. Note that &SYSLIST cannot appear without a subscript unless it is preceded by the number attribute reference N'; this is discussed later.

---

EXAMPLE 9

The following tables list the values of &SYSLIST(*n*) and &SYSLIST(*n*,*m*) for various values of *n* and *m* with respect to this macro instruction:

```
CONTINUE  EXAMPLE   ONE,KEY=X,TWO,,(FOUR,,SIX),SEVEN
```

| *n* | **&SYSLIST(*n*)** | **Notes** |
|---|---|---|
| 0 | CONTINUE | Symbol in name entry. |
| 1 | ONE | First positional operand. |
| 2 | TWO | Second positional operand. |
| 3 | null | Third positional operand is omitted. |
| 4 | (FOUR,,SIX) | Fourth positional operand is a sublist. |
| 5 | SEVEN | Fifth positional operand. |
| 6 | null | Reference beyond the end of the operand list. |

| *n,m* | &SYSLIST(*n,m*) | Notes |
|---|---|---|
| 4,1 | FOUR | First entry of fourth positional operand. |
| 4,2 | null | Second entry of fourth positional operand is omitted. |
| 4,3 | SIX | Third entry of fourth positional operand. |
| 4,4 | null | Reference beyond the end of the sublist. |
| 2,1 | TWO | Second positional operand, even though it is not a sublist. |
| 2,2 | null | Second positional operand is not a sublist. |

## SELF-TEST EXERCISES

4. What statements are generated by the macro instruction

```
CALL  SUB,(DATA)
```

if it appears immediately after the macro instruction that was given in Figure 18.12? (The CALL macro was defined in Figure 18.11.)

5. Consider the macro prototype

```
TEST   &A,&B=(12,-1)
```

and the macro instruction

```
TEST   (XY,-2,,W)
```

Indicate what each of the following represents within the definition of TEST when the macro instruction is expanded. Assume that the macro instruction is the first one that the assembler encounters in your program.

**a.** &A
**b.** &A(2)
**c.** &A(1)&A(2)
**d.** &A(1).&A(4)
**e.** &A.(1)
**f.** &A(3).4
**g.** &A(5)
**h.** &A.V.(3)
**i.** &A(4)&SYSNDX
**j.** &B(2)
**k.** &B
**l.** &B(3)
**m.** &SYSLIST(1)
**n.** &SYSLIST(2)
**o.** &SYSLIST(1,2)
**p.** &SYSLIST(1,3)
**q.** &SYSLIST(2,1)

### *The MNOTE and MEXIT Directives*

Use MNOTE to issue warnings or as a debugging tool.

The directive MNOTE generates a message in the macro expansion; using MNOTE, you can issue warnings about erroneous macro instructions or determine the value of a variable symbol during preassembly time. MNOTE can be summarized as follows:

| Name | Operation | Operand | Instruction Name | Action |
|---|---|---|---|---|
| *sequence symbol* or *blank* | **MNOTE** | [*n*,]'*message*' | MACRO NOTE | Generates a *message* in the macro expansion. |

If *n* is an asterisk or is omitted, MNOTE generates the character string *message* as a comments statement. If *n* is a number between 0 and 255, then MNOTE issues *message* as an error message with a **severity code** of *n*. Typically, a severity code of 5 or greater prevents execution of the assembled program. The *message* can contain variable symbols; the current value of each variable symbol in *message* replaces the variable symbol when MNOTE generates the comments statement or error message. Thus, you can use MNOTE as a debugging tool.

If you want an ampersand or an apostrophe to appear in the message that MNOTE generates, you must write it in duplicate in *message*, as Example 10 demonstrates.

---

EXAMPLE 10

```
MNOTE *,'AT THIS POINT, &&X = &X'
```

If the variable symbol &X has a value of ABC when the assembler encounters this MNOTE, then the following comments statement appears in the macro expansion:

```
*,AT THIS POINT, &X = ABC
```

---

Use MEXIT to exit a macro definition.

The MEXIT directive terminates the processing of a macro definition. It can be summarized as follows:

| Name | Operation | Operand | Instruction Name | Action |
|---|---|---|---|---|
| *sequence symbol* or *blank* | **MEXIT** | ignored | MACRO EXIT | Terminates the processing of the macro definition. |

It is best to use MNOTE or MEXIT with the branching instructions in the conditional assembly language. You will see the branching instructions in the next section, with another example of MNOTE and MEXIT.

## *The System Variable Symbols &SYSDATE and &SYSTIME (OS only)*

The date and time of assembly

The system variable symbols &SYSDATE and &SYSTIME provide the date and the time, respectively, of the assembly of your source program. They are available within all macro definitions and remain constant; you cannot change their values. &SYSDATE represents an 8-character string in the form *mm/dd/yy*, where *mm* is the month, *dd* is the day, and *yy* is the year. &SYSTIME represents a 5-character string in the form *hh.mm*, where *hh* is the hour on a 24-hour clock and *mm* is the minutes. Two common uses of &SYSDATE and &SYSTIME are within the TITLE and DC directives: you can use them to generate either a title for the assembly listing, or a constant within the program that includes the date and time of assembly.

EXAMPLE 11

```
DC      C'ASSEMBLED ON &SYSDATE AT &SYSTIME'
```

If you assemble the source program that contains this DC instruction on May 20, 1987 at 2:48 P.M., then the following character constant will be defined:

ASSEMBLED ON 05/20/87 AT 14.48

## The Conditional Assembly Language within Macro Definitions

The utility and power of macro definitions increase greatly when you use the conditional assembly language. You can use most of the features of the conditional assembly language in the open code as well, but its use in the open code is much less important than its use within macro definitions.

### *SET Symbols*

SET symbols are another type of variable symbol; like all variable symbols, they have values at preassembly time. You can change or assign the values of SET symbols much like you would change or assign the value of a variable in a high-level programming language. SET symbols can represent values within model statements; can be used with the AIF directive to determine which model statements are processed; or can be subscripts for sublists or other SET symbols that themselves are subscripted. The chapter will discuss subscripted SET symbols later; ignore them for now.

There are three types of SET symbols: arithmetic, Boolean, and character. **Arithmetic SET symbols (SETA symbols)** have values that are signed 32-bit binary integers. **Boolean SET symbols (SETB symbols)** have values that are either 0 for false or 1 for true. **Character SET symbols (SETC symbols)** have values that are character strings whose length does not exceed 255.

**LCL*x* and GBL*x* declare and initialize SET symbols.**

*The LCL*x *and GBL*x *Directives.* Regardless of type, SET symbols can have local or global scopes. A **local SET symbol** is valid only within a single macro definition. However, you can make a **global SET symbol** available in any or all macro definitions. You must declare local SET symbols within the macro body before you can use them. (In DOS, you must declare all SET symbols immediately after the macro prototype statement, and you must declare global SET symbols before local SET symbols.) You declare local SET symbols by writing LCL*x* directives, where *x* is A for arithmetic, B for Boolean, or C for character. You declare global SET symbols by writing GBL*x* directives within each macro definition that references the SET symbols. Here, *x* is the same as for LCL*x*. The LCL*x* and GBL*x* directives also initialize the SET symbols to certain values that depend upon the type of SET symbol.

The directives to declare nonsubscripted SET symbols can be summarized as follows:

| Name | Operation | Operand | Instruction Name | Action |
|---|---|---|---|---|
| *blank* | {LCLA, LCLB, LCLC} | *variable symbol, . . .* | DECLARE LOCAL SET SYMBOLS | Declares the variable symbols in the operand entry to be local SET symbols that are either arithmetic (LCLA), Boolean (LCLB), or character (LCLC); initializes arithmetic and Boolean SET symbols to 0, and character SET symbols to the null string. |
| *blank* | {GBLA, GBLB, GBLC} | *variable symbol, . . .* | DECLARE GLOBAL SET SYMBOLS | Declares and initializes global SET symbols in the same way as the LCL*x* directives. |

Initialization of a particular global SET symbol only occurs the first time that the assembler processes a GBL*x* instruction that declares the symbol. Subsequent GBL*x* instructions do not change the value of the symbol.

The variable symbol that you choose for a particular SET symbol may not begin with &SYS, and must differ from any other SET symbol (regardless of type) or symbolic parameter that you have defined within the same scope. However, within the same source program, you can use the same variable symbol in more than one macro definition as local SET symbols, which differ in value or meaning. For example, in the following macro definitions, &X in M1 differs from &X in M2:

```
MACRO                                   MACRO
M1                                      M2
LCLA  &X                                LCLA  &X
.                                       .
.                                       .
.                                       .
```

Similar comments are true for symbolic parameters and sequence symbols—both of which have local scopes.

**SETA assigns a value to a SETA symbol.**

*The SETA Directive.* You assign new values to arithmetic SET symbols by writing the SETA directive. It can be summarized as follows:

| Name | Operation | Operand | Instruction Name | Action |
|---|---|---|---|---|
| *variable symbol* | **SETA** | *arithmetic expression* | ASSIGN VALUE TO SETA SYMBOL | Evaluates the *arithmetic expression* and assigns the resulting signed 32-bit value to the SETA symbol that appears in the name entry. |

You form an **arithmetic expression** from variable symbols; self-defining terms; numeric attribute references (which will be defined shortly); the operators +, −, *, and /; and parentheses. Variable symbols that are permitted in an arithmetic expression are SETA symbols; SETB symbols; SETC symbols whose values are unsigned decimal self-defining terms; symbolic parameters whose values are self-defining terms; &SYSLIST references whose values are self-defining terms; and &SYSNDX.

---

EXAMPLE 12

Assume that you have declared &S and &CON as arithmetic SET symbols by writing

```
LCLA    &S,&CON
```

The following describes the effect of a *sequence* of SETA instructions:

| Instruction | | | Effect |
|---|---|---|---|
| &S | SETA | 3 | Assigns the value 3 to &S. |
| &S | SETA | &S+1 | Increments the value of &S by 1, so that it becomes 4. |
| &CON | SETA | 2*(1−&S) | Assigns the value −6 to &CON. |

When you use a SETA symbol that has a negative value in a model statement, a minus sign is not generated in the macro expansion. Thus, if the model statement is

```
DC    F'&CON'
```

where &CON has a value of −6, then

```
DC    F'6'
```

appears in the expansion.

---

EXAMPLE 13

Assume that &A is a SETA symbol and that &LIST is a symbolic parameter. Consider the following statements within a macro definition:

```
&A      SETA   3
        L      R8,&LIST(&A)
        AR     R8,R&A
```

If the value of &LIST is (X,Y,Z), then these statements expand to:

```
+       L      R8,Z
+       AR     R8,R3
```

---

**SETC assigns a value to a SETC symbol.**

*The SETC Directive.* You assign new values to character SET symbols by writing the SETC directive. It can be summarized as follows:

| Name | Operation | Operand | Instruction Name | Action |
|---|---|---|---|---|
| *variable symbol* | **SETC** | *'string'* | ASSIGN VALUE TO SETC SYMBOL | Assigns the character string that the character expression *'string'* represents to the SETC symbol that appears in the name entry. |

A **character expression** *'string'* consists of a sequence of characters and variable symbols, whose values are interpreted as characters, all of which are enclosed in apostrophes. Signs and leading zeros in the values of arithmetic variable symbols are ignored. You can use the concatenation character within an expression; if you want a period to appear within the generated character string, you must write two periods. You can use character expressions in the operand entry of the SETC directive.

The operand entry of the SETC directive also may consist of either a type attribute reference, which is not enclosed in apostrophes; or a substring; both the type attribute and substrings are discussed later in this chapter. You can concatenate character expressions, substrings, or both in the operand entry.

---

EXAMPLE 14

Assume that &C is a SETC symbol or symbolic parameter with the value XY, and that &A is a SETA symbol or symbolic parameter with the value −51. The following indicates the values of various character expressions—each of which can appear in the operand entry of a SETC directive:

| Expression | Value | Notes |
|---|---|---|
| 'XY Z' | XY Z | The value is simply the character string between the apostrophes. A blank is a valid character within a string. |
| '&C.Z' | XYZ | The value of the variable symbol &C is concatenated with the character Z. |
| 'Z&C' | ZXY | The concatenation character is not required here. |
| '&C&C' | XYXY | You can concatenate the values of two variable symbols. |
| '&C&A' | XY51 | The absolute value of &A is represented as a character string. |

---

EXAMPLE 15

Suppose that you want to control a simple BCT loop with two macros—REPEAT and ENDREPT. Assume that the loop will be executed *n* times, and that *n* is in Register 3. The instructions within the loop should appear between two macro instructions, as follows:

The REPEAT macro must construct a label for the beginning of the loop by using &SYSNDX, and must generate a statement such as

```
LP0005    EQU    *
```

You must make this label and the register name that is specified in the REPEAT macro instruction available to the ENDREPT macro so that it can construct the required BCT instruction. You accomplish this step by using global SET symbols, as demonstrated in Figure 18.13.

The symbols &LOOP and &COUNTER are declared as global SET symbols in both macro definitions. In REPEAT, the symbols are assigned values for use in ENDREPT. You could define &COUNTER as a SETC symbol instead of a SETA symbol in both macro definitions. If you do so, you also would replace the SETA directive in the definition of REPEAT by

```
&COUNTER SETC   '&REG'
```

Figure 18.14 lists a sample expansion of these macros.

```
         MACRO
         REPEAT &REG=9
.** INITIALIZATION FOR A REPEAT LOOP.  &REG IS A LOOP COUNTER.
         GBLC   &LOOP              USED TO PASS LOOP LABEL TO ENDREPT
         GBLA   &COUNTER           USED TO PASS &REG TO ENDREPT
&LOOP    SETC   'LP'.'&SYSNDX'     CONSTRUCT LOOP LABEL
&COUNTER SETA   &REG               MAKE REGISTER NAME GLOBAL
&LOOP    EQU    *                  LABEL FIRST STATEMENT IN LOOP
         MEND
         MACRO
         ENDREPT
.** END OF REPEAT LOOP.  SETS UP CORRECT BCT.
         GBLC   &LOOP              LOOP LABEL
         GBLA   &COUNTER           LOOP COUNTER
         BCT    &COUNTER,&LOOP     LOOP CONTROL
         MEND
```

**Figure 18.13**
The definitions of the REPEAT and ENDREPT macros, as described in Example 15.

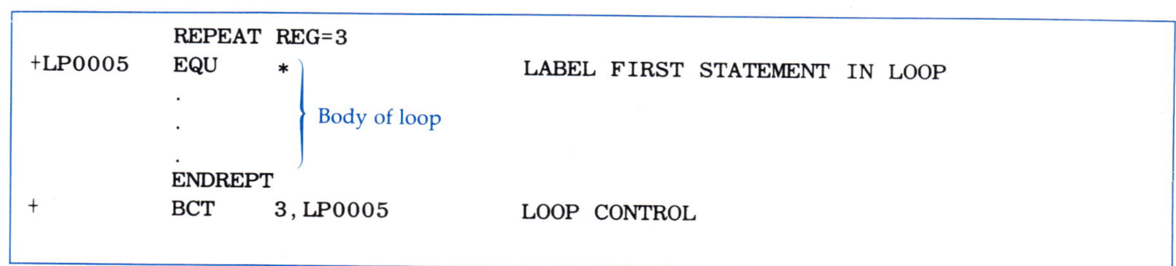
```
          REPEAT REG=3
+LP0005   EQU    *                  LABEL FIRST STATEMENT IN LOOP
          .
          .      Body of loop
          .
          ENDREPT
+         BCT    3,LP0005           LOOP CONTROL
```

**Figure 18.14**
A sample expansion of the REPEAT and ENDREPT macros that were defined in Figure 18.13.

**SETB assigns a value to a SETB symbol.**

*The SETB Directive.* You assign new values to Boolean SET symbols by writing the SETB directive. It can be summarized as follows:

| Name | Operation | Operand | Instruction Name | Action |
|---|---|---|---|---|
| *variable symbol* | **SETB** | (*logical expression*) or 0 or 1 | ASSIGN VALUE TO SETB SYMBOL | Assigns the value in the operand entry to the SETB symbol that appears in the name entry. |

A **logical expression** can be either two arithmetic expressions that are separated by one of the relational operators EQ, NE, LT, LE, GT, or GE; or two character expressions—or anything that is valid as the operand of a SETC instruction—that are separated by a relational operator. Logical expressions also can consist of either a SETB symbol; two logical expressions that are separated by one of the Boolean operators OR, AND, OR NOT, or AND NOT; or a single logical expression that is preceded by NOT. Each of the relational or Boolean operators just defined must be preceded and followed by at least one blank. You can enclose any logical expression within parentheses.

---

EXAMPLE 16

Assume that &A, &B, and &C are an arithmetic SET symbol, a Boolean SET symbol, and a character SET symbol, respectively, whose values are defined by the statements

```
&A          SETA   4
&B          SETB   1
&C          SETC   'XYZ'
```

The following are examples of logical expressions and their values.

| Logical expression | Value | Notes |
|---|---|---|
| `&A LE 15` | 1 | $4 \leq 15$ |
| `NOT &B` | 0 | NOT 1 |
| `'&C' EQ 'XYZ'` | 1 | The character strings have equal values. |
| `'&C' EQ ''` | 0 | `''` denotes the null string |
| `(NOT &B) AND (&A LE 15)` | 0 | 0 AND 1 = 0 |
| `(&A GT 0) AND (&A LT 50)` | 1 | 1 AND 1 = 1 |
| `&B OR ('&C' EQ 'YES')` | 1 | 1 OR 0 = 1 |
| `&B AND NOT (&A GT 5)` | 1 | 1 AND NOT 0 = 1 |

Each of these logical expressions can appear—within parentheses—in the operand entry of a SETB directive. For example, each of the following statements assigns the value 1 to &B:

```
&B          SETB    ('C' EQ 'XYZ')
&B          SETB    ((&A GT 0) AND (&A LT 50))
```

---

## SELF-TEST EXERCISES

**6.** Classify each of the following according to its validity within the operand entry of a SETA directive, a SETB directive, or a SETC directive. Assume that &A is a SETA symbol with the value 4; &B is a SETB symbol with the value 0; &C is a SETC symbol with the value ABC; &X is a symbolic parameter with the value R; and &Y is a symbolic parameter with the value 15. &X and &Y are, respectively, the first and second positional parameters.

| | |
|---|---|
| **a.** &C | **k.** '&A' |
| **b.** &X.'5' | **l.** '&B' |
| **c.** ('&X' EQ '') | **m.** (&C) |
| **d.** &A | **n.** (&Y LT &A) |
| **e.** &B | **o.** NOT (&Y = 15) |
| **f.** &X | **p.** '&A+&Y' |
| **g.** &Y | **q.** (&A+&Y) |
| **h.** &A&B&C&X&Y | **r.** &SYSLIST(2) |
| **i.** (&A) | **s.** &SYSLIST(1) |
| **j.** (&B) | **t.** 1 |

**7.** Consider this macro definition:

```
        MACRO
&LABEL  SQ    &EVEN=2,&N,&ANS
        LCLA  &ODD
&ODD    SETA  &EVEN+1
&LABEL  L     &ODD,&N
        MR    &EVEN,&ODD
        ST    &ODD,&ANS
        MEND
```

What macro expansions are generated by each of the following instructions?

**a.** `SQ    =F'26'`
**b.** `SQ    X,Y`

## *Branching*

By using the conditional assembly branch directives AIF and AGO, you can affect the order in which the assembler processes statements at preassembly time. With these directives, you can select the model statements that the assembler uses to generate the macro expansion. By branching to a statement at preassembly time, you tell the assembler to process that statement next. Such a statement must contain a sequence symbol in its name entry. Recall that a sequence symbol is formed just like a variable symbol—except that a sequence symbol begins with a period instead of an ampersand. With the exception of the GBL*x*, LCL*x*, MACRO and EQU directives (and other directives not covered in this text), the macro prototype instruction, and, under DOS, the DSECT statement, you can write sequence symbols in any name entry that is not already in use. When the name entry of the desired statement does contain another symbol, you can label that point in the program with a sequence symbol by preceding the statement with the ANOP directive. The ANOP directive will be discussed later in this chapter.

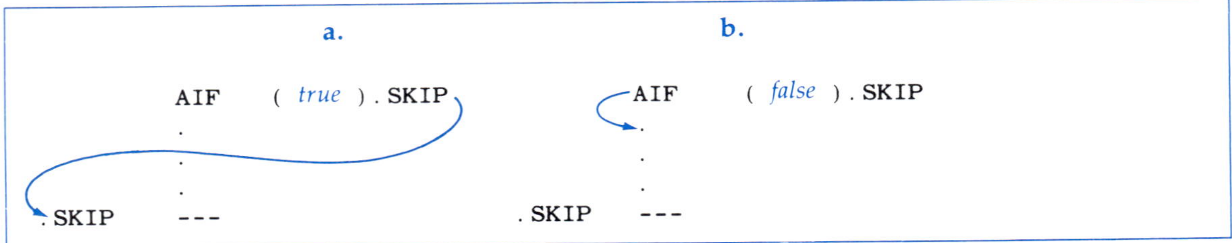


Figure 18.15
The effect of the AIF directive when the logical expression is, **a**. true and, **b**. false.

AIF performs a conditional branch at preassembly time.

*The AIF and AGO Directives.* The AIF directive tells the assembler either to branch or not to branch according to conditions that AIF tests. You use AIF either to skip or to repeat the processing of model statements. The directive can be summarized as follows:

| Name | Operation | Operand | Instruction Name | Action |
|---|---|---|---|---|
| *sequence symbol* or *blank* | **AIF** | *(logical expression) sequence symbol* | ASSEMBLY-TIME IF | Directs the assembler to process the statement that is labeled with the sequence symbol that appears in the operand entry if the logical expression is 1 (true); directs the assembler to process the next sequential statement if the logical expression is 0 (false). |

Figure 18.15 illustrates the effect of the AIF directive.

You can branch forward or backward within a macro definition by using an AIF directive, but you cannot branch from one macro definition to another.

---

EXAMPLE 17

```
AIF    (&K LT 10).LOOP
```

This AIF instruction directs the assembler to process the statement at .LOOP, if &K has a value that is less than 10. If &K has a value that is greater than or equal to 10, the assembler processes the statement that follows this AIF.

---

EXAMPLE 18

The AIF directive enables you to rewrite the CALL macro definition in Figure 18.11 to accommodate any subprogram that does not have an argument list. Figure 18.16 gives the new definition and a sample macro expansion. The AIF statement compares '&ARGS' to the null string. An equal comparison implies that the macro instruction does not specify an argument list, and causes the assembler to generate a BALR instruction next. If the macro instruction does contain an argument list, the macro expansion is

```
         MACRO
&LABEL   CALL   &ENTRY,&ARGS
.** CALLS THE SUBPROGRAM AT &ENTRY.  DEFINES AND PASSES AN ARGUMENT
.** LIST MADE UP OF THE ARGUMENTS THAT ARE DESIGNATED BY &ARGS, BUT
.** ONLY IF &ARGS IS SPECIFIED IN THE OPERAND.
         LCLC   &NDX
&NDX     SETC   '&SYSNDX'
&LABEL   L      15,=V(&ENTRY)
         AIF    ('&ARGS' EQ '').NONE
         LA     14,RET&NDX
         CNOP   2,4
         BALR   1,15
         DC     A&ARGS
RET&NDX  EQU    *
         MEXIT
.NONE    BALR   14,15
         MEND
         .
         .
         .
         CALL   SUB ◄──────────── Macro instruction
+        L      15,=V(SUB)  }
+        BALR   14,15       }  Macro expansion
```

**Figure 18.16**
A revised definition of the CALL macro and a sample expansion, as described in Example 18.

similar to the one that was given in Figure 18.12. Notice the way that you can use the MEXIT directive to exit the macro definition.

You can use the SETC symbol &NDX to avoid writing RET&SYSNDX in a name entry. Although RET&SYSNDX is legal, it is more than 8 characters and, therefore, violates the customary alignment of fields.

---

**AGO performs an unconditional branch at preassembly time.**

The AGO directive permits unconditional transfers within a macro definition. AGO can be summarized as follows:

| Name | Operation | Operand | Instruction Name | Action |
|---|---|---|---|---|
| *sequence symbol* or *blank* | **AGO** | *sequence symbol* | ASSEMBLY-TIME GO TO | Directs the assembler to process the statement that is identified by the sequence symbol that appears in the operand entry. |

The range of permitted branches is the same as the range for AIF. Notice that MEXIT is equivalent to an AGO to the MEND statement.

**Use ANOP to label a point within a macro definition.**

*The ANOP and ACTR Directives.* While the ANOP directive does not perform an operation, it provides you with an alternate way to label a point in a program with a sequence symbol. If you want to branch to an instruction whose name entry contains a symbol other than a sequence symbol, you can precede that statement with an ANOP. It can be summarized as follows:

| Name | Operation | Operand | Instruction Name | Action |
|---|---|---|---|---|
| *sequence symbol* or *blank* | **ANOP** | ignored | ASSEMBLY-TIME NO OPERATION | No operation. |

**SELF-TEST EXERCISES**

8. Write statements that print an error message with a severity code of 16 if the register name that corresponds to the symbolic parameter ® is not an even number.
9. Write the definition for a macro REGEQU that equates the symbols R0, R1, and so on to R15, to the integers 0 through 15, respectively.
10. Write a definition for a macro INCR that increments a designated register by a specified amount. When INCR is first called, the macro should zero the designated register. If a register is not designated in the macro instruction, use Register 2. If an increment amount is not specified, use a value of 1.

---

EXAMPLE 19

When inserted immediately after the LCLC declaration in the definition of the CALL macro in Figure 18.16, the following statements will issue an error message if the entry point is missing:

```
         AIF    ('&ENTRY' NE '').PROCEED
         MNOTE 8,'MISSING ENTRY POINT. NO CODE GENERATED'
         MEXIT
.PROCEED ANOP
```

The ANOP directive is necessary because the SETC instruction that follows in the macro definition contains a variable symbol in its name entry.

---

ACTR limits the number of AIF and AGO directives that are processed in a single macro definition.

The assembler counts the number of AIF and AGO instructions that it processes within each macro definition. If the number for a particular macro definition exceeds 4096, the assembler stops processing that definition. You can change the limit of 4096 for a particular macro definition by writing an ACTR directive within that definition. ACTR can be summarized as follows:

| Name | Operation | Operand | Instruction Name | Action |
|---|---|---|---|---|
| *sequence symbol* or *blank* | **ACTR** | *arithmetic expression* | ASSEMBLY-TIME COUNTER | Limits the number of AIF and AGO directives that the assembler processes within the macro definition to the value that the operand entry specifies. |

---

EXAMPLE 20

You can rewrite the ADD macro definition of Figure 18.10 to permit sublists of a length that you specify. Figure 18.17 shows this type of a revision. The macro instruction specifies a value for &N, which the AIF instruction uses

**Figure 18.17**
A revised definition of the ADD macro that uses a sublist of a specified length, and a sample expansion, as described in Example 20.

```
         MACRO
&L       ADD    &LIST,&N,&REG,&RESULT
.** COMPUTES THE SUM OF THE &N FULLWORD BINARY INTEGERS
.** IN THE SUBLIST &LIST.
.** &REG = A WORK REGISTER
.** &RESULT = A FULLWORD IN STORAGE FOR THE SUM
         ACTR   50                   LIMIT NO. OF AIF AND AGO
         LCLA   &J                   COUNTER AND SUBSCRIPT
&L       L      &REG,&LIST(1)        LOAD FIRST ENTRY
&J       SETA   2                    POINT TO SECOND ENTRY
.* WHILE &J <= &N
.LOOP    AIF    (&J GT &N).DONE      ALL ELEMENTS PROCESSED?
         A      &REG,&LIST(&J)       ADD NEXT ENTRY
&J       SETA   &J+1                 INCREMENT COUNTER
         AGO    .LOOP                REPEAT
.* END WHILE
.DONE    ST     &REG,&RESULT         STORE SUM
         MEND
         .
         .
         .
SUM      ADD    (X,Y,=F'16'),3,2,ANSWER  <------ Macro instruction
+SUM     L      2,X                  LOAD FIRST ENTRY
+        A      2,Y                  ADD NEXT ENTRY
+        A      2,=F'16'             ADD NEXT ENTRY
+        ST     2,ANSWER             STORE SUM
```

to generate the correct number of Add instructions. The ACTR instruction effectively limits the value of &N to 25 because the assembler processes two AIF and AGO instructions during each cycle of the loop.

---

### *Attributes*

The assembler assigns **attributes** to the ordinary symbols and the variable symbols that represent constants, data areas, and instructions. Attributes are certain characteristics of the represented data. There are six attributes: length, number, count, type, scaling, and integer. You can denote attribute values by using the following notations:

| Notation | Name of attribute |
|---|---|
| L′ | Length |
| N′ | Number |
| K′ | Count |
| T′ | Type |
| S′ | Scaling |
| I′ | Integer |

When attached to an ordinary symbol or a variable symbol, this notation forms an **attribute reference.** For example, the length attribute reference L′X denotes the length attribute of the ordinary symbol X, and K′&Y denotes the count attribute of the variable symbol &Y.

**Figure 18.18**
The applicability of attributes within macro definitions.

| | Attributes | | | | | | | | |
|---|---|---|---|---|---|---|---|---|---|
| | *Under OS* | | | | *Under DOS* | | | | |
| | **L,S,I** | **K** | **N** | **T** | **L** | **S,I** | **K** | **N** | **T** |
| Symbolic parameters | X | X | X | X | X | X | X | X | X |
| &SYSLIST | — | — | X | — | — | — | — | X | — |
| &SYSLIST(*n*) | X | X | X | X | X | X | X | X | X |
| &SYSLIST(*n,m*) | X | X | — | X | X | X | X | — | X |
| SET symbols | — | X | — | X | — | — | — | — | — |
| System variable symbols except &SYSLIST | — | X | — | X | — | — | — | — | — |
| Ordinary symbols | X | — | — | X | X | — | — | — | — |

X indicates that the attribute is applicable.

You can use certain attribute references within arithmetic expressions and logical expressions of the conditional assembly language, but not within character expressions. The length attribute reference, which was discussed in Chapter 10, is the only attribute reference that you can use outside of the conditional assembly language; therefore, it is the only one that is available at assembly time—all other attribute references have meaning only at preassembly time. All attributes are defined for symbolic parameters and some form of &SYSLIST. The attributes of &SYSLIST(*n*) and &SYSLIST(*n,m*) are the attributes of the relevant positional operand or sublist entry. Only the type attribute under OS is defined for all ordinary symbols or all variable symbols. Figure 18.18 summarizes the applicability of the attributes.

**The length in bytes of a data item**

*The Length Attribute (L').* As discussed in Chapter 10, the length attribute of an ordinary symbol is the length in bytes of the data that the symbol represents. The length attribute also is valid for symbolic parameters, &SYSLIST(*n*), and &SYSLIST(*n,m*), if they ultimately represent a symbol in the name entry of a statement in the open code. The length attribute is available at preassembly time only if you use it within arithmetic expressions that are associated with conditional assembly language statements; if you do not use it there, it is not available until assembly time.

---

EXAMPLE 21

Consider this macro instruction that moves an arbitrarily long field at X to the field at Y:

```
MOVE      X,Y
```

When the field at X does not exceed 256 bytes in length, the move is accomplished with a single MVC instruction. For example, if X has a length attribute of 10, then the MOVE macro generates the single instruction

**Figure 18.19**
A portion of the definition of the MOVE macro and a sample expansion, as described in Example 21.

```
          MACRO
          MOVE   &FROM,&TO
.** MOVES FIELD OF ARBITRARY LENGTH FROM FIRST OPERAND
.** LOCATION TO SECOND OPERAND LOCATION.
          LCLA   &LEN
&LEN      SETA   L'&FROM
          AIF    (L'&FROM GT 256).SKIP
          MVC    &TO.(&LEN),&FROM
          MEXIT
.SKIP     ANOP
          .
          .
          .
          MEND
          START
          .
          .
          .
          MOVE   X,Y  <-------- Macro instruction
+         MVC    Y(10),X <----- Macro expansion
          .
          .
          .
X         DC     C'ABCDEFGHIJ'
Y         DS     CL256
```

```
     MVC     Y(10),X
```

The portion of the macro definition that generates this MVC instruction is listed in Figure 18.19. The symbolic parameter &FROM corresponds to X in the given macro instruction. To test the length of X, you can test L'&FROM by using the AIF directive.

The model statement for the MVC instruction uses a SETA symbol &LEN, but you can write the model statement without a SET symbol in a form that is not accepted by older assemblers, as shown here:

```
     MVC     &TO.(L'&FROM),&FROM
```

In this form, L'&FROM becomes L'X when it is expanded at preassembly time: thus, the assembler generates the statement

```
     MVC     Y(L'X),X
```

L'X then has a value of 10 at assembly time.

---

**The number of entries in a sublist**

*The Number Attribute (N').* The number attribute is defined only for macro instruction operands and, therefore, is applicable to symbolic parameters, &SYSLIST, and &SYSLIST(*n*). The number attribute of either a symbolic parameter or &SYSLIST(*n*) is equal to the number of entries in a sublist that is written as the corresponding macro instruction operand. This number includes skipped entries, and is equal to the number of commas plus 1. If the operand is not a sublist, the number attribute is 1; if the operand is omitted, the number attribute is 0. N'&SYSLIST is the number of positional operands, which includes skipped operands, that are written in the corresponding macro instruction. A sublist is counted as one operand, and keyword operands are ignored. (Note that this is the only place that you can write &SYSLIST without a subscript.)

---

EXAMPLE 22

The following lists the number attribute for each value of a second positional operand that corresponds to a second positional parameter &B:

| Second positional operand | Value of N'&B or N'&SYSLIST(2) |
|---|---|
| (W,X,Y,Z) | 4 |
| (W,,,Z) | 4 |
| (W,X) | 2 |
| (W) | 1 |
| W | 1 |
| Omitted operand | 0 |

---

EXAMPLE 23

Consider this macro prototype statement:

```
NUM    &A, &KEY=, &B, &C
```

The following lists the number attribute of &SYSLIST for each macro instruction that corresponds to the given prototype:

| Macro instruction | N'&SYSLIST | Notes |
|---|---|---|
| NUM    W, X, (Y, Z) | 3 | There are 3 positional operands. |
| NUM    X, , Z | 3 | Skipped positional operands are counted. |
| NUM    W, KEY= (R, S, T) , (X, Y) | 2 | Keyword operands are ignored. The third positional operand is omitted, so it is not counted. |

---

The number of characters in a value

*The Count Attribute (K').* The count attribute is equal to the number of characters in the value that is represented by a variable symbol within a macro definition.

---

EXAMPLE 24

The macro instruction operands in the following list correspond to the first positional parameter &A in a macro prototype. The count attribute of each operand is listed here:

| Macro instruction operand | K'&A or K'&SYSLIST(1) | Notes |
|---|---|---|
| (W,X,Y,Z) | 9 | All characters are counted. |
| DATA | 4 | |
| 'DATA' | 6 | The apostrophes are counted. |
| Omitted operand | 0 | |

---

EXAMPLE 25

The count attributes of several SET symbols are listed here:

| Set directive | | | Count attribute of SET symbol | Notes |
|---|---|---|---|---|
| &A | SETA | 153 | 3 | Value contains 3 digits |
| &B | SETB | 0 | 1 | |
| &C | SETC | 'DATA' | 4 | The value is DATA; apostrophes are ignored. |

---

EXAMPLE 26

K'&SYSLIST(2,*m*) for various values of *m* are listed here. Assume that the second positional parameter in the macro definition corresponds to the operand (ABC,'WXYZ',,12).

| *m* | &SYSLIST(2,*m*) | K'&SYSLIST(2,*m*) |
|---|---|---|
| 1 | ABC | 3 |
| 2 | 'WXYZ' | 6 |
| 3 | null | 0 |
| 4 | 12 | 2 |

---

EXAMPLE 27

Note the difference between the count attribute and the length attribute. Suppose that, in a macro instruction, DATA is the operand that corresponds to the symbolic parameter &X, and is defined as follows:

```
DATA      DC    C'ABCDEFGHIJ'
```

K'&X is 4 because there are 4 characters in the symbol DATA, whereas L'&X is 10 because DATA represents a 10-character field.

---

The type of data as a one-letter code

*The Type Attribute (T').* The type attribute of a symbol is a letter code that indicates the type of data represented by the symbol. For example, if the symbolic parameter &X corresponds to the operand CONSTANT where

```
CONSTANT DC    F'98'
```

**Figure 18.20**
The type attribute of symbols that are in the name entry of, **a**. DC or DS directives and, **b**. other statements.

| Type attribute | Type of data in DC or DS |
|---|---|
| A | A-type address constant, implicit length |
| B | Binary constant |
| C | Character constant |
| D | Long-form floating-point constant, implicit length |
| E | Short-form floating-point constant, implicit length |
| F | Fullword binary integer constant, implicit length |
| G | Binary integer constant, explicit length |
| H | Halfword binary integer constant, implicit length |
| K | Floating-point constant, explicit length |
| L | Extended-form floating-point constant, implicit length |
| P | Packed-decimal constant |
| R | Address constant, explicit length |
| V | V-type address constant, implicit length |
| X | Hexadecimal constant |
| Z | Zoned-decimal constant |

**a.**

| Type attribute | Type of statement |
|---|---|
| I | Executable instruction |
| J | CSECT, START, COM, or DSECT |
| M | Macro instruction |
| N | Macro instruction operand that is a self-defining term |
| O | Omitted macro instruction operand |
| T | EXTRN |
| U | Several statements not assigned another type attribute. |

**b.**

then the value of T'&X is F, since CONSTANT represents the address of a fullword. The type attribute of a sublist is equal to the type attribute of the first element in the sublist. Figure 18.20 lists most type attribute codes.

**The number of places to the right and to the left of a number**

*The Scaling (S') Attribute and the Integer (I') Attribute.* The scaling attribute and the integer attribute are applicable—either together or separately—to symbolic parameters, &SYSLIST(*n*), &SYSLIST(*n*,*m*), and, under OS, to ordinary symbols within a macro definition. These attributes are relevant only to binary integer constants (types F and H), floating-point constants (types E, D, and L), and decimal constants (types P and Z).

As defined in Chapter 15, the scaling attribute and the integer attribute for decimal constants are the number of decimal digits to the right and to the left, respectively, of the assumed decimal point after the constant is assembled. Although you cannot write scaling attribute references or integer attribute references within an assembler language statement, you can assign their values to ordinary symbols by using the SETA directive. The following shows how to do this with a scaling attribute reference:

```
&SCALE    SETA   S'X
SX        EQU    &SCALE
```

SX represents the scaling attribute of the decimal field at X; you can use SX within assembler language statements as you did in Chapter 15. You can use this technique within macro definitions or the open code for either the scaling attribute or the integer attribute.

This text does not discuss scaling attributes and integer attributes of binary and floating-point constants.

---

EXAMPLE 28

Consider the following macro prototype and corresponding macro instruction:

```
TEST   &A, &B, &C                  ← Prototype
TEST   PACKED, STARS, (2, ZONED)   ← Macro instruction
```

Assume that PACKED, STARS, and ZONED are defined as follows:

```
PACKED    DC     P'1234.56'
STARS     DC     5CL10'*'
ZONED     DC     Z'123.1'
```

The following lists the applicable attributes of several variable symbols:

| | Attributes of variable symbol | | | | | |
|---|---|---|---|---|---|---|
| **Variable symbol** | **L'** | **N'** | **K'** | **T'** | **S'** | **I'** |
| &A | 4 | 1 | 6 | P | 2 | 5 |
| &SYSLIST(2) | 10 | 1 | 5 | C | – | – |
| &C | – | 2 | 9 | N | – | – |
| &SYSLIST(3,2) | 4 | – | 5 | Z | 1 | 3 |

---

EXAMPLE 29

You can rewrite the ADD macro definition of Figure 18.17 to permit sublists of arbitrary length. Figure 18.21 presents such a revision. You can use K'&LIST to determine whether the sublist is missing so that you can issue an error message with an MNOTE directive. Assuming that a sublist exists, you define a SETA symbol &J, and use it as the subscript of a sublist and as a counter to control the number of generated instructions in the macro expansion. The AIF instruction and the AGO instruction direct the assembler to repeat the processing of the same model statements for each entry in the sublist. The AIF instruction determines when the assembler exits the loop by comparing the counter &J with the number of entries in the sublist, which is equal to the number attribute N'&LIST.

You can use the count attribute K'&RESULT to determine whether the third operand is missing: if it is, skip the Store instruction and leave the result in the register. Notice that you could also use the number attribute instead of the count attribute to determine if an operand is missing.

Figure 18.22 lists several expansions of this macro.

**Figure 18.21**
A revision of the ADD macro that permits sublists of arbitrary length, as described in Example 29.

```
          MACRO
&L        ADD    &LIST,&REG=2,&RESULT
.** COMPUTES THE SUM OF FULLWORD BINARY INTEGERS IN
.** THE SUBLIST &LIST.
.** &REG = A WORK REGISTER
.** &RESULT = A FULLWORD IN STORAGE FOR THE SUM.
.** IF &RESULT IS OMITTED, THE ANSWER IS LEFT IN &REG.
.** IF &LIST IS OMITTED, AN ERROR MESSAGE IS ISSUED.
          LCLA   &J                  COUNTER AND SUBSCRIPT
.* TEST FOR MISSING SUBLIST OPERAND:
          AIF    (K'&LIST NE 0).OK
          MNOTE  9,'MISSING SUBLIST.  NO CODE GENERATED.'
          MEXIT
.* INITIALIZE:
.OK       ANOP
&L        L      &REG,&LIST(1)       LOAD FIRST ENTRY
&J        SETA   2                   POINT TO SECOND ENTRY
.* WHILE &J <= N'&LIST
.LOOP     AIF    (&J GT N'&LIST).DONE
          A      &REG,&LIST(&J)      ADD NEXT ENTRY
&J        SETA   &J+1                INCREMENT COUNTER
          AGO    .LOOP               REPEAT
.* END WHILE
.* IF &RESULT IS MISSING, QUIT, ELSE STORE:
.DONE     AIF    (K'&RESULT EQ 0).EXIT
          ST     &REG,&RESULT        STORE SUM
.EXIT     MEND
```

**Figure 18.22**
Sample expansions of the ADD macro that was defined in Figure 18.21.

```
 CONTINUE ADD    (A,B,C,D),REG=R10,SUM
+CONTINUE L      R10,A               LOAD FIRST ENTRY
+         A      R10,B               ADD NEXT ENTRY
+         A      R10,C               ADD NEXT ENTRY
+         A      R10,D               ADD NEXT ENTRY
+         ST     R10,SUM             STORE SUM
*
          ADD    (A,B)
+         L      2,A                 LOAD FIRST ENTRY
+         A      2,B                 ADD NEXT ENTRY
*
          ADD    ,ANSWER,REG=R3
+    9,MISSING SUBLIST.  NO CODE GENERATED.
```

---

EXAMPLE 30

The SSS macro definition in Figure 18.23 demonstrates the use of &SYSLIST, the type attribute, and the number attribute. The macro treats each operand as if it were a sublist. There can be an arbitrary number of operands in the macro instruction, and any operand can be a sublist of arbitrary length. For each sublist, the macro squares the sum of the fullword or halfword binary integers that the entries in the sublist specify. The macro then computes

```
         MACRO
&LABEL   SSS
.** SQUARES THE SUM OF THE FULLWORD OR HALFWORD ENTRIES IN EACH
.** SUBLIST OPERAND AND COMPUTES THE SUM OF THESE SQUARES.
         LCLA  &NOPS                 NUMBER OF OPERANDS
         LCLA  &NENTS                NUMBER OF SUBLIST ENTRIES
         LCLC  &T                    TYPE OF OPERAND/ENTRY
&LABEL   SR    0,0                   CLEAR ACCUMULATOR
&NOPS    SETA  N'&SYSLIST            GET NUMBER OF OPERANDS
.* WHILE THERE ARE OPERANDS:
.OUTLOOP AIF   (&NOPS EQ 0).DONE
&NENTS   SETA  N'&SYSLIST(&NOPS)     ASSUME NO. OF ENTRIES IS > 0
&T       SETC  T'&SYSLIST(&NOPS,&NENTS) ASSUME TYPE IS F OR H
.* - IF &T = 'H', LEAVE AS IS, ELSE SET TO NULL
         AIF   ('&T' EQ 'H').LOAD
&T       SETC  ''                    SET TO NULL IF FULLWORD
 .* - END IF
.LOAD    L&T   3,&SYSLIST(&NOPS,&NENTS) LOAD ENTRY
.*   COMPUTE SUM OF ENTRIES IN SUBLIST.  IF NOT A SUBLIST,
.*   SUM IS THE SINGLE OPERAND:
.* - WHILE THERE ARE MORE ENTRIES IN A SUBLIST:
.INLOOP  AIF   (&NENTS EQ 1).SQUARE
&NENTS   SETA  &NENTS-1              DECREMENT COUNTER
&T       SETC  T'&SYSLIST(&NOPS,&NENTS) ASSUME TYPE IS F OR H
.* - - IF &T = 'H', LEAVE AS IS, ELSE SET TO NULL
         AIF   ('&T' EQ 'H').ADD
&T       SETC  ''                    SET TO NULL IF FULLWORD
.* - - END IF
.ADD     A&T   3,&SYSLIST(&NOPS,&NENTS) ADD NEXT ENTRY
         AGO   .INLOOP
.* - END WHILE
.SQUARE  MR    2,3                   SQUARE THE SUM
         AR    0,3                   ADD IT TO ACCUMULATOR
&NOPS    SETA  &NOPS-1               DECREMENT COUNTER
         AGO   .OUTLOOP
.* END WHILE
.DONE    MEND
```

**Figure 18.23**
The definition of the SSS macro, as described in Example 30.

the sum of these squares and places the sum into Register 0, under the assumption that no computation exceeds 32 bits. For instance, suppose that A, B, C, D, E, and F are ordinary symbols that represent the addresses of either fullword or halfword binary integers. Then the macro instruction

```
SSS   (A,B,C),D,(E,F)
```

generates instructions that evaluate the following expression:

$$(A + B + C)^2 + D^2 + (E + F)^2$$

You can use the type attribute to distinguish halfwords from fullwords, and to generate the proper instructions.

The statements in the macro definition process the operands backwards, by beginning with the last one and assuming that no operands are missing. Sublist entries are also processed backwards. Registers 0, 2, and 3 are used in the expansion; the macro does not save their prior contents.

**Figure 18.24**
A sample expansion of the SSS macro that was defined in Figure 18.23.

```
* A, B, D, AND F ARE FULLWORDS; C AND E ARE HALFWORDS
         SSS   (A,B,C),D,(E,F)
+        SR    0,0                  CLEAR ACCUMULATOR
+        L     3,F                         LOAD ENTRY
+        AH    3,E                         ADD NEXT ENTRY
+        MR    2,3                  SQUARE THE SUM
+        AR    0,3                  ADD IT TO ACCUMULATOR
+        L     3,D                         LOAD ENTRY
+        MR    2,3                  SQUARE THE SUM
+        AR    0,3                  ADD IT TO ACCUMULATOR
+        LH    3,C                         LOAD ENTRY
+        A     3,B                         ADD NEXT ENTRY
+        A     3,A                         ADD NEXT ENTRY
+        MR    2,3                  SQUARE THE SUM
+        AR    0,3                  ADD IT TO ACCUMULATOR
```

The expansion of the macro instruction just given appears in Figure 18.24; it assumes that A, B, D, and F are fullwords, and that C and E are halfwords. The remarks in the expansion are not aligned: this is due to the lengthy operand entries in the model statements that generate the Load and Add instructions. You can align the remarks entries by replacing each occurrence of &SYSLIST(&NOPS,&NENTS) in Figure 18.23 by a SETC symbol that has the same value. (See Self-Test Exercise 14 below.) While this change allows sufficient room to align the remarks, it obscures the logic of the macro definition and may not be worth the advantage of aligned remarks.

## SELF-TEST EXERCISES

**11.** Assume this macro prototype, its corresponding macro instruction, and these DC directives:

```
         TEST  &ONE,&TWO             ← Prototype
         TEST  PACK,(PACK,CHARS)     ← Macro instruction
PACK     DC    P'1.2345'
CHARS    DC    C'ABCDEFG'
```

Indicate the values of all attributes that are applicable to the following:

**a.** &SYSLIST(1) **c.** &SYSLIST(2,1)
**b.** &TWO **d.** &SYSLIST(2,2)

**12.** Given the definition of the ADD macro in Figure 18.21 (Example 29), what does this macro instruction generate?

```
ADD    REG=3,ANSWER
```

**13.** Modify the definition of the ADD macro in Figure 18.21 so that ® is a positional parameter. If the corresponding operand is omitted from the macro instruction, use Register 2 as the register in the expansion.

**14.** Replace &SYSLIST(&NOPS,&NENTS) in Figure 18.23 by a SETC symbol so that you can align the remarks entries.

## *Subscripted SET Symbols*

**A SET symbol can be an array.**

You can use a subscripted SET symbol to represent an array of values that is analogous to an array in a high-level programming language. To declare a SET symbol as a subscripted SET symbol, you specify a dimension in the LCL*x* directive or the GBL*x* directive. You can declare both subscripted and nonsubscripted SET symbols in the same LCL*x* and GBL*x* directives. They can be summarized as follows:

| Name | Operation | Operand | Instruction Name | Action |
|---|---|---|---|---|
| *blank* | **LCLA** / **LCLB** / **LCLC** | *variable symbol*[(*dimension*)], . . . | DECLARE LOCAL SET SYMBOLS | Declares and initializes local SET symbols as described earlier. The *dimension* is an optional self-defining term that, if present, indicates that the SET symbol is an array with *dimension* elements. |
| *blank* | **GBLA** / **GBLB** / **GBLC** | *variable symbol*[(*dimension*)], . . . | DECLARE GLOBAL SET SYMBOLS | Declares and initializes global SET symbols as described earlier. The *dimension* has the same meaning as for the LCL*x* directive. |

The *dimension* is an optional decimal self-defining term that is greater than 0 but is a maximum of 32,767 (4,095 in DOS). A global array must have the same dimension each time that you declare it. These directives initialize each element of an array with the same values that the directives use to initialize nonsubscripted SET symbols.

You reference the array values by using subscripts that are arithmetic expressions whose values are greater than 0. You write the subscripts, enclosing them in parentheses, immediately after the variable symbol. You can use subscripted SET symbols wherever you can use nonsubscripted SET symbols.

---

EXAMPLE 31

The following notes the effect of each statement in the given *sequence*:

| Statement | Effect |
|---|---|
| `LCLA &A,&X(4)` | Declares local arithmetic SET symbols &A and &X. &X is an array that contains 4 elements: &X(1), &X(2), &X(3), and &X(4). Initializes &A and all elements of &X to 0. |
| `GBLB &Y(3)` | Declares a global Boolean subscripted SET symbol &Y with elements &Y(1), &Y(2), and &Y(3). Initializes each element to 0. |

| Statement | | | Effect |
|---|---|---|---|
| | LCLC | &Z(12) | Declares a local character subscripted SET symbol &Z with elements &Z(1), &Z(2), and so on to &Z(12). Initializes each element to the null string. |
| &X(3) | SETA | 1 | Sets the third element of &X to 1. |
| &Y(2) | SETB | (&X(&A+3) LT 2) | Sets the second element of &Y to 1. &X(&A+3) is &X(3) because &A equals 0. Since &X(3) equals 1 and 1 is less than 2, the Boolean expression is true. |
| &Z(&A+1) | SETC | '&A.(&X(3))' | Sets the first element of &Z to the character string 0(1). Note the distinction between concatenation and the subscript notation. |

### *Substrings*

You can reference characters within a character string by using a substring notation of the form

*'string'*(*s1*,*s2*)

Here, *'string'* is a character expression, and *s1* and *s2* are arithmetic expressions that are used as subscripts. The first subscript *s1* points to the first character of the substring within the given string. The second subscript *s2* indicates the number of consecutive characters in the substring. You can use substring notation either in the operand entry of a SETC directive or in a logical expression.

EXAMPLE 32

Assume the following declarations:

```
LCLC    &R,&S(9),&T,&U
GBLB    &V
```

The following *sequence* of statements demonstrates the use of substring notation:

| Statement | | | Notes |
|---|---|---|---|
| &R | SETC | 'ABCDEFGH'(2,3) | Sets &R to the substring BCD. |
| &S(3) | SETC | 'ABCD'(2,1).'XY' | Sets the third element of &S to BXY. The concatenation character is optional. |
| &T | SETC | '&R'(1,2) | Sets &T to the substring BC. (&R is BCD.) |

| Statement | | | Notes |
|---|---|---|---|
| &U | SETC | '&S(3)'(2,1) | Sets &U to the substring X. (&S(3) is BXY.) |
| &V | SETB | ('&R'(1,1) EQ 'B') | Sets &V to 1 since the Boolean expression is true. (&R is BCD, so '&R' (1,1) is B.) |
| AIF | ('&R'(1,1) EQ 'B').OUT | | Branches to the sequence symbol .OUT since the Boolean expression is true. |

---

EXAMPLE 33 The macro ARRAY in Figure 18.25 demonstrates a simple application of substrings. It generates an array of &N fullword constants at increments of &INCR that begin with zero. The symbolic parameters &N and &INCR are

```
           MACRO
           ARRAY &N,&INCR
.** DEFINES AN ARRAY OF &N FULLWORD CONSTANTS AT INCREMENTS OF &INCR
.** THAT BEGIN WITH ZERO.
           ACTR  2000              LIMIT NO. OF AIF AND AGO INSTRUCTIONS
           LCLA  &I                INCREMENT IN NUMERIC FORM
           LCLA  &CON              CONSTANT VALUE
           LCLA  &J                COUNTER
           LCLC  &TEMP             INCREMENT WITHOUT MINUS SIGN
.* IF INCREMENT IS POSITIVE:
           AIF   ('&INCR'(1,1) EQ '-').NEG  IS THERE A MINUS SIGN?
.* - THEN:
&I         SETA  &INCR             POSITIVE INCREMENT IN NUMERIC FORM
           AGO   .AHEAD            BRANCH AHEAD
.* - ELSE:
.NEG       ANOP
&TEMP      SETC  '&INCR'(2,10)     EXTRACT MAGNITUDE OF INCREMENT
&I         SETA  -&TEMP            NEGATIVE INCREMENT IN NUMERIC FORM
.* END IF
.AHEAD     ANOP
&CON       SETA  0                 SET CONSTANT TO FIRST VALUE
&J         SETA  1                 SET COUNTER TO 1
.* WHILE &J <= &N DO:
.LOOP      AIF   (&J GT &N)).DONE TEST IF DONE
.* - IF &CON < 0
           AIF   (&CON GE 0).POS
.* - - THEN:
           DC    F'-&CON'
           AGO   .CONTIN
.* - - ELSE:
.POS       DC    F'&CON'
.* - END IF
.CONTIN    ANOP
&CON       SETA  &CON+&I           INCREMENT CONSTANT
&J         SETA  &J+1              INCREMENT COUNTER
           AGO   .LOOP             REPEAT
.* END WHILE
.DONE      MEND
```

**Figure 18.25**
The definition of the ARRAY macro, as described in Example 33.

assumed to have values that are decimal self-defining terms. For example, the instruction

```
ARRAY 3,-2
```

generates these instructions:

```
DC    F'0'
DC    F'-2'
DC    F'-4'
```

To simplify the definition of the macro, assume that positive operand values are unsigned.

Since &INCR represents a character string, you must use a substring notation to determine if the value of the string contains a minus sign. You can then define a SETA symbol &I that represents the increment as a signed numeric quantity.

The SETA symbol &CON represents the value of the next constant that is generated. Since &CON can have a negative value and since, if it does, F'&CON' would not generate a minus sign, you must test &CON and branch to the appropriate DC statement.

The ACTR directive limits the array to approximately 500 constants, since four AIF and AGO directives are processed during each cycle of the loop.

---

EXAMPLE 34

The ATIME macro in Figure 18.26 defines a character constant that contains the time that your program was assembled. The time is in either 24-hour or 12-hour notation. If you write

```
ATIME   24
```

then the generated constant has the form *hh:mm* in 24-hour notation. Since the value that &SYSTIME provides has the form *hh.mm*, you simply replace the period by a colon. If you write ATIME without an operand, then the time that &SYSTIME provides is converted to 12-hour notation, and one of the following suffixes is included in the constant: AM, PM, NOON, or MID.

The definition of ATIME does not include a symbolic parameter in the operand entry of the prototype statement, although the definition could. Therefore, you refer to the operand by using &SYSLIST(1) within the macro definition. You use substring notation to isolate the hours and minutes in the character string that &SYSTIME provides. To generate the constant in 24-hour notation, you concatenate the hours, a colon, and the minutes. To convert the time to a 12-hour notation, you must perform some arithmetic on the hours by using the SETA symbol &H. Notice that &HR represents the hours in character form, while &H represents them in numeric form. The minutes portion of the time is also represented in two forms, although this is not required. After you have adjusted the hours, if necessary, you concatenate the hours, a colon, the minutes, and the proper suffix to form the desired character constant.

The following pairs of macro instructions illustrate the nature of the generated constants for various assembly times:

```
         MACRO
&LABEL   ATIME
.** DEFINES A CHARACTER STRING THAT CONTAINS THE TIME OF ASSEMBLY
.** OF THIS PROGRAM IN EITHER 24-HOUR OR 12-HOUR NOTATION.
.** SPECIFY 24 FOR 24-HOUR NOTATION; OMIT OPERAND FOR 12-HOUR NOTATION
         LCLC  &T                    TIME FROM &SYSTIME
         LCLC  &AMPM                 SUFFIX (AM, PM, NOON, MID)
         LCLC  &HR,&MIN              HOUR, MINUTES IN CHARACTER FORM
         LCLA  &H,&M                 HOUR, MINUTES IN NUMERIC FORM
         LCLC  &BLNK                 1 BLANK CHARACTER
&BLNK    SETC  ' '
&T       SETC  '&SYSTIME'            GET TIME OF ASSEMBLY (HH.MM)
&HR      SETC  '&T'(1,2)             GET HOUR
&MIN     SETC  '&T'(4,2)             GET MINUTES
         AIF   ('&SYSLIST(1)' EQ '24').HR24  24-HR NOTATION DESIRED?
.* IF OPERAND IS NOT 24, THEN CONVERT TIME TO 12-HOUR NOTATION:
&H       SETA  &HR                   CONVERT HOUR TO NUMERIC
&M       SETA  &MIN                  CONVERT MINUTES TO NUMERIC
&AMPM    SETC  'MID'                 SET SUFFIX; ASSUME MIDNIGHT
         AIF   ((&H EQ 0) AND (&M EQ 0)).MID ADJUST HR IF MIDNIGHT
&AMPM    SETC  'AM'                  SET SUFFIX; ASSUME AM
         AIF   (&H LT 12).DC         IF AM, ALL SET
&AMPM    SETC  'NOON'                SET SUFFIX; ASSUME NOON
         AIF   ((&H EQ 12) AND (&M EQ 0)).DC  IF NOON, ALL SET
.* TIME IS PM:
&AMPM    SETC  'PM'                  SET SUFFIX; TIME IS PM
         AIF   (&H EQ 12).DC         NO NEED TO ADJUST HOUR IF IT IS 12
&H       SETA  &H-12                 CONVERT FROM 24- TO 12-HR NOTATION
         AGO   .DC                   GO DEFINE CONSTANT
.MID     ANOP
&H       SETA  12                    12 MIDNIGHT
.DC      ANOP  ,                     GENERATE CONSTANT; 12-HR NOTATION
&LABEL   DC    C'&H:&MIN&BLNK&AMPM'
         MEXIT
.HR24    ANOP  ,                     GENERATE CONSTANT; 24-HR NOTATION
&LABEL   DC    C'&HR:&MIN'
         MEND
```

**Figure 18.26** The definition of the ATIME macro, as described in Example 34.

| Instruction and generated constant | Assembly time |
|---|---|
| `ATIME` | 1:09 A.M. |
| `+ DC C'1:09 AM'` | |
| `ATIME 24` | 1:09 A.M. |
| `+ DC C'01:09'` | |
| `*` | |
| `ATIME` | Midnight |
| `+ DC C'12:00 MID'` | |
| `ATIME 24` | Midnight |
| `+ DC C'00:00'` | |
| `*` | |
| `ATIME` | 3:50 P.M. |
| `+ DC C'3:50 PM'` | |
| `ATIME 24` | 3:50 P.M. |
| `+ DC C'15:50'` | |

Since the definition uses the arithmetic SET symbol &H for the hours portion of the 12-hour constant, leading zeros do not appear; however, since the character SET symbol &HR appears in the 24-hour constant, leading zeros do appear. &MIN is used in both 12-hour and 24-hour constants so that leading zeros do appear.

Finally, notice that you can omit the SETA symbol &M. Such a change requires that you replace the logical expression (&M EQ 0) by ('&MIN' EQ '00') in two AIF instructions.

---

EXAMPLE 35

The macro definition in Figure 18.27 demonstrates subscripted SET symbols and substring notation. This macro also illustrates that you can perform a substantial amount of computation at preassembly time. The macro sorts a string of letters and digits into alphanumeric order; the macro creates a character constant from the ordered string. You specify the letters and digits in any order in the operand entry of the macro instruction. For example, if you write

```
CHARSORT    ZT5AXB
```

then the macro generates the following:

```
DC        C'ABTXZ5'
```

The macro definition begins by using substring notation to isolate each character in the given operand, and places each character into an array element of a subscripted SET symbol. After the macro sorts the array, it concatenates the ordered characters to form the desired constant.

---

## SELF-TEST EXERCISE

15. What are the values of the SET symbols after the assembler processes the following *sequence* of instructions?

```
             LCLA   &J(3),&K
             LCLB   &FLAGS(4)
             GBLC   &T(5)
&FLAGS(2)    SETB   ('&T(3)' NE 'NULL')
&J(2)        SETA   &J(&K+1)+4
&FLAGS(4)    SETB   (&FLAGS(&J(2)-2))
&T(2)        SETC   '&K.(1&J(2),&J(1)+2)'
&T(1)        SETC   'ABCDEFGHIJ'(4,5)
&T(3)        SETC   '&T(1)'(2,3)
&FLAGS(1)    SETB   ('&T(3)'(1,1) EQ 'F')
&T(4)        SETC   '&T(3)'(3,1).'&T(1)'(4,2)
&K           SETA   -021
&FLAGS(3)    SETB   (&K LT 0)
&T(5)        SETC   '5&K'(1,3).'&K+1'
```

```
         MACRO
&LABEL   CHARSORT &CODES
.** DEFINES A STRING OF CHARACTERS IN ALPHANUMERIC ORDER FROM
.** UNORDERED CHARACTERS IN THE OPERAND.
         LCLC  &C(36)               ARRAY OF CHARACTERS
         LCLC  &TEMP                WORK VARIABLE FOR SORT
         LCLC  &CONST               GENERATED CONSTANT
         LCLA  &K                   POINTER
         LCLB  &INORDER             FLAG FOR BUBBLE SORT
         LCLB  &TRUE,&FALSE         CONSTANTS TO ASSIGN TO FLAG
&TRUE    SETB  1                    &TRUE = 1, &FALSE = 0
&K       SETA  1                    INITIALIZE POINTER
.** CONVERT OPERAND TO AN ARRAY OF CHARACTERS:
.* REPEAT:
.LOOP1   ANOP
&C(&K)   SETC  '&CODES'(&K,1)       PLACE NEXT CHARACTER INTO ARRAY
&K       SETA  &K+1                 INCREMENT POINTER
         AIF   (&K LE K'&CODES).LOOP1  REPEAT FOR ALL CHARACTERS
.* END REPEAT
.*
.** SORT ARRAY OF CHARACTERS (BUBBLE SORT):
.* REPEAT:
.LOOP3   ANOP
&INORDER SETB  (&TRUE)              SET FLAG TO TRUE
&K       SETA  1                    INITIALIZE POINTER
.* - FOR &K = 1 TO K'&CODES-1:
.LOOP2   ANOP
.* - - IF ARRAY ELEMENTS ARE OUT OF ORDER:
         AIF   ('&C(&K)' LE '&C(&K+1)').OK  SKIP AHEAD IF IN ORDER
.* - - - THEN INTERCHANGE ARRAY ELEMENTS:
&TEMP    SETC  '&C(&K)'
&C(&K)   SETC  '&C(&K+1)'
&C(&K+1) SETC  '&TEMP'
&INORDER SETB  (&FALSE)             ARRAY WAS OUT OF ORDER; SET FLAG
.* - - END IF
.OK      ANOP
&K       SETA  &K+1                 INCREMENT POINTER
         AIF   (&K LT K'&CODES).LOOP2  REPEAT UNTIL END OF ARRAY
.* - END FOR
.* UNTIL &INORDER IS TRUE
         AIF   (NOT &INORDER).LOOP3  IF ARRAY IS NOT ORDERED, REPEAT
.* END REPEAT
.*
.** ARRAY IS IN ORDER; CONCATENATE CHARACTERS TO FORM A STRING:
&K       SETA  1                    INITIALIZE POINTER
.* REPEAT:
.LOOP4   ANOP
&CONST   SETC  '&CONST&C(&K)'       PLACE NEXT CHAR. ON RIGHT OF STRING
&K       SETA  &K+1                 INCREMENT POINTER
         AIF   (&K LE K'&CODES).LOOP4  REPEAT FOR ALL CHARACTERS
.* END REPEAT
&LABEL   DC    C'&CONST'            GENERATE CONSTANT
         MEND
```

**Figure 18.27**
The definition of the CHARSORT macro, as described in Example 35.

## Additional Features of Macro Definitions

You can use the features that are described in this section within macro definitions, but they are not part of the conditional assembly language.

### *Inner Macro Instructions*

**Macro calls within a macro definition**

You can call a macro from within a macro definition. A macro instruction that you write within a macro definition is called an **inner macro instruction,** or a **nested macro instruction.** Operands of inner macro instructions may include symbolic parameters and SET symbols that are defined in the containing macro definition, and system variable symbols. An inner macro instruction may call recursively the macro definition that contains it.

The use of inner macro instructions allows you to reorganize a macro definition into smaller portions. The resulting definition should be easier to understand, and the component macro definitions should be easier to write. In this respect, the macro definitions are analogous to subprograms.

Note that you cannot nest macro definitions: you cannot define a macro within the definition of another macro.

---

EXAMPLE 36

Consider the SSS macro definition that was given in Figure 18.23. A portion of this definition computes the sum of the entries in a sublist. You can isolate this portion as a separate macro ADD2, as is done in Figure 18.28. Both the SSS macro definition and the SSS2 macro definition produce the same expansion—although the remarks in the SSS2 expansion are aligned.

Notice that &LABEL is a name field parameter and .DONE is a sequence symbol in both macro definitions. These elements are local to each macro definition: thus, &LABEL and .DONE within the SSS2 macro differ from &LABEL and .DONE within the ADD2 macro.

---

### *The System Variable Symbol &SYSECT*

**Use &SYSECT to access the name of the current control section.**

The assembler assigns a value to the system variable symbol &SYSECT, which appears within a macro definition. This value is equal to the symbol that names the control section, dummy section, or common section containing the macro instruction that calls the macro definition. For example, you can use &SYSECT when you define an address constant that you use to establish addressability of the section. In addition, imagine that a macro expansion interrupts the present control section by defining another control section, dummy section, or common section; you can then write &SYSECT in the name entry of a CSECT, DSECT, or COM directive to resume the definition of the original section.

```
         MACRO
&LABEL   SSS2
.** SQUARES THE SUM OF THE FULLWORD OR HALFWORD ENTRIES IN EACH
.** SUBLIST OPERAND AND COMPUTES THE SUM OF THESE SQUARES.
         LCLA  &NOPS               NUMBER OF OPERANDS
&LABEL   SR    0,0                 CLEAR ACCUMULATOR
&NOPS    SETA  N'&SYSLIST          ASSUME > 0
.* WHILE THERE ARE OPERANDS:
.OUTLOOP AIF   (&NOPS EQ 0).DONE
         ADD2  &SYSLIST(&NOPS),3   ADD SUBLIST ENTRIES
.SQUARE  MR    2,3                 SQUARE THE SUM
         AR    0,3                 ADD IT TO ACCUMULATOR
&NOPS    SETA  &NOPS-1             DECREMENT COUNTER
         AGO   .OUTLOOP
.* END WHILE
.DONE    MEND
.*
         MACRO
&LABEL   ADD2  &LIST,&REG
.** COMPUTES THE SUM OF THE FULLWORD OR HALFWORD ENTRIES IN A
.** SUBLIST OPERAND
         LCLA  &NENTS              NUMBER OF SUBLIST ENTRIES
         LCLC  &T                  TYPE OF OPERAND/ENTRY
&NENTS   SETA  N'&LIST             ASSUME NO. OF ENTRIES IS > 0
&T       SETC  T'&LIST(&NENTS)     ASSUME TYPE IS F OR H
.* IF &T = 'H', LEAVE AS IS, ELSE SET TO NULL
         AIF   ('&T' EQ 'H').LOAD
&T       SETC  ''                  SET TO NULL IF FULLWORD
.* END IF
.LOAD    L&T   &REG,&LIST(&NENTS) LOAD ENTRY
.* COMPUTE SUM OF ENTRIES IN SUBLIST.  IF NOT A SUBLIST, SUM IS
.* THE SINGLE OPERAND:
.* WHILE THERE ARE MORE ENTRIES IN A SUBLIST:
.INLOOP  AIF   (&NENTS EQ 1).DONE
&NENTS   SETA  &NENTS-1            DECREMENT COUNTER
&T       SETC  T'&LIST(&NENTS)     ASSUME F OR H
.* - IF &T = 'H', LEAVE AS IS, ELSE SET TO NULL
         AIF   ('&T' EQ 'H').ADD
&T       SETC  ''                  SET TO NULL IF FULLWORD
.* - END IF
.ADD     A&T   &REG,&LIST(&NENTS) ADD NEXT ENTRY
         AGO   .INLOOP
.* END WHILE
.DONE    MEND
```

**Figure 18.28**
The definitions of the SSS2 and ADD2 macros, as described in Example 36.

---

EXAMPLE 37

The macro definitions in Figure 18.29 demonstrate the effect of &SYSECT when you use inner macro instructions. Here, the macro MAC1 defines a control section, and names it with the symbol in the name entry of the macro instruction that calls MAC1. Within this new control section, MAC1 defines an address constant that is equal to the address of the control section from which MAC1 is invoked. MAC1 then calls MAC2. MAC2 defines an

```
         MACRO
&SECTION MAC1
.** DEFINE A CONTROL SECTION THAT CONTAINS AN ADDRESS CONSTANT
&SECTION CSECT ,                       DEFINE A NEW CONTROL SECTION
         DC    A(&SYSECT)              ADDRESS OF CALLING CONTROL SECTION
         MAC2
         MEND
.*
         MACRO
         MAC2
.** DEFINE AN ADDRESS CONSTANT
         DC    A(&SYSECT)              ADDRESS OF CALLING CONTROL SECTION
         MEND
```

**Figure 18.29**
Using &SYSECT in an inner macro instruction, as described in Example 37.

```
ONE      START ,                      BEGIN A CONTROL SECTION
         MAC2  ,                      CALL MAC2; NO NESTING
+        DC    A(ONE)                 ADDRESS OF CALLING CONTROL SECTION
TWO      MAC1  ,                      MAC1 CALLS MAC2
+TWO     CSECT ,                      DEFINE A NEW CONTROL SECTION
+        DC    A(ONE)                 ADDRESS OF CALLING CONTROL SECTION
+        DC    A(TWO)                 ADDRESS OF CALLING CONTROL SECTION
```

**Figure 18.30**
Sample expansion of the MAC1 macro and the MAC2 macro that were defined in Figure 18.29.

address constant that is equal to the address of the control section from which MAC2 is invoked.

The macro expansions in Figure 18.30 illustrate the behavior of these two macros. When MAC2 is called from the control section ONE, &SYSECT has the value ONE within the definition of MAC2. This fact is reflected in the address constant that appears in the macro expansion. The call to MAC1 defines a new control section named TWO. Since MAC1 is called from the control section ONE, &SYSECT has a value of ONE within the definition of MAC1. When MAC2 is called from within the definition of MAC1, the call is from the control section TWO. Thus, &SYSECT has the value TWO within the definition of MAC2. Therefore, the expansion of MAC1 defines a control section that contains two address constants: the first contains the address of the control section from which MAC1 was called, and the second contains the address of the new control section.

EXAMPLE 38

The macro definition in Figure 18.31 illustrates the use of &SYSECT to resume the definition of a control section. The CALLSUB macro calls an external subprogram, and generates the subprogram itself the first time that you use the macro.

A key to the logic of the macro definition is the global SETB symbol &INCLUDE. By testing &INCLUDE, you can decide whether or not to generate the subprogram. Initially, the value of &INCLUDE is 0. The first time that the macro definition is processed, you generate a control section that contains the subprogram and you generate a calling sequence to the subprogram. You also set &INCLUDE to 1: subsequent uses of CALLSUB result in only the calling sequence to the subprogram. Since the control section that constitutes the subprogram interrupts the other control section that contains the CALLSUB macro instruction, you must resume your original control section by writing &SYSECT in the name entry of a CSECT directive.

**Figure 18.31** The definition of the CALLSUB macro, as described in Example 38.

```
          MACRO
&LABEL    CALLSUB &ENTRY,&ARGS
.** GENERATE A CALLING SEQUENCE TO A SUBPROGRAM.  GENERATE THE
.** SUBPROGRAM THE FIRST TIME THAT THIS MACRO IS CALLED.
          GBLB  &INCLUDE           FLAG INDICATES IF SUBPROGRAM IS
.*                                 INCLUDED.  FLAG IS INITIALLY FALSE.
          AIF   (&INCLUDE).SKIP    IF SUBPROGRAM IS ALREADY INCLUDED,
.*                                   THEN SKIP AHEAD; ELSE INCLUDE THE
.*                                   SUBPROGRAM AND SET FLAG TO TRUE:
&ENTRY    CSECT   }
          .       }
          .       }  Subprogram
          .       }
          BR    14}
&SYSECT   CSECT ,                  RESUME ORIGINAL CONTROL SECTION
&INCLUDE  SETB  1                  SET FLAG TO TRUE FOR NEXT TIME
.SKIP     ANOP  ,                  GENERATE CALLING SEQUENCE
&LABEL    L     15,=V(&ENTRY)      LOAD ENTRY POINT  }
          .                                          }  Calling sequence
          .                                          }  as in Figure 18.11
          .                                          }
          MEND
```

## *The System Variable Symbol &SYSPARM*

**Use &SYSPARM to communicate between your program and an option that you specify in the JCL.**

The system variable symbol &SYSPARM allows you to pass a character string from the JCL to the source module. You do this by writing one of the following JCL statements:

| System | Statement |
|---|---|
| OS | // EXEC    ASFMCLG, PARM.ASM='SYSPARM(*string*)' |
| DOS | // OPTION SYSPARM='*string*' |
| CMS | ASSEMBLE *file* (SYSPARM(*string*)) |

&SYSPARM has the value *string*, and is available as a constant throughout all macro definitions in your source program. You can use &SYSPARM either to select options or to set parameters within a macro definition.

**SELF-TEST EXERCISE**

**16.** Modify the definition of the MAC1 macro in Figure 18.29 (Example 37) so that the original control section from which MAC1 is called is resumed after the address constants are defined.

## The Conditional Assembly Language within Open Code

Occasionally, the conditional assembly language can be useful within the open code. For example, you can generate a long series of DC directives by using a conditional assembly loop—thereby avoiding the tedium of writing each DC separately. Often, it is convenient to define translation tables in this manner.

When you use conditional assembly language statements within the open code, remember the following comments:

- The AIF and AGO directives must branch within the open code; it is illegal to branch from the open code to a macro definition.
- Attribute references to ordinary symbols are restricted to type, length, scaling, and integer. Although scaling and integer attribute references may not appear directly in assembler language statements, you can use them in open code SETA directives, as was discussed earlier.
- You cannot use &SYSNDX, &SYSLIST, &SYSECT, or symbolic parameters within the open code: they are local to macro definitions. However, you can use &SYSDATE, &SYSTIME, and &SYSPARM.
- Under DOS, the GBL*x* and LCL*x* directives must appear between the source macro definitions and the start of the first control section.
- Under OS, you can use MNOTE in the open code.

---

EXAMPLE 39

You can use the statements in Figure 18.32 to generate powers of 3 as an array of fullword integers within the open code.

```
         LCLA  &CON,&J
&CON     SETA  3               SET CONSTANT TO FIRST VALUE
&J       SETA  1               INITIALIZE COUNTER
.* REPEAT 20 TIMES:
.LOOP    DC    F'&CON'
&J       SETA  &J+1            INCREMENT COUNTER
&CON     SETA  3*&CON          COMPUTE NEXT POWER OF 3
         AIF   (&J LE 20).LOOP REPEAT
.* END REPEAT
```

**Figure 18.32**
Instructions in the open code that generate powers of 3 as an array, as described in Example 39.

## Debugging Hints

1. A common oversight is to omit the LCL*x* and GBL*x* declarations—particularly when the SET*x* directives are used to assign values to SET symbols. The SET*x* directives are analogous to assignment statements: separate declarations of the SET symbols are necessary.
2. Remember to distinguish between the preassembly phase, the assembly phase, and the execution phase of a program. You must do this especially when you use the conditional assembly language, since its similarity to high-level programming languages can make you forget that a macro is expanded before the program is assembled, well before it is executed.
3. You can use the MNOTE directive as a debugging tool to verify the values of variable symbols at preassembly time.

## Stylistic Notes

1. While you can use symbols for register names within macro definitions, reconsider this practice when you write macro definitions that other programmers will use. Your macro definitions are more general if you use self-defining terms for register names since the users of your macros will not have to supply EQUs for symbols that they might not otherwise use.
2. When a macro instruction represents executable instructions, you should consider its effect upon the length of the object program. Typically, macros are advantageous when they represent a modest number of instructions. Long sequences of instructions are best organized into a subprogram that the program branches to. However, it is appropriate to define the call to such a subprogram as a macro.

## Summary

1. Source macro definitions precede the first control section of your program. You delimit each definition with MACRO and MEND directives, and write the prototype statement and the macro body between these directives. In general, the macro body consists of model statements and conditional assembly language statements.
2. You invoke a macro by writing a macro instruction that the assembler replaces with the macro expansion at preassembly time.
3. Variable symbols begin with an ampersand and take on values that affect the macro expansion. Sequence symbols begin with a period: they are used as statement labels within the context of the conditional assembly language.
4. There are three types of variable symbols: symbolic parameters, SET symbols, and system variable symbols.
   a. You write symbolic parameters in the prototype statement to represent the input operands of the macro instruction. These symbolic parameters can be positional or keyword parameters. The name field parameter appears in the name entry of the prototype statement, and represents the symbol, if any, in the corresponding macro instruction.
   b. To affect the macro expansion, you use SET symbols that take on arithmetic values, Boolean values, or character values within the context of the conditional assembly language. SET symbols can have a local scope or global scope. They may also be subscripted and, as such, are analogous to arrays of a high-level language.
   c. System variable symbols begin with &SYS and represent values that are defined for you. The available system variable symbols are &SYSNDX, &SYSLIST, &SYSDATE, &SYSTIME, &SYSECT, and &SYSPARM.
5. A sublist is an operand in a macro instruction that consists of a list of items, which are separated by commas; the list is enclosed in parentheses. You can reference the entries within a sublist by using a subscript notation.

6. You use the MEXIT directive to terminate the processing of a macro definition.
7. You use the MNOTE directive to generate a warning message within a macro expansion.
8. You form an arithmetic expression from self-defining terms; SETA symbols; SETB symbols; SETC symbols whose values are unsigned decimal self-defining terms; symbolic parameters whose values are self-defining terms; &SYSLIST references whose values are self-defining terms; &SYSNDX; numeric attribute references; the operators +, −, *, and /; and parentheses.

   You can use an arithmetic expression in the operand entry of the SETA directive; within a logical expression; as a subscript for either a SET symbol, symbolic parameter, or &SYSLIST; and in the notation for a substring.
9. A character expression consists of a sequence of characters and variable symbols, whose values are interpreted as characters; the entire sequence is enclosed in apostrophes. You can use a character expression in the operand entry of the SETC directive, within a logical expression, or in the notation for a substring.
10. A logical expression can be either two arithmetic expressions that are separated by one of the relational operators EQ, NE, LT, LE, GT, or GE; or two character expressions (or anything that is valid as the operand of a SETC instruction) that are separated by a relational operator.

    Logical expressions also can consist of either a SETB symbol; two logical expressions that are separated by one of the Boolean operators OR, AND, OR NOT, or AND NOT; or a single logical expression that is preceded by NOT. You can use a logical expression in the operand entry of either the SETB directive or the AIF directive.
11. You use the AIF and AGO directives to alter the order in which the assembler processes statements at preassembly time. Using these directives, you can branch to statements that you have labeled with a sequence symbol.
12. You use the ANOP directive to label a point in the program with a sequence symbol. This is necessary when the instruction to which you must branch already has a symbol in its name entry.
13. Ordinary and variable symbols have attributes. They are length (L′), number (N′), count (K′), type (T′), scaling (S′), and integer (I′).
14. You can reference a substring of a character string with a double subscript notation. The subscripts denote the beginning position and the length of the substring, respectively.
15. Macro definitions can contain inner macro instructions.
16. With a few restrictions, you can use the conditional assembly language in the open code. However, its major application is within macro definitions.

## New Instruction Summary

| Name | Operation | Operand | Instruction Name | Action |
|---|---|---|---|---|
| *blank* | **MACRO** | ignored | BEGIN MACRO DEFINITION | Initiates a macro definition. |
| *sequence symbol* or *blank* | **MEND** | ignored | END MACRO DEFINITION | Terminates a macro definition. |
| *blank* | {**LCLA** / **LCLB** / **LCLC**} | *variable symbol* [(*dimension*)], . . . | DECLARE LOCAL SET SYMBOLS | Declares the variable symbols in the operand entry to be local SET symbols that are either arithmetic (LCLA), Boolean (LCLB), or character (LCLC); initializes arithmetic and Boolean SET symbols to 0, and character SET symbols to the null string. The *dimension* is an optional self-defining term that, if present, indicates that the SET symbol is an array with *dimension* elements. |

| Name | Operation | Operand | Instruction Name | Action |
|---|---|---|---|---|
| *blank* | {GBLA, GBLB, GBLC} | *variable symbol* [*(dimension)*], . . . | DECLARE GLOBAL SET SYMBOLS | Declares and initializes global SET symbols in the same way as the LCL*x* directives. However, initialization of a particular SET symbol only occurs the first time that the assembler processes a GBL*x* instruction that declares the symbol. Subsequent GBL*x* instructions do not change the value of the symbol. |
| *variable symbol* | **SETA** | *arithmetic expression* | ASSIGN VALUE TO SETA SYMBOL | Evaluates the *arithmetic expression* and assigns the resulting signed 32-bit value to the SETA symbol that appears in the name entry. |
| *variable symbol* | **SETB** | *(logical expression)* or 0 or 1 | ASSIGN VALUE TO SETB SYMBOL | Assigns the value in the operand entry to the SETB symbol that appears in the name entry. |
| *variable symbol* | **SETC** | *'string'* or T'*symbol* or *'string'(s1,s2)* | ASSIGN VALUE TO SETC SYMBOL | Assigns the character string that the character expression *'string'* represents to the SETC symbol that appears in the name entry. The entries *s1* and *s2* are arithmetic expressions, and *symbol* is an ordinary or variable symbol. |
| *sequence symbol* or *blank* | **AIF** | *(logical expression) sequence symbol* | ASSEMBLY-TIME IF | Directs the assembler to process the statement that is labeled with the sequence symbol that appears in the operand entry if the logical expression is 1 (true); directs the assembler to process the next sequential statement if the logical expression is 0 (false). |
| *sequence symbol* or *blank* | **AGO** | *sequence symbol* | ASSEMBLY-TIME GO TO | Directs the assembler to process the statement that is identified by the sequence symbol that appears in the operand entry. |
| *sequence symbol* or *blank* | **ANOP** | ignored | ASSEMBLY-TIME NO OPERATION | No operation. |

| Name | Operation | Operand | Instruction Name | Action |
|---|---|---|---|---|
| *sequence symbol* or *blank* | **ACTR** | *arithmetic expression* | ASSEMBLY-TIME COUNTER | Limits the number of AIF and AGO directives that the assembler processes within the macro definition to the value that the operand entry specifies. |
| *sequence symbol* or *blank* | **MNOTE** | [*n*,]'*message*' | MACRO NOTE | Generates a *message* in the macro expansion: if *n* is between 0 and 255, sets a severity code to *n* and generates an error message; if *n* is omitted or is an asterisk, generates the message as a comments statement. |
| *sequence symbol* or *blank* | **MEXIT** | ignored | MACRO EXIT | Terminates the processing of a macro definition. |

## Exercises

1. Classify each of the following according to their validity within the operand entry of a SETA directive, a SETB directive, or a SETC directive. Assume that &A is a SETA symbol with the value −8; &B is a SETB symbol with the value 1; &C is a SETC symbol with the value 51; &X is a symbolic parameter with the value 5; &Y is a symbolic parameter with the value ABC; and W is an ordinary symbol that represents the address of an F-type constant.

   a. '&C'
   b. T'W
   c. '&C'(&A,2)
   d. &C(1,2)
   e. '&Y'
   f. '&Y'(1,2)
   g. '&C'.'&Y'(1,2)
   h. 'RST.&C'
   i. '&C&Y'
   j. '&A'.'&X&Y'
   k. &C
   l. '&SYSLIST(2)'
   m. &Y
   n. '&X&Y'.'Z'
   o. '16'
   p. −2
   q. &SYSLIST(1)
   r. &X
   s. '&X'
   t. (&X EQ 0)
   u. ('&X' EQ '0')
   v. (&Y EQ ABC)
   w. ('&Y' EQ 'ABC')

2. Define a macro BGE that branches when a comparison is "greater than or equal to." Define similar macros BLE (≤), BGT (>), and BLT (<).

3. Define macros that behave as if they were RX format instructions that are analogous to the instructions LTR, LPR, LNR, and LCR.

4. Define a macro FLTEQU that equates the symbols F0, F2, F4, and F6 to the integers 0, 2, 4, and 6, respectively.

5. Define a macro that calls either or both of the macros REGEQU (Self-Test Exercise 9) and FLTEQU (Exercise 4) according to the status of a keyword parameter. In the macro instruction, let the keyword operand be G if you want to generate the EQUs for the general registers; F if you want them for the floating-point registers, and FG or GF if you want both sets of EQUs. The macro also should generate both sets of EQUs if you omit the keyword operand.

6. Revise the DOUBLE macro in Figure 18.6 so that it will work for halfword or fullword integers, and short-form, long-form, or extended-form floating-point numbers.

7. What is wrong with using LP&SYSNDX instead of &LOOP in the definitions of the REPEAT and ENDREPT macros of Figure 18.13?

8. Define a macro SUB that is invoked with an instruction of the form SUB *R1,E2*. *R1* specifies a register, and *E2* represents an RX operand designation that addresses a fullword in storage. The macro should subtract the binary integer in the register from the binary integer in storage, and should replace the storage operand with the difference. The contents of all registers should remain unchanged.

9. Define a macro BASE that loads and declares one or more base registers. The operand should consist of any number of base register names that are separated by commas. The base addresses that the macro defines should differ by multiples of 4096.

10. Define a macro FLAG that sets bit *n* of Register 3 to 0 or 1, according to whether the second positional operand is OFF or ON. For example, the instruction FLAG 4,ON sets bit 4 of Register 3 to 1.
11. Revise the ADD macro in Figure 18.21 so that there are no symbolic parameters in the operand entry of the prototype statement, and only positional operands in the macro instruction. The revised macro should have the same effect as the original macro when operands are missing.
12. Revise the ADD macro in Figure 18.21 so that the sublist can contain halfword and fullword integers.
13. Revise the ADD macro in Figure 18.21 so that the sublist can contain both short-form and long-form floating-point numbers.
14. Revise the ADD macro in Figure 18.21 so that the sublist can contain halfword and fullword integers, and short-form and long-form floating-point numbers. Compute the sum by using long-form floating-point arithmetic.
15. Revise the macro CHARSORT in Figure 18.27 so that another macro that CHARSORT calls performs the sort. Note that this new macro does not generate assembler language statements.
16. Revise the statements in Figure 18.32 so that they generate one DC instruction to define all of the constants.

## Programming Problems

1. Revise the CALL macro in Figure 18.16 so that the macro instruction has no comma between the subprogram name and the sublist of arguments, such as in the following instruction:

```
CALL  SUB(A,B)
```

2. Revise the ARRAY macro in Figure 18.25 so that you can specify the first constant in the generated array as a macro operand. Allow for both positive and negative operand values. Also, permit optional plus signs in the specifications of the initial constant and the increment.
3. Define a macro that converts a reference to an element in a two-dimensional array of fullwords, into the index value that is necessary to address that element. For example, the effect of the following macro instruction would load Register 9 with the index that is required to address the I,J element of the array ARRAY:

```
INDEX 9,ARRAY,(I,J)
```

(For the formula that is necessary to compute the index value, see Programming Problem 6 in Chapter 7.)
4. Repeat Programming Problem 3, omitting the comma between the array name and the subscripts.
5. Without using the MVCL instruction, complete the definition of the MOVE macro in Figure 18.19 so that it handles fields that are greater in length than 256. Do this in two ways: iteratively and recursively.
6. Define a macro ENTER that you can use at the beginning of a program to generate instructions in the following form:

```
B     b(15)
DC    X'ℓ'
DC    CLℓ'name'
DC    CL8'mm/dd/yy'
DC    CL5'hh.mm'
```

Here, *name* is the name of the control section; there are ℓ characters in *name*. The date and time of assembly are *mm/dd/yy* and *hh.mm*, respectively. To branch around the constants, use an appropriate value of *b*.
7. Define a macro that you can use instead of the GET macro. The first time that your macro is called, it should generate the necessary OPEN instruction and a GET instruction. Subsequent calls should just generate a GET.
8. Define a macro ADATE that is called with an operand entry that contains either a blank or the word JULIAN. If there is no operand, ADATE should generate a character constant that contains the assembly date of the program in the form *mmddyy*, where &SYSDATE defines *mm*, *dd*, and *yy*. (However, notice that &SYSDATE places slashes between these numbers.) If JULIAN is specified, generate the date in Julian form, *yynnn*, where *nnn* is the number of the day in the year. For example, if the date of assembly is Feb. 1, 1988, then the Julian form is 88032.
9. Define a macro that generates a pattern for the ED instruction and the EDMK instruction. The macro instruction operand is a character string, which is enclosed in apostrophes, that pictures the desired edited result. Use 0 to indicate each digit; X to indicate the first significant digit, if any; and other message or fill characters as

desired. The following are examples of operands and resultant patterns:

| Operand | Pattern |
|---|---|
| ' 0,00X.00' | X'40206B2021204B2020' |
| ' 0.X0–' | X'40214B202060' |

Your macro can define each pattern character with a separate DC. As a refinement, define the pattern with one DC.

10. Extend Programming Problem 9 so that the macro issues a warning message if the pattern contains an even number of digit selectors and significance starters.

11. Define a macro that generates a translation table for the TRT instruction. The macro should assign the first operand value to all table entries that subsequent macro operands do not define. Subsequent macro operands are sublists with two or three entries in the form *(byte,value)* or *(byte1,byte2,value)*. The entry *byte* designates the byte in the table: when you add *byte* to the beginning address of the table, you get the address of the desired byte. The entries *byte1* and *byte2* are similar to *byte*, but designate a range of table bytes. The value that will be assigned to the byte or bytes in the table is *value*. Assume that all operand designations use self-defining terms. For example, the macro instruction

```
TRTTAB    X'0',(C',',X'1'),(C'A',C'F',X'2')
```

defines a table with a 1 in the byte that corresponds to a comma, a 2 in each of the bytes that correspond to the letters A through F, and zeros in all other bytes.

# Appendices

# APPENDIX A Answers to Self-Test Exercises

## Chapter 2

1. **a.** 27, **b.** 60, **c.** 117, **d.** 166, **e.** 670
2. **a.** 1B, **b.** 3C, **c.** 75, **d.** A6, **e.** 29E
3. **a.** 77, **b.** 346, **c.** 3431, **d.** 11976, **e.** 199103
4. **a.** 1001101, **b.** 101011010, **c.** 110101100111, **d.** 10111011001000, **e.** 110000100110111111
5. **a.** 11001, **b.** 100101, **c.** 100101000, **d.** 111000011, **e.** 11001011100
6. **a.** 19, **b.** 25, **c.** 128, **d.** 1C3, **e.** 65C
7. **a.** 101000, **b.** 101001, **c.** 1001010, **d.** 1010000, **e.** 01001, **f.** 010001, **g.** 010111, **h.** 010010
8. **a.** 661, **b.** 18AB, **c.** D00E, **d.** 168ACD, **e.** 20121, **f.** 4BF, **g.** 4BF, **h.** 6047, **i.** 30F8B6, **j.** 0FEEF
9. **a.** 0B40, 00000B40, **b.** FE3A, FFFFFE3A, **c.** 0082, 00000082, **d.** FE53, FFFFFE53, **e.** 01C5, 000001C5, **f.** FED4, FFFFFED4
10. Sign-magnitude: **a.** 00000111, **b.** 10000001, **c.** 10011011, **d.** 00000000, overflow, **e.** 11000000, **f.** 10000000, overflow
    2's complement: **a.** 00000111, **b.** 11111111, **c.** 11100101, **d.** 10000000, overflow, **e.** 11000000, **f.** 10000000
11. Sign-magnitude: **a.** 0110011, **b.** 1010011, **c.** 0010011, **d.** 0000001, overflow, **e.** 1000001, overflow
    2's complement: **a.** 0110011, **b.** 1101101, **c.** 0010011, **d.** 1000001, overflow, **e.** 0111111, overflow
12. 1000111, −7
13. 1101111, −17
14. **a.** 63A2, **b.** 2031, **c.** D15E, **d.** FCF7, **e.** 2EF1

## Chapter 3

1. Reg. 0 = 2468ACF0, Reg. 1 = 76543210, Reg. 2 = 11111111, Reg. 3 = 3579BE01
2. BF5D00 (dw, fw, hw), 07DAB2 (hw), 000D14 (fw, hw), 001000 (dw, fw, hw), 07D9B4 (fw, hw), 07D9AE (hw). The integral boundaries are designated as follows: dw = doubleword, fw = fullword, hw = halfword
3. **a.** 005004, Reg. 3 = 56789ABC, **b.** 005008, Reg. 3 = DEF01234, **c.** Yes; 005008
4. **a.** 1AB5A8, 1AB5B0, 1AB5AC, **b.** Reg. 4 = 00000008, Reg. 1 = E0470004 (overflow), Reg. 0 = 65000005
5. **a.** 006, **b.** 00A

## Chapter 4

1. b, c, e, h, i, l
2. **a.**
   ```
   DC  H'11'
   DC  H'12'
   DC  H'13'
   ```
   **b.**
   ```
   DC  X'B'
   DC  X'C'
   DC  X'D'
   ```
   **c.**
   ```
   DS  0H
   DS  832X
   ```
   **d.**
   ```
   T  DS  0F
      DC  X'00ABCDEF'
   ```
3. **a.** 0A00FFFFFFFF000000000031
   **b.** 0404000012121212
   **c.** FFFB0000012ABC012ABC
4. Absolute: a, e, h, k, m, n
   Relocatable: b, c, i, l
   Invalid: d, f, g, j
5. c, d, h, k, m
6. Second operand entries: **a.** 156(0,12) **b.** 160(0,12) **c.** 156(3,12) **d.** 160(3,12) **e.** 152(2,12)
   Machine language instructions: **a.** 5880C09C **b.** 5A80C0A0 **c.** 5B83C09C **d.** 5083C0A0 **e.** 5882C098
7. **a.** Y **b.** Y(3) **c.** Y+4 **d.** Y+4(2) **e.** Y−2 **f.** Y−2(3)
8. **a.** `X  EQU  X'AB'`
   **b.** `Y  EQU  X`
   **c.** `Z  EQU  WORD-2`
9. The EQU defines an absolute symbol R whose value is 4. The DC defines a fullword constant whose value is 4.
10. **a.**
    ```
    05C0
    5850C00E
    1A55
    5050C012
    07FE
    0000
    FFFFFFFF
    FFFFFFFF
    ```
    **b.**

    | Symbol | Value | Type |
    |---|---|---|
    | BASE | 2 | R |
    | PROG | 0 | R |
    | R5 | 5 | A |
    | R12 | C | A |
    | X | 10 | R |

    **c.** FFFFFFFFFFFFFFFE

## Chapter 5

1. **a.** 3, **b.** 2, **c.** 2, **d.** 0, **e.** 3, **f.** 1, **g.** 2, **h.** 1, **i.** 1, **j.** 2, **k.** 0, **l.** 1, **m.** 1, **n.** 1, **o.** unchanged, **p.** unchanged
2. **a.** 3, **b.** 7
3. **a.** 14, **b.** 6
4. **a.** ≠, **b.** ≥, **c.** =, **d.** ≥, **e.** ≤
5. **a.** 0 result or overflow, **b.** no overflow, **c.** overflow,

d. positive result or overflow, e. nonzero result or overflow, f. result ⩾ 0 or overflow, g. result ⩽ 0 or overflow

6. a. FFFFFFFF FFFFFFE0 (−32)
   b. 00000000 00000038 (56)
   c. FFFFFFFF FFFFFFE8 (−24)
   d. 00000000 00000100 (256)
   e. 00000000 00000010 (16)

7.
```
         L     R3,THREE
         M     R2,X
         L     R5,FOUR
         M     R4,Y
         AR    R3,R5
         ST    R3,Z
         ...
THREE    DC    F'3'
FOUR     DC    F'4'
```

8.
```
LR   R7,R6
MR   R6,R6
LR   R6,R7
```

9.
```
LR   R5,R3
MR   R2,R3        n^2
S    R3,ONE       n^2 - 1
MR   R4,R3        n * (n^2 - 1) = n^3 - n
```

10. a, c, e, f

11. a. 00000003 FFFFFFFF (3, −1)
    b. FFFFFFFC 00000000 (−4, 0)
    c. FFFFFFFF 00000001 (−1, 1)
    d. 00000003 C0000001 (3, $-2^{30} + 1$)

12.
```
L    R3,X
M    R2,ONE
D    R2,THREE
ST   R3,RESULT
L    R3,Y
M    R2,ONE
D    R2,FOUR
A    R3,RESULT
ST   R3,RESULT
```

13.
```
LR   R7,R6
SR   R6,R6
D    R6,MINUS3
ST   R7,RESULT
```

14.
```
M    R10,ONE
DR   R10,R0
ST   R10,REMAIN
```

15. a.
```
L    R3,L
A    R3,TWO
M    R2,ONE
D    R2,K
S    R3,THREE
M    R2,N
ST   R3,RESULT
```
b.
```
L    R3,X
A    R3,ONE
L    R4,Y
S    R4,FIFTEEN
MR   R2,R4
L    R4,Z
S    R4,THREE
DR   R2,R4
ST   R3,RESULT
```

## Chapter 6

1. a. BC mode: CC = 1, IA = E2B184, Mask = F, ILC = 2, Interruption code = 0008
   b. EC mode: CC = 1, IA = 01A9BE, Mask = 8
   c. 370-XA mode: CC = 3, IA = 00F94DA2, Mask = F
   d. BC mode: CC = 2, IA = F28A06, Mask = C, ILC = 1, Interruption code = 0005

2. a. $800E4F7C_{16}$, $10_2$, $EC160_{16}$, $00_{16}$, $00_2$
   b. No: the first bit of the program mask is 0.

## Chapter 7

1. a. R1 = 000054A8, b. R2 = 00000004, c. R3 = 00000006, d. R4 = 000054AC, e. R5 = 00000006, f. R6 = 000054AC, g. R7 = 00000004, h. R8 = 00000008, i. R9 = 00000007, j. R10 = 00000011, k. R11 = 000054AC

2. a. 4110C4A6, b. 41200004, c. 5832C4A6, d. 4142C4A6, e. 58540000, f. 41640000, g. 41720000, h. 41822000, i. 41900007, j. 41A23007, k. 41B7C4A6

3. a. R0 = 000A54F1, branch to LOOP; b. R2 = 00008C05, branch to LOOP+4; c. R4 = FFFFFFFE, branch to LOOP; d. R6 = FFFFFFFF, branch to LOOP; e. R8 = 00000000, no branch; f. R0 = 000A54F1, branch to 8C06; g. R8 = 00000000, no branch; h. R9 = 00000003, branch to 8C06; i. R9 = 00000003, no branch; j. R6 = FFFFFFFF, branch to 8C06; k. R6 = FFFFFFFF, no branch

4. a. 1, b. 3, c. $2^{32}$, d. $2^{31}$

5. a. R6 = 00000010, yes; b. R8 = 0000001C, no; c. R7 = 00000004, yes; d. R2 = 00000010, no; e. R2 = FFFFFFFC, no; f. R2 = 00000014, no; g. R9 = FFFFFFF8, yes; h. R7 = 00000018, yes; i. R9 = FFFFFFFC, no; j. R2 = 0000001C, yes; k. R9 = 00000004, yes; l. R9 = 00000008, no; m. R8 = 00000010, yes; n. R7 = FFFFFFF8, no

6. a. 1, b. 3, c. 3

## Chapter 8

1. a. CDCDCDCC, 9B9B9B9B; b. CDCDCDCE, 6E6E6E6C; c. 07373737, 9B9B9B9B; d. 07373737, 39B9B9B9; e. 80000000, 9B9B9B9B; f. 00000000, 9B9B9B9B; g. 80000000, 00000000; h. 73737373, 9B9B9B9B; i. 00000000, 73737373; j. 73737373, 00000001; k. 0000000E, 9B9B9B9B; l. 60000000, 9B9B9B9B

2.
```
SLL   2,9
SRL   2,10
ST    2,DATA
```

3.
```
SLL   5,10
SRDL  4,10
ST    5,WORD
```

4.
```
L     8,X
SRDL  8,19
SRL   9,13
```

5.
```
SLL   5,0(3)
```

6.

| | R4 | R5 | CC |
|---|---|---|---|
| a. | A5A5A5A4 | 1F1F1F1F | 1 |
| b. | 96969690 | 1F1F1F1F | 3 |
| c. | 80000000 | 1F1F1F1F | 3 |
| d. | D2D2D2D2 | 7C7C7C7C | 2 |
| e. | D2D2D2D2 | 1F1F1F00 | 3 |
| f. | D2D2D2D2 | 00000000 | 3 |
| g. | F4B4B4B4 | 1F1F1F1F | 1 |
| h. | FFFFFFFF | 1F1F1F1F | 1 |
| i. | FFFFFFFF | 1F1F1F1F | 1 |
| j. | D2D2D2D2 | 03E3E3E3 | 2 |
| k. | D2D2D2D2 | 00000000 | 0 |
| l. | FFD2D2D2 | D21F1F1F | 1 |
| m. | D2D2D21F | 1F1F1F00 | 3 |
| n. | FFFFFFFF | FFFFFFFF | 1 |
| o. | 80000000 | 00000000 | 3 |
| p. | 80000000 | 1F1F1F1F | 3 |

7. SLDA 10,6 Fixed-point overflow exception; condition code is set to 3.

8.
```
M      6,=F'5'
SRDA   6,3
```

## Chapter 9

1. **a.** AREA = 00000000 11111111 22222222 76543210
   **b.** AREA = FFFFFFFF 00000000 11111111 22222222
   **c.** AREA = EEEEEEEE FFFFFFFF FEDCBA98 76543210
   **d.** R14 = ABCDEF01, R15 = 23456789, R0 = FEDCBA98, R1 = 76543210
   **e.** R1 = ABCDEF01, R2 = 23456789, R3 = FEDCBA98, R4 = 76543210
   **f.** R15 = ABCDEF01, R0 = 23456789
2. **a.** R0 = 00000000, cc = 0; **b.** R2 = 80000000, cc = 1; **c.** R3 = 0000FFFF, cc = 2; **d.** R6 = 7FFFFFFF, cc = 2; **e.** R0 = FFFFFFFC, cc = 1; **f.** R5 = 80000001, cc = 1; **g.** R0 = 00000004, cc = 2; **h.** R6 = 80000000, cc = 3; **i.** R3 = 7FFFFFFF, cc = 2; **j.** R5 = 7FFFFFFF, cc = 2; **k.** R6 = 00000000, cc = 0; **l.** R2 = 0000FFFF, cc = 2; **m.** R3 = FFFFFFFC, cc = 1; **n.** R0 = FFFF0001, cc = 1; **o.** R4 = 8000000C, cc = 1; **p.** R4 = 00000000, cc = 0; **q.** R0 = 80000001, cc = 1; **r.** R3 = 80000001, cc = 1; **s.** R3 = 00000004, cc = 2; **t.** R0 = FFFF0001, cc = 1; **u.** R4 = 80000000, cc = 3; **v.** R4 = 00000000, cc = 0; **w.** R0 = 80000001, cc = 1; **x.** R3 = 7FFFFFFF, cc = 2
3.
```
LTR   9,9
BZ    ZERO
BM    NEG
```
4. **a.** W = 4321; **b.** X = 00001111; **c.** X = 88880000; **d.** Z = 4321FFF8; **e.** R1 = FFFFFFFC; **f.** R1 = FFFFFFFF; **g.** R2 = FFFF8888; **h.** R2 = 00007777; **i.** cc = 1; **j.** cc = 1; **k.** R1 = 8764CBA9, cc = 1; **l.** R2 = ABCD2222, cc = 1; **m.** R1 = 87654325, cc = 1; **n.** R2 = ABCD0001, cc = 1; **o.** R2 = 50CC0000; **p.** R2 = 54330000
5.
```
         LH    2,H1
         CH    2,H2
         BL    STORE
         LH    2,H2
STORE    STH   2,H3
```
6. 8000
7. **a.** 8000000E, 1; **b.** 8000000E, 3; **c.** 7FFFFFFE, 3; **d.** 7FFFFFFE, 2; **e.** 7FFFFFFF, 3; **f.** 7FFFFFFF, 2; **g.** 00000000, 2; **h.** 00000000, 0
8. **a.** R2 = 0000BF18, R3 = 0000000A, R4 = 0000BF08; **b.** Replace the first * with a symbol that labels LA. Replace the second * with ARRAY + 10.
9. **a.** POINTB, **b.** BR B BR(5)
10. The displacements are off by 2.

## Chapter 10

1. **a.** R4 = 40F1F2F5; **b.** R4 = 40F1F2F6; **c.** DATA = F3F6F7F8; **d.** DATA = F5F6F3F8; **e.** F5F6F7F3; **f.** R4 = F5F1F2F6, cc = 1; **g.** R4 = 40F5F6F7, cc = 1; **h.** R4 = 40F100F3, cc = 0; **i.** R4 = 40F1F2F3, cc = 0; **j.** R4 = 405B5CF3, cc = 2; **k.** DATA = 40F1F3F8; **l.** DATA = F5F2F7F8; **m.** DATA = F3F6F7F8; **n.** DATA = F1F2F7F8; **o.** DATA = 40F3F7F8
2. 4247C4A8, BE4DC4A8
3. **a.** STCM 6,B'1111',W **b.** STCM 2,B'11',H **c.** STCM 2,B'1',C
4. **a.** ICM 6,B'1',BYTE **b.** adv: sets cc: disadv: nonindexable
5. The bytes at X and Y are given as characters: **a.** ABZDEF **b.** ABC EF **c.** CDEFEF **d.** ABABAB **e.** RSTDEF **f.** AB$$$$ **g.** EDCDEF **h.** ABCCBA
6. Both set BYTE to $5B_{16}$. MVI: SI, 4 bytes long, C'$' is a self-defining term. MVC: SS, 6 bytes long, =C'$' is a literal.
7.
```
MVC   TEMP(5),DATA
MVC   DATA+3(5),TEMP
```
8.
```
MVC   HEADING(10),=C'0123456789'
MVC   HEADING+10(110),HEADING
```
9. **a.** 1, **b.** 2, **c.** 1, **d.** 1, **e.** 0, **f.** 2, **g.** 0, **h.** 1, **i.** 2, **j.** 1, **k.** 2, **l.** 2, **m.** 0
10.
```
     LA    2,0
     LA    3,100
     LA    4,STRING
LOOP CLI   0(4),C','
     BNE   SKIP
     LA    2,1(2)
SKIP LA    4,1(4)
     BCT   3,LOOP
```
11.
```
     LA    2,0
     LA    3,238
     LA    4,STRING
LOOP CLC   0(3,4),=C'ABC'
     BNE   SKIP
     LA    2,1(2)
SKIP LA    4,1(4)
     BCT   3,LOOP
```

12. A = 000012000012, B = 00000C, C = 5C40405C4040, D = C1, E = 23, F = 00000003, G = 00000012, H = 000BF1CA, I = 000BF1CF, J = 0BF1C4, K = F0F0F0F0F0F0F0F0
13. A = 2, B = 2, C = 3, D = 3, E = 1, F = 4, G = 5, H = 1, I = 20, J = 4, K = 1, L = 5, M = 1
14. Replace the first instruction with L R3,=A(DATA). Replace the two instructions at OUT with
```
OUT      S    R3,=A(DATA).
```
15. **a.** 80, **b.** 80, **c.** 80, **d.** 1, **e.** 4, **f.** 1, **g.** 4, **h.** 4, **i.** 1
16. **a.** MVC Y(8),=CL8' ' **b.** CLC Z(5),=5C'0'

## Chapter 11

1. **a.** R4 = 0000000C, cc = 1
   **b.** R5 = 00000000, cc = 0
   **c.** R6 = 0000000C, cc = 1
   **d.** R6 = FFFFFFFE, cc = 1
   **e.** R6 = 0000000C, cc = 1
   **f.** R6 = 0000000C, cc = 1
   **g.** R4 = FFFFFFF3, cc = 1
   **h.** R5 = 0000000C, cc = 1
   **i.** R6 = 00000000, cc = 0
   **j.** R6 = AB00000D, cc = 1
   **k.** R6 = 00000000, cc = 0
   **l.** R6 = 00000004, cc = 1
   **m.** R6 = AB000008, cc = 1
2. **a.** 1, FFCDEF; **b.** 1, AB49EF; **c.** 1, ABCDEF; **d.** 1, 0000EF; **e.** 0, 000000; **f.** 1, ABCDEF; **g.** 1, 543210
3. **a.** N 4,=4X'AA' **b.** OC D(8),=8X'55'
   **c.**
```
N    2,=X'CFFFFFFF'
O    2,=X'0F000000'
X    2,=X'003F8000'
```
4. X 5,=X'FFFFFFFF'
5. **a.** XI GROUP1,CHAR7
   **b.** OI GROUP2,CHAR5+CHAR8
   **c.**
```
NI   GROUP1,DELETE-CHAR2
NI   GROUP2,DELETE-CHAR2
```
   **d.** NC GROUP1(2),=2X'BF'
   **e.**
```
TM   GROUP1,CHAR3+CHAR5
BZ   NEITHER
```
   **f.**
```
TM   GROUP2,CHAR1+CHAR4
BM   ONE
```
   **g.**
```
TM   GROUP1,CHAR5+CHAR6
BNO  MISSING
```
6. **a.** A*bbbbbbbbb* **b.** ABCDE*bbbbb* **c.** ABCDE*bbbbb* **d.** ABCDEF*bbbb*
7. IC 2,=X'7A'
8. The TR instruction translates digits from EBCDIC to numeric form and translates each nondigit to #.
9. TR HEX(8),=C'0123456789ABCDEF'
10.
```
TR   ALPHA(50),T
where T      DC     256C' '
             ORG    T+C'A'
             DC     X'010203040506070809'
             ORG    T+C'J'
             DC     X'0A0B0C0D0E0F101112'
             ORG    T+C'S'
             DC     X'131415161718191A'
             ORG
```
11.
```
MVC  REVERSE(10),=X'09080706050403020100'
TR   REVERSE(10),STRING
```
12. L'TABLE is 1.
13. **a.** R1 = 0000BF20, R2 = ABCDEF02, cc = 1; **b.** R1 and R2 are unchanged, cc = 0; **c.** R1 = 0000BF24, R2 = ABCDEF09, cc = 2; **d.** R1 = 0000BF23, R2 = ABCDEF09, cc = 1
14.
```
TRT  DIGITS(100),T
BZ   YES
where T      DC     256X'FF'
             ORG    T+C' '
             DC     X'0'
             ORG    T+C'0'
             DC     10X'0'
             ORG
```
15.
```
         LA    1,INPUT-1
         SR    3,3
LOOP     LA    4,INPUT+78
         SR    4,1
         EX    4,TRT
         BZ    OUT
         LA    3,1(3)
         BM    LOOP
OUT      ...
TRT      TRT   1(0,1),TAB
TAB      DC    256X'0'
         ORG   TAB+C','
         DC    X'1'
         ORG
```
16. **a.** FIELD1 contains FIELD2 followed by 2 blanks, R0 = A(FIELD1 + $200_{16}$), R1 = 0, R2 = A(FIELD2 + $1FE_{16}$), R3 = 40000000, cc = 2; **b.** FIELD1 contains the first $200_{16}$ bytes of FIELD3, R0 = A(FIELD1 + $200_{16}$), R1 = 0, R4 = A(FIELD3 + $200_{16}$), R5 = 40000300, cc = 1; **c.** FIELD2 contains first $1FE_{16}$ bytes of FIELD3, R2 = A(FIELD2 + $1FE_{16}$), R3 = 40000000, R4 = A(FIELD3 + $1FE_{16}$), R5 = 40000302, cc = 1; **d.** FIELD1 = FIELD4, R0 = A(FIELD1 + $200_{16}$), R1 = 0, R6 = A(FIELD4 + $200_{16}$), R7 = 40000000, cc = 0; **e.** FIELD3 is FIELD1 padded with $300_{16}$ bytes of 0's, R4 = A(FIELD3 + $500_{16}$), R5 = 40000000, R0 = A(FIELD1 + $200_{16}$), R1 = 0, cc = 2
17. **a.** cc = 2, R0 = A(FIELD1 + 5), R1 = 40000007, R2 = A(FIELD2 + 5), R3 = 40000000; **b.** cc = 0, R2 = A(FIELD2 + 6), R3 = 40000000, R4 = A(FIELD3 + 6), R5 = 40000000

## Chapter 12

1. **a.** No, **b.** Yes, **c.** No, **d.** No, **e.** No
2. STMTS 4, 9, and 10. Displacements would exceed 4095.
3. Replace STMT 5 with BASE1 L R11,=A(BASE1+4096). Use LTORG to ensure addressability.
4. **a.** No, **b.** Yes, **c.** No, **d.** Yes, **e.** Yes, **f.** No, **g.** No
5. **a.** STMT 3: R12, 5: R11, 6: R11, 7: R12, 8: R11
   **b.** 4: R11, 6: R12, 7: R12
   **c.** All use R12
   **d.** 3: R12, 6: R11, 7: R11, 11: R10, 13: R12, 14: R11, 15: R10

## Chapter 13

1.
```
        LA     R1,ARGS
        L      R15,=V(SWAP)
        BALR   R14,R15
        ...
ARGS    DC     A(S1)
        DC     A(S2)
```
2.
```
SWAP    CSECT
        STM    R14,R12,12(R13)
        BALR   R12,0
        USING  BASE,R12
BASE    LM     R2,R3,0(R1)
        XC     0(50,R2),0(R3)
        XC     0(50,R3),0(R2)
        XC     0(50,R2),0(R3)
        LM     R14,R12,12(R13)
        BR     R14
        END
```
3. Replace R3 with R0. Delete both the L instruction at SKIP and the ST instruction. Label the LM instruction with SKIP.
4.
```
SUB1    CSECT
        STM    R14,R12,12(R13)
        BALR   R12,0
        USING  BASE,R12
BASE    L      R15,=V(SUB2)
        BALR   R14,R15
        LR     R2,R0
        LA     R1,8(R1)
        BALR   R14,R15
        OR     R0,R2
        LM     R14,R12,12(R13)
        BR     R14
SUB2    CSECT
        STM    R14,R12,12(R13)
        USING  SUB2,R15
        LM     R2,R3,0(R1)
        IC     R0,0(R2)
        IC     R3,0(R3)
        NR     R0,R3
        LM     R14,R12,12(R13)
        BR     R14
        END
```
5. a.
```
        L      R15,=V(MIN)
        LA     R14,RET
        CNOP   2,4
        BALR   R1,R15
        DC     A(A,C,F)
RET     ST     R0,M1
```
b.
```
        L      R15,=V(MIN)
        LA     R14,RET
        CNOP   2,4
        BALR   R1,R15
        DC     A(A,B,D,E,F)
RET     ST     R0,M2
```
6. a. `CALL MIN,(A,C,F),VL`

b. `CALL MIN,(A,B,D,E,F),VL`

7. Replace the STM instruction with
```
SAVE   (R14,R12)
```
Replace the instruction sequence LM, LM, BR with
```
SAVE   (R0)
RETURN (R14,R12)
```
8. There are addressability errors in the first control section at =F'−1' and CON, and in the second control section at WORD.
9.
```
AL      DSECT
AX      DS     A
AY      DS     A
AZ      DS     A
X       DSECT
Y       DSECT
Z       DSECT
MAX     CSECT
        STM    R14,R12,12(R13)
        USING  MAX,R15
        USING  AL,R1
        LM     R4,R6,AL
        USING  X,R4
        USING  Y,R5
        USING  Z,R6
        L      R3,X
        C      R3,Y
        BNL    SKIP
        L      R3,Y
SKIP    ST     R3,Z
        LM     R14,R12,12(R13)
        BR     R14
        END
```
10.
```
SUM     CSECT
        STM    R14,R12,12(R13)
        BALR   R12,0
        USING  BASE,R12
BASE    L      R11,=A(ARRAY)
        USING  ARRAY,R11
        LA     R4,50
        SR     R0,R0
        SR     R3,R3
LOOP    A      R0,ARRAY(R3)
        DROP   R11
        LA     R3,4(R3)
        BCT    R4,LOOP
        DROP   R12
        LM     R14,R15,12(R13)
        LM     R1,R12,24(R13)
        BR     R14
ARRAY   COM
        DS     50F
```
11. In the solution to Self-Test Exercise 10, replace COM with DSECT. Insert EXTRN DATA after CSECT and replace ARRAY in the L instruction with DATA.
12.
```
SUB     CSECT
        ...
        L      R11,=A(DATA)
        USING  DATA,R11
        ...
DATA    COM
X1      DS     CL8
X2      DS     CL6
Y       DS     CL6
        END
```

13. Retain the dummy sections for X and Y in Figure 13.23.

```
SUB      CSECT
         EXTRN  DATA
         . . .
         L      R11,=A(DATA)
         USING  DATA,R11
```

## Chapter 14

1. a. 908C
   b. 012C
   c. 0000000C
   d. 0007408D
   e. 408D
   f. F1F2D3
   g. F0F1F9D8
   h. C7C7
   i. F1C9
   j. F0F0C0
2. a. 2, 1; b. 4, 4; c. 6, 2; d. 3, 3; e. 2, 2
3. a. A = 12345C
   b. A = 000012345C
   c. A = 345C
   d. B = 000012345C
4. a. A = F1F2F3F4C5??
   b. A = F3F4C5??????
   c. A = F0F1F2F3F4C5
   d. B = F0F1F2F3F4C5
   e. B−2 = FFF3F3F4C5
5. a. $L1 < [L2/2] + 1$, b. $L1 < 2*L2 - 1$
6. a. R2 = FFFFFF02
   b. R3 = 0000002A
   c. R4 = FFFFFFFF; data exception
   d. X = 00000000 0000091C
   e. Y = 00000000 0000004D
   f. Z = 00000000 0000001D
7. a. 40F9F8F7F6F5, cc = 1, SI on
   b. 404040F8F0F2, cc = 2, SI off
   c. 4040F16BF0F9F84BF0F7, cc = 1, SI on
   d. 404040404040F14BF0F0, cc = 2, SI off
   e. 40F6F06BF0F0F04BF0F0, cc = 1, SI on
   f. 404040404040404040F4, cc = 2, SI off
   g. 40F9F06BF0F0F04BF0F860, cc = 1, SI on
   h. 40404040F5F0F04BF4F240, cc = 2, SI off
   i. 40404040F1F2F34BF0F560, cc = 1, SI on
   j. 4040404040F4F64BF0F040, cc = 2, SI off
   k. 404040404040F14BF9F960, cc = 1, SI on
   l. 40404040404040404BF0F240, cc = 2, SI off
   m. 40F9F06BF0F0F04BF0F860, cc = 1, SI on
   n. 40404040F5F0F04BF4F240, cc = 2, SI off
   o. 40404040F1F2F34BF0F560, cc = 1, SI on
   p. 4040404040F4F64BF0F040, cc = 2, SI off
   q. 404040404040F14BF9F960, cc = 1, SI on
   r. 404040404040F04BF0F240, cc = 2, SI off
   s. 5C5CF94BF15C5CF54BF0F0, cc = 1, SI on
   t. 5CF1F24BF3605C5C4BF0F1, cc = 2, SI off
   u. 5C5CF04BF05C5C5C4BF9F0, cc = 1, SI on
8. a. 402020202020
   b. 4020214B202020
   c. 4021204B202020
   d. 402020204B2020
   e. 40202020204B20
   f. 4020202020204B
9. a. 5CF9F8F76BF6F5F44BF3, R1 = A(P+1), cc = 2
   b. 5C5C5CF16BF0F0F04BF0, R1 = A(P+3), cc = 1
   c. 5C5C5C5C5CF5F0F24BF8, R1 = A(P+5), cc = 1
   d. 5C5C5C5C5C5C5C5C4BF2, R1 is unchanged, cc = 1
10. The bytes at RESULT in character form are as follows.

| With Fig. 14.15: | With Fig. 14.16: |
|---|---|
| a. $12345.67 | a. *b*12345.67 |
| b. *bbb*$12.34 | b. *bbbb*12.34 |
| c. *bbbb*$1.23 | c. *bbbbb*1.23 |
| d. *bbbb*$0.12 | d. *bbbbb*0.12 |

11. a. 404021206B202020
    b. 4021206B2020204B
    c. 4040202020204B20
    d. 40214B2020202060
12.

```
*CONVERT C(R3) TO PRINTABLE FORM
         CVD    R3,PDN
         EDMK   P(11),PDN+2
         BCTR   R1,0
         MVI    0(R1),C'+'
         LTR    R3,R3
         BNM    DONE
         MVI    0(R1),C'-'
DONE     ----
PDN      DS     D
P        DC     X'4020202020202020202020'
```

13. Each field can affect R1, but the final value of R1 applies to the rightmost field that affects R1. When the last field does not affect R1, you cannot set a default value for R1 to use because an earlier field can destroy R1.

## Chapter 15

1. a. A = 1234634C, cc = 2
   b. A+2 = 634C, cc = 2
   c. B+1 = 4C, cc = 3
   d. A+1 = 05433D, cc = 1
   e. B = 500D, cc = 3
   f. A+3 = 0C, cc = 0
   g. B = 500D, cc = 1
   h. B = 167C, cc = 2
   i. cc = 0
   j. cc = 2
   k. cc = 1
   l. cc = 2
   m. A = 0000067C, cc = 2
   n. A = 067C, cc = 2
   o. B = 567C, cc = 2

p. B = 007C, cc = 2
q. A = 0034567C, cc = 2
r. A+1 = 00000C, cc = 0
s. A = 1234567C, cc = 2

2. a. U = 0000480D
b. data exception
c. U = 0000080D
d. data exception
e. data exception
f. specification exception
g. data exception
h. U = 003D004C
i. specification exception
j. decimal divide exception
k. specification exception
l. U = 00020D0C
m. decimal divide exception
n. decimal divide exception

3. a.
```
ZAP    WORK(4),=P'198'
MP     WORK(4),=P'10'
```
b.
```
ZAP    WORK(10),=P'12345678912345678'
MP     WORK(10),=P'-2'
```
c.
```
ZAP    WORK(4),=P'501'
DP     WORK(4),=P'-50'
```
d.
```
ZAP    WORK(6),=P'4591'
DP     WORK(6),=P'123456789'
```

4. a. W = 345678900D, cc = 3
b. W = 234567890D, cc = 3
c. W = 001234567D, cc = 1
d. W = 000123457D, cc = 1
e. Z = 0987654C, cc = 2
f. Z = 0098766C, cc = 2
g. Z = 8765430C, cc = 3

5. a. W = 09876543FD
b. Z = 456789DF
c. W = 000123456D
d. W = 6789D6789D
e. Z = 92745638
f. W+1 = 32527292
g. Z+3 = 3C
h. Z = 1836547F
i. W+1 = 1416181D
j. Z+3 = 0F

6. a. `SRP Y(4),64-5,0`
b. `SRP Y(4),64-6,0`
c. `SRP Y(4),64-1,5`
d. `SRP Y(4),64-2,5`
e. `SRP Y(4),1,0`
f. `SRP Y(4),6,0`

7. a.
```
MVO    Y(4),Y(1)
```
b.
```
MVO    Y(4),Y(3)
MVO    Y(4),Y(1)
```
c.
```
ZAP    TEMP(16),=P'5'
MVN    TEMP+15(1),Y+3
AP     TEMP(16),Y
MVO    Y,TEMP(15)
```
d.
```
ZAP    TEMP(16),=P'50'
MVN    TEMP+15(1),Y+3
AP     TEMP(16),Y
MVO    TEMP(16),TEMP(15)
MVO    Y,TEMP(15)
```
e.
```
       ZAP    TEMP(16),Y
       NI     TEMP+15,X'F0'
       MVO    Y,TEMP(16)
       ...
TEMP   DS     PL16
       DC     XL16'0'
```
f.
```
       MVO    TEMP(16),Y
       MVI    TEMP+15,X'00'
       MVO    Y,TEMP+2(16)
       ...
TEMP   DS     PL16
       DC     XL16'0'
```

8.
```
       ZAP    Z,X
       SRP    Z,4,0
       AP     Z,Y
       SRP    Z,64-1,5
       ...
Z      DC     PL5'.0000'
```

9. a.
```
ZAP    Z(2),Y
SRP    Z(2),1,0
AP     Z(2),X
```
b.
```
ZAP    Z(3),Y
SRP    Z,1,0
SP     Z,W
XI     Z+2,X'01'
SRP    Z,64-1,5
```
c.
```
ZAP    Z(5),W
MP     Z(5),X
SRP    Z(5),64-2,5
```
d.
```
ZAP    Z(5),W
SRP    Z(5),2,0
DP     Z(5),Y
```

## Chapter 16

1.
```
IN    DCB    DSORG=PS,MACRF=GM,DDNAME=INDD,
             RECFM=FB,LRECL=80,BLKSIZE=1600
```
2.
```
OPEN    (IN,INPUT)
CLOSE   (IN)
```
3.
```
GET     IN,DATA
PUT     OUT,DATA
```
4.
```
PUT     OUT
LR      R2,R1
GET     IN,(R2)
```
5.
```
//INDD    DD    DSNAME=EX5,DISP=(OLD,KEEP),
             UNIT=TAPE,VOL=SER=TP1
```
6. This answer is the same as the answer to Exercise 5, except that UNIT=SYSDA and VOL=SER=D1.

7.
```
TEMP   DCB    DSORG=PS,MACRF=PM,DDNAME=TDD,
              RECFM=FB,LRECL=80,BLKSIZE=1600
//TDD    DD    DSNAME=SCR,DISP=(NEW,DELETE),
              UNIT=SYSDA,SPACE=(TRK,(2,1))
```
8.
```
IN    DTFSD    DEVADDR=SYS001,IOAREA1=BUF1,
               RECFORM=FIXBLK,RECSIZE=80,BLKSIZE=
               1600,TYPEFLE=INPUT,WORKA=YES
```

9.
```
OPEN    IN
CLOSE   IN
```
10.
```
GET     IN,DATA
PUT     OUT,DATA
```
11.
```
PUT     OUT  ASSUME IOREG=(2) IN DTF AT OUT
GET     IN,(R2)
```
12.
```
// TLBL IN,'INPUT-DATA',100,TP1
```
13.
```
// DLBL IN,'INPUT-DATA',100,SD
```
14.
```
TEMP DTFSD DEVADDR=SYS002,IOAREA1=BUF1,
   RECFORM=FIXBLK,RECSIZE=100,BLKSIZE=
   1008,TYPEFLE=OUTPUT,WORKA=YES
// DLBL TEMP,'SCRATCH',1,SD
// EXTENT SYS002,D1,1,,65,5
```
15.
```
//GO.OUTPUT DD UNIT=TAPE,VOL=SER=TP001,
   DSNAME=MYDATA,DISP=(NEW,CATLG)
```
16. Replace DTFSD with DTFMT. Replace the DLBL statement and EXTENT statement with
```
// TLBL OUTFILE,'MYDATA',100,TP1
```
17. In Fig. 16.20, replace GET and PUT with
```
GET     INFILE
LR      R2,R1
PUT     OUTFILE
MVC     0(80,R1),0(R2)
```
Change the value of the MACRF parameter in the DCBs at INFILE and OUTFILE to GL and PL, respectively. In Fig. 16.21, replace GET and PUT with
```
GET     INFILE
PUT     OUTFILE
MVC     0(80,R2),0(R3)
```
In the DTFCD instruction, replace WORKA=YES with IOREG=(R3). In the DTFSD instruction, replace WORKA=YES with IOREG=(R2).

18. In Fig. 16.24, replace the four instructions at LOOP with
```
LOOP    PUT    OUTFILE
        LR     R2,R1
        GET    INFILE,0(R2)
```
Change the value of the MACRF parameter in the DCB at INFILE to GM. In Fig. 16.25, replace the three instructions at LOOP with
```
LOOP    PUT    OUTFILE
        GET    INFILE,0(R3)
```
In the DTF at INFILE, replace IOREG=(R2) with WORKA=YES.

19. Insert `PUT PRINT,RECORD-1` after the first GET, and insert `DC C' '` before RECORD. In OS, insert
```
PRINT    DCB    DSORG=PS,MACRF=PM,DDNAME=
   SYSPRINT,RECFM=FA,LRECL=81,BLKSIZE=81
```
In DOS, insert
```
PRINT DTFPR DEVADDR=SYSLST,DEVICE=3203,
   IOAREA1=PBUF,RECFORM=FIXUNB,BLKSIZE=
   81,WORKA=YES,CTLCHAR=ASA
PBUF    DS      CL81
```
20.
a. `READ  DECB1,SF,D1,B1`
b. `WRITE DECB2,SF,(5),(8)`
c. `CHECK DECB2`
d.
```
DCB1   DCB      BUFNO=3,...
       GETBUF   DCB1,(4)
```
21. Replace the four instructions at LOOP with
```
LOOP    READ    DECB1,SF,INFILE,BUF
        READ    DECB2,SF,INFILE,BUF2
        CHECK   DECB1
        WRITE   DECB3,SF,OUTFILE,BUF
        CHECK   DECB2
        WRITE   DECB4,SF,OUTFILE,BUF2
        CHECK   DECB3
        CHECK   DECB4
```
Insert NCP=2 into both DCB instructions. Define BUF2 as 80 bytes of storage.

22. Delete the GETBUF, FREEBUF, and FREEPOOL instructions. Delete BUFNO=2 from the DCB instruction. Define BUF1 and BUF2 as 80 bytes of storage each. In the READ and WRITE instructions, replace (R2) with BUF1 and (R3) with BUF2.

23. Insert `GETBUF DISK,(R2)` after OPEN. Replace BUF in the READ instruction with (R2). Insert BUFNO=1 into the DCB at DISK. Replace L'BUF in the LA instruction with 240. Delete `LA R2,BUF` and the DS instruction that defines BUF. Insert the following after CLOSE:
```
FREEBUF     DISK,(R2)
FREEPOOL    DISK
```
24. In Figure 16.32:
```
INLOOP WRITE   DECB2,SF,PRINT,(R2)
       CHECK   DECB2
```
In Figure 16.33:
```
LOOP1    LA      R7,4(R4)
         READ    DECB2,SF,INFILE,(R7)
         CHECK   DECB2
```

## Chapter 17

1. **a.** $.4\overline{C}$, **b.** .C, **c.** $1B.B\overline{5C28F}$, **d.** $10.\overline{9}$
2. **a.** .0618, **b.** 3.4
3. **a.** 10100100.000100001111, **b.** .001011
4. **a.** 40F98765
   **b.** 43100ABF
   **c.** C2ABCDEF
   **d.** 3DF160E0
   **e.** BB12A000
5. **d.** 3DF160E0 00000000, **e.** BB12A000 00000000
6. **d.** 3DF160E0 00000000 2F000000 00000000
   **e.** BB12A000 00000000 AD000000 00000000
7. **a.** C0C00000
   **b.** 421BB5C3
   **c.** C04CCCCD
   **d.** 3E800000
   **e.** C0666666
8. **a.** C0C00000 00000000
   **b.** 421BB5C2 8F5C28F6
   **c.** C04CCCCC CCCCCCCD
   **d.** 3E800000 00000000
   **e.** C0666666 66666666
9. **a.** C0C00000 00000000 B2000000 00000000
   **b.** 421BB5C2 8F5C28F5 34C28F5C 28F5C28F

c. C04CCCCC CCCCCCCC B2CCCCCC CCCCCCCD
d. 3E800000 00000000 30000000 00000000
e. C0666666 66666666 B2666666 66666666

10. a. 144
b. −1.5
c. −.0195312
d. .0001831
e. $-.625 \times 16^{-64}$

11. a. C0428F5C 28F5C28F
b. 41BE6666
c. 40199999 99999999 32999999 9999999A

12. a. 442F0000
b. 8112AB00
c. 2EF40000
d. AEABC000

13. $16^{-70}$ to $16^{63}$

14. a. F2 = 3E111111 9ABCDEF0
b. F2 = 41F00000 9ABCDEF0
c. F6 = 3E111111 22222222
d. F6 = 12345678 9ABCDEF0
e. X = 12345678 22222222
f. X = 3E111111 12345678
g. X = 41F00000 66666666

15. a. C213B332, C213B333 33333332, C213B333 33333333 B4333333 33333332
b. C310A7FF, C310A7FF FFFFFFFF, C310A7FF FFFFFFFF B5FFFFFF FFFFFFFF
c. C1EFFFFA, C1EFFFFF FFFFFFFA, C1EFFFFF FFFFFFFF B3FFFFFF FFFFFFFA

16. a. F0 = 42146668 66666666, cc = 2
b. F0 = 42146669 56667665, cc = 2
c. F0 = C2F00FFA 66666666, cc = 1
d. F4 = C2F00FFF FFFFFFFA, cc = 1
e. F6 = 80000000 00000000, cc = 1, exponent overflow
f. F0 = C2F01000 00000001, F2 = B4999999 9999999A, cc = 1
g. F0 = 42146663 66666666, cc = 2
h. Significance exception. If the last bit of the program mask is 0, F6 = 0 and cc = 0.
i. F0 = 42146663 76665666, cc = 2
j. F4 = C3118DCC 66666666, cc = 1
k. F4 = C3118DCC CCCCCCCC, cc = 1
l. F6 = FF800000 00000000, cc = 1
m. F0 = 43118DCC CCCCCCCC, F2 = 35E66666 66666666, cc = 2

17. a. F4 = C0888888 00000000
b. F4 = 40888888 88888888
c. F0 = C02468AC A8642000
d. F4 = C02468AC F13579BD
e. F4 = C02468AC F13579BD, F6 = B2B97530 ECA86420
f. F4 = C0888888 88888888, F6 = B2000000 00000000
g. F4 = 00000000 00000000, F6 = 00000000 00000000
h. F0 = C02468AC F13579BD, F2 = B2DDDDDD DDDDDDDD

18. a. F4 = C0888888 22222222
b. F4 = 40888888 88888888
c. Divide exception
d. F6 = 00000000 00000000
e. F4 = C0888888 22222222
f. F4 = C0888888 88888888, F6 = B2888888 88888888
g. F6 = C1111111 00000000
h. F6 = C1111111 11111111

19. a. F4 = BEDCBA98 87654321
b. F0 = 2FEDCBAA FFFFFFFF
c. F4 = CD100000 87654321
d. F4 = CD100000 00000000

20. a. cc = 0
b. cc = 2
c. cc = 2
d. cc = 2
e. cc = 0
f. F0 = 42300000 98765432, cc = 2
g. F0 = 42300000 00000000, cc = 2
h. F4 = 00FEDCBA 00000000, cc = 2
i. F4 = 00FEDCBA 98888888, cc = 2
j. F4 = 80FEDCBA 00000000, cc = 1
k. F6 = C2300000 00000000, cc = 1
l. F0 = C2300000 98765432, cc = 1
m. F0 = 00FEDCBA 98888888, cc = 2

21.
```
MDR   2,2
SD    2,=D'1'
DD    2,=D'7'
STD   2,Z
```

22.
```
LE    2,N
MER   2,2
LRER  2,2
STE   2,NSQ
```

23.
```
LE    2,X
MER   2,2
LE    4,Y
MER   4,4
ADR   2,4
MD    2,=D'3'
DD    2,=D'4'
LRER  2,2
STE   2,W
```

24. a. F4 = 31002244 9988FFFF, cc = 2
b. F2 = 31001129 B988FFFF, cc = 2
c. Significance exception. If the last bit of the program mask is 0, F4 = 00000000 9988FFFF and cc = 0.
d. Significance exception. If the last bit of the program mask is 0, F6 = 00000000 FFFFFFFF and cc = 0.
e. F6 = 31000000 00770000, cc = 2
f. F6 = 2F000099 FFFFFFFF, cc = 2
g. F2 = C0800000 00000000, cc = 1

## Chapter 18

1. Add ® to the prototype in Figure 18.4. Replace each occurrence of 2 with ®.
2. Replace the prototype in Figure 18.4 with
```
&LABEL   DOUBLE   &NUMBER,&RESULT,&REG=2
```
Replace each occurrence of 2 with ®.

3. &A is null, &B is X, &C is null, &D is Y, &KEY1 is null, &KEY2 is 3, &KEY3 is 0, and &KEY4 is 8.
4. The statements are like those in Figure 18.12; but R0008 replaces R0007, and DATA replaces X,Y,Z.
5. a. (XY, −2,,W)
   b. −2
   c. XY−2
   d. XYW
   e. (XY, −2,,W)(1)
   f. 4
   g. null
   h. (XY, −2,,W)V.(3)
   i. W0001
   j. −1
   k. (12, −1)
   l. null
   m. (XY, −2,,W)
   n. null
   o. −2
   p. null
   q. null
6. Valid in SETA: d, e, g, i, j, q, r, t
   Valid in SETB: c, i, j, n, q, t
   Valid in SETC: k, l, p
7. a.
```
         L     3,=F'26'
         MR    2,3
         ST    3,
```
   b.
```
         L     3,X
         MR    2,3
         ST    3,Y
```
8.
```
         AIF   ((&REG/2)*2 EQ &REG).OK
         MNOTE 16,'ODD-NUMBERED REGISTER'
.OK      ANOP
```
9.
```
         MACRO
         REGEQU
         LCLA  &R
.LOOP    ANOP
R&R      EQU   &R
&R       SETA  &R+1
         AIF   (&R LE 15).LOOP
         MEND
```
10.
```
         MACRO
         INCR  &REG=2,&VAL=1
         GBLB  &FLAG
         AIF   (&FLAG).SKIP
         SR    &REG,&REG
&FLAG    SETB  1
         MEXIT
.SKIP    A     &REG,=F'&VAL'
         MEND
```
11.

| | L' | N' | K' | T' | S' | I' |
|---|---|---|---|---|---|---|
| a. | 3 | 1 | 4 | P | 4 | 1 |
| b. | 3 | 2 | 12 | P | – | – |
| c. | 3 | – | 4 | P | 4 | 1 |
| d. | 7 | – | 5 | C | – | – |

12.
```
+        L     3,ANSWER
```
13. Replace ®=2 in the prototype with &R. Declare ® in a LCLA statement. Insert the following after MEXIT:
```
&REG     SETA  2
         AIF   (K'&R EQ 0).OK
&REG     SETA  &R
```
14. Replace each of the four occurrences of &SYSLIST(&NOPS,&NENTS) with &S. Declare &S in a LCLC statement. Insert the following after the LCLC statement:
```
&S       SETC  '&SYSLIST(&NOPS,&NENTS)'
```
15. &J: 0 4 0
    &K: −21
    &FLAGS: 0 1 1 1
    &T: DEFGH 0(14,0+2) EFG GGH 52121+1
16. Insert &SYSECT CSECT after MAC2 within the definition of MAC1.

# APPENDIX B References and Selected Bibliography

## Books and Articles


Abel, P. *Programming Assembler Language,* 2d ed. Reston, Va.: Reston Publishing Company, 1984.

Archibald, R. G. *An Introduction to the Theory of Numbers.* Columbus, Ohio: Charles E. Merrill Publishing Company, 1970.

Berry, H. *Assembly Language for IBM-Compatible Processors: A Systematic Primer.* Boston: PWS Publishers, 1984.

Booth, T. L. *Introduction to Computer Engineering: Hardware and Software Design,* 3d ed. New York: John Wiley & Sons, 1984.

Burian, B. J. *A Simplified Approach to S/370 Assembly Language Programming.* Englewood Cliffs, N.J.: Prentice-Hall, 1977.

Deitel, H. M. *An Introduction to Operating Systems.* Reading, Mass.: Addison-Wesley Publishing Company, 1983.

Department of Consumer Affairs. "The Rule of 78's or What May Happen When You Pay Off a Loan Early." Philadelphia: Federal Reserve Bank of Philadelphia, 1986.

Feingold, C. *Introduction to Assembler Language Programming.* Dubuque, Iowa: Wm. C. Brown Publishers, 1978.

Gruenberger, F., and T. Jaffray. *Problems for Computer Solution.* New York: John Wiley & Sons, 1965.

Hannula, R. *Computers and Programming: A System/360-370 Assembler Language Approach.* Boston: Houghton Mifflin Company, 1974.

Helman, P., and R. Veroff. *Intermediate Problem Solving and Data Structures.* Menlo Park, Calif.: The Benjamin/Cummings Publishing Company, 1986.

Johnson, D. L. *Structured Assembly Language for IBM Computers.* Palo Alto, Calif.: Mayfield Publishing Company, 1983.

Keil, K. *Exercises for IBM Basic Assembler Language.* Chicago: Science Research Associates, 1985.

Knuth, D. E. *The Art of Computer Programming.*
 Vol. 1, *Fundamental Algorithms,* 2d ed. 1974.
 Vol. 2, *Seminumerical Algorithms,* 2d ed. 1981.
 Vol. 3, *Sorting and Searching,* 1973.
 Reading, Mass.: Addison-Wesley Publishing Company.

Kudlick, M. D. *Assembly Language Programming for the IBM Systems 360 and 370 for OS and DOS,* 2d ed. Dubuque, Iowa: Wm. C. Brown Publishers, 1983.

Kuo, S. S. *Assembler Language for FORTRAN, COBOL, and PL/1 Programmers.* Reading, Mass.: Addison-Wesley Publishing Company, 1974.

Massie, P. *Programming IBM Assembly Language.* Santa Rosa, Calif.: Burgess Communications, 1985.

McQuillen, K. *System/360-370 Assembler Language (OS).* Fresno, Calif.: Mike Murach & Associates, 1975.

Overbeek, R. A., and W. E. Singletary. *Assembler Language with ASSIST and ASSIST/I,* 3d ed. Chicago: Science Research Associates, 1986.

Rudd, W. G. *Assembly Language Programming and the IBM 360 and 370 Computers.* Englewood Cliffs, N.J.: Prentice-Hall, 1976.

Savitch, W. J. *Pascal: An Introduction to the Art and Science of Programming,* 2d ed. Menlo Park, Calif.: The Benjamin/Cummings Publishing Company, 1987.

Stark, R. H., and D. W. Dearholt. *Computer Concepts and Assembler Programming: 360/370 Systems.* New York: Academic Press, 1975.

Stern, N., A. Sager, and R. A. Stern. *Assembler Language Programming for IBM and IBM-Compatible Computers,* 2d ed. New York: John Wiley & Sons, 1986.

Silver, J. L. *Structured Assembly Language Programming for the IBM 370.* San Francisco, Calif.: Dellen Publishing Company, 1986.

Stoddard, S. D. *Principles of Assembler Language Programming for the IBM 370.* New York: McGraw-Hill Book Company, 1985.

Struble, G. *Assembler Language Programming: The IBM System/370 Family,* 3d ed. Reading, Mass.: Addison-Wesley Publishing Company, 1984.

Tuggle, S. K. *IBM Assembler Language Programming: A Systems Approach,* 2d ed. Chicago: Science Research Associates, 1987.

Uspensky, J. V., and M. A. Heaslet. *Elementary Number Theory.* New York: McGraw-Hill Book Company, 1939.

Weiderman, N. H., and B. M. Rawson. "Flowcharting Loops without Cycles." *ACM SIGPLAN Notices,* Vol. 10, No. 3, April 1975: 37–45.

## IBM Reference Manuals

### General

*System/360 Principles of Operation*, GA22-6821
*System/370 Principles of Operation*, GA22-7000
*System/370 Extended Architecture Principles of Operation*, SA22-7085
*OS/VS-DOS/VSE-VM/370 Assembler Language*, GC33-4010
*System/370 Reference Summary*, GX20-1850

### OS/VS1

*OS/VS1 JCL Reference*, GC24-5099
*OS/VS1 Data Management Macro Instructions*, GC26-3872
*OS/VS1 Data Management Services Guide*, GC26-3874
*OS/VS1 Supervisor Services and Macro Instructions*, GC24-5103
*OS/VS1 System Codes*, GC38-1003

### OS/VS2

*OS/VS2 JCL*, GC28-0692
*OS/VS2 MVS Data Management Macro Instructions*, GC26-3873
*OS/VS2 MVS Data Management Services Guide*, GC26-3875
*OS/VS2 MVS Supervisor Services and Macro Instructions*, GC28-0683
*OS/VS2 MVS/370 Message Library: System Codes*, GC38-1008

### DOS

*DOS/VS Supervisor and I/O Macros*, GC33-5373
*DOS/VSE System Control Statements*, GC33-5376
*DOS/VS Data Management Guide*, GC33-5372
*VSE/Advanced Functions Applications Programming Macro Reference*, SC33-6197
*VSE/Advanced Functions System Control Statements*, SC33-6198
*DOS/VS Messages and Codes*, SC38-0272

### CMS

*VM/370 SCP CMS Command and Macro Reference*, GC20-1818
*VM/370 SCP CMS User's Guide*, GC20-1819
*VM/370 SCP CP Command Reference for General Users*, GC20-1820
*VM/SP CMS Command and Macro Reference*, SC19-6209
*VM/SP CMS User's Guide*, SC19-6210
*VM/SP CP Command Reference for General Users*, SC19-6211

### VSAM

*VSAM Primer and Reference*, G320-5774
*OS/VS Virtual Storage Access Method (VSAM) Programmer's Guide*, GC26-3838

### I/O Devices

*3380 Direct Access Storage: General Information*, GC26-4193
*3380 Direct Access Storage: Planning and Use*, GC26-4208
*3803 Model 2, 3420 Models 4, 6, and 8: Magnetic Tape Subsystems Description*, GA32-0021
*3480 Magnetic Tape Subsystem User's Reference*, GC35-0099

## Additional References


Asimov, I. *Asimov's Biographical Encyclopedia of Science and Technology*, 2d ed., 343. Garden City, N.Y.: Doubleday & Co., 1982.

Broadbent, T. A. A. "George Boole." In *Dictionary of Scientific Biography*, Vol. II, edited by C. C. Gillespie, 293-298. New York: Charles Scribner's Sons, 1970.

Brock, G. W. *The U. S. Computer Industry: A Study in Market Power*. New York: Ballinger Publishing Co., 1975.

Buchholz, W. "The Word Byte Comes of Age." *BYTE*, February 1977: 144.

Capron, H. L., and B. K. Williams. *Computers and Data Processing*, 2d ed. Menlo Park, Calif.: The Benjamin/Cummings Publishing Company, 1984.

Ceruzzi, P. E. *Reckoners: The Prehistory of the Digital Computer, from Relays to the Stored Program Concept*. Westport, Conn.: Greenwood Press, 1983.

Eves, H. W. "Arabic Numerals." In *The World Book Encyclopedia*, Vol. 1, 547. Chicago: World Book, 1986.

*14K Days: A History of the Poughkeepsie Laboratory*. Poughkeepsie, N.Y.: IBM Data Systems Division, 1984.

Hofmann, J. E. "Leibnitz, Gottfreid Wilhelm." In *Dictionary of Scientific Biography*, 140-168. New York: Charles Scribner's Sons, 1973.

Hopper, G. M. "The First Bug." In *Annals of the History of Computing*, Vol. 3, No. 3, July 1981: 285-286.

"IBM Shocks the Plug-Compatibles." *Business Week*, June 18, 1979: 107-108.

"IBM's New Line Confirms the Rumors." *Business Week*, July 4, 1970: 21.

"IBM's Surprising New Computer." *Business Week*, September 26, 1970: 31.

"IBM Thinks up a New Generation." *Business Week*, June 13, 1970: 32.

Junge, C. W. "Numeration Systems." In *The World Book Encyclopedia*, Vol. 14, 450a-453. Chicago: World Book, 1986.

Kneale, W. "Boole and the Revival of Logic." *Mind*, Vol. 57, 1948: 149-175.

Mackenzie, C. E. *Coded Character Sets, History and Development*. Reading, Mass: Addison-Wesley Publishing Company, 1985.

McLaughlin, R. A. "The IBM 704: 36-Bit Floating-Point Money-Maker." *Datamation*, Vol. 21, No. 8, August 1975: 45-50.

Mendelson, S. E. "ASCII Code." In *Encyclopedia of Computer Science and Technology*, 272-278. New York: Marcel Dekker, 1975.

Moreau, R. *The Computer Comes of Age*. Translated by J. Howlett. Cambridge, Mass.: MIT Press, 1984.

"No. 1's Awesome Strategy." *Business Week,* June 8, 1981: 84-90.

Pugh, E. *Memories that Shaped an Industry.* Cambridge, Mass.: MIT Press, 1984.

*Rand McNally 1985 Road Atlas,* 27. Chicago: Rand McNally & Company, 1985.

Rosen, S. "Digital Computers." In *Encyclopedia of Computer Science,* 463-495. New York: Van Nostrand Reinhold Company, 1976.

Rosen, S. "IBM 360-370 Series." In *Encyclopedia of Computer Science,* 625-628. New York: Van Nostrand Reinhold Company, 1976.

Sanders, D. H. *Computers Today,* 2d ed. New York: McGraw-Hill Book Company, 1985.

Schmid, H. *Decimal Computation.* New York: John Wiley & Sons, 1974.

*A Supplement to the Oxford English Dictionary.* Oxford: Clarendon Press, 1972.

Stibitz, G. R., and J. A. Larrivee. *Mathematics and Computers.* New York: McGraw-Hill Book Company, 1957.

Tropp, H. "George Boole." In *Encyclopedia of Computer Science,* 177-178. New York: Van Nostrand Reinhold Company, 1976.

Tropp, H. "Whence the 'Bug'?" In *Annals of the History of Computing,* Vol. 6, No. 4, October 1984: 409.

Uttal, Bro. "How the 4300 Fits IBM's New Strategy." *Fortune,* July 30, 1979: 58-64.

Weil, U. *Information Systems in the 80's.* Englewood Cliffs, N.J.: Prentice-Hall, 1982.

"Why Cores Could Become Just a Memory." *Business Week,* December 26, 1970: 60-61.

Wise, T. A. "IBM's $5,000,000,000 Gamble." *Fortune,* September 1966: 118-123, 224-228.

Zuse, K. "The Outline of a Computer Development from Mechanics to Electronics." 1962. In *The Origins of Digital Computers,* edited by B. Randell, 172. New York: Springer-Verlag, 1973.

APPENDIX C

# Extended Mnemonic Instructions

| RX Format Instructions | | | | RR Format Instructions | | | | |
|---|---|---|---|---|---|---|---|---|
| Extended | | Equivalent | | Extended | | Equivalent | | Meaning |
| B | *S2* | BC | 15,*S2* | BR | *R2* | BCR | 15,*R2* | Branch Unconditionally |
| NOP | *S2* | BC | 0,*S2* | NOPR | *R2* | BCR | 0,*R2* | No Operation |
| *After comparing the first operand A with the second operand B:* | | | | | | | | |
| BE | *S2* | BC | 8,*S2* | BER | *R2* | BCR | 8,*R2* | Branch on Equal (A = B) |
| BH | *S2* | BC | 2,*S2* | BHR | *R2* | BCR | 2,*R2* | Branch on High (A > B) |
| BL | *S2* | BC | 4,*S2* | BLR | *R2* | BCR | 4,*R2* | Branch on Low (A < B) |
| BNE | *S2* | BC | 7,*S2* | BNER | *R2* | BCR | 7,*R2* | Branch on Not Equal (A ≠ B) |
| BNH | *S2* | BC | 13,*S2* | BNHR | *R2* | BCR | 13,*R2* | Branch on Not High (A ≤ B) |
| BNL | *S2* | BC | 11,*S2* | BNLR | *R2* | BCR | 11,*R2* | Branch on Not Low (A ≥ B) |
| *After arithmetic instructions:* | | | | | | | | |
| BZ | *S2* | BC | 8,*S2* | BZR | *R2* | BCR | 8,*R2* | Branch on Zero |
| BP | *S2* | BC | 2,*S2* | BPR | *R2* | BCR | 2,*R2* | Branch on Plus |
| BM | *S2* | BC | 4,*S2* | BMR | *R2* | BCR | 4,*R2* | Branch on Minus |
| BO | *S2* | BC | 1,*S2* | BOR | *R2* | BCR | 1,*R2* | Branch on Overflow |
| BNZ | *S2* | BC | 7,*S2* | BNZR | *R2* | BCR | 7,*R2* | Branch on Not Zero |
| BNP | *S2* | BC | 13,*S2* | BNPR | *R2* | BCR | 13,*R2* | Branch on Not Plus |
| BNM | *S2* | BC | 11,*S2* | BNMR | *R2* | BCR | 11,*R2* | Branch on Not Minus |
| BNO | *S2* | BC | 14,*S2* | BNOR | *R2* | BCR | 14,*R2* | Branch on No Overflow |
| *After the TM instruction:* | | | | | | | | |
| BO | *S2* | BC | 1,*S2* | BOR | *R2* | BCR | 1,*R2* | Branch if Ones |
| BZ | *S2* | BC | 8,*S2* | BZR | *R2* | BCR | 8,*R2* | Branch if Zeros |
| BM | *S2* | BC | 4,*S2* | BMR | *R2* | BCR | 4,*R2* | Branch if Mixed |
| BNO | *S2* | BC | 14,*S2* | BNOR | *R2* | BCR | 14,*R2* | Branch if Not Ones |
| BNZ | *S2* | BC | 7,*S2* | BNZR | *R2* | BCR | 7,*R2* | Branch if Not Zeros |
| BNM | *S2* | BC | 11,*S2* | BNMR | *R2* | BCR | 11,*R2* | Branch if Not Mixed |

# APPENDIX D Tables: Character Codes; Hex and Decimal Conversions; and Powers of 2 and 16†

## Table of Character Codes

| Dec. | Hex | Inst. (RR) | Graphics and Controls BCDIC | EBCDIC‡ | ASCII | Binary |
|---|---|---|---|---|---|---|
| 0 | 00 | | | NUL | NUL | 0000 0000 |
| 1 | 01 | | | SOH | SOH | 0000 0001 |
| 2 | 02 | | | STX | STX | 0000 0010 |
| 3 | 03 | | | ETX | ETX | 0000 0011 |
| 4 | 04 | SPM | | SEL | EOT | 0000 0100 |
| 5 | 05 | BALR | | HT | ENQ | 0000 0101 |
| 6 | 06 | BCTR | | RNL | ACK | 0000 0110 |
| 7 | 07 | BCR | | DEL | BEL | 0000 0111 |
| 8 | 08 | SSK | | GE | BS | 0000 1000 |
| 9 | 09 | ISK | | SPS | HT | 0000 1001 |
| 10 | 0A | SVC | | RPT | LF | 0000 1010 |
| 11 | 0B | | | VT | VT | 0000 1011 |
| 12 | 0C | | | FF | FF | 0000 1100 |
| 13 | 0D | BASR | | CR | CR | 0000 1101 |
| 14 | 0E | MVCL | | SO | SO | 0000 1110 |
| 15 | 0F | CLCL | | SI | SI | 0000 1111 |
| 16 | 10 | LPR | | DLE | DLE | 0001 0000 |
| 17 | 11 | LNR | | DC1 | DC1 | 0001 0001 |
| 18 | 12 | LTR | | DC2 | DC2 | 0001 0010 |
| 19 | 13 | LCR | | DC3 | DC3 | 0001 0011 |
| 20 | 14 | NR | | RES/ENP | DC4 | 0001 0100 |
| 21 | 15 | CLR | | NL | NAK | 0001 0101 |
| 22 | 16 | OR | | BS | SYN | 0001 0110 |
| 23 | 17 | XR | | POC | ETB | 0001 0111 |
| 24 | 18 | LR | | CAN | CAN | 0001 1000 |
| 25 | 19 | CR | | EM | EM | 0001 1001 |
| 26 | 1A | AR | | UBS | SUB | 0001 1010 |
| 27 | 1B | SR | | CU1 | ESC | 0001 1011 |
| 28 | 1C | MR | | IFS | FS | 0001 1100 |
| 29 | 1D | DR | | IGS | GS | 0001 1101 |
| 30 | 1E | ALR | | IRS | RS | 0001 1110 |
| 31 | 1F | SLR | | ITB/IUS | US | 0001 1111 |
| 32 | 20 | LPDR | | DS | SP | 0010 0000 |
| 33 | 21 | LNDR | | SOS | ! | 0010 0001 |
| 34 | 22 | LTDR | | FS | ‖ | 0010 0010 |
| 35 | 23 | LCDR | | WUS | # | 0010 0011 |
| 36 | 24 | HDR | | BYP/INP | $ | 0010 0100 |
| 37 | 25 | LRDR | | LF | % | 0010 0101 |
| 38 | 26 | MXR | | ETB | & | 0010 0110 |
| 39 | 27 | MXDR | | ESC | ' | 0010 0111 |
| 40 | 28 | LDR | | SA | ( | 0010 1000 |
| 41 | 29 | CDR | | SFE | ) | 0010 1001 |
| 42 | 2A | ADR | | SM/SW | * | 0010 1010 |
| 43 | 2B | SDR | | CSP | + | 0010 1011 |
| 44 | 2C | MDR | | MFA | , | 0010 1100 |
| 45 | 2D | DDR | | ENQ | - | 0010 1101 |
| 46 | 2E | AWR | | ACK | . | 0010 1110 |
| 47 | 2F | SWR | | BEL | / | 0010 1111 |
| 48 | 30 | LPER | | | 0 | 0011 0000 |
| 49 | 31 | LNER | | | 1 | 0011 0001 |
| 50 | 32 | LTER | | SYN | 2 | 0011 0010 |
| 51 | 33 | LCER | | IR | 3 | 0011 0011 |
| 52 | 34 | HER | | PP | 4 | 0011 0100 |
| 53 | 35 | LRER | | TRN | 5 | 0011 0101 |
| 54 | 36 | AXR | | NBS | 6 | 0011 0110 |
| 55 | 37 | SXR | | EOT | 7 | 0011 0111 |
| 56 | 38 | LER | | SBS | 8 | 0011 1000 |
| 57 | 39 | CER | | IT | 9 | 0011 1001 |
| 58 | 3A | AER | | RFF | : | 0011 1010 |
| 59 | 3B | SER | | CU3 | ; | 0011 1011 |
| 60 | 3C | MER | | DC4 | < | 0011 1100 |
| 61 | 3D | DER | | NAK | = | 0011 1101 |
| 62 | 3E | AUR | | | > | 0011 1110 |
| 63 | 3F | SUR | | SUB | ? | 0011 1111 |

| Dec. | Hex | Inst. (RX) | Graphics and Controls BCDIC | EBCDIC‡ | | ASCII | Binary |
|---|---|---|---|---|---|---|---|
| 64 | 40 | STH | SP | SP | SP | @ | 0100 0000 |
| 65 | 41 | LA | | RSP | | A | 0100 0001 |
| 66 | 42 | STC | | | | B | 0100 0010 |
| 67 | 43 | IC | | | | C | 0100 0011 |
| 68 | 44 | EX | | | | D | 0100 0100 |
| 69 | 45 | BAL | | | | E | 0100 0101 |
| 70 | 46 | BCT | | | | F | 0100 0110 |
| 71 | 47 | BC | | | | G | 0100 0111 |
| 72 | 48 | LH | | | | H | 0100 1000 |
| 73 | 49 | CH | | | | I | 0100 1001 |
| 74 | 4A | AH | | ¢ | ¢ | J | 0100 1010 |
| 75 | 4B | SH | . | . | . | K | 0100 1011 |
| 76 | 4C | MH | □) | < | < | L | 0100 1100 |
| 77 | 4D | BAS | [ | ( | ( | M | 0100 1101 |
| 78 | 4E | CVD | < | + | + | N | 0100 1110 |
| 79 | 4F | CVB | ‡ | \| | \| | O | 0100 1111 |
| 80 | 50 | ST | & + | & | & | P | 0101 0000 |
| 81 | 51 | | | | | Q | 0101 0001 |
| 82 | 52 | | | | | R | 0101 0010 |
| 83 | 53 | | | | | S | 0101 0011 |
| 84 | 54 | N | | | | T | 0101 0100 |
| 85 | 55 | CL | | | | U | 0101 0101 |
| 86 | 56 | O | | | | V | 0101 0110 |
| 87 | 57 | X | | | | W | 0101 0111 |
| 88 | 58 | L | | | | X | 0101 1000 |
| 89 | 59 | C | | | | Y | 0101 1001 |
| 90 | 5A | A | | ! | ! | Z | 0101 1010 |
| 91 | 5B | S | $ | $ | $ | [ | 0101 1011 |

†Reprinted, by permission of International Business Machines Corp., from *System/370 Reference Summary* (GX20-1850), 1984.
‡Two columns of EBCDIC graphics are shown. The first gives IBM standard U.S. bit pattern assignments. The second shows the T-11 and TN text printing chains (120 graphics).

## Table of Character Codes

| Dec. | Hex | Inst. (RX) | BCDIC | EBCDIC‡ | ASCII | Binary |
|---|---|---|---|---|---|---|
| 92 | 5C | M | * | * * | \ | 0101 1100 |
| 93 | 5D | D | ] | ) ) | ] | 0101 1101 |
| 94 | 5E | AL | ; | ; ; | ∧ | 0101 1110 |
| 95 | 5F | SL | Δ | ¬ ¬ | — | 0101 1111 |
| 96 | 60 | STD | - | - - | ` | 0110 0000 |
| 97 | 61 | | / | / / | a | 0110 0001 |
| 98 | 62 | | | | b | 0110 0010 |
| 99 | 63 | | | | c | 0110 0011 |
| 100 | 64 | | | | d | 0110 0100 |
| 101 | 65 | | | | e | 0110 0101 |
| 102 | 66 | | | | f | 0110 0110 |
| 103 | 67 | MXD | | | g | 0110 0111 |
| 104 | 68 | LD | | | h | 0110 1000 |
| 105 | 69 | CD | | | i | 0110 1001 |
| 106 | 6A | AD | | ¦ | j | 0110 1010 |
| 107 | 6B | SD | , | , , | k | 0110 1011 |
| 108 | 6C | MD | %( | % % | l | 0110 1100 |
| 109 | 6D | DD | γ | — — | m | 0110 1101 |
| 110 | 6E | AW | \ | > > | n | 0110 1110 |
| 111 | 6F | SW | ⧻ | ? ? | o | 0110 1111 |
| 112 | 70 | STE | | | p | 0111 0000 |
| 113 | 71 | | | | q | 0111 0001 |
| 114 | 72 | | | | r | 0111 0010 |
| 115 | 73 | | | | s | 0111 0011 |
| 116 | 74 | | | | t | 0111 0100 |
| 117 | 75 | | | | u | 0111 0101 |
| 118 | 76 | | | | v | 0111 0110 |
| 119 | 77 | | | | w | 0111 0111 |
| 120 | 78 | LE | | | x | 0111 1000 |
| 121 | 79 | CE | | ` | y | 0111 1001 |
| 122 | 7A | AE | ƀ | : : | z | 0111 1010 |
| 123 | 7B | SE | #= | # # | { | 0111 1011 |
| 124 | 7C | ME | @' | @ @ | ¦ | 0111 1100 |
| 125 | 7D | DE | : | ' ' | } | 0111 1101 |
| 126 | 7E | AU | > | = = | ~ | 0111 1110 |
| 127 | 7F | SU | √ | " " | DEL | 0111 1111 |

| Dec. | Hex | Instruction and format | BCDIC | EBCDIC‡ | ASCII | Binary |
|---|---|---|---|---|---|---|
| 128 | 80 | SSM S | | | | 1000 0000 |
| 129 | 81 | | | a a | | 1000 0001 |
| 130 | 82 | LPSW S | | b b | | 1000 0010 |
| 131 | 83 | Diagnose | | c c | | 1000 0011 |
| 132 | 84 | WRD SI | | d d | | 1000 0100 |
| 133 | 85 | RDD SI | | e e | | 1000 0101 |
| 134 | 86 | BXH RS | | f f | | 1000 0110 |
| 135 | 87 | BXLE RS | | g g | | 1000 0111 |
| 136 | 88 | SRL RS | | h h | | 1000 1000 |
| 137 | 89 | SLL RS | | i i | | 1000 1001 |
| 138 | 8A | SRA RS | | | | 1000 1010 |
| 139 | 8B | SLA RS | | { | | 1000 1011 |
| 140 | 8C | SRDL RS | | ≤ | | 1000 1100 |
| 141 | 8D | SLDL RS | | ( | See Note | 1000 1101 |
| 142 | 8E | SRDA RS | | + | See Note | 1000 1110 |
| 143 | 8F | SLDA RS | | + | | 1000 1111 |
| 144 | 90 | STM RS | | | | 1001 0000 |
| 145 | 91 | TM SI | | j j | | 1001 0001 |
| 146 | 92 | MVI SI | | k k | | 1001 0010 |
| 147 | 93 | TS S | | l l | | 1001 0011 |
| 148 | 94 | NI SI | | m m | | 1001 0100 |
| 149 | 95 | CLI SI | | n n | | 1001 0101 |
| 150 | 96 | OI SI | | o o | | 1001 0110 |
| 151 | 97 | XI SI | | p p | | 1001 0111 |
| 152 | 98 | LM RS | | q q | | 1001 1000 |
| 153 | 99 | | | r r | | 1001 1001 |
| 154 | 9A | | | | | 1001 1010 |
| 155 | 9B | | | } | | 1001 1011 |

Note: This character is an EBCDIC superscript character.

| Dec. | Hex | Instruction and format | BCDIC | EBCDIC‡ | ASCII | Binary |
|---|---|---|---|---|---|---|
| 156 | 9C | See below | | ¤ | | 1001 1100 |
| 157 | 9D | See below | | ) | See Note | 1001 1101 |
| 158 | 9E | See below | | ± | | 1001 1110 |
| 159 | 9F | See below | | ■ | | 1001 1111 |
| 160 | A0 | | | — | See Note | 1010 0000 |
| 161 | A1 | | | ~ ° | | 1010 0001 |
| 162 | A2 | | | s s | | 1010 0010 |
| 163 | A3 | | | t t | | 1010 0011 |
| 164 | A4 | | | u u | | 1010 0100 |
| 165 | A5 | | | v v | | 1010 0101 |
| 166 | A6 | | | w w | | 1010 0110 |
| 167 | A7 | | | x x | | 1010 0111 |
| 168 | A8 | | | y y | | 1010 1000 |
| 169 | A9 | | | z z | | 1010 1001 |
| 170 | AA | | | | | 1010 1010 |
| 171 | AB | | | └ | | 1010 1011 |
| 172 | AC | STNSM SI | | ┌ | | 1010 1100 |
| 173 | AD | STOSM SI | | [ | | 1010 1101 |
| 174 | AE | SIGP RS | | ≥ | | 1010 1110 |
| 175 | AF | MC SI | | ● | | 1010 1111 |
| 176 | B0 | | | $^0$ | See Note | 1011 0000 |
| 177 | B1 | LRA RX | | $^1$ | See Note | 1011 0001 |
| 178 | B2 | See below | | $^2$ | See Note | 1011 0010 |
| 179 | B3 | | | $^3$ | See Note | 1011 0011 |
| 180 | B4 | | | $^4$ | See Note | 1011 0100 |
| 181 | B5 | | | $^5$ | See Note | 1011 0101 |
| 182 | B6 | STCTL RS | | $^6$ | See Note | 1011 0110 |
| 183 | B7 | LCTL RS | | $^7$ | See Note | 1011 0111 |
| 184 | B8 | | | $^8$ | See Note | 1011 1000 |
| 185 | B9 | | | $^9$ | See Note | 1011 1001 |
| 186 | BA | CS RS | | | | 1011 1010 |
| 187 | BB | CDS RS | | ┘ | | 1011 1011 |
| 188 | BC | | | ┐ | | 1011 1100 |
| 189 | BD | CLM RS | | ] | | 1011 1101 |
| 190 | BE | STCM RS | | ≠ | | 1011 1110 |
| 191 | BF | ICM RS | | – | | 1011 1111 |

**S Format**

9C00 – SIO, 9C01 – SIOF, 9C02 – RIO, 9D00 – TIO, 9D01 – CLRIO, 9E00 – HIO, 9E01 – HDV, 9F00 – TCH, 9F01 – CLRCH, B200 – CONCS, B201 – DISCS, B202 – STIDP, B203 – STIDC, B204 – SCK, B205 – STCK, B206 – SCKC, B207 – STCKC, B208 – SPT, B209 – STPT, B20A – SPKA, B20B – IPK, B20D – PTLB, B210 – SPX, B211 – STPX, B212 – STAP, B213 – RRB, B218 – PC, B219 – SAC

**RRE Format**

B221 – IPTE, B223 – IVSK, B224 – IAC, B225 – SSAR, B226 – EPAR, B227 – ESAR, B228 – PT, B229 – ISKE, B22A – RRBE, B22B – SSKE, B22C – TB

| Dec. | Hex | Inst. (SS) | BCDIC | EBCDIC‡ | ASCII | Binary |
|---|---|---|---|---|---|---|
| 192 | C0 | | ? | { | | 1100 0000 |
| 193 | C1 | | A | A A | | 1100 0001 |
| 194 | C2 | | B | B B | | 1100 0010 |
| 195 | C3 | | C | C C | | 1100 0011 |
| 196 | C4 | | D | D D | | 1100 0100 |
| 197 | C5 | | E | E E | | 1100 0101 |
| 198 | C6 | | F | F F | | 1100 0110 |
| 199 | C7 | | G | G G | | 1100 0111 |
| 200 | C8 | | H | H H | | 1100 1000 |
| 201 | C9 | | I | I I | | 1100 1001 |
| 202 | CA | | | SHY | | 1100 1010 |
| 203 | CB | | | | | 1100 1011 |
| 204 | CC | | | ⑁ | | 1100 1100 |
| 205 | CD | | | | | 1100 1101 |
| 206 | CE | | | ⑂ | | 1100 1110 |
| 207 | CF | | | | | 1100 1111 |

## Table of Character Codes

| Dec. | Hex | Inst. (SS) | Graphics and Controls BCDIC | EBCDIC‡ | | ASCII | Binary |
|---|---|---|---|---|---|---|---|
| 208 | D0 | | ! | } | | | 1101 0000 |
| 209 | D1 | MVN | J | J | J | | 1101 0001 |
| 210 | D2 | MVC | K | K | K | | 1101 0010 |
| 211 | D3 | MVZ | L | L | L | | 1101 0011 |
| 212 | D4 | NC | M | M | M | | 1101 0100 |
| 213 | D5 | CLC | N | N | N | | 1101 0101 |
| 214 | D6 | OC | O | O | O | | 1101 0110 |
| 215 | D7 | XC | P | P | P | | 1101 0111 |
| 216 | D8 | | Q | Q | Q | | 1101 1000 |
| 217 | D9 | MVCK | R | R | R | | 1101 1001 |
| 218 | DA | MVCP | | | | | 1101 1010 |
| 219 | DB | MVCS | | | | | 1101 1011 |
| 220 | DC | TR | | | | | 1101 1100 |
| 221 | DD | TRT | | | | | 1101 1101 |
| 222 | DE | ED | | | | | 1101 1110 |
| 223 | DF | EDMK | | | | | 1101 1111 |
| 224 | E0 | | ‡ | \ | | | 1110 0000 |
| 225 | E1 | | | NSP | | | 1110 0001 |
| 226 | E2 | | S | S | S | | 1110 0010 |
| 227 | E3 | | T | T | T | | 1110 0011 |
| 228 | E4 | | U | U | U | | 1110 0100 |
| 229 | E5 | See below | V | V | V | | 1110 0101 |
| 230 | E6 | | W | W | W | | 1110 0110 |
| 231 | E7 | | X | X | X | | 1110 0111 |

**SSE Format**
E500 – LASP
E501 – TPROT

| Dec. | Hex | Inst. (SS) | Graphics and Controls BCDIC | EBCDIC‡ | | ASCII | Binary |
|---|---|---|---|---|---|---|---|
| 232 | E8 | MVCIN | Y | Y | Y | | 1110 1000 |
| 233 | E9 | | Z | Z | | | 1110 1001 |
| 234 | EA | | | | | | 1110 1010 |
| 235 | EB | | | | | | 1110 1011 |
| 236 | EC | | | ⑂ | | | 1110 1100 |
| 237 | ED | | | | | | 1110 1101 |
| 238 | EE | | | | | | 1110 1110 |
| 239 | EF | | | | | | 1110 1111 |
| 240 | F0 | SRP | 0 | 0 | 0 | | 1111 0000 |
| 241 | F1 | MVO | 1 | 1 | 1 | | 1111 0001 |
| 242 | F2 | PACK | 2 | 2 | 2 | | 1111 0010 |
| 243 | F3 | UNPK | 3 | 3 | 3 | | 1111 0011 |
| 244 | F4 | | 4 | 4 | 4 | | 1111 0100 |
| 245 | F5 | | 5 | 5 | 5 | | 1111 0101 |
| 246 | F6 | | 6 | 6 | 6 | | 1111 0110 |
| 247 | F7 | | 7 | 7 | 7 | | 1111 0111 |
| 248 | F8 | ZAP | 8 | 8 | 8 | | 1111 1000 |
| 249 | F9 | CP | 9 | 9 | 9 | | 1111 1001 |
| 250 | FA | AP | | \| | | | 1111 1010 |
| 251 | FB | SP | | | | | 1111 1011 |
| 252 | FC | MP | | | | | 1111 1100 |
| 253 | FD | DP | | | | | 1111 1101 |
| 254 | FE | | | | | | 1111 1110 |
| 255 | FF | | | EO | | | 1111 1111 |

## Hexadecimal and Decimal Conversions

*From hex:* locate each hex digit in its corresponding column position and note the decimal equivalents. Add these to obtain the decimal value.

*From decimal:* (1) locate the largest decimal value in the table that will fit into the decimal number to be converted, and (2) note its hex equivalent and hex column position. (3) Find the decimal remainder. Repeat the process on this and subsequent remainders.

*Note:* Decimal, hexadecimal, and binary equivalents of all numbers from 0 to 255 are listed in the code tables.

| HEXADECIMAL COLUMNS | | | | | | | | | | | |
|---|---|---|---|---|---|---|---|---|---|---|---|
| 6 | | 5 | | 4 | | 3 | | 2 | | 1 | |
| HEX | DEC | HEX | DEC | HEX | DEC | HEX | DEC | HEX | DEC | HEX | DEC |
| 0 | 0 | 0 | 0 | 0 | 0 | 0 | 0 | 0 | 0 | 0 | 0 |
| 1 | 1,048,576 | 1 | 65,536 | 1 | 4,096 | 1 | 256 | 1 | 16 | 1 | 1 |
| 2 | 2,097,152 | 2 | 131,072 | 2 | 8,192 | 2 | 512 | 2 | 32 | 2 | 2 |
| 3 | 3,145,728 | 3 | 196,608 | 3 | 12,288 | 3 | 768 | 3 | 48 | 3 | 3 |
| 4 | 4,194,304 | 4 | 262,144 | 4 | 16,384 | 4 | 1,024 | 4 | 64 | 4 | 4 |
| 5 | 5,242,880 | 5 | 327,680 | 5 | 20,480 | 5 | 1,280 | 5 | 80 | 5 | 5 |
| 6 | 6,291,456 | 6 | 393,216 | 6 | 24,576 | 6 | 1,536 | 6 | 96 | 6 | 6 |
| 7 | 7,340,032 | 7 | 458,752 | 7 | 28,672 | 7 | 1,792 | 7 | 112 | 7 | 7 |
| 8 | 8,388,608 | 8 | 524,288 | 8 | 32,768 | 8 | 2,048 | 8 | 128 | 8 | 8 |
| 9 | 9,437,184 | 9 | 589,824 | 9 | 36,864 | 9 | 2,304 | 9 | 144 | 9 | 9 |
| A | 10,485,760 | A | 655,360 | A | 40,960 | A | 2,560 | A | 160 | A | 10 |
| B | 11,534,336 | B | 720,896 | B | 45,056 | B | 2,816 | B | 176 | B | 11 |
| C | 12,582,912 | C | 786,432 | C | 49,152 | C | 3,072 | C | 192 | C | 12 |
| D | 13,631,488 | D | 851,968 | D | 53,248 | D | 3,328 | D | 208 | D | 13 |
| E | 14,680,064 | E | 917,504 | E | 57,344 | E | 3,584 | E | 224 | E | 14 |
| F | 15,728,640 | F | 983,040 | F | 61,440 | F | 3,840 | F | 240 | F | 15 |
| 0 1 2 3 | | 4 5 6 7 | | 0 1 2 3 | | 4 5 6 7 | | 0 1 2 3 | | 4 5 6 7 | |
| BYTE | | | | BYTE | | | | BYTE | | | |

### Powers of 2

| $2^n$ | $n$ |
|---|---|
| 256 | 8 |
| 512 | 9 |
| 1 024 | 10 |
| 2 048 | 11 |
| 4 096 | 12 |
| 8 192 | 13 |
| 16 384 | 14 |
| 32 768 | 15 |
| 65 536 | 16 |
| 131 072 | 17 |
| 262 144 | 18 |
| 524 288 | 19 |
| 1 048 576 | 20 |
| 2 097 152 | 21 |
| 4 194 304 | 22 |
| 8 388 608 | 23 |
| 16 777 216 | 24 |
| 33 554 432 | 25 |
| 67 108 864 | 26 |

| | |
|---|---|
| $2^0 = 16^0$ | |
| $2^4 = 16^1$ | |
| $2^8 = 16^2$ | |
| $2^{12} = 16^3$ | |
| $2^{16} = 16^4$ | |
| $2^{20} = 16^5$ | |
| $2^{24} = 16^6$ | |
| $2^{28} = 16^7$ | |
| $2^{32} = 16^8$ | |
| $2^{36} = 16^9$ | |
| $2^{40} = 16^{10}$ | |
| $2^{44} = 16^{11}$ | |
| $2^{48} = 16^{12}$ | |
| $2^{52} = 16^{13}$ | |
| $2^{56} = 16^{14}$ | |
| $2^{60} = 16^{15}$ | |

### Powers of 16

| $16^n$ | $n$ |
|---|---|
| 1 | 0 |
| 16 | 1 |
| 256 | 2 |
| 4 096 | 3 |
| 65 536 | 4 |
| 1 048 576 | 5 |
| 16 777 216 | 6 |
| 268 435 456 | 7 |
| 4 294 967 296 | 8 |
| 68 719 476 736 | 9 |
| 1 099 511 627 776 | 10 |
| 17 592 186 044 416 | 11 |
| 281 474 976 710 656 | 12 |
| 4 503 599 627 370 496 | 13 |
| 72 057 594 037 927 936 | 14 |
| 1 152 921 504 606 846 976 | 15 |

## APPENDIX E Nonprivileged Instructions

| Mnemonic | Operand† | Format | Op Code | Instruction Name | Cond. Code‡ | Action |
|---|---|---|---|---|---|---|
| A | *R1,S2(X2)* or *R1,D2(X2,B2)* | RX | 5A | ADD | *a* | $C(R1) \leftarrow C(R1) + C(E2)_{0\text{-}31}$ |
| AD | *FPR1,S2(X2)* or *FPR1,D2(X2,B2)* | RX | 6A | ADD DOUBLE | *b* | $C(FPR1)_{0\text{-}63} \leftarrow C(FPR1)_{0\text{-}63} + C(E2)_{0\text{-}63}$ |
| ADR | *FPR1,FPR2* | RR | 2A | ADD DOUBLE REGISTERS | *b* | $C(FPR1)_{0\text{-}63} \leftarrow C(FPR1)_{0\text{-}63} + C(FPR2)_{0\text{-}63}$ |
| AE | *FPR1,S2(X2)* or *FPR1,D2(X2,B2)* | RX | 7A | ADD SHORT | *b* | $C(FPR1)_{0\text{-}31} \leftarrow C(FPR1)_{0\text{-}31} + C(E2)_{0\text{-}31}$ |
| AER | *FPR1,FPR2* | RR | 3A | ADD SHORT REGISTERS | *b* | $C(FPR1)_{0\text{-}31} \leftarrow C(FPR1)_{0\text{-}31} + C(FPR2)_{0\text{-}31}$ |
| AH | *R1,S2(X2)* or *R1,D2(X2,B2)* | RX | 4A | ADD HALFWORD | *a* | $C(R1)_{0\text{-}31} \leftarrow C(R1)_{0\text{-}31} + F[C(E2)_{0\text{-}15}]$ |
| AL | *R1,S2(X2)* or *R1,D2(X2,B2)* | RX | 5E | ADD LOGICAL | *f* | $C(R1) \leftarrow C(R1) + C(E2)_{0\text{-}31}$ |
| ALR | *R1,R2* | RR | 1E | ADD LOGICAL REGISTERS | *f* | $C(R1) \leftarrow C(R1) + C(R2)$ |
| AP | *S1(L1),S2(L2)* or *D1(L1,B1),D2(L2,B2)* | $SS_2$ | FA | ADD PACKED | *a* | $C(E1)_{L1} \leftarrow C(E1)_{L1} + C(E2)_{L2}$ |
| AR | *R1,R2* | RR | 1A | ADD REGISTERS | *a* | $C(R1) \leftarrow C(R1) + C(R2)$ |
| AU | *FPR1,S2(X2)* or *FPR1,D2(X2,B2)* | RX | 7E | ADD UNNORMALIZED SHORT | *b* | $C(FPR1)_{0\text{-}31} \leftarrow C(FPR1)_{0\text{-}31} + C(E2)_{0\text{-}31}$ |

†See Operand Notes, p. A.34 ‡The notation in the condition code column is defined on p. A.34

(Continued)

| Mnemonic | Operand[†] | Format | Op Code | Instruction Name | Cond. Code[‡] | Action |
|---|---|---|---|---|---|---|
| AUR | *FPR1,FPR2* | RR | 3E | ADD UNNORMALIZED SHORT REGISTERS | *b* | $C(FPR1)_{0\text{-}31} \leftarrow C(FPR1)_{0\text{-}31} + C(FPR2)_{0\text{-}31}$ |
| AW | *FPR1,S2(X2)*<br>or *FPR1,D2(X2,B2)* | RX | 6E | ADD UNNORMALIZED DOUBLE | *b* | $C(FPR1)_{0\text{-}63} \leftarrow C(FPR1)_{0\text{-}63} + C(E2)_{0\text{-}63}$ |
| AWR | *FPR1,FPR2* | RR | 2E | ADD UNNORMALIZED DOUBLE REGISTERS | *b* | $C(FPR1)_{0\text{-}63} \leftarrow C(FPR1)_{0\text{-}63} + C(FPR2)_{0\text{-}63}$ |
| AXR | *FPR1,FPR2* | RR | 36 | ADD EXTENDED REGISTERS | *b* | $C(FPR1,FPR1+2) \leftarrow C(FPR1,FPR1+2) + C(FPR2,FPR2+2)$ |
| BAL | *R1,S2(X2)*<br>or *R1,D2(X2,B2)* | RX | 45 | BRANCH AND LINK | — | With 24-bit addressing:<br>C(*R1*) ← ILC, cond. code, prog. mask, IA<br><br>With 31-bit addressing:<br>C(*R1*) ← 1, IA<br><br>With either 24-bit addressing or 31-bit addressing, branches to the effective address *E2*. |
| BALR | *R1,R2* | RR | 05 | BRANCH AND LINK REGISTER | — | Loads *R1* in the same way as BAL. Branches to the address in *R2* if $R2 \neq 0$. |
| BAS | *R1,S2(X2)*<br>or *R1,D2(X2,B2)* | RX | 4D | BRANCH AND SAVE | — | $C(R1) \leftarrow C(PSW)_{32\text{-}63}$<br>Branches to *E2*. |
| BASR | *R1,R2* | RR | 0D | BRANCH AND SAVE REGISTER | — | $C(R1) \leftarrow C(PSW)_{32\text{-}63}$<br>Branches to C(*R2*) if $R2 \neq 0$. |
| BASSM | *R1,R2* | RR | 0C | BRANCH AND SAVE AND SET MODE | — | $C(R1) \leftarrow C(PSW)_{32\text{-}63}$<br>$C(PSW)_{32\text{-}63} \leftarrow C(R2)$ if $R2 \neq 0$ |
| BC | *M1,S2(X2)*<br>or *M1,D2(X2,B2)* | RX | 47 | BRANCH ON CONDITION | — | If the condition code is as specified by *M1*, branches to the effective address *E2*; if not, sequences. |
| BCR | *M1,R2* | RR | 07 | BRANCH ON CONDITION REGISTER | — | If the condition code is as specified by *M1*, branches to the address in *R2*; if not, sequences. Does not branch if $R2 = 0$. |
| BCT | *R1,S2(X2)*<br>or *R1,D2(X2,B2)* | RX | 46 | BRANCH ON COUNT | — | $C(R1) \leftarrow C(R1) - 1$<br>Branches to *E2* if $C(R1) \neq 0$. |

| | | | | | | |
|---|---|---|---|---|---|---|
| BCTR | *R1*,*R2* | RR | 06 | BRANCH ON COUNT REGISTER | — | $C(R1) \leftarrow C(R1) - 1$<br>Branches to the address in *R2* if $C(R1) \neq 0$ and $R2 \neq 0$. |
| BSM | *R1*,*R2* | RR | 0B | BRANCH AND SET MODE | — | $C(R1)_0 \leftarrow C(PSW)_{32}$ if $R1 \neq 0$<br>$C(PSW)_{32\text{-}63} \leftarrow C(R2)$ if $R2 \neq 0$ |
| BXH | *R1*,*R3*,*S2*<br>or *R1*,*R3*,*D2*(*B2*) | RS | 86 | BRANCH ON INDEX HIGH | — | $C(R1) \leftarrow C(R1) + C(R3)$<br>Branches to *E2* if $C(R1) > \begin{cases} C(R3) \text{ if } R3 \text{ is odd.} \\ C(R3+1) \text{ if } R3 \text{ is even.} \end{cases}$ |
| BXLE | *R1*,*R3*,*S2*<br>or *R1*,*R3*,*D2*(*B2*) | RS | 87 | BRANCH ON INDEX LOW OR EQUAL | — | $C(R1) \leftarrow C(R1) + C(R3)$<br>Branches to *E2* if $C(R1) \leqslant \begin{cases} C(R3) \text{ if } R3 \text{ is odd.} \\ C(R3+1) \text{ if } R3 \text{ is even.} \end{cases}$ |
| C | *R1*,*S2*(*X2*)<br>or *R1*,*D2*(*X2*,*B2*) | RX | 59 | COMPARE | *c* | Compares $C(R1)$ with $C(E2)_{0\text{-}31}$ |
| CD | *FPR1*,*S2*(*X2*)<br>or *FPR1*,*D2*(*X2*,*B2*) | RX | 69 | COMPARE DOUBLE | *c* | Compares $C(FPR1)_{0\text{-}63}$ with $C(E2)_{0\text{-}63}$ |
| CDR | *FPR1*,*FPR2* | RR | 29 | COMPARE DOUBLE REGISTERS | *c* | Compares $C(FPR1)_{0\text{-}63}$ with $C(FPR2)_{0\text{-}63}$ |
| CDS | *R1*,*R3*,*S2*<br>or *R1*,*R3*,*D2*(*B2*) | RS | BB | COMPARE DOUBLE AND SWAP | *d* | Compares $C(R1,R1+1)$ with $C(E2)_{0\text{-}63}$<br>$C(E2)_{0-63} \leftarrow C(R3,R3+1)$ if comparison is equal<br>$C(R1,R1+1) \leftarrow C(E2)_{0\text{-}63}$ if comparison is unequal |
| CE | *FPR1*,*S2*(*X2*)<br>or *FPR1*,*D2*(*X2*,*B2*) | RX | 79 | COMPARE SHORT | *c* | Compares $C(FPR1)_{0\text{-}31}$ with $C(E2)_{0\text{-}31}$ |
| CER | *FPR1*,*FPR2* | RR | 39 | COMPARE SHORT REGISTERS | *c* | Compares $C(FPR1)_{0\text{-}31}$ with $C(FPR2)_{0\text{-}31}$ |
| CH | *R1*,*S2*(*X2*)<br>or *R1*,*D2*(*X2*,*B2*) | RX | 49 | COMPARE HALFWORD | *c* | Compares $C(R1)$ with $F[C(E2)_{0\text{-}15}]$ |
| CL | *R1*,*S2*(*X2*)<br>or *R1*,*D2*(*X2*,*B2*) | RX | 55 | COMPARE LOGICAL | *c* | Compares $C(R1)$ with $C(E2)_{0\text{-}31}$ |

*(Continued)*

| Mnemonic | Operand† | Format | Op Code | Instruction Name | Cond. Code‡ | Action |
|---|---|---|---|---|---|---|
| CLC | *S1*(L),*S2*<br>or *D1*(*L*,*B1*),*D2*(*B2*) | $SS_1$ | D5 | COMPARE LOGICAL CHARACTERS | *c* | Compares $C(E1)_L$ with $C(E2)_L$ |
| CLCL | *R1*,*R2* | RR | 0F | COMPARE CHARACTERS LONG | *c* | Compares the two fields whose starting addresses and lengths are in the even-odd register pairs that *R1* and *R2* designate. |
| CLI | *S1*,*I2*<br>or *D1*(*B1*),*I2* | SI | 95 | COMPARE LOGICAL IMMEDIATE | *c* | Compares C(*E1*) with *I2* |
| CLM | *R1*,*M3*,*S2*<br>or *R1*,*M3*,*D2*(*B2*) | RS | BD | COMPARE LOGICAL UNDER MASK | *c** | Compares bytes of *R1*, which are selected according to *M3*, with the consecutive bytes at *E2*. |
| CLR | *R1*,*R2* | RR | 15 | COMPARE LOGICAL REGISTERS | *c* | Compares C(*R1*) with C(*R2*) |
| CP | *S1*(*L1*),*S2*(*L2*)<br>or *D1*(*L1*,*B1*),*D2*(*L2*,*B2*) | $SS_2$ | F9 | COMPARE PACKED | *c* | Compares $C(E1)_{L1}$ with $C(E2)_{L2}$ |
| CR | *R1*,*R2* | RR | 19 | COMPARE REGISTERS | *c* | Compares C(*R1*) with C(*R2*) |
| CS | *R1*,*R3*,*S2*<br>or *R1*,*R3*,*D2*(*B2*) | RS | BA | COMPARE AND SWAP | *d* | Compares C(*R1*) with $C(E2)_{0\text{-}31}$<br>$C(E2)_{0\text{-}31} \leftarrow C(R3)$ if comparison is equal<br>$C(R1) \leftarrow C(E2)_{0\text{-}31}$ if comparison is unequal |
| CVB | *R1*,*S2*(*X2*)<br>or *R1*,*D2*(*X2*,*B2*) | RX | 4F | CONVERT TO BINARY | — | $C(R1) \leftarrow$ The two's complement binary equivalent of $C(E2)_{0\text{-}63}$ |
| CVD | *R1*,*S2*(*X2*)<br>or *R1*,*D2*(*X2*,*B2*) | RX | 4E | CONVERT TO DECIMAL | — | $C(E2)_{0\text{-}63} \leftarrow$ The packed-decimal equivalent of C(*R1*). |
| D | *R1*,*S2*(*X2*)<br>or *R1*,*D2*(*X2*,*B2*) | RX | 5D | DIVIDE | — | $C(R1+1) \leftarrow$ Quotient of $C(R1,R1+1) \div C(E2)_{0\text{-}31}$<br>$C(R1) \leftarrow$ Remainder of $C(R1,R1+1) \div C(E2)_{0\text{-}31}$ |
| DD | *FPR1*,*S2*(*X2*)<br>or *FPR1*,*D2*(*X2*,*B2*) | RX | 6D | DIVIDE DOUBLE | — | $C(FPR1)_{0\text{-}63} \leftarrow C(FPR1)_{0\text{-}63} \div C(E2)_{0\text{-}63}$ |
| DDR | *FPR1*,*FPR2* | RR | 2D | DIVIDE DOUBLE REGISTERS | — | $C(FPR1)_{0\text{-}63} \leftarrow C(FPR1)_{0\text{-}63} \div C(FPR2)_{0\text{-}63}$ |

| | | | | | | |
|---|---|---|---|---|---|---|
| DE | *FPR1,S2(X2)* or *FPR1,D2(X2,B2)* | RX | 7D | DIVIDE SHORT | — | $C(FPR1)_{0\text{-}31} \leftarrow C(FPR1)_{0\text{-}31} \div C(E2)_{0\text{-}31}$ |
| DER | *FPR1,FPR2* | RR | 3D | DIVIDE SHORT REGISTERS | — | $C(FPR1)_{0\text{-}31} \leftarrow C(FPR1)_{0\text{-}31} \div C(FPR2)_{0\text{-}31}$ |
| DP | *S1(L1),S2(L2)* or *D1(L1,B1),D2(L2,B2)* | $SS_2$ | FD | DIVIDE PACKED | — | $C(E1)_{L1\text{-}L2} \leftarrow$ Quotient of $C(E1)_{L1} \div C(E2)_{L2}$<br>$C(E1+L1-L2)_{L2} \leftarrow$ Remainder of $C(E1)_{L1} \div C(E2)_{L2}$ |
| DR | *R1,R2* | RR | 1D | DIVIDE REGISTERS | — | $C(R1+1) \leftarrow$ Quotient of $C(R1,R1+1) \div C(R2)$<br>$C(R1) \leftarrow$ Remainder of $C(R1,R1+1) \div C(R2)$ |
| DXR (*370-XA only*) | *FPR1,FPR2* | RRE | B22D | DIVIDE EXTENDED REGISTERS | — | $C(FPR1,FPR1+2) \leftarrow C(FPR1,FPR1+2) \div C(FPR2,FPR2+2)$ |
| ED | *S1(L1),S2* or *D1(L1,B1),D2(B2)* | $SS_1$ | DE | EDIT | *g* | $C(E1)_{L1} \leftarrow$ Zoned and edited packed-decimal field, or fields, at *E2*. |
| | Pattern characters: Digit Selector = X'20', Significance Starter = X'21', Field Separator = X'22' | | | | | |
| EDMK | *S1(L1),S2* or *D1(L1,B1),D2(B2)* | $SS_1$ | DF | EDIT AND MARK | *g* | $C(E1)_{L1} \leftarrow$ Zoned and edited packed-decimal field, or fields, at *E2*.<br>C(Register $1)_{8\text{-}31} \leftarrow$ Address of the first nonzero digit selected unless a previous Significance Starter forced the digit's significance. (In 31-bit addressing, bits 1–31 contain the address, and bit 0 is set to 0.) |
| EX | *R1,S2(X2)* or *R1,D2(X2,B2)* | RX | 44 | EXECUTE | — | If $R1 \neq 0$, executes the target instruction at *E2* as if its second byte had been ORed with $C(R1)_{24\text{-}31}$; the target instruction is unchanged in storage. If $R1 = 0$, executes the target instruction as is without modification. |
| HDR | *FPR1,FPR2* | RR | 24 | HALVE DOUBLE REGISTER | — | $C(FPR1)_{0\text{-}63} \leftarrow C(FPR2)_{0\text{-}63} \div 2$ |
| HER | *FPR1,FPR2* | RR | 34 | HALVE SHORT REGISTER | — | $C(FPR1)_{0\text{-}31} \leftarrow C(FPR2)_{0\text{-}31} \div 2$ |
| IC | *R1,S2(X2)* or *R1,D2(X2,B2)* | RX | 43 | INSERT CHARACTER | — | $C(R1)_{24\text{-}31} \leftarrow C(E2)_{0\text{-}7}$ |
| ICM | *R1,M3,S2* or *R1,M3,D2(B2)* | RS | BF | INSERT CHARACTERS UNDER MASK | *h* | Loads bytes in *R1*, which are selected according to the mask *M3*, from consecutive bytes at *E2*. |
| IPM | *R1* | RRE | B222 | INSERT PROGRAM MASK | — | $C(R1)_{0\text{-}7} \leftarrow 00$, cond. code, prog. mask |

*(Continued)*

| Mnemonic | Operand† | Format | Op Code | Instruction Name | Cond. Code‡ | Action |
|---|---|---|---|---|---|---|
| L | $R1,S2(X2)$ or $R1,D2(X2,B2)$ | RX | 58 | LOAD | — | $C(R1) \leftarrow C(E2)_{0\text{-}31}$ |
| LA | $R1,S2(X2)$ or $R1,D2(X2,B2)$ | RX | 41 | LOAD ADDRESS | — | With 24-bit addressing: $C(R1_{0\text{-}7} \leftarrow 0$; $C(R1)_{8\text{-}31} \leftarrow E2$<br>With 31-bit addressing: $C(R1)_0 \leftarrow 0$; $C(R1)_{1\text{-}31} \leftarrow E2$ |
| LCDR | $FPR1,FPR2$ | RR | 23 | LOAD COMPLEMENT DOUBLE REGISTER | *b* | $C(FPR1)_{0\text{-}63} \leftarrow -\ C(FPR2)_{0\text{-}63}$ |
| LCER | $FPR1,FPR2$ | RR | 33 | LOAD COMPLEMENT SHORT REGISTER | *b* | $C(FPR1)_{0\text{-}31} \leftarrow -\ C(FPR2)_{0\text{-}31}$ |
| LCR | $R1,R2$ | RR | 13 | LOAD COMPLEMENT REGISTER | *a* | $C(R1) \leftarrow$ The two's complement of $C(R2)$ |
| LD | $FPR1,S2(X2)$ or $FPR1,D2(X2,B2)$ | RX | 68 | LOAD DOUBLE | — | $C(FPR1)_{0\text{-}63} \leftarrow C(E2)_{0\text{-}63}$ |
| LDR | $FPR1,FPR2$ | RR | 28 | LOAD DOUBLE REGISTER | — | $C(FPR1)_{0\text{-}63} \leftarrow C(FPR2)_{0\text{-}63}$ |
| LE | $FPR1,S2(X2)$ or $FPR1,D2(X2,B2)$ | RX | 78 | LOAD SHORT | — | $C(FPR1)_{0\text{-}31} \leftarrow C(E2)_{0\text{-}31}$ |
| LER | $FPR1,FPR2$ | RR | 38 | LOAD SHORT REGISTER | — | $C(FPR1)_{0\text{-}31} \leftarrow C(FPR2)_{0\text{-}31}$ |
| LH | $R1,S2(X2)$ or $R1,D2(X2,B2)$ | RX | 48 | LOAD HALFWORD | — | $C(R1)_{0\text{-}31} \leftarrow F[C(E2)_{0\text{-}15}]$ |
| LM | $R1,R3,S2$ or $R1,R3,D2(B2)$ | RS | 98 | LOAD MULTIPLE | — | $C(R1), C(R1+1), \ldots, C(R3) \leftarrow C(E2), C(E2+4), \ldots$ |
| LNDR | $FPR1,FPR2$ | RR | 21 | LOAD NEGATIVE DOUBLE REGISTER | *b** | $C(FPR1)_{0\text{-}63} \leftarrow -\ \lvert C(FPR2)_{0\text{-}63}\rvert$ |
| LNER | $FPR1,FPR2$ | RR | 31 | LOAD NEGATIVE SHORT REGISTER | *b** | $C(FPR1)_{0\text{-}31} \leftarrow -\ \lvert C(FPR2)_{0\text{-}31}\rvert$ |
| LNR | $R1,R2$ | RR | 11 | LOAD NEGATIVE REGISTER | *a** | $C(R1) \leftarrow -\ \lvert C(R2)\rvert$ |

| | | | | | | |
|---|---|---|---|---|---|---|
| LPDR | *FPR1,FPR2* | RR | 20 | LOAD POSITIVE DOUBLE REGISTER | *b** | $C(FPR1)_{0\text{-}63} \leftarrow \lvert C(FPR2)_{0\text{-}63}\rvert$ |
| LPER | *FPR1,FPR2* | RR | 30 | LOAD POSITIVE SHORT REGISTER | *b** | $C(FPR1)_{0\text{-}31} \leftarrow \lvert C(FPR2)_{0\text{-}31}\rvert$ |
| LPR | *R1,R2* | RR | 10 | LOAD POSITIVE REGISTER | *a** | $C(R1) \leftarrow \lvert C(R2)\rvert$ |
| LR | *R1,R2* | RR | 18 | LOAD REGISTER | — | $C(R1) \leftarrow C(R2)$ |
| LRDR | *FPR1,FPR2* | RR | 25 | LOAD ROUNDED DOUBLE REGISTER | — | $C(FPR1)_{0\text{-}63} \leftarrow C(FPR2,FPR2+2)_{0\text{-}127}$ rounded |
| LRER | *FPR1,FPR2* | RR | 35 | LOAD ROUNDED SHORT REGISTER | — | $C(FPR1)_{0\text{-}31} \leftarrow C(FPR2)_{0\text{-}63}$ rounded |
| LTDR | *FPR1,FPR2* | RR | 22 | LOAD AND TEST DOUBLE REGISTER | *b* | $C(FPR1)_{0\text{-}63} \leftarrow C(FPR2)_{0\text{-}63}$ |
| LTER | *FPR1,FPR2* | RR | 32 | LOAD AND TEST SHORT REGISTER | *b* | $C(FPR1)_{0\text{-}31} \leftarrow C(FPR2)_{0\text{-}31}$ |
| LTR | *R1,R2* | RR | 12 | LOAD AND TEST REGISTER | *a** | $C(R1) \leftarrow C(R2)$ |
| M | *R1,S2(X2)* or *R1,D2(X2,B2)* | RX | 5C | MULTIPLY | — | $C(R1,R1+1) \leftarrow C(R1+1) * C(E2)_{0\text{-}31}$ |
| MC | *S1,I2* or *D1(B1),I2* | SI | AF | MONITOR CALL | — | If $C(\text{Control Reg. } 8)_{16+I2} = 1$, then C(Loc. 148) ← 0, C(Loc. 149) ← *I2*, C(Loc. 156) ← *E1*, and a monitor-event program interruption occurs. *I2* must be ≤ 15. |
| MD | *FPR1,S2(X2)* or *FPR1,D2(X2,B2)* | RX | 6C | MULTIPLY DOUBLE | — | $C(FPR1)_{0\text{-}63} \leftarrow C(FPR1)_{0\text{-}63} * C(E2)_{0\text{-}63}$ |
| MDR | *FPR1,FPR2* | RR | 2C | MULTIPLY DOUBLE REGISTERS | — | $C(FPR1)_{0\text{-}63} \leftarrow C(FPR1)_{0\text{-}63} * C(FPR2)_{0\text{-}63}$ |
| ME | *FPR1,S2(X2)* or *FPR1,D2(X2,B2)* | RX | 7C | MULTIPLY SHORT | — | $C(FPR1)_{0\text{-}63} \leftarrow C(FPR1)_{0\text{-}31} * C(E2)_{0\text{-}31}$ |
| MER | *FPR1,FPR2* | RR | 3C | MULTIPLY SHORT REGISTERS | — | $C(FPR1)_{0\text{-}63} \leftarrow C(FPR1)_{0\text{-}31} * C(FPR2)_{0\text{-}31}$ |

(*Continued*)

| Mnemonic | Operand[†] | Format | Op Code | Instruction Name | Cond. Code[‡] | Action |
|---|---|---|---|---|---|---|
| MH | *R1,S2(X2)* or *R1,D2(X2,B2)* | RX | 4C | MULTIPLY HALFWORD | — | $C(R1)_{0\text{-}31} \leftarrow C(R1)_{0\text{-}31} * C(E2)_{0\text{-}15}$ |
| MP | *S1(L1),S2(L2)* or *D1(L1,B1),D2(L2,B2)* | $SS_2$ | FC | MULTIPLY PACKED | — | $C(E1)_{L1} \leftarrow C(E1)_{L1} * C(E2)_{L2}$ |
| MR | *R1,R2* | RR | 1C | MULTIPLY REGISTERS | — | $C(R1,R1+1) \leftarrow C(R1+1) * C(R2)$ |
| MVC | *S1(L),S2* or *D1(L,B1),D2(B2)* | $SS_1$ | D2 | MOVE CHARACTERS | — | $C(E1)_L \leftarrow C(E2)_L$ |
| MVCIN | *S1(L),S2* or *D1(L,B1),D2(B2)* | $SS_1$ | E8 | MOVE INVERSE | — | $C(E1)_L \leftarrow C(E2-L+1)_L$ in reverse order |
| MVCL | *R1,R2* | RR | 0E | MOVE CHARACTERS LONG | *i* | Each of two even-odd register pairs that *R1* and *R2* designate contains the starting address and length of a field in storage. Replaces the first field with copies of bytes that are in the second field, which is extended on the right if necessary by copies of $C(R2+1)_{0\text{-}7}$. |
| MVI | *S1,I2* or *D1(B1),I2* | SI | 92 | MOVE IMMEDIATE | — | $C(E1) \leftarrow I2$ |
| MVN | *S1(L),S2* or *D1(L,B1),D2(B2)* | $SS_1$ | D1 | MOVE NUMERICS | — | Numerics of $C(E1)_L \leftarrow$ Numerics of $C(E2)_L$ |
| MVO | *S1(L1),S2(L2)* or *D1(L1,B1),D2(L2,B2)* | $SS_2$ | F1 | MOVE WITH OFFSET | — | $C(E1)_{0-(8*L1-5)} \leftarrow C(E2)_{L2}$ |
| MVZ | *S1(L),S2* or *D1(L,B1),D2(B2)* | $SS_1$ | D3 | MOVE ZONES | — | Zones of $C(E1)_L \leftarrow$ Zones of $C(E2)_L$ |
| MXD | *FPR1,S2(X2)* or *FPR1,D2(X2,B2)* | RX | 67 | MULTIPLY EXTENDED FROM DOUBLE | — | $C(FPR1,FPR1+2) \leftarrow C(FPR1)_{0\text{-}63} * C(E2)_{0\text{-}63}$ |
| MXDR | *FPR1,FPR2* | RR | 27 | MULTIPLY EXTENDED FROM DOUBLE REGISTERS | — | $C(FPR1,FPR1+2) \leftarrow C(FPR1)_{0\text{-}63} * C(FPR2)_{0\text{-}63}$ |
| MXR | *FPR1,FPR2* | RR | 26 | MULTIPLY EXTENDED REGISTERS | — | $C(FPR1,FPR1+2) \leftarrow C(FPR1,FPR1+2) * C(FPR2,FPR2+2)$ |

| | | | | | | |
|---|---|---|---|---|---|---|
| N | $R1,S2(X2)$ or $R1,D2(X2,B2)$ | RX | 54 | AND | *e* | $C(R1) \leftarrow C(R1)$ AND $C(E2)_{0\text{-}31}$ |
| NC | $S1(L),S2$ or $D1(L,B1),D2(B2)$ | $SS_1$ | D4 | AND CHARACTERS | *e* | $C(E1)_L \leftarrow C(E1)_L$ AND $C(E2)_L$ |
| NI | $S1,I2$ or $D1(B1),I2$ | SI | 94 | AND IMMEDIATE | *e* | $C(E1) \leftarrow C(E1)$ AND $I2$ |
| NR | $R1,R2$ | RR | 14 | AND REGISTERS | *e* | $C(R1) \leftarrow C(R1)$ AND $C(R2)$ |
| O | $R1,S2(X2)$ or $R1,D2(X2,B2)$ | RX | 56 | OR | *e* | $C(R1) \leftarrow C(R1)$ OR $C(E2)_{0\text{-}31}$ |
| OC | $S1(L),S2$ or $D1(L,B1),D2(B2)$ | $SS_1$ | D6 | OR CHARACTERS | *e* | $C(E1)_L \leftarrow C(E1)_L$ OR $C(E2)_L$ |
| OI | $S1,I2$ or $D1(B1),I2$ | SI | 96 | OR IMMEDIATE | *e* | $C(E1) \leftarrow C(E1)$ OR $I2$ |
| OR | $R1,R2$ | RR | 16 | OR REGISTERS | *e* | $C(R1) \leftarrow C(R1)$ OR $C(R2)$ |
| PACK | $S1(L1),S2(L2)$ or $D1(L1,B1),D2(L2,B2)$ | $SS_2$ | F2 | PACK | — | $C(E1)_{L1} \leftarrow$ Packed version of $C(E2)_{L2}$ |
| S | $R1,S2(X2)$ or $R1,D2(X2,B2)$ | RX | 5B | SUBTRACT | *a* | $C(R1) \leftarrow C(R1) - C(E2)_{0\text{-}31}$ |
| SAC | $D2(B2)$ | S | B219 | SET ADDRESS SPACE CONTROL | — | $C(\text{EC-mode PSW})_{16} \leftarrow C(E2)_{23}$ |
| SD | $FPR1,S2(X2)$ or $FPR1,D2(X2,B2)$ | RX | 6B | SUBTRACT DOUBLE | *b* | $C(FPR1)_{0\text{-}63} \leftarrow C(FPR1)_{0\text{-}63} - C(E2)_{0\text{-}63}$ |
| SDR | $FPR1,FPR2$ | RR | 2B | SUBTRACT DOUBLE REGISTERS | *b* | $C(FPR1)_{0\text{-}63} \leftarrow C(FPR1)_{0\text{-}63} - C(FPR2)_{0\text{-}63}$ |
| SE | $FPR1,S2(X2)$ or $FPR1,D2(X2,B2)$ | RX | 7B | SUBTRACT SHORT | *b* | $C(FPR1)_{0\text{-}31} \leftarrow C(FPR1)_{0\text{-}31} - C(E2)_{0\text{-}31}$ |
| SER | $FPR1,FPR2$ | RR | 3B | SUBTRACT SHORT REGISTERS | *b* | $C(FPR1)_{0\text{-}31} \leftarrow C(FPR1)_{0\text{-}31} - C(FPR2)_{0\text{-}31}$ |
| SH | $R1,S2(X2)$ or $R1,D2(X2,B2)$ | RX | 4B | SUBTRACT HALFWORD | *a* | $C(R1)_{0\text{-}31} \leftarrow C(R1)_{0\text{-}31} - F[C(E2)_{0\text{-}15}]$ |

*(Continued)*

| Mnemonic | Operand† | Format | Op Code | Instruction Name | Cond. Code‡ | Action |
|---|---|---|---|---|---|---|
| SL | *R1,S2(X2)* or *R1,D2(X2,B2)* | RX | 5F | SUBTRACT LOGICAL | *f** | $C(R1) \leftarrow C(R1) - C(E2)_{0\text{-}31}$ |
| SLA | *R1,D2(B2)* | RS | 8B | SHIFT LEFT ARITHMETIC | *a* | Shifts $C(R1)_{1\text{-}31}$ to the left by $n = E2$ (mod 64) bits. Bits shifted out of the left are lost; zeros fill in vacancies that are created on the right. The leftmost bit (bit 0) of *R1* remains unchanged. |
| SLDA | *R1,D2(B2)* | RS | 8F | SHIFT LEFT DOUBLE ARITHMETIC | *a* | Shifts $C(R1,R1+1)_{1\text{-}63}$ to the left by $n = E2$ (mod 64) bits. Bits shifted out of the left of *R1* are lost; zeros fill in vacancies that are created on the right of $R1+1$. The leftmost bit (bit 0) of *R1* remains unchanged. |
| SLDL | *R1,D2(B2)* | RS | 8D | SHIFT LEFT DOUBLE LOGICAL | — | Shifts $C(R1,R1+1)$ to the left by $n = E2$ (mod 64) bits. Bits shifted out of the left of *R1* are lost; zeros fill in vacancies that are created on the right of $R1+1$. |
| SLL | *R1,D2(B2)* | RS | 89 | SHIFT LEFT LOGICAL | — | Shifts $C(R1)$ to the left by $n = E2$ (mod 64) bits. Bits shifted out of the left are lost; zeros fill in vacancies that are created on the right. |
| SLR | *R1,R2* | RR | 1F | SUBTRACT LOGICAL REGISTERS | *f** | $C(R1) \leftarrow C(R1) - C(R2)$ |
| SP | *S1(L1),S2(L2)* or *D1(L1,B1),D2(L2,B2)* | $SS_2$ | FB | SUBTRACT PACKED | *a* | $C(E1)_{L1} \leftarrow C(E1)_{L1} - C(E2)_{L2}$ |
| SPM | *R1* | RR | 04 | SET PROGRAM MASK | *x* | Condition code $\leftarrow C(R1)_{2\text{-}3}$<br>Program mask $\leftarrow C(R1)_{4\text{-}7}$ |
| SR | *R1,R2* | RR | 1B | SUBTRACT REGISTERS | *a* | $C(R1) \leftarrow C(R1) - C(R2)$ |
| SRA | *R1,D2(B2)* | RS | 8A | SHIFT RIGHT ARITHMETIC | *a** | Shifts $C(R1)_{1\text{-}31}$ to the right by $n = E2$ (mod 64) bits. Bits shifted out of the right are lost; copies of bit 0, which remains unchanged, fill in vacancies that are created on the left. |
| SRDA | *R1,D2(B2)* | RS | 8E | SHIFT RIGHT DOUBLE ARITHMETIC | *a** | Shifts $C(R1,R1+1)_{1\text{-}63}$ to the right by $n = E2$ (mod 64) bits. Bits shifted out of the right of $R1+1$ are lost; copies of bit 0, which remains unchanged, fill in vacancies that are created on the left of *R1*. |

| | | | | | | |
|---|---|---|---|---|---|---|
| SRDL | *R1,D2(B2)* | RS | 8C | SHIFT RIGHT DOUBLE LOGICAL | — | Shifts C(*R1,R1*+1) to the right by $n = E2$ (mod 64) bits. Bits shifted out of the right of *R1*+1 are lost; zeros fill in vacancies that are created on the left of *R1*. |
| SRL | *R1,D2(B2)* | RS | 88 | SHIFT RIGHT LOGICAL | — | Shifts C(*R1*) to the right by $n = E2$ (mod 64) bits. Bits shifted out of the right are lost; zeros fill in vacancies that are created on the left. |
| SRP | *S1(L1),D2(B2),I3* or *D1(L1,B1),D2(B2),I3* | $SS_2$ | F0 | SHIFT AND ROUND PACKED | *a* | Shifts $C(E1)_{L1}$ by $\|n\|$ places where $n = E2$ (mod 64) represents a signed value. The shift is to the left if *n* is positive, and to the right if *n* is negative. *I3* is the rounding digit for right shifts. |
| ST | *R1,S2(X2)* or *R1,D2(X2,B2)* | RX | 50 | STORE | — | $C(E2)_{0\text{-}31} \leftarrow C(R1)$ |
| STC | *R1,S2(X2)* or *R1,D2(X2,B2)* | RX | 42 | STORE CHARACTER | — | $C(E2)_{0\text{-}7} \leftarrow C(R1)_{24-31}$ |
| STCK | *S2* or *D2(B2)* | S | B205 | STORE CLOCK | *j* | $C(E2)_{0\text{-}63} \leftarrow \begin{cases} \text{TOD clock, if the clock is either in the set, stopped, or in a not-set state} \\ \text{0, if the clock is in either the error or the not-operational state} \end{cases}$ |
| STCM | *R1,M3,S2* or *R1,M3,D2(B2)* | RS | BE | STORE CHARACTERS UNDER MASK | — | Stores bytes of *R1*, which are selected according to the mask *M3*, into the consecutive bytes at *E2*. |
| STD | *FPR1,S2(X2)* or *FPR1,D2(X2,B2)* | RX | 60 | STORE DOUBLE | — | $C(E2)_{0\text{-}63} \leftarrow C(FPR1)_{0\text{-}63}$ |
| STE | *FPR1,S2(X2)* or *FPR1,D2(X2,B2)* | RX | 70 | STORE SHORT | — | $C(E2)_{0\text{-}31} \leftarrow C(FPR1)_{0\text{-}31}$ |
| STH | *R1,S2(X2)* or *R1,D2(X2,B2)* | RX | 40 | STORE HALFWORD | — | $C(E2)_{0\text{-}15} \leftarrow C(R1)_{16\text{-}31}$ |
| STM | *R1,R3,S2* or *R1,R3,D2(B2)* | RS | 90 | STORE MULTIPLE | — | $C(E2), C(E2+4), \ldots \leftarrow C(R1), C(R1+1), \ldots C(R3)$ |
| SU | *FPR1,S2(X2)* or *FPR1,D2(X2,B2)* | RX | 7F | SUBTRACT UNNORMALIZED SHORT | *b* | $C(FPR1)_{0\text{-}31} \leftarrow C(FPR1)_{0\text{-}31} - C(E2)_{0\text{-}31}$ |

(*Continued*)

| Mnemonic | Operand[†] | Format | Op Code | Instruction Name | Cond. Code[‡] | Action |
|---|---|---|---|---|---|---|
| SUR | *FPR1,FPR2* | RR | 3F | SUBTRACT UNNORMALIZED SHORT REGISTERS | *b* | $C(FPR1)_{0\text{-}31} \leftarrow C(FPR1)_{0\text{-}31} - C(FPR2)_{0\text{-}31}$ |
| SVC | *I* | RR | 0A | SUPERVISOR CALL | — | Causes a supervisor-call interruption with an interruption code of 0*I*. |
| SW | *FPR1,S2(X2)* or *FPR1,D2(X2,B2)* | RX | 6F | SUBTRACT UNNORMALIZED DOUBLE | *b* | $C(FPR1)_{0\text{-}63} \leftarrow C(FPR1)_{0\text{-}63} - C(E2)_{0\text{-}63}$ |
| SWR | *FPR1,FPR2* | RR | 2F | SUBTRACT UNNORMALIZED DOUBLE REGISTERS | *b* | $C(FPR1)_{0\text{-}63} \leftarrow C(FPR1)_{0\text{-}63} - C(FPR2)_{0\text{-}63}$ |
| SXR | *FPR1,FPR2* | RR | 37 | SUBTRACT EXTENDED REGISTERS | *b* | $C(FPR1,FPR1+2) \leftarrow C(FPR1,FPR1+2) - C(FPR2,FPR2+2)$ |
| TM | *S1,I2* or *D1(B1),I2* | SI | 91 | TEST UNDER MASK | *k* | Tests bits of C(*E1*) that are selected according to *I2*. |
| TR | *S1(L),S2* or *D1(L,B1),D2(B2)* | $SS_1$ | DC | TRANSLATE | — | Translates *L* bytes as follows:<br>$C(E1) \leftarrow C(E2 + C(E1))$<br>$C(E1+1) \leftarrow C(E2 + C(E1+1))$<br>and so on. |
| TRT | *S1(L),S2* or *D1(L,B1),D2(B2)* | $SS_1$ | DD | TRANSLATE AND TEST | *x* | Each of a maximum of *L* consecutive argument bytes at *E1*, which are considered from left to right, references a function byte in the table at *E2* in exactly the same manner as the TR instruction, except that the arguments are unchanged. This referencing continues until one of the following occurs.<br>1. A nonzero function byte is referenced:<br>$C(\text{Reg. }1)_{8\text{-}31} \leftarrow$ Address of the argument byte that references the nonzero function byte.<br>(With 31-bit addressing, the address is placed in bits 1–31 of Register 1 and bit 0 is 0.)<br>$C(\text{Reg. }2)_{24\text{-}31} \leftarrow$ Contents of the function byte. |

$$\text{Condition code} = \begin{cases} 1, \text{ in case the argument byte is not the last (rightmost) one in the first operand} \\ 2, \text{ in case the argument is the last one in the first operand} \end{cases}$$

2. All arguments are considered and all function bytes are zero:

   Condition code = 0
   Registers 1 and 2 remain unchanged.

| | | | | | | |
|---|---|---|---|---|---|---|
| TS | $S2$ or $D2(B2)$ | S | 93 | TEST AND SET | $x$ | Condition code $\leftarrow C(E2)_0$<br>$C(E2) \leftarrow FF_{16}$ |
| UNPK | $S1(L1),S2(L2)$ or $D1(L1,B1),D2(L2,B2)$ | $SS_2$ | F3 | UNPACK | — | $C(E1)_{L1} \leftarrow$ Zoned version of $C(E2)_{L2}$ |
| X | $R1,S2(X2)$ or $R1,D2(X2,B2)$ | RX | 57 | EXCLUSIVE OR | $e$ | $C(R1) \leftarrow C(R1)$ EX. OR $C(E2)_{0\text{-}31}$ |
| XC | $S1(L),S2$ or $D1(L,B1),D2(B2)$ | $SS_1$ | D7 | EXCLUSIVE OR CHARACTERS | $e$ | $C(E1)_L \leftarrow C(E1)_L$ EX. OR $C(E2)_L$ |
| XI | $S1,I2$ or $D1(B1),I2$ | SI | 97 | EXCLUSIVE OR IMMEDIATE | $e$ | $C(E1) \leftarrow C(E1)$ EX. OR $I2$ |
| XR | $R1,R2$ | RR | 17 | EXCLUSIVE OR REGISTERS | $e$ | $C(R1) \leftarrow C(R1)$ EX. OR $C(R2)$ |
| ZAP | $S1(L1),S2(L2)$ or $D1(L1,B1),D2(L2,B2)$ | $SS_2$ | F8 | ZERO AND ADD PACKED | $a$ | $C(E1)_{L1} \leftarrow 0 + C(E2)_{L2}$ |

## *Operand Notes*

1. You can write an RX instruction's second operand entry in implicit form without an index register as *S2*.
2. In addition to the forms of the operand entry that are indicated for the $SS_1$ instructions given earlier, you also can write one of the following:
   *S1,S2*
   *S1(L),D2(B2)*
   *S1,D2(B2)*
   *D1(L,B1),S2*
3. In addition to the forms of the operand entry that are indicated for the $SS_2$ instructions given earlier, you also can write one of the following:
   *S1,S2*
   *S1,D2(L2,B2)*
   *S1(L1),D2(L2,B2)*
   *D1(L1,B1),S2*
   *D1(L1,B1),S2(L2)*

## *Condition Code Settings*

The following notation indicates the condition code settings for the instructions given in this appendix. When an asterisk appears in the condition code column of a particular instruction, certain settings differ for that instruction. These differences are noted here.

*a* 0 if the result = 0
1 if the result < 0
2 if the result > 0
3 if overflow occurs
* LNR: only 0 or 1
LPR: not 1
LTR: not 3
SRA: not 3
SRDA: not 3

*b* 0 if the result fraction = 0
1 if the result < 0
2 if the result > 0
* LNDR and LNER: not 2
LPDR and LPER: not 1

*c* 0 if the comparison is equal
1 if the comparison is less than
2 if the comparison is greater than
* CLM: also 0 if *M3* = 0

*d* 0 if operands are equal
1 if operands are unequal

*e* 0 if the result is zero
1 if the result is nonzero

*f* 0 if no carry, zero result
1 if no carry, nonzero result
2 if carry, zero result
3 if carry, nonzero result
* SL and SLR: not 0

*g* 0 if the last field edited is zero, or if no Digit Selector or Significance Starter codes are encountered while editing the last field
1 if the last field edited is nonzero and the Significance Indicator is on at the conclusion of the instruction
2 if the last field edited is nonzero and the Significance Indicator is off at the conclusion of the instruction

*h* 0 if the inserted bytes are zero or if *M3* = 0
1 if the leftmost bit of the inserted bytes is 1
2 if the inserted bytes are not zero, but the leftmost bit is 0

*i* 0 if $L_1 = L_2$
1 if $L_1 < L_2$
2 if $L_1 > L_2$
3 if no bytes are moved due to destructive overlap

*j* 0 if set state
1 if not-set state
2 if error state
3 if stopped state or not-operational state

*k* 0 if all selected bits are 0's or if *I2* = 0
1 if some selected bits are 0's and other bits are 1's
3 if all selected bits are 1's

*x* Condition code settings appear in the Action column

# APPENDIX F Assembler Directives

| Name† | Operation | Operand† | Directive Name | Action |
|---|---|---|---|---|
| *seq-symbol* or *blank* | ACTR | *arith-expr* | ASSEMBLY-TIME COUNTER | Limits the number of AIF and AGO directives that the assembler processes within the macro definition to the value that the operand entry specifies. |
| *seq-symbol* or *blank* | AGO | *seq-symbol* | ASSEMBLY-TIME GO TO | Directs the assembler to process the statement that the sequence symbol in the operand entry identifies. |
| *seq-symbol* or *blank* | AIF | (*log-expr*) *seq-symbol* | ASSEMBLY-TIME IF | If the logical expression has a value of 1, directs the assembler to process the statement that the sequence symbol in the operand entry identifies. If the logical expression has a value of 0, directs the assembler to process the next sequential statement. |
| *seq-symbol* or *blank* | ANOP | none | ASSEMBLY-TIME NO OPERATION | No operation |
| *any-symbol* or *blank* (Name entry in DOS: *seq-symbol* or *blank*) | CNOP | *byte,group* | CONDITIONAL NO-OPERATION | If necessary, generates No-Op instructions to force alignment to the byte number that is indicated by *byte* within a fullword (*group* = 4) or doubleword (*group* = 8); *byte* and *group* are absolute expressions. Only *byte* values 0, 2, 4, and 6 are permitted. |
| *any-symbol* or *blank* (Name entry in DOS: *blank*) | COM | none | DEFINE COMMON SECTION | Initiates or resumes a common section. |
| *blank* | COPY | *symbol* | COPY LIBRARY | Inserts into the source module a copy of source statements from a portion of a library; *symbol* identifies this portion. |
| *any-symbol* or *blank* | CSECT | none | DEFINE CONTROL SECTION | Initiates or resumes a control section. |

| Name† | Operation | Operand† | Directive Name | Action |
|---|---|---|---|---|
| *any-symbol* or *blank* | CXD†† | none | CUMULATIVE EXTERNAL DUMMY SECTION LENGTH | Reserves a fullword into which the loader will store the total length of all external dummy sections. |
| *any-symbol* or *blank* | DC | *dtLn'c'* or *dtLn(c)* | DEFINE CONSTANT | Defines *d* copies of the constant *c* of type *t* and length *n*; *d* and L*n* are optional. (Use parentheses instead of apostrophes to enclose *c* when *t* = A, Y, S, V, or Q.) |

| *t* | Alignment | Constant | Truncation/ Padding |
|---|---|---|---|
| B | byte | unsigned binary digits | left |
| C | byte | characters | right |
| X | byte | unsigned hex digits | left |
| F | fullword | signed binary integer | left |
| H | halfword | signed binary integer | left |
| E | fullword | short floating-point | right |
| D | doubleword | long floating-point | right |
| L | doubleword | extended floating-point | right |
| P | byte | packed-decimal | left |
| Z | byte | zoned-decimal | left |
| A | fullword | value of address | left |
| Y | halfword | value of address | left |
| S | halfword | base-displacement address | — |
| V | fullword | externally defined address value | left |
| Q | fullword | symbol that defines a DXD or DSECT | left |

| Name† | Operation | Operand† | Directive Name | Action |
|---|---|---|---|---|
| *seq-symbol* or *blank* | DROP | *R1*[,*R2*, . . .] or *blank* | DROP BASE REGISTERS | Removes the listed registers from the pool of available base registers. (Or, if the operand entry is blank, removes all registers from the pool.) |
| *any-symbol* or *blank* | DS | *dtLn'c'* | DEFINE STORAGE | Reserves storage as described by the operand entry, which has the same meaning as in the DC directive. However, DS does not define constants. (*'c'* is optional.) |
| *any-symbol* or *blank* (Name entry in DOS: *symbol* or *var-symbol*) | DSECT | none | DEFINE DUMMY SECTION | Initiates or resumes a dummy section. |
| *any-symbol* | DXD†† | *dtLn'c'* | DEFINE EXTERNAL DUMMY SECTION | Defines an external dummy section. The operand entry is the same as for DS. |
| *seq-symbol* or *blank* | EJECT | *blank* | SKIP TO A NEW PAGE | Prints the next line of the source program at the top of a new page. |
| *seq-symbol* or *blank* | END | *rel-expr* or *blank* | END SOURCE MODULE | Signals the end of a source module. The *rel-expr* identifies the entry point. |

| Name† | Operation | Operand† | Directive Name | Action |
|---|---|---|---|---|
| *seq-symbol* or *blank* | ENTRY | *rel-symbol, . . .* | IDENTIFY ENTRY SYMBOLS | Declares the symbols that are listed in the operand entry to be entry symbols. |
| *symbol* or *var-symbol* | EQU | *expression* | EQUATE SYMBOL | Defines *symbol* and assigns to it a value that is equal to *expression*, which is either absolute or relocatable. |
| *seq-symbol* or *blank* | EXTRN | *rel-symbol, . . .* | IDENTIFY EXTERNAL SYMBOLS | Declares the symbols that are listed in the operand entry to be external symbols. |
| *blank* | {GBLA GBLB GBLC} | *var-symbol*[(*dimension*)], . . . | DECLARE GLOBAL SET SYMBOLS | Declares the variable symbols in the operand entry to be global SET symbols that are either arithmetic (GBLA), Boolean (GBLB), or character (GBLC). Initializes arithmetic and Boolean SET symbols to 0, and character SET symbols to the null string. The *dimension* is an optional self-defining term that, if present, indicates that the SET symbol is an array with *dimension* elements. |
| *blank* | ICTL | *b* or *b,e* or *b,e,c* | INPUT FORMAT CONTROL | Defines the begin (*b*), end (*e*), and continue (*c*) columns of all source statements that follow. |
| *blank* | ISEQ | *l,r* or *blank* | INPUT SEQUENCE CHECK | Initiates sequence checking of source statements by examining columns *l* through *r*. Terminates sequence checking when the operand entry is *blank*. |
| *blank* | {LCLA LCLB LCLC} | *var-symbol*[(*dimension*)], . . . | DECLARE LOCAL SET SYMBOLS | Declares and initializes local SET symbols in the same way as the GBL*x* directives. |
| *any-symbol* or *blank* | LTORG | *blank* | LITERAL ORIGIN | Positions the literal pool—which was created since the beginning of the program or since the last LTORG—at the next doubleword boundary after the occurrence of the LTORG in the program. |
| *blank* | MACRO | none | BEGIN MACRO DEFINITION | Initiates a macro definition. |
| *seq-symbol* or *blank* | MEND | none | END MACRO DEFINITION | Terminates a macro definition. |
| *seq-symbol* or *blank* | MEXIT | none | MACRO EXIT | Terminates the processing of a macro definition. |

*(Continued)*

| Name† | Operation | Operand† | Directive Name | Action |
|---|---|---|---|---|
| *seq-symbol* or *blank* | MNOTE | [*n*,]'*message*' | MACRO NOTE | Generates a *message* in the macro expansion. If *n* is between 0 and 255, sets a severity code to *n* and generates an error message. If *n* is omitted or is an asterisk, generates the message as a comments statement. |
| *symbol* | OPSYN†† | *opcode* or *blank* | OP CODE SYNONYM | Assigns to *symbol* the meaning of *opcode*; or when the operand entry is blank, invalidates *symbol* as an op code. |
| *any-symbol* or *blank* (Name entry in DOS: *seq-symbol* or *blank*) | ORG | *rel-expr* or *blank* | ORIGIN | Sets the location counter to the value of *rel-expr.* If the operand entry is omitted, resets the location counter to the highest value attained so far. |
| *seq-symbol* or *blank* | POP†† | PRINT or USING or PRINT,USING or USING,PRINT | RESTORE PRINT/ USING STATUS | Restores the status of PRINT or USING that the most recent PUSH saved. |
| *seq-symbol* or *blank* | PRINT | [ON / OFF] [GEN / ,NOGEN] [NODATA / ,DATA] | PRINT DETAILS | Controls the amount of detail in the assembly listing.<br>ON/OFF: Prints or does not print a listing<br>GEN/NOGEN: Prints or does not print macro expansions<br>DATA/NODATA: Prints all bytes or leftmost 8 bytes of constants. |
| *seq-symbol* or *blank* | PUNCH | '*string*' | PUNCH A CARD | Punches the characters in *string* into a card. |
| *seq-symbol* or *blank* | PUSH†† | (same as POP) | SAVE PRINT/ USING STATUS | Saves the current status of PRINT and USING. |
| *seq-symbol* or *blank* | REPRO | none | REPRODUCE CARD | Punches the data that follows REPRO into a card. |
| *var-symbol* | SETA | *arith-expr* | ASSIGN VALUE TO SETA SYMBOL | Evaluates the arithmetic expression and assigns the resulting signed 32-bit value to the SETA symbol that appears in the name entry. |
| *var-symbol* | SETB | (*log-expr*) or 0 or 1 | ASSIGN VALUE TO SETB SYMBOL | Assigns the value in the operand entry to the SETB symbol that appears in the name entry. |
| *var-symbol* | SETC | '*string*' or T'*symbol* or '*string*'(*s1*,*s2*) | ASSIGN VALUE TO SETC SYMBOL | Assigns the value in the operand entry to the SETC symbol that appears in the name entry. The entries *s1* and *s2* are arithmetic expressions, and *symbol* is an ordinary or variable symbol. |

| Name† | Operation | Operand† | Directive Name | Action |
|---|---|---|---|---|
| *seq-symbol* or *blank* | SPACE | *n* | INSERT BLANK LINES | Inserts *n* blank lines into the listing of the source program. If *n* is omitted, assumes *n* = 1. |
| *any-symbol* or *blank* | START | *blank* or *self-defining term* | DEFINE FIRST CONTROL SECTION | Initiates the first control section. Initializes the location counter to the value, if any, in the operand entry. |
| *any-symbol* or *blank* | TITLE | *'string'* | CREATE HEADER | Provides a heading for each page of the assembly listing; *string* consists of up to 100 characters. |
| *seq-symbol* or *blank* | USING | *S,R1*[*,R2,R3*. . .] | DECLARE BASE REGISTERS | Adds the listed registers to the assembler's pool of available base registers. The assembler assumes that *R1* contains the address *S*, *R2* contains the address *S* + 4096, *R3* contains the address *S* + 8192, and so on. |
| *seq-symbol* or *blank* | WXTRN | *rel-symbol*, . . . | IDENTIFY WEAK EXTERNAL SYMBOLS | Same as EXTRN, but does not search libraries. |

† Here is a summary of the notation used:

| | |
|---|---|
| *symbol* | ordinary symbol |
| *seq-symbol* | sequence symbol |
| *var-symbol* | variable symbol |
| *any-symbol* | ordinary symbol, sequence symbol, or variable symbol |
| *rel-symbol* | relocatable symbol |
| *arith-expr* | arithmetic expression |
| *rel-expr* | relocatable expression |
| *log-expr* | logical expression |

†† OS only

APPENDIX G

# Summary of Program Exceptions and Interruption Codes

| Interruption Code | Name of Exception | Cause | Relevant Instructions |
|---|---|---|---|
| | Access: | Reference to an operand that is in a protected portion of storage, or reference to an invalid address. | Any instruction that references storage. |
| 0004 | Protection | | |
| 0005 | Addressing | | |
| 0010 | Segment translation | | |
| 0011 | Page translation | | |
| 0012 | Translation specification | | |
| 0007 | Data | Any of the following: | |
| | | • Invalid digit or sign codes in the fields that are specified by either operand of AP, SP, MP, DP, or CP; the first operand of SRP, ED, or EDMK; or the second operand of ZAP or CVB. | AP, CP, CVB, DP, ED, EDMK, MP, SP, SRP, ZAP |
| | | • An invalid rounding digit in SRP, even if it is not used. | SRP |
| | | • Improper field overlap in AP, SP, MP, DP, CP, or ZAP. | AP, CP, DP, MP, SP, ZAP |
| | | • The MP instruction when its first operand field does not contain *L2* bytes of leading zeros. | MP |
| 000B | Decimal Divide | The DP instruction when any of the following is true:<br>• The quotient exceeds *L1* − *L2* bytes.<br>• The divisor is zero.<br>• The leftmost digit of the dividend is not zero. | DP |
| 000A | Decimal Overflow | The first operand field cannot contain the results of the operation. | AP, SP, ZAP, SRP |
| 0003 | Execute | The target instruction of an EX is an EX instruction. | EX |
| 000C | Exponent Overflow | The correct characteristic exceeds $7F_{16}$. | Floating-point Add, Subtract, Multiply, Divide, or Round |
| 000D | Exponent Underflow | The correct characteristic is less than zero. | Floating-point normalized Add, normalized Subtract, Multiply, Divide, or Halve |

| Interruption Code | Name of Exception | Cause | Relevant Instructions |
|---|---|---|---|
| 0009 | Fixed-Point Divide | Either of the following: | |
| | | • The divisor is 0 or the quotient exceeds 32 bits. | D, DR |
| | | • The result exceeds 32 bits. | CVB |
| 0008 | Fixed-Point Overflow | Either of the following: | |
| | | • The carry into the leftmost bit position differs from the carry out of that bit position. | A, AH, AR, LCR, LPR, S, SH, SR |
| | | • The leftmost bit differs from any bit that is shifted out. | SLA, SLDA |
| 000F | Floating-Point Divide | The divisor has a zero fraction. | DD, DDR, DE, DER, DXR |
| 0001 | Operation | Attempting to execute an instruction that has an invalid op code. | All invalid op codes |
| 0002 | Privileged Operation | Attempting to execute either a privileged instruction while the CPU is in the problem state or a semiprivileged instruction without authorization while the CPU is in the problem state. | All privileged and semiprivileged instructions |
| 000E | Significance | The fraction of the result is zero. | Floating-point Add or Subtract |
| 0006 | Specification | Any of the following is true: | |
| | | • The IA portion of the PSW contains an odd address. | All Branch instructions |
| | | • The first register operand is odd-numbered. | CLCL, D, DR, M, MR, MVCL, SLDL, SLDA, SRDL, SRDA |
| | | • The target address is not a halfword boundary. | EX |
| | | • $L2 > 8$ or $L2 \geqslant L1$. | DP, MP |
| | | • A floating-point register operand entry is not 0, 2, 4, or 6; an extended-precision register operand entry is not 0 or 4. | All floating-point instructions |
| | | • The storage operand is not on an appropriate integral boundary. | CDS, CS |
| | | • Bits 8–11 of the instruction are not 0's. | MC |
| | | • Bits 20–22 of the second operand address are not 0's. | SAC |
| | | *The following apply to the IBM 360:* | |
| | | • The storage operand is not a halfword. | AH, CH, LH, MH, SH, STH |
| | | • The storage operand is not a fullword. | A, AE, AL, AU, C, CE, CL, D, DE, L, LE, LM, M, ME, N, O, S, SE, SL, ST, STE, STM, SU, X |
| | | • The storage operand is not a doubleword. | AD, AW, CD, CVB, CVD, DD, LD, MD, SD, STD, SW |

# APPENDIX H The Conversational Monitor System (CMS)

## Introduction

In addition to OS, DOS, and their virtual memory variations, IBM also offers **VM.** VM is not an operating system like OS and DOS: it provides a virtual System/370 on which you can run any operating system that you choose, including another copy of VM. The **control program (CP)** component of VM provides the facilities of a system console that controls the virtual machine. The CP also provides powerful tools for debugging any program, including an operating system, that runs on the virtual machine.

The **Conversational Monitor System (CMS)** is a simple interactive, single-user operating system that runs on the virtual machine that VM defines. CMS provides almost all of the facilities of OS, an interactive editor, its own file system, additional assembler macros that take advantage of the interactive environment, and a set of its own debugging tools. With certain restrictions, you may run unmodified OS assembler language programs or programs that you modify to use CMS macros. To take maximum advantage of the debugging tools that CMS and VM provide, you must know both the location of your program in the memory of the virtual machine, and the contents of the registers of the virtual machine at any time during program execution. You can do this easily under OS by looking at an assembly listing.

## Command Environments

The virtual machine can be in one of the following states:

- **CP command environment,** in which the machine expects a CP command.
- **CMS command environment,** in which the machine expects a CMS or a CP command.
- **CMS edit environment,** in which the machine expects additions or changes to a program file.
- **CMS debug environment,** in which the machine expects debug subcommands.
- **Executing a CMS program.**
- **Virtual console read environment,** in which the machine expects input in response to a request by a CMS program.

Initially, your virtual machine is in the CP command environment. When in this environment, you can use only CP commands. If the virtual machine is in another environment, you can temporarily enter the CP command environment either by typing #CP or by pressing the Attention key. To return to the original environment and begin execution of the virtual machine, you can type CP BEGIN.

To enter the CMS command environment from the CP environment, type CP IPL CMS. Normally, you would do this only once per terminal session. If you want to execute a CP command while you are in CMS mode, you type #CP, followed by at least one blank and the CMS command. While your machine is in CMS mode, you can enter either the edit environment to create or modify a file, or the debug environment. This appendix does not describe the CMS editor, but you can learn about it by consulting the following IBM reference manuals: *CMS User's Guide* and *CMS Command and Macro Reference.*

When the virtual machine is executing a command or a program, you must press the Attention key to halt execution and to change to the CMS command environment before you can enter a command. You then can do one of the following:

- Enter a null line to continue execution.
- Enter HX to stop program execution permanently and to return to the CMS command environment. This is the typical way to halt a program that is in an infinite loop.
- Enter either HT to halt the terminal display and to resume execution, or RT to resume the terminal display.
- Enter other CMS commands. The system stacks these commands, resumes program execution, and processes the stacked commands after program execution is complete.
- Enter #CP followed by a blank and a CP command. The virtual machine will execute this command and then resume execution of the task that was halted earlier.
- Enter #CP to place the machine into the CP command environment.

When your program requests an input record, the machine enters the virtual console read environment. You cannot enter CMS commands because the program will

When your program requests an input record, the machine enters the virtual console read environment. You cannot enter CMS commands because the program will treat them as input. However, you can enter #CP followed by a blank and a CP command. The machine executes this command and the environment then changes back to virtual console read.

## The CMS File System

A virtual machine normally has several **virtual disks** that resemble real disks in their logical structure, but have a much smaller capacity. The machine can create additional virtual disks that are temporary. Although a virtual disk has a virtual hardware address, you usually designate the disk by using a letter identifier. All of the examples in this appendix use the letter A as an identifier and, thus, use the **A-disk.** The A-disk is the primary user disk for read/write operations. CMS automatically accesses the A-disk when you begin a terminal session.

You can create a CMS file either by using the CMS editor or by running a program under CMS. To read or write a CMS file, you must reference it by its name, called the **file identifier,** which consists of three fields: the **filename,** or **fn;** the **filetype,** or **ft;** and the **filemode,** or **fm.** The filename and the filetype each consist of one to eight alphanumeric characters. Although there are no reserved filenames, you should not use a CMS command name or a CP command name as a filename because you will often use a filename to name a user-defined command. Certain filetypes, called **reserved filetypes,** have special meaning to CMS. For example, the filetype of a program that you will assemble must be ASSEMBLE. The filemode consists of one or two characters: a letter that specifies the virtual disk and an optional digit that specifies the **access mode.** Typically, you will omit the digit: CMS will assume an access mode of 1, which indicates unrestricted read access and write access to the file. If you omit the filemode, CMS uses the A-disk.

To a CMS program, a CMS file may appear to have any of the formats of sequential, partitioned, or direct data sets. However, the files are actually in a system-specified format that CMS converts as necessary. For this reason, CMS cannot obtain the block size from an existing blocked data set: you must specify the block size in such cases. CMS can also read but not write OS sequential and partitioned files that are located on OS disks. This capability is beyond the scope of this appendix and will not be discussed further.

**The TYPE command.** You can display all or a portion of a CMS file by using the TYPE command. Its format is as follows:

TYPE *fn ft* [*fm*] [*rec1*] [*rec2*] [(*options*]

The command displays records whose record numbers range from *rec1* to *rec2*. If you omit *rec1*, CMS assumes a value of 1; if you omit *rec2*, CMS displays records until it reaches the end of the file. TYPE displays the file in EBCDIC unless you specify HEX as one of the *options*—in which case, TYPE displays the hexadecimal representations of the EBCDIC characters. You can also specify COL *xxxxx-yyyyy* as an option: this causes TYPE to display only columns *xxxxx* through *yyyyy* of each record in the designated range. (Although you can write a closing parenthesis after *options*, it is not required.)

## Assembling and Running OS Assembler Programs

Suppose that you have created a file that contains the source statements of your program by using the CMS editor. The filetype must be ASSEMBLE.

**The GLOBAL command.** By using the GLOBAL command, you must make available to CMS any macro libraries that your program needs during assembly.

Once per terminal session and before you assemble a program, enter the following command:

```
GLOBAL MACLIB CMSLIB OSMACRO OSMACRO1
```

This command defines the following macro libraries: CMSLIB, which contains the CMS macros; OSMACRO, which contains the OS macros that are simulated by CMS; and OSMACRO1, which contains the other OS macros that you can use under CMS.

**The ASSEMBLE command.** You invoke the VM assembler by writing the command

ASSEMBLE *fn*

You can abbreviate ASSEMBLE as A. (This appendix will indicate abbreviations by boldfacing them, as was done here.) The assembler creates two files: *fn* TEXT, which contains the object module, and *fn* LISTING, which contains the assembly listing. The assembler places both files on the same disk on which you placed the source file *fn* ASSEMBLE. Assembly time error messages appear both at the terminal and in the file *fn* LISTING. You correct errors by using the CMS editor and then by assembling your program again.

**The LOAD command.** After assembly, you must load the object module by writing the command

LOAD *fn*

This command loads the file named *fn* TEXT into virtual memory at the address $20000_{16}$. If you must load several object modules that result from separate assemblies, write the filenames of the corresponding TEXT files, separated by blanks, in the operand entry of a single LOAD command. Any unresolved external references will produce an error message at the terminal.

**The START command.** To begin execution of your program, write the command START. Any nonzero completion code will appear at the terminal.

## Using OS Macros for I/O

When you use CMS to develop programs that you intend to run in an OS batch environment, it is helpful to use the standard OS macros for I/O. CMS simulates many of these macros, including all of the QSAM macros and BSAM macros that Chapter 16 describes.

**The FILEDEF command.** You use the FILEDEF command to logically connect a data set to a device or file. The command has the following form:

FILEDEF *ddname device* [(*optionA* [*optionB*]]

This notation is defined as follows.

- *ddname* is the symbol that identifies the file in your program. This symbol appears in the DDNAME portion of the DCB macro.
- *device* has one of the following values:

PRINTER specifies the spooled printer.
TERMINAL specifies your terminal. Terminal I/O uses unblocked records and input records can be no longer than 130 characters.
DISK *fn ft* [*fm*] specifies a CMS file on a virtual disk.
DUMMY indicates that no I/O takes place for this data set.
CLEAR removes any definition that might exist for the *ddname*.

- *optionA* has one of the following values:

PERM retains the present definition until you clear or change it by using another FILEDEF command.
RECFM *a* specifies the file's record format, where *a* is any of the formats that Chapter 16 describes.
LRECL *nnnnn* is the logical record length.
BLKSIZE *nnnnn* is the block size.

- *optionB* appears only when *device* is DISK. It has one of the following values:

DISP MOD specifies that you will add records at the end of an output file.
MEMBER *membername* specifies the name of a member of a partitioned data set.

---

EXAMPLE 1

**Terminal Input and Output by Using QSAM Macros**

Assume that you have used the CMS editor to create the file named DEMO ASSEMBLE A, which contains the program shown in Figure H.1. If you have not already done so, you should type the GLOBAL command that was described earlier. To assemble, load, and execute the program, type the following commands:

```
A DEMO
FILEDEF IN T (LRECL 20
FILEDEF OUT T
LOAD DEMO
START
```

Note that you must specify LRECL in the FILEDEF command for the input file because LRECL does not appear in the DCB at FILE1 in Figure H.1. (Here, CMS determines the block size and record format by default.) However, since LRECL does appear in the DCB at FILE2, you omit LRECL from the FILEDEF command for the output file.

When your program executes a GET, CMS sends a prompt character—often a period—to your terminal. You type the input record and then press a carriage return. The program responds by writing the record, which it just read, on your terminal. Pressing a carriage return without an input record creates an end-of-file condition that the program in Figure H.1 recognizes as a signal to terminate execution. If you want the final version of this program to be interactive, you should include a prompt that describes the input data.

---

EXAMPLE 2

**CMS File Input and Output by Using QSAM Macros**

Reconsider the program in Figure H.1, but read input records from the file DEMO INPUT A instead of from the terminal. Assume that you have created the file DEMO INPUT A by using the CMS editor, and that you specified the logical record length as 20. The program will write its output records on the file DEMO OUTPUT A. To assemble, load, and execute the program, type the following commands:

```
A DEMO
FILEDEF IN DISK DEMO INPUT A (RECFM F
FILEDEF OUT DISK DEMO OUTPUT A
LOAD DEMO
START
```

```
** COPY FILES BY USING QSAM
DEMO     CSECT
     (standard entry)
         OPEN   (FILE1,INPUT,FILE2,OUTPUT)
* NOTE THAT THERE IS NO PROMPT FOR INPUT, SINCE THE FINAL
* VERSION OF THIS PROGRAM WILL NOT BE INTERACTIVE.
* REPEAT UNTIL END-OF-FILE:
LOOP     GET    FILE1,BUF            READ
         PUT    FILE2,BUF            WRITE
         B      LOOP                 REPEAT
* END REPEAT
FIN      CLOSE  (FILE1,,FILE2)
     (standard exit)
BUF      DS     20C                  INPUT BUFFER
FILE1    DCB    DDNAME=IN,DSORG=PS,MACRF=GM,EODAD=FIN
FILE2    DCB    DDNAME=OUT,DSORG=PS,MACRF=PM,RECFM=F,LRECL=20,BLKSIZE=20
         END    DEMO
```

**Figure H.1**
A program that performs I/O, as described in Examples 1 and 2.

While the system can obtain the logical record length of the input records from the existing input file, you must specify RECFM since the record format is not available otherwise.

You can look at the resulting output file by typing the command

```
TYPE DEMO OUTPUT A
```

## Using CMS Macros for I/O

If you design your program to run interactively, then you can use special CMS macros to perform I/O. Since you will replace the DCB macro by a CMS macro, you will not need the FILEDEF command. Furthermore, because CMS macros do not alter Registers 2 through 14, your program will not need a save area if it does not call external subprograms or use OS macros.

The most useful of the CMS macros are as follows:

FSREAD — Reads a record from a CMS disk file and places it into an I/O buffer.

FSSTATE — Determines whether a particular CMS file exists.

FSWRITE — Writes a record from an I/O buffer to a CMS disk file.

LINEDIT — Converts a two's complement binary number into EBCDIC or hex, and inserts the result into a terminal message.

RDTERM — Reads a line from the terminal and places it into an I/O buffer.

WRTERM — Writes a line to the terminal.

You specify many of the operand entries in the macro instructions in a keyword format as *keyword*=*option*.

**The FSREAD macro.** You can write a FSREAD macro instruction to read a record from a CMS disk file. The instruction has the following form:

*optional-symbol*  FSREAD  *fileid*,*keyword*=*option*[,...]

You can specify the CMS file identifier *fileid* either as '*fn ft fm*' or as a register name between 2 and 15, enclosed in parentheses. Such a register must contain the address of an 18-character identifier: 8 characters for filename, 8 characters for filetype, and 2 characters for filemode. The possible choices for *keyword*=*option* are as follows:

- BUFFER=*buf* specifies the address of the buffer.
- BSIZE=*size* specifies the number of bytes to be read. Usually the buffer is *size* bytes long. If a fixed-length input record is shorter than the buffer, the record is left-justified in the buffer and the rest of the buffer is unchanged. If a fixed-length record is longer than the buffer, an error message will occur. However, CMS truncates a variable-length record that is longer than the buffer.
- NOREC=*num* specifies the number of records for the next read operation so that you can read a block. If you omit this keyword, its default value is 1.
- ERROR=*erraddr* specifies the address to which the operating system will branch if an error occurs. However, if you omit this keyword, the next sequential instruction in your program will execute as if no error had occurred, and Register 15 will contain a code that indicates the nature of the error. These codes are listed in the *CMS Command and Macro Reference* manual.

You can specify *buf, size,* and *num* each as a decimal self-defining term or as the name of a register in parentheses that contains the desired value.

After a successful read operation, Register 0 will contain the number of bytes that were read and Register 15 will contain 0.

The following FSREAD instruction reads one 30-byte record from the CMS file DEMO IN A and places it into the buffer at INPUT:

```
FSREAD 'DEMO IN A',BUFFER=INPUT,BSIZE=30,ERROR=FIN
```

Although the only anticipated error is an end-of-file condition, *any* error will cause a branch to the instruction at FIN.

**The FSSTATE macro.** You can use the FSSTATE macro to determine whether a particular CMS file exists. The macro has the following form:

*optional-symbol* FSSTATE *fileid*,ERROR = *erraddr*

The operand entries have the same meanings as they do for FSREAD. If the specified file exists, then FSSTATE loads Register 15 with 0. If an error occurs, FSSTATE loads Register 15 with an error code.

**The FSWRITE macro.** You use a FSWRITE instruction to write a record, which is in an I/O buffer, to a CMS disk file. The instruction has the following form:

*optional-symbol* FSWRITE *fileid,keyword* = *option*[,...]

The *fileid* and the keyword parameters BUFFER = *buf* and ERROR = *erraddr* have the same meanings as they do for FSREAD. Other keyword parameters have the following meanings:

- NOREC = *num* specifies the number of records that you want to write. Normally, *num* is 1. However, if you want to write a block of records by using a single FSWRITE, *num* specifies the number of records in the block.
- BSIZE = *size* specifies the number of bytes that you want to write. If you write one record, then *size* is the length of the record. However, if you write a block of *num* records, then *size* specifies the number of bytes in the block.
- RECFM = *format* specifies the record format. To specify fixed-length records, either omit this keyword or write RECFM = F. To specify variable-length records, write RECFM = V.

If no errors occur during the write operation, Register 15 will contain 0. However, if an error occurs, Register 15 will contain an error code.

The following FSWRITE instruction writes 400 bytes from the buffer at MSGS to the file SAMPLE OUT A, and treats the bytes as a block of five 80-byte records:

```
FSWRITE 'SAMPLE OUT A',BUFFER=MSGS,BSIZE=400,NOREC=5
```

Since ERROR = is omitted, the next sequential instruction is always executed, even if an error occurs.

**The LINEDIT macro.** You can use the LINEDIT macro instruction to convert a two's complement binary number into EBCDIC or hexadecimal, and to insert the result into a message that is displayed at your terminal. The instruction has the following form:

*optional-symbol* LINEDIT TEXT = '*message*',SUB = (*list*)
or TEXTA = *address*,SUB = (*list*)

TEXT = '*message*' specifies the text of the message that you want to edit and display at the terminal. Alternatively you can specify the address of the message text by writing TEXTA = *address*, where *address* is either a symbolic address or the name of a register from 2 through 14, which is enclosed in parentheses, that contains the address. When you use TEXTA to specify the address of the message text, the first byte of the text must contain the number of bytes in the message.

SUB = (*list*) specifies a list of substitutions made by LINEDIT for each set of periods that occur within the message text. The *list* indicates both the type of substitution and the value that will replace the periods. You can specify either this value directly or its address. Some possibilities for *list* are as follows:

| | | |
|---|---|---|
| HEX,(*reg*) | or | HEX,*expression* |
| DEC,(*reg*) | or | DEC,*expression* |
| HEXA,*address* | or | HEXA,(*rega*) |
| DECA,*address* | or | DECA,(*rega*) |

HEX or HEXA converts the specified value to hexadecimal; DEC or DECA converts the specified value to decimal. You specify the value by writing either *expression*, (*reg*), (*rega*), or *address*: *expression* is a symbol or a symbolic address whose value is converted; *address* is the address of a fullword whose contents are converted; *reg* is the name of a register from 2 to 14 whose contents are converted; and *rega* is the name of a register from 2 to 14 that contains the address of a fullword whose contents are converted.

LINEDIT replaces each period in a sequence of periods by one character. If there are more characters in the text than there are periods, characters are truncated on the left. Negative decimal values appear with a minus sign.

The following instruction displays the message REG 5 = 456, assuming that $000001C8_{16}$, which is $456_{10}$, is in Register 5.

```
LINEDIT TEXT='REG 5 = ....',SUB=(DEC,(5))
```

The next macro instruction displays the message VALUE AT 020008, assuming that BUF represents the hex address 00020006:

```
LINEDIT TEXT='VALUE AT ......',SUB=(HEX,BUF+2)
```

**The RDTERM macro.** The RDTERM macro reads a line that you type at your terminal into an I/O buffer. It has the following form:

*optional-symbol* RDTERM *buffer*,PRBUFF=*addr*,PRLGTH=*length*

To specify the address of the buffer that will contain the line that RDTERM reads, you write *buffer*, either as a symbolic address or as the name of a register, which is enclosed in parentheses, that contains the address of the buffer. RDTERM assumes that the buffer is 130 bytes long. As an option, you can also use PRBUFF and PRLGTH to specify the address and the length, respectively, of a prompt message that RDTERM displays before the read operation. Following the read, Register 0 will contain the number of bytes read and Register 15 will contain 0 unless an error occurs— in which case, Register 15 will contain an error code.

**The WRTERM macro.** The WRTERM macro writes a line at the terminal. It has the following form:

*optional-symbol* WRTERM *line*,*length*,EDIT=NO

You specify the line that you want to write by writing *line* in one of three ways: as the actual text enclosed in apostrophes; as a symbol that represents the address of the text; or as the name of a register, enclosed in parentheses, that contains the address of the text. You specify the number of characters in the line by writing *length*. It is either the name of a register, enclosed in parentheses, that contains the length; or it is a self-defining term. You can omit *length* if you specify *line* as a character string enclosed in apostrophes. EDIT=NO will leave trailing blanks and omit a carriage return. You can remove trailing blanks and add a carriage return by omitting EDIT=NO.

---

EXAMPLE 3

### Terminal Input and Output by Using CMS Macros

The instructions in Figure H.2 have the same effect as the instructions in Figure H.1 of Example 1, but use only CMS macros instead of QSAM macros to perform the I/O. Assume that you have used the CMS editor to create the file named BDEMO ASSEMBLE A that contains the instructions in Figure H.2. If you have not already done so, you should type the GLOBAL command as given earlier in this appendix. To assemble, load, and execute the program, type the following commands:

```
A BDEMO
LOAD BDEMO
START
```

Notice that you do not use FILEDEF commands.

When you type an input record, which you follow with a carriage return, in response to a prompt by RDTERM, the instructions in Figure H.2 write the record on your terminal. RDTERM places the number of bytes that it reads into Register 0. By using the LTR instruction, you can test for zero bytes read, which is an end-of-file condition. If you do not do this, you can terminate program execution only by pressing the Attention key and then by typing HX.

---

EXAMPLE 4

### File Input and Output by Using CMS Macros

The instructions in Figure H.3 have an effect that is similar to the effect of the instructions in Figure H.1, as Example 2 describes. However, these instructions use only CMS macros instead of QSAM macros to perform the I/O. The instructions copy a file and append 10 bytes of blank characters to each record. As in Example 2, assume that you want to copy the file DEMO INPUT A, which has logical records of length 20, onto the new file DEMO OUTPUT A.

The FSREAD instruction requests 30 bytes; but since each input record is only 20 bytes long, the instruction reads 20 bytes and loads Register 0 with 20. When an end-of-file condition occurs, FSREAD loads Register 15 with the error code 12. You can test for this situation and for any other error that might occur during the read operation. The instructions here terminate program execution when a read error occurs, and produce a message at the terminal for any error other than an end-of-file.

To assemble, load, and execute this program, you should create a file that contains the instructions in Figure H.3, and type commands that are analogous to the ones given in Example 3.

---

## Debugging Aids Provided by CP

The control program (CP) component of VM provides commands to stop program execution so that you can either display at your terminal, or alter the contents of storage or

**Figure H.2**
A program that performs terminal I/O, as described in Example 3.

```
** ECHO TERMINAL INPUT BY USING CMS MACROS
DEMO     CSECT
    (EQUs that define register notation)
         SAVE    (R14,R12)
         BALR    R12,0
         USING   *,R12
* REPEAT UNTIL END-OF-FILE:
LOOP     RDTERM BUF,PRBUFF=PROMPT,PRLGTH=6      PROMPT AND READ
         LTR     R0,R0               ZERO-LENGTH INPUT?
         BZ      FIN                 IF YES, EXIT LOOP
         WRTERM BUF,20               WRITE RECORD
         B       LOOP                REPEAT
* END REPEAT
FIN      RETURN (R14,R12)
BUF      DS      CL130               INPUT BUFFER.  RDTERM READS 130
*                                      CHARACTERS
PROMPT   DC      C'INPUT: '          PROMPT MESSAGE
         END     DEMO
```

**Figure H.3**
A program that performs file I/O, as described in Example 4.

```
** COPY FILE BY USING CMS MACROS
DEMO     CSECT
    (EQUs that define register notation)
         SAVE     (R14,R12)
         BALR     R12,0
         USING    *,R12
         LA       R3,OLDFILE        ADDR. OF FILE NAME
         FSSTATE  (R3),ERROR=NTF DOES FILE EXIST?
* IF FILE EXISTS, REPEAT UNTIL END-OF-FILE:
LOOP     FSREAD   (R3),BUFFER=BUF,BSIZE=30   READ RECORD
         C        R15,=F'12'        END-OF-FILE?
         BE       FIN               IF YES, EXIT LOOP
         LTR      R11,R15           OTHER ERRORS?
         BNZ      ERR               IF YES, WRITE ERROR CODE
         FSWRITE  'NEW DATA A',BUFFER=BUF,BSIZE=30   WRITE RECORD
         B        LOOP
* END REPEAT
NTF      WRTERM   MSG,L'MSG         MISSING FILE: WRITE MESSAGE
         LA       R15,16            SET RETURN CODE FOR ERROR
         B        RET
ERR      LINEDIT TEXT='ERROR CODE .... IN READING FILE',SUB=(DEC,(R11))
         LA       R15,8             SET RETURN CODE FOR ERROR
         B        RET
FIN      LA       R15,0             NORMAL RETURN CODE
RET      L        R14,12(R12)
         RETURN   (R0,R12)
BUF      DS       CL20              INPUT BUFFER
         DC       10C' '            10-BLANK PAD
OLDFILE  DC       CL8'OLD',CL8'DATA',C'A '  FILE IDENTIFIER
MSG      DC       C'FILE NOT FOUND'         ERROR MESSAGE
         END      DEMO
```

of registers. You can direct large storage dumps to the printer. In addition, you can resume program execution at any instruction and trace the program's execution. This section describes the following CP commands:

| | |
|---|---|
| ADSTOP | Stops program execution at a virtual address that you specify. |
| BEGIN | Resumes program execution. |
| DISPLAY | Displays registers or storage at your terminal. |
| DUMP | Prints a register and a storage dump on the printer. |
| STORE | Changes the contents of registers or storage. |
| ·PER | Traces up to 255 events during program execution. |

**The ADSTOP command.** You can use the ADSTOP command to specify a hexadecimal virtual **stop address** at which program execution will stop. In this way, you can use other commands either to examine the contents of registers and storage, or to alter their contents. You use ADSTOP after you load your program into storage, but before you execute it. The command has the following forms:

| | | |
|---|---|---|
| | ADSTOP | *stop-address* |
| or | ADSTOP | OFF |

ADSTOP flags the instruction at the *stop-address,* and causes program execution to stop just prior to execution of this instruction. OFF clears a flag that an earlier ADSTOP command has set.

Only one stop address can be in effect at a time. You can obtain the necessary instruction address by examining the assembly listing file: remember that the program begins at virtual address $20000_{16}$. When the flagged instruction ultimately is executed, the flag that ADSTOP sets will be cleared. Therefore, if later you need to stop execution at that same instruction, you must issue another ADSTOP command.

**The BEGIN command.** After program execution stops at a stop address, you can resume execution by issuing a BEGIN command. The command has the following forms:

| | | |
|---|---|---|
| | BEGIN | *address* |
| or | BEGIN | |

BEGIN resumes program execution with the instruction either at *address* or—if there is no operand entry—at the address in the virtual PSW. The address in the virtual PSW is usually the stop address that ADSTOP set earlier. Note that BEGIN places *address,* when present, into the virtual PSW.

**The DISPLAY command.** You can display at your terminal the contents of either registers or storage by typing a DISPLAY command. It has the following forms:

| | | |
|---|---|---|
| | DISPLAY | [T]*hexloc1*[-*hexloc2*] |
| or | DISPLAY | [T]*hexloc1.bytecount* |
| or | DISPLAY | G\|Y*reg1*[-*reg2*] |
| or | DISPLAY | G\|Y*reg1.regcount* |
| or | DISPLAY | G\|Y |
| or | DISPLAY | PSW |

You use the hexadecimal virtual addresses *hexloc1* and *hexloc2* to specify either a single address or a range of addresses. You can also specify a block of *bytecount* consecutive addresses that begin at *hexloc1* (*bytecount* is a hex number). You can precede *hexloc1* with T to obtain an EBCDIC translation of the specified locations. G*reg1* displays general register *reg1,* while G*reg1-reg2* displays general registers *reg1* through *reg2;* G*reg1.regcount* displays *regcount* consecutively numbered registers, beginning with *reg1.* You can display floating-point registers by replacing G with Y in the operand entries just described. You can display either all general registers or all floating-point registers by writing G or Y, respectively. You can display the virtual PSW by writing PSW.

You can write several operand entries in one DISPLAY command by separating them with blanks. For instance, the following command displays storage locations 20010, 20040, and 20200 through 2023F; General Register 4; and all floating-point registers:

```
DISPLAY    20010 20040 T20200.40 G4 Y
```

This command causes locations 20200 through 2023F to be displayed both in EBCDIC and in hexadecimal.

**The DUMP command.** By using the DUMP command, you can print a register and a storage dump on the printer. The command has the following forms:

| | | |
|---|---|---|
| | DUMP | *hexloc1-hexloc2* |
| or | DUMP | *hexloc1.bytecount* |

DUMP prints the contents of the PSW, the general registers, the floating-point registers, the storage keys, and the virtual storage locations that you specify in the operand entry. The notation here has the same meaning as it does for the DISPLAY command. If *hexloc1* is not divisible by 32, DUMP rounds it down to the next lower address that is divisible by 32. Note that if you use DUMP in CMS mode, type #CP DUMP so that the dump will preserve the machine's virtual registers. If you do not precede DUMP by #CP, the dumped registers will be those of the CMS command processor.

**The STORE command.** You can change the contents of either registers or storage by using the STORE command. It has the following forms:

| | | |
|---|---|---|
| | STORE | *hexloc hexword1 [hexword2]...* |
| or | STORE | G\|Y*reg hexword1* [*hexword2*]... |
| or | STORE | S*hexloc hexdata* |
| *or* | STORE | PSW [*hexword1*] *hexword2* |

You can use STORE to store the hex constants *hexword1, hexword2,* and so on, into the fullwords at the hex address *hexloc,* which STORE, if necessary, rounds down to the next fullword address. If you write either G*reg* or Y*reg* instead of *hexloc*, the constants are stored into consecutive general registers or floating-point registers, respectively, beginning with Register *reg*. STORE with the operand entry S*hexloc hexdata* stores the hex constant *hexdata* into the bytes that begin at the address *hexloc* without boundary alignment. STORE with the operand entry PSW *hexword1 hexword2* stores the fullwords *hexword1* and *hexword2* into the PSW. If you specify only *hexword2*, STORE replaces only the second fullword of the PSW.

The following are examples of the STORE command:

| | |
|---|---|
| `STORE 21025 11 AB` | Stores the hex constant 00000011000000AB into locations 21024 through 2102B. |
| `STORE G3 12 34` | Stores the two hex constants 00000012 and 00000034 into General Registers 3 and 4, respectively. |
| `STORE S21025 11AB4F` | Stores the hex constants 11 at location 21025, AB at 21026, and 4F at 21027. |
| `STORE PSW 123456` | Stores the hex constant 00123456 into the second fullword of the PSW. |

**The PER command.** The PER command traces a choice of events during program execution. It has the following forms:

| | Event | Specific option | General options |
|---|---|---|---|
| PER | INSTRUCT | DATA *hexdata* | RANGE *address-range* |
| PER | BRANCH | INTO *address-range* | STEP *n* |
| PER | STORE | INTO *address-range* | RUN |
| PER | STORE | INTO *addr* DATA *hexdata* | PASS *n* |
| PER | MASK | INTO *addr* DATA *mask* | CMD *commands* |
| PER | G*reg1-reg2* | DATA *hexword* | |

You can specify several events with their options in a single PER command. For each event, you can specify its **specific option** and any of the **general options.** The following describes these events and the event-specific options.

PER I traces all instructions. You can restrict the instructions that PER traces by specifying options. For instance, PER I DATA 1845 traces all LR 4,5 instructions. (The machine language form of LR 4,5 is 1845.) PER I DATA 1935 I DATA 078E traces all CR 3,5 instructions and all BZR 14 instructions. PER I DATA 1935078E traces the sequential pair of instructions CR 3,5 and BZR 14.

PER BR traces all instructions that actually branch. With the option INTO, PER traces only branches into the indicated address range and, when such a branch occurs, PER displays the previous five branches. You specify address ranges as you do for the DISPLAY command.

PER ST traces all instructions that place values into storage. Either PER ST INTO 0-20 or PER ST INTO 0.21 traces only instructions that store into the range of addresses 0 to 20. PER ST INTO 20124 DATA F1F2F3 traces instructions that place the hex data F1F2F3 into bytes that begin at the address 20124.

PER M INTO *addr* DATA *mask* traces instructions that change bits that are in the bytes at the address *addr*. These bits correspond to the 1's in *mask*. For instance, PER M INTO 1C0 DATA 8001 traces instructions that change either the first bit or the last bit of the halfword at the address 1C0.

PER G traces instructions that change the contents of any general register. PER G10-12 restricts the trace to Registers 10 through 12, and PER G10 restricts the trace to Register 10 only. You can use DATA to look for certain hex values: for instance, PER G14-F DATA 5 traces instructions that change either Register 14 or Register 15 to 00000005.

You can specify one or more of the general options after the specific option for any event. These options are described as follows. RANGE restricts the trace to instructions whose first byte lies within a range of addresses that you specify in the same way as you specified the ranges in the DISPLAY command. You can write up to eight ranges for a single command. For instance,

```
PER ST G R 20000-20050 R 20100.26
```

traces instructions that are within either of the two address ranges 20000 to 20050 or 20100 to 20125, and that either place values into storage or change any general register.

STEP *n* halts program execution after *n* displays of trace output for the event. This can accelerate tracing without loss of information because, without STEP, program execution halts after every event, and the system enters the CP command environment. For instance,

```
PER M INTO 20220 DATA FF R 20000.101 STEP 8
```

traces all instructions within the address range 20000 to 20100 that change any bit in the byte at 20220. After eight of these events, the program halts for user commands.

RUN suppresses all execution halts.

PASS *n* suppresses the display of *n* events and then resets *n* to zero. You can use PASS to skip the first *n* events. For instance, PER I PA 753 halts after execution of 754 instructions.

CMD *commands* specifies commands that you want to execute just after the event occurs. CMD must be the last option that you write on a line. You must type ''# to separate multiple commands. For instance,

```
PER ST INTO 20100 RUN CMD DISPLAY 20100 ''# STORE 20100 4
```

traces all stores into location 20100, displays the value stored, stores 00000004 into location 20100, and continues execution.

There are other ways to use the PER command. PER COUNT counts events without producing trace output. This is useful if the error that you seek occurs after many instructions. QUERY PER displays the current count and lists all trace elements, with each element preceded by a number. PER by itself displays the current count and terminates counting. PER END *n* terminates tracing of element *n* only. PER END ALL terminates all PER tracing.

EXAMPLE 5

### Interactive Debugging in CP

The program in Figure H.4 should protect itself from input records that are longer than 10 characters by ignoring these records and printing an error message. A null input should terminate execution. However, the program contains an error, which can prevent normal termination. Suppose that you are at the point where a null input causes the program to display the "too long" error message and to request more input. Take the following steps:

1. To stop execution at the Compare instruction, enter the command #CP ADSTOP 2002E. (You can determine that the Compare instruction is at the address 2002E by looking at an assembly listing.)
2. Respond to the program's request for input with, for example, JKL.
3. When the program halts at the address 2002E, enter D G0 to display the input length in Register 0. (JKL has length 3.) Then determine the value of the literal constant that =F'10' defines by entering D 20160. You will find that the literal constant is C3F4400A, a negative value that causes all input values to appear too long.
4. To determine when the program destroys the literal constant, first restore the constant to its correct value of 10 by entering ST 20160 A. Then, to display the two values that the Compare instruction compares, enter PER I R 2002E RUN CMD D G0 ''# D 20160. To halt execution when the literal constant changes, enter PER ST INTO 20160 R 20000.158 CMD D 20160.
5. To resume execution at the RDTERM instruction, enter BEGIN 20006. Enter input values of length 14 and then values that have lengths from 1 to 12. Notice that the program detects the first long input value and correctly handles input values of length less than 10. An input value of length 10 changes the literal constant from 0000000A to 4000000A, so that now all input values are acceptable.
6. Resume execution by entering BEGIN. Notice that an input of 11 or more characters not only is acceptable, but also causes the program to store the eleventh input character into location 20160, the twelfth character into 20161, and so on until it stores the last character of the input string. The program then stores a blank ($40_{16}$) after this last character.
7. Because of the error, the program always stores a blank after the correct input string. When the input is of length 10, this blank destroys the first byte of the literal constant. The error is compounded as described in Step 6. The program stores the blank because the MVC instruction moves one character too many. To correct the error, either subtract 1 from Register 2 before using it in the EX instruction or reserve 11 bytes for BUF2.

## Debugging Aids in CMS

CMS provides commands that set **breakpoints**—which are similar to stop addresses—in programs at which execution will stop. You then can either display or alter the contents of storage or of general registers. You also can direct large storage dumps to the printer. In addition, you can resume program execution at any instruction and trace the program's execution. You also can display the meaning of error messages. The following CMS commands are available:

| | |
|---|---|
| HELP | Explains designated error messages. |
| DEBUG | Enters the CMS debug environment. |

**The HELP command.** HELP *mess-id* displays an explanation of either CMS or CP messages, where *mess-id* is the seven-character message identifier.

**The DEBUG command.** You enter the debug environment from the CMS environment when one of the following occurs: you issue the command DEBUG; you cause an external interrupt by typing #CP EXT; or the system encounters a breakpoint, which you set with the BREAK subcommand, during program execution. While in the debug environment, you can use only either CP commands that you precede with #CP or DEBUG subcommands. This section describes the following subcommands:

| | |
|---|---|
| **BR**EAK | Stops program execution at a specified virtual address. |
| **DU**MP | Prints a register and storage dump. |
| GO | Leaves the debug environment and resumes program execution. |
| GPR | Displays the contents of general registers. |
| HX | Leaves the debug environment, which the machine entered due to an interruption. |
| PSW | Displays the PSW. |
| RETURN | Returns to the CMS command environment. |
| SET | Changes the contents of the PSW or of the general registers. |
| **ST**ORE | Changes the contents of virtual memory. |
| X | Displays the contents of virtual memory. |

Since you can invoke DEBUG after an unanticipated abend, CMS can provide an ex post facto dump. The CMS commands that display or change the contents of storage and general registers are useful only if you are able to select the proper breakpoints. Although CMS does not have the elaborate trace facilities that the PER command provides, you can trace program execution by setting breakpoints at appropriate places and examining all relevant variables. However, you cannot display or change the contents of the floating-point registers.

**Figure H.4**
A program that contains an error, as described in Examples 5 and 6.

```
** ECHO INPUT OF 10 OR FEWER CHARACTERS.  IGNORE LONGER
** INPUT.  HALT ON NULL INPUT.
DEMO     CSECT
     (EQUs that define register notation)
         SAVE     (R14,R12)
         BALR     R12,0
         USING    *,R12
* REPEAT:
LOOP     RDTERM   BUF,PRBUFF=MSG1,PRLGTH=L'MSG1     READ
         C        R0,=F'10'         INPUT LENGTH > 10?
         BH       ERR               IF YES, ERROR
         LTR      R2,R0             INPUT LENGTH = 0?
         BZ       FIN               IF YES, FINISHED
         EX       R2,MOV            MOVE INPUT TO BUF2
         LA       R3,L'MSG2(R2)     R3=LENGTH OF OUTPUT LABEL
*                                      AND BUFFER
         WRTERM   MSG2,(R3)         WRITE INPUT RECORD
         B        LOOP              REPEAT
ERR      WRTERM   'INPUT TOO LONG - IGNORED'
         B        LOOP              REPEAT
* END REPEAT
* STANDARD RETURN
FIN      RETURN   (R14,R12)
MOV      MVC      BUF2(0),BUF       TARGET FOR EX
BUF      DS       CL130             INPUT BUFFER
MSG1     DC       C'TYPE 10 OR FEWER CHARACTERS: '  PROMPT
MSG2     DC       C'THE INPUT IS: ' OUTPUT LABEL
BUF2     DS       CL10              OUTPUT BUFFER
         END      DEMO
```

**The BREAK subcommand.** After you load your program into storage and before you execute it, you can set breakpoints by using the BREAK subcommand. Program execution will then halt just before execution of the instruction at the breakpoint so that you can either examine or alter the contents of registers and storage. The subcommand has the following form:

BREAK *id hex-address*

BREAK sets a breakpoint at *hex-address* and identifies it with *id*, which is a decimal integer from 0 to 15. Remember that you determine *hex-address* by examining an assembly listing. You can have a maximum of 16 breakpoints in effect at one time. When the flagged instruction is executed, the flag that BREAK sets is cleared. Therefore, if you later need to stop execution at that same instruction, you must issue another BREAK subcommand.

**The DUMP subcommand.** By using the DUMP subcommand, you can print a register and storage dump on the printer. The dump will contain the contents of the general registers, the floating-point registers, the PSW, and virtual memory in the hex address range *hexloc1* to *hexloc2*. The subcommand has the following form:

DUMP *hexloc1-hexloc2*

**The GO subcommand.** After program execution stops at a breakpoint, you can resume execution by using the GO subcommand. It has the following forms:

GO *hex-address*
or GO

GO resumes program execution with the instruction at either *hex-address* or—if there is no operand entry—the address in the virtual PSW. The address in the virtual PSW is usually the address of the instruction at which execution stopped. Note that GO places *hex-address,* when present, in the virtual PSW. If you enter the debug environment by using the DEBUG command, then GO must have an operand entry.

**The GPR subcommand.** The GPR subcommand displays the contents of general registers. You can specify either one register *reg1* or a range of registers from *reg1* to *reg2*. GPR has the following form:

GPR *reg1* [*reg2*]

**The HX subcommand.** If an interrupt causes the machine to enter the debug environment, you can return to the CMS environment by typing the HX subcommand, which has no operands.

**The PSW subcommand.** You can display the current contents of the old PSW by typing the PSW subcommand, which has no operands.

**The RETURN subcommand.** If you used the DEBUG command to enter the debug environment, you can return to the CMS environment by typing the RETURN subcommand, which has no operands.

**The SET subcommand.** You can use the SET subcommand to change the contents either of the old PSW or of one or two general registers. SET has the following forms:

```
      SET   PSW hexdata1 [hexdata2]
or    SET   GPR reg hexdata1 [hexdata2]
```

Each of *hexdata1* and *hexdata2* specify 1 to 4 bytes of hex data. SET stores *hexdata1* left-justified into either the leftmost fullword of the PSW or Register *reg*. SET stores *hexdata2*, when specified, left-justified into either the rightmost fullword of the PSW or Register *reg* + 1.

**The STORE subcommand.** You can use the STORE subcommand to change the contents of a maximum of 12 bytes of virtual memory. STORE has the following form:

```
STORE    hex-address hexdata1 [hexdata2] [hexdata3]
```

Here, *hexdata1*, *hexdata2*, and *hexdata3* each specify 1 to 4 bytes of hex data. These bytes form a single string of bytes that are stored at *hex-address*.

**The X subcommand.** You can display a maximum of 56 consecutive bytes of virtual memory beginning at *hex-address* by using the X subcommand. It has the following form:

```
X     hex-address [n]
```

If you omit the byte count *n*, X displays 4 bytes.

---

## EXAMPLE 6

### Interactive Debugging under CMS

Consider the program in Figure H.4 that was described in Example 5. Suppose that, after a null input, the program displays the "too long" message. You can take the following steps to locate the error:

1. Enter the debug environment by typing either #CP EXT or DEBUG. Then set a breakpoint at the Compare instruction by typing BREAK 1 2002E.
2. Type GO 20006 to execute the read instruction again. Respond to the program's request for input with, for example, JKL.
3. When the program halts at the address 2002E, enter GPR 0 to display the input length in Register 0. (JKL has length 3.) Then determine the value of the literal constant that =F'10' defines by typing X 20160. You will find that the literal constant is negative, so that all input values appear too long.
4. Since CMS cannot trace instructions, you must use breakpoints to determine when the program destroys the literal constant. Therefore, set breakpoints at the instructions C, BZ, and LA, and at the addresses ERR and FIN. Then, restore the literal constant and resume execution at the RDTERM instruction. You can accomplish the steps just given by typing:

```
BR 1 2002E
BR 2 20038
BR 3 20040
BR 4 20066
BR 5 2009E
ST 20160 0000000A
GO 20006
```

You can proceed as in Steps 5, 6, and 7 of Example 5 by substituting GO for BEGIN.

---

# APPENDIX I A Job Control Language Primer

This appendix provides a brief overview of the control statements that you will need to run a program. Since several aspects of these statements depend on the particular computing system and operating system that you are using, there may be differences between what you read about here and what is required for your particular situation.

## OS

Jobs that run under OS use the job control statements that are presented in Figure I.1. These statements follow rules similar to those of assembler language statements, except that the first two columns usually contain two slashes (//). Immediately following the slashes is a symbol, which can be optional. An operation appears next, which must be preceded and followed by at least one blank. There are only three possible operations: JOB, EXEC, or DD. Following the operation entry is the operand entry.

The **JOB statement** signals the beginning of the job; gives it a name, which begins in column 3 and which is EXAMPLE in Figure I.1; and specifies installation-dependent accounting information and certain options. The **EXEC statement** signals the beginning of a job step. It names the program—such as the assembler or the linkage editor—to be executed during the job step. It also names options that, for example, affect the assembly listing or point to a library of macro definitions. A job may contain several EXEC statements—one statement for each job step. For instance, assembling, link editing, and executing a program requires three job steps and, therefore, three EXEC statements. Alternatively, an EXEC statement may name a **catalogued procedure** instead of a program name. A catalogued procedure is a sequence of JCL statements that entirely define one or more job steps. These JCL statements are stored in a library of the operating system. By using a single catalogued procedure instead of the three EXEC statements mentioned earlier, you could specify the three steps that are necessary to assemble, link edit, and execute a program. The procedure ASMFCLG in the EXEC statement of Figure I.1 is commonly used for this purpose. The name entry of a procedure is optional, but the three EXEC statements that the procedure ASMFCLG represents have name entries ASM, LKED, and GO. You can supplement or alter statements within this procedure by using these names as references. The statements in Figure I.1 that contain ASM and GO demonstrate how you do this.

**Data Definition,** or **DD, statements** define the data sets that the job steps require. In Figure I.1, the third statement

```
//ASM.SYSIN   DD    *
```

defines the input data set to the job step named ASM, which is the assembly step. The input to the assembler is the source program, and the * indicates that the source program appears in the same data set as the JCL statements; this data set is called the **job stream.** The last DD statements

```
//GO.SYSPRINT DD      SYSOUT=A
//GO.SYSUDUMP DD      SYSOUT=A
//GO.SYSIN    DD      *
```

define data sets that your program uses during execution. The first DD indicates that the program's output will be printed. The second DD is optional; it indicates that if the program terminates abnormally, the resulting dump will be printed. The last DD indicates that the input to the program is in the job stream.

Finally, the /* statement in Figure I.1 is a delimiter that indicates the end of a data set within the job stream.

Note that the assembler language instructions that appear in Figure I.1 include the **standard entry** to and the **standard exit** from an assembler language program. You must write these instructions in each program that you run under OS.

## DOS

Jobs that run under DOS use the job control statements that are presented in Figure I.2. The functions of these statements are similar to those just described for OS. The first two columns usually contain slashes. At least one blank must precede and follow the operation. In the JOB statement, the job name follows the operation JOB—an order that is unlike the order of the analogous OS statement. A single blank separates the job name from the accounting information. The OPTION statement specifies certain job options. For example, LINK indicates that the object module is to be link edited. You must specify this option if an EXEC LNKEDT statement appears in the job stream, as it does here. The DUMP option indicates that if the program terminates abnormally, then a dump will be printed.

```
//EXAMPLE       JOB    accounting information
//              EXEC   ASMFCLG
//ASM.SYSIN     DD     *
          CSECT
* STANDARD ENTRY:
          STM    R14,R12,12(R13)
          BALR   R12,0
          USING  BASE,R12
BASE      ST     R13,SAVE+4
          LA     R13,SAVE
          .
          .
          .                              Source program
* STANDARD EXIT:
          L      R13,SAVE+4
          LM     R14,R12,12(R13)
          BR     R14
*
SAVE      DS     18F
          .
          .
          .
          END
/*
//GO.SYSPRINT DD     SYSOUT=A
//GO.SYSUDUMP DD     SYSOUT=A
//GO.SYSIN    DD     *

     (Data, if any)

/*
```

**Figure I.1**
Typical OS control statements to assemble and execute a program.

The ASSGN statement assigns logical I/O units to physical devices. See Chapter 16 for more information about this statement.

Of the EXEC statements in Figure I.2, the first invokes the assembler; the second invokes the linkage editor; and the third initiates the execution of the program. The /* statements signal the end of the source program and the end of the input data set, and the /& signals the end of the job.

The assembler language instructions that appear in Figure I.2 indicate the **standard entry** to and the **standard exit** from an assembler language program. The instruction EOJ terminates program execution and returns control to the operating system.

## CMS

CMS does not use JCL statements. Under CMS, you can use an editor to create a file that contains a source program. Then, by using a sequence of CMS commands—such as those listed in Figure I.3—you can assemble the program and execute it interactively. The GLOBAL MACLIB command identifies the macro libraries that are necessary for the assembly process. In Figure I.3, the macro libraries are CMSLIB, OSMACRO, and OSMACRO1. The ASSEMBLE command causes the named file—EXAMPLE, in this case—to be assembled. The LOAD command initiates the linking and loading processes; START begins program execution. See Appendix H for further details about CMS.

```
//   JOB   EXAMPLE accounting information
//   OPTION   LINK,DUMP
//   ASSGN devices
//   EXEC   ASSEMBLY
            CSECT                          )
* STANDARD ENTRY:                          |
            BALR   R12,0                   |
            USING  BASE,R12                |
BASE        LA     R13,SAVE                |
            .                              |
            .                              |
            .                              |
* STANDARD EXIT:                           }  Source program
            EOJ                            |
*                                          |
SAVE        DS     9D                      |
            .                              |
            .                              |
            .                              |
            END                            )
/*
//   EXEC   LNKEDT
//   EXEC

     (Data, if any)

/*
/&
```

**Figure I.2**
Typical DOS control statements to assemble and execute a program.

```
GLOBAL MACLIB CMSLIB OSMACRO OSMACRO1
ASSEMBLE EXAMPLE
LOAD EXAMPLE
START
```

**Figure I.3**
Sample CMS commands to assemble and execute a program.

# Index